D0382571

EUROPE

ASIA

AFRICA

INDIAN

OCEAN

EASTERN HEMISPHERE

Civilization—Past and Present

VOLUME TWO

CIVILIZATION—

VOLUME TWO: from the beginnings of the modern era to the midst of the Second World War. About 1650 A.D. into the fifth decade of the twentieth century

A survey of the history of man—his governmental, economic, social, religious, intellectual, and esthetic activities—from the earliest times to the present, in Europe, in Asia, in Africa, and in the Americas

PAST AND PRESENT

by T. WALTER WALLBANK

and ALASTAIR M. TAYLOR

THE UNIVERSITY OF SOUTHERN CALIFORNIA

Scott, Foresman and Company

CHICAGO ATLANTA DALLAS NEW YORK

Copyright, 1942, by Scott, Foresman and Company

PRINTED IN THE UNITED STATES OF AMERICA

Preface

TO VOLUME TWO

THIS VOLUME covers a time span of approximately 300 years, from about 1650 to 1942. A continuation of *Civilization—Past and Present,* Volume I, it utilizes the same approach and techniques. In brief it attempts a global synthesis of modern history. This volume constitutes the text for the second half of a general survey course in history and is required, for example, of all freshmen at the University of Southern California. The purpose has been to offer to all students some idea about how the world in which they live came to be. To achieve this end the developments of the past 300 years in Latin America, the United States, western Europe, the British Dominions, Africa, India, China, Japan, and Oceania are discussed as part of an interdependent and integrated world civilization.

The authors believe that this global treatment, in the light of recent developments, fulfills a definite need and that, therefore, it carries its own motivation. Furthermore, everything has been done to make the material understandable and assimilable by the student. It has been blocked out into fifteen chapters, each designed for one week's study. Groups of related chapters are then introduced and held together by interchapters. The chronological aspects of each chapter can be quickly grasped by reference to the chart which begins each chapter. About 65 maps have been prepared, using new interpretive techniques, and some 175 photographs and diagrams have been used to make the narrative more vivid and meaningful. Several features at the end of the book will assist students in their study. A master chronology on pages 512-515 shows parallel lines of development throughout the world. Tables of Cultural History (pages 516-519) present under six main headings concise résumés of developments in government, economics, religion, social life, thought, and art. Special pains have been taken to provide comprehensive and usable bibliographies. In addition a bibliographical essay has been included which can appropriately be used as the basis for exercises in the effective use of library materials.

While retaining politics as the most obvious strand in the development of human affairs, considerably more emphasis than is customary has been placed upon art, science, economics, religion, and thought. Man, it is presumed, is just as important in his role of worker, worshiper, artist, and thinker as in that of citizen.

This volume contains relatively more material on the twentieth century than is ordinarily the case. While not neglecting earlier periods, almost half of the book relates to developments of the closing decades of the nineteenth century and the forty-odd years of the twentieth century. It is the authors' belief that the average student, while recognizing the need for a general knowledge of the configuration of the remote past, is more vitally interested in his own age and with those immediate causal factors that helped give it form.

Any emphasis upon twentieth-century history inevitably raises the problem of interpretation. This time span constitutes a complex pattern in process of change, with the ultimate configuration still very much in doubt. Few periods have seen such drastic and rapid changes. Because so much of our civilization is in flux, the authors have tried at all times not to lay down *ex parte* or pontifical judgments and evaluations. It is believed that the desirable and logical course was to try to present facts as accurately and objectively as possible, leaving the matter of interpretation and evaluation to each classroom, where the interests of teacher and students would decide the appropriate line of approach.

While assuming complete responsibility for all facts and interpretations throughout the book, the authors wish to express their thanks to the following persons for many penetrating suggestions at various stages of their work, either in manuscript, galley proof, or page proof: to Professor H. F. MacNair of the University of Chicago for checking over the material on China, Japan, and the Pacific islands; to Professor G. V. Bobrinskoy of the University of Chicago for the material on India; to Professor C. W. de Kiewiet of Cornell University for Chapters 1, 2, and 3; to Professor S. William Halperin of the University of Chicago for Chapters 1 through 15; to Mr. Francis J. O'Malley of Notre Dame University for Chapters 1 through 15; to Professor Ross Berkes of The University of Southern California for assistance in preparing the material on Latin America in Chapters 7 and 12; and to Professor E. A. Wolfram of St. John's College for the preparation of the Chart of Contemporary Events and the Tables of Cultural History.

The authors are especially indebted to Dr. A. S. Raubenheimer, Dean of the College of Letters, Arts, and Sciences, The University of Southern California, for making it possible to offer a vital and comprehensive history of world civilization and for advice and encouragement throughout the project. They would also like to express their appreciation to the freshman class at The University of Southern California for helpful reactions and suggestions during the years when this work was being formed.

We express our thanks also to the following persons for various kinds of work on the book: to Mr. R. M. Chapin, Jr., for the continuation of his work on the maps and to Mary Herrick Porter for the large amounts of research that went into them; to Miss Charlotte Speight for her continued assistance in selecting art illustrations and suggesting methods of textual integration; to Mr. Barney Moore for the initial drawings for each chapter; and to Dr. Otto Bettman for his diligent selection of pictures to enliven the past.

Finally, we express our appreciation to the following publishers from whose books quotations have been made. Such quotations are indicated in detail in the Bibliography beginning on page 544: George Allen & Unwin, London; D. Appleton-Century Company, New York; George Bell & Sons, London; A. & C. Black, London; Cambridge University Press, London; Carnegie Endowment for International Peace, New York; F. S. Crofts & Co., New York; Events Publishing Co., New York; Foreign Policy Association, New York;

Ginn and Company, Boston; Harcourt, Brace and Company, New York; Harper & Brothers, New York; D. C. Heath and Company, Boston; Henry Holt and Company, New York; Houghton Mifflin Company, Boston; Kegan Paul, Trench, Trubner & Co., London; Alfred A. Knopf, New York; J. B. Lippincott Company, Philadelphia; Longmans, Green & Co., New York; The Macmillan Company, New York; McGraw-Hill Book Company, New York; Methuen and Company, London; The New York Times, New York; W. W. Norton & Company, New York; Oxford University Press, New York and London; Oskar Piest, New York; Scott, Foresman and Company, Chicago; Simon and Schuster, New York; University of California Press, Berkeley; D. Van Nostrand Company, New York; The Viking Press, New York.

T. W. W.
A. M. T.

Los Angeles, California
August 1, 1942

Contents: Volume Two

List of Maps

List of Illustrations

1. New Ways of Life

2. Science, Reason, and Enlightenment

3. When in the Course of Human Events

4. *Factories, Owners, and Workers*

5. *Nationalism and Democracy Advance*

6. *All's Right with the World*

7. *New Europes Overseas*

8. *Dominion over Palm and Pine*

9. *Explosion in Europe*

10. *A Quest for World Order*

11. *New Patterns in Statecraft*

12. *Democracy on Trial*

13. The Orient Astir

14. A World Divided

15. *Forging a New World*

Paleolithic man had not freedom from want and fear. The fight for food and a place to sleep took nearly all his attention, but he had time to paint the walls of his cave.

Glancing Back from 1650

The ***history of man*** might be called the greatest show on earth. It has been running continuously since it opened about a million years ago in a Paleolithic setting with its principal character arrayed in skins and emitting guttural sounds. It is an epic of endurance and ambition, of struggle for survival against the elements, a tragedy of wars, disasters, and privations, a comedy of man's pleasant, humorous, and even ludicrous moments. The drama of man's history can highlight only the more salient aspects of his activity upon this earth—how he created civilizations in one age only to destroy them in another, how he examined the mystery of his own creation and of his universe, and how he learned with increasing success to control and utilize his environment. But it is well to remember that the real story of man is his unbroken, day-by-day existence extending over a million years and on every continent of the earth.

During Paleolithic times man discovered how to make use of fire, how to work with fist hatchets and other primitive tools, how to hunt more effectively with harpoons and spears, and even how to decorate in a crude sort of way the cave dwellings that protected him. In Neolithic times he domesticated important animals and plants, learned to build wooden houses by the shores of lakes, to fashion pottery, and to use the bow and arrow, thus greatly increasing his fighting effectiveness. Also among man's Neolithic accomplishments belong the introduction of weaving, the fashioning of the first rude boats, and the beginnings of commerce. About 5000 B.C. the Age of Metals began, when our ancestors discovered the use of copper in making tools. Later, they became adept in working with bronze and iron. The Age of Metals also saw the invention of sailing ships and the wheel. Transportation on an important scale was now made possible. Man had advanced a long way from his Paleolithic cave shelters.

The first great civilizations appeared in the valleys of certain rivers. In these regions the fertility of the soil enabled agricultural pursuits to be carried on profitably. At the same time a substantial population developed. Villages and cities emerged, bringing with them problems of government and social action. River transportation was cheap and permitted traders to sell their wares in quite distant places, thus bringing new contacts among peoples. These initial river civilizations were widely scattered. Egypt grew up along the banks of the Nile, Mesopotamia developed between the Tigris and Euphrates in what is now called the Near and Middle East, India began along the Indus and the Ganges, and China in the region of the Wei and the Hwang Ho. Despite the fact that these four civilizations emerged more or less independently of one another and differed in language, literature, and political and religious philosophies, their similarities were just as striking as their differences. Each civilization produced intricate social organizations, invented alphabets and calendars, introduced new crafts, and developed commerce. Each achieved outstanding success in literature and art and formulated complex religious and philosophical systems.

One of Egypt's contributions to civilization was the art of writing, although it remained for the Phoenicians to develop the first true alphabet. The Egyptians devised a workable calendar very early, partly at least for the purpose of keeping a more accurate tab on the rise of the Nile. The flooding of this river necessitated frequent land measurements, and as a result the Egyptians gained great proficiency in geometry. They built such imperishable stone monuments as the pyramids and the Sphinx, while their temples displayed architectural skill of a high order. Their literature abounded in lofty religious sentiment, but the land suffered from a too powerful and reactionary priestcraft which stifled the aspirations of the people. The people of the Nile valley maintained their own government for thousands of years but finally fell under the control of the Roman empire.

While the Egyptians were passing from a stone to a metal culture, clusters of people in the Tigris-Euphrates valley were also building up rich and varied civilizations. The old Babylonians had a well-established city life and nearly 2000 years B.C. formulated the first great law code—that of Hammurabi. The Hittites of Asia Minor made clever use of iron, the Phoenicians invented an alphabet and carried on extensive commercial operations in the Mediterranean, and the Hebrew people thought out some of the loftiest religious concepts the world has known—including the belief in one god, or monotheism. Before the Persians arose to bring the entire area under one centralized control between the sixth and fourth centuries B.C., the Assyrians coupled with their ruthless military might a surprising proficiency in sculpture and architecture. The Chaldeans made themselves famous by their irrigation projects in Babylonia, Nebuchadnezzar's celebrated hanging gardens, and their proficiency in mathematics and astronomy. The Persians added to the history of religious thought through the moral and ethical contributions of their teacher, Zoroaster, while in the realm of political science they are to be remembered for the efficiency with which they provided provincial administration and linked up their far-flung empire by a vast system of military roads.

Some 4000 years B.C. there developed in northwest India an advance civilization comparable to those in Egypt and Mesopotamia. The Indus valley civilization, so-called because it grew up along the banks of the Indus River, had a complex city culture, as is proved by the remnants of such excavated towns as Mohenjo-Daro and Harappa. Although we know next to nothing of the inhabitants of these cities, it is well established that they possessed remarkable artistic ability and even installed in their carefully planned-out towns a drainage system far superior to anything found in Europe until modern times. The Indus valley civilization perished about 2500 B.C. through unknown causes.

The next important event in the history of India was the influx of invaders through the northwest passes. These newcomers were Indo-Aryans belonging to the great Indo-

European-speaking family, whose other main branch migrated westward at this time to Greece and the shores of the Mediterranean. The Indo-Aryans conquered northern India over a period of hundreds of years, driving southward the Indo-Negroid peoples already established there. The Indo-Aryan conquerors were at first hard-fighting nomadic tribes, but in time they settled down in villages and cities. Early in their new homes they built up a caste system and a complex philosophical-religious system which have persisted down to the present. Among their age-old beliefs was the principle of the unity of life, reincarnation, and the law of cause and effect—*karma.* During the sixth century B.C. was born the greatest of all Indian religious teachers, Gautama Buddha. He attempted to purge Indian religious life of superstitions and impurities, and his philosophy of self-reliance and self-deliverance from illusion became in time the principal creed in Burma, Ceylon, Tibet, China, and Japan. By the time of his death, India had established firmly the chief religious, social, economic, and intellectual foundations of her "timeless" civilization. This intricate culture was to endure with surprisingly little change through centuries which saw entire civilizations rise and fall in the west.

In India around 100 B.C. *the life story of a reformer, Gautama Buddha, was carved on the wall of a sacred building.*

About 3000 B.C., while the Indus valley civilization was flourishing in India, a new culture was being born in China where the Hwang Ho is joined by its tributary, the Wei. Although the history of the next thousand years in China is a complex mixture of fable and fact, it seems certain that during this time the Chinese were making use of domesticated animals, had spread eastward along the Hwang Ho, and had established a stable government, well organized under the rule of the emperor, and were already proficient in agricultural pursuits, in raising silkworms, and working in bronze. Bronze masterpieces are especially identified with the Shang dynasty, which lasted from the eighteenth through the twelfth centuries B.C. The longest reigning dynasty in China's history was the one succeeding the Shang—the Chou dynasty (1122-249 B.C.), when many of China's most important institutions took form. The new civil service was administered by men who had proved their ability in scholarship, irrespective of social background. A strict code of manners in court circles evolved, while the towns saw the evolution of the guild system. Splendid objects of art were fashioned from jade, and good poetry was written. But the Chou period made its chief claim to immortality by giving to China the country's most important philosophers, Lao-tse, Confucius, and Mencius. Lao-tse urged that life's inner processes be sought in nature to attain knowledge and individual tranquillity, and he exerted a profound influence upon Chinese art as a result. Confucius laid down important moral and ethical codes, being much more concerned with the practical and humanistic side of life than were the philosophers of India, for example, who sought along mystical lines to explain the nature of the universe. Mencius interested himself in the philosophy of government and was remarkably democratic and modern in much of this thought. From these and other philosophers the Chinese people received a practical, urbane, and "down to earth" attitude towards daily living which has not left them to the present day. As in the case of India, by this time China had established her principal cultural foundations firmly, and her civilization was to endure with a stability unknown to western civilizations.

Indian and Chinese civilizations continued to defy the onslaughts of time and destruction, but those of the Near and Middle East were not so fortunate. They declined in importance before the rise of the two civilizations to which our own culture is most heavily indebted—Greek and Roman. One branch of the Indo-European-speaking peoples migrated to India; Greece and Rome were the products of the migration of the other main branch. Tribes of these conquerors filtered into the Aegean world for a thousand years prior to 1200 B.C., some taking up their abode in the Greek peninsula and neighboring islands, others marching on to Italy, there to build up in time the Roman world.

The Greek newcomers were indebted to Egyptian and Mesopotamian culture, largely through the medium of the rich Cretan civilization which was flourishing as the Greek marauders swarmed into the Aegean region. But the Greeks early proved themselves to be a highly, even stubbornly, independent people both in the political and intellectual spheres. They cut themselves free from the stultifying traditionalism and priestcraft of the Near East and experimented for themselves. The results were startling and beneficial. Athens, the principal Greek city-state, achieved (about the fifth century B.C.) something new in political science, a democracy. Greek philosophers broke with the past and attempted to give a rational explanation of the universe along naturalistic lines. In addition, thinkers like Socrates worked out rules of moral conduct for man, Plato formulated his views of the ideal social state, and Aristotle united with his many profound observations on natural laws a new system of logical deduction. With their emphasis upon the life and problems of man, the Greeks wrote mighty epics about heroic exploits, great tragedies and comedies concerned with subtle psychological and moral situations. In sculpture they idealized the human figure as the perfect embodiment of beauty and grace. The Athenian Greeks did little in experimental science, but the Greeks living in Alexandria made many memorable discoveries in physics, medicine, and geography. So freedom-loving and individualistic were the Greeks that they never really learned the art of cooperation and literally destroyed themselves. But this individualism set a new note of human dignity which influenced all future generations in western history, while the Greek spirit of intellectual skepticism broke the shackles of traditionalism and opened up new channels of human enquiry.

The Romans borrowed heavily in thought and art from their Greek teachers. But whereas the Greeks were adept at speculation and esthetic expression, the Romans were an intensely practical people. They adopted and preserved a culture which might otherwise have perished when the Greek city-states fell. The Romans thus became the great disseminators of classical knowledge for western Europe and thus stamped indelibly the pattern of things to come. The history of Rome is largely an account of the expansion of a village on the muddy banks of the Tiber until it became the proud empress of the entire Mediterranean world by the second century B.C. It is also a story of the evolution of governmental, administrative, and legal processes over a period of many centuries, as man learned the most efficient means of governing a mighty empire. Roman contributions in the art of government and in law may well constitute their finest gifts to us. But these supremely practical people produced more than administrators like Julius Caesar and Hadrian. Virgil composed the epic *Aeneid,* Lucretius wrote a remarkable philosophical poem *On the Nature of Things,* Terence and Plautus were gifted dramatists, and Pliny and Plutarch distinguished themselves as historians. In architecture the Romans took over the basic Greek forms, but they contributed the basilica, the triumphal arch, and the amphitheater. Above all else, the

The Romans excelled in political theory and were great builders. Yet within the walls of the Colosseum they sent forth men to fight against beasts; they cheered brutal gladiators and watched the Christians die.

Romans were a monumental-minded people who did everything on a lavish scale, whether it was the building of a public forum or an empire.

Internal decay and external attack at length destroyed the Roman world. For centuries prior to the fifth century A.D., the empire had been undergoing a process of "barbarization" as Germanic peoples filtered into Roman territory and gradually modified its life. As conditions became increasingly chaotic, with irresponsible soldiers capturing the government, commerce declining, and the middle class deteriorating, people looked about them for solace. Some found relief in oriental cults or philosophical schools like Epicureanism and Stoicism. But into the Roman world now came the faith—Christianity—that was to color and direct the western world for more than the next thousand years. The Christian religion spread largely through the missionary efforts of Paul, the needs of the times, and the organizational framework of the Roman empire. After the "fall" of the empire, the Christian Church was an invaluable agent in fusing Roman and barbarian and in perpetuating the classical heritage. While Europe underwent a rather drab period of transition and reorganization until it achieved a position of greater stability in the ninth century under the rule of Charlemagne, the Church was the principal preserver of learning and the great disseminator of culture in the west.

Civilization appeared to retrogress at this time in Europe, especially as compared with the feats of the Greeks and Romans. But in this very period of the so-called "dark ages" four highly advanced civilizations were flourishing in scattered parts of the world. Standing on the crossroads of the east and west was the city which the Roman emperor Constantine had formally dedicated in 330 A.D., Constantinople. Until its capture by the Turks over a thousand years later in 1453, this magnificent city was the center of the rich and varied Byzantine civilization. The Byzantines were not so much the originators of cultural innovations as the transmitters of Greek learning and scholarship. They were an urban-dwelling, sophisticated people who showed themselves particularly adept in commerce and industry, and whose pastimes and interests indicated their penchant for living dangerously. Many notable milestones were erected in Byzantine history. During the reign of Justinian in the sixth century, Roman law was codified, and the vast cathedral of Saint Sophia, embodying a new architectural principle, was erected. In the ninth and tenth centuries the Eastern Church converted the Slavic world to Christendom. Altogether, the civilization centering about Constantinople was as colorful and stimulating as its bazaars, piled high with the luxuries of the occident and orient.

Constantinople fell before the frenzied attack of the Mohammedans. Mohammed, who died in 632 A.D., was a product of the Arabian desert who by the power of his teachings welded his people together and laid the foundations of a mighty and powerful civilization. Like the Jews and the Christians, the followers of Mohammed believed in one God and received ethical teachings of a high order. In the centuries following the Prophet's death, a great Mohammedan civilization spread until it stretched from Spain to India. Its cultural zenith was reached during the Abbasid dynasty (750-1258) and especially in the tenth and eleventh centuries. In medicine, philosophy, geography, and mathematics the Moslems proved highly gifted. The unity of Moslem thought was largely preserved by the universal use of Arabic in all religious and intellectual matters. The richness of Mohammedan culture stemmed from its genius to adopt and synthesize the contributions of the many civilizations with which it came in contact in the occident and orient. From China the Moslems learned about paper-making, while they took from medieval India the all-important numeral system which we today call Arabic. Mohammedan scholars preserved classical Greek manuscripts, and Avicenna and Averroës wrote learned commentaries on Aristotle—commentaries which were to color profoundly the thought of medieval Europe.

The Moslem caravans and ships carried on a brisk and lucrative trade with the flourishing civilizations of medieval India and China. But the Indians and Chinese had been adding to their culture long before the advent of Mohammed and his faith—in fact, they had never stopped growing since the days of Gautama Buddha and Confucius, centuries before the coming of Christ. In the third century B.C. India was fortunate enough to have one of the most enlightened and progressive monarchs in the world's history, Asoka. He advanced the arts of peace and helped establish Buddhism as a major religion. The next great period in Indian history, the Golden Age of the Guptas, took place from the fourth to the seventh centuries A.D. This was the age of Hindu supremacy, in which science, literature, and art flourished. Mathematicians wrote the most abstract equations in verse, and the numeral system was formulated, later to be adopted by the Moslems. Sculpture and painting far superior to anything then being produced in Europe came from Indian hands, while Kalidasa, the Indian Shakespeare, wrote immortal dramas. Hindu culture suffered a serious setback from the twelfth century on, when Mohammedan invaders overran the country and persecuted rival faiths. But out of this clash of opposing cultures was fused a unique pattern of living which, despite numerous modifications, was to endure with unabated vitality until the British took over control in modern times.

Civilization in medieval China likewise had periods richer than anything which contemporary Europe had to offer. Chinese culture showed for the two thousand years following Confucius a happy ability to assimilate foreign influences and impacts without losing its indigenous pattern. Governmental administration, poetry, and art during one dynasty in particular were so splendid and the country enjoyed such material prosperity that this period of Chinese history (618-906 A.D.) has since been known as the Golden Age of the T'angs. To medieval China we owe the invention of paper and printing as well as the creation of what may well be the world's finest porcelain (in the Sung dynasty). The account

The common people of the Middle Ages lived in towns huddled close to a feudal castle for protection against warring nobles and outlaws. They were born into the Church and in it they died, for this was the Age of Faith.

of Marco Polo in the thirteenth century bears eloquent witness to the richness of China's civilization at a time when medieval Europe was engulfed by petty wars and constricted by many cultural limitations.

Yet for the thousand years extending from the fifth through the fifteenth centuries, which roughly designate the Middle Ages in Europe, life was not so sterile or constricted as to prevent medieval civilization from advancing along richly creative paths. The Middle Ages were neither barren of thought nor static, as they have been so often wrongly described. Out of the chaos and confusion following the collapse of the Roman empire and the infiltration of numerous groups of barbarians, a period marked by the disintegration of governmental order and security, Europe slowly developed new patterns of living. To bring back greater political stability, the system of feudalism evolved, based on land tenure and a strict social hierarchy. Linked with feudalism was the manorial system by which Europe lived on an agrarian economy of almost self-sufficiency. The shackles of this localism were gradually loosened by the growth of towns and the quickening of trade and industry. With the rise of cities developed the future arbiters of European life, the middle class. In the towns life quickened, new ideas accompanied the influx of products from foreign lands, the townspeople became proud of their hard-won urban privileges and helped undermine the power of the conservative feudal landowners.

The most important institution of the Middle Ages was the Church. Everyone in Christendom was automatically born into the Church, and practically everyone believed implicitly in its teachings, obeyed its commands, and trusted in its power to assist the individual in winning everlasting salvation. The Church had a comprehensive administrative system extending from the Pope at Rome to the humble parish priest who knew each member of his community. As a result the

Renaissance times were as lavish, enthusiastic, and free as this painting by Breughel. Gradually the otherworldliness of medieval Europe was slipping away, and realism and individuality were taking its place.

Church was intimately connected with the daily life of the people. They celebrated its feast days, used its offices at such solemn occasions as baptism, marriage, and death, and found the Church a place of refuge, a social center, and a source of artistic activity. The most magnificent expressions of medieval art had religious motivation, whether it was the sculpturing of saints, the fashioning of stained-glass windows, the illuminating of manuscripts, or the erecting of mighty cathedrals. The Church as no other institution in the Middle Ages unified the minds and hearts of our medieval ancestors and, in an age when Europe was hopelessly split up into petty political groups, gave history a glimpse of international cooperation.

Medieval intellectual interests also stemmed mainly from a religious source. Philosophers tried to reconcile faith and reason in order to make all knowledge fit in with Church theology. Scholars translated Greek works out of Arabic into Latin so as to use the writings of Aristotle for theological purposes. The Church monopolized education in the Middle Ages, and with the passing of centuries and the quickening of cultural activities in the medieval environment, the university evolved. Science began to advance at an ever-increasing tempo during the later Middle Ages. Doctors learned to dissect and became relatively skillful at diagnosing disease. Leprosy was all but stamped out of Europe, and such public health measures as quarantines were introduced. The magnetic compass came into use, geographical knowledge increased as men traveled farther afield, and even the alchemists in their fruitless search after the Philosopher's Stone stumbled upon many important chemical discoveries.

The tempo of European culture had been "stepped up" progressively during the later

An ex-Buddhist monk established the Ming ("brilliant") dynasty in China, during which, early in the fifteenth century, the Forbidden City of Peking, rich with lacquer work, colored tiles, marble, and alabaster, was built.

Middle Ages, and in the period from 1200 to 1650, forces which had been long at work culminated in sweeping changes. In the political sphere national states evolved out of feudalism in England, France, and Spain, resulting in the establishment of a powerful centralized royal administration with a royal legal system, royal armies, and royal treasuries. In Italy, and elsewhere in Europe later, intellectual and artistic pursuits took a spectacular turn. Petrarch and other Humanists repudiated the medieval attitude of "otherworldliness" and proclaimed loudly the importance of man as an individual and a free agent. They delighted in discovering classical manuscripts and imitating the Latin style of Cicero, at the same time deriding the Latin of the medieval scholars. The chief glory of this new era in Italy, known as the Renaissance, was its art. Frescoes of splendid proportions filled the walls of churches, new edifices in a modified classical style were erected in the Italian cities, imposing equestrian statues dotted town squares, and patrons vied with one another to procure the services of famous painters. The Renaissance culminated in the achievements of such geniuses as Leonardo da Vinci, Raphael, and Michelangelo. It was an age of rich accomplishments in other countries also. The Dutch Humanist, Erasmus, revealed the superstition and ignorance prevalent in high quarters. The Spaniard Cervantes wrote his immortal *Don Quixote* to satirize the bankrupt feudal ideology still holding sway over his country. In France Montaigne wrote polished, urbane essays, while Rabelais made fun of hypocrisy with prodigious humor and earthy speech. In England Francis Bacon championed the inductive method as the best scientific procedure, and Shakespeare wrote his immortal plays.

Changes in European thought were soon apparent also in the religious field. The unity and supremacy of the medieval Church were shattered by a great Religious Revolt. In the thirteenth and fourteenth centuries the

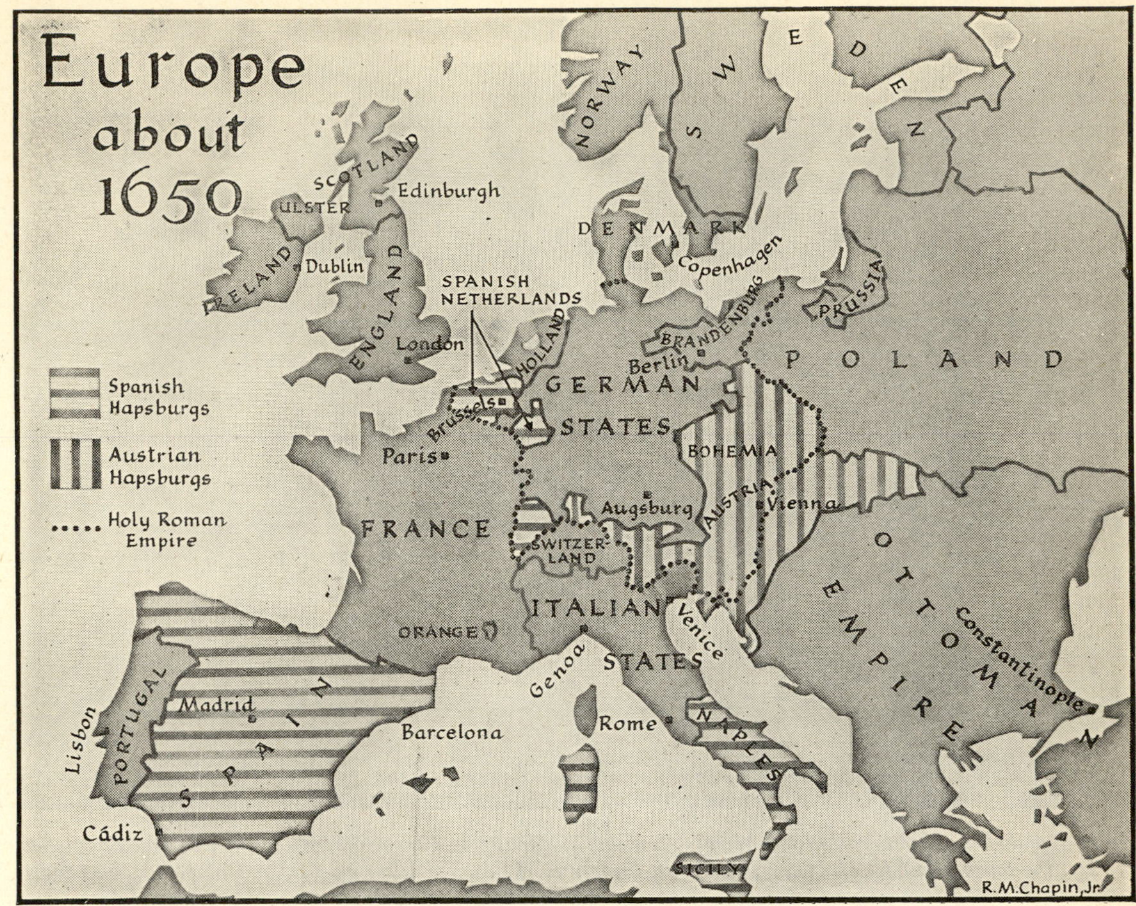

Church had suffered internally from discord among some of its leaders and externally from attacks on its temporal claims by the aggressive monarchs of France and England. But the real religious revolution broke out in 1517 when a German monk, Martin Luther, attacked important aspects of Church doctrine. Eventually Europe was split up into Protestant and Catholic factions, and in the sixteenth and seventeenth centuries the religious problem was often used to mask bitter political rivalries and ambitions.

The Renaissance was likewise the great period of exploration. One remarkable achievement was the rounding of Africa. This was followed by Vasco da Gama's voyage to India. Meanwhile Columbus had discovered America, and after 1500 the European countries had begun the great race for colonial possessions. Spanish *conquistadores* gained control of the lands of the Aztecs, Mayas, and Incas in Central and South America. England and France established rival posts in eastern Canada, while English settlers emigrated to the Atlantic seaboard. Portuguese vessels bearing hard-fighting soldiers and hard-bargaining merchants established lucrative trading ports in India and the Spice Islands, and European ships began to make their appearance in the estuaries of Chinese and Japanese rivers. The empires built up in the Western Hemisphere were colonized by European settlers, but in the east, where the native populations far outnumbered the newcomers and highly developed cultures were already in existence, the areas taken over were of commercial value only.

In this swift résumé of historical developments it has been shown how civilizations appeared first in river valleys, then around the shores of the Mediterranean. Now, by 1650, men had struck out across oceans, circumnavigated the globe, and established overseas empires. It has also become apparent that culture is a cumulative process; from primitive beginnings men increased in knowledge and with growing sureness learned to control their environment. Whole civilizations rose and fell, and their contributions often appeared to be permanently destroyed. But knowledge once won was seldom totally lost, and subsequent generations built upon the stones of the past.

Civilization and "progress" were never the monopoly of the people of the occident. In the two major cultural streams of the east and west, the one embracing India and China was fully equal in creativeness and complexity to the one in which our western culture has developed. In fact, prior to 1650 eastern civilizations were in many respects superior to their western counterparts. Whereas the west was often the victim of historical cataclysms, the east achieved a unique stability and permanency. The civilizations of India and China learned how to assimilate outside influences without being themselves destroyed. Their people acquired a long-range perspective and attained a poise which the western peoples apparently lacked. In their religious life the Indians and Chinese became highly contemplative and emphasized introspection to an unusual degree. Often this attitude degenerated into a state of existence so otherworldly as to be static. This proved a stumbling block for the east in Renaissance times when it was invaded and partially subjugated by the ill-mannered but more aggressive and alert west.

The year 1650, then, saw a world which had been circumnavigated but whose cultural interdependence was not yet global. But as we come into modern times, we can see that men were in the position for the first time in history to begin to break down the age-old barriers separating east and west and to correlate world culture.

As we reach the era of modern times, we can see by our résumé also that the most aggressive region of the world—although by no means necessarily the most civilized—was Europe. Political expansionist ambitions, commercial attempts to satisfy a growing desire at home for overseas products, scientific advances which put more powerful weapons and techniques in the hands of Europeans, and an insatiable curiosity to discover and conquer the rest of the world—all these factors help explain why the history of the world in modern times has been largely the chaotic but thrilling account of the Europeanization of the world.

PART ONE

Charting the Present

CHAPTER 1

New Ways of Life

CHAPTER 2

Science, Reason, and Enlightenment

CHAPTER 3

When in the Course of Human Events

CHARTING THE PRESENT

During the period of history known as "early modern times" the economic aspect of man's civilization came to play an increasingly important role. Commerce grew in volume and variety; industry was soon to evolve new inventions and new techniques of production and distribution. All of this brought about the triumph of the capitalistic middle class, employing new techniques in banking and finance and gradually ousting the landed aristocracy from its control of economy. There were also important changes in the political sphere. The growing middle class, and ultimately the common people, demanded greater representation in government and dethroned wherever possible those kings who refused to give in.

The development of commerce and industry enticed more and more people to cities, which became increasingly important. Modern life became in large measure an urban life with a livelier tempo. In the following chapters, then, we shall see man charting the present, making revolutionary discoveries in commerce, industry, science, philosophy, religion, education, literature, art, and politics which made possible the pattern of life which we follow today.

The era of geographical explorations brought into Europe new products from overseas and established colonial empires. At first Spain and Portugal enjoyed the richest fruits of this commercial expansion, but in time the trade centers shifted to northern Europe. Holland, France, and especially England forged to the front. The growth of commerce stimulated the rise of capitalism, as did the importation of precious metals from the New World. While capitalism had its roots deep in the past, its commercial aspects became especially strong in the seventeenth and eighteenth centuries.

The breakdown of traditional authority, the storm and stress of the Religious Revolt, and the influence of geographical discoveries also brought about a rapid advance in science. Europe embarked upon an era of scientific discovery that eclipsed anything seen in the world's history prior to that time. Modern medicine was established, astronomy threw off the shackles of obsolete ideas, dozens of indispensable scientific instruments were developed, and chemistry, physics, and geology were founded as exact sciences.

The dispassionate and analytical attitude of the new science was transferred to the realm of human relations, giving rise to an active period of stocktaking. Philosophers scrutinized social institutions in an effort to improve them. The

Deists sought to bring religion into alignment with the physical sciences. Many other thinkers made use of mathematics and the implications of natural laws to build new philosophies. Outworn and inhumane aspects of society were condemned by those who sought to broaden the educational system and introduce more humane legal codes. This searching scrutiny by European thinkers reached its greatest intensity during the eighteenth century in the Age of Reason.

During the Age of Reason, or the Enlightenment, the arts were also dominated by precision of thought and technique. Swift, Pope, and Johnson in England, Voltaire in France, Schiller and Goethe in Germany, all tended to emphasize the superiority of mind over emotions. Modern music was born. Among the illustrious composers were Johann Sebastian Bach, the great master of counterpoint, Haydn, Handel, and Mozart. Each of these men developed new musical forms. Painting and architecture were generally patterned along neo-classical lines, although some highly original artists flourished early in the period under discussion.

Social philosophers in early modern times were incensed at many aspects of prevailing political institutions. Such men as Hugo Grotius were alarmed at the unscrupulous machinations of absolute governments, bent primarily on enhancing their prestige or seizing territory. In early modern times what we now speak of as power politics was born. Government was generally despotic. European absolutism was best symbolized by the régime of Louis XIV, who governed France as he personally saw fit. But a new philosophy of government was emerging in England in which the king had to share his power with Parliament, a body composed in part of elected representatives of the people.

The English idea that government must be based upon the consent of the governed crossed the Atlantic in the eighteenth century and resulted in the independence of the American colonies in 1783. The impact of new political ideals was especially strong in France, where in 1789 an effete and corrupt monarchy fell before the onslaughts of an aroused populace.

The next three chapters survey the development of European culture during a period whose main emphasis lies approximately between the years 1650 and 1800, or 1815 in the case of politics. We shall have to go back as far as the year 1500 in some instances to lay a foundation for the rise of new institutions. However, we are primarily concerned with the changes occurring in Europe during the seventeenth and eighteenth centuries, for it was during this period that our own pattern of living took shape.

Rise of Modern Business

1500-1750	Increased trade result of exploration, Church's changed attitude, rise of national states, etc.	
	Trade shifts from Mediterranean to Atlantic	Italian cities, Hanseatic League decline
	Domestic system in industry	Industrial capitalism begins
1500-1575	Portuguese commercial prosperity	
1531	First *bourse*, exchange, in Antwerp	
16th century	Rise of banking	Fuggers and Welsers, German bankers
1550-1600	Heyday of Spanish empire, commerce	Mercantilism, policy of all colonial powers
1563	England enacts statute of apprentices	
1563-1598	Poor Laws passed in England	
1576	Spanish sack Antwerp	Trade supremacy passes to Amsterdam
1580	Spain annexes Portugal	Portuguese trade dwindles
1588	England defeats Philip II's Spanish Armada	
1589-1715	Economic development in France	Richelieu's and Colbert's reforms
1600	Commercial advances in Europe	Double-entry bookkeeping, use of checks
1600-1675	Holland foremost commercial power	Displaces declining Spain
1602	Dutch East India Company formed	J. P. Coen
1609	Bank of Amsterdam founded by local merchants	
1621	Dutch West India Company formed	
1650	Cromwell has Navigation Acts passed	
1652-1672	Commercial wars, England vs. Holland	
1666	Great Fire in London	Fire insurance companies formed
1668	Marine insurance	Lloyd's of London
1672	Hudson's Bay Company formed	
1684	First mutual insurance company	Friendly Society in England
1685	Revocation of Edict of Nantes	Causes flight of industrious French Huguenots
1690	England founds trading post at Calcutta	Nucleus of Indian empire
1694	Parliament establishes Bank of England	
1698	First modern stock exchange in London	
1700-1750	Agricultural reforms in England	Crop rotation, scientific breeding
1713	England gains *asiento* from Spain	Monopoly of slave trade
1720	Wild-cat speculation in England and France	South Sea and Mississippi Bubbles

CHAPTER 1

New Ways of Life

THE economic history of modern times can be roughly separated into two periods. The age from 1500 to about 1750 was characterized by changes and developments in commerce, while the age from about 1750 to the present has witnessed striking changes in industry. Therefore we can call the first age the commercial era, and the second the industrial era. It is with the first era only that we shall concern ourselves at present.

The commercial era was accompanied by three "revolutions," each of which had a distinct effect upon it. These were the political revolution, which saw the breakdown of feudalism and the medieval Church and the substitution of national states and churches; the intellectual and moral revolution, as witnessed in the Renaissance and Religious Revolt and later in the development of science and rationalism; and the geographical revolution, which opened up the world to seemingly unlimited European expansion, and in turn modified the economic and social life of Europe itself. The cumulative effect of these three revolutions gave to the commercial era its distinctive characteristics.

A discussion of the commercial era is not limited to the exchange of goods between men or nations and the growth of trade and trade practices. It is true that commerce (in this narrow definition of the term) will be discussed, as will such related subjects as mercantilism and the rise of commercial companies and monopolies. But there are other topics which will have to be investigated. One is the development of capitalism and the growth of such capitalistic phenomena as banking, stock exchanges, insurance, and accounting, as well as financial crises and "bubbles" which affected capitalism's development. Changes in industry and agriculture must also be noted, as well as changes in the relative strength of the aristocracy, the middle class, and the common people. Lastly, these economic developments all shared in modifying the customs, manners, and spirit of the people who lived in these early modern times, as will be seen.

The Growth of Commerce

Effects of the political revolution. The political revolution—the emergence of national states operated by a powerful centralized authority which could subjugate the feudal nobility and medieval Church—had far-reaching effects on commercial development. The tendency from now on was to introduce uniform taxes, laws, currencies, weights and measures, and to build roads and bridges to suit the needs of a nation, not just those of a parish or fief. Trade was thus made easier, while the administration of justice made the lot of the trader more safe and dependable.

The ambition of rulers, the desire for glory and territorial expansion, the quarrel over New World lands, and religious conflicts all combined to make war "almost a normal relationship among national states." But these wars cost great sums of money, because many men were used, armaments were more expensive, and campaigns were not short, as the usual feudal wars had been. Furthermore, kings had to rely not on the old feudal levies but often upon hired troops who sold their services to the highest bidder. The powers along the Atlantic seaboard had to build fleets to protect their sea-lanes and inflict damage on one another's commerce. Ways and means had to be found to meet these new expenses. The kings tried various means, such as depreciating the currency, selling titles to *nouveau riche* commoners, levying new direct and indirect taxes, and despoiling the Roman Catholic Church of its valuable property. When these sources of wealth proved insufficient to pay for foreign wars and extravagant court life, the rulers had to borrow from wealthy merchants. Thus arose the great loan markets of Europe, controlled by a new merchant-banker group which lent money to the monarchs but exacted trade monopolies and other privileges in return. The kings found themselves forced to protect and advance the interests of a rising middle class which was furthering its control over commerce and finance. This was not so true in France, where royal sponsorship of commercial interests was only spasmodic, but it was particularly the case in England and Holland, where the middle class secured so many privileges that it exercised a powerful influence in governmental affairs.

Effects of the intellectual revolution. The intellectual and moral revolution had definite economic effects. The invention of printing during the Renaissance resulted in an ever-growing trade in books and stimulated activity in all other fields. The Renaissance also whetted the desire for luxuries among the rich so that there arose a large demand for new furniture, art objects, and costly wearing apparel and foodstuffs imported from the orient or the New World.

The Religious Revolt had economic repercussions, especially in northern Europe. Henry VIII dissolved the English monasteries in 1534 and 1539 and gave the lands and buildings to favored nobles. Similar restrictions took place in northern Germany and Scandinavia, while large annual sums paid formerly to the Pope were no longer sent by the Protestant nations. The Protestant doctrine of individualism at the same time was an important source of encouragement to the rising middle class. The medieval Church had frowned on the practice of usury. (While in modern times the word "usury" connotes the lending of money at exorbitant rates of interest, in the Middle Ages the word meant simply the lending of money at any rate of interest.) Now, although Luther condemned it because it resulted in the exploitation of the poor, other reformers like Calvin praised the use of money interest "as a just reward for the service rendered by a loan." Similarly, whereas the medieval Church had maintained that man's finest efforts should be directed toward otherworldly ends, the reformers praised the virtues of industry and thrift. Calvin even made it righteous to accumulate money, so that poverty was no longer the mark of the saint but of the sinner. Justification of the practices of the rising capitalist class led to an early alliance between Calvinism and capitalism. This led G. K. Chesterton to make the clever (if not exact) epigram that the Religious Revolt was "the revolution of the rich against the poor."

Effects of exploration. The geographical revolution was inevitably to affect the economic life of Europe. We should not exaggerate the importance of this revolution because, despite the discovery of new lands and sea routes, trade remained predominantly European. Furthermore, commerce and industry would have developed in the sixteenth and seventeenth centuries even if there had been no geographical discoveries. Nevertheless, the discovery of the sea route to the east by Vasco da Gama had a sweeping effect. It allowed a greater volume of goods to be carried at a smaller cost. During the fifteenth and sixteenth centuries the efficiency, reliability, and carrying capacity of ships were increased. Maritime trade was cheaper than land trade because, although the sea-lanes might be infested with pirates and enemies, they were not infested with customs barriers. One continuous sea journey supplanted the countless handlings and loadings that accompanied land caravans from the orient to Europe. At once the volume of trade increased enormously—perhaps the most striking feature of the commercial era. Whereas in the past Europe had carried on a limited trade with the orient in spices and such luxury goods as silks, aromatic woods, tapestries, and precious stones, now these products were imported in large quantities.

The spice trade was especially profitable because there was no refrigeration for foods at this time, and slightly spoiled food could be made edible by cooking it with cloves, cinnamon, or pepper. Portugal and later Holland controlled the spice trade, and through monopolies managed until the eighteenth century to maintain high prices. Cloths from the orient became popular. Calicoes, chintzes, and ginghams began to be used to cover the chairs, cushions, and beds of prosperous Europeans. New, inexpensive textiles "tended to promote the habit of wearing underclothing and carrying handkerchiefs," with consequent improvement to health. So incensed did the textile workers of England become at the invasion of their industry by the orient that eventually they demanded a prohibition on the import of such fabrics, maintaining that they were "tawdry, pie-spotted, flabby, ragged, low priced, made by a parcel of heathens and pagans that worship the Devil and work for ½d. a day."[1] Among other imports from Asia were carpets, rugs, porcelain, brassware, and the all-important beverages, coffee and tea.

From Africa came gold and ivory. Guinea, Abyssinia, and Madagascar provided gold. The most lucrative—and notorious—branch of African trade dealt in human misery. Slavers sailed to the Guinea coast, where they bought or stole their human freight. "A woman slave might change hands for a gallon of brandy, six beads; a man slave might cost eight guns, one wicker-covered bottle, two cases of spirits, and twenty-eight sheets."[2] The voyage across the Atlantic to America cost the lives of ten to twenty-five per cent of the misery-stricken Africans, but the rest were profitably disposed of. One authority estimates that in three centuries some 20,000,000 Negroes were brought to the American labor market, and the Spanish king made the delivery of slaves to Spanish America a monopoly, known as the *asiento,* which he granted to a given group of traders from time to time. The respectability which this business enjoyed during the age comes as a shock to us today and at the same time gives us an insight into the callousness of society in early modern times.

The opening up of the New World brought a flood of native products back to Europe. Five of these products, especially, modified European tastes enormously: cocoa, cotton, potatoes, tobacco, and to a lesser extent, corn. Cocoa, which was the sacred beverage of the Aztecs, soon found its way to Spain and thence throughout Europe during the seventeenth century. This drink, along with coffee and tea, reduced the consumption of beer and wine. Cotton, which came somewhat later, made cheap, easily washed clothes available to all, while the food supply of Europe was greatly increased by the addition of potatoes. Tobacco affected British commerce considerably during the seventeenth century. Colonists in Virginia had a profitable commodity to sell in England; British shipping was stimulated and the national revenue increased.

The New World gave Europe other commodities of importance. A more abundant supply of fish came from New England and the Grand Bank of Newfoundland, greatly in-

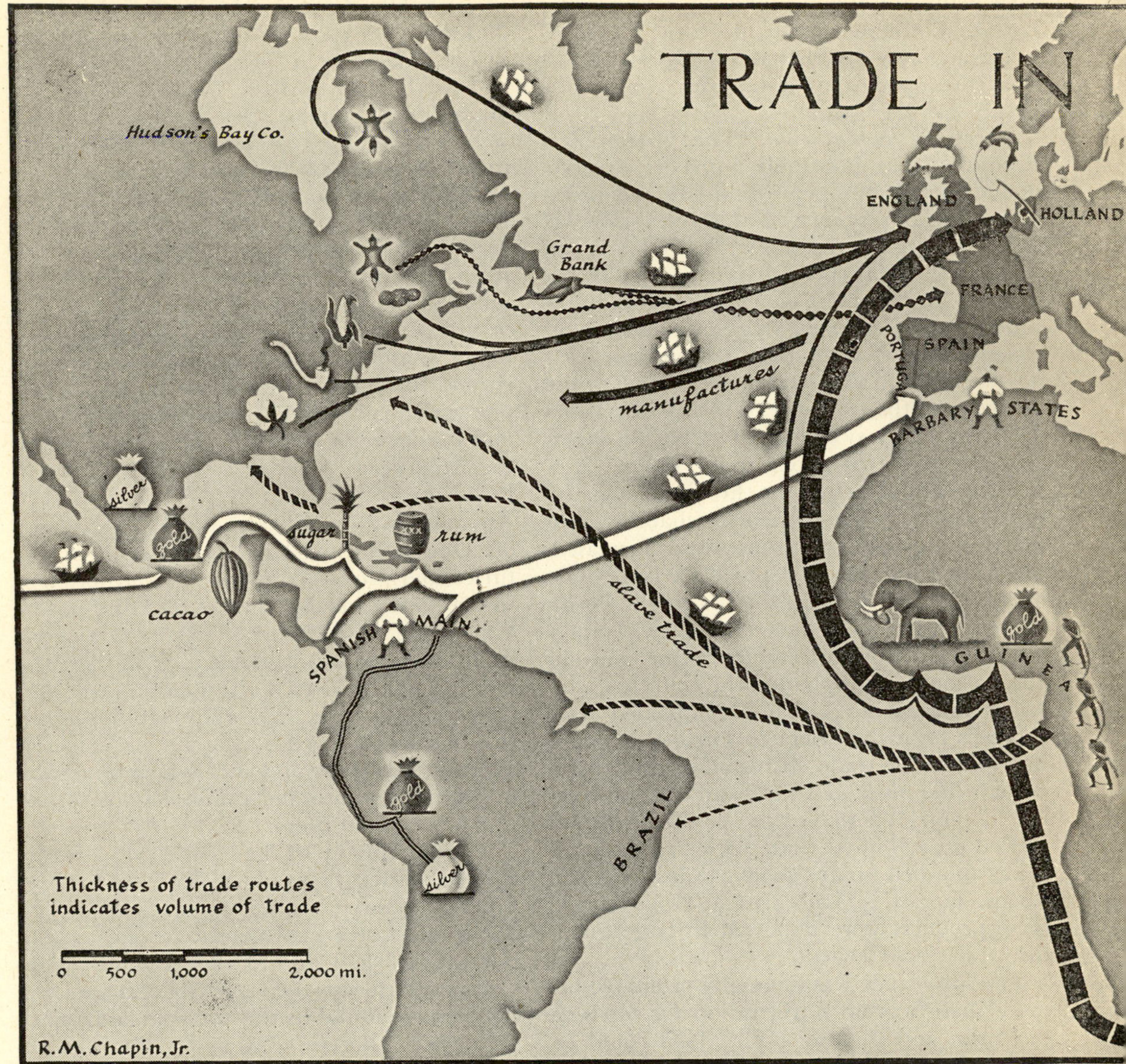

The lad who went to sea in early modern times was heir to the accumulated knowledge of those romantic explorers who searched for the Seven Cities of Cibola and the mythical kingdom of Prester John. For the sailor of 1700 life was made easier by improvements in navigation, the charting of seas, and the knowledge that good hard gold and silver or precious silks and spices rather than legends and will-o-the-wisps lay in far-off ports. Yet as far north as Iceland roamed the Barbary pirates, plundering merchant vessels and ravaging the coasts in search of slaves and booty. While governments bought immunity for their own shipping, the pirates played one nation against another. In the Carribbean the buccaneers visited destruction on Spanish shipping and colonies in the islands and on the Spanish Main. Everywhere commercial rivalries between nations flared out in the roar of cannon, and merchant vessels traveled in fleets like modern wartime convoys.

The blessings of free trade were unknown; Adam Smith and Cordell Hull were yet unborn. Each country monopolized the trade of a particular far-off region, at the same time trying to edge in on its neighbor. The spice trade was handled by the Dutch, the gold and silver supply from the New World was a Spanish monopoly, the slave trade to the Spanish colonies was owned by the Spanish government and farmed out to whatever group of traders was in favor at the time. Inevitably there was much smuggling, piracy, and bloodshed.

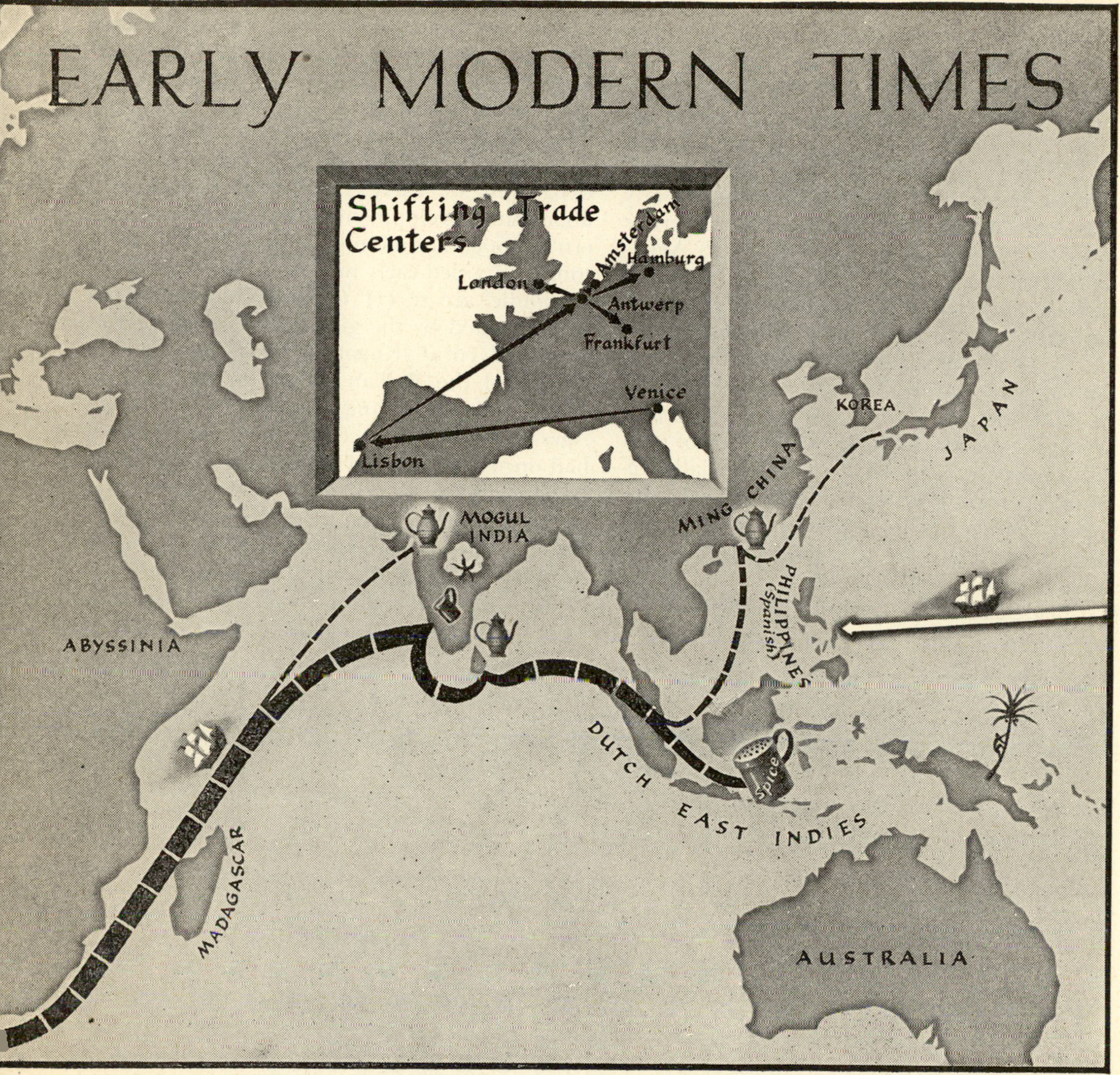

Another phase of monopoly was the granting of exclusive trading privileges to a single company. The Dutch, French, and British East India companies each had a monopoly in its own country on trade in the East Indies; no merchant outside the membership could trade there. It was the same in other parts of the world. The Muscovy Company had exclusive right to exploit Russia for the English. The rivalries of commercial companies had important political overtones and were reflected in national political rivalries. Inordinate wealth and power was achieved by the successful companies. It was the custom, in England at least, to give trading companies extensive governmental powers. In Canada the Hudson's Bay Company for two hundred years governed a territory four or five times the size of the English and French Canadian colonies. Selfish and irresponsible government was the result. This was especially true in British India.

By 1700 trade, primarily ocean-borne, had become worldwide. Contrast this with trade in medieval times (Volume One, pages 328-329), when slow and costly pack-caravans traveled interminably over ancient routes and only the hardy Italians in the Atlantic and the fearless Arab traders in the Indian Ocean braved the dangers, real and fabulous, of sea-borne trade. The products featured in international trade were in the main consumers' goods—spices, foods, cloths and hides, and gold and silver to spend at home—having great value in small bulk.

creasing the volume of food and variety of diet. Valuable furs were to be obtained by trappers willing to penetrate the interior of the North American continent. From the West Indies came dyes and hard woods such as mahogany. Sugar was grown in the West Indies and soon became so popular in Europe that it supplanted honey, which had been universally used down to the seventeenth century. Shrubs and flowers were imported from North America and Africa to add loveliness to European gardens, while tropical fruits from Central and South America were introduced into southern Europe. Probably the most important commodity which flowed from the New World to the Old was the supply of precious metals. Between 1521 and 1660 some 200 tons of gold and 18,000 tons of silver were officially recorded in their journey from the Americas to Spain. "Much of this new supply of gold and silver was minted by the Spaniards, or their subjects in the Netherlands; it was they who first made the dollar famous along with doubloons and pieces of eight."[3] The influx of these new amounts of gold and silver into Europe upset the old price level, affected wages, created more currency, aided in the creation of a new banking and credit system, and played a part in the growth of capitalism.

Europe's economic areas. The commercial expansion of early modern times brought about the development of the principal modern European economic powers. Herbert Heaton has divided early modern Europe into four economic areas: (1) Certain countries were little affected by the growth of commerce and remained rural—Russia, Prussia, Austria, Poland, and the Balkan states; (2) two regions with lucrative trading powers in the Middle Ages were outstripped by areas which they had once served—the Hanseatic towns and the Italian city-states; (3) two countries were first in the new commercial field and built up large empires only to lose them to more aggressive neighbors—Portugal and Spain; (4) three nations in particular after 1600 took the ascend-

A French encyclopedia printed this detailed drawing of a Newfoundland station for curing and drying codfish. Observe the three-masted vessel and the hooded fisherman in the foreground.

ancy in commercial enterprise and carved out powerful colonial empires—Holland, France, and England.[4]

Decline of the Hanseatic League. During the Middle Ages the wealthy trading confederacy of towns in the Baltic area known as the Hanseatic League had acted as the distributor for all northern Europe. After the fifteenth century, however, the League's power had declined, due to rivalry from the merchants of such countries as England, Holland, and Scandinavia. The shift in oriental trade from Venice to Lisbon deprived the German towns of rich commerce which had previously flowed northward over the Alps from Italy. A shift in the spawning ground of the herring from the Baltic to the North seas and the development of the new locality by Dutch fishermen broke the old monopoly held by the League. Another factor contributing to the fall of the League was the Thirty Years' War (1618-1648), which devastated Germany both socially and economically. An effort to revive the Hanseatic League at its last general assembly (1669) was a failure. Another factor was the absence of protection by a strong central government in Germany, while in other countries traders were being given increasing protection and political conditions were becoming stabilized.

Italian trading cities. Italian cities had grown wealthy through Mediterranean commerce. Venice had fallen heir to the commercial empire of Byzantium and had entered into numerous trade treaties, with centers in the Black Sea, Syria, Egypt, and the Balkans. The crusades had been a stimulus to Italian commercial expansion, and the Fourth Crusade, which pillaged Constantinople in 1204, made Venice the chief trading center in Europe. Genoa in the thirteenth century arose to challenge Venetian supremacy in the Near East and the Black Sea. The fourteenth century was marked by bitter struggles between the two rivals, Venice finally winning out, while the following century witnessed conflicts between Venice and other powers, including the Turks. The Venetians continued to act as the great middlemen of Europe because they still controlled the lucrative Asiatic trade.

The new sea route to India was the major cause of the downfall of Italian trade. Ships from Portugal began to sail directly to the east around the Cape of Good Hope, while the Portuguese now obstructed the passage of goods by way of the Red Sea and the Persian Gulf. Soon the trade over the mountain passes to Germany dwindled, the last Venetian galleys sailed to Flanders in 1532, and the Turks allowed French, Dutch, and English shipping in their ports. Deprived of their main source of wealth, the Italians turned from an economy geared to commerce and concentrated on their luxury industries. The Italians maintained their supremacy longest in international finance. This will be taken up at length later when we consider the fortunes of the Medici and other Italian banking families whose business dealings extended throughout western Europe until the seventeenth century.

But on the whole, the economic decline of the Italian cities was far advanced. Their commerce had been diverted to seaboard powers on the Atlantic, their luxury industries were rivaled by those in France and Holland, and the wealth accumulated through banking operations benefited only a few privileged families. Unable and unwilling to achieve national unification, the Italian city-states had little chance of holding their own in European power politics, and by the sixteenth century Italy had become a battleground for rival European powers. These invasions had a disastrous effect upon the prosperity of the city-states. Furthermore, Italian armies and navies no longer proved a match for the strength of the new national states, and they lost out in the struggle for overseas possessions and commerce.

Portugal. Initiative and daring had enabled Portugal to carve out a great commercial empire in the Far East. The early success of this undertaking was largely due to the tireless efforts and administrative genius of Alfonso de Albuquerque, most famous of Portuguese governors. Soon Portugal had settlements fringing the coasts of Africa and Asia, and along the coast of Brazil. But the country had a diminishing population to administer an empire spread over three continents. "Of the thousands who went out, not one in ten returned; the rest perished, or deserted, or disappeared on strange adventures. Plague and famine also did their work, and, added to this curse of excessive emigration, reduced the population, during the sixteenth century, from two millions to hardly more than one."[5] The

Portuguese had all they could do to transport cargoes back to Lisbon and had to leave to others the profitable business of distributing the goods through northern Europe. Antwerp was now the central port of distribution, and foreign ships (principally Dutch) were often in possession of the cargoes by the time Antwerp was reached. After Spain annexed Portugal in 1580, the Dutch and English regarded Portuguese possessions in the Far East as lawful prizes to be won from their Spanish enemies. When Portugal regained its independence in the seventeenth century, it possessed only Goa, Macao, and a few other small possessions in the Far East, together with some trading posts on the African coasts, its islands in the mid-Atlantic, and Brazil—which belonged to Portugal until 1822. The economic power of Portugal ebbed away, not primarily because of any lack of initiative, but because the task was too great to be borne by a nation so limited in resources and industries.

Spain's apparent power. The decline of Spain's commercial might cannot be so simply explained. This nation had everything—and failed. The conquistadors had won the New World with all its riches and endless potentialities, so that during the sixteenth century more gold and silver was brought into Spain than had been accumulated anywhere else up to that time. Thanks to these discoveries and a series of fortunate marriages in the royal family, Spain was at the zenith of her material greatness when Philip II (1556-1598) came to the throne.

The economic decay of Spain. Spain's economy crumbled in the sixteenth century, when this nation, the most powerful in all Europe and possessing a great army, navy, and overseas empire, appeared on the surface to be immeasurably rich in gold and resources. What caused Spain's rapid economic decline in the face of so much apparent prosperity? One reason was the neglect of farming and the overemphasis placed upon sheep herding. The crown had given the sheepowners many privileges. In summer sheep were sent to the valleys in the northwest to graze, and in winter were driven south to graze on the plains. The sheepowners were permitted to drive through the lands of the farmers, thus injuring crops. Meanwhile, the prices for grain made the labor of the farmer relatively unprofitable. The government burdened the industrial guilds with so many regulations that more harm than good resulted. The expulsion of the Jews and Moors undoubtedly had a detrimental economic effect. For centuries these people had been the financiers and craftsmen of Spain, and their going seriously crippled commerce and industry.

Other factors were contributing to Spain's impoverishment. One was the costly and fruitless foreign wars which the Spanish Hapsburg kings waged with the French, Dutch, and English. So severe was the strain of these conflicts and the recklessness with which they were waged that they helped exhaust the income from America and eventually forced the government to increase domestic taxes, raise large loans (and default on their payment), and even debase the currency after 1598. The ensuing periods of sharp inflation and deflation that occurred in the seventeenth century were among the most important causes of Spain's economic decline. The taxes which the Hapsburgs imposed on the country realized but small returns. This was due to the general corruption of the tax collectors, the confused state of the nation's economy, and the poverty of the common people. By the time Philip II died in 1598, the Spanish royal debt amounted to some $160,000,000. The financial system was hampered by the fact that the upper classes were exempt from certain forms of taxation, as was the Church, so that a disproportionate share of the tax burden fell on the shoulders of industry.

We now come to a most interesting paradox—the poverty of sixteenth-century Spain despite the large influx of precious metals from the New World. On the surface, the import of precious metals made Spain the envy of all Europe and gave men the false idea that the more gold a nation possessed the richer she was. In reality the nation was in a serious economic plight. Mining in the New World was carried on by private interests, and the state gained only a *quint*, or tax of twenty per cent (and sometimes only ten per cent). The influx of precious metals brought about a rise in the general level of prices. Spanish prices in 1601 were between three and four times as high as in 1501. This price revolution wreaked havoc in many ways. It caused suffering among the workers, whose wages lagged behind prices. Those citizens whose income was fixed also suffered in purchasing power, as their incomes could no longer purchase the same amount of commodities. The rise in prices was higher in Spain than anywhere else in Europe, and this condition made it natural for manufactured products to stream in from Holland, France, and England, to the advantage of those countries but to the detriment of Spanish manufacturers. Spain not only lost out in manufacturing; she lost the gold and silver also in having to give them to foreign merchants in exchange for commodities, many of which she could, and should, have been making herself.

In the decades after 1600, Spanish industry and commerce diminished steadily, and her population likewise decreased. But the influence of Spain on the world was by no means concluded with her economic decline. There will be frequent occasions to notice how she made her idiom the idiom of a large part of the New World, and how her customs and manners have endured in the lives of millions of people throughout the Old and New Worlds even to this day.

The shift in European trade centers. To this point we have seen an important shift in the trade axis of Europe. Commerce was diverted from the Mediterranean to the Atlantic, from the Italian cities to Portugal and Spain. The shift had repercussions in Germany, for the drying up of trans-Alpine trade helped bring about a decline of the Hanseatic League. Now a second shift of trade had also been in progress, from southern to northern Europe, centering in the sixteenth century in Antwerp. The most important center in northwestern Europe prior to this time had been Bruges, but its trade restrictions and the silting up of its harbor had diverted trade to Antwerp. To this city came the Fuggers and the Welsers, because these German bankers realized that the commercial axis had shifted from the Mediterranean and central Europe to the Atlantic seaboard (as did the Venetian bankers who also flocked to Antwerp). English, French, Scandinavian, and Dutch merchants, moneylenders, and manufacturers made Antwerp the commercial capital of Europe. The city authorities facilitated matters by creating a toll-free port and a perpetual fair. "Soon it was said that Antwerp did as much business in one month as Venice in two years. In the town there were about a thousand business houses, while every week fifty vessels sailed into port, not to speak of eight or nine hundred fishing-boats. Customs duties brought in 726,000 florins a year."[6]

Many institutions of modern capitalism were developed here. The first stock exchange, or "bourse," was established in 1531. Life insurance and insurance on ships and cargoes came into extended use. Foreign exchange, speculation, and attempts to corner the market were used daily. But the spectacular prosperity of Antwerp was almost as short lived as the fortunes of some of its speculating inhabitants, for during the wars of the Netherlands against Spain it was sacked in 1576. From this time on, Antwerp's trade was largely appropriated by such rising centers as Amsterdam, London, Hamburg, and Frankfurt (see map inset page 9).

Holland's herrings. The Dutch at this period had acquired a reputation for industry. To quote a Venetian ambassador, "These people are so inclined to industry and toil that there is no task so difficult that they will not undertake to finish it. . . . They were born to toil and to deny themselves, and all do work in one way or another."[7] Hanseatic control over the herring industry was broken by the shift of the spawning-ground and by the inroads of Dutch fishermen who used improved boats which could carry up to fifteen men and enabled the catch to be salted on board. The results were far-reaching for Holland's prosperity, and by 1610 some 2000 boats were sweeping the North Sea and pushing up into the Baltic. Thus arose the expression that Amsterdam was "built on herringbones."

Dutch trade and industry. Dutch commerce now extended to Scandinavia in one direction and to the Mediterranean and Iberian ports in the other. After war broke out between Spain and the seven northern provinces, later known as Holland, the Dutch ships were excluded in 1580 from Lisbon and Cadiz. Cut off from trade with the Portuguese Spice Islands by this action, the Dutch decided to invade Spain's private preserve by sending fleets along the sea routes around the Cape of Good Hope. At the same time the Dutch attempted to find a northwest and northeast passage to Asia. Henry Hudson's voyage in 1609 was one such attempt.

In 1602 there was formed the famous and profitable Dutch East India Company, which possessed a monopoly on Holland's Asiatic trade, the backing of its government, and powers to maintain an army and navy and to found colonies. The driving force behind the com-

In the opulent warmth of a Dutch kitchen geese are plucked and a child watches the roasting meat and fowl in the fireplace. A Bible picture in the background illustrates the story of Mary and Martha.

pany's successful career was J. P. Coen, who entered its service in 1607 and served until his death in 1630. Thanks to him, the Dutch founded Batavia and began the policy which by the middle of the seventeenth century had made the East Indies Dutch. In 1621 the West India Company was founded to exploit the Americas. The company also captured some islands off the Spanish Main and founded Dutch Guiana in South America.

By 1650 Holland was the principal commercial, financial, and manufacturing country in Europe. This was due partially to the supremacy of Dutch shipping. Hollanders built their ships better and operated them more efficiently than their rivals, and the savings enabled them to offer lower freight rates. Dutch industry flourished. To Amsterdam came the diamond-cutting industry. Other specialized industries included the grinding of lenses (a task which the philosopher Spinoza performed), the making of pendulum clocks, and the designing of instruments for navigation. Delftware pottery, famous for its white glaze and blue painting, made Dutch pottery popular, while printing brought both profits and learning to Holland.

Dutch engineers showed great skill in reclaiming large areas of their country which lay below water. Their reclamation projects stimulated Dutch agriculture. The most famous crop was tulips, which became the center of a wild speculation which crashed in 1637, bringing disaster and misery to thousands of people in all walks of Dutch society. The prosperity of the country as a whole, derived from commercial, industrial, agricultural, and financial pursuits, is reflected in the paintings of the Dutch masters (see pages 70 and 71). Holland, unlike Portugal and Spain, had built up a sturdy middle class which gloried in its industry and thrift and whose art reflects its love of herring boats, butcher shops, windmills, and barrels of beer.

Holland's limitations. Nevertheless, Holland, like Portugal, was a comparatively small nation. and it was probably inevitable that larger neighbors should one day overtake it. Rivalry between England and Holland resulted in three wars in the latter half of the seventeenth century (1652-1654, 1665-1667, and 1672-1674). These conflicts were mainly fought on the sea and somewhat weakened Dutch sea power and commerce. Because the country managed to remain more or less neutral during the great conflicts between France and England from 1688 to 1815, Holland was not too badly hit. But the Dutch declaration of war against England in 1780 proved a blow. England captured much shipping, while Holland's powerful East India Company and Bank of Amsterdam crashed. Yet Dutch skill, together with its retention of the East Indies, enabled Holland in the nineteenth century to become once again a significant partner in world commerce.

France attains leadership. When Spain lost its predominance in European affairs, France took over authority. The age which we are studying marked the wise rule of Henry IV, the ambitious policies of Richelieu and Mazarin, the dazzling splendor of the reign of Louis XIV, and the eighteenth-century conflict with England. France had a population of some 15,000,000 in the seventeenth century and possessed rich agriculture and large industrial and commercial resources, yet she lost out in the race against her arch-enemy, England. Perhaps the chief cause of this loss was the unhealthy political condition of the kingdom from about 1450, when the French succeeded in expelling the English from French soil, to the time they staged a successful revolution against themselves in 1789. The economic resources of an industrious people were squandered by the ambitious political policies of an absolute government. It has been estimated that between 1685 and 1715 France lost a million subjects, due to almost unbroken conflict, the loss of valuable colonial territories, and the drain of emigration. Meanwhile the reverses created by the disastrous Seven Years' War (1756-1763) reduced foreign trade by one half.

Henry IV (1589-1610), perceiving the relationship between commercial prosperity and good transportation, had rivers linked by canals and excessive tolls eliminated. Sully, the economic minister of Henry IV, built and improved roads. Overseas commerce was not so integral a part of French economic life as in Holland and England, for most French trade was with her neighbors—Italy, England, Spain, and the Baltic states. It was not that France made no attempt to stimulate colonial trade, for Henry IV, Richelieu, and Louis XIV's minister Colbert were interested in the settlement of colonies in Canada and in the rich sugar-producing islands of the Caribbean. The following statements of Colbert indicate at once his plans and economic philosophy: "It is necessary to reduce all the activities of your (Majesty's) subjects, as soon as possible, to those which are useful for (our) great plans. These are agriculture, industry, land commerce and sea commerce. Reduce all (your) subjects to these four, and (you) can become master of the world."[8] To stimulate trade, Colbert, "the work-ox of Louis XIV," established the East India and West India companies in 1664, the Levant Company in 1670 (to trade with the Near East), and the Senegal Company in 1673 (for African commerce). Unfortunately for France, the English and Dutch were too firmly established in all these places, and the Seven Years' War ruined France's empire and the trade that went with it. However, France's main commerce had been with European neighbors and the Near East, and its total foreign trade increased some 500 per cent between 1716 and 1787, or from $43,000,000 to $230,000,000.[9]

Loss of supremacy. Yet France did not attain the high economic levels of which it was capable, and this was due not only to the policies which hindered its commerce but also to the handicaps imposed upon its industry. Many industries were subsidized and nurtured by the government, such as textiles, porcelains, and tapestries, but the numerous decrees laid down by the government proved more of a handicap than an aid. Furthermore, the brilliant court life placed an emphasis among the French upon the creation of luxury commodities for the benefit of the upper classes, while the Dutch and English supplied the common people and so won a huge and profitable market. Lastly, the destruction of the great Protestant middle-class craftsmen, the Huguenots, proved a hard blow to French economic life, for the Huguenots were outstanding in banking, shipping, industry, and trade and had always constituted a hard-working, loyal class of citizens. When the Edict of Nantes was revoked in 1685, the fleeing Huguenots took their capital and skill to neighboring Protestant countries. Their flight proved a hard blow to France's economic life, just as the expulsion of the industrious Jews and Moors from Spain had crippled that nation's economy.[10]

The rise of England's sun. England was inferior to France in area, fertility of soil, and population. On the other hand the English had in their favor factors which more than compensated for these disadvantages. In 1500 the Tudors were on the throne, a dynasty favoring the rising middle class and opposed to the old feudal régime. No invasion or serious military disaster shook the kingdom or ruined its commercial structure. The country was united in a way that the provinces of France were not, and, after the union of England and Scotland in 1707, domestic trade flourished in the "largest customs-free area in western Europe." London was at once the political and economic capital of the kingdom and served to keep politics and trade united. The aristocracy and middle class which controlled Parliament controlled the principal trading and banking companies, with the result that the progress of new enterprises was more complete and peaceful than anywhere else in Europe. Finally, the gradual control of the seas, made possible by the defeat of the Spanish Armada in 1588 but not fully realized until the end of the seventeenth century, together with a judicious policy of taking possession of overseas territory as its share of booty won in successful European wars, enabled England to build the world's largest empire and to gain its commercial benefits.

English commercial expansion. England in the fifteenth century was an insignificant commercial nation. What foreign trade she had was in the hands of foreigners. The next century, however, saw an increase of native commerce. Certain developments on the continent made the lot of the English trader much more advantageous. The decline of the Hanseatic

To prevent rutting the muddy roads, George II *ruled that the wheels of mail coaches must be at least nine inches wide. For non-compliance the coachman was made to forfeit a horse.*

League opened up the markets in northern Europe. The attempt to find a northeast passage resulted in trade relations with Russia. Changes in politics among the Italian cities gave England new markets in Pisa, Florence, Venice, and Genoa. In 1579 England obtained permission to trade directly with the Turkish empire, thus increasing its Near East commerce. Friendly intercourse with Portugal gave English merchants an access to oriental goods.

During the seventeenth century, English merchants pushed into the rich trading areas of India and established posts (Madras, 1639, and Calcutta, 1690) from which they could later move to conquer the country. Trading stations were also established on the Guinea coast of Africa, and a profitable trade in slaves progressed, culminating in 1713 when England gained the coveted *asiento*. After 1763, when Canada was conquered and the way was opened for the conquest of India, England's commerce reigned supreme in every ocean.

English commercial expansion was due in large measure to the changes in the nature of trade and the commercial legislation that went with them. Up to the fifteenth century the export trade had been mostly in raw materials such as tin, wool, and cereals. But from 1500 to 1750 a large increase occurred in home industries, so that finished woolen cloth became the chief export. To keep this profitable manufacturing at home the government forbade the export of raw wool, particularly to Flanders, and during the reign of George III sheep-shearing was forbidden within a radius of five miles from the coast to restrict smuggling. Although public taste demanded the colorful Indian cottons which the East India Company was importing, the government put a ban on the import of these goods, at the demand of a coalition of sheep farmers and cloth manufacturers.

England's industries. Mining and metallurgy increased strikingly during this period. The output of coal in 1550 was only 200,000 tons but in 1700 it had jumped to nearly 3,000,000. The manufacturing of iron, steel, brass, and copper articles increased also. The cutlery industry was already well established, while Birmingham by 1750 was specializing in hardware of all varieties. Commerce was bound to flourish when England's ever-increasing manufactures were finding a ready market on the continent and in the colonies. England during this period was still predominantly agricultural, and during the seventeenth century cultivation expanded and the government passed laws — the Corn Laws ("corn" in England applies to wheat and other grains)—designed to encourage exports and maintain prices to protect the grain grower. But after the middle of the eighteenth century there was a succession of poor harvests, and as the population was increasing, exports became negligible, while imports increased. Commerce in agricultural commodities had swung the other way, and England was no longer self-sufficient in her food supply.

England's merchant marine. The growth of England's merchant marine was phenomenal. Down to about 1450 English foreign trade was almost entirely in the hands of foreign shippers. But during the period under discussion individual merchants, companies, and even town governments took pride in building fleets of vessels. The government gave strong encouragement to shipbuilding. As early as 1485 a law was enacted that wines from France must be imported in English vessels, manned for the most part by Englishmen. Elizabeth continued this policy, while in 1651 Cromwell had the famous Navigation Act passed, a statute reënacted by later governments. By the Navigation Act all goods imported into England from Africa, America, or Asia must come in vessels belonging to English owners, built in England, and manned by English sailors, while all goods exported from England to these localities had to observe the same rules. The authorities also aided the merchant navy by making harbors deeper and wider, building lighthouses on dangerous promontories, and improving marine charts. The government sponsored settlements abroad which would furnish outlets for English goods. Thus took place the "plantation of Ulster," when English and Scottish settlers were "planted" in the north of Ireland between 1610 and 1620, the settlement of the east coast of North America and the development of the thirteen colonies, the emigration from England to the rich islands of the British West Indies, and the later colonizing of Canada.

English commercial supremacy. The predominance of exports over imports during this period gave England a large favorable balance of trade. By 1750 England had already outstripped all European rivals in commerce and had laid the foundations of its economic domination of the world in the nineteenth century. While the increase of English foreign trade from 1500 to 1750 was considerable, we shall find that it was relatively small compared with the increase that came after 1750 when the Industrial Era brought England undisputed supremacy in commerce and industry. Thus in 1600 England's exports had a total value of about $10,000,000, in 1700 they were worth about $32,000,000, and in 1750 they rose to about $63,000,000. But in 1802 England's exports had jumped to the commanding figure of $207,000,000, while the imports were valued at about $157,000,000.[11]

Commercial companies. The preceding sketch of the commercial growth of leading European nations has shown that the expansion of foreign trade was stimulated chiefly by two factors: commercial monopolies in the form of privileged groups or companies, and the active participation by governments in economic policies. The new commerce was by its nature most advantageously handled through a few well-regulated companies. Piracy and enemy attacks made the voyage of single merchant ships decidedly risky, so that it was far safer for ships to travel in groups. But flotillas could be equipped best only through powerful companies. Again, it was desirable that the trade with distant foreign places should be centralized under one or two corporations because this made the task of supervision and taxation much easier for the state. As a result the seventeenth and eighteenth centuries saw the rise of commercial monopolies everywhere.

The companies were of two main types—regulated and joint-stock. In the regulated company individuals financed their own businesses but abided by definite rules which had been accepted by the group to protect the trade in which they had a mutual interest. The majority of earlier companies were of this nature, including in England the Russia, Morocco, and Guinea companies. The most famous English regulated company was that of the Merchant Adventurers. Later companies, however, were of the joint-stock variety. Here was an association of capital as well as men, for the members put their money into a common fund and gave the management of the company to a board of directors. The joint-stock company became universal because it proved itself so beneficial to the new commerce. It had several advantages. As many people as wanted could contribute capital. The joint-stock company had a permanent legal personality that did not expire, whereas the regulated company was not a legal entity and each of its members must sue and be sued individually. Stock in a joint-stock company might be transferred as its owner wished. At the same time the policy of the company underwent no serious change. The great corporations of today grew out of this early business organization.

The English and Dutch East India companies both started as regulated companies but were afterward reorganized as joint-stock groups. French joint-stock companies also operated in Canada, the West Indies, west Africa, Madagascar, and the East Indies. It has been estimated that at least one hundred joint-stock companies were organized in early modern times for the purposes of developing trade, promoting colonies, and dealing in manufactures and mining.

Mercantilism. The growth of the national state system had brought political unification under the leadership of a strong centralized authority that dictated all major policies. Now, with the rise of commerce, it was natural that the centralized authority should want to bring about economic unification under its own guidance. The means used to bring about a strong, self-sufficient economic state as a natural partner of the strong, self-sufficient political state has been called mercantilism. Some writers have called mercantilism a "system," but this is a mistake, for it was never a definite body of thought to which a group of theorists might commit themselves. Different countries at different times made use of various techniques to further the aims of mercantilism: the strengthening of the state through the concentration of national economic life under the control of the central government and at the expense of rival national powers.

The tenets of mercantilism. Mercantilism had certain features which should be noted here. First, it stressed the importance of accumulating precious metals, because gold and silver were believed to be indispensable to a nation's wealth. Mercantilists were fond of saying, "Money is the sinews of war," while Louis XIV's financial minister, Colbert, maintained, "It is only the abundance of money in a state that determines its greatness and power." But as we have seen in the case of Spain, this view was founded on a fallacy. Money does not necessarily spell wealth, for money itself is only a measure of value and a means of exchanging real wealth. To understand the fetish for hoarding, let us remember that gold and silver were necessary for coinage and the payment of armies and navies, while the rich treasures garnered by Spain coincided with her predominance in European affairs.

Secondly, if a nation was not in a position to mine the precious metals, they could be obtained through a favorable balance of trade. It was thought that a nation must export more than it imports so that foreign nations would have to pay the difference in precious metals. This placed an emphasis on trade, especially on the export of goods. On the other hand, each nation sought to minimize the import of foreign goods to make the favorable balance as large as possible. Only raw materials which could not be obtained at home were to be imported, and then exported after they had been manufactured into finished goods. Exports of manufactured articles were thus encouraged as much as possible, and subsidies and bounties were always being given to increase home production.

Thirdly, it was believed that when the raw materials were native, the profit to the country was one hundred per cent. Therefore, if the country could not supply the materials itself, it should possess colonies from which they could be procured without giving any advantage to a rival power. Furthermore, colonies were advantageous in that they not only constituted sources of supply for raw materials but also furnished markets for finished products. This was foreseen back in 1583 in an English document favoring colonies: "it is well known that all savages . . . will take marvellous delight in any garment, be it never so simple, as a shirt, a blue, yellow, red, or green cassock, a cap, or such like, and will take incredible pains for such a trifle, . . . which being so, what vent for our English cloths will thereby ensue. . . ."[12]

Lastly, this belief in the peculiar economic value of colonies implied a definite colonial policy. Colonies must be protected adequately, and hence large navies were built. On the other hand the colonies must not engage in any manufacturing, as this would interfere with the industries of the mother country. And as the mother country was to exploit the economic resources for her own interest, it followed that foreign countries should be excluded from colonial markets and the colonies prohibited from trading with the foreign powers.

We have already seen examples of mercantilist policy. Spain and Portugal attempted to forbid alien merchants and colonists from intercourse with their empires. England forbade the export of raw wool so that the cloth industry might be nurtured at home, while the navigation laws were designed to stimulate English shipping and manufactures (and became one of the chief causes of the American Revolution). France embarked upon an extensive system of government regulation of quantity and quality of merchandise. This policy was developed especially by Colbert in the seventeenth century, and stringent state control of manufacture is still termed "Colbertism." Other nations embarked on mercantilism. In Prussia it was called cameralism and was designed to strengthen national existence through state control of domestic industry. Cameralism aided greatly in the development of scientific agriculture in Germany. Sweden in 1724 passed a Navigation Act, while Holland, like Spain and Portugal, tried to keep foreigners from poaching on her rich imperial possessions.

Mercantilism at home. Thus far the manifestations of mercantilism in foreign commerce have been emphasized. However, it also had important effects upon economic activity within a nation. The government rigidly controlled domestic industry and trade. The emigration of skilled artisans was forbidden, the quality of goods was often prescribed, and the use of certain foreign commodities was forbidden. In medieval England, for example, there were meatless periods in which the law prescribed the eating of fish in order to encourage the important English fishing industry. Examples of the operation of mercantilistic policy can be seen in the Elizabethan Poor Laws enacted between 1563 and 1598. These statutes provided for state regulation of poor relief, for the training of poor children in regular trades, and for the punishment of chronic idlers. In 1563 there was also enacted the famous Statute of Apprentices. This covered the whole field of labor. It stipulated the length of apprenticeship, hours of labor, and wages. Men not trained as artisans had to work as agricultural laborers on demand. To summarize, the long arm of governmental regulation under mercantilism controlled all aspects of national economy, both external and internal.

Mercantilism reached its zenith in the eighteenth century and then declined. But it did not decline in all countries simultaneously. The more important commercial powers, such as England, France, and Holland, had been among the first to embark upon mercantilistic policies and, similarly, began to discard them first. The more backward economic powers, however, such as Prussia, Russia, and the Scandinavian countries, were still favoring mercantilism after England and France had turned to new doctrines.

Development of Banking and Commercial Practices

The rise of banks. Banking, one of the most important characteristics of our present-day economy, arose in the late Middle Ages. The word "bank" is derived from the Italian *banco*, "bench." Moneylenders in medieval Italy used to sit on benches in the market place to carry on their business. When one of the fraternity failed, the people would break his bench, and from this custom came the word "bankrupt," "broken bench." Moneychangers and moneylenders were to be found at medieval fairs and towns. Since the Church frowned on usury, banking in the early Middle Ages was in the hands of Jews, who were not under Church jurisdiction. In fact there arose the rather ludicrous situation of moneylenders becoming indispensable to the kings of England and France and being forbidden to be converted. But moneylending became indispensable to the administration of the Church itself during the late Middle Ages and began to be countenanced officially. With this change of attitude banking passed from Jewish to Christian control.

Italian bankers. Large-scale banking was first developed in the Italian cities, because they had been the first to profit from the expansion of commerce after the crusades. Wherever Italian merchants took their wares their financial practices went with them. Merchant-bankers speculated in bullion, arranged bills of exchange, and negotiated loans. At the same time they performed a valuable service for the Church by collecting revenues all over Europe, charging five per cent or more for the trouble. As early as the twelfth century the Popes were employing Italian bankers to collect papal dues in England. The bankers were now lending money as well to various kings, and even to the Popes themselves. The Italian lenders were called Lombards since they came largely from cities in Lombardy. The great financial district in London today is located on Lombard Street, so called because the early bankers congregated there.

Florence was one of the earliest banking centers. The town had derived wealth from its wool trade, and since 1252 had issued annually from 300,000 to 400,000 gold florins of standard weight and value. The florin was a beautiful coin, pure gold, "weighing 54 grains, about twice the weight of the American gold dollar of 1932." These florins were soon in use all over Europe, and other centers began to issue florins also. Venice in 1284 was coining ducats which also became popular in trading. "By 1400 the Venetian mint coined annually a million ducats."[13] By 1350 there were some eighty banking houses in Florence, and certain families grew wealthy as bankers. The two outstanding families were the Bardi and Peruzzi, with branches scattered from England to Asia Minor. But Edward III, as a result of reverses in the Hundred Years' War, defaulted on loans they advanced to him, and the two houses went bankrupt.

The Medici. In the fifteenth century the great Florentine banking family was the Medici. Giovanni de'Medici (1360-1429) started the family fortune by spreading his banking activities throughout Flanders and France and acting as financial agent for the Popes. Cosimo de'Medici (1389-1464) added to the family wealth by creating branches all over western Europe and became the financial giant of the age. Under his son Lorenzo (1449-1492) the Medici fortunes reached their apex. Called Lorenzo the Magnificent, this banker was a gifted scholar and poet, politician (he ran Florence like a political boss), and outstanding patron of the arts. Lorenzo died in 1492, the year of Columbus' epoch-making discovery which was to destroy Italy's commercial supremacy, and the Medici family began to decline. It is ironic that this proud family, whose coat of arms had six red balls emblazoned on a field of gold, is today partly remembered by an adaptation of that same coat of arms—the three golden balls of the humble pawnbroker.

The Fuggers. The Medici of the fifteenth century represented a new capitalist class which treated money as a commodity to be bought and sold in much the same way that merchants bought and sold wool, and who could even dictate political policies to princes and Popes. This trend is further represented by another powerful banking house which reached its greatest power in sixteenth-century Germany—the Fuggers, originally weavers near Augsburg. Johann Fugger and his descendants built up a huge fortune out of commerce and banking. The most famous member of the family was Jacob the Rich (1459-1525), who acquired the latest trading and accounting techniques at Venice. He set up counting houses and merchandise depots in Venice, Rome, Antwerp, Lisbon, and other cities. He bought mines and eventually controlled the silver, copper, and iron markets of central Europe and the silver and mercury mining of Spain. Added to all this was the role he played in international finance and politics. In return for mining concessions he made large loans to the German princes and the Hapsburgs. To ensure that a Hapsburg would be returned to the imperial throne upon the death of the emperor Maximilian in 1519, the Fuggers loaned the half million gold florins which bribed the "right people" to elect Charles v. We have figures for the year 1527 to show the resources of the Fugger family. The figures are in florins, each of which would be worth about eight dollars today.

Mines (Tyrol, Hungary)	270,000
Other real estate (city and country)	150,000
Merchandise (copper, silver, brass, textiles)	380,000
Cash (in home office and 14 factories)	50,000
Loans	1,650,000
Private accounts of associates	430,000
Various current affairs	70,000
	3,000,000[14]

For a while after Jacob's death in 1525, the fortunes of the Fuggers increased. The loaning of money was most lucrative, the Fuggers for decades making an average yearly profit of over 30 per cent. But several governments defaulted on their loans, and the Fugger concern became bankrupt in 1607.

Banks throughout Europe. While the Fuggers were the greatest banking house of the sixteenth century, there were numerous others spreading throughout Europe all this time. By 1600 modern banking practices were in operation in the Mediterranean area. Private banks made loans to merchants under state regulation, and public banks took deposits and catered to public or private needs. Some banks were allowing checks to be used, while in Naples depositors were sometimes given receipts which could be used as currency.

Public banking made its way northward, and in 1609 the Bank of Amsterdam was founded by local merchants to put an end to prevailing financial disorders. Among its duties was the conversion of various currencies into credits called bank money, which because of its standard value came to be preferred to coins. The Bank of Amsterdam was patterned after the banks of Venice and was forbidden to make loans. Unfortunately it evaded this rule and made large loans to the Dutch East India Company. In the early nineteenth century both enterprises crashed.

The Bank of England. The English banking system was not placed on a sound basis until 1694, when the Bank of England was established by an act of Parliament. This famous institution, the "Old Lady of Threadneedle Street," was formed through the proposal of William Paterson, a Scotsman, who proposed that the financially distracted government borrow £1,200,000 at eight per cent interest. In return for putting up the money the subscribers could form a bank "with power to issue notes, buy and sell bullion, discount bills, and make loans." The new bank gave financial stability to the nation. It did not compete with private companies for the accounts of the general public, but became the bankers' bank and a semiofficial institution which marketed the government's securities and administered the currency.[15]

New banking methods. With modern banking there naturally evolved new financial techniques. Business transactions in medieval times were carried on through barter or the medium of cash. But medieval communication was poor and the risks of carrying money were great. Therefore there developed the use of bills of exchange. A branch or agent of a banking firm in one town would receive a merchant's money and issue a bill of exchange which could be redeemed in some other city where there was another branch or agent. This practice evolved in Italy and was in general use in other European nations during the thirteenth century. Despite the increase in precious metals after 1500, the supply could not keep up with the increase in trade, and there arose the practice of payment in checks against a sum of money held on deposit in a bank. This scheme greatly facilitated business transactions and meant that the means to carry on transactions could be expanded far beyond the bounds imposed by a cash system. Today most of our business transactions are carried on through checks, and cash has given way in large measure to paper tokens. Likewise bank notes rather than bulky and heavy metal are used for the larger sums of currency.

The financial development of modern times was greatly facilitated also by the progress made in commercial arithmetic and bookkeeping. In Florence in 1202 there appeared Leonardo da Pisa's *Abbaci,* which "laid the foundations of correct calculation." Yet as late as 1299 people were still objecting to the use of Arabic numerals even though they were by far the best means of quick and accurate calculation. But in the fourteenth century the science of reckoning made some progress in Italy. In the fifteenth and sixteenth it spread to northern Europe. Books on arithmetic be-

Jacob Fugger's secretary drew this picture of himself and his "boss" at work before the filing cabinet with its correspondence from the Fugger offices in Nuremberg, Venice, Lisbon, and other cities.

gan to be distributed widely. Florence, for example, had schools attended by some 1200 boys who were instructed in "the abacus and the elements of commercial arithmetic." Lübeck (an important Hanseatic center) was the first German town to have an arithmetic school.

As early as the thirteenth century simple bookkeeping had been developed. Double-entry bookkeeping was not much later in coming into use. In the year 1340 Genoa's city government kept its accounts in this way, while in the fifteenth century both private and public accounts were kept by the new double-entry technique. The perfection of the system and the first theoretic treatise on double entry came from the pen of Luca Pacioli in 1494. Because double-entry bookkeeping relates all transactions in terms, not of moral or qualitative values, but of profit and loss, it both represented and stimulated the rising spirit of translating all activities primarily into money evaluations. "By 1500 the double-entry method of bookkeeping was well known in Italy and by 1600 in western Europe."[16]

Insurance. Shakespeare, writing around 1596, had this to say in *The Merchant of Venice* concerning the dangers which merchants must undergo when they sent their vessels abroad: "But ships are but boards, sailors but men: there be land-rats and water-rats, water-thieves and land-thieves, I mean pirates; and then there is the peril of waters, winds, and rocks."[17] Therefore it was very desirable for merchants to figure out some method by which risks could be minimized. The solution lay in insurance. As the risks were great and the loss of his vessel might well ruin a merchant, it came to be the practice to distribute losses among a group of traders. Interested merchants would draw up an agreement by which each was responsible for a percentage of any possible loss. They signed their names at the bottom of this document, and the practice came to be known as underwriting.

Since the first part of the fourteenth century it had been a common practice to insure for both marine and land risks, and insurance grew up in such large commercial centers as Venice, Genoa, Milan, and Barcelona. Later companies arose which specialized in marine insurance, the first being set up in 1668 in Paris. The most famous of all marine insurance groups is Lloyd's in London. This unusual enterprise began through the congregation of London shipowners and underwriters at a coffee house owned by Edward Lloyd. Lloyd's is really not a company but an association of individual underwriters, and it has become the authority for the world on matters of ship classification. It publishes *Lloyd's List* daily to show the whereabouts of all ships, and the ringing of a bell signifies that a vessel is officially missing or destroyed. Lloyd's has also branched out into other forms of insurance. Its members have to keep a large deposit on hand so that they will not default on any obligation which they have underwritten.

Following the disastrous Great Fire of 1666 which destroyed much of London, a number of fire insurance companies were started. Also during this period certain companies began to specialize in life insurance. The first mutual company was the Friendly Society, organized in 1684. A mutual insurance company is one in which policyholders receive a certain share of the profits. Today there are thousands of life insurance companies all over the world, and their huge investments of capital have made their effect upon modern finance almost as important as that of banks.

Stock exchanges. The convenience of the stock exchange was of course unknown in early modern times, but the first produce and stock exchanges fulfilled much the same need as their descendants today. The produce exchange, descendant of the medieval fairs, is a market for dealing in various products such as wheat, wool, rubber, cotton, and metals, while a stock exchange is a market for buying, selling, or exchanging stocks, shares, bonds, and debentures. The earlier exchanges acted in both capacities. In the fifteenth century there were exchanges, or bourses, in Bruges and elsewhere, but the first really modern, international bourse was at Antwerp. Speculation and attempts to corner the market were not uncommon, and there developed the all-important practice of making exchanges through paper certificates representing commodities. Exchange was now a relatively simple matter, but the temptation arose to speculate upon the fluctuating prices of commodities—a temptation which caused many failures in 1929.

The creation of joint-stock companies at this time gave impetus to the new exchange system because stock was issued in shares which could easily be transferred from one person to another like any other commodity. Toward the end of the seventeenth century the exchange of joint-stock shares was so prevalent that a bourse independent of the produce exchange was seen to be desirable, and the stock exchange came into existence. While, as we are soon to see, the stock exchange encouraged in the eighteenth century a wild mania of speculation, it performed certain valuable tasks for capitalism, including the easy amalgamation of capital from a thousand and one different sources, enabling large commercial companies to be formed, and the creation of facilities for investment.[18]

The growth of speculation. The rapid increase of trade during the last decades of the seventeenth century brought about an avalanche of speculation in the joint-stock companies that were developing everywhere. At this time Colbert in France was organizing many new trading companies to compete with the powerful Dutch and English concerns, especially the two East India companies. In England and Scotland new concerns were also promoted. Thus in 1670 the famous Hudson's Bay Company was established, as was the Royal African Company two years later.

The great years of company promotion, nevertheless, were from 1713 to 1720. One authority comments on the fantastic nature of some of these wild-cat schemes "which promised to earn great dividends by trading in human hair, making square cannon balls, getting butter from beech trees, marketing an air pump for the brain, perfecting a wheel for perpetual motion, searching for rich wrecks off the Irish coast, or importing jackasses from Spain."[19]

The greatest financial disasters occurred in 1720 when two huge speculative "bubbles" were pricked, bringing financial ruin to thousands in England and France. The first of these crises was the notorious South Sea Bubble in England; the second was the Mississippi Bubble in France. Such disastrous financial crashes retarded the growth of banking and credit organization, for the public was justifiably suspicious of all business promotion for many decades.

The Development of Industry

Mercantilism fosters industry. The most impressive characteristic of the economic evolution of early modern times was the expansion of commerce. But industry made rapid advances also from 1500 to 1750, due largely to the impetus of the commercial revolution. We have already seen in the economic evolution of Europe's leading commercial powers how various industries were fostered under a mercantilist policy so that each nation would be as self-sufficient as possible and export manufactured products to acquire a favorable balance of trade. Overseas colonies also stimulated industry, for they were sources of raw materials and markets for the mother country's finished goods. Some of the most important manufactured products of European nations were the following: silks, laces, and velvets in Italy; woolen cloth, linens, pottery, navigation and optical instruments, and ships in Holland; silks, tapestries, furniture, and specialized luxury goods in France; and woolen cloth, cottons, ships, and hardware (such as muskets, swords, tools, nails, and hoes) in England.

The textile industry especially was highly developed and flourished in all the leading European nations. Increase in textile manufacture was due in no small measure to the growing demand on the part of colonists and the natives overseas for woolens and a cloth called fustian. Fustian began to be made in the late Middle Ages, and from the latter half of the sixteenth century it was exported from England. The fabric was made with a linen warp and a cotton weft. Fustian proved popular in the tropics and was exported in large quantities to Africa and the plantations in the Indies. As raw cotton began to be imported in ever larger amounts, a thriving industry sprang up in the manufacture of calico, chintz, and underclothing, although the woolen manufacturers did everything possible to stifle it. In the nineteenth century cotton became the chief English textile, but during the period under discussion woolens dominated the market. In fact Daniel Defoe, the author of *Robinson Crusoe,* maintained that the woolen industry in England was "the richest and most valuable manufacture in the world"—of greater value to England, even, than were the rich mines of Peru and Mexico to Spain.[20]

New industrial methods. As industry increased under the impetus of the expansion of commerce and investment, important changes occurred in the organization of industry itself. In the Middle Ages industry had been carried on under the guild system, where the master craftsman bought the raw materials, turned them into finished goods at his own shop through the labor of himself, his family, and his employees, and usually sold the product on his own premises. But due to the growing exclusiveness of the craft guilds and their inability (because of their local organization) to cope with world-wide industrial demands, there grew up a new industrial system. This was the domestic, or putting-out, system, which was in operation in Italy as early as the thirteenth century, later finding its way along the valley of the Rhine into Flanders and across the Channel into England.

The domestic system appeared in England as early as 1464. It was most common in the woolen industry. Under the domestic system a merchant capitalist, or entrepreneur, would buy raw materials and give them to artisans to be worked up in their own homes for specified wages. Then he would take the finished product and sell it for whatever price he could get. This new system brought many changes. First, it interposed a middleman between producer and consumer—a middleman who did not work like the master craftsman of the guild system but spent his time in purchasing raw materials and selling finished products at a profit, thus accumulating in time large supplies of capital. Secondly, production was no longer confined to trained workmen working under a single roof as in the case of guilds, but was now spread over wide areas.

A third change brought about by the domestic system concerned the status of labor. The gulf between employer and employee widened to an extent unknown under the guild system, where the master and apprentice worked together. Under the domestic system the worker sometimes owned his own tools and even furnished the raw materials, but as time advanced, the worker became more dependent upon the entrepreneur. While the later factory system brought the worst evils in labor's working conditions, many abuses existed under the domestic system. Child labor was common as was that of women before and after marriage, with wages exceedingly low. The hours of labor lasted from dawn to dusk, and occupational diseases began to take a serious toll.

The domestic, or putting-out, system had both advantages and disadvantages. It was an advantage to some agricultural tenants, who could now augment the bare subsistence they won from their bits of ground by working at home at a task that did not monopolize their entire attention. Again, the worker at this time had more independence than his nineteenth-century factory descendant and was more or less removed from the worst evils of factories and slums. But the employee's loss of freedom, and the long hours of labor for men, women, and children were disadvantageous.

The employer also had to face serious problems. He could not supervise his scattered workmen, who often took advantage of his absence by refraining from work altogether or by substituting inferior substances for the raw material he had sent them, selling the stolen material to unscrupulous brokers. But even more important was the waste of time and money which came from having to send the material around the countryside and then collecting the finished product. Central shops began to appear even before the advent of the factory system proper.

The domestic system reached its widest application in England among the textile industries and was in force from the sixteenth century until the advent of the factory system two hundred years later. On the continent, however, while the domestic system was established in certain localities, the guild system persisted.

The Development of Agriculture

Importance of agriculture. So far in this chapter we have discussed the development of commerce and industry. But agriculture all during this period continued to occupy the chief place in the economic life of Europe. Even today agriculture provides occupations for the majority of people, but four hundred years ago the proportion was even greater. Agriculture was profoundly affected by the commercial era and the rise of modern capitalism. The discovery of new lands resulted in the exchange of products between Europe and the colonies. To the New World went the horse, ox, sheep, poultry, and various vegetables and fruits, while to the Old World traveled the potato, tomato, tobacco, cocoa, vanilla, dye and cabinet woods, and various flowers. Meanwhile northern Europe was slowly learning scientific agriculture from Italy and Spain, forests were being cleared, regions were being reclaimed from the sea by the Dutch, and everywhere land was being turned to sheep farming because of the great wool trade.

The change in agricultural conditions in England was hastened by certain political and economic factors. Land there has usually been considered the most desirable form of ownership, while "to engage in trade" lowers social standing. This attitude of course goes back to feudal times when the possession of land was the mark of the noble, both socially and economically. The new commercial society naturally wished to imitate and even merge with the landed aristocracy and hence bought up large tracts of land to gain social prestige. There was now a new relationship between commerce and land. The new capitalistic class largely controlled both, and they also controlled Parliament. Therefore they passed laws which would make it profitable to raise wheat and to export it abroad. Before they were repealed in the nineteenth century, these statutes, the famous Corn Laws, brought great riches to the upper classes and much misery to the common people.

New farming methods. Although the new commercial landowners tended to ape the aristocracy in many respects, they were not content to retain primitive farming techniques. They applied vigorous business attitudes to their newly acquired estates and during the eighteenth century brought about a revolution in agriculture. New tools, new crops, new ideas in stock breeding, new soil developments were introduced. The agricultural innovators founded scientific groups interested in bettering agricultural conditions. One of the pioneers was Jethro Tull (1674-1741). Up to this time little or nothing had been done to work up the soil about the roots of crops and to eliminate weeds. Tull advocated this procedure: after plowing the land carefully, plant seeds in a row by use of a drill which he had invented, and then keep the plants well hoed. Despite his many mistakes, the tradition of experimentation which Tull established was an important one. His book on agriculture, scorned in his lifetime, is now considered a valuable source.

Another important agriculturist was Viscount Townshend (1674-1738). "Handsome, well connected, confident in himself, and industrious, he was given one post after another, ambassador, secretary, and virtually prime minister."[21] After a lengthy political career this noble retired in 1730 to his estate, largely worthless sand and swamp. Through the use of a mixture of clay and lime, he made the land fertile. He then rotated the planting of wheat, turnips, barley, and clover to produce food for human and animal consumption in alternate years. At once Townshend had eliminated the wasteful business of a third of the ground being forced to lie fallow each year, and had found in turnips a fodder for livestock. This new food supply increased the size of herds, made more animal products available in winter, and increased the supply of fertilizer. So enthusiastic was the viscount over his pet crop that he was nicknamed "Turnip Townshend."

Townshend had solved the problem of feeding animals, but the problem of breeding had not yet been scientifically attacked. The man responsible for the change was Robert Bakewell (1725-1795). Animals had always been allowed to run together in a common pasture so that breeding was haphazard. The sheep and cattle were inferior in build, sheep weighing only 28 to 40 pounds and cattle only about 370 pounds. Bakewell, through careful inbreeding of choice animals, improved the types of cattle and sheep, adding to their size and improving the quality of their meat. By 1800 the average beeves weighed 800 pounds and the average sheep 80 pounds, while the milk of the animals had also improved.

Popular adoption of new methods. Bakewell's methods were gradually adopted, as were those of Tull and Townshend, by the gentleman farmers and landlords who found it both fashionable and profitable to engage in agricultural experiments. George III himself had part of his lands made into a farm and is said to have enjoyed being termed the "Farmer King."

The most ardent publicist of the changes in agriculture was Arthur Young (1741-1820). Although he had tried unsuccessfully to run three farms, Young wrote continuously on the subject, touring England, Ireland, and France and making observations wherever he went. He showed, through writings that were translated into many foreign tongues, the advantages to be gained from well-equipped farms and scientific techniques. "It was his greatest contribution to have written the declaration of independence of English agriculture, and to have preached it as long as health and strength served: independence of ancient methods that were both wasteful and unprogressive."[22]

Another stimulus to more efficient farming was the rapid increase in population in the latter half of the eighteenth century. That fact, along with poor harvests, made imperative the intensive cultivation of all available lands. The resulting high prices made capitalistic farming profitable indeed, and led a contemporary writer to remark that war prosperity had transformed the farmer into a person with a "fox-hunting horse, polished boots, a spanking trot to market, a 'Get out of the way or by God I'll ride over you' to every poor devil on the road, wine at his dinner, a servant (sometimes in livery) to wait at his table, a painted lady for a wife, sons aping the young squires and lords, and a house crammed up with sofas, pianos, and all sorts of fooleries."[23]

The enclosure movement. Meanwhile another agricultural development had been taking place in England since Tudor times. This was the practice of enclosing open lands. The primary purpose of enclosure was to fence in open land which had once been held as communal property. The manorial system will be recalled, with its open-field system, scattered tenancies, joint labor, and the holding of waste and pasture lands in common. The defects of that system were many, and with its decline the rising group of land tenants seized every opportunity to obtain compact holdings which could be fenced in and operated independently. During the fourteenth and fifteenth centuries the enclosure of arable lands went forward as a steady development. On the whole this new development proved beneficial to farming. But another type of enclosure that caused distress among the English people was the conversion of arable land into pasture. The reason for this type of enclosure was the growing demand for wool in the rich woolen industry of England. Both types of enclosure were inevitable and both could be justified from the economic standpoint. "Probably the net result of the enclosure movement, at least on the technical side, was the more careful use of a greater amount of land than had been available before, including especially the waste land."[24] But the second type—the enclosing of land for purposes of sheep raising—had unfortunate social effects. Sheep raising required fewer hands, and the enclosure of large areas often meant the uprooting of whole villages and the eviction of their inhabitants who, because they could not be re-absorbed into the sheep-raising industry, were left without land or work. These farm laborers, deprived of their land, drifted into the cities, where they glutted the supply of labor.

The agricultural revolution resulted in a speed-up of the enclosure movement. The new methods of stock breeding and crop rotation could not be practiced on unfenced land. During the eighteenth century, therefore, enclosures were carried on at a rapid rate. Many people were forced off the land with much consequent suffering. But, on the other hand, English agriculture became more efficient and the food supply was increased to keep pace with the rapidly growing city population.

Capitalism in Early Modern Times

Early capitalism defined. When we examine the principles underlying the evolution of banking and commercial practices, the commercial expansion of Europe, and the development of industry and agriculture in early modern times, we find a significant common denominator existing throughout. It is this, simply stated: Wealth is being used on a large scale for the definite purpose of securing an income, or profit. Wealth which is set aside for the purpose of gaining an income (or additional wealth) is called capital. The system based on this principle is known as capitalism. Let us examine our previous discussion in the light of this concept to obtain a clear picture of the economic philosophy of early modern times. For the present we can dispense with the social aspects of capitalism since, as we shall discover in time, they became important not so much in the commercial era (1500-1750) as in the industrial era (1750 to the present).

Commerce and capitalism. Great geographical discoveries stimulated the growth of commerce. Soon merchants found it profitable to invest capital in ships and to secure additional wealth by carrying profitable cargoes from one land to another. Thus commercial capitalism arose. Important trading companies were started in the major European countries with the idea of capturing great wealth through the ownership of commercial monopolies. The economic policy known as mercantilism was in some measure an aspect of commercial capitalism, for it strove by various techniques to use the wealth of a state to augment the national income.

The Medici and the Fuggers were lending their wealth (money) in order to gain income (interest). Similarly the shares which people bought in speculative companies represented the investment of wealth to gain further wealth. Thus began what has been called financial capitalism. The existence today of banks, stock exchanges, "Wall Streets," and financial companies of all sorts shows how important this type of capitalism has become.

Industry and capitalism. Commerce had fostered industry, with textile goods especially increasing in quantity. The failure of the medieval craft guilds to meet the needs of expanded markets led to the domestic, or putting-out, system. A man with capital would purchase raw materials, give them out to artisans to be made into finished articles at their homes, then sell the finished articles to the public at a profit. Thus began industrial capitalism, whereby the entrepreneur invests his wealth in raw goods and in wages, with the object of reaping profits from the transaction. However, industrial capitalism was to assume its tremendous importance only after the application of steam to machinery, the creation of the factory system, and the more complete divorce of the worker from the ownership of the tools by which he earned his daily wage.

Agriculture and capitalism. Agriculture was also becoming capitalistic. The manorial system of the Middle Ages was primarily based on a barter and self-sufficiency economy. But in the fourteenth and fifteenth centuries the nobles often would lease their lands to tenants in return for money rentals. Agriculture was now motivated largely by the profit motive, for the breakdown of the manorial system saw the change from production for consumption to production for profit. The enclosure movement in England also stimulated agricultural capitalism. We have just seen how the growing demand for textiles stimulated both industry and commerce. The raising of sheep for wool became so lucrative that men with capital invested in lands and changed their normal economy from crop raising to sheep raising for the sake of large profits. The eighteenth century saw an extension of agricultural capitalism when new tools, crop rotation, and stock breeding made farming more efficient and profitable.

A copper engraving depicts the shop of a seventeenth-century Paris shoemaker. The master is both foreman and stylist, with the three journeymen filling orders. His wife is helping, too.

Much of this development was nourished under the mercantilistic philosophy. In the last decades of the eighteenth century and in the nineteenth century the capitalistic system became emancipated from mercantilism, that is, from governmental regulation. Such freedom or "rugged individualism," became the very bedrock of nineteenth-century capitalism.

Daily Life in Early Modern Times

Classes of society. So far this chapter has shown the economic development of early modern Europe—how men made their living. It remains to glance at the way they spent their money, how they lived from day to day, what things they liked and disliked. Since it is not possible to investigate the interesting habits of the whole of Europe, this glimpse will be directed chiefly at England in the late seventeenth century, then a nation of a little over five million people. Of these, four million lived in the country and were dependent upon agriculture. At the top of the social scale were the nobility and the country gentry. Living from the produce and the rents of their lands, this class enjoyed a fortunate existence, dominating English society and government.

Unlike the French nobility, the English gentry was not an exclusive caste. There was frequent marriage of commoners into the families, and the younger sons often went into business. The English country gentlemen were widely traveled. It was common for them to top off their college training with a grand tour of one or two years on the continent. Returning home the young aristocrats would often bring back paintings by old masters to hang in their stately manor houses, and trunks of fine books to add to their libraries. Established in

A delicate cartoon in porcelain ridicules the height attained by an ornate hairdress of the rococo period. The observer must have a spy-glass in order to see the top of milady's head.

their manor houses the squires would interest themselves in the new agriculture, dispense justice and counsel to their tenants and the workers of the locality, and also have much time for foxhunting and drinking. This squirearchy was often boorish, intolerant, and interested chiefly in horses. But on the whole these gentlemen farmers supervised their estates efficiently, carried the responsibility of local government, and at times carved out brilliant careers in Parliament.

In the country, midway between the gentry and the farm laborers, were the yeomen, sturdy small landowners. Unfortunately this class became practically extinct in the eighteenth century as a result of the enclosure movement.

The agricultural laborers comprised about half the country's total population. On the whole, the lot of these people was quite miserable. The average weekly wage of a farm worker was only two dollars, and usually his wife and the older children had to work to supplement the family income. The diet was inadequate; meat was seldom eaten and milk was little used. The laborer's cottage consisted of two rooms, a living room and bedroom, in which large families were often packed. Windows were small and the bare earth was the floor.

Turning to the city we would find merchants and shopkeepers, skilled artisans, and common laborers. As yet, industrial workers constituted a small percentage of the working population. This was to be radically changed with the advent of the Industrial Revolution and the rise of the factory system. Artisans enjoyed a better standard of living than the farm laborer. There were many wretched and poor people in the cities, but European visitors often remarked upon the well-being and luxuries enjoyed by English skilled craftsmen.

Early modern London. London by this time was already the greatest city in Europe and the world's commercial and financial center. This city of the late seventeenth century was evidently a fascinating place.

The Great Fire of 1666 had proved a blessing to the city. It had destroyed thousands of plague-ridden wooden houses. The evil-smelling sewer called the Fleet River had been converted into a clean New Canal, and the streets were gradually being made wider and cleaner. The houses of the middle class were becoming more comfortable. There were several bedrooms, at least one of which had a carved bedstead with a canopy, curtains, and a looking glass. The house might have two parlors, one elaborately furnished with tapestry curtains, a carpet, tables, a clock case, a leather chair, several cloth chairs, and a stool. In the kitchen the material used most for dishes and plates was pewter; chinaware was kept in the parlor cupboard. The house might have a tiled roof, glass windows, and perhaps even some rugs from the Near East and wallpaper from China. Plumbing was simple at this time, but an occasional owner who could afford to do so was installing bathtubs, even though the majority of people only washed their hands and faces, making up for their deficiencies of hygiene by copious use of perfumes. From such a home the merchant would saunter out in the morning after a breakfast of cold meat, oatcakes, and a small beer. He would perhaps drop by the coffee house at ten, then transact business at his office till noon. He might next go to the Exchange until two, after which he would revisit the coffee house until four. At this hour he would enjoy his dinner, then go off to his club or visit the theater. Generally he was home around ten, when he had some supper to keep his digestive system active during the lonely hours of the night.

A visit to London about 1700. Perhaps we can imagine ourselves residents. We are awakened early in the morning by numerous street cries. Sticking our head out of the window we see that the weather is threatening and decide to put on our second-best wig. Down the street the inn signs are swinging noisily, a signal that the wind is rising. After a hearty breakfast we sally forth into the street.

There is no sidewalk where we walk, but iron posts separate us from traffic. However, our stockings are bound to be splattered by mud flung from carriage wheels, while in the narrower lanes we have to be careful. There are marks along the brickwork from the hubs of the carriages, and we are forced to hug the wall when a carriage careens through the passageway.

Dress. Thanks to the geographical discoveries and the commercial revolution, women can now buy furs from Canada, silks from southern France and Italy, and even ostrich feathers from Africa. Many men wear wigs. Wigs hide whether a man is bald or whether his hair is gray, and they conceal the vermin that lurk in everybody's hair. The more important the man, the more expensive will be his wig. Wigs are costly, and to have a big wig is a proof of being a "bigwig." But the fops and dandies have gone to absurd lengths with this fashion, some even attempting to wear wigs that trail around the knees. The nobles and wealthier merchants are resplendent in white satin coats, knee breeches, gold-braided hats, ruffles, and silk stockings. They carry carved canes and expensive snuffboxes. Like the ladies, they possess pocket mirrors which they consult frequently. Ladies' dresses are mountainous and their fashions bewildering. Beautiful imported brocaded dresses, parasols, mirrors, ivory fans, and much gold and silver lace produce a gaudy picture. They make up a great deal, and one cynic has described a fading beauty in the following unkind terms: "Her teeth were made on the Blackfriars, both her eyebrows in the Strand, and her hair in Silver Street. . . . She takes herself asunder when she goes to bed into some twenty boxes; and about noon next day is put together again like a great German clock."[25]

Lloyd's of London began in the frank and homey confines of Edward Lloyd's coffee house. The man with raised eyebrows appears to have received some shocking news.

Not all people, however, are able to wear such costly and fashionable attire. The common people dress simply. They have few changes, wear no waistcoat, carry no sword, and have buttons of black horn. The mechanics often wear an apron over their blue-cloth frocks, and their stockings are made of wool.

Coffee houses. The coffee house is distinctly masculine in flavor, caters to all types of men, and represents the growing urbanity in manners. There are all sorts of these resorts for men who want to discuss business, politics, religion, literature, new discoveries in medicine and science, or court gossip.

The story of the new beverages also deserves our attention. Coffee came first from Arabia but it was later transplanted by the Dutch to the East Indies and by the Portuguese to Brazil. Tea has been extremely popular ever since being introduced into Europe by the Dutch in 1606. Its early exponents in London maintained that it was good for the memory, stomach, liver, and lungs. Men like to gather in their favorite coffee house, and they esteem those among themselves who have an ability for apt phrases and witty discussion. We can see that the coffee house is bringing a new elegance of manners together with a greater sophistication and urbanity of thought among the prosperous classes.

Alcoholic beverages. But we can also see by the countenances and paunches of the passers-by that not everyone is confining his tastes to non-alcoholic beverages. Tea is still just a fashion and luxury, and even small children are given beer as a matter of course. Ales, wines, and beer are the popular beverages, but the wealthy like punches and cordials. We notice that the lower classes are taking to gin. There are even establishments which guarantee to get a man drunk for a penny and dead drunk for twopence. The effect of gin upon the working classes is to be even more detrimental in the future decades of the eighteenth century and will require bills of Parliament to try to stop its ravages.

Foods. Thanks to the additions from overseas, diet lately has been enriched. We now can have potatoes, tomatoes, lima beans, yams, rice, maize, cane sugar, pineapples, bananas, watermelons, dates, turkey, peanuts, and a more plentiful supply of fish, besides the new beverages, tea, coffee, and cocoa. Nevertheless roast beef is still a mainstay of the people although the dandies scorn the native dishes in favor of exotic variations from abroad.

In foreign vests the gaudy Fops may shine,
And on dissected frogs politely dine.

Amusements. If we were to go to Kensington Gardens we might happen upon a duel, for this is still the genteel way of settling differences between gentlemen. Even the clergy sometimes indulge in it. While affairs of honor are settled in parks, gardens, and even taverns, the most fashionable rendezvous is admitted to be the Field of the Forty Footsteps behind Montague House (where the British Museum is one day to be located).

A very popular sport at this time is cock-fighting. At Westminster, Drury Lane, and behind Gray's Inn eager crowds gather to watch the birds tangle amid shouts of encouragement and much betting. Baiting of all sorts is also well received at this time. On one occasion an evening's amusement consists of the following: "the baiting of a tiger by six bull and bear dogs, for £100; a bull and a bear driven mad by being covered all over with lighted fireworks; and, to conclude, six young men to play at blunts, that is, at fighting with sticks, he to get the prize who broke most heads." We might also see such other sports as wrestling, boxing, sword-play, and tennis, or go boating on the Thames.

If we so wish we can pursue yet more amusements. We can journey over to Hampstead Spa. The leisured class goes there, there may be something interesting to see, and anyway the waters will do us no harm. Some of our friends derive amusement by journeying to Bedlam, the London madhouse, to laugh at the antics of the inmates. Richard Steele, the famous essayist, has taken friends at times to Bedlam, and as late as 1770 the revenue from the admission of visitors is some £400. We are told that the private asylums are even more wretched, because relatives often bribe keepers to hold perfectly sane people in perpetual confinement. However, we might visit Old Bailey, the law courts, to watch a trial or two. We would probably not choose to enter the notorious prison, Newgate, where conditions are reputed to be scandalous. Prisoners there suffer from fever and die in appalling numbers. Of course not all men are sentenced to prison for their offences. Some are placed in the stocks or pillory and exposed to the public's ridicule. Others are publicly whipped as punishment to themselves and a warning to would-be offenders. But the punishment that meets most with public approval is the hanging of criminals at Tyburn. This is quite a gala affair, and certain days are set aside for the festivities. Hanging is surprisingly common. The death penalty is invoked for a host of crimes, both major and minor, which include at this time murder, treason, coining money, arson, rape, piracy, forgery, burglary, highway robbery, house breaking, stealing, or picking pockets above 1 shilling, shoplifting above 5 shillings, shooting at a revenue officer, stealing horses, cattle, or sheep, and sacrilege. Great crowds gather at Tyburn to watch the poor offender's last convulsions and to compare notes as to his composure and *savoir-faire.*

After dark. London's streets at night are the envy of all other capitals because they are considered to be remarkably well lighted. The most important thoroughfares have oil lamps which are lit until eleven o'clock, when they are allowed to go out because all respectable citizens are then in bed. However, despite this we need a link-boy to go before us and guide us to our destination. If we wish, we can attend the masquerades which are held among the wealthy, who are fond of donning strange costumes. If we are in a mood to hear music and enjoy dancing we can go to a favorite night spot—Vauxhall

Cutpurse, dandy, rake, and gambler mingle with solid citizens and a deaf old man in Hogarth's "Cockpit." The begrimed chimney sweep is stealing some snuff while its owner watches the fight.

Gardens. Displays of fireworks are given, lamps hang in festoons among the trees, and romance is carried on beneath the moon. We might want to go to the theater. Five o'clock is the time to attend the plays, but if we wish to be ultrafashionable and make a conspicuous entrance we had better be late. Everybody has deserted the coffee house to attend the opening of a new play. Inside we are amazed by the conduct of the spectators, for evidently the play itself is of minor importance. In the gallery the footmen and servants shout, fight, catcall, and hiss to their hearts' content. In the pit people chatter, flirt, laugh, and make social engagements. After the play we call a sedan chair, give our address to the men, and make our way home. After a supper washed down with wine, we pick up our candle and make our way to bed.

Elsewhere in Europe. This picture of English life and times holds true in many ways for much of Europe, especially Holland. There were, of course, many important differences. In most of the European countries strong evidences of political feudalism survived. The nobles still retained many privileges long forgotten in England. The manorial system was very much in evidence, and serfdom, then a thing of the past in England, was quite common in Europe. The middle class was slowly emerging but in most areas had little influence.

We often refer to the expansion of the capitalistic system and industrialism from Europe over much of the world. This was primarily the accomplishment of the people of the westernmost fringe of Europe. We often forget, therefore, that the advance of industrialism and the emergence of the middle class to power were trends that only slowly obtained a foothold in eastern Europe. In countries such as Poland and Hungary, a species of feudal landholding has survived down to the present day.

Summary

In this chapter we have discussed the economic transformation of early modern times and its effect upon social life and manners. We have called the period under discussion the commercial era because Europe's economic life was particularly affected by the enormous increase in trade, an increase due in large measure to exploration. New products, the slave trade, new social habits brought overseas to Europe, the increase in precious metals, the establishment of colonies to supply raw products and buy finished articles, and the rise of powerful national empires are all directly attributable to the era of discovery.

During the Middle Ages the chief economic centers had been the Hanseatic League in northern Europe and the Italian trading cities. But with the outburst of geographical discoveries and the creation of changed trade routes, the Atlantic seaboard assumed the dominant trade position. The first great colonial empires were built up by Spain and Portugal. But these powers were eventually superseded in commercial brilliance by Holland, France, and England. Of these three, England became preëminent in the eighteenth century.

The importance of the commercial transformation of Europe was not lost upon the governments of the participating states, who set about passing laws which controlled commerce to make the state self-sufficient and to weaken its rival powers. This policy was known as mercantilism, a movement which reached its zenith in the eighteenth century.

It was this era also that saw the development of banking and commercial practices. Italy led the way in the evolution of large-scale banking, and likewise in the minting of reliable coinage—florins and ducats. The Fuggers and the Medici built up great fortunes in banking in the fifteenth and sixteenth centuries. By the seventeenth century important banking institutions had been founded throughout Europe. Indispensable commercial practices, double-entry bookkeeping, marine and fire insurance, stock exchanges, and the joint-stock company, all were popularized in this period.

Industry and agriculture kept pace with commerce. In England men learned how to rotate crops scientifically, how to cultivate and reclaim the soil, how to improve stock by careful breeding. Industry—particularly English textile industry—was accelerated by the introduction of the putting-out, or domestic, system.

The quickening of Europe's commercial, agricultural, and industrial life could not fail to stimulate changes in existing morals, manners, and social customs. People were tending to become increasingly secular, urban, and sophisticated. This trend was to intensify in the nineteenth and twentieth centuries. That is why we term the age from 1500 to 1750 "early modern times."

TRADESMEN IN THE CITY OF LONDON

The Scientific Method

1575-1650	Descartes, Bacon demand facts, not opinions	*Discourse of Method, Novum Organum*
	Scientific instruments are developed	Barometer, pendulum clock, air pump
	Mathematics uses new devices	Decimals, logarithms, calculus, etc.
1662-1666	Royal Society and French Academy founded	
	Astronomy becomes a science:	
1473-1542	Heliocentric theory developed by Copernicus (also Brahe and Kepler)	*Concerning the Revolutions of Heavenly Bodies*
1564-1642	Galileo popularizes Copernican theory	*Dialogues . . . Two Great Systems of the World*
1642-1727	Newton discovers law of gravity	*Principia Philosophiae Naturalis Mathematica*

Philosophy Constructs New World Views

1596-1650	Descartes' philosophical dualism	
1632-1677	Spinoza's pantheism	*Ethics*
1646-1716	Leibnitz' monads theory	Forerunner of atomic theory
1632-1704	Locke's empiricism, Berkeley, Hume	*Essay Concerning Human Understanding*
1724-1804	Kant's philosophical idealism	*Critique of Pure Reason*
18th century	Religion feels influence of Age of Reason	Rationalism of Deism appeals to educated
	Pietism, a reaction from Deism	Quakers, Methodists, etc.
1750-1800	Humanitarianism and education:	di Beccaria, Howard, Rousseau

The New Sciences

18th Century	Chemistry revolutionized by new discoveries	Boyle, Priestley, Lavoisier, Franklin
	Geology proves earth not static	Werner, Hutton
	Biology, botany, zoology systematized	Gesner, Linnaeus, Buffon
16th-18th Centuries	Foundations of scientific medicine	Paracelsus, Vesalius, Paré, Harvey, Auenbrugger, etc.

The Arts

1600-1800	Precision in English poetry and prose	Dryden, Pope, Swift, Addison, etc.
	French drama, romanticism, *philosophes*	Molière, Racine, Rousseau, Voltaire
	Golden age of German drama	Schiller, Goethe
	Music becomes monophonic: opera, symphony	Handel, Bach, Haydn, Mozart
	Italian baroque architecture replaced by rococo	Bernini, Versailles Palace
	English architecture: neo-classicism	Wren, Addam brothers
	Spain develops outstanding painting	El Greco, Murillo, Velásquez
	Netherlands painters add realism	Rubens, Vernier, Rembrandt
	French effeminacy in painting	Watteau
	English painting superficial, class art	Reynolds, Gainsborough
	Nonconformists in art satirize evils of day	Hogarth, Goya

CHAPTER 2

Science, Reason, and Enlightenment

MEDIEVAL life in western Europe had been almost completely transformed by the close of the sixteenth century. The Renaissance, the Religious Revolt, and the geographical explorations all worked toward this transformation. In the previous chapter we saw how the medieval economic structure was being revolutionized by the growth of commerce, the development of capitalism, and the rise of an energetic and ambitious middle class.

In the fields of thought, art, literature, and science the old was likewise giving way to the new. So important are these changes in European thought in early modern times, from the latter part of the seventeenth century through the eighteenth century, that they constitute what is known as the Enlightenment. During this epoch the mind, not faith, was regarded as the best source of guidance. Reason was elevated above everything else, and there was little use for what was regarded as emotion, myth, and supernaturalism. The main support of the new rationalism was science. Thinkers of the Enlightenment were so positive that reason could solve all human problems that their whole approach to man and society was colored by a vigorous optimism. Faith in the improvability of mankind caused scholars to evince a strong solicitude for the downtrodden, for the exploited and poverty-stricken. Faith in reason, exaltation of science, and belief in humanitarianism led writers and thinkers of the eighteenth century to carry on a strenuous campaign of stock-taking in all aspects of society. In a word, the Enlightenment was a period of inventory. Beginning in earnest about 1685, what Preserved Smith has called "a vast spiritual revolution" got well under way early in the eighteenth century and reached its culmination by 1750 in the period known as the Age of Reason.

During the Enlightenment the progress of science was especially rapid. The development of inductive methods in the laboratory, the advance of mathematics, and the encouragement afforded by new scientific societies did much to foster this advance. The old geocentric theory was dethroned by Copernicus, Newton gave the world his law of gravitation, Lavoisier made chemistry a full science, William Harvey and Vesalius established medicine on a firm basis, and Hutton revolutionized the study of geology.

In religion a movement called Deism, reflecting the vogue of science, tried to reduce worship to an intellectual formula. In some respects Deism was more of a challenge to established religious thought than the Religious Revolt of the sixteenth century had been. Deism in turn gave way to a religious movement called Pietism which sought to return to emotionalism, to fervor, and even to mysticism.

Literature and music, art and architecture were all profoundly affected by the Enlightenment. Here the cult of reason played a dominant role. In writing and music it led to a neo-classicism, in art to the grandiose baroque style. Everywhere there was a serene confidence in reason, a tendency to minimize spirit and emotion, and a close attention to classical forms and rules that were considered "good taste." Despite its formalism, however, the artistic accomplishments of the Age of Reason in music, art, and literature were mighty ones. In the following pages we will encounter men like John Locke, Rembrandt, Johann Sebastian Bach, Samuel Johnson, and—most representative of all—Voltaire.

New Mathematics and Astronomy

Advance of science. Building on the contributions of scholars of the late Middle Ages and especially taking advantage of Moslem learning, science advanced in the sixteenth and seventeenth centuries at a pace little short of miraculous. There were several reasons for this rapid growth. The passing of feudalism had created the strong national state which assured more political stability and law and order, conditions which are prerequisite if intellectual activity is to flourish. At the head of these national states were kings and queens who brought prestige to their dynasties by attracting scientists and writers to their courts. Charles II of England made science respectable and fashionable by dabbling in chemistry. Frederick the Great of Prussia for a time was the patron of the French philosopher Voltaire, and Catherine of Russia was the benefactor of the writer Diderot.

Enlightened despots were not alone, however, in aiding the advance of science and letters. There were merchant princes whose wealth enabled them to engage in the pastime of gathering specimens for private scientific collections, to build laboratories on their country estates, and to enjoy reflected glory by acting as the patrons of famous scientists. Science also benefited by the forces that were at this time transforming men's minds. In spite of setbacks due largely to the Religious Revolt, the secular tradition of the Renaissance was forging ahead. The medieval outlook, dominated by fear of the supernatural, preoccupied with theology, and lacking interest in nature, was steadily being replaced by skepticism toward the supernatural, impatience with theological dogma, and an almost fanatical zeal to probe into the laws of the natural world.

Finally, geographical discoveries were exercising a decisive influence upon the thought of Europeans. The discovery of new continents gave scholars a mass of novel and startling information—new types of people, thousands of new plants, strange fossils and geological formations, unknown animals, medicinal remedies heretofore nonexistent to European doctors, and strange social customs, forms of government, and economic organization.

Progress in scientific method. The remarkable progress made by science was stimulated by several trends: the clear exposition of the method which must be utilized in scientific inquiry, the invention of scientific instruments, the aid of higher mathematics, the popularization of science and establishment of societies devoted to the promotion of science, and the zeal for collecting scientific data from all over the world, made possible largely through the support of European governments, especially England.

The fundamental weaknesses of Greek science were its neglect of experimentation, its lack of instruments, and its over-reliance upon brilliant theorizing. The great scientists of early modern times usually collected facts first and formulated opinions after they had meticulously studied the data. This is the experimental, or the inductive, method of inquiry. It consists of several essentials: the necessary instruments to carry on experiments, suitable places, such as laboratories, dissecting theaters, and observatories, where such experiments can be conducted, a superior standard of exact observation and skill in experimental technique, tentative hypotheses based on experiments tested by further experiments and, if substantiated, formulated into basic principles and scientific laws.

The great achievement of the seventeenth century was that it started science well on its way in the new inductive, experimental method, with all that this implies. The basic features of the new method, which has guided scientific procedure in the past three hundred years, were most clearly and eloquently expressed by Francis Bacon and René Descartes. In his *Discourse of Method,* Descartes—a French soldier of fortune, philosopher, and mathematical genius—enjoined all men claiming to be scientists to begin their research by doubting traditional dogmas, by eliminating individual prejudices, and by demanding facts before opinions.

Sir Francis Bacon. Bacon, as an exponent of scientific methodology, was more illustrious than his younger contemporary, Descartes. Born in London in 1561, this apostle of the new science entered Parliament in 1583 and was appointed lord chancellor of England by James I in 1618. During this long career of public service Bacon wrote his precise *Essays* and seven scientific works which proclaimed the possibilities of the new science. Bacon's conception of a Utopia in the *New Atlantis* was constructed in accordance with scientific principles. In his *Novum Organum* one finds the famous Baconian Idols, which the author maintains are the major obstacles to human progress. The first, the Idols of the Tribe, refer to the tendency to see only those facts which support an opinion one wishes to entertain, and to the ease with which emotion dominates reason in most men. The Idols of the Cave refer to the peculiar mental or physical composition of each individual, his birth, childhood, education, and social and economic status. Bacon would have us beware of our individual biases.

Idols of the Market Place relate to the confusion in mental processes caused by words—the media by which thought is transferred. But word symbols often represent different meanings to different people. Care must be taken, therefore, that in writing, conversation, and argumentation words convey a precise and commonly accepted meaning. Finally, there are the Idols of the Theater. By this Bacon meant that men have a tendency to become attached to particular theories, schools of thought, and philosophies, and render tenacious allegiance long after logical basis for the continuance of these theories and philosophies has disappeared.

New scientific instruments. Beginning with the invention of the telescope and microscope by spectacles makers in Holland, a flood of new instruments poured forth to serve science. The micrometer was designed and perfected between 1640 and 1666, the barometer was invented (1647-1648) by Torricelli and Pascal, the pendulum clock by Huygens, and the air pump by von Guericke. Von Guericke astounded his observers with an experiment in which sixteen horses were required to pull apart two hollow iron hemispheres from which the air had been pumped. (See the picture on page 51.) The eighteenth century contributed the centigrade and the Fahrenheit thermometers, the chronometer, the sextant, and the anemometer, a device for measuring the force of wind.

Better methods of calculation. The most obvious mathematical need about the year 1600 was for quicker methods of calculation. Cumbrous tables to help shorten the process of computation had been devised, but these were not adequate. A mathematician had invented the slide rule in 1622, and the first adding machine was developed in 1645 by Pascal.

The invention of decimals did much to simplify calculation. A Dutch mathematician is given credit for this discovery in a work published in 1585 entitled: "The Decimal, teaching with unheard-of ease how to perform all calculations necessary among men by whole numbers without fractions."

A Scotsman, John Napier, published *A Description of the Marvellous Rule of Logarithms* in 1614. Logarithms reduced the time and effort heretofore entailed in solving intricate mathematical problems, and it has been said that by halving the time necessary to solve problems Napier doubled the lives of his fellow mathematicians.

Descartes, while most of Europe was shaken by the Thirty Years' War, found time to reflect upon mathematics and philosophy. In mathematics his most important achievement was the blending of geometry and algebra into what we know as analytic geometry.

Infinitesimal, or fluxional, calculus, the greatest mathematical achievement of the seventeenth century, was the work of Sir Isaac Newton (1642-1727), the famous English scientist, and Gottfried Leibnitz (1646-1716), a German scholar of remarkable versatility. This new calculus dealt with the idea of variation within limits and with infinitesimal elements. It enabled mathematicians, for the first time, to consider quantitatively such problems as the motions of stars and the movement of heat, and to compute quickly the content of circles and the calculation of stresses.

Scientific societies. An important feature of the progress of science in early modern times was the establishment of scientific societies. The first, the Academy of Experiments, was founded in Florence and patronized by the Medici. The Royal Society of England was organized by admirers of Francis Bacon and received its royal charter in 1662 from Charles II. Three famous names on its roster in the seventeenth century are Newton, Robert Hooke, the discoverer of the cellular structure of plants, and the diarist Samuel Pepys. The French Academy of Science was established in 1666 and had an illustrious group of supporters.

These societies concentrated upon the collection of scientific data and the promotion of experimentation. Questionnaires relating to the newly discovered lands across the seas were given to ship captains and other travelers. Sailors before their voyages received specific instructions for astronomical and geographical observations. Museums and botanical gardens were also established. Under the good offices of governments and societies dozens of trained herbalists, geographers, and physicians were sent on expeditions to conduct investigations and collect specimens.

Science takes to the heavens. It was in astronomy that science made its most spectacular advance. For over a thousand years western Europe had accepted the view of Claudius Ptolemy, a Greek scholar of the second century A.D., as presented in his work the *Almagest,* that the earth is stationary and the sun, stars, and planets move around it every twenty-four hours. The Ptolemaic system, or geocentric theory, was incorporated into the scholastic system of the Church. By the close of the Middle Ages a mass of data relating to movements of planets had been collected, placing a heavy strain upon the Ptolemaic theory. The so-called doctrine of epicycles—small circles whose centers moved round in the circumference of a larger circle—had been utilized to account for the varying positions of the planets, but thoughtful men found it more and more difficult to square the traditional theory with the facts.

Before this confused thinking in the astronomical world could be removed, four things were essential: improvement in the technique of celestial observation, the development of more accurate instruments, refined methods of mathematical computation, and finally a revolution in men's conceptions of the heavens. These objectives were attained for civilization chiefly through the labors of five great minds: Copernicus, a Pole; Brahe, a Dane; Kepler, a south German; Galileo, an Italian; and Newton, an Englishman.

The early career of Copernicus. Copernicus was born in 1473, a contemporary of Martin Luther and Christopher Columbus. The father having decided that his son should enter the Church, Copernicus at nineteen was sent to the University of Cracow. He was fascinated by the study of mathematics and astronomy. Following the completion of his studies, he was elected a canon of a cathedral in his homeland in 1497. The ecclesiastical career of Copernicus, however, was postponed by a leave of absence for three years of advanced study at the University of Bologna in Italy. He read widely in the classical authors and was much impressed with the Pythagorean school of ancient Greece.

In the midst of these labors Copernicus was forced to return to Poland, his quest for truth not satisfied. Presently he received permission to study medicine and law. Again he returned to Italy and established himself at the University of Padua, which enjoyed an unrivaled reputation for its medical faculty and its Humanistic tradition. Several years of study made him an excellent doctor, but Copernicus did not neglect his first love—the study of the heavens. He returned to Poland with an astounding knowledge of astronomy and with serious doubts as to the validity of the Ptolemaic theory.

The heliocentric theory. The more Copernicus studied the heavens, the more convinced he was of the absurdity of the geocentric theory. By concentrating on the movements of the planet Mars he finally concluded that the sun, not the earth, was the center of our planetary system. This discovery came to be known as the heliocentric theory. In 1522 he wrote a brief and popular account of his theory which attracted considerable attention. By this time his fame as an astronomer had become widespread. But Copernicus, with reason, feared the consequences of the publication. Luther had already denounced vehemently what little he had heard about the new theory, and the papacy would hardly deal kindly with one of its sons who challenged principles upon which the Church had established its thought. So Copernicus was in no hurry to publish his theory with all the supporting data.

In 1542 the aged astronomer, now in his seventieth year, was persuaded by a young professor from the University of Wittenberg to publish his work. Just before his masterpiece came off the press in 1543, Copernicus suffered a series of strokes. On the twenty-fourth day of May, after a long period of unconsciousness, he awakened to see a messenger standing at his bedside with his book. The dying astronomer happily glanced at the title page, attempted to thumb the contents of the book, smiled, and breathed his last.

In 1615 the Roman Inquisition formally condemned the teachings of Copernicus, and in 1616 his book was banned in the *Index of Prohibited Books,* from which it was not removed for a century and a half. Copernicus was dead, but his theory was to give him immortality.

A woodcut from the works of Tycho Brahe shows the Danish astronomer in his observatory at Prague. A modern scientist might have been photographed in a similar pose for his readers.

Significance of Copernicus. The title of the book Copernicus wrote was *Concerning the Revolutions of the Heavenly Bodies.* Its thesis was that the earth rotated every twenty-four hours about its axis from west to east, that it was accompanied by the other planets as it made an annual movement around the sun, and that the sun, therefore, was the center of the planetary system. It is true that Copernicus still adhered to the old notion of epicycles, but this does not detract from his accomplishment. Copernicus worked under almost insuperable handicaps. He was short-sighted and he had no telescope. His theory was the fruit of brilliant analytical thought utilizing a slender body of facts. The publication of his book in 1543 has been regarded by many as the beginning of modern science.

Tycho Brahe (1546-1601). Before the truth of the Copernican theory could be demonstrated, a vast amount of meticulous data had to be procured. This need was supplied by Tycho Brahe, a Dane who had studied at the universities of Copenhagen and Leipzig. In 1576 Brahe was given funds by Frederick II to establish an observatory on an island in Danish waters. The new establishment was called Uraniborgg—the castle of the heavens—and was remarkably well equipped with library, printing press, workshops, and several observatories. For twenty-one years Brahe carried on accurate daily observations and carefully ascertained the positions of 800 stars. While a splendid observer and collector of data, Brahe did little with the vast amount of facts he had accumulated. This was to be the work of the brilliant German, Johann Kepler.

Johann Kepler (1571-1630). Kepler obtained a position as Brahe's assistant, and in 1602 succeeded him as official astronomer of the Holy Roman Empire. Kepler secured the huge collection of data his chief had accumulated over a period of twenty years. On these records Kepler concentrated for twenty-five years. Brahe had never accepted the theory of Copernicus, but Kepler, after wading through the records of his master and applying his mathematical insight, confirmed the general validity of the theory. He abandoned the idea of epicycles and proved that the earth and the planets do not have circular orbits but travel in an ellipse, and that as they approach the sun their pace accelerates. The cause for this variance in planetary motion was not understood by Kepler, but it presented a problem of fundamental importance. To solve this question was to ascertain the law or force that controlled the universe.

Galileo (1564-1642). Galileo Galilei, a contemporary of Kepler, popularized the Copernican theory and discovered many facts which demonstrated its validity. Galileo at the age of twenty-five secured a professorship in mathematics at the University of Pisa. Here his unconventional teaching and advanced views aroused the resentment of the faculty, and Galileo moved to the University of Padua, where he remained for eighteen years. For some time Galileo had accepted the Copernican theory, but news in 1600 of the burning at the stake of Giordano Bruno, a zealous popularizer of the heliocentric doctrine, so shocked him that he imparted his ideas only to a few friends. Hearing of the invention of a Dutchman who arranged lenses in a tube to magnify objects, Galileo made a telescope for himself, ready for use in 1609. Armed with this new instrument, Galileo discovered mountains on the moon, sun spots, the satellites of Jupiter, the rings of Saturn and its phases. The grandeur of these discoveries so thrilled Galileo that he forgot his customary caution and began to publicize his findings. In 1616 the College of Cardinals formally condemned the Copernican doctrine and forbade Galileo to teach or subscribe to the theory.

In 1630 Galileo could no longer stifle the urge to prove the truth of his ideas. He published the work entitled *Dialogues about Two Great Systems of the World.* Three characters in the dialogue discuss the relative merits of the Ptolemaic and Copernican systems. This device was used so that the author could deny having either supported or denied the latter theory. In addition, to disarm the censor, Galileo included a very pious introduction in which, with tongue in cheek, he heaped ridicule on the doctrine of Copernicus. But Galileo's reading public was not deceived. Europe laughed at the trick, and the Pope was highly indignant at the author's duplicity. In October 1632, Galileo was hailed before the Inquisition, and was examined on four different occasions over a period of four years. In the last trial, torture was applied to the old scientist, now seventy. His spirit was thoroughly broken, and a complete renunciation of all his ideas was exacted from him. There has persisted the story, which cannot be substantiated, that after the confession in which he had renounced the idea of the movement of the earth Galileo whispered to himself, *"E pur si muove!"* ("But it does move!")

Opposition to the heliocentric theory. In the foregoing discussion of astronomy, the Roman Catholic Church may have appeared to have been the major obstacle to science. This, however, is an over-simplification. The truth is that the discoveries of such men as Copernicus and Galileo set off a struggle within European thought in which the whole traditional group mentality sought to prevent acceptance of new, disturbing ideas. The whole train of events following the momentous year 1543, when the Copernican theory appeared, illustrates a common feature of history—that people are usually reluctant to change their mental habits. The advent of the new science precipitated a widespread contest between those, undoubtedly a majority at first, who saw no reason to change their fundamental ideas regarding the nature of the universe, and those who believed that these ideas no longer fitted the facts.

The Church was only one, albeit the most powerful, of many organizations to attempt to halt the advance of science. Here the majority of Protestants and Catholics saw eye to eye. Even many intellectuals—Francis Bacon, Pascal, and Milton—refused to accept the Copernican theory. The Roman Catholic Church assumed the leading role in this controversy primarily because it was the strongest and most widespread religious organization. Furthermore, it had for centuries functioned as the traditional arbiter in the verities of thought; it had also acted as the main prop of stability and the relentless foe of anything considered to be capricious change.

As the facts of science became better known, each succeeding generation felt less aversion to the new discoveries and gradually fitted them into a system of thought in which religion and science were harmoniously dovetailed. By 1650 Europe had been largely won over to the Copernican system. What was originally suspect had now become part of the mental habits of most Europeans, and the Catholic Church gradually accepted the accomplished fact. All reference to the ban heretofore imposed on works containing Copernican thought was omitted in the Catholic *Index of Prohibited Books* issued in 1757.

Sir Isaac Newton (1642-1727). Great as had been the contributions of Brahe, Kepler, and Galileo, their individual discoveries had yet to be united into one all-embracing principle or law which would explain the motion of all bodies in the planetary system and present the world as one great unity operating according to unalterable principles. This achievement was realized in the career of Sir Isaac Newton, the most illustrious figure in science in the momentous century and a half from 1650 to 1800.

Newton was born just a year after Galileo's death and a century after the passing of Copernicus. His parents were small farmers, but by procuring a scholarship he was able to attend the University of Cambridge. Here he astounded his professors with his mathematical skill. Euclidean geometry seemed quite obvious to him, and he quickly mastered the works of such mathematicians as Descartes and Kepler. At the age of only twenty-four he had made all of his important discoveries, which included the law of gravitation, the principles of calculus, and the compound nature of light. At twenty-seven the youthful genius was given a professorship in mathematics at the University of Cambridge.

We are indebted to Voltaire for the story that the concept of gravitation first occurred to Newton as he happened to see an apple fall from a tree in his garden. Although he had discovered his law as early as 1666, he was unable to prove it mathematically until 1685. In 1687, therefore, Newton's momentous work was published in Latin under the title *Philosophiae Naturalis Principia Mathematica* (Mathematical Principles of Natural Philosophy). At last the numerous contributions of previous astronomers were synthesized in a master principle for the universe, the law of gravitation. This universal law was expressed by Newton in a concise and simple mathematical formula, that "every particle of matter in the universe attracts every other particle with a force varying inversely as the square of the distance between them and directly proportional to the product of their masses."

The publication of the *Principia* was the climax of nearly one hundred fifty years of struggle of scientists against static tradition and intolerant authority. Newton was now showered with honors. France made him a member of her Academy of Sciences, his native land made him a knight and president of the Royal Society. Pope wrote:

Nature and Nature's laws lay hid in night:
God said, Let Newton be! and all was light.

Newton died in his eighty-fifth year and was buried among England's most illustrious dead in Westminster Abbey, "like a king," commented Voltaire, "who had done good to his subjects."

The perfection of the Newtonian system. Another significant astronomer was William Herschel (1738-1822), who had come to England from Germany as a lowly military bandsman. While still following music as a career, he became interested in astronomy and taught himself higher mathematics and telescopic observation. The efforts of this amateur star gazer were amply rewarded in 1781 by the discovery of the planet Uranus. The following year

Herschel published an important work entitled *Motion of the Solar System in Space.* These achievements were recognized by his appointment as royal astronomer in 1782 by George III. Other eighteenth-century astronomers, especially Pierre Simon de Laplace (1749-1827), did important service in sounding out the Newtonian system.

Science and the New Philosophy

The necessity of a new world view. Men have never accepted life without question or interpretation. From early times, beginning especially with the Greeks, there has been the attempt to answer the "how" and the "why," to probe into the laws that control the universe, to discover the essence of matter, to explain the riddle of life and death, and to fit the facts, as far as they are known, into some kind of unified and understandable explanation.

In the Middle Ages, philosophers, conditioned by the ideas of their day, constructed an intricate theological philosophy whose main purpose was to explain the fundamental doctrines of the Universal Church. Philosophy was for a thousand years the servant of theology.

The impact of the new science, however, could not be ignored by European philosophers. Newton, Copernicus, and Galileo made a new world view and a revaluation of existing thought inevitable. Inspired by science, many philosophers emancipated themselves from theology, became unchristian, and at times even antichristian. With reason, not faith, as their guide, they took up anew such problems as the nature of reality, the meaning of matter, the problems of knowledge. Now "all scientists of the time were inclined to be philosophical, and all philosophers to be 'scientific.' "

Giordano Bruno (1548-1600). An Italian philosopher, Giordano Bruno was perhaps the first to apply the Copernican theory to philosophy. This spirited champion of the new truth, who was intoxicated by the immensity of the universe which the scientist had opened to his mind, and who bravely proclaimed a philosophy of pantheism throughout Europe until he was burned at the stake, maintained that the universe "is a great organism, whose dwelling-place is the infinite reaches of space." Everything in the universe is alive; God is everywhere. The earth is ruled not by man but by the sun, "with the life which breathes in common through the universe."

Descartes' dualism. René Descartes, (1596-1650), besides his mathematical contributions, was really the first of the modern philosophers. This pioneer thinker sought to harmonize medieval thought with scientific progress by picturing a mechanistic world in which supernatural phenomena are impossible, and in which everything can be explained rationally, preferably in mathematical terms. Apart from this mechanistic world, however, according to Descartes, is another world—that of God and spirit—which is beyond and apart from the reach of science.

All of Descartes' thinking was permeated by the mathematical approach. He was always emphasizing that sound thinking must follow the logical processes utilized in mathematics. Above all Descartes believed philosophy should be practical. "Philosophy," he maintained, "is a perfect knowledge of all that man can know, as well for the conduct of his life as for the preservation of his health and the discovery of all the arts."[1] The essence of Descartes' philosophical system was that mind, or God, and man, or nature are distinct one from the other. The theory is known as philosophical dualism. According to Descartes, reason is the chief source of knowledge. By logical methods of thought the nature of reality, the existence of God, and the existence of the human self can be demonstrated.

Spinoza's pantheism (1632-1677). Baruch Spinoza was deeply influenced by Descartes but could not accept his dualism. Born in Amsterdam of well-to-do Jewish-Portuguese parents, he first studied Jewish theology but found it little to his liking. So dissatisfied was young Spinoza that he renounced Judaism and was promptly excommunicated by the Jewish elders. He now was compelled to leave Amsterdam and went to The Hague, where he managed to earn a meager living by grinding lenses. His poverty did not prevent him from carrying on his studies, especially of religion and philosophy. So important were his writings that he was offered the post of professor of philosophy at the University of Heidelberg, provided he tone down some of his rather radical ideas. Spinoza refused this offer; to him independence of thought was preferable even if it had to be enjoyed amid poverty. Following the methods of Descartes, Spinoza strove to build a mathematical philosophy. His work *Ethics* is filled with geometric axioms, postulates, and theories. The dualistic system of Descartes was rejected by Spinoza, to whom mind and matter were manifestations of one substance—nature or God. In other words, the Universe and God are one. The idea that God is everything and everywhere is known as pantheism. While Spinoza was alive both Jews and Christians despised him as an atheist. In more recent times his true spirituality has become better understood, and instead of being branded an atheist he has been called "the God-intoxicated man." In the year 1677 Spinoza died, impoverished and persecuted.

Leibnitz's philosophy. Another interesting attempt to reconcile philosophy and science is seen in the work of the German Leibnitz, who also was a renowned mathematician. Spinoza believed in one universal substance; Leibnitz, on the other hand, created a philosophical system in which there existed an infinite number of substances. The philosophical system of Leibnitz anticipated to an astonishing degree the modern scientific conception of the universe. To Leibnitz the elemental substance in the world is force, or energy. The universe is, therefore, made up of an infinite number of centers of force called monads, each throbbing with energy. The monads of Leibnitz were strikingly similar to our modern conception of atoms made up of electrons.

John Locke (1632-1704) and empiricism. The continental philosophers in the main were rationalists who believed that knowledge is gained through reasoning. English thinkers of the period tended toward practicality and hard-headedness. They believed that knowledge came only from sensory experience, a school of thought known as empiricism. Its founder was John Locke, who had studied philosophy, science, and medicine at Oxford. Locke's opinion was that there had been too much abstruse and flighty thought in Europe and that someone should work out a reasonable and simple philosophy. This belief was strengthened when he joined a group to discuss philosophy and the group got nowhere. There was no agreement on definitions or concepts and, after a long evening of discussion, the philosophers would leave with the knowledge that everybody there had been in complete disagreement with everybody else. Locke wrote a book called *An Essay Concerning Human Understanding* which sought to analyze the human mind. According to Locke, the mind at birth is like a blank tablet. Experience gained through the senses writes on this tablet. Unlike the rationalist school on the European continent, Locke maintained that mind of itself has no innate power to grasp reality. In analyzing the source of knowledge, Locke leaned heavily on the theory that the mind is not completely passive but that knowledge is due to perception plus reflection. By the process of association the new and the old react one on the other, blending into a new idea.

The successors of Locke, however, carried his empiricism to greater extremes. We find Bishop Berkeley (1685-1753) declaring that reality can exist only in the mind, outside which there is no material universe. David Hume (1711-1776), the Scottish historian and philosopher, even challenged the reality of the mind.

Immanuel Kant (1724-1804). Immanuel Kant was meanwhile living a serene and contemplative life as professor of philosophy at the University of Königsberg. Never ruffled, kindly, high-minded, and above all methodical, this quiet dreamer, who never ventured more than forty miles from the university in his life of eighty years, was thoroughly aroused at the exaggerated skepticism and materialism of Hume. He determined to shift philosophy back to a more sensible position without necessarily giving up too much of its "rational" basis. Kant's answer, contained in the *Critique of Pure Reason,* marked the end of eighteenth-century natural philosophy and ushered in philosophical idealism, so important in the first part of the nineteenth century.

While agreeing with Locke on the importance of the senses in acquiring knowledge, Kant denied that the mind is "mere passive wax," because all sensations must be sifted and interpreted through patterns of the mind which are the product of reason. To resolve the conflict between mind and matter, Kant resorted to dualism. Beyond the realm of physical nature to which the laws of science can be applied, lies the world of "things-in-themselves," which science can never penetrate. It is, therefore, the proper domain of philosophical inquiry. Kant agreed with his contemporaries that the existence of God could not be demonstrated scientifically but declared that man's moral sense compels him to believe in the immortality of the soul and in the presence of God.

Religion in the Age of Reason

Religion and reason. The Enlightenment worshiped reason and attempted to reduce all human interests and activities to rational analysis. The Religious Revolt had split the unity of the medieval church, but fundamentally religious thought had been little changed. Both Protestants and Catholics still clung tenaciously to their dogmas and creeds.

Deism. To the intellectual of the eighteenth century, traditional Christianity with its occasional excesses of intolerance seemed at variance with the findings of the new science. Religions must be simplified, stripped of their superfluities, and made to accord with reason. The solution offered by the eighteenth-century philosophers was Deism. God was thought of as the impersonal Force of scientific law and became the "first cause," the custodian of the world-machine, the master "clock-winder" of the universe. This God had been necessary to create the universe, but once the universe was in motion its immutable laws could not be altered. It was regarded as useless, therefore, to invoke the intercession of God in order to cause the laws of nature to deviate from their ordered course. Men must rely upon reason to solve the problems of society.

Underlying Deistic thought was the concept of a natural religion, including God as master of the universe, the necessity of worshiping God, the atonement by man for his sins, the doctrine of immortality, and the view that the aim of religion was virtue or sensible living. All religions were to be based on these simple and rational essentials. Anything additional was extraneous and not worth squabbling about. Deists maintained that if all creeds would incorporate these fundamentals and give up, or at least minimize, what was left, religious intolerance and bigotry would cease. The God of Deism was universal and acceptable to all. It mattered little what he was called. In the words of Pope:

> Father of all! in every age,
> In every clime adored,
> By saint, by savage, and by sage,
> Jehovah, Jove, or Lord!

The French "philosophes." France in the mid-seventeenth century had been the intellectual center of Europe, but by the end of the century the reputation of Newton and the fame of England's advanced governmental system made her the exponent of a new system of politics and science. Due largely to two famous French thinkers, Voltaire and Montesquieu, however, English thought was transferred to the continent. Early in the eighteenth century France again enjoyed the intellectual supremacy of Europe. Here a group of thinkers and writers, known as the *philosophes,* brought the Age of Reason to its climax. The term *philosophes* cannot be translated as "philosophers," because the thinkers to whom it referred were not, strictly speaking, philosophers, but rather students of society, expressing its evils and advocating reforms. Foremost of these *philosophes* were Voltaire and Diderot, whose influence will be noted in this chapter, and Rousseau and Montesquieu, whose importance in political reform will be discussed in the following chapter.

Voltaire (1694-1778). Voltaire, more than any other thinker, personified the skepticism of the eighteenth century toward traditional religion and the evils of the time. Born of middle-class parents, François Marie Arouet (his real name) was reared in Paris where he attended a Jesuit secondary school, one of the best in France. Following this schooling, the "crasher of noble gates" gave up his family name, assumed the more aristocratic "Monsieur de Voltaire," and became a member of a club of young intellectuals who drank freely, talked incessantly, and scoffed at the illogical customs of their time. The young Voltaire was clever, witty, and inordinately vain. Above all he enjoyed exercising a caustic pen. By criticizing the stupidities of high officials and members of the nobility he soon ran afoul of the law and twice was imprisoned in the Bastille. On one occasion he received a cruel beating at the hands of the servants of a nobleman he had ridiculed and, finally, was banished to England for three years.

Voltaire put his time to good use writing and gathering ammunition for a relentless attack on the abuses of his day. He championed tolerance, popularized the science of Newton, fought for personal liberty and freedom of the press, and was an influential propagandist of the natural religion of Deism. Returning to the continent from exile, Voltaire lived for fifteen years in Lorraine, a little country wedged between Germany and France. Always fearful of offending the authorities, Voltaire felt secure in this frontier zone. Here amid his books, manuscripts, and laboratory equipment —for like all eighteenth-century thinkers Voltaire liked to think himself a scientist—he acted the part of host to the many intellectuals who came to his door, and turned out a prodigious amount of writing in the form of histories, plays, pamphlets, essays, and novels. Modern editions of his works and letters fill about ninety volumes. His correspondence alone is estimated at ten thousand letters, in which he wittily spread the gospel of rationalism, and attacked the abuses of the old régime without pity. After the death of his mistress, Voltaire went to the court of Frederick the Great in Berlin for three years, but the "statesman who wanted to be a poet" and the "poet who wanted to be a statesman" got on each other's nerves. Following a violent quarrel with his royal patron, Frederick, Voltaire wandered over Europe for two years, finally settling down near Geneva, where he passed the remaining twenty-three years of his life. On his deathbed the old scoffer cackled that he was dying because of having drunk 250,000 cups of coffee, for he had been an inveterate drinker of this beverage all his life.

As the most relentless critic of the established churches, Protestant and Catholic alike, Voltaire achieved his greatest fame. He was sickened by the intolerance of organized Christianity and disgusted by the petty squabbles which seemed to monopolize the time of many priests and clergymen. Yet in spite of his vituperation against Christianity, Voltaire was not a wrecker of religion. He once said that if a God did not exist it would be necessary to invent one. Voltaire wished to induce men to worship a God of nature.

Although much of Voltaire's writing was clever rather than profound, superficial rather than sincere, and in his attack on existing abuses he often failed to suggest alternative substitutes, he is to be remembered as a truly great figure.

Denis Diderot (1713-1784). Voltaire had many disciples and imitators, but his only rival in spreading the gospel of rationalism and deism was a set of books. This was the famous French *Encyclopedia,* edited by Denis Diderot, who in some respects was more original and influential in his thought than Voltaire. As planned by the editor, the purpose of the *Encyclopedia* was not only to serve as a repository of knowledge but also to function as a weapon against traditional authority. Its seventeen volumes, therefore, contained articles whose writers—tradesmen as well as scientists and philosophers—criticized in a moderate tone such evils as unfair taxation, the slave trade, and the cruelty of the existing criminal code.

Deism evaluated. In studying the literature of Deism one runs across many conflicting estimates of its worth. Some critics declare it taught what people should not believe but offered nothing in the place of traditional worship. They also argue that it destroyed reverence for the Church and engendered indifference to religion. Other writers hail Deism as a major step in mankind's emancipation from superstitious dogma. It is true that Deism at its best in the eighteenth century produced more tolerant and enlightened clergymen and encouraged moderation and good sense. But its appeal was mainly to the educated upper classes, not to the common people, who got little satisfaction and solace from its cold rationalism. In England, particularly, the established Church had become formal, lifeless, and de-spiritualized. Spiritual emotion was all but extinct. The poorer classes got little inspiration from sermons that were in the main philosophical discourses. Churches were, as a result, mainly patronized by the well-to-do, who sat in pews surrounded by curtains well suited, as Swift, the satirist, has said, for "lodging folks disposed to sleep."

Quakers, Methodists, and Pietists. In England Deism had overreached itself and the Church stood in urgent need of re-spiritualization. A pioneer in this movement was George Fox (1624-1691), whose teachings formed a foundation for the later reaction against Deism in the mid-eighteenth century. Fox was the founder of the religious sect called the Friends, or Quakers. It was his belief that the external aspects of Christianity—dogma, organization, and ritual—were unimportant as compared with the "inner light," the spiritual experience of the individual. The Quakers took a strong stand against war and also severely criticized religious intolerance.

It was not until the time of John and Charles Wesley that the reaction against rational religion known as Pietism, got well under way in England. Following a trip to the new colony of Georgia where the Wesleys tried to convert the Indians, the brothers began in 1738 to preach in a new way to the English people. The cold formalism of the old Church was discarded for a glowing emotionalism. Stilted sermons were laid aside for extemporaneous appeals filled with intense religious fervor. The Wesleys stressed methodical devotion, regularity of conduct, and frequent prayer. At first a term of derision, the word "Methodist" came to be the respected and official name of the movement. Following the death of John Wesley in 1791 the Methodists officially broke away from the Anglican Church. In England the new denomination became one of the most important religious forces in the national life.

On the European continent, a German Lutheran named Philipp Spener (1635-1705) stressed what he called "the religion of the heart" rather than that of unimportant externals. It is said that the philosophers Leibnitz and Kant, referred to earlier in this chapter, were influenced by the teachings of Spener. Another European Pietist was Emanuel Swedenborg (1688-1772), the brilliant son of a Swedish professor of theology. After an intense religious experience in 1745, Swedenborg devoted himself to writing religious works tinged with a strong mystical spirit. After his death his followers established the "Church of the New Jerusalem" which has come down to the present day and has retained its mystical, Pietistic character.

New religious attitudes. With the end of the eighteenth century, the religious life of Europe had been beset by almost continuous strife and uncertainty for three hundred years. This was only part of the general adjustment being made in European life and thought as medieval ideas and institutions gave way to those of the modern age. By the year 1800 a more balanced Christianity was emerging from the suffering brought about by the wars of the Religious Revolt, the excesses of the science versus religion controversy, and the repercussions of Deism and Pietism. Intolerance and undue emphasis upon dogma and form were giving way to tolerance and to the practical application of Christ's teachings. Undue belief in the helplessness of man and the depravity of human nature was superseded by an understanding of man's mental and moral dignity and the desire to evaluate religion by the test of its "reasonableness and utility in this life."

During the Religious Revolt and the succeeding wars intolerance was the mark of Catholic and Protestant alike. Persecution raged between sects because men were passionately interested in religious matters. How did religious tolerance come about? There were two causes, one material, the other intellectual. The devastating religious wars had ruined Germany and undermined the economic strength of Spain. Religious intolerance hindered freedom of commerce. But Holland, a tolerant nation for whom unhampered trade was possible, had prospered enormously. Men were coming to see that it paid rich dividends to overlook another's creed if his credit was good.

Intellectually, tolerance grew for a number of reasons. As we have shown, the warring sects saw that they could not wipe each other out; therefore they had to learn to endure one another. Then again, the religious wars had gradually shifted men's interest from purely theological matters to those of politics and nationalism. And of course the rise of the scientific spirit and of intellectual skepticism gradually permeated the thought of the seventeenth century, until by the following century tolerance had manifested itself in a lessening of persecution of such minority groups as the Jews, the atheists, and the Quakers.

A very healthy sign in the late seventeenth century was the slow but sure dying out of demonology and its cruel witch-hunting. The sixteenth century, which had witnessed the birth of modern science, also marked the flourishing of perhaps the darkest age of superstition. This appears to be a strange paradox, but the reason is not difficult to find. As reason rebelled against blind faith, faith tried by all means possible to retain its power. One means was playing upon the superstitious credulity of the people. Astrology held a wide popularity, including among its champions such famous men as Milton and Kepler. On the other hand, Montaigne, Francis Bacon, and Molière heaped ridicule on astrologers and their adherents. But although astrology, like alchemy, tended to decline in popular favor, one superstition was readily accepted in the sixteenth century—demonology.

The need for humanitarianism. There were many social evils that cried aloud for rectification. Negro slavery was legal, a barbarous criminal code inflicted physical torture upon wrongdoers, prisons were breeding places for disease, the insane were treated like animals, the poor laws were inadequate, and some religious intolerance still persisted. There had been much improvement in the past five hundred years, but European people were more than ever aware of the need of widespread reform. Rationalism and, more particularly, Deism and Pietism were the driving forces behind reform in the eighteenth century. Deism provided the intellectual protest against intolerance and cruelty, while Pietism led to a strong urge to succor and bring comfort to the oppressed and downtrodden.

In 1764 Cesare di Beccaria, an Italian nobleman interested in social reform, published his *Essay on Crimes and Punishments.* This work established the science of criminology with its insistence that prison terms should be deterrents to crime rather than punishment for crime. Beccaria's ideas soon were widely recognized and in many countries new criminal codes were based on his principles. Torture in obtaining evidence, and such punishment as whipping, branding, and slitting of ears were gradually eliminated from most codes.

John Howard and prison reform. John Howard (1726-1790) was the outstanding prison reformer of eighteenth-century England. The son of a wealthy merchant, Howard lived off his inheritance and spent his days in reading and study, in building model cottages for the common people, and in constructing schools. After he became a sheriff, in 1773, he began inspecting the prisons of his area and was astonished to find that the jailers did not receive a regular salary but had to collect their remuneration in fees from their unwilling boarders. In some cases Howard found that persons who had been acquitted by a jury had not been released because they had no funds to pay for their "board." In 1774 Howard gave evidence before a committee of the House of Commons which resulted in an act providing pay for jailers. In 1777 Howard's important book, *The State of the Prisons in England and Wales,* appeared. This work stressed the need for efficient prison administration. It further maintained that the main aim of imprisonment should be reformation of the criminal. In the last five years of his life, Howard devoted himself to a study of the plague, making trips to the European continent for this purpose. On his last journey he made his way to Russia, where, observing the ravages of a contagious disease, he contracted it and died.

Education in the seventeenth century. The growth of tolerance was connected (though all too slightly) with the growth of education in the seventeenth century, a function of the Church in Catholic countries and often of the state in Protestant lands. But these government controlled schools demanded religious and political obedience from their pupils. Most of the institutions were designed to educate the sons of gentlemen and gentry. Nevertheless, in Scotland and especially New England primary education was made universal and in the latter region even obligatory, as enacted by the laws of 1642 and 1647 in Massachusetts.

Meanwhile an educational expansion occurred in the Catholic Church. The development was largely the work of the Jesuits, and their schools, often called colleges, gave a thorough education not only to their own members but also to outsiders. The first Jesuit school to be opened to the public was the Collegium Romanum in 1551; by 1626 the Jesuits could count more than 13,000 pupils in Paris alone, and in both Europe and America many colleges had been founded.

Despite setbacks from the religious wars of the sixteenth and seventeenth centuries, the universities continued to grow and develop. Unfortunately, universities in all countries were too hidebound to allow much real progress to be made either in science or in tolerance. There was no wholesome student life, and courses of study were extremely conservative.

Eighteenth-century schools. By the eighteenth century educational thought had begun to reflect the humanitarianism of the age, particularly in the movement to provide schools for the common people. Schools had been all too few, the subjects taught often bore no relation to the needs of actual life, and the common idea seemed to be that beatings in the classroom should be as frequent as possible. The English poet George Crabbe wrote:

Students like horses on the road,
Must be well lashed before they take the load:
They may be willing for a time to run,
But you must whip them ere the work be done.

One of the most important influences in education was Jean Jacques Rousseau, whose literary and political significance will be discussed later. Rousseau wrote a treatise called *Emile* which challenged the current practice of making little boys and girls miniature adults. "Let the child be himself," was Rousseau's message. The aim of education should be self-expression, not repression; education must be many-sided to appeal to different children; and, Rousseau maintained, the pupil, not the subject matter, is most important.

Other educational reformers in the late eighteenth and early nineteenth century tried to follow the teachings of *Emile*. One was Johann Heinrich Pestalozzi, born in Switzerland in 1746. This teacher first translated Rousseau's general recommendations into specific teaching methods. Pestalozzi believed that the classroom should reflect kindliness and love, not harshness and repression. In England the Sunday-School movement, sponsored mainly by the Methodists, was a pioneer attempt to bring the rudiments of learning to the poor.

Early in the nineteenth century the influence of Rousseau and of Pestalozzi made itself felt in a rapid advance of educational opportunities for the children of the common people. From now on schooling in the United States and in certain parts of Europe was in the direction of free, public, and compulsory education.

Belief in progress. Humanitarian reforms were an important feature of the Age of Reason. Thinking men believed that by the application of intelligence to human problems man could be improved. The eighteenth century originated what we refer to as the modern idea of progress, a buoyant optimism in mankind's possibilities. An expression of this belief is to be found in Marquis de Condorcet's (1743-1794) *Historical Sketch of the Progress of the Human Mind* (1794). In this work the French thinker asserts there are no limits to human perfectability and declares that progress will come by abolishing inequalities between nations, by securing equality for all men within nations, and by improving, "grading up," the human race in mind and body.

Scientific Progress Continues

Old and new sciences. By the end of the seventeenth century important discoveries had been made in mathematics and astronomy, and their impact on philosophy and religion was profound. Meantime, scientific progress was being made in other areas. Older sciences were being reshaped by the impact of the new methods of inquiry, by more efficient instruments for experiment, and by the recently stimulated spirit of inquisitiveness among Europeans. Totally new discoveries were destined to remake the lives of all people.

The science of chemistry in the sixteenth and early seventeenth centuries seemed to have suffered from arrested development. Men followed the will-o'-the-wisps of alchemy and magic. The real beginnings of modern chemistry hinged around the unraveling of the phenomenon of combustion. An explanation was advanced by Georg Ernst Stahl (1660-1734) to the effect that in all things that burn there is a "combustible substance, a principle of fire, but not fire itself." This invisible and highly combustible substance was called "phlogiston" (from Greek "to set on fire"). Although later disproved, it was the first important chemical theory and did much to turn the attention of chemists from magic and alchemy.

Boyle, father of modern chemistry. Robert Boyle (1627-1691), the son of an Irish nobleman, is considered the father of modern chemistry. This inveterate experimenter was the first to emphasize the difference between a compound, whose constituent parts have been unified by chemical action and cannot be dissociated without chemical change, and a mixture, in which various ingredients are merely brought together by mechanical means. In 1660 he enunciated the law that the volume of a gas varies inversely with the pressure. The term "gas" had first been used by a Belgian, van Helmont, who had discovered the chemistry of gases. The range and diversity of Boyle's researches are amazing. They include experiments on the rusting of metals, fire, respiration, fermentation, and evaporation. Perhaps most important was his book *The Sceptical Chymist* (1661), in which he fulminated against alchemy and urged the use of the true method of inductive inquiry in chemistry.

***Priestley* (*1733-1804*).** Joseph Priestley, the chemist-preacher, was an enthusiastic amateur who divided his loyalty between his congregation and his crucible. He discovered muriatic acid, now used for cleaning metals and in manufacturing glue and gelatine. He also isolated ammonia, the gas which in modern times has come to play an important role in the refrigeration process. In 1774 Priestley discovered a gas which he called "dephlogisticated air," later to be given the name of oxygen. A fearless reformer and liberal, Priestley was the center of a distinguished group of intellectuals in Birmingham who composed the Lunar Society. Two of the "Lunatics," as they called themselves, were James Watt, inventor of the steam engine, and Erasmus Darwin, grandfather of the scientist who announced the theory of evolution. In 1791, as a result of his sympathies with the French Revolution, a mob attacked Priestley's house and destroyed his laboratory. Three years later the chemist came to the United States and settled in Pennsylvania, where he carried on his studies. His last important experiment, in 1799, was the production of carbon monoxide gas. Much of the gas used in our homes for cooking and heating purposes is made by the method first devised by Priestley. His home has now been made into a permanent memorial by the chemists of America. Here one can see the flasks, retorts, and vials with which he conducted so many epochal experiments.

***Henry Cavendish* (*1731-1810*).** A fellow countryman of Priestley's, but a member of one of England's most wealthy and venerable families, Henry Cavendish might have domi-

An apothecary is distilling chemicals. The absence of Bunsen burners—standard equipment for chemists—is the more obvious for the stacks of fuel and the bellows. But retorts and flasks are rather modern-looking.

nated the clubs and smart society of London. But he was a shy misanthrope, "shabby, awkward, nervous," a woman-hater who has been called the "wisest of all rich men and the richest of all wise men." He led the existence of a recluse, devoting all his time to chemical experiments. In 1766 he discovered that hydrogen gas is entirely different from ordinary air; in 1781 he demonstrated that water was a compound of two gases. One hundred years later two British chemists studying the memoirs of Cavendish, in which the results of his many experiments were related, came across a clue which led them to discover four new elements: argon, neon, krypton, and xenon.

Through Boyle, Priestley, and Cavendish chemistry had come a long way from the fruitless medieval alchemy, but the tyranny of the phlogiston theory still remained. No scientist as yet had been able to dethrone it. Priestley, in spite of his discovery of oxygen, defended phlogiston to the end. Chemistry could not hope to attain the status of a true science until Stahl's theory of combustion had been discarded.

Lavoisier dethrones the phlogiston theory. Antoine Lavoisier (1743-1794) as a young man demonstrated unusual ability in the sciences. At nineteen he was recognized as an authority on illumination; at twenty-five he was admitted to the French Academy. In 1775 the French government appointed him head of the state powder works. One of Lavoisier's assistants, a young man named Eleuthère du Pont, fled from Paris during the French Revolution, came to America, and in 1802 established the firm of Dupont.

Lavoisier led a busy, fruitful, and happy life. His official duties were heavy, but he found time to carry on experiments in his chemical laboratory and to write a text, *Elementary Treatise on Chemistry*, which revolutionized chemistry. He also kept up a voluminous correspondence with scientists in America and Europe and conferred with scholars from foreign lands, such as Priestley and Franklin.

Lavoisier's most important work was his singlehanded destruction of the phlogiston theory. The supporters of this doctrine had maintained that "phlogiston" was removed during combustion. By introducing the balance, scales used by chemists for weighing, Lavoisier proved that nothing was given off, but, on the contrary, something was added. Certain metals were carefully weighed and then burned. Placed upon the balance after combustion they were found to be heavier after being burned. The metals then were burned in a sealed vessel and here it was found that the total weight in the sealed vessel, that is of the air and of the metals both before and after combustion, was the same. From these facts Lavoisier reasoned that burning is a process in which the "dephlogisticated air" discovered by Priestley is taken from ordinary air and unites with the substance consumed. Lavoisier conclusively proved this when he reversed the above experiment, taking the red powder resulting from burned mercury and decomposing it. The loss of weight of the powder was exactly equivalent to the weight of the dephlogisticated air given off. To the element so essential in combustion Lavoisier gave a new name —oxygen. In the face of such incontrovertible facts, the phlogistonists had to lay down their arms. The phlogiston theory was now discredited, and chemistry was ready for real achievement.

Law of the conservation of matter. In his experiments on combustion Lavoisier also discovered the law of the conservation of matter —that matter cannot be created or destroyed. Chemistry had now become an exact science, with knowledge that weight was a constant and that the scientist, aided by his balance, could accurately determine by weight the chemical substances in any compound. Lavoisier, now only fifty-one, was at the full height of his powers, ready for even greater contributions to science, but the career of this "Newton of Science" was cut short by the fury and intolerance of the French Revolution. Lavoisier had been an official of Louis XVI's despised government, had come from a wealthy family, and had married the daughter of a wealthy plutocrat. In the eyes of the revolutionists he was, therefore, no friend of the people. Arrested by soldiers of the Revolutionary Tribunal, he was falsely convicted and condemned to the guillotine.

The beginnings of electricity. A discovery that has probably exercised more influence in shaping our lives in the twentieth century than any other single agency was that of electricity, the efficient donor of light, heat, power, and the most important element in our modern system of communication—telegraph, telephone, and radio.

Only three hundred years ago practically nothing was known of electricity and its seemingly magical potentialities. Knowledge of the power of the lodestone, or magnet, to attract small pieces of iron, however, goes back to ancient times. In addition to observing the peculiar properties of magnetic ore, the ancients had also pondered over the fact that amber when rubbed possessed the power of attracting other bodies. The world, however, had to wait until the seventeenth century before anything substantial was done toward investigating magnetism. William Gilbert (1540-1603) is usually given credit for having founded the modern science of electricity. His *De Magnete* appeared in 1600, after seventeen years of experimentation. In this volume the attraction between magnets is studied, as well as the forces created when such bodies as amber are rubbed. Gilbert was first to use the term "electricity," deriving it from the Greek word for amber *(elektron)*. Gilbert's studies were all the result of experimentation. In the introduction to his famous book the author dedicates it "alone to the philosophers, the ingenuous minds, who not only in books but in things themselves look for knowledge."

Other early discoveries. The next important step in the history of electricity was the creation of a crude machine to produce it. In 1660, Otto von Guericke, the scientist whose air pump we have already discussed, invented a machine consisting of a globe of sulphur set in a glass sphere mounted on a revolving axis. When rubbed by a cloth, it produced both sound and light. This scientist also discovered that an electric current could be sent from one end of a thread to the other. This was the first hint of the possibility of the electrical transmission which in our own day makes possible the great power lines carrying light to thousands of cities and power to the wheels of factories.

The discovery of the Leyden jar in 1745 enabled investigators to accumulate in a glass phial the electricity produced by their primitive friction machines. Bands of showmen now began to tour Europe showing off this new marvel of magic. Amusement and astonishment was aroused when pompous townsfolk and priests joined hands in a demonstration of the powers of the Leyden jar.

Benjamin Franklin (1706-1790). The next important advance in electricity is credited to

Von Guericke's famous experiment of pulling two hemispheres apart, after the air had been pumped out of them, is shown in this engraving. The feat, demonstrating the power of air pressure, required 16 horses.

Benjamin Franklin, America's first great name in science. He was an author, diplomat to France, signer of the Declaration of Independence, and participant in the Constitutional Convention, as well as a scientist. A letter written to a learned society in Philadelphia in 1745 by a fellow of the English Royal Society was the means of getting Franklin interested in electricity. Believing that the static electricity in the Leyden jar was identical with lightning, Franklin carried out his famous kite experiment in June 1752.

Franklin's kite experiment was one of the most daring and brilliant in the annals of science. It gave a rational explanation for what had been an awe-inspiring and terrifying phenomenon of nature for thousands of years. The experiment led to the invention of the lightning rod. Soon all important buildings were being equipped with the new device. Franklin, of course, received universal acclaim. He was given honorary degrees by many British universities and made a fellow of the Royal Society.

Alessandro Volta (1745-1827). Between 1752, the year of the kite experiment, and 1800, the most illustrious name in electricity was Alessandro Volta. Up to this time friction machines were used to give a static charge to some insulated body, such as the Leyden jar. If a conducting circuit was formed by joining the machine with the earth, a flow of electricity could be produced. But in a friction machine the amount of electricity sent out along a wire was so small that it was difficult to detect it. It was the momentous achievement of Volta to make available to science a new kind of electricity, "current electricity," the kind manufactured today.

Volta, a university professor, became interested in electricity following some experiments by Luigi Galvani, also a professor, on the action of an electric current upon the nerve and muscles of a frog's leg. In 1800 Volta sent to the English Royal Society a complete report of a remarkable achievement. He had found a new way of generating electricity that flowed continuously, instead of discharging itself in one spark, as was the case in the Leyden jar. Volta's apparatus consisted of a series of tumblers containing water with a little sulphuric acid. In each glass two plates, one copper and one zinc, were immersed in the solution. The copper plate of one glass was wired to the zinc of the next; only the zinc plate of the first tumbler and the copper plate of the last were unconnected. Volta found that electricity flowed through the connecting wires of his apparatus and that the free copper plate carried a positive charge and the free zinc plate, a negative charge. Thus Volta's machine produced electricity simply but effectively. It was a direct ancestor of modern electric cells and batteries.

Volta became famous overnight. The journals of his time are filled with the marvels of the new instrument. He was called to lecture before Napoleon I, emperor of France, who gave him a gold medal and a substantial pension. At the end of the eighteenth century the idea of sending messages by electricity was being widely discussed and the stage was now set for the amazing development of electricity in the nineteenth century. The name of Alessandro Volta has been immortalized in the term we use for a unit of electrical measurement, the volt.

Geology. Another science which developed remarkably in the eighteenth century was geology. For two thousand years mankind had been intrigued with the study of planets millions of miles distant but had given little thought to the structure of the earth. There were a few exceptions among the Greeks. Such thinkers as Herodotus, Aristotle, and Strabo, discounting the idea that the earth was ruled by capricious gods who unleashed floods and earthquakes at will, made intensive observations of rocks, fossils, and erosion. As a result the theory was advanced that stratified rocks represented the floors of ancient oceans.

After this encouraging beginning, little progress was made for a thousand years. Not until the time of Leonardo da Vinci, in the fifteenth century, was the old Greek theory concerning the formation of rock strata revived. Leonardo apparently had little influence, for two centuries later the few men who concerned themselves with studying rocks and earth strata reverted to a pseudo-scientific approach, with little relation to scientific facts.

The catastrophic theory. In 1765 the first mining school in Europe was established in Germany. Nine years later there came to the new institution a professor named Abraham Werner, whose great learning and efficient teaching methods made this school the greatest center of mineralogy studies in the world.

Werner made the study of minerals a fascinating experience for his students, but unfortunately he indoctrinated them with unsound ideas in geological theory. Werner believed that the earth's surface as now constituted was the result of sudden, catastrophic changes and that originally it had been dissolved in a great ocean out of which the strata of rock had been deposited as the water evaporated.

James Hutton (1726-1797). For a generation Werner's ideas were unchallenged, but, meanwhile, there was a Scotsman quietly working out a theory which was to disprove Werner's as conclusively as Copernicus had overthrown Ptolemy. James Hutton was born in Edinburgh in 1726, and after studying medicine in Paris and the Netherlands he returned to Scotland, where he became a gentleman farmer. Putting his extensive education to good use, he farmed on a scientific basis, introducing important innovations. Hutton became interested in mineralogy as he studied soils. Travel abroad and extensive field trips in the British Isles gave him an acquaintance with many different types of geological formations. At first it seemed to Hutton that the earth's surface presented only a jumble of complex, diverse, and unrelated features. But after long study he concluded that behind this diversity lie a few simple processes which explain how the world today came to be what it is, and that these same basic forces are, at the present time, making the earth what it will be in the future.

In 1785 Hutton, before the Royal Society of Edinburgh, read a preliminary statement of his theory which was expanded into a two-volume work ten years later. In brief he maintained that two fundamental processes are behind all the various formations of the earth's surface and that these basic forces work in a constant and relatively imperceptible manner, rather than in catastrophic fashion as Werner claimed. The two processes are disintegration, or decay, and reconstruction, or repair. The former, utilizing the action of water and wind and chemical decomposition, continually wears away the earth's surface. The resulting material is carried off and deposited on ocean, lake, and valley floors, where new strata are formed.

Hutton emphasized that the best way to understand what has happened in the past is to observe what is taking place in the present. He thus removed the conception of the earth as a static thing. Finally, by emphasizing the immensity of geological time, he gave the world an entirely new time perspective.

Advance in biology. Biology, the science of life, treats of the basic functions and structure of all living things. Its two main branches are botany, dealing with plants, and zoology, dealing with animals. Natural history, as the study of plants and animals used to be called, was practically forgotten after the days of Aristotle and Pythagoras until the sixteenth century. One of the first natural scientists in modern times was Konrad Gesner (1516-1565), a Swiss, who made important contributions in botany and zoology. His work, the *Catalogue of Plants,* did much to stimulate interest in botany, and his *History of Animals* started modern zoology. Stephen Hales (1677-1761), an Englishman, also did notable work in botany. The old idea of plant nutrition was that vegetation absorbed food from the ground in a ready-made form. Hales in 1727 published a work called *Vegetable Statick,* in which it was shown that plants obtain food from the air and that leaves play an important role in the process.

Linnaeus and botany. The seventeenth and eighteenth centuries brought to light a tremendous body of new information on plant and animal life, material gravely in need of sorting and classifying. But it was necessary, too, that the science of classification, or taxonomy as it is called, be placed on a scientific basis. The old method designated all living things as fish, birds, and beasts. It classified plants as either trees, herbs, or shrubs. The system was, naturally, quite inadequate to cope with the wealth of new data. The Swedish naturalist, Carolus Linnaeus, made a trip of some five thousand miles collecting specimens. In 1735 there appeared his *Systema Naturae,* in which he worked out a logical system of plant classification. He divided the plant kingdom into classes, orders, genera, and species. The system of classification worked out by Linnaeus has been amended in modern times, but many of the scientific names, usually Latin, that he applied to both plants and animals are still used.

Buffon and zoology. In the field of zoology the French scientist Georges Buffon (1707-1788) performed the same function as Linnaeus had in botany. As keeper of the Royal Museum and

Botanical and Zoological Gardens at Paris, Buffon had an excellent opportunity to collect information. In 1748 there appeared the first volume of his encyclopedia, *Natural History of Animals,* which ran to more than forty volumes before it was finished. Both this work and the *Systema Naturae* of Linnaeus had wide popularity and did much to stimulate the collection of specimens, both plant and animal.

Doctors, Diseases, and Drugs

Backwardness of medieval healing. As the Middle Ages drew to a close, public health, sanitation, and the general state of medicine were in a deplorable condition in practically all European localities. The few existing hospitals were terribly filthy. In one of the most important, for example, the Hotel Dieu in Paris, four or five patients were crowded into a single bed. Ailing infants, consumptives, typhus patients, and women in child labor were all intermingled. The hospital was filled with foul smells, since little attention was paid to sanitation, and the bodies of the dead were often allowed to remain for as long as a day beside those still living. Diet was also neglected. On some days there would be shortage of food; on others the patients would be allowed to gorge themselves and even to get drunk. In western Europe at this time there was no satisfactory anesthesia to deaden pain, the plague was a constant menace, the germ theory of disease was unknown, most patients preferred to die rather than undergo the torments of surgery and its uncertain results, and obstetrics was in the hands of ignorant midwives. The state of public health can be realized by the fact that the plague called the Black Death may have carried off fifty million people during the twelfth and thirteenth centuries.

Early surgery. During much of the medieval period in Europe, healing was in the hands of churchmen who practiced medicine but not surgery, as the Church forbade them to shed blood. Surgery was therefore, in most places, turned over to unscrupulous charlatans and barbers, whose chief work was to pull teeth and bleed the sick. These so-called doctors were with reason suspected of being more interested in fees than in their patient's cure. For many centuries blood-letting was the most important remedy for any disease. At the barber-surgeon's shop the patient would be bled for indigestion, fits, insomnia, colds, and a host of other maladies both serious and superficial. The modern barber's sign, the red and white pole, dates back to the Middle Ages when the pole represented a patient's arm. The red stripes represent the bleeding flesh and the white signify the tourniquet used to control the flow of blood. Not until the thirteenth century did governments begin to concern themselves in the improvement of medicine. Surgery first became a real profession in France, and in 1515 this fact was recognized when the faculty of the University of Paris grudgingly admitted the surgeons as a department. From now on the professions of barber and surgeon were differentiated, barbers being allowed only to cut hair and pull teeth.

Drugs and cures. By the sixteenth century much of the medical power of the barbers had been removed so that medicine was in the hands of three corporations, or guilds: the apothecaries, the physicians, and the doctors. The first group did about as much harm as good with their vile and ridiculous nostrums. The general principle of druggists at this time might well have been based on an old Chinese saying to the effect that "if a medicine does not stir up a commotion in the patient, the disease will not be cured by it." One famous prescription concocted by an English physician was made up almost entirely of precious stones: gold, silver, pieces of sapphire, emeralds, and shavings of ivory mixed with honey and roses. Concerning this wonderful remedy, its inventor declared: "Kings and nobles have used this for their comfort. It causeth them to be bold-spirited, the body to smell well, and ingendereth to the face a good color."[2]

The dawn of scientific medicine. In the sixteenth century many of the evils prevailing in medicine were swept away and it became a real science, mainly through the work of three outstanding men. Paracelsus inaugurated a new era in internal medicine; Vesalius created the modern science of anatomy; and Paré placed surgery on a rational foundation. All three lived colorful and even romantic lives. Paracelsus, christened Philipp Theophrastus Aureolus Bombastus von Hohenheim, was born in Switzerland. Even this long-winded appellation did not suffice, for later von Hohenheim added Paracelsus, with which he signed most of his medical works. At the age of sixteen he entered a university and soon was absorbed in the study of medicine. Seven years later, apparently annoyed with Scholasticism and the tyranny of tradition which dominated even the study of medicine, Paracelsus began traveling. On the eve of travels that took him to most of the countries of Europe, he sagely remarked, "If a man wishes to become acquainted with many diseases he must set forth on his travels. If he travels far, he will gather much experience, and will win much knowledge."[3]

The life of Paracelsus was one long journey, for he was never permitted to stay long in one place. He was egotistical, and his writings seemed so opinionated that from his middle name, Bombastus, is derived the synonym for a high-sounding and inflated style of expression. For a time Paracelsus was a professor at the University of Basel, where he began by burning in public the works of Galen, Hippocrates, and Avicenna. The other faculty members were further shocked when he lectured in German, not in Latin as was the custom. He ridiculed the reliance of his contemporaries upon classical authorities and urged instead recourse to experimental science.

Such sentiments soon forced him to leave the university and take up his journeys again. In spite of his quarrels, his fame as a healer became widespread. Of this Paracelsus bitingly remarked, "I pleased no one except the sick whom I healed."

Chemicals for medicine. The gist of Paracelsus' teachings was that since the human body was basically chemical in its operations, only the prescription of the proper chemicals could cure disease. In short, chemistry must be utilized in the service of medicine. Paracelsus improved the preparation of many drugs and exposed the foolishness of time-honored remedies. He was the first to advocate the use of metals such as lead, antimony, and iron in prescriptions. The zinc oxide ointment commonly used today for treatment of skin diseases was introduced by Paracelsus. He also introduced opium in a new form, laudanum. Although three hundred years separates modern research workers in biological chemistry and related fields from Paracelsus, they can be regarded as carrying on his work. The use of insulin, thyroxin, concentrated vitamins, sulphanilamide, and many other drugs and medicines are a logical unfolding of the methods advocated by Paracelsus.

Vesalius, founder of modern medicine. If Paracelsus was the forerunner, the real founder of modern medicine was Vesalius (1514-1564), a native of Brussels. The Netherlander, while studying medicine at the university, became disgusted with the teaching, especially in anatomy. In this subject, his professors too often referred to pages in Galen instead of resorting to their scalpels. Dogs, not cadavers, had to serve the dissecting needs of the class. Vesalius complained that a medical student might just as well work in a butcher's shop to learn anatomy. In disgust, the young medical student left the university and launched upon a feverish hunt for cadavers, naturally a dangerous pursuit and one forbidden by the Church.

Fear of persecution led Vesalius to Italy, where he became a professor of anatomy at the University of Padua. Under his inspira-

The amputation scene is a familiar one in all contemporary pictures of early medicine. Instruments were like carpenter's tools, and the patient had no anesthetic.

tion the university became the foremost medical center in Europe. In 1543 he published a folio composed of seven books entitled *Fabric of the Human Body*. His work exposed numerous discrepancies in classical anatomy, and its publication is a landmark in the history of medical science.

Ambroise Paré. Vesalius showed the true structure of the human body and exposed the errors in anatomy made by such authorities as Galen and Hippocrates; Ambroise Paré introduced a rational procedure for surgeons who wished to operate on the body. Paré was a Frenchman, born in Brittany in 1517. At an early age he was apprenticed to a Paris barber, and at nineteen he became an army surgeon. Attached to the French army, Paré saw many bloody battles and gained practical knowledge in how to extract bullets, treat sword cuts, and amputate limbs. After one battle, the boiling oil customarily used to cauterize wounds and stop bleeding was used up. Paré prepared a salve of egg yolk, attar of roses, and turpentine and used the mixture to treat the wounds of those not treated by the hot oil. The next morning Paré made his sick rounds, and to his surprise found that those treated with his salve were much better off than those doused with the hot oil. But a problem soon presented itself. Soothing salves might be a good substitute for oil, but how could they take the place of hot oil as a cautery for stopping the flow of bleeding? Paré began to employ ligatures to arrest hemorrhage. It has been said that surgery presents three basic problems: how to ease pain, how to prevent infection, and how to stop bleeding. By employing the ligature, Paré solved the bleeding problem. Not until the nineteenth century were scientists able to introduce the other two solutions: asepsis and anesthesia.

William Harvey (1578-1657). The founder of modern physiology, William Harvey, attended Cambridge University in 1595 and following graduation entered the University of Padua in Italy as a student of Fabricius, a disciple of Vesalius. After four years of study, Harvey returned to England, where he was recognized as an outstanding doctor. Becoming interested in the circulation of the blood, Harvey plunged into painstaking research which was in 1628 incorporated into a small book of 72 pages with the title *Anatomical Exercise on the Motion of the Heart and Blood in Animals*. In this classic study it was clearly explained that blood is pumped from the heart through the arteries, that it comes back to the heart through the veins, and that blood therefore moves ceaselessly in a circle in the body.

Harvey's discovery furnished a unified explanation for the functions of the body. All the basic physical functions of the body depend upon the fundamental circulating fluid, the blood. After food has been digested in the stomach, it is the blood which carries its nutriment through the body. When energy is being used, or "burned up," as we say, the waste products are thrown into the blood and carried to the kidneys and lungs. When the blood passes through the lungs it extracts the vital properties from the air that has been inhaled. Harvey's demonstration of the circulation of the blood was a kind of master key to unlock the many doors leading to an understanding of how the human body functioned. In surgery Harvey's work was, of course, of great value, for here there is always the danger of bleeding to excess—hemorrhage—and it would be impossible to control this menace without a detailed knowledge of how the blood circulates.

Harvey's claim to immortality in the annals of medicine does not rest alone in his work on circulation. He also founded the science of embryology. Up to his day the traditional view had been that at the time of conception an animal was a tiny but exact copy of the adult form ultimately to be achieved. This was called the preformation doctrine. In his *Exercise on the Generation in Animals* (1651), Harvey argued that the embryo went through definite stages of development and that its form progressively changed until the time of birth arrived.

Auenbrugger (1722-1809) and lung diseases. When a doctor examines the chest after a bad cold by tapping here and there with his fingers, he is using an important technique of diagnosis developed in the eighteenth century by Leopold Auenbrugger, a Viennese physician. It was fortunate for medicine that this doctor was also a good musician, interested in acoustics, and that he applied his knowledge of sound to the study of medicine. He started on the principle that the chest when struck makes a sound and that the sound varies with the condition of the chest. The more air in the lungs the lower the sound. If the normal cavities are filled with the fluid of disease, the note is higher in pitch. In 1761 this doctor-musician published *The New Invention, which enables the physician from the percussion of the Human Chest to detect the Diseases hidden within.*

The stethoscope. Another device of great importance in diagnosis was the stethoscope, invented by a Breton physician, René Laënnec. While attached to a large hospital in Paris he became interested in diseases of the chest. On one occasion he had a woman patient so fat that he despaired of hearing her heart beat, yet something was obviously the matter with it. Laënnec went for a walk into the gardens of the Louvre, and there mused while he watched the children at play. One group of youngsters was having a hilarious time. The doctor saw that they were playing with a wooden plank. One child would put his ear to one end and at the other his playmate would scratch the plank with a pin the sound of which would be transmitted to the other end. Laënnec hurried back to the hospital with a new idea. Fashioning a piece of rolled paper into a cylindrical shape, he used this to examine the chest of his patient, and in his own words "was not a little surprised and pleased to find that I could thereby perceive the action of the heart much more clear and distinct than I had ever been able to do by the immediate application of the ear."[4]

Laënnec devised a wooden stethoscope and showed it to many doctors, native and foreign, who realized its great importance in studying diseases of the chest.

Still another diagnostic discovery of the eighteenth century was the study of blood pressure, one of the most important means of discovering disease. This diagnostic technique was developed by Stephen Hales (already mentioned in connection with his work in chemistry), who made the first measurement of blood pressure in the year 1710. His method was crude, consisting of a tube attached to a blood vessel which enabled him to discover just how high the blood would rise in the tube. But it was the forerunner of modern apparatus.

Literature in Early Modern Times

Seventeenth-century English literature. The religious revolt naturally had an effect upon the literature of the age. The old medieval romances, which the Renaissance had merely pronounced ridiculous, were termed immoral by the Reformers. Roger Ascham, Queen Elizabeth's tutor, stated that the pleasure of *La Morte d'Arthur* "stood in two special points—open manslaughter and bold bawdry." Cervantes had ridiculed medieval knight-errantry and the outmoded ideals of chivalry. The plays of Shakespeare had exhibited the universality of man's nature and of human problems. But some of the literature in England during the next fifty years shows how the religious struggle affected the writings of poets and authors. The great Puritan poet and theologian John Milton (1608-1674) clearly shows the change and at the same time epitomizes the spirit of Calvinism in his epic masterpiece *Paradise Lost.* This story of the fall of Adam and Eve, printed in 1667, for which Milton received £5 down and £5 when the first 1300 copies had been sold, makes of the universe a battleground between the forces of good and evil.

It is significant that Milton in his portrayal of the universe shows that he is acquainted with the Copernican theory, but he side-steps the astronomical controversy, probably because, while he must have been aware of the logic of the heliocentric view, he must have also been profoundly aware of the dangers of the theory when applied to the theology of his day. The poem is magnificent in its cosmic sweep, regardless of its orthodox dogmas, and the portrait of Satan as a majestic figure of pride and power is easily the finest in the poem. That very fact has led critics of Milton's psychology to point out that the "hell and brimstone" emphasis of Puritanism naturally made it possible for Milton to portray Satan and the losing of Paradise much more forcibly than God or the regaining of the heavenly kingdom.

After the gay Restoration came to England in 1660, but before the adherents of Puritanism had all passed away, another Englishman, John Bunyan (1628-1688), wrote *Pilgrim's Progress,* published in 1678. It is an allegory in which the hero, Christian, leaves the City of Destruction and, after traversing the Slough of Despond, the Valley of Humiliation, the Valley of the Shadow of Death, Vanity Fair, and other places of temptation, comes finally to the Celestial City. The book is simply but powerfully written, and its appeal was so universal that it has been translated into one hundred eight different languages and dialects.

In the latter part of the seventeenth century in England notable developments were made in literature. Writers became infatuated with the latest discoveries of science. The Restoration, a reaction against the religious revolt in England, produced such names as Samuel Pepys (1633-1703), whose irrepressible *Diary* is a vivid keyhole view of contemporary everyday life in London inns, quaysides, and the sophisticated and immoral court of Charles II, and John Dryden (1631-1700), the brilliant playwright and poet laureate, whose numerous works set the keynotes of English classicism—formal style, criticism of existing institutions, and devotion to natural science.

Eighteenth-century classicism. European religion, philosophy, and science, as we have seen, were revolutionized by the overthrow of traditional ideas. But strangely enough literature and art almost reverently worshiped classical models. The eighteenth century prided itself on its rationalism, sophistication, balance, and self-control. Science pictured a world based on immutable law; hence literary forms must follow definite rules and conventions. These were to be found in classical antiquity, especially in the works of Aristotle, Horace, and Cicero. The Enlightenment felt spiritually akin to Rome's Augustan age, with its stability, refined polish, and absence of unrestrained emotion. The literature of much of the eighteenth century, therefore, sprang from the intellect, not the heart, from reason, not emotion, and it slavishly imitated classical forms. Style of expression was all-important, and content often inconsequential. Old ideas sufficed as long as they were polished in form or elegantly expressed. Orators such as Burke accepted Demosthenes as a model, letter writers like Lord Chesterfield turned to the epistles of Cicero for inspiration, and writers of both prose and poetry, shunning enthusiasm and moral earnestness, imitated the polished regularity of Horace.

Alexander Pope (1688-1744). The foremost exponent of the classical spirit in the Age of Reason was an English poet, Alexander Pope, who with deft ease voiced the spirit of the age in the so-called heroic couplet. These lines, from the *Essay on Criticism,* in which Pope expounded the rules of classical literary theory, illustrate the dignity and sonorousness of the heroic couplet.

Some to conceit alone their taste confine,
And glittering thoughts struck out at every line;
Pleased with a work where nothing's just or fit;
One glaring chaos and wild heap of wit.
Poets like painters, thus unskilled to trace
The naked nature and the living grace,
With gold and jewels cover every part,
And hide with ornaments their want of art.
True wit is nature to advantage dressed,
What oft was thought, but ne'er so well expressed;
Something, whose truth convinced at sight we find,
That gives us back the image of our mind.

As a Roman Catholic and the son of a retired linen merchant, Pope was at first excluded from elevated English society. To the handicaps of a suspect religion and low social status was added the fact that the poet was a malformed cripple. Undaunted by these obstacles, Pope by the sheer force of his intellect and poetical genius made a brilliant literary success as England's foremost classical poet. Perhaps his most famous work was *The Essay on Man.* Published in 1733, this poem discussing man's relation to the universe was acclaimed throughout Europe.

Pope had a faculty for creating subtle epigrams which have become almost proverbial. For example: "To err is human, to forgive divine"; "fools rush in where angels fear to tread."

Fair tresses man's imperial race ensnare,
And beauty draws us with a single hair.

Jonathan Swift (1667-1745). In prose, not poetry, however, English neo-classicism made its most important contributions. Like the poetry of the period it was ornamental and polished. It tended to use long-winded sentences filled with classical allusions. But it did achieve a powerful and direct style, later to be used in the familiar essay and in the novel. One of England's outstanding prose writers in the first half of the eighteenth century was Jonathan Swift, born in Dublin of English parents. Probably disappointment in not obtaining a high position in the Church and misery resulting from a brain disease were important influences on Swift's writing. He was obsessed by a sense of the follies and vices of mankind and of man's inhumanity to man. Swift described man as: "The most pernicious race of little odious vermin that nature ever suffered to crawl upon this earth." He excelled at biting satire, often coarse, savage, and bitterly funny. It is ironical that his most devastating satire, *Gulliver's Travels,* because of its absorbing adventures and strange characters, should become, in adapted form, a favorite book for children. Much of the work of Swift consists of controversial pamphlets dealing with the evils of his time. One of them, the *Modest Proposal,* exposing the degradation of the Irish peasantry, suggests ironically that the children of the poor should be eaten by their parents to save them from the miseries of a life of poverty and disease.

In *Gulliver's Travels* Swift ridicules the pettiness of man's quarrels, wars, and vices. In the fictitious country of Lilliput, for example, Captain Gulliver finds two opposing factions: The Big-endians who passionately maintain that eggs must be opened at the big end, and the Little-endians, who are equally vehement that the small end should be used. This absurd quarrel referred to a petty religious dispute raging in England at that time. In the strange land of Lilliput, where men are only six inches high, we are "shown ourselves as pygmies, through the wrong end of a telescope as it were," and our affairs, now so diminutive, appear inconsequential and ridiculous.

Addison and Steele. Of comparable importance with Swift in influencing English prose were the essayists Sir Richard Steele (1672-1729) and Joseph Addison (1672-1719). Writing in the *Tatler* and *Spectator,* ancestors of modern journals of opinion, Steele and Addison sought to improve the morals and standards of their age. Unlike Swift, their style was restrained and delicate, using gentle irony and quiet humor.

Genesis of the novel. The most distinctive literary form of the eighteenth century was the modern novel, a fictitious, unified narrative of some length, with believable characters and considerable plot. The novel, like inventions in any field of endeavor, was not an instantaneous creation but was indebted to Old Testament stories, medieval romances, Elizabethan pastoral narratives, allegory, and satire. Daniel Defoe (1661-1731) is sometimes regarded as the first English novelist. His most celebrated work was *Robinson Crusoe,* a book which has brought joy to countless thousands of young readers, although its sententiousness makes it hard going now for adults.

More important in the development of the novel was Samuel Richardson (1689-1761), whose *Pamela* is more correctly regarded as the first real English novel. Richardson's novels were long-winded, often running to seven or eight volumes, and extremely sentimental.

With Henry Fielding (1707-1754) the novel achieved full stature. Disgusted with the "goody-goodness" of Richardson, Fielding achieved fame by parodying the smug sentimentality of *Pamela* in his *Joseph Andrews.* This book was followed by *Tom Jones.* Fielding was a master of plot and a realist, and unlike Richardson injected a robust sense of humor into his novels.

Samuel Johnson (1709-1784). England's literary dictator of the mid-eighteenth century was the renowned Samuel Johnson. Important for his *Dictionary of the English Language,* his edition of Shakespeare, and the *Lives of the Poets,* his fame rests above all on his genius for conversation, his unique personality, and the fact that James Boswell selected him as the subject for the best known of all biographies. Boswell's *Life of Samuel Johnson, LL.D.* provides a graphic picture of Johnson as the center of a brilliant coterie of intellectuals revolving around the famous Literary Club, whose headquarters was in London. The roster of this organization included Edmund Burke, Sir Joshua Reynolds, Oliver Goldsmith, and James Boswell.

Oliver Goldsmith (1728-1774). Goldsmith produced in *The Vicar of Wakefield* a novel more widely read than any other fiction of the eighteenth century, with the exception of *Robinson Crusoe.* This story has a simple charm, and its main character, the vicar, has become one of the most famous characters in English fiction. Much of English drama in the eighteenth century was either dull or indecent, but the humor of *She Stoops to Conquer* was gentle and at the same time penetrating. In addition to his successes in the novel and drama, Goldsmith wrote one of the most famous poems in the English language, *The Deserted Village.* Outstanding in three fields—prose, poetry, and drama—Goldsmith well deserved the tribute of his friend, Dr. Johnson: "He left almost no kind of writing untouched, and touched nothing that he did not adorn."

French prose. The strength of French literature in the eighteenth century was not in fiction or poetry but in the controversial writing of the *philosophes.* One of the few important contributions to prose fiction was made by Alain René Le Sage in his *Gil Blas.* The hero of this vagabond tale is a youth of seventeen who, mounted on his mule, sets out for the University of Salamanca. He never gets there. But failure to become a university student does not prevent him from getting an education, of a sort. He hobnobs with thieves, cavorts with actors and politicians, and becomes the protégé of a lady of fashion. The escapades of this rogue exerted a strong influence upon eighteenth-century English novelists, especially Fielding.

Another important prose contribution was the famous romance, *Manon Lescaut,* written by Abbé Prévost. This story reveals keen insight into feminine psychology. It is the passionate love story of a hero who sacrifices everything for love and of a heroine who, because of desire for riches and splendor, proves unfaithful to her lover.

French drama. The classical age in literature came to its finest fruition in France at the end of the seventeenth century in the brilliant plays of Corneille (1606-1684), the satirical comedies of Molière (1622-1673), the tragedies of Racine (1639-1699), and the matchless fables of La Fontaine (1621-1695). The output of these writers made the era of Louis XIV envied throughout the western world. So strong was the influence of these French writers that it became fashionable in Germany and England to speak French and to read French literature in the original.

Drama achieved little distinction in France during the eighteenth century. The most important plays were written by the versatile Voltaire who, in such tragedies as *Oedipe* and *Merope,* achieved some success. But on the whole his plays, while brilliant and clever, are cold and lifeless. French drama was saved from utter mediocrity by the comedies of Pierre Augustin Caron (Beaumarchais). In 1775 his *Barber of Seville,* with its interesting plot, amusing surprises, and sallies of wit, brought fame to its author. Eight years later, Beaumarchais produced the *Marriage of Figaro.* This brilliant comedy is full of political satire and did much to spread the seeds of discontent against the old régime in France. For example, in alluding to the freedom of the press, Beaumarchais has Figaro say: "As long as I write nothing against the government, religion, politics, morality, officials, or anyone who has a claim to anything, I am free to print what I choose—under the inspection of two or three censors."[5] These two comedies have gained additional importance in being adapted to the opera, *The Barber of Seville* by Rossini and *The Marriage of Figaro* by Mozart.

Rousseau and romanticism. Jean Jacques Rousseau (1712-1778) was one of the first to express indignation at the social injustices of his time. (His political and social writings will, therefore, be more appropriately discussed along with the French Revolution in the next chapter.) He was also in the vanguard of writers who rejected the purely rational in literature, appealing instead to the imagination, to the emotions. He was, in other words, a romanticist. His autobiography is contained in his *Confessions,* a discussion of the author's vices and faults with a frankness little short of amazing. Descriptions of scenery and sketches of rural life place Rousseau apart from his fellow classicists. In the charming story *Emile,* referred to earlier, Rousseau expounds his educational theories, as we have seen (page 48), and in *The New Héloïse* he becomes a sentimental moralist. This last tale of domestic virtue received wide acclaim, over seventy editions being printed in the eighteenth century, and exercised profound influence upon the development of French romanticism.

Voltaire and French literature. French poetry in the eighteenth century was of little consequence. Voltaire was regarded as the foremost poet, but his epic poems *The Henriade* and *Pucelle* lack poetical imagination. Although it was not realized in his own day, Voltaire's most important literary contribution lay in other fields. His short fictional satire *Candide,* a biting attack on the easy optimism of Leibnitz and his view that this is the best of all possible worlds, is now judged his masterpiece. On an extended journey,

Candide, accompanied by his tutor, finds this "best world" of Leibnitz's to be rent and disturbed by earthquakes, famines, plagues, greed, and injustice.

Italian literature. The glories of the Renaissance had a disappointing sequel in Italy. In the seventeenth century cultural life was decadent, and much of the eighteenth was characterized, especially in literature, by the dominance of lifeless classicism. Poetry and drama grew more and more stale. But in the latter part of the century a decided improvement is illustrated in the works of Alfieri, one of Italy's greatest playwrights. Alfieri was a prolific writer of tragedies, nearly all of which reveal his hatred of tyranny. One of his plays was dedicated to George Washington.

German literary revival. Intellectual activity in Germany was seriously hampered by the destruction and horrors resulting from the Thirty Years' War. Such German literature as survived was rendered lifeless by its dependence upon French classical models. Intellectual sterility, however, gave way early in the eighteenth century to a period of intense cultural activity, the German counterpart to the Enlightenment in France and England. The German cultural rebirth resulted in the founding of new universities, in a demand for magazines, plays, and novels, and most important, in a revolt against foreign domination in literature.

In this literary revolution many writers championed the idea that Germany should develop a distinctive national literature of her own. Gotthold Lessing (1729-1781), a versatile playwright, scholar, and critic, was the first to use a German character as the central figure in a comedy. Building on these achievements, the literature of the German Enlightenment reached its height in the contributions of Schiller and Goethe.

Schiller (1759-1805). Through all the writing of Schiller runs a passionate belief in liberty. Although he produced several histories and philosophical studies and many poems, Schiller gained his greatest fame as a dramatist. In *The Robbers* he was so outspoken against tyranny that he gained the displeasure of at least one ruling duke. In his later years, Schiller gave the world a series of great dramas, most famous of which is *Wilhelm Tell.* Dealing with the struggle of the Swiss for their national independence, this play makes an impassioned attack on tyranny and is regarded as Schiller's masterpiece.

Goethe (1749-1832). Great as was the genius of Schiller he was surpassed by his friend Johann Wolfgang von Goethe. As a lyrical poet Goethe gave the Germans their greatest songs. Born in Frankfurt of a wealthy merchant family, Goethe received an unusually thorough education. He read and was delighted with such English writers as Shakespeare, Goldsmith, and Gray. Largely as a result of these new influences, in 1773 he published *Goetz with the Iron Hand,* a prose drama dealing with medieval chivalry. This play carried on the movement of Lessing to emancipate German literature from foreign domination. For the first time a German character was used as the central figure in a dramatic tragedy.

The following year there appeared Goethe's *The Sorrows of Werther,* a sentimental novel narrating the tragic life of a love-sick youth who, disappointed in love, kills himself with the pistol of his successful rival. This tale had an enormous success all over Europe where romanticism, now superseding rational classicism, welcomed the opportunity of joyfully shedding tears over the death of lovelorn Werther.

In 1775, at the invitation of the young ruler, Charles Augustus, Goethe made his home at Weimar, the capital of a small grand-duchy in Germany. Here he assumed an important role as an official in the government of his patron, became the director of the state theater, and worked indefatigably on plays, novels, and verse. Under the benevolent rule of Charles Augustus, whose love of the arts led him to encourage intellectual pursuits of all kinds, especially the work of Goethe, Weimar became the intellectual center of Germany, known as the "poets' city" and the "German Athens."

Goethe's Faust. The greatest and the last work of Goethe, on which he worked intermittently for fifty-eight years, was his *Faust.* This drama, written in verse, is based on an old German legend which relates the story of a man, Faust, who made a compact with the devil, Mephistopheles, that in return for twenty-four years of unmitigated pleasure Faust would then give his soul to the devil. As adapted by Goethe, the legend is enlarged on a magnificent scale and becomes the vehicle for a philosophical discussion of the intellectual history of the human soul. The play is a poetic interpretation of Goethe's own life, with his aspirations, doubts, and triumphs, and is shot through with underlying meaning and symbolism. Only a small part has been adapted for the stage, and this portion has been made the basis for Gounod's opera *Faust.*

Music in Early Modern Times

Polyphonic music. Throughout the Middle Ages music was polyphonic, not monophonic, in form. In monophonic music a single melody or tune may be supported by an accompaniment of chords or by dividing the notes of the chords among three or four voices, in which the "air" is usually carried by the sopranos. In the polyphonic form several melodies are joined so as to contrast or support each other in a melodious patchwork of sound in which no single melody predominates. In polyphony there is often a shuttling back and forth from one tune to another—musical counterpoint. Music passed through the polyphonic period before it came to the less complex monophonic period. The reason for this was that musical composition in the Middle Ages was dominated by the Church, which required not a straightforward and logical music based on one dominant theme, but rather a highly organized and complex product in which several melodies blending into an intricate web of glorious sound created the essential ethereal and majestic atmosphere desired by the Church.

Palestrina. Polyphonic music had developed so far that at the end of the Middle Ages as many as twenty-four parts were combined into one intricate stream of music. This musical form reached its highest perfection in the works of Giovanni da Palestrina (1526?-1594), an Italian, who is regarded as the last of the medievalists and at the same time, because he wrote much of the new monophonic choral music, the first of the modernists in music. With Palestrina's church music the polyphonic style of combining several voice melodies into an even flow of music created a powerful emotional effect.

Start of modern music. By Palestrina's time music was ready for a remarkable advance. The application of printing to music had of necessity regularized and simplified musical notation, and Protestant church music was making a new contribution. The shift from the polyphonic to the monophonic form is best seen in the genesis of dramatic opera in Florence. About 1580 a circle of Florentines studying Greek drama came to the conclusion that the speeches of the characters were declaimed with a musical accompaniment. A single character, however, declaiming his lines would be lost amid the welter of melodies if the traditional polyphonic form be used. Out of the experiments of this Florentine circle, therefore, came a new musical form, the opera, in which the music was subordinated to the words of the main characters.

Spread of opera. Claudio Monteverde (1567-1643), who lived and worked at Venice, is regarded as the first master of classical tragic opera. His most famous operas were *Arianna* and *Orfeo.* The new type of dramatic music, in which the music became all-important and the words incidental, became the rage throughout Italy and by about 1630 three opera houses had opened at Venice. Other Italian cities quickly followed suit. Italian opera now conquered Europe and became the favored ward of princes and kings. The rulers of the time saw in opera a diverting amusement; it would give them the reputation of patronizing the arts. The new musical form also owed much of its rapid development to the support rendered it by the rich and cultured bourgeoisie. At Hamburg, especially, the old merchant families possessed fine libraries and music rooms. With their support Handel produced an important opeia as early as 1705.

Handel (1685-1759). The first half of the eighteenth century is known as the age of Handel and Bach. George Frederick Handel, born in 1685, came of lowly parents, his father being a barber-surgeon. While a boy in his teens Handel showed unusual musical precocity but was opposed in his interests by his father. Fortunately for the world of music, a music-loving nobleman, appreciating the promise of the boy, persuaded the father to let him continue his musical studies. In 1703 young Handel went to Hamburg to seek his musical fortune. Earning the respect and support of a circle of culture-loving merchants, Handel produced two operas and gained much fame. Following a sojourn in Italy he became court musician to the Elector of Hanover, later George I of England. When the Elector George became king of England, Handel established himself permanently in London and became a naturalized British subject. Turning Covent Garden into an opera house, Handel wrote over forty operas, all more or less modeled upon the stiff and conventional classical style of the day. For some time Handel was the musical idol of London. Then, as interest in opera diminished, his popularity waned. Spurred on by financial reverses and by broken health, he sought to recoup his fortunes and succeeded when he turned to the oratorio. At first this was merely a religious opera dating from about 1600 in Italy, where such compositions were performed in the oratory of a Roman church. As time elapsed it took on more and more of a choral character until by the time of Handel the oratorio was a musical composition based on a Biblical subject in which a chorus, vocal soloist, and orchestra combined, and in which there was no action and no scenery. The *Messiah* is best known of all Handel's oratorios; indeed it is still the most frequently offered choral composition.

Bach **(*1685-1750*).** Johann Sebastian Bach came from a distinguished musical family and was given a thorough musical education, especially as an organist. At fifteen a choirboy, at twenty-three court organist to the Duke of Weimar, he soon attracted wide attention by his organ compositions and church cantatas. Finally, in 1723, Bach became the organist and choir master at the Church of St. Thomas at Leipzig, positions he held until his death in 1750. Earning a rather meager livelihood, and comparatively unknown during his lifetime, this unassuming organist turned out as part of his job a prodigious number of musical compositions in every form except opera. So obscure was he that few of his compositions were published for more than one hundred years after his death. The standard edition of his collected works issued in the latter part of the nineteenth century consists of fifty large volumes.

Bach achieved a rare proficiency in his organ playing and introduced new methods of keyboard fingering. His great organ fugues have never been surpassed, while he reached his greatest inspiration in his choral compositions, such as the *Mass in B Minor* and the *St. Matthew Passion.*

Bach, it should be remembered, cannot be catalogued as belonging to the prevailing classical and secular-minded school of the eighteenth century. His deep religious conviction, his mysticism, and his use of the polyphonic style of the medieval church set him apart from his contemporaries, who hardly realized his existence.

Franz Joseph Haydn **(*1732-1809*).** About 1760 Italy ceased to dominate in music and a new capital arose at Vienna. The supremacy of this city is associated with the contributions of a great musical triumvirate, Haydn, Mozart, and Beethoven. Beethoven will be discussed in Chapter 6. Haydn was born in Austria in 1732 and, as the protégé of one of the empire's richest noblemen, gained the admiration of all Europe by composing a large number of songs, operettas, orchestral and chamber pieces. In the first half of the century the composition of the orchestra had been revolutionized owing to the demands made upon it by the new opera. The whole violin family had been created from the earlier viols in the seventeenth century, the violin being in use as early as 1608. The great evolution in the violin took place in the seventeenth century and culminated in the work of the Amati and Stradivarius families, whose skill in making musical instruments was passed on from generation to generation. By 1700, violin-making had reached a perfection which has never been surpassed. Taking advantage of the progress in instrumentation, Haydn composed over one hundred symphonies and perfected as a result

Mozart strikes a somewhat formal pose with his father and sister in this lithograph of a family concert.

a balanced orchestra consisting of strings, wood-winds, brasses, and percussion sections.

Mozart (1756-1791). Wolfgang Mozart was born in Austria, where his father was a court musician. He could pick out little tunes on the clavier at four, compose at five, perform in public at six, and read any music at sight for clavier, organ, and violin at the age of ten. The Mozart family made their first musical tour of Europe when their son was only six years of age.

Following his tours, young Mozart became the concertmaster of a rather disagreeable archbishop at a salary of twenty shillings a year. For nine years the young genius poured forth a flood of church and concert music. Early in 1781, at the invitation of the Elector of Bavaria, Mozart composed his first opera, hailed as the best in existence. This success encouraged him to break with his unappreciative patron, the archbishop, and set himself up as a musical freelance in Vienna, where he received the encouragement of Haydn, the friend of all struggling musicians. In 1786 his *Marriage of Figaro* appeared and became a model for all subsequent comic operas. A fine future seemed assured for the promising young musician. But his marriage was not happy, and his income while not small did not suffice to cover his many extravagances. In a few years, the young musician's habits became dissolute. In 1788 his opera *Don Giovanni* and three years later *The Magic Flute*, another operatic work, brought his work to a climax. The brilliant young man wrote forty-nine symphonies, four of which are often played today. In the midst of these great accomplishments Mozart, only thirty-five years of age, died and was buried in the common grave of the city's paupers.

Art in the Age of Reason

Italian baroque architecture. In art, as in other aspects of eighteenth-century life, formality was characteristic and the classical style was an important influence. Because Italian Renaissance architects had used classical forms, eighteenth-century Europeans turned to Italy for their models. The influence of Italian architecture, like that of Italian opera, spread all over the continent.

However, Italian architecture, although based primarily on classical forms, did not reproduce them exactly. After Michelangelo there was a strong tendency in both architecture and art in Italy toward exaggeration in style and overuse of ornamentation. This particular style is known as baroque. It was the logical development of the decorative Renais-

SANTA MARIA DELLA SALUTE, VENICE

COURT OF SAINT PETER'S CATHEDRAL, ROME

VERSAILLES PALACE FROM THE GARDEN

sance style, characterized by free use of curving, non-structural elements and overly elaborate decoration. This tendency is evident in the Venetian church Santa Maria della Salute.

Rome became the capital of the new baroque architecture. In the Roman villas architects strove to give the effect of vastness of size and richness of ornamentation. Giovanni Lorenzo Bernini (1598-1680), the most renowned seventeenth-century architect of the school, designed the colonnade and square outside St. Peter's illustrated opposite. This grandly composed approach to the church is typical of the baroque use of vast spaces and curving lines. Bernini also erected the heavily ornamented canopy of twisting columns and bronze hangings over the high altar of the cathedral (see Volume One, page 447).

Spanish baroque. The Italian baroque style permeated all Europe in the sixteenth and seventeenth centuries. In Spain it was developed particularly by José Churriguera, who made distinctive use of luxuriant detail and elaborate filigree work. This type of baroque, known as churrigueresque, was brought to Mexico and Latin America, where it was utilized in a modified form in churches.

French baroque. In France baroque architecture was characterized by formality and magnificence of decoration. The palace of Louis XIV at Versailles, symbol of his glory and ostentation, is built in the baroque style. In the extent of its imposing buildings and the luxury of its interiors, Versailles was an ideal which nearly every European prince hoped to attain, if only in miniature. The baroque features of Versailles are particularly to be noted in the sweeping composition of its vast formal gardens, with their pools reflecting the great buildings, imposing fountains, formal statuary, and elegant rows of hedges. The baroque love of ornamentation is expressed in the details of the palace. In the interior the silk and velvet drapes, rich marbles, and gilded carvings created a background for profuse painted decoration.

While the baroque style originated in Italy, the French form became the prevailing model

SANS SOUCI, PALACE OF FREDERICK THE GREAT AT POTSDAM

throughout Europe in the eighteenth century. In Germany after 1730, as a result of the tremendous prestige of French soldiers and French civilization, Italian influence in architecture gave way to the prevailing French fashion. Frederick the Great of Prussia built his Sans Souci palace at Potsdam on a French design and tried to make it another Versailles. Compare the two and note the heaviness of the German decoration. Other sovereigns in Europe followed suit in copying the Versailles mode.

Rococo. As the eighteenth century progressed, there was a reaction against the elaborate and heavy baroque style. Rococo, as the new style was called, was dainty and artificial. In the designing of interiors, the pomposity of French baroque was replaced by delicate paneling and ornamental scroll designs. The rococo style reflected the decadence, artificiality, and blasé elegance of the French aristocracy in the heydey of Madame Pompadour and Louis XV. Rococo was widely copied elsewhere in Europe.

Christopher Wren (1632-1723). English architecture was strongly influenced by the Italian Renaissance, as was baroque architecture everywhere, but the English adaptation of Renaissance forms was more restrained than that of the continent. Sir Christopher Wren, a distinguished architect of the baroque period, is famous for his London churches. After the fire of London in 1666 he was commissioned to rebuild numerous churches, the largest of which was the cathedral of St. Paul. Wren proposed to construct St. Paul's "after a good Roman manner" and "not to follow the Gothick Rudeness of the old Design." Wren's smaller churches had to be sandwiched in among the shops and business establishments of a congested London. In order to set them apart from their secular competitors, he concentrated upon their spires, which rose against the sky from amid stores and offices. The spire was a form carried over from the Gothic period.

The return to classical style. In England a return to a purer classical style appeared early. The trend resulted partly from the numerous discoveries of classical ruins and the publication of Renaissance drawings of Roman buildings. The new architectural style

ADDAM: INTERIOR OF ENGLISH COUNTRY HOUSE

DOORWAY OF THE BOCKMAN TAVERN

emphasized close imitation of classical models rather than the free adaptation of the baroque and rococo. The last half of the eighteenth century was the heyday of the English aristocracy. While making their "grand tours" on the continent the sons of the English gentry became familiar with the classical architecture of Rome and Greece and found it much to their liking. The influence of Rome can be seen in the homes of the aristocracy. The brothers Addam, fashionable architects of English country houses, used classic motifs for decoration. The interior shown above has walls decorated with Roman figures, urns, and classic garlands. The curling, leafy decoration on the ceiling is like that on the Forum of Trajan (Volume One, page 173). In France the architect Jacques Soufflot and others followed the same fashion.

Since England was the first country to develop modern administrative buildings on classical lines, it was natural for transplanted Englishmen in colonial America to use a classical type of architecture for their country homes and public buildings. The colonial builders adapted classical details to wood. On the door of the Bockman Tavern, notice the pilasters and the gable modeled after the Greek temple roof. Beautiful though their buildings were, it seems a long way from a marble temple in Greece to the frame doorway of a tavern in colonial America.

The home of our first president at his Mount Vernon estate is an adaptation in wood of classical forms, as is the stately mansion of Thomas Jefferson at Monticello. This interest in the classic style carried over through the nineteenth century, and today in the United States many courthouses, libraries, and legislative buildings are classical in derivation. Architecture through the Italian Renaissance and the seventeenth, eighteenth, and nineteenth centuries is occupied almost entirely with decorative, stylistic, and compositional, as opposed to structural, features. Not until the late nineteenth century do structural experiments in architecture appear as the influence of the classic style via the Renaissance begins to wane.

Baroque painting. Italy, with such masters as da Vinci, Michelangelo, and Titian, had been preëminent in European painting in the

EL GRECO: THE AGONY IN THE GARDEN

TIEPOLO: CHARIOT OF VENUS

sixteenth century. Post-Renaissance painters, using the techniques of modeling, *chiaroscuro* (light and shade), and perspective developed during the Renaissance, painted without the imagination or the message of the Renaissance masters. The same trend toward exaggeration and floridness characteristic of baroque architecture is evident in the painting of the period. The decline of the Venetian school, whose painters used characteristically rich colors and atmosphere, can be seen in the work of such men as Tiepolo (1696-1770), who made meaningless use of classic subjects combined with exaggerated perspective and atmosphere. The "Chariot of Venus" employs exaggerated perspective to give the effect of great distance and height. The artist is most interested in grand composition and in painting the human figure in unusual poses. Note the flying figure at the top of the picture.

Spanish painters. Seventeenth-century Spain was outstanding in painting. The influence of Italy can be seen strongly in early painters. But El Greco's (1548?-1614) expression was truly Spanish. Although he was influenced by Italian painters such as Tintoretto in the use of color and exaggerated *chiaroscuro,* he used them in distinctively Spanish fashion. His paintings, their subjects depicted with attenuated heads, noses, and fingers, and their eyes burning feverishly, express the religious intensity of the period. (Spain, it will be remembered, was the leading Catholic country and a center of the Inquisition and the Catholic reformation.) El Greco used the traditional oil-glaze technique, but his distortion of human bodies for emotional effect was a departure which greatly influenced later painters. In comparison with painters of his age he appears amazingly "modern" in approach.

The painter Bartolomé Murillo (1617-1682) was the master of sentimentalism and Catholic devotion. His portraits of the Virgin are especially famous; he often portrayed her gazing in rapt adoration toward heaven, surrounded by happy cherubs and resting one foot upon a crescent moon.

Diego Velásquez (1599-1660) painted court groups and battle scenes. Velásquez had a strong influence on later art, for he used direct-oil painting, probably the most common painting technique from his time on. The oil paint is applied thickly without tempera underpainting, and the brush strokes in the oil paint are much more noticeable than in the earlier thin glazes. This method, called impasto, can be seen in the detail of the "Infanta Margaret." Velásquez painted what he saw, with no attempt at commenting or at creating dramatic compositions like those of El Greco: Compare the emotional distortion of sky, drapery, and figures in "The Agony in the Garden" with the objective, undistorted type of representation used by Velásquez in the detail from

VELÁSQUEZ: INFANTA MARGARET (DETAIL)

RUBENS: DECORATION FOR MARIA DE' MEDICI

"Infanta Margaret." The beauty of Velásquez' paint application, the color and atmosphere it produced, and his objective approach show an affinity with the later French Impressionist school.

Painting in the Netherlands. The baroque influence penetrated the Netherlands in the seventeenth century. In the Spanish Netherlands, one artist stands out prominently--Peter Paul Rubens (1577-1640). This painter, whose brush was prolific, whose subject matter was both pagan and Christian, whose style was sensuous and robust, and whose fame brought him commissions and wealth from such patrons as Henry IV of France and James I of England, was one of the most celebrated Flemish artists. Rubens succeeded in combining to a great extent the realism of the north and the grandiose compositional ability of the southern baroque painters. The picture shown is one of a series painted for Maria de' Medici. In this allegory can be seen the sensuous treatment of flesh, fabrics, and other textures, combined with a composition of sweeping lines.

In the northern Netherlands flourished a school of painting which depicted the life of its prosperous country. The typical Dutch burgher was little interested in wars or religious scenes; he liked his pipe, his profitable shipping business, and pictures which reminded him of his comfortable and spotless house, his cronies drinking at the tavern, and

REMBRANDT: ENTOMBMENT

VERMEER: SOLDIER AND LAUGHING GIRL

RUISDAEL: LANDSCAPE WITH WATERFALL

his hardworking spouse surrounded by industrious maids. With such an attitude the thrifty Dutch burghers were little likely to spend good money on church decorations. Instead they built unpretentious churches but imposing banks, stock exchanges, town halls, and private homes. They decorated their homes with beautiful gardens and paintings of scenes which they loved.

Jan Vermeer van Delft (1632-1675), whose few paintings each command a king's ransom, used colors sensitively to obtain wonderful effects of depth, light, and atmosphere. He painted the comfortable life of the Dutch burghers in a realistic manner and his subjects were simple, everyday ones. His pictures were painted without comment but possessed great beauty of color, texture, and play of light and shade, as may be seen in the "Soldier and Laughing Girl" illustrated on page 70. Franz Hals (about 1580-1666) is an equally famous painter of the period. He painted realistically the life and people about him, from cavaliers to fishwives.

Jacob van Ruisdael (1628?-1682) painted the lovely Dutch landscapes which the burgher never tired of contemplating. He is one of the earliest landscape painters. Until his time landscape had usually been merely incorpo-

WATTEAU: LOVE IN THE FRENCH THEATER

THE GOBELIN TAPESTRY

rated as background in figure compositions. In the "Landscape with Waterfall" the small figures became incidental to the landscape (so incidental as to disappear completely in our reproduction. Compare this treatment of landscape with that of Giorgione in the Renaissance, Volume One, page 451). This interest in landscape as a subject has continued until the present day.

Rembrandt (1606-1669). One of the greatest of all the painters of northern Europe was an obscure, poverty-ridden, and unhappy artist called Rembrandt Harmens van Rijn. Instead of pandering to the superficial tastes of patrons who wanted to be flattered, or indulging in religious sentimentality, Rembrandt endured poverty and abuse in order that he might paint in a straightforward fashion the environment in which he lived. He could describe equally well a lesson in human anatomy, an old woman cutting her nails, Christ at Emmaus, a windmill before a bright sky and dark clouds, and a huge beef hanging in a butcher's shop. Perhaps no other man achieved such mastery as Rembrandt over the effects which are to be produced from a skillful blending of lights and shadows. Rembrandt was the only one of the Dutch painters of this period to paint pictures with any real religious sense. In his "Entombment" (page 70) can be seen a strong touch of the dramatic. Notice especially the vigorous handling of the light and dark pattern. The figures in this painting are Dutch, but compare it with the Vermeer illustration next to it to see how Rembrandt broke away from the more realistic painting of his compatriots.

French painting. French artists, influenced by the lavish court and the decorated baroque and rococo architecture, painted in a more frivolous manner. These qualities were in keeping with the elegance and make-believe of the prevailing tinsel life of the nobility, with its fetes and pageants, its salons and boudoirs, and its perfumed and bewigged ladies and gentlemen.

Jean Antoine Watteau (1684-1721) illustrates the ultra-refinement and effeminacy which characterized French painting in the reign of Louis XV. Watteau's painting exhibits a lack of vitality, an undue restraint, and a delicate artificiality which, though quite charming, mirror the decadent age of the French nobility in which he lived. Watteau's dominating interest in the love life, fine costumes, and fetes of the aristocracy is reflected in "Love in the French Theater," illustrated on page 71.

The atmosphere of the French court appears in the tapestries which were used to decorate the walls of the palaces. The Gobelin tapestry illustrated opposite shows the way in which the tapestry-makers of the eighteenth century imitated the technique of painting in the woven cloth. Compare this with the tapestries of the Gothic period, Volume One, page 393, whose design and execution allow the warp-and-woof pattern of the weaving to be revealed.

English court painting. It has often been remarked that, while England has fostered important developments in architecture and produced a great literature, she has never had any painters of the first rank and her contributions to sculpture have been negligible. Perhaps a partial explanation lies in the fact that the rich promise of English medieval art was dealt a crippling blow by the intolerant spirit which swept over England and Scotland following the Protestant Revolt. With the restoration of the pleasure-loving Stuarts to the English throne and the rise of a wealthy and influential class of gentry, the arts were revived. The nobility acquired some taste for art, which expressed itself in a desire for portraits painted in the "grand manner." Painting in England, therefore, became a narrow and rather superficial class art dominated by the taste of the gentry.

The aristocracy imported distinguished foreign artists, such as Holbein, as portrait painters, and native painters were neglected. This monopoly by foreigners was finally ended in the mid-eighteenth century, and native painters came into their own. Sir Joshua Reynolds (1723-1792) painted the portraits the fashionable world demanded. The most famous beauties of the day and many prominent men sat for the wealthy and famous Sir Joshua.

Thomas Gainsborough (1727-1788), another English portrait painter, demonstrated a vivacity and sincerity not so obvious in the work of Reynolds. He was commissioned to paint attractive portraits of the English upper classes, and he succeeded admirably in this. Gainsborough was a master in depicting fresh complexions, bright eyes, and gleaming fabrics. His use of landscape background accorded with the English love of the countryside. "Mrs. Mordey and Her Children," illustrated below, is typical of his portraits of the wealthy families of England.

GAINSBOROUGH: MRS. MORDEY AND HER CHILDREN

HOGARTH: THE SHRIMP GIRL

Satirists Hogarth and Goya. Watteau in France and Reynolds in England are symbolic of the rather artificial aristocratic painting of the day. But there were some nonconformists who refused to mirror the hollow pomp of the aristocracy and instead strove to reproduce the life around them in the gutter, the tavern, and the royal court. They even used their art to draw attention to the evils of the day. Outstanding in this regard were Hogarth in England and Goya in Spain.

William Hogarth (1697-1764) began his career as a commercial artist in London, where he found the life of the great city fascinating. It was a crude age. Hogarth was more interested in depicting the people he saw in the

GOYA: MARIA LUISA

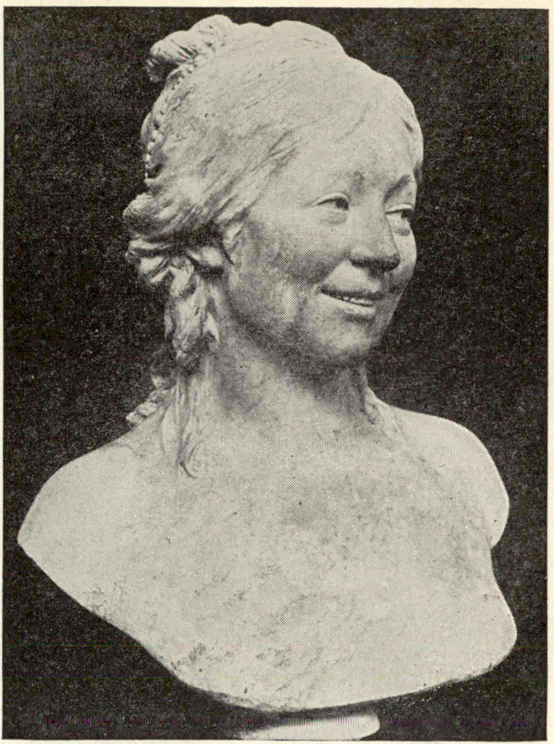

HOUDON: PORTRAIT OF HIS WIFE

London streets and taverns (see his engraving of a cock fight on page 31) than in supplying the nobility with meaningless portraits, although he painted portraits successfully. In 1731 appeared a series of engravings called "A Harlot's Progress," followed by "The Rake's Progress" and "Marriage à la Mode." In these series Hogarth showed himself a pictorial pamphleteer shrewdly and truthfully exposing the vices of the London middle class. He sought to achieve reality, not to escape from it.

Although Hogarth's satires are particularly interesting and are able pieces of work, he reached a greater height of artistic expression in his painting. "The Shrimp Girl" certainly places him on a level with the great artists on the continent. Observe the free handling and lack of nonessentials. This picture, with its free brush strokes, has all the freshness of the Gainsborough painting, but it is not artificial.

Goya (1746-1828), the Spanish counterpart of Hogarth, reveals a side of Spain which the fashionable painters glossed over. The Spain of his day (he was painting a century and a half later than El Greco and Velásquez) was morally and culturally bankrupt. Much of Goya's work was designed to reflect the hypocrisy of the Spanish Church, the degeneration of the government, and the rottenness of society in general. In Goya's portraits of the royal family and the nobility he scarcely concealed his disdain for their viciousness and corruption. His portrait of Maria Luisa shows his keen insight into character. In a series of etchings called "The Horrors of War" he portrayed this curse of humanity in all its bestiality and misery, while other artists were covering its horror with a gallant and patriotic embroidery of brass buttons, vivid uniforms, and prancing steeds.

Eighteenth-century sculpture. In sculpture most of the productions were imitations of classic forms, exhibiting an emptiness of conception. The subject matter consisted mostly of nymphs, Venuses, or other such classic personages. When an art turns to the past for its sole inspiration, and for its models, it cannot escape lifelessness. The French portrait sculpture was more original. Of this Houdon's "Portrait of His Wife" is a well-known example. This statue was made of baked clay, or terra cotta. The vitality of portraiture in this work was due to the fact that it was inspired by nature rather than by classic remains.

Summary

In the years between 1543 and 1800 European science made remarkable progress. National governments capable of maintaining law and order had replaced feudalism. Art and science were patronized by kings and by the prosperous new middle class. Geographical discoveries and the changes which they effected in everyday life encouraged men to be skeptical of old notions, to seek new ideas as well as new lands.

The development of the method of scientific inquiry known as the experimental, or inductive, method was revealed in the *Discourse of Method* by the French Descartes, and in Francis Bacon's *Novum Organum.* In astronomy Copernicus, Galileo, and Kepler proved that the sun, and not the planet earth, is the center of the universe. Newton established the theory of gravitation. A new era in medicine opened with the work of Paré the surgeon, Vesalius the anatomist, and Paracelsus, the doctor who employed the findings of chemistry to effect healing.

Chemistry as a science was established by Robert Boyle in the seventeenth century. Building on his work, Priestley and Cavendish in England constructed a real modern science. The experiments of Lavoisier in chemistry were the most outstanding in the eighteenth century. It was he who finally overthrew the phlogiston theory and proved that matter cannot be destroyed. The science of electricity was first expounded in *De Magnete,* a work published by William Gilbert in the year 1600. The invention of the Leyden jar, Franklin's kite experiment, and Volta's invention—a machine which produced a continuous flow of electricity—were momentous steps in the understanding of electricity. Geology, botany, and zoology became sciences as a result of the studies of James Hutton, Carolus Linnaeus, and Georges Buffon.

The progress in Europe's intellectual and esthetic life in early modern times was comparable to the amazing advance made in science. The many-sided manifestations of cultural quickening—in philosophy, art, literature, and music—are often collectively referred to as the Enlightenment; and the period in which it reached its most fruitful expression, the mid-eighteenth century, is known as the Age of Reason. Although the Enlightenment had its genesis in England in the early seventeenth century, intellectual supremacy soon passed to France. Here the Age of Reason, in the activities of the *philosophes,* most important of whom were Voltaire, Diderot, and Rousseau, found brilliant and significant expression. A steady stream of pamphlets and books emanating from France proclaimed the supremacy of science and reason.

Philosophy ceased to be the tool of religion. In fact, it often became antichristian. Despite the efforts of such reconcilers as Descartes, Leibnitz, Spinoza, and Kant, philosophy in the hands of Locke, Berkeley, and Hume became more and more skeptical and materialistic. The Deistic movement demanded that God be reduced to "a scientific principle" and that denominational dogma be swept away and replaced by a natural religion.

Deism in the long run proved too formal and philosophical for most people. The reaction took the form of Pietism, which stressed emotion and fervor and sometimes leaned in the direction of mysticism. A humanitarian movement was manifested by such reformers as John Howard, who sought to improve conditions in the prisons, and Beccaria, who founded a more humane and scientific procedure in criminology.

Literature, unlike other aspects of the Enlightenment, did not break away from tradition but tended to follow the pagan models of Greece and Rome. Disdaining emotion and any romantic feeling, writers for the most part expressed themselves in faultlessly phrased, elegant, and cold writing. This "neo-classicism" in literature reached its height in the poetry of the Englishman Alexander Pope. Drama and poetry in the Age of Reason were on the whole not of a high order. This period is rather one of great prose. Swift, Addison, Steele, and Samuel Johnson exercised an important influence upon the development of a vigorous English prose style. The novel attained full stature in Fielding's *Tom Jones.* French drama in the seventeenth century, from the pens of Corneille, Racine, and Molière, achieved a brilliance in keeping with the age of Louis XIV, and French literature, like French architecture and French manners, became the fashion in Europe. In eighteenth-century France and in Italy drama and poetry were generally mediocre, but in prose Voltaire's histories and his novel *Candide* have won immortality. Germany managed to throw off French classical dominance and established, in the late eighteenth century, a vigorous school of national literature best represented by Goethe and Schiller.

Music, like literature, usually followed classical forms and, while often uninspiring in the hands of ordinary musicians, achieved new perfection and beauty in the works of Bach, Haydn, and Mozart. Architecture and painting, like the other arts, were classical in inspiration. Architecture assumed the pompous and decorative style referred to as baroque. There were no new structural contributions. Painting, exemplified in France by the artist Watteau, reflected in its elegance and superficiality the meaningless life of the nobility of the time. As in France, the canvases of Reynolds and Gainsborough in England were dominated by the world of fashion. Hogarth exposed the vices of the urban middle class, while Goya depicted the rottenness in the Spanish ruling classes. In this period may be seen the germ of the modern school in painting. Velásquez developed the direct-oil technique, and El Greco's canvases were very "modern" in approach. In the Netherlands the life of the burghers was depicted realistically by such men as Vermeer, while Rembrandt brought a strong religious sense to his painting.

	Absolutism	
1624-1661	Richelieu, Mazarin power behind French throne	Consolidate royal power
1640	Puritans revolt in England	Charles II deposed, executed
1642-1654	Commonwealth and Cromwell in England	
1660-1688	Restoration in England: Charles II, James II	Kings pro-Catholic, autocratic
1661-1715	Louis XIV rules France as the Grand Monarch	Wars to secure "natural boundaries"
1682-1721	Peter the Great westernizes Russia	Gains from Sweden window on Baltic
1689-1697	League of Augsburg withstands Louis	Treaty of Ryswick
1702-1713	War of Spanish Succession (Queen Anne's War)	Treaty of Utrecht
1713-1740	Frederick William I rules Prussia	Establishes efficient government
1740-1748	Frederick the Great—War of Austrian Succession	Gains Silesia by Treaty of Aix-la-Chapelle
1756-1763	France eclipsed in America and India	Peace of Paris
1762-1796	Catherine the Great strengthens Russia	Gains from Turks window on Black Sea
1772	Poland partitioned by Prussia, Russia, Austria	Frederick annexes Polish Corridor
1793-1795	Second and third partitions of Poland	Ceases to exist as independent state
	Revolution	
1679	Parliament passes Habeas Corpus Act	Landmark in constitutional history
1688	Glorious Revolution in England	William and Mary offered crown
	Bill of Rights guarantees supremacy of Parliament	Toleration Act for Protestants
1690	Intellectual revolt against absolutism	Locke, Montesquieu, Rousseau
1721-1742	Walpole first English prime minister	Establishment of cabinet government
1777-1783	American Revolution	Treaty of Paris
1789	French Revolution	National Assembly makes sweeping changes
1791-1792	Limited monarchy in France	Ends in massacre of king
1792	France declares war on Austria	Fears intervention to restore king
1793-1795	France at war with Europe	First coalition
1793-1794	Reign of Terror	Ended by execution of Robespierre
1795-1799	Directory incompetently governs France	
	Napoleonic Period	
1797	Napoleon defeats Austria	Treaty of Campo Formio
1798	English stop Napoleon in Battle of Nile	
1799	Napoleon seizes government	Creates Consulate, becomes chief consul
1801	Concordat with Pope	Reestablishment of Church
1804	Civil Code systematizes law	Local government, education reorganized
1805-1808	Napoleon, emperor—conqueror of Europe	Ulm, Austerlitz, Jena
1812	Invasion of Russia backfires	Disastrous retreat from Moscow
1813-1815	Napoleon on the run, Waterloo, St. Helena	Battle of Nations, The Hundred Days

CHAPTER 3

When in the Course of Human Events

THIS chapter is a discussion of the political aspects of western Europe's culture from 1650 to 1815. In this period were laid the foundations of western political life, as they were to become established late in the nineteenth century, foundations which came into being as a result of the following trends: the perfection of the national-state system, the operation of power politics, the culmination of absolutism in France and its defeat in England in the seventeenth century, and in the following century the development of political liberalism in France and America. The rise of militarism in Prussia and the expansionist tendencies of Russia are also important features.

The influence of great persons looms large in the unfolding of European politics from 1650 to 1815. In the following pages we will encounter the scholarly Hugo Grotius, father of international law; we will see the mighty edifice of French absolutism rising under the direction of the astute Cardinal Richelieu; and we will note the beneficiary of the cardinal's labors, Louis XIV, posing in his grand palace of Versailles as the divinely ordained master of Europe. We will discover the crafty Frederick the Great of Prussia, and Russia's mighty czarina, Catherine, two rulers who specialized in international banditry, or as it is more politely termed, power politics. More appealing figures will be John Locke and Jean Jacques Rousseau, thinkers who provided philosophical justification for revolution against despotic kings, and George Washington, the first great hero of a new political entity, the United States of America.

The political narrative from 1650 to 1815 reveals a long succession of wars. In the age of the Religious Revolt an epidemic of religious wars had been precipitated. Ending about 1650, the wars of religion were followed by another epidemic of wars which sprang mainly from the ambitions of rulers to seize territory, to obtain colonies and trade, or to advance their power in other ways. A study of politics from 1650 to 1815 necessitates a knowledge of the chronology of these wars. It may be helpful, then, to remember that Louis XIV was engaged in four conflicts: the War of Devolution against the Spanish Netherlands (1667-1668), a second war of conquest against Holland (1672-1678), the War of the League of Augsburg (1689-1697), and the War of the Spanish Succession (1702-1713). Following an interim of comparative peace, war again broke out in western Europe in 1740 and there was little peace on the distracted continent until Napoleon was defeated at Waterloo in 1815. Wars that should be especially noted are: the War of the Austrian Succession (1740-1748), the Seven Years' War (1756-1763), and the French revolutionary wars, which extended from 1792 to 1815. In addition to these conflicts between various states there were at least three revolutions which overthrew absolutism in some form. The French Revolution (1789-1799) soon expanded from a domestic struggle to a great European conflict. In addition there were the Glorious Revolution of 1688 in England, and the War of American Independence (1775-1783), in which the colonists threw off the rule of George III.

The National-State System and Power Politics

Medieval idea of unity. During the period from the Peace of Westphalia to the Congress of Vienna (1648-1815) the modern state system assumed permanent shape. During the Middle Ages, all Europeans considered themselves as members of one great, unified, Christian commonwealth. All men, and even governments, owed obedience to the universal Church. The papacy was a great international power. On many occasions the Pope acted as arbiter between disputing kings. In 1298, for example, the Pope intervened in a quarrel between Philip IV of France and Edward I, the English sovereign; and in 1494 the colonial controversy between Spain and Portugal was finally decided with the Treaty of Tordesillas. In politics as in religion the ideal of unity held an important place. Over a large part of Europe the belief was held that one international organization, the Holy Roman Empire, should be supreme. Lamenting the passing of its power, Dante maintained in his *De Monarchia* (1309): "Whole heaven is regulated by a single ruler—God. It follows that the human race is at its best state when it is ruled by a single prince and one law. So it is evidently necessary for the welfare of the world that there should be a single monarchy or princedom, which men call the Empire."[1]

The national state. The hope for European unity was vain. The tradition of political and religious unity was destroyed by the rise of the national state and by the successful Protestant revolt from Rome. Instead of heeding the appeal of Dante, the kings and princes followed the advice of a later Italian, Machiavelli. They found his book *The Prince* an excellent guidebook. In it rulers were shown how best to gain their ends without any regard for religious or ethical scruples. "A wise ruler," urged Machiavelli, "for the sake of the state, removes without scruple or mercy every obstacle he finds in his way." By the seventeenth century, national states, disdaining the Holy Roman Empire and the Church, claimed to be the supreme and sole judges of their actions, and hence a law unto themselves. This characteristic of independence, termed national sovereignty, has come to be regarded as the very heart of the modern state system.

Power politics. Exercise of national sovereignty inaugurated the practice of what is termed power politics. More and more the idea of a unified cooperative European commonwealth faded away in favor of a new political system in which national states competed against each other without restraint and with few or no scruples for land, commerce, and power. Although war had been prevalent enough in the Middle Ages, the lack of strong nationalism and the existence of a powerful international agency, the Church, to which all men belonged, had tended to reduce the possibilities and the extent of armed conflict. But now with the rise of power politics, war became the conscious and deliberate tool of national policy. Egged on by a rising spirit of national egoism and a craving for glory and conquest, the rulers embarked upon an undisguised program of power politics in which might made right and war was the chief measure of national power.

A period of international anarchy followed the inception of the national-state system. In the sixteenth century England fought Spain and French Bourbon kings engaged in a series of bitter wars with the Holy Roman Empire. The seventeenth century saw the terrible Thirty Years' War devastate Germany and in the latter part of this century the aggressions of Louis XIV of France set off another string of wars ending in 1713. Conflict continued in the eighteenth century as the European nations carried their rivalries to America and even to the Far East. These national struggles often intensified the wars within nations between men belonging to the same political systems. In this connection one has only to recall the Huguenot civil war in France, the hostilities between the Lutheran German princes and their emperor, and the Dutch struggle for freedom against Spain.

Hugo Grotius (1583-1645). Many thoughtful Europeans appreciated the menace to civilization of these wars. One was a Hollander, best known by the Latinized version of his name, Hugo Grotius. The son of a Dutch burgomaster, Hugo at an early age gave promise of unusual mental powers. He wrote Latin verses at the age of nine, entered a university when he was twelve, and was a qualified scholar at the age of fifteen. After receiving his LL.D. he wrote dramas and poems in Latin and practiced law. At the age of twenty he was appointed official historian by the government of Holland.

When the Thirty Years' War broke out, Grotius actively campaigned for religious toleration and peace between the opposing factions. His views were rewarded with a sentence of life imprisonment. While in prison, he was permitted to continue his studies. Many chests of books were passed by his guards into Grotius' prison study. In 1621, his wife, who was with her scholar husband in prison, smuggled him out of the fortress in a chest supposedly containing dirty linen and books. Following his escape Grotius made his way to Paris where he continued his studies and was granted a modest pension by Louis XIII.

In 1625 appeared *De jure belli ac pacis* (*On the Law of War and Peace*). This book gained instant fame for Grotius and lasting recognition as the founder of international law. Explaining the reasons which caused him to write his treatise, Grotius declared:

"I saw prevailing throughout the Christian world a license in making war of which even barbarous nations would have been ashamed; recourse being had to arms for slight reasons or no reason; and when arms were once taken up, all reverence for divine and human law was thrown away, just as if men were thenceforth authorized to commit all crimes without restraint."[2]

In his famous work Grotius endeavored to set forth a new code of conduct, "a principle of right which should govern the relations of states." This was not to be based upon the authority of the Church but on what the author termed the fundamental idea of the law of nature which in turn was founded on the dictates of right, reason, morality, and justice.

Grotius tried to show that if civilization was to endure there must be consideration for others, humanity and reason in the relations between nations. According to him, wars are justifiable only to repel invasion or to punish an insult to God. In the event that conflicts are justified, Grotius insisted that humane considerations must be followed in the conduct of fighting.

This intelligent appeal of Grotius, however, fell largely upon deaf ears. *The Prince*, by Machiavelli, enjoyed more popularity in European palaces than *On the Law of War and Peace*. National states did little to restrain their rivalries and conflicts. A continuous state of war, however, obviously menaced the very existence of civilization. The development of trade and commerce in Europe brought home to the nations the need for some form of international cooperation. It soon became quite apparent that the menace of war must be reduced, that machinery must be developed for the peaceful settlement of disputes between nations, that negotiations whenever possible should be in the hands of the diplomat, not the soldier. A crude and makeshift compromise was devised, therefore, which recognized the need for some degree of cooperation between states. Yet, at the same time, it gave ample opportunity for the nations to resort to war. Commercial relations and amicable cooperation between sovereign nations were encouraged by the development of numerous agreements and treaties which formed a crude system of international law. Furthermore, the increasing contact between nations and their interdependence, especially in trade, were recognized by the growth of consular services for commercial matters and diplomatic services for political negotiations.

The rise of modern diplomacy. From early times the medieval Church had followed diplomatic practices. Popes sent envoys called legates to reside at the courts of various kings. Papal ambassadors were maintained at the Byzantine court. Modern diplomatic practice had its real birth in northern Italy where in late medieval times a number of small independent city-states, such as Milan, Venice, and Genoa, were continually at war with each other. They created alliances and practiced a kind of Lilliputian balance of power. These city-states were really rehearsing and developing a kind of international diplomacy which was soon to be practiced on a grander scale by the great European powers.

The republic of Venice was particularly active. Venice has been called "the school and touchstone of ambassadors." Its authorities began to register treaties, to maintain diplomatic archives, and to advise their representatives in various parts of Europe by means of elaborate reports. Venetian ambassadors were famous for their skill. Their long reports have been preserved and throw interesting light on the Europe of their day. Florence was not far behind Venice. In the thirteenth and fourteenth centuries she counted in her diplomatic service such famous characters as Dante, Petrarch, and Boccaccio. In the thirteenth century Venetian ambassadors were forbidden to take their wives with them on diplomatic missions for fear they might divulge state secrets. Diplomats were further instructed to take along personal cooks to safeguard against poisoning. It is believed that the first permanent embassy in history was sent by the duke of Milan, in 1455, to act as his agent at Genoa. Within a short time most of the important nations followed suit and posted representatives in the capitals of Europe.

The development of the technique and machinery of diplomacy undoubtedly encouraged negotiation rather than war on many occasions. On the other hand, its methods so often involved deceit and treachery that diplomacy often fanned rather than dampened the fires of national hostility. An Englishman of the seventeenth century defined an ambassador as "an honest man sent to lie abroad for the good of his country." Diplomacy during the past three hundred years has done little to improve this definition.

Virile versus decadent states. In the political world which grew up in early modern times where, as we have seen, war was the main instrument of national policy, where might made right, and where there was no effective body of international law to restrain the aggressor, wars were not continuous but they were frequent. The prevalence of war, the failure of mankind to establish for nations a code of conduct based upon reason and justice is civilization's most conspicuous failure. The tendency on the part of national states to enhance their power at the expense of their neighbors was further strengthened because a large number of nations in Europe in the seventeenth and eighteenth centuries were in a state of decline. Such was true of Poland, Holland, Sweden, Spain, and Turkey. England, Russia, France, and Prussia especially, however, were aggressive and virile and readily took advantage of the decadent powers.

Louis XIV and the Peak of Absolutism

Monarchical absolutism. The seventeenth and eighteenth centuries saw monarchical absolutism reach its height. Practically everywhere the power of the nobles had been destroyed, the government centralized, and all power lodged in the hands of absolute kings. Only in England, Swiss cantons, and the Netherlands were there governments which rested even to a limited degree on the consent of the governed.

Political absolutism based on divine right was by no means an innovation of the seventeenth century. It had a history going back as far as the ancient empire of Egypt, the government of Alexander the Great, and the empire of the Caesars. But in the seventeenth century absolutism attained its most exaggerated form and its most fulsome philosophical expression. Such political philosophers as the Frenchmen Bodin and Bossuet and the Englishman Hobbes extravagantly defended the divine right of kings. According to Bossuet, (1) a king is above all law and is the image of God, (2) he is responsible only to God, and (3) it is a grievous sin for any subject to question the acts of his sovereign.

The prevalence of absolutism in government made national conflicts and power politics more acute. The policies of nations were dictated by their rulers; the common people had little or no influence in affairs of state. Disregarding the wishes and the interests of their subjects, these absolute kings in their desire to advance the prestige of their dynasties embarked frequently upon unnecessary wars.

Absolutism and revolution. This propensity for war and the failure of kings and their aristocratic courts to extend to the middle classes an adequate voice in government finally discredited political absolutism. In western Europe, and in England and France in particular, the merchant classes in the cities were rapidly growing in wealth. The expansion of trade following the period of geographical explorations and the opening up of the New World had brought about an economic revolution. The middle class now forged to the front, wealthy and ambitious, and resentful that capricious monarchs still managed affairs of state. A struggle for power, therefore, was precipitated within the various nations, at the same time that power politics was bringing about numerous conflicts between the European states. The political struggle, in which the rising middle class challenged divine right, precipitated three great upheavals. These were the Puritan Revolution and the Glorious (sometimes called Bloodless) Revolution in England in the last half of the seventeenth century, the American Revolution in the eighteenth, and, most important, the French Revolution at the end of the eighteenth century. Out of these events were born the ideas of nationalism and democracy which were to become dominant in the nineteenth century and almost universal in the first quarter of the present century. From this point on we will be mainly concerned with conflicts between nations. This will set the stage for our discussion in the latter part of the chapter, of the struggle for political power within nations, notably in England, British colonial America, and France.

France under Henry IV. The best example of political absolutism is offered by seventeenth-century France in the reign of Louis XIV. This proud Bourbon monarch inherited a realm, strong and prosperous, which it had taken a century and a half to produce. The sixteenth century had been a sorry period in France's history. Conflicts with Charles V, the emperor of the Holy Roman Empire, and Philip II of Spain, as well as civil war at home, had weakened the country. The accession of Henry IV in 1589, however, brought better times. By 1610, when this king fell a victim to assassination, disorder had disappeared. Prosperity and strong government were everywhere in evidence. Henry IV with his gay manner and warm heart endeared himself to the hearts of his people. Modern biographers do not miss the opportunity of emphasizing that his favorite pastime was the pursuit of women. But his affairs in no way deterred him from his main objective—to make France strong and prosperous.

Richelieu promotes absolutism. The death of Henry left Louis XIII, a boy of nine, on the throne and an incompetent queen-mother as regent. For fourteen years the work of Henry of Navarre was undermined. Fortunately for France, in 1624 Cardinal Richelieu became the real power behind the throne. For "eighteen years the biography of Richelieu is the history of France." As chief adviser to Louis XIII "the grim cardinal" set about restoring and furthering the work of his royal master's father. His basic objective was to exalt the power of the monarchy, to make Louis' power unchallengeable.

The structure of absolutism quickly took shape under Richelieu's direction. Castles of the nobility were torn down, their power as governors in the local districts was eliminated, local officials, called *intendants,* superseded the governors, and finally the Estates-General —a representative body that might have challenged the power of the king—was shelved. In foreign affairs, Richelieu was equally successful. His intervention in the Thirty Years' War struck a staggering blow against Hapsburg power and made France the greatest power in Europe.

Richelieu was Machiavelli's "prince" in action. Though he was handicapped by a frail body and wasted with disease, his will and determination were yet inflexible. His haughty manner and relentless campaign against the unruly nobles made him a hated figure among the aristocracy, but against these opponents he knew no mercy. He met deceit with deceit and opposition with relentless vengeance.

Mazarin. Richelieu died in 1642, just a year before the passing of Louis XIII. Again the throne of France was occupied by an infant, Louis XIV, who was less than five years old. But Richelieu had anticipated this emergency. Before he died he had carefully schooled a promising young Italian to carry on his work. This was Cardinal Mazarin, who governed France with a firm and efficient hand during the minority of the king. Following the death of Mazarin in 1661, Louis XIV, now twenty-three years old, took over the personal management of state affairs. He found an obedient and docile people to govern. Henry IV, Richelieu, and Mazarin had done their work well. During the incredibly long reign of Louis XIV the French people "worked, fought, lived, conquered for him alone."

Louis XIV, the sun king. In personal appearance Louis XIV was well qualified to play the role of absolute king. He was regal and dignified whether in his dressing gown or in his most magnificent robes of state and has been described as "the greatest actor of majesty that ever filled a throne." While not possessing a creative mind, the young king was of much more than average intelligence. He certainly was far superior to his mediocre father and to his degenerate great-grandson, Louis XV. Louis XIV worked assiduously at what he described as "the business of being king." His duties in the council chamber and the many documents which accumulated on his desk demanding attention took from six to eight hours of his time every day. This did not include Louis' attendance at court ceremonies and palace fetes.

A burning ambition to make his reign glorious possessed Louis. Believing implicitly in the divine right of kings, he chose the sun as the symbol of his power. There was no one to curb his inordinate pride. His fawning courtiers dubbed him *le 'roi-soleil* (sun king) and he became known throughout Europe as the Grand Monarch. The palace of the Louvre in Paris had been good enough for his predecessors, but Louis wanted a more magnificent symbol of his greatness.

Versailles. Nine miles from Paris, midst barren marsh land, the king began in 1669 to build the palace of Versailles. (It is illustrated on page 65.) At one time more than thirty thousand men were employed on this project, and the total cost of construction probably exceeded one hundred million dollars. André Lenôtre, the master gardener of his time, transformed the marsh land into the most beautiful park in Europe. Versailles when completed had a façade over a quarter of a mile in length. Its interior consisted of great rooms richly decorated with gilding, carvings, tapestries, and statues. The most famous of these rooms were the Salon of Apollo, with a solid silver throne, and the Grand Hall of Mirrors. The latter has seen much history. Besides its association with the military glories of Louis, in this room Bismarck proclaimed the new German empire after the defeat of France in 1871. In 1919 the great mirrors reflected an equally momentous occasion when the representatives of Germany signed the Treaty of Versailles.

Versailles Palace is a depressing place today. The huge building seems lifeless, a symbol of royal elegance and tinsel court life that has no place in our modern world. But two hundred years ago Versailles was the most fashionable spot in Europe. Here during the day the French nobles promenaded with their king among the woods, terraces, and fountains of the park. Or they hunted and hawked in the nearby woods and meadows. At night thousands of candles transformed Versailles into a blaze of light. Lords and ladies, in powdered wigs, silks, and laces, now attended balls, masquerades, and concerts. Or if the weather was unusually fine, aquatic carnivals were held on the Grand Canal in the park.

Perhaps the most interesting aspect of life at Versailles was its "cult of majesty." Palace etiquette was carried to ridiculous extremes. The king was treated practically as a god. Life at Versailles was a continuous pageant and Louis as the symbol of the state was the center of it. The nobles now lived a purposeless existence, dependent upon the favor of the king and in no position to challenge his word. Surrounded by fawning toadies and satellites, Louis' every action was made a regal ceremony based on the strictest precedent. For example, a nobleman of designated rank was required to dry the king after his bath, and only a very illustrious noble could hand the king his royal shirt or breeches during the public ceremony of dressing.

Colbert. When Louis XIV undertook to govern France in 1661 he had in his hands a prosperous land and a fairly efficient system of government. Here was an opportunity to follow the path of economic and social progress which had been indicated by his predecessors. But instead, Louis chose the path of military glory. He undid the work of Henry IV by revoking the Edict of Nantes, driving thousands of industrious Huguenots out of France. For a number of years, Louis had the fortune to possess as one of his ministers Jean Baptiste Colbert. Called the work-ox of the king, Colbert labored to advance France's economic interests. New industries were encouraged, colonies founded, the navy strengthened, and a surplus accumulated in the treasury. But all this work went for naught in the face of the king's reckless expenditure of money at Versailles and his costly wars.

Louis' thirst for conquest kept Europe in almost constant turmoil for nearly fifty years. Fortified by the knowledge that he possessed the strongest army in existence and the most capable generals of the age, he embarked on a career of conquest whose basic objective was to attain for France her "natural boundaries." This meant extending French territory on the north at the expense of the Spanish Netherlands, and on the east to the Rhine.

Wars against the Netherlands. Without any justification Louis attacked the Spanish Netherlands in the so-called War of Devolution (1667-1668). Carrying all before them, the French armies were on the point of annexing this rich territory when Holland, alarmed at the growing power of France, succeeded in forming a coalition of European powers to thwart Louis' design. As a result he had to be content with the seizure of only a few towns along the northern frontier of France. Irritated at Holland's interference with his plans, Louis next declared war against the Dutch in 1672. Deserted by their former allies, who had

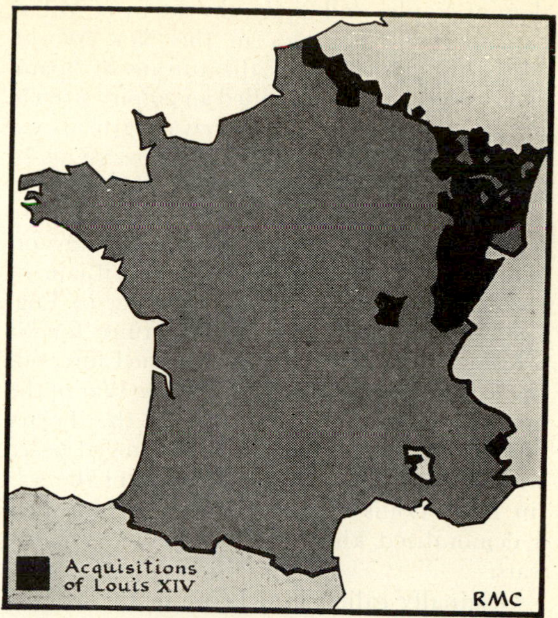

been bought off with French gold, the Dutch were for a time in desperate straits. The inspired leadership of William of Orange and the return of Holland's allies to her aid, however, saved the day for the Dutch and checkmated Louis' aggression. The conflict was ended in 1678 by the Treaty of Nimwegen.

The War of the League of Augsburg. Notwithstanding the heavy cost of these conflicts in lives and money, Louis XIV precipitated yet another war by seizing certain German border districts along the Rhine. Europe by this time was thoroughly aroused by the fear that Louis wanted to dominate the continent. In response to this threat, a coalition of powers called the League of Augsburg was formed in 1686, and for nine years following the outbreak of hostilities in 1689, French armies fought against those of England, the German empire, Sweden, and Holland. Finally in 1697, when both sides were exhausted, the Treaty of Ryswick (giving France a few small additions of territory) brought the war to a conclusion.

The War of the Spanish Succession. The end of this useless warfare was not in sight. At a time when all nations feared the extension of French power, Louis defied Europe by accepting the throne of Spain for his grandson. Spain, while not so powerful as in the days of Philip II, was still important. Its king not only controlled the kingdom of Spain proper but also the southern Netherlands, the Kingdom of Naples and Sicily, the duchy of Milan, Sardinia, and colonies in the New World. With his grandson on the throne of Spain, Louis would have controlled an empire stretching from Holland to Sicily, rivaling in its extent and power the Hapsburg possessions of Charles v in the sixteenth century. In answer to what was to be Louis' last menacing gesture to dominate Europe, another alliance was organized under the leadership of William of Orange, who had now become king of England. From 1702 to 1713 French armies fought a losing battle against the combined forces of the European coalition. In 1713 the War of the Spanish Succession was ended by the Treaty of Utrecht, by which the allies arranged peace with France. Shortly after the end of the war (in 1715) Louis xiv died, leaving behind him a demoralized kingdom bled white by costly wars.

Originally called into being in the Middle Ages by widespread feudal anarchy, the strong monarchy had become all-powerful and irresponsible. The reign of Louis xiv was indicative that absolutism had outlived its usefulness. Leaving behind a record of misery and discontent, Louis paved the way for the French Revolution and the bloody downfall of his dynasty.

The balance of power. During the numerous wars which agitated Europe from 1667 to 1713 there evolved what was to become the guiding principle of international diplomacy in modern times, the concept of the balance of power. To prevent France from dominating Europe, coalition after coalition was formed to resist the aggression of Louis xiv. From now on European diplomacy is to be explained largely in the refusal of the various powers to permit any single state or combination of nations to exercise too much power. In maintaining this delicate diplomatic equipoise, England, as we shall see, because of her relative geographical isolation from the continent, assumed the role of diplomatic balance wheel, throwing her support first to one side and then to the other in order to maintain the balance of power on the continent.

Another important development was that wars were becoming worldwide in scope. In the War of the Spanish Succession the struggle was carried on by fleets in the Mediterranean and Atlantic and by armies along the Rhine and in Spain, Italy, and even far-off colonial America. Warfare from now on became less and less localized and hence more dangerous and destructive to civilization.

The Treaty of Utrecht. Of the several treaties which ended the wars of Louis xiv, the Treaty of Utrecht was most important in shaping the map of modern Europe. This peace settlement, made in 1713, is comparable in its importance to the Peace of Westphalia, concluded in 1648. The Treaty of Utrecht arranged with France a relatively moderate settlement. No nation was excessively weakened, no single power was made too strong, and a fairly satisfactory balance of power was maintained without any major conflicts for nearly thirty years. The terms of the Treaty of Utrecht were as follows:

(1) Louis' grandson was permitted to remain king of Spain so long as the thrones of France and Spain were not united.
(2) England obtained important colonies: Nova Scotia, Newfoundland, and Hudson Bay, and valuable naval bases in the Balearic isles and Gibraltar in the Mediterranean.
(3) The Duke of Savoy, an Italian ruler, was given the title of king, and Sicily was added to his possessions.
(4) To Austria the allies gave Naples, Milan, Sardinia, and the Spanish Netherlands—the last to discourage the further expansion of France.
(5) The Dutch were allowed to regain certain important fortresses on their southern frontier as a protection from any future aggression from France.
(6) The Hohenzollern elector of Brandenburg was recognized as "king in Prussia."
(7) France was allowed to retain most of the conquests along her boundaries made in preceding years. This gave her more defensible frontiers.

The significance of several provisions in this peace should be noted. The acquisition of important colonies and naval bases marks a significant stage in the rise of England to world power. The Treaty also gave recognition to two aggressive ruling families, the House of Savoy and the House of Hohenzollern. In the nineteenth century, the House of Savoy succeeded in unifying Italy politically, and the Hohenzollerns did the same for Germany, as we shall see.

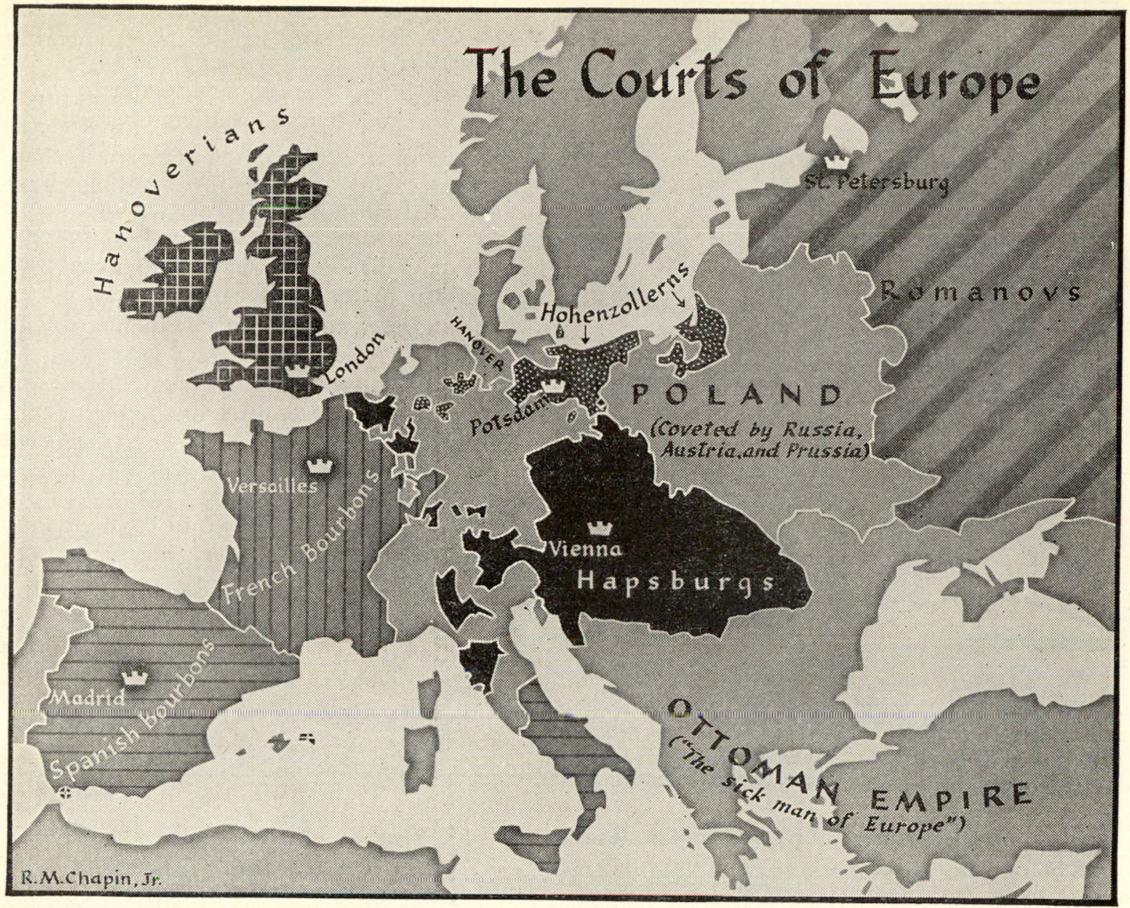

Power Politics in Operation

The "Big Five." The European state system at the beginning of the eighteenth century was dominated by the "Big Five." Great Britain, which had just led a triumphant coalition over France, was the greatest naval and commercial power in the world. France, in spite of her recent defeat, was still a first-class power and her civilization was universally admired and imitated on the continent. Far to the east a new state was beginning to loom on the horizon. This was Russia, which was being energetically transformed into a modern state by some capable Romanov monarchs. Most of the German states north of the Danube, belonging to the loosely organized and impotent Holy Roman Empire, were too weak to play a dynamic role in European affairs. But Prussia was an important exception. Led by one of the most efficient ruling houses in all history, the Hohenzollerns, Prussia became a great power in the eighteenth century, intimidating its weaker neighbors and expanding its territory by unscrupulous diplomacy and military force. The archdukes of Austria, belonging to the Hapsburg dynasty, were emperors of the Holy Roman Empire. As such they possessed little power. But as rulers of a vast hereditary empire, composed of Austria, Bohemia, Hungary, lands in Italy, and the Austrian Netherlands, the Hapsburg lands constituted one of the "Big Five" in Europe. The map above shows the leading dynasties and their holdings about 1740.

Other states. In addition to these five important powers there was a medley of minor states. Spain was now becoming decadent, her economic life stagnant, and her rulers corrupt. Italy, lacking any unifying national feeling, was fragmented into petty city-states largely under Austrian domination. High in the Alps the small but proud republic of Switzerland

A Russian artist lampoons the cutting off of beards in Russia after the decree of the czar, Peter the Great, who wanted to modernize his country. This picture was originally printed from a woodcut. A conversation between the two men has been written in Russian.

enjoyed political liberty and economic prosperity. Somewhat similar to this Alpine confederation in its love of liberty was Holland, which had gained its freedom from Spain in the Peace of Westphalia. In 1700 Sweden was apparently a very powerful state, as all of the islands and much of the coast of the Baltic Sea were in her possession. But this power was illusory. The extensive territories could be kept intact only by military force, which was rapidly draining Swedish resources. The eighteenth century therefore witnessed the collapse of the Swedish empire.

Extending from Hungary to the Baltic lay the great country of Poland. Ranking third in size among the states of Europe, it had a population of over eleven million. For several hundred years Poland had played an important role in European politics, but about 1675 its power and ability to defend itself rapidly declined.

The Ottoman empire in the seventeenth century included most of Hungary, the Balkan peninsula, much of Asia Minor, and Egypt, and was attempting further conquest in Europe. But in 1683 the Turkish steam roller was turned back at the gates of Vienna and in 1699 Hungary was reconquered by Austria. After 1700 the decline of the Ottoman empire was rapid. Plans for its partition were made by Austria and Russia, a design which was averted by the outbreak of the French Revolution. The carving up of the "Sick Man of Europe" was postponed until the nineteenth century, at which time this question precipitated many diplomatic crises and even wars between the major European powers.

Russian beginnings. The emergence of Russia and Prussia as great powers, largely at the expense of weaker nations, forms one of the principal themes of politics in the eighteenth century. The nucleus of modern Russia was the principality of Muscovy (the small dark area on the first map, page 89), whose princes had managed, in the late Middle Ages, to secure the allegiance of all Russians. In 1613 Mikhail Romanov was chosen as czar and founded the Romanov dynasty, which was to occupy the throne until the assassination of Nicholas II in 1917. Russia in the seventeenth century was culturally isolated from Europe. Commerce was negligible, illiteracy universal, the laws inhumane, and "the peasants were to be used and abused at pleasure." Russia at this time appeared semi-oriental, for the men wore long beards and flowing robes, and the women lived in a secluded atmosphere.

Policies of Peter the Great. Peter the Great, grandson of the first Romanov, made Russia a great nation. Coming to the throne in 1682, Peter had three objectives: (1) to Europeanize his people, (2) to obtain an outlet, or "a window," on the sea, and (3) to make the power of the czar absolute. After a visit to Europe, Peter the Great returned to Moscow and began an aggressive program of westernization. Printing presses were set up, art masterpieces collected, the study of foreign languages encouraged, long beards taxed, and the seclusion of women ended. Women were now to be seen in Russia, if not heard. Peter molded the structure of Russia to his imperious will. The Church was subordinated and, along with the army, made a bulwark of autocracy. All vestiges of local government were removed, and the mass of people confirmed in serfdom. This situation was to remain little changed until the Bolshevik Revolution in 1917.

In foreign affairs, Peter resolved to obtain

an all-year port on the Baltic, but Sweden at this time controlled most of the Baltic coast. Hoping to take advantage of the fact that Sweden was ruled by Charles XII, a boy of fifteen, Peter with several allies attacked the young king's territories in 1699. Russia was assisted in her design by Poland and Denmark. The Great Northern War resulted. To the consternation of the allies, the intended victim refused to be victimized. Charles, called the Swedish Meteor, won battle after battle. But his egotism, cruelty, and impetuosity proved his undoing. Peter bided his time, and in 1709 the Swedish army was annihilated. "Now by God's help," cried the czar, "are the foundations of St. Petersburg securely laid for all time." In 1721 the Treaty of Nystad confirmed the collapse of the Swedish empire and Russia obtained an important strip of coastline bordering the Gulf of Finland, and at tremendous cost St. Petersburg was built as a "window" on the Baltic (see middle map).

Catherine the Great. The continuation of Peter the Great's policies had to wait until Catherine, also called the Great, became czarina (1762-1796). Catherine, a German princess, married the Russian heir to the crown and found him half insane. Catherine tacitly consented to his murder, and it was announced that he died of "apoplexy." Brilliant and unscrupulous, she had two objectives: the extension of Russian territory into Europe at the expense of Poland, and the acquisition of lands around the Black Sea.

Sensing the weakness of the Ottoman empire, Catherine waged war against the Turks from 1768 to 1774. Following numerous defeats the Turks consented to a peace by which

An etching by Le Prince (1733-1781) shows a peasant's home in the time of Catherine the Great. Apparently the food vessels are being scraped clean. There is a small household shrine at the right.

Russia became the primary power on the Black Sea. Catherine had gained a second "window" for her country (see third map).

Catherine the Great was a most interesting historic character. She had only one objective, the strengthening of Russia's power. Utterly devoid of conscience, she felt quite at home in the battle of power politics. Crafty in diplomacy, the czarina was frankly immoral

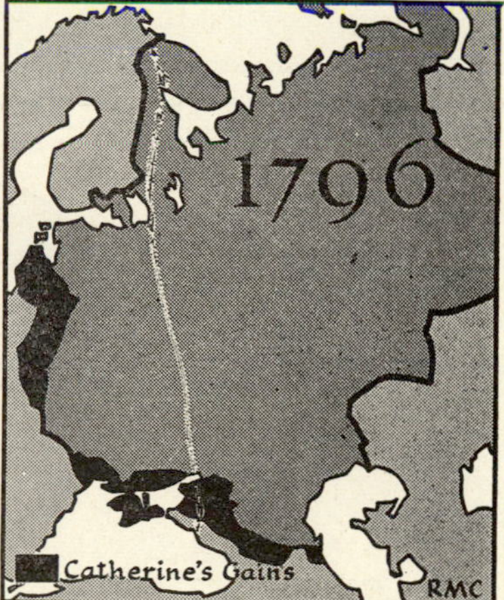

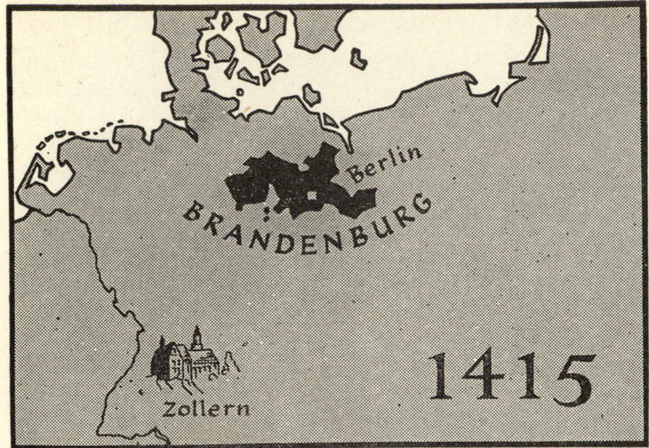

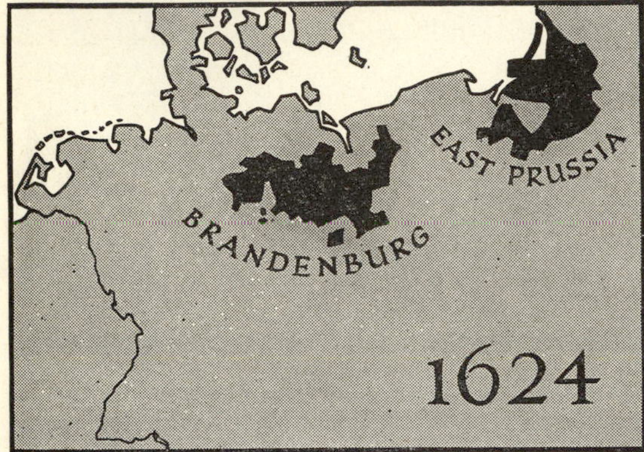

in her own private life, and scandalous stories of her conduct were common all over Europe. It was said that "her male favorites were as openly paraded as the female favorites of King Louis xv."

The rise of Hohenzollern power. If the rise of Russia was remarkable, the development of Prussia was even more amazing. Prussia was manufactured by its ruling house, the Hohenzollerns. History has scarcely a parallel example of the manner in which this royal house, by fair means or foul, expanded its territory and exalted its power. The Hohenzollerns in the eleventh century were petty nobles occupying a castle on the heights of Zollern in south Germany; in 1870 they were the rulers of a world power, the German empire (compare the first map on the left with the second on page 177). The first notable advance made by the Hohenzollerns was in 1415, when they received Brandenburg as a gift from the emperor of the Holy Roman Empire. This territory was a border province centering around its small town of Berlin. In 1618, as a result of a marriage alliance, East Prussia was acquired and about the same time valuable lands along the Rhine were obtained.

The Great Elector and the "barrack king." Prussia owed its meteoric rise to three men. The first, Frederick William (1640-1688), The Great Elector, laid the necessary foundations by encouraging industry and (unlike recent rulers of Germany) by assisting industrious refugees from other lands to settle in Berlin. The second, Frederick William I (1713-1740), the "barrack king," believed in the maxim "order, discipline, and work." He regarded himself as the father of his people who alone knew what was best for them. Once he declared, "Salvation belongs to the Lord, everything else is my business." To this man, more than anybody else, modern Germany owes its deep-rooted tradition of subordination of the individual to the state and of efficient government from above. A highly trained army was created and Berlin became "the Sparta of the north." Frederick William I had only one luxury. He scoured all Europe for giants over six feet whom he would cajole and bribe to join his Potsdam Guards regiment.

The right to call Brandenburg a kingdom was recognized in 1701 and from then on the Hohenzollerns were kings in Prussia, taking their new title from the province they obtained in

1618. The weakness of the new kingdom was that its territory was not contiguous (see maps). It became the policy to acquire the lands between the scattered Hohenzollern holdings. This will explain the ruthless annexation of the Polish Corridor in 1772.

Frederick the Great. Frederick William I was disappointed in his son, who devoted his youth to verse making and flute playing. Horrified, the militarist father subjected the boy to ten years' rigorous discipline. In 1740 he died, well content, for the once namby-pamby poet had been transformed into that cynical politician and tireless servant of the state, Frederick the Great, the third great ruler of Prussia.

War of the Austrian Succession. The new king soon showed his true colors. In 1740 he invaded the Austrian empire, ruled by beautiful, young Maria Theresa. This was done in spite of Prussia's and all Europe's guarantee to Maria Theresa's late father, in the document called the Pragmatic Sanction, that the lands of the young empress would be respected. Frederick's action precipitated the War of the Austrian Succession. He soon conquered the rich territory of Silesia. Other nations—France, Saxony, and Spain—thereupon threw in their lot with Frederick in order to obtain a share in the loot. The war slogan of these nations might well have been "What is an obligation to an opportunity?" In 1742 Frederick showed there is no honor even among international thieves by deserting his allies and making a separate peace with Austria. By this agreement Maria Theresa concurred in the Prussian occupation of Silesia. In 1744, however, fearing that Austria was becoming too strong because of English assistance, Frederick broke his engagement with Austria and again entered the fray. A year later, the Prussian king made his peace with Maria Theresa, although other belligerents continued the war for three more years. In 1748 the Treaty of Aix-la-Chapelle brought the struggle to an end. By this peace Maria Theresa, who had fought so valiantly in defense of her lands, retained most of her empire. There was little exchange of territory. Only the wily Frederick came out of the struggle with a rich prize—Silesia (see fourth map).

Brandenburg and Prussia. The seizure of Silesia by Frederick the Great is an important commentary on the character of international politics in the mid-eighteenth century, but the partition of Poland even transcends the crime committed against Maria Theresa. The events relating to the partition of Poland are highly significant, bearing as they do upon the Polish Corridor dispute, which was the immediate cause of the conflict that broke out in Europe in 1939. Back in the Middle Ages the Teutonic Knights, a crusading order, conquered and Christianized a Slavic people called the Borussians (Prussians). In 1466 this order gave the western part of Prussia (roughly corresponding to the modern Polish Corridor) to Poland but retained East Prussia as a fief under the suzerainty of the king of Poland. Following a marriage alliance between the ruling family of Brandenburg and that of East Prussia, in 1618 the latter territory came into the possession of the Hohenzollerns. Later the great-grandfather of Frederick the Great persuaded the Polish king to give up his overlordship over East Prussia and thus the Hohenzollerns gained complete title to this territory.

Poland partitioned. A glance at the third map on page 90 shows that when Frederick became king the province of East Prussia was separated from the main block of Prussian territory by West Prussia, held by Poland—the Polish Corridor. After his annexation of Silesia, Frederick turned his attention to this problem. He found fellow conspirators at hand in Austria and Russia. Poland, without natural barriers to aid her defense, was at this time governed by a corrupt nobility. Taking advantage of this situation, the three above states seized large areas of Polish territory in 1772 (as shown on the map below). In

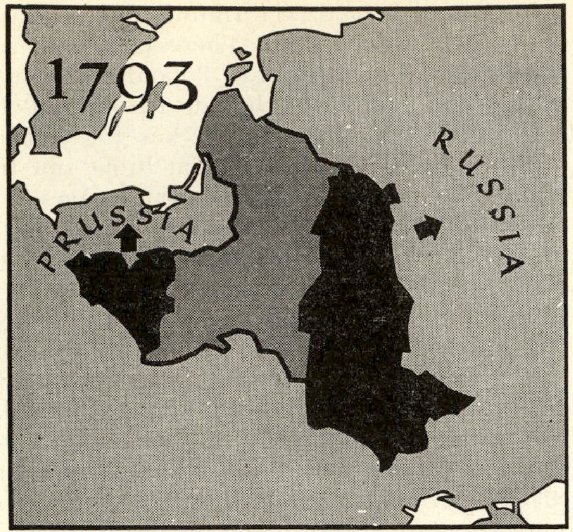

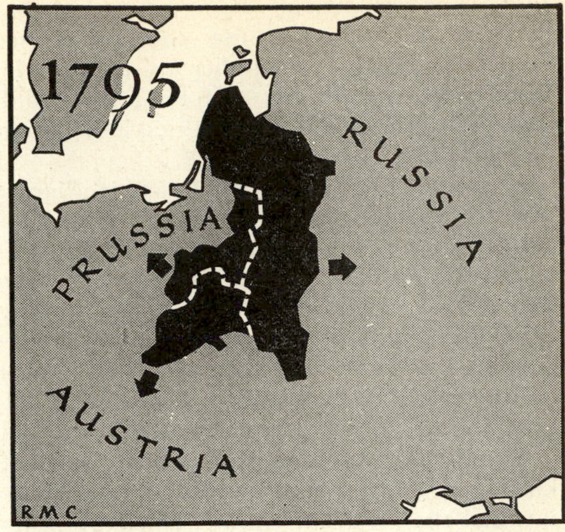

this manner Frederick "ironed out" the Polish Corridor and made East Prussia a contiguous part of his realm (see fourth map, page 90). Maria Theresa, it is said, declared Frederick's proposal of partition immoral, but faced with the fact that her abstention would allow Prussia and Russia to annex all of Poland, the empress reluctantly joined in the territorial surgery. Cynical Frederick, hearing that Maria Theresa deplored the seizure of Polish territory, remarked, "She wept, but she kept on taking." In 1793 and again in 1795 Polish territory was annexed (see the two maps above). In the third partition Poland ceased to exist as an independent state. Although dismembered and under the alien rule of three different governments, Poland still continued to live in the hearts of the Poles, who hoped for her resurrection. Their faith was rewarded after the World War of 1914-1918 through the leadership of two great heroes of Poland—Józef Pilsudski and Ignace Paderewski.

Franco-English rivalry. The operation of power politics in Europe from the days of Louis XIV to the time of Frederick the Great precipitated many wars, as we have seen. The most widespread and protracted of the conflicts in the eighteenth century was that waged between England and France.* At first England pitted herself against France in a desire to preserve the balance of power in Europe, but the issue between the two nations increasingly became that of colonies and trade. Between 1700 and 1740 the English and French became intense commercial rivals in five regions of the world: in India, Canada, the Mississippi valley, the West Indies, and Africa (shown on the map on page 93). The growth of France's sugar trade, the extension of its fur trade, and the advance of its fisheries gave the English cause for alarm. Then, too, the French, using Canada as a base, were extending their power into the Mississippi valley. This would prevent the English colonists from expanding west of the Appalachians, give the French control of the heart of North America, and relegate the English colonies to a narrow strip of land along the Atlantic coast. In all the European wars which have been discussed above, England and France were on opposite sides. Hostilities also were extended to the colonies. We refer, for example, to the War of the Spanish Succession as Queen Anne's War in American history.

As England came to realize that her main concern consisted not in checkmating French ambitions in Europe but in destroying French commerce and sea power in North America and India, the English adopted a shrewd diplomatic policy. This was the practice of obtaining allies to keep the French occupied in Europe while at the same time the bulk of British troops and especially sea power was concentrated on the task of conquering the

* In the eighteenth century Great Britain and France were at war in (1) the War of the Spanish Succession, 1702-1713; (2) the War of the Austrian Succession, 1740-1748; (3) the Seven Years' War, 1756-1763; (4) during the American Revolution, 1775-1783; and (5) the Revolutionary and Napoleonic wars, 1789-1815.

colonies and destroying the commerce of the French. The French, on the other hand, divided their energies by trying to play the game of power politics in Europe and at the same time endeavoring to compete with England over colonies. The result was that France failed in both policies.

The Seven Years' War. The duel for world empire between England and France reached a decisive stage in the Seven Years' War (1756-1763). The Treaty of Aix-la-Chapelle ending the War of the Austrian Succession had left Maria Theresa thirsting for revenge against Frederick the Great. The Austrian empress, therefore, turned to her country's hereditary enemy, France and suggested to Louis xv that the two countries form an alliance against Frederick of Prussia. As an inducement, France was to receive Frederick's Rhenish provinces. At first the French king refused. But the capable Austrian diplomat Kaunitz enlisted the assistance of Louis' mistress, Madame de Pompadour, who was infuriated at Frederick's frequent allusion to her as "Mademoiselle Poisson," for Pompadour was reputed to be the daughter of a fish wife. Pompadour's influence at the French court was important, but probably the decisive factor in Louis' decision to accept the Austrian offer was that he understood that England, not Austria, was now his most dangerous rival.

The Diplomatic Revolution. In order to checkmate France, England immediately made an alliance with its recent foe, Prussia. So completely had the diplomatic tables been turned that we refer to this new alignment of nations as the Diplomatic Revolution of the eighteenth century. While Frederick, assisted by British subsidies, fought against heavy odds in Europe, England, following the brilliant leadership of her prime minister, William Pitt, gained victory after victory in the New World and in India. The struggle in North America ended in British victory over the French general Montcalm at Quebec in 1759. On the sea the English also won decisive naval victories, and the power of the French in India was destroyed when Robert Clive gained a complete victory over the French and their Indian allies at the Battle of Plassey (1757).

England's triumph. After seven years of fighting, the Peace of Paris ended hostilities in 1763. To England France lost Canada and all the territory east of the Mississippi River, and ceded to Spain all of Louisiana west of the Mississippi and New Orleans. In the West Indies the English acquired several important islands from France, and in India the French were forced to recognize the English conquest of the important province of Bengal and to agree that the small trading posts kept by the French would not be fortified. England was

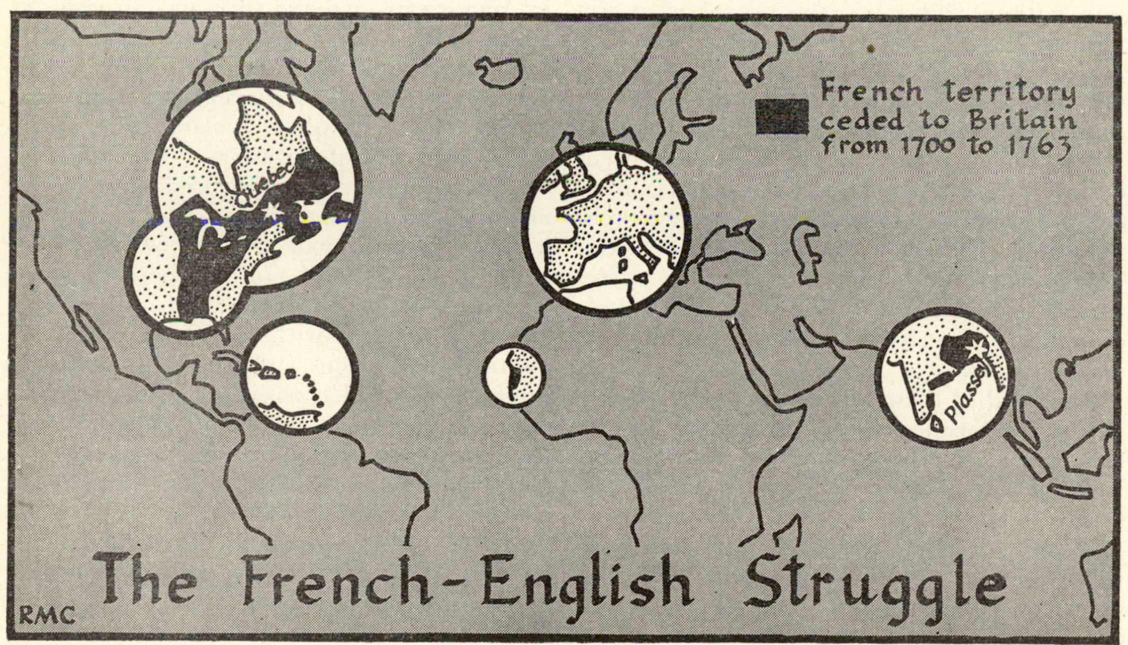

now the greatest colonial, commercial, and naval power in the world. Louisiana was to change hands several times before she became part of the United States. By the Second Treaty of San Ildefonso (1800) France again secured Louisiana from Spain. Three years later Napoleon sold Louisiana to the United States.

Wars, then and now. The story of international relations in the eighteenth century makes it clear that religion had long ceased to count as a motive, or even as an excuse, for war. The stakes of diplomacy were now colonies, territory, and commerce. It is also apparent that the nation which had the most cannon stood the best chance of success in competing for trade and colonies. War, therefore, was now the basic instrument of national policy. It is ironic that, while citizens were expected to order their lives according to certain basic ethical and moral standards of conduct, each nation remained free to conduct its affairs as it saw fit. The eighteenth century had more than its share of wars. But there was a difference between the conduct of wars then and now. Wars were largely conducted by professional soldiers. The great mass of people were not concerned, and the average civilian was able to live a fairly normal life while his nation's professional soldiers bore the brunt. This is in marked contrast with the conditions under which war is now waged.

King versus Parliament

The rise of representative government. Up to this point, the narrative of European politics in the seventeenth and eighteenth centuries has been concerned with the clash between European states for power and territory. In this process political absolutism played an important part. We saw how French policy, guided by Louis XIV, was the best example of national power politics in operation. But while numerous wars were raging between the European nations in the seventeenth and eighteenth centuries, an equally important struggle was making itself manifest within certain nations. This was the rise of what we term representative, or constitutional, government. Originally the kings had allied themselves with the middle class to make common cause against the common foe—the feudal nobility. But once political feudalism had been destroyed, the kings interfered with the interests of the middle class as much as, and even more than, had the feudal lords. Heavy taxes were levied on business, restrictions were placed on trade, and the whole foundation of economic prosperity was often jeopardized by needless wars.

Resentful of these hindrances to their prosperity, the business classes determined to obtain a more effective voice in government. The result was the development of representative government. This may be defined as a political system in which certain fundamental rights are guaranteed to the people by a constitution. In addition, a legislature made up of representatives selected by voters makes the laws of the land, and the executive branch of the government is expected to lead the nation in accordance with these laws and in conformity with the will of the electorate as expressed by their representatives in the legislature.

Extension of political privileges. Although the germs of this middle-class movement for greater political power go back to the Middle Ages, it was not until the Glorious Revolution of 1688 in England that the movement won its first momentous victory. Comparable revolutions in which the middle class played an important role took place in the British colonies in America in 1776 and in France in 1789. It is important to keep in mind that representative government does not necessarily mean democracy. The three revolutions mentioned above, which will form the main theme of the remaining pages of this chapter, were directed by the wealthy and influential classes who monopolized political power after absolutism had been overthrown. But the process of expanding the basis of political power continued. Politics in the nineteenth century was largely concerned with the development of political liberalism and the representative principle by which political privileges, obtained in the first instance by the middle class, were gradually extended to the common people. Beginning as a rather selfish class movement, representative government—as we shall see later—passed into a more democratic phase offering effective citizenship to all, regardless of social or economic status.

Cavaliers and Roundheads. For hundreds

of years England had been slowly working in the direction of constitutional government. From the Anglo-Saxon assembly through *Magna Charta* and the rise of Parliament, English representative principles had slowly developed. During the Wars of the Roses (1455-1485), parliaments controlled by predatory cliques of nobles temporarily halted the progress of constitutional government. During the period of Tudor rule (1485-1603) the English people were willing to be governed by such benevolent despots as Henry VII, Henry VIII, and Elizabeth, because they maintained law, order, and national prosperity. But when the last proud Tudor died, when Elizabeth was succeeded by James I of the House of Stuart, struggle broke out between Parliament and the crown. The quarrel was complicated by religious differences. During the reign of James it was restricted in the main to fiery speeches and resolutions in the House of Commons, but during the reign of the second Stuart, Charles I, a civil war broke out in 1642. For seven years Roundheads and Cavaliers, as the soldiers of Parliament and the king were respectively called, fought each other. The Roundheads were finally triumphant. In 1649 the king was beheaded; England became a republic and remained so for eleven years. But during this kingless decade the people were far from content. The Puritans, champions of liberty against the former king, were, ironically, forced to rule the English republic in an even more autocratic fashion than had the autocrat they had beheaded. Following the death of Cromwell, the chief Puritan leader, in 1658, it became evident that the revolution had gone too far, that too many traditions part and parcel of English life had been destroyed, and that the people wanted the reëstablishment of kingship.

The restoration of Charles II. In May 1660, the dark and handsome son of the king who had been executed by the Puritan government entered London amid the rejoicing of its people. The Restoration placed him upon the English throne as Charles II, one of the most interesting monarchs of his day. To his subjects he exposed an infectious smile, a debonair attitude welcomed by his subjects only lately repressed and inhibited by the blue laws of the Puritan régime. Dubbed as a ruler who "never said a foolish thing or did a wise one," Charles gave the impression of being little more than a royal playboy, but this masked his designs to reintroduce Catholicism in England and make the royal power supreme. The new king, while believing in divine right like his father, was much more astute and adroit in his statesmanship. His one aim was to avoid going on his travels again, as he had been forced to do during the civil war.

Behind the backs of his anti-French subjects, the king negotiated a secret treaty with Louis XIV of France. In return for an annual subsidy from the French government, making him financially independent of Parliament, Charles agreed to reëstablish Catholicism in England. The English king also promised to support Louis in a war against Holland. This agreement, made in 1670 and called the Treaty of Dover, was one of the most scandalous actions ever committed by an English king. After Charles had collected a substantial sum from Louis, he had the effrontery to persuade Parliament to grant him money for waging war against the French king, his secret ally. No ruler has ever been able to give a better performance of running with the hare and hunting with the hounds and making everybody like it.

Although the Restoration had ended the Puritan republic and brought back the Stuarts, England did not return to the constitutional position existing before the civil war. The monarchy no longer possessed arbitrary courts, taxes were expressly forbidden without parliamentary consent, and making laws by royal proclamation was illegal. In theory, at least, Charles II could not be so absolute as his father had been. The king, however, still wielded considerable power. He could veto laws, he commanded the militia, and unless he committed a very serious breach of the constitution warranting his deposition, Parliament had no weapon to compel him to do its will. In short, power was now shared between the crown and Parliament. As long as they cooperated with each other the situation was satisfactory.

To carry out his shady bargain with Louis, Charles by royal command in 1672 suspended the operation of laws directed against English Catholics. As the English had come to associate Catholicism with the menace of strong foreign foes and with despotic government, a political crisis was precipitated by the king's action. The following year Parliament passed a law, the Test Act, excluding all Catholics from public office. It also endeavored to exclude James, a staunch Catholic, from succeeding to the throne upon the death of his brother Charles.

The rise of political parties. Two significant consequences of this controversy between Charles and Parliament should be noted. First was the rise of political parties as we know them today. To thwart Charles's pro-Catholicism, members of the House of Commons, with headquarters at a London tavern, formed the Green Ribbon Club. This in time became the Whig Party, which stood for the supremacy of Parliament, the interests of the business classes, and Protestantism. The Whig motto was "life, liberty, and property." In opposition there developed the Tory Party, supported by the landed gentry, which championed "the king, the church, and the land." Although factional grouping existed in the earliest times and in many places, England can be considered the ancestral home of modern political parties. Since political parties are an indispensable part of the machinery of representative government, the organization and tactics of the Whig and Tory parties were later imitated in free countries all over the world.

Habeas corpus. The second important constitutional contribution of the reign of Charles II was the passage of the Habeas Corpus Act in 1679. Anyone who thought himself unjustly imprisoned could obtain a writ of *habeas corpus*, which compelled the government to explain why he had been deprived of his liberty. This safeguard against arbitrary imprisonment was later incorporated in the American constitution.

James II. In the latter part of the reign of Charles, his astute tactics outmaneuvered Parliament, and the king in effect set up a royal despotism. When the king died in 1685 and his brother James ascended the throne, the cause of popular liberty seemed in danger of extinction. But fortunately for the English people "this second James was as tactless as the first; without the latter's erudition; as stubborn as his father, the first Charles, with none of his more attractive qualities; while in politics he was a fool as compared with his older brother."[3]

At the outset of his reign James tried to coerce Parliament to repeal the Test and Habeas Corpus acts. In 1687 he suspended by royal order all laws against Catholics. This was followed by attempts to intimidate the courts and to appoint Catholics to office. In the face of such unpopular acts the English laid aside all factionalism and determined to remove James from the throne. An invitation was therefore extended to William of Orange, ruler of the Dutch, to assume the English crown.

William and Mary. This choice was dictated by two factors. William was considered the champion of Protestantism in Europe, and he was the husband of Mary, the older daughter of James II, the Protestant next in line to the throne. In November 1688 William set sail for England and landed without opposition. Forsaken by his army, the discouraged James escaped to France, and on December 19, 1688, William entered London. Parliament offered the crown to William and Mary as joint sovereigns. This offer was contingent on their acceptance of a declaration of rights, later enacted as the Bill of Rights.

The Bill of Rights. Rivaling in importance *Magna Charta,* this declaration provided that, (1) the king could not suspend the operation of laws, (2) no money was to be levied without consent of Parliament, (3) freedom of speech in Parliament was to be assured, (4) bail was not to be excessive, (5) the king must be a Protestant, and (6) Parliament ought to be held frequently. These provisions have exercised a tremendous influence in the development of constitutional government. Many clauses of the Bill of Rights were embodied in the new state constitutions in America after 1776, and the first ten amendments to the Constitution of the United States and the French Declaration of the Rights of Man show their debt to the English declaration of 1688.

The Glorious Revolution and its results. The events which placed William and Mary on the English throne are referred to by Englishmen as the Glorious, or Bloodless, Revolution. Without bloodshed Parliament had deposed the old line of kings and laid down the conditions under which English sovereigns of the future were to rule. By the Revolution of 1688 the long duel between kings and Parliament had been brought to a conclusion. The theory of divine right had been discredited in England, and Parliament had become the dominant agency in government. The Glorious

Revolution was also attended by other important results. By the Toleration Act of 1689 Protestants not belonging to the established Church of England were given the right of public worship, but full political privileges were not secured until early in the nineteenth century. In 1693 the first debate on freedom of the press took place in Parliament. This body refused to pass the customary licensing act which had been used by the government to muzzle the press. From now on freedom of the press became an important aid in representative government. In foreign affairs the events of 1688 caused England to switch from the heretofore pro-French policy of Charles II and James II. William, the champion of Protestantism on the European continent, was now king of England and immediately proceeded to use its great resources to checkmate the designs of Louis XIV.

The importance of the Glorious Revolution, significant as it was, should not be overemphasized, for in essence it was narrowly political and did nothing to eliminate many social and economic abuses existing in England. While the Bill of Rights and the Toleration Act guaranteed to the common people certain fundamental rights, the nation was now governed by a small and wealthy minority of merchants and gentry.

Modern politics take form. The constitutional development of England from 1689 down to the middle of the eighteenth century mainly concerned the perfection of political parties and the rise of the cabinet system of government. The deposition of King James in 1688 had made Parliament all-powerful. Instead, therefore, of trying to get the king in their control as political factions had done in the past, the new political parties now saw that the way to influence governmental policy was to elect a majority of their representatives to the House of Commons. This was a unique development in European politics. The middle class and influential gentry, anxious to shape governmental policy so that it would foster their economic interests, were forced to take a more active interest in elections. The newspaper and pamphlet, barely a half-century old, were now enlisted in the rough-and-tumble process of electioneering. Modern politics as we know them were thus taking form.

The first prime minister. In spite of the growing importance of political parties and the development of all the paraphernalia which we now associate with elections, it became obvious in the reign of William and Mary that something was still wrong with the machinery of government. Since the reign of Charles II it had been customary for the king to have a small committee, or cabinet, to assist him in carrying on the government. William carried on this custom but tried to select his cabinet from both political parties, which caused much wrangling between the king and Parliament. During the reign of George I (1714-1727) the principle was established that the king select as his main adviser, or prime minister, the statesman who could command a majority of the votes in the House of Commons.

George was the first of the Hanoverian line of kings. He was more German than English. In fact he could not speak the language of his new subjects, and this handicap plus his lack of interest in English politics caused him to turn over the task of administration to his chief, or prime, minister. George I rarely attended cabinet meetings, and in the reign of his successor, George II, this custom hardened into precedent and the king was well on his way to being a mere ceremonial figurehead.

During a large part of the reigns of these two sovereigns Robert Walpole served as the real head of the government and as head of the House of Commons (1721-1742). Walpole is therefore regarded as the first real prime minister in English history. In 1742, following the loss of his majority in the House of Commons, Walpole resigned. By this act recognition was given to the principle that the executive branch of the government, in theory the king but actually the prime minister, must resign when his actions are no longer approved by the House of Commons, by now more important than the House of Lords. This precedent effectively removed the danger of conflict between the legislative and executive branches of government. The essence of cabinet government, therefore, is that the executive is responsible to the legislature. In most of the representative systems which grew up mainly in the nineteenth century, the British system of cabinet government was followed. The principal exception was the United States.

Corrupt "popular" government. By the mid-eighteenth century the cabinet system of responsible government was well on its way to perfection in England. Students of government living in France, Spain, and other countries on the continent were prone to speak of the glories of the English system. But the truth is that, although England was far in advance of her neighbors, her government if judged by modern standards was still backward. Corruption was rampant. Walpole, it is said, once looked over the House of Commons and said, "Every man has his price." Wealthy leaders of the Whig and Tory parties kept their followers in line by distributing fat sinecures or outright bribes. At one time it was estimated that more than fifty per cent of the House held pensions or well-paid sinecures. Members of the Commons were elected by a franchise system which included only ten per cent of the adult males as voters.

The five hundred sixty members of the House of Commons represented either counties or boroughs. Each county had the right to elect two representatives, and the same usually held true of the borough or town. Many of the boroughs, once flourishing towns, had lost most of their inhabitants to other parts of the country, and in some cases the borough had become partly inundated by the sea. These so-called "rotten boroughs" still continued to send their representatives to Parliament. The most famous example was Old Sarum, situated on the site of the ancient city of Salisbury. Not a single building remained of the original settlement, but when election time came, the owner would pitch a tent for election purposes and cast the necessary votes. In some of the boroughs, even with a large population, it was possible for an interested party to buy up enough votes to swing the election. These were the "pocket boroughs" controlled by patrons similar to "ward heelers" and political bosses in the United States.

The height of parliamentary corruption was reached in the reign of George III (1760-1820). It was the ambition of this monarch to recover the royal prerogatives surrendered by his two predecessors, the first and second Georges. In particular George III was out to destroy the cabinet system of government. But George was wise enough not to challenge openly the rights of Parliament. The execution of Charles I in 1649 and the Glorious Revolution in 1688 warned him of this danger. He used instead the weapon of bribery. The pocket and rotten boroughs gave him ample opportunities. In no time George III succeeded in building up a servile body of henchmen in the House of Commons, known as the King's Friends, ready at any time to do their royal master's bidding. George III was misguided and foolish in most of his policies. The quarrel with the American colonies reached a crisis during the reign of this obstinate king.

The Intellectual Assault on Absolutism

Criticism of existing governments. It has been pointed out that eighteenth-century thought was characterized by the belief that all aspects of civilization—art, religion, literature, music, government—should be based on reason, the ultimate touchstone of perfection. The scholars of the Enlightenment found much that was irrational and indefensible in the institutions of their day. It will be recalled that the movement called Deism sought to eliminate from organized religion all denominational dogma and what was thought to be mere superstition. Absolutism in government was also called to trial. Keen-minded scholars like Voltaire studied the causes and results of the Glorious Revolution in England and were moved to inquire why France and other European countries were so far behind the English in the theory and practice of government. The Glorious Revolution was a challenge to men everywhere in the western world to throw off their tyrants, to obtain constitutions, and to introduce representative institutions.

Merchants, lawyers, doctors, shopkeepers, and bankers were particularly desirous of bringing about sweeping changes in government. Although religion played an important part in the Puritan and Glorious revolutions in England, it was the ambition of the urban middle class that gave both these movements their greatest strength. As we shall soon see, the middle class was of equal importance in the French and the American revolutions.

John Locke (1632-1704). The middle-class drive against intrenched monarchical authority was greatly assisted by ammunition from the great thinkers of the day, for what was inimical to business also seemed to be repugnant to common sense. John Locke was the first important thinker to supply the middle class with the necessary intellectual arguments to justify revolution. One of the most eminent men of his day, Locke was an Oxford graduate, a practitioner of medicine, a member of the Royal Society, a political scientist, and a famous philosopher. We have already discussed his philosophy in Chapter 2.

Locke's *Two Treatises of Government*, published in 1690, was a defense and justification of the Glorious Revolution. In France Locke's ideas of natural rights and social contract became the basis for the attack on absolutism, and in America the colonists considered the "great Mr. Locke" as the fountain-head of their revolutionary ideas. The *Two Treatises of Government* expounded the following principles:

(1) Before government was established, all men, living in a "state of nature," possessed certain "natural rights." These were inherent in the very order of nature and consisted principally of the right to life, liberty, and property. Alexander Hamilton was thinking of these rights when he declared:

"The sacred rights of mankind are not to be rummaged for among old parchments or musty records. They are written as with a sunbeam in the whole volume of human nature, by the hand of the Divinity itself, and can never be erased or obscured by mortal power."[4]

The concept that men possess certain natural, inalienable, and sacred rights did not originate with Locke but can be traced back as far as Aristotle and Roman law. In the English civil war of the seventeenth century, however, the idea of natural rights received its first effective impetus.

(2) Life in the state of nature was not satisfactory. The strong oppressed the weak, and there was no impartial judge to settle disputes. Locke agreed with another English philosopher, Thomas Hobbes, that the state of nature is one of "continual fear and danger of violent death; and the life of man solitary, poor, nasty, brutish, and short."

(3) Government is, therefore, necessary to maintain order and guarantee the enjoyment of man's natural rights. By common consent an agreement, or compact, is entered into by which a sovereign is set up with power to govern and enforce his will.

(4) Through this contract the people give up some of their rights to the government but their basic natural rights are in no way surrendered.

(5) The social contract, which does away with the chaotic state of nature and establishes an organized society with a government, is bilateral, or binding upon both parties. The government, for its part, can demand the obedience of the people, but the people may also expect that the government will keep its part of the contract by not abridging, in any way, the natural rights of the people. If these rights are violated, if the government rules unwisely and tyrannically, the people have a perfect right to overthrow their rulers. In short, the people are the real rulers, the custodians of "popular sovereignty." It was the great achievement of Locke to give, for the first time, a clear and comprehensive exposition of what we call the doctrine of popular sovereignty, which gives the people the right of revolution.

The doctrines of social contract and natural rights reached their most influential expression in the writings of the French *philosophes* in the mid-eighteenth century, whose influence in religion and other fields of inquiry have already been noted. Such men as Montesquieu and Rousseau carried Locke's political philosophy to its logical culmination, and by reason of their lucid and appealing style of writing reached a far greater audience than did their English teacher.

Montesquieu (1689-1755). Montesquieu was a French nobleman and judge who first achieved distinction by his *Persian Letters* in 1721. This work purports to be the letters of two rich Persians describing to their friends in Persia their reaction to conditions in France. The whole is a brilliant satire which slyly and humorously exposes the evils of the old régime in France.

After twenty years of study, Montesquieu completed his *Spirit of Laws*. This was one of the most important books of the eighteenth century. Montesquieu's method of studying government was different from Locke's and more in accord with modern ideas. Locke built up a philosophical justification of revolution which was not based on historical fact. We have no record of primitive people, possessing no political organization, suddenly deciding to meet together to supply the defect. Locke's technique was deductive; that of Montesquieu inductive. Montesquieu painstakingly collected facts about the various governments which are recorded in history. These he then classified and analyzed. Following this comparative approach, Montesquieu laid down the dictum that there is no one best type of government. Governments must conform to the features of geography, economic resources, and race with which they are associated.

Of great importance to American students is Montesquieu's idea of the separation of powers in government. By dividing the machinery of government into three departments—legislative, executive, and judicial—and preventing encroachment or intimidation of one on the other, Montesquieu believed that autocratic government would be prevented. The fathers of the American constitution adopted this plan as a basic element in the federal government of the United States. Montesquieu was moderate in his writings. His books show a strong admiration for constitutional, or representative, government, especially as exemplified by the English system; and his advocacy of popular sovereignty was lucid and sincere.

Rousseau (1712-1778). Jean Jacques Rousseau was one of the most enigmatic, strange, and yet significant figures of the eighteenth century. Rousseau has been called a rogue, cheat, hypocrite, and madman, yet he exercised a tremendous influence upon his age, an influence that was wholesome and most worth while.

Of French Huguenot stock, Rousseau was born in Geneva in 1712 of humble parents. Without the care of his mother, who had died at his birth, and neglected by his father, the boy grew up undisciplined and untrained. At the age of sixteen he took to the open road, and for twenty years he wandered as servant, tutor, music teacher, and secretary. Finally he arrived in Paris.

The fame of Rousseau rests upon four books. In 1760 he published *The New Héloïse,* a romantic novel. In this he launched the back-to-nature vogue. Inveighing against the inhibitions and restraints of what he believed to be an artificial and decadent civilization, Rousseau preached the return to a simple life. In 1762 *Emile* appeared, in which Rousseau outlined his ideas on education. It contains the modern idea that education should be child-centered. The aim of education, according to Rousseau, was to develop the innate potentialities of the individual, not to encumber him with a lot of useless knowledge.

A third book upon which the fame of Rousseau is based is his *Social Contract,* published in 1762. The famous opening sentence declares, "Man is born free, but is everywhere in chains." Taking the political philosophy of Locke, Rousseau expressed it with fervor, imagination, and emotional intensity that made it a much more effective piece of propaganda than the dry tomes of Locke. "All the rulers of the earth," cried Rousseau, "are mere delegates of the people, who, when they are displeased with the government, have the right to alter or abolish it."

The *Confessions,* published after his death, was another work which contributed materially to Rousseau's immortality. One of the frankest autobiographies ever written, it reveals the complex and baffling character of the author.

The influence of Rousseau was enormous. His *Social Contract* has been called the Bible of the French Revolution, which broke out just fourteen years after his death. The watchwords of this revolt—"liberty, equality, and fraternity"—were taken from the *Social Contract.* Rousseau's back-to-nature idea became a popular fad, his educational ideas became the basis for modern pedagogy, and the middle class in France used his political teachings as a justification for revolution.

The American Revolution

Democratic ideas in the colonies. The effects of the Glorious Revolution of 1688 were felt not only by Englishmen but by their compatriots in the American colonies. The Puritan Revolution had also made a deep impression upon American opinion. Some of its advanced political ideas did not make much impression in conservative England but found a fertile soil in the colonies. A faction in Oliver Cromwell's army called the Levelers espoused democratic ideas. "The meanest man in England," they maintained, "had the right to a share in the election of his rulers."

Such ideas and John Locke's philosophy of natural rights and social contract became the political testament of the colonists, who throughout the eighteenth century gained more and more voice in governmental affairs.

Middle-class interests in the colonies. The American Revolution was not so much a revolt against the tyranny of the English king, George III, as a revolt of the American middle class against the selfish economic policy of the mother country. England was controlled by a commercial oligarchy which wished to "use" the colonies economically. According to mercantilistic views prevailing in Europe, a colony should be primarily a source of economic wealth to its mother country. As early as 1650, England had begun to enact navigation laws which forced the colonists to trade only with England and prohibited them from competing with English manufactured goods. For one hundred years these acts were not rigidly enforced. The colonists, therefore, were able to carry on a lucrative illicit trade without much interference.

Great Britain's new taxation. After the Seven Years' War England found herself saddled with a debt of nearly $700,000,000. Meantime, a serious uprising of Indians in the northwest in 1763 showed the need for a strong force of British regulars in America for defense purposes. George Grenville, the prime minister, decided, therefore, that it was only fair that the colonists should assist in carrying the imperial economic burden. Plans were made to reduce the rates of the Navigation Acts but at the same time to enforce them rigidly (1764), a stamp act on colonial newspapers and legal documents was passed (1765), and an act for quartering English troops in America was enacted.

Much has been made of the colonists' slogan "No taxation without representation," but it should be remembered that the English government tried to get the colonial governments to raise the necessary taxation themselves. This, however, the colonists refused to do, and the English government proceeded with their taxation measures. The truth of the matter is that the American people were averse to paying any taxes, either to their own legislatures or to the imperial Parliament. As H. A. L. Fisher says, "The English have always quarreled over money and the English colonists in America who resisted Grenville's stamp tax were faithful to the habits of their ancestors."[5]

Revolt of the colonies. Following the imposition of the stamp tax, events moved rapidly in the direction of open hostilities between the colonies and the mother country. American students are familiar with such events as the First Continental Congress (1774), the first clash of arms in 1775, the Declaration of Independence in 1776, the heroic struggle of the Continental army from 1776-1783, the courage and patience of George Washington, and, finally, victory and independence recognized in the Treaty of Paris in 1783.

Reasons for revolution. Although England's taxation measures precipitated the revolution, it would be a mistake to interpret the American Revolution as solely, or even primarily, the effect of economic causes. For example, although the American commercial classes were mainly interested in freeing themselves from English trade regulation, they justified their revolt by resorting to the political philosophy of the Puritan and Bloodless revolutions. Economic self-interest and sincere political liberalism were blended, and economic issues were translated into a crusade against despotic government.

As in all great historical movements the American Revolution was a complex phenomenon. In addition to the British taxation policy, there were other factors which help explain why the American colonies broke away from their mother country.

There was little real patriotism for England in the colonies. Many colonists had suffered religious persecution in the mother country and had little love for their homeland. In 1775, out of a population of nearly 3,000,000, almost forty per cent were of non-English stock, mainly from Ireland and south Germany. "To many Americans," remarks L. M. Larson, "England had been an arbitrary and unkind mother; to a greater number she had never been a mother."[6]

The colonists were different from the people living in England. In America a rugged spirit of independence rapidly developed which would tolerate little restraint and interference with fundamental personal liberties. Life on the frontier nourished a strong belief in the equality of man.

Political conditions in England also form an important background for the American Revolution. Not only were there irritating and arbitrary acts by royal officials in America, but there was the same tendency to abridge political liberties in England. George III had been reared with one maxim ringing in his ears: "George, be a king." By bribery and craft he gained control of the cabinet and Parliament. Many Englishmen, therefore, who opposed the king's arbitrary policies at home supported the cause of the American colonists as their own. For this reason the American Revolution has been called "a civil war within the British Empire." Edmund Burke (1729-1797), the great Irish orator and member of Parliament, spoke eloquently for conciliation and consideration for the colonies. In discussing the crisis he declared: "The question with me is not whether you have a right to render people miserable; but whether it is not your interest to make them happy." And he warned the government that "Magnanimity in politics is not seldom the truest wisdom; and a great empire and little minds go ill together."

The problem of governing a great empire was too difficult for the mediocre statesmen who were George's henchmen. Slowness of communication in 1750 made it difficult to govern remote colonies. Given the marine telegraph, fast steamers to bring dispatches, and the radio, English statesmen might have avoided some of their blunders, but they did not intelligently use the facilities at hand.

Undoubtedly there was a large class of people in the colonies who were against any governmental authority. They were poor and discontented and saw in any revolution the chance for a "reshuffle" which might be to their benefit. This section of radical opinion was utilized by the commercial middle class to assist it in escaping from the irksome English Navigation Acts. When independence was finally achieved, the conservative merchant classes established a new régime based upon law, order, and the sanctity of property, not at all liked by the colonial proletarians.

What the American Revolution meant. It is quite clear that the American Revolution cannot be explained by recourse to any single cause. But refusing to interpret the events of 1776 solely by the "tyranny formula" does not

"A Peep into the Antifederal Club," drawn by an unknown artist in 1793, is a fierce satire on the Jacobins, as the Jeffersonians were called. The man in the center is debating whether it is better to "knock down dry goods with this hammer or with this head contrive some means of knocking down a government."

in the least detract from the tremendous significance of the American Revolution to world civilization. (1) If it did not result immediately in the attainment of democracy, it made its attainment inevitable in America. (2) For the first time, a great nation set up a republic. (3) In the field of government, the United States began a remarkable experiment in a federal system of government designed for a large land area. (4) A written Constitution, for the first time (if we except the Puritan Instrument of Government, which was of brief duration), became the basic law of a country. (5) As Charles A. Beard says, the revolution "started a dislocation of authority" in a heretofore-aristocratic social structure. Voting qualifications soon became more liberal, land privilege was ended by the breaking up of large estates, the criminal code became more humane, and established churches were soon the exception rather than the rule. (6) No matter how complicated the issues underlying the American Revolution now seem to scholars, the revolt of the colonists and the classical exposition of their cause in the Declaration of Independence was a symbol of hope and inspiration to oppressed people the world over. The fall of the Bastille in Paris occurred only six years after the United States obtained its independence in 1783.

The French Revolution

The old régime in Europe. Western Europe in the middle of the eighteenth century presented many contrasts with conditions prevailing in medieval times. Science was revolutionizing man's conceptions of society and the natural universe. Geographical discoveries had opened up new lands for European settlement and trade. Commerce was increasing the wealth and ambitions of the middle class. On every hand critical thinkers were assailing institutions and ideas which they considered outworn and illogical. Although progress in the past four hundred years had been remarkable, many political and social absurdities still persisted.

Certain phases of feudalism still lived on. Continental Europe was plagued by a parasitic nobility which exacted onerous personal services and financial dues from the peasants. Now that the political power of the nobility had been broken by the king, in most of Europe the monarchs were absolute rulers, disclaiming any responsibility for their actions. Not only were governments despotic, but frequently they were corrupt and inefficient. It is estimated that the higher clergy and the nobility represented not more than one per cent of Europe's population. Yet these classes controlled a vast amount of wealth, escaped from taxation, and exercised an influence disproportionate to their limited numbers. Such was the old régime, as European society in the eighteenth century is termed. Resentful of the power and privileges of the clergy and nobility, the rising middle class aspired to seize governmental power.

Enlightened despots. The injustices of the old régime were not ignored by all the European rulers. A remarkable group of monarchs called "enlightened despots," influenced by the writings of the French *philosophes*, sincerely endeavored to eliminate some of the evils in European society. In fact this period has been termed "the monarch's age of repentance." Among the enlightened despots were Frederick the Great of Prussia, Catherine II of Russia, Gustavus III of Sweden, and Joseph II of Austria. Each of these rulers regarded himself as the first servant of the state. Sincerely desirous of promoting the best interests of their nations, they based their absolute power on efficiency. The wise monarch alone knew what was good for his people, they believed. Under their rule commerce was extended, new industries established, harsh law codes amended, and agriculture improved.

In spite of achieving many desirable reforms, the enlightened despots failed to effect any basic reforms in the old régime. They were continually hampered by the selfish interests of the nobles and clergy. They hesitated to initiate any really sweeping and drastic changes, such as the abolition of serfdom. Another serious weakness of enlightened despotism was that there was no guarantee that an efficient and well-meaning monarch would be followed by a capable successor. In many instances thriftless and incompetent rulers destroyed much of the work bequeathed them by their competent predecessors.

Joseph II of Austria illustrates the failure of enlightened despotism. An enthusiastic devotee of Rousseau, he wished to make "philosophy the legislator of his empire." Sweeping reforms were initiated. But Joseph was in too much of a hurry. As Frederick the Great commented, "Joseph always wishes to take the second step before he has taken the first." Nobles, clergy, and the peasantry misunderstood his intentions and opposed his reforms. After a reign embittered by many failures, Joseph II died a broken-hearted man, realizing that he had satisfied few of his subjects and alienated the majority. The aim of the despotic reformers was to perpetuate the old régime in a modified form, but it contained so many features at variance with new intellectual currents that there could be no compromise.

France in 1789. Incompatibility between the rationalistic temper of the Age of Reason and the evils of the old régime was most acute in France. This country, as we have seen, was a hotbed of criticism against the old régime, but no important reforms, such as had been carried out by enlightened rulers elsewhere, had taken place. Superficially France enjoyed an enviable position in 1789. The brilliance of her philosophers and the glitter of her royal court at Versailles were the envy of the continent. France had just assisted America in humbling Great Britain in the New World, her population was nearly three times as great as England's, and her foreign trade had increased 500 per cent since the year 1700. But underneath this apparently satisfactory situation were many problems that urgently demanded solution.

Weak French kings. France had become a despotism to escape the evils of feudalism and expected two things from her kings: an effective foreign policy and good internal government. In the eighteenth century French absolutism failed in both. The century had started with the legacy of the costly wars of Louis XIV. The next monarch, Louis XV (1715-1774), had been indifferent to matters of government. Preoccupied with his mistresses, notably Madame de Pompadour and Madame du Barry, Louis allowed his country to become entangled in a disastrous foreign policy which involved France in the War of the Austrian Succession and the Seven Years' War. As a result, in 1763 France was forced to cede her most important colonies to England. At the end of his reign one of the king's ministers wrote, "The opinion gains ground that absolute monarchy is the worst conceivable form of government."[7]

The French people hoped for better things when Louis XVI ascended the throne. Although the young monarch was well meaning, he was ill-educated, indolent, and shy. Shirking matters of state, Louis spent his happiest hours in a workshop tinkering with locks and, passionately fond of hunting but too lazy to join the chase, he had deer driven by a palace window where he shot them down. Louis XVI married Marie Antoinette of Austria, who had little of the vision and strength of character of her mother, Maria Theresa. The queen gained the reputation of being frivolous and much too extravagant. She did little to encourage her husband in affairs of state and interfered in government only when she wished to obtain a concession for one of her favorites. "If the court of France was a corrupt ring living on the country," comments Edward J. Lowell, "Marie Antoinette was not far from being its centre."[8]

Obsolete governmental structure. In addition to the incompetency of her kings, France was encumbered with an obsolete and inefficient government. Administration was unduly centralized in the hands of the king, a satisfactory plan when the ruler was intelligent and hard working. But when the king was incompetent, the whole system of government was deranged. In the classical land of royal absolutism little vestige of self-government remained in the local districts. As a result, a mass of petty and inconsequential requests and reports from local officials poured into Paris, cluttering up the central government.

In the process of building the French national state, the kings had added land bit by bit. But as these small territories were added to the realm, they had been allowed to retain their local customs and administrative machinery. In consequence, France was a hodge-podge of conflicting legal codes, tariff boundaries, and overlapping governmental agencies. Every locality had its own system of weights and measures, its code of laws, its special customs duties, and its own rate of taxation.

The Estates-General. In contrast with the constitutional situation in England, where Parliament had developed into an important agency for the expression of public opinion and was in fact more powerful than the monarchy in determining governmental policy, France had not established any comparable institution. To be sure, an assembly similar to the first English Parliament of 1295 had been called by the French king in 1302. This was known as the Estates-General.

The term *estate* has been used in history to refer to a political class, as the English Lords or Commons. In France the Estates-General consisted of three classes: the first estate, made up of the representatives of the clergy, the second, consisting of the nobility, and the third, recruited from the rest of the population. The Estates-General soon became impotent and was dominated by the powerful French kings. In 1614 it held its last meeting for a period of 175 years. The discontent of the people, denied any legitimate opportunity for venting its aspirations, was driven underground, where it gathered strength and waited for an opportunity to strike for freedom. At the meeting in 1614 one of the representatives of the third estate had declared, "The people are weary of being the anvil; let others have a care lest they become the hammer."[9]

The system of privilege. Thoughtful Frenchmen were irked at the confusion prevailing in government; they were enraged at the discriminations and injustices prevailing in the social structure. Under the old régime, birth, not intelligence or achievement, assured success and social position. Out of France's twenty-five million people only 200,000 belonged to the privileged classes. These were the clergy and nobility, comprising the first and second estates, who controlled nearly half the nation's land, monopolized the best positions in the Church, army, and government, and evaded much of the taxation.

Owning property valued at nearly a billion dollars, the clergy was exempt from taxation, although from time to time free gifts were made to the government. The highest ranks of the Church were often filled by nobles who had no interest in religious affairs. Enjoying huge incomes, these church dignitaries paid subordinates to perform their duties while they enjoyed a life of frivolity at the royal court. The second estate, numbering about 110,000 nobles, represented a privileged group similar to the clergy. Exempt from the *taille,* an especially heavy tax, yet recipients of the income from about one fifth of the land, the nobles failed to contribute their fair share toward the maintenance of the state. Many nobles were absentee landlords whose properties were managed by stewards, while their masters squandered their rents in ostentatious expenditure at Versailles.

Burdens of the peasants. More than ninety-five per cent of the people belonged to the third estate, or underprivileged class. This group comprised the peasants, the middle class, or bourgeoisie, made up of merchants, bankers, and professional men, and the city artisans. Eighty per cent of the population, the peasants, were saddled with intolerable burdens. The *taille,* a land tax, the tithe levied by the Church, the *gabelle,* a levy on salt, a poll and an income tax took away nearly fifty per cent of a peasant's income. Although serfdom had practically disappeared, the peasants yet suffered from many vestiges of their medieval subordination. Fishing, hunting, and the keeping of pigeons were exclusively reserved for the nobility. Game might destroy crops, but the peasants were forbidden to molest the deer and rabbits. Grainfields were often trampled underfoot by noble hunting parties, and swarms of pigeons from noble dovecotes gobbled up newly planted seed. The lords still collected feudal dues in money, and they also required onerous physical service from the peasants. The hearts of the peasantry were filled with rancor against selfish and rapacious lords.

A discontented bourgeoisie. Although belonging to the underprivileged class, the bourgeoisie were better off than the peasants. The middle class was prosperous and its wealth was rapidly increasing. Representing the first educated class in France, the bourgeoisie resented playing second fiddle to a parasitic nobility. Practical and businesslike in viewpoint, they were disgusted at the inefficiency of government. The middle class wanted a system in which people should hold office by reason of merit, not because of birth. The extravagance of the royal court, the unfair methods of tax collection, and the absence of a sound system of national bookkeeping especially called forth censure. The middle class sought economic freedom and above all a constitutional monarchy in which they would be the dominant force.

Culture lag and revolution. Conditions in France were not the worst in Europe. France had the most prosperous middle class outside of England, and her peasants were better off than in any other continental country. The revolution came to France because the common people in France were sufficiently alert to realize the evils of the old régime. France in 1789 exhibited all the characteristics of an advanced case of culture lag on a national scale. Economic, political, and social institutions no longer met the needs of the French people. A small clique who profited by the retention of outworn conditions tenaciously blocked any reform. If there is one thing that history teaches, it is the inevitability of change and the necessity of the continual adaptation of institutions to meet changing conditions. When those at the head of the state are wise enough to realize that institutional reforms must be made, tensions, unrest, and institutional incongruities are avoided, but if this is not done, the repressed urge for reform breaks out and revolution is the result. In France such statesmanship was absent, and force was introduced.

The financial crisis. The immediate cause of the French Revolution was the inability of the monarchy to avert the danger of national bankruptcy. Participation in the American Revolution on the side of the colonists had cost France almost four hundred million dollars. The credit of the government became so poor that it had to pay a rate of twenty per cent on its loans, whereas England paid only four per cent. By 1789 the government was faced with an annual deficit of twenty-seven million dollars, and interest payments on the national debt took half of the total national revenues.

Heedless though he usually was to problems of government, even Louis appreciated the danger of bankruptcy. In 1774 he appointed the capable scholar and statesman Turgot as his chief finance minister, a step which might have done much to rehabilitate the government's finances. But Turgot's financial reforms pinched too many noble toes, and the influence of the queen and her court forced the king to dismiss him in 1776. A succession of ministers was now called in to perform financial miracles, but the nobles would not contribute their fair share to the national treasury and little was done to check extravagance at the court of Versailles.

In 1787 Louis in desperation convened the Assembly of Notables, composed of representatives of the two privileged classes. This body, however, could propose no solution. Only one course, therefore, was left open to the king, the calling of a body which would represent the whole nation. Such an institution lay at hand in the Estates-General. The king and the nobles decided to convene the body. The sole purpose of such action was to get additional revenue. But the middle class had been impatiently awaiting an opportunity to make its voice heard. The king did not realize it, but his decision to call this body initiated the French Revolution.

The National Assembly. The calling of the Estates-General in 1789 precipitated a demand for reform all over France. For the guidance of the delegates to the body, *cahiers*, or notebooks, of grievances were prepared by the people. In tone these were moderate; there was no disloyalty expressed against the monarchy. The *cahiers*, however, did demand personal liberty, a national legislature to make the laws, a jury system, freedom of the press, and abolition of unfair taxation. On May 5, the Estates-General was formally convened with 308 clergy, 285 nobles, and 621 of the third estate in attendance. According to custom the three estates were expected to vote by orders. This would mean that any schemes of reform formulated by the third estate could always be defeated by a two to one vote at the hands of the clergy and nobility. After six weeks of wrangling on the question of whether voting should be by order or by head, the third estate, joined by many clerics and some noblemen, solemnly took the Tennis Court Oath, June 20, 1789. They declared that they would not disband until a constitution had been drawn up. Louis, in a blustering mood, then tried to coerce the members of the third estate, but the leader Mirabeau defiantly shouted to the king's minister, "Sir, go tell your master that nothing but bayonets will drive us out of here." Louis weakly acquiesced and the Estates-General now made itself into a National Constituent Assembly.

The collapse of absolutism. All over France millions of eyes were watching the events at Versailles. Peasants and city workers grew bold at the capitulation of the king, and disorders and riots broke out throughout the country in July 1789. Houses of nobles were sacked in the cities, peasants demolished the castles of their lords, and everywhere it was manifest that royal government was collapsing in France. Paris seethed with radical and revolutionary opinion. Pamphlets exhorted the people to revolt, and radical political organizations, such as the Jacobin and Cordelier clubs, fanned the flame of discontent. Following a rumor that the king was concentrating troops at Versailles as a means of browbeating the Assembly, a Parisian mob attacked the Bastille, hated symbol of the old régime. This grim fortress had been built to guard one of the gates of the city of Paris. As the city grew, the Bastille expanded far beyond the original walls and came to be used as a prison. Kings banished political enemies to its grimy dungeons. Late in the eighteenth century, apparently, the Bastille was no longer the horrible place it was supposed to be, for it contained in 1789 just seven prisoners: four counterfeiters, one habitual drunkard, and two lunatics.

The fortress was stormed and its defenders slain. On hearing this, King Louis is said to have remarked to the messenger, "This is a revolt." "No, Sire," was the reply, "it is a revolution." Again, in October, came another disquieting instance of mob violence. Suffering from lack of food and aroused at the news that the king was unwilling to cooperate with the reformers in the Assembly, a Parisian mob composed of women and a few men dressed as women marched on Versailles, where they encamped near the palace land. The mob was adamant that the royal family return to Paris, and after a night of terror, the king agreed. The next day a procession of more than thirty thousand people marched with the royal coach back to Paris yelling, "We have the baker and the baker's wife and the little cook-boy, now we shall have bread."

Reforms of the National Assembly. The National Constituent Assembly which accompanied the king to Paris was in session from June 1789, until October 1791. During this period the Assembly passed more than two thousand laws, effected a peaceful and permanent revolution, and modernized France. The Declaration of the Rights of Man was one of its most notable achievements. This document ranks with the Declaration of Independence of the United States and with the English *Magna Charta* in historical importance. In it are reflected the philosophy of Locke, Rousseau's concept of popular sovereignty, and

A cartoon depicts the emancipation of the French press during the Revolution. The rebels are displaying their own journals—"The Friend of Our Country," "The Mirror," "The Journal of Free Men."

ideas borrowed from American sources. Some of the most important provisions were: "Men are born and remain free and equal in rights. . . . Liberty consists in the power to do anything that does not injure others. . . . Society has the right to require of every public agent an account of his administration."

Among the most important achievements of the National Assembly were: (1) the abolition of absolutism and the establishment of a new constitution, (2) the ending of feudal dues, (3) the abolition of all social privileges, (4) the confiscation of church lands and the subordination of this institution to the state, (5) the creation of a uniform system of local administration, (6) the dissolution of the medieval guilds, and (7) the thorough reconstruction of the system of justice. Referring to the accomplishments of the National Assembly, C. J. H. Hayes declares, "No other body of legislators has ever demolished so much in the same time period."[10]

The Legislative Assembly. The new constitution established by the National Assembly provided for a Legislative Assembly, with the king in the role of a constitutional monarch. Despite the protestations of political equality in the Declaration of the Rights of Man, the new government denied the vote to the common people. The Legislative Assembly, elected under the new constitution, therefore, was dominated by the bourgeoisie who, having assumed the political power formerly wielded by the king and aristocracy, were anxious not to have the revolution go any further in the direction of radicalism. But this is just what happened. The limited monarchy represented by the Legislative Assembly lasted for scarcely one year, from 1791 to 1792. It was doomed to failure. The people, denied political rights, maintained that the middle class had cheated them. Reactionary nobles sought to discredit the Legislative Assembly and to reëstablish the system of privilege of the old régime. The rigorous and sometimes ill-advised measures taken by the new government to correct abuses in the Church also earned the enmity of the Catholic clergy. Another group composed of radical intellectuals asserted that the revolution had not gone far enough. It was their resolve to overthrow the monarchy and establish a republic in its place. Most prominent in this clique were Marat, Danton, and Robespierre. Much might have been done by the king. Apparently Louis did not understand that if the Legislative Assembly failed, representing as it did a moderate solution of France's problems, the revolution would take a radical turn and the monarchy be swept away. Instead of rallying to the support of the new government, the king had tried to flee the country. Many people also suspected that the king was in league with the enemies of France.

The outbreak of war. Under such circumstances the limited monarchy had little chance of success, but it was the shock of foreign war that precipitated its downfall. All over Europe absolute monarchs were watching with alarm the course of events in France. The brother of Marie Antoinette, Leopold of Austria, was especially concerned over the safety of his sister. In August 1791, the sovereigns of Austria and Prussia had issued a declaration stating that the restoration of order in France was of "common interest to all sovereigns of Europe." Such a pronouncement implied the intervention of foreign arms to restore the old régime in France. Undaunted by the prospect, the radicals in the Legislative Assembly succeeded in influencing this body to declare war upon Austria in April, 1792. The radicals believed that war would discredit the monarchy, bring out the treachery of the aristocrats, and result in a republic.

In the face of foreign invasion a wave of nationalistic fervor spread through France. Bands of patriots marched through France singing a stirring new song, the *Marseillaise*. But enthusiasm soon turned to dismay when the unprepared armies of France fled in complete rout before the allied forces of Austria and Prussia.

The end of the monarchy. On July 25 the allied commander issued a manifesto demanding that no harm come to the king, that the allies treat French soldiers as traitors to their king, and that royal authority be reëstablished. This convinced the French people that the monarchy and the menace of foreign invasion were one and the same threat. During the ninth and tenth of August, therefore, the radicals in Paris, supported by the common people, seized control of the government. The royal palace of the Tuileries was stormed, the Swiss guards of the king were massacred, and the royal family was turned over to the Commune of Paris, which imprisoned them in the tower of the palace of the Templars. Having formally suspended the king, the Legislative Assembly called a National Convention to create a new constitution.

During the interim between the deposition of the king and the convening of the National Convention in September, a provisional government under Danton ruled France. Under his leadership the country prepared to meet the foes of the revolution, both at home and at the front. New drafts of volunteers rushed to the battle front and stemmed the tide of foreign invasion. To crush opposition at home, Danton resorted to a policy of terrorism. During September, wholesale massacres of royalists were carried out. Anyone suspected of royalist leanings was butchered—priest, woman, or child. The news of these indiscriminate executions spread over Europe, doing much to discredit the revolution. On September 21, the National Convention met. Two days later it declared a republic, and in January 1793, it condemned the king to death.

France against Europe. Upon the heels of the royalist massacres came word to the European governments of the determination of France to bring liberty and the blessings of revolution to the entire continent. The French revolutionists had now defied the old régime all over Europe. While impelled to a large extent by the new revolutionary ideals of liberty, equality, and fraternity, the French leaders did not hesitate to combine them with certain national interests. It soon became apparent that the French in bringing liberty to their suppressed neighbors were also thinking of extending their national boundaries. In the face of a growing French imperialism which threatened the balance of power and aimed at destroying monarchy all over Europe, a coalition composed of Great Britain, Austria, Spain, Holland, Prussia, and Sardinia was formed to wage war on the French republic.

Of all the allies arrayed against France, Great Britain was to be the most implacable foe. These powers were at war almost continuously from 1793 to 1815. In the first phase of the French Revolution, when the moderate reforms seemed a French version of the Glorious Revolution, many Englishmen welcomed the stirring events across the Channel. But the execution of Louis XVI and later the excesses of the Reign of Terror shocked conservative opinion in England. Then when French armies threatened the Low Countries, England prepared for war. It had long been a cardinal point of English foreign policy since the days of Louis XIV that no great power should control the Netherlands. Later, when French armies controlled most of Europe, England continued to fight because she believed that France as in the days of Louis XIV was determined to dominate the entire continent.

To meet the professional armies of her enemies, republican France forged a new weapon, the nation in arms. Compulsory military service was introduced. Military seniority was discarded and brilliant young generals were given the highest commands. Results were demanded from these officers. It was victory or the guillotine. During 1794-1795 the new French armies carried out a series of great campaigns. Belgium was annexed and Holland was forced into close alliance. The Rhine was now in French hands from the sea nearly to its source. In three years the republic had gained "natural frontiers" that had been the objective of French monarchs for hundreds of years. Treaties made in 1795 ended hostilities with half the members of the First Coalition. Only Great Britain, Austria, and Sardinia remained at war. (The map on this page shows the First Coalition against which France fought, and the territorial situation after the settlements of 1795.)

The Reign of Terror. Meanwhile in France, while victory was crowning the revolutionary armies, a despotism of liberty had been devised in order to destroy the despotism of kings. The attack of the First Coalition found

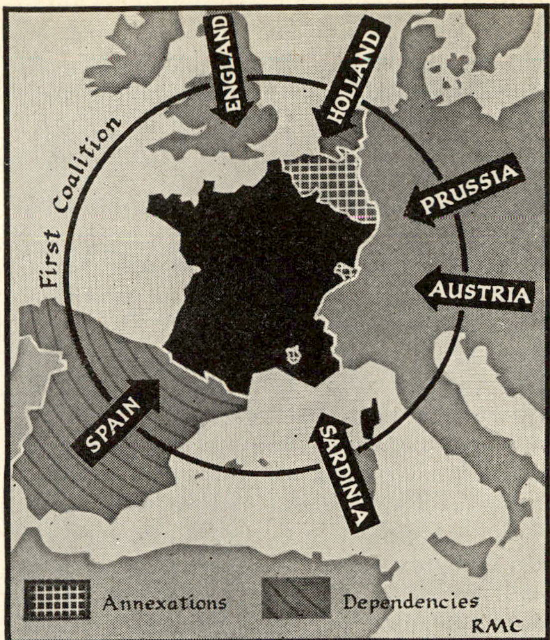

the French nation in serious straits. Food was not plentiful, the people were tired of political crises, and in many parts of France civil war had broken out. To meet this threat the National Convention entrusted its power to a small body called the Committee of Public Safety. It in turn relied upon the Committee of General Security to ferret out traitors, and upon the revolutionary tribunal to judge and execute them at the hands of "Madame Guillotine." During the Reign of Terror (1793-1794) more than 10,000 French people died thus.

Terrible as the Terror was, perhaps it was the only way of obtaining unanimity in France when the First Coalition threatened its very existence. But certain fanatics, especially Robespierre, continued the executions after the foreign foe had been defeated. Factionalism broke out among the French leaders. While a bewildered Paris looked on, Madame Roland, Camille Desmoulins, and Danton—all courageous leaders of the revolution—were executed. The disillusioned Danton just before his death declared, "I would rather be guillotined than guillotine others. . . . I am sick of the human race."[11] Robespierre was now dictator, and each citizen feared that he might be the next to be declared an enemy of the republic. Disgusted at the unnecessary bloodshed instigated by Robespierre, the members of the convention revolted from his leadership, arrested him, and sent him to the guillotine, where so many of his innocent victims had already met an unjust fate. With the death of Robespierre in 1794, Frenchmen now hoped that the long period of excesses was over, that the nation could bind up its wounds and settle down to a period of tranquillity and repose.

The Napoleonic Period

Reforms of the National Convention. The Convention had not spent all its energies hunting suspects during the Reign of Terror. It accomplished certain very important reforms. Most notable were the plan for a national system of education, the ending of Negro slavery in French colonies, the establishment of a metric system of weights and measures, and the abolition of primogeniture, the exclusive right of inheritance for first-born children. In addition to these reforms the National Convention drafted a new system of government composed of two legislative chambers and an executive body of five members, called directors.

The Directory and Napoleon. Assuming power in 1795, the Directory soon proved to be an incompetent and even venal government. The directors were mediocre politicians who engaged in an orgy of graft. While the middle class profited under this bourgeois government, the poor lacked employment and the necessities of life. Determined to smash the remnants of the First Coalition, the Directory commissioned three armies to invade Austrian territory. Two of these forces failed, but the one led by an obscure young general, Napoleon Bonaparte, crossed the Alps in 1796 and crushed the Sardinians and the Austrians. With a French army at the gates of Vienna, the Austrians were forced to accept the Treaty of Campo Formio (1797). Only Great Britain, protected by its fleet, remained at war with France. Following his triumph over Austria, Napoleon obtained consent of the Directory to invade Egypt, his purpose being to menace England's great colony in the Far East, India. Evading the English fleet, Napoleon and his

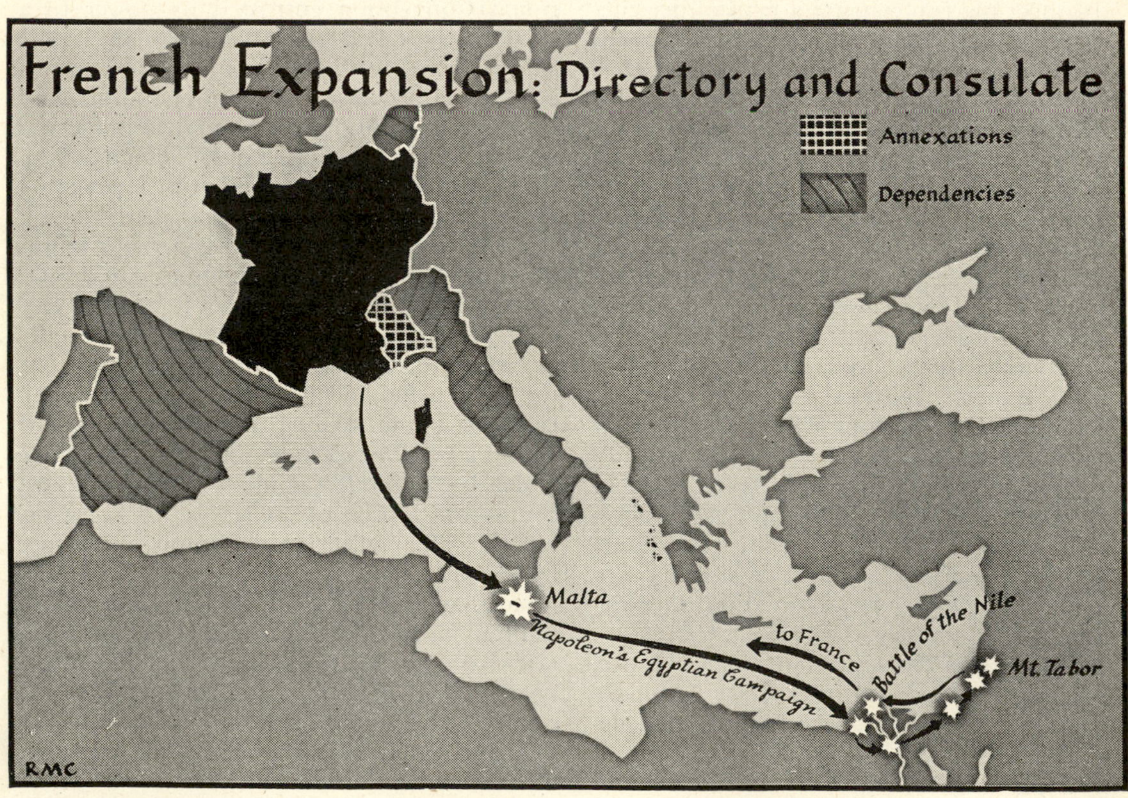

army landed in Egypt and won some initial battles. Efforts to crush Turkish forces, however, were not successful and, in the meantime, the English Admiral Nelson had destroyed Napoleon's Mediterranean fleet in the Battle of the Nile in 1798. (See map opposite.)

Napoleon's coup d'état. Hearing that the Directory was becoming more and more incapable of coping with France's problems, Napoleon deserted his army and managed to get to France. Avoiding all reference to his defeats, the popular young general thrilled the French people with the glories of his Egyptian campaign. The country in 1799 was in a bad way. A Second Coalition had been formed against France, and invasion seemed imminent. Financial bankruptcy had precipitated revolution in 1789 and even yet the finances of the country had not been put on a firm basis. Faced with ruin and invasion, the French turned to the one man they thought might save the day, Napoleon. "What France now needed was not so much popular sovereignty, not democracy, not liberty," comments Albert Hyma, "but order, efficiency, and victories."[12] Hence in the year 1799 the French acclaimed as their political savior the man who called himself Napoleon Bonaparte, the "man of destiny." Sensing the mood of France, he swept the effete Directory from power and created a new government called the Consulate. Ostensibly a republic, nearly all power was centralized in the first consul, Napoleon.

What manner of man was this "Savior" of France? Born in Corsica in 1769, the young "Napoleone" was the son of a family belonging to the Corsican lower nobility, of Italian origin. At the age of nine Napoleon received a scholarship in a French military school. Apparently a boy of unusual personality, the young Corsican was described by one of his teachers as "taciturn, preferring solitude, capricious, haughty, and inordinately self-centered," and with ambitions "that stop at nothing."[13] After graduation, Napoleon made several attempts to free Corsica from French rule but was unsuccessful. When the revolution broke out in France, he joined the revolutionary French army determined to make a name for himself. In a short time he became recognized as a young officer of unusual brilliance. His marriage to the widow Josephine de Beauharnais, who had much influence with the directors, gained him his first big chance, command of the army of Italy. His spectacular career was now under way. Napoleon was supremely certain of his destiny. He was sure that he had been called to play a great part in Europe's affairs. In character he was unscrupulous and calculating. He once remarked, "I am no ordinary man, and the laws of propriety and morals are not applicable to me." Physically and mentally, too, he was well adapted to play a dominating role. Napoleon had a tremendous reservoir of energy which enabled him to be in the saddle all day and over his maps most of the night.

After his seizure of power as first consul, Napoleon soon scattered the forces of the Second Coalition. Austrian forces were defeated and the Austrian government was compelled to sign the Treaty of Lunéville (1801). Great Britain was a different matter, but in 1802 a temporary peace was patched up between France and England.

Napoleon's domestic reforms. The first consul now turned his attention to domestic reforms, and here he made his most enduring contributions. In the field of local government, the system was reorganized to provide for a completely centralized structure. Prefects appointed by the central government had almost complete charge of local affairs. This made for efficiency at the expense of liberty. Next, Napoleon grappled with the financial problem. Graft and inequality in tax collection were ended, economies in public expenditures were effected, and, most important, the Bank of France was established.

In matters of religion the French revolutionaries had made some serious mistakes. In their enthusiasm to abolish the evils practiced by the clergy they were not content to reform the Church but became so anti-religious that they threatened the very existence of Christianity in France. Napoleon, while quite irreligious himself, as a wise statesman realized that the people demanded the reëstablishment of the Church. This was accomplished in the Concordat (1801), an agreement with the Pope in which Napoleon stated that the republic would pay the salaries of the clergy. The Catholic Church was now restored in France, but without much of its former power.

Before 1800 scarcely 25,000 children in France were attending elementary school. To remedy this situation Napoleon created a system of public education, providing for an edu-

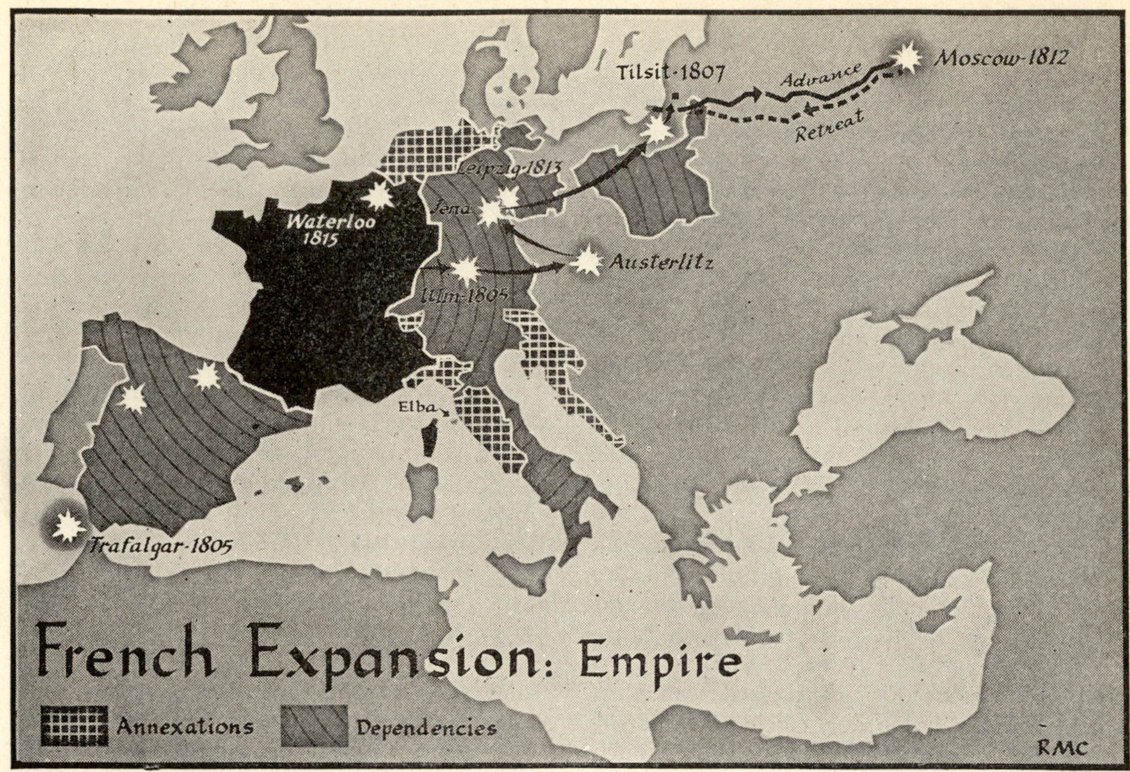

cational pyramid beginning with public elementary schools, secondary institutions, *lycées,* special schools for technical training, and the University of France.

Most famous of Napoleon's accomplishments was his codification of the French law, which brought order out of legal chaos. The great Civil Code was finished in 1804. Written with precision and clarity, it guaranteed many of the achievements of the French Revolution, such as religious toleration, equality of inheritance, and the abolition of serfdom. A code of civil procedure and one relating to criminal cases were also made. These codes have exerted profound influence upon the codes of other countries. Napoleon could say at St. Helena, "My true glory is not that I have gained forty battles. Waterloo will efface those victories. But that which nothing can efface, which will live forever, is my Civil Code."[14] A grateful and contented people approved Napoleon's action declaring himself emperor, in 1804. The republic was now no more.

Napoleonic expansion. Just before Napoleon assumed the crown of emperor, war was renewed between Great Britain and France. Napoleon welcomed it. His meteoric rise from a nonentity to the first citizen of France had not satisfied his lust for glory. During 1803-1804, extensive preparations were made to invade England. The inability of Napoleon's naval forces to gain control of the approaches to England and the formation of the Third Coalition, composed of Great Britain, Russia, Austria, and Sweden, compelled Napoleon to forego his projected invasion of England. Instead, he suddenly marched eastward against his continental enemies, and, in victory after victory—at Ulm and Austerlitz—he effectively destroyed the armies of the Third Coalition. The following year he defeated Prussia decisively and reorganized territory taken by Prussia in the partitions to form a French dependency. (See map above.)

Napoleon now reached the height of his power. In 1807, at Tilsit the Russian emperor agreed to assist France in disposing of the French emperor's last and most stubborn antagonist—England. By 1808, Napoleon ruled over a France which extended from the North Sea to the Pyrenees and included much of Italy. Several of his relatives had been placed on the thrones of nearby countries. Prussia and Austria were impotent before French power, and Russia appeared to be only a Napoleonic satellite.

Napoleon on the defensive. Invincible as the Napoleonic empire appeared, from 1808 to 1814 it was increasingly forced upon the defensive. The following factors explain its decline. Napoleon's mental and physical powers seemed to deteriorate rapidly after his destruction of the Third and Fourth Coalitions. From then on he was a tired man, fast becoming corpulent and lethargic. And if the emperor was tired, the French people were also suffering from war weariness. Another factor was the effect of the French invasions throughout Europe. The armies of Napoleon which at the outset had been utilized to "liberate" subject peoples in Europe, had disseminated the French revolutionary ideals of liberty, equality, and fraternity. As Napoleon became more and more imperialistic, the people he had "emancipated" realized that they had merely exchanged one despotism for another. Napoleon in posing as the champion of the French Revolution had sown the seeds of nationalism and liberty which were to prove his undoing.

By 1808 it became apparent that the Napoleonic empire could not survive unless it defeated England. Lord Nelson's victory at Trafalgar (1805) had established Great Britain's supremacy on the seas. Safe behind warships, English factories turned out more and more manufactures. British commerce and wealth increased, while French trade declined. Napoleon sought to crush England's economy by prohibiting the entry of vessels into countries under his control. Great Britain imposed a counter-blockade. Fundamentally, the war was now a struggle between English sea power and industrial superiority and French military power on the continent.

Napoleon's decline. Napoleon's decline when once started was rapid. Unwise occupation of Spain and Portugal caused a national uprising in these countries. All over Germany

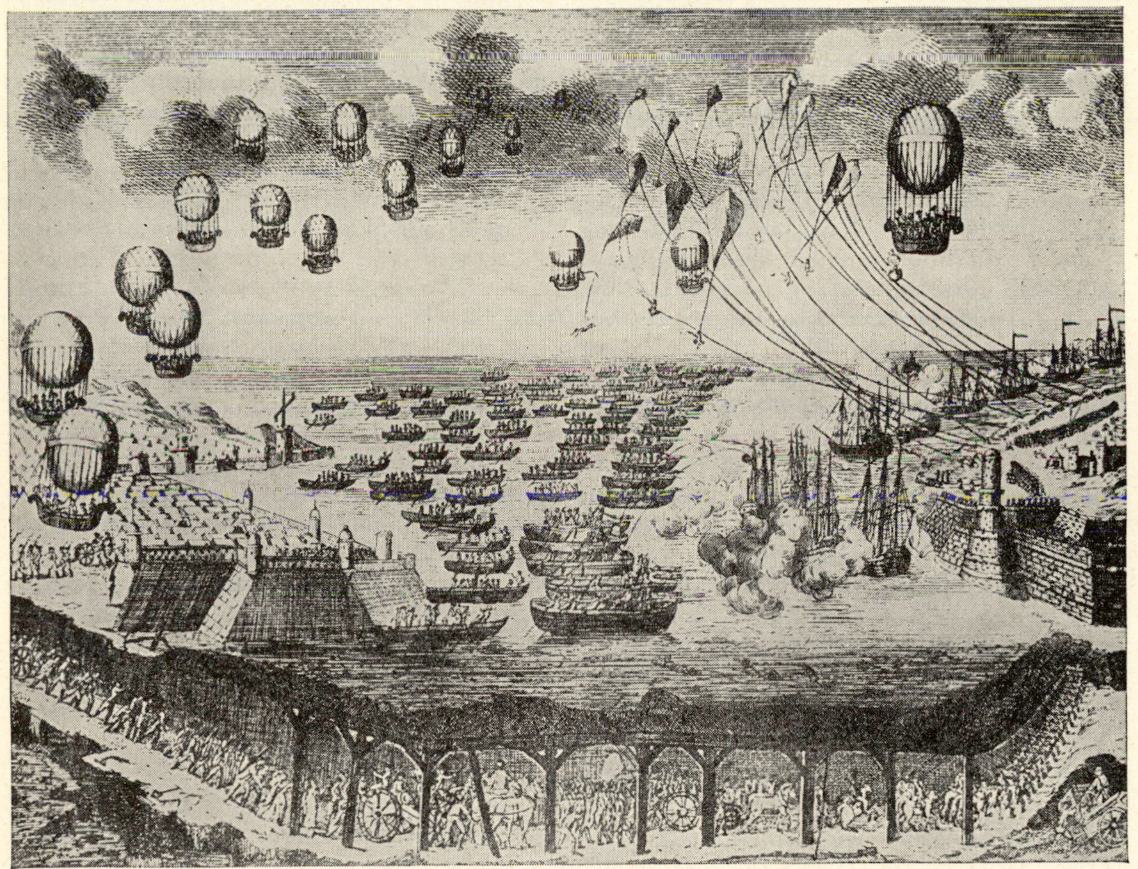

A contemporary artist drew this satire on Napoleon's dream of invading England in 1803. He pictures the army tunneling under the English Channel while a fleet of balloons fly over it.

a wave of nationalism stirred the people to prepare for a war of liberation. Napoleon's first major misstep was his quarrel with Alexander I of Russia and the consequent invasion of the czar's realm in 1812. The campaign was a catastrophe. Out of 600,000 men who managed to reach Moscow barely 100,000 were able to make their escape from Russia to Germany.

The nations of Europe now struck relentlessly at the tottering Napoleonic giant. English troops under Wellington cleared French armies out of Spain, and in 1813 the allies inflicted a disastrous defeat upon Napoleon's main army in the Battle of the Nations at Leipzig. The empire of Napoleon now "tumbled like a house of cards." In March 1814, allied forces entered Paris. Two weeks later the French emperor abdicated his throne, receiving in return sovereignty over the little island of Elba, where he was to end his days with a liberal annual pension. In February 1815, however, Napoleon eluded the British fleet and landed in France. After a tumultuous welcome, he entered Paris and raised another army.

An allied army was hastily mobilized under the leadership of Wellington and marched toward France. The issue was decided at Waterloo. Here, near this sleepy Belgian town, combined British and Prussian forces decisively defeated the French army. Following this reverse, Napoleon sought refuge on board a British warship. Taking no chances, the allies shipped the ex-emperor to the island of St. Helena, about 1200 miles off the west coast of Africa. Here he died in 1821.

Accomplishments of Napoleon. Napoleon's rise to power is one of the most remarkable stories in all history. He was an uncompromising militarist, with unbridled ambition. But it would be incorrect to dismiss Napoleon's historical significance with this negative verdict. It is true that his wars killed between three and six million people, but his interference throughout Europe spread French revolutionary ideals and kindled nationalism. In France, Napoleon expanded and safeguarded many of the social and economic gains of the Revolution, such as legal equality and the land settlement which had benefited the peasants. Outside of France his rule swept away many of the obsolete institutions of the old régime. Because of Napoleon the first step toward the national unification of Germany was achieved. The multiplicity of German states had been a barrier to national unity throughout the middle ages. To create a defensive barrier on France's eastern frontier, Napoleon wiped out more than one hundred petty German states and merged them with large states. Another important obstacle to unification was removed in 1806 when Napoleon did away with the Holy Roman Empire. He is important chiefly because he preserved and disseminated many aims of the French Revolution. His boast that he was "The Son of the Revolution" is in part justified. Perhaps no better evaluation of Napoleon has ever been given than de Tocqueville's: "He was as great as a man can be without virtue."[15]

Causes of Napoleon's collapse. More specifically, the downfall of Napoleon was due partly to the fact that his immense empire was the creation of one man's military and administrative genius. When the physical vigor and the mental brilliance of the creator began to flag as a result of the ravages of disease (Napoleon died of cancer six years after Waterloo), the empire began to fall apart. In addition, the resurgence of nationalism in Europe was bound to destroy any dictator who first stimulated it by prating about liberty, equality, and fraternity, and then ended by putting the people he liberated in chains. Students of warfare can point out that the defeat of Napoleon is mainly explained by the relative importance, in that day, of seapower on the one hand and landpower on the other. British command of the sea, these strategists aver, finally led to the Napoleonic collapse. Finally, there are those who see the Little Corporal's greatest blunder in his Russian alliance, which boomeranged and ended with the retreat from Moscow.

Summary

In this chapter we have observed now a new political system, the national state, shattered the medieval ideal of religious and political unity. The national states prided themselves on their sovereignty—the right of any state to act as it pleased, unhindered by any superior authority. Naturally this led to conflict. In vain, thinkers like Hugo Grotius pleaded for honesty and justice in international affairs. Machiavelli was more popular. Some rulers, however, realized that constant warfare would destroy European civilization. There developed, consequently, a code of suggested behavior called international law and a system of negotiation between nations known as diplomacy.

Absolute monarchy, partner of the national state, was best exemplified in the person of Louis XIV of France, known throughout Europe as the Grand Monarch. Louis, though not unintelligent, had an insatiable desire for power and fame. As a result he embarked upon a series of wars so disastrous that absolutism was seriously discredited. In the eighteenth century it suffered a staggering blow in the French Revolution; in the nineteenth it was to topple before the advance of democracy.

From the attempts of various alliances of nations to prevent Louis XIV from dominating Europe the principle of the "balance of power" in diplomacy crystallized. Checkmating Louis, however, did not end conflict in Europe. In 1740, callously disregarding the Pragmatic Sanction, Frederick the Great of Prussia attacked and secured Silesia, a rich province belonging to the territories of Maria Theresa, the Hapsburg empress. This aggression, bad as it was, was outdone by the partition of Poland. With no excuse save national self-interest, Prussia, Austria, and Russia appropriated large slices of Poland in 1772 and 1793. The third partition, in 1795, obliterated Poland as an independent state.

The question of who should control the colonies and commerce of the New World engaged England and France in a gigantic duel. France, to her detriment, tried to engage in both the European and the colonial struggles. Great Britain wisely concentrated upon the colonial issue and contented herself with subsidizing her allies on the European continent. As a result France lost most of her colonial possessions in the Peace of Paris, 1763, and England became the foremost power in the world.

As early as the seventeenth century, the middle class in several countries of Europe began to feel that absolutism was a menace to its interests. From this time on, therefore, the bourgeoisie engaged in a determined struggle for political supremacy. In some nations success was not achieved, as we shall see, until the nineteenth century, but in France, England, and the American colonies, revolutions were successfully undertaken. The Glorious Revolution was the starting point for the middle-class drive for political power, its roots being in the Puritan Revolt and the English Civil War (1642-1649), which gave England a premature republic. Following the restoration of the Stuart kings in 1660 the constitutional struggle broke out again. The final outcome was the deposition of King James II in 1688 and the assumption by Parliament of a dominant position in political affairs. In the eighteenth century upper- and middle-class control of the English government was made more effective by the establishment of the cabinet. Henceforth the supremacy of Parliament, now controlled by the landed and propertied, was unquestioned.

The philosophy which Englishmen utilized in 1688 as justification for their revolution found ready acceptance among the individualistic and liberty-loving colonists in

British America. It was only a question of time until certain factors, such as the vexatious interference of the mother country with American economic activity, should cause the colonists to embark on a revolution of their own. The conflict broke out in 1775, and eight years later a new nation—the United States of America—came into being. Meanwhile, on the European continent, liberals and their bourgeois supporters were becoming more and more restive under absolute government. This was especially true in France. Here the monarchy and the ruling class seemed most inept, and the government hovered on the brink of bankruptcy. Here also criticism against the old régime, directed by such men as Montesquieu and Rousseau, was the most caustic.

The calling of the Estates-General in 1789 gave the French bourgeoisie their long-awaited opportunity. Transformed into the National Constituent Assembly, this body between 1789 and 1791 effected a comprehensive and reasonable revolution. The attempt to establish a constitutional monarchy proved a failure. Moderate solution was doomed by the treachery of the royal family, the perfidy of nobles, and the demand of the radicals for a republic. As a result, from 1792 to 1794 France was convulsed with bloody purges, bizarre social experiments, and a desperate struggle with foreign foes. As an attempt to return to normalcy, a weak and corrupt republican form of government, called the Directory, was set up in 1795. From now on, the fate of the republic was largely in the hands of an inordinately ambitious military genius, Napoleon Bonaparte.

Taking advantage of his tremendous popularity as a military hero, Napoleon became the real head of the state in 1799. In 1804 he became emperor. Although he introduced many noteworthy reforms in France, their good effects were more than overshadowed by the horrible wars which resulted from his ambition to dominate Europe. The misery caused by these wars was soon forgotten, and their by-product—the spread of the revolutionary gospel—was to kindle the fires of nationalistic revolt in such countries as Belgium, Poland, Greece, and Hungary.

Of the three revolutions discussed in this chapter the influence of the French, from 1789 to 1815, was most profound, although, paradoxically, certain basic ideals of the revolution, such as constitutional government, were not fully realized in France until later. The French, more than the English and the American revolutions, was social as well as political. Its ideology represented the most radical departure from that of the old régime. For the first time, the goal of universal manhood suffrage had been envisaged. The French Revolution also constituted the first great stimulus to dynamic nationalism in Europe. Intellectual and religious freedom was given strong emphasis. Finally, liberty was projected from the political to the economic realm. Henceforth under the doctrine of *laissez faire* men were to be free to conduct their business affairs as they wished.

Much of the history of the nineteenth century was to concern the realization and the amplification of these three basic principles: democracy, intellectual and religious freedom, and *laissez faire*.

PART TWO

The Optimistic Age

THE OPTIMISTIC AGE

THE PRECEDING CHAPTERS traced the beginnings of modern times, especially in Europe. They indicated the commercial quickening, the rise of modern capitalism, the surging to the fore of an aggressive middle class, and the sweeping social changes which accompanied these important economic developments. Likewise, in the seventeenth and eighteenth centuries, science advanced mightily in method and new discoveries. Innovations of a progressive nature were also brought about in philosophy and religion, in literature, art, and music, and in education and prison reform. Sweeping changes were also undertaken in politics, where entrenched royal absolutism fell before popular insistence in England, America, and France for greater political privileges.

The accompanying belief in progress, formulated in the eighteenth century, was taken up by the next century with great enthusiasm. As a result, the period we are about to discuss can be called the Optimistic Age. That much of this optimism was ill-founded and false will be readily seen from the perspective of a later, more critical century. But the fact remains that the nineteenth century regarded itself rather complacently as highly progressive and enlightened. It maintained an easy optimism and showered favors on those who proclaimed that theirs was the greatest of all ages.

The economic changes which took place from about 1500 to 1750 were largely of a commercial nature. In the latter part of the eighteenth century, however, an epoch-making revolution occurred through the application of steam-power to machines. As a result, a new and far-reaching industrial era was inaugurated. The urbanization of society, already under way in England and some other countries, was accelerated through the establishment of immense new factory towns. This movement engendered social problems—slums, the exploitation of women and children, long hours and starvation wages—which the nineteenth century did relatively little to solve. Meanwhile, a new economic philosophy, *laissez faire,* had arisen to justify the attitudes of middle-class capitalists who owned the new steam machines and controlled the national economy. In opposition to this philosophy arose the socialistic ideology of Marx, Engels, and others, who preached with varying degrees of intensity the doctrine of class struggle and encouraged the workers to unite and restrain their "exploiters." Dickens and other writers pointed out the evils of the existing economic order, but the widespread misery of so great a part of the population was largely forgotten by the comfortable element, who complacently pointed to the giant strides being made in industrial expansion.

GREAT POLITICAL REVOLUTIONS had lately been fought against absolutism in England, America, and France. The ideals of the French revolutionists—"liberty, equality, fraternity"—made an especially strong appeal to the nineteenth century. The dominant middle class in England fought relentlessly to gain and keep political emancipation for themselves, though before the end of the century the entire male population had the ballot. Other countries experienced similar trends. The unfolding of modern political democracy in the nineteenth century hinged upon a series of struggles, some peaceful, others violent, to obtain three fundamentals: first, a constitution, usually written, which outlined the structure of government and provided for the protection of individual liberties; second, representative government; third, universal manhood suffrage which, in theory at least, meant that the policies of the government represented the wishes of a majority of the people. Democratic evolution in the nineteenth century often entailed an accompanying drive for universal and free education and the elimination of the clergy's interference with the government.

Hand in hand with nineteenth-century democracy went nationalism, largely a product of the French Revolution, through which the people united to repel those who tried to nullify the gains of the Revolution. It is said that the French Revolution made important for the first time in the history of nations a national flag, a national anthem, and national holidays. Nationalism is not easily defined. It may be described as the mutual feelings of a group of people held together by common ties of language and history and cultural traditions. Each national group desires above all else to be independent, free to pursue its own destiny. Nationalism tends to nurture the belief that the nation to which one belongs is superior to other nations in its endowments and virtues. Nationalism also assumes loyalty on the part of its members and is frequently based on the notion that a nation can do no wrong and that self-interest is the only test for its behavior.

The intellectual and artistic achievements of the nineteenth century did much to justify its spirit of optimism and complacency. The age produced such great men as the scientists Darwin, Pasteur, and Koch; the writers Victor Hugo, Tennyson, and Dostoevski; the composers Beethoven, Brahms, Verdi, and Wagner, and the painters Manet, Turner, and Cézanne. The Age of Optimism was in fact an age of opulence in almost every way.

Beginning of Modern Industry

1764-1846 New textile machinery: spinning jenny (1764); water frame (1769); spinning mule (1779); cotton gin (1792); sewing machine (1846)

1765-1856 Power for new machinery: Watt's steam engine (1765); principle of dynamo (1831); first practical dynamo (1873); Diesel engine (1897); puddling process for wrought iron (1784); steam engine used in smelting (1788); Bessemer converter for steel (1856)

1807-1914 Transportation: Fulton's steamship (1807); Stephenson's railroad engine (1814); first English railroad (1825); Erie Canal (1825); steamships cross Atlantic (1838); Suez Canal (1869); German canals—Dortmund-Ems, Kiel (1870); improvements in ships open great North Atlantic service (1875); Panama Canal opened (1914)

1840-1896 Communication: penny post in England (1840); Universal Postal Union (1875); Western Union (1856); Bell invents telephone (1876); Marconi patents wireless (1896)

Industrialism Spreads

1774-1870 France: Turgot breaks guilds' power (1774-1776); all business on license basis (1791); guild regulations repealed (1815); industrial advance under Third Republic (1870)

1818-1900 Germany: Zollverein organized by Prussia (1818); improved methods in metallurgy (1850); unification brings industrialism (1870); acquisition of Alsace-Lorraine (1871); French war indemnity provides capital (1871); maker of four fifths of world's dyestuffs (1900)

1860-1905 Russia: emancipation of serfs increases labor supply (1860); Witte invites investment of foreign capital (1893); Trans-Siberian railway completed (1905)

Belgium: becomes heavily industrialized, produces coal, iron, laces, carpets, cotton

Sweden: uses hydroelectricity to make fine steel

1865-1914 America: rapid industrialization, railroads, business trusts

1870-1914 Japan: industrializes rapidly; low wages, large labor market; specializes in textiles

Consequences of Industrialism

1750-1914	Trend toward urbanization	Regional shifts in population
	Increased population in Europe	Malthus' theory of population
	Factory system and working conditions	Child labor, tenements, long hours
	Industrial capitalism	Banks, insurance, corporations
	Rise of big business, especially in United States	Pools, trusts, and cartels
	Laissez-faire economic theory	Adam Smith's *Wealth of Nations* (1776)
	Manchester school of economic liberalism	Bentham, James Mill, J. S. Mill
	Free trade in England	Repeal of Corn Laws (1846)

New Thought and Reform

1750-1850	Utopian socialism and Christian socialists	Saint-Simon, Fourier, Owen, Kingsley
1848	Scientific socialism—communist Manifesto	Marx's *Das Kapital*
1891	State socialism	Erfurt Program, Fabian Society
1833-1881	Reforms in England: Factory Act	Ten Hour Law, right to unionize
1883-1889	Social legislation in Germany	Sickness and old-age insurance
1909	Liberal party in England makes social reforms	Minimum wage, housing, unemployment insurance
1914	Workmen's compensation and child-labor laws in U. S.	

CHAPTER 4

Factories, Owners, and Workers

WHEN the explorer, the merchant, and the financier were coming into their own in Europe from 1500 to 1750, they were establishing themselves as the most potent economic elements of early modern times. Yet the basic social structure of the vast majority of Europe's population had not materially altered. The overwhelming mass of the people still lived in the parish where their ancestors had always lived, gaining livelihood from the same soil and in practically the same way. Even industrial workers carried on their new tasks under the putting-out system, working in their own cottages. Life was still as provincial and as easy-going as the carts which rumbled past the sleepy village inn and out into the pastures in the early morning hours. Europe was both rural and rustic.

But during the century and a half following the year 1750, the economic and social structure in many parts of the world was completely revolutionized. The rural and relatively static culture of the early eighteenth century gave way to a quickly changing industrial and urban economy. Sleepy villages, the stage coach, the sailing vessel, the town crier, and the hand loom were to be gradually superseded by huge industrial cities, transcontinental railroads, steamships, newspapers, and large factories. These important industrial changes occurred first in England, then spread throughout the western world. They are even now transforming the orient. By the very nature of events, therefore, much of this chapter will be concerned with the history of industrial growth in the British Isles.

Four factors brought about an extraordinary increase in the means by which man was able to control his environment. They were: new machinery by which man's productive capacity has been increased to an almost unlimited extent; new kinds of power to motivate the machinery; new methods of extracting and using metals, which industry now had need of in ever-increasing amounts, and the application of new discoveries in pure science to the technological needs of industry, thus bringing about greater production, new occupations, and new wares.

These factors have revolutionized our manufacturing, transportation, and communication systems, and with them our whole social structure. There is not a continent that has been left unaffected by them. And, because the changes thus brought about have been of such incalculable effect, the entire movement has been labeled the Industrial Revolution. The term Industrial Revolution was originally applied by its author, Arnold Toynbee, to cover the economic history of England between 1760 and 1830, but research has shown that the word "revolution" suggests a change far too drastic and sudden. For a long time prior to 1760 men were making use of machinery, and since 1830 there have been inventions and technological changes which have dwarfed those prior to that time. Taking the figure of speech which one authority uses, we can say that for two hundred years prior to 1750 economic change was in "low gear." Gradually there was sufficient "pick-up" to shift into "second," and this occurred during the period about which Toynbee is speaking, that is, from 1760 to 1830. Finally, the economic machine gathered enough speed to warrant changing into "high"—and we have been traveling in high ever since.

There is another reason why the term Industrial Revolution should be used sparingly. So far the figure of speech has applied only to the machine. But a great deal of this chapter will be devoted to the classes of society which have been affected by it. The middle class came to own the machine and has been able to keep the driver's seat. The common people have been employed as mechanics to keep the machine in running order yet have had to pay the driver for riding in it. And lastly, more than one mechanic has decided that he has the right also to occupy the driver's seat.

Technological Changes

Industrial expansion in England. The economic history of early modern times showed the eventual commercial supremacy of England. Now we are about to discover that we must again focus our main attention on England. Why is this so? The changes that occurred in the industrial era took place first in England for several reasons. England possessed a strongly centralized and stable government which catered to the interests of the commercial classes. The revolution of 1688 had put an end to royal interference and unjust taxation, and Parliament now guaranteed property rights. The foreign situation also favored England's economic evolution. The royal navy protected the country from invasion and, at the same time, kept open the trade routes and ensured the supremacy of England's mercantile fleet. The military situation on the continent from 1793 to 1815 stimulated English industry especially. The European nations involved in the Napoleonic wars were not able to devote time to expanding home industry but had to rely heavily on English goods. So effective was this industrial aid to Napoleon's enemies that James T. Shotwell could say "the wars against Napoleon were not won at Leipzig or Waterloo, but rather in the cotton factories of Manchester and iron mills of Birmingham."[1]

The commercial prosperity of England had created a large supply of surplus capital which could be invested in the new industrial enterprises. England also possessed an abundance of labor, particularly unskilled labor. The enclosure system in agriculture had thrown great numbers of peasants off their holdings, and they wandered to the cities to furnish cheap labor. The country was blessed with rich deposits of coal and iron, both vital to the new industrial order, while the quality of its wool was unsurpassed. England specialized particularly in staple goods, and these were readily adaptable to mass production in factories, whereas France manufactured luxury and high-quality goods which demanded individual technique. Finally, numerous scientific discoveries made in England during the eighteenth and nineteenth centuries were adapted to the needs of English manufacturing.

Inventions prior to 1700. The invention of machinery did not occur suddenly in the eighteenth century. It appears that as early as the fourteenth century machines driven by horse or by water power were in use in the silk industry in a number of Italian cities. The modern world has recently become conscious of ideas that sprang from the fertile mind of Leonardo da Vinci, such as roller bearings, universal joints, lathes, gears, flying machines, a needle-polishing machine, and turbines. While most of these ingenious plans remained imprisoned in da Vinci's notebooks, they stimulated scientific activity and certainly proved beyond all doubt that invention is not the monopoly of the past two hundred years. In the last years of the sixteenth century an Englishman invented a machine by which woolen stockings were knitted a hundred times as fast as by hand. A story written about 1600 describes a wool factory as follows, showing that such institutions existed much earlier than most people have thought:

Within one roome, being large and long,
There stood two hundred loomes full
  strong.
Two hundred men, the truth is so,
Wrought in these loomes all in a row.
By every one a prettie boy
Sat making quils with mickle joy;
And in another place hard by,
An hundred women merrily
Were carding hard with joyfull cheere,
Who singing sat with voyces cleere.[2]

Men were also developing new means of harnessing water, wind, and animal power and were experimenting with better pumping methods for mines.

Eighteenth-century machines. Prior to the eighteenth century, however, machines were but a relatively minor factor in industry. This was due to their crudity and imperfections, the lack of adequate power facilities, and the governmental restrictions placed everywhere on new mechanisms which might hurt some vested interest. But in the eighteenth century the mass of inventions accumulated, the restrictions by government weakened as manufacturers saw the possibility of mass production, and the concomitant advances made in technology, power, metals, and science all combined to make the machine the dominant factor in industry—which it has remained until the present day. In the eighteenth century, therefore, and especially after 1750, there was an avalanche of new ideas. Men took to the air with the first balloon in 1783; others talked about submarines and horseless carriages.

Textile industry. The textile industry was the first to be revolutionized by machines. This industry is one of the world's most important, because it caters to the basic need of man to clothe himself ". . . the preparation of clothing from the raw materials is a difficult process, requiring special implements and consuming a great amount of time if all the work is done in the household."[3] In 1738 the first important weaving innovation was accomplished. John Kay invented the flying shuttle. This device allowed one person to weave a wide cloth, whereas formerly two had been required. Prior to Kay's invention, the weaver required five or six spinners to provide his yarn. Now the weaver needed the yarn of eight to ten spinners. Something had to be done to increase the output of spinning.

New textile machinery. In 1764 a carpenter named James Hargreaves invented the spinning jenny. This machine, according to one story, was the outcome of an idea Hargreaves had when his wife's spinning wheel overturned and kept revolving on the floor with the spindle in a vertical position. At any rate the spinning jenny (so named in honor of Hargreaves' wife) was inexpensive and easy to operate and allowed one person to spin eight, then sixteen, and finally as many as eighty threads at once.

The spinning mule, most efficient of the early machines, was so arranged that a few men could keep a roomful of machinery in operation. But it spun thread faster than it could be woven.

Hargreaves' jenny had one defect, however. The yarn was coarse and loose, so that flax had to be mixed with the cotton. About 1769 a former hair dyer and wig maker named Sir Richard Arkwright appropriated the idea of using the principle of rollers, which other inventors had developed, and patented his "water frame." The yarn was stronger and finer, and now, for the first time, a pure cotton yarn could be used, thus replacing the old half-linen yarn. The climax came in 1779 when a spinner named Samuel Crompton combined the spinning jenny and water frame into the famous spinning "mule"—so called because of its hybrid origin. This machine could be run by power like the water frame but was lighter and easier to operate, while the thread which it spun was so strong and fine that muslins, cambrics, and other sheer materials could now be woven. Arkwright amassed a huge fortune, but Crompton received as an original reward only three hundred dollars and died in poverty, while his invention enabled manufacturers to become wealthy.

Spinning had now outstripped weaving, and the hand loom could no longer weave cloth as fast as the machine could spin yarn for it. A power loom was needed. This machine was invented by Edmund Cartwright. The power loom definitely began to supplant hand weaving. While in 1813 there were only some 2300 power looms in operation, by 1833 this number had increased to over 100,000. Cartwright was one inventor who obtained recognition during his lifetime, the British government voting him a subsidy amounting to nearly fifty thousand dollars. With spinning and weaving on a mechanical basis, the growth of the textile industry was assured.

The growth of cotton manufacturing placed a heavy burden on the supplying of raw cotton. Although the spinning jenny could now produce many times its former capacity, the only method for separating cotton seed from its fiber was hand picking. The best hand-workers could prepare not more than five or six pounds a day. In 1792 a young Yale graduate named Eli Whitney invented a cotton gin which enabled a man to clean as much as 1000 pounds of cotton a day. "In 1793 the United States exported less than half a million pounds of raw cotton; in 1795 over 6,000,000 pounds; in 1801 over 20,000,000; in 1803 over 40,000,000; in 1810 over 90,000,000; and in 1820 over 120,000,000 pounds; in 1832 over 300,000,000."[4] This revolutionary invention persuaded the southern states to give greater attention to "King Cotton," and the resulting specialization of the South in cotton agriculture meant the extension of Negro slavery. It took a civil war to dethrone the "King" and to emancipate his slaves.

Other textile inventions were appearing all this time. In 1783 a Scotsman improved on the old method of printing calicoes. About 1820 a Frenchman invented a crude sort of sewing machine, but he was plagued by Parisian seamstresses, and his invention was not readily adopted. In 1846 an American perfected a workable sewing machine. Later in the century a stronger type of sewing machine was used for the making of boots and shoes.

Steam power to run machines. Improvements in machinery would have been useless without corresponding improvements in motive power, which had been supplied up to this time by oxen, horses, and water mills. "One little mill is said to have been operated by a Newfoundland dog."[5] Water power has always been one of the cheapest sources of energy. It was used, for example, to drive Arkwright's water frame. But water power is not always accessible to raw materials or ready markets, nor is it always available in sufficient strength to run all the machines in a given district.

The solution came in the harnessing of steam power. Steam power, however, was not an eighteenth-century discovery. "Hero of Alexandria had developed a device similar to the steam reaction turbine or the common lawn sprinkler of the present day. Society had no use for it except for such a trivial application as to turn the spit in the kitchen."[6] Thomas Newcomen about 1705-1706 devised an engine in which a piston was raised by injected steam, the steam was condensed, and the atmospheric pressure returned the piston. Newcomen's invention, used to pump water from mines, doubled the depth at which coal could be worked. "This invention marks the effective beginning of the utilization of the new sources of power with which scientists and inventors had been struggling actively for about a century. Although the active source of pressure was the atmosphere, the actual operation turned upon the production of steam and practically all the engines were coal burners."[7] But it consumed enormous quantities of coal, which the mines could supply cheaply but which factories could not. Another type of engine had to be invented.

Watt's steam engine. The transformation of the atmosphere engine into the true steam engine was the contribution of James Watt (1736-1819). This Scottish genius was employed at the University of Glasgow as its mathematical instrument-maker. One day he was asked to repair the University's Newcomen engine. Studying it, Watt was surprised to see how inefficient and cumbersome the machine was. Especially was he struck by the waste of steam that resulted from the

The calico printing machine, looking not unlike the printing press of a modern newspaper, had reached this stage of development in 1840. The design of the striped cloth is characteristic of the period.

alternate heating and chilling of the cylinder, and he set about to improve the engine. Watt found that at least four fifths of the steam used was lost in heating the cold cylinder, and only one fifth performed service by acting on the piston. He saw the possibility of employing steam to force the piston back and forth inside a closed cylinder instead of having to make use of the atmosphere through a continual cooling of the cylinder. With this novel idea of using steam power as the principal energy, Watt also devised a separate condenser to control and apply the steam. Watt's own words as to when he got the "flash" that introduced the age of steam are interesting:

"I had gone to take a walk on a fine Sabbath afternoon, early in 1765. I had entered the green by the gate at the foot of Charlotte Street (Glasgow), and had passed the old washing-house. I was thinking upon the engine at the time, and had gone as far as the herd's house, when the idea came into my mind that as steam was an elastic body it would rush into a vacuum, and if a communication were made between the cylinder and an exhausted vessel it would rush into it, and might be there condensed without cooling the cylinder. . . . I had not walked farther than the golfhouse when the whole thing was arranged in my mind."[8]

Watt made other improvements to his engine, including the automatic governor, by which the flow of steam into the cylinder is regulated to take care of the needs of the machine either when pulling a load or idling. Still another innovation was his crank and shaft arrangement. The first engines were used for pumping, but in 1785 they were introduced into a cotton mill and still later were adapted to the needs of the steam locomotive and the steamship. It was a Watt engine that drove the *Clermont* up the Hudson in 1807.

In the latter half of the nineteenth century a further development took place in steam with the invention of the steam turbine. This new device made use not of the piston but of a series of blades that revolved inside a closed cylinder. The turbine does not lose energy through the constant reversal of motion which takes place with the piston. "The development of the large turbines has thus resulted in fuel economies roughly proportionate to the economies realized by Watt's engines in comparison with the Newcomen engine."[9] The turbine has a smooth pull which makes it of particular value in propelling steamships.

Electricity for power. While the age which we are discussing made particular use of steam, two other modes of power which are especially popular today were being experimented with at that time. Many men, including Benjamin Franklin, had amused themselves with electricity. In 1831 Faraday came upon the principle of the dynamo and demonstrated how electricity could be obtained mechanically. Not until 1873, however, was a really practical dynamo available when "at the Vienna exhibition . . . it was accidentally discovered that (a certain) dynamo was, in fact, a reversible engine and could be used as a motor."[10] From this time on, electrical engineering made rapid progress. The steam turbine proved of great value in propelling dynamos, while France and Italy took advantage of the waterfalls in the Alps to harness their waterpower.

Gasoline for power. The development of the internal-combustion engine has also revolutionized modern life. The power in the gasoline engine is created through the explosion of vaporized gas by an electric spark within the cylinder. But because gasoline is expensive, Rudolf Diesel in 1897 invented a machine making use of a cheaper and heavier oil which is sprayed into the cylinders. "The efficiency of this engine excited the greatest interest. Three tons thirteen hundred weight of oil costing twelve dollars delivered more power through a Diesel engine than twelve tons fifteen hundred weight of coal costing fifty dollars burned under a steam boiler."[11] The Diesel engine has been extensively used in modern ocean liners and the new streamlined trains which make speeds in excess of a hundred miles an hour. Diesel engines are also taking their place in the automobile industry, being used increasingly in trucks because of the cheapness of their fuel.

England's iron and coal industries. Just as the invention of new textile machinery required the introduction of new power processes to drive them, so the machines needed an increased production of iron and coal. Therefore it was inevitable that the English iron and coal industries should witness radical changes. Fortunately for England, her northern and north-central portions have rich iron and coal deposits. Until the beginning of the eighteenth century, however, the utilization of these resources was meager because of the primitive methods employed in obtaining them. Heretofore vast quantities of timber were used to produce charcoal, the fuel used in smelting. This seriously menaced the forest resources of such countries as England and Sweden. In 1709, Abraham Darby made use of coke for smelting. In 1760 John Smeaton devised a cylinder-blowing machine to force air on the coke, and, after 1788, the steam engine was used to produce the blast.

The iron which was being manufactured up to 1784 was cast iron, which contained impurities, would break rather than bend, and was too brittle to withstand hard strains and blows. The new machinery needed wrought iron, devoid of impurities. Henry Cort came upon a method of making wrought or malleable iron. By it the impurities were burned out, and the iron left was clean and tough. Because the molten iron was stirred, or "puddled," with a long rod, the technique was called the puddling process. This process enabled Great Britain to produce by far the cheapest wrought iron. To show the rapid increase of the English iron industry, here are the figures for the output of pig iron in thousands of tons:

Year	Amount
1740	17
1788	68
1796	125
1806	258[12]

Steel production. Steel is an alloy of iron possessing less than one per cent of carbon and is both stronger and more elastic than other forms of iron. To obtain steel, a process had to be devised which could extract more carbon than the puddling process was able to extract. In 1856 in England, the son of a French refugee, Sir Henry Bessemer, hit upon a scheme. He poured molten iron into a large egg-shaped container (converter) in the bottom of which were numerous holes. Through these holes air was sent into the liquid iron; the oxygen combined with the carbon and silicon and the impurities were automatically burned out. To the pure iron was then added the right quantity of carbon and manganese needed to make steel. The Bessemer converter allowed steel to be manufactured quickly and cheaply; in fact, between 1856 and 1870 British steel fell to one half the price formerly charged for the best grades of iron, while production increased sixfold.[13]

Coal-mining improvements. Hand in hand with the advance of metals went the development of the coal-mining industry. But much as coal was needed, it could never have been mined unless certain problems had been solved. Death lurked constantly below the surface. Obviously something had to be done to curb the terrible percentage of fatalities among the miners. Again, devices had to be created to enable men to hew more coal per day and also to carry the hewn coal more quickly to the surface of the mine. The steam engine was able to pump out water and also to sink deeper shafts, but the deeper the shaft was sunk, the greater the danger from suffocation through chokedamp and explosion from coal dust. Ventilation was improved through the sinking of a second shaft containing a fire, which made an upward draft and drew fresh air down the first shaft. The use of large fans also facilitated matters. But explosions were the great danger, for miners needed illumination, and their lamps created explosions. In 1815 Sir Humphry Davy introduced his famous safety lamp, which materially lessened the danger of underground explosions.

To get more coal out of a seam, mine owners began to replace the pillars needed to support the roof (these pillars were formerly made of coal) with brick and wooden props. However, roofs often caved in, a danger which even today results in heavy loss of life. Mechanical picks were introduced to help miners hew more coal, but the use of machines spread slowly. In the early days in England, women and children were employed to carry the coal in baskets up long flights of stairs and ladders to the surface. This inhuman labor was replaced by the sliding of trucks along parallel boards of wood. Later, rails of metal replaced the wood.[14]

Transportation. Means of production were revolutionized, but this revolution would have been worthless unless the means of distribution had also undergone complete transformation. The English textile industry was now concentrated in northwest England, yet it would soon have perished without better means of transportation to facilitate the shipment of goods all over the world. We find transportation achievements taking place in four fields: (1) roads, (2) canals, (3) railroads, and (4) steamships.[15]

Roads. The highways of England in the seventeenth century were extremely bad. They were trails in whose ruts lumbering coaches were painfully hauled by straining horses, and which became bogs in wintertime, infested with highwaymen. Daniel Defoe could write of one highway that it "is not passable but just in the middle of summer, after the coal carriages have beaten the way; for the ground is a stiff clay, so after rain the water stands as in a dish, and the horses sink in it up to their bellies."[16] During the first half of the eighteenth century there was little improvement in the roads, despite the passage of turnpike acts, authorizing private individuals to build roads and charge tolls as compensation.

Scientific road building began with the elimination of steep grades and the building of good foundations for roads. But the problem of an adequate top surface remained to be solved. The solution came as a result of the researches of Telford and McAdam. Both Telford and McAdam employed the principle of correct drainage and proper materials, and their labors revolutionized road building. The stagecoach, which had once required fourteen days to lumber from Edinburgh to London, could now make the trip in forty-eight hours. Speeds had increased impressively, "but when the Liverpool-Manchester coach did one journey of about thirty miles at fourteen miles an hour there were loud calls for a judicial inquiry into this attempted manslaughter."[17]

Canals. Canal building played an important role in pre-railroad days not only in England but also on the continent and in America. Canals have always been important in world history: the Grand Canal in ancient China helped unite that vast country; the Egyptians constructed a canal to link the Red Sea with one of the mouths of the Nile delta. In recent times several exceedingly important ditches have been dug. The Suez Canal links the Mediterranean and Red seas and is part of the British empire's lifeline. The Panama Canal joins the Atlantic and Pacific oceans and constitutes America's lifeline. In recent years the Soviet Union has engaged in an extensive program of canal building, including the linking of the Volga and Don rivers and the Baltic and White seas, materially strengthening the country's waterways system. Canals provide inexpensive freight costs and safety and smoothness of travel. While the railroad with its greater speed has largely superseded the canal for purposes of modern business, we can readily understand the value of canals in the period immediately preceding the advent of the railroad.

Modern canal building in England began in 1759 with the authorization by Parliament of the construction of a canal from the third Duke of Bridgewater's colliery to Manchester, a distance of seven miles. As a result of this project the price of coal in Manchester was cut in two and all England became "canal conscious." Projects multiplied so that England by 1830 had nearly 4000 miles of improved rivers and canals.

During the nineteenth century great canal schemes were put into motion in other countries. In 1825 the Erie Canal, which linked the Hudson River and New York City with the Great Lakes, was finished, thus making New York the commercial capital of the United States. After 1870 canal building flourished in Germany. Among the most important projects completed have been the Dortmund-Ems Canal, which provides a German outlet through the Rhine to the sea, the Mittelland Canal, which allows vessels to steam from the Rhine to the Vistula, and the Kiel Canal, which connects the Baltic and North seas.

The steam locomotive. We have seen how iron rails came to be used in coal mines to facilitate the hauling of loads. Besides these private tramways used in mines, there were also public tramways built near such towns as London and Munich. Upon payment of a toll anyone could make use of these tramways, the carts and coaches being drawn by mules, horses, or oxen. Naturally it was not long before man devised an engine propelled by steam to travel on these iron rails. The man to whom honor must go for having first applied steam to the hauling of loads upon a railway is Richard Trevithick, an engineer. In 1808, Trevithick erected a steam railroad near London. Unfortunately his locomotive accidentally went off the track (after having worked successfully for several weeks), and the impoverished inventor found no more funds with which to repair the damage.

The man who has won chief fame as the inventor of the steam locomotive is George Stephenson. This son of a poor colliery fireman attended night school at eighteen in order to learn to read, but by 1814 he had constructed a "travelling engine" to haul coal at four miles an hour between a colliery and a shipping port nine miles away. In 1825 the first English railroad was opened, the famous Stockton and Darlington. The engine was driven by Stephenson himself at the dizzy speed of over four miles an hour. A signalman on horseback dashed in front to warn spectators of the approach of the iron monster, its chimney red-hot and belching forth clouds of smoke and sparks. But it was a real engine. Another line opened in 1830, this time from Liverpool to Manchester, and Stephenson's *Rocket* made what was then the terrifying speed of 29 miles an hour.

A contemporary account of the speed of the first trains strikes us as amusing: "It was anticipated that the speed at which the locomotive could run upon the line would be about nine or ten miles an hour; but the wisest of the lawyers and the most experienced engineers did not believe this to be practicable, and they laughed outright at the idea of an engine running twenty miles in an hour. But very soon after the railway was opened for traffic, passengers were regularly carried the entire thirty miles between Liverpool and Manchester in little more than an hour."[18] The future of the railroad was assured. Whereas in 1838 England had only 500 miles of track, in 1890 it possessed 20,000 miles, while other European countries had made similar strides forward. The effect of the railroad upon such vast territories as the United States, Canada, and Russia can hardly be exaggerated; the Union Pacific, the Canadian Pacific, and the Trans-Siberian railroads literally united these nations with bands of steel. Of tremendous economic and political significance during the twentieth century was the start of two other huge railroads—the Cape-to-Cairo railway, which was designed to span Africa from north to south and keep British dominion there supreme, and the equally famous Berlin-to-Bagdad railway, a prewar German enterprise by which that country hoped to win hegemony over the Balkans and the Near East.

Steamships. Ocean transportation was improved precisely as the railroads had been: through the use of iron in the construction of ships, and the use of steam in their propulsion. It was not until after 1840 that a skeptical world began to accept the idea that iron ships would float and that they were safer than ships of wood. Great Britain evolved the steel steamship at the same time that the United States was perfecting the wooden sailing ship—the famous clippers that brought back tea cargoes from the orient, whose beauty and speed have been so often praised. Despite the achievements of the splendid Yankee clippers, however, the age of wood and sail was replaced by the less romantic but more practical age of steel and steam.

An 1840 caricature suggests these safety clothes for railroad travel for man, woman, or beast. Railroads were for many years considered a devilish invention.

Various men have been involved in the creation of steamships, but the man who has reaped the lion's share of glory is Robert Fulton of the United States. Fulton bought a Watt engine and placed it in the *Clermont* which, in 1807, traveled 150 miles up the Hudson in thirty-two hours, to the consternation of some skeptics who then saw "the Devil on the way to Albany in a saw-mill."[19] Here are Fulton's own words (in a letter to a friend) commenting on the memorable journey:

"The power of propelling boats by steam is now fully proved. The morning I left New York there were not perhaps thirty persons in the city who believed that the boat would ever move one mile an hour, or be of the least utility; and while we were putting off from the wharf, which was crowded with spectators, I heard a number of sarcastic remarks. This is the way in which ignorant men compliment what they call philosophers and projectors."[20] In 1819 the *Savannah,* a sailing ship with an auxiliary engine, crossed the Atlantic in twenty-nine and one half days—but used steam for only eighty hours of that time. Not until 1838 did ships cross the Atlantic entirely by steam power.

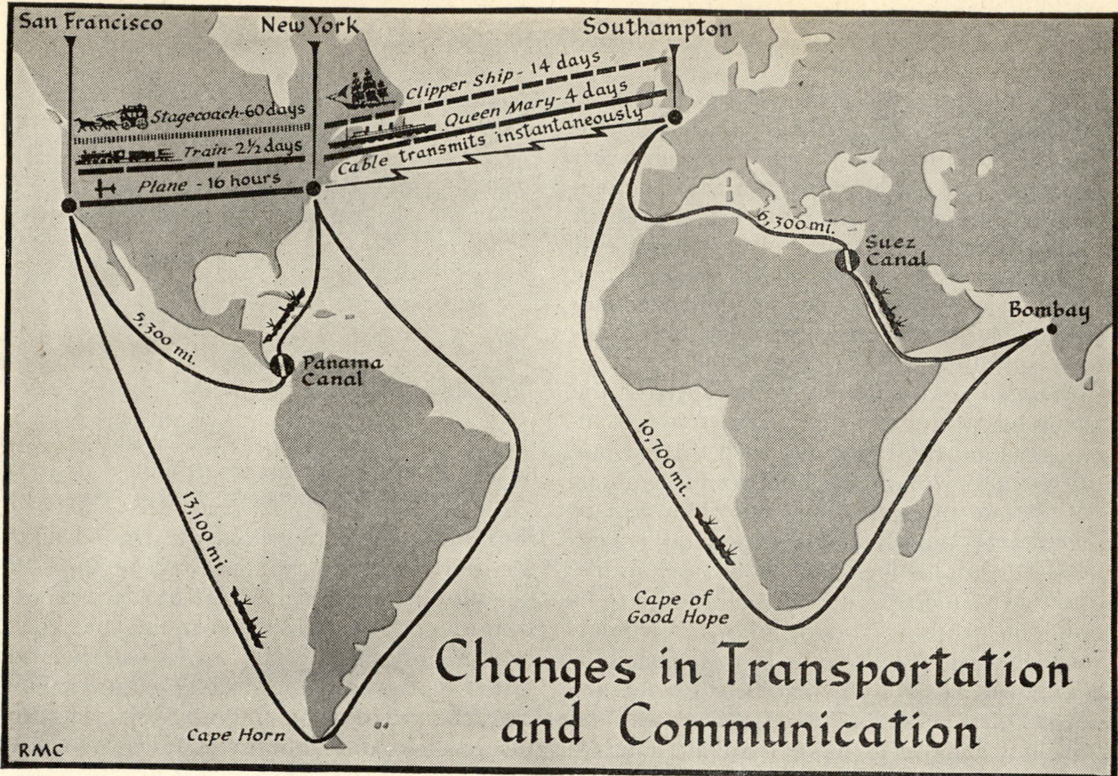

Changes in Transportation and Communication

The steamship was aided by various improvements: the use of steel hulls, the invention of the screw propeller which replaced the old side-wheel or stern-wheel paddles, and the innovation of compound engines, which proved more economical and efficient. These improvements in ships made possible the development of the great north Atlantic passenger service. By the last quarter of the nineteenth century large numbers of American tourists were being transported to Europe by a fine fleet of ships, and hundreds of thousands of European immigrants were being brought back to the New World. The advent of grain and refrigerator ships also played an important part in making food supplies easily available for the European countries.

Within the present century we have seen the growing use of Diesel engines and fuel oil, cleaner and cheaper than coal fuel. In the past hundred years we have also witnessed an increase in the size and speed of ocean-going ships. The *Great Western* was the marvel of its day, yet its tonnage was only 1340. The tonnage of the pre-war *Normandie* is 83,423, its length 981.3 feet. Whereas it took the *Great Western* some two weeks to cross the Atlantic in 1838, certain modern liners have spanned the distance in a fraction over four days. Shipping routes were shortened when the Suez Canal was opened in 1869 and the Panama Canal in 1914. The great improvement in steam navigation has resulted in a decrease of shipping rates by fifty per cent in the past fifty years. The romance of the gallant sailing vessel has been sacrificed for the utility of the steam vessel.

Communication revolutionized. Not only have the transportation facilities of modern life been revolutionized; there has been a corresponding revolution in communication facilities. The year 1840 saw the inauguration of the penny post in England, while in 1875 the Universal Postal Union was created to facilitate the passage of mail from one country to another. Meanwhile, certain men, including Samuel F. B. Morse, the American, had a share in perfecting the telegraph. The first British telegraph company was formed in 1846, and in 1856 the Western Union Company was organized. Within ten years, Cyrus W. Field had successfully laid a cable across the Atlantic Ocean. Today cables span every ocean, while telegraph wires cross every continent and country, thus making the news of one portion of the globe the instant knowledge of the rest. Modern communication likewise depends on the telephone, wireless, radio, and electrical transmission of pictures and soon will make wide use of television. While these marvels are more or less the products of the twentieth century, Alexander Graham Bell first transmitted his voice by telephone in 1876. Wireless telegraphy was the invention of Guglielmo Marconi, an Italian scientist, who obtained a British patent for his discovery in 1896. He succeeded in sending a wireless message from England to Newfoundland, and in 1909 Marconi's momentous achievement in the realm of communication earned for him the Nobel prize in physics.

Industrialism and world markets. The industrial era could not have advanced very far without the advances in transportation and communication just described. The nineteenth century saw industrialism primarily concentrated in western Europe and, in the last decades of the century, the United States and Japan (see map, page 135). This localization of industry meant that adequate transportation agencies were required to carry the manufactured articles from the centers of productivity to markets all over the world. Then again, Europe and Japan, and even the United States in some instances, did not have the raw materials out of which manufactured goods are produced. Vast quantities of cotton, rubber, jute, copper, lumber, oils, and tin—and many other materials—had to be imported. This would not have been possible without the existence of cheap and efficient transportation. Industrialism also brought about a growth of population. England and Japan in particular could not grow enough food to meet their needs. The new transportation enabled overcrowded centers of population to obtain adequate and cheap supplies of grain, fruit, beef, mutton, and other food products. The amazing advances in postal and telegraph facilities also made it possible for businessmen all over the world to keep in touch with each other when buying, selling, and paying accounts.

Industrialism Becomes World-Wide

Challenge to England. We saw earlier the reasons why industrialization came first to England. This process, which brought radical changes to that country in the years following 1750 and gave her economic supremacy for the next century and a half, inevitably spread to adjoining areas during succeeding decades. It was not to be expected that the continental countries should submit forever to England's control of the textile trade or that the United States should remain only an agricultural nation, when she had more natural resources for becoming a highly industrialized power than England herself. However, it was not until after 1870 that such leading nations as Germany, France, the United States, and Japan found themselves in a position to challenge England's industrial rule.

England enjoyed a virtual monopoly up to that time, not only by reason of her accumulation of machines, capital, and markets, but also because various political circumstances prevented rival nations from turning wholeheartedly to an industrialized economy. Germany was not united politically until 1870-1871, the United States underwent a civil war in the sixties, and Japan did not embark upon her era of westernization until the seventies. However, when industrial changes did occur in those nations, they took place in a fifteen- or twenty-year period, whereas a full century had been required for the transformation in England. Industrialism was transplanted almost *en bloc* from England, which served as a working model for all such innovations.

But the newer industrial nations have not been content merely to imitate England. They have profited by her mistakes, and, because they entered the field more recently, they have been in a position to adopt more modern techniques. For example, whereas England built up her industrial greatness on steam, nations like Germany and the United States have adapted their technology largely to electricity. Nations which entered the industrial world late had the advantage of being able to make use of the most modern techniques without having to scrap costly "dated" machinery and processes. This advantage in large measure compensated for their being late-comers in the race for world markets.

Slow tempo in France. At the opening of the nineteenth century France was overwhelmingly agricultural. Prior to the French Revo-

Highway travel in nineteenth-century France was hazardous, according to this artist, who puts all the reportorial vividness of a Paris journal into his racy painting of a mailcoach robbery.

lution there had been some improvement in farming techniques. Nevertheless, "the great prizes of the time were offered not to those who served society but to those who served a government which lived to exploit society. The government of the old régime drained from the country both the capital and the men needed for industrial progress."[21] The French Revolution and the Napoleonic era saw the abolition of feudal dues, the improvement of the rural population's social status, and the increase of small holdings through the sale of nobles' estates and church lands. Whereas in 1789 the yield of wheat was 93,000,000 bushels, by 1848 it had increased to 152,000,000, and the making of wine had jumped from 374,000,000 to 924,000,000 gallons. The peasants also improved their economic status by producing more corn, beets, potatoes, tobacco, and wool. A corresponding increase in the number of new bridges, roads, and canals also contributed to their well-being. However, the French peasant has always been noted for his conservatism. He likes his few acres of fertile soil, the nearby village where he goes to Mass on Sunday, and where he sips his wine and smokes his pipe with cronies when his labor permits him. He is a painstaking son of the soil, and his mixture of conservatism and provincialism has made him slow to adopt modern machinery even when he has been able to afford it.

French industry also showed a tardiness in adopting machines. Prior to the Revolution it was controlled by the guilds, despite the attempts of Turgot in 1774-1776 to break up the power of these associations by permitting every man to choose his own occupation. The guild system had broken down in some places before the onslaughts of the putting-out system, but restriction rather than freedom was the rule. In 1791 the National Assembly opened all fields of business to anyone securing a license. Napoleon restored some of the guilds, such as those of the bakers and butchers, to improve the quality of goods and regulate prices, but after 1815 the guild regulations were generally repealed, although one or two guilds lasted until 1870.

The overthrow of the guild system ushered in an era of free competition and machinery. While France was the first country on the continent to become industrialized, it lagged far behind Great Britain. A census taken in 1851 showed that some fifty-seven per cent of the people were following agriculture, only twenty-five per cent were engaged in manufacture, and of these, three fourths were engaged merely in local handicrafts.

Like many other nations, France made its greatest industrial advance during the decades following 1870-1871, when the Third Republic was created. This advance took place despite the loss of the rich industrial regions of Alsace-Lorraine to Germany, following a disastrous war. However, despite creditable gains, French industry lagged behind that of such rivals as Great Britain, Germany, and the United States.

Industrial restraints in Germany. The history of industry in Germany is more spectacular. In the eighteenth century this country was split up into a multitude of small, jealous states whose economy was little changed from that of the Middle Ages. Agriculture was all-important. The industries that did exist were checked by the persistence of the guild system (very much as in France during the same period). Not until the middle of the nineteenth century was the guild system permanently extinguished by the granting to workers of complete freedom of action and the allowing of competitive initiative to industry. Besides the fettering hold of the guild system, there were such other handicaps as political and territorial disunity, inadequate transportation facilities, lack of foreign markets or resources, absence of capital in sufficient amounts to create large industrial enterprises, and the general impoverishment of the region through the effects of the Napoleonic wars. In 1803 eighty per cent of the population lived as farmers, and not until 1820 had serfdom disappeared in most of the German states.

Advance of German industry. The basis of future industrial greatness was laid during the years between 1815 and 1871. One of the major forward steps was the economic unification of the German states. In 1800 Prussia alone had sixty-seven different tariffs. In 1818 that kingdom created one uniform tariff throughout its territory and asked other states to join in a tariff union, called the Zollverein. By 1834 seventeen states had entered the Zollverein (see map, page 175), and other states joined later. Any member of this union could send its goods to any other member without having to pay duties. The motto was "Freedom of trade through unity," and it acted as a great stimulus to commerce and industry. Another factor in Germany's increasing prosperity was a long period of peace. Machines began to be imported from England, and rapid strides were made, especially in the textile industry—woolen, linen, and silk manufacturing. Not until the century was half over did German iron production show signs of real advancement. After 1850 improved methods in metallurgy were introduced, and the output from German furnaces increased fourfold between 1850 and 1870. Likewise coal mining made striking advances. In 1846 about 3,000,000 metric tons were mined in Prussia, and in 1871 the total had jumped to 25,950,000 tons.

Important as these advances were in the years prior to 1871, they were dwarfed by Germany's attainments in the decades that followed. The final unification of the German empire (recounted in the next chapter) was one factor responsible for this industrialization. Other factors included the acquisition from France in 1871 of the extremely rich iron and manufacturing districts of Alsace and Lorraine, the payment by France of a war indemnity of 5,000,000,000 francs which gave Germany a great increase of capital for industrial purposes, the rapid growth of population (from forty-one million in 1871 to almost sixty-five million in 1910), and the entrance of Germany into the world race for foreign markets. The German government played a decisive role at home in this expansion of industry. Tariffs were designed to aid the new industries, educational facilities were provided for the training of youth along technical lines, and the psychology of salesmanship was carefully studied so as to cater most effectively to the needs of customers in other lands. In recent years we have learned of the painstaking methods which German salesmen have used to capture rich South American markets, principally at the expense of American and British interests.

Unlike the situation in certain other European countries, especially England, where agriculture had been neglected as a result of industrialization, in Germany farm production was expanded and made more efficient. By means of protective tariffs and application of scientific methods, Germany greatly increased its agricultural productivity in the latter part of the nineteenth century. Of course the most phenomenal economic advances made in Germany were in industry. In addition to advances in already established industries, the nation concentrated also on the development of such new industries as the dye, chemical, and electrical groups. Naturally, this industrial development brought with it the factory system, whereby large population shifts occurred from the country to the cities. This system will be discussed presently.

The manufacture of iron and steel has been the foundation of Germany's modern industrial greatness. The chief iron resources were found in Silesia, Lorraine, and regions along the Rhine, and the iron industry is still located in the rich Ruhr valley. German iron production was held back for decades because so much of the nation's ore contained phosphorus. However, the Thomas-Gilchrist process freed iron from phosphorus, and from 1868 onward Germany's iron production leaped forward, helped also by the growth in transportation facilities and the establishment of large capitalistic enterprises. Whereas Germany in 1872 was producing 1,927,000 tons of iron, in 1900 the figure had reached 8,469,000, and by 1914 only the United States surpassed Germany in the output of iron. The remarkable progress made by Germany in the coal and iron industries and its resulting threat to British supremacy are graphically shown in the accompanying tables (the figures represent round millions of tons):

	Germany	England	France
Coal			
1875	28	99	11
1913	273	287	40
Increase	x10	x3	x4
Pig Iron & Steel			
1875	2	6	1
1913	14	8	2
Increase	x7	x1	x2[22]

The textile industry also made extensive strides forward, although Germany still lagged far behind Great Britain in this respect. In 1911 Germany had 10,500,000 spindles, while Great Britain had 55,000,000. But in the chemical industry the Germans held undisputed first place, so that by 1900 four fifths of the world's dyestuffs were produced by them. In the electrical industry also Germany came to hold an enviable place, her skilled technicians working to produce intricate electrical equipment destined for all countries.

Backwardness of industry in Russia. It is scarcely to be wondered at that Russia should have lagged behind England, France, and Germany. It was overwhelmingly an agricultural country, rich in arable lands which the illiterate peasants tilled by primitive methods on the great estates of the nobles. The country is enormous, sprawling across Europe and Asia, from the Arctic Ocean to the borders of Persia, but its size proved a burden in the days when Russia's transportation system was almost nonexistent. The government was bureaucratic, inefficient, reactionary, and undemocratic. Not until the 1860's were the serfs emancipated.

Not until the nineties did the imperial government seriously undertake to build up the nation's industries. There were several reasons for this sudden interest in industrial progress at the close of the century. The emancipation of the serfs had increased the labor supply, and the growth of education made more people capable of fitting themselves into an industrial life. Another reason lay in the appointment by Nicholas II of Count Sergius Witte in 1893 to the ministry of finance and commerce. This energetic and progressive noble saw that agriculture alone could not make a nation strong and self-sufficient. He decided on the construction of railroads and factories and the development of Russia's vast natural resources. But the country had not the capital with which to embark upon such an ambitious program. Witte invited foreign capitalists to invest in Russian industries, and thus began that era of investment on a huge scale by French, Belgian, German, and other capitalists—an era cut short when Russia was transformed into the Union of Soviet Socialist Republics. Despite depressions, Russia advanced industrially in the years leading up to the First World War. Not only did factory production and numbers of workmen employed increase, but between 1885 and 1905 there was an increase in railway mileage from 16,155 to 40,500. Finally, in 1905, the famous Trans-Siberian Railway was completed, and Russia was linked by steel from St. Petersburg to the Pacific. But despite these changes Russia at the outbreak of war in 1914 was still preponderantly agricultural. Its real period of industrialization began when in 1928 the Soviet Union put into operation the first of its Five-Year plans.[23]

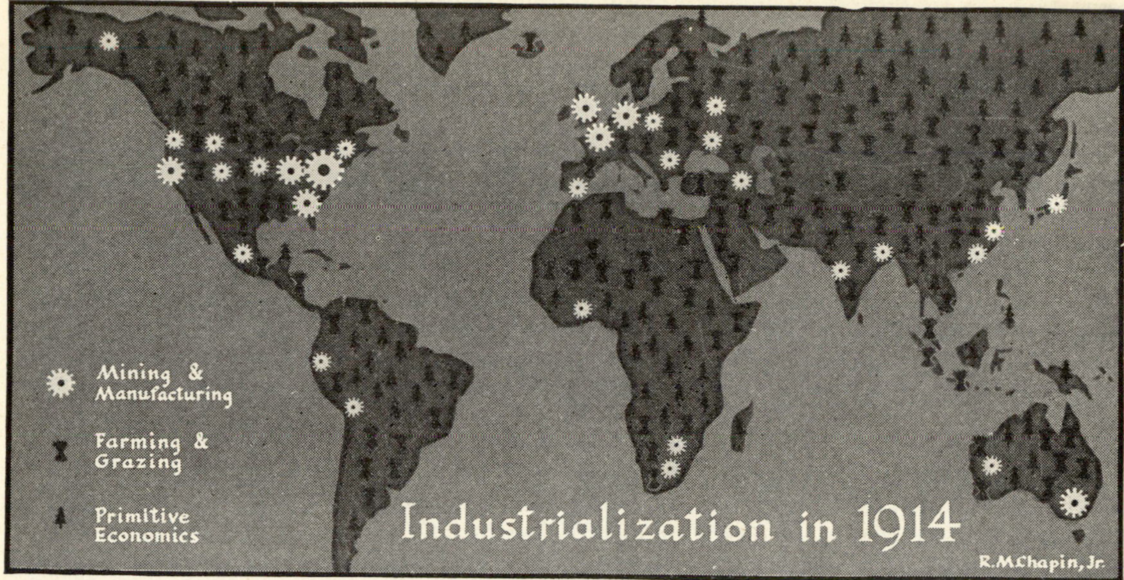

Industry in other European nations. Italy's industrial program was also thwarted until 1870 by her political disunity. The lack of sizable iron and coal deposits has been a serious hindrance to real industrial expansion, even though Italy has made splendid use of the hydroelectric resources which her mountains provide. The Italians built up a considerable textile industry, the manufacture of silk playing an important role in the national economy.

Switzerland is a small nation, but its water-power resources and specialization in such trades as the making of clocks and watches, electric locomotives, and dyes have brought comparative prosperity to this beautiful and proud mountain region.

After 1830 the Industrial Revolution began to make itself evident in Holland. Important advances were made in such manufacturing as shipbuilding, fine porcelain, cigar making, diamond cutting, and brewing. Holland's economic importance, however, was not in her industries but rather in her commerce. A tremendous amount of trade was handled in her harbors and transshipped to other European centers. In 1914 Holland's foreign trade was nearly equal to that of France.

Belgium's industrial growth is quite unique, in that this small nation as early as the first quarter of the nineteenth century was introducing machinery of the latest type for its textile industry. As early as 1830, also, Belgium was mining about 6,000,000 tons of coal a year, and this figure increased as time went on. Yet even this amount was not sufficient to sustain Belgium's other industries, and coal had to be imported after 1840 from England. A network of railroads was built, and canals also aided the process of industrialization. Belgium, despite her small size, was producing nearly as much coal and iron as France at the end of the nineteenth century, and her fine laces, carpets, cottons, and linens were produced in great quantities and sold throughout the world.

Of the three Scandinavian nations Sweden made the greatest industrial advances. Although it lacks sufficient quantities of coal, Sweden has cheap hydroelectric power which it has used for manufacturing fine steel products, such as hardware. This steel is made from iron ore found north of the Arctic Circle in Sweden. Of outstanding quality, this ore is one of the most important of Swedish products, and in 1907 Sweden produced 700,000 tons of iron. Sweden built its first railroad in 1856, and by 1914 over 8000 miles of track had been constructed through this mountainous and lake-filled land.

In 1870 Danish agriculture was in a poor state, but in the next three decades the farmers turned away from the traditional crops of wheat and rye and concentrated upon dairy and poultry products. Between 1881 and 1914 the butter exports increased six hundred per cent. Much of the success of Danish intensive farming was due to the organization of farmers' cooperatives, organizations which studied improved methods of farming and also provided efficient central-sales methods.

It was natural that the fiord-studded coast of Norway should have encouraged Norwegians to depend upon the sea for their livelihood. The Industrial Revolution with its demand for greater shipping facilities and more food for industrialized nations gave the Norwegians a profitable economic outlet. One hundred thousand fishermen sailed the seas, and a merchant marine of four million tons helped carry the commerce of the world.

Industry in the Far East. The economic transformation of the world spread presently to Asia, chiefly to Japan. Japan had to accustom herself to the conditions of the occident largely as a protection against the policy of ruthless exploitation which the west was beginning in the Far East. The changes in the social, political, and economic life of Japan which occurred after 1870 were many and radical. Here we will discuss industry only.

Japan made swift industrial progress for a number of reasons. The labor market was large, and workmen could always be found to work at a low wage, enabling the Japanese manufacturer to undersell his rivals in other nations. The government aided industrialization by subsidizing railroads and steamship lines. Large supplies of coal which the island empire possesses were a real advantage in the transformation of industry. Japan specialized in textiles. Where prior to 1880 there were no cotton mills, by 1897 over 750,000 spindles had been set up, and this figure had increased by 1914 to nearly 2,500,000. Such a successful advance created serious competition for the mills of Manchester, which began the modern machine age. Other important industries which Japan fostered have been paper, matches, toys, and, in recent times, rayon.

The rapid industrial progress of the Japanese during the last decades of the nineteenth century had immediate economic and political effects. It gave the country more wealth and power and prompted the government to look across at China with eager eyes, because of China's rich though undeveloped resources and its vast possibilities as a market for Japanese manufactures.

China itself did not westernize its economy during the nineteenth century and was unable to resist aggressive exploitation.

Industrial growth in the United States. The United States made even greater industrial strides in the nineteenth century than did Germany or Japan. Before the Revolutionary War, the American colonies had been primarily an economic accessory of England. The economy of the colonies had to serve that of the mother country. Following independence in 1783, the new nation boldly struck out to achieve a new economic destiny. The shutting off of imports from Europe during the Napoleonic wars aided the process. During the period from 1783 to 1860 the factory came to America, and the textile, iron, steel, and shoe industries were established. Tariffs were enacted to protect the infant industries. Machinery was brought from Europe, as well as a large supply of skilled labor. Industry was also aided by many American inventions.

After 1865 the industrialization of the United States proceeded at an even more rapid pace. "The production of pig iron first passed 1,000,000 long tons in 1870. By 1880 it was nearly 4,000,000, by 1890 over 9,000,000, and in 1900 almost 13,800,000. This growth continued, though not steadily, to a high point of over 42,600,000 tons in 1929."[24] Great business trusts were formed, transcontinental railroads were built, and huge industries were initiated. Rich mineral and forest resources poured out an increasing stream of materials for hungry factories and mills. In 1860 the total value of American manufactures was less than two billion dollars. By the end of the century the figure had jumped to nearly seven times this amount.

Consequences of Industrialism

Population trends. The effects of the new industrialism were deep and widespread not only in productive methods but also in the lives of the people. This is illustrated by the change in population trends. The general tendency was for people to leave the country and come to the city. Here the new machines demanded thousands of workers. Ever since the late Middle Ages the city had been slowly emerging as an important factor in civilization. Now the process was accelerated. The trend toward urbanization became more and more apparent. First in England, then in Belgium, France, and Germany, and later in other parts of the world, old cities outgrew their boundaries, and many new ones were founded. In general, we may say that, from 1750 down to the present, people have more and more tended to concentrate in cities, while population in the country has declined. In addition, there were often regional shifts in population. For example, in England there was a shift of population from the south to the north. Ever since the beginning of English history the bulk of the people had resided south of the river Thames. The industrial transformation changed this radically. Coal and iron were discovered in the north, and numerous industrial centers were founded in the vicinity of the basic raw materials. Cities like Birmingham and Manchester, became the great industrial centers, and both of these are north of London.

Population increases. In addition to the shift from country to city and from one region to another, the industrial era was accompanied by a substantial and continuous increase in population. It has been estimated that Europe in 1800 had about 175,000,000 people, whereas by 1900 it had 400,000,000, and this figure in turn had risen in 1930 to 505,000,000. Why? Up to early modern times, populations were checked by food scarcity—famines, crop failures, inability to transport food from distant places to the stricken areas—and by pestilence and high infant mortality. Now the growing economic productiveness of European countries, through greater industrial capacity, the draining of swamps, the introduction of intensive farming, and the techniques of scientific agriculture, enabled larger populations to be supported. Europe was also able now to import more foodstuffs from other continents, as a result of the increase in transportation facilities.

Another reason for the growth of population was the reduction of the death rate. Modern medicine and public hygiene slowly but surely conquered the dreaded plagues—such as cholera, typhus, and small-pox—and in our own century have assailed the scourge of tuberculosis. Medical progress and the combating of insanitary conditions have also reduced infant mortality. In the eighteenth century it was by no means uncommon for a mother to bear ten children and lose seven of them. The birth rate in recent times has fallen sharply, yet during these times the death rate has fallen even more sharply, so that there has been in general a continuous growth in population.

Need for world markets. Another important result of industrialism was the increase in the productivity of man's economic equipment. The new machines poured forth textiles, sheet iron and rails, pottery, cutlery, and a host of other commodities. Comparative statistics show that in certain industries productivity was increased a hundredfold and in others as much as a thousandfold. This amazing increase in the flow of manufactured commodities had an important effect upon the extent of the market. It soon became apparent that the home market could not absorb the goods produced, and it became necessary to search for trade outlets all over the world. This required a network of world transportation, a need which was satisfied by such inventions as the steamship and telegraph. The world was becoming an integrated economic unit connected by strands of international commerce.

Imperialism. Closely allied to this need for world markets was imperialism. Isolated and primitive natives were brought into touch with western culture by traders who desired to create markets. Often these backward natives in Africa and other tropical areas were conquered by aggressive western powers. Thus in the nineteenth century the great industrial nations carried out a program of imperialism, the creation of great colonial empires, which will be discussed at length in a later chapter. The search for colonies to serve as markets or as sources for essential raw materials had, as we shall see in our discussion of the First World War, important consequences in the field of international politics. The struggle for markets and for colonies frequently poisoned international relations and had much to do with the outbreak of war in 1914.

The factory triumphs. The most important agent or symbol of the new industrial order was the factory, for here was the site of the new machinery and power that made industrialism possible.

The factory system did not replace the domestic system overnight; the two existed side

A textile mill—without benefit of a labor relations board—is the subject of this English woodcut, dated 1853. A broken thread frequently meant a beating.

by side for decades, with the former waging a winning fight all the time. We can trace the victory of the factory system in the English textile industry. In former times the making of yarn and the weaving of cloth had been entrenched in the domestic system. However, once inventions had adapted the processes to factory production, the change came about. It might still be possible for a man to install a new machine in his own home, but when the transformation in power came about and machines capable of turning out huge quantities of goods were created, it was no longer possible for the ordinary worker to buy and maintain these machines. The hand worker now tried to compete with the expensive machine, but the machine could turn out goods in greater amounts and for a cheaper price. The result was inevitable; the hand worker was forced to go to those communities where the new factory was located.

Factory conditions. The first factories which were thrown up during the extraordinary rise of such industrial centers as Manchester and Birmingham were lacking in the most elementary principles of sanitation. The buildings were dingy, low-ceilinged, without proper ventilation or light. The new machines were not fenced off, with the result that the most horrible cases of mangling were a common occurrence among the factory hands. Any accident which the worker might suffer was considered a result of his own negligence, for which the employer could not be held responsible. There was no compensation or health insurance, and anyone so injured was liable to be thrown out in the street destitute, while his position was taken by another hand recruited from the thousands who had flocked to the new cities in search of employment.

Despite the innovation of "labor-saving" machinery, the worker was certainly not saved any labor. The factory bell summoned him to long hours of monotonous drudgery every day, and his work was disciplined by a long series of stringent regulations.

The mills employed some children four and five years of age, and in the coal mines children were employed to help carry baskets of coal up ladders. Employers sometimes contracted with public officials for the assignment of pauper children to the factories, where, working ostensibly as apprentices, they were treated as slaves. As a West Indian slavemaster summed up the matter: "I have always thought myself disgraced by being the owner of slaves, but we never in the West Indies thought it possible for any human being to be so cruel as to require a child of nine years old to work twelve and a half hours a day, and that, you acknowledge, is your regular practice."[25] The youngsters often worked in relays, so that the beds in which they slept never cooled, as one batch followed another in sharing the piles of vermin-ridden rags. Women would be forced by poverty to work to a day or two before delivery of their children and then to report back to work within another two or three days after the child was born. Lung trouble, asthma, rheumatism, and distortion of limbs were common ailments which beset the workers as a result of the unhealthful factory conditions and the monotonous hours of toil.

Contemporary accounts of the workers' quarters in the new industrial centers fill us with loathing and infinite pity. If we had visited a working-class district in Manchester early in the nineteenth century, we should see whole sections of "jerry-built" houses thrown up by speculators, built back to back so that the rear rooms had no windows, while the houses faced on narrow, unpaved alleys or courts in which garbage and sewage would be dumped. Proof of the awful conditions is to be found in one account which states: "A carpenter and builder unite to buy a series of building sites (i.e., they lease them for a number of years) and cover them with so-called houses. In one place we found a whole street following the course of a ditch, because in this way deeper cellars could be secured without the cost of digging—cellars not for storing wares or rubbish but for dwellings for human beings. *Not one house of this street escaped the cholera.*"[26]

Walking down the street we should have seen workers wretchedly fed and dressed. Men and women could not afford to buy anything but cheap cotton goods, which gave them scant protection against the damp climate, while their food was conducive not to nourishment and health but to malnutrition and disease. According to one contemporary authority, "The potatoes which the workers buy are usually poor, the vegetables wilted, the cheese old and of poor quality, the bacon rancid, the meat lean, tough, taken from old, often diseased cattle, or such as have died a natural death, and not even fresh then, often half decayed."[27] Naturally epidemics were frequent and their toll appalling. In the year 1843 in Glasgow 32,000 persons were seized with typhus, of whom thirty-two per cent perished.

Children employed in the mills received almost no education, for this was not compulsory or free, the facilities for obtaining even the most rudimentary training were insufficient, and evening schools were of little benefit to children who had to toil twelve hours during the day. One Children's Employment Commission's report showed some amazing results: one boy of seventeen could not even tell what two plus two equaled, other boys had never even heard of London, and several did not know who the queen was and were ignorant of such names as Nelson, Wellington, and Bonaparte, while one child "does not know who Jesus Christ is, but had heard the name; had never heard of the twelve Apostles, Samson, Moses, Aaron, etc."

Though we saw little education, we should see other aspects of living in which the masses overindulged. On all the streets could be found a multitude of public-houses where men and women spent their meager wages on gin, cheap whiskey, and beer. It is estimated that in Glasgow some thirty thousand workingmen got drunk every Saturday night, while in 1840 in certain slum areas one house in ten was a public-house. There were no movies, parks, or libraries for healthful relaxation, while the hovels in which these workers lived and the factories in which they drudged were fit only to be forgotten—by drink, if necessary. Naturally crime and vice ran unchecked in such an environment, but these evils were due as much to the wretched wages which the mill workers received as to the filthy and dreary slums in which they had to spend their lives.

The factory system created what has been described as a new list of seven deadly sins—insanitary factories, urban slums, long hours, unemployment, low wages and an unpropertied working class, child labor, and the exploitation of women. The condition of the working people was most wretched in England, but the advent of industrialism in other countries was followed by similar conditions. The evils of the factory system were not entirely escaped in the United States, but here an expanding frontier and free land softened the impact of industrialism. Not until after 1825 was there any serious attempt to remedy these evils, and the past hundred years have by no means seen their elimination.

Industrial capitalism. The advent of the factory system in the early nineteenth century led to the development of industrial capitalism. In early modern times, the profits of capitalism had been mainly obtained through the buying and selling of commodities. That period, corresponding roughly to the sixteenth, seventeenth, and the early eighteenth centuries, is known as the era of commercial capitalism, in contrast to the industrial capitalism which followed in the wake of the factory system after 1750.

Controlled and administered by the mill owners, the new industrial capitalism soon resulted in important changes in business organization. Banks increased in size, and insurance took on added importance, but above all the corporation became the characteristic form of business organization. Other forms of business organization, such as individual proprietorship and partnership, proved inadequate to meet the needs of industrial capitalism. The corporation possessed many advantages over other forms of business organization. It could accumulate large sums of capital by the sale of its shares of stock. It possessed what is known as limited liability. That is, the owner of a share of stock, in the case of corporation failure, need only lose what he had paid for it, whereas in the partnership investors were obliged to pay, if necessary, all the liabilities of the company. Another advantage of the corporation was the ease with which its shares could be transferred from one investor to another.

The corporate revolution. In the latter part of the nineteenth century, corporations grew in number and in size. So rapid and important was this growth that some economists refer to it as the corporate revolution. The development of what is known as big business was especially marked in the United States. In 1904 two per cent of the factories turned out thirty-eight per cent of the total manufactured wares. While the total output of each industry increased, the number of individual firms decreased. Those that remained grew larger and larger.

Pools, trusts, cartels. Big business in industrial capitalism did not stop with the creation of super-corporations. Other gigantic organizations were created. In the United States the business pool was developed. Its purpose was to obtain agreement among competing units engaged in the same industrial processes. The pool in turn gave way to the trust, in which various companies in an industry gave up the majority of their stock to a central board of trustees, who dictated the policies for all the subscribing members. The holding company was then developed. Instead of placing authority in a board, as in the case of the trust, a separate company was incorporated to hold the stock of the interested companies.

In Germany various other forms of business integration or union were practiced. These were generally known as cartels. The trend toward consolidation of business units was less hurried in England than in the United States and Germany, but at the beginning of the twentieth century it was well advanced in England. By 1914 the trust and cartel movement had transcended national boundaries, for there were international cartels in such industries as electric globes, aluminum, shipping, and railroads.

Bourgeoisie and proletariat. Since the Middle Ages a new social class, the merchants and burghers of the cities, had been rising to power despite the opposition of the feudal nobility. The Industrial Revolution made the triumph of this class complete and allowed them to dominate society. A new kind of "nobility" arose to supersede the landed gentry—iron masters, captains of industry, steel kings, coal barons, and railroad magnates. Bourgeoisie and middle class are terms used synonymously—that group in society which owned the agents (principally machines) of production and got profits, not wages, as a reward. The new businessmen managed the great factories and controlled the capital that built them. Hence the middle class, the factory owners, are often referred to as capitalists. In contrast to the owners of the new machinery was the great army of workers. These men could not own machines of their own and therefore had to sell their labor to the factory owner, in return for which they received wages. This working, wage-receiving class is often referred to as the proletariat.

It is true that the Industrial Revolution divided society into two general classes, but the demarcation between the two was not sharp. Between the middle class and the proletariat were the "not-so-rich and not-so-poor individuals," small-shop keepers, governmental officials, lawyers, doctors, independent farmers, and teachers. The existence of this borderline class has caused some economists to divide the middle class into the upper bourgeoisie (*haute bourgeoisie*) and the lower bourgeoisie (*petite bourgeoisie*). For purposes of simplification, however, when we refer to the middle class in this chapter we refer to the capitalists and mill owners, the upper bourgeoisie.

Middle class triumphant. Social and moral as well as political standards were dictated by the middle class. In England in particular the businessmen supposedly looked down upon the old nobility. In secret, however, the bourgeoisie envied the aristocrats and often tried to emulate them. They bought estates, married into titled families, and tried to cut handsome figures in society. The new plutocracy in America had no aristocracy at home to imitate; so they sought to bring European refinement home, by buying it if need be. The results were sometimes ludicrous, as Charles and Mary Beard have pointed out in their book.

"The armor of medieval knights soon stood in the halls of captains of industry whose boldest strokes were courageous guesses on the stock market or the employment of Pinkerton detectives against striking workingmen; while Mandarin coats from Peking sprawled on the pianos of magnates who knew not Ming or Manchu and perhaps could not tell whether their hired musicians were grinding out Wagner or Chopin. Grand ladies, who remembered with a blush the days when they laundered the family clothes, shone idly resplendent in jewels garnered by a search of two hemispheres. European tutors were imported to teach the 'new people' and their offspring 'parlor and table etiquette,' music and 'appreciation,' as Greek preceptors had served Roman families in the time of Cicero. European artists were brought over to design and decorate for them as the artists of Athens were summoned to beautify the homes of Trimalchio's contemporaries. Private libraries of the "sets," rare editions, and rich bindings were quickly assembled in job lots to give tone to establishments —a diversion that afforded gratifying appearances of culture with none of its laborious penalties."[28]

In addition to a desire to be admitted to the best social circles and to make alliances with old families, the middle class made a determined effort to gain control of government. We shall see in the following chapter that much of the political history of the nineteenth century, with its electoral reforms and even revolutions, was mainly the activity of the ambitious bourgeoisie.

The triumph of laissez faire. With this political and social triumph of the middle class in the nineteenth century, we also find the triumph of the economic philosophy, called *laissez faire,* which it so warmly championed. To understand the significance of this philosophy better, we must think of the movements on foot in Europe during the latter half of the eighteenth century, when it was brought to the fore. This was an age when heavy emphasis was placed on individual liberty and natural law. Men looked upon authority imposed from above as something to be destroyed. The American colonies revolted against a king who forbade them adequate representation and stifled their commercial life by mercantilistic regulations. A little later the French people revolted against despotic authority. This was an age when a man like Jean Jacques Rousseau went so far as to state that all the regulatory institutions of civilized society were evil and that man should return to nature in order to regain his individual liberty and happiness. The eighteenth century was also "natural law" conscious. Everywhere men talked about the omnipotence of the laws of nature and believed that there was a natural order which regulated man's actions. Let men conform to this natural order, and they would automatically be happier, but allow them to interfere with nature's laws by legislating laws of their own, and misery would inevitably follow. The best government, therefore, was that which governed least.

The French physiocrats. Thinkers began to apply the theories of individual liberty and natural law in the field of economics, to the detriment of mercantilism. The first thinkers to come to the attack in a serious way were the French physiocrats. This group owed their name to the title of a book written by one of their members, Du Pont de Nemours, *Physiocracy, or the Natural Constitution of That Form of Government Most Advantageous to the Human Race* (1767). The physiocrats conceived a body of beliefs which stressed the natural rights of man and the natural order of society and condemned the passage of all restrictive laws as unnatural and adding to man's misery. To these thinkers, the duty of government should be limited to the protection of persons and property, public works, and public education. Social legislation was regarded as dangerous since it would interfere with the working of natural economic laws. The physiocrats maintained that land furnished the raw materials of all industry, and that commerce was only a branch of the tree of agriculture. Therefore, since it was to everyone's interest that the soil should produce as much as possible, all obstructions to agriculture in the form of restrictive legislation should be at once removed. There should be complete freedom of cultivation and trade and, at the same time, complete freedom of individual initiative.

Smith's Wealth of Nations. The philosophy of the physiocrats had an important influence upon a thinker who has long been considered the first great systematic writer on political economy. He was Adam Smith (1723-1790), a Scotsman who had been educated at the Universities of Glasgow and Oxford. After leaving Oxford in 1746, Smith gave lectures and for some years taught logic and moral philosophy at Glasgow University. For three years he traveled on the continent as the companion and tutor of an English duke. When he returned to Britain in 1766, he started work on his most famous book, *An Inquiry into the Nature and Causes of the Wealth of Nations*, which was published in 1776.

Smith showed his indebtedness to the physiocrats in regard to the problems of personal liberty, natural law, and the position of the state as a regulatory medium, but he differed with them regarding the importance of agriculture in national economy. Rather he stressed that the labor of a nation is the source from which it derives all the necessities and luxuries of life. He also advanced the theory that rapid production largely depends on division of labor, and he taught that each individual in society should perform the work for which he is best fitted. Then, by a wise division of labor, each member of society will perform quickly and efficiently those tasks for which he has an aptitude and will have a large field in which to exchange the results of his own labor for commodities produced by the labor of others.

Laissez faire. The philosophy of *Wealth of Nations* can be summed up in one phrase—*laissez faire,* which might be translated "Let well enough alone" or "Hands off!" It meant that government should avoid placing any restrictions on private trade or industry. Smith stated that every individual is motivated by prudent self-interest, and, to use his own words, "The natural effort of every individual to better his own conditions, when suffered to exert itself with freedom and security, is so powerful a principle that it is alone, and without any assistance, not only capable of carrying on the society to wealth and prosperity, but of surmounting a hundred impertinent obstructions with which the folly of human laws too often encumbers its operations."[29] Smith looked on all fixing of wages, trade unions which limit apprenticeship, tariffs, and governmental interference as injurious to trade, and he scoffed at the mercantilists' view that the wealth of a nation depends on the surplus of exports, the amassing of bullion, and the crippling of neighboring countries. Smith pointed out that one nation cannot thrive at the expense of another, for trade works to the benefit of both countries.

Although the Scottish economist died before the real industrialization of England had taken place, his views were accepted and expanded by other economists. Thinkers who followed Smith elaborated on *laissez faire* and, at the same time, showed a marked growth of pessimism regarding the possible ameliorating of social evils, because they said this would conflict with economic "laws." Such men as Ricardo, McCulloch, and Malthus thought that so little could be done to improve the economic life of the common people and held out so gloomy a future for them that economics came to be known as the "dismal science."

Theories of wages. David Ricardo (1772-1823) made a famous contribution to economic thought—his "subsistence theory of wages." In this theory Ricardo maintained that labor has a natural price and also a market price. The natural price is that "which is necessary to enable the laborers . . . to subsist and to perpetuate their race without either increase or diminution." The market price depends on the law of supply and demand. When labor is scarce and in demand, it gets well paid; when it is plentiful, it is poorly paid.

Whenever the supply of capital available is large and the labor supply is not large, the market price exceeds the natural price. The result is prosperity for the laborer. The opposite situation (a limited supply of capital and a large labor supply) brings about a reverse situation, and the result is poverty for the laborers.

Unfortunately, said Ricardo, labor tends to increase faster than available capital, with the result that wages fall to the lowest point at which labor can subsist. Although varying circumstances might qualify the situation, by and large it was an iron wage law which nothing could change. "Like all other contracts, wages should be left to the fair and free competition of the market, and should never be controlled by the interference of the legislature."[30]

Malthus. Thomas Robert Malthus (1766-1834) was an English clergyman whose fame depends most of all on his *Essay of Population* (1798). Briefly stated, Malthus' proposition runs as follows: under normal conditions population increases faster than food, the former by geometrical progression, the latter only by arithmetical. It appeared obvious from this situation that misery was the inevitable lot of mankind, because the birth rate outran the food supply. In the past the population was checked by war and disease, but any remedial legislation to aid the people would ultimately do no good, for it would only help increase their misery. Malthusian thought was one of the main pillars of the subsistence theory of wages. Malthus' only solution to what he believed to be a permanent problem was the practice of self-restraint in reproduction. The postponing of early marriages seemed to Malthus an excellent means of preventing the people from having too many children. There was a glad acceptance of this doctrine by the middle class in the nineteenth century. Malthus could point correctly in his own day to a comparatively limited food supply and a population that was increasing by leaps and bounds.

Economic liberalism. Other writers who popularized *laissez-faire* doctrines, or what has been called economic liberalism (one of the doctrines of the French physiocrats) were Jeremy Bentham, James Mill, John Stuart Mill, and the so-called Manchester School. Jeremy Bentham was a rich philosophical writer who interested himself in such subjects as law, prisons, ethics, and education. Bentham has given us the doctrine of utilitarianism, based on the two concepts of utility and happiness. He correlated these two terms by saying that each individual knows what is best for himself and that all human institutions should be measured according to the amount of happiness they give. Bentham thought that happiness could thus be measured quantitatively, and his belief was that the function of government should be the securing of as great a degree of individual freedom as possible, for freedom made for happiness. Utilitarianism has been defined as "The greatest happiness for the greatest number." James Mill popularized these views and tried to show that economically they could only be accomplished through acceptance of the principles of economic liberalism. His son, John Stuart Mill, modified these views considerably, at length maintaining that, while the processes of production should be allowed to operate undisturbed according to natural law, the processes of distribution should be open to human social legislation. This idea allowed the regulation of wages, rent, and profits. The Manchester School was the name given a group of politicians who strove in Parliament to spread and foster the ideals of economic liberalism. They advocated the repeal of the Corn Laws, the adoption of free trade, and a foreign policy based on economic cooperation rather than imperialistic rivalry. During the middle portion of the nineteenth century the policies of these men won wide acceptance and made supreme the economic and political prestige of a middle class thoroughly devoted to economic liberalism.

When we amalgamate the views of these men, we obtain the following political, economic, and social philosophy of the middle class (not only in England but eventually for all the western world): (1) Every man knows what is best for himself, and if every person is free to do those things for which he is best fitted, society will obtain the total maximum contributions from the human agents of which it is composed. (2) There should be as little regulation of business by government as possible. The economic structure should consist of freely competing units "held in equilibrium by the force of competition, much as the material universe is held together by the attraction of gravitation." (3) If competition is allowed to work unimpeded, weak and inefficient firms will be forced out of business. Society should not have to support economic parasites. The force of competition will also remove the antisocial businessman who adulterates his products or cheats the public in other ways. The consumer will buy only from the ethical businessman. (4) If the forces of supply and demand are allowed to work at will, prices will tend to reach an equilibrium which will be fair both to the producer and to the consumer. In the long run the extreme, the unfair price, will be thus avoided. (5) Freedom in the business world offers rewards commensurate with a person's ability, sacrifices, and application. In a phrase, unimpeded self-interest will be the "dynamo of progress." Goods will become better, new commodities will be introduced, and startling inventions will be perfected because there will be no limit to the rewards offered to the intelligent and to the persevering. (6) The middle class felt, at the outset at least, that there was an alliance between wealth and virtue. Businessmen sincerely believed that poverty was not their concern, for it was mainly the consequence of improvidence, shiftlessness, immorality, laziness. (7) Finally, it was believed that the government should be used only to protect the nation from foreign aggression, to maintain peace and order at home, to protect foreign investments, to enforce contracts, and above all to protect private property.

The middle class wanted no governmental interference in their affairs. But it cannot be said that the nineteenth-century businessman, therefore, was not interested in participating in the government. In England, for example, the middle class wished to remove the tariffs that still remained as a vestige of the mercantilistic system. These duties, mainly on imported wheat, had as their main purpose the protection of the agricultural interests. The businessmen, however, were not interested in profits for the landed interests but rather in cheap raw materials for their factories and cheap bread for their workers. The heart of industrial England, Manchester, organized the Anti-Corn Law League and after a brilliant campaign of propaganda succeeded in 1846 in having the government remove the Corn Laws from the statute books. England was now a free-trade country. In theory, at least, the middle class was interested in maintaining *laissez faire* in both the domestic and the international field. In most countries, however, the middle class was satisfied with business freedom at home but forced the government more and more to interfere in foreign commerce by enacting lop-sided tariff laws.

The Challenge of the Workers

Injustices appear. In theory the philosophy of the middle class, *laissez faire,* had seemed logical and indeed a positive aid to social and economic progress. As we have seen from the discussion of conditions under the factory system, however, a wide gulf soon appeared between theory and practice. The operation of competition did not always ensure fair prices, because of monopolistic practices and secret collusion between competitors. Nor did competition ensure the survival of honest and efficient business. Underhanded and unfair competition often wrecked the more ethical and scrupulous firms. And the general public was not able to obtain the information necessary for judging whether or not goods were adulterated or stock watered. It also became increasingly difficult to reconcile the great wealth enjoyed by a few with the poverty borne by the many. It became obvious that poverty is not necessarily a result of personal improvidence. The working class became embittered against the factory owners.

In England after the Napoleonic wars the misery of the people caused rioting and bloodshed on several occasions. In 1819, for example, a large number of people congregated in an open space at Manchester to discuss their grievances. The authorities called out soldiers, who charged upon the meeting, killing a dozen people and wounding several hundred. Repression seemed the order of the day, and the workers could only nourish their grievances secretly. On the European continent there were also evidences of unrest.

The socialist doctrine. Yet the workers were not without able friends who began to raise their voices. Certain individuals already were challenging the doctrines of economic liberalism and the right of the middle class to control affairs. Some of these intellectuals were known as socialists, that is, they endorsed a social and economic philosophy known as socialism, which believes that land, natural resources, and the instruments of production should be publicly owned and managed in the interests of the people as a whole and not for private profit. They charged that although many persons had to cooperate to produce an article there was not a just method of distributing the rewards of such industry because relatively few (the employer class) received too big a proportion of the profits, while the workers (at whose expense, they charged, these profits were made) had to content themselves with a wage barely sufficient to keep body and soul together. The socialists also charged that capitalism was chaotic and wasteful. It overproduced one year, underproduced the next, and from this lack of plan came depressions and panics. The socialists charged that discontent created by the denial of the workers' demands resulted in class struggle and the subjection of the laboring group by the middle class, which now controlled the major economic, political, and social power. True democracy, claimed the socialists, was not possible until the people as a whole owned the means of production and reaped the rewards of their own labor. Thus, socialism called for something more than a mere transfer of the ownership of property; it demanded a complete change in the social as well as the economic structure of a nation.

Utopian socialism. The first important socialistic movement is known as the Utopian (named after the book *Utopia,* by Sir Thomas More) and was inspired largely by the French Revolution. Its proponents sought to give the people more economic liberty in keeping with the political emancipation which they had won. The first of the Utopian socialists was a sincere, poverty-stricken French nobleman, Claude Henri, Comte de Saint-Simon (1760-1825). While his views were quite misty and ill-formed, Saint-Simon influenced such prominent thinkers as Auguste Comte with his belief that the society of the future must be cooperative and concerned with the exploitation of nature, rather than competitive and replete with the exploitation of man.

François Fourier (1772-1837) believed too that future society must be cooperative, and he spent much time in working out what he considered an ideal plan for communal living, which he termed "phalanstery." Some 1800 persons were to work and live together in an economic "phalanx" which would be composed of agricultural laborers, mechanics, artisans, and so forth. Each person in the phalanstery was to pursue that type of work which best suited his taste. This view was endorsed by many prominent thinkers of the day. The famous Brook Farm colony in the United States was one of several short-lived attempts to establish Utopian communities in the nineteenth century.

A more practical Utopian socialist was Robert Owen (1771-1858), a successful mill owner in Scotland. Owen really led the way in factory reform. He gave his workers good wages, decent factory conditions, schools for their children, and healthful houses for themselves. Owen, after having brought about factory reforms in Parliament, came to Indiana in 1825, where he founded too a short-lived Utopian colony called New Harmony. Utopian socialism failed to achieve the goal for which its advocates had labored, partly because of the impracticality of such colonies as New Harmony and partly because it made no practical attempt to meet the problems of the working classes as a whole.

Christian socialists. A group of Christian socialists arose in the nineteenth century who aimed at showing that the economic doctrines of the Sermon on the Mount were primarily socialistic in character. In England the leaders were drawn largely from the Broad Church party of the Church of England, the Methodists, the Unitarians, and the Quakers. The most outstanding Christian socialists were John Frederick Denison Maurice, generally credited as the founder of Christian socialism in England, who advocated mass education, and the famous novelist and reformer Charles Kingsley, whose indictment of current social evils appeared in his novels *Alton Locke, The Water Babies,* and *Yeast.* The Christian socialists stimulated interest in cooperative societies and working-class reforms, and they made a genuine attempt to instill in organized Christianity a realization of the social aspects of the teachings of Christ.

Karl Marx and scientific socialism. A more radical, belligerent, and precise philosophy was known as scientific socialism. This revolutionary doctrine was the work primarily of a German intellectual of penetrating mind and realistic purpose, Karl Marx (1818-1883). Adam Smith stands out as the great exponent of the philosophy of private initiative; Marx is to be remembered as the most outstanding champion of socialism. Excellently educated, influenced early by the Utopian socialists, and forced to spend his life in perpetual exile as a result of his lifelong associations with revolutionary movements, Karl Marx finally wound up in London where he wrote his famous *Das Kapital,* as epochmaking an economic treatise in its own way as Smith's *Wealth of Nations.* But before its publication Marx and his friend Friedrich Engels had collaborated in 1848 in issuing the Communist Manifesto, which has been described as the "birth-cry of modern socialism" and which called on the workers to unite and overthrow their exploiters.

The following constitute the principal tenets of Marxian socialism: (1) Economic conditions have been the principal means of changing the course of history, and such problems as those arising out of patriotism, religion, and culture are only "ideological veils" to obscure the fundamental economic forces. Thus Marxian socialism is materialistic in its philosophy. (2) As the Manifesto put it, the history of all former societies has been that of class struggle. The workers must become "class conscious" and recognize their undying antipathy toward all capitalistic interests. From class consciousness will come class solidarity, and this will ultimately make possible a world revolution which will overthrow the bourgeoisie and result in a classless society. (3) All commodities are produced by human labor, and the real value of any commodity must be measured by the amount of labor necessary to produce it. But the laborer only gets a portion back (in the form of wages) of what he produces. The rest is "surplus value," which the employer takes as profits. What is needed, therefore, is to take away the possibility of exploitation by establishing a socialistic system of distribution which would dispense with any middle-class profits and allow the workers to receive all the value created by their own productivity. (4) Because the workers create more goods than their wages will allow them to consume, surpluses pile up which cause overproduction, crises, and unemployment. Wealth is concentrated in fewer and fewer hands, while more and more people get less and less. (5) Finally, out of self-defense, the workers will have to take over the means of production and distribution, by peaceful methods if possible and forcible methods if need be. When labor is driven to such a desperate plight, then, says the Manifesto: "The knell of capitalism is sounded. The expropriators are expropriated." The interests of the proletariat are fundamentally the same the world over. Therefore workers should unite, for their real enemy is not some particular nation but the bourgeoisie with whom they all have a common conflict. Only by an international union of workers can permanent peace be realized.[31]

State socialism. Socialists were agreed on condemnation of capitalism but disagreed as to what system should take its place. Not long after the death of Marx in 1883, socialists began to quarrel among themselves. One wing, orthodox Marxists, kept scrupulously to the exact tenets of their leader. Another group, calling themselves Revisionists, began to feel that some of the doctrines of Marx were not tenable. The Revisionists called for cooperation with existing governments, bourgeois or not, to enact reforms. They declared the workers could not wait until "the roast pigeons of the socialist revolution would fly into their mouths."[32] In 1891 the moderate German socialists adopted the Erfurt Program, which became a model for less extreme socialists all over the world. While not giving up the ultimate aim of governmental ownership and control of industry, this program demanded universal suffrage, an eight-hour day, free education, high income and inheritance taxes, and extensive factory reforms.

The views of the Revisionist school are sometimes called state socialism. While believers in state socialism did not agree on details, generally speaking they favored the attainment of the democratic socialist state by means of the ballot. Perhaps the most famous exponents of this type of socialism were the Fabians of England, a society founded in 1884, deriving its name from the cautious Roman general, Fabius Maximus Quintus, who wore down his enemy, Hannibal, by a policy of watchful waiting and by being content with small gains. The Fabian Society has included such outstanding British intellectuals as George Bernard Shaw, Sidney and Beatrice Webb, and H. G. Wells.

Anarchism and syndicalism. The nineteenth century produced other schools of proletarian thought. One important movement was anarchism. Anarchism and socialism stand poles apart. Where the latter stresses complete governmental control, philosophical anarchism denounces all authority from state, Church, or any other source. Such thinkers as the Frenchman Pierre Joseph Proudhon and the Russian Michael Bakunin maintained, in the words of the latter, that "the liberty of man consists solely in this, that he obeys the laws of nature because he himself has recognized them as such and not because they have been imposed upon him externally by a foreign will, human or divine, collective or individual."[33] The anarchists favored the abolition of all classes and compulsion. Men should work together only through mutual cooperation, and the products of their combined labor should be shared mutually. Anarchism is really the ultimate in individualism, but the anarchists fought the *laissez-faire* individualists as the chief exploiters of society. Anarchism often degenerated into violence and bomb throwing and contributed little of a constructive nature to the improvement of the workers' lot.

Still another school, one which became strong in workingmen circles, was syndicalism. Many people felt that the state socialists' plan to make changes via parliamentary methods was a waste of time. The syndicalists, like the anarchists, repudiated the state as the weapon of exploitation and preferred to put their trust in what they called "direct action." This was to be done by taking over the trade unions (to be discussed later in this chapter) to unite all workers, while the chief weapons at their disposal were the strike and sabotage (from the French *sabot,* a wooden shoe, which early strikers were said to have thrown into machinery to ruin it). The syndicalists strengthened the trade-union movement, but their hope that general strikes would bring about a complete revision of the economic and social order has not been realized.

The Compromise

The "June Days." The evils of the factory system gave rise to the development of class consciousness among the proletariat, that is, the workers increasingly tended to believe that the interests of their class were opposed to those of the bourgeoisie. In 1848, the same year in which Marx and Engels published their Communist Manifesto, an armed clash took place between the bourgeoisie and the proletariat in Paris. The French king, Louis Philippe, had just been overthrown by a revolution in which the proletariat had joined with the bourgeoisie in ousting the ruler. As a reward for this assistance, the city workers of Paris expected the new government of the republic to guarantee them the "right to work" by establishing national workshops, with fair wages for all, the plan of Louis Blanc, a French socialist. But the bourgeoisie had no intention of encouraging socialistic experiments; the national workshops were disbanded after little more than a month. Infuriated at what they believed was bourgeois treachery, the Parisian workers rose in rebellion against the new government, crying "Bread or lead." During the terrible "June Days" desperate street fighting took place in the streets of Paris. Hundreds of workingmen lost their lives in futile resistance to the military forces.

This outbreak had important consequences. To many Europeans it signalized the beginning of a bitter struggle between workers and the middle class. The "June Days" have been selected by some historians as the true beginning of modern times. They demonstrated that the era of conflict between the rising bourgeoisie and the landed aristocracy was over. The triumph of the middle class brought a new alignment of economic classes—the bourgeoisie versus the working class. During the next two decades, following the outbreak of 1848, other clashes took place between what soon came to be called capital and labor. In 1871, for example, another bloody conflict was recorded in Paris between the workers and bourgeoisie, and even in the United States, where an abundance of free land had tended to prevent the development of a militant class consciousness among the people, the year 1877 saw the outbreak of armed hostilities between workers and capital. This was a great railroad strike which involved pitched battles between the strikers and state militia.

The Compromise. The latter part of the nineteenth century and the decade preceding the First World War did not, however, see an intensification of the struggle between capital and labor. On the contrary, while instances of industrial warfare did crop up, there was a definite improvement in the situation, which might be called the Compromise. In many countries that had felt the influence of industrialization, a strong humanitarian movement developed which demanded that the evils of the factory system be remedied.

The demand for reform. The writings of such "esthetic rebels" in England as Thomas Carlyle, Charles Dickens, John Ruskin, and Charles Reade brought home to the reading public the necessity of reform, while Ralph Waldo Emerson in America, George Sand in France, and Leo Tolstoy in Russia accomplished similar results. Dickens showed the pitiful conditions of the working classes, Carlyle reviled the industrialists for their materialism and love of Mammon, Ruskin resented the filth and sordidness of factory towns which were transforming England from a land of green scenery to one of smoke-grimed smokestacks. Sand popularized the doctrines of early socialism in her novels, while Tolstoy went so far as to advocate the repudiation of the new industrialism and a return to an agrarian economy based on cooperative principles.

Support for economic reforms came from other sources. In England, for example, the Tory landowners resented the rise of the *nouveau riche* mill owners in the cities, and they were quite willing to advocate the passage of factory acts which would curb the power of the middle-class entrepreneurs. Among the factory owners there were many who came to see the necessity of measures aimed at improving the lot of the workers. With some this desire was mainly altruistic, with others it came from a shrewd belief that in the long run much trouble would be avoided if the people were better taken care of. In the latter part of the nineteenth century and just before the First World War, there were also outstanding statesmen, such as Theodore Roosevelt, Lloyd George, and Otto von Bismarck, who believed in the extension of governmental control to protect the working people.

Early child-labor legislation. It is not possible here to give a complete account of the reform legislation that ameliorated the lot of the workers in all the important industrial countries, but how indicative the trend was can be shown by a brief analysis of social reconstruction in nineteenth-century England, the home of the new industrialism. As early as 1802 an act had been passed forbidding the employment of children for more than twelve hours a day, exclusive of time for meals, and night work was prohibited in some cases. But because supervision was in the hands of local authorities, little benefit resulted. In 1819 another attempt was made to help the plight of children under nine years of age and to limit to twelve hours a day the work of youngsters whose ages ranged from nine to sixteen.

Unfortunately, no real provision was made in this case, either, for the enforcement of this anything-but-radical reform. Conditions in the factories remained so brutal, unhealthful, and inhuman that finally an aroused public demanded a complete investigation in 1831. The appalling statistics and accounts disclosed by the royal commission led to the passage in 1833 of the first effective factory act in British history. The men most responsible for this factory reform were Tory squires who had little use for democracy but possessed a deep humanitarian spirit and resented the callous indifference toward human rights on the part of the urban mill owners.

The act of 1833 forbade the employment in textile factories of children under nine. It also restricted the hours of labor for children between nine and thirteen to forty-eight a week and the hours of children from thirteen and eighteen to sixty-eight, while no one under eighteen was allowed to work at night. Government factory inspectors were to help administer the act, a piece of legislation which strikes us today as anything but radical but which prompted such manufacturers as John Bright to exclaim it was "most injurious and destructive to the best interests of the country" and violated "the liberty of the subject" and "freedom of contract"—as though children of nine had liberty or freedom of contract in bargaining with mill owners.

While the textile-factory conditions were improved, those of the mines remained ghastly. Children of six and seven were employed underground twelve hours a day to open and shut doors which provided ventilation and even harnessed "like dogs to a go-cart" to haul coal wagons. In 1842 a law was passed forbidding the labor of women, and of girls and boys under ten in the mines. Then, in 1846, the Ten-Hour Law was enacted to limit the work of women and children in textile factories to ten hours a day, and succeeding years saw other improvements in factory conditions.

Advance of trade unionism. In 1799 and 1800 Parliament passed a series of laws known as the Combination Acts. In effect they forbade trade unions on the grounds that they restrained trade. Strikes were classed with conspiracies, and strikers were harshly punished. In 1824 the Combination Acts were repealed, thus making trade unionism possible once more. The following year a new act somewhat limiting union activities superseded the Act of 1824. But the measures of 1824-1825 meant that the workers had been granted legal recognition to organize in unions. During the period 1871-1876 a series of acts was passed granting extensive rights to trade unions.

The trade union aided the laboring class to bargain for higher wages, shorter hours, and more healthful conditions of work. The failure of the workers in 1848 to achieve greater political and economic rights, which will be discussed in the next chapter, made them turn more and more to the trade union as a means of enforcing their demands. Finally, through unions, British workers became part of the Labor Party, established in 1900, and with the rapid rise in power of this party in the twentieth century, came to be adequately represented directly in Parliament.

Trade unionism also made rapid progress in other countries. In France the workers were allowed by law in 1864 to combine for strikes, and in 1884 were granted freedom of organization. Trade unionism now spread rapidly, and in 1895 there was organized the General Confederation of Labor, composed of nearly all the French unions and dedicated to the purpose of uniting "the workingmen in the economic field with the bonds of class solidarity to struggle for their integral emancipation." During the sixties trade unionism made progress in Germany, as it did in the United States, where between 1861 and 1865 the number of local unions multiplied almost fourfold. In 1869 a powerful labor group bearing the florid name Noble Order of the Knights of Labor was organized. In 1881 there was founded a trade union whose membership soon numbered millions and which became the most powerful voice in the ranks of American workers—the American Federation of Labor. For decades this union was headed by Samuel Gompers, and it has remained to this day an active champion of labor in the industrial world.

German social reform. An important reflection of the movement to ameliorate the condition of the people was the advent of social legislation, laws to protect the working class and improve its conditions by offering such facilities as better housing, free medical service, unemployment insurance, compensation for industrial accidents, and old-age pensions. The first comprehensive program of social legislation was introduced into Germany by Bismarck, the chancellor. This statesman was thoroughly aroused at the advance made by socialism in Germany. To Bismarck the interests of both capital and labor were subordinate to the state. If the workers were discontented, it was the duty of the government to intervene. This meant the passage of laws designed to keep the workers happy and, what was most important to Bismarck, docile and loyal to the state. "Give the workingman the right to work as long as he is healthy," Bismarck declared in 1884, "assure him care when he is sick, and maintenance when he is old . . . then the socialists will sing their siren song in vain, and the workingmen will cease to throng to their banner."[34] Following this policy, Bismarck had a sickness insurance bill passed in 1883. The following year saw provision for accident insurance, and in 1889 old-age insurance was introduced.

English social reform. In the early twentieth century Great Britain followed suit with an even more ambitious code of social insurance. The Liberal Party led the attack on *laissez faire* in Great Britain. A Parliamentary commission made a monumental report on the condition of the English people in 1909. Some forty volumes compiled by the commission painted a gloomy picture of the workers' lot in Great Britain. Twelve per cent of the population received half of the national wealth, and over thirty per cent of the adult male workers got a starvation wage of less than seven dollars per week. With such pitifully small wages it was impossible for the workers to lay aside any savings for intermittent periods of unemployment, which seemed to be occurring with more and more frequency. Confronted with this widespread economic injustice, the Liberal Party under the leadership of such men as Winston Churchill, Lloyd George, and Herbert Asquith carried through Parliament an ambitious program of social reform. This provided for national labor-employment bureaus, a minimum wage act, housing and town planning, sickness and accident insurance, and, above all, unemployment insurance. Thus in England, the mother of the Industrial Revolution and the citadel of *laissez faire,* the old doctrine of noninterference in business was discarded in favor of rigorous governmental control.

Reform in the United States. By 1914 social-insurance systems existed in ten European countries. France had set up sickness and accident insurance late in the nineteenth century and in 1910 had created an old-age-pension system. Meanwhile, the advance of industrialism in the United States gave rise to many of the problems that had followed the emergence of the factory in England and on the European continent. In 1836 Massachusetts passed the first act regulating child labor. This state was the pioneer, and by 1889 it forbade the employment of children under fourteen. By 1914

Workers returned after the long day in mill and factory to these tightly fenced back yards and endless lines of wash in the London slums.

every state in the Union had some kind of child-labor regulation.

After the Civil War numerous laws were passed relating to safety devices, fire prevention, and sanitary inspection in factories. The payment of accident compensation to workers came relatively late in the United States. Maryland made a start in 1902, Montana followed in 1909, and the first important act was passed by New York in 1910. During the next decade many other states followed, although much difficulty was experienced in framing compensation laws that would not be declared unconstitutional by the courts. Another important landmark was the introduction of the minimum-wage principle for women in Massachusetts in 1912. As yet the United States has not succeeded in obtaining a federal child-labor law, though some federal legislation does provide certain checks on child labor.

Philanthropic reform. Philanthropy helped improve the conditions of the people by bringing them opportunities in higher education, free hospitals, libraries, and other facilities. George Peabody, for example, gave $700,000 in 1862 to provide housing facilities for English workers and in 1867 established a fund of three million dollars for education in the American southern states.

Another giant of philanthropy was Andrew Carnegie, who distributed ninety per cent of his fortune. Grants were made to colleges and universities, churches, and libraries. Social-service centers were established in Great Britain and the United States. In 1885 Toynbee Hall was founded in London, and in 1889 Jane Addams began her remarkable social-settlement work at Hull House in Chicago. Another munificent donor was John D. Rockefeller, whose benefactions for numerous causes amounted to hundreds of millions.

Recognition of trade unions, factory legislation, social legislation, and middle-class philanthropy were responsible for achieving some degree of reconciliation between the proletariat and the bourgeoisie. While the middle class still occupied a dominant position in most industrialized nations, this class by 1900 began to see that the doctrine of pure *laissez faire* was no longer applicable. Since the days of Ricardo and Malthus, the middle class had come to realize that protective legislation on the part of government and philanthropy on the part of capital were essential if the capitalistic system was to be perpetuated. The workers were not completely satisfied but were willing in most instances to cooperate with management in the hope that the future would see more substantial gains. Describing this partial reconciliation, Ferdinand Schevill remarks: "The majority [of society] is so constituted that its members are always ready to abate something of their extreme demands in the interest of social peace. They will seek a compromise; and compromise has, on the whole, been the most characteristic feature in the relation of the two classes, employers and employees, carried to the front by the Industrial Revolution."[35]

Summary

The period under discussion, 1750 to 1914, saw the most amazing economic revolution in the history of mankind. It had been made possible by the utilization of new power resources, mainly steam and then electricity. Further, it had been brought about by the ingenuity of inventors who were able to devise machines for making goods run by the new power. England was the home of the Industrial Revolution, and what happened here was more or less duplicated in all those other regions that became industrialized. The progress of industrialization depended upon adequate transportation to serve expanding markets and to make raw materials available.

The Industrial Revolution had important social consequences. The factory system created two classes, the wage earner and the factory owner and manager. The former suffered from low wages, unemployment, child labor, inadequate housing, and a host of other evils. Such problems were of little concern to the middle class early in the nineteenth century, for they developed a philosophy, *laissez faire,* or economic liberalism, which permitted them to witness evils with the belief that these were not of their doing and could not be remedied even if they desired. *Laissez faire* implied that out of unrestricted competition the strong would survive and society would benefit.

In the face of want and poverty the workers began to protest and at times to rebel, and this trend was strengthened by the coming of the socialist movement. Karl Marx urged the workers to become class conscious and prepare for the day when capitalistic exploitation should be removed, by force if necessary. By 1850 a clash between worker and manager seemed imminent, but the latter part of the nineteenth century saw the advent of reform, which prevented this outcome. Factory laws, social legislation, and philanthropy all played their part. In most countries a compromise was achieved.

The story of the industrial era is mainly the narrative of the rise of the middle class to power. This class played the dynamic role in nineteenth- and early twentieth-century history. The middle class increasingly dominated polite society, dictated standards of morality, and patronized arts and letters. Much criticism has been leveled against bourgeois indifference to misery and exploitation. We should remember, however, that such criticism comes from hindsight. The pace of industrialism a century ago was so fast, the game of the new business so absorbing, that businessmen had little thought for the social consequences of their actions. Then, too, the philosophy of *laissez faire* seemed quite logical and conducive to society's good. The businessman of the nineteenth century certainly had a blind spot which seemed to make him impervious to suffering among his fellow men, and for this he has received his full share of criticism. At the same time, however, when the evils of pure *laissez-faire* doctrine became manifest, the middle class did play a part in their removal, or at least their partial rectification.

It is always difficult to evaluate any great movement such as the Industrial Revolution, for one is at a loss to know at what point in time the judgment should be made. An evaluation in 1850 would show that the industrialization had brought great riches to the few and much misery to the many. In 1900 some of the evils were being counterbalanced by such gains as the reduction of the hours of work and the increase of leisure, the reduction of the prices of manufactured goods, and a general advance in the standard of living. One hardly dares ponder what judgment may be made in 1975. All that can safely be said now is that the Industrial Revolution with its tremendous technological contributions constitutes the foundation of our twentieth-century machine age with all its accomplishments and shortcomings.

	Congress of Vienna Enthrones Reaction	
	Peace settlement: reaction rules	Metternich, Castlereagh, Talleyrand
1815	Bourbons restored in France, Spain, Naples	Restorations in Piedmont, and Holland
	Protective belt around France	Netherlands, Rhineland, Savoy
	Austria given Lombardy-Venetia	Compensation for Netherlands
	Sweden given Norway	Compensation for Finland
	England retains colonies captured	Ceylon and Cape Colony
	Nationalism disregarded	Germany, Italy, Norway, Belgium, Poland
1815	Quadruple alliance	Austria, Prussia, Russia, England
1818	Holy Alliance of little importance	Proposed by Alexander
	France and revolution	
1815	Bourbon restoration	Louis XVIII, Charles X
1830	Paris rebels against reaction	Charles deposed, other revolts in Europe
1848	Revolution and Second republic	Workers fight bourgeoisie
1851-1870	Second French empire	Louis Napoleon seizes power
1870	Third French republic	Republican constitution
	England and gradualism	
1832	Reform bill by new Whig government	Transferred balance of power to bourgeoisie
1833	Slavery abolished; Factory Act	
1865-1867	Disraeli introduces Second Reform Bill	
1868-1874	Gladstone's reforms	Forster Education Act, Ballot Act
1884	Third Reform Bill	Enfranchises agricultural workers
1911	Parliament Bill weakens House of Lords	House of Commons supreme
	Elsewhere in Europe	
1848	Revolution fails in Germany	
1855-1861	Alexander II tries liberalism in Russia	Serfdom abolished, zemstvos
1863	Alexander turns reactionary	Crushes Polish revolt
1905	Nicholas II promises constitutional rule	Sets up *Duma* but breaks promises
1831	Belgium gains liberal constitution	
1844-1845	Switzerland the peer of democracies	Referendum, initiative introduced
1848	Italy tries parliamentary government	Liberal constitution granted
1909-1913	Norway, the most democratic monarchy	Manhood, woman suffrage
	Victory for Nationalism	
1815-1848	Germany begins to unite	Confederation, Zollverein, Frankfurt Assembly
1829	Greece wrests independence from Turkey	European powers lend aid
1852-1860	Cavour gains Lombardy, northern papal states	*Risorgimento*, war with Austria
1860	Cavour annexes Kingdom of Two Sicilies	Garibaldi's Red Shirts
1864-1870	Bismarck unites Germany	Wars with Austria, France
1866-1870	Italy acquires Venetia, occupies Rome	Unification complete
1871	German empire proclaimed in Paris	North, south Germany united

CHAPTER 5

Nationalism and Democracy Advance

THE defeat of Napoleon on the battlefield of Waterloo in 1815 found the people of Europe impoverished and dazed by almost twenty-three years of constant warfare (1792-1815). Hundreds of thousands of men had lost their lives, and the nations had been kept in almost constant turmoil. It was natural, then, that most people were dominated by a desire for peace and the creation of a new order of things that would perhaps end war and bring a better social structure to mankind. There must be freedom to participate in one's government, to worship and think as one pleased, to engage in business and trade without interference from the government, and, if ruled by an alien people, to try to establish an independent national government. The history of the nineteenth century almost exclusively concerns the unfolding of these forces.

As a background for our survey of the development of democracy and nationalism, this chapter will begin with a description of the work of the Congress of Vienna, for the diplomats in this conference in 1815 made decisions which influenced the development of European politics throughout the nineteenth century. With the work of the Congress of Vienna well in mind, we then will discuss the rise and progress of democracy in nineteenth-century Europe. Among the great powers France and Great Britain succeeded in attaining the most democratic institutions in Europe by the beginning of the twentieth century. In France the advance of democracy alternated between violent revolutions and despotic interludes, such as the rule of the emperor Napoleon III. In England, on the other hand, progress was slow but was accompanied by little or no violence.

Having followed the progress and eventual triumph of political liberalism in France and England, we will next focus attention upon political developments in Germany and Russia. Here democracy had little success, for the end of the nineteenth century saw the German kaiser ruling as a benevolent despot, similar in some respects to his forebear, Frederick the Great, and the Russian czar ruling as a despot, with little that was benevolent in his régime. Among the lesser powers of Europe we shall note several conspicuous successes in the achievement of democratic institutions. The Scandinavian countries and Switzerland especially come to mind. Spain and Portugal, among the less powerful states of Europe, did manage to obtain the outward form of democracy, but in reality these countries were governed by irresponsible political cliques whose corruption brought misery and poverty to the people. In Italy the functioning of parliamentary machinery left much to be desired, being manipulated frequently by self-seeking politicians.

The remaining sections of this chapter deal with the nineteenth century's second basic political force: nationalism. As in the case of democracy, our starting point will be the work of the Congress of Vienna. Much of our discussion will hinge around efforts to undo arrangements made at Vienna that violated the principle of nationalism. The period from 1815 to 1848 constitutes the first phase in the unfolding of European nationalism. During this time we will note that Greece and Belgium succeeded in obtaining their national independence but that nationalism achieved little success in Poland, Italy, Austria, and Germany, where people longed to be free from foreign rule. After 1848 a new epoch in nationalism was ushered in, ending in 1871 with the unification of Italy and Germany as sovereign national states. These two countries had heretofore constituted the most important violations of the principle that people of one nationality should be united under their own government. But the unification of Germany and Italy still left many nationalistic problems in Europe. The Irish chafed under British rule, the French in Alsace-Lorraine looked for the day of emancipation from their German masters, the Czechs in Bohemia desired their freedom from Austria, and Slavs in the Balkans likewise dreamed of national independence.

Reaction at Vienna

The Congress of Vienna. In September 1814, a brilliant gathering of diplomats and rulers assembled at Vienna to remake the map of Europe after Napoleon's defeat. Representatives from every nation in Europe, except Turkey, were in attendance. The Austrian government played the part of a lavish host to the treaty makers. There was a round of festivals, hunts, balls, and musicales. Beethoven conducted the première of his "Seventh Symphony." For ten months kings, lords, and diplomats, with their ladies, dined and danced and worked not too industriously at the task of reconstructing Europe after the Napoleonic wars. In this atmosphere of high society, and what frequently turned out to be low diplomacy, intrigue and spying flourished. The Congress as such never met! There were a few formal meetings of the more important representatives, but generally speaking, the new map of Europe was made in small, secret conferences, concealed behind the pomp of balls, masques, and pageants: "At a ball, kingdoms were enlarged or sliced up—at a dinner an indemnity granted—a constitution sketched while hunting; occasionally a *bon mot*, or a witty idea, brought an agreement where conferences and notes failed."[1]

The chief actors. The leading delegates at the conference were the czar Alexander I, Lord Castlereagh of Great Britain, Talleyrand representing France, and Prince von Metternich, the representative of Austria. The czar was a queer mixture of liberalism, mysticism, and personal ambition. The English delegate, Castlereagh, was sound and practical. It was he who counseled that "no arrangement could be wise that carried ruin to one of the countries between which it was concluded." This moderate attitude goes far to explain why France was treated so fairly. Talleyrand, the spokesman for France, was one of the most astute and unscrupulous diplomats of his day.

The "prince of diplomats," the most important figure at the Congress, however, was Prince Metternich. Born of a noble family, educated in the best schools, and associated from early youth with the elegant society of aristocratic Austria, Metternich grew up to be the most charming, suave, and competent statesman of his day. During the Napoleonic period he had become an inflexible opponent of the French emperor. After Waterloo, Metternich was resolved that there should be no return of the revolutionary ideas exported from France between 1792 and 1815. Referring to the French Revolution, he declared it was "the disease which must be cured, the volcano which must be extinguished, the gangrene which must be burned out with the hot iron."[2] Most of the rulers attending the Congress agreed wholeheartedly with these sentiments. The king of Prussia declared, "The whole world is mad and wants new constitutions."

The task confronting the Congress. The task confronting the diplomats at the Congress of Vienna was threefold: What was to be done with France? What basic principles should be utilized in reconstructing the old governments and political boundaries so ruthlessly swept aside by Napoleon in the countries of Europe? And, finally, what should be the attitude regarding the radical ideas that had been developed by revolutionary France? Many people in Europe were hopeful that the peace settlement would be guided by two principles that had grown rapidly during the stormy days from the outbreak of the French Revolution in 1789 to the fall of Napoleon in 1815. These were nationalism and democracy. The first principle, in brief, promised all people the right to rule themselves free of the control of outside nations. The second offered to men the right to participate in their government, the right to enjoy political liberty. Unfortunately, the Congress of Vienna was in no mood to respect the aspirations of the people. Reaction, not progress, was the keynote of the assembly that met in 1815. Much of the discontent and political turmoil of European history in the nineteenth century was owing to the efforts of the Congress to go back and restore the old rather than to pioneer and introduce the new.

The treatment of France. In solving the first question, the future of France, the Congress proved to be sensible and moderate. The Treaty of Paris signed by French representatives in May 1814 had given France about the same boundaries she possessed in 1792, and no indemnity was required. Following this treaty, however, Napoleon had escaped from the island of Elba, where he had been exiled, and during his so-called "Hundred Days" of freedom again led French armies against the allies, while the diplomats at Vienna awaited events with much trepidation. After Waterloo and the banishment of Napoleon to St. Helena, a second and more severe treaty was imposed upon France. This second treaty of November 1815 somewhat reduced French territory, but even with this reduction France's frontiers were larger than they had been in 1789. A war indemnity was imposed, and a number of strategic fortresses were to be occupied by allied troops for a maximum period of five years.

Reconstruction of European politics. In the solution of the second great problem, the reestablishment of the European political order, three principles were followed: (1) legitimacy, (2) encirclement, and (3) compensations. It was agreed at the Congress that, wherever possible, the legitimate rulers who were in power before their deposition by Napoleon should have their thrones restored to them. Following this principle, all of the rulers that had been established by Napoleon were removed except Bernadotte of Sweden who, because he had been loyal to the allies, was permitted to keep his throne. The old Bourbon line of kings in France, in the person of Louis XVIII, was restored by the Congress. Other Bourbon rulers were put back on their thrones in Spain and in the kingdom of Naples. The House of

Savoy reigned again in Piedmont, and the House of Orange was restored in Holland.

In the reconstruction of the political boundaries of Europe, reaction was again the keynote. France was, as we have seen, reduced from an empire to substantially her former size; Spain, Holland, and other Napoleonic possessions were restored to independence. The map of Europe looked much as it had before the French Revolution (compare the map above with that of 1740, page 87). But certain features of the map were modified in accordance with the principle of encirclement. The allied statesmen were resolved that a protective belt (represented on the map by the dotted line and arrows) should surround France to hem her in and prevent any future aggression on her part. The Austrian Netherlands were turned over to Holland, making Holland a stronger barrier on France's north. Prussia was also given extensive territory along the Rhine for the same reason. The kingdom of Savoy was enlarged in order to block any French invasion of Italy. Switzerland was given back three small cantons which had been recently incorporated into France, and in addition Swiss neutrality was guaranteed by the European powers.

Compensations to states surrendering territory were another factor modifying the map of Europe. Austria, for example, was compensated for giving up the Austrian Netherlands by acquiring Lombardy and Venetia in northern Italy and some Adriatic coast as well. In such fashion the diplomats at Vienna portioned out the spoils so that no important power was slighted. When Sweden agreed to give Finland to Russia, her compensation was the acquisition of Norway. England's share was the retention of colonies captured in the wars, notably the Dutch Ceylon and Cape Colony.

Napoleon's own reorganization of Europe was responsible for some differences between the maps of 1789 and 1815. The Polish state he had set up under his control was turned over in its entirety to Russia instead of being restored to its former rulers, Austria and Prussia. The Holy Roman Empire remained dissolved, and the thirty-eight states set up by Napoleon were retained in place of the hundreds existing in pre-Revolutionary times.

Violations of nationalism. The most serious mistake in the territorial settlements made at Vienna was the disregard of the principle of nationalism. During the great war against Napoleon, there had arisen in Europe, especially in Italy and Germany, a new kind of patriot and nationalist who envisaged belonging to a strong and united nation. But the nationalistic aspirations of these patriots were disregarded. Austria did not want a united Italy. In Metternich's words, Italy must remain only a "geographical expression," and it was, therefore, further split up into petty states, some of which had Hapsburg rulers. Italy in its disunity was helpless under Austrian control. Norway was arbitrarily given to Sweden, and again the principle of nationalism was violated when the Belgians were turned over to the Dutch. The Poles in Poland and Finns in Finland simply exchanged masters.

A large and militant group of the German people were particularly incensed and disappointed at the refusal or the inability of the Congress to work toward unifying Germany. It is true that no attempt was made to return to the chaos of the Holy Roman Empire with its hundreds of little states. But in the face of the demand of many German patriots who wished to see a strong, united Germany arise from the political anarchy of the past, a weak and loosely organized Germanic Confederation of thirty-eight states was established, with Austria at its head. This was largely Austria's doing, for she saw in a united Germany a threat against her dominance in central Europe. It was logical that the spirit of nationalism should move the German people in the direction of national unification under one central government. Inability to obtain this unity later challenged a masterful character, Bismarck, to obtain this objective by force and, in the process, to foster the militaristic tradition in Germany. But had national unity been achieved in 1815, German political liberalism might have developed in the direction of democracy instead of becoming overwhelmed by the "blood and iron" tactics of those who utilized war for nationalism's sake later in the nineteenth century.

Quadruple and Holy alliances. So much for the territorial changes made in 1815. The most difficult problem facing the Congress, however, was not the allocation of land but how to check the growth of revolutionary ideas. The prevailing fear of liberalism is illustrated by the following incident. A nobleman is reputed to have congratulated the Austrian emperor on having a "good physical constitution." The emperor retorted with some heat, "A good constitution? Let me never hear that word again. Say my robust health, my strong bodily system, or my good physical condition, but never say my constitution. I have no constitution; and I never will have one. I'd perish first. No one but the Devil has a constitution, or has need for any."[3] Metternich, "The Gibraltar of the old régime," was the champion of reaction at the Congress, and he had little difficulty in persuading his colleagues that every effort must be made to return to the status quo as it existed before the French Revolution. This not only meant restoring the old lines of kings but reëstablishing the supremacy of autocracy and benevolent despotism.

On November 20, 1815, as a result of Metternich's influence, the "Big Four," composed of Austria, Prussia, Russia, and England, signed the Quadruple Alliance. The object of this document was stated to be the maintenance of "tranquillity" in Europe, and for this purpose the members were to meet from time to time to agree on the proper measures to be taken. In 1818 France was admitted to the compact, making it a Quintuple Alliance. Great Britain early withdrew its support from the league. It was soon to become apparent after 1815 that the real purpose of the alliance was to crush relentlessly any growth of political liberalism.

Another famous document was also written at Vienna, the Holy Alliance. This was proposed by the visionary Alexander I of Russia and was signed by most of the powers attending the Congress. They agreed to a declaration that they would base their policies on those of that "holy religion, namely, the precepts of justice, Christian charity, and peace." No one was quite sure just what Alexander meant by this pact, and there was much joking by the diplomats at his expense. Castlereagh described the Holy Alliance as "a piece of sublime mysticism and nonsense." The opponents of reaction at this time confused the Holy Alliance with the Quadruple Alliance and regarded the former as the instrument which was responsible for the reaction and repression following the Congress. Actually, however, they were the consequence of Metternich's Quadruple Alliance.

Results of the Congress. The arrangements made at the Congress of Vienna shaped the course of political events in Europe during most of the nineteenth century, just as the provisions of the Treaty of Versailles influenced post-war developments in Europe after 1919. The Congress of Vienna placed Italy under the influence of Austria. This was to lead to a vigorous nationalistic movement in Italy, which finally triumphed in 1870. In 1815 the Hohenzollern House in Prussia was strengthened by the addition of valuable territory. More than ever Prussia resented Austria's dominance of central Europe. Armed conflict resulted and ultimately brought unification of Germany under Prussian auspices. Belgians, Norwegians, Poles, and Finns were not content to be placed under alien governments, and during the nineteenth century these people struggled for national liberty.

Above all, the diplomats at Vienna by their Quadruple Alliance created and set in motion machinery designed to stifle and discourage the development of democracy. This resulted in three important series of revolutions that engulfed Europe—in 1820-1821, 1830-1831, and 1848. Another manifestation of the revolt in Europe against the ideas of Metternich and his fellow statesmen occurred in Russia in 1905.

The Democratization of France

Monarchy restored in France. In 1815 constitutional monarchy was established in France in the person of Louis XVIII, who gave his subjects a constitution. Louis was a believer in strong monarchy, but he was shrewd enough to appreciate that after the Revolution the French people would accept no ruler who did not at least grant them a constitution. The constitution guaranteed many of the gains of the French Revolution. Religious freedom and the liberty of the press were now enjoyed by French citizens, serfdom was a thing of the past, and the privileges of the nobility were not restored.

The government of Great Britain was more liberal than the régime set up in France in 1815, but there was not one really democratic government in existence in Europe at this time. Louis XVIII's constitution made it possible for only one man in seventy to vote. This was not to the liking of the lower middle class, the intellectual groups, and the workers, who were determined to obtain a more liberal constitution. On the other hand, the established Church, the nobles, and the traditionally conservative peasant class were determined that the constitution should not be further liberalized. France was to go through many tribulations and several bloody revolutions before she was to realize a really democratic régime under the Third French Republic. While Louis XVIII reigned, he sincerely tried to be moderate and restrained the reactionary tendencies of the Ultras, the royalist party.

The revolutions of 1830. Following the death of Louis XVIII in 1824, the French throne was occupied by Charles X. Historians have little to say of this monarch except in denunciation. A man of mediocre mind, he was a staunch exponent of divine right, did not believe in religious freedom, and possessed a fanatical urge to rule France arbitrarily. In a word, Charles X was the reincarnation of the stubborn and reactionary aristocrat of the mid-eighteenth century. In July 1830 he issued a series of ordinances gagging the press and limiting the franchise.

Galled by this violation of the constitution, Paris arose in rebellion. The streets of Paris were choked with overturned carts, boxes, tables, and paving-stones. Behind these barricades crouched the armed revolutionaries, who returned the fire of the soldiers with good effect. From the roofs of the houses descended tile and rocks, thrown with enthusiasm upon the soldiery by the families of those who manned the barricades below. Again and again in nineteenth-century revolutions, such barricades succeeded in toppling despotism.

After three days the revolutionists took over the government, and Charles fled ignominiously to England. The "July days" were the signal for other revolutions all over Europe. They led to the Great Reform Bill in Great Britain, to a successful revolt in which the Belgians obtained freedom from Holland, and to several unsuccessful uprisings in Italy. In the German states several rulers were forced to

give their subjects constitutions. The year 1830 is an important landmark in European political development. It marks a definite weakening of the Metternich system. By this time Great Britain was no longer a member of the Quintuple Alliance, the Monroe Doctrine protected the Spanish colonies in the New World, the Bourbon king had been ejected from France, and the Belgians had achieved their national independence.

Nineteenth-century liberalism. With the revolutions of 1830 marking the first important break against the system of the Congress of Vienna, it is pertinent to examine what we have so far called the democratic movement. It is part of what is known as nineteenth-century liberalism, a movement that had received great impetus in the eighteenth century from such thinkers as Voltaire, Locke, and Rousseau. The crux of their philosophy was individual liberty, and the middle class in their drive against aristocratic privilege and monarchical despotism eagerly turned to this thought for intellectual ammunition. Nineteenth-century middle-class liberals held such beliefs as freedom of thought, the right of the individual to worship as he sees fit, *laissez faire*, or economic individualism, representative government, and, at times, the right of suppressed peoples to gain their national independence. This last cause was often supported because it resulted in new, favorable commercial arrangements with the liberated peoples. It also often happened that the bourgeois demand for political reform enlisted the support of intellectuals, artists, and writers.

The revolutions in nineteenth-century Europe are often described as democratic. It is more correct to point out that they were primarily a bourgeois movement. To be sure, in many instances of political reform, by force or through constitutional means, the middle class secured the support of the common people. The people believed that they too would soon share in the political gains. It soon became evident, however, that by representative government the middle class meant the government of the state by bourgeois representatives. By 1860 the middle class, in some countries, had obtained wide power in both economic and political spheres. But just as in the previous chapter we have seen the middle class being forced to make concessions in economics, it was also forced to relinquish much ground in politics. In championing the cause of political liberty for themselves the bourgeoisie soon found that they had initiated a movement that could not be stopped. After 1860 the right to vote was extended gradually to the workers. In fact the common people won a far more complete victory in politics than they secured in business, for by 1914 manhood suffrage was becoming quite usual in most industrialized states.

Liberalism of the nineteenth century is a term used to describe the political program of the middle class and is so used in this chapter. It should be pointed out, however, that liberalism is also often used in a general way to refer to the program of one who advocates a course of moderate reform in politics, economics, or any other form of human activity. This view is in contrast to that of the conservative, who defends the status quo. At the extremes stands the reactionary, who often demands a return to conditions that existed prior to the status quo, and the radical, who sees little or no good in existing or prior conditions and consequently champions sweeping and drastic changes.

Louis Philippe, citizen-king. The July Revolution gave France a new king, Louis Philippe (1830-1848), a ruler who prided himself on being the representative of the business interests of his country. The suffrage was extended, but it did not yet include the lower middle class or the common people. Louis made a point of parading in democratic simplicity as an ordinary businessman in the streets of Paris, "in a frock coat and top hat and carrying an umbrella, the symbols of the new régime, as wig, kneebreeches, and sword had been of the old."[4] It soon became apparent that the July monarchy had little concern with the lower classes. "Work, get rich, and then you can vote," was the government's advice. The new régime was the first bourgeois government to be set up in Europe. Discontent rapidly grew among the working classes. Louis Blanc, leader of the workers, demanded state factories in which all the workers could obtain employment and where they would be allowed to divide among themselves the fruits of their labors. Blanc maintained: "To the able-bodied citizen the state owes work; to the aged and infirm it owes aid and protection. This result cannot be obtained except through a democratic power."[5] Louis Philippe gave France a smug prosperity but little glory. "Business before national honor" seemed to be his policy in foreign affairs.

The people began to yearn for national glory and turned back to the immortal deeds of the great Napoleon. Here was the genesis of the Napoleonic legend, which was later to place another Bonaparte at the head of the French government. In the face of rising opposition, the king turned to a policy of coercion. Barricades again rose in the streets of Paris in February 1848. A republic was proclaimed, and Louis Philippe fled to England. The new republic was to have a brief and inglorious existence. Soon after its proclamation, strife broke out among the workers, who demanded that a national system of state workshops be established, as advocated by Louis Blanc. Fighting broke out in the French capital, which was put down after much loss of life. This left among the workers a bitter memory of hatred against the bourgeoisie and, among the bourgeois elements, a deep fear of radicalism.

Louis Napoleon and the Second empire. Taking advantage of the magic appeal of his name, Louis Napoleon, the nephew of Napoleon I, successfully campaigned for the presidency of the Second Republic. In his mind burned the imperial traditions of his great uncle, and in December 1851, while serving as president, Louis Napoleon showed his hand by forcibly dissolving the government. Anticipating the methods of modern dictators, he then carried out a plebiscite, which gave almost unanimous support to his action. Again, in 1852, Napoleon carried out a sweeping change in the government by proclaiming himself emperor of the French. The Second Republic was no more. The ideals of the French Revolution seemed farther away than ever.

The period of the Second French Empire, from 1852 to 1870, saw fateful developments in France. The emperor seemed destined to fulfill all the best projects that had been initiated by his illustrious relative. For eighteen years the "emperor-boss" gave France nearly everything a great nation could desire, except liberty. The government was made extremely complex to hide its despotism. Paris was becoming the artistic and intellectual capital of the world. The city was beautified, and the economic system improved. But all these benefits were nullified by Louis Napoleon's disastrous foreign policy. He was no match for the Prussian statesman, Bismarck. Defeat in the Franco-Prussian War swept away the government of Napoleon, and in 1870 a republic was again declared in Paris.

The Third Republic. The Third French Republic had the bitter task of making peace with Prussia. After this was accomplished, it became apparent that the members of the new national assembly were more monarchical than republican in their leanings. But a great personality emerged to save the republic, Léon Gambetta, a man of magnificent presence, an eloquent orator, and a devoted servant of republicanism. Largely owing to his efforts the monarchical threat was met successfully.

During this period of uncertainty a republican constitution was drawn up and adopted in 1875, providing for the election, by manhood suffrage, of representatives to the Chamber of Deputies, the influential lower house. The political rights of the people thus were recognized, and France had gone a long way from the bourgeois government of 1830.

By 1880 the Third French Republic appeared safe. Statesmen pushed forward the work of making the country's defenses strong, colonies were acquired, educational reform was carried out, and industries were developed. In the last two decades of the nineteenth century the republic was placed on the defensive by a series of scandals, the most serious of which was the Dreyfus case. A Jewish officer in the French army was wrongly accused of selling military secrets to a foreign power. The Dreyfus case not only raised the issue whether racial intolerance and rank injustice would be countenanced in France, but more significantly, "It was a bloodless civil war between friends and foes of the Republic of which Dreyfus happened to be the symbol and the victim."[6] This "detective story on a national scale" caused Emile Zola to write his famous *J'accuse,* which was the first advance made in the ultimate exoneration of Dreyfus.

It had been apparent during the Dreyfus scandal that the established Church was one of the most active supporters of the anti-Dreyfusards. The alliance between the Church and the army led to a strong anticlerical movement in France in the early years of the twentieth century. In particular, French liberals in the government were determined that in the educational system the influence of the Church should be eliminated. In 1901 a law was passed resulting in the closing of thousands of church schools, and in 1905 the drastic step was taken of separating Church and state. In the words of Aristide Briand, one of the main sponsors of the Separation Law, "The State must remain neutral in respect to all religions. It is not anti-religious, for it has not the right to be so; it is merely non-religious."[7]

Democracy established in France. By 1900 France had attained a stable, prosperous, and respected republic, but only after a century of wars and revolutions. By the end of the nineteenth century, the old régime of 1789, with its denial of liberty, self-government, and equality, was entirely dead. The Third French Republic was now the most important democracy in continental Europe. All Frenchmen possessed suffrage without educational tests or taxpaying requirements. The Republic had vanquished its enemies, especially the royalists, established a public-school system, and restored the country's strength after the debacle of 1870-1871.

Political Liberalism in England

Democracy in Great Britain. In the first decades of the nineteenth century Great Britain lagged in governmental reform. This was attributable in part to the bloody excesses of the French Revolution, which shocked and antagonized men in England. Edmund Burke published in 1790 his *Reflections on the French Revolution,* which was equally critical of despotic and of democratic government and championed the rule of benevolent aristocracy based on constitutional government.

For nearly fifty years the specter of the French guillotine hindered the progress of democracy in Great Britain. But in 1832 the process of political reform recommenced, and a trend was begun which was to make Great Britain, by 1900, the most democratic great power in western Europe. The achievement of political democracy in England stands in sharp contrast to the same process in France. In the latter, there were wars and revolutions; in the former, the keynote was evolution, political gradualism, not revolution. Great Britain has had an instinct for keeping intact her old political framework and adapting it to new uses with changing conditions. This explains why Great Britain has been able to keep her ancient monarchy and yet fit it into the structure of a modern political democracy.

Tory repression. Reaction was in full swing in England immediately after 1815. The Tory party, controlling the government, followed the doctrine of "peace, law, order, and discipline." Unemployment and starvation were the cause of much social unrest and riots. These were crushed with force by the ruling class, with little sympathy for the misery prevalent in the country. In 1816 a mass meeting in London, which passed a resolution calling attention to the intolerable economic condition of the people, was forcibly dispersed. There was also a serious epidemic of strikes in the industrial areas, and in 1819 a large meeting demanding universal suffrage held in St. Peter's Fields in the city of Manchester was dispersed by a cavalry charge, with the loss of several lives. The ruling class, terrified by what they believed to be the imminence of revolution, enacted repressive acts which restricted public meetings, sought to stamp out liberal newspapers, and imposed heavy fines on "seditious literature." This was in addition to the suspension of the Habeas Corpus Act in 1817.

The July Revolution of 1830 in France contributed the impetus necessary for political reform in Great Britain. By this time not only was the working class thoroughly incensed against the system of privilege which ruled it, but the businessmen were determined to break the monopoly of the aristocracy in government. In this year the Duke of Wellington, now prime minister, made a fateful speech in which he declared that the constitution of the country was quite satisfactory for all its needs. This so aroused public opposition that the Iron Duke was forced to resign, and Charles Grey, the leader of the Whig party, now became head of the government. This ended sixty years of almost continual Tory rule, which had been based upon the maintenance of the status quo.

The new government under Grey immediately set about reforming the government. There was a crying need for such action. The House of Lords was dominated by the great nobles, while the House of Commons was almost completely under the control of the landed gentry. Representation in the House of Commons had virtually no relation to the population. It has been estimated that three per cent of the population dictated the election of the members. Of its 571 members, 82 were elected by the counties controlled by the landed aristocracy, and the remaining 489 members came from incorporated towns, called boroughs. As we have noted in a previous chapter, pocket, or nomination, boroughs were under the control of "borough mongers," political bosses who dictated the election of representatives. In the rotten boroughs members of Parliament were often elected to represent areas which no longer contained any inhabitants. On the other hand, new and rapidly growing industrial towns, such as Manchester with 140,000 inhabitants and Birmingham with 100,000, had no representatives.

Reform Bill of 1832. Supported by the rising middle classes, who were determined to break the aristocracy's political monopoly, and also by the workers, Grey's government introduced a bill to abolish the rotten boroughs and give representation to the new industrial towns. Defeated in the Commons at the outset, it was again introduced and passed, only to be defeated in the House of Lords. Revolution now seemed imminent. After the Reform Bill had been introduced a third time but drastically changed by the upper house, the king finally threatened to create enough new peers to pass the measure in the House or Lords. These new peers would become members of the House of Lords, selected by the king on the advice of the prime minister. Thus they could vote for the passage of the Reform Bill in the upper house. Confronted by this threat, the upper house passed the measure on July 7, 1832. The measure as enacted did not represent a radical political change. In essence, it transferred the balance of power from the landed gentry to the upper middle classes, the well-to-do businessmen of England.

The working classes were keenly disappointed at their failure to obtain the franchise. This discontent was soon to be reflected in the Chartist Movement. The important fact of the Great Reform Bill is that, while in its immediate effects it did not represent a substantial widening of the franchise (only one male in thirty was given the right to vote), it did constitute an initial step in breaching the wall of political privilege. It foreshadowed future political reforms such as the second Reform Bill in 1867 and the third in 1884. The Reform Bill of 1832 did not introduce democracy into England, but it did make democracy ultimately possible.

Additional reforms. Immediately following the first Reform Bill, several other notable reforms were enacted. Slavery was abolished in the British Empire in 1833. The first important Factory Act was passed in the same year, and in 1834 improvements were made in poor-law administration. The Municipal Corporations Bill was enacted in 1835. Up to this time the towns had been frequently governed by small exclusive bodies that often filled their pockets with the taxes. The new act gave all towns a uniform system of town government. Municipal government was democratized by substituting popularly elected bodies for the heretofore exclusive municipal corporations.

The Chartist Movement. For a decade following the enactment of the Reform Bill of 1832, Parliament pressed the progress of reform; then it rested on its laurels. The middle class was now in possession of the vote, slavery had been abolished, and new factory acts and laws dealing with the relief of the poor did much for the common people. England was a different, and certainly a more liberal, land in 1840 than it had been in 1815.

The Industrial Revolution which was making England the workshop of the world was also bringing prosperity to the country. Even the working people shared somewhat in this economic advance. Concern with domestic reform was superseded by interest in foreign affairs. This was primarily the work of "Old Pam" (Lord Palmerston), a dashing and colorful statesman, who prepared to substitute glory and excitement for political and economic reform.

In the midst of the preoccupation with foreign affairs, however, there was an important indication that discontent still smouldered among the lower classes. This was the radical Chartist Movement, which received wide support from the workers. In 1838 it published its People's Charter, containing six demands: universal suffrage, secret voting, no property qualifications for members of Parliament, payment of members so that poor men could seek election if they wished, annual elections for Parliament, and equal electoral districts. In 1839 they presented their petition, with over a million signatures, to the House of Commons. Again in 1842, a procession two miles long marched through the streets of London and presented a similar petition. The third and last petition was prepared and passed on to the government in 1848. After this date the movement rapidly declined. During its lifetime it had apparently accomplished little, for the government ignored its demands, but the next hundred years were to see all but one of the Chartist planks, annual elections to Parliament, become part of the law of the land.

The Victorian Compromise. By 1865 Great Britain had reached the end of an era having its origin in the Reform Bill of 1832. This period is often described as the Victorian Compromise, which meant that the aristocrats and the middle class agreed to bury the hatchet in order to keep the lower classes in their stations. The years between 1832 and 1865 saw middle-class political liberalism at its height in England. With the landed gentry, the bourgeoisie

The Sphinx and Disraeli exchange winks as the premier acquires controlling shares in the Suez Canal project. Queen Victoria was overjoyed at this bold move. It is said this was the first time Disraeli saw her smile.

dominated the government. Some political and social reforms were granted, but these were exceptions in the general atmosphere of middle-class complacency.

Gladstone and Disraeli. The death of Palmerston in 1865 and the entry of two new political leaders into the limelight of government heralded the beginning of a new era in British affairs. For a generation English politics is little more than the biographies of William Ewart Gladstone (1809-1898) and Benjamin Disraeli (1804-1881).

The son of a rich Liverpool merchant, Gladstone had every advantage that wealth and good social position could bestow. As a student at Eton College and later at Trinity College, Oxford, it was his first ambition to enter the English Church and combine this clerical career with scholarly pursuits. But Gladstone became interested in politics, entering Parliament in 1833 at the age of twenty-four. In short order the young politician made a name for himself as one of the greatest orators of his day, on one occasion holding the attention of the house for five hours while he expounded the intricacies of the national budget. At first Gladstone was a conservative in politics, a follower of the Tory leader Robert Peel. But gradually he shifted his allegiance to the Liberal Party, which he headed for the first time as prime minister in 1868. Gladstone was a staunch believer in *laissez faire*, the belief that government should not interfere in business. His record as a reformer in social and economic fields, therefore, was not imposing. But in political reforms his accomplishments were noteworthy.

The great rival of Gladstone, Benjamin Disraeli, had few advantages of birth and social position. The son of a cultured Jew who had become a naturalized British subject in 1801, Disraeli belonged to a race whom many despised, and he was consequently barred from the best social circles. The young Jew first made a name for himself as a novelist when his *Vivian Grey* appeared in 1826. Unlike Gladstone, Disraeli began his political career as a radical and ended it as a conservative. All his life somewhat a fop and dandy, Disraeli created a furor when he first appeared in the staid House of Commons attired in a yellow vest and green trousers. His language was grandiloquent and florid, and his first speech was received with derision and laughter. This setback did not dim Disraeli's confidence in his own powers, and he steadily forged ahead to become the leader of the Conservative Party. Disraeli was responsible for rekindling the flame of imperialism in the hearts of Englishmen. Interest in colonies had lagged following the loss of the American colonies in 1783, and this apathy continued well past the middle of the nineteenth century.

Disraeli's political reforms did not equal Gladstone's, but in social reform he outshone his rival. Disraeli was not a defender of middle-class interests. In fact, his whole political philosophy was based on the theory that the landed gentry in the Conservative Party should make an alliance with the workers against the businessmen, "the government by the classes in the interest of the masses." This was called by Disraeli "Tory Democracy." Acting on his desire to woo the support of the people, the Conservative Party passed a number of important reforms between 1874 and 1880, including the improvement of public health, the liberalizing of restrictions against labor unions, and the inauguration of housing schemes. Disraeli is generally remembered for his imperialistic exploits, but perhaps his best claim to the regard of the English is that he pointed the way toward the enactment of a comprehensive scheme of social legislation.

Disraeli introduced a new reform measure which was enacted in 1867. This second Reform Bill added a little more than a million voters to the electoral rolls. Its result was to enfranchise the artisans and workers in the cities, although the agricultural laborers were still excluded from the franchise. This reform aroused much criticism. Thomas Carlyle, the famous historian, called it "Shooting Niagara," and one statesman described it as "a leap in the dark." Despite these criticisms the progress of reform continued.

Gladstone's political reforms. One of the most famous periods in English reform was the first ministry of Gladstone (1868-1874). Prime minister for the first time, he eagerly pressed forward a number of reforms. The Forster Education Act of 1870 had a close connection with the development of English democracy, for this measure was the first step taken in the direction of establishing an adequate system of public education. The enfranchisement of the city workers in 1867 had made such a step imperative. In 1870 Gladstone took action which introduced competitive examinations for government positions. This was the beginning of the English civil service.

Before the enfranchisement of the urban workers, it had not been so essential to have secret balloting, for only the rich could vote, and a rich man had few superiors who could intimidate him. But open balloting exposed the workers to all sorts of pressure from their employers, landlords, and others. The Ballot Act of 1872, therefore, was just as important for the functioning of democracy in England as was the Education Act of 1870.

In 1884 Gladstone was responsible for a further extension of democracy in Britain. In this year the third Reform Bill was passed, a measure which brought England to the verge of universal manhood suffrage. By this act the franchise was extended to the agricultural workers.

Four years after the third Reform Bill, the passing of the County Councils Act (1888) democratized the system of local county government in Great Britain. Since the days of the Tudors, government in the local districts had been under the dominance of the landed gentry as justices of the peace. The new act created elective boards which assumed most of the administrative duties heretofore performed by the landed gentry.

Recession of Lords' power. The latter part of the nineteenth century and the first decades of the twentieth saw the fulfillment of political democracy in Great Britain. For some time there had been grumbling and criticism against the House of Lords. The House of Commons was responsible to the people, but its will could be thwarted by the irresponsible upper house, whose members sat in the august body only because of accident of birth. On several occasions the legislative program of the Liberals was obstructed by the Lords. The climax was reached in 1909, when the upper house refused to pass the budget prepared by the chancellor of the exchequer, David Lloyd George. Although the budget was finally passed by the Lords, the House of Commons, dominated by Liberals and Laborites, decided that an irresponsible upper house was an anachronism in a democracy.

The result was the Parliament Bill of 1911. Before this was passed, it was necessary for Asquith, the prime minister, to announce, as had been done in 1832, that the king had promised if necessary to create enough peers to pass the bill in the House of Lords. The bill took away from the Lords all power of absolute veto. They could not veto any money bill, and any other measure passing the Commons in three successive sessions would become law without the assent of the Lords, provided that two years had elapsed since its first introduction.

After 1911 the will of the people as expressed in the Commons could no longer be blocked by the House of Lords. The Lords were left with power only to slow up and force reconsideration of legislation of which they did not approve. When Parliament had consisted of two houses, both possessed of important powers, the English legislature was bicameral, but now it was, in large measure, a one-house, or unicameral, national legislature.

England in 1914. Political liberalism in the hands of the middle class had since 1832 thoroughly overhauled the English system of government. By 1914 the House of Commons, responsible to the people, was the dominant legislative body. The provision for payment of salaries to members of the House of Commons now enabled poor men to enter national politics. Free and compulsory education in the elementary grades and greater opportunities for secondary and university education were measures that strengthened political democracy.

In addition to political reform, middle-class liberalism by the end of the nineteenth century came to recognize that political reforms were not enough, that social and economic changes must also be made, as we have seen in the previous chapter. This departure from *laissez faire,* first begun in Germany and then adopted by numerous other nations, is one of the most important happenings in modern times. If the nineteenth century had been primarily the era of political reform, it seemed in 1900 that the next century would be mainly concerned with the advance of social legislation, sometimes referred to as economic democracy.

England by 1914 was to all intents a political democracy. But there still remained a few vestiges of privilege. The right to vote was still a middle-class conception based on the ownership or occupation of property. Domestic servants, bachelors living with their parents and paying no rent, and all others with no fixed abode could not vote. English women were becoming restive at being denied the franchise. Just before the First World War the suffragette movement demanding "Votes for Women" carried on an extensive campaign. In the social realm England still perpetuated a class system in which the nobility and the landed gentry, and to some extent the middle class, held themselves aloof from the people in general.

Parliamentary and presidential democracies. There were certain basic differences between the systems of democratic government evolved in Great Britain and France in the nineteenth and twentieth centuries and that existing in the United States. In England and France the cabinet with its leader, the prime minister, represents the executive branch, which is dependent for its tenure upon the support of the legislature. This is called responsible government. At any time public opinion, as reflected in the legislature by a vote of "no confidence" or by the defeat of a major bill, can force the resignation of the cabinet. The executive is simply a committee of the legislature.

In a presidential government, however, such as we have in the United States, power is divided among the various departments of government. The tenure of the executive, the president, is for a stipulated term and it is not dependent upon the support of the legislature.

Germany and Russia Reject Democracy

German democratic backwardness. If Great Britain and France, among the great powers of Europe, represent the nearest approach to political democracy in the nineteenth century, the German and the Russian empires constitute, among the first-class European states, democracy's greatest failure. During the late Middle Ages, England and France had become united national states, and by 1800 both had gone far in directions which ultimately matured into democratic government. Germany had made little progress in either nationalism or political liberalism. Under the Holy Roman Empire, the Germanies had been a hodgepodge of states in which few traces of constitutionalism existed. It took the shock of the Napoleonic wars to arouse the Germans from their lethargy.

This is seen especially in Prussia, where the great patriot-statesman Baron vom und zum Stein abolished serfdom in 1807 and in the year following instituted a system of local self-government. Stein's ultimate object, never achieved in Germany, was to establish a constitutional limited monarchy on the English model. This "regeneration" of Prussia had much to do with Napoleon's final defeat.

The Germans were political enemies of the French, but liberals eagerly assimilated French revolutionary ideas. In 1815 the states in the Germanic Confederation, successor to the Holy Roman Empire, had parliaments dominated by the aristocracy, and only a few had written constitutions. After 1815 a remarkable liberal movement developed, deriving much of its strength from young university students and their professors. The students organized societies demanding a free and a united fatherland. In 1817 a great celebration was held by the liberals. Thoroughly alarmed, Prince Metternich convened a conference in 1819 which with repressive decrees stifled liberalism for thirty years.

Failure of revolution. In 1830 the outbreak of revolution in France caused similar revolts in the Germanies (see map, page 159), and several small states obtained constitutions. The revolutionary outbreaks of 1848 had more significant consequences. Riots occurred in Berlin, several citizens were killed, and the Prussian king was forced to pay his respects to these martyrs in public and to promise a constitution. The promising liberal movement in Prussia and in other German states failed, however. In Prussia this was largely because the army proved loyal to the king and to the aristocracy. Thousands of liberals fled the country, many of whom became citizens of the United States. In 1850 the Prussian king granted a constitution, but it did little to reduce his powers.

Germany after 1871. As we shall see later, the Germanies were transformed into the German empire in 1871. The attainment of this national unification did little to advance the cause of democracy. It is true that universal manhood suffrage was introduced for elections to the Reichstag, the imperial lower house, but this legislative body had little power in comparison with that of the *Bundesrat,* the upper house, whose members were personal nominees of the rulers of the various states in the empire. Superficially, the chancellor in the imperial government was analogous to the British prime minister, but, as the principle of ministerial responsibility was not accepted, the chancellor could defy the wishes of the Reichstag.

In the German federal union of twenty-five states, Prussia exerted the preponderant power. This explains why political absolutism could exist in a parliamentary government. The chancellor took his orders only from the Prussian king, and any constitutional amendment could be blocked by the large Prussian delegation in the federal legislature. The Prussian king not only controlled the imperial government, but he also was all-powerful within Prussia itself. The old constitution granted to the Prussian people in 1850 was in force when war broke out in 1914. Under it, representatives to the Prussian *Landtag*—legislative body

—were elected by an illiberal franchise system. One third of the members of the *Landtag* were chosen by a few wealthy individuals who paid one third of the taxes. Another third were selected by a slightly larger group of economically powerful men who paid another one third of the state's taxes. The peasants and working people were given the right to elect the final one third of the representatives.

Reasons for despotism. Many Germans keenly resented the undemocratic features of their constitution. There were several reasons why despotism existed in such a prosperous and advanced country. The influence of the army was important. The country had a militaristic tradition. It had achieved its unity by "blood and iron." Any liberal movement would, if necessary, be crushed relentlessly by the armed forces who were passionately loyal to the Hohenzollern dynasty.

What we may term the German tradition also played its part. Benevolent despotism took strong hold on Prussia in the early days of its national life, especially in the reign of Frederick the Great. The people were taught to serve the state unquestioningly, to look to their leaders for guidance. As the Germans expressed it, "*Alles kommt von oben*" (Everything comes down from above). This negation of political individualism and the doctrine of the supremacy of the state were also strengthened by the teachings of such philosophers as Hegel and the historian Treitschke.

The people also gave their government unquestioning loyalty because it was efficient and solicitous of their material welfare. Bismarck introduced a comprehensive system of unemployment insurance and health and accident insurance in order to keep them contented. About the rejection of democracy in the German empire Charles Hazen has written:

"The German state was the most autocratic in western Europe; it was also the most militaristic. Fundamental individual liberties, regarded as absolutely vital in England, France, America, and many other states, had never been possessed by Germans, nor were they possessed in 1914. Germany was rich, vigorous, powerful, instructed. It was not free."[8]

This description applies even more forcefully to the German Nazi régime which came into power in 1933.

In summary, Germany at the end of the nineteenth century was a benevolent despotism in which efficiency and a paternal solicitude were the order of the day. The workers were given employment or in its absence unemployment benefits, but physical welfare was enjoyed at the expense of political liberty.

Russia's static condition. Among the great powers of Europe, Russia was politically the most backward in the nineteenth century. Russia until modern times had not been much influenced by those great movements, the Renaissance, the French Revolution, and the Industrial Revolution, which had done so much to sweep away obsolete institutions and ideas in western Europe. Russia until almost the twentieth century remained isolated and aloof, sealed in "granite conservatism."

In the first decades of the nineteenth century the Russian czar, Alexander I, dabbled somewhat in the new ideas of his time and cautiously flirted with political liberalism. But the growth of revolutionary trends in his empire caused him to become a convinced reactionary and a firm ally of Prince Metternich.

In 1825, Nicholas I became czar of all the Russias. The new ruler was an unimaginative militarist who administered his empire with unbelievable cruelty, according to a program of "discipline, order, and the maintenance of the status quo." In his reign Russia became a "frozen country," sealed from all contacts with the outside world. No foreign books containing liberal ideas were permitted to come into the country, suspicious travelers were debarred from entrance, spies were everywhere, and even musical compositions were censored. The weakness of this despotic and reactionary régime was manifested in the Crimean War (1854-1856), when Russia suffered a severe defeat at the hands of France and Great Britain.

Alexander II, who came to the throne in 1855, was determined to be a liberal ruler. His reign saw three important reform measures introduced. Serfdom was abolished in 1861. There was a radical remodeling of the judicial system, which heretofore had dispensed justice in an arbitrary fashion. Finally, the people were given a measure of local government. This was provided for by the creation of *zemstvos*, local assemblies having control over such matters as roads, bridges, prisons, and poor relief. But these reform measures did not prevent the growth of revolutionary ideas, and

Alexander II, quite alarmed, swung toward reaction. In 1863 he repressed the Polish revolt with great cruelty. Plots now were made against his life and against high Russian officials by Russian radicals, and in 1881 Alexander fell a victim to assassination.

Nihilism. Alexander III, feeling his father had been too liberal, followed the system of Nicholas I and devoted his efforts to preserving autocracy. Reaction and repression again became the order of the day. The growth of radicalism, however, continued. Its most fertile soil was among the young educated Russians, many of whom were known as nihilists from Latin *nihil,* meaning "nothing." The new movement believed most Russian institutions were outworn and that nothing of the old order should be retained. The novelist Turgenev defined a nihilist as "a man who does not bow before any authority whatsoever, does not accept a single principle on faith, with whatever respect that principle be endowed."[9] After attempting to obtain political reforms by peaceful means, the nihilists were forced to assume terroristic methods. In "underground Russia" they carried on their propaganda, fought with the dreaded secret police of the czar, and planned assassinations of members of the Russian bureaucracy.

The climax of this radical movement came during the reign of Nicholas II, who ascended the throne in 1894. In 1904 Russia became involved in a costly war with Japan. This conflict bared the graft and incompetency of the czar's régime. Unrest and discontent spread throughout the country. In January 1905, a peaceful delegation of peasants and workers, who had gone to the czar's palace to present a petition requesting political and economic reforms, was fired upon, and many were killed.

A general strike immediately followed, and the country was paralyzed. This amazing demonstration of proletarian opinion forced the czar to issue his October Manifesto, promising constitutional government and civil rights. A *Duma,* or legislative body, was thereupon set up, but the czar broke his promises and refused to abide by the *Duma's* deliberations. In desperation a group of the legislators convened in Finland and appealed for the support of the country. The people did not respond to this appeal, and the liberal movement collapsed.

The triumph of repression. Supporting the czar were the army and the governing classes. The people were ignorant and illiterate. The peasants generally gave filial devotion to the czar, whom they called "Little Father," and the secret police ruthlessly stamped out liberal views. The first attempt to establish a constitutional government in Russia failed. The czar should have learned a lesson from the spontaneous uprising of his subjects in 1905. But repression was again introduced after the liberal movement's failure, and the stage was set for a second but much more violent uprising that would later destroy every vestige of czarism in Russia.

Middle-class weakness. In Russia, because of the slow progress of industrialization, there was no opportunity for the middle class to become powerful enough to dominate the government. While businessmen spoke for the state in countries like Great Britain and France, the landed aristocracy had little trouble in running Russian affairs for the czar. This absence of a strong middle class was one of the most important of Russian characteristics in 1914 and throws much light on the events that took place after the First World War.

Democratic Struggles in Other European Areas

Contributions of small states. The small states of Europe, often overshadowed by their larger neighbors, nevertheless have made many contributions to civilization and illustrate the maxim that a country does not need to be large to be truly great. During the nineteenth century (before the advent of totalitarian warfare) the small nations of Europe served as buffer states between the great powers. Wedged between the great powers, these little states prevented dynamic and often jealous states from having contiguous boundaries. In the nineteenth century, when international law was supposed to have some validity, the recognition of the neutrality of such a country as Switzerland meant that great powers bordering on this "neutralized area" could assume that no attack would come from this quarter.

These second- and third-rate political powers also made many intellectual contributions—in art, literature, and music. One has only to think of Maeterlinck (Belgium), Ibsen (Norway), Grieg (Norway), and Hans Christian Andersen (Denmark). The Scandinavian countries in particular in the latter part of the nineteenth century began that interesting development which was to make them sociological laboratories, where "few should have more than they need, and fewer still should have less than they need." Certain of the small European countries have also made their mark on democratic institutions. The enfranchisement of women was first introduced in Norway, proportional representation had its first trial in Belgium, and Switzerland invented the use of the referendum and the initiative.

Holland. In the nineteenth century, democracy made important gains in most of the countries of Europe, and where its progress was retarded, there were signs that political liberalism would soon be in the ascendancy. In Holland, for example, the people were first granted a constitution during the revolutionary period of 1848. This was not a democratic document. The king still wielded large powers, and the franchise was restricted. The main constitutional theme in Holland from this time until the outbreak of the European conflict in 1914 was the demand for a more liberal franchise. Some concessions were won in 1887 and again in 1896, but Holland was not a complete democracy even in 1914. Forty per cent of her adult males still were without the vote, as were all women. Although the Dutch constitutional system gave the people an efficient and reasonably liberal régime, of all the west-European nations in 1914 Holland had the least democratic franchise.

Belgium. Holland's next-door neighbor, Belgium, adopted, in 1831, the most liberal constitution then in existence in Europe. English principles of responsible government were adhered to, but the franchise was based on high property qualifications. The government was in essence that of the well-to-do. Belgium is, for its size, the most highly industrialized country in the world. Karl Marx once referred to it as "the paradise of the capitalists." Social legislation lagged behind England's, and a discontented proletariat formed a Socialist Party determined to democratize the franchise. General strikes were frequently resorted to. These had some effect, for in 1893 the vote was given to all men over twenty-five. The use of plural voting, which gave some individuals more than one vote, however, robbed the people of the fruits of their victory. In 1899 a concession in the direction of a government by the people was granted in the form of proportional representation. But down to the First World War, the retention of a privileged franchise marred Belgium's claim to a truly democratic government.

Switzerland. Switzerland in the nineteenth century developed a democratic government without a peer in the world. The Swiss in 1844 introduced the democratic instrument known as the referendum, which allows a bill passed by the legislature to be given to the voters for their approval. In 1845 the Swiss introduced the initiative. This is the practice of giving the voters the right to propose laws and present them to the lawmaking body for enactment. The initiative and referendum have been copied by other governments in many parts of the world. In certain of the local units, or cantons, where no legislatures existed, pure democracy was followed. All the citizens attended meetings to transact business and make laws. This procedure is similar to our New England town meeting.

No better statement of Swiss democracy can be given than the following words of Lord Bryce:

"Among the modern democracies which are true democracies, Switzerland has the highest claim to be studied. . . . It contains a greater variety of institutions based on democratic principles than any other country. . . . The most interesting lesson Switzerland teaches is how traditions and institutions, taken together, may develop in the average man, to an extent never reached before, the qualities which make a good citizen—shrewdness, moderation, common sense and a sense of duty to the community."[10]

Italy, Spain, Portugal. Brief reference must be made to the Latin trio of Italy, Spain, and Portugal. Democracy made certain gains in these lands, but its record in the nineteenth century was far from promising. After Italian unification in 1871, the country's government was modeled on the liberal constitution granted by Charles Albert, the king of Sardinia, to his subjects in 1848. It established a representative monarchical government.

Italian parliamentary government, however, worked under great difficulties. The people lacked experience in constitutional government and did not understand the workings of the political-party system. Further, there was missing a well-informed and vigorous electorate which could keep close watch on political leaders. In 1861 seventy-five per cent of the population was illiterate, and in addition the franchise was very restricted. As late as 1904 only twenty-nine per cent of the adult male population could vote, and of these only thirty-eight per cent actually went to the polls. The consequence was that too many men rose to political power whose only thought was self-gain. One Italian prime minister named Depretis became notorious for the utilization of a device known as *Transformismo*, that is, the bribing of the opposition leaders in order to eliminate all parliamentary opposition. J. E. Gillespie has summarized the situation thus:

"Italian political life was characterized by regionalist tendencies, lack of experienced leaders, and factiousness of officials. Party discipline was lacking; parties centered mainly around individuals; platforms were vague. Coalitions were extremely unstable, and statesmen were noted more for their ability to manipulate parliament adroitly than for the legislation they sponsored. Deputies spent most of their time currying favor with their constituents by intriguing for government positions and state pensions."[11]

Early in the twentieth century, however, there were manifestations of discontent among the people against this sort of political system. From 1900 to 1914 there was a definite movement toward democratic reform. This liberal trend was strengthened by a rising socialist movement. Liberals joined socialists in demanding such reforms as universal suffrage, payment of members of parliament, compulsory education, freedom of the press, and social legislation which would ensure better working conditions for the masses. As a result of this emerging liberalism, laws were passed in 1912 providing for universal suffrage and for payment of deputies in parliament.

Spain was the scene of many civil wars and revolutions during the greater part of the nineteenth century. The country had a monarchy which, after 1876, was supposedly a responsible government. The franchise until 1890 was a narrow one based on high property qualifications. Spain had a constitution, parliamentary government, and the franchise—at least for the upper classes. But these adjuncts of democracy functioned even worse than those in Italy. In Spain, rotativism was carried to the extreme; that is, by a secret understanding, the politicians of the opposing political parties agreed as to how each party was to alternate in power. Elections were held, of course, to fool the people. A vicious land system, an intrenched and powerful Church, and a weak monarchy also contributed to the failure of democracy in Spain.

Portugal's history, as far as governmental affairs go, has been a close imitation of Spain's unenviable record. Revolution, graft, and political anarchy were prevalent during most of the nineteenth century. Unlike Italy and Spain, which retained their monarchies, the Portuguese monarchy was overthrown in 1910, and the government became a republic. This change, however, did little to improve conditions. The people showed little capacity for good government.

Scandinavian countries. The Scandinavian states have a much better record than the Latin trio. In these far-northern monarchies, the franchise was broadened and the principle of responsible government developed. In Denmark the king claimed the right to control the ministry, but in 1901 he finally agreed to the principle that his ministers must be chosen in accordance with the will of the legislature.

Norway came to be called the most democratic monarchy in the world. The suffrage was given to women taxpayers in 1907, and in 1913 it was granted to all women. Manhood suffrage was introduced before Norway's separation from Sweden in 1905. It will be remembered that the Congress of Vienna had united Norway with Sweden, an arrangement irksome to the Norwegians, who were much more democratic than the Swedes.

In Sweden democratic development lagged behind that in Norway and Denmark. In 1909 manhood suffrage was granted, but until 1914 the cabinet was not responsible to the popularly elected lower house, and the king exercised considerable power, including an absolute veto.

Workers in politics. Thus far a general survey has been presented of the advance of political liberalism in various European countries. This advance was first noted in political gains secured by the middle class, later in advantages obtained by the workers. Having secured the right to vote, the workers, to ensure the effective organization of their political power, proceeded to form socialist parties which hoped to compel the bourgeois state to enact reforms for the working classes.

In 1863 Ferdinand Lassalle organized the General Workingmen's Association in Germany. By merging with a Marxist labor organization, it became the Social Democratic Party in 1875. The German workers in 1871 had only two representatives in the German Reichstag, but in 1912 the Social Democrats polled 4,250,000 votes and secured 110 seats in the lower house. The workers now had the largest single political party in Germany, developed in the face of Bismarck's determination to crush what he chose to call the "red peril."

In France the United Socialist Party was set up in 1905 out of smaller socialistic groups, and by 1914 this party controlled 1,500,000 votes and 102 seats in the Chamber of Deputies. Other countries also had their socialist parties: Russia organized such a party in 1903, Belgium as early as 1885, Austria in the 1880's, and Italy in 1891. England saw the Labor Party emerge in 1900. The Labor Party became so strong that the Liberal Party was dependent upon Labor support to stay in office.

By the end of the first decade of the twentieth century, it appeared that middle-class political liberalism was passing into a new phase in which manhood suffrage and the objectives of moderate socialism were merging into a working-class instrument. Many leaders of the workers believed that the next few decades would see the laboring classes, especially in Germany, Great Britain, and France, in a position to dominate the governments and thus by constitutional means secure many socialist measures. In 1914, however, in the face of imminent war, the workers in Great Britain, France, and Germany forgot their common class ties with each other, shelved their socialism, and prepared for the fray.

The Stirring of Nationalism (1815-1848)

The nationalistic movement. If democracy was a potent force behind the history of the nineteenth century, nationalism was equally important. It was not until the French Revolution, when the entire people arose *en masse* to fight a common invader, that modern nationalism was born. Before this time, patriotism—a term almost synonymous with nationalism—was primarily the possession of the upper classes. The great mass of people permitted their country's wars to be fought by professional soldiers and took little interest in the foreign affairs of their rulers. The French Revolution changed all this. The people now felt that they had a stake in the struggle against the invaders, who wished to nullify the gains of the Revolution. The French Revolution made important for the first time in the history of nations a national flag, a national anthem, and national holidays.

Nationalism, being a state of mind, a feeling, or an emotion, is somewhat difficult to define, but it may be described as a feeling on the part of a group of people that they are held together by certain ties, such as a common language, history, and cultural traditions, which mark them off from other national groups. Nationalism is also based on the belief that the national group to which one belongs is superior in its endowments and virtues to any other group. Nationalism implies, furthermore, a willingness on the part of an individual to "live and die for his country," to accept no loyalty higher than his devotion to the state. It also is frequently based on the notion that a nation can do no wrong, that self-interest is the only test for its behavior.

In 1815 the Congress of Vienna almost totally ignored the nationalistic sentiments of many of the European peoples. The Germans wanted a strong and united fatherland, and the Belgians desired their national independence, as did the Poles, Danes, Finns, and other subject peoples. In Italy many patriots resented the facts that the northern provinces of Lombardy and Venetia were under Austrian rule and that throughout the peninsula Austrian rulers sat on Italian thrones.

As we trace the development of European nationalism, it will become apparent that this movement assumed two forms. The first involved the unification of separate states, inhabited by people of the same nationality, into one large national state. The classic examples of this form of the nationalistic movement are the unification of Germany and of Italy. The second form of nationalism was the striving for independence against alien rule of such submerged nationalities as the Greeks, Irish, Norwegians, Serbs, Poles, and Czechs.

Greek independence. One of the first important nationalistic movements originated in Greece, which together with all the Balkan peninsula was under Turkish rule. During the French Revolution many Greeks had become imbued with nationalism and longed to see their land once more free and independent. In 1814 a secret organization resolutely made preparations for the revolution, which occurred in 1821. The fighting was hard and bitter. Large numbers of Greeks were massacred by their Turkish overlords.

The struggle went on for six dreary years. If Metternich had had his way, nothing would have been done for the Greeks. But European public opinion demanded intervention. The wonderful heritage of ancient Hellas counted for something, and intellectuals everywhere asked that Greece be freed. Many volunteers came to assist the Greeks. The most famous, Lord Byron, gave his life for the cause. Even in America, remote from European affairs, Henry Clay urged support for the Greeks. Acting on this widespread sympathy, the European powers intervened, and a Turkish fleet was annihilated by an allied naval squadron. In 1829 the sultan granted independence to Greece and a measure of self-government to certain areas in the Balkan peninsula.* European governments were also motivated by selfish reasons to intervene. The Russian czar wished to extend his control over the Balkans; the French king, Charles x, wanted military glory, and Great Britain, suspecting Russian designs, was unwilling to see her intervene alone in the Greek crisis.

In the development of Greek nationalism, a literary revival exerted an important influence. Adamantios Coraes (1748-1833), a patriot and student of ancient Greek, undertook to arouse enthusiasm among his countrymen for the idea that they were a great people with a noble past, the descendants of the once mighty race that peopled the city-states of Athens, Thebes, and Sparta. Coraes took the language of ancient Greece and translated it into a language midway between the pure Attic original and the common speech then in use. A new language "helped to call into being a new nation." In the development of the nationalistic movement among the Greeks and other European peoples, literature often proved a valuable ally. The rediscovery of legends, the collection of folklore, and the writing of histories and poetry glorifying the past—all of these did much to quicken pride and revive love for old traditions and heroes.

Belgium freed. Belgium was a mere pawn in European diplomacy in 1815. Without consideration for the wishes of its people, it was handed over to Holland. This was a most unnatural union. Speech, religion, and economic interests were quite different in the two countries. William, the Dutch king, quickly alienated his new subjects. Their press was muzzled, the schools rigidly controlled, and Dutch made the official language. This resulted in intense resentment, and in November 1830, barricades were erected in Brussels. The people proclaimed their independence from Holland and named a German prince as their king. In 1831 the new state was officially recognized by France and Great Britain, and the Dutch were forced to agree to Belgian independence. Later, in 1839, Belgium was recognized as a perpetually neutral state, an arrangement that was to have momentous consequences in the summer of 1914.

The Unification of Italy

Carbonari and Mazzini. Italy in the early nineteenth century was disunited and impotent, under the thumb of Austria, not a nation but only a "geographical expression." French occupation during the revolutionary wars had done much to generate a desire for unity and liberty, but this was stifled at Vienna in 1815. The first attempt to realize these aims was undertaken by the *Carbonari*, a secret revolutionary organization. It was poorly organized, tried to solve problems by merely resorting to force, and soon proved to be a failure.

In the thirties a new movement in the development of Italian national unity was inaugurated called the *Risorgimento* (Resurrection). This centered around the activities of a

*Throughout the nineteenth century there were numerous other nationalistic outbreaks in the Balkans. As these were intimately connected with the story of European diplomacy, they will be reviewed in Chapter 9, dealing with the First World War (1914-1918).

group of students and patriots led by Giuseppe Mazzini (1805-1872). A society called Young Italy was formed. Mazzini exhorted his followers to be missionaries for liberty and national unity. As in Greece, the emphasis upon nationalism was reflected in a rich literary renaissance. Mazzini was first and foremost an idealist. It was his contribution to spread the cause of nationalism in Italy, but he lacked the shrewd and calculating qualities necessary to bring his ideas to completion. The failure of the Young Italy movement was shown in 1848, Europe's great year of revolutions. Revolts against Austrian rule broke out in many parts of Italy (see map, page 159), thanks to the growing strength of nationalism and liberalism. But there was no united action. Only the kingdom of Sardinia, assisted by three other small Italian states, carried on a vigorous struggle against the Austrian armies. The inevitable result was defeat. The courageous Sardinian king, Charles Albert, abdicated and left his son Victor Emmanuel II to carry on the struggle for Italian unity when the opportunity should arise.

The small kingdom of Sardinia-Piedmont was to be the nucleus of Italy, as we know it.

Count Cavour. A new phase of the Italian *Risorgimento* began with the career of Count Cavour (1810-1861), who stands with Lincoln, Bismarck, Gladstone, and Gambetta among the important statesmen of the nineteenth century. Cavour was born of a noble family in the Italian kingdom of Sardinia and was educated for a military career. Travel in Switzerland, France, and England completely changed his outlook upon life. He became a thorough liberal and began to ponder on how best to free Italy from Austrian domination.

By means of his newspaper, the *Risorgimento,* he spread his views, and in 1852 he became the prime minister of Sardinia. In making his plans, Cavour realized that his little state of Sardinia could not fight Austria unaided and thus achieve Italian unification. An ally was indispensable. In order to advertise his cause and "put Sardinia on the map," Cavour astonished Europe by joining Great Britain and France in their fight against Russia in the Crimean War (1854-1856). This seemed a ridiculous step to take, but it enabled Cavour at the peace conference to make a speech calling attention to the grievances of Italy.

The Austro-Italian war, 1859. Where to find an ally? This was answered when Cavour and Napoleon III, emperor of France, met in France in 1858. Here it was agreed that, if Cavour could trick Austria into war, France would come to her assistance. With Austria ejected from the Italian provinces of Lombardy and Venetia, Sardinia was then to rule over all of north Italy. In return, France was to receive Nice and Savoy from Sardinia.

Within a year Cavour had tricked Austria into war and had done it so cleverly that all Europe believed that Austria was the aggressor and instigator of the conflict. Two bloody battles were fought, and the Austrian troops were driven out of Lombardy by Sardinian and French soldiers. During the progress of the fighting, Napoleon III was acclaimed by Italians as their savior and liberator. But just before the allied armies started to invade Venetia, the French emperor—without consulting Cavour—made a separate peace with Austria. Napoleon III realized too late that he had started a movement destined to unite not just north Italy but the whole peninsula, creating a strong rival on the borders of France.

Other reasons influencing Napoleon's action were that the French emperor feared some German military action on the Rhine frontier while he was occupied in Italy. A further worry was that Cavour had designs against the Papal States. This last move would

alienate the support of the French Catholics. Cavour was furious, but peace was made in 1859, by which Lombardy was added to the kingdom of Sardinia.

In the following year, largely through the auspices of a friendly Great Britain, plebiscites were conducted in neighboring states, all of which voted to join Sardinia. Sardinia thus acquired Tuscany, Modena, and Parma.

Garibaldi and his Red Shirts. The center of interest now shifted to southern Italy and to a new Italian leader. Giuseppe Garibaldi (1807-1882) was a follower of Mazzini and a member of the Young Italian movement. His revolutionary plots forced him to flee the country, and in 1836 he emigrated to South America. In 1848 he returned to Italy and took part in the unsuccessful liberal movement of 1848. Again he was forced to become an exile and did not return to his native land until 1854. Secretly subsidized by Cavour, Garibaldi recruited one thousand tough adventurers, his immortal Red Shirts, and in 1860 invaded the island of Sicily.

His audacious plan worked, and next he turned to the mainland and attacked the forces of the king of Naples, reputed to be 100,000 strong. These troops, however, were not loyal, and Garibaldi had little trouble in conquering the kingdom and entering Naples in triumph. He planned to set up a separate democratic government in the Kingdom of Naples and Sicily—a serious detriment to the creation of a united Italy. Cavour therefore rushed troops to Naples, and Garibaldi surrendered his power to Victor Emmanuel. November 1860 saw the annexation of the Kingdom of Naples and Sicily and all of the remaining papal territory except Rome and its surrounding territory known as the Patrimony of St. Peter.

Garibaldi was a romantic nationalist and a daredevil adventurer, but he had little of the diplomat in him. Not realizing the danger of his action, he resolved, after conquering Naples, to move on the territories still under papal rule and force them to come into a united Italian kingdom.

Cavour knew that such an action would alienate Catholics all over the world and probably precipitate war with France, since Napoleon had stationed French troops at Rome to protect the Pope. In order to avoid this danger, Sardinian troops in 1862 forcibly restrained the Garibaldian volunteers from attacking Rome. This disgusted Garibaldi, the fire-eater, who had little use for, or understanding of, high diplomacy.

"Victor Emmanuel offered him rewards: the Order of Annunciation, a castle, an endowment, a ducal title. He would have none of them. On 9 November he sailed . . . avoiding all public demonstration, with bloodshot and angry eyes, a flame in his breast, an evil and unbridled tongue; yet great and fine at this moment of his life, for after six months of uncontrolled dictatorship he carried away with him nothing but a sack of flour, a box of red herring, four crowns, a morsel of cheese, and a small crust of bread."[12]

Unity achieved. Italy's first parliament met in 1861. A new nation counting 22,000,000 citizens had been created. But the task was not fully completed. Austria still controlled Venetia, while Rome and the immediate surrounding territory were still under papal control. It was during the war between Prussia and Austria in 1866 that Italy, acting as an ally of Prussia, obtained Venetia. And when the Franco-Prussian War broke out in 1870 and French troops were withdrawn from Rome, the last chapter in Italian unification was written as Italian troops took possession of Rome.

The main architect for united Italy did not live to see the full fruits of his work. Cavour died in 1861, but he realized that a united Italy was not far off. There are many who have criticized the duplicity and trickery of Cavour. He made no attempt to hide the true nature of his methods. "If we did for ourselves," he once said, "what we do for our country, what rascals we should be."[13]

The Unification of Germany

The German Confederation. In place of the old Holy Roman Empire, the Germanies in 1815 belonged to a German Confederation consisting of thirty-eight states. This was a loose organization of sovereign states, with no common executive or lawmaking body. The Diet, made up of representatives sent by the various rulers in the Confederation, (with its rule that a two-thirds vote was necessary to carry any proposed action) was nothing more than "a center of inertia." Such an ineffectual union far from satisfied many patriots, who desired to see all the German states in a close political union. Little progress was made in this direction, however, until 1848, when revolutionary movements occurred throughout central Europe (see map, page 159).

The Frankfurt Assembly. In 1848 representatives in Germany were elected to a national constitutional convention meeting in Frankfurt. The presiding officer announced that its purpose was to create a constitution for Germany. For thirteen months the delegates labored at their task. There were too many divergent views regarding the nature of the new united Germany, too much fruitless discussion about abstract rights of man. But a plan was finally formulated for an empire which would include all the German states and, in addition, the German-speaking sections of the Austrian empire. The emperorship was offered to the Prussian king, but heeding the warnings of Prussian reactionaries, fearing the reprisal of Austria, and yielding to his aversion for all things liberal, he refused. Thereupon the Frankfurt Assembly voted for revolution, but it was disbanded by armed forces.

The middle-class liberals at Frankfurt in 1848 represented some of the best minds in Germany, but they had failed in their purpose of establishing national unity for the Germans.

"It is one of the tragedies of modern history that this Assembly, launched on a vast surge of national enthusiasm, was unable to accomplish its self-appointed task and that the union of Germany was achieved, not by the give-and-take of Parliamentary argument, but by the blood and iron of civil and foreign wars."[14]

Growth of German nationalism. The creation of the German Confederation, in 1815, while not establishing a close union did not, at least, return to the political anarchy existing in the Germanies before 1789. The second important advance toward unification was the creation of the Zollverein by Prussia in 1834. The Zollverein was a customs union whereby Prussia was able to enforce free trade within the German Confederation. By 1842, most of the German states were members of the Zoll-

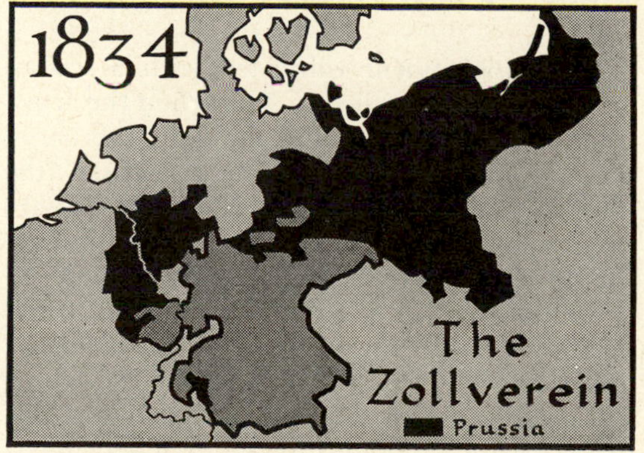

verein. The tariff union demonstrated that it was good business for the various states to develop closer measures of economic cooperation.

Another factor in stimulating the movement toward unification was the Italian war of 1859. One of its by-products was the formation of a German patriotic society whose stated purpose was "achieving the unity of the fatherland and the development of its liberties." The activities of a group of remarkable German historians also accelerated German nationalism. Such scholars as Johann Gustav Droysen, Heinrich von Sybel, and Heinrich von Treitschke wrote eloquently of the historic achievements of German heroes and urged the union of all Germans under the leadership of Prussia. "We have no German Fatherland," declared Treitschke, "the Hohenzollerns alone can give us one."

Otto von Bismarck (1815-1898). The unification of Germany was finally made possible through the genius of a consummately brilliant statesman, Otto von Bismarck. A Prussian, a member of the landed aristocracy, the future chancellor of all Germany grew up to be a typical Prussian Junker, an enemy of all liberal ideas, and a fanatical supporter of the state and its king. While at the university, Bismarck made little impression on his professors but astonished his student comrades by his beer-drinking capacity and gained renown as a duelist.

Returning from the university, Bismarck entered the Prussian civil service but found this occupation too monotonous. Resigning his post, he returned to his estate and in 1847 entered politics, an activity more to his liking. Soon he entered the Prussian diplomatic service and did valuable service in France and in Russia. In 1862 he was called to be chancellor.

His appointment coincided with a serious crisis. The king wished to strengthen the army, but the legislature would not pass the necessary appropriations. Bismarck advised the king to defy parliament and levy the necessary taxes without its consent. At the head now of the Prussian government, Bismarck soon appreciated that his greatest contribution would be the union of the German states under the leadership of Prussia.

The difficulties standing in the way of this project were almost insuperable. There was a strong tradition of state rights among the various German kingdoms. How could they be induced to give up their sovereignty and individual existence? Could the Prussian army hope to be equal to the serious fighting that must come in the process of unification? Another serious problem was whether the Prussian people would be willing to fight against their blood brothers in Austria if the necessity should arise. And finally, France would have to be weakened and its opposition to union destroyed.

Bismarck's "blood and iron." With meticulous care and craftiness Bismarck prepared his master plan. He was even more unscrupulous than Cavour. No statesman in modern times even approached his cunning and success until the advent of the totalitarian despots of our own day. Not only was Bismarck a superb master of diplomatic intrigue, but he worshiped force. "Germany," he announced, "does not look to Prussia's liberalism, but to her power. . . . The great questions of the day are not to be decided by speeches and majority resolutions—therein lay the weakness of 1848 and 1849—but by blood and iron."[15]

In 1864 he invited Austria to join Prussia in waging war on Denmark, the issue being the status of two duchies, Schleswig and Holstein, claimed by Denmark and the German Confederation. Following the defeat of Denmark, Bismarck next proceeded to isolate Austria. This was essential because he understood that until Austria's influence was removed from the German Confederation, Prussia could never unify Germany. Italy was promised Venetia if she would assist Prussia when war came. The French emperor was induced to be neutral, in return for which Belgium was to be given to France.

It was not difficult for Bismarck to provoke a war with Austria. Hostilities broke out in 1866 but lasted only seven weeks. At the battle of Sadowa the Austrian army was defeated by superior Prussian forces, which had been made into the most efficient fighting machine in the world, largely through the work of two men, Roon and von Moltke. A moderate peace, avoiding the humiliation of Austria, was imposed, ending the old German Confederation. In its place the North German Confederation was formed, excluding Austria and four southern German states, and dominated by Prussia (see first map, page 177).

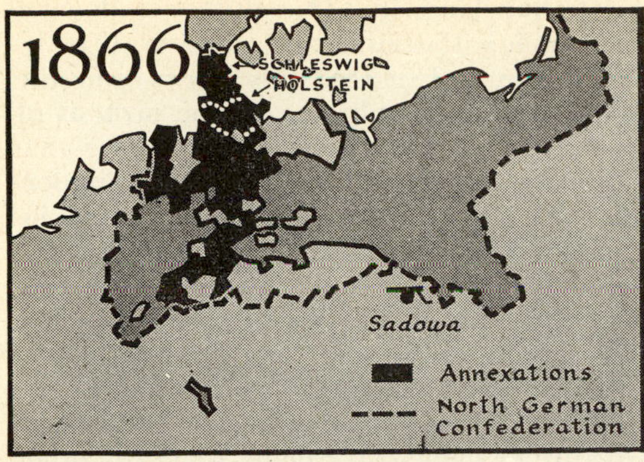

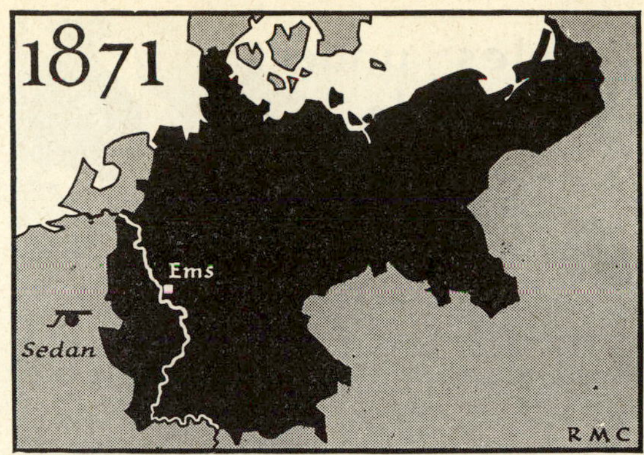

The Franco-Prussian War. Too late Napoleon III realized that a great rival power was in the making. It would no longer be possible for France to dominate Europe. "Revenge for Sadowa" became a common cry in France. Historians point out that at this time there were no real grievances between France and Prussia. France in trying to thwart the culmination of nationalism in Germany was not acting in accordance with the ideals of her historic French Revolution. The French emperor, and even more his empress, did not work hard for peace, because they felt the French imperial house must have martial glory. Bismarck also welcomed war. He believed that so long as a powerful France existed it would be a menace to the fulfillment of German unification. Such a conflict, according to Bismarck's point of view, would also stimulate a common patriotism in the hearts of all Germans, irrespective of the state in which they lived.

War came over a trivial incident with regard to the succession to the Spanish throne. As the throne was vacant, it was offered to Leopold, a Hohenzollern prince. This would represent, in the eyes of the French government, an unwelcome extension of Prussian influence which appeared more and more formidable. As a result of French protests the prince withdrew his candidacy. Then the French government made a fatal mistake. The French ambassador was sent to Ems to demand that the Prussian king promise that no Hohenzollern should ever sit on the Spanish throne. A polite refusal was given to this unreasonable request, and the king thereupon directed that a dispatch be sent to Bismarck acquainting him of the results of the interview.

Bismarck was depressed when he believed, on first thought, that the French had been allowed to "get by" with their discourteous demand. Reading the dispatch more carefully, he saw that there was still a chance to trick the French. Taking his pen, he paraphrased the dispatch so that it appeared the French ambassador had insulted the Prussian king and that the ruler had thereupon retaliated and insulted the ambassador. The dispatch was then published.

In France it infuriated the people; in Prussia it did likewise. France declared war. Amid wild enthusiasm and shouts of "On to Berlin," the French regiments marched to the front. It soon became apparent that the French system of mobilization was inefficient and chaotic and that there was no comparison between the superbly trained Prussian hosts and the army of Napoleon III. The French suffered reverse after reverse. The crowning disaster was the surrender at Sedan, where an entire French army and the emperor were forced to capitulate.

As we have previously noted, this defeat ended the Second French Empire and created the Third French Republic. Upon the shoulders of this new republic fell the terrible task of meeting the harsh Treaty of Frankfurt and raising France again to something of its old power and glory.

During the conflict the southern German states had joined the North German Confederation in its fight against France. This common struggle removed the last obstacle to national unification. (See map above.) On January 18, 1871, at the palace of Versailles, in the famous Hall of Mirrors, King William of Prussia was proclaimed German emperor.

As a by-product of German nationalism, the ambitions of Cavour were realized in 1870, as we have seen. In this year, faced with defeat, Louis Napoleon hurriedly evacuated a French garrison from Rome. The French emperor, trying to secure the support of French Catholics at home, had maintained French forces at Rome in order to prevent the last part of the Papal States from being absorbed by the new Italian kingdom. Immediately following the French withdrawal, an Italian army occupied Rome, and in 1871 this city became the capital of united Italy despite the protests of the Pope.

Bismarck's methods. Bismarck's most important work was completed by 1871, although he remained the chancellor of the German empire until 1890. He had used terrible means, but perhaps, as in the case of Cavour, he felt that circumstances left him no alternative. With the exception of Frederick the Great, Bismarck did more in shaping the policy and structure of modern Germany than any other man. It was a tragedy for the world that blood and iron seemed to Bismarck absolutely essential in forging a united Germany, for it strengthened the notion that war is a national business that can be made to pay big dividends. Further, from the time that Bismarck defied the will of the Prussian parliament in 1862, there was no opportunity for German public opinion to unseat the executive or to control governmental policy. The German state was now thoroughly set in the mold of benevolent despotism, a constitutional situation that continued until the end of the Hohenzollern dynasty in 1918.

Submerged Nationalities (1870-1914)

Danes, Poles, French in Germany. National unification was triumphant in Germany and in Italy, but after 1870 there still existed submerged nationalities (see map above) living under the government of an alien race. Germany, having realized its nationalistic aspirations in 1871, refused to consider the rights of any of those non-German races included in the German empire. The Danes in Schleswig were not a serious problem, as they numbered only about 140,000 people. But they resented German rule and kept demanding the right of a plebiscite on the question of joining Denmark.

The four million Poles in the empire were a far more serious problem. The German government was determined to Germanize this large racial minority. This necessitated the destruction of the Polish nationalistic spirit. The obvious way to try to weaken any national culture is to obliterate the language which enshrines its history, poetry, and traditions. The German government, therefore, set about discouraging the use of the Polish tongue in every way possible. All public meetings had to be addressed in German, and in the public schools only the German tongue was permitted. Polish school children would often refuse to recite in German and would resort to strikes despite the punishment which was sure to follow. A cartoon of the day showed a Polish school boy saying: "If I say my prayers in German, my father beats me; if I say them in Polish, my teacher beats me; if I don't say them at all, my priest beats me."[16] In 1886 the German government commenced buying land in the Polish areas in order to establish colonies of Germans. A law gave the government the right to expel Poles from their land, and in such cases the landowner usually was not fairly indemnified.

Another serious nationality problem facing the Germans was that of the French in Alsace-Lorraine. It is said that when these two provinces were taken from France in 1871 the emperor of Austria sent to the German ruler a telegram which read: "I congratulate you on the annexation of an open sore to your empire." Following the annexation, thousands of French families fled to France. The government did everything possible to stifle the pro-French sentiments of the Alsatians. Use of the French language was discouraged, and a strict censorship was applied to all news coming from France. These measures did little to weaken Alsatian nationalism, and on every occasion the representatives sent by Alsace-Lorraine to the German legislature protested against their annexation and by various means did everything possible to embarrass the government.

Russification. The great empire of Russia had numerous subject peoples, especially Jews, Poles, and Finns. It was during the reign of the czar Alexander III (1881-1894) that a ruthless policy of Russification was introduced. Alexander was determined that all his subjects should be essentially Russian in feeling and outlook. The most vigorous attempts were made to stamp out any evidences of foreign nationalism. The Russian language was made compulsory, and all vestiges of local government in the submerged areas were done away with. The Poles and the Finns felt the heavy hand of the Russification policy, but both peoples strenuously clung to their traditions, their language, and the hope that one day in the future they would gain their independence.

Suppressed peoples in the Balkans. Austria had more discontented and submerged peoples than any other government in Europe. Until 1867 the dominant people had been the Germans, living mainly in Austria, but the disasters suffered by Austria in 1859 (the Italo-Austrian War) and 1866 (the Austro-Prussian War) compelled the Germans, who had heretofore monopolized the government, to make concessions to the Hungarians (also called Magyars), the next most powerful group. In 1867 an agreement called the *Ausgleich* created the dual monarchy of Austria-Hungary. This arrangement provided for a virtual free hand for the Hungarians in their own affairs, while matters relating to foreign policy and defense were placed in the hands of a joint body called the Delegations, composed of German Austrians and Hungarians. This union between the German Austrians and the Hungarians was basically a selfish one. Its purpose was to enable the two ruling minority races to dominate a great mass of subject peoples and suppress any attempts they might make to establish their nationalities.

"Dropping the Pilot," the famous cartoon from "Punch" (1892) represents the young kaiser's dismissal of the iron chancellor who had, in his own ruthless way, served the German state so long and faithfully.

In the Austro-Hungarian empire the two ruling races represented less than half of the total population. The remaining subject peoples were principally Slavs, who comprised such racial groups as Czechs, Poles, Moravians, Serbians, and Croatians. In one region of the Alps was also a considerable number of Italians under Austro-Hungarian rule. In effect, under the *Ausgleich,* the Germans told the Hungarians, "You rule your barbarians, and we will take care of our own." The subject races were deprived of political rights, especially in Hungary, the use of their language was restricted, and every attempt was made to crush their national culture.

These inequalities tended to encourage rather than discourage the nationalistic aspirations of Italians, Poles, and Czechs. Full rights were vehemently demanded "in school, in office, and in public life." In Bohemia, Czech nationalism grew with great rapidity. Its most important manifestation was a renaissance of the Czech language. Palacky, Bohemia's great historian, wrote a patriotic history of Bohemia. Czech dictionaries were compiled, and poets sang of the beauty and grandeur of their native land.

In Turkey likewise Slavs and other nationals were restive. The racial make-up of this country was perhaps even more complicated than that of Austria-Hungary. Turkey had within its borders Serbs, Bulgarians, Rumanians, Greeks, Albanians, and Montenegrins, as well as Turks, all intermingled. A single province might contain Greeks, Serbs, Bulgarians, and five or six other peoples. The weakness of the decadent Turkish government invited revolt and tempted other powers interested in controlling that area to meddle in Turkish affairs. The cross-currents of politics and nationalism in the Balkans and the consequent wars and hatreds they produced during the years 1870-1914 were to prove one of the basic causes of the First World War.

During the Middle Ages English kings, believing that an island as near them as Ireland must be a menace unless under their own rule, tried to conquer Ireland, but their attempts were never strong or sustained enough to subjugate the Irish. They simply aroused Irish hatred and kept the Irish from learning to govern themselves. The Protestant Revolt was a tragedy in Anglo-Irish relations. Ireland remained Catholic; England became Protestant. For two hundred years Ireland was the center of plots against England, emanating from her enemies on the continent who were usually Catholic.

In the latter part of the seventeenth century, savage laws were passed against the Irish, restricting their political, economic, and religious freedom. Large numbers of Scottish emigrants were planted in the north of Ireland, in Ulster, where they developed into a strong Protestant settlement. Another injustice was the abolition of the Irish parliament by the Act of Union in 1801. By this act the Irish had to send their representatives to the Parliament in London.

Irish history in the nineteenth century is the story of the struggle of the Irish people to force the British government to remove these disabilities. In 1829 the Act of Catholic Emancipation, largely the work of the great Irish leader Daniel O'Connell, granted political rights to the Catholics in Ireland. Another victory was the disestablishment of the Anglican Church in Ireland in 1869, thus abolishing the use of Irish tax money in supporting a church to which seventy-five per cent of the population did not belong.

One of the most glaring injustices to the people of Ireland was to be found in the land situation. After numerous English conquests, Irish land had been confiscated and distributed among the victors. The Irish thus became a nation of tenants paying rents to an army of landlords living in England. The rents paid were often too high, and refusal to pay was followed by eviction by the landlord without compensation to the tenant for any improvements he may have made. In 1870 the British government introduced the first of a series of land acts which did much to remove such unjust practices, and in a few years measures were taken to assist the Irish farmers to own their own lands. Generous financial assistance resulted in greatly reducing the numbers of cases of absentee landlordism. It is estimated that by 1914 about half the soil of Ireland was owned by the people.

Gladstone and Irish reform. If England in early modern times was guilty of following a harsh and inhumane policy in Ireland, from the middle of the nineteenth century it must be acknowledged that a sincere attempt was made to make amends for the past. This policy is associated especially with the reforms of William Gladstone, the leader of the Liberal Party, whose avowed object was to pacify Ireland. Important land and religious reforms were the work of Gladstone, but his greatest struggle was on the question of home rule for Ireland.

The Irish, led by Charles Stewart Parnell, asked for the right to govern themselves, with the understanding that matters relating to defense and foreign policy should remain with the British Parliament. In 1886 and in 1893 Gladstone introduced measures for home rule, but both were defeated. In 1914 the third home-rule bill was passed, but the outbreak of war prevented it from being put into operation. These measures caused much resentment in northern Ireland. In Ulster the

Protestant Irish were determined not to cut loose the British connection. The efforts of Gladstone and other British statesmen to solve Ireland's political, land, and religious problems went far to rectify Irish injustices. But unfortunately these concessions came too late. It was only natural that the Irish, imbued with a dynamic national spirit, should have become more and more determined to obtain their political freedom as a state independent and separate from Great Britain.

Summary

Nationalism and democracy were the two major political movements of the nineteenth century. For the purpose of simplification, they were given separate treatment in this chapter, but actually they were very closely connected. In 1848, for example, the German people not only demanded the grant of liberal government but at the same time strove to satisfy their aspirations for a united Germany. In Italy and Austria-Hungary, democratic yearnings and nationalistic ambitions were closely blended. The new Europe constructed in 1815 at the Congress of Vienna paid little attention to the principles of democracy and nationalism. Territorial arrangements were carried out to suit the ambitions of the great powers, and under the leadership of Prince Metternich steps were taken to crush the growth of political liberalism. Democracy and nationalism, however, were too dynamic and potent to be obstructed by the reactionary diplomats at Vienna, and much of the history of the next hundred years revolves around alterations in the political structure created by the peacemakers in 1815. Democracy, or political liberalism, was the program of the middle class, who sought to end the aristocrats' dominance of government. After achieving this end, however, the middle class in many countries had to grant political concessions to the common people.

The growth and triumph of the democratic movement are best illustrated by France and Great Britain. France passed through a series of revolutions and domestic convulsions before stable, self-governing institutions were established under the Third Republic. In Great Britain, democracy's victory was no less complete, but it was the product of evolution, not revolution. The bloody excesses of the French Revolution had dealt a severe blow to the progress of reform in Great Britain. But in 1832 the passage of the great Reform Bill signalized the beginning of a slow reform movement that transformed the country from an aristocratic oligarchy to a real political democracy. Important steps in this process after 1832 were the second Reform Bill of 1867 and the third Reform Bill in 1884. Another very significant advance in democratizing the government was the Parliament Bill of 1911, which made the House of Commons superior to the aristocratic House of Lords.

Among the smaller nations of Europe, democracy made important gains. This was notable in Denmark, Norway, Sweden, and Switzerland. On the other hand, political liberalism made only a sorry showing in Italy, Spain, and Portugal. In Germany a vigorous liberal movement showed great promise early in the nineteenth century, only to fizzle out in the Frankfurt Assembly of 1848. From this time on, largely because of Bismarck's influence and the dominant position of Prussia in the German empire, benevolent despotism grew at the expense of political liberalism.

In Russia, the great empire of the czars, absolutism and political tyranny were the order throughout the nineteenth century. The exposure of the weakness and inefficiency of the Russian bureaucratic government during the conflict with Japan brought about revolution in 1905. A constitutional government providing for a *Duma* was thereupon granted by the czar, but division among the liberal ranks, the illiteracy of the peasants, and the loyalty of the army to the czar soon crushed the democratic movement and made the *Duma* a farce.

The first great victory for nationalism was the Greek achievement of national independence in 1829. Two years later the Belgians succeeded in freeing themselves from Dutch control. From 1850 to 1871 the advance of the principle of nationality is best illustrated by the events taking place in Germany and Italy. A comparison of the process of unification of these two countries shows certain interesting parallels and also dissimilarities. In both, the methods utilized were Machiavellian. Force, trickery, and treachery were the implements used in the creation of the new states. The process of unification owed much to the genius of great leaders—Bismarck in Germany and Cavour in Italy. The germs of national enthusiasm in Italy and Germany were spread by idealistic liberal organizations. A nucleus for unification also existed in both Italy and Germany. The kingdoms of Sardinia and Prussia were the nuclei and the agents of unification. Prussia was strong enough to accomplish its task unaided, whereas Sardinia had to secure the aid of an outside power, France. Both Italy and Germany had to remove Austrian control before national union could be secured. It is interesting to note the part played by France in this historical movement. In Italian unification, France actually waged a war to assist Sardinia, but Germany's unification resulted from a great French defeat. A final point to be observed is that the existence of the Papal States constituted a serious obstruction in the path of Italian unification, which was not true in Germany.

Nationalism triumphed in Germany and Italy, but it was frustrated in many other European areas. The Germans tried to stifle the national cultures of the Danes, Poles, and French within their borders. The Russians engaged in a harsh crusade of Russification against their subject races. In Austria-Hungary the two dominant races, the Austrians and Magyars, united in order to repress the nationalism of a great mass of submerged people. Ireland has been regarded as the British government's greatest failure. The confiscation of land, the passing of severe penal laws, and the restriction of political liberties made the Irish little more than a nation of serfs. During the nineteenth century Great Britain made belated attempts to make amends. The land situation was improved, and religious disabilities were removed. The greatest problem proved to be that of home rule. After two failures, a measure giving Ireland self-government was passed in 1914. But by this time Irish nationalism had grown too strong to be contented with anything short of full national independence.

All nationalistic movements were strengthened and inspired by literary and linguistic revivals. This was particularly true in Bohemia and Ireland. For seventy-five years following the French Revolution, nationalism was strongly tinged with liberalism and a spirit of moderation. But in the last quarter of the nineteenth century it became apparent that it was changing into an intolerant, unreasonable, and belligerent force, involving the very existence of European civilization. Nations, having gained their own freedom, savagely repressed the national culture of their minority races. Even the old nations, created long ago, became imbued with a new type of fanatical nationalism, or super-patriotism. This resulted in a cult of national superiority and the inclination to intimidate and threaten other national states. We will return to this alarming aspect of nationalism in our discussion of the First World War.

DAUMIER: EUROPEAN BALANCE OF POWER

Science

1802	Chemical research discovers atoms, molecules	Dalton, Avogadro
1830	Geology transformed into true science	Lyell's *Principles of Geology*
1830	Biology uses microscope	Schwann's cell theory
1842-1892	Medical progress: ether, chloroform, germs	Pasteur, Koch, Lister
1843	Advances in physics	Joule, Helmholtz
1859	Darwin formulates theory of evolution	*Origin of Species*
1895	X-ray and radium	Roentgen, the Curies
	Electrical study on scientific basis	Ohm, Ampère, Faraday
1900	Studies in heredity—Mendel's law	de Vries' mutation theory

Philosophy

1770-1831	Hegel's idealistic philosophy	
1825-1850	British practicality—Utilitarianism	Bentham, Mill
1844-1900	Nietzsche—war and the will to power	Influenced German National Socialism
1820-1902	Spencer applies principle of evolution	

Literature

1800-1830	Romanticism in English poetry and prose	Byron, Shelley, Keats, Scott, etc.
1850-1900	The spirit of Victorianism	Tennyson, Browning, Kipling
	Trend to realism in the novel	Dickens, Eliot, Butler, Hardy
	Critics and essayists	Carlyle, Macaulay, Ruskin
	American literature grows up	Irving, Longfellow, Emerson, Whitman, Twain, etc.
	French romanticism shifts to realism	Hugo, Dumas, de Maupassant, Zola
	German romanticism	Goethe, Schiller, Heine
	Russia: Dostoevski, Tolstoy	Pushkin, Gogol
	Scandinavia: Andersen, Ibsen	Björnson, Strindberg
	Italy: Manzoni, Giacosa	

Music

1770-1827	Beethoven revitalizes music	Mood and tone rather than composition
1809-1849	Chopin develops resources of piano	
1833-1897	Brahms, successor to Beethoven	
	French develop orchestra, organ	Berlioz, César Franck
	"The Five" in Russia, and Tschaikowsky	
19th Century	Development of national opera	Wagner, Gounod, Bizet, Verdi, Rossini

Art

19th Century	From Classicism to romanticism, then realism	Delacroix, Corot, Millet, Manet
	Impressionism, Post-Impressionism	Monet, Renoir, Cézanne
	Individualists	Gauguin, Van Gogh
	English landscape painters	Constable, Turner
	Architecture: classicism, Gothic Revival	Influenced by Hugo, Scott, Ruskin
	Sculpture	Carpeaux, Rodin
	American Art	Stuart, Whistler, Saint Gaudens

CHAPTER 6

All's Right with the World

It has been the fashion among many people to patronize the nineteenth century, to call it prudish, hypocritical, and stuffy. They deride the smug attitude of the Victorians on social and moral issues, and they accuse our grandparents of exhibiting bad taste in art and literature. Whereas the nineteenth century was complacent in its belief that it was the most enlightened of all ages in history, the twentieth is by no means so optimistic in its outlook.

The optimism of the Victorians came from several sources. We saw in previous pages how gigantic were the industrial and economic strides which the nineteenth century made, thanks to the multitude of new inventions which occurred all during this period. In the political arena the Europeans of the nineteenth century believed there was much for which to be grateful. Their armies and navies carved out for leading powers vast colonial empires possessing unlimited raw resources.

The present chapter possesses no character wading through blood to a throne, but it tells about a score of geniuses who labored ceaselessly to conquer nature and not their fellow men. To rid the world of disease, superstition, and ignorance—this was the goal of the doctors, the physical and social scientists. To give the world more pleasure and beauty—this was the ideal of the authors, painters, and composers whom we shall soon meet. And in the attempts of some of these men to accomplish what they set out to do we shall witness feats of character infinitely more arresting than those performed by most of the world's loudly heralded soldiers. The scientists made rich discoveries and opened up new avenues of scientific research; the doctors mastered scourges which hitherto had kept mankind in dread; the philosophers contributed what appeared to be conclusive theories regarding the mysteries of the universe; and the poets, painters, and composers immeasurably enriched the artistic heritage of man.

The history of political ambitions and economic rivalries centers about national achievements; the story of the nineteenth century's intellectual and artistic accomplishments is international. So rich was the nineteenth century in the great men and new ideas which it produced that we cannot hope in a few pages to do justice to more than a handful of the outstanding figures and their contributions. With each fresh discovery and invention came a host of ramifications, so that we find whole new fields of science being explored for the first time, as well as remarkable philosophical and artistic activity.

Science of the Nineteenth Century

Mathematics and astronomy develop. During the nineteenth century, while most mathematicians did work according to Euclidean geometry and traditional algebra, several outstanding thinkers perceived their limitations. Niels Abel, a brilliant young mathematician, proved that ordinary algebra was incapable of solving higher equations, while Professor Nikolai Lobachevski of Russia published a book in 1840 which demonstrated the limitations of Euclidean geometry and laid the foundation for non-Euclidean and hypergeometry. Building on these innovations, twentieth-century mathematicians like Einstein and Planck were able to revise the Newtonian concepts of physics and astronomy.

Closely linked with mathematics were developments in astronomy. Urbain Leverrier, the director of the Paris observatory, showed by mathematical computation that beyond Uranus in the solar system there must exist another planet. Proof was forthcoming in 1846 when this planet, called Neptune, was observed almost exactly in the location figured out in advance by Leverrier and by the Englishman Adams, also, in 1843.

Progress in the science of optics enabled larger and more accurate telescopes to be fashioned. A new astronomical instrument in particular—the spectroscope—was invented, bringing astronomy and physics together in what is called astrophysics. Now for the first time scientists could examine minute fixed stars and determine their chemical composition by an analysis of the light received from them. Still later, astronomy was immeasurably benefited by photography, which could record on a sensitive plate thousands of celestial objects which the unaided human eye could never pick out. Today it is said that ninety per cent of all observations are made photographically.

The new geology. While astronomers were focusing their attention upon the heavens, geologists were burying themselves in the mysteries of this planet. We may recall that in 1785 there had appeared a book called *Theory of the Earth,* by James Hutton, which ascribed the origins of the earth to natural rather than supernatural causes. After the publication of this volume more data was gathered. In 1830-1833 appeared an epoch-making work by Sir Charles Lyell, which he called *Principles of Geology, an attempt to explain the former changes of the Earth's surface by reference to causes now in operation.* Lyell's *Principles,* so influential that by 1872 it had gone through eleven editions, transformed geology into a true science. In it he showed that the earth had achieved its present appearance through earthquakes, volcanoes, erosion, and the continuous rising and sinking of land surfaces.

A separate branch of geology, known as paleontology, was founded by a French natural scientist, Baron Georges Cuvier. This science, which is concerned with the study of fossils or extinct forms of life on the planet, enabled men to reconstruct gradually the history of geological ages.

Progress of physics. Physics made phenomenal progress during the nineteenth century. Especially important was the work done in thermodynamics and electricity. Thermodynamics is the science which deals with the relations between heat and motive power, and it attracted much attention because of the importance of steam engines. Until about 1798, the view prevailed that heat was a mysterious fluid called "caloric." In that year, however, an American loyalist who had gone to Great Britain in 1776 and was later known as Count Rumford, disproved this theory. Later Sir Humphry Davy carried out a test in which he melted two blocks of ice by friction in an atmosphere below freezing. Such a result was contrary to the caloric theory, and in the decades that followed, men worked out a new law which showed that friction generates heat in proportion to the amount of work expended. In 1843 a Manchester brewer-scientist, James Joule, determined the mechanical equivalent of heat, that is, the mechanical energy needed to raise the heat of any given body by a certain amount. This unit of energy was called the "joule." Joule pointed the way toward the converting of energy into heat; a German physicist, Hermann von Helmholtz, presented to the world the principle of the conservation of energy. This principle means that the sum total of the energy in the universe is a constant energy and cannot be created or destroyed; it can only be transformed from one form to another.

Other scientists were engaged in the converse problem of transforming heat into energy and noting its effects. This problem was of especial interest to engineers who sought to make the steam engine more efficient. In 1824 Nicolas L. Sadi Carnot showed that heat could never be completely converted into energy. From this arose the principle of the dissipation and degradation of energy. According to this principle, although the total amount of energy in the universe remains constant, the amount of energy actually available is always diminishing through its transformation into nonavailable, or dissipated, heat.

Advance in electricity. Benjamin Franklin had aided the study of electrical phenomena in the eighteenth century, as had Galvani and Volta. But it remained for the next century to place electrical investigation upon a genuinely scientific basis. In 1819, a Danish scientist, H. C. Oersted, discovered that an electric current deflected a magnetic needle. G. S. Ohm, a German, discovered the nature of electric conductors and measured mathematically the resistance in the conduction of electric currents. A French scientist, A. M. Ampère, had meanwhile taken up Ohm's discovery and showed that a current produced a mechanical effect not merely on magnets but also on other currents.

Probably the most prominent figure in the study of electricity during this century was Michael Faraday, son of a London blacksmith. He showed that electric currents produce a magnetic field and described the principles of electromagnetic induction. He invented the first electric dynamo when he produced an electric current by having a copper disk rotate between the poles of a magnet. This simple dynamo experiment made possible the use of the electric motor, the transmission of large currents over long distances, the electric telegraph, the telephone, and electric lighting. These benefits took time to evolve, but their foundation had been laid.[1]

Electromagnetism was further advanced by the English scientist James Maxwell, who elaborated exact mathematical equations covering Faraday's discoveries. Maxwell performed a notable service when he showed that light waves are of the same nature as those sent out by oscillating electric discharges. Thus Maxwell linked up optics and electricity and maintained that light, radiant heat, and invisible ultraviolet radiation were all electromagnetic phenomena. Soon the science of radiation became a part of electrodynamics, and from an application of the principles evolved by Maxwell and the German physicist Heinrich Hertz, Marconi invented wireless telegraphy.

The electromagnetic theory of wave motion helped explain other forms of radiation which were discovered in the last quarter of the century. In 1895 Wilhelm Konrad Roentgen discovered a ray that could penetrate a nontranslucent mass. He called it X-radiation, as he did not know the nature of this strange phenomenon, while other scientists suggested the term Roentgen ray. In 1898 Pierre Curie and his Polish wife, Marie Curie, extracted radium from pitchblende, and the world at last became conscious of the potency of radioactivity.[2]

Progress in chemistry. The seventeenth and eighteenth centuries had contributed to the advance of chemistry, and the industrial inventions of the nineteenth greatly accelerated fresh research. At the base of nineteenth-century chemistry was the all-important atomic theory. In 1802 an English schoolteacher, John Dalton, proved that if two substances combined to form compounds chemically different the mass compositions were in simple arithmetical ratio. From this discovery he argued that every element was composed of extremely minute particles called atoms, which cannot be further divided. Furthermore, these elements combine with one another, atom by atom, and in definite simple proportions by weight. About the same time an Italian professor, Count Amadeo Avogadro, showed that gases consist of minute particles which he called molecules, and he set forth Avogadro's Law, that "equal volumes of all gases, under the same conditions of temperature and pressure, contain the same number of smallest particles, or molecules."[3]

Chemists now investigated the atomic weights of the elements, arriving at the tabulation of the Periodic Law. When the elements are grouped according to their atomic weights, they arrange themselves in groups of eight. Thus the eighth element will have characteristics similar to those possessed by the first. Gaps in this sequence seemed to point to the existence of undiscovered elements. This theory was substantiated by the discovery of gallium in 1871, scandium in 1879, and germanium in 1886.

Toward the end of the century scientists probed a prevailing belief concerning the indivisibility of the atom. Sir William Crookes and J. J. Thomson showed that the atom contained negatively charged particles, which became known as electrons, while in the early years of the twentieth century positively charged particles, protons, were discovered. This discovery had far-reaching results in both science and philosophy.

Biological developments. During the nineteenth century notable advances were made in biology, the science of living organisms. The invention of the microscope in the thirties of the century enabled Theodor Schwann to work out his cell theory. Schwann and his successors showed that all living creatures have a cellular structure and that the "many-celled organism begins its existence as a fertilized egg cell, which divides and redivides to form an embryo." Hugo von Mohl in 1844 called the "plastic, nitrogenous living matter" within these cells protoplasm.

Bacteriology. A separate biological science known as bacteriology came into being in the seventies. Louis Pasteur, son of a humble French tanner, investigated microscopic organisms which are present in the air, water, and earth. He showed how these bacteria are responsible for many diseases. Concrete results of his experimentation included the stamping out of certain silkworm diseases, the prevention of hydrophobia, and the pasteurization of milk, while his research on fermentation resulted in complete changes in the wine-making and brewing industries.

Robert Koch was a German country doctor, who placed bacteriology upon a firm foundation. Koch isolated the tuberculosis and cholera bacilli, discovered the value of steam sterilization, systematized the method for cultivating and classifying bacteria, and established the science of immunology. Koch became professor of hygiene and bacteriology at the University of Berlin and received the Nobel Prize in 1905.

The theory of evolution. The nineteenth century witnessed the spread of a doctrine which had far-reaching effects at once on science, philosophy, and western religion. This was the theory of evolution, namely, that all living organisms on this earth developed, through the operation of natural causes, from simple early forms and that no species is fixed and changeless. Some of the classical philosophers had seen the reasonableness of such an hypothesis. Heraclitus, for example, had stressed that growth and constant change lay at the bottom of universal processes, while the Roman poet-scientist, Lucretius, in his cosmological poem *De Rerum Natura* conceived of a vast evolutionary scheme in which the universe was based upon an atomic system and motivated by natural causes.

Little more was done with this trend of thought until the eighteenth century, when various thinkers drew significant conclusions from their observations. The Swedish botanist Linnaeus set forth a system for classifying organic life which appeared to suggest a common origin for various existing species. The naturalist Buffon perceived the effect of environment upon the differentiation of species, a thesis developed still further by Erasmus Darwin, the grandfather of Charles Darwin.

During the nineteenth century evidence kept accumulating to indicate that organic and inorganic matter alike had evolved according to natural causes. Sir Charles Lyell's *Principles of Geology* showed that the earth was formed and modified by natural agencies and that these processes were going on under men's very eyes. In 1802 the hypothesis of an organic evolution was set forth by a French nobleman, Jean Baptiste de Lamarck. His doctrine of evolution stated that every organism tends to develop new organs in order to adapt itself to the changing conditions of its environment and that the development of organs is in constant ratio to their use. The changes which have thus taken place in an organism are transmitted through heredity to its descendants who, inheriting these characteristics, are thereby changed in structural form. Lamarck took as his example the giraffe, which he said had to develop a long neck to reach the high leaves and branches of the trees on which it fed, and the slight gain made by each generation was handed on to the next.[4]

Charles Darwin. The man most responsible for the furthering of the evolutionary hypothesis was Charles Darwin (1809-1882). This remarkable English scientist arrived at his conclusions after many years of investigation. Between 1831 and 1836 he acted as a naturalist on board a surveying ship called the *Beagle,* which voyaged along the coast of South America and among the South Sea Islands. After his return to England, Darwin studied the specimens he had collected on his voyage, meanwhile having been deeply impressed by two books in particular. The first was Lyell's *Principles of Geology,* which showed, as we have already noted, that changes could come about through natural causes. The other book was Malthus' *Essay on Population.* This work suggested to Darwin that Malthus' concept regarding the relationship between human population and the struggle for survival could be extended to all of nature. Darwin made a sketch of his theory in 1842 but did not publish his views until 1859, when they appeared under the title *On the Origin of Species by Means of Natural Selection, or the Preservation of Favored Races in the Struggle for Life.* This book was published as the result of a strange coincidence. Another Englishman, Alfred Russel Wallace, had traveled to the Amazon and East Indies, also as a naturalist. In 1858, while ill with fever in the Moluccas, Wallace also started reflecting on Malthus' *Essay on Population* and also arrived at the idea of the survival of the fittest. After working out his views in essay form, Wallace sent them to Darwin, the outstanding naturalist in England. After reading Wallace's views, Darwin wrote to Lyell:

"I never saw a more striking coincidence; if Wallace had my manuscript sketch written out in 1842, he could not have made a better short abstract! Even his terms now stand as heads of my chapters."[5]

Darwin read Wallace's essay and his own before a London society, giving the younger scientist full credit for his share of the doctrine, and the world heard for the first time of the Darwinian hypothesis. In 1871 Darwin published *The Descent of Man and Selection in Relation to Sex,* which elaborated upon some of the views expressed in the *Origin of Species* and also applied the law of natural selection to human beings.

There are three main points in the Darwinian hypothesis of evolution. First, all existing vegetable and animal species are descended from earlier and, generally speaking, more rudimentary types. Secondly, evolution involves "natural selection." Every species produces more young than will grow to maturity. In the struggle to survive, the fittest will win out at the expense of their rivals. They will be the most capable of adapting themselves to their environment. This fitness will be transmitted to subsequent generations. Here we see the influence of Malthus' population theory and Lamarck's theory of the inheritance of acquired characteristics. Thirdly, the Darwinian hypothesis contended that differentiation among the species was also brought about by sexual selection. But this point was soon discarded by scientists as of little or no worth.

Darwinian theory modified. By the close of the nineteenth century scientists were in virtual agreement regarding the general validity of the Darwin hypothesis. However, several new discoveries had been made which altered some of its tenets. For example, a German professor of zoölogy named August Weismann showed in his *Essays upon Heredity and Kindred Biological Problems* that there is a continuity of the germ plasma and that acquired characteristics cannot be transmitted as maintained by Lamarck and accepted by Darwin. Despite the controversy which ensued over Weismann's hypothesis, his views gradually displaced the older concept.

Meanwhile an Austrian monk, Gregor Mendel, had been experimenting with the crossing of garden peas and had formulated definite laws of heredity. Mendel published his important findings in an obscure scientific journal in 1866, and they were overlooked until 1900. Mendel's laws not only proved a valuable help in scientific breeding of plants and animals, but they made the problem of the evolution of different species more complex than had been deduced by Darwin.

At the turn of the century a Dutch botanist, Hugo de Vries, was working on heredity, and from his experiments came the mutation theory in 1901. This doctrine showed that there existed mutations, that is, sudden and unpredictable variations in heredity, and that these acted as the source of numerous new species.

Rapid strides of medical science. Among the more remarkable advances in nineteenth-century medicine was the development of anesthetics. In 1800 Sir Humphry Davy discovered the anesthetic value of nitrous oxide, or laughing gas, but little more was done on the subject until decades had passed. Then in 1842 an American physician in Georgia, Dr. Crawford W. Long, performed an operation involving the use of ether. In 1846 a Boston dentist, W. T. G. Morton, gave ether as a general anesthetic. When another Bostonian, Charles T. Jackson, disputed with Morton as to whom the credit should go for its use, it was proposed that the two should have statues erected on a common pedestal with the inscription "e(i)ther."

In 1847 a professor at the University of Edinburgh, James Simpson, told the scientific world of his discovery of the value of chloroform. The use of chloroform by Queen Victoria in childbirth in 1853 and 1857 popularized its use tremendously.

The nineteenth century conquered the dread puerperal fever, a malady perpetually raging. A Hungarian physician assisting in the Vienna General Hospital, Ignaz Philipp Semmelweiss, observed that uncleanliness lay at the root of the disease. He ordered medical students to wash their hands in chlorine water before coming into his hospital ward, with the result that puerperal fever almost died out in the Vienna infirmary. But when in 1857 Semmelweiss published *The Prevention of Childbed Fever,* he was persecuted by his colleagues, who were furious at the suggestion that their unwashed hands might be contributing to the toll of puerperal-fever victims. Finally, Semmelweiss' mind broke down under the bombardment of ridicule and hostility, and this champion of a new order, "the saddest figure in the history of medicine," as he has been called, died in a Vienna asylum in 1865.

Joseph Lister (1827-1912). The introduction of asepsis into surgery was another step of the first magnitude. An English Quaker surgeon, Joseph Lister, introduced techniques of surgery which are commonplace today but which were revolutionary when he began. He did away with the filthy "surgeon's coat" which was used at operation after operation, substituting a fresh linen apron; he used dressings treated with carbolic acid instead of bandages left over from a previous operation. Lister also introduced carbolic acid to cleanse the wound and to purify the operating room and used the rubber drainage tube.

The germ theory of disease. Asepsis is the method of preventing the entry of bacteria into a wound, while antisepsis is the method of disinfecting wounds so as to destroy dangerous bacteria. Both spring from a knowledge of the germ theory of disease, another notable accomplishment of the nineteenth century. For this discovery we are indebted in large measure to Lister's brilliant friend, Louis Pasteur, whom we have already discussed in connection with bacteriology as a separate science. This Frenchman showed for the first time that small organisms are the cause of fermentations, and from this discovery came the theory that microbes are the cause of disease. In 1882 Robert Koch, as we have seen, discovered the germ of tuberculosis, while the germs of many other diseases have since been recognized and combatted.

The Russian scientist Elie Metchnikoff proved that white corpuscles in the blood fight the germs that enter the body, and we now know that the pus in a wound is composed principally of dead white corpuscles. Science also discovered that some germs generate antitoxins, which tend to nullify the effect of the toxins, or poisons, of the germs. This led to serum-therapy, that is, the taking of antitoxins from persons or animals suffering from a disease and injecting them into a patient to strengthen his resistance to the same disease. In 1892 von Behring discovered an antitoxin for diphtheria, and since that time similar antidotes have been developed for many other diseases.

By the close of the century the world had been made conscious of the value of preventive medicine. Communities began to stress the need of proper sewage-disposal systems, the purification of water, the pasteurization of milk. People were educated to the necessity for individual drinking cups and towels and to the danger of spitting in public places.

Philosophy and the New Social Sciences

The dogma of progress. The impact of science upon nineteenth-century thought was bound to be far-reaching. Research in electrodynamics, the discoveries in the new life sciences, and the confirmation of the hypothesis that evolution exists in both the inorganic and organic worlds naturally modified contemporary philosophies. The universe was now looked upon as dynamic and changing, as a great machine in perpetual motion that acted according to definite laws. Furthermore, scientists thought that they understood these laws quite completely and that they were on the threshold of unraveling the mysteries of the universe. The nineteenth century was sure that progress was a universal fact, even as it was sure that Newton's laws explained all the mysteries of gravitation. The Darwinian hypothesis seemed to prove the doctrine of progress conclusively. Everything was evolving biologically, and change was considered progress.

The dogma of progress seemed to be substantiated in other ways. Science had discovered laws which led to a thousand and one inventions. Surrounded by new comforts of life and enjoying a higher standard of material living than had hitherto ever existed, people placed their faith in the apostles of science as never before. This spirit of adulation, in fact, infected the intellectuals as well. Philosophers might question whether science could unravel all the universal mysteries, but they admitted that it was supreme in matters relating to the physical world. Scholars specializing in such subjects as history, economics, geography, and anthropology termed their fields social science and even tried to formulate what they thought were definite laws like those existing in physics and chemistry. Religion was also profoundly affected by the new discoveries in the physical sciences.

Idealistic philosophy—Hegel. Philosophy took a distinctly scientific turn during the century, especially the latter half. For the first decades, thought continued along the lines laid down by the German Idealists. These philosophers developed the idea that the entire universe is an expression of mind or spirit. Idealistic philosophy reached a climax in the works of Georg Wilhelm Friedrich Hegel (1770-1831), who ruled the world of philosophy during the last years of his life. Hegel's philosophy is obscure and not easily defined. Hegel maintained that nothing is unknowable. To him thought and reality were identical; the reality of a thing depended upon its intelligibility to us, and it became intelligible only as it entered into concrete experience. Every element of experience, he held, is connected with a rational whole, and this rational whole in its entirety is God, or the Absolute. It is for philosophy to show how each factor of experience is related to the rational whole to which it belongs. Hegel made use of a dialectic technique of "thesis-antithesis-synthesis" to evaluate experience. We have an idea which at first we think is self-complete, but its very incompleteness brings forth its opposite, or antithesis, thus showing that we have grasped as yet only a portion of reality. There follows a clash between the two, out of which develops a synthesis of the true elements of each viewpoint. This synthesis gives us reality and progress. Subsequent thought was profoundly affected by Hegel's theory, and we have only to read Karl Marx (a disciple of Hegel) for confirmation. The class-struggle theory, in which we find bourgeoisie and proletariat ranged against one another with the inevitable clash out of which emerges a classless society, is Hegelian in its nature.

British empiricism. The German Idealists dealt with absolutes and attempted by logic to show that God must exist at the base of all universal processes. While the Germans were deducing their abstract systems, British philosophy was developing along quite different lines. It was empirical; that is, it said that no knowledge could be gained except through the senses and by experience. It was natural that British thought should have had this practical bent during the early nineteenth century, for England was concerned with such down-to-earth matters as the growth of industrialism, with its far-reaching social consequences, and with the democratization of English politics and society.

Jeremy Bentham started out with the view that the only thing which is real is the particular instance. Furthermore, the sole end of man's actions is the preservation of pleasure and the avoidance of pain. Now, said Bentham, particular pleasures and pains can be measured quantitatively according to their intensity, duration, certainty, and propinquity. The determination of the moral quality of any act comes from the measuring by these standards of its effect in terms of pleasures and pains upon all members of the community. Thus the criterion of the goodness of a law depends upon the principle of utility: "It is the greatest happiness of the greatest number that is the measure of right and wrong." Bentham's was the philosophy of Utilitarianism. Since the motive of an act is always self-interest, according to Bentham, it is necessary for education and law to teach the individual how he can serve the best interests of both the community and himself.

John Stuart Mill modified Utilitarianism. He began as a warm exponent of Bentham and of economic liberalism, but his studies in science, psychology, and sociology led him to advocate what was called the "new liberalism": an acceptance of the general principle of individualism tempered by the need of such sociological reforms as the emancipation of women, the betterment of the workers' lot, and the nationalization of land. His most permanent contribution to philosophy itself was his *System of Logic.* This monumental work appeared in 1843 and was an attempt to create an inductive logic of scientific inquiry similar to that which Aristotle had provided for formal logic.

Nietzsche and the "superman." Despite the optimistic spirit inherent in the thought of the English Utilitarians, certain philosophers on the continent had a decidedly pessimistic outlook on life. One of these was Friedrich Nietzsche (1844-1900). This neurotic thinker, whose attacks on Christianity were made with savage scorn, had extraordinary influence upon contemporary thought. He advanced the concept of the will to power. To Nietzsche the only type of person fit to exist is he who has the power to attain authority, no matter how ruthless the means. The man who should rule is the superman, whose virtues consist of bravery, strength, egoism, arrogance, ruthlessness.

War is praised as the theater where such virtues manifest themselves. Nietzsche challenged the world with "You say, 'A good cause sanctifies even war,' but I say, 'A good war sanctifies every cause.' " Nietzsche thought of Christianity with contempt, because he looked upon gentleness as weakness and humanitarianism as the protection of the unfit and spineless. Democracy and socialism were likewise to be ridiculed for protecting the worthless and weak and hindering the strong from succeeding.

His most famous work was *Thus Spake Zarathustra,* which maintained that progress has been kept back for ages by a false belief in "the good, the true, and the beautiful" and advocated the doctrine of the will to power and the rise of the superman. It is significant to note that Nietzsche profoundly influenced Wagner and that his views became a cornerstone in the National Socialism of Hitlerian Germany.

Auguste Comte's positivism. The Frenchman Auguste Comte (1798-1857) was the first in the nineteenth century to build an important philosophical system upon the assumptions of science. Comte became secretary to Saint-Simon, and from him he received many ideas regarding the need for placing social matters upon a scientific basis and of bettering the lot of mankind. Between 1851 and 1854 Comte published the four volumes of *Positive Philosophy,* in which was set forth his system of thought. This was founded on an evolutionary basis and stressed the all-importance of science.

Positivism as a philosophy gave up the attempt to find out about universal first causes and stressed instead the gathering and classifying of all knowledge in the physical and social world. Comte believed it necessary to classify all the sciences according to their complexity. He undertook to crown these natural sciences with one dealing with the facts of man's social life: the positive science of society, or sociology. It was the task of this new social science to take the findings of the natural sciences and then to reorganize man's political, social, and religious institutions accordingly.

Herbert Spencer's scientific philosophy. Another philosopher who placed his trust in science was an Englishman, Herbert Spencer (1820-1903). During Spencer's youth, English thought was being stirred by the advance of biology, the implications involved in Lyell's work on geology, and the increasing interest in the theory of evolution. Even before Darwin spoke, Spencer wrote an essay on "The Development Hypothesis," but the appearance of Darwin's *Origin of Species* in 1858, with its detailed documentation of the evolutionary hypothesis, strengthened Spencer's views. It was Spencer who coined the phrase "survival of the fittest," which so aptly summed up Darwin's law of natural selection. Spencer labored for nearly forty years on his ten-volume *Synthetic Philosophy*. In it he applied the principle of evolution to four fields—biology, psychology, sociology, and ethics.

Spencer looked on society as a living organism. "The organic conception of society is now a commonplace, and Spencer did much to bring this about."[6] He made use of the doctrine of survival of the fittest to justify the theory of economic individualism and competition, although he protested against many of its evils.

English Literature

Backgrounds of romanticism. The three passionately proclaimed ideals of the French Revolution were "Liberty, Equality, and Fraternity." They symbolized a new emphasis upon the importance of man and his rights, as well as a new emphasis upon the importance of human emotions. This was expressed by a love of nature, the growth of humanitarian movements, and a mystical form of philosophy often referred to as transcendentalism—the gaining of knowledge by intuition instead of empirical means, sometimes involving the belief that man could unite himself with the deity through a love of nature. From these roots grew romanticism, an emotional approach to life and art.

Burns, Wordsworth, Coleridge. Writers in Great Britain were turning away from the classicism and intellectualism that marked the Enlightenment in the eighteenth century. Robert Burns (1759-1796), the Scottish bard, all his life sounded the new note of the dignity and worth of the common man, vehemently decrying political inequality, economic oppression, and religious bigotry. Burns won the love of his countrymen for all time not only by his championing of the downtrodden but also by his lyrics and such rollicking tales as "Tam o' Shanter" and "The Jolly Beggars."

Burns and the new romanticism had a deep effect upon two young English poets, William Wordsworth (1770-1850) and Samuel Taylor Coleridge (1772-1834). These writers, deep friends and companions for years, together published *Lyrical Ballads* in 1798. In it Coleridge stated that his "endeavours should be directed to persons and characters supernatural or at least romantic," while Wordsworth took it upon himself "to give the charm of novelty to things of every day." It was a revolutionary book of verse, for it rebelled completely against the artificiality of the literature of the day, contained absolute simplicity of subject and diction, and stressed among other matters a deep-rooted love of nature.

Byron, Shelley, Keats. In Lord Byron, Percy Bysshe Shelley, and John Keats, romanticism reached its height. All three had strong natural poetic gifts and deep-rooted convictions about the sanctity of human rights. Likewise, all three suffered much from personal humiliation or frustration, and each of them died young and abroad from England.

Lord Byron (1788-1824) had the misfortune to be at the same time a genius, handsome, clubfooted, and the unbalanced scion of unbalanced parents. He rebelled against the strange mixture of love and hatred which his mother showered upon him and, conditioned in such an environment, continued the rest of his short life to rebel against all symbols of authority. When the Greeks revolted against the Turks in 1823, Byron joined the cause of independence and died of fever in Greece. The poetry of Byron was just as tempestuous and uneven as his personal nature. The work which brought him initial fame was a long autobiographical poem, *Childe Harold's Pilgrimage,* in which appeared his famous description of the night before Waterloo. Probably his masterpiece was *Don Juan,* in which he criticized the foibles of human nature with consummate artistry.

Shelley (1792-1822) was more a visionary than a rebel, although he was condemned by his contemporaries because he would not conform to any accepted social or intellectual pattern. He believed in the perfectability of mankind but felt that it would come only through complete freedom of thought and action. Before he was drowned in Italy (with a volume of Sophocles in one pocket and Keats's poems in the other), Shelley had established himself as one of the world's greatest lyric poets. Such poems as "To a Skylark," "The Cloud," and "Ode to the West Wind" are resplendent in imagery and brilliant in style.

Keats (1795-1821) was one of the shortest-lived of England's poets; he was also one of her greatest literary figures. Born the son of an innkeeper and destined by consumption to an unhappy life and early death, Keats still found time enough to sing splendidly of beauty and its philosophy. Keats's attitude toward his mission as a poet is expressed in the following words:

Beauty is truth, truth beauty—that is all
Ye know on earth, and all ye need to know.

While Keats wrote many long poems, his popularity rests on some of his more outstanding short pieces.

Early nineteenth-century novelists. Prose flourished in England during the early nineteenth century. The two foremost novelists were Sir Walter Scott and Jane Austen. Scott (1771-1832) was a prolific writer who excelled especially in the field of the historical romance,

Sauciness and good humor characterize this little portrait of Victoria (1899), by Oliver Herford. "Q Is for Queen" is one of a series of alphabet drawings.

although he attained popularity also as a poet. Few people have not heard of his long narrative poems *The Lady of the Lake* and *Marmion.* But this Scottish romancer devoted his time and talents principally to the novel after the publication in 1814 of his first *Waverley.* Twenty-eight followed, including *Ivanhoe, Quentin Durward, Rob Roy, The Antiquary, The Bride of Lammermoor, The Talisman,* and *The Fair Maid of Perth.*

Jane Austen (1775-1817) wrote an altogether different type of novel. She portrayed the life of the middle class of her own day, delicately satirizing its shortcomings. Her two most famous novels are *Sense and Sensibility,* which first appeared in 1811, and *Pride and Prejudice* (1813). Jane Austen's popularity has continued to the present day, and many readers still find enjoyment in her analysis of early-nineteenth-century society and its foibles.

"Victorian" explained. Queen Victoria came to the throne in 1837 and remained there until 1901. During her important reign England saw a vast increase in economic power and empire, the rise of the bourgeoisie to political control, a rapid improvement in the standard of living, and a large output of revolutionary scientific concepts and inventions. The Victorian era began in romanticism and ended in realism. "Victorian" is the term used to mark what was characteristic of the Queen's reign. As we have mentioned earlier, the age saw an improvement in material matters. There was also an improvement in morality and concepts of decency, compared with the reigns of George IV and William IV. From all this came the so-called Victorian attitude: a sense of high moral purpose, a deficiency in sense of humor, and a rather stilted desire to be always "edifying" and "respectable."

Victorian poets. A poet who epitomized the Victorian spirit was England's poet laureate, Alfred, Lord Tennyson (1809-1892). It has been fashionable in recent years to "debunk" Tennyson because he mirrored so closely the Victorian age. However, Tennyson was a skillful poet and a popular one. "The Lady of Shalott," "The Lotos-Eaters," and "Frater Ave atque Vale" show Tennyson as a consummate craftsman. He is an extremely quotable poet, a master of words and rhythm. Most of us can recall lines from "The Charge of the Light Brigade," "The Brook," and "Crossing the Bar."

A much deeper thinker than Tennyson was his contemporary Robert Browning (1812-1889). It is true that Browning was not Tennyson's equal in versification, and he indulged in such liberties as rhyming "fabric" with "dab brick," but he displayed a piercing insight into human emotions. This was demonstrated by his development of the dramatic monologue, in which the poet allowed the subject of the monologue to reveal his character completely in what he said. Some of Browning's most famous dramatic monologues are "My Last Duchess," "Fra Lippo Lippi," and "The Bishop Orders His Tomb at Saint Praxed's." Browning lived much of his life in Florence, and he found in the history of the Italian Renaissance rich opportunities for character analysis. His masterpiece was *The Ring and the Book*, a long poem based on the story of an old murder case that occurred in Rome, about which Browning read in a parchment-covered tome he picked up in a market stall in Florence. Skillfully, Browning analyzed the psychological aspects of the murder from the viewpoint of each of the characters involved. Despite Browning's interest in abnormal aspects of human nature, he was intensely optimistic in his philosophy, and in this respect he largely mirrored the spirit of his age.

Rudyard Kipling (1865-1936), famous as both a poet and as a novelist, epitomized England's spirit of power, prestige, and imperialism. It was his self-appointed task to sing of England's mission as civilizer of backward peoples, to thank fate for her "dominion over palm and pine," and to relate stories of the bravery of her "thin red lines" of gallant Tommies. Kipling was superficial and jingoistic, but the lilt of his verses brought him a great deal of popularity. His best-known books of verse came largely out of his exposure to conditions in India, where he was born, and are entitled *Departmental Ditties* and *Barrack-Room Ballads.*

Charles Dickens, social novelist. The most widely read novelist of the Victorian age was Charles Dickens (1812-1870), who peopled the pages of literature with a vast array of characters portrayed in vivid detail. Among his best-loved novels are *Pickwick Papers, David Copperfield, The Old Curiosity Shop, Dombey and Son, Oliver Twist, A Tale of Two Cities,* and, of course, *A Christmas Carol.* Dickens wrote to instruct as well as amuse. He attacked the evils attending England's industrial expansion: slum conditions, the misery of the poor, and the inhuman debtors' prisons.

Thackeray, Kingsley, Eliot. Another novelist was William Makepeace Thackeray (1811-1863). His particular forte was the satirizing of England's upper classes, which he did with superb wit and urbanity. Perhaps his most famous novel is *Vanity Fair* (1848), with its clever but unscrupulous heroine, Becky Sharp. Thackeray wrote other brilliant novels, including *The Newcomes, The History of Henry Esmond,* and *The Virginians.*

Charles Kingsley (1819-1875) we have met before in connection with Christian socialism. He was a forceful novelist who showed his sympathies with the working classes in *Yeast* and *Alton Locke*, the latter dealing with the Chartist movement. *The Water Babies,* ostensibly a fairy tale about a chimney sweep who falls into the river and is turned into a water baby, has a strong social import. *Westward Ho!* Kingsley's most successful novel, is a historical romance set in Elizabethan times.

The most gifted woman novelist of the day was George Eliot (1819-1880). She wrote with penetrating power concerning human emotions and the effects of pain and suffering upon the personality. Eliot won her reputation on such works as *Adam Bede, The Mill on the Floss,* and *Silas Marner.*

Meredith, Butler, Hardy. Novelists who saw the century out showed an increasing tendency toward realism. Objective character studies and a frank facing of social issues became the vogue. George Meredith made his mark with character studies in *Beauchamp's Career* and *Diana of the Crossways,* while Samuel Butler (1835-1902) won fame as the author of *The Way of All Flesh.* This brilliantly ironic work levels a stinging indictment against middle-class concepts of family life, religion, and morality.

Probably the most pessimistic of this group of novelists was Thomas Hardy. Living for eighty-eight years without any particular blow of fate to break his spirit, admired and respected by the literary world, and dwelling in the lovely countryside of southwestern England, Hardy yet exhibited a remarkably negative attitude toward life. He wrote from the viewpoint that man is but a pawn in the hands of circumstance and environment, which are callously indifferent to his ideals. Hardy's novels display a fascinating array of characters, and he affords us a penetrating insight into the daily life of the countryside he loved so well. His fame rests principally on such novels as *Tess of the D'Urbervilles, The Return of the Native,* and *Jude the Obscure.*

Critics and essayists. The Victorian age abounded in excellent essayists and literary critics. Thomas Carlyle (1795-1881) was a trenchant critic of the complacent spirit that pervaded mid-Victorian political and social thought. He maintained in vitriolic language that the mere expansion of the ballot would not solve democracy's problems, and he railed against the evils of contemporary industrialism. This hard-headed Scot with grim humor and tortuous literary style attacked the materialism and sham of his day and felt that the hope of humanity lay in the heroic deeds of strong men. Besides his essays on this subject, Carlyle wrote widely read histories on the French Revolution, Frederick the Great, and Oliver Cromwell.

While Carlyle was assailing his fellow Victorians, Thomas Babington Macaulay (1800-1859) was gratifying them with brilliantly styled essays having the underlying thesis that theirs was the most wonderful and progressive of all ages. Macaulay's chief claim to fame, however, lies in his *History of England from the Accession of James* II. This work vividly depicts the characters of the time. Unfortunately it is a biased history, for it was penned from a Whig and Protestant point of view and coincides with Macaulay's own political philosophy.

John Ruskin (1819-1900), along with Dickens, Kingsley, and Carlyle, fought against the misery and ugliness brought about by nineteenth-century industrialism, a protest often called the esthetic revolt. Ruskin decried the new, sprawling, filthy factory towns, the ruin of the beautiful English countryside, and the misery of the factory workers. His solution lay in socialistic reforms and greater education for the people. Ruskin also wrote voluminously on art, defending such artists as Turner and the Pre-Raphaelites. His literary reputation is based chiefly on his *Seven Lamps of Architecture* and *The Stones of Venice,* which praise Gothic architecture and decry "the pestilent art of the Renaissance."

American Literature

Early dependence on England. The United States during the first half of the century was still suffering from growing pains which came from the expansion westward and the consolidation of its continental territory. America had not grown up, and this fact was reflected in much of its literature. The country might proudly boast of its independence from British political domination, but it was still indebted principally to the United Kingdom for its main intellectual and social inspirations. Washington Irving (1783-1859) has left us delightful short stories and essays in his *Sketch-Book* and *Knickerbocker's History of New York.* Though his settings are often laid in America, his style and outlook are fundamentally so English that it is little wonder he was accepted by the English reading public as a transplanted English writer. Other American writers of the period show the same indebtedness to English influences. James Fenimore Cooper (1789-1851) placed his *Leatherstocking Tales* in America, but he patterned his romances on those of Sir Walter Scott, and indeed he has been called the American Scott. The first American poet of ability was William Cullen Bryant (1794-1878), who has left us some excellent poems, including "Thanatopsis." Bryant was a poet of nature, who wrote about the American scene much as Wordsworth would have written had he come to New England.

American romanticism. The period from 1830 to 1860 represents the triumph of romanticism in American literature, and its center was New England, where lived and wrote the New England school—an appropriate name, for these poets and essayists were still largely following English patterns and adapting them to a New World environment. The most gifted of the New England poets was Henry Wadsworth Longfellow (1807-1882), who held a place in the popular American mind of the day akin to that held by Tennyson across the ocean. Like Tennyson, Longfellow was an excellent craftsman but given to moralizing and sententiousness.

The outstanding author of philosophical essays in New England was Ralph Waldo Emerson (1803-1882), a friend of Thomas Carlyle, who brought back to America a modified German idealism call transcendentalism. Emerson preached the doctrine of self-reliance and individualism, declaring that America's "long apprenticeship to the learning of other lands draws to a close." But there were only a few to answer his plea for individuality.

Literary individualists. A few American writers were not primarily imitators of European models. One such writer was Edgar Allan Poe (1809-1849). Concerned with the bizarre and abnormal in his tales and poetry, Poe revealed his vivid imaginative powers in a medium which he developed to a remarkable degree—the short story. Later writers both in America and abroad were to profit by Poe's brilliant contribution.

The most American poet of the nineteenth century was Walt Whitman (1819-1892), who stands in direct contrast to the romantic New England school, with its polished style and "respectable" subject matter. Whitman brought a new and dynamic force to American letters. He rejected the accepted patterns of verse writing and refused to confine himself to traditional subjects. Whitman was romantic in his idealism but realistic in his frank and earthy presentation of American life. He wrote poems about the Brooklyn Ferry, or

The varied and ample land, the South and the North in the light, Ohio's shores and flashing Missouri,
And ever the far-spreading prairies covered with grass and corn.

Like Burns a century before in Scotland, Whitman was the great apostle of the dignity and brotherhood of man. His outspoken frankness, which shocked his contemporaries, was consciously democratic.

While the New England school continued to maintain its general popularity throughout the nineteenth century, the literary aspirants of the twentieth century found their inspiration in the originality of writers like Poe and Whitman.

Humorists. American humor is exuberant and spontaneous, whereas that of the English is restrained and inclined to understatement. The exaggeration of the Americans may have developed during America's westward expansion, when restraints tended to be broken and the vastness and vitality of the movement entered into the national life. Certainly the many humorists of the period found fertile territory for creative writing west of the Mississippi.

Undoubtedly the finest humorist of the age was Mark Twain (1835-1910), famous for his description of life on the Mississippi and such classics as *The Adventures of Tom Sawyer* and *Huckleberry Finn.* Mark Twain could be bitterly satirical at times but is remembered mainly for his jocular analysis of the American scene, which he knew intimately.

Other humorists of genuine ability have also contributed to this attractive phase of American letters, including Bret Harte (1839-1902), whose poems and stories are laid in California, particularly during the gold rush of Forty-Nine and the years following. Again, in Bret Harte, we find exaggeration as well as emphasis upon the picturesque and bizarre in the American scene.

Literature of the Continent

French literature. The literature of France was abundant during the nineteenth century. During the first part of the age it was dominated by romanticism, for the influence of the French Revolution and Rousseau colored all thought. The internal political dissensions which racked the country all during the century, together with the bitter disillusionment brought about by the disastrous Franco-Prussian War, resulted in a reaction, however, and the last decades were marked by a stern and even savage realism.

French romantic poets. Alphonse de Lamartine (1790-1869), poet and statesman, won fame as a champion of liberty. Lamartine earned attention by his attractive style, sentimentalism, and delicacy of expression. He published poems of a mystical nature called *Meditations* (1820), followed by *New Meditations* in 1823. But Lamartine showed superficiality of thought, and his verse was not sufficiently vigorous and original to warrant his being ranked among the greatest romantic poets.

Alfred de Vigny (1797-1863) has been called the most restrained of all the French romanticists. Born of a distinguished family, de Vigny was educated for the army but resigned and devoted himself to literature. Owing to personal disappointments, including deception by an actress of whom he was fond, de Vigny withdrew from his circle of friends. His poetic works include *Poems, Ancient and Modern,* which have classical restraint yet are romantic in their vocabulary. They are evidence of de Vigny's strong intellectual gifts. De Vigny also wrote a historical novel of the period of Louis XIII called *Cinq-Mars* and a play entitled *Chatterton.*

Whereas de Vigny was restrained, Alfred de Musset (1810-1857) gave free reign to his emotions and moods and for this reason has been called by some critics the Byron of French literature. By the time he was seventeen years old, de Musset was winning prizes for his poetry, and at an early age he met the famous Victor Hugo, who encouraged him to write. In 1833-1834 he ran off to Italy with the gifted woman novelist, George Sand, but the tempestuous love affair quickly ended, and de Musset fell into despair. Within the next few years, however, he had written a group of splendid lyrics entitled *Nights.* Like Byron, de Musset was often careless as to detail and refused to polish phrases, perhaps because it was felt among the romanticists that revision destroyed the original flow of inspiration.

Victor Hugo. By far the most commanding French writer of the period, and for that matter probably the most outstanding literary figure in France during the entire century, was Victor Hugo (1802-1885). When only fifteen he was awarded honorable mention by the French Academy for his poem "On the Advantages of Study," and in 1826 he published a book, *Odes and Ballads.* Thereafter a steady stream of poems, dramas, novels, essays, and histories flowed from his tireless pen. He combined with a fertile imagination a magnificent command of language, so that he could express any of his many moods with appropriate words and phrases.

In 1838 Hugo was made an officer of the Legion of Honor, and in 1841 he was elected to the French Academy. In 1845 he went into politics as a fervent exponent of the principles of democracy. When Louis Napoleon engineered a *coup d'état* to gain the throne, Hugo denounced the political trick to such an extent that he was forced into exile. Not until 1870 did Hugo return to his native land, writing in the meantime some of his finest novels as well as a violent satire against Louis Napoleon, whom he called "*Napoléon le petit.*" When he died in 1885, Victor Hugo was a great national figure. His funeral was in itself a most magnificent spectacle, and his body was interred in the Panthéon in Paris. His greatest novel was *Les Misérables* (1862), a superbly told story of the misery and degradation of the common people, involving the theme of sin and redemption. In his poetry Hugo praised the beauty of nature, the goodness of God, and the progress of man.

Alexandre Dumas. The first half of the century was enriched by numerous other novelists. The best-known romantic novelist, after Hugo, was Alexandre Dumas the elder (1802-1870), a master of the historical novel and a storyteller *par excellence.* His father was one of Napoleon's generals whose mother had been a West Indian Negress, and from his grandmother Dumas inherited characteristics which Stevenson describes: "the ventripotent (gluttonous) mulatto, the great eater, worker, earner and waster, the man of much and witty laughter, the man of the great heart and alas! of the doubtful honesty." However fair may be this judgment, there is no denying the vividness of the swashbuckling tales he wrote (or helped write, for in many instances he gave the ideas, and hack-writers filled in the details). Everyone is acquainted with his masterpieces, *The Three Musketeers, Twenty Years After,* and *The Count of Monte Cristo.*

French realists: Balzac. Realism as a literary philosophy found an early champion in Honoré de Balzac (1799-1850). This prolific writer (in twenty years he turned out eighty-five novels) lived most of his life in poverty and loneliness. In his *Comédie Humaine,* a series of a hundred novels containing some five thousand characters, Balzac portrayed minutely and realistically the whole framework of French society. He has been often criticized for glorying in the crudities and frailties of mankind.

Gustave Flaubert. The age of the Second Empire (1852-1870) saw the decline of romanticism and the growth of realism. By far the most prominent of the novelists was Gustave Flaubert (1821-1880), who cherished art for art's sake, hated the bourgeoisie for their concepts of morality and art, and was a stylist who labored ceaselessly to perfect every sentence he wrote. So careful a craftsman was he that he once said, "I have worked sixteen hours to-day and have at last finished my page." His most famous novel was *Madame Bovary*, regarded by many as the masterpiece of realistic fiction. The tragedy of the unhappy wife of a country doctor who sought in various ways to give rein to her romantic nature and who so degraded herself that she finally committed suicide, *Madame Bovary* is almost photographic in its realism. For this work Flaubert has been called a literary surgeon who "dissected passion and conducted post mortem examinations of the human heart."

The humiliation suffered by France in its disastrous war with Prussia and the terrible days of the Communes brought romanticism to a final close. In the midst of so much national melancholy it was impossible that the romantic philosophy of progress and Utopianism should continue to exist. Men sought instead a "down-to-earth" philosophy in which doubt, uncertainty, and even gloom had their place. Science and skepticism were the keynotes of the new realism. Authors were now supposed to look at everything in life—beauty and ugliness, good and evil—quite dispassionately. Theirs was the job, theoretically at any rate, to chronicle without comment, to be photographic without "touching up." Flaubert the realist stated the dictum of the new school, "An artist ought no more appear in his work than God does in nature."

Paul Verlaine, poet. One of the most prominent of the Third Republic poets, and certainly one of its most musical, was Paul Verlaine (1844-1896). Verlaine was an extraordinary character who spent his life in the café, gutter, jail, and hospital, and who has been described as an "absinthe-sodden poet," but he captivated his readers with his exquisitely musical verse. Melancholy and volatile, Verlaine would express in subtle phrases his ever-changing moods and could quickly change from an antisocial roisterer to a profound mystic, honoring Jesus and the Virgin with ecstatic lyrics.

Guy de Maupassant. Guy de Maupassant (1850-1893) stands out as the great master of the short story. Between 1880 and 1892, this nephew of Flaubert wrote a dozen volumes of short stories and half a dozen full novels. An utter realist who portrayed dispassionately mankind's virtues and vices alike, Maupassant was content to allow the reader to draw any conclusions he wanted. He has been called "a great artist with low ideals," but this accusation is probably unjust. His aim was to entertain rather than instruct.

Emile Zola. In the works of Emile Zola (1840-1902), realism reached an extreme called naturalism. The realist was bound to write only what he observed, but the naturalist felt it his duty actually to experience the environment of his characters for himself. In order to get "slices of life," the naturalist often became a miner or farmer and might even have himself put in prison to get the right atmosphere. The most famous writer of this school was Zola, who wrote a twenty-volume series (*Rougon-Macquart*) describing in complete detail the sociological history of a middle-class family living under the Second Empire. There is much justice in the accusation leveled against Zola that he overemphasized the sordid and regarded man only as a human beast, but he came magnificently to the defense of a wronged innocent man, Captain Dreyfus, in *J'accuse*, a letter which pleaded for justice at a time when French courts were playing politics (see page 161).

Anatole France. A literary craftsman who saw the century out and who won universal fame for his writings was Jacques Anatole Thibault, known better as Anatole France (1844-1924). When he was but twenty-four, he made his literary debut with a biographical study of Alfred de Vigny, and in the years that followed he wrote many masterpieces in flawless language. Anatole France was a Frenchman of the best intellectual type: witty, analytical, skeptical, urbane, delicately ironic, yet tolerant and kindly. His most famous novel may be *Penguin Island*. It is a satirical tale in which the author adroitly picks apart the religious, artistic, moral, and political foibles of his native land. He closed the novel with a picture of society ruined by social inequality, plunged into revolution, and faced with the task of rebuilding civilization.

German literature. Romanticism found a dominant place in nineteenth-century German literature. As the century opened, however, the stage was monopolized by two great figures who were only partially influenced by the new movement. One was Johann Friedrich von Schiller (1759-1805), the other Johann Wolfgang von Goethe (1749-1832). These two fast friends were deeply influenced by Rousseau's revolt against conventions and interest in nature, but they always retained a classical approach to literature.

The greatest of the lyric poets in Germany was Heinrich Heine (1797-1856), a Jew who lived the last years of his life in Paris, the victim of many personal misfortunes including almost complete paralysis during his last eight years. Heine was gifted with a wonderful lyric ability and piercing wit. He used the vocabulary of folk poetry a great deal, and his lyrics are simple in expression and melody. Many of them have been put to music by composers.

The greatest German dramatist of his age was Christian Friedrich Hebbel (1813-1863). Rising out of direst poverty, Hebbel gained a position of eminence with such dramas as *Judith, Maria Magdalene,* and a trilogy centering around German folk-lore, *Die Nibelungen.* Hebbel was primarily concerned with problems in the field of abnormal psychology, and this interest proved a drawback to his success as a practical dramatist, who has to present his story in as simple a manner as possible.

Richard Wagner (1813-1883), poet and musician, combined his talents in the creation of great music-dramas. It was his belief that both music and story should blend into a stirring work of art. He would take a mythological subject, sketch out the drama, next write the verse, and from this structure be inspired to compose appropriate music. Wagner was fond of German folk literature and conceived from it *Der Ring des Nibelungen,* consisting of the operas *Das Rheingold, Die Walküre, Siegfried,* and *Götterdämmerung.* We shall have more to say about Wagner when we summarize the development of music in the nineteenth century.

Russian poetry. Nineteenth-century Russian literature had a substantial number of poets and novelists of the first order. The greatest poet was Alexander Pushkin (1799-1837), born the son of a noble and destined by circumstances and his own personality to a wild, exciting, but short life, dying in a duel at St. Petersburg. Pushkin has been called the Russian Byron, and for his English contemporary he held the highest regard. In fact, Byron opened Pushkin's eyes to literary horizons that were fresh and vivid. But Pushkin was no mere imitator. Rather he became the poet of his native land. He painted in brilliant lyric poetry the beauty of the Russian landscape and the wealth to be found in Russian folklore. He described everyday life among his countrymen so strikingly that he remains their most beloved bard. Pushkin wrote a novel in verse, *Eugene Onegin,* the story of a citizen of St. Petersburg. This work, described as the "first Russian novel," is brilliantly witty and arresting and, like *Hamlet,* has lent itself to endless quotations. Pushkin also wrote a tragic dramatic poem, *Boris Godunov,* the story of a pretender to the throne who claimed to be the son of Ivan the Terrible. This work was made into a well-known opera by Moussorgsky (see page 204).

Russian novelists. A great satirist and writer, considered most responsible for the development of modern Russian prose, was Nikolai Gogol (1809-1852). Gogol is known to English readers chiefly for the translation of his novel *Dead Souls,* a satire of provincial Russian society. It was the custom for Russian landlords to pay poll taxes on each of their serfs, of whom a census was made once every ten years, and this tax was paid during the interval even though a serf died. An adventurer named Chichikov acquires these "dead souls" from their owners and deposits the title to them in a bank which still believes them alive as security for loans he makes. The various characters of the book are portrayed with much humor. Gogol's greatest drama was *The Inspector-General,* which satirizes Russian government officials and the corrupt bureaucracy of the day.

Ivan Sergyeevich Turgenev (1818-1883) blended a strong sense of humor with facility of description. He gained his reputation with *The Diary of a Sportsman,* which contained lifelike representations of the Russian serfs and which had some effect in gaining their emancipation. His best-known novel was *Fathers and Sons,* which describes the conflict between the younger generation with its scientific and social ideology and the older group with its love of the status quo. The novel is an artistic triumph in that Turgenev skillfully blended imaginative writing with a social theme.

Feodor Dostoevski (1821-1881) was a master of the psychological novel. Born an epileptic amid poor surroundings and condemned for political activities to hard labor in the Siberian mines from 1849 to 1855, Dostoevski was well qualified to write realistically. He probed unflinchingly "the dark places of the human spirit" to ferret out motives and abnormal emotions, and there is little humor in his masterpieces. Such novels as *The Brothers Karamazov* and *Crime and Punishment* ensure Dostoevski's reputation as one of the world's greatest novelists. *Crime and Punishment* is the unvarnished tale of a poor student who, out of egotism and a resentment against life in general, commits murder. His sweetheart persuades him to confess his crime. He is sent to Siberia, where he is joined by the girl, and through her devotion he is redeemed. It was Dostoevski's philosophy that suffering brings about humanity's salvation.

Count Leo Tolstoy (1828-1910) was an extraordinary character. Born of wealthy and aristocratic parents and having seen military service in the Crimean War, Tolstoy in his later years experienced a profound spiritual conversion, though not of an orthodox nature, for he was actually excommunicated by the Greek Orthodox Church. Tolstoy came to the conclusion that the only philosophy worth while was the teaching of Jesus, stripped of all ecclesiastical authority. He lived a most simple life; in fact he was a pacific anarchist who preached the doctrine of love and nonresistance. His two greatest novels were *War and Peace* and *Anna Karenina.* The first is a historical novel in the Russia of the Napoleonic wars. The plot is complex and disorganized, but Tolstoy's characterizations are superb. In it he not only shows the horror and futility of war but glorifies the simple, natural life at the expense of the sophisticated, artificial one which our civilization has created. *Anna Karenina* is the powerfully written tragedy of a woman who leaves her pompous husband for a vain and brilliant lover, who tires of her, and of her condemnation by the world until there is no solution but suicide. It ranks high among the world's classics.

Scandinavian writers. Denmark was the home of Hans Christian Andersen (1805-1875), known to all for his fairy tales and other stories for children. But Norway probably produced the most outstanding Scandinavian writers of the century. A brilliant dramatist was Henrik Ibsen (1828-1906), satirist of modern middle-class society and student of social and psychological problems. *Peer Gynt,* called "the most Norwegian of his plays," ridicules Ibsen's countrymen by portraying what he thinks to be their basic shortcomings. Some of Ibsen's other well-known plays include *Hedda Gabler, The Lady from the Sea,* and *A Doll's House,* in which Ibsen assails prevailing views concerning the life of the family and the relationships between men and women and parents and children. That Ibsen was also a fine poet is shown by "The Eider-Duck," written when leaving Norway for Italy.

Björnstjerne Björnson (1832-1910) was also a Norwegian poet and dramatist, but, unlike Ibsen, his approach to life was by way of the emotions rather than the intellect. He wrote a dramatic trilogy called *Sigurd Slembe,* taken from the history of Norway. He also composed stories which stressed social progress and Björnson's faith in the common people. It has been said that Ibsen exemplifies the mental make-up of the Norwegian, while Björnson has an emotional impetuosity akin to that of the ancient Vikings.

The most famous Swedish writer of the nineteenth century was Johan August Strindberg (1849-1912), proficient in such diversified fields as drama, fiction, and history. Strindberg in his literary philosophy was motivated by realism and naturalism, while the passing of years changed his political views from democratic radicalism to Nietzsche's theory of the superman, and his religious views from orthodoxy to atheism. Strindberg attained notoriety because of his pronounced aversion to women, a hatred to be found in such of his dramas as *Countess Julia* and *Creditors.* He won deserved fame for the excellence of his poetry, fiction, and short stories.

Italian writers. One of the most gifted Italian writers was Alessandro Manzoni, a dramatist and novelist. Two of his historical tragedies were *Carmagnola* and *Adelchi.* However, he won chief fame for the historical novel *The Betrothed* (*I Promessi Sposi*), which Sir Walter Scott declared the best ever written. Poetry for much of the century was influenced by the popular theme of Italian unification and patriotism, and poets like Giosuè Carducci, author of *Odi Barbare,* attained eminence for glorifying the unified kingdom. Giuseppe Giacosa, chiefly because of the delicacy and penetration of his work, has been rated the most capable Italian dramatist of the nineteenth century. His first plays were written under the influence of the romantic school, but he became interested more and more in social problems with the coming of realism. Giacosa shows his indebtedness to the Norwegian dramatist Ibsen, in some of his work. The librettos for Giacomo Puccini's operas were composed by Giacosa.

Developments in Music

Eighteenth- and nineteenth-century music. The eighteenth century had evolved a style of music in keeping with its intellectual and social pattern. We think of this age as one in which poets laid stress upon rigid form and philosophers praised the intellect above the emotions. It was the age of the salon and of the landed aristocracy. It was also the age of the minuet and saw the development of the clearly defined, formalized sonata form. When we listen to the music of Haydn and Mozart, we are struck by its graceful quality and "good taste," but we are not likely to be deeply stirred emotionally. It is known that Haydn was quiet and completely self-possessed when he composed his music and liked to be neat and wearing his best clothes when at work upon his more serious numbers, while Mozart, although able to write music down as quickly as most people write a letter, never felt so impassioned that he could not take part in a conversation at the same time. It was typical also of these polished, urbane days that the orchestra which played the compositions of Mozart and Haydn was small; it consisted mostly of stringed instruments and contained few solo brasses or percussions.

The nineteenth century, however, changed music radically. Europe had now embarked upon new political developments as a result of forces put into operation by the French Revolution, including the growth of parliamentary practices and national patriotism, while the new order of machines and factories had brought tremendous social and economic results. The intellect was challenged by the emotions, the aristocracy by the bourgeoisie, and the salon by the counting house. Nineteenth-century music was too full of new forces and ideas to be fettered by the rigidity of the minuet or forced to half-express itself through the limited medium of the small chamber orchestra of the eighteenth century.

German music—Beethoven. The genius who broke the classical mold and vitalized music was Ludwig van Beethoven (1770-1827). This tempestuous, moody, misery-ridden composer was born the son of a poor musician, and his early life was passed in hardship. He soon showed great ability at extemporizing, and his promise attracted favorable notice from Haydn, under whom he studied awhile, although the older man never appreciated fully the radical tendencies of his brilliant pupil. Beethoven's later life was filled with much ill-fortune, culminating in stone-deafness. Throughout his stormy life Beethoven was a sincere lover of nature. He would range the countryside, sometimes lying on his back and staring into the sky with delight, sometimes pacing along, humming snatches of melody, pausing to jot down notes. Beethoven at the same time possessed a tremendous love for the common people and for democratic principles. He had written his third symphony in honor of Bonaparte and was about to dispatch it to Paris when news came that Napoleon had made himself emperor. Beethoven tore off the page bearing the soldier's name and nearly destroyed the symphony itself. But when it was finally produced, it bore the significant words, "*Sinfonia Eroica,* in memory of a great man."

Beethoven's versatility was great; he was proficient in almost all kinds of musical expression. The symphonies alone are sufficient to ensure Beethoven's fame. Of these the Fifth is perhaps best known. In his First symphony Beethoven shows the influence of Haydn, but later compositions show successively his deeply original nature.

Beethoven performed many valuable services in the evolution of music. He added flexibility by breaking many conventions of composition: he modified the character of the rondo and scherzo and, in fact, changed the dominating factor in music from an emphasis upon regulations of composition to the expression of mood and tone. He developed new harmonies, enlarging the scope of the orchestra to handle them, giving new importance, for example, to the woodwinds, brasses, and percussion instruments. Despite the assertion of a contemporary critic that Beethoven's music was the "obstreperous roaring of modern frenzy," the composer performed a twofold task: he freed music from formalism and lifeless laws, and he brought it out of the fashionable salons, where only a few aristocratic persons could hear it, giving it to the world at large. "Beethoven's whole art is the triumph of power over material, a triumph of function over substance, subject over object."[7]

The German romantics. Beethoven acted as a bridge between classicism and romanticism, and there now arose in Germany a number of composers who accepted the new musical philosophy. Karl Maria von Weber (1786-1826) lived during the days which saw the overrunning of the German states by Napoleon's armies, and he became a deep-rooted patriot. His music has in it melodies which came from German folk songs, and his appeal was to nationalistic emotions. His greatest triumph was the opera *Der Freischütz,* which was written in the German tongue and is completely German in all characteristics. Its success was immediate and sensational. With this work began the era of the national opera for the German people.

Franz Schubert (1797-1828) created German romantic concert music. To Schubert we are indebted for the perfecting of the modern song, or *lied,* as the Germans call it. In his eighteenth year Schubert composed an almost flawless song, "The Erlking," and from this time on, songs poured almost ceaselessly from his pen. Besides writing over six hundred fifty songs, many of which are known all over the world, Schubert composed numerous instrumental works. Of his symphonies, the most frequently played are No. 7 in C major and No. 8 in B minor, known familiarly as the "Unfinished" symphony.

Another romanticist, one extremely popular in his own day, was Felix Mendelssohn-Bartholdy (1809-1847). Using classical forms to express his romantic sympathies, Mendelssohn wrote music that was fresh and charming but certainly not soul-stirring. By the time he was seventeen, Mendelssohn had written the incidental music to *A Midsummer-Night's Dream,* and in his short life he also composed two piano concertos, a violin concerto, three oratorios (including *Elijah*), four symphonies, and numerous songs and incidental works.

Robert Schumann (1810-1856) was prominent as a composer, conductor, critic, and essayist. He was the founder and editor of the influential *Neue Zeitschrift für Musik* (New Journal for Music), and the great friend and champion of Johannes Brahms. Schumann's last years were clouded by insanity; in 1854 he failed in an attempt at suicide. He died two years later. Schumann was a romanticist, but his style was formalized, for he looked on Bach as his master. Schumann's works include many vocal compositions and pieces for the piano, of which he was particularly fond; his piano concerto in A minor has always been popular. He also wrote four symphonies and the opera *Genoveva.*

Johannes Brahms. In 1853 a young man of twenty came to the home of Schumann, armed with a letter of introduction. When he sat down to the piano to play one of his compositions, Schumann interrupted him by saying, "Clara must hear this," and when his wife came into the room, "Here, dear Clara, you will hear such music as you never heard before; now, begin again, young man!"[8] From that moment the future of Johannes Brahms (1833-1897) was assured. Schumann wrote to a leading musician of the day, "This is he that should come," and proclaimed in an article in his *Neue Zeitschrift für Musik* that Brahms was the true successor of Beethoven. Brahms lived up to Schumann's prophecy. Some critics consider the three outstanding geniuses in the history of music to be Bach, Beethoven, and Brahms.

Brahms was master of the art known as thematic development. He could take a quite unpretentious theme and, with his complete knowledge of every harmonic and contrapuntal resource, create an effect of entrancing beauty. Brahms has been ranked among the romantic composers in that his work strongly shows his own moods and personality. But the austerity and restraint of emotion and sensuousness take him out of this school and place him as one apart. His appeal is to the serious and even somber moods, rather than the humorous and carefree. Brahms studied German folk music and wrote many beautiful accompaniments for cycles of songs in addition to his instrumental works.

French music. To this point we have concentrated upon the advances made by nineteenth-century German composers, especially their orchestral music and innovations in instrumentation and harmony. Other nations at this time were producing their quota of gifted orchestral composers. France was the home of Hector Berlioz (1803-1869), a precocious genius who had the trait of shocking people in everything he said and did. As a romanticist he rebelled against conventions of all sorts. It is said that his ability at discovering orchestral timbres was equaled only by his ability at making enemies. "Ah, me!" he wrote in his *Memoirs,* "what was the good God thinking when He dropped me down in this pleasant land of France?" Berlioz was responsible in large measure for the development of the orchestra's latent qualities. He helped free instrumental music from traditionalism, and his theories of orchestration were revolutionary. Typical of the "bigness" of the romantic school, Berlioz maintained that his ideal orchestra should consist of four hundred sixty-seven instruments. Among his best-known works are the symphony *Romeo and Juliet,* the oratorio *The Damnation of Faust,* and the opera *Benvenuto Cellini.*

Of a completely different mold was César Franck (1822-1890). Born in Belgium, Franck passed most of his life in Paris, almost in obscurity, playing the organ at Sainte Clotilde and teaching at the Conservatoire. But Franck was oblivious to the slights of fame and fortune; he was a religious mystic who lived for his music, and the sincerity of his simple life is reflected throughout his compositions. His works for the organ are extremely fine, for he was particularly fond of this instrument. He composed only one symphony, the D minor, but its fame is universal.

The five Russians. The defeat of Napoleon in his campaign of 1812 kindled in nineteenth-century Russians a fervent patriotism which affected their arts. Music became tinged with added emotionalism and romanticism, and the composers of the period were decidedly nationalistic. A group of young composers made themselves famous by building on the rich folk music and historical settings of their native land. They are known as "The Five" and consist of Mili Balakirev, César Cui, Alexander Borodin, Nikolay Rimski-Korsakov, and Modest Moussorgsky.

Balakirev was the founder of this group and inspired the others by his own enthusiasm and accomplishments. He not only made a splendid collection of old Russian folk songs, but he composed for the piano and orchestra. Cui was the first convert to the new movement, and he wielded his pen bravely in defending and publicizing the cause; he is thus remembered more as a pamphleteer than as a composer.

Borodin was a versatile person. By profession he was an army physician and chemist, and he also attained distinction as an author, educator, and philanthropist. But as a composer he enriched his country's culture by writing piano pieces, songs, a symphonic poem, two symphonies, and the famous opera *Prince Igor.* Borodin imbued his music with rich coloring and an oriental spirit, and the dances from *Prince Igor* attest to the virile qualities of his music.

Rimski-Korsakov spent the early years of his life as a naval cadet. However, he turned to music and became one of the greatest masters of orchestration that the history of music has known. His rich gifts in orchestration are evident in the strikingly oriental symphonic poem *Scheherazade.* Rimski-Korsakov also composed three symphonies and some outstanding operas, including *The Snow Maiden* and *The Golden Cockerel.*

The most gifted composer of "The Five" was Modest Moussorgsky, who wrote many songs (of which "The Flea" is popular), symphonic music, and operas. The repertoire of the modern orchestra includes his brilliant tone poem *A Night on Bald Mountain* and *Pictures at an Exhibition.* This latter work was originally written for the piano, but later composers like Maurice Ravel orchestrated it because of its rich possibilities in that field. Moussorgsky, however, is most famous for his stirring music drama, *Boris Godunov,* which is set in medieval Russia and is a fascinating blend of wild Cossack folklore and sensuous Byzantine music.

Tschaikowsky. The world at large looks on Peter Ilich Tschaikowsky (1840-1893) as Russia's most outstanding composer. He stood apart from the "Five," who were much more Russian both in subject matter and technique. Tschaikowsky, on the other hand, followed traditional German methods and was an out-and-out romanticist. Everyone is acquainted with such melodious songs as "None but the Lonely Heart," the "1812 Overture" and "Marche Slav," the symphonic poem *Romeo and Juliet,* and the ever-popular *Nutcracker Suite.* In addition he wrote the opera *Eugene Onegin* and six symphonies. The last three are best known, and of these the *Pathétique* has attained a world-wide popularity.

Chopin's graceful music. Every student of the piano is intimately acquainted with the works of Frédéric Chopin (1809-1849). Polish by birth, Chopin lived most of his life in Paris after 1831. His life was rather uneventful except for a short and not-too-happy love affair with the illustrious woman novelist George Sand. This gifted master of the piano was singularly self-contained in an age when Paris was the scene of revolution and the romantics were going to extremes. Rejecting everything except what he himself desired, Chopin wrote music at once gentle and graceful and marked by strict craftsmanship. His greatest contribution, aside from composing a great deal of music, was the development of the resources of the piano as an instrument. "His originality is so compelling, every one of his ideas and phrases has such unique aroma, that perhaps no other composer can be so quickly identified."[9]

Development of opera. Prior to the nineteenth century the opera had been highly conventionalized, but now composers attempted with increasing success to correlate such varied elements as vocal parts, orchestration, and dramatic action, a goal that is best attained in the music dramas of Richard Wagner and Modest Moussorgsky.

In Germany Karl Maria von Weber created national opera and also correlated vocal and instrumental music in his *Der Freischütz.* In France there grew up a national opera due to the efforts of Charles Gounod, Camille Saint-Saëns, Georges Bizet, and Jules Massenet. Gounod in his work possessed the charm of poetic sentimentality, of being "sensuous but not sensual," and this quality permeated nineteenth-century French opera. Gounod's masterpiece was *Faust,* while *Romeo and Juliet* is probably his next best. Saint-Saëns made his mark in the operatic field with the popular *Samson and Delilah,* from which comes the song "My Heart at Thy Sweet Voice." Bizet is always remembered for *Carmen,* as popular as any opera in existence. It was most unfortunate for the history of opera that within three months after *Carmen* had been performed for the first time in Paris its young composer died. Massenet also combined rich melodies and appropriate orchestration in his operas. His best-known works are *Manon, Thaïs,* and *Le Jongleur de Notre Dame.*

Italian opera. By far the most outstanding Italian composer was Giuseppe Verdi (1813-1901). His parents were peasants and innkeepers, but Verdi's untutored father gave the boy a spinet and encouraged him to cultivate his natural genius. A merchant of the town gave him the opportunity to go on with his musical education, and later Verdi married his patron's daughter, by whom he had two children. His wife and family died tragically, however, and Verdi for a time gave up all composing. When he had overcome his grief, he resumed work and throughout his long life composed famous operas—*Rigoletto, Il Trovatore, La Traviata, Aïda* (written for the khedive of Egypt), *Otello,* and *Falstaff.* It was a phenomenon that Verdi composed some of his finest work when almost eighty.

In the field of the comic opera, another Italian composer achieved notable success. He was Gioachino Rossini (1792-1868), the son of a trumpeter and a baker's daughter. Rossini did much to modernize Italian opera, both of the serious and comic variety. He did away with the old practice of allowing the *prima donna* to monopolize the opera with florid solos and improvisations, and he was the first Italian to assign leading roles to contraltos and basses. He also made each dramatic scene a continuous musical movement and amplified the finale. His most famous opera, one which is still enthusiastically received whenever played, is *The Barber of Seville.*

English music. A unique type of comic opera was developed in the nineteenth century by a pair of Englishmen, Gilbert and Sullivan. Their work is completely English in spirit and subject matter. Among their many operas are *H.M.S. Pinafore, Iolanthe, The Yeomen of the Guard,* and *Pirates of Penzance.* Sir William S. Gilbert, who wrote the words, was a witty satirist who lampooned "Toryism" in the army, navy, House of Lords, and law courts and also parodied existing social and literary movements, such as the esthetic "sunflower" school of Oscar Wilde. Sir Arthur Sullivan wrote music which acted as a perfect foil to the patter of Gilbert, with the result that the Gilbert and Sullivan operas have become almost as sacred an English institution as the "sacred cows" which they lampooned.

Other than the work of these two men, however, nineteenth-century England produced little music of outstanding merit, although Sir Edward Elgar wrote some serious works which have stood the years. Orchestras today play his interesting *Enigma Variations,* while military bands throughout the British Commonwealth can always get a cheer out of their audiences by playing that unofficial national anthem, the *Pomp and Circumstance* march.

Wagner, the individualist. The most individualistic musical figure in the entire century was Richard Wagner (1813-1883). In many respects he stands as the culmination of the romantic school, with his tremendous emotional drive and stirring nationalistic appeal. On the other hand, the many innovations which Wagner made in the special field of his genius, the music-drama, stamp him as a composer apart and place him in that select group of musicians whose works have transcended the limitations of environment and time—men like Bach, Mozart, Beethoven, and Brahms. Wagner was an individualist in everything he did. He was a political rebel who had to flee into exile for years and a social rebel who shocked contemporaries by his unconventional life. He believed wholeheartedly in Nietzsche's doctrine of the superman, and was extremely nationalistic. It is not very difficult to understand that Hitler became a fervent admirer of Wagner.

Most of his music-dramas are still performed today. *Tannhaüser* and *Lohengrin* Wagner called romantic operas, and this appellation fits them both. *Tristan and Isolde,* based on an old Celtic legend, is unsurpassed in its simple, intensely emotional presentation of a tragic love story. *Die Meistersinger von Nürnberg* is sometimes called Wagner's one comic opera, but it is not so amusing as Rossini's *Barber of Seville,* which in several respects it resembles. Rather it lacks the tragic elements to be found in Wagner's other works. *Parsifal* is his most religious opera and represents the merging in Wagner's mind of the dramatic qualities surrounding Christ's life with the mystical concepts which the composer got from his studies of Buddhism and the philosophy of Schopenhauer.

Wagner was fascinated by the old German epic, the *Nibelungenlied,* and over a period of years he composed his memorable *Der Ring des Nibelungen* consisting of the following music dramas: *Das Rheingold, Die Walküre, Siegfried,* and *Götterdämmerung.* These are easily the most popular of Wagner's works, especially with audiences which respond to large, stirring themes of strong emotional content, sometimes gaudy and pompous.

Painting, Architecture, and Sculpture

Trends in painting. Art in the nineteenth century reflected the rather stormy course of history. The painting, architecture, and sculpture of the period reveal many new influences, for it was a century of revolution in the arts as well as in politics. At the beginning of the century the classic style held sway. It was a stricter classicism than that of the Renaissance, and severity and simplicity were the mode. Later in the century, as reaction gave way to liberalism in politics and the French Revolution came to be regarded less as a catastrophe and more as a struggle for freedom, there developed a great interest in the struggles of the individual in society, which was manifested in art as the romantic school. The romantic artist often liked to escape from the dreary world of cities and factories which he saw around him. Revivals of the styles of other periods were popular, especially in architecture. Romantic architects built houses, factories, and bridges with medieval towers and arches and decorative details, while painters and sculptors found enchanting subject matter in medieval legends. The painter was drawn to the picturesqueness of the Near East. But along with the picturesque trappings, artists were becoming more interested in the individual, and many were deeply moved by the political struggles of the day. The writings of Rousseau were widely read, and much interest was shown in his back-to-nature movement. Painters began to go outdoors to paint and became interested in the country, just as the romantic poets had rediscovered nature.

In the last decades of the nineteenth century another revolt appeared. As a reaction against the subjective and emotional romantic school, artists concerned themselves with objective representation, depicting just what they saw with little literary or political comment. These painters, the Impressionists, made many important technical experiments.

Classicism. Among the painters influenced by the classic style at the beginning of the century was Jacques Louis David. His portrait of

Madame Récamier below shows the affected simplicity and severity typical of the art of the period. Notice the "classic" details such as the bare feet, the simple white robe, and the lamp at the side. The picture shows how artists used the superficial decorative details of the classic style without catching any of the essential Greek attitude. In technique this type of painting is lacking in beauty of paint application and in any real compositional ability. Compare it with the works of such painters as El Greco (page 68), Velásquez (69), or Hogarth (74).

Romanticism. The romanticists had a dramatic approach to painting which was expressed in their use of strong color and generally exciting compositions. Eugène Delacroix was a painter whose turgid and melodramatic canvases illustrate the emotional approach of the romanticists. He liked to paint bloody battle scenes, calamitous storms at sea, galloping horses, and human beings in the throes of emotional conflict. In his "Massacre of Scio" (page 208) can be seen his great interest in eastern subjects and his concern with individual reactions to situations. Delacroix never portrayed the individual in a contemporary setting or dispensed with the elaborate trappings of romanticism. As with other romanticists both in painting and literature, the exaggerated emotional intensity of his work made melodrama of its dramatic elements.

The influence of Rousseau showed itself in such artists as Corot and Millet, who left their studios to paint outdoors, choosing as subject matter the countryside and people around them. Millet painted peasants in idealized fashion, while Corot chose peaceful landscapes of rivers and trees. These painters suggested to later artists that the everyday life around them was subject matter worth using. A comparison of any of their works with David's portrait of "Madame Récamier" will illustrate the shift in emphasis begun by Corot and Millet.

Realists Courbet and Daumier. Other French artists too were rebelling against the artificialities of the academicians who painted "respectable" canvases to suit the taste of the upper classes. (The term "academician" was applied to those who clung to the old ideas in

DAVID: MADAME RECAMIER

DELACROIX: MASSACRE OF SCIO

art, refusing to sanction any changes. The term developed in France, where at a later date experimenters had to start their own salon in order to obtain a place to exhibit their work.) Such a rebel was Gustave Courbet, who lived in Paris, painting everyday scenes with intense realism. Courbet was the kind of artist who "didn't paint angels, because he never saw one," who preferred to record life as it actually appeared to him. Courbet was speaking for his times when he said, "It is better to paint railway stations . . . engine-houses, mines, and factories, for these are the saints and miracles of the nineteenth century."[10]

One of the most powerful satirists of French society was Honore Daumier, an artist who knew Parisian life intimately. He chose his subject matter from the poor of Paris; the washerwomen along the Seine were favorite subjects of his paintings. His lithographs, which appeared in periodicals, are also very well known. They were biting satires of the politics of the day, the law courts, and the life of the bourgeoisie. A lithograph is drawn on a base of finely ground limestone with a special wax crayon. By a process of etching, the sections of the stone not covered by the crayon are desensitized to the ink, so that when the stone is inked the part drawn in crayon is printed. Daumier's black-and-white lithographs evidenced his expert handling of light and shade. The cartoon below depicts an innocent family slaughtered by soldiers who, wandering through discontented Paris in 1834, had become irked by snipers. It shows that political and social cartoons can have great artistic value.

Edouard Manet. Edouard Manet (1832-1883) was an experimenter who had a strong influence on the impressionists. His innovations were misunderstood by the academicians, and some of his paintings created an uproar of protest. From studying Spanish masters he had acquired a taste for bright colors and the technique of laying them on in broad strokes. Manet painted all sorts of everyday subjects in brilliant colors. This choice of subjects, the vitality of his canvases, and his use of strong color influenced other progressive painters. "The Fifer" (page 210) is an example of the way in which Manet used almost flat areas of one color contrasted with other brilliant colors. Compare its subject matter with that of David's "Madame Récamier" (page 207) and Watteau's "Love in the French Theater" (page 71).

Impressionism. A new school of painting came to the fore in the seventies, characterized by objectivity of expression and a new technique in the handling of light and atmosphere. The impressionists, as these painters were called, aimed to catch the first impression made on the artist's vision by a scene of nature and to do it in terms of light and color rather than solidity of form. The impressionists found that a much more vivid and lively effect of light could be obtained by placing one bright area of color next to another without any transitional tones, while shadows could be shown not as gray but as composed of colors complementary to those of the objects casting the shadows. At close range an impressionist picture is simply a splotch of unmixed colors, but at the proper distance the eye mixes them, and a vibrating sense of light emerges. This technique was not altogether unique with the French impressionists. Medieval artists had placed bright unmixed colors next to each other in their stained-glass windows, and the English painters Constable and Turner had experimented with this "broken color" technique (pages 212-213). The scientific application of the new technique on the part of

DAUMIER: RUE TRANSNONAIN

MANET: THE FIFER

French impressionists brought about a tremendous change in nineteenth-century painting.

Claude Monet (1840-1926) was in some respects the most typical of the impressionists. He surpassed his friends in the importance which he attached to color phenomena. He concentrated on landscapes and was always concerned with catching "impressions" of the fleeting moment. In 1874 he exhibited a small painting which was roundly derided by the traditionalists, who threw the term "impressionists" contemptuously at the new artists for daring to set aside the formal traditions of the day. But the term summed up the philosophy underlying their works, and "impressionism" became a permanent word in the vocabulary of artists. Another famous impressionist was Hilaire Edgard Degas, whose paintings of ballet girls combine impressionism with a very strong sense of line.

CÉZANNE: THE PORTRAIT OF A PEASANT

Renoir and Cézanne. Auguste Renoir (1841-1919) painted all sorts of subjects—nights at the opera, landscapes, houseboat parties on the Seine, and life in the boulevard cafes, and all of them reveal his rich sense of color. There is little or nothing of the spirit of revolution, of "social significance" in the paintings of Renoir. He loved gay scenes and fresh colors. The sunlight plays across his paintings, giving one a sense of a passing moment caught in paint. "The Luncheon of the Boating Party" is one of these (page 211). Renoir employed broken color, giving his canvases a glowing quality which, combined with his individual handling of brush strokes, makes his work extremely rich. The objects in his paintings show more solidity than those of most impressionists, and his soft colors are admirably set off by rich black areas.

Paul Cézanne (1839-1906) departed further from impressionist techniques. He was the moving figure in what became known as post-impressionism. Cézanne studied the works of masters in the Louvre and developed a strong sense of structure and design. Although as a student he had learned the principles of impressionism and had thereby added richness of color to his work, Cézanne believed that the school's greatest weakness lay in its lack of solidity and design. Maintaining that "I always keep one foot in the Louvre" and "I want to make impressionism something solid and permanent like the old masters," Cézanne emphasized the value of planes and their relationship to color. He worked with the problem of space organization, feeling that the apparent chaos in nature must be put in order instead of being painted exactly as seen. This was opposed to the more objective attitude of impressionist painters. "The Portrait of a Peasant" shows his interest in the planes which build up an object. Notice the way in which the planes of light and dark colors are simplified. Cézanne himself said that everything in nature adheres to the cone, the cylinder, and the cube. This was a step toward abstractionism and cubism. Compare Cézanne's painting with Picasso's cubist "Woman with Mandolin" (Chapter 15) to see how the cubists carried these experiments even further. Cézanne was more interested in showing the solidity of objects than were the impressionists, and he broke the object into planes in order to achieve this solidity. Young artists at the turn of the century looked upon Cézanne as their teacher and imitated him extensively.

Gauguin and Van Gogh. Two other prominent nineteenth-century artists were influenced by impressionism, but their strong individualism placed each in a category by himself. They were Paul Gauguin (1848-1903) and Vincent Van Gogh (1853-1890). Gauguin did not use the usual impressionist broken-color technique. He maintained, "A meter of green is greener than a centimeter if you wish to express greenness. . . . How does that tree look to you? Green? All right, then use green, the greenest on your palette. And that shadow, a little bluish? Don't be afraid. Paint it as blue as you can." He thus allowed his imagination to dispense with the restraints which straight copying placed upon the artist.

Vincent Van Gogh was born in Holland but is always identified with the French impressionist school. In Paris he found the impressionists in control. The particular fashion

RENOIR: THE LUNCHEON OF THE BOATING PARTY

VAN GOGH: LA BERCEUSE

of the day was pointillism, in which dots of broken color were applied to the canvas. Van Gogh elongated the dots into sharp brush lines which followed the form of the object. This technique is seen in such paintings as "La Berceuse." The extraordinary intensity of Van Gogh's personality expressed itself in the violence of his colors, which he used in large flat areas. In the picture shown, there is a great deal of character and psychological understanding of the model, but the painting is treated as a decorative canvas, and there is no attempt at realism. With this, as with most of the impressionist paintings, much of the beauty of the canvas is lost in black and white reproduction. But although these painters did not use the *chiaroscuro* of earlier periods (compare their work with that of da Vinci, Volume One, page 449, and Rembrandt, page 70), dark and light patterns were not neglected. Note the strong pattern in "La Berceuse."

English landscape painters. Although France predominated in nineteenth-century painting, artistic activity was not lacking in other coun-

TURNER: PORT RUYSDAEL

CONSTABLE: HAMPSTEAD HEATH

tries. Landscape painting was popular in England. John Constable (1776-1837) was in some respects the creator of the modern school of landscape painting. He considered it primary that the sketch be made directly from nature at a single sitting. Having made his sketch, Constable would then work leisurely on the large canvas, believing that the vitality of the initial impression could be retained. His choice of color was revolutionary in the eyes of his contemporaries, for he used greens freely in his landscapes, an innovation considered audacious by men who had stressed the necessity of painting nature in browns. Constable made his greens bright and vivid by skillful juxtaposition of different tones. Compare "Hampstead Heath" with Ruisdael's landscape (page 71) to see the more nearly impressionistic approach of the former.

An English landscape artist who created a great stir in the nineteenth century because of his originality was Joseph Turner. Whereas Constable had set himself the task of faithfully reproducing what he saw, Turner painted imaginatively. Many of his paintings are almost abstract in their pattern and lack of realistic detail. He was particularly interested in soft, moist, atmospheric effects, as in "Port Ruysdael" (page 212), and most of his canvases are misty. He used an almost impressionistic color technique, experimenting with principles of broken color later used by the impressionists.

The Pre-Raphaelites. In 1848 a group of artists revolted against the ugliness of industrial England and went back to the art of the early Renaissance for beauty. They painted in an early Renaissance manner and in general practiced what we now call escapism. Their crafts were covered with Italian ornamentation. Instead of molding everyday objects into good design, they attempted to disguise function by decoration. The Pre-Raphaelites stimulated the rebirth of handicrafts, although their actual productions are not considered of great artistic importance. Although their principle that everyday objects should be beautiful was sound, their idea of beauty was narrow and imitative. The books designed at this time were largely influenced by early Renaissance painting and decoration, but the new interest in bookmaking led later to a sincere contemporary approach to typography and design.

The artist and the public. In painting and in sculpture there was evidence of a definite break between the artist and the public. Very few murals were executed, and on the whole the artist did not paint on commission. The public seemed taken up with other activities, and the artist was content to withdraw and work in isolation. This situation was in marked contrast to the Renaissance period, when few paintings or statues were done except on commission and with a definite setting in mind.

Architecture in the nineteenth century. Instead of searching for new building methods appropriate to the period, architects in the nineteenth century merely imitated Roman classical styles and medieval Gothic architecture. The result was "pseudo" and artificial. Until about 1830 architecture in Europe and America centered around classical models. In France, for example, Napoleon encouraged neo-classicism, and the old Roman triumphal arches were emulated by the huge Arch of Triumph commemorating Revolutionary and Napoleonic military victories. The Church of La Madeleine in Paris (page 215) was built for a Catholic congregation in imitation of a temple of antiquity. Although there was little imagination in such imitations, Napoleon's monumental boulevards and great vistas (below) led the way to modern city planning which in the twentieth century has turned to such practical uses as rehousing. England and other nations were likewise erecting neo-classical structures; the national Capitol in Washington and the statehouses in many American states were built in the spirit of Rome or Greece and not that of native culture.

After 1830, there was in architecture a "Gothic Revival" in which the towers and pointed arches of the Middle Ages were the chief source of inspiration. In France the writing of *Notre Dame de Paris* by Victor Hugo gave the movement a powerful impetus. The Gothic Revival was stimulated in England not only by the medieval romances from the pen of Sir Walter Scott but also by the sturdy defense written by the popular art critic John Ruskin. America, far removed as it was from the sources, did not escape the Gothic revival. American architects used it for buildings of all types and produced the contradiction of using Gothic forms in wood. Gothic was developed as a small-stone construction, and the forms translated into wood or stones superimposed on steel skeletons are meaningless. Many American university campuses were designed in imitation of the Gothic buildings of Oxford. The Smithsonian Institution in Washington is an example of this imitation of Gothic in a country and age far

CARPEAUX: THE DANCE

CITY PLANNING AROUND ARCH OF TRIUMPH

NINETEENTH-CENTURY GOTHIC REVIVAL IN AMERICA: THE SMITHSONIAN INSTITUTION

removed from the forces which inspired it. The results of a new world's scientific thought and experiment are housed in a building inspired by the ecclesiastic thought of the old.

However, the period was not entirely lacking in original architecture. The necessity for housing large industrial plants and the invention of new facilities for large-scale construction of steel and glass combined to bring drastic changes in architectural concepts. Some of the large expositions of the century had huge structures designed for the purpose. The London International Exhibition of 1851 was housed in a steel and glass building called the Crystal Palace. Even more spectacular is the Eiffel Tower, a steel monument 1000 feet high erected for the Paris Exposition of 1889. The tower was an engineering feat which foreshadowed steel-skyscraper construction. In America the Columbian Exposition of 1893 used many imitative motifs, but it showed what could be done with monumental planning of groups of buildings. Louis Sullivan's transportation building at this exposition was one of the earliest functional buildings in America.

Sculpture. France again led the way in nineteenth-century sculpture. The classical ideal persisted during the first decades, but later Jean Baptiste Carpeaux attained fame for his romantic work. His most outstanding group is an allegory, "The Dance," which was commissioned for the Paris Opera House façade.

CHURCH OF LA MADELEINE, PARIS

Auguste Rodin (1840-1917) carried the spirit of experimentation into sculpture. He was interested in the psychological interpretation of his subjects, and in spite of the rigidity of his medium he conveyed a diversity of moods and feelings. His handling of bronze and stone was impressionistic, and in some cases his impressionism overstepped the limitations of his rigid material. Perhaps this characteristic can best be understood by comparing "St. John the Baptist" with the work of a later sculptor, Aristide Maillol (Chapter 15). Maillol's sculpture is bound by the solidity of the material, and although there is a mood of sorrow in the war monument, the mood does not destroy the solidity called for by the medium.

American art. Art in America had made some progress in colonial times, but it was on the whole modeled on the fashionable art in England. Of the most polished painters Gilbert Stuart (who did some famous studies of George Washington), John Trumbull, and Benjamin West are the best known. These men painted ably, producing portraits for wealthy patrons, historical scenes, and allegorical compositions, but their work was almost completely European in approach and method, as comparison with that of an English portraitist such as Gainsborough will reveal.

There were some self-taught artists who, although their work was crude and naïve, worked with a freshness which was in keeping with the spirit of a new world. They were often itinerant painters who traveled from town to town painting portraits or farmers who carved wood in their spare time. The woodcarving of Henry Ward Beecher (below) is the work of an unknown artist who must have been much impressed by this fiery preacher. The artist was more interested in expressing the spirit of the abolitionist than in making his work finished in the European manner.

In the nineteenth century American artists drew more inspiration from the French school than from the English. James McNeill Whistler was strongly influenced by the impressionists and lived and worked most of his life in

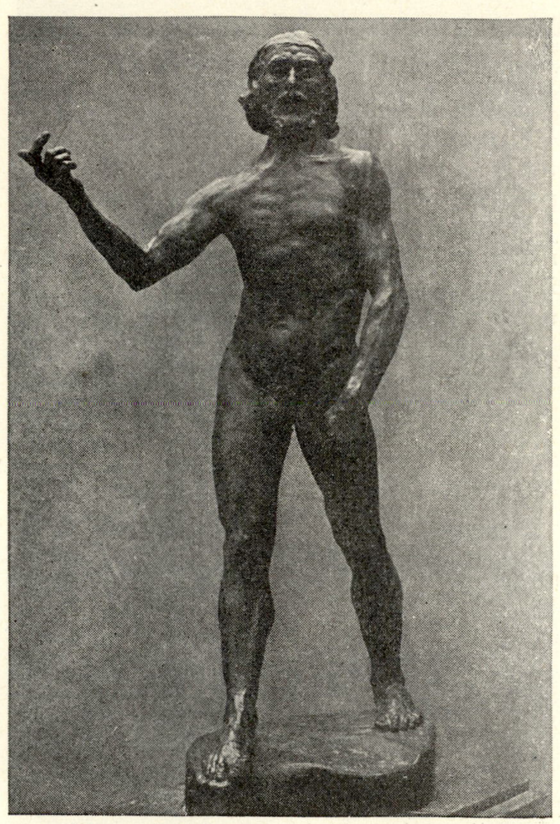

RODIN: ST. JOHN THE BAPTIST

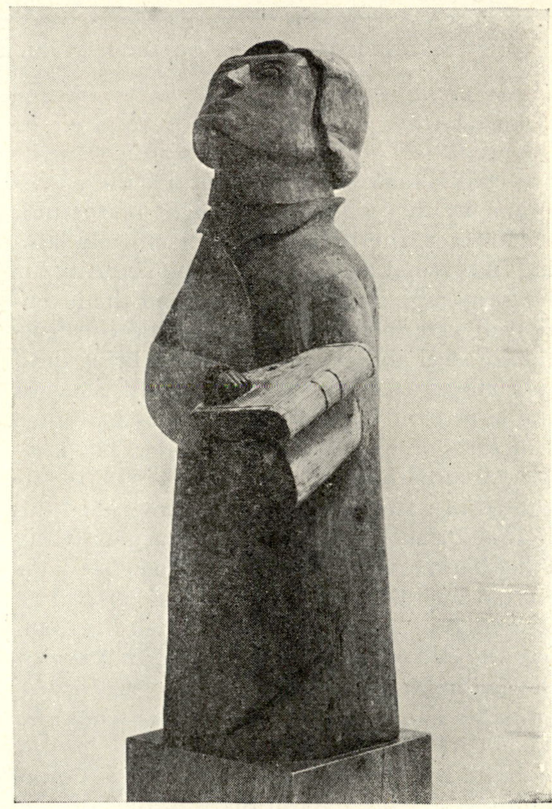

WOODCARVING OF HENRY WARD BEECHER

EAKINS: WALT WHITMAN

WHISTLER: OLD BATTERSEA—NOCTURNE, BLUE AND GOLD

Europe. In his night scenes particularly, such as "Old Battersea—Nocturne, Blue and Gold," can be seen the impressionist interest in mood and color, rather than the romantic interest in the human drama of a scene, or the social commentator's interest in the social conditions represented. "Old Battersea" also shows the influence of the Japanese print on Whistler's design in the simplicity of the silhouettes and the rather unusual perspective. However, his use of hazy atmospheric perspective is very different from the Japanese linear technique.

Toward the end of the century American artists became more interested in what their own country had to offer in subject matter. The newer, cruder life around them called for a different treatment. The polished academic painting of the English tradition no longer seemed right, and the very refined and rather specialized approach of the impressionists likewise seemed wrong. In painting, men like Thomas Eakins, Inness, and La Farge turned to their own country for inspiration, and a painting such as Eakins' "Walt Whitman" seems to catch the spirit of a new country more than the work of Europeanized painters. These men turned the knowledge gained from Europe to more national subjects. In sculpture Augustus Saint-Gaudens, whose work was more like that of European artists, produced a portrait of another great American, Lincoln.

The academic approach and the rather meaningless copying of European movements were certainly not dead, but men were beginning to realize that the life around them could provide them with subject matter just as worthy of attention as the academic European subject matter. With this came a more clearly understood application of the lessons taught them by the old world rather than a dead imitation of old-world methods.

Summary

Science was the hallmark of the Victorian period. In pure science, theories relating to the nature of heat and light were advanced and perfected. Principles explaining electrical phenomena were formulated, thus making possible the use of electricity for both power and illumination. Pasteur and Koch did much to establish the germ theory of disease, and Lister demonstrated the supreme importance of antisepsis in surgery. The most important single theory developed by science in the nineteenth century was that of evolution. This resulted in much controversy between thinkers who defended its validity and those who believed it was incompatible with traditional religious beliefs.

Influenced by the development of science, philosophy in the nineteenth century stressed the dogma of progress and evolution. Hegel, at the beginning of the century, was little influenced by the new science and emphasized subjective reality. A more practical philosophy, utilitarianism, was formulated by the British empiricists, Bentham and Mill. On an entirely different track was the German Nietzsche, a pessimist who advanced the concepts of the will to power and the superman. The all-importance of science was the basis of Comte's positivism and of Spencer's evolutionary philosophy.

Literature was one of the enthusiasms of the nineteenth century. In its youthful exuberance it expressed its love of life and of nature in the writing of the romanticists, who rebelled against the cold formalism of the Age of Reason. But by the middle of the century literature was becoming more realistic, turning away from romanticism to social criticism. In this respect we think of the novels of Dickens, Balzac, and, above all, Zola and Anatole France. One of the interesting features of literary development in the nineteenth century was the astonishing productivity of Russian men of letters. Tolstoy, Turgenev, and Dostoevski made profound contributions to world literature. Not to be ignored also are the contributions of Hebbel, the German dramatist, and in this same field those of the Norwegian, Henrik Ibsen.

In the hands of Beethoven, Brahms, Tschaikowsky, Verdi, and Wagner—to mention some of the most important names—music flourished as it had never done before. Operas, symphonies, songs, and concertos poured forth.

In art the Victorian era was a period of revolt and change. The twentieth century considers itself a century of artistic progress, but without the groundwork laid by the nineteenth century we should have none of our new developments. In architecture the revival of past styles was carried to its ultimate absurdity. But toward the end of the century new influences appeared which paved the way for the functional rather than stylistic approach. And although stations were disguised as picturesque castles and banks as temples, engineers were developing new methods of construction which were to be used more frankly later on. Painting and sculpture were revolting against the sterile academic approach. Delacroix led the romanticists in giving new life to painting, and later on, the impressionists broke even further away from accepted academic standards. Toward the end of the century Cézanne and the post-impressionists emphasized structure and design, of considerable influence on contemporary art. In America artists took their cue mainly from the prevailing European mode, but the beginnings of a more constructively American school were evident.

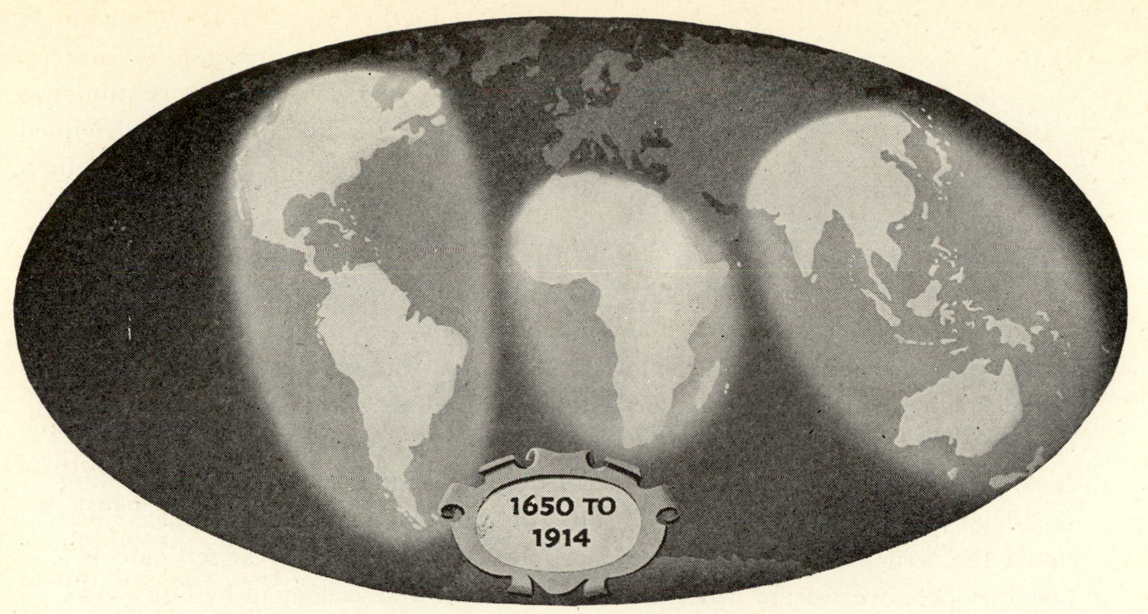

PART THREE

Triumph of the West

CHAPTER 7

New Europes Overseas

CHAPTER 8

Dominion over Palm and Pine

THE FOREGOING CHAPTERS have shown how the Industrial Revolution placed the middle class in the driver's seat in Europe and created factories with amazing productivity, how nationalism and democracy influenced nineteenth-century European politics, and how this century was notable for remarkable achievements in science, philosophy, literature, and art. Now a new theme—the expansion of Europe—calls for attention.

European expansion has been one of the most significant forces in molding the shape of world civilization. Through it much of the world's surface came under the actual control of European peoples. They created great settlements—new Europes—overseas; or, where the climate prohibited settlement by Europeans, they set up commercial and sometimes political rule over areas inhabited by Asiatic, African, or other non-European peoples. Settlement colonies populated by people from Europe were located largely in temperate zones, while the commercial or exploitation colonies were situated in the tropics.

But European expansion means much more than mere annexation and control of areas. As one travels over our six continents, there is overwhelming proof of the expansion of western culture in all lands, whether or not they have been controlled or actually settled by Europeans. African natives now ape the European in trying to do the latest dance step; the Japanese businessman has given up the kimona for an ordinary suit; Gandhi, the apostle of the nonmaterialistic east, tours India in a Ford; Chinese students avidly absorb western ideas at American universities; and the Filipinos have nourished their aspirations for self-government by quoting Patrick Henry's "Give me liberty or give me death."

The actual transplanting of settlers from Europe began as early as 1493 in South America by the Spaniards, 1608 in Canada by the French, and 1607 by the English in the earliest of the thirteen American colonies. The Dutch also established a permanent settlement in Africa at the Cape of Good Hope in the middle of the seventeenth century. Early in the nineteenth century another great area was opened up as a habitat for Europeans, consisting of Australia, New Zealand, and the islands of the South Pacific.

Where Europeans have controlled countries without actually settling in them the situation is called imperialism. One of the earliest and most important instances of imperialism was the Dutch acquisition of the rich islands of the East Indies in the seventeenth century. Another was the conquest of India by Great

Britain in the eighteenth. Then for more than half a century the imperialistic process was largely halted by Europeans. But by 1880 it was in full swing again. Africa, China, and many odds and ends of land, such as small Pacific islands, were penetrated or even gobbled up by the great powers.

The shifting and transplanting of peoples has been one of the most important influences in bringing about new historical movements and combinations in human affairs. The rise and fall of nations, the expansion of commerce, the diffusion of culture traits, the discovery of new lands—all accompany the shifting of populations. So it was in the creation of European settlements in North America. Starting with a mere trickle of hardy colonists early in the seventeenth century, the transfer of population from the old world to the new reached a million a year between 1900 and 1914. History has never seen such a vast drama of people in motion, crossing the Atlantic, entering an undeveloped continent and moving westward, taking possession of the land, harnessing its powers and garnering its riches, until the Pacific slope was reached.

Although our pattern of culture is largely derived from Europe, in many details it is quite different from the original product. Millions of people with varying national cultures, from Ireland, the Scandinavian countries, England, Germany, France, and many others, have been poured into the American melting pot. At times, of course, these ingredients did not blend readily into a uniform product. Tension and strain were apparent, but generally speaking the process was remarkably successful. The end-product was European in essence, but because different blends of European culture were included and because they were shifted to an environment foreign to Europe, the new strain was far from being a replica of the European pattern. It had become American.

Our survey of European expansion will first cover the various areas where widespread settlement was the rule—the United States, Canada, Australia, New Zealand, South Africa, and Latin America. The following chapter will show how European nations secured control of extensive areas in the tropics, particularly in India, China, Japan, and Africa.

The Making of America

1689-1763	French-British struggle for North America	Ended by Peace of Paris, French defeat
1776-1783	Thirteen colonies win independence	French alliance, Treaty of Paris
1781-1789	Articles of Confederation make loose union	"Critical period in American history"
1789	Constitution creates a new democracy	Popular sovereignty, limited government
1812-1814	Naval war with Great Britain	Treaty of Ghent
1823	Monroe Doctrine encourages internal growth	Warns against European intervention
1803-1848	Westward movement—the lure of the frontier	Louisiana purchase, Texas, Oregon, California
1861-1865	Civil War settles slavery question	Trend toward industrialism
1865-1914	Rapid industrialization—rugged individualism	Shady finance, economic inequality

The British Dominions

1689-1763	Canada won by British	French defeated at Quebec
1774	Quebec Act	*Magna Charta* of French-Canadians
1837	Durham's Report	Results in responsible government
1867	British North America Act	Creates federal union
1788-1840	Australia colonized by political prisoners	Sydney, New South Wales
1850	Liberal self-government granted	
1851-1860	Discovery of gold quickens development	Population doubles in decade
1901	Commonwealth formed	Six provinces, responsible government
1837-1914	New Zealand settled, pioneer in reform	Secret ballot, social legislation
1651-1806	South Africa colonized by Dutch	
1815	Congress of Vienna confirms British conquest	Known as Cape Colony
1834	Great Trek of Boers northward	Establish Transvaal, Orange Free State
1885	Discovery of gold in Transvaal	Immigration, British domination
1899	Boer War results in British victory	Annexation of Transvaal, Orange Free State
1909	Union of South Africa	Boer and Briton cooperate

Latin America

1814-1824	Revolutionary wars	San Martin, Bolivar
1824-1862	Age of dictators	Political fragmentation
1891	Republican constitution in Brazil	Replaces empire
1861-1867	French intervention in Mexico	Maximilian
1890-1914	United States dollar diplomacy	Political finance
1898	Protectorate over Cuba	Platt Amendment
1902-1903	Venezuela dispute	Germany, Great Britain, Italy
1904	Roosevelt's corollary to Monroe Doctrine	"Big Stick" policy
1903	Panama Canal diplomacy	Revolt engineered in Panama
1889-1914	Pan-Americanism sponsored by United States	Distrusted by Latin America

CHAPTER 7

New Europes Overseas

TODAY more than two hundred million people live outside of Europe yet speak European languages and possess a pattern of culture which is European in most of its traits. How European ways of thought and life came to exist in much of the Americas, South Africa, Australia, and New Zealand is one of the most significant and interesting movements in world history. This chapter will explain how and why it took place and consider briefly the nature and development of these new Europes overseas.

In the case of the United States, most of the thirteen colonies were politically and culturally part of England for the entire period from 1607 to 1783. Even when political independence came, the basic pattern of life still remained very much what it had been. But the influence of the New World environment and the impact of national cultures brought in later by millions of non-British immigrants gradually modified the original English pattern and made American civilization a rich and distinctive blend. In tracing the development of the United States this chapter will give particular attention to the American Revolution, the westward movement, the Civil War, industrial expansion, and the progressive movement.

The British Dominions reveal an early history somewhat different from that of the United States. The French, not the English, were the original settlers in Canada, and the Dutch preceded the English in South Africa. Later, Canada, like the United States, was faced with the problem of absorbing people of non-British origin, but Australia and New Zealand, which were not colonized until the first half of the nineteenth century, were settled by the British in the beginning and thus never had to adjust themselves to an influx of other European peoples. All of these new Europes have achieved, on the whole, a notable record of progress and stability.

This has not been so much the case in Latin America, the other great area of intensive European colonization. Here the Indian problem was far greater than it was in the United States, and here also relations between the two races were very different. From the time of the successful revolt against Spain in the first quarter of the nineteenth century, the history of Latin America has been marked by civil wars and local struggles for political power. As this chapter discloses, threats from the outside and attempts to gain economic if not political control of Latin America by other powers did much to retard the rate of growth of Latin America as a whole. Nevertheless in many parts of Latin America a high degree of stability and prosperity has been achieved, and the cultural patterns that developed there are a unique and valuable component of world civilization.

The Making of a New Nation

Early English colonizing. A significant example of the transplantation of European civilization from the parent continent to a remote new world is found in the history of the United States of America. For a period of over three hundred years Europeans have been attracted to North America by its rich natural resources, ample land, and temperate climate. From a puny settlement in Virginia, the United States has become a nation of well over 130,000,000 people. It is a blend of the basic features of an older European culture and of new culture traits that have developed and flourished independently in the New World. The colonization of the New World, the struggle for political independence, the epic sweep of the pioneers westward to the Pacific, the exploitation of rich natural resources, and the subsequent building of the world's most extensive industrial structure are all parts of one of the most absorbing stories in world history.

It was in the days of such Elizabethan seamen as Sir Francis Drake and Sir John Hawkins that Englishmen first began to interest themselves in exploration and plunder in the New World. This interest was encouraged by an active propagandist, Richard Hakluyt, who urged his countrymen to build new Englands overseas. Thus it was that between 1578 and 1583 Sir Humphrey Gilbert made several attempts to establish colonies on the eastern coast of North America. He never succeeded in doing so, and after his death by shipwreck in his last venture, the task of colonization was carried on by his half brother, Sir Walter Raleigh.

Jamestown. It was not many years, however, before a permanent colony was founded in Virginia. In April 1607, a small fleet outfitted by the London Company, a group of men interested in colonization, landed an exploration party and established a colony which they named Jamestown. For a number of years the colonists suffered from lack of food and other privations, but they were tided over this initial crucial period by America's first hero, Captain John Smith, whose romantic rescue from death at the hands of the Indians by the beautiful maiden Pocahontas is one of our oldest legends. The charter granted to the colonists by the English king contained one important provision. Article sixteen stated: "All and every the Persons, being our Subjects, which shall dwell and inhabit within every and any of the said several Colonies and Plantations, and every of their children . . . shall have and enjoy all Liberties, Franchises and Immunities within any of our Dominions . . . as if they had been abiding and born within this our Realm of England."[1] This remarkable promise made possible the transplantation of the English common law to the New World and, even more important, the establishment of representative government. In 1619 the governor called a representative assembly to assist in the tasks of government. This body, which later became the legislature of the state of Virginia, is now the oldest representative assembly in existence with the exception of the parent Parliament in London.

New England. For one hundred twenty-five years after the establishment of Jamestown a steady stream of English colonists crossed the Atlantic and set up additional settlements until by 1733 thirteen colonies existed along the Atlantic seaboard. In 1620 the Puritans founded a settlement at Plymouth, and eight years later the Massachusetts Bay Company established colonies elsewhere in New England. During the arbitrary rule and religious persecution of the English Stuart king Charles I, some fourteen thousand Puritans emigrated to New England. This movement, called the Great Migration, had important consequences upon American development. It brought to the New World a number of educated and responsible people whose courage and intelligence aided the colonization of New England greatly. The influence of such leaders as John Winthrop, Thomas Dudley, and Thomas Hooker did much to shape the new society set up in America.

The end of the first stage of development. The founding of Georgia in 1733 brought the number of colonies to thirteen. By this time the experimental and crucial phase of colonization was ended. The southern colonies were becoming prosperous by cultivating tobacco, indigo, and rice, while those in the north began to develop a flourishing shipbuilding industry and to carry on a profitable three-cornered-trade between the New England colonies, Africa, and the West Indies. The first slaves to be imported were brought into Virginia in 1619. At the beginning only a few thousand were used to work the tobacco and rice fields of the southern colonies, but by the end of the eighteenth century, their number had grown to half a million. By the middle of the nineteenth century the existence of this large body of slaves became a serious national problem.

The defeat of France in America. In 1700 the colonial population numbered 200,000 and in 1760 it was approaching two million, or close to one third that of England. In this first phase of American history foreign affairs played an important part. Between 1689 and 1763 the colonists were involved in a series of conflicts waged by Britain and France. This long period of war began as an effort on the part of England and her European allies to thwart the French king's apparent desire to dominate the continent, but the struggle between France and England soon shifted to a widespread conflict over world trade and colonial empire. In four separate wars, King William's War (1689-1697), Queen Anne's War (1702-1713), King George's War (1744-1748), and the Seven Years' War (1756-1763), the American colonists fought shoulder to shoulder with British regulars against French armies in the settlements France had established in Canada and the Mississippi valley. The issue of supremacy in the New World was decided at the battle of Quebec in 1759.

The defeat of France in America was of great significance in our national history. So long as France was entrenched in the Ohio and Mississippi valleys, the American colonists were cooped up along the Atlantic seaboard and expansion to the west was impossible. Furthermore, had France won, it is doubtful that the American colonists could have maintained their independence. The extension of French political dominance would have been assured, and with it would have come French political ideas, legal customs, culture, and language to revolutionize the development of American civilization.

American independence. The Battle of Quebec and the Treaty of Paris which ended the Seven Years' War ensured the fact that English, not French, civilization was to be dominant on the North American continent. Yet not long afterward a serious problem arose involving the relationship between the thirteen colonies and England. Following the great struggle with France, Great Britain tightened her regulations governing the trade of the empire. As we have already noted in Chapter 3, her object in doing so was to make the colonies contribute to the policing and protection of the empire and, further, to regulate colonial economic activity in order to prevent it from competing with that of the mother country.

This new policy of the British government had disastrous results in America. Such measures as the Sugar Act (1764), the Stamp Act (1765), and the Quartering Act (1765) generated strong resentment in some colonies and among some colonists, which soon culminated in a general determination to secure independence from the English. July 4, 1776, the date of the Declaration of Independence, represents the birthday of the American nation.

From then on there was no turning back. For seven years the struggle was carried on with courage, determination, and skill by such leaders as Washington, Franklin, Madison, and Hamilton. The defeat of the British general Burgoyne in October 1777 and the alliance with France the following year turned the scales in favor of the colonies. In 1783 the mother country granted independence to the thirteen colonies, which were now free to make their own destinies, unhampered by constraints from Europe.

From 1607 until 1776 the American colonies had been part of the British Empire, and practically all the forces shaping and influencing the development of civilization in America came from England. The period of the Revolution did little to alter the fundamentals of society that had been transplanted from England during the long period of incubation as part of the empire. The Revolution did not displace the English language, the common law, and the religion, philosophy, and literary influences that had been brought from the motherland. Thus it is that Shakespeare, Milton, Cromwell, and Locke are now much more a part of our heritage than men of similar stature in the nations on the European continent.

The Articles of Confederation. Just before the conflict with Great Britain ended, the American colonies ratified the Articles of Confederation (1781). The Articles set up a loose league of sovereign states in which the central government possessed little authority, had no army or navy, and little money. Under this system the colonies began their national existence. They were anything but united. Civil strife and confusion arose, and serious tariff and boundary disputes raged between the states. As Washington said, "We are fast verging to anarchy and confusion." This period has well been termed by historians "the critical period in American history," because it seemed then that the victory over Great Britain was about to be lost. At this juncture a group of public-spirited men, including such leaders as Hamilton, Madison, Washington, and Jay, determined to establish a strong central government. Their efforts finally led to the Constitutional Convention, which met in Independence Hall in Philadelphia from May to September 1787 in a momentous session. After much debate and even acrimonious disagreement a brilliant compromise was reached between the advocates of a strong central government and those favoring sovereign states. The compromise assured the supremacy of the federal government without making mere puppet governments of the states. When this plan was incorporated in a Constitution for the United States of America, it aroused much opposition. Finally, however, the required number of states ratified the new Constitution, and on April 30, 1789, George Washington took the oath of office as president in New York.

The Constitution. The new Constitution was certainly a political anomaly in 1789. Nothing quite like it had ever been seen before. The English had gone a good distance in the direction of political freedom and representative government in their Glorious Revolution of 1689, but there were still many traces of political and religious inequality in the English system. The American Constitution represented a clean break with the past and a promise of complete democracy in the near future. Manhood suffrage was not realized under the Constitution in America for several decades, but this delay does not detract from the importance of the advanced democratic philosophy which became the law of the land in 1789.

The American system. This new system, which was to be widely imitated by other peoples throughout the nineteenth century, embodied certain fundamental principles. The first was the doctrine of popular sovereignty. This meant that all power ultimately resided in the people. Recognition of this fact appears in constitutional provisions requiring the participation of the people in amending the Constitution and denying this right to the national government acting alone. Another principle, revolutionary in its day, was that of limited government, which safeguarded the rights of the people by setting up definite bounds and restraints on the actions of their public officials. A third important feature was the principle of federalism. In most governments all power resided in the national government. But in the United States power was divided between the state governments and the national government. The principle of federalism became one of America's greatest contributions to government.

Separation of powers was a fourth fundamental aspect of the new Constitution. In the field of the national government, the powers and duties of legislature, judiciary, and executive are carefully defined. Thus Congress makes the laws, the president applies and enforces them, and the courts interpret them. However, by a fifth feature, a system of checks and balances, careful provision was made so that no one of the three governmental departments could become too independent or powerful. The president, for example, can veto laws passed by Congress. But the legislature can by a two-thirds vote pass bills over the president's veto. In like manner, the Supreme Court stands as an ultimate safeguard because it has the power to declare any law unconstitutional.

Finally, the Constitution contained a sixth basic principle, the protection of the rights of the individual, although in reality this principle appears as the Bill of Rights in the first ten amendments to the Constitution instead of in the Constitution proper. No laws can be made encroaching upon freedom of religion, press, and speech, and all persons are safeguarded from arbitrary arrest and imprisonment.

Popular sovereignty, limited government, protection of the rights of the individual—these and other important features of liberal government came into operation in 1789. Upon such principles the American people built a governmental system that came to be the most outstanding example of democracy the world had yet seen and the inspiration of people the world over who still labored under some form of political inequality.

Early years of the young nation. What kind of civilization had been developed in the colonies by 1790? Including the slaves, the new nation now had a population of about 4,000,000. Cities were few and far between. Only six had a population of 8000 or more, and they contained only three per cent of the total population. The remainder were in little villages or scattered in isolated farms over the countryside. As yet much of the country was covered with thick forest, and only in part of New England and in the middle colonies did the cleared land exceed the wooded areas. The Appalachians were still a barrier of considerable consequence. Roads were poor, and every journey was an exciting and at times a dangerous venture in which the traveler might land in a quagmire, lose his way on a lonely road, or find himself at the mercy of cutthroats in an unscrupulous landlord's tavern. Today America enjoys an enviable reputation in matters of sanitation and cleanliness, but the colonies in the late eighteenth century were considered by Europeans dirty and unhealthful.

Early growth and struggles. In 1790 a national patriotism hardly existed. Men were Virginians, Carolinians, or New Yorkers. America was not yet a nation, and there were many prophesies of failure by critics of liberal government in Europe. Nevertheless there were men with vision who grasped the significance of the American experiment and had some appreciation of the greatness that could be America's. In 1778 the famous French statesman Turgot wrote a letter declaring:

"This people is the hope of the human race. It may become the model. It ought to show the world by facts that men can be free and yet peaceful and may dispense with the chains in which tyrants and knaves of every color have presumed to bind them, under pretext of the public good. The Americans should be an example of political, religious, commercial and industrial liberty. The asylum they offer to the oppressed of every nation, the avenue of escape they open, will compel governments to be just and enlightened; and the rest of the world in due time will see through the empty illusions in which policy is conceived."[2]

Shortly after the inauguration of the new Constitution in the United States, a long period of war and revolution broke out in Europe. The French Revolution began the very year of Washington's inauguration, and in a few years the rise of Napoleon's power precipitated a war in which France and Great Britain were the principal antagonists. In the face of this warring world, American statesmen tried to preserve their country's neutrality, though in 1798 the United States nearly went to war with republican France. In 1812 the annoyances and losses occasioned by the British naval blockade of Europe resulted in hostilities which were brought to a conclusion by the Treaty of Ghent in 1814. During the struggle the Americans found out that the British on the sea were not so invincible as they claimed to be and that in a rough and tough soldier named Andrew Jackson they had a leader good enough to defeat the British veterans of the Napoleonic campaigns in Europe.

The Monroe Doctrine. After Napoleon had been sent to St. Helena and various monarchs were restored to their thrones in Europe by the Congress of Vienna, the old world formed a Quadruple Alliance to stifle liberalism in Europe and reëstablish the power of the Spanish monarchy over its rebellious colonies in South America. Great Britain, although then dominated by conservative statesmen, was in no mood to aid repression in the New World. Now that the Spanish colonies were free, Great Britain wanted to increase her trade with them, and she was aware that the return of Spanish authority would mean restrictions on trade by Madrid. George Canning, the British foreign secretary, suggested that Great Britain and America make a joint declaration warning against any intervention in South America on the part of European powers. After much study with his secretary of state, John Quincy Adams, and with the ex-presidents Jefferson and Madison, President Monroe set forth what has become known as the Monroe Doctrine in his message to Congress in December 1823. In effect it contained two declarations: (1) There was to be no further colonization in the western hemisphere, a prohibition aimed at Russia, which had lately claimed all land along the Pacific coast as far south as the fiftieth parallel, just north of the present American-Canadian boundary line, and (2) a plain warning was given to the Quadruple Alliance not to try to compel the South American republics to return to their old Spanish allegiance.

The influence of this doctrine upon American history is incalculable. The United States was able to concentrate all her efforts upon internal development, knowing that the weight of the British fleet could be relied on to enforce the doctrine. Great Britain supported the doctrine not out of any desire to assist the United States but merely because it was to her interests to do so. For more than a century thereafter, the western hemisphere, the United States in particular, was sheltered from the storms of European power politics. This fact was not appreciated by most Americans, but in 1940 the possibility of a British defeat at the hands of Hitler aroused this country to the grave responsibilities involved in the defense of the New World should this burden have to be borne by the United States alone.

Democratic influence of the frontier. In 1783 the United States could not be called a democracy. Josiah Quincy once remarked that it took fifty years after the Declaration of Independence "to reach a vital belief that the people and not gentlemen are to govern this country." In 1789 only one male in seven possessed the franchise. Test oaths, religious requirements, and property qualifications effectively kept many of the common people from participating in governmental affairs. For the first forty years the new government was largely in the hands of established families from the south, such as those of Washington and Jefferson, or of men of wealth and substance from the middle class of the north, such as Madison and Adams. But the influence of the western frontier helped awaken faith in the common man, to discredit the belief in the innate superiority of the social or economic élite, and to move America close to the position of a full democracy.

Even while the Articles of Confederation were in force, thousands of pioneers followed in the wake of Boone and Sevier across the mountains into the "western country." By 1800, 50,000 families had settled along the banks of the Ohio, 100,000 had gone into Tennessee, and twice this number into Kentucky. Here land was to be had for the asking, and there was no economic privilege such as existed in the old colonies along the seaboard. It was the individualist, the dissenter, the man wishing to better his lot, and the youth seeking adventure who migrated to the west. On the frontier there was no social caste; one man was as good as another. The things that counted were not birth or wealth but vigor, courage, and self-reliance. Throughout most of the nineteenth century, as pioneers moved westward, the west was to be a source for new movements, especially those of a liberal character, which reacted on the more conservative settled areas of the country and did much to prevent American democracy from becoming stratified or complacent. In the words of Frederick J. Turner, who did much to demonstrate the importance of the frontier in American history: "The western man believed in the manifest destiny of his country . . . the frontiersman's dream was prophetic. In spite of his rude, gross nature, this early western man was an idealist withal. He dreamed dreams and beheld visions. He had faith in man, hope

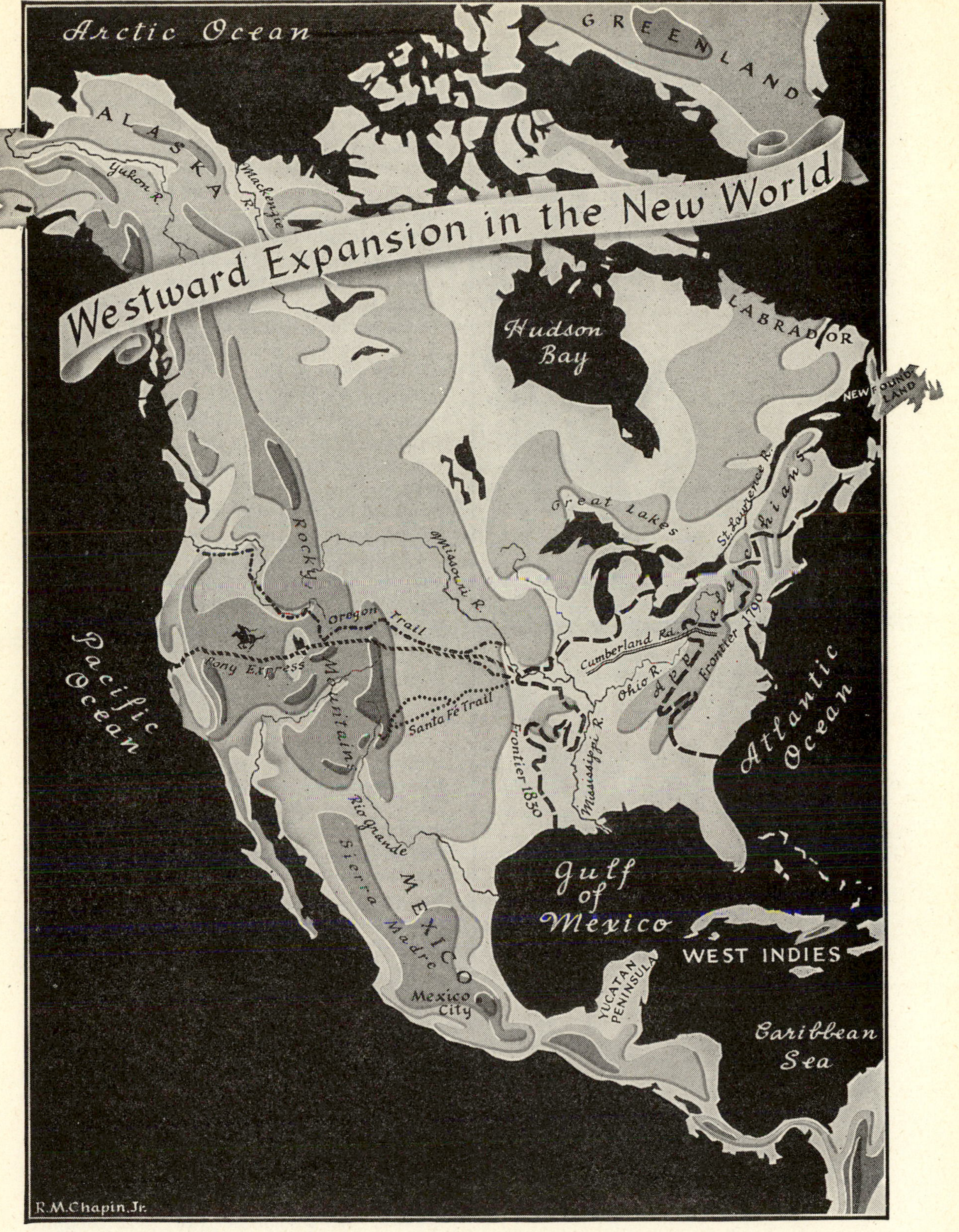
Westward Expansion in the New World
Arctic Ocean
GREENLAND
ALASKA
Yukon R.
Mackenzie R.
Hudson Bay
LABRADOR
NEWFOUNDLAND
Great Lakes
St. Lawrence R.
Appalachians
Rocky Mountains
Missouri R.
Oregon Trail
Pony Express
Santa Fé Trail
Cumberland Rd.
Ohio R.
Frontier 1790
Frontier 1830
Mississippi R.
Pacific Ocean
Atlantic Ocean
Rio Grande
Sierra Madre
MEXICO
Mexico City
Gulf of Mexico
WEST INDIES
YUCATAN PENINSULA
Caribbean Sea
R.M.Chapin, Jr.

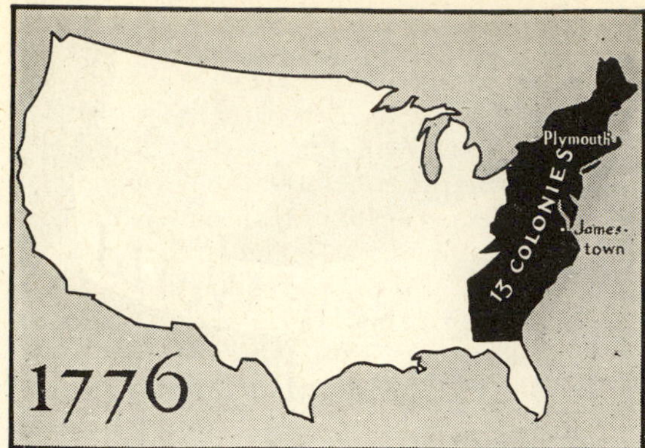

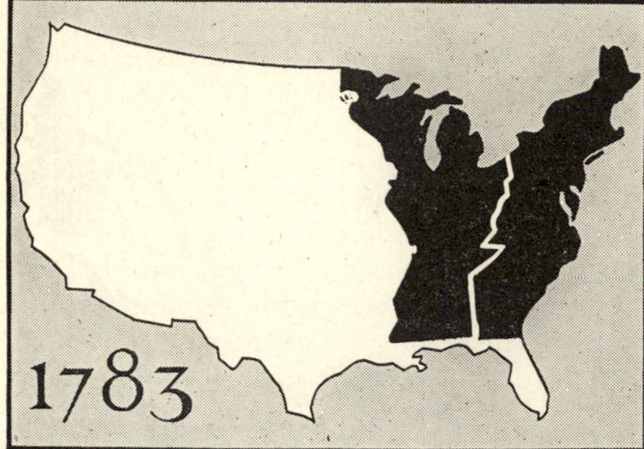

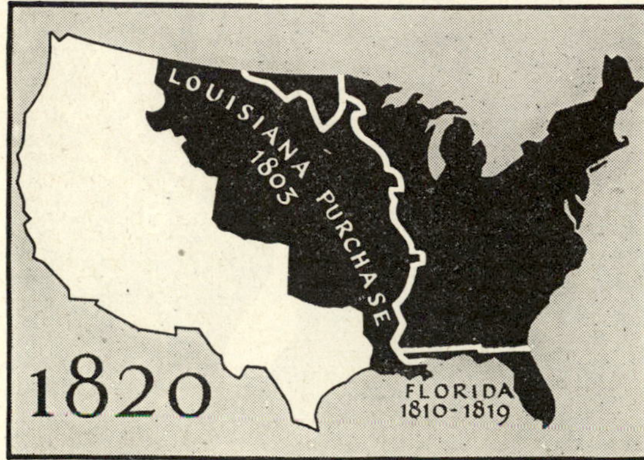

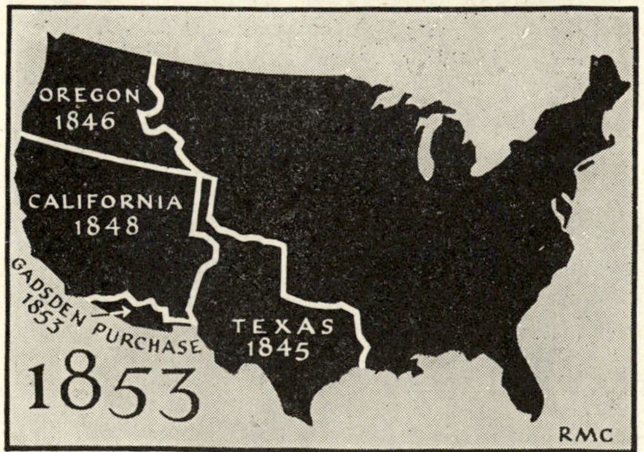

for democracy, belief in America's destiny, unbounded confidence in his ability to make his dreams come true."[3]

Long-distance emigration to the west was made easier by the completion of the Cumberland Road from Maryland through Pennsylvania and Ohio and by the increasing success with which steamboats were able to conquer the "western waters." In the six years following the War of 1812 five new states were added to the Union, and by 1820 there were nine states west of the Appalachians. The democratic nature of constitutions of the western states tended to liberalize political practices somewhat back east, and in the thirties especially the process of democratization was rapid. As time went on, the election of officials came more and more into the hands of the people, and the privileged middle-class system was superseded by a society in which government was the instrument of the common man. In 1828 Andrew Jackson was elected to the presidency in a campaign featuring the slogan "Down with the aristocrats!" All presidents before him had come from propertied families, and all of them except Washington had received a college education. Jackson was born of poverty-stricken parents in South Carolina. Nobody knows where he got the rudiments of his learning, and although he later became a well-educated man, all through his life he continued to speak the language of the common people. With the election of this man came the idea of "Jacksonian democracy," the idea that any man in America, by virtue of being an American citizen, was worthy of holding any office in the land.

Acquisition of new lands. From 1800 to 1860 the westward movement proceeded at an amazing pace. In 1803 President Jefferson purchased the Louisiana territory from France for $14,500,000. This acquisition doubled the size of the United States and offered a tempting field for the land-hungry pioneers who were beginning to move west. The annexation of Texas in 1845 was followed by war with Mexico in 1846. Two years later Mexico signed a peace whereby she ceded California, all title to Texas, and also the country between California and Texas to the United States. The discovery of gold in California in 1849 did much to attract new settlers to the Pacific coast. The same year that war broke out with Mexico, the Oregon territory was occupied after the settlement of a serious disagreement with Great Britain. As a result of these acquisitions, the area of the United States had been increased nearly one hundred per cent over what it was in 1840. (See maps, page 230.)

The slavery issue. The acquisition of so much new territory raised the question whether slavery should be allowed in these areas. At the same time the whole issue of slavery was raised by the growth of a crusading spirit in the North against the institution. Henry Clay's Missouri Compromise of 1820 satisfied both sides temporarily, but the antislavery forces grew more insistent. In the senatorial campaigns of 1858 Abraham Lincoln became famous for his exposition of the slavery issue. Lincoln declared: " 'A house divided against itself cannot stand,' I believe this government cannot endure permanently half slave and half free. I do not expect the Union to be dissolved—I do not expect the House to fall—but I do expect it will cease to be divided. It will become all one thing, or all the other."

The Civil War. Soon after the inauguration of Lincoln as president, the southern states seceded from the Union, formed the Confederacy, and the first shot of the Civil War was fired. Four agonizing years of conflict followed, and on a score of battlefields thousands of men lost their lives. The Confederacy finally collapsed before the overwhelming Northern superiority in man power, industrial resources, and wealth. The Civil War ended when General Lee surrendered to General Grant in April 1865, but a few days later the joyful North was stunned by the assassination of President Lincoln. Had Lincoln lived, his deep sense of justice and his broad humanity would probably have prevented the humiliation and the unfair treatment meted out to the defeated South in the period of reconstruction following the Civil War. It is also possible that the position of the liberated Negroes in American life would have been clarified.

Industrial expansion. The victory of the North signified the overthrow of slavery and the maintenance of the federal union. It also foreshadowed an irresistible trend toward industrialism. In its lasting effects the economic revolution in America which followed the

Currier and Ives, American lithographers, produced this "Satire on the Feminist Movement" in Civil War times (1868). The suffragette, leaving her child in the care of a submissive male, is off to attend a political rally.

Civil War was more significant than the conflict itself, for revolutionary changes took place in American life. The conflict which had raged from 1861 to 1865 was fundamentally a duel between two contrasting economic systems: a static agricultural South and a dynamic industrial North. With the South in no position to contest their decisions or question their policies, the leaders of the North after 1865 proceeded to advance the cause of triumphant industrialism. Railroads were built across broad prairies. The first transcontinental railroad, the Union Pacific, was completed in 1869. Thousands of settlers advanced to the west. Forests were cut down, great lumbering concerns started, mines sunk, telegraph lines extended, stock and produce exchanges established. Cities multiplied amazingly, and immigrants came by the hundreds of thousands.

Throughout the country the number of cities with a population of 50,000 or more doubled between 1850 and 1880. Clothing and food products ceased to be made in homes and were now produced by factories. The number of men employed in industry increased fifty per cent. In 1865 there were 35,000 miles of railway in the country. This was more than doubled in the next eight years, and by 1900 the trackage was estimated to be about 200,000 miles, more than in all of Europe. In 1860 little more than a billion dollars was invested in manufacturing, but by 1900 this figure had risen to twelve billion, and the value of manufactured products in this same period was fifteen times what it had been thirty years before. In 1870 the production of iron and steel was far below that of France and England. Twenty years later America had outstripped them and was producing about one third of the world's iron and steel.

The age of rapid industrialism following the Civil War was one of materialistic expansion in which many who pursued profits lost sight of ethical principles both in business and in government. The notorious Tweed Ring cost the city of New York at least one hundred million dollars in graft between 1865 and 1870. The unbelievable activities of such financial manipulators as Jay Gould and Jim Fisk menaced the financial stability of the nation, and during General Grant's administration as president, the country was shocked by scandals and railroad frauds. A new rich class, elevated to power and wealth overnight, was unable or unwilling to appreciate its responsibilities to society. Corruption in business —defalcations, stock-watering, railway wrecking, and unfair competition—were features of the new economic order.

For roughly a century following the establishment of the new nation the gospel of America had been one of "rugged individualism." Government interference in business was unwelcome because it was felt that the individual should be free to follow his own inclinations, run his own business, and enjoy the profits of his labors. In an expanding nation where free land, jobs, and opportunity beckoned from every corner there was little to indicate that the system would not work indefinitely. By 1880, however, there were signs that America was becoming a mature nation. The end of the frontier was in sight. Free land of good quality was becoming scarce, the country was filling up, life was becoming more complicated and less free, and the frontier was no longer an adequate safety valve ready to release the pressure of unemployed or discontented populations from the east.

The evils of industrialism. The new nation had made itself the most powerful state in the Western Hemisphere, increased its national wealth between 1850 and 1900 from seven to eighty-eight billion dollars, established a fine system of public education, and made certain the enjoyment of civil liberties. But there were many disturbing signs. Unemployment became common in the rapidly growing industrial areas, and child labor was prevalent. Industrial accidents occurred with increasing frequency. The slums in large cities and the appearance of disease among the poorer people were further evils needing correction. The country experienced its first really serious industrial conflict in 1877 when bloody riots broke out at Pittsburgh. In 1892 a bitter strike accompanied by violence occurred in the works of the Carnegie Steel Company, and two years later another clash between labor and capital in the great Pullman strike showed that tension was developing in the structure of American society.

Not only in the great cities did a new proletariat challenge their employers. The western farmers, weighed down by depressions, poor crops, and mortgages, began to criticize the injustice of the prevailing economic order. Forming the Populist Party, they pressed for reform, declaring in their platform in 1892: "We meet in the midst of a nation brought to the verge of moral, political, and material ruin. Corruption dominates the ballot box, the Legislatures, the Congress, and touches even the ermine of the Bench. The people are demoralized. . . . The fruits of the toil of millions are boldly stolen to build up colossal fortunes for a few. . . . From the same prolific womb of governmental injustice we breed two classes—tramps and millionaires."[4]

America had obtained her freedom in 1783, become a political democracy early in the nineteenth century, and prevented the collapse of the federal union between 1861 and 1865; but a new challenge had arisen by 1890, that of economic democracy. In referring to this period John M. Harlan of the Supreme Court has said that "there was everywhere among the people generally a deep feeling of unrest. The nation had been rid of human slavery . . . but the conviction was universal that the country was in real danger from another kind of slavery, namely the slavery that would result from aggregations of capital in the hands of a few."[5]

The progressive movement. At this point, however, as had happened in England and elsewhere at about the same time (see Chapters 4 and 5), a powerful movement was started whose object was the removal of economic inequalities. It strove for the elimination of sweatshops, of exploitation of foreign labor, and of waste of the nation's natural wealth. This was the so-called progressive movement. Various statesmen endeavored to eradicate the conditions which they believed were menacing American democracy. Magazines and books also took up the crusade. It was the era of the so-called muckrakers, roughly from 1890 to 1910. Thorstein Veblen thundered against the "conspicuous consumption" of the wealthy classes. In his *Looking Backward* Edward Bellamy pictured America as it might be. Jacob Riis disclosed the existence of the slum dwellers in *How the Other Half Lives.* John Spargo denounced child labor in *The Bitter Cry of the Children.* Lincoln Steffens exposed graft in municipal politics in his *Shame of the Cities,* Ida Tarbell unearthed the unscrupulous practices of the great trusts, and many others took up their pens in the serious attack on injustices.

The success of the progressive movement was reflected in the constitutions of new states admitted to the Union and in the introduction of the direct primary, the initiative and referendum, and the direct election of senators. All these measures tended to give the common man more effective control of his government. As President of the United States, Theodore Roosevelt (1901-1909) launched an aggressive campaign against the trusts, did much for the conservation of national resources, and extended the regulation of the national government over the railroads, food, and drugs. In the prewar year of 1913 President Wilson inaugurated a militant campaign of reform which he called the "New Freedom." Thus it was that the tariff was reduced because it was too much the instrument of special economic privilege, that banking reform was effected by the Federal Reserve Act in 1913, and that the regulation of business by the national government for the protection of public interests was further extended by the enactment of the Clayton Anti-Trust Act and the establishment of the Federal Trade Commission. After the enactment of the Interstate Commerce Act in 1887, which brought the railroads under national control, a steady expansion of governmental regulation of industry began.

The United States in 1914. The United States had experienced phenomenal growth. In 1914 it was the most populous, rich, and influential of all the new Europes that had sprung from motherlands in Europe. The population of the young nation in 1790 had been just under four million; the census of 1910 showed it to be nearly ninety-two million. During the nineteenth century and in the first decade of the twentieth, more than twenty-five million immigrants had made America their new home. The United States had once been primarily a frontier country, but by 1890 the frontier had practically disappeared. The once vacant spaces were now rich meadow and crop lands. Since the days of George Washington the national wealth had increased at least a hundredfold. Once only the producer of raw materials, the United States in 1914 was the greatest industrial power in the world. In 1900 it was turning out more steel than Great Britain and Germany combined; and one of its concerns—United States Steel—was capitalized for $1,460,000,000, a sum greater than the total estimated wealth of the country in 1790. In spite of this amazing growth many people in the United States and in the rest of the world failed to appreciate its significance. Only the great World War in 1914 could give tangible proof to all the world that one of the young nations in the New World had outstripped the mother country and other nations from which it had sprung.

The Dominion of Canada

Other British colonies. We have seen in the previous section of this chapter how thirteen colonies of Great Britain cut the connection between themselves and their mother country and embarked upon a new existence, separate and independent from the old world. There were other colonies founded by English-speaking peoples or taken from other Europeans by Great Britain which also illustrate the transplanting of British culture to remote parts of the world. In this connection we think of the Dominion of Canada, the Commonwealth of Australia, New Zealand, and the Union of South Africa. As we shall see, one of the most interesting aspects of the story of these new Britains overseas is that they finally arrived at a status of full national independence or sovereignty comparable to that now possessed by the United States, without recourse to arms. At the same time they remained closely associated and allied with the mother country as members of the British Commonwealth of Nations. Because of our increasing ties with Canada and the fact that its political development was a model for other English colonies, our main emphasis will be placed upon Canadian history, with only a brief mention of the other three Dominions.

The exploration of Canada. Until the start of the sixteenth century Canada was practically an unknown land, populated by some 200,000 Indians. In 1497 John Cabot, sailing from England, reached Labrador or Newfoundland. In 1524 Verrazano, employed by France, sailed along the American coast and called the area around the mouth of the St. Lawrence New France, a name later used to refer to all French territory in the New World. During the first half of the sixteenth century many venturesome fishermen from England, France, and Portugal came to the Grand Bank of Newfoundland to fish.

The story of the French in Canada really begins with Jacques Cartier. Making three voyages between 1534 and 1541, he sailed up the St. Lawrence River to an Indian settlement on the site of Montreal. After Cartier, the French neglected Canada for more than half a century, but a new impetus came with the work of Samuel de Champlain. In July 1608, Champlain founded Quebec, the center and capital city of New France for nearly two hundred years. The new settlement grew very slowly, however, because of plots hatched by discontented colonists in Quebec and the intrigues of enemies in Paris.

Meanwhile numerous Frenchmen, spurred on by love of adventure and the promise of rich profits in the fur trade, were exploring the interior of Canada. French missionaries were also important in opening trails into the wilderness. The first mission was established in 1615, and ten years later the Jesuit order came to Canada to carry on their mission of converting the Indians. Their activities were marked by heroism, zeal, and hardships. One of their number, Jean de Brébeuf, worked for twenty-five years among the Hurons and finally died at the martyr's stake in an Indian village. Everywhere the Jesuit mission went, it was a center for the diffusion of French civilization and influence. In 1673 Father Marquette and the trader Joliet began exploring the Mississippi, the great "Father of Waters." The greatest of all the French explorers, René Robert Cavalier de La Salle, completed the exploration of the Mississippi and reached the Gulf of Mexico in 1682.

French Canada. Unlike the English-speaking settlements in the New World, the French colony of Canada was supervised very rigidly by the home government. All trade activities were carefully regulated. The Catholic Church monopolized education and censored the reading of the colonists, and few Protestants were allowed to enter and settle in New France. An attempt was made to introduce European feudalism. The French king granted huge tracts of land to nobles, who in turn parceled their estates out to peasant farmers. Although this feudal system had some good features, on the whole it seriously retarded the development of the colony. The peasant farmer lived a simple and frugal life. During the long winters he spent much of his time going from house to house in the little village in which he lived to while away the time in singing and dancing.

In 1763, on the eve of the British conquest, there were only sixty-five thousand people in New France. This figure was just five per cent of the total population of the American colonies. Agriculture was conducted along primitive lines, industry was almost nonexistent, and fur trading was the most important economic activity.

The French-British quarrels. No one can say how rapidly development would have taken place in French Canada had it been allowed to continue an independent existence. Quite early in its history, however, England's activities in North America plainly endangered the future of New France. In addition to English interest in settlements along the Atlantic seaboard of the United States, attention had early been directed toward regions adjacent to French Canada. English sailors made frequent use of Newfoundland in their fishing expeditions, and in 1670 the Hudson's Bay Company was founded to carry on trading activities, especially in furs, with the Indians in the territory around Hudson Bay. Many disputes occurred between English and French trappers in the far north, and there were many other differences of opinion between the French settlers and the inhabitants of the English colonies. When war broke out between England and France in the old world, their colonies went to war in the new, fighting the series of wars already mentioned (page 92). The ultimate victory of England in the struggle for the New World was foreshadowed by the Treaty of Utrecht (1713). In this treaty France was forced to cede Acadia, later known as Nova Scotia, to give up all her claims to Newfoundland, and to recognize the Hudson's Bay territory as British.

The peaceful activities of the colony were again rudely interrupted by the renewal of the duel between Great Britain and France. The war ended in a complete victory for Britain. In 1763, by the Peace of Paris, Canada passed into British hands, but care was taken by the victors to assure the loyalty of the French Canadians by means of a royal proclamation guaranteeing the Catholic religion and the political rights of the inhabitants. In 1774 the British government passed the famous Quebec Act which has been termed the "*Magna Charta* of the French Canadian race." This again guaranteed Catholicism and perpetuated French law and custom. However, no representative assembly, such as existed in the English-speaking colonies, was provided for, because the French lacked experience in self-government and were little interested in it. The opinion of the English administrators at this time was that Canada was and should remain French in race, language, and institutions.

Canada's formative period. The conquest of Canada by Great Britain ushered in what we may call Canada's formative period. It lasted from 1763 to 1867 and was characterized by the following important developments: the addition of an English-speaking population, the repulse of a serious attempt at conquest on the part of the United States, the grant of local self-government, or, as it is called, responsible government, and, finally, the confederation of Canada into a Dominion in 1867.

The addition of an English population to French Canada came as a result of the American Revolution. During this conflict with the mother country, colonists led by Richard Montgomery and Benedict Arnold tried to conquer Canada, but the French remained loyal, largely because of the liberal concessions of the Quebec Act, and the invasion failed. A large number of people in the American colonies were not in favor of separation from Great Britain. These Tories, as they were called, suffered at the hands of the patriots, and a large number of them went to Canada. The emigrants, known as United Empire Loyalists, settled in Nova Scotia, along the St. Lawrence River, and north of the Great Lakes.

The newcomers did not relish the absence of representative government in their new home and immediately began to agitate for a meas-

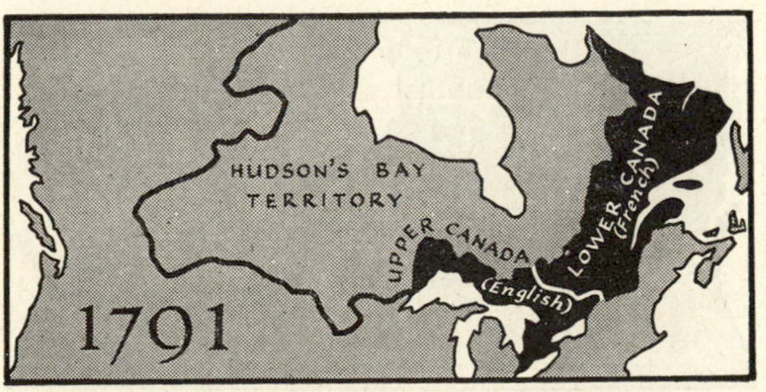

ure of self-government. The presence of the English also caused many racial controversies between the French Canadians and the newly arrived Loyalists. To meet this situation the British government in 1791 divided Canada into two separate provinces called Upper and Lower Canada (see map, page 235) and granted each a representative assembly. The quarrel between the French and English still continued but was shelved temporarily during the War of 1812 when American troops invaded Canada. The two decades following this conflict saw a return of racial strife and also a growing discontent with the government in both provinces of Canada. Open rebellion in 1837 was quelled only after some serious fighting.

Responsible government granted Canada. Realizing the seriousness of the situation, the government in London dispatched a special commissioner, Lord Durham, to study the problem and make recommendations. Durham was a statesman with vision who realized that if the home country was to hold the loyalty of her colonies a much larger degree of self-government must be granted. The basic recommendation of Durham's Report was that responsible government be granted to the Canadian people. Certain matters of imperial concern, such as the control of foreign relations, were to be left to the discretion of the mother country, but Canada alone was to control her domestic affairs. At first the Report was received with little enthusiasm in London, and Durham died a few years later. His last words are reputed to have been "I would fain hope I have not lived altogether in vain. Whatever the Tories may say, the Canadians will one day do justice to my memory."[6] Lord Durham was soon justified. By the middle of the nineteenth century responsible government was granted to Canada. Students of the British Empire now lavish eloquent praise upon the Durham Report because it enabled Canada to start on the road to complete self-government. Unlike the original American colonies, who severed their connection with the mother country, Canada achieved independence without revolution and remained loyal to the home country, thanks to Durham's statesmanship.

The next problem after the winning of responsible government was the union of the various political units in British North America. Fear of the United States, the need for a common tariff policy, and a concerted effort to develop natural resources led the Canadians in the direction of political confederation. After much controversy a plan of union was drawn up, approved by the British government, and passed in 1867 by the Parliament in London as the British North America Act. This act united Canada, then divided into the provinces of Quebec and Ontario, and two other colonies, Nova Scotia and New Brunswick. Canada was now a federal union composed of four provinces, somewhat similar in its political organization to the United States. Unlike our system, however, the Canadian government utilized the cabinet with its principle of ministerial responsibility. The Canadian premier, unlike our chief executive, the president, was not elected for a stipulated period. His tenure of office depended on the support of a majority in the Canadian House of Commons. Whenever this was not forthcoming he had to resign. As a symbol of Canada's connection with the mother country, provision was also made in the governmental structure for a governor-general who was the personal representative of the British king.

Obstacles to Canadian development. With the British North America Act Canada's career as a nation really began. The early economic progress of Canada was disappointing. If the population increase of the 1820's had been maintained, Canada would have had a popu-

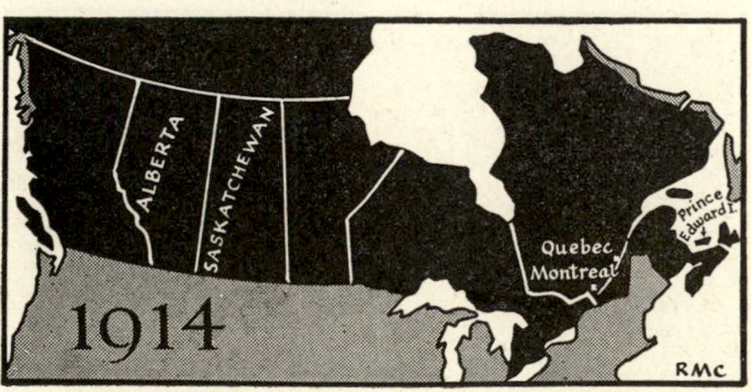

lation of 16,000,000 by 1880. Actually there were only four and a half million by this date, because many Canadians moved south to the United States, and European emigrants preferred this country to Canada. Canadian business was slow in growing because England abandoned her tariff system beginning in 1846. Thus many Canadian products, formerly given preference in the English home market over goods from countries outside the empire, were now forced to contest for British trade on equal terms with those of any and all nations.

When the Canadian provinces were united into a federal union in 1867, this new nation found itself confronted with numerous obstacles to national development. Communications were poor. Far off on the Pacific coast a new colony, British Columbia, joined the Dominion four years after confederation (see map, top page 236), but there was no transcontinental railroad to connect this Pacific province with those in eastern Canada. Another disturbing element was the lack of cordial relations with the United States. During the Civil War a conflict had at one time seemed imminent between Great Britain and the government at Washington. After the Civil War, anti-British sentiment was fanned by Irish patriots in the United States who conducted armed forays over the Canadian border on several occasions. Fortunately the major points of difference between Canada and the United States were ironed out in the Treaty of Washington in 1871, which can be considered as a landmark in the use of arbitration to remove differences between nations. The need for better cooperation between the English and French peoples in the Dominion was present at all times.

Canada's national development. Under the leadership of the Dominion's first prime minister, Sir John A. Macdonald, Canadians resolutely set about the task of national development. Bounties were offered to new industries, a railroad was completed across the continent from the east to British Columbia in 1885, and an active propaganda for immigrants was pursued. By 1890 Macdonald's national policy was already achieving results. In 1911, 100,000 immigrants from the United States alone crossed the Canadian border, and between 1897 and 1912 Canada received two and a quarter million new citizens. New provinces were also carved out of land formerly controlled by the Hudson's Bay Company so that in 1914 the Dominion consisted of nine provinces (see map, bottom page 236).

The Hudson's Bay Company. Canada owes much to the Hudson's Bay Company, which had been incorporated in 1670 as the Company of Gentlemen Adventurers of England Trading into Hudson's Bay. Early in the nineteenth century the company established posts throughout the Canadian west, and all of the vast territory extending from what is now the province of Ontario to British Columbia on the Pacific was administered by this great trading organization. The company built a fort at Vancouver in 1824, the nucleus for the later province of British Columbia, and then pushed south into the territory of Oregon. Here the serious boundary dispute that developed between the company and American settlers caused Americans to raise the cry "54-40 or fight" and "All of Oregon or none." Fortunately the controversy was settled amicably when Great Britain and the United States accepted a boundary of 49°. The history of the Canadian west and even our own, it can be seen, was greatly influenced by this English trading company, and while the company no longer possesses its former administrative powers, it still continues to play an important part in the economic life of Canada.

Unrest in Canada. After 1906 certain problems began to appear as the result of Canada's rapid growth. The advance of industrialism produced labor problems and some discontent among the common people. The influence of big business began to permeate the halls of the Canadian parliament. In the far west the farmers were having a difficult time. The competition of wheat from Russia, South America, and the United States, and the vagaries of the climate had serious economic effects on the Canadian farmer. This period, then, saw the rise of agrarian unrest rather similar to the movement called Populism in western America about 1890. Canada was becoming a mature nation, with all the accompanying problems of the maldistribution of wealth, depressions, and the need of governmental restraint of business. In 1904 the Canadian government created a body for regulating the railroads similar to our own Interstate Commerce Commission.

Early in the twentieth century Canada had achieved a population of a little more than seven million people. The fundamentals for a great and powerful state had been laid under the direction of Sir John A. Macdonald, and the work of this outstanding leader was carried on by Sir Wilfrid Laurier, who as prime minister dominated Canadian politics from 1896 until 1912. The responsibilities of Canadian statesmen were greatly increased early in the twentieth century by the realization that a conflict was looming between Germany and Great Britain.

Australia, New Zealand, and South Africa

The history of Australia. In discussing the growth of new Britains, the major emphasis has been placed on Canada, but some reference must also be made to its sister dominions, New Zealand, South Africa, and Australia. In these three countries there have been interesting similarities to problems and historical trends found in both the United States and Canada. The challenge of exploring the huge continent of Australia set in train a fascinating story of exploration. Following the example of Canada and the United States, the Australian states finally joined in a federal system of government in many respects similar to our own. Economic sectionalism has been a serious problem in Australia as in Canada and is similar to our own economic cleavage between the agricultural west and the industrial and financial east.

Discovery and settlement. The discovery of Australia, the smallest of the continents or largest of the islands, dates back to the seventeenth century when numerous Dutch explorers, notably Abel Tasman, sighted its shores, but it was the voyage of the famous English explorer, Captain Cook, to the South Seas in 1769 that paved the way for English settlement. Touching the eastern shore of the great island, Captain Cook's expedition brought back to England a glowing account of this new land. In 1788 a group of English convicts were transported to Australia and settled at Sydney. From the parent colony of Sydney, later called New South Wales, five other settlements were founded. Although the first European inhabitants of Australia were convicts transported from England, many of them were not criminals but political prisoners and debtors. After seven years of servitude, many of the convicts were liberated and as "emancipists" entered civil life and became valuable citizens. Quite early in the nineteenth century many free settlers came to Australia of their own accord and soon began to agitate for the termination of the transporting of convicts. The first step in this direction was taken by the mother country in 1840. In 1842 the parent colony, New South Wales, was granted a large measure of self-government similar to that recommended for Canada in the Durham Report, and by 1850 the Australian colonies were enjoying a liberal form of self-government.

The Australian colonies grew slowly during the first half of the nineteenth century. A great deal of effort was expended in exploring a continent whose interior contained hundreds of miles of deadly salt marshes and trackless sandy wastes and whose climate ranged all the way from the temperate regions of the south to the tropical areas of the north. Sheep raising became the principal basis of economic prosperity, and in 1851 the discovery of gold greatly quickened the tempo of development. The population of the country was about 400,000 in 1850; a decade later it had reached nearly 800,000. Pastoral and farming activities continued, however, to be the mainstay of Australia's economic life. Railway mileage was

An aboriginal Australian drawing on bark pictures a kangaroo hunt. The hunted animal has been made disproportionately large to emphasize his importance in the situation. It is interesting to compare this representation with primitive European cave drawings (Volume One, page 16).

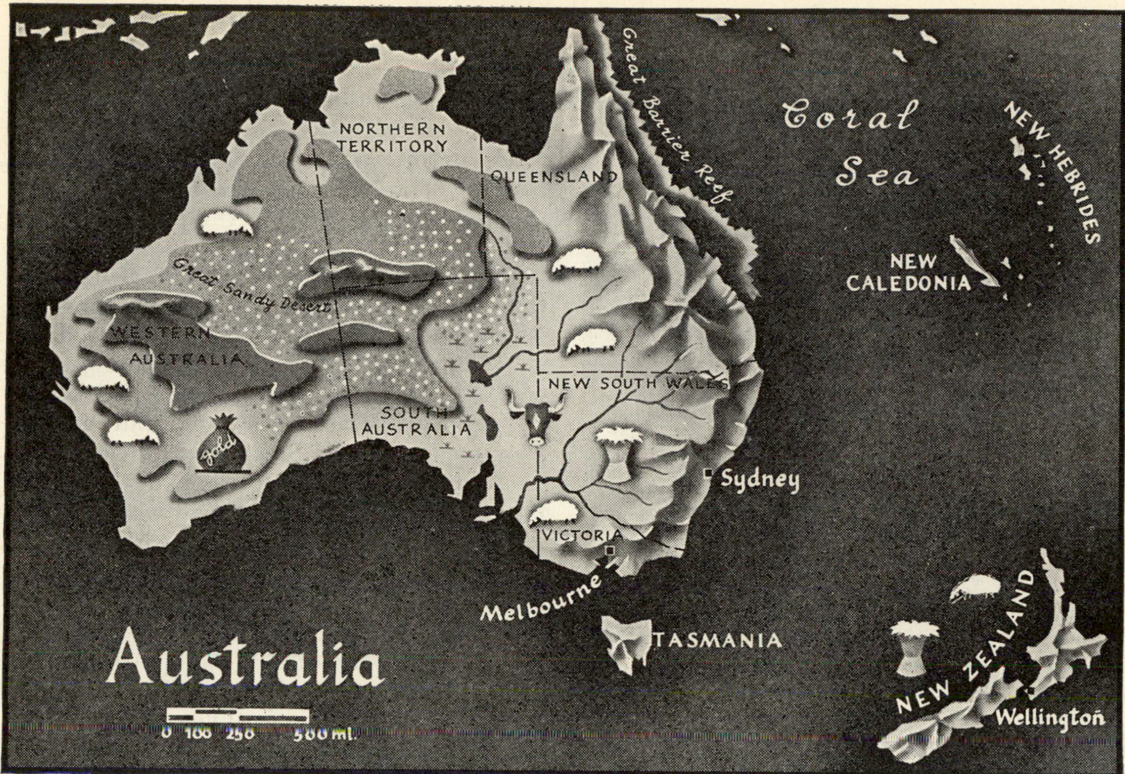

expanded, and large amounts of foreign capital flowed in to assist the young nation in developing her resources. In the decade preceding 1914 the population increased from just under four million to five million people.

The Commonwealth formed. In the latter part of the nineteenth century the six Australian colonies became apprehensive about their security in the South Pacific, largely because of the advance of Germany as a colonial power. They also felt the need of a common railroad and tariff policy. As a result of these factors the various states consented to form a federal union to be known as the Commonwealth of Australia. In 1901 the Commonwealth came into being, bearing many resemblances to our own American system of government. The Commonwealth has a legislature composed of a House of Representatives and a Senate. The members of the latter house, six for each state, are elected regardless of population, while the lower house is made up of members elected by each state in accordance with its population. As in Canada, however, the Commonwealth government makes the chief executive, the prime minister, responsible to the legislature and thus does not provide him with the fixed tenure guaranteed the American president.

New Zealand's development. About a thousand miles from the Australian mainland is a group of small islands, two of which are of particular importance. These lonely projections of European influence in the South Pacific constitute the self-governing Dominion of New Zealand. The total population of this country, which has an area five sixths the size of Great Britain, is just a little over one and a half million. The earliest settlers were desperate convicts who had escaped from the penal settlements in Australia. In 1837 a group of colonial enthusiasts formed the New Zealand Company with the purpose of establishing settlements. The activity of the colonizers forced the British government to assume protection of the islands. This was done in 1840, and a treaty was signed by British agents guaranteeing certain rights, especially in land, to the indigenous peoples.

These natives, the Maoris, were a splendid race. Some scholars have evaluated their state of development as being roughly equivalent to that of the Germanic tribes about the time of their invasion of the Roman empire in the

A South African Negro of the Dahomey tribe carved this Christian-influenced Crucifixion scene. It has the same quiet reverence which is found in early medieval sculpture, and the simplicity and distortion of technique emphasize the religious feeling.

fifth century. In spite of careful planning to avoid any difficulties, some differences did arise between the settlers and the Maoris, and several costly wars followed. The Maoris are exceptional in that they have been able to survive the impact of European culture better than most peoples whose life and institutions have been destroyed and uprooted by the alien invader.

New Zealand is a rich pastoral, farming, and fruit-raising country. Farm products, especially wheat and wool, are her chief exports. The development of refrigeration has enabled her to send large quantities of meat to foreign markets, especially to Great Britain. This Dominion is aptly termed the "Great Britain of the South." Its founders were independent and resolute settlers who came to their new world to establish an England of their own. The aim of the New Zealand Company, as defined by its directors in 1847, was "to transplant English society with its various gradations in due proportions, carrying out our laws, customs, associations, habits, manners, feelings—everything of England, in short, but the soil."[7]

The Dominions' social advance. New Zealand and Australia have been termed sociological laboratories by reason of their pioneer activities in labor reform, social legislation, and democratic government. As early as 1855 the colony of Victoria introduced the secret ballot in its elections. The Australian ballot was later introduced in both Great Britain and the United States, and indeed all over the world. By 1893 New Zealand introduced woman suffrage. In New Zealand a program of "land for the people" was carried out by taxing heavily large tracts of land held by absentee landlords. This dominion also introduced compulsory arbitration in labor disputes, and in Australia laws were enacted guaranteeing workmen's compensation and old-age pensions.

New Zealand is too small and its people of European stock are too close and dependent upon the culture of the mother country to have made many distinctive achievements in literature, art, and music. The educational system is outstanding for its high standards. Any boy or girl can obtain an elementary and secondary education without cost. It is said that New Zealand is the best per capita book market of any country in the British Empire. This reading public depends upon Great Britain and the United States for its books, since few outstanding works of fiction have been produced in New Zealand. Perhaps the best known of New Zealand writers and intellectuals was Katharine Mansfield (Kathleen Beauchamp).

Dutch settlement of South Africa. The Union of South Africa is located at the tip of what most people think of as a black man's country. Here some two million Europeans have made their home far from their motherland of Europe. The land first came within the ken of Europe when Bartholomew Diaz reached the Cape of Good Hope in 1487. Twelve years later Vasco da Gama rounded the Cape on his way to the Indies. In the seventeenth century, when large fleets of merchantmen from Holland made their way around Africa to the Indies to trade for spices and oriental wares, the Cape became of great importance as a place to obtain fresh water for the ships' crews and to revictual ships.

Thus it was that in 1651 Jan van Riebeek left Holland with orders from the Dutch government to establish a settlement at the Cape of Good Hope. After a voyage of 104 days the destination was reached and the fort of Good Hope was built, around which were laid out vegetable gardens to supply the ships on their way to the East Indies. The new settlement of Cape Town grew slowly. There was much discontent among the local inhabitants with the arbitrary administration of the Dutch East India Company, and as the Dutch settlers pushed into the interior, they came into conflict with the Kaffirs, or Bantu native people, who put up stout resistance against the expansion of the whites.

British rule. The Dutch period of South African history came to an end when Great Britain acquired the colony in 1806 during the Napoleonic wars. The British conquest was confirmed by the Congress of Vienna in 1815, and Cape Colony became part of the British Empire. From the beginning of English rule there was bad blood between the two European races. The English were not especially disposed to cater to the sensitivities of the Dutch burghers, or Boers, who were a proud and independent people. The Dutch had large numbers of slaves, and the British emancipation of all slaves in the empire in 1833 caused much ill-feeling. Moreover the Boers disliked the pro-native attitude of the missionaries, who were continually accusing the Dutch of abusing the natives.

In 1834 the Boers began an epic journey in their great ox-drawn wagons to a new country where they could pursue their way of life without interference. This Great Trek was a folk movement similar in its importance to the covered wagon epic of our own west. For six years the Boers were on the march. Finally, on the high veldt, they established two little republics far away from the British, the Orange Free State and the Transvaal. The British, in the meantime, extended their settlement along the eastern coast north of the Cape and had founded the colony of Natal.

The Great Trek did little to solve the difficulties of the Boers. In the mid-nineteenth century there was much fighting with the natives, who got out of hand at times. This fighting forced the British government to intervene because any native warriors when once out to "blood their spears" would make no distinction between Boer and Briton. For a time the British actually took over the administration of the Orange Free State. In 1852 and 1854, the British government made treaties with the Boers, acknowledging their independence but retaining a shadowy right to have a voice in the foreign affairs of the two little republics.

Many Englishmen and Boers in South Africa believed that some form of political union between the English and the Dutch states should be the ultimate goal. Unfortunately any hopes for a peaceful union of South Africa were destroyed by the increase of friction between the British government and the Boers between 1860 and 1885. During this period the British annexed the Transvaal, and the Boers inflicted a serious defeat on a small English army. In 1884 the British government again recognized the Transvaal as an independent state.

The Boer War. It was the discovery of gold in the Transvaal in 1885 that brought on the Boer War. Thousands of Englishmen and people of other nationalities thronged to the mines, where in a few years the boom town of Johannesburg grew to be a city of over a hundred thousand. President Kruger of Transvaal distrusted the British and was determined that the alien element should not get control of affairs. The miners, or Uitlanders, were heavily taxed, and all materials imported for the mines were charged heavy customs duties. Much of this money went to buy military equipment. The Uitlanders complained that they paid taxes but that their children were denied adequate educational facilities and that it was almost impossible to become a natural-

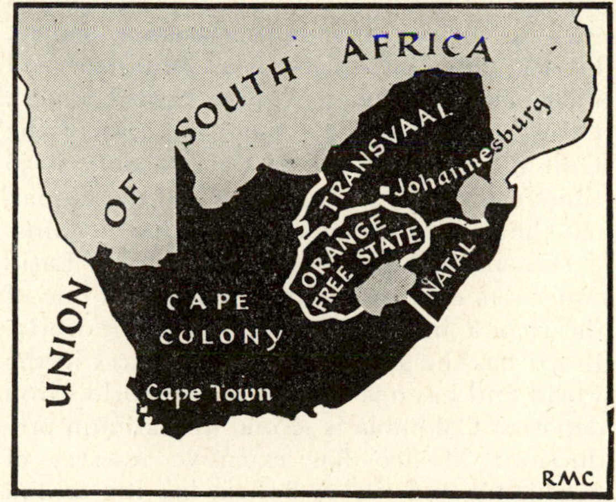

ized Boer citizen. In their anger the Uitlanders began to appeal to the British authorities for assistance. At this point a complex plot was hatched which included a revolt of the Uitlanders in "Jo-Burg." The plan went awry and the Boer leaders, especially Kruger, became all the more determined to resist any further British intervention. Relations between Boer and Briton went from bad to worse, and hostilities broke out between the two republics, the Orange Free State and Transvaal, and Great Britain in the fall of 1899.

For some months the British had been sending reinforcements to South Africa, and a large force of regular troops was on hand to meet the Boer attack. The world was amazed at the war which followed. The Boers were crack shots and splendid horsemen. Knowing every inch of the ground on which they fought, they frequently outmaneuvered the British troops. The tide turned in 1900 when Lord Roberts and General Kitchener managed to inflict several disastrous defeats upon the Boers.

Formation of the Union. In 1902 the Dutch surrendered, and their victor treated them magnanimously. Loans were procured to rebuild burned farmhouses and purchase cattle. In 1906 the Transvaal was given self-government, which two years later was extended to the Orange Free State. The Liberal government in Great Britain then permitted the Dutch and English states to unite and form the Union of South Africa in 1909. Boer and Briton, only seven years after the war, joined hands in creating a new self-governing dominion in the tradition of Canada and Australia. The first prime minister of the Union was Louis Botha, who had been a Boer general in the late war. It was Botha's prime purpose to remove the causes of misunderstanding between the two European nations. The aim was to create not an English or a Dutch nationality but a blend of the two in a new South African patriotism.

Latin America Struggles toward Greatness

The nature of Latin America. Extending south and east 7000 miles from the border dividing the United States and Mexico—as far as from London to Cape Town, South Africa—is a continuous stretch of territory comprising Mexico, Central America, and South America. This huge area, Latin America, consists of twenty republics: Mexico, six states in Central America, three in the West Indies, and ten in South America proper (see map, page 249). Though usually not considered as part of Latin-American culture, in the area extending south from Mexico are numerous European colonies such as British Honduras, Jamaica, Dutch, French, and British Guiana, Trinidad, and Puerto Rico (belonging to the United States). Latin America is three times the area of the United States, and South America alone is 56 times the size of France, once and three quarters the size of Europe, and twice that of China.

Dimensional greatness is only one of Latin America's characteristics. This area is one of the richest in natural resources in the world. Brazil has the greatest timber resources in the world and has one quarter of the world's iron deposits; Colombia is second in platinum production; Mexico has extensive reserves of petroleum and silver; Bolivia has the second largest tin deposits in the world; and Argentina is famous for the tremendous output of agricultural products and meat. Latin America is a land of striking contrasts. Here one can visit some of the most beautiful cities in the world. Buenos Aires, progressive capital of Argentina, and Rio de Janeiro, capital of Brazil, rival famous European cities. Rio, built around a magnificent harbor guarded by Sugar Loaf Mountain, has opera, handsome schools, department stores, and luxurious homes. Along the Rua de Ouvidor one can patronize shops as elegant as any in upper Fifth Avenue. But in contrast to this sophistication, many parts of Latin America are still primitive and poor. Only by studying the history of the Latin Americans can we understand the illogicality of poverty amid abundance and follow the attempts of these people to play a part in world civilization in keeping with their potentialities.

Spanish and Portuguese conquest. Latin-American civilization, like that in the United States and in the British Dominions, came as the result of the transplanting of Europeans from their homeland, in this case mainly from the Iberian peninsula. These Europeans came to Latin America a good century before the

English and French came to North America, for the first permanent Spanish settlement was made in 1493 in the Caribbean islands. During the next few decades explorers came to the coast of South and Central America, among them Amerigo Vespucci and Ferdinand Magellan. By 1530 most of the coast of the South Atlantic had been charted.

Following hard on the heels of the explorers came the conquistadors, the great conquerors, who in the name of the king of Spain subjugated the New World. Lured by the abundance of precious metals and by love of adventure, these explorers performed deeds of bravery and endured great hardships. But their treatment of the Indians left much to be desired. One conquistador, Hernando Cortes, conquered Mexico between 1519 and 1521, and a decade later Francisco Pizarro brought Peru and its Incas under his control. These Spanish conquerors reached out in all directions, founding such settlements as Buenos Aires (1535) and Santiago (1541).

Meanwhile the Portuguese had not been idle. Early in the sixteenth century they made several settlements along the coast of Brazil, among them Rio de Janeiro.

By 1575 some 32,000 Spanish families had been established. They began to work the mines and to exploit the rich agricultural possibilities of the country. The Spanish conquistadors were given large land grants by the king and the right to use the original inhabitants as a labor force. While these Indians were technically not considered slaves, their status on these huge estates was little else than outright slavery. However, Negroes were brought in as slaves in large numbers. In Latin America the Indian population was much more numerous than in the territory which became the United States, nearly 25 million as against not much more than half a million. During the period of conquest large numbers of the native population were exterminated by the Spanish and Portuguese, but the great bulk of the Indian population lived on as laborers in the mines or on the estates. Unlike Anglo-Saxon colonization in North America, there was much racial fusion between the Latin conquerors and the natives. Spanish colonial society early came to be composed of four basic elements: the *mestizos,* or half-breeds, who were the result of the union of Indian and European blood, the Creoles or pure Europeans born in America, the so-called Peninsulars, who were born in Spain and held the highest governmental posts, and the native Indians.

Like English settlement in Australia, the United States, and other areas, Spanish colonization meant the diffusion of culture traits from the motherland to the area of colonization. In 1493 the first horse was brought to the Western Hemisphere, and domestic pigs, cats, and dogs soon followed. Wheat and barley, oranges, and many vegetables were likewise brought by the new settlers. Also, the Spanish, as they penetrated into their new world, brought their language, religion, and political institutions.

Literature and the arts. In 1551, eighty-five years before the founding of Harvard, two universities were established in Latin America—one in Mexico City and the other in Lima, Peru. The first printing press was started in Mexico as early as 1538. During the colonial period, when Latin America was ruled from Europe, literature and learning did not thrive. There was too much repression by the authorities, and literature languished under the burden of fifteen press laws regulating the book trade. Conditions were somewhat different in the field of art. In early Spanish colonization there was a strong religious fervor which stimulated art as an accessory to worship. On hillsides and in every village plaza rose churches which were designed to be both beautiful and appropriate as places of worship. The Indians showed considerable artistic ability, and their services were often utilized by the Church.

By 1800 the population of Spanish America was fifteen million, with another three million in Portuguese Brazil. By this time the culture traits of the Iberian peninsula had been widely disseminated and had taken root. The *siesta* was now the rule, and courting was regulated with the same care and precision required of the young people in Madrid. Amusements consisted of bullfights, cockfights, horsemanship, and much singing to the accompaniment of the guitar.

Discontent with Spanish rule. Spanish rule in America was paternalistic, repressive, and highly centralized. One of the first governmental agencies set up in the New World was the *audiencia,* which combined administrative with judicial functions. By the end of the sixteenth century nine such bodies had been set

Eight Spanish colonies had gained independence by 1826, and Brazil had broken with Portugal.

up. Back in Spain a Council of the Indies was created to exercise supreme control in political matters affecting Spanish America. After 1535 an official called the viceroy became all important in the administrative machinery. By 1776 the Spanish colonies had been divided into four administrative areas, each under a viceroy. The Spanish officials in these viceroyalties rigidly supervised immigration, open only to Spaniards and to Catholics in good standing. Every precaution was taken to supervise economic activity in the colonies. Following an even more exaggerated mercantilistic policy than that which England practiced in dealing with the thirteen colonies, Spain held her new world in economic bondage. Heavy taxation and restrictive measures prevented the healthy expansion of trade between the Spanish colonies themselves and between the colonies and the mother country. The natural results of this restriction were much resentment and considerable smuggling.

A strong feeling against the mother country had been developing among the Creoles, who resented the Spanish commercial restrictions and the fact that the best governmental posts were usually given to the Peninsulars. Below the Creoles, who constituted a kind of middle class, were the heavily taxed, resentful masses. During the last half of the eighteenth century discontent and even open revolt became apparent. For a century political liberalism had been filtering in from England, France, and the thirteen colonies. The writings of John Locke, Voltaire, and Rousseau were eagerly read by the discontented colonists.

Rebellion and independence. Instead of seceding quietly from the mother country, the Spanish colonies in America achieved their independence only at the expense of deep-seated European interest and diplomatic intrigue. Latin-American independence was, in fact, the child of European politics. Napoleon's invasion of Spain in 1808 and dethronement of the Spanish royal house not only laid the foundation for his own downfall but also for the crumbling of Spain's empire in America. Taking advantage of the temporary eclipse of their king in Spain, the Spanish American rebels set up independent *juntas* (revolutionary councils) to replace the bewildered provincial governments of the crown. Questioned as to their ultimate intentions, many of the *juntas* professed allegiance with varying intensity to the Spanish Bourbons. However, when Ferdinand VII was restored to the throne in 1814, they found him blindly unreceptive to needed colonial reforms. Having once enjoyed the benefits of independence, especially the widened horizons of an international trade free from the stifling, selfish restrictions of Spain's mercantile policy, the revolutionary *juntas* refused to turn back the clock and instead marched on along the precarious way toward acknowledged independence.

After the return of the legal king to the Spanish throne, the revolutionary war broke out in earnest in Spanish America and continued until 1824, when the royalist troops suffered a last decisive defeat. In the struggle for independence the rebels were fortunate in possessing such great leaders as San Martín and above all Simon Bolivar. The Spanish government recognized the independence of some of the colonies in 1826, and eight new political units emerged (see map above). In this same decade Brazil declared its independence from Portugal (1822). A liberal constitution was established which, however, did not abolish the monarchical system in Brazil. By 1823, therefore, nothing remained of the huge American holdings of Spain and Portugal but a few islands in the Caribbean, mainly Cuba and Puerto Rico, which were destined to remain in Spanish hands until the Spanish-American War three quarters of a century later.

British-American policy. Independence once achieved was not so easily maintained. In the post-Napoleonic period Spain joined the autocratic, reactionary clique of European monarchies engineered by Metternich—the Quadruple Alliance. Too weak to undertake the task of retrieving control over its lost American colonies alone, Spain solicited the aid of the other powers. France appeared especially eager to help, and the prospect of restoration seemed bright in the early 1820's. They had not reckoned with Great Britain and the United States, however, and it was not to the interests of either of these powers that Spanish America be returned to Spain. To Great Britain it would have meant not only the loss of newly won markets of great potentiality but also added prestige and power in European politics for the reactionary alliance. Neither of these prospects was at all palatable to the trade-conscious and less autocratic British. To the United States it would have meant not only a blow to trade possibilities and to the democratic tradition—for Spanish America had gone republican—but even a threat to its own security and newly won way of life.

While hardly the most compatible of bedfellows at the time, in view of the War of 1812, Great Britain and the United States found themselves agreed in their intent to see the youthful republics of Spanish America successfully embarked. Mutual suspicions prevented a joint Anglo-American stand, but while Great Britain warned France and cajoled Spain, the United States took up a British suggestion, modified it, and in 1823 announced to the world its famous Monroe Doctrine. As we have already seen, the doctrine in essence was a warning that the United States would not tolerate the resumption of European control over, the extension of the European "system" to, or the future colonization of the independent states of Latin America. If it was a seeming impertinence that some 10,000,000 Yankees dared the combined and powerful monarchies of all Europe to keep their hands off an entire continent four times the size of their own country, it may be recalled that the British government was in substantial accord. Without committing herself to guarantee the doctrine, Great Britain by her naval supremacy throughout the nineteenth century was possibly more responsible than was the United States for the success of the Monroe Doctrine. While the stirring military achievements of the rebel armies under Bolivar, San Martín, and others should not be underemphasized, it was British and American sympathy that helped the Spanish American republics attain independence.

Difficulties of independence. Latin America was now free, but events soon demonstrated that its people lacked experience in self-government. The majority of people were illiterate, and the new constitutions were drafted by idealists who had been given little opportunity to gain political experience under the paternalistic Spanish régime. In addition to absence of experience in managing self-governing institutions, there was much rivalry between the leaders throughout the emancipated areas. A growing sectionalism appeared which caused interregional rivalry, and further, the colonial population, now freed from their old masters, began to split into antagonistic groups, mainly the *mestizos* and the Creoles.

During the Spanish revolutionary wars it had been the hope of Simon Bolivar that a large part of South America would merge into one great political unit. But in Latin America political liberty brought about fragmentation, not unity. By 1850 the eight original Spanish states had split into fifteen republics (compare the maps on pages 244 and 249). Some of these at times temporarily broke up into several divisions. The process of political fragmentation often took place because of ambitious leaders, usually military men, who sought to advance their personal power. This period of political turbulence is known as the age of dictators. In Mexico, for example, from 1824 to 1876 there were fifty-seven presidents and one emperor. The period ended in various states at different times. In Chile the age of dictators was over as early as 1833, while in Argentina it lasted until 1862. While civil war and revolution tended to decrease toward the end of the nineteenth century, they have persisted in numerous Latin-American republics even down to the present time.

Brazil was more fortunate. In the emperor Pedro II (1831-1889) it had an enlightened ruler who introduced many reforms, including the abolition of slavery, and gave his country peace for many years. In 1889, however, the empire came to an end, and a republican constitution was adopted in 1891.

Latin America in the industrial era. The chronic political instability prevailing in Latin America not only hindered domestic progress but also had equally important repercussions in relations with the outside world. The Industrial Revolution began to get into its full stride just after the Latin-American republics were born. The great industries of western Europe, and later those of the United States, demanded more and more raw materials and new markets in which to sell the completed products. Capital accumulated and investors eagerly sought opportunities to place their money where high rates of interest could be obtained. This drive for markets, raw materials, and outlets for surplus capital led to the movement known as economic imperialism. As the following chapter shows, imperialism was particularly active in Asia and Africa, but South America did not escape unscathed.

The continual disorder and the lack of strong governments gave businessmen ample opportunity to obtain rich concessions and float huge loans. Many of the Latin-American governments, created by revolution and interested only in filling their own pockets, often resorted to the vicious practice of selling concessions to foreign corporations for ready cash. Political bosses bartered away the economic heritage of their land, for Latin America was rich in minerals, oil, and other important resources. Sometimes the foreign investor acted in good faith, providing capital at a reasonable rate of interest to Latin-American régimes who, it developed, had no intention of fulfilling the contract. On other occasions unscrupulous capitalists took full advantage of officials in the ignorant or helpless governments. In many cases defaults occurred and controversy ensued.

The protection of nationals. The foreign investor usually appealed to his government to intercede in his behalf, and an unending stream of diplomatic correspondence over debt claims was begun, for neither the United States, Great Britain, Germany, France, Italy, nor Spain—the chief investor states—would see its nationals mistreated in their foreign-investment dealings.

For a time the United States merely ranged itself with the rest of the powers in drafting futile diplomatic protests, unaware of the potential danger and approaching dilemma inherent in the bickering relationship of Latin America with the European powers. The first big warning occurred in 1861 when, satiated with Mexican irresponsibility, France, Spain, and Great Britain jointly determined upon armed intervention. Faced by the prospect of European armies on Mexican soil, the government of Benito Juárez yielded to their demands. While Spain and Great Britain departed satisfied, France under Napoleon III marched straight to Mexico City, ousted Juárez, and set up an Austrian Hapsburg, Maximilian, as puppet emperor. Engaged as it was in civil war, the United States was temporarily unable to do more than look on in amazement at this bold and calculated violation of its sacrosanct Monroe Doctrine. For five years Secretary of State Seward vainly protested.

The fickle Louis Napoleon began to back down, however, when upon the conclusion of the Civil War American troops commenced to assemble on the Mexican border. In 1866-1867 the French troops reëmbarked for France, leaving Maximilian to his fate. With Mexico once again restored to the Mexicans, the United States breathed a sigh of relief, but the core of the danger—international irresponsibility—remained.

Roosevelt and the Monroe Doctrine. The climax occurred in 1902-1903 when a similar dispute between Venezuela and a coalition of Germany, Great Britain, and Italy provoked the three European powers into blockading Venezuela and even firing upon coastal fortifications to remind the recalcitrant Venezuelan dictator of obligations he had contracted with some of their nationals. At first reluctantly resigned to sit by and cross its fingers when faced by this European threat to the Monroe Doctrine, the United States soon lost its patience. Suspicious of German intentions, President Theodore Roosevelt matched threat with threat and the American Admiral Dewey's fleet with any assemblage of warships the kaiser might care to leave cruising in Caribbean waters. Germany thereupon quickly retreated with her other two partners into the safer field of international arbitration. The Venezuelan imbroglio vanished, leaving the United States and President Roosevelt with an increasing determination never again to allow Europe so much rope in the Western Hemisphere, no matter how just the cause.

The next step was already chiseled out. If Europe was to be prevented by the Monroe Doctrine from pursuing the legitimate task of protecting its nationals—even to the employment of force—then it was natural for Europe to charge the United States with the responsibility of protecting European creditors as well as its own. Barely a year passed after the Venezuelan affair before a new outbreak of the old malady occurred. This time the scene was the Dominican Republic, where the government defaulted on its debts. In 1904 the American president proclaimed the "Roosevelt Corollary" to the Monroe Doctrine. This doctrine frankly and clearly stated that chronic wrongdoing on the part of Latin-American governments might force the United States to exercise an international police power. Picturesquely described as the policy of treading softly but carrying a big stick, the Roosevelt *pronunciamento* thus launched the era of the Big Stick. Under its banners the United States not only established a customs receivership in the Dominican Republic but exercised similar control in Nicaragua and Haiti.

By the beginning of the twentieth century, the United States had just completed twenty-five years of rapid industrialization following the Civil War. Like the older industrial nations she now became acutely conscious of the need for raw materials and markets. The Monroe Doctrine was now used not so much for its original purpose of keeping out European political interference in Latin America but rather as an agency for expanding the commercial interests of the United States.

Cuba becomes a protectorate. After the war with Spain, American expansion led to a protectorate over Cuba, to the building of the Panama Canal, and to the operation of dollar diplomacy, to be discussed presently. In 1898 Spain and the United States became involved in war. For a long time many Americans had been shocked at the evils of Spanish rule in Cuba, but this altruism was also linked with the plain fact that American investors now held large concessions in this rich sugar island.

The Spanish-American War was very nearly over before it was well under way, and the United States found itself almost unwittingly the heir to a conglomeration of islands large and small in the Pacific Ocean and the Caribbean Sea.

If it is true that it was years before the United States could even locate all of its legitimate spoils of war, it is equally true that Washington was acutely aware of the presence of at least one vociferous war baby in her back yard, Cuba. Sensitive of accusations of outright imperialism in Cuba, the government dared not risk its political future by exercising the privilege of acquisition. Instead, Cuba was offered an imperfect, closely tutored independence, and the Cubans were obliged to acknowledge by law the right of the United States to intervene for the "preservation of Cuban independence" and the "maintenance of a government adequate for the protection of life, property, and individual liberty." These and other meaningful restrictions to Cuban independence were embodied in the so-called Platt Amendment, in the new Cuban constitution under the authority of which the United States established its first American protectorate.

The Panama Canal. Another manifestation of American policy made its appearance almost simultaneously. The acquisition of a Pacific as well as a Caribbean empire, the growing importance of the Pacific coast, and the increasing stature of the United States in international affairs generally, all conspired to lead the American government into the sponsorship of an interoceanic canal across the American isthmus. Strategically and commercially imperative, the project had not only its problems in engineering but also its complications in diplomacy. The impatience of Theodore Roosevelt would tolerate neither failure nor delay, however, and once the choice of Colombia's province of Panama had been made for the site, even a Colombian hold-out for better terms could not stop him. On November 3, 1903, the Panamanians revolted against Colombia. United States warships gave them their support. The new republic of Panama was thereupon established. Three days later it was recognized by the United States. On November 18 a treaty was signed arranging for the cession of rights essential for the construction of the canal. The canal diplomacy of the United States was eminently successful, for out of it was gained an exclusively controlled canal and another strategically located protectorate.

Dollar diplomacy. The next and final manifestation of the imperialistic mood of the United States has been appropriately called dollar diplomacy. Briefly defined as political finance, dollar diplomacy referred to the coordinated activities of American foreign investors and their Department of State. American investors backed by their government sought and obtained concessions in various parts of the world. In particular, however, dollar diplomacy found its most fertile field in the Caribbean region.

The power of the United States government over the struggling Caribbean republics, exerted by various kinds of financial and political manipulation, often proved a profitable safeguard and encouraging stimulus to the investment bankers in the United States, eager to sell money even to the bankrupt Caribbean states, provided the security was adequate.

This finance diplomacy of the period from 1890 to 1914 acutely affected nearly a dozen of the Latin-American republics. The United States government, for reasons of both finance and political strategy, could in the last analysis —and at times did—control the policies of these states.

The "Colossus of the North." The growing and multiple-headed assertiveness of the United States in the Western Hemisphere was accompanied by increasing alarm among the Latin Americans. If they had ever felt a grateful appreciation for the protection afforded by the Monroe Doctrine, its benign aspect was forgotten in their concern over what they now chose to call the Colossus of the North. Yet even before imperialism and its dollar diplomacy had clouded the horizon of inter-American amity, the United States had encountered a vision of the fraternity of the Americas indissolubly linked by common bonds of geography, heritage, and ideals.

While this vision was admittedly to be exploited mainly in the interests of trade and commerce, it seized the American imagination, and out of it came the Pan-American movement, sponsored and carefully nursed by Washington officialdom. Expressed by periodic conferences, the first of which was held in 1889, and the establishment of a permanent secretariat in Washington known as the Pan American Union, Pan-Americanism appeared as a sentiment of continental brotherhood and cooperation.

Barely a decade had passed since the inauguration of Pan-Americanism in 1889-1890 before Yankee imperialism utterly shook the foundations of the new movement. Recognizing the familiar stamp of "made in the U. S. A.," the more suspicious Latin Americans began to see Pan-Americanism as a "skillful move in the expansionist policy of the North, and a suicidal tendency of the simple-minded South."[8] By 1913 the general resentment evoked such charges of hypocrisy that an important South American diplomat undiplomatically felt prompted to state in all sincerity that "There is no Pan-Americanism in South America. It only exists in Washington."[9] More satirical colleagues gave vent to their feelings by referring to the Pan American Union as the Colonial Division of the Department of State.

Latin America in 1914. Thus, by 1914, Latin America's relations with the outside world were neither healthy nor comforting. Added to its traditional difficulties was the new and disturbing factor of the emergence of the United States as the politically and economically predominant power in the New World, an emergence which crept up with a Big Stick and burst upon the southern neighbors in a spirit of self-interested paternalism. Internationally, Latin America's troubles were basically economic and financial. If in the early nineteenth century the southern republics became "the financial colonies of Europe," they hardly felt comforted by the growing aspiration of the United States after 1890 to become their sole creditor. Providing the battleground for an international competition of exploiting foreign-investment syndicates, Latin America looked on sullenly when, as in Mexico, British oil interests fought United States oil interests and used competing political factions as implements of warfare.

Although a century of independence had elapsed, Latin America still lingered "on the margin of international life." Regarded as potential colonies by most of the European powers (provided some method could be found to emasculate the Monroe Doctrine) the southern republics were given so little acknowledgment in the world of diplomacy that in sending invitations to the first peace conference at The Hague in 1899 the powers included only

Cuba
Jamaica
Haiti
Dominican Republic
Puerto Rico
BR. HONDURAS
HONDURAS
NICARAGUA
COSTA RICA
PANAMA
Caracas
Trinidad
VENEZUELA
BRITISH GUIANA
DUTCH GUIANA
FRENCH GUIANA
gold
COLOMBIA
ECUADOR
Amazon R.
Equator (marked at 500 mi. intervals)
PERU
B R A Z I L
coffee
rubber
silver
Lima
BOLIVIA
Plateau of Matto Grosso
PARAGUAY
Paraná R.
Rio de Janeiro
São Paulo
CHILE
(nitrates, copper)
ARGENTINA
URUGUAY
Valparaiso
Santiago
Buenos Aires
Montevideo
SOUTH AMERICA
Strait of Magellan
Cape Horn
R.M.Chapin, Jr.

Mexico and Brazil. Thanks to the sponsorship of the United States, which found common cause with Latin America after the Venezuelan imbroglio in opposing the forcible collection of debts, Latin America was ably represented at the second Hague Conference in 1907. Nonetheless, Latin America was finding the United States increasingly imperialist and Europe increasingly uninterested on the eve of the First World War. Left to shift for themselves in the face of a future shaded by Yankee imperialism, Latin America saw only a hard road ahead in its relations with the outside world.

Summary

The process of European settlement in lands outside the mother continent comprised three periods. In the initial phase, falling in the sixteenth century, more than 30,000 Spanish families migrated to Mexico, Central America, and South America; the Portuguese established a settlement in Brazil. During the next period, from 1600 to 1700, Europeans from north Europe settled in three important areas. The English settled America along the Atlantic seaboard; the French set up centers of colonization along the great St. Lawrence River and outposts in the country west of the English colonies along the Ohio and Mississippi rivers; and at the southernmost tip of Africa the Dutch established a permanent settlement. In the eighteenth century the relationship of these various colonies with their mother governments was considerably modified. There was much discontent and restlessness.

The relationship between the American colonies and England was drastically changed by revolution; the relationships between French and Dutch colonists and their respective home governments were changed by war. The Seven Years' War (1756-1763) made French Canada a British possession; the Napoleonic wars made Dutch South Africa part of the British Empire. These same Napoleonic struggles, which ended only in 1815, also set off a series of revolts that extinguished Spanish and Portuguese authority in Latin America. But European settlement of unexplored lands continued well into the nineteenth century, for the process of colonizing Australia hardly got under way before 1830. In New Zealand it did not take place until 1850.

As a result of this mass movement of people which began about 1500, new Europes dot the world, in which politics, social customs, literature, religion, and language function much as they do in the continent of their origin. Yet the cultures in these new Europes are not completely European. In Canada, the existence of French and English people living side by side has given Canadian national life certain original characteristics. The medley of many European nationalities in the United States has created a distinctive national product in our own land. And in Latin America the final form of the culture pattern in many countries may not be dominantly European but instead a blend of Spanish, Portuguese, and Indian. Perhaps the culture of New Zealand and Australia is more like that in the parentland than that in any other of the new Europes, because these settlements are isolated from other large masses of Europeans.

Of all these new Europes, Latin America had the largest percentage of non-European stock. The presence of this mainly illiterate and politically inexperienced mass goes far in explaining the political instability and many revolutions from which Latin America suffered during the nineteenth century.

In this same period the western world became increasingly industrialized. It was inevitable that the aggressive nations of the world would make increasing contacts with Latin America, for here were rich economic resources. Several European powers, especially Britain and Germany, supported their citizens in making heavy investments in Latin America. It remained, however, for the United States to become the most influential power in dominating the political and economic fortunes of her southern neighbors, and by 1914 throughout Latin America there was much distrust and fear of the "Colossus of the North."

	Africa	
1876-1882	Leopold of Belgium claims Congo	Stanley obtains 900,000 square miles
1881-1884	Tunisia acquired by French	Equatorial Africa claimed on de Brazza's explorations
1882	British assume administration of Egypt	Natives revolt, French withdraw
1884	Berlin conference called by Bismarck	Powers disregard rules set up
1884-1885	Germans claim west and east Africa	Work of Karl Peters
1886-1890	German-British claims settled	Helgoland to Germany
1896	Abyssinia defeats Italians	Retains independence
1898-1900	Great Britain acquires Nile headwaters	Buy Nigeria from Niger Company
1911	Morocco made French protectorate	Madagascar annexed
1911-1912	Italy acquires Tripoli	Declares war on Turkey
	India	
1690-1761	Mogul decline	Fanatic Moslem rule, lavish royal tastes
1757	British rule, French ousted	Clive wins battle of Plassey
1818	British East India Company master of country	
1857	Sepoy rebellion results in reforms	East India Company's rule ended
1885	Indian National Congress formed	Rising nationalistic feeling
	Oceania	
1602-1798	Dutch East India Company exploits islands	
1802	Ceylon acquired by British from Dutch	Treaty of Amiens
1819	British secure Singapore	Influence of Raffles
1823-1885	Burma annexed by British	After commercial wars
1857-1887	French appropriate Indo-China	Siam remains independent
1909	British get additional Malay states	Transferred by Siam
1867	Midway Islands occupied by United States	
1897	Hawaii annexed	Queen deposed by engineered revolt
1898	Spanish-American War	U. S. gets Philippines, Guam, Puerto Rico
	China	
1796-1908	Decline of Manchus	
1839-1860	Opium Wars with Great Britain	Hong Kong ceded, Shanghai, Yangtze opened
1861-1908	Manchu rule preserved by Tzu Hsi	The dowager empress
1860-1914	European powers acquire concessions	Macao, Dairen, Weihaiwai, Kwangchow
	Japan	
1854	Perry opens trade with west	Treaty of Kanagawa
1867	Overthrow of *shogunate*	New emperor, Meiji Tenno
1868	Westernization, industrialization	Feudalism abolished
1889	New constitution on German model	Work of Prince Ito's commission
	Literature and art	Formalized simplicity

CHAPTER 8

Dominion over Palm and Pine

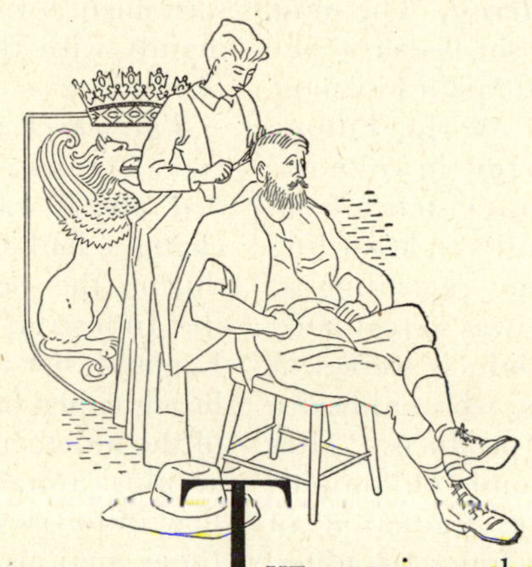

THE previous chapter dealt with one phase of European expansion, the wholesale transplanting of European communities to sparsely settled areas located primarily in temperate zones outside of Europe. In these territories the primitive inhabitants were either exterminated or subjugated by the conquering Europeans, who proceeded to create permanent and flourishing communities. In this chapter we come to a different type of European expansion. In the tropical areas of the world the climate constituted an insuperable obstacle to permanent European settlement. Thus the white man became a planter, a missionary, a trader, or a colonial administrator rather than a permanent settler, whereas in the temperate zones of the world the European culture pattern was transferred more or less intact. In the tropics the European culture pattern and that of the native peoples came into headlong collision and the institutions and ways of life of the natives generally gave way. In India and China the force of the impact between east and west greatly modified but did not destroy these advanced civilizations of ancient lineage.

When one talks about the white man's activities in the backward areas of the world the word "imperialism" invariably crops up. Imperialism is one of those omnibus terms everyone uses. It has numerous meanings and is, therefore, often misunderstood. In its most general usage it means the extension of the authority or control, direct or indirect, of one country over another. Thus the Nazi program of dominating western Europe in the Hitlerian New Order is one evidence of imperialism. The determination of Japan to dominate China is another. And Uncle Sam's indirect but effective control of the Caribbean area is still another. As the term imperialism is used here it refers primarily to the control exercised by advanced powers over less powerful peoples found mainly in the tropics.

This chapter is concerned mainly with the story of imperialism in the nineteenth century and the first decade of the twentieth. We shall consider the factors that led to a revival of imperialism about 1880, the scramble for colonies in Africa, the rise of great colonial empires in southeastern Asia and the Malay Archipelago, the extension of British power in India, and the impact of imperialism upon China and Japan.

The What and Why of Imperialism

The waning of colonial interest. The most recent phase of imperialism began about 1880. After Great Britain and Spain lost most of their colonies in the New World, Europe as a whole began to lose interest in colonization. The colonial empires in existence from 1450 to 1763 had been administered according to the mercantilist philosophy prevailing at the time. Their economic life was so regulated that their most important products were sent only to the mother countries, who enjoyed a monopoly in selling these products. After 1763 *laissez faire*, a new economic philosophy, which stressed freedom, not regulation of trade, gradually came to the fore. Its adherents argued that there was no advantage in possessing colonies, that the cost of administering and defending colonies was a burden to those who had them. The whole world was to be opened to free trade, and it was pointed out that England's trade with the United States was greater after the thirteen colonies achieved their independence than before.

In England in particular there was little enthusiasm for colonies in the earlier nineteenth century. The British were the unrivaled industrialists of the world, and their products went in large quantities to every part of the globe unimpeded by tariffs. There was no need to worry about access to colonial markets when goods could be sold anywhere without let or hindrance. Great Britain seriously considered freeing Canada and certain other colonial possessions. In fact the new territories the British acquired, such as Cape Colony in South Africa, Ceylon, and Malta, were obtained primarily as naval bases to protect British commerce rather than colonies for trade or settlement.

Other nations were too busy with domestic problems to interest themselves in colonies. In Italy and Germany the thoughts and efforts of statesmen for many decades were concerned mainly with the problem of national unification.

The search for new markets. By 1880, however, Germany and Italy had each become unified, and it was apparent that great economic changes had occurred in the western world during the preceding half century. Because the Industrial Revolution took place first in England, her export trade developed first and brought her handsome profits in the first half of the nineteenth century, enabling her to lend surplus capital to other nations. To help their new industries compete with British factories, these nations introduced protective tariffs. The free-trade world of the early nineteenth century disappeared as tariff walls appeared in the United States, Russia, Germany, and France. Great Britain began to lose her old markets, so she and the newly industrialized nations now producing a surplus of manufactured goods began to search vigorously for trade outlets. As tariff barriers were raised, Great Britain and her new competitors realized that one method of obtaining new markets was to obtain colonies. Here, it was believed, there were millions of potential customers eager to exchange valuable tropical products for the wares of western factories.

Socialist critics of the nineteenth century's new capitalism gave their own interpretation to the growing interest in colonies. They said that the wages of the workers did not represent purchasing power sufficient to absorb the increased output of machines. The acquisition of new markets was therefore indispensable if a glut of goods and consequent economic depression were to be avoided. In the words of Marx and his collaborator Engels: "The need of a constantly expanding market for its products chases the bourgeoisie over the whole surface of the globe. It must nestle everywhere, settle everywhere, establish connections everywhere."[1]

Raw materials; investments. After 1880 there was a growing demand for tropical products as well as for new markets. The industrialized western nations demanded greater quantities of cotton, rubber, palm oil, tin, sisal, coffee, sugar, and petroleum. Surplus capital also did much to bring about the new imperialism. Capital was scarce in undeveloped areas of the world. In China, Africa, and India twenty per cent might be realized on investments while at home the return might be only three or four per cent. In 1875 the European nations had comparatively little capital invested overseas. In 1914, however, England had four billion pounds, France fifty billion francs, and Germany twenty-eight billion marks.

The European population problem. In the middle of the eighteenth century the people of Europe numbered about 140,000,000 but by 1914 this figure had increased to 463,000,000. From 1800 to 1900, for example, Great Britain's population increased from 16,000,000 to 41,000,000; Germany's from 21,000,000 to 56,000,000; Austria-Hungary's from 23,000,000 to 45,000,000; and Italy's from 18,000,000 to 32,000,000. Millions of Europeans left their homelands for new homes overseas, where they had heard that land was more plentiful and jobs were easier to secure. Many of these emigrants settled in the United States and in South America. In such areas the loyalty and support of these sons and daughters of Germany, Italy, and other nations was lost to the homeland. Some of the statesmen of Europe, however, thought of the acquisition of new colonies as a means whereby their surplus population could be settled in vacant lands without escaping the political control of the motherland. This was the attitude particularly in Italy and Germany.

Nationalism as a factor. Although economic causes were perhaps most important in explaining the renewed interest in colonies, there were other causes as well. Among these was nationalism. Fresh from their successes in achieving national unification, Germany and Italy were eager to give further evidence of their national strength. Both demanded a place in the sun. In Great Britain there was a strong nationalist spirit ready to take on any antagonist who stood in the way of imperial expansion. In the late seventies, the most popular ditty heard in London music-halls was:

> We don't want to fight,
> But by Jingo if we do,
> We've got the ships, we've got the men,
> We've got the money too.

The possession of colonies came to be regarded as necessary for any power desiring to be "great." Some ardent nationalists believed that it was the sacred destiny of a great nation to spread its culture—its language, ideals, and customs—over as much of the surface of the globe as possible. The new imperialist spirit even touched a limited group in the United States. An editorial published in the *Washington Post* just before the Spanish-American War declared:

"A new consciousness seems to have come upon us—the consciousness of strength—and with it a new appetite, the yearning to show our strength. . . . Ambition, interest, land hunger, pride, the mere joy of fighting, whatever it may be, we are animated by a new sensation. We are face to face with a strange destiny. The taste of Empire is in the mouth of the people even as the taste of blood in the jungle. It means an imperial policy, the Republic, renascent, taking her place with the armed nations."[2]

The military factor. Closely allied to nationalism was the military factor in imperialism. A nation to be great had to be strong to defend its interests. This meant that colonies had to be acquired as naval bases or as buffer states to protect an important colony against the designs of another imperialist power. During the nineteenth century, for example, Great Britain endeavored to control Afghanistan and make it a buffer state to keep back Russian influence on the northern frontier of India. Colonies were thought of in terms of troop reservoirs, where large native armies could be recruited. This idea appealed especially to France, whose population lagged behind that of her traditional enemy, Germany, and in the late nineteenth century France introduced conscription into some of her colonies as a means of offsetting the greater manpower of her neighbor across the Rhine.

The white man's burden. Nevertheless the acquisition of colonies cannot be explained on economic, political, or strategic grounds alone. A number of statesmen sincerely believed that the rule of their government would bring law and order to colonial areas heretofore suffering from the ravages of intertribal warfare. Colonial administrators often became imbued with the idea that they were carrying the "white man's burden," that it was a fine and sacred task to bring the best western civilization to their backward wards. Even the public was moved by a strong humanitarian sentiment. Many Americans supported the Spanish-American War because they detested the oppressive rule of Spain in Cuba, and Great Britain annexed New Zealand largely because renegade whites were selling liquor to the natives and stealing their land. In the middle of the nineteenth century the *kanaka,* or "blackbirding" trade, a form of slave traffic carried on by unscrupulous European traders in the islands of the Pacific, brought about the intervention of several European governments in order to stamp out this inhuman practice.

The religious motive was likewise especially strong in the new imperialism. In the nineteenth century British missionaries were particularly active. Soon organizations such as the London Missionary Society were actively engaged in religious endeavors in India, Africa, China, and other non-Christian areas. Large numbers of missionaries from France and Germany were also sent to these regions.

The most eloquent propagandist for the white man's burden was Rudyard Kipling, the man who coined this phrase. Born in India in 1865, young Kipling traveled widely over India and became thoroughly convinced of the blessings of British rule to the Indians. When he began to write he pictured the British colonial administrators and soldiers as men who did their duty, lived by their code, and even died for a cause which they might not always understand but which they instinctively felt to be right. Over the jungles of Africa and through the treacherous defiles of the north Indian frontier marched Kipling's Soldiers Three, lovable mercenaries with hearts of gold, led by lieutenants with amazing courage, keeping guard over their homeland's interests and protecting the backward native peoples.

The Race for Colonies in Africa

The exploration of Africa. Africa is the best area in which to follow the course of nineteenth-century imperialism. Nowhere else on the globe were colonial empires achieved so quickly. A great continent four times the size of the United States, with nearly 150,000,000 people, came almost completely under the control of European powers (see map, page 261).

The opening of Africa began in earnest late in the eighteenth century. By 1835 most of northwestern Africa had been mapped by Europeans. However, the greatest of all African explorers was David Livingstone, who spent thirty years traversing barren wastes and jungles from the Cape of Good Hope to the equator and from the Atlantic to the Indian Ocean.

In 1853 "the very great doctor," as the natives called him, began his series of explorations. After his death in 1873 his exploration of the interior was carried on by H. M. Stanley, who had located him in the jungle when others had believed him lost. By the end of the century Africa was no longer the dark continent. The source of the Nile had been discovered, the courses of the Niger and Congo had been traced, and the world had begun to realize the rich resources of Africa.

On the eve of the European scramble for Africa only ten per cent of the continent was under the control of western nations. In 1875 the two most important European holdings were Algeria, administered by France, and Cape Colony, held by Great Britain. In South Africa there were Dutch farmers in two little republics, the Orange Free State and the Transvaal. Most of the other European holdings were mere coastal ports. The interior still remained a mysterious land inhabited by primitive black men.

Belgian interest in Africa. Stanley's explorations galvanized the European nations into action. When he returned to Europe to interest businessmen in Africa's immense economic possibilities, he found little support for his ideas at first, except from the king of the Belgians. Leopold II was so much impressed with Stanley's views that he organized the International African Association in 1876, composed of scientists and explorers from all nations. Ostensibly the association was to serve humanitarian purposes. According to the crafty Leopold, who had other pur-

AFRICA
Mediterranean Sea
Red Sea
Gulf of Aden
Sahara
Senegal R.
Niger R.
Nile R.
gold
GUINEA COAST
SUDAN
Congo R.
Equator
(marked at 500 mi. intervals)
Atlantic
Ocean
rubber
Zambezi R.
gold
MADAGASCAR
Indian Ocean
Cape of Good Hope
R.M.Chapin, Jr.

This expressive wooden mask with its exaggeratedly wrinkled forehead symbolizes the god of wisdom. It comes from the Cameroons in Africa.

poses in mind, it was "a crusade worthy of the century of progress." As an agent of the association, Stanley went to the Congo region, where he made treaties with several African chiefs and obtained, by 1882, over 900,000 square miles of territory.

The British in Egypt. Meanwhile important developments were taking place in the Nile valley. Shortly before the completion of the Suez Canal in 1869, Ismail, the khedive, or ruler, of Egypt undertook to modernize his country. He borrowed enormous sums from French and English bankers at high rates of interest. When he became involved in financial difficulties in 1875, he was forced to sell his block of 175,000 shares in the Suez Canal. These were snapped up by the astute Disraeli, prime minister of Great Britain, who realized that such a large block of stock would give Great Britain practical control in the management of this strategic highway between Europe and the east. The sale of the stock did little to improve the state of Egyptian finances, which could not stand the combined strain of Ismail's extravagance and corruption in the administration of revenues. In 1876 the khedive repudiated his debts, and Great Britain and France assumed joint financial control over Egypt, forcing Ismail to abdicate in favor of his son, Tewfik.

Foreign intervention was not relished by the Egyptian ruling classes, and in 1882 a serious revolt broke out. Many Europeans lost their lives in riots in the city of Alexandria. France withdrew her fleet at this point, but Great Britain decided to quell the revolt and assume responsibility for the administration of Egypt.

To reorganize Egyptian finances, eliminate corruption from the administration, and improve the cotton industry Great Britain sent Sir Evelyn Baring, later Lord Cromer, who was actual ruler from 1883 to 1907. This administrator reduced political corruption and curbed the use of forced labor. The fertility of the country was improved by the construction of huge dams, and the system of government was overhauled. Indeed it has been said that if imperialism has any justification, its best record is to be found in Egypt. The entry of Great Britain into Egypt was brought about primarily by concern for her own financial interests and the knowledge that control of the Nile valley would ensure the protection of the Suez Canal, but British rule was not harsh, and the average peasant profited by the occupation. Nevertheless, the twentieth century barely got under way before the Egyptians voiced a growing demand for self-government.

The organization of imperial policy. The occupation of Egypt was the first move in what soon came to be a precipitous and undignified scramble for African territory. French, German, and Italian agents now appeared in Africa, and it became apparent that friction and even war might ensue if the new imperialist activities were not guided by careful diplomacy. Bismarck therefore convened a conference in Berlin in 1884 to discuss the African problem. This assembly of diplomats paid lip service to humanitarianism by condemning the slave trade, prohibiting the sale of liquor and firearms in certain areas, and expressing concern for proper religious instruction for the natives. Then the diplomats turned to more important matters. They laid down the rules of fair competition by which the great powers were to be guided in seeking colonies. They agreed that the area along the Congo was to be administered by Leopold of Belgium, that it was to be neutral territory, and that trade and navigation were to be free in this area. No nation was to peg out claims in Africa without first notifying other powers of its intention. No territory could be claimed unless it was effectively occupied, and all disputes were to be settled by arbitration. In spite of these encouraging declarations, however, the competitors ignored the rules they laid down when it was convenient to do so, and war on several occasions was avoided only by a hair's-breadth.

The Belgian Congo. Shortly after the Berlin conference Leopold organized his African territories as the Congo Free State. He squeezed out other interested parties and ruled a vast colony subject to no control, not even that of the parliament of Belgium. Thereupon he began to exploit the economic resources of the Free State by granting concessions to private companies and reserving for his own administration an extensive rubber area, ten times as large as Belgium. A system of forced labor was introduced, and soon stories of filthy work camps, horrible whippings, and other atrocities leaked out of the Free State, now undergoing the process of "civilization." In England, societies like the Aborigines Protection Society began to attack Leopold, and two British subjects, Sir Roger Casement and Edmund Morel, did much to arouse world opinion by their exposures. In the face of a rising tide of international indignation, Leopold was forced to turn over the Free State to the Belgian government in 1908. Under the direct administration of the government conditions improved in the colony, now known as the Belgian Congo.

German interest in Africa. In Germany during the seventies there was a growing demand for imperial expansion, to which Bismarck, the chancellor, was at first deaf. By 1882, however, he had been converted to the gospel of imperialism, and the Germans began to look about them for "a place in the sun." Obtaining the promise of German protection from Bismarck, a merchant named Lüderitz sent an agent to southwest Africa to negotiate with the natives for a suitable port. The agent succeeded in acquiring some three thousand square miles of territory in exchange for 500,-200 rifles and a quantity of toys. This German port was near enough to the British Cape Colony to produce a feeling of uneasiness among the British, but nothing could be done after Bismarck declared a formal protectorate over the region in 1884. While German merchants were thus establishing a protectorate in southwest Africa, the chancellor had sent Gustav Nachtigal in a warship to sail along the west coast, assuring the British government meanwhile that Nachtigal was merely collecting commercial information. At a port on the north coast of the Gulf of Guinea Nachtigal discovered that the British were about to take over this region. He hastily declared the area to be under German protection. He then turned east along the coast to the corner of the Gulf of Guinea. By the time the British had dispatched an official to forestall further German annexations, Nachtigal had negotiated a treaty with the chiefs of the area and proclaimed it German territory.

It was on the east coast of Africa, however, that the most important German acquisitions were made. German penetration there was largely the work of Karl Peters. After attending several German universities, this man had gone to England to study British methods of colonization. He returned to Germany to organize a colonization company, and in 1884 he and three other colonial enthusiasts, disguised as English workingmen, set out on a secret mission to east Africa. Peters made his way into the interior and succeeded in obtaining treaties from chiefs giving him control of 60,000 square miles. In 1885 Bismarck proclaimed a protectorate over the region claimed by Peters.

The British-German African settlement. The British were not completely taken by surprise by German activity. Sir Harry Johnston, a famous English explorer and colonial official, had been busy in the meanwhile pegging out English claims to the region directly north of Peters' concessions, and in 1885 a group of English merchants organized the British East Africa Company to exploit the area explored by him. German and British claims were settled by an agreement in 1886. Four years later another important agreement was made by the two powers. Germany received several concessions from Great Britain, notably a strategic island in the North Sea

and a favorable adjustment of the boundary of her territory in southwest Africa. Great Britain got an exceptionally fertile region to the west of her east African holdings.

The British flag followed trade. Reluctant as the British government may have been to go beyond its intervention in Egypt, activities of the Germans and the French finally persuaded Great Britain to take an active part in the race for colonies. For some time the British government lagged behind its merchants, who staked out claims in Africa and administered valuable territory for several years before the home government indicated its willingness to take over. In Africa, time and time again, bourgeois interests compelled governments to annex territory. Trade did not follow the flag. The flag followed trade. In 1884 Great Britain obtained control over a stretch of African coast fronting on the Gulf of Aden. This protectorate was of great strategic value inasmuch as it guarded the lower approach to the Suez

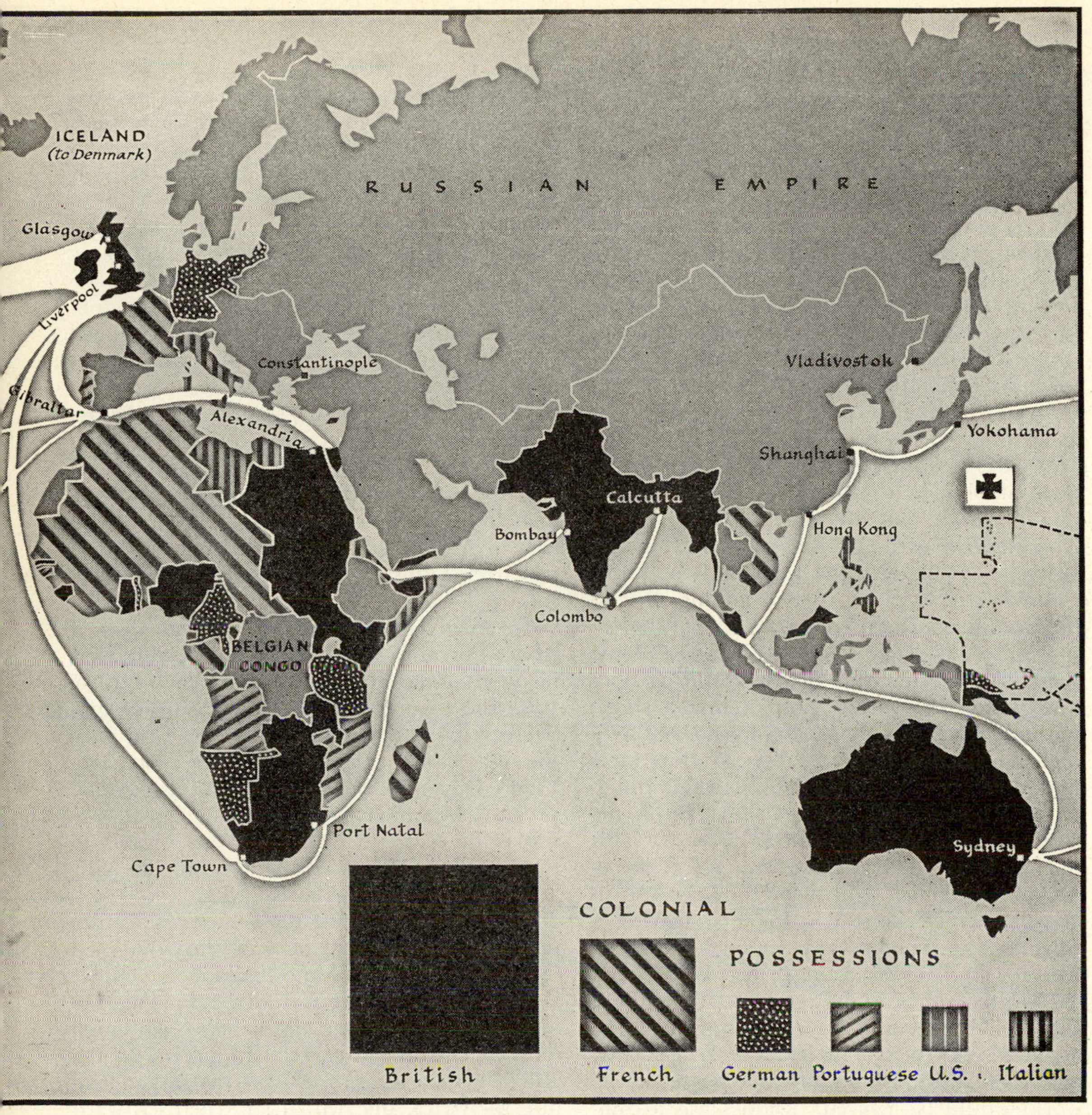

Canal. Even more important were the headwaters of the Nile, situated in the Sudan. In 1898 a British expedition conquered this strategic area also.

On the west coast of Africa Great Britain retained the several trading posts she had established in the seventeenth and eighteenth centuries and enlarged her holdings by acquiring some adjoining hinterlands. Among her new acquisitions on the African west coast the most important was the territory around the mouth of the Niger, stretching back toward the Sudan, which had been opened up to European influence by a private trading concern, the Royal Niger Company. In 1900, after having secured for the British crown an area of nearly 400,000 square miles containing 19,000,000 people, the Niger Company sold its equipment and buildings to the British government.

Cecil Rhodes, empire builder. Great Britain's influence in Africa expanded northward from Cape Colony almost to the equator, where it reached the German east African territory. In this drive north the main impetus came from Cecil Rhodes, who dreamed of an uninterrupted corridor of British territory from the Cape to Cairo. Rhodes, born in England in 1853, was the youngest of five sons of an Anglican vicar. Because of poor health he was sent to join his brother in southern Africa. Shortly after his arrival diamonds were discovered north of Cape Colony, and Rhodes and his brother immediately set out to make their fortunes. In time Rhodes became the leading figure in the fabulously wealthy diamond syndicate of De Beers and the owner of many valuable gold-mining properties in the Transvaal. His annual income was estimated to be at least $5,000,000 by 1890.

Rhodes was interested in money not for its own sake but as a means of extending British power throughout the world, especially in Africa. He was the prime figure in extending British control over the rich lands of south central Africa, more than doubling British holdings in southern Africa.

By 1890, as prime minister of Cape Colony, Rhodes' one remaining task was uniting Boer and Briton in southern Africa into a single nation. The facts of geography made this a logical objective, but since the two white races had never been able to compose their differences, Rhodes made the fatal mistake of conspiring to use force to achieve his ends. This only widened the breach between the two peoples and did much to bring on the Boer War in 1899. In 1902 Cecil Rhodes died leaving a huge legacy to endow 175 scholarships at Oxford for students from the British Dominions, the United States, and Germany. He believed that if harmony and understanding could be achieved between the United States, Germany, and the British Dominions the peace of the world would be assured. Rhodes was a complex combination of astute financier, fanatical nationalist and empire builder, and confused seeker after world peace.

French colonies in Africa. The first important colonial acquisition of France in Africa had been made long before the eighties. In the 1820's, during the reign of Charles x, French statesmen had seen in north Africa a chance to counterbalance political unrest at home. For some time France had been complaining of alleged piratical activities of the Algerians and when in 1827 the Algerian ruler insulted the French consul in public by hitting him on the head with a fly-swatter, France was furnished with a good pretext for intervention. In 1830 a large army was dispatched to occupy the country, but seventeen years elapsed before the French succeeded in subduing the fierce Berber tribes. Algeria was made an integral part of the French state.

For several decades following the conquest of Algeria, there was little French activity elsewhere in Africa. But the activities of de Brazza, a famous French explorer who obtained concessions in the Congo region in 1877 and 1878, enabled France by 1884 to claim a huge section of equatorial Africa along the right bank of the Congo River. Three years earlier France had obtained Tunisia in north Africa. The repudiation of interest payments on large loans and the charge that wild tribesmen from Tunisia crossed the border to pillage in Algeria gave the French an excuse to take over Tunisia. It is said that Bismarck encouraged the French to go into Tunisia in order to divert their minds from the loss of Alsace-Lorraine, which had been ceded to Germany after the Franco-Prussian War of 1870. With the acquisition of Algeria, Tunisia, and strategic posts along the west coast, and with the right bank of the Congo in her possession, France began to develop an ambitious colonial program by which a great west African empire was to be created, stretching from Algeria to the Congo and from the Atlantic to the Nile, and perhaps even to the Red Sea.

From her posts along the west coast, France pushed into the interior and thus obtained most of the basins of the Senegal and Niger rivers, while expeditions from Algeria and Tunisia were penetrating the Sahara. Although the French did not succeed in getting to the Nile, by 1900 they controlled the largest empire in Africa, one which stretched eastward from the Atlantic to the western Sudan, and south to the Congo River. In addition the French annexed the large island of Madagascar in the south Indian Ocean and in 1911 made Morocco a French protectorate despite the opposition of Germany.

Italy's African ventures. If overpopulation, lack of trade, and widespread poverty constitute the most compelling reasons for obtaining colonies, Italy should have gained the most extensive areas in Africa. But she came out of that scramble with very little territory. When

Tunisia became a protectorate of France in 1881, the Italians, their ambitions in the same area blocked, turned to east Africa, where they obtained a piece of Red Sea coast and a slice of barren and desolate land on the Indian Ocean. However, these areas were of little value without the rich plateau of Abyssinia (Ethiopia) in the hinterland. An attempt to annex this ancient empire in 1896 ended in the destruction of an Italian army by Abyssinian warriors. After this Italy shifted her attention to the Turkish territory of Tripoli. This she managed to acquire with the secret consent of Spain, France, Great Britain, and Russia. In 1911 she declared war on Turkey, forcing her to cede this area in 1912.

Africa under European control. This event temporarily marked the end of Italian expansion and likewise the end of the race for colonial empires by European powers. The following table shows the shares of African territory taken by the various states during the nineteenth century and the first decade of the twentieth:

	AREA	POPULATION
France	4,200,000	25,000,000
Great Britain	3,300,000	35,000,000
Germany	1,100,000	12,000,000
Belgium	900,000	7,000,000
Portugal	800,000	8,000,000
Italy	600,000	1,000,000
Spain	75,000	200,000

The economic wealth of Africa surpassed the expectations of the most avid imperialist. By the first decade in the twentieth century it was the world's greatest producer of gold and diamonds. In addition rich resources of tin, phosphates, and especially copper were uncovered. From the once dark continent also poured rubber, coffee, sisal, palm oil, and cotton. Such products became more and more essential for the great industrial nations of the world.

While Europe was profiting from the economic exploitation of Africa, what was happening to the more than 150,000,000 people living on this continent? European control did bring some blessings. The old slave trade was extirpated, intertribal warfare was often eliminated, and the scourges of plague were lessened by modern medicine. European contact also brought missionaries who did much to remedy conditions that had caused suffering and backwardness among the natives. However, these blessings were by no means unmixed. In many colonies the natives were forced off their land, their chiefs deposed, and European officers substituted in their places. Taxation forced natives out of their villages to earn money. The natives in some areas were looked upon only as a cheap labor supply for European mines and plantations. In general one may say that their lives were radically changed and their rights not always carefully looked after.

The European Sahib Masters India

Europe and the Far East. The remainder of this chapter deals with imperialism in India, China, Japan, and the Pacific islands. These lands were unlike Africa and other primitive areas. Ancient civilizations flourished and a high level of culture prevailed in most of these regions. Nevertheless they were backward industrially and in the arts of war, and their relatively static cultures had not experienced the revolutionary changes brought about by the rise of science and the Industrial Revolution. We shall see that India came completely under European domination, that China did so in a large measure, and that only Japan and Siam were able ultimately to resist western encroachment fairly effectively.

The Mogul ruler Aurangzeb. During the Mogul era in the seventeenth century the first Europeans came to India to establish trading posts. At the same time that European infiltration was going on, Mogul authority was declining rapidly. In fact one Hindu historian describes the Mogul empire at this period as "a system of organized brigandage." The reign of Shah Jahan marked the height of Mogul power, as we have seen. His successor, Aurangzeb (1658-1707), was a cunning, ruthless, and fanatical ruler who ascended the throne at the age of forty with the firm intention of getting rid of all art, vice, and heretical views. However, to govern a large Hindu empire on the "principles of an ascetic Muslim saint" was impossible. Aurangzeb was a brilliant warrior, able administrator, and upright individual, but he was a complete failure as a ruler. He ordered every Hindu school closed, smashed hundreds of Hindu temples and their priceless art objects, revived the hated poll tax which Akbar had abolished, terrorized millions of his subjects by his fanaticism, and alienated the loyalty of the Rajputs. From 1681 to his death in 1707 he waged war in the Deccan with the powerful Marathas, and by 1690, when territorial expansion reached its greatest point, the Mogul empire stretched the length and breadth of the Indian peninsula.

Decline of the Moguls. This period of power was followed by one of decline. The Deccan campaign drained the imperial treasury, and the country was too vast for one man to handle alone, as Aurangzeb insisted upon doing. At the time of his death, his empire seethed with corruption, oppression, and revolt, and within half a century the great Mogul empire crumbled and perished. The condition of India during this time "may be summed up in one word—misery." Nobles bent on gaining power, marauding armies, and officials who oppressed the people brought anarchy to India. The Sikhs and Marathas fought the tottering Moguls, and Delhi was sacked in 1739 by invaders from Persia and again in 1757 by marauders from Afghanistan. Until 1858 (after the Sepoy Rebellion) the Moguls kept their title of emperor, but the dynasty was a mere shadow of its former grandeur and strength. By 1761 the empire had ceased to exist.

It is not difficult to understand why the Mogul power declined. The Moguls were foreigners in race and religion ruling an empire the majority of whose inhabitants looked upon them as usurpers. The policy of religious toleration by which Akbar (1542-1605) won his subjects was replaced by the fanatical Moslem rule of Shah Jahan and Aurangzeb which won only the hatred of the people. Aurangzeb's long absence from Delhi and the invasion of the Deccan weakened his government at home and sapped his military strength in the field. The lavish tastes of Shah Jahan and other sultans eventually ruined the land and resulted in privation for the people. The line which had produced Babur, Akbar, Shah Jahan, and Aurangzeb lost its virility and produced a group of weaklings and debauchees at the very time when the empire had most need of strong rulers. In the end civil wars and lawlessness of all descriptions prevailed, until, as in the beginning, India was reduced to virtual anarchy.

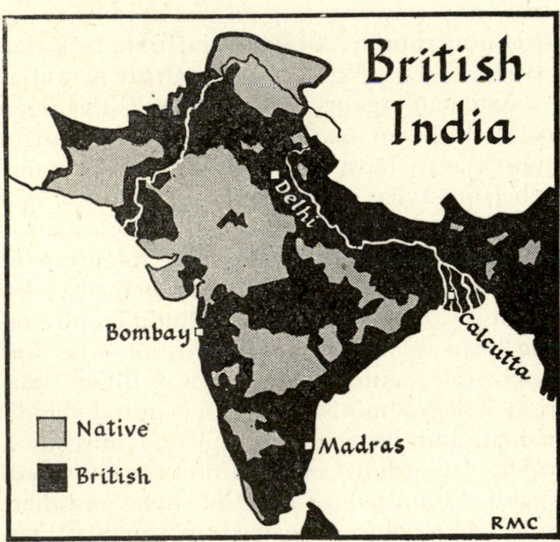

The English East India Company. The collapse of the central government left the field open to a new authority. For more than one hundred years English and French trading companies had fought one another for supremacy, and by the middle of the eighteenth century a great struggle for colonies and trade was taking place between England and France in Europe, in America, in the islands of the Caribbean, and along the eastern coast of India (see map, page 93). While British regulars and American militiamen were fighting the French in America, a similar struggle for mastery was going on in India. During the Seven Years' War (1756-1763), which saw the British victorious in America at Quebec, Robert Clive, the British leader in India, settled the issue in his country's favor by defeating the French and their Indian allies at the decisive battle of Plassey (1757). This victory ushered in a new period in Indian history, that of British rule.

The most important problem facing the English East India Company after the elimination of the French was its relationship with the Indian people. As the Mogul emperor became more and more a puppet ruler anarchy spread until the company was forced to accept the role of policeman in India. Soon the entire subcontinent came under the company's influence. Some local rulers were forced to accept its overlordship, others were deprived of their territories. Where an Indian ruler was allowed to retain his throne the company obtained the right to control his foreign policy in return for a guarantee of internal independence. Thus it is that modern India consists of British India, some 1,000,000 square miles in extent, which the British administer directly, and Indian India, about 700,000 square miles, where native dynasties are perpetuated under British supervision (see map).

Dual governmental control. By 1818 the English East India Company was practically master of India. For some time the British government had realized the anomaly of a great business concern, interested primarily in profits, controlling the destinies of millions of people. In 1773, therefore, Parliament passed an act which gave it the power to control the policies of the company. Again in 1784 another act permitted the company to continue its commercial operations and to use its armed forces and officials in carrying on the business of administration, but gave to the government at London the authority to appoint the highest company official in India, the governor-general. This system of dual control—the government of a huge country by a private corporation under the supervision of the British government—lasted from 1784 until 1858. In 1833 the trading rights of the company were revoked, and from then on its task was one of governing only.

British reforms in India. Early in the nineteenth century a strong humanitarian movement swept England. This led to many social and economic reforms at home, and likewise led the English to consider what might be undertaken in India. In a debate on Indian affairs in Parliament in 1833, the historian Macaulay stated, "We are trying to give a good government to a people to whom we cannot give a free government." During the administration of Lord William Bentinck, governor-general from 1828 to 1835, many significant reforms were introduced. The practice of *suttee,* in which widows burned themselves on the funeral pyres of their deceased husbands, was prohibited, the custom in some areas of killing girl babies was combated, and a notorious group of murderers called thags (hence our word thug) was hounded down by the British secret police. At the same time a comprehensive educational system including secondary schools and universities was introduced, in which English language, literature, and history were given chief emphasis.

The mutiny against Great Britain. The progress of reform was suddenly interrupted in the spring of 1857 by a mutiny which jeopardized the very existence of British rule in India. It is now known that this uprising was mainly a mutiny of the Indian troops, called sepoys, who formed the bulk of the company's armed forces. The immediate cause of the revolt was the religious sensibilities of the sepoys, who complained that a new cartridge issued to them was smeared with the fat of cows and pigs. This infuriated the Hindus, who regarded the cow as a sacred animal, and horrified the Mohammedans, who considered the pig as unclean. The mutiny would have come in all probability without the incident of the greased cartridges, because there was unrest and discontent throughout India. The British had been building railroads, stringing up telegraph wires, and in general introducing many disturbing western methods. Moreover, the Hindus feared that the British were going to assist missionaries to spread Christianity so that ultimately it would triumph over Hinduism. The mutiny was a dreadful and bloody affair. Fortunately for the British, many areas in India remained loyal or at least quiescent, and after fierce fighting the revolt was crushed.

Changes in administration. One consequence of the mutiny was the final eclipse of Mogul authority. In 1857 Bahadur Shah, the last of the Mogul emperors who had been permitted to maintain a court at Delhi, had been proclaimed by the mutineers as their leader. After order had been restored Bahadur Shah was exiled by the British to Burma. Another result of the mutiny was the termination of the system of dual control. The British government relieved the East India Company of its political responsibilities and after 258 years of existence the company terminated its rule.

Shortly after the company retired from the Indian scene, the British government overhauled the administrative system. The police force was reorganized, the criminal code was revised, and the Indian central government at Calcutta, as well as the local governments at Bombay and Madras, were given small legislative councils containing nominated Indian members. A trained civil service was recruited from honor graduates of British universities, and these men, most of them devoted to their duty, sincerely tried to rule India benevolently and efficiently. Great dams were built, railroad lines spanned the country, machinery for food distribution was created to eliminate famine, and an efficient postal system was introduced.

The growth of Indian nationalism. For a generation after the mutiny British administration functioned smoothly and Indian public opinion remained passive. But by 1880 it was apparent that nationalism was growing rapidly. In 1885 the Indian National Congress was formed with the aid of several Englishmen who had interested themselves in Indian political ambitions. Once the nationalist revival got under way, it grew rapidly. The railroads, a cheap postal service, the telegraph, and a free press were convenient agencies for spreading the doctrine of India for the Indians.

One of the most potent forces back of the new movement was the British educational policy. Since the days of Lord Bentinck (1828-1835), the educational system in India had been western in its content and English in its outlook. Indians became acquainted with the story of the rise of self-government in England and were introduced to *Magna Charta,* Oliver Cromwell, the Glorious Revolution, and the Bill of Rights. It was therefore quite natural that a desire for political freedom should appear among the youths in the classrooms of Bombay, Madras, and Calcutta. Furthermore, the prestige of the white man was diminished when an Italian army was cut to pieces in 1896 in Abyssinia and a heretofore almost unknown Asiatic kingdom, Japan, defeated Russia in 1904-1905. Because British educational policy stressed literary training at the expense of agricultural and technical education, the schools were filled to overflowing with young men, who had only one aim—to obtain a degree in order to get into government service. Consequently there were always more applicants than openings, and thousands of young men unable to obtain "white collar" employment and disdainful of manual labor joined the ranks of an educational proletariat and turned against the government in wrath. Ardent young patriots manufactured bombs, procured revolvers and ammunition, and assassinated several British judges and administrators. The twentieth century in India, as we shall note in a later chapter, saw nationalism become even more insistent.

Southern Asia and Oceania

The southeastern regions. Southern Asia and the Pacific Islands comprise another great area of western expansion which in some ways is even more important than Africa. This area includes Ceylon, Burma, British Malaya, and French Indo-China in southeastern Asia and a group of large islands called the East Indies. The most important of this island group are the Netherlands East Indies and the Philippines. Farther east in the Pacific Ocean there are hundreds of smaller islands, the most important being Samoa and the Hawaiian and Fiji groups.

Ceylon. The island of Ceylon, located immediately southeast of the southernmost tip of India, had its golden age, accomplished mainly by the Singhalese rulers of northern India, between 500 B.C. and 300 A.D. But the golden age was dimmed by the invasions of the Tamil people who came from south India. For centuries a conflict raged in Ceylon and Tamil Land between Hinduism and Buddhism. In the sixteenth century Portuguese and Dutch adventurers occupied the chief ports of the country. During the wars of the French Revolution, in 1796, the British forced the Dutch to give up their holdings in Ceylon, and the island was granted to Great Britain in the Treaty of Amiens (1802).

As the nineteenth century unfolded Ceylon became one of the most valuable colonies controlled by Great Britain. With the exception of India it was the first tropical region to be developed extensively by the British and soon became one of the most important tea producers in the world. It produces the best grade of cocoa and ranks next to the Netherlands East Indies and the Malay Peninsula in the production of rubber. The British also began to mine lead ore and sapphires. Later the island became one of the most important exporters of coconuts in the world.

Burma. Burma adjoins India on India's eastern land frontier. Early in the nineteenth century Burma came into conflict with the British, who claimed that the Burmese king was interfering with English commerce and threatening the Indian province of Bengal. After two wars (1823-1825 and 1851-1852) independent Burmese territory was reduced to a small fragment.

While this British penetration took place the French extended their holdings in the

In the famed ruins at Angkor Wat in French Indo-China can be found this battle scene, a carved stone relief. Note the stylized flatness of treatment, appropriate to relief, and the rhythmic line of soldiers.

proximity of Burma, using their recently acquired holdings in Indo-China (see page 268) as a base of operations. To escape European conquest the Burmese king tried to play off the French against the British, but before France could come to his aid the British suddenly invaded his territory in 1885 and annexed what was left of the Burmese kingdom.

As in the case of Ceylon, British capital was poured into Burma to exploit its riches. The country is now the greatest source of teak, a very valuable wood used in shipbuilding, and the majority of its 10,000,000 inhabitants are engaged in agriculture, principally the growing of rice. British conquest brought the Burmese in closer contact with European culture, particularly in such cities as Rangoon, where young men of the upper classes obtained an English education and were employed in the British governmental service or in European firms. In the rural areas, however, with the exception of those who worked on European plantations, the majority of the Burmese peasants continued to cultivate their family

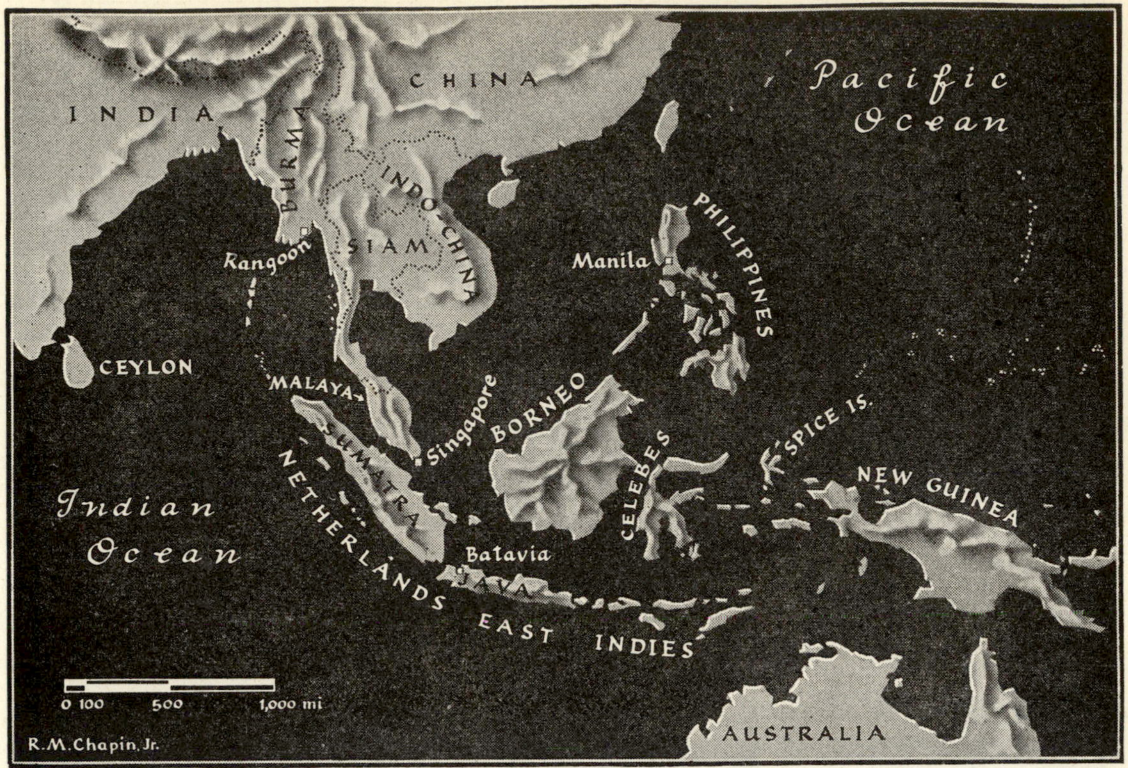

holdings and were not greatly affected by European influences.

French Indo-China. While French explorers were pegging out important colonial holdings in tropical Africa a new empire was in the process of creation in the rich peninsula of Indo-China. As early as 1787 France had secured the rights to a port from the most important native ruler in Indo-China. Little French activity followed thereafter until the middle of the nineteenth century, when the murder of a Spanish missionary brought a Franco-Spanish naval flotilla to the peninsula in 1857. During the next thirty years the French expanded their holdings in the peninsula, by annexation and by the declaring of protectorates over successive areas. In the process France came into conflict with China (1883-1885), who had for many years received annual tribute from certain regions in the peninsula. The Peking government was finally forced to recognize French supremacy in Indo-China. Later France took territory in the south away from Siam, her neighbor to the west.

By the beginning of the twentieth century France had succeeded in creating a compact empire in Indo-China nearly fifty per cent larger than the mother country. Its 17,000,000 people are mainly Annamese and follow a form of Buddhism. Indo-China became especially important for the production of rice. Tin, pepper, coal, and cotton were also produced in large quantities as time went on. French colonial administrators regarded their Asiatic empire as one of great economic importance, both as a market for French goods and as the main source of rice for France. As one of these French imperialists declared: "No French colony is more populous than the Indo-Chinese Empire, none has a richer soil. . . . The resources to exploit are immense."[3]

Siam. Colonial expansion of the British in Burma and the French in Indo-China seriously endangered the independence of the small nation of Siam, a country nearly as large as France with a population of 9,000,000. Siamese territory was pared down by both Great Britain and France but it succeeded in maintaining its existence. This was owing in part to the fact that both France and Great Britain welcomed the retention of an independent Siam which would act as a buffer between British and French Asiatic possessions, and partly to the marked ability of the royal house of Siam.

British Malaya. British Malaya was the southern part of the long peninsula which begins at southern Asia and edges down to the coast of the Dutch island of Sumatra, leaving only a small channel of communication between the Pacific and Indian oceans. This narrow waterway between the Malay Peninsula and Sumatra is one of the most strategic highways in the world. British influence in the Malay Peninsula dates back to 1786. In 1796 a coastal strip was obtained, and in 1819 Sir Thomas Stamford Raffles, an energetic English colonial official, secured the uninhabited island of Singapore from a Malay sultan. Raffles saw that the island could dominate the commercially significant strait between the Malay Peninsula and Sumatra.

British influence was gradually extended northward up the peninsula. In the latter part of the nineteenth century four independent sultanates became British protectorates, and in 1909 Siam transferred to Great Britain the control and administration of additional states. These acquisitions brought British Malaya in contact with the frontiers of Siam proper.

British Malaya had an area slightly less than that of England and in 1942 had a population of 5,494,264. It is one of the richest colonial areas in the world, particularly in tin and rubber. The period from 1874 to 1900 was largely concerned with the development of tin mining. Exports of this metal rapidly increased, and in 1907 the Malay Peninsula produced 52 per cent of the world's supply. After 1900 increased attention was given to the growing of rubber, and the peninsula became one of the most valuable rubber producers.

The economic development of the Malay Peninsula has been mainly the work of Chinese and Indian immigrants. The Malayan natives live contentedly in their great jungle forests where luxuriant tropical growth easily supplies most of their wants. Consequently they have little interest in hard work. The mines, plantations, and commercial enterprises are dominated by the Chinese. In the southern Malay Peninsula the Chinese not only outnumber the Malayan natives but also monopolize higher education and dominate such professions as medicine and law. From the very beginning one of the problems of British colonial administration had been that of safe-

A Chinese sage strokes his stone beard in the temple of Wat Poh at Bangkok, Siam (Thailand). The treatment of drapery denotes the Chinese influence.

guarding the Malayan native from the aggressive Chinese immigrant.

Raffles' appreciation of the importance of Singapore was fully confirmed by the end of the nineteenth century. The island city became one of the greatest ports in the world. Many of the ships passing east and west between Europe and Asia used its dock and coaling facilities, and as long as Great Britain controlled this island she could dominate the seas surrounding southern Asia.

The East Indies islands. Extending southward from the Malay Peninsula and Indo-China is the Malay Archipelago, or the East Indies, the largest group of islands in the world. Endowed with rich natural resources and populated by relatively backward peoples, it is natural that this area should have become the scene of active western imperialism. The majority of the islands came under Dutch influence, and that part of the archipelago under their control was known as the Netherlands East Indies (see map, page 268). On several of these islands control was shared with other European powers. Great Britain had possessions in Borneo, part of another island belonged to Portugal, and Australia controlled the eastern part of New Guinea. North of this great Dutch island empire—but still part of the Malay Archipelago—were the Philippine Islands, which came under the rule of the United States at the close of the nineteenth century.

The Netherlands East Indies. The story of the Netherlands East Indies begins in 1596, when the first Dutch fleet reached Sumatra. Until Spain obtained control of Portugal in 1580, the Portuguese had monopolized the rich spice trade of the East Indies. They brought the spices to Europe, where they were distributed by the Dutch, who acted as middlemen. The temporary and partial union of Portugal and Spain and the Dutch struggle for independence from Spain caused the Dutch to set about securing contact with the spice trade at its source.

In 1602 the Dutch East India Company was organized to exploit the resources of the Spice Islands, and by the middle of the seventeenth century it had eliminated all rivals in this area. For the next hundred years this company enjoyed great prosperity, although much of it came at the expense of the rights of the natives. Forced labor and other hardships caused a widespread insurrection to break out on the island of Java in 1749, which was crushed only by strong military and naval action.

Dutch influence in the East Indies declined and wavered from 1750 to 1816. The old trading company became corrupt and its trade declined. In 1798 it was abolished, and all Dutch holdings were transferred to the Dutch crown. During the Napoleonic wars Holland was dominated by France, and the Netherlands East Indies were considered a part of the Napoleonic empire. In 1810, therefore, a British expedition captured several important Dutch islands, and in the following year a fleet from India gained control of Java. The British occupation lasted from 1811 to 1816, when the islands were returned to the Dutch authorities in accordance with a treaty made in 1814.

Dutch systems of agriculture. The spice trade had been declining for some time, and the Dutch in consequence set about raising new products. At first they gave their attention to tea and coffee, for which there was an expanding market. In the 1830's the so-called culture system was introduced into the islands, under which one fifth of all native land was set aside to raise crops for the government and one fifth of all the natives' time was required to till these lands. The production of tobacco, sugar, coffee, tea, indigo, pepper, and cinnamon increased enormously, and in the first twelve years of the operation of the culture system products worth $700,000,000 were raised by the natives for the government.

The culture system had some advantages for the native, for in the long run it gave the islands a prosperous agricultural system and a body of workers who had been trained and forced to work. But because it was based on forced labor, it often prevented the natives from having enough land for their own use. In 1860 the culture system was thoroughly discredited in a novel written by Edward Dekker, *Max Havelaar,* which exposed the evils of colonial administration. Liberal sentiment in Holland demanded reform and gradually, from 1860 to 1880, the culture system was abolished. From then on Dutch administration improved. Steps were taken to protect native rights, free labor superseded the culture system, and Dutch rule now sought to be humanitarian.

By 1900 the Dutch were in complete control of the various islands in their southern Pacific empire. In no other colonies was there such careful application of science and administration to the task of tropical development. In Java intensive agricultural development took place with the help of free native labor under the direction of Dutch experts. Rubber, sugar, coffee, and tea were the most important products at the start of the twentieth century and in addition kapok, tobacco, tapioca, sisal, and coconuts were exported. Later tin, oil, and chinabark, from which quinine is prepared, likewise became important.

Problems of Dutch rule. By 1900 the evils of the culture system had been remedied, and the native peoples enjoyed certain benefits. But, as in Africa, India, and other areas where European influence had penetrated, Dutch rule also brought problems with it. The appearance of the European in the Indies eventually created two worlds. In one there was the great number of natives who lived largely as their ancestors had lived for hundreds of years. In the main their lives continued untouched by alien influences. In the other world there were the natives who had adopted European culture, gone to Dutch schools, and largely substituted European customs for those of their ancestors. As greater and greater numbers of natives went to school and became absorbed in European commerce or in the governmental service, the Europeanized native tended to look down on his fellows who still followed the traditional way of life. The villagers no longer understood the strange ways of their young men who had taken up a new life in Batavia. Europeanization also presented the Dutch colonial administrators with an even more perplexing problem. Among the natives exposed to European traditions a strong political consciousness developed. Demands were made for a share in the government of the country.

People of the Netherlands East Indies. Under Dutch administration the population of the Netherlands East Indies had increased at a rapid rate. In Java, for example, the population was about 3,000,000 in 1800. By 1880 it was 20,000,000, and by 1900, 29,000,000. This increase of population continued in the twentieth century, so that today the Netherlands East Indies constitute one of the most densely populated areas in the world. In 1940 it was estimated that the total population was 70,000,000.

The people of the Netherlands East Indies include some 137 tribes and groups. Malay stock is dominant, but in the eastern islands there are large groups belonging to the Melanesian racial group known as Papuans. The civilization of the people of the Netherlands East Indies is often referred to as Indonesian because of the strong culture influences that radiated from India in the past. During the period from 600 to 1400 Indian rulers succeeded in establishing great kingdoms on the islands. They erected magnificent temples and forced Hinduism upon the people. Buddhism was also introduced and led to the building of many temples, one of which, Boro-Budur, ranks among the architectural marvels of the world. In the fifteenth century Arab invaders brought a new culture, which gradually became dominant, and this process of Islamization had just been completed when the first European traders came to the Indies. The religion of the majority of the people today is Mohammedanism.

The Javanese and Balinese and the natives of Sumatra are light brown in color, while the Papuans of New Guinea are dark, with frizzy hair and large noses. The Javanese, in particular, are noted for their fine features and graceful carriage. Hard-working people, the natives of the Netherlands East Indies toil unremittingly on their rice patches. Every inch of ground must be cultivated. The landscape is carefully terraced so that the natives can carry their rice cultivation high up the mountainside. All planting is done by hand, and at harvest time each rice stalk is cut separately with a special knife. The social unit is the village. All matters relating to irrigation, cattle breeding, work in the communal cemetery, and the making of terraces are administered by the elders of the village.

The Philippine Islands. Little more than 250 miles north of the Netherlands East Indies is the southernmost large island of the Philippine group. This latter group consists of eleven large islands and more than 3000 small ones. The Philippine Islands became known to Europeans when the noted Portuguese explorer Magellan discovered them in 1521. The Chinese had traded in the islands for centuries. After much rivalry with the Portuguese, Spanish control was firmly established in the Philippines, thanks to the pioneering enterprise of Miguel López de Legazpi, the conquistador who founded the first permanent Spanish settlement in 1565. In 1571 the city of Manila was established. By the time of Legazpi's death in 1572 Spanish authority had been extended over a large area, trade was developing, and the colony had been placed on a firm basis.

During the next two centuries the Spanish administration concerned itself principally with Christianizing the Filipinos. The lure of gold and silver in Latin America which resulted in forced labor and other harsh practices for the Indians was absent in the Philippines, where colonial officials were able to follow a more humane policy. If the Spanish were liberal in their religious and educational policies, they were not liberal in politics. The Filipinos were given no more opportunity to participate in government than were other non-European peoples, or even European colonists, in areas ruled by Europeans prior, say, to the late eighteenth century. In 1872 there was a serious uprising. Discontent continued, especially among educated liberals, and another widespread revolt occurred in 1896.

The most prominent of Filipino leaders who demanded reform was José Rizal (1861-1896). Destined to become the national hero of the Philippines, Rizal as a youth attended a college in Manila, later studied in Madrid, where

he obtained a degree in medicine, and finally went to Germany for further study. In a few years after his return to the Philippines, Rizal had established a wide reputation as a champion of political reform, a scientist, and a writer. To draw attention to the evils of the Spanish régime he wrote two novels, *The Social Cancer* and *The Reign of Greed.* These books give an excellent picture of the life and times of the nineteenth-century Filipinos and the excesses of Spanish rule. During the revolt of 1896 Rizal was arrested and executed by the authorities.

United States imperialism. While Spain wrestled with Filipino discontent a new imperialist power was emerging in the Pacific. During much of the nineteenth century the United States had been occupied in the westward movement, which ultimately carried American power from the Appalachian Mountains to the Pacific. The Civil War occupied all the energies of the young nation in the sixties and this crisis was followed by a hectic period of industrialization and economic expansion. By 1890 the United States was a great industrial power, more and more conscious of the importance of world markets, international investments, and raw materials. This consciousness later was responsible for the expansion of American interest and influence in Latin America and the rise of dollar diplomacy.

The new expansionist spirit was reflected not only in the Caribbean and in Central America but in the Pacific as well. As early as 1842 Daniel Webster had told the people of the Hawaiian Islands that the United States would not permit any foreign power to annex their territory.[4] In 1867 the Midway Islands, a thousand miles west of Hawaii, were occupied by naval forces of the United States. In the 1880's the upward surge of imperialism nearly involved us in war as a result of the interest of Great Britain, Germany, and the United States in Samoa. For several years the three powers negotiated and disputed, and civil war raged in Samoa between pro-British and pro-German partisans. In 1889 Bismarck threatened to land troops. President Cleveland was resolved to use force if necessary to prevent this step. The crisis was reached in 1889 when British, American, and German warships were dispatched to Samoa. At this juncture a terrible hurricane swept the island,

In "The Boy Stood on the Burning Deck" Charles Nelan ridicules the stubborn Spanish régime in Cuba (personified by the premier, Sagasta), which refuses rescue from the European powers.

destroying nearly all the vessels. Thus what seemed to be an inevitable war was averted, and in 1889 a treaty was arranged. This agreement provided for the withdrawal of Great Britain, leaving the United States and Germany to divide Samoa.

The annexation of Hawaii. The next advance of the United States was in the Hawaiian Islands. During the nineteenth century Europeans and Americans had developed large sugar plantations in this fertile group. American capital and American businessmen continued to pour into the islands, and by 1881 an American Secretary of State could speak of the Hawaiian Islands as part of the "American system." Because of this economic tie and the desire of many Americans to continue residence in the islands and simultaneously to live on American soil, a revolt was engineered in 1893 which deposed the Hawaiian queen and set up a republic. United States marines assisted in the uprising. The desire of the pro-American faction in the islands for annexation was blocked when President Cleveland refused to send the annexation treaty to the Senate. The President, however, had no choice but to recognize the republic of Hawaii. In 1897, when McKinley had succeeded Cleveland, Hawaii was annexed by joint declaration of both houses of Congress and became a Territory of the United States.

The Spanish-American War. In 1898 the United States went to war against Spain. Strong resentment of United States citizens against the harsh rule of Spain in Cuba, large American investments in this great sugar island, and the mysterious destruction of the battleship Maine in Havana harbor contributed to the outbreak of war. In the Pacific Admiral Dewey had little difficulty in destroying the Spanish fleet at Manila in May 1898. American soldiers were then landed in the Philippines. Cooperating with these troops were Filipino patriots under the direction of their leader Aguinaldo. Spanish resistance here as in Cuba quickly crumbled, and in the treaty of December 1898, Spain agreed to cede to the United States the Philippines, Guam, and Puerto Rico. The next year the United States occupied the small Pacific outpost of Wake Island.

America and the Philippines. Aguinaldo had no wish merely to exchange masters and to see the United States acquire the Philippines. Fighting broke out between his forces and American troops in the spring of 1899. Hostilities lasted for three years, and 60,000 troops were employed before the revolt was crushed. The ironic spectacle of American forces being used in a second conquest of the Philippines brought about a strong revulsion against imperialism in many quarters in the United States. However, regardless of what can be said for or against this second conquest, American colonial administration in the first decade of the twentieth century in the Philippines was for the most part liberal and well intentioned. Every effort was made to establish an adequate school system, and ultimately an opportunity was afforded the Filipinos for participation in their own government. In 1913 the legislature became dominantly native, although final authority in the most important matters was still reserved for the United States Congress. The Philippine tariff was shaped to favor American trade, and large amounts of capital from the United States were invested in the islands.

The population of the Philippines in 1903 was estimated to be nearly 8,000,000, the majority of whom belonged to the Malayan racial group. American occupation speeded up the process of westernization, which had been in operation for nearly three hundred years. Increased educational opportunities caused many young men to leave their ancestral lands to become teachers, lawyers, and businessmen. Among these educated and traveled Filipinos developed the desire for national independence. In their eyes American government in the Philippines, no matter how efficient or humanitarian, was no substitute for self-government.

Imperialism in China (1650-1895)

The Manchu dynasty. The Manchus were in part descendants of a group of Tatars who wrested northern China from the Sungs, only to be defeated in turn by the forces of Genghis Khan. These warriors had lived for centuries in Manchuria, recently named Manchukuo (country of the Manchus). The Manchus (who came to power in 1644) appreciated the Chinese civilization and adopted a conciliatory attitude toward their subjects. They kept the civil service examinations which the Mings had reintroduced, retained most of the Chinese administrative officials, honored Confucianism, kept Buddhism and Taoism as national religions, and patronized Chinese literature and art. However, they refused to allow intermarriage with the Chinese, for the Manchus realized that they would soon be assimilated and conquered unless they strictly maintained their blood difference. They also kept garrisons throughout the land to impress the Chinese with the inadvisability of revolting, and to keep them conscious of submission the Tatars forced the Chinese to shave the front of the head and wear the hair in queue fashion, a style of hairdress common to the Tatars. By and large, however, the Manchus became Chinese in their habits and attitudes.

The Manchu emperors were remarkable conquerors. When the dynasty came to the throne, it held only four provinces in the north. But the Manchus were so efficient as militarists and administrators that they won an empire (see map opposite). Although outlying regions had only nominal relations with the imperial court at Peking, they were nevertheless definitely affected by Manchu rule.

The greatest scholarly feat during the rule of the Manchus was the compilation of the huge dictionary of the Chinese language, the

Dictionary of K'ang Hsi. It contains 44,439 characters, with the pronunciation of each. It represents the work of thirty scholars, who worked upon it for years, and is still the final authority on the meaning of Chinese characters.

Manchu China and the west. For some 150 years relative prosperity and well-being existed in China. The Ch'ien Lung reign (1736-1796) is of special importance. The emperor put down numerous revolts and attained suzerainty over eastern Turkestan, Burma, and Tibet.

Meanwhile at Canton and other southern ports trade had been developing on an increasing scale between Chinese and European merchants. While the Portuguese traded at Macao, British, French, Dutch, Danes, Swedes, and Germans came to Canton to purchase porcelains, silks, cottons, and tea. Friction arose, however, from the high import and export duties which foreigners had to pay and from other irritating restrictions. Another cause of friction was the growing opium evil, which the imperial government tried to curb. But foreign merchants continued to get the profitable product of the poppy into the country by one means or another. To settle difficulties, the British government sent a diplomatic mission that reached Peking in 1793. Commercial overtures failed, however, and matters at Canton got worse instead of better. The tone of the letter which the Ch'ien Lung emperor sent in reply to George III's request for trading privileges with China is both amusing and significant as indicating the attitude of official China toward aliens:

"I set no value on objects strange and ingenious, and have no use for your country's manufactures. . . . I have expounded my views in detail and have commanded your tribute envoys to leave in peace on their homeward journeys. It behooves you, O King, to respect my sentiments and to display even greater devotion and loyalty in the future, so that, by perpetual submission to our throne, you may secure peace and prosperity for your country hereafter."

Factors in Manchu decline. Eventually able rulers were followed by weak monarchs who reigned but could not rule. The great ruler of the Ch'ien Lung era was succeeded by the Chia Ch'ing emperor (1796-1820), "churlish, sordid, and uncouth," whose reign was not auspicious for China. The mandarinate became more and more corrupt, and one powerful statesman was found to have amassed a private fortune estimated at $105,000,000. Secret societies conspired against the government, especially in the south, where, as indeed throughout China, the Manchus were looked upon as foreign usurpers. Unrest was increased by a series of national disasters, and the great drought of 1817 made even the government wonder if it was losing the mandate of heaven. Piracy increased.

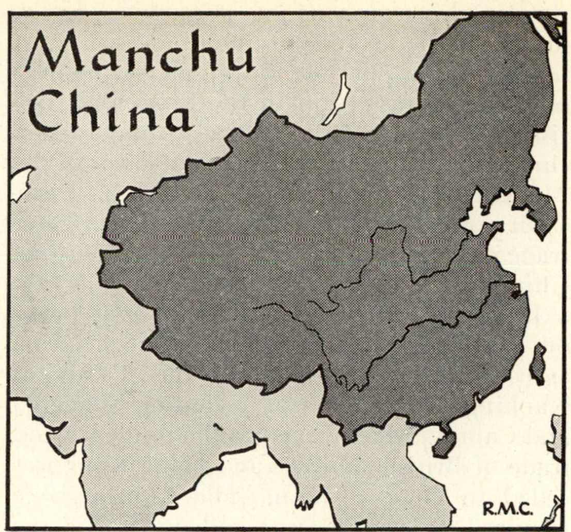

The opium problem became increasingly grave. In 1800 the imperial government forbade the importation of the drug, but the trade continued to flourish. Although the English East India Company prohibited the transportation of opium in its own ships, the company continued to produce the drug in India for Chinese consumption and allowed other ships under its control to take opium to Macao and Canton. Privately owned vessels of other countries, including the United States, as well as those of British registry, continued to make huge profits out of the helplessness of growing numbers of Chinese addicts, and because many corrupt Chinese and Manchu officials were bribed, the traffic expanded, and the edicts of the central government became as ineffective as did the prohibition laws in the United States a hundred years later.

The Tao Kuang emperor (1821-1851), who occupied the imperial throne during the first war between Great Britain and China, tried in vain to curb the opium traffic, inasmuch as three of his own sons had succumbed to the drug. He checked corruption in his own court but could not put an end to the growing evils of bad administration in the provinces. Uprisings in many of the provinces under Manchu government showed that the power of the Manchus was crumbling from within. European powers pressed from without for greater trade concessions in China, often disregarding Chinese jurisdiction and sovereignty.

War and western exploitation. War broke out with England in 1839, and in 1842 China agreed to the provisions of the Treaty of Nanking. Certain ports, including Shanghai and Canton, were opened to the residence and trade of British subjects, and Hong Kong was ceded to Great Britain. The Chinese were required to pay a large indemnity for the opium destroyed by Chinese officials and to pay the expenses of the war. In the years immediately following, other western powers, including the United States, France, and Russia, secured trading privileges also, and China appeared well on the way to ultimate physical dismemberment and economic vassalage.

Defeated, China's rulers still refused to cooperate with the great powers, preferring instead to use obstructionist tactics whenever possible. Furthermore, the foreign merchants were continually scheming to obtain larger trade concessions and to have more cities opened to commerce. With relations at a breaking point, a trivial incident provoked a second war in 1856, in which by 1860 China was again vanquished. By the Treaty of Tientsin in 1858, supplemented by the conventions of 1860, six new ports were opened for trade and residence, the Yangtze was made a waterway for foreign merchants, foreigners with passports were permitted to travel anywhere in the interior, Christians, practically speaking, had the right to propagate their faith wherever they wished, diplomatic relations were inaugurated between London and Peking, and Great Britain received some territory across from Hong Kong.

Still other privileges were wrested from the defeated Chinese and Manchus. Three of these privileges which caused bitterness for many years among the Chinese were: (1) extraterritoriality, (2) customs regulation, and (3) the right to station foreign warships in Chinese waters. Extraterritoriality provides the citizen of a foreign nation with the right to be tried in his own country's consular court whenever he is involved in a dispute with a Chinese. This practice has been defended on various grounds, among them that the Chinese concept of justice was more rigid and harsh than that of the west, but the Chinese argue that extraterritoriality not only is humiliating to China's sovereignty but discriminates in favor of the western nations.

Difficulties of the Manchus. The concessions which the Manchus had been forced to grant the "foreign devils" resulted in a loss of prestige for the ruling house. Serious domestic difficulties further diminished their hold on the country, and the rebellion of 1850-1864 almost overthrew the dynasty. This revolt was suppressed with the aid to a minor degree of an army under the consecutive command of an American, General Frederick Townsend Ward, and a Scotsman, Major Charles George "Chinese" Gordon, later killed in the Sudan. The Manchus, more indebted to the foreign powers than ever, had managed to weather this internal struggle, but the time was not far distant when they were to founder before more powerful tempests of revolt.

The Manchu dynasty survived another half century, in large measure because of the statecraft of a remarkable woman, Tzu Hsi, the dowager empress, popularly known as "Old Buddha." She was the real power behind the throne from 1861 to her death in 1908. By vigorous policy, relatively astute statecraft, and often unscrupulous actions, Tzu Hsi not only put down internal revolts but helped restore a measure of prestige to her country. But Tzu Hsi, being Manchu and limited by the viewpoint of the Forbidden City, felt that security for China lay in adhering to ancient traditions and customs, and she encouraged anti-foreign sentiment.

Encroachments of foreigners. Immigration of Chinese to foreign countries, especially the United States, caused trouble both here and abroad. Anti-Chinese riots broke out in the western American territories or states, and further immigration of the Chinese to America was prohibited. Trouble lay even nearer home, for various powers were slicing off bits of territory on the periphery of China. By 1860 Russia had annexed the entire area north of the Amur River, by 1885 France had taken Indo-China, by 1886 Great Britain had seized Burma, and in 1887 China was forced officially to agree to the cession to Portugal of Macao which had already become predominantly Portuguese.

Other powers now proceeded to take still more away from China. Germany got control of Kiaochow Bay plus some adjacent territory, Russia got leases to Dairen and Port Arthur on the tip of the Liaotung peninsula, Great Britain received the naval base of Weihaiwei, while the French were given Kwangchow in southern China (see map, page 414). Besides these outright cessions of territory, the European powers captured rich economic concessions at the expense of the helpless Chinese people.

In the words of G. N. Steiger:

"By the great majority of the officials and by the overwhelming mass of the Chinese people the West was hated, despised, and feared. Although they realized China's inability to resist foreign demands, the officials and literati felt that the introduction of foreign ideas and methods would result in the destruction of the very foundations of their own civilization, while the mass of the common people, often knowing the foreigner only as a purveyor of strange and disturbing religious doctrines, resented his upsetting influence in the affairs of the town or village community. . . . In 1894, therefore, as fifty years earlier, the Manchu government was chiefly desirous of keeping the foreigner at arm's length, and in this policy it had the approval of the nation at large."[6]

Japan Accepts the West (1650-1890)

Japanese culture in isolation. Many of the imperialistic activities we have discussed were noted with alarm by the Japanese, particularly the western conquests in India, the Netherlands East Indies, and the Philippines. The result in Japan in the seventeenth century was the ousting of European Christian missionaries and traders with the exception of a few Dutch on one of the islands, and the closing of ports to foreign commerce. For more than two hundred years the *shoguns*, who ruled nearly all of Japan, like the Manchu emperors of China, endeavored to remain isolated from the rest of the world.

Japan opens her doors. On July 7, 1853, a squadron comprising two steam frigates and two sloops of war steamed into the bay near the city of Yedo, later named Tokyo. The fleet's commander, Commodore Matthew Calbraith Perry, had been sent by the United States government to induce the Japanese rulers to conclude a treaty whereby trading relations between the two nations might be opened. Perry was instructed to be tactful, but in all likelihood he would have used force if it had been necessary. The *shogun* and his advisers were well aware that the empire's defenses were weak and that the American warships carried armament which could not be ignored. Perry tactfully sailed away to China after a short call, leaving the Japanese officials to wrangle over their predicament, but when the commodore returned in February 1854 with even greater forces, there was no doubt as to the course of procedure. On March 31, 1854, Japan agreed to the Treaty of Kanagawa, "the first formal treaty with any western country." By its terms shipwrecked sailors were guaranteed hospitable treatment, foreign vessels were allowed to stop for provisions, and two ports, "the two worst harbors in the country," were opened to American ships. It was not long before Great Britain, Russia, and Holland had obtained similar privileges.

The Tenno restored to power. Nippon would have suffered the fate of China or worse had not her leaders quickly learned to act far differently from the Manchu rulers. For fifteen years following the signing of the Treaty of Kanagawa, confusion among Japan's leaders caused endless friction. For hundreds of years the real ruler of the kingdom had not been the Tenno, or Heavenly King (called at times Mikado in the west), who lived in seclusion in central Japan, but the *shogun*, who conducted the affairs of state at his palace in Kamakura, or finally in Yedo (Tokyo). Since 1603 the *shoguns* had come from the house of Tokugawa, but at this time its power and prestige were steadily declining. The Tokugawa *shogunate* was associated with the signing of the treaty with Perry, and this was used by anti-foreign forces to overthrow the *shogunate* system and restore the throne's supreme authority. In September 1866, one *shogun* died and was succeeded by a *shogun* named Keiki. Six months later, the Tenno died and was succeeded by the boy Mutsuhito, afterward to be known as Meiji Tenno. The feudal chiefs now urged the new *shogun* to restore the administration to the emperor so that the kingdom might be united to meet its common dangers. Keiki resigned his power to the emperor, who accepted the *shogun's* resignation in the following curt words: "Tokugawa Keiki's proposal to restore administrative authority to the Imperial Court is accepted by the emperor."[7] With the transfer of power back to the Tenno, a new era opened for Japan.

The adoption of western ideas. The official change began in January 1868 with the adoption of the word Meiji, meaning "enlightened government." Meiji Tenno ruled until 1912, and with his reign are associated those epoch-making events which transformed Nippon from a sleepy oriental island kingdom into a dynamic, semimodernized power which the European nations had to recognize as an equal. The restoration of the throne's supreme authority was aided by the *daimyo's* (chieftain's) voluntary abolition of his feudal rights, and in 1871 the abolition of the feudal system became an official, although far from an actual, fact. The *daimyo* retired on an income of one tenth of the feudal revenues, and 400,000 *samurai* were pensioned. However, they were no longer to be the only soldiers of the country, for in 1876 national conscription went into effect and every element of society became liable for military or naval service.

Here we can but catalogue some of the many reforms which now began to transform Japan. Railways, telegraphs, lighthouses, and dockyards were soon constructed, a postal system was organized in 1870, a mint was established to coin new money, a bimetallic system of currency and a system of national banks were instituted, orders were placed in England for the construction of warships. American advisers were consulted regarding national education and imperial universities were founded in several parts of the country. Other foreign experts were brought in to teach the Japanese about medicine, engineering, and agriculture. Beginning January 1, 1873, the Gregorian calendar was adopted. The Japanese continued to mark their chronology officially from the reputed accession of Jimmu Tenno in 660 B.C., although it probably took place some six centuries later. ("History" begins in Japan about the fifth century A.D.)

Governmental reconstruction. The political reconstruction of the empire may be said—for convenience—to have commenced with the creation of a senate in 1875. Three years later an edict set forth the formation of elective assemblies for cities and prefectures. In 1881 an imperial decree announced that a national parliamentary government would be inaugurated within ten years' time. Six months later a party, led by Ito Hirobumi (subsequently Prince Ito), one of the greatest statesmen in Japanese history, set forth to study the world's various governmental systems. Ito was particularly impressed by the German plan as developed by Bismarck.

The Ito mission returned in 1883 and set to work framing the new constitution. The cabinet system was reorganized in order to give the premier a position analogous to that held by the chancellor in Germany. The cabinet included nine ministers, each controlling a state department, and it was made responsible not to the diet but to the emperor alone. The army and navy alone could appoint their respective ministers, and, since no statesman could form a cabinet without a war minister and the army could overthrow any cabinet by simply withdrawing him, final control of policies rested in the hands of the military group. The army was for many years dominated for the most part by the Choshu clan, and the navy by the Satsuma clan, two of the four feudal clans which helped overthrow the *shogunate* and restore the Tenno to power.

The constitution provided for a diet, divided into the House of Peers and the House of Representatives. The latter body was made elective, but the property qualifications at first limited the electorate to a small number. While the cabinet is independent of the diet, the latter body wields a modicum of power in financial matters because it can in peace times hold up an unpopular budget by refusing to vote supplies. In the event of such action, the government is forced to stay within the limits of the budget of the previous financial year. On February 11, 1889, the constitution was promulgated, marking the apparent adoption of certain western political ideas and a partial severance with the ideology of the past. The constitution stressed the position and powers of the emperor. In its articles it stated that "the Emperor is sacred and inviolable, . . . is the head of the empire, combining in himself the rights of sovereignty, and exercises them according to the provisions of the present Constitution, . . . has supreme command of the Army and Navy, . . . declares war, makes peace, and concludes treaties," . . . and alone initiates amendments to the constitution.[8]

Japanese literature. Japan's period of isolation was not entirely one of stagnation. The seventeenth and eighteenth centuries witnessed some remarkable advances in literature. Modern drama appeared in various forms. Japanese poetry also came to the fore in the seventeenth century in the creation of *hokku,* poems of seventeen syllables. Still later the novel developed as a medium of expression for the sentiments of social classes other than the aristocracy, who had heretofore dominated literature.

Nipponese art. Japanese art showed strict adherence to formal patterns. Within these patterns, dictated by custom and religion, the artist found his scope in the perfection of design and detail, and it is in the details of his work that we must look for charm and beauty. Domestic architecture, before it became Europeanized, maintained a high standard of efficiency and beauty. Simplicity was always the theme. The paper-walled houses were divided into rooms by sliding or folding screens, so that the size and shape of rooms could be changed according to need. There was little furniture. Decoration appeared on the painted screens, in flower arrangements, small statues, and pottery. The home owner did not care to have many furnishings. Rather he was interested in creating a simple background for one or two perfect objects, no matter how small. In the picture can be seen the simplicity of the houses, setting off the few decorations.

Landscape gardening was an art with the Japanese, and no house or temple was complete until every detail of the landscape around it was in harmony with the building. We have seen many imitations of Japanese gardens, which appear very artificial, so that it is a pleasant surprise to find now natural-looking most of the gardens really are. This naturalness may have been carefully planned. The Japanese concentrated on improving nature, not destroying it. Bridges were an important feature of their gardens, sometimes focusing attention upon a building. In the picture on page 281 the round stepping stones are arranged to enhance the natural loveliness of the stream, water hyacinths, and trees.

The Japanese use of sliding walls and screens and the elimination of cumbersome furniture might solve many of our modern living problems. The grass matting on the floor is kept fragrant and fresh by frequent changing.

The Japanese love of nature appeared in the painting of the pre-Europeanized period. Such men as Okyo, Sosen, and Hokusai painted animals and nature in a meticulous and life-like manner. The Japanese sense of formalization, however, can be seen in even the most realistic painting.

The drama in Japan. Unquestionably the most outstanding Japanese dramatic form has been the *No* play. In the beginning it consisted only of a religious dance performed before a Shinto temple, but by the end of the fifteenth century four types of *No* were discernible, each with its own subject matter and purpose. In a full *No* program five or six plays were given in which appropriate selections from the four types were chosen. The style of the *No* is exceedingly formalized. Even the masks of the actors and their body movements must be in accord with strict tradition, the language is stilted, a chorus must be employed (sometimes to interpret the action in the manner of the chorus of the Greek drama), and the stage is quite bare and limited to a surface twenty-five feet square. The purpose of the *No* drama is primarily to create an atmosphere far more subtle than might ordinarily be obtained by mere physical action. Its highly ritualistic nature practically hypnotizes a sympathetic audience.

The masks which were made for the *No* drama were, in many cases, of great artistic merit. The strict limitations which the artist had to respect kept him from attempting a completely realistic interpretation. As in all formalized arts there was a period when the restrictions served to help the artist, but eventually the rules and formulas became overly important, and character was lost.

Poetry. Japanese poetry is terse, exquisite, and full of wonder over the beauties of nature and the seasons. It is confined to a relatively few syllables and a relatively few topics, but within its limits it is unsurpassed. Two main types of poems are the *minyo,* or folksongs, and the *hokku,* or seventeen-syllable verse. The most famous exponent of this style of poetry was the great Basho (1644-1694). *Minyo* contains few nature poems, but, like the folk poetry of all peoples, is concerned primarily with themes of daily toil, festivities, and love. These are typical *minyo* poems:

THE DAWN

With the rustling birds
The day is faintly breaking;
And the bells too are ringing
In temples far and near.

THE BON SONGS

One who never dances,
At the ball of *Bon,*
Is a wooden Buddha,
A Buddha of bronze,
A stone Buddha!

THE PARTING

The ship casts off her mooring:
The sea gulls homeward fly;
The waves ashore are rolling,
While the day makes ready to die.

BETWEEN THE TWO

Is it the ringing of the bell?
Or is it the hammer of the bell?
No, 'tis between the two it rings.

PARENTAL LOVE

All over the world
Parents may their children seek,
But rare are the children
Who their parents ever seek.

Imperialism Evaluated

The extent of empires in 1914. By the close of the nineteenth century the great powers could indeed be satisfied with their acquisitions. Practically all of Africa had come under European control, India was a British dependency, southeastern Asia was controlled by Great Britain and France, the Dutch had a great island empire in the Netherlands East Indies, and the United States had acquired the Philippines, Puerto Rico, and Hawaii. In addition, by 1900 vast but prostrate China seemed to be on the verge of complete dissection at the hands of imperialist powers.

A glance at the map on pages 260-261 will show the vast extent of empires in 1914. The greatest empire was that of Great Britain, which controlled one fourth of the habitable area of the world and more than a quarter of the world's population. The smallest was that of Italy. Spain, once the leading nation in

Europe and the possessor of rich and vast areas abroad, had now not even one of the first six empires.

The two sides of imperialism. Like all great historical movements, imperialism was a complex phenomenon in which there were good and bad elements alike. It is true that *suttee* was abolished in India and that British law and order superseded the disorder attending Mogul decline. It is equally true that intertribal war and the old slave trade in Africa were largely abolished. Notwithstanding these desirable features many informed people believe that in nineteenth-century imperialism the bad far outweighed the good. The aggressive powers obtained valuable raw materials and pushed the sale of their manufactured wares with scant attention to the desires and welfare of the people under their control. Millions of helpless natives felt the heavy hand of economic exploitation. The European people also paid dearly. So rich were the prizes of colonies, so eager were the leading nations for plunder that international relations in the latter part of the nineteenth century became more and more poisoned by the imperialist rivalries of the great powers. As we shall see in the following chapter, this had much to do with bringing on the First World War.

It has been impossible to discuss all the many colonies and other manifestations of imperialism. The West Indies, for example, contained numerous islands controlled principally by European powers. Holland, France, and Great Britain possessed small holdings in Latin America. Russia and Great Britain enjoyed certain imperialist concessions in Persia, and over the globe there were hundreds of islands, most of which formed a part of some nation's empire.

Summary

We have seen in this chapter that the expansion of European culture consisted not only of the creation of permanent settlements in the world outside Europe but also of the extension of European control in tropical areas where white settlement was impossible because of climatic handicaps. The general term used to describe the establishment of

The round stepping stones in this garden in central Japan, zigzag across the stream, an arrangement which it is said, kept the evil spirits from following the crosser.

one country's power over other nations is imperialism. In the history of imperialism we can go back to the very dawn of the human race, to the days of the Assyrians, Persians, Egyptians, and Romans. But modern imperialism, the control of backward peoples in the tropics, began in relatively recent times. Quite early in the seventeenth century the Dutch secured control of a great island empire off south Asia, and late in the eighteenth century the British began the complete subjugation of all India through the agency of the British East India Company. However, the real contest for the control of the tropics did not fully get under way until about 1880. In the following twenty-five years huge colonial areas were annexed by Great Britain, France, Germany, and the United States.

The new imperialism of the 1880's was primarily due to economic causes, but nationalism, humanitarianism, and military considerations also played an important part. Humanitarianism, sometimes symbolized by the phrase "the white man's burden," caused some statesmen, colonial officials, explorers, missionaries, and others to believe quite sincerely that they were bringing the blessings of a superior civilization to the backward races.

In Africa, industry, commerce, and finance became interested in the tremendous economic potentialities of the continent. In the mid-nineteenth century David Livingstone and H. M. Stanley were the advance guard of an army of explorers, traders, and European officials who often obtained concessions and treaties from ignorant natives. By 1900 practically the entire continent had come under European control. Great Britain and France secured the lion's share, Germany was not quite so successful, and Italy obtained only a few crumbs.

In the Far East empire-building in such areas as the Malay Peninsula, Indo-China, and the Netherlands East Indies was similar in method to that in Africa. In India, China, and Japan ancient and advanced civilizations did not prevent the penetration of European control. Only Japan succeeded in thwarting the designs of the western nations. We shall see in a later chapter that, having done this, Japan herself inaugurated one of the most aggressive programs of imperialism in history.

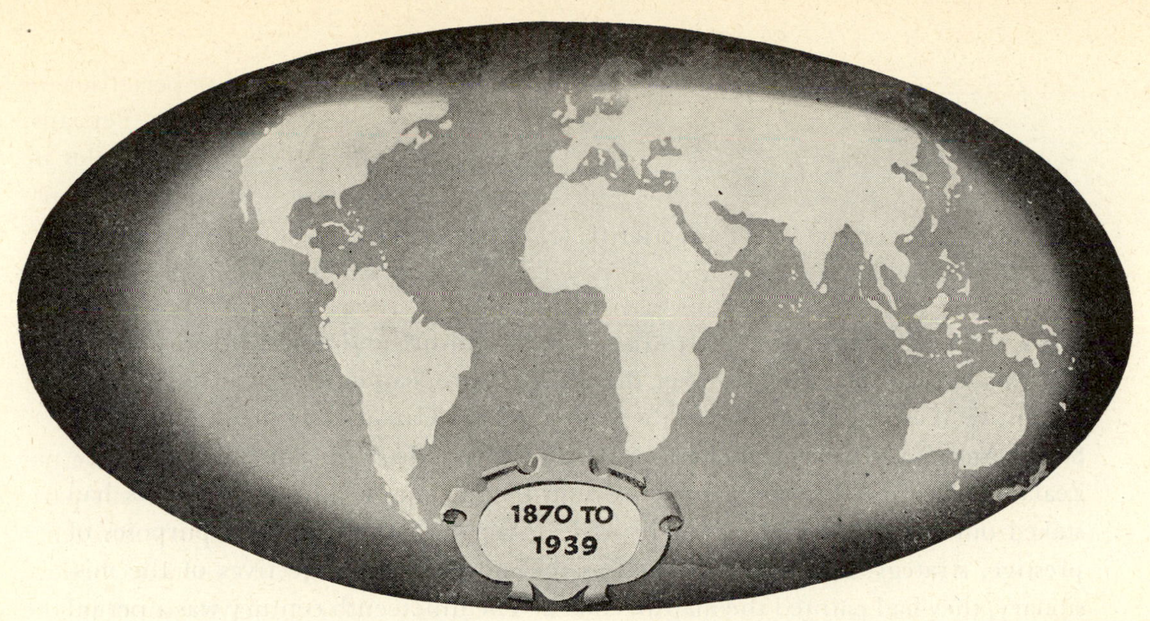

PART FOUR

The World in Turmoil

By the end of the nineteenth century the culture and power of Europe had made themselves felt all over the world. European culture was spread over the entire Western Hemisphere: the United States, Canada, Mexico, Central and South America. It permeated South Africa and was basic in Australia and New Zealand. Nor did Europe's influence stop there. Major European powers had staked out vast territorial claims in Africa, Asia, and Oceania. For purposes of prestige, strategy, and trade (as well as the more sincere objectives of the missionary) they had painted the map all colors. The nineteenth century was a period of aggressive imperialistic expansion, but the European justified his actions by maintaining that he had taken up the "white man's burden"—he was bettering the lot of backward peoples by giving them the benefits of European civilization.

But Europe was soon to reveal to the rest of the world that its pretentions to superiority of culture were based on fallacious grounds. From 1870 on, the major European powers entered into a suicidal rivalry among themselves. The stakes were high: colonial possessions, lucrative world markets, and prestige at the conference table. In this hotly contested race they jockeyed for better positions and to gain them were not above indulging in shady tactics. Finally the race narrowed down to two principal contestants, the Triple Alliance—composed of Germany, Austria, and Italy, and the Triple Entente—made up of Great Britain, France, and Russia. After many years of "incidents" in which war was only narrowly averted, the great struggle known as the First World War exploded in Europe. At tremendous cost and after the United States had entered the war, the Germans, Austrians, and their followers were defeated.

Now followed a futile quest for world order. The Treaty of Versailles (1919) was designed to make the world safe for democracy, but it left unsettled some major problems, accentuated others, and was phrased in such a manner as to give demagogues in the defeated countries a chance to warp its limitations into an excuse for violent revision. Meanwhile, as part of the new framework of the war settlement, the League of Nations was established. This institution, chiefly the offspring of Woodrow Wilson's idealism, was the first real attempt in world history to create an international agency for the settlement of differences among nations and to ensure world peace.

Meanwhile, certain countries had started to experiment with new patterns of government. The corrupt and reactionary régime of the czars in Russia first revealed its incompetence during the Russo-Japanese war of 1905. Russian reverses in the First World War convinced the people that a drastic change was essential. The outcome was the Revolution of 1917 and the resulting Communist government. Later a new socialistic order was established.

Soon after the war another important experiment in government began with the triumph of Mussolini's philosophy of Fascism. This ideology established strict governmental regulation over capital and labor for purposes of national planning and building up Italy's power.

Early in the thirties Germany accepted a brand of Fascism with the rule of Hitler and his National Socialist party. Hitler too believed in national planning, pledged himself to wipe out the Treaty of Versailles, and undertook to make Germany the supreme power in Europe.

THE DEMOCRATIC NATIONS had won the First World War, and the attendant treaty was of their shaping. While Great Britain and France accepted the League of Nations (the United States refused to do this) with its program for peace, in reality they appeared little interested in trying to change the *status quo*. Democracy in the twenties and thirties became complacent and static, for it did little to rectify many economic and social maladjustments, and it neglected to prepare defense against the aggressive ideologies bent upon its destruction.

The failure of western civilization in the twentieth century to live up to its self-proclaimed ideals of the nineteenth caused profound reverberations all through Asia. Despite the obvious fact that western science and invention had put in the hands of the white race the most powerful weapons and industrial techniques, the European had "lost face" in the eyes of the Asiatic. The Indians saw in British rule not the political emancipation which it had promised them but only imperialistic exploitation. The Chinese attempted to enlist western support in their struggle for national unity and independence but saw their efforts thwarted time and again by the unwillingness of the occidental powers to relinquish vested interests. The Japanese were swift to see the value of adopting western technology as a means of reorganizing the political and economic life of their country. But they also knew that the occidental nations were not invincible; Japan's smashing defeat of Russia in 1905 convinced them of that. Therefore, their statesmen planned through the decades of the twentieth century how best to drive the western powers out of Asia and build up a vast Japanese-controlled empire.

In 1931 Japan started upon its program of conquest, inaugurating a series of events which threw the entire world into a state of turmoil, which was to culminate in the Second World War.

1870-1914	**Events Leading up to World War I**	
	Non-political international cooperation	
1856	European Danube Commission	
1864	International Red Cross	
1868	International Telegraphic Union	
1874	Universal Postal Union	
1888	International Copyright Union	
1899-1907	Hague Peace Conferences	
1877-1878	Russo-Turkish war in Balkans	Treaty of San Stefano
1878	Congress of Berlin	Reduces Russian war gains
1884-1885	Berlin Conference	Made rules for partition of Africa
1873	Bismarck's Three-Emperors' League	With Russia and Austria-Hungary
1879	Bismarck makes Dual Alliance with Austria	
1881-1887	Three Emperors' League revived	
1882	Italy joins alliance, making it the Triple Alliance	
1887-1891	Reinsurance Treaty between Germany, Russia	Tries to keep both Austria, Russia allies
1889	First Pan American Conference	Three more conferences held before War
1894	Franco-Russian alliance	
1898	Fashoda incident	British-French rivalry in upper Nile
1899	Boer War in South Africa	British victory
1894	Sino-Japanese War	
1902	Anglo-Japanese alliance	
1903	Berlin-to-Bagdad railway	Germany seeks hegemony in Near East
1904-1905	Russo-Japanese War	
1904	Entente Cordiale	France and Great Britain
1907	Triple Entente	Great Britain, France, Russia
1908	Austria annexes Bosnia-Herzegovina	With approval of Germany
1911	Second Moroccan crisis	Bargain made by France, Germany
1911-1912	Turco-Italian War	Libya gained by Italy
1912-1913	First and Second Balkan wars	Balkan countries quarrel over spoils
1914	Assassination of Austrian archduke	By Serbian nationalists
	Austria's ultimatum	Clever Serbian reply
	Austria declares war on Serbia	Russian mobilization
1914-1918	**The First World War**	
	Allies: France, Great Britain, Russia, Japan	
	Central Powers: Germany, Austria-Hungary, Turkey	
1914	Battle of the Marne saves France	Germans advance on Paris
1915-1918	Trench warfare	Little large-scale movements
1915	Rout of Russians on eastern front	Battle of Tannenberg, Germany victory
	Italy joins Allies	Secret Treaty of London
	U. S. helps finance war, sends materials	
	Sinking of Lusitania	Stirs United States against Germany
	Bulgaria joins Central Powers	
1916	Battles of Verdun and Somme	Huge Allied losses
	Rumania joins Allies	Soon forced to capitulate to Bulgaria
1917	Russian revolution	Treaty of Brest Litovsk with Germany
	United States entry into war	U-boat campaign immediate cause
1918	Wilson's Fourteen Points	
	German offensive	Allied counterattack
	Germany collapses, asks armistice	

CHAPTER 9

Explosion in Europe

FEW periods in history have been graced with so much promise, worth-while accomplishment, and consequent optimism as the last half of the nineteenth century in Europe. In the span of one century Europe's population had more than doubled to reach a figure of over four hundred million in 1910. Europe was now, more than ever, the center of the world, the richest area in material wealth, and the most fruitful in artistic and intellectual achievement. The spread of public-school systems made illiteracy less prevalent; the expansion of public libraries and the publication of inexpensive books and periodicals made literature the property of the people; and applied science blessed the life of civilized man with such new inventions as the telephone, the telegraph, the modern locomotive, and gas illumination. Governments also showed more solicitude for their peoples. "It seemed as if statesmen had now at last learned the lesson that politics is the art of human happiness."[1]

In increasing number laws protecting the workers from industrial accidents and assuring them adequate medical service and support during unemployment found their way onto the statute books. A kind of cultural internationalism pervaded Europe, with music, art, and literature transcending political boundaries. In the field of government, too, the omens were promising. The franchise was broadened, parliamentary government began to crowd out aristocratic plutocracy, and everywhere political liberty was on the march. The progress of industry made the nations increasingly interdependent as strands of railroads, cables, and shipping bound the world into a single unit. Science and business appeared to be heralding the approach of the world community in which cooperation and not conflict would prevail among nations. Yet, despite numerous instances of cooperation between nations, there was a lamentable absence of idealism, justice, and generosity in their dealings with one another. Fundamental forces were at work making the nations more bellicose and selfish. If men could be said to have reached a position just lower than the angels in their intellectual and scientific attainments, their tactics in international relations fell considerably short of this mark.

This chapter reveals what happened because nations knew and accepted no laws higher than their own narrow interests. Our discussion surveys the forces working for world cooperation, the fundamental causes of the conflict of 1914, the diplomatic history of western Europe from 1871 to 1914, the operation of the system of rival alliances, and the First World War. In this connection attention is also given to the factors that brought the United States into the conflict in 1917.

Economic Progress and World Interdependence

The new industrialism and its results. A previous chapter has already outlined the industrial changes that began to transform life in England in the latter part of the eighteenth century and later revolutionized economic life in many other parts of the globe. As the nineteenth century drew to a close, a new phase of the Industrial Revolution, even more intense and breath-taking than its predecessor, took place. New machines for production, new instruments for transportation, and new devices for communication made the inventions and discoveries of Arkwright, Stephenson, Fulton, and Morse seem old-fashioned and inefficient. This new phase began to gather force shortly after 1850 and was most evident in the United States and Germany. In the United States the rapid progress of the new industrialism was characterized by the introduction of mass-production methods. In Germany the rapid advance of industry was assisted especially by the skillful utilization of chemistry. While Germany and the United States made the most phenomenal industrial advances, progress was also recorded in such countries as France, Belgium, Sweden, Japan, and Great Britain.

The new industrialism brought about many changes, of which the following may be singled out as of major importance: (1) Machinery became more complicated and more automatic in its operation. (2) Parts for machine-made goods became standardized so that repairs could be obtained cheaply and readily by the consumer. (3) New forms of power were developed, especially electricity and oil. (4) Products of nature were created artificially by chemical processes, and even products heretofore unknown to nature were likewise developed. Perfumes, flavoring extracts, fats, explosives, fertilizers, and many other things now came out of test tubes.

(5) Great new industries began to compete with the textile industry and other giants that had been born earlier. Shortly before the American Civil War drilling for oil was perfected in the United States. This was the beginning of an amazing industry that soon developed large refineries, transportation systems, factories to manufacture by-products, and great corporations to guide the many manufacturing processes connected with petroleum. Rubber is another example. As early as 1825 rubber had been used to waterproof textiles, but its extensive industrial application was not possible until the process of vulcanization was discovered in 1839. In Ireland in 1888 J. B. Dunlop hit upon the principle of the pneumatic tire, a discovery which created a tremendous demand for rubber shortly thereafter. The appearance of horseless carriages in the latter part of the nineteenth century led to the development of yet another great new industry. By the first decade of the twentieth century it was apparent that the automobile would soon radically change older modes of transportation and at the same time become one of the most important of all industrial enterprises.

(6) Another major result was the creation of ever larger business organizations, some of which were corporations capitalized at more than one billion dollars, having annual sales totaling the same amount. Capitalism by 1900 had already passed through two basic stages

Inevitably the old horse-drawn lorry had to try to show up its competitor, the new steam-driven passenger vehicle. The "self-acting steam omnibus" is getting the better of it in this London race.

of development—commercial in the fifteenth, sixteenth, and seventeenth centuries and industrial in the eighteenth and nineteenth. Now it was entering the third stage—finance capitalism, in which the banker and financier rather than the manufacturer became the dominant figure. To create and operate huge industrial organizations required larger sums of capital than the manufacturer could ordinarily provide. Hence these sums had to be secured from great investment banks or financial houses. More and more the control of industry came into the hands of the financiers.

Increase in productivity. All these new changes in the economic life of men and nations brought significant results with them. There was an enormous increase in industrial productivity. The new automatic machines, for example, enabled one man to turn out 500 pounds of nails daily. In 1780 the output had been only five pounds. In the eighteenth century the daily output of one man in a coal mine had been one half a ton. Now it was four tons. In 1865 the production of iron by the main industrial nations was nine million tons. In 1910 it had reached sixty-six million tons, and in the same period the output of coal increased from 180 million tons to one billion and a quarter.

This increase in industrial productivity brought about a need for new markets and new sources for raw materials. These demands in turn gave rise to a vast network of international communication and transportation. Telephone, telegraph, and cable linked the many countries of the world and facilitated business transactions. Transcontinental railroads, canals, and fleets of cargo vessels carried a stream of commodities around the globe (see map, pages 260-261). In 1860 world trade was worth slightly more than seven billion dollars; in 1913 it was worth nearly forty-two billion.

Economic interdependence. It seemed as if the world would soon become one great integrated business unit in which the people would be held together by bonds of common economic interdependence. An era of world economy seemed just around the corner. New inventions increased industrial efficiency. Although there was a noticeable trend in the direction of higher tariffs, up to the First World War tariffs were relatively low and consequently no serious detriment to the flow of goods across national boundaries. People were still fairly free to move about and came by the millions from Europe to the New World. This movement tended to ease Europe's economic problems and at the same time assisted in the development of the countries of the New World. International trade was based on a stable world monetary system, the gold standard. There was little tinkering with national currencies, and world trade profited thereby. Moreover, in this era of economic expansion, the world was relatively peaceful. Investors did not hesitate to invest capital all over the world. These investments, for the time being at least, brought profitable returns to the capitalists, who lived for the most part in the industrialized countries, and helped develop the resources of other areas, mainly in economically backward countries.

International cooperation. Despite the fact that national boundaries divided the world into some sixty independent political units, there was some measure of international cooperation. A habit of political collaboration apparently was developing among the European powers. Ever since the Congress of Vienna, the great powers had frequently conferred among themselves whenever the peace of the continent was jeopardized. This practice of consultation, called the concert of Europe, had helped on several occasions to keep the peace. Following the revolt of the Belgians, a conference met at London in 1831 to work out a suitable arrangement for Belgian independence. A congress met in Geneva in 1864 to organize the international Red Cross. Again in 1868, at St. Petersburg, and in 1874, at Brussels, conferences took place to secure more humane agreements regarding the conduct of war.

The Congress of Berlin in 1878 averted war between Russia and her opponents, Great Britain and Austria. The Berlin Conference of 1884-1885 drew up rules regulating the partition of Africa, and in 1906 on the initiative of the United States a conference was held at Algeciras to prevent the French and Germans from coming to blows over Morocco. In 1912-1913 the European powers met in London to work out terms for ending the Balkan wars. In the Western Hemisphere the first Pan American Conference, consisting of eighteen countries, assembled in 1889 at Washington, D.C. Matters of common economic interest were discussed as well as problems pertaining to the maintenance of peace in the Western Hemisphere. Before the First World War other conferences were held at Mexico City (1901), Rio de Janeiro (1906), and Buenos Aires (1910).

The examples just given deal only with cooperation among nations in the realm of international politics. Although nations continued to retain their national identities, there was ample recognition among them of the fact that the forces of industrialism and modern science were pushing them in the direction of a world community in other fields as well. In 1865 a conference met at Paris to discuss the coordination of telegraph lines and the problem of rates. This resulted in the establishment of the International Telegraph Union, formed by twenty countries, who created a permanent office in Switzerland in 1868. The Universal Postal Union was set up in 1874 to facilitate the handling of mail all over the world. In 1886 an international copyright union was formed. It drew up an agreement for the protection of authors which was subsequently ratified by nineteen nations. During the period from 1880 to 1914 there were similar agreements regarding cables, weights and measures, and the protection of birds. One of the most important examples of international cooperation was the formation and operation of the European Danube commission. This commission, established in 1856, policed the lower Danube, kept boat facilities in order, and established rates for river commerce. In the interests of international commerce and cooperation, Rumania, through which the lower Danube flowed, surrendered a portion of its sovereign right to police and control "its own river."

The idea of international cooperation became apparent in the minds and actions of peoples as well as governments. World-wide religious movements and scientific congresses and societies appeared, and a world parliamentary union was formed. In general, men were being drawn together on the basis of universal needs and desires, particularly in matters which were nonpolitical in character.

The movement for peace. Moreover, there was a consistent interest in the maintenance of peace, although the desire for it was perhaps stronger among the people than it was among their governments. Starting in England as early as 1816, the peace movement had grown steadily until by the end of the century it was a vigorous and powerful movement. Alfred Nobel, a Swedish manufacturer, devoted much of his fortune to the advancement of peace, and an American philanthropist, Andrew Carnegie, subsidized internationalism by building a "temple of peace" at The Hague. In this edifice, in 1899 and in 1907, two great peace conferences were held in an attempt to achieve some limitation in armaments. This aim was not achieved, but the conferences established a court of international arbitration and agreed to certain rules for the humane conduct of warfare. Many individuals wrestled with the problem of the elimination of war, and many writers devoted their attention to this subject. One book which made a deep impression in 1898 maintained that war would mean the end of civilization. In *The Great Illusion,* a work by Norman Angell, the author declared that the world was becoming so unified and its economic structure so sensitive that the shock of war would bring disaster to victors and vanquished alike—in short, that in modern war there could be no complete victory for either side.

The Causes of the Great War

The forces of antagonism. At the same time that some forces were working to bring about closer cooperation between nations and peoples, other forces were operating to bring about distrust and rivalries. These forces of antagonism finally proved to be more potent than those working for cooperation, and Europe and most of the world with it were plunged into war in 1914. Back of this great conflict were some six basic causes: (1) the national-state system and power politics, (2) militarism, (3) the system of rival alliances, (4) secret diplomacy, (5) economic imperialism, and (6) the emotion of nationalism.

National states and power politics. Organized under the national-state system, Europe in 1914 consisted of some twenty independent political units who recognized no authority higher than their own. International law had no force behind it adequate to guarantee its continuous enforcement, although the rules of international law were obeyed for the most part if they did not clash with a nation's fundamental interests. It was the aim of the governments in Europe, as elsewhere, to advance national interests. Questionable methods were frequently employed and ethics ignored because each state was answerable to no higher authority. In fact, all nations regarded war as an instrument of national policy to be used in obtaining their ends when peaceful methods failed.

Often departing from ethical standards, subordinated to no higher law, and always ready to utilize force, the nations of the world lived in a system of "international anarchy." Power became an end in itself. In the nineteenth century, the operation of the "concert of Europe" and the growth of an active sentiment for international peace camouflaged the fact that power politics were as strong as ever. Great Britain and France, for example, discussed the possibility of carving up the Turkish empire on several occasions; on the eve of the First World War Germany and Great Britain were making plans to divide the Portuguese colonial empire; and France, Great Britain, and Italy in 1906 made an agreement looking to the division of Abyssinia. The undignified scramble for Chinese territory in the last decade of the nineteenth century was merely another reflection of power politics.

Militarism. When war is the ultimate arbiter in international affairs, armed forces become extremely important. Bismarck showed his neighbors in three wars leading up to the unification of Germany what could be done with an efficient fighting force. The German army was based on the conscription of all the nation's manpower, and this practice was likewise prevalent in the rest of Europe. Only Great Britain, protected by its fleet, refused to introduce conscription. The latter part of the nineteenth century saw Europe being transformed into an armed camp. From 1870 to 1910 about one billion dollars was spent yearly on arms. In 1913 the figure had reached nearly two billion dollars.

With the growth of these huge national armies, augmented by the most scientific equipment, war became a science. Trained specialists were needed by the thousands, a complex system of mobilization had to be worked out, and intricate plans had to be laid for conquest or against invasion. This condition gave rise, more than ever before, to a powerful class of professional soldiers or militarists. Some thinkers in Europe, influenced by the concept of the survival of the fittest, developed a kind of neo-Darwinian theory in which they saw war as the instrument for weeding out the decadent and exalting the strong nations. One organization in Germany announced:

"War is the noblest and holiest expression

of human activity. For us, too, the glad hour of battle will strike. Still and deep in the German heart must live the joy of combat, and the longing for it. Let us ridicule to the utmost the old women in breeches, who fear war and deplore it as cruel and revolting. No! War is beautiful."[2]

Such sentiments were found in nearly all European states; no one nation had a complete monopoly of militarism. Germany, however, seemed to be the most blatantly militaristic. Here the adulation of war was most intense and the prestige of the Prussian military clique most elevated. "Eternal peace is a dream," declared Moltke, one of Germany's military heroes, "for war is part of God's world ordinances. . . . In war, the noblest virtues flourish that otherwise would slumber and decay. The experience of war stays with a man, and steels him all his life."[3] Nations increased their armaments so as to be reassured that their neighbors would not be tempted to attack them. Meanwhile these neighbors had interpreted the increase not as a defensive but as an offensive measure which left them no alternative but to increase their own armaments. Thus the armament race began, and the faster it went, the higher tension and distrust mounted.

Rival alliances. Living in this "international anarchy," where no nation could trust its neighbors, no state felt strong enough to rely upon its own military resources for protection. Nations whose interests ran along parallel lines joined together so that in union they could command more fighting power. But this, in turn, provoked nations outside the alliance to form a union capable of matching strength with strength. The creation of two great rival alliances was a feature of European diplomacy after 1871 (see map, page 299), but it did not offer any more security to the states involved. In fact it made the prospects of war more horrible because it was now unlikely that any conflict between two nations in Europe could be localized. Immediately—as members of two opposing alliances—the aid of their allies would be invoked, and the whole continent would be at war. This is what happened in the summer of 1914.

Secret diplomacy. Another basic cause of the war and one closely connected with the system of alliances was the practice of secret diplomacy. The two rival diplomatic combinations were vitally concerned in weakening each other's ranks. And since allies in the same alliance did not always completely trust each other, there were often rumors that attempts were being made to wean one state away from its diplomatic friends. While the majority of people remained ignorant of what was going on, jockeying for power, threats and intimidations, and offers of gifts, often involving the territory of another power, went on unrestrained. The activities of spies, secret reports, and unscrupulous methods employed by the foreign offices of Europe poisoned the atmosphere and heightened the tension.

Economic imperialism. The tremendous increase in industrial productivity and the expansion of world trade between 1870 and 1914 have already been noted. At the same time a contest developed between business groups of rival nations over the lion's share of the new riches. To the extent that industry and finance now controlled their governments or were influential in the formation of policy, various nations competed among themselves to secure economic advantages for their respective groups. *Laissez faire* and the absence of governmental interference in business began to decline in the last decades of the nineteenth century. Governments now began to raise their tariffs and to use their diplomatic power and even the force of arms to secure control of areas rich in essential raw materials or valuable as markets for manufactured goods. Thus *laissez faire* gave way to a new kind of mercantilism in which governments acted as aggressive champions for their own business interests. One of the most significant features of this neo-mercantilism was economic imperialism, which mainly concerned the struggle for the control of the backward or colonial areas of the world.

Economic imperialism brought many nations to the verge of war. Great Britain and Germany had serious disputes over the partition of Africa in the 1880's. These nations also nearly came to blows over Samoa in 1889, and German support of the Boers in South Africa, involving as it did an obstacle to British plans of control in this region, also caused much ill will between Great Britain and Germany. Another serious clash of British and German imperialism took place in Asia Minor. Here in 1903 German capitalists had secured from Turkey the right to construct a railroad connecting Constantinople with Bagdad and thence to the Persian Gulf (see map, page 299). Forming a junction at Constantinople with German controlled railroads that led north to the Baltic Sea, the Berlin-to-Bagdad railroad would have enabled German businessmen to control a great corridor from the Baltic through middle Europe down into Mesopotamia to the Persian Gulf. The German scheme created much alarm in British political and financial circles. The British government was also fearful that access to the Persian Gulf might enable Germany to threaten the security of India. Although the British government was able to block completion of the railway, for several years the Berlin-to-Bagdad railroad scheme was a serious source of friction between Great Britain and Germany.

Great Britain and Russia also had their differences, mainly in the Balkans and Afghanistan. Great Britain sought to prevent Russian domination of the Straits and encroachment in the vicinity of the Indian northern frontier. From 1880 to 1900 Great Britain and France were rivals in southeast Asia and in Africa, where France envisaged an empire stretching from the Atlantic to the Red Sea. Such an empire would give her control of the headwaters of the Nile and seriously interfere with Great Britain's program of creating a continuous stretch of British territory from the Cape to Cairo. British and French armies almost came to blows along the upper Nile in 1898, but a battle was averted when France gave way.

There were several other occasions on which various powers found themselves blocked by others, but before the First World War the most serious crises concerned the control of Morocco. On two occasions (1905 and 1911) German and French rivalry very nearly brought Europe into open conflict (see page 298).

In some cases war did occur. In 1894 Japanese designs upon the Asiatic mainland brought about war with China, and in 1899 Great Britain became engaged in war with the Boer republics of South Africa. Japan and Russia fought over Manchuria in 1904-1905, and Italy wrested Tripoli from Turkey after the war of 1911-1912 (see map, page 299).

The emotion of nationalism. In the opinion of many people the most important fundamental cause of the First World War was nationalism. National pride and inflated patriotism became a new religion, the emotional adjunct to power politics. Nationalism fattened on the acquisition of colonies, took pride in the defeat of enemies, and refused to believe that a nation could ever be wrong. History, as taught in schools, was frequently distorted in order to glorify a nation's past achievements and gloss over its shortcomings. National self-glorification became the objective of numerous writers in various countries who exalted their own particular country's culture and often heaped ridicule and odium on that of others.

The polyglot Balkans. Notwithstanding the unification of Germany and Italy, Europe still contained many danger spots in 1914, submerged peoples having strong nationalistic aspirations. Reference has already been made (Chapter 5) to the problem of nationalism in the Balkans. In 1914 nationalism in this area had grown acute enough to bring on the war. Nowhere else in Europe was the connection between power politics, secret diplomacy, and instability in international relations better illustrated.

The Balkan peninsula in 1815 was ruled mainly by the Turkish empire (see map, page 156). The Turks were only a minority ruling caste, the great majority of the people being Christian Slavs. In Austria-Hungary a similar situation obtained. Under the *Ausgleich,* as we have seen, a number of national groups, principally Slavic peoples, were ruled by the Austrian Germans and the Hungarians. More nationalities were found in the Balkans than anywhere else in Europe, most of them cherishing nationalistic aspirations. These aspirations were aggravated by the interests of the great powers in the Balkans.

In the nineteenth century the geography of the Balkan area made it of supreme strategic importance in power politics. Since the days of Peter the Great the dominant policy of Russia had been to obtain warm-water ports, for many of her harbors are frozen in winter. Peter the Great had bequeathed his country a window on the Baltic, but this of itself did not solve the problem, for here again ice hinders shipping at certain periods of the year. The logical place for Russia to secure a good exit to the outside world was in the south via the Black Sea (see map, page 299). But this body of water is connected with

In 1871 the long historical trend toward the growth of national states was apparently ended with the unification of Germany and Italy. The map of Europe looked complete. Then the trend began to reverse itself. Out of the old Turkish empire appeared the Balkan states (see inset); after the First World War the trend to more and smaller states continued (see page 317).

the Mediterranean by two narrow straits, the Bosporus and the Dardanelles, and these were under Turkish control. It was the policy of Russia, therefore, to weaken and even dismember Turkey so that she could obtain the Straits. But again the factor of geography intruded itself. Most Englishmen as individuals detested the corrupt rule of the sultans, but the British government supported Turkey in the nineteenth century for reasons of national self-interest. If Russia obtained the Straits, she would become a naval power in the eastern Mediterranean. This, so the British diplomats argued, would menace the safety of the Suez Canal, which had become of prime strategic importance to Great Britain. Perhaps no other area in the world presents a better example of the influence of geography upon history, and more specifically on political strategy, than does the Straits.

Russia in the Balkans. The discontent of the various submerged nationalities in the Balkans gave Russia an excellent opportunity to interfere in this region in the nineteenth century. The first people to escape from Turkish thralldom were the Greeks in 1829 (see page 172). Some twenty-five years later the Rumanians gained a measure of self-government. Disguising her interest in obtaining the Straits, Russia began to pose as the protector of her brother Slavs in the Balkans. Following 1870 numerous nationalist revolts occurred throughout the peninsula. These were put down with great ferocity by the sultan, Abdul Hamid, and Russia thereupon in 1877 declared war on Turkey. Gaining a complete victory, Russia forced upon her defeated foe the Treaty of San Stefano (1878). This gave additional territory and complete independence to the Serbians, Rumanians, and Montenegrins, and it further provided for the creation of a large Bulgarian state under the thumb of Russia.

This arrangement was not to the liking of the two other most interested powers, Great Britain and Austria. Threatening war, these nations forced Russia to agree to a congress, held at Berlin in 1878, where Russia's peace treaty was reëxamined. Bulgaria was reduced in size and the two important Turkish provinces of Bosnia and Herzegovina were given to Austria, whose aim was to push her control in the direction of the Aegean Sea. While Russia's ambition of domination of the Balkans had been thwarted, she was permitted to retain certain towns in the Caucasus and also a strip of Rumanian territory. The Congress of Berlin left a legacy of hatred. The Serbians were enraged at the action of Austria, the Bulgarians resented having their new state whittled down, and Irredentist movements flourished all over the peninsula. Irredentism, a term used by the Italians to refer to their "unredeemed Italy" still under Austrian rule, generally refers to a nation's desire to secure territory inhabited by people of the same nationality and under alien rule.

Germany and Austria in the Balkans. It soon became clear that both Germany and Austria were determined to extend their influence in the Balkans. German motives were largely economic. The Germans envisaged a great continuous economy stretching from the Baltic to the Persian Gulf. The Austrian concern in the Balkans was primarily defensive. Austria-Hungary was a polyglot empire containing millions of Slavs. If Serbia, egged on by Russia, should extend an Irredentist movement into the southern part of the Austrian empire, many Slavs might be lost and ultimately the operation of nationalism would result in the destruction of the whole empire. The Austrians were thus determined that Pan-Slavism, of which the Greater Serbia movement was a manifestation, should be checked before it became too dangerous.

Raven Hill's cartoon, "The Boiling Point," represents the great powers—among them Austria, Germany, and England—attempting to retain their influence in the troublesome Balkans. The picture was printed in "Punch."

Hence they acquired Bosnia and Herzegovina outright in 1908 (see map, page 299).

Balkan wars (1912-1913). Following the Russo-Turkish War of 1877-1878 Balkan affairs continued to give much worry to the European diplomats, and, in fact, a European war was narrowly averted in 1908 and 1913. In 1912, under the leadership of the famous Greek prime minister Venizelos, an alliance was formed by Greece, Bulgaria, Serbia, and Montenegro for the purpose of waging war on Turkey.

War followed, in which the allies were completely successful, and a conference was held at London to arrange the peace. Here the allies illustrated the viciousness of power politics as they began to quarrel over the spoils. Bulgaria's claims ran counter to those of Greece. Serbia wanted Albania because the territory would give her access to the sea, but this desire clashed with Austria-Hungary's ambition of pushing back Slav expansion. Denied Albania, Serbia demanded as compensation territory that Greece and Bulgaria wanted. Finally the erstwhile allies began to fight each other. Greece, Serbia, and Montenegro fought Bulgaria, and, to complicate this second Balkan war, vanquished Turkey and Rumania joined in to see what spoils they could obtain.

In 1913 the second war came to an end, but no permanent solution had been found for the Balkan problem. The Serbians had been prevented by Austria from obtaining Albania. Backed by Russia the Serbs began to carry on active propaganda among the Slavs in Austria to undermine their loyalty to the dual monarchy of Austria-Hungary. Russia was more determined than ever to try to obtain the Straits. This resolution ran counter to German interests, whose Berlin-to-Bagdad railway project in turn caused the British much alarm. The Bulgarians nourished a bitter hatred against Serbia, Greece, and Rumania. Truly the Balkans in 1914 were a witches' cauldron of international discord.

Other national groups. There existed also numerous nationalistic sore spots in Europe outside the Balkans (see map, page 178). The Italians wanted to free their kinsmen from Austrian rule. In France the spirit of revenge was directed toward the reincorporation of Alsace-Lorraine in the French domain, and in Austria Poles, Czechs, Slovaks, Croats, and Slovenes all yearned for freedom. Danes, Finns, and Irish in other parts of Europe also represented discontented nationalities, waiting for the hour of deliverance.

The Coming of the Great War (1871-1914)

The isolation of France. Following its defeat by Germany in 1870-1871, France was isolated diplomatically for twenty years. Bismarck fully realized that France would hope some day to defeat Germany and regain her lost provinces in Alsace-Lorraine, and he therefore determined to prevent France from obtaining any allies. "As long as France has no alliances," Bismarck observed, "she is not dangerous to Germany."[4]

In 1873 Bismarck made an alliance with Russia and Austria-Hungary known as the Three Emperors' League. By this agreement in the event of threat of war the signatories agreed to consult "in order to determine a common course of action." Germany and Russia specifically promised mutual support in case of attack. In 1877 the Russo-Turkish War occurred, and, following the demands of Austria and Great Britain, Russia was forced to agree to a European conference on the Balkan problem to be held at Berlin. Up to this point Bismarck had had few diplomatic worries. Great Britain was following the policy of "splendid isolation," Russia and Austria were the allies of Germany, and Italy was unimportant. But at the Congress of Berlin (1878) Bismarck was forced to choose between supporting the claims of Austria or those of Russia in the Balkans.

Bismarck's diplomacy. Bismarck chose to support Austria because he apparently believed that it was impossible to have both countries as close allies and because he trusted Austria more than Russia. The Germans in Vienna were his kinsmen, whereas he was somewhat suspicious of Slav loyalty, and in any event Austria was too close to Germany for comfort in any capacity other than as an ally. Furthermore Bismarck was afraid that supporting Russia would alienate Great Britain and cause her to make an alliance with Austria. Russia for her part was resentful over Bismarck's support of Austria's Balkan ambitions at the Congress of Berlin. The year after the Congress of Berlin (1879), Bismarck negotiated the Dual Alliance with the Austrian government. Three years later in 1882 a new partner was secured, Italy, thus bringing into operation the Triple Alliance (see map on page 299). By its terms the three powers promised not to enter into any alliance against each other. Further, it was provided that in the event of an unprovoked French attack upon either Italy or Germany both allies would wage war on France. And if any member or members of the alliance were attacked by two or more great powers, all three allies were pledged to make war.

The choice of Austria as a close ally in preference to Russia did not mean that Bismarck was reconciled to the loss of the latter's friendship. In 1881 the Three Emperor's League was renewed and continued to 1887, when rivalries between Austria and Russia in the Balkans made it impossible for these two powers to be in the same group. Bismarck therefore negotiated a separate alliance with Russia called the Reinsurance Treaty. Many diplomats pondered how Germany could at one and the same time be the ally of Russia and Austria, and Bismarck's tactics were described as "keeping five balls in the air at once."

The Franco-Russian alliance. Under the masterful hand of Bismarck Germany retained hegemony over the European continent from 1871 to 1890. In 1890, however, young William II, the new German kaiser, dismissed the old chancellor (see cartoon, page 179), and German foreign policy now passed into his hands. The kaiser allowed the Reinsurance Treaty to lapse, thus permitting Russia to seek new allies, and France, isolated and smarting from her diplomatic impotency, immediately began to woo Russia. In 1891 a French naval squadron visited Russia, and the czar agreed to a military alliance which, however, did not go into effect until 1894. Russia was badly in need of loans to help construct the Trans-Siberian railway and for military purposes. Millions of French francs went to buy Russian bonds, and France received what she had wanted for twenty years, a strong military ally.

England's position. The diplomatic history of the next seventeen years (1890-1907) concerns the development of a great alliance system including Great Britain, France, and Russia, to offset the Triple Alliance of Germany, Austria, and Italy (see map, page 299). The most important nation in this development was Great Britain. As long as she followed her policy of "splendid isolation," Germany's Triple Alliance and the Russo-French combination were fairly equally matched. But if Great Britain were to join the Russians and the French, the balance of power would shift at once and make this combination supreme. In the 1890's Great Britain began to question the wisdom of having no allies. At this time she was engaged in active and sometimes bitter colonial rivalry with Russia and France. In 1898 in the Fashoda incident Great Britain and France narrowly averted war when the rival expeditions of General Kitchener and Colonel Marchand both claimed the region of the upper Nile. Again, during the Boer War all the great powers in Europe were anti-British. Only the supremacy of England's fleet effectively discouraged the development of an interventionist movement. More and more, Great Britain became disquieted by her policy of diplomatic isolation.

It was this circumstance which explained British overtures to Germany in 1898 and again in 1901. The exponent of Anglo-German friendship and concord was Joseph Chamberlain, the father of Neville Chamberlain, late prime minister of Great Britain. The Germans were not favorably impressed by the offer of a British alliance and interpreted it as a sign of British weakness. Most important: (1) Germany felt strong enough to be able to dispense with allies; and (2) she believed she could get an alliance on her own terms.

Meanwhile Anglo-German relations steadily grew worse. The Germans were jealous of the great empire the British had built up before Germany had succeeded in attaining national unity. The kaiser himself contributed to Anglo-German misunderstanding by his bellicose and threatening speeches. The British, on the other hand, were alarmed at the tremendous strides made by German industry. The new naval program, more than anything else, made Germany and Great Britain enemies. Great Britain's dependence upon the outside world for most of her food supply had always made command of the seas an indispensable feature of her defense strategy. The British had no quarrel with the size of the German army, but when the German Reichstag in 1900 passed a naval law providing for the construction by 1920 of a fleet strong enough to jeopardize Great Britain's naval supremacy, England was seriously alarmed.

The Entente Cordiale (1904). Rebuffed by Germany, England turned elsewhere for friends. In 1902 she made a treaty of alliance with Japan, and two years later England and France settled their outstanding differences. This rapprochement was made possible, in some degree, by the popularity in France of Edward VII and his enthusiasm for all things French. An Entente Cordiale between these two countries thus ended England's traditional policy of isolation and brought her into the diplomatic combination pitted against Germany's Triple Alliance. Great Britain's desire to settle all outstanding differences with France and Russia was accentuated by alarming developments in her relations with Germany. In 1905 Great Britain began the construction of a new type of warship, the dreadnought, which rendered all existing ships largely obsolete by its heavy armor and twelve-inch guns. The advent of this new type of battleship enabled the Germans to carry on the naval race on equal terms with their British rivals, as all existing ships were now outmoded. The British suggested a naval holiday to the German government, but the kaiser and his admiral, von Tirpitz, were determined to push their naval building program. Two years after laying the keel of the dreadnought, Great Britain settled its problems with Russia, thereby establishing the Triple Entente. Great Britain made no definite military commitments in her agreements with France and Russia. She retained theoretically her freedom of action but, for all this, was now part of the alliance system.

Diplomatic crises: 1905-1914. For a decade before the First World War, from 1905 to 1914, Europe experienced a series of crises. In each of these diplomatic duels both sides managed to come out without losing too much prestige and without going to war. France thought her safety and economic interests demanded the exclusion of German interests in Morocco, Austria wanted a free hand in the Balkans—an objective resolutely opposed by Russia—Germany resented Great Britain's opposition to her economic penetration into the Near East, and England was determined to maintain her naval supremacy against Germany in the North Sea. With each new crisis war seemed inevitable, but the diplomats somehow managed to control the machinery of diplomacy. But it was almost certain that a crisis would soon be precipitated, unleashing forces that could not be stopped.

The first Moroccan crisis (1905). The first serious diplomatic crisis concerned Morocco, a backward area under an independent sultanate. By obtaining control of this territory France would have a stretch of contiguous dependencies from the north Atlantic across the north African coast to Tunisia. The German government thought it saw in the Moroccan question a chance to weaken the Anglo-French Entente. Russia had just suffered a decisive defeat by Japan and could not be expected to assist her ally France. Carefully timing his moves, the German chancellor arranged for the kaiser to visit the Moroccan port of Tangier, where he declared that all powers must respect the independence of the country. The French were forced to give up their immediate plans for taking over Morocco and agree to Germany's suggestion that an international conference be called at Algeciras (1906) to discuss the matter. At this meeting the German hope that a rift might appear between the British and French did not materialize. On the contrary, all the nations in attendance—even Italy—supported France rather than Germany. Only Austria remained at the side of Germany. It was agreed that Morocco should still enjoy its sovereignty but that France and Spain should be given certain rights to police the area.

European tension. The events at Algeciras and the British agreement with Russia the following year (1907) filled the Germans with dread. The diplomatic hegemony enjoyed by Germany under Bismarck was completely gone. Italy could not be trusted. Germany had no friend except her ally, Austria. The Germans spoke of this situation as the encirclement policy. In 1908 another crisis occurred, this time in the Balkans, where Austria annexed the two provinces of Bosnia and Herzegovina (see map, page 299). Serbia was furious at this incorporation of what she considered her Slavs in the Austro-Hungarian empire. The Russian government moved to throw its armed might in support of Serbia but was forced to back down when it became apparent that full German support had been pledged to Austria. If Algeciras had been a defeat for Germany, Austria and Germany had managed to secure a victory for the Triple Alliance in 1908.

In 1911 the scene shifted back to Morocco again, where France had sent an army "to maintain order." Germany countered by dispatching the gunboat *Panther* to the Moroccan port of Agadir. Russia was still weak from her defeat at the hands of the Japanese, but Great Britain came out with the plain warning that all her power was at the disposal of France. It was now Germany's turn to back down, although this was done without loss of prestige. A diplomatic bargain was struck. France got a free hand in Morocco in return for which Germany was given grants of French holdings in equatorial Africa.

Following the second Balkan war in 1913 (see pages 295-296) Europe faced the future with uncertainty and dread. One German general remarked, "There is a smell of blood in

the air." The American statesman, Colonel House, then touring Europe, reported: "Everybody's nerves are tense; it only needs a spark to set the whole thing off."

Assassination of the archduke. This fateful spark came on June 28, 1914, when the Archduke Francis Ferdinand, the heir to the Austrian throne, and his wife were assassinated in the town of Sarajevo in Bosnia.

This deed was the work of a young Bosnian student, Gavrilo Princip, who was inspired by the Greater Serbia propaganda. He and his two associates had received assistance from high Serbian officers, and although the direct complicity of the Serbian government has not been proved, nevertheless it seems unlikely that it could have been ignorant of the plot. Count Berchtold, the Austrian foreign minister, believed that the assassination justified crushing, once and for all, the anti-Austrian propaganda and terrorism emanating from Serbia. Austria could take no action, however, without securing the support of its ally, Germany. Berchtold thereupon prepared a letter to the kaiser and succeeded in getting the Austrian emperor's signature. This letter, received by the kaiser, declared:

"The crime against my nephew is the direct

consequence of the agitation carried on by Russian and Serbian Pan-Slavists, whose sole aim is to weaken the Triple Alliance and shatter my empire. . . . The aim of my government must henceforth be to isolate and diminish Serbia."[5]

The German emperor was genuinely moved by this appeal. The news of the assassination had shocked him deeply, and he viewed the Bosnian terrorists as little more than fanatical savages. William decided to assure the Austrian government of his full support. Berchtold thus obtained a "blank check" from Germany. Austria was Germany's only reliable ally. Everything possible must be done to prevent her from being weakened by such forces as Serbian terrorism. Germany agreed with Austria that military action against the Serbs was necessary. Vienna wanted only a local Austro-Serb war, and Germany favored quick action to forestall intervention. But the possibility of Russian intervention was not ignored by the German and Austrian governments.

The Austrian ultimatum. The Austrian foreign minister proceeded with his plans of subjugating Serbia. On July 23 an Austro-Hungarian ultimatum was presented to Serbia. The terms were harsh. All anti-Austrian activities in Serbia must cease, textbooks unfriendly to Austria could not be used in the schools, and the assistance of Austro-Hungarian officials was to be accepted in putting down any "revolutionary movement directed against the territorial integrity of the Dual Monarchy." Furthermore it was demanded that all officials in the Serbian army and governmental service "guilty of propaganda" against the Austrian government should be removed. The ultimatum, which was intended to be turned down, contained ten demands in all, and Berchtold demanded unconditional acceptance within forty-eight hours. In answer, on July 25, the Serbians penned a very clever reply. Only two demands were accepted in their entirety, and most of the others were neatly sidestepped by diplomatic qualifications. This reply was announced as unsatisfactory, and mobilization of the armed forces in the Austro-Hungarian empire was ordered.

Russia, meanwhile, was following developments in the Balkans closely. She realized that, if the Austrians succeeded in humbling Serbia, Russian prestige in this area would suffer tremendously. Even before the Austrian ultimatum had been presented, Sergei Sazonov, the Russian foreign minister, had plainly told the Austrian representative at St. Petersburg that "Russia would not be indifferent to any attempt to humiliate Serbia; Russia could not permit Austria to use menacing language or military measures against Serbia."[6] The French in the meantime assured the Russians of their full cooperation and urged strong support for Serbia.

Grey's peace efforts. Sir Edward Grey, the British foreign minister, began his efforts to maintain peace as early as July 20, before the ultimatum to Serbia had been served. He advised negotiations between the Russians and Austrians to avoid the problem of dangerous demands upon Serbia. On July 24, Grey proposed that England, France, Germany, and Italy should agree to exercise a "moderating or mediating influence" simultaneously in St. Petersburg and Vienna. The Germans agreed, but the French opposed the plan, saying they would collaborate if Germany first exerted pressure on Vienna. A third peace proposal came from Grey on July 26, but this had no more success than its predecessors. While the diplomats worked for peace, Berchtold was fearful that Serbia would escape from his clutches. On July 27 he succeeded, thanks in part to falsehood, in convincing the emperor that war was the only way out, and the following day a formal declaration of war was announced against Serbia.

Russian mobilization. Berchtold's decision made a general European conflict almost inevitable, but there was still the hope that Germany could restrain its ally. The kaiser had been satisfied with Serbia's reply to the Austrian ultimatum. The German chancellor, Bethmann-Hollweg, urged Austria to negotiate with Russia. As the possibility of a general European war loomed, several frantic telegrams were sent by Berlin to Vienna. The German ambassador was instructed to tell Berchtold, "As an ally we must refuse to be drawn into a world conflagration because Austria does not respect our advice."[7] At this critical stage, when German pressure on Austria might have opened a path to peace, an event took place which wrecked any further attempts at negotiation. This was the Russian mobilization on July 30.

Up to this time Bethmann-Hollweg, the

German chancellor, had sought peace, but the mobilization of Russia caused an abrupt halt to his efforts. The significance of mobilization in modern warfare must be understood to appreciate the import of the Russian action. Modern armies constitute millions of men. To call out the reserves to join their regiments, to hand out equipment, and to reach previously assigned strategic positions is a task requiring several days and careful timing. To allow a dangerous rival to mobilize before you do would be to enable him to inflict defeat before your mobilization was complete. In the case of Germany the mobilization question was especially vital, because in the event of war with Russia and France she would be confronted with enemies on two fronts. The best plan seemed to be to launch a lightning attack against France, crush her, and then turn to meet Russia, who could ordinarily be expected to mobilize rather slowly (see map, page 303). To allow Russian mobilization to proceed would jeopardize this strategy, called the **Schlieffen** Plan.

World war. Faced by the Russian action, the German government decided upon war July 31. Ultimatums were sent to Russia and France demanding from the former cessation of mobilization and from the latter a pledge of neutrality. Failing to receive satisfactory replies, Germany declared war on Russia August 1 and on France August 3. On August 2 an ultimatum was delivered by the German ambassador in Brussels announcing Germany's intention of sending troops through Belgium. The Belgian cabinet refused to grant permission for this transit and appealed to Russia, France, and Great Britain for aid in protecting her neutrality.

The position of Great Britain during these momentous days had been obscure. She was under no definite obligation, by the agreements of 1904 and 1907, to furnish military aid to her allies. Sir Edward Grey was in an embarrassing position. A majority in the cabinet were not in favor of war. But the news of the German ultimatum to Belgium turned the tide in favor of entering the war on the side of France and Russia. The invasion of Belgium, declared Lloyd George, "set the nation on fire from sea to sea. . . . Before then the cabinet was hopelessly divided. After the German ultimatum to Belgium the cabinet was almost unanimous." It should not be thought that Great Britain entered the war because Belgium was invaded. The basic reason was the maintenance of the balance of power and the protection of the buffer states of Belgium and Holland along the English Channel and North Sea. "In this crisis of British policy," declares a recent volume produced by a group of British scholars, "Belgian neutrality was wholly subordinate to the wider issues, the ambitions of Germany and the fate of France. . . . Great Britain would not have remained neutral even if Belgium had not been violated."[8] Sir Edward Grey sent an ultimatum to Germany demanding that Belgian neutrality be respected. This Germany refused to do, and on August 4 Great Britain declared war.

Italy refused to carry out her engagements under the Triple Alliance on the basis that Germany and Austria were not waging a defensive war and remained neutral for the time being. In the latter part of August Japan joined the Allies, and in October Turkey, fearing the designs of Russia, threw in her lot with the Central Powers, Germany and Austria.

The responsibility for the war. During the terrible years between 1914 and 1918 when hatred ran high, the two sides accused each other of bringing on the war. The Allies charged that Germany was guilty of provoking the conflict. The structure of the Treaty of Versailles, as we shall see later, rested in large part on the "war guilt" of Germany. Scholars and laymen alike in the Allied countries sincerely believed when the Treaty was first written that Germany was completely responsible for the war. As a more realistic perspective developed in the light of new evidence, it became increasingly clear that the problem was more complex than had been originally thought. Today, most historians agree it is next to impossible to try to explain the war in terms of any one great power's actions. Rather, all the major participating nations must own, in some measure, responsibility for the outbreak of the First World War.

It is conceivable that inspired statesmanship, the right kind of leadership, and a good measure of luck might have avoided war in 1914. It is also conceivable that certain of the European powers must bear more of the responsibility for the outbreak of the conflict than other nations. Yet even if we were to grant all this, it is foolish to try to apportion the blame for the tragedy, because it was inherent in the prevailing order of international anarchy. As J. W. Swain says: "When once the Archduke Francis Ferdinand had been assassinated, nothing could be done. The French seizure of Morocco, the Agadir crisis, the Turco-Italian War and the Balkan wars, chauvinism, militarism, and preparedness, political demagogues and heroic newspaper editors had brought Europe to such a state of excitement that the insane act of three ill-balanced youths could set the world on fire."[9] War came in 1914 because it was the logical outcome of the political arrangements and ambitions of the time.

The First World War

Strategy in 1914. Both sides anticipated a quick victory in 1914. Allied strategy was to launch two simultaneous offensives—one by the French against Alsace, the other by the Russians against East Prussia. The German high command put their trust in the famous Schlieffen Plan (see map). This was a brilliantly conceived maneuver designed to crush the French armies. A great enveloping movement was to be launched through Belgium. Wheeling through France, the German armies would outflank the French and push them against Alsace-Lorraine, where they would be met by another German army. Hemmed in on both the east and west, capitulation must take place. With France smashed, the main German forces would then be transported to East Prussia, where a relatively small German army had been given the task of holding the Russians at bay. The reinforcements then would fall on the Russians and destroy their forces, and the war would be over.

Battle of the Marne. In the west the German strategy unrolled with clocklike precision. Belgian resistance was smothered by the fire of immense siege artillery. A small British expeditionary force tried unsuccessfully to halt the German onrush in Belgium. Meanwhile disaster had overtaken the French, whose offensive against Alsace fizzled out. Nearer and nearer the German forces came to the French capital. At the beginning of September they were within twenty-five miles of Paris. At this moment the German high command made a fatal blunder. Somewhat weakened by the dispatch of troops to East Prussia to meet a Russian attack, the German command directed its east flank to pass to the east of Paris. The original plan had been to encircle Paris from the west. This tactic left the right flank of the German forces exposed, a fact not lost to Joffre, the French commander, and his advisers. On September 5, Joffre decided to initiate a bold counter-offensive, and so began the Battle of the Marne. For five days a titanic battle raged, but in the end the Germans had to retreat, and France was saved. A race to the sea followed, the object being to reach the important ports along the English Channel. The Channel ports were saved, and by December 1914, the western front had been stabilized. A huge system of trenches stretched from the English Channel to Switzerland. Open warfare now ceased, and trench warfare replaced it until the last few months of the conflict in 1918.

The eastern front. On the eastern front, the Russian armies had little trouble in overrunning East Prussia. It seemed likely that the Russian "steam roller" might smash its way to Berlin. At this moment Paul von Hindenburg was brought from retirement and made head of the German forces in Prussia. In the Battle of Tannenberg (August 26-31) the Germans surrounded and dispersed one Russian army under General Samsonov, who committed suicide. Hindenburg then turned his attention to the other Russian army and inflicted a severe loss. While the Battle of the Marne was raging, the Russians under General Brusilov launched a successful offensive against the Austrians at the same time that an Austrian attack on Serbia was being repulsed.

The Dardanelles campaign. The year 1915 dawned with both the Allies and the Central Powers supremely confident of the outcome of the war. The aim of the Allies was to widen Germany's battle front and reëstablish communication with Russia. The entrance of Turkey on the side of Germany had closed the Dardanelles to Allied shipping, and much needed munitions and other supplies could now be sent to Russia only via Archangel, a port ice-locked much of the year. Therefore Great Britain tried to force the Dardanelles,

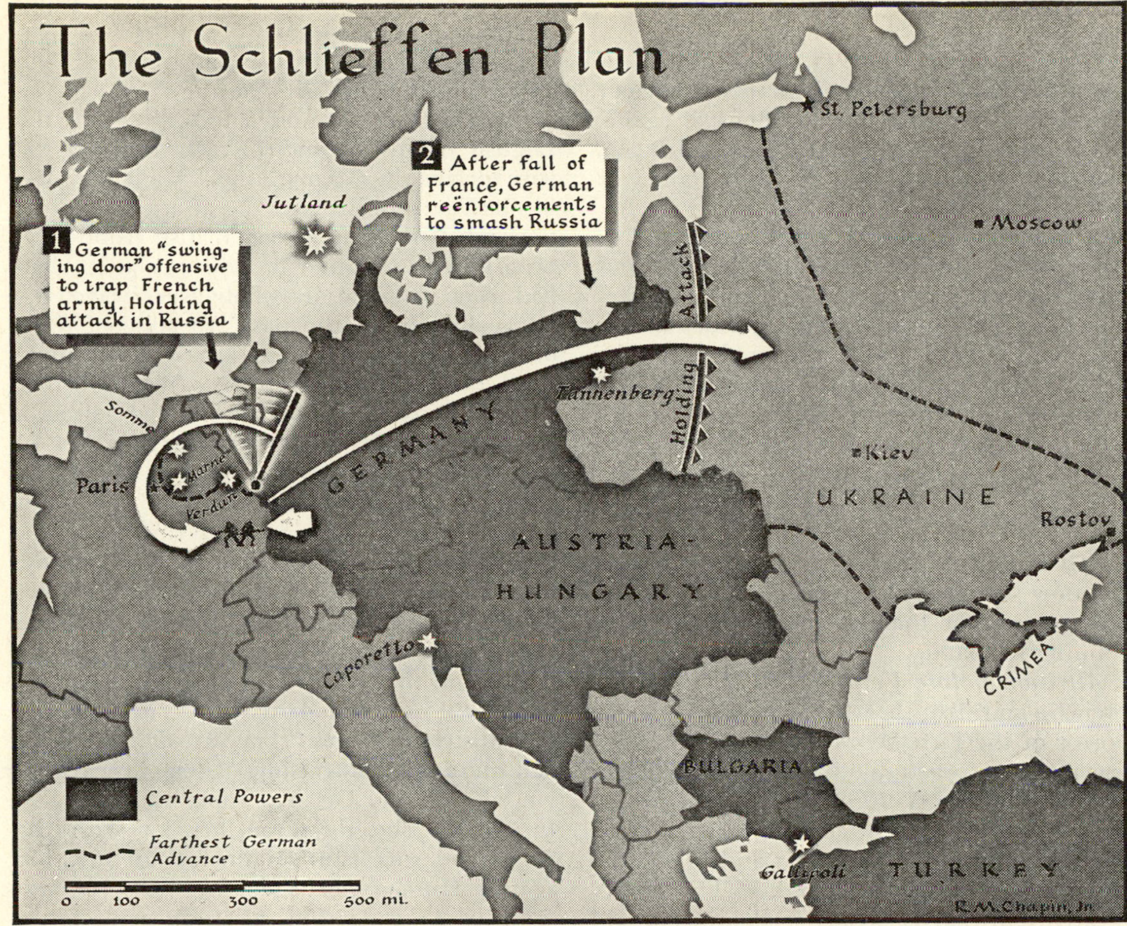

a plan attributed largely to Winston Churchill. Other objectives of this campaign were to lessen the possibility of attack on Egypt and Suez, to isolate Turkey, and to win over the Balkan neutrals. The campaign was a series of blunders and ghastly failures. As if to furnish the Turks with advance information regarding their intentions, the Allies sent a naval squadron to make a preliminary attack in November 1914 and followed this up by a determined naval attack in March. In the engagement three battleships were sunk, and the Allies withdrew. We know now that at this moment the Turkish batteries were practically out of ammunition. Had the attack been pressed, the Straits must have fallen.

During the latter part of April Australian and New Zealand troops forced a landing on the Gallipoli peninsula (see map above). In the face of machine-gun nests and concealed barbed wire, the "Anzacs" waded ashore from small boats and charged up the beach, suffering tremendous losses. For the remainder of the year the British troops clung to their precarious foothold but were finally evacuated in January 1916.

Italy joins the Allies. The attempt of the Allies to widen Germany's battle front brought Italy into the war. From December 1914 to April 1915, both sides wooed Italy. The Allies were successful because in the secret Treaty of London they made the most generous promises, including a promise to turn German-speaking people in the southern Tyrol over to Italy after the war ended. As the British statesman Balfour remarked, "This is the sort of thing you have to do when you are engaged in war." Italy entered the war on what she believed was the winning side in 1915 in spite of her earlier commitments to the Triple Alliance. The entrance of Italy on their side was the only victory achieved by the Allies in 1915. Everywhere else there was a series of melancholy defeats.

German successes in 1915. The Germans, on the other hand, went from victory to victory. They carried out a terrific offensive against the Russian forces in May 1915, in which 700,000 shells paved the way for the infantry attack. The Russian trenches simply melted away. Soon the czar's army was in rapid retreat, which quickly degenerated into a rout. More than 1,200,000 were killed and wounded. The Germans captured nearly 900,000 prisoners. Russia never fully recovered from this debacle. On all sides criticism began to grow against the government, and the morale of the nation began to break down.

Serbia was the next victim. The conquest was made all the easier because Bulgaria entered the war on the side of Germany and Austria-Hungary in September 1915. Serbia was now surrounded by enemies and thus unable to prevent them from completely overrunning her land.

Attrition before Verdun. To all Germans, French, and British who went through the horror of the First World War, the year 1916 was made unforgettable by the blood baths of the Somme and Verdun. It was the Allied strategy to restrict attacks on the western front to intermittent nibbling and to concentrate upon the naval blockade. This policy of attrition, that is, steady weakening, would in the end result in starvation in Germany. Germany, on the other hand, resorted to another kind of attrition and applied it to France. The plan was to concentrate a gigantic attack on Verdun. This move would attract hundreds of thousands of French troops, terrible losses would result, and French morale would be steadily worn down. All during the spring and summer of 1916 the Germans pounded the forts of Verdun with thousands of shells and threw wave after wave of infantry against the French positions. In the face of these attacks the French stubbornly resisted. The cry of the French *poilu* was "Ils ne passeront pas!" ("They shall not pass!") The result of this fighting around Verdun was attrition for both sides. The Germans alone suffered the loss of 300,000 men.

The Somme. To ease the tremendous pressure against Verdun and also to discourage the Germans from sending fresh troops against Russia, the British army began a great offensive along the Somme on the western front. For seven days a tornado of artillery fire battered and wrecked the German trenches; then on the morning of July 1, as the shrill whistles of British officers sounded the zero hour, the English troops advanced slowly through the wire toward the German lines. A terrible blast of machine-gun fire met the attackers, and by the end of the day 60,000 British troops had been killed or wounded, more casualties than had been suffered in whole wars waged by Great Britain in the past. In spite of these heart-breaking losses the attack was continued until heavy rains in October made further efforts impossible. The British had gained a few square miles of territory at the cost of over 400,000 killed and wounded.

Russia and Rumania, 1916. A bright spot for the Allies in the midst of all this gloom was the thrust of the Russian commander Brusilov, who in June 1916 struck the Austrian lines with the force of a thunderbolt, capturing 300,000 prisoners. The assistance of German troops and the lack of war materials, however, halted the Russian drive before it destroyed the Austrian armies. The Russian offensive had one important result. Rumania was convinced that the German cause was hopeless. In August she threw in her lot with the Allies and successfully launched an invasion against Hungary. Her success, however, was short-lived. Bulgarian and German forces simultaneously attacked the Rumanian armies, which proved to be quite inferior, and Rumania was forced to capitulate. Vast stores of oil and grain, urgently needed by the Central Powers, were obtained.

Allied offensives, 1917. The tremendous cost of the fighting in men and materials became apparent early in 1917, especially in Russia and Germany. On the western front, however, the French and British were approaching the height of their fighting strength. Military conscription in Great Britain had enabled her to train and equip an army of two million men. This force during April and May carried out a successful offensive against German positions. In April the French army also made a large-scale attack. The new French commander in chief, General Nivelle, who had succeeded Joffre, confidently expected an audacious attack to break the German lines. The attack was a complete failure. Thousands of French lives were lost. The army was thoroughly disgusted by the failure of their leader, and ten divisions mutinied rather than continue what they considered useless slaughter. This disaster forced the British army to take over large sections of the front which had hitherto been defended by various units of the French army.

The meaning of modern war. In the First World War, as in the Second, the burden was carried not only by the soldiers in the field but by entire nations. From the vigorous young men in the trenches to the women at work in the munitions factories ran a continuous link touching the lives of practically every adult in a nation at war. Old women knitted socks and sweaters for the soldiers, scientists put aside their research to work on new gases or explosives, men too old for active military service worked behind the lines in labor battalions, and even school children were expected to till school gardens to help produce the necessary food.

On the western front there was enacted a drama of horror never before witnessed by man. In a line of trenches almost 600 miles long two opposing bodies of troops faced each other. Between the trenches was no-man's-land, crisscrossed with barbed wire and spotted with craters where lay the dead. During the day the soldiers crouched in their dugouts, using periscopes to peer over the parapets, for sharpshooters were a constant menace. At night, while the men tried to gain a little fitful sleep, the sentries peered anxiously into the darkness on the watch for raiding parties. Machine-gun fire, the menace of gas, the flame thrower, the risk of attack from marauding airplanes, the sudden death from the salvo of big guns—these became the lot of the soldiers in the trenches.

The United States and the War

The policy of the United States. After Italy entered the war on the side of the Allies, America was the only great power remaining neutral. The outbreak of the war came as a staggering surprise to most Americans, who had little understanding and knowledge of the conditions in Europe. The overwhelming sentiment in this country was for peace. On August 4, 1914, President Wilson announced the neutrality of the United States and declared that the people "must be impartial in thought as well as in action." The events of the next two years showed that this was no easy task.

A type of combat new in its day—trench warfare—characterized a large part of the fighting in the First World War. The tank, looking thin by comparison with present-day models, was also introduced.

A German airplane boils black smoke as it plunges toward earth, shot down by an Allied fighter. Note the characteristic Maltese-cross markings on the under wings of the German plane.

Our economic stake in the Allied cause. As the war got under way, it became apparent that the British blockade would permit our trade and commerce to be carried on with the Allies only, and it was not long before our factories and farmers were producing munitions and food exclusively for Great Britain and France. Our industry expanded and began to enjoy a prosperity dependent upon the continuance of Allied purchases. During 1915 and 1916 about one and a half billion dollars of Allied bonds were sold in America. ". . . to those who sponsored and participated in these loans, whose financial reputation and whose principal and interest depended upon the continued solvency of the debtor nations, it was not a matter of indifference which side won the war."[10] The financial stake of the United States in the Allied cause has in recent times received much attention. But careful students point out that, although this certainly influenced our final decision to go to war, "the financial community as a whole . . . favored American neutrality rather than American participation; for neutrality afforded Wall Street all the profits of war without the compensating sacrifices and taxation. And there is not a shred of evidence to support the allegation that Wilson was at any time influenced by the financial 'stake' in his relations with Germany. . . ."[11]

The German U-boat campaign. The immediate cause of the entry of the United States into the war on the side of the Allies was undoubtedly the German submarine campaign. At the outbreak of hostilities, Great Britain immediately imposed a tight naval blockade against Germany. Neutral ships were brought into British ports for examination, and the list of contraband goods was expanded despite the existing rules of international law. For the first nine months of the war it was the British blockade, more than anything else, that evoked protests from our state department. During this period we had little trouble with Germany. But the kaiser's government was getting desperate as a result of the pressure of

Great Britain's blockade. There was only one method of retaliation—the submarine. The German government, therefore, announced unrestricted submarine warfare in February, 1915. On May 1, 1915, the *Gulflight* was torpedoed with the loss of several of her American crew. On May 7, 1915, came the horrible disaster of the sinking of the *Lusitania*, one of the largest and most luxurious liners of the Cunard line. The *Lusitania* had on board a large number of civilian passengers, and, in addition, it is generally recognized that she was carrying ammunition. However, it is still debated whether she was armed. Sunk by a torpedo in the Irish Sea, she went to the bottom with the loss of over one thousand lives, including more than one hundred Americans. Public opinion in America never recovered from the horror of this tragedy.

In March 1916, the unarmed French steamer *Sussex* was sunk without warning, and several Americans were killed. Following this act, an ultimatum demanding the cessation of the submarine campaign was sent by the government of the United States to Germany. In reply the Germans made pledges that in the future merchant vessels would not be sunk without warning and that provision would be made for the safety of passengers and crew. President Wilson had apparently won an important diplomatic victory.

American entry into the war. In the fall of 1916, Wilson was reëlected to the presidency. One of the important claims made during the campaign was that "he kept us out of war." This claim, however, was soon swept away by the force of events. In January of the next year another crisis in our diplomatic relations with Germany appeared with the renewal of submarine warfare. In February diplomatic relations were broken off. The discovery of German plots to embroil Mexico in a war against us added more fuel to the fire. Finally, on April 2, 1917, the President asked Congress to declare war against Germany. Resolutions to this effect passed both houses, and on April 6, 1917, war was declared.

If the immediate cause of our entry in the war was unrestricted submarine warfare, there were less obvious but nevertheless potent factors that motivated public opinion in America to war on the side of the Allies. It should not be overlooked that, by and large, American opinion from 1914 was favorable to France, Great Britain, and their allies. There was the strong tradition of friendship for France because of that country's help to the struggling American colonies during the Revolutionary War. Hence "Colonel Stanton's 'Lafayette we are here' was something more than dramatics." Despite the fact that there had been much "twisting of the British Lion's tail" in America since the days of the Revolution and the War of 1812, there persisted strong cultural links between the two Anglo-Saxon peoples. There was similarity of language, literature, law, and political institutions.

In the case of Germany American opinion had been profoundly shocked by the invasion of Belgium in 1914 and the sinking of the *Lusitania.* Even before the war German-American relations had been none too cordial. The German government had, unlike Great Britain, refused to sign one of Secretary of State Bryan's arbitration treaties. Many Americans were disgusted with the "sabre-rattling" speeches of the kaiser and found little to their liking in the mode of government in the German empire. In 1914 it was virtually inconceivable that we would ever join Germany against France and Great Britain, but it was not unthinkable that we might eventually join the cause of the Allies.

The Wilsonian blueprint for peace. Whatever the cause—our economic stake, our common traditions, the U-boat campaign—America was now fighting on the side of the Allies. President Wilson was convinced that America was fighting for national security, justice,

Despite its flimsiness, the "orange crate" airplane of World War I *(here dropping a torpedo) proved that air power would be all-important in future wars.*

honor, and democracy in the world. The conflict, in his words, was "a war for freedom and justice and self-government amongst all the nations of the world, a war to make the world safe for the peoples who live upon it and have made it their own, the German people themselves included."[12] In January 1918 President Wilson therefore enunciated his famous Fourteen Points as the basis for a lasting peace. These provided for:

1. Open covenants openly arrived at.
2. Freedom of the seas in peace and in war alike.
3. The removal of all economic barriers and the establishment of an equality of trade conditions among all nations.
4. Reduction of national armaments.
5. A readjustment of all colonial claims in which the interests of the population concerned must have equal weight with the claims of the government whose title is to be determined.
6. The evacuation of Russian territory and the independent determination by Russia of her own political development and national policy.
7. The evacuation and restoration of Belgium.
8. The evacuation and restoration of France and the return of Alsace-Lorraine.
9. A readjustment of the frontiers of Italy along national lines.
10. Self-determination for the peoples of Austria-Hungary.
11. Evacuation of Rumania, Serbia, and Montenegro and access to the sea for Serbia.
12. Self-determination for the peoples under Turkish rule and freedom of the Dardanelles under international guarantees.
13. The independence of Poland, with free access to the sea guaranteed by international covenant.
14. The formation of a general association of nations under specific covenants for the purpose of affording mutual guarantees of political independence and territorial integrity to great and small states alike.

This program represented the Wilsonian blueprint for a new and just world order. The spell of his idealism and the challenge of his speeches caused a great welling of idealism in America. No matter what causes had operated to bring America in, she was now fighting, in the words of her President, "to make the world safe for democracy."

Allied weakness in 1918. American help was needed desperately. In March 1917 a revolution in Russia deposed the czar. For a few months the new government endeavored to carry on the war, but in November it was overthrown by the Bolsheviks under Lenin. In December the Bolsheviks agreed to negotiate a separate peace with Germany and in March 1918 were forced to sign the Treaty of Brest Litovsk, a harsh settlement. The Russians agreed to cede 500,000 square miles of territory and nearly 70,000,000 people (see map, page 317). The Allies had already suffered a severe blow in the fall of 1917 when the Italians had been crushed at the battle of Caporetto. Only the arrival of British and French troops saved Italy from collapse.

Ludendorff's last effort. While the United States mobilized its tremendous resources in manpower and materials, the German government decided the war must be won at any cost before American aid became effective. General Ludendorff, freed from the necessity of fighting on the Russian front, transferred every available man to France and launched in March 1918 what he hoped would be a knockout blow against the British fifth army. Carrying all before them, the German shock troops, outnumbering the British four to one, made a large dent in the Allied line. A breakthrough, however, was not achieved. Another blow was made by Ludendorff against the British in another sector. Again impressive gains were made but not the rout which the German command had expected. A third desperate offensive was launched against the French forces, but fresh American troops thrown into the struggle halted the advance. Ludendorff now made a last supreme effort. Launching a "Peace Drive" against the French, Ludendorff declared, "If my offensive succeeds, we have won the war." By this time, however, the German troops had suffered heavy losses since they had assumed the offensive in March. The Allies created a unified command of all their armies under General Foch, Great Britain sent every available man to France, and American troops were now arriving in large numbers. Between March

and July 1918 more than one million landed in France. The advantage in manpower and equipment was now with the Allies, and Ludendorff's "Peace Drive" failed after an advance of some three miles.

German collapse and armistice. Hardly had the German drive been halted when Foch counterattacked on July 18. For three weeks the Second Battle of the Marne raged. Outnumbered and without adequate supplies, the Germans had to retreat to their Hindenburg Line, the position held before they began their great offensive in March. Foch gave no respite. With fresh American troops in France the reinvigorated Allied armies advanced along the whole Hindenburg Line. The German line bent, broke, and then fell back in rapid retreat. By the end of October the German forces had been pushed out of most of France, and Allied armies were advancing through Belgium.

On October 1, Hindenburg notified the kaiser that Germany must sue for peace. Three days later the German chancellor sent a note to President Wilson requesting peace. The President's reply notified the German government that peace was impossible as long as the autocratic régime in Germany existed. The German chancellor tried to retain the monarchy by introducing certain liberal reforms, but it was too late. Revolution broke out in many parts of the country, and on November 9 the kaiser abdicated, and the republic was proclaimed. On November 5 Wilson had already notified the German government of the willingness of the Allies to initiate peace negotiations. Two days later, German delegates entered the Allied lines and were given the armistice terms by General Foch, the supreme Allied commander. Then at five o'clock on the morning of November 11, in a dining car in the Compiègne Forest, the two German delegates signed the terms of the armistice. At eleven o'clock the same day hostilities were halted. The world was now at peace, confronted with the task of binding up its wounds and removing the scars of conflict. All over the world the news of the armistice was received with an outburst of unrestrained joy.

While Germany was staggering under the relentless pounding of Foch's armies, her allies were suffering even greater misfortunes. Bulgaria surrendered on September 30, Turkey capitulated a month later, and Austria gave up the struggle against Italy on November 3.

Ramifications of the war. Only the barest sketch of the great war has been given. It was a world war fought on land, sea, and in the air. To study this conflict adequately we should have had to describe the Japanese conquest of the German colony in China, to follow the activities of South African and Indian troops in their capture of German colonies in Africa, note the expeditions sent from Australia and New Zealand against the German colonies in the Pacific, study the successes of British forces led by General Allenby in the Turkish empire and the escapades of the romantic Lawrence of Arabia, and, finally, follow the many sea battles that reached a climax in the great naval encounter at Jutland between the high-seas fleets of Great Britain and Germany. There were few parts of the world where some manifestation of the great struggle had not occurred.

Summary

The progress of the second phase of the Industrial Revolution promised a new era of economic prosperity for the world. The closest cooperation between nations was demanded to ensure the harmonious operation of an increasingly integrated world economic structure. In spite of the retention of old political boundaries and the idea of national sovereignty, the great powers recognized this fact in some measure. In the political field attempts were made to eliminate the danger of war, and attention was given to technical and economic problems through the formation of several international unions. To a certain extent, peoples as well as nations banded together to solve national and international problems, although most of these attempts were concerned with nonpolitical matters.

These cooperative efforts could not cope with other forces that made for international rivalry and war. The national-state system, power politics, secret diplomacy and its rival alliances, militarism, economic imperialism, and emotional nationalism finally led Europe to war in 1914 and most of the world with it as well.

The immediate cause of the 1914 conflict was nationalism in the Balkans. Serbian Irredentism menaced the existence of the polyglot Austrian empire. Russia backed Serbia because this move suited her designs in the Near East. In turn Russia received the support of France because France hoped to compel Germany to cede her the "lost provinces." Germany was committed to back Austria, who was her only reliable ally. Great Britain tried to remain aloof from the system of alliances but was finally drawn in. She could not afford to see Germany triumph, because German success would alter the European balance of power to the detriment of Great Britain.

The war became a world conflict fought on land, sea, and in the air and inaugurated what we now refer to as "total war." The distinction between soldier and noncombatant tended to become nonexistent. The immediate cause of America's entry into the war was the submarine campaign, but behind this cause were a strong tie with Great Britain and France, tactless German diplomacy, an economic stake in an Allied victory, and finally the realization that a German victory would endanger American security. Although there are many conflicting opinions on why the United States entered the war, the people themselves believed that they had embarked on a great crusade "to make the world safe for democracy."

In the first years of the war—1914-1916—Germany appeared likely to win. Even the entrance of Italy on the side of the Allies in 1915 did not add greatly to Allied strength. Although British and French forces had begun to make impressive gains by 1917, the help of the United States was desperately needed when the German U-boat campaign at last precipitated American entry into the war early the following year. By October 1918 the Germans had been pushed out of France; a month later they surrendered to the Allies.

The Peace Settlement

1918	Personnel of the peace conference	Wilson, Lloyd George, Clemenceau
1919	Treaty of Versailles (involves compromises)	Germany humiliated
	Treaty of St. Germain with Austria	Carves up Austro-Hungarian empire
	Treaty of Sèvres with Turkey	Turkey refuses harsh terms
1923	Treaty of Lausanne	Turkey obtains more favorable terms
	Treaty of Trianon with Hungary	Loses territory, people
	Treaty of Neuilly with Bulgaria	Did not suffer as much as Hungary

The League of Nations

1919	Covenant adopted	Headquarters at Geneva, Switzerland
	Organization—Assembly, Council, Secretariat	Permanent, non-permanent members
1920	The World Court	Located at The Hague
	The International Labor Organization	Governing Body and Labor Office
	Membership—forty-two nations	Rose to 65 in 15 years
	U. S. refuses to join League	Wilson's collapse
1921-1927	Boundary settlements	Vilna controversy
1922-1928	Resettlement of refugees of Greco-Turkish War	
1923	Corfu incident	War averted at cost of League prestige
1924	Aland affair	Victory for League
	Financial assistance to Austria and Hungary	

Security and Disarmament

1922-1927	French system of alliances	Known as Little Entente
	With Poland, Czechoslovakia, Rumania, Yugoslavia	Directed against Germany
1922	Washington Conference	5:5:3 ratio
1923	French occupation of the Ruhr	Result of reparations dispute
1924	Dawes' plan for reparation	
1925	Locarno Treaties	Guaranteed Rhine
1927	Geneva Conference	
1928	Kellogg-Briand Pact	Renunciation of war as instrument of national policy

Tariff Barriers and War Debts

1922	Fordney-McCumber tariff in U. S. makes war debt payment difficult	Highest rates ever in U.S.
	Smoot-Hawley tariff causes retaliatory tariffs in other countries	Rates raised to almost highest in world
1929	Young Plan for reparations payments	Bank of International Settlements established

Depression and International Finance

1929	Stock market crash in U. S.	Ended wild speculation
1931	Hoover moratorium on debts	
1931-1933	Great Britain and United States go off gold standard	World trade becomes barter
1932	Lausanne conference	Reparations practically canceled
1932-1934	War debt payments cease	Finland continues to pay
1932	Germany stops reparations payments	
	Great Britain goes off free trade	Enacts high tariff
1932	Ottawa Imperial Economic Conference	Principle of imperial preference
1933	World economic conference in London	
1934	U. S. reduces gold content of dollar	Other countries also devaluate currency

CHAPTER 10

A Quest for World Order

LAYING down its arms in 1919, the world looked to the Peace Conference to repair the damage of the conflict. The war had lasted for 1565 days. During this time over sixty million men had donned uniforms. About nine million of these were killed, twenty-two million were wounded, and, in addition, about ten million civilians lost their lives as a direct or indirect result of the war. Furthermore, billions of dollars' worth of property had been used up or destroyed by the warring armies. The statesmen at the conference had two basic tasks. The first was to reverse the trend toward international anarchy that had brought on the First World War. It was imperative to remove or at least lessen such factors as nationalism, secret diplomacy, economic imperialism, and militarism—all of which had helped to bring war in 1914. The second task was to repair the extensive economic damage wrought by war and to endeavor to continue the world's economic progress. This problem demanded the reduction of barriers to world trade and cooperation among the nations in solving their mutual economic problems.

This chapter records the attempts to perform these tasks during the postwar decade. It will be seen that the peace was not based on President Wilson's Fourteen Points, as the Germans hoped, and that vindictiveness and selfish national interests conspired from the beginning to defeat Wilsonian idealism. One result of the Great War was the establishment of a league of nations. For the first time in history, the world was to have a powerful agency, composed of representatives from nearly all the nations existing, to compel states to arbitrate their differences, protect nations from aggression, and endeavor to eliminate the various causes that had in the past brought on wars. Some attention will be given to the League of Nations and its activities, and the reader will see why and how both national and international efforts to achieve security and disarmament failed in their purpose.

Problems of postwar economic reconstruction form the last half of the chapter. The impossible financial burden of reparations placed on Germany and the failure of the Allied nations to come to some agreement regarding inter-Allied debts revealed themselves as serious obstacles in the path of reconstruction, and with them appeared an increase of tariffs, a contraction of international trade, and a world depression in 1930. In general the world was no more successful in its search for economic prosperity than it was in the quest for political security.

Making the Peace

The armistice terms. The armistice terms accepted by Germany on November 11, 1918, compelled her to evacuate Alsace-Lorraine, Luxemburg, Belgium, and the northern part of France. Within a month Allied troops were to occupy the German territory west of the Rhine. A large number of units of the German fleet were to be surrendered, locomotives, trucks, and other equipment turned over, and all Allied prisoners released. While these terms were being carried out by the new German government that had taken over after the kaiser's abdication, delegates from the Allied nations from all over the world were converging on Paris, where the greatest Peace Conference in the world's history was to be held.

Personnel of the conference. The thirty-two Allied powers all sent delegations, some numbering more than a hundred, which included statesmen and experts of various kinds, secretaries, and clerical help. The vanquished nations—Germany, Austria-Hungary, Turkey, and Bulgaria—were not accorded representation. At the conference Woodrow Wilson, David Lloyd George, and Georges Clemenceau dominated the proceedings. Wilson, in a number of truly great speeches, had already formulated the hopes and aspirations of a war-weary world, and in the eyes of the peoples of Europe he was a veritable Messiah. However, it soon became apparent after his arrival in France in December 1918 that he would be unable to prevent his ideals and promises from being sabotaged. Wilson's idealism was challenged not only by the Allied statesmen in Paris but back home in America as well, where certain factions in Congress were preparing to repudiate his program for a more just and a better ordered world. Wilson was preëminently the scholar and idealist, and so thoroughly convinced was he of the validity of his own ideas that he often refused to consider the possibility of merit in those of his opponents. A farseeing "armchair statesman," handicapped by a cold and imperious personality, Wilson had little chance of holding his own against the wily Lloyd George and the cynical Clemenceau.

Lloyd George, the prime minister of Great Britain, came to the conference just after a triumphant victory at the polls in which the electorate had been promised the "hanging of the kaiser" and the "squeezing of the German lemon until the pips squeaked." He was determined to destroy the commercial and naval power of Germany, to acquire the German colonies, and to compel Germany to pay a large share of the cost of the war. Lloyd George was not a scholar, but he was a consummately clever politician who could use the arts of diplomatic bargaining with rare skill. His greatest asset was an engaging personality that thawed many a stubborn opponent.

The strongest personality of the conference was an old man of seventy-seven years. Clemenceau was the sole survivor of the French Assembly that had protested against the loss of Alsace-Lorraine in 1871. His one burning ambition was to secure conditions ensuring the security of France in the future. The "Old Tiger" was shot in the chest by a madman during the peace negotiations, but so strong was his desire to live that he quickly rallied after the shooting and, for a time, dominated the conference from his bedside.

Pre-armistice peace principles. The Germans had not surrendered unconditionally, but only with the understanding that the peace would follow in the main the Fourteen Points and in general coincide with the speeches of Wilson. In February 1918, the President had announced "There shall be no annexations, no contributions, no punitive damages," and on July 4 he had said that every question must be settled "upon the basis of the free acceptance of that settlement by the people immediately concerned." Some of the Allies saw the question of the peace in a different light, and before the armistice was signed, three reservations to the Fourteen Points were made by the European Allied powers. One sprang from Great Britain's attitude toward the freedom of the seas, another came from the demand that Germany must be made to pay for all damage done to Allied civilians, and the third appeared because of the dissatisfaction of the peoples of Austria-Hungary with mere autonomy within the Hapsburg empire. Subject to these reservations the victorious Allies were pledged to work out a peace based on Wilsonian principles.

The conference. With two hundred newspaper men reporting the conference, the statesmen assembled in their first plenary meeting on January 18, 1919, the anniversary of the date on which the German empire had been proclaimed in Paris in 1871. It became evident at once that little progress could be made if business was carried on in the full conference. The Council of Ten was therefore set up. It consisted of the two ranking delegates of the five great powers—the United States, Great Britain, France, Italy, and Japan. Soon this was narrowed down to the Big Four, minus Japan, and when the Italian delegates went back to Rome after a quarrel with Wilson, the Big Three carried on the work of the conference. The lesser powers counted for little, although their representatives often delivered long addresses before the Council of Ten, "who for the most part sat in bored silence."

The League Covenant. The first difficulty in the peace conference arose over the question of a league of nations. As early as March 1918 a draft plan had been prepared in England, and drafts were later prepared by Colonel House, the close personal friend and adviser of Wilson, and General Smuts, the premier of the Union of South Africa. In Paris a special committee was assigned to draw up a definite scheme. Wilson was insistent that the first work of the conference must be to agree upon a covenant of a league of nations and that this must be made a part of the peace treaty. After much disagreement the Covenant was approved by the full conference in April 1919. In order to gain support for his league idea, Wilson had to give way on other matters. This compromising meant a partial repudiation of his Fourteen Points, but he felt that it was better to have an imperfect treaty incorporating the League than a perfect one without it.

Redrawing German boundaries. Redrawing German boundaries was another task of the conference (see map, page 317). Alsace-Lorraine was turned over to France without question, in accordance with one of the Fourteen Points. Three districts formerly belonging to Germany were given to Belgium, after a dubious plebiscite conducted by Belgian officials, and another plebiscite gave half of Schleswig back to Denmark. Clemenceau and General Foch were determined that a buffer state consisting of the German territory west of the Rhine should be established under the domination of France. In the eyes of the American and British representatives, such a crass violation of the principle of self-determination would only breed future wars, and a compromise was therefore offered Clemenceau, which he accepted. The territory in question was to be occupied by Allied troops for a period of from five to fifteen years, and, further, a zone fifty kilometers east of the Rhine was to be demilitarized. In addition, Wilson and Lloyd George agreed that the United States and Great Britain would guarantee France against aggression, and two treaties were drawn up and signed. Although Clemenceau also claimed the Saar Basin, a rich coal area, this was not given outright to France but placed under the administration of the League instead. The French were given the ownership of the mines to compensate for the destruction of their own in northern France. It was agreed, however, that after fifteen years a plebiscite would be conducted to determine whether the region wished to continue under League supervision, become part of France, or return to Germany.

Along Germany's eastern frontier the creation of the Polish Corridor raised grave problems. Large sections of German territory in

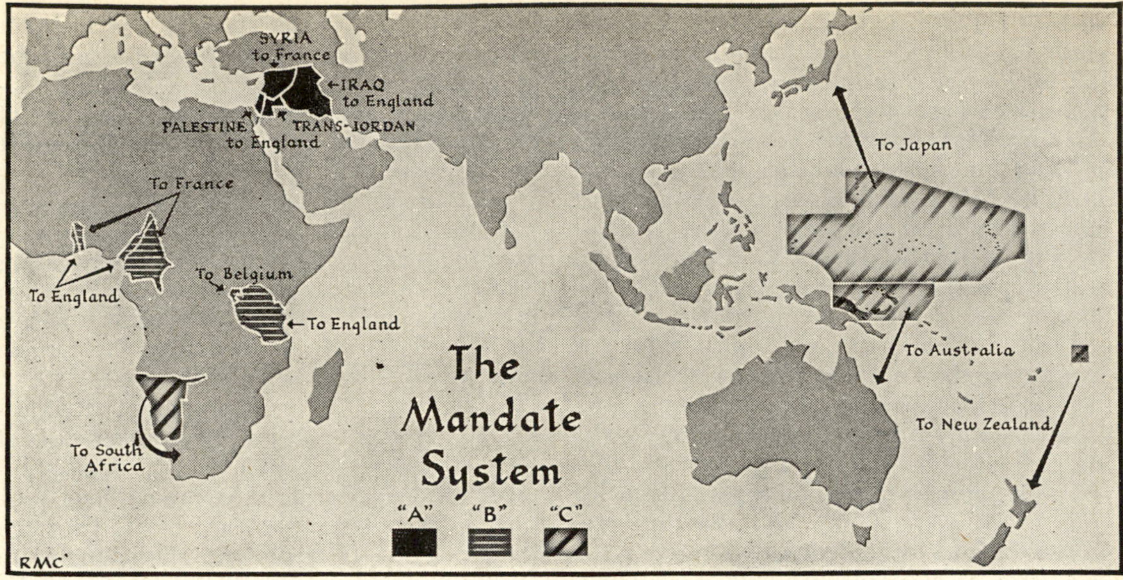

which there were Polish majorities but also a goodly number of Germans were turned over to Poland (see map, page 321), and Danzig, a German city, was handed over to the League for administration. Although many Germans were turned over to Poland by this arrangement, the land in question had been taken from Poland by Prussia in the eighteenth century. A section of Silesia was likewise given to Poland, but only after a plebiscite, and a small section of East Prussia was placed in 1923 under the control of Lithuania. All in all, Germany lost 25,000 square miles inhabited by some six million people.

The mandate system. A curious mixture of idealism and revenge determined the allocation of the German colonies and certain territories belonging to Turkey. Because outright annexation would look too much like unvarnished imperialism, it was suggested that the colonies be turned over to the League which in turn would give them to certain of its members to administer (see map above). The colonies were to be known as mandates, and praiseworthy precautions were taken that the mandates would be administered for the well-being and development of the inhabitants. Once a year the mandatory powers were to present a detailed account of their administration to the permanent mandates commission of the League.

"A" mandates, such as Syria, Palestine, and Iraq, were regarded as territories able to achieve full statehood in the not too distant future. "B" mandates, such as most in central Africa, represented peoples whose progress had not reached a point where admission to statehood was possible for a long time to come. "C" mandates, in southwest Africa and the South Pacific islands, were regarded as locations where size, proximity to the mandatory power, or remoteness from civilization made control by others the best safeguard of the natives' rights and welfare. The mandate system, as such, was a step forward in colonial administration, but Germany nevertheless had been deprived of all her colonies on the excuse that she could not rule them justly or efficiently.

Reparations. Germany had accepted the armistice terms with the understanding that she was to pay for all damage done to the civilian population of the Allies. At the conference the British and French delegates went much further by demanding that Germany pay the total cost of the war including the pensions. The American representatives maintained that such a claim was contrary to the pre-armistice Allied terms and succeeded in arriving at a compromise. It was agreed that Germany was not to pay the entire cost of the war, except in the case of Belgium, but only for war damages which included damage to civilians and the cost of pensions. These payments, called reparations, were exacted on the ground that Germany was responsible for the

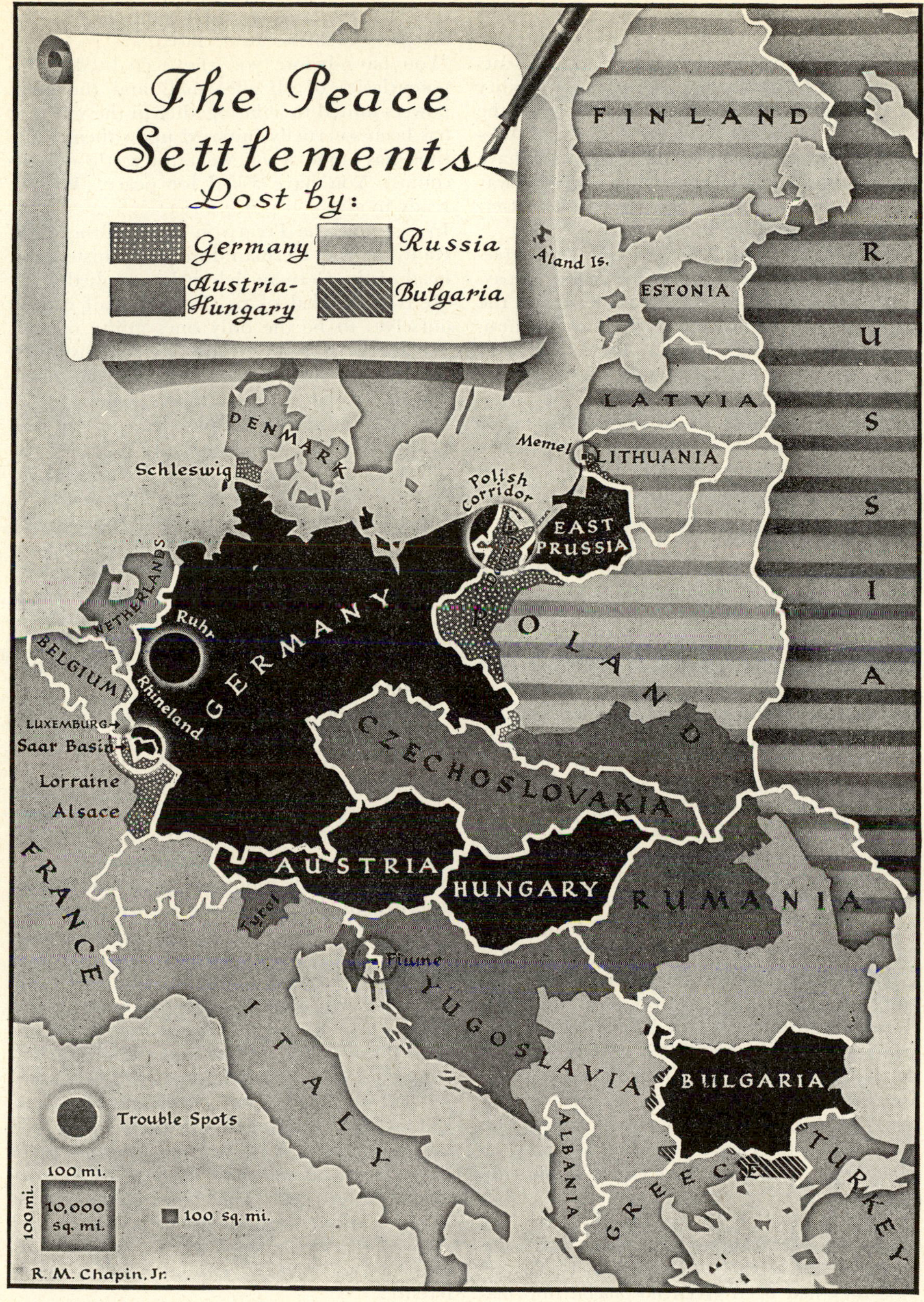
The Peace Settlements
Lost by:
Germany
Russia
Austria-Hungary
Bulgaria
FINLAND
Aland Is.
ESTONIA
LATVIA
RUSSIA
Memel
LITHUANIA
Polish Corridor
EAST PRUSSIA
POLAND
DENMARK
Schleswig
NETHERLANDS
Ruhr
BELGIUM
Rhineland
GERMANY
LUXEMBURG
Saar Basin
Lorraine
Alsace
CZECHOSLOVAKIA
AUSTRIA
HUNGARY
RUMANIA
FRANCE
Tyrol
Fiume
YUGOSLAVIA
ITALY
BULGARIA
ALBANIA
GREECE
TURKEY
Trouble Spots
100 mi.
100 mi.
10,000 sq. mi.
100 sq. mi.
R. M. Chapin, Jr.

war. In fact, the war guilt clause (Article 231) in the Treaty of Versailles said explicitly:

"The Allied and Associated Governments affirm and Germany accepts the responsibility of Germany and her allies for causing all the loss and damage to which the Allied and Associated Governments and their nationals have been subjected as a consequence of the war imposed upon them by the aggression of Germany and her allies."

Although the Allies were in complete agreement that Germany should be made to pay, they were completely unable to decide on the sum. Some demands ran as high as two hundred billion dollars. Finally they decided to let a committee fix the amount and report to them not later than May 1921. In the meantime Germany was to commence payments which were to total the equivalent of nearly five billion dollars by the time the reparations committee's report was ready.

Other Allied demands. Germany was required to hand over all her merchant ships over 1600 tons and fifty per cent of all those between 1000 and 1600 tons and in addition to construct for the Allies one million tons of new shipping. Vast amounts of equipment, tools, and machinery were also to be delivered by Germany to the Allies, and over twenty-two million tons of coal were to be given to France, Belgium, and Luxemburg over a ten-year period. In matters regarding Germany's fighting strength, the demands were even more drastic. Germany was permitted a standing army of only 100,000 men, the size of her fleet was drastically reduced, possession of military airplanes was forbidden, and her munitions plants were to be placed under close supervision. The treaty also provided that the kaiser was to be tried by a tribunal "for a supreme offense against international morality and the sanctity of treaties," and over 800 German officials were cited for trial for war atrocities. But the kaiser fled to Holland after the German revolution, and when that country refused to surrender him, no further steps were taken by the Allied governments, who had inserted the clause providing for the punishment of the kaiser largely for home consumption.

German reaction to the Treaty. The German delegation came to Paris in April 1919 to receive the Treaty of Versailles. Up to this time they had been given no official information as to its terms. In addressing the German delegates Clemenceau declared:

"You have before you the accredited plenipotentiaries of all the small and the great powers united to fight together in the war that has been so cruelly imposed upon them. The time has come when we must settle our accounts. You have asked for peace. We are ready to give you peace."[1]

In receiving the Treaty on May 7, Brockdorff-Rantzau, the German foreign minister and head of the German delegation, replied:

"It is demanded of us that we shall confess ourselves to be the only ones guilty of war. We are far from declining any responsibility, . . . but we energetically deny that Germany and its people . . . were alone guilty. In the last fifty years the imperialism of all the European states has chronically poisoned the international situation. You will find us ready . . . with a firm intention . . . of repairing . . . any wrong that may have been committed—principally the wrong to Belgium, and to show to mankind new aims of political and social progress. . . . Only if the gates of the League of Nations are thrown open to all who are of good will can the aim be attained, and only then the dead of this war will not have died in vain."[2]

During the 1920's and the early 1930's the majority of scholars were inclined to agree with the German complaint that the terms of the peace made at Versailles were unnecessarily severe. The course of Nazi imperialism in the Second World War, however, has tended to cause a revaluation of the Treaty of Versailles. The following quotation is characteristic of this new attitude:

"After all the Peace Treaty was less catastrophic than [German] nationalism likes to portray it. Certainly it was a punitive peace, garnished with many senseless humiliations which operated as constant irritants; but it was not a Punic Peace, such as Imperial militarism, gone stark mad, tried to impose on temporarily defeated Russia and Rumania in Brest Litovsk and Bucharest (1917-1918) or as Nazi militarism, as briefly, we hope, forced upon Czechoslovakia and Poland (and other conquered countries). The Peace settlement of 1919 left intact Germany's national unity and allowed the defeated nation to work out its own internal solution without manifest interference."[3]

The Treaty of Versailles signed. After obtaining the Treaty the German government balked at what it considered its outrageous terms. The menace of Allied invasion gave it no alternative but to sign, and the government therefore instructed its delegates to accept the Treaty for Germany "without abandoning her view in regard to the unheard of injustice of the conditions of the peace." On June 28, on the anniversary of the assassination of Archduke Francis Ferdinand and in the Hall of Mirrors at Versailles where the German empire had been proclaimed in 1871 by the victorious hosts of Bismarck, the ceremony of signing the Treaty was carried out.

During the last stages of the conference Lloyd George apparently began to realize how unfair some of the clauses in the Treaty really were. Another statesman, General Smuts, was outspoken in his criticism of the Treaty. On May 30 the general sent Wilson a communication in which he declared, "I think we should all give the gravest consideration to the question whether our Peace Treaty is within the four corners of your speeches of 1918. Frankly I do not think this is so, and I think the Germans make out a good case. . . . All the one-sided provisions . . . and all the pinpricks, with which the Treaty teems, seem to me to be both against the letter and the spirit of your Points."[4]

Other World War treaties. Treaties were also concluded with the rest of the Central Powers. In the case of Austria-Hungary these legalized the nationalist movements of Czechs, Poles, and Slavs and transformed the empire into the states of Austria and Hungary (see map, page 317). By the treaty of Saint Germain Austria was reduced from 116,000 to 32,000 square miles and in population from 28,500,000 to 6,000,000. *Anschluss*, or union of the Germans in Austria with their kinsmen in the new German republic, was forbidden. The disposition of former Hapsburg territory at the conference created a serious controversy. Italy, taking her stand on the secret Treaty of London, wanted the Adriatic as an Italian lake. In order to achieve this the cession of a slice of the Dalmatian coast and especially the port of Fiume was necessary. This city, however, was the natural port for the newly created state of Yugoslavia and had not been promised to Italy in 1915. Wilson declared that the Italian claim was in flat contradiction to the principle of self-determination, and a controversy ensued which nearly wrecked the Peace Conference. The question of Fiume was finally settled in 1924 by direct Italo-Yugoslav negotiations. Austria also ceded to Italy the south Tyrol district containing 250,000 Germans, an arrangement likewise violating the principle of self-determination. Hungary by the Treaty of Trianon lost territory to Czechoslovakia, Yugoslavia, and Rumania (see map, page 317). Under these arrangements one third of the Hungarian population was placed under foreign rule (see map, page 321). The motto of Hungary following the peace was "No, no, never!"

The Treaty of Sèvres with Turkey required Turkey to give up Arabia, Palestine, Mesopotamia, and Syria and to relinquish control of the Straits, which were to be demilitarized and internationalized. After these terms had been announced an English paper declared, "After five hundred years the Turkish power disappears for all practical purposes." But Turkey refused to accept the terms, and under its great leader Kemal Ataturk succeeded in obtaining more favorable terms by the Treaty of Lausanne in 1923. The Balkans thus continued to be full of international discord as they were before the war.

The Treaty of Neuilly cut off Bulgaria from the Aegean Sea (see map, page 317), imposed an indemnity, and provided for compulsory demilitarization. Bulgaria lost nearly one million of her subjects but did not suffer so severely as Hungary in the loss of land.

The gap between aims and achievements. Such was the general outline of the settlement worked out by the victorious Allies at Paris. The possibility of a permanent peace foundered on the rocks of secret treaties and national interests, and on the whole the peace settlement was inadequate and unrealistic. In the signing of the treaties, "the statesmen had not been equal to the grandeur of events." Nevertheless in evaluating what the Allies did to their foes, one must also consider what the victorious Germans meted out to Russia in the Treaty of Brest Litovsk. Of the great powers who drafted the Treaty of Versailles, the United States alone received no concessions of territory and asked no reparations, but only the payment of loans made during the war.

Results of the war. Out of the conflict democracy seemingly emerged stronger than ever before. In 1914 there had been only two important republics in Europe (France and Switzerland); after the peace settlement there were seventeen. Wilson's insistence upon the self-determination of nations had resulted in an almost universal victory for the principle of national self-determination. For five hundred years larger nations had swallowed their weaker neighbors. In 1750 there were some 350 independent states in Europe. By 1815 this number had been decreased to about sixty, and in 1914 there were only about twenty. Enthusiastic adoption of the principle of self-determination at the Peace Conference, however, reversed this process of unification, and the peace treaties of 1919 increased the number of states in Europe by nearly fifty per cent. While many people welcomed the emancipation of the heretofore submerged nationalities, others were disturbed at what they described as the "Balkanization of Europe."

Moreover the peacemakers at Versailles had not been able to liberate all Europeans from alien rule. The Italians had been given Yugoslavs and Germans, the Poles had within their frontiers a large number of Germans and Russians, nearly a million Bulgars had been distributed among Bulgaria's neighbors, and three million Magyars (Hungarians) had been detached from Hungary (see map). The political frontiers of Europe coincided better than ever before with racial boundaries in 1919, but there were exceptions that in time became sources of infection in Europe and which German leaders later used to advantage.

The war also radically altered the political balance of power. France, not Germany, now enjoyed undisputed political dominance on the continent. After 1919 it was France's desire to maintain the status quo as laid down in the Treaty of Versailles. From a world viewpoint, the war weakened the relative strength of Europe as a whole in comparison with other areas in the world. After 1919 the United States became recognized as the strongest and wealthiest of all nations. The countries of South America and the self-governing dominions of the British Empire assumed a new importance in world affairs. Japan also came out of the First World War with increased influence and prestige, and an appetite for imperial expansion.

Organization and Function of the League of Nations

Development of the League idea. The League of Nations came into existence in the spring of 1919. At that time Sir Eric Drummond was given $500,000 to employ a staff and proceed with the task of building the machinery of the League. Soon the League Secretariat and library were established in a large hotel in Geneva, Switzerland. People all over the world followed these events with keen interest, for this was the first time that such an ambitious scheme in international cooperation had been launched.

The actual organization of the League of Nations was novel, but the idea of such a body had been in the minds of idealists and prophets for hundreds of years. In ancient Palestine the Jewish prophet Isaiah had already prophesied a day when "Nation shall not lift up sword against nation, neither shall they learn war any more." At the close of the Middle Ages, Dante, the Italian scholar and poet, in his work *De Monarchia* (1313) outlined a plan for a united Europe under one benevolent ruler. About the same time the French scholar Pierre Dubois proposed a plan for the abolition of war by means of a league and an international court. Hugo Grotius, whom we have already noted as the founder of international law, discussed methods for utilizing arbitration in international disputes in his treatise *On the Law of War and Peace*. Another landmark in the development of the league of nations idea was William Penn's suggestion, in 1603, that Europe should have a general parliament with arbitration powers. In 1786 the noted English political philosopher Jeremy Bentham published his *Plan for an Universal and Perpetual Peace*. This work suggested the formation of an international court of justice, the limitation of arms, and the abolition of secret diplomacy. The great German philosopher Immanuel Kant, whom we have already met in our discussion of the Age of Reason, wrote two important tracts on the problem of war and peace. Believing that despotic rulers often caused wars, this thinker advocated that democratic government should supersede absolut-

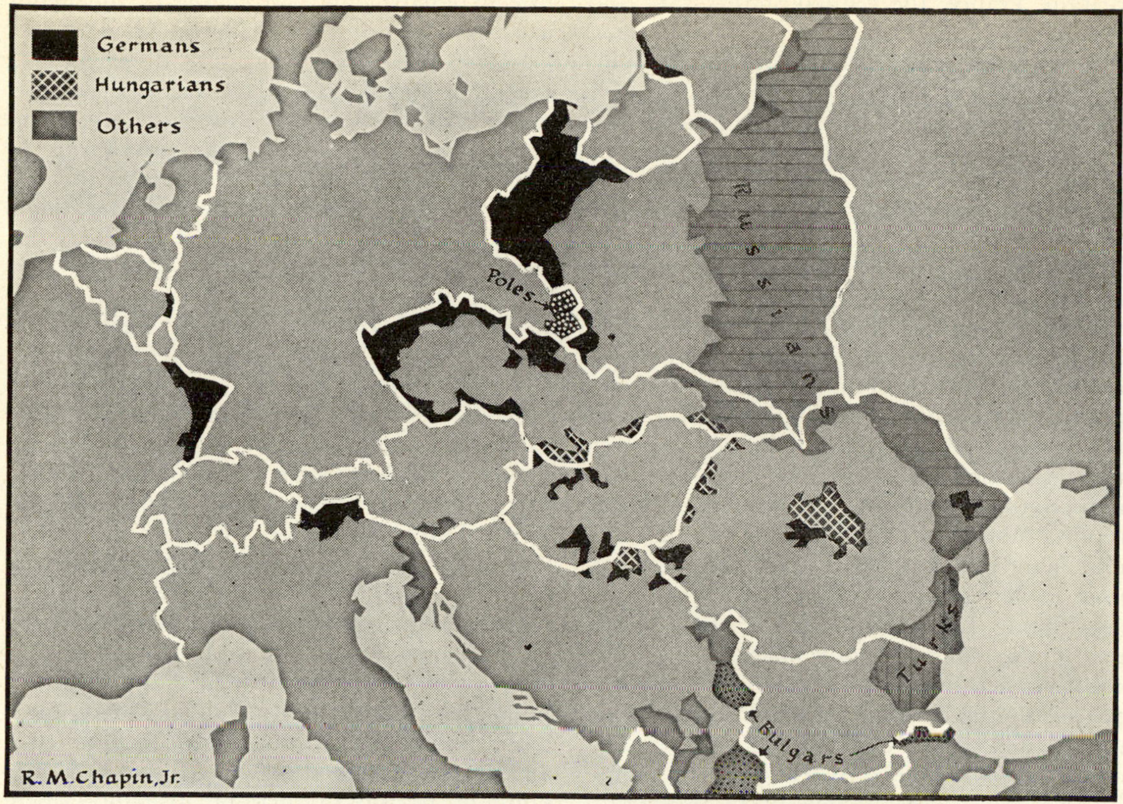

TROUBLE SPOTS IN POSTWAR EUROPE—THE SUBMERGED MINORITIES

ism, standing armies be abolished, and the nations federated into one large group.

During the nineteenth century the peace movement grew rapidly. In 1828 William Ladd formed the American Peace Society. Twelve years later he wrote an important work entitled *Essay on a Congress for the Adjustment of International Disputes without Resort to Arms.* By 1914 there were about 150 peace organizations in the world. During the Great War many of these groups in England and America discussed the possibility of creating some kind of international league following the termination of hostilities. A committee appointed by the British government worked out an elaborate plan for a league of nations. To this scheme were also added the ideas of Woodrow Wilson and General Smuts of South Africa. The British and American contributions were finally merged into a third draft which, with certain changes, became the Covenant of the League of Nations. The Covenant, the constitution of the League, consisted of a preamble and twenty-six articles.

Organization of the League. The three principal organizations of the League of Nations as set up by the Covenant were the Assembly, the Council, and the Secretariat. The first body contained representatives of every member state and held annual sessions at Geneva, usually on the second Monday in September. The Assembly determined the budget of the League, admitted new members, elected the judges of the World Court in cooperation with the Council, and might consider "any matter within the sphere of action of the League or affecting the peace of the world." The Assembly could not make any important decisions without the unanimous consent of its members, and every nation represented in the Assembly had one vote. The public was admitted to plenary sessions of the Assembly upon presentation of cards which might be secured upon request.

The Council of the League of Nations as originally planned was to consist of five permanent and four nonpermanent members, the former representing the great powers (Great

Britain, France, the United States, Italy, and Japan) and the latter the smaller states. Changes were later made in the rules regulating the membership of the Council, so that the permanent members came to number five (without the United States) and the nonpermanent members, nine. In 1936 two nonpermanent seats were added, and the withdrawal of Japan, Germany, and Italy between 1935 and 1939 left the number of permanent members of the Council at three—Great Britain, France, and Russia. After 1929 the Council held four regular meetings each year, usually at Geneva. The general scope of the powers of the Council corresponded to that of the Assembly, except that the former was given more specific duties. Among these were the reduction of arms, the study of the annual reports submitted by the nations holding colonial mandates, and the formulation of measures to be taken to protect any state from aggression. Like the Assembly, the Council might also consider "any matter within the sphere of action of the League or affecting the peace of the world." Each member state represented on the Council had only one representative and one vote. The rule of unanimity prevailed here also except in procedural matters. A smaller body which met more frequently than the Assembly, the Council dealt with most of the emergencies that occurred in international affairs.

The Secretariat represented the civil service of the League. At the head of this permanent staff was the secretary-general, who was assisted by one deputy and three undersecretaries. The personnel of the Secretariat, numbering about 700, constituted the first example in history of an international civil service whose loyalty was pledged to no single nation but to the interests of all nations in common. In 1938 the head of the Secretariat was Joseph Avenol, a Frenchman, assisted by two deputies, one Spanish and the other Italian. The undersecretary-general was British, and a citizen of Uruguay held the post of legal adviser. The chiefs of the principal departments of the Secretariat consisted of two Englishmen, two Italians, an American, a South African, a Dutchman, a Pole, a Swede, a Greek, a Frenchman, and a Dane. The Secretariat handled a tremendous amount of correspondence. All treaties made by members of the League had to be registered with the Secretariat, and its fifteen departments had charge of the many matters of administrative routine arising from mandates, questions relating to disarmament, health problems, the protection of racial minorities, and any other problems, general or special, which the League was considering.

The World Court. In addition to the Assembly, the Council, and the Secretariat, there were two other important bodies which derived from the Covenant of the League. The first of these was the Permanent Court of International Justice, commonly referred to as the World Court. Empowered by article XIV of the League Covenant, a committee drew up a draft for an international court in 1920. Adopted unanimously by the Assembly, the plan provided for a permanent court consisting of eleven judges chosen for nine-year terms. Later the number of judges was raised to fifteen. The Hague was selected as the site of the tribunal. Unlike the court of the first Hague peace conference in 1899, the new World Court was not one of arbitration. Its main purpose was to "interpret any disputed point in international law and determine when treaty obligations had been violated," and it was also competent to give advisory opinions to the Council or Assembly when they asked for them. By 1937 forty-one states had agreed to place before the Court all disputes to which they were a party concerning the interpretation of treaties, questions on international law, problems arising from breaches of international obligations, and the question of reparations arising from such breaches.

The International Labor Conference. The second international body stemming from the Covenant was the International Labor Conference. Pledged "to secure and maintain fair and humane conditions of labor for men, women, and children," this institution consisted of three organizations: the general conference, the governing body, and the international labor office. The general conference was similar in organization to the League Assembly. Each member state sent four representatives to its annual meetings. Two of these four represented the government of the sending state, one represented the employers, and one represented labor. Each delegation voted individually. The most important work of the general conference was in passing recommendations called "draft conventions" relating to working hours, forced labor in colonies, workmen's compensation, labor organization, and many other allied problems. These conventions were then presented to the various governments represented in the International Labor Conference for ratification.

The governing body, which met every three months, and the International Labor Office were similar to the League Council and the Secretariat in organization and function. The governing body was composed of thirty-two members, sixteen representing the governments, eight the employers, and eight the workers. The International Labor Office had a permanent staff which was responsible for research and investigation in labor problems and for the publication of important findings.

Purposes of the League. Some attention has been given to the organization of the League of Nations because, in 1920, it was the first time in history that a carefully planned scheme for the encouragement of international cooperation had been established. Following the Great War the world stood in dire need of such an agency. Misery and confusion were prevalent in Europe. In Poland the peasants were faced with famine, in Russia typhus and cholera stalked through the land, and even the victorious French were faced with the immense task of restoring their devastated regions. At one time more than seventy-five million people were dependent on supplies given by the Allies, mainly the United States. The political scene also reflected chaos. In 1920 Russia and Poland fought a bitter war. The new Russian government was also fighting desperately to eject the pro-czar "White Russian" armies from the country. Greek armies invaded Turkish Asia Minor, civil war caused turmoil in India and Ireland, and in Hungary a Rumanian army had just crushed a strong Communist movement. It was these facts General Smuts had in mind when he declared, "Unemployment, starvation, anarchy, war, disease, and despair stalk the land . . . a large part of Europe is threatened with disaster and decay."

The postwar world, especially Europe, obviously presented serious problems. But it was generally felt that political anarchy and economic confusion rife in certain areas of the globe would gradually be removed by the constructive efforts of the League of Nations. Before tracing the achievements and failures of the League in the decade following the Great War it will be useful to see just how the framers of the League intended it to operate as an agency of international reconstruction. Its purposes may be thought of as fourfold: (1) to prevent war and punish aggression, (2) to organize peace, (3) to assume certain duties connected with the operation of the peace treaties, and (4) to stimulate international cooperation for the removal of economic and social evils and for general humanitarian and cultural purposes.

Preventing war. By Article x of the League Covenant, the member states agreed "to respect and preserve as against external aggression the territorial integrity and existing political independence" of all states belonging to the League. Other articles enjoined the members to accept arbitration in the case of international disagreements, to accept any verdict reached by arbitration, and not to embark on war in defiance of the verdict of the Council.

In answer to any nation embarking on such a belligerent course, Article xvi specifically required the members "immediately to subject it to the severance of all trade or financial relations." The imposition of these "economic sanctions" on an aggressor could also be made more drastic by a decision of the Council recommending military or naval measures against the wrongdoer.

Organizing peace. The second main purpose of the League was to carry on positive activities for peace. The World Court was to be used as a judicial agency to which states could bring their differences. The menace of secret treaties was to be removed by the rule that all League members were to present their treaties to the Secretariat, which was then to arrange for their publication. A very far-seeing clause in the Covenant (xix) recognized that there were certain features in the postwar settlements made at Paris that would sooner or later have to be changed. The Assembly, therefore, "from time to time" was "to advise the reconsideration by members of the League, of treaties which have become inapplicable and the consideration of international conditions whose continuance might endanger the peace of the world." Finally, in its positive and long-term efforts for peace, the League was to strive for arms limitation. The members were, in the words of the Covenant, to "recognize that the maintenance of peace re-

The extreme isolationist sentiment of the twenties is reflected in this cartoon. A salesman offers advice to Yankees embarrassed by international problems, in the form of an etiquette book telling how to behave at a League of Nations party.

quires the reduction of national armaments to the lowest point consistent with national safety."

Other duties of the League. Certain duties connected with the operation of the peace treaties represented a third type of League activity. It was to conduct plebiscites in Schleswig, East Prussia, and Silesia and to be responsible for the administration of the Free City of Danzig; it was to govern the Saar territory for a period of fifteen years, at which time a plebiscite was to be held. It also acted as a supervising body for the mandate system. Each year the nations administering mandates were to present to a permanent mandates commission of the League a full account of their administration of the mandated areas.

The fourth basic purpose of the League was to carry on international humanitarian activities and encourage all types of intellectual and social welfare cooperation among nations. To this end special agencies were established as part of the League machinery, such as an economic and financial organization. Other agencies were created in the interests of health, intellectual cooperation, and the opium evil.

United States' refusal to join the League. In 1919, the year of its establishment, the League, with its high purposes and comprehensive machinery, constituted a most promising agency for improving the status of mankind everywhere. At the very outset, however, the League suffered a blow when the United States refused to enter its membership. During the war Americans took pride in the world-wide acclaim of President Wilson's proposals for a new world order. But the peace settlement as finally worked out pleased few people. Chauvinists found it too lenient, and liberals found it too harsh. Republicans, seeking to discredit Wilson, agitated against it. Returning to the United States in July 1919, President Wilson immediately pressed the Senate for a ratification of the Treaty of Versailles, carrying with it membership in the League of Nations, of course. A strong group of isolationists in the Senate successfully blocked ratification. In desperation, and faced with the wreckage of all his visions of a new world united in a common effort to outlaw war, President Wilson toured the country in September 1919, appealing to the people to support the League of Nations. Not yet fully recuperated from his exertions at the Peace Conference, Wilson could not stand the heavy strain of his whirlwind campaign. He suffered a complete physical collapse and was stricken with paralysis, and with his collapse the opportunity to build a new world order disappeared. Although the retiring President appealed to the nation from his sickbed to make the presidential campaign of 1920 a "solemn referendum" on the question of the League, the election was in no sense clear-cut on this issue. Harding, the Republican candidate, both praised and criticized the League in one and the same breath. As one historian has said, "His masterly obfuscation of the issue was perhaps his supreme intellectual achievement."[5]

Following the Republican victory at the polls in 1920, Wilson lived in retirement until his death in 1924. One cannot help feeling the deep anguish and bitterness in his few last public utterances. Speaking over the radio in November 1923, Wilson declared:

"The only way in which we can worthily give proof of our appreciation of the high significance of Armistice Day is by resolving to put self-interest away and once more formulate and act upon the highest ideals and purposes of international policy. Thus, and only thus, can we return to the true traditions of America."

These words, in most part, fell upon deaf ears. The chaos in international affairs that was to come in the 1930's and the coming of World War II were hidden in the future. Following the easy slogan "Back to normalcy," the mass of Americans lapsed into complacent isolationism and optimistic economic prosperity.

United States' cooperation with the League. The cooperation of the United States with the League was not, however, denied completely. During the postwar period American observers at Geneva followed the deliberations of the Council and Assembly and kept their government at Washington informed. Many of the important conferences held under League auspices, such as those on disarmament, were attended by official representatives from the United States. The United States began to cooperate with the advisory opinion committee as early as 1923 and took a vigorous part in the activities dealing with the protection of women and children. Membership was also accepted in the International Labor Conference, and representatives from the United States made valuable contributions to its work. In February 1939, in a note to the League, the United States said in part: "The League, however, has been responsible for the development of mutual exchange and discussion of ideas and methods to a greater extent and in more fields of humanitarian and scientific endeavor than any other organization in history. The United States Government is really aware of the value of this type of general interchange and desires to see it extended."[6]

The League of Nations in Action

Growth of the League. The refusal of the United States to join the League of Nations was a serious impediment to the successful functioning of the new body. Despite this handicap, however, the membership of the League increased rapidly. In 1920 the original membership was forty-two nations. In 1921 three Baltic states joined, in 1922 Hungary, in 1923 the Irish Free State and Abyssinia, in 1926 Germany. Later, in 1932, Mexico joined the League. Russia entered in 1934. The roster of League membership in 1935 reached the total of sixty-two states.

The Aland Islands affair. The record of the League from 1920 to 1930 was neither a dismal failure nor a complete triumph. In the matter of attempting to prevent war, the League achieved some outstanding successes in certain international disputes and failed miserably in others. The Aland Islands affair can be cited as an example of the former. Lying between Sweden and Finland, the Aland Islands dominate the entrance to the Gulf of Bothnia. These islands and Finland once belonged to Sweden but came under Russian rule in 1809. In 1917, when Russia collapsed, Finland became an independent state and extended her control over them. The following year, Sweden recognized the independence of Finland and made no objection to Finnish control. The Alanders, however, are mainly Swedish and commenced an agitation for union with Sweden. Two unofficial polls showed that a large majority of the inhabitants were not content to remain under Finnish rule. The movement for union with Sweden grew rapidly, and open revolt seemed imminent. The arrest of many of the agitators by the Finnish authorities angered Swedish opinion, and prospects of war became lively.

In June 1920 the League investigated the dispute, and in the spring of 1921 the Council gave its decision. Accepted by both Sweden and Finland, the decision permitted Finland to retain its sovereignty over the Aland Islands. The inhabitants were given local self-government, the use of Swedish in the schools was guaranteed, and the islands were demilitarized. The settlement without recourse to war was indeed a notable achievement of the League.

Boundary settlements. Many of the disputes presented to the League of Nations for settlement concerned boundary problems raised by the peace treaties. After an inconclusive plebiscite in Silesia, the Council assumed the task of determining the boundary between Poland and Germany in this area. Following the investigation of a committee appointed by the Council, the larger part of the area was turned over to Germany, although the most valuable economic resources were awarded to Poland.

In 1921 a serious boundary dispute occurred between Yugoslavia and Albania. Yugoslavian troops crossed into Albanian territory, and there was danger of another Balkan war. The League threatened to impose an economic blockade on the aggressor, whereupon Yugoslavia agreed to accept the boundary line drawn by a delimitation committee of the League.

Two additional boundary disputes were brought to the attention of the League. A serious disagreement in 1924 between Great Britain and Turkey over Mesopotamia, rich in oil, was settled successfully by the action of the Council, and in 1925 the menace of war between Greece and Bulgaria was likewise removed.

When the disputants were small powers, the League was generally able to enforce its decision. When the dispute concerned a major power, the League was not so successful. The success obtained by the League in the British-Turkish dispute was not a conclusive test of its strength because the verdict had been favorable to a great power—Great Britain.

The Corfu incident. Perhaps the most significant test of the League's power in the decade following the Peace Conference was the Corfu incident of 1923, involving Greece and Italy. An international commission had been sent to the Balkans to settle the Greco-Albanian boundary line. During its labors four Italian members of the commission were killed in Greek territory by unknown assailants. Mussolini immediately dispatched a stiff ultimatum to Greece demanding a full apology, a salute to the Italian flag, an inquiry by Greece with the assistance of an Italian official, and the payment of a large reparation. Mussolini had been dictator of Italy at this time for less than a year and saw in the outrage an opportunity to obtain national glory and a diplomatic triumph for the Fascist régime. Greece refused to accept all the terms of the ultimatum, denouncing the demands as "outraging the honor and violating the sovereignty of the State," and appealed to the League. Mussolini thereupon ordered an Italian naval squadron to the Greek island of Corfu to bombard the harbor. Fifteen civilians were killed and many wounded, and Italian marines landed and took possession of the port. Mussolini let it be known that Italy would refuse to be bound by any action taken by the League.

Confronted by this defiance on the part of a great power, the League sought to escape from a serious situation by turning the dispute over to a council of ambassadors. This non-League body ordered a commission to investigate the controversy. In September 1923 the commission presented its report to the council of ambassadors without having discovered who had been guilty of the murders. The council then ordered Greece to pay Italy the sum of 50,000,000 lire. This amount was duly paid, and the Italian forces evacuated Corfu. War had been averted, but many members of the League Assembly were indignant over the handling of the whole affair because the League had allowed Italy to defy it. And many suspected that the evidence obtained by the commission of investigation did not warrant the imposition of such a large indemnity upon Greece. This failure of the League to function successfully in a dispute involving a major power in 1923 was a portent of what was to happen in the period of international anarchy following 1930.

Other League political activities. The effectiveness of the League as a peace agency following the Great War is debatable, but certain of its activities deserve only the highest praise. It supervised the exchange and repatriation of nearly half a million prisoners of war. More than a million Greek refugees expelled as a result of the Greco-Turkish War of 1922 were saved from starvation by the League. By 1928 it had been instrumental in erecting 76,000 houses in Greece for these refugees and settling 143,000 families in the land. Several important loans were floated by Greece under League auspices.

Following the war, Austria and Hungary were faced with financial bankruptcy. In 1922 it became evident that Austria was in danger of imminent economic collapse. Responding to an appeal for assistance, the Council immediately investigated the situation. In October 1922 the League announced that the governments of Great Britain, France, Italy, and Czechoslovakia would guarantee a loan of $135,000,000 to Austria, that a special bank to handle Austrian currency would be set up, and that during the period of the rehabilitation of Austrian finances the various measures recommended by the League to attain this end would be supervised by a commissioner-general who was to be a League official. Valuable assistance was also afforded Hungary. A fifty million dollar loan was obtained, and a special League official was sent to Hungary to supervise certain features of Hungarian finance. Other examples of the League of Nations' financial activities were foreign loans arranged for Bulgaria to enable her to take care of 200,000 refugees, loans to Estonia to assist her in placing her currency on a gold basis, and financial aid to the Free City of Danzig.

Of importance also in assisting the economic reconstruction of war-worn Europe was its work in administering the region of the Saar Basin and the Free City of Danzig. In the Saar until 1926 a pro-French commission created resentment and discontent among the inhabitants. Upon the insistence of Great Britain the situation was investigated, and a Canadian was appointed by the League to head the commission responsible for the administration of the Saar. From this point on, conditions in the Saar improved, and the German inhabitants relaxed their criticisms. In the Free City of Danzig a popular assembly of 120 members and a senate of 22 members were established by the League to administer the city. The port facilities of Danzig were placed under the administration of an equal number of Poles and German Danzigers.

Nonpolitical efforts of the League. More successful than its work in the political field were the League's efforts in the fields of health, humanitarian, and intellectual activity. The health organization at Geneva concerned itself in perfecting hygienic techniques to decrease epidemics in the various nations. Studies of the cause and control of such diseases as smallpox, anthrax, cancer, and tropical maladies were stimulated by the League. The League also investigated the existence of slavery in certain sections of the world, sought to control the traffic in dangerous drugs, and stood ready to offer assistance when great disasters brought suffering and destruction to any portion of the world's population. It published books and periodicals dealing with national and international problems of all kinds, broadcast important information, particularly in the field of health, from its own radio station, and generally was of extreme usefulness in its own technical work. The budget for all its activities, which was subscribed to principally by the members, was more than six million dollars a year.

Problems of Security and Disarmament

The search for security. Following the First World War there was a universal desire of nations for security. France hoped that she could make herself strong enough with the aid of allies and the League to discourage Germany forever from attacking her. Great Britain still retained her faith in a great navy to protect her. Germany was determined to build up her power again so that she could regain her former prestige. In central Europe new states such as Czechoslovakia and Poland, apprehensive of Germany and Russia, also sought to obtain security for themselves. Poland feared Germany and Russia from the start, while Czechoslovakia was worried about Hungarian revisionism immediately after 1920. Despite this common desire of all nations for security it soon became evident that what one nation regarded as security for herself was invariably considered by others as a menace to them.

German response to Versailles. What was the German conception of security? It could hardly be expected that she would remain content with an inferior role in Europe after having been the strongest military power on the continent from 1871 to 1914. Her population was a third larger than that of either France or Great Britain, and her industry was more efficient than that of any country in Europe with the exception, in certain instances, of Great Britain. She was resolved to break the iron ring of unfriendly powers that had been established at Versailles, to rearm, to cancel reparations, to get back her colonies, and to obtain some of the territory—such as the Saar Basin, Danzig, and the Polish Corridor—taken away from her in 1919. Germany never ceased believing that the Treaty of Versailles was unjust, and this belief helped shape her foreign policy to gain strength enough to force a revision of its clauses. When the Treaty was first presented to Germany in 1919, Philipp Scheidemann, the chancellor, declared:

"This treaty is, in the view of the German government, unacceptable, so unacceptable that I am unable to believe that this earth could bear such a document without a cry issuing from millions and millions of throats in all lands, without distinction of party: 'Away with this murderous scheme.' "

Middle Europe's dissatisfaction. In 1920 the attitude of Hungary, Bulgaria, Turkey, and Austria coincided in general terms with the German view. They, too, interpreted security as the right to rearm and regain some of the territory that had been taken away from them. Bulgaria and Hungary, especially, were determined to get back land that had gone to build up the new state of Yugoslavia and enlarge their old rival Rumania. In addition, Hungary had also been forced to cede territory to Czechoslovakia. Turkey was fairly content. Of all the defeated nations, she alone (as will be shown in Chapter 11) had been able to defy the harsh peace terms imposed on her and obtain much fairer treatment in a new agreement. Austria was not so bellicose and bitter as Germany over her peace terms. But there were many Austrians who believed that their country's destiny lay in union with Germany. Furthermore, there were some in Austria who wanted to restore the House of Hapsburg and secure a union with Hungary.

Fear in France. If Germany and her former allies interpreted security as the right to break the peace terms of 1919, France believed that security meant a rigid enforcement of these same terms. The plain truth was that France was afraid. During the past half century German armies had tramped on French soil on two occasions. The disparity between the population of Germany and that of France gave the French great concern as they contrasted their thirty-nine million people with the sixty-two million across the Rhine. As Wilson once said, "France feels an almost superstitious awe of Germany." In view of these conditions, security in French eyes was to be achieved only by keeping Germany disarmed and surrounded by powerful neighbors allied to France.

The new and enlarged states of Europe were the logical allies of France. They, too, feared an Austro-German union and the menace of a rearmed Germany. Czechoslovakia had a few million Germans within her borders. Poland had been rebuilt out of areas previously seized by Russia, Germany, and Austria-Hungary. Rumania had absorbed a large number of Hungarians.

Great Britain's isolation. After the war Great Britain tended to return to the "splendid isolation" she had maintained throughout most of the nineteenth century. Her task had been accomplished when she had joined France and Russia in preventing Germany from becoming too powerful. Now Germany's naval might had been destroyed and her commercial menace to the British Empire removed. Great Britain, therefore, was not greatly concerned with her security. Protected by her great fleet, her far-flung empire and world commerce had little to fear, and as a great industrial power she was anxious that central Europe and Germany should achieve a measure of economic prosperity as soon as possible in order to furnish her with a market for manufactured goods.

Italy's jealousy. Italy was torn by conflicting diplomatic purposes. It was to her interest to uphold the Austrian treaty settlements of 1919, for Austria now constituted a convenient buffer state between Italy and Germany. But many features of the peace settlement nettled the Italians. They were angry with their former allies for not giving Italy a greater share of the spoils and were especially jealous of France's claims in the Mediterranean. During the postwar decade, then, Italy tried to run with the hare and hunt with the hounds. She usually sided with her former allies but was not averse to associating herself with Germany at times.

Thus it was that each of the nations gave a different meaning to "security." In their attempts to achieve it they sometimes acted alone and sometimes made alliances against those they feared. On several occasions they attempted to negotiate directly with their rivals. In the end none of the methods employed produced enduring results in spite of the pacts, alliances, and conferences inside and outside of the framework of the League.

French efforts to weaken Germany. In 1919 France in her quest for security had two objectives: to make Germany pay the costs of the war and to render Germany incapable of challenging the Treaty of Versailles. The first aim, discussed at length later in this chapter, led France to occupy the German territory of the Ruhr in 1923. This action brought about very strained relations between France and Germany during 1923 and 1924. The second aim led France to secure from Great Britain and the United States in June 1919 a guarantee that these two nations would aid France in the event of German aggression. Upon the return of Wilson to the United States, however, the American Senate refused to ratify this pact, whereupon the British also withdrew their ratification.

Overwhelmed by this blow to their hopes, the French set about obtaining allies on the continent. In 1920 a defensive alliance was made with Belgium. Overtures were then made to Poland. This country owed much to France. In 1920 General Weygand and a group of French military experts had helped save Poland from the Bolshevik armies, and at Paris in 1919 France had supported Polish claims in Silesia. After a preliminary agreement in 1921, France and Poland concluded an outright military alliance in 1922 directed against any future danger from Germany. This agreement was buttressed by large French loans and by the assistance of military experts from France.

After the visit to Paris of President Thomas Masaryk and Foreign Minister Benes of Czechoslovakia a treaty was signed with France in 1924. This pact pledged the signatories to take concerted measures in the event of a union between Germany and Austria or an attempt on the part of either Germany or Hungary to restore their ruling houses. Not content with these allies, the French foreign office negotiated similar pacts of alliance with Rumania in 1926 and with Yugoslavia in 1927. These smaller states not only made pacts with France but during 1920 and 1921 also made treaties of mutual assistance among themselves. This diplomatic bloc was known as the Little Entente, and its power rested upon extensive French loans and military collaboration. In place of the perilous diplomatic equilibrium created by the Triple Alliance and the Triple Entente in the years prior to 1914, the new system of alliances dominated by France now tipped the scales heavily in favor of the French (see map, pages 330-331).

The Locarno Conference and conciliation. For five years following the peace settlements, Europe was little more than an armed camp. In 1925 conditions suddenly improved in international affairs. Aristide Briand came to the foreign office in France. Gustav Stresemann held the same position in Germany, and in Great Britain foreign affairs were now handled by Sir Austen Chamberlain. All of these men believed in pursuing a policy of conciliation in European affairs. Stresemann had been a bitter foe of France during the war, but he was now eager to try cooperating with his former enemies. British statesmen for some time had been deploring France's harsh attitude toward Germany, and Briand in Paris was now ready to offer the olive branch to Berlin. In the spring of 1925 Stresemann proposed to Briand that France, Germany, Great Britain, and Italy should guarantee the existing Franco-German and German-Belgian frontiers and agree to settle their differences by arbitration and that Germany and her neighbors should conclude treaties of arbitration. This proposal paved

POSTWAR EUROPE
French alliances encircling Germany
NORWAY
SWEDEN
Oslo
Stockholm
NORTHERN IRELAND
EIRE
GREAT BRITAIN
Manchester
Birmingham
London
North Sea
DENMARK
Baltic Sea
The Hague
HOLLAND
BELGIUM
Berlin
GERMANY
Warsaw
English Channel
Paris
Rhine R.
Prague
CZECHOSLOV
FRANCE
Munich
Vienna
AUSTRIA
SWITZERLAND
Geneva
HUNGAR
Milan
YUGOSL
Belgrade
Marseilles
Lisbon
PORTUGAL
Madrid
SPAIN
ITALY
Adriatic Sea
Corsica
Rome
Balearic Is.
Sardinia
Corfu
Sicily
(Spanish)
MOROCCO (French)
ALGERIA
TUNISIA

White Sea
KARELIA
Archangel
FINLAND
Helsinki
Leningrad
ESTONIA
LATVIA
THUANIA
Vilna
WHITE RUSSIA
R. S. F. S. R.
Gorki
Moscow
Samara
Chelyabinsk
Ural R.
Volga R.
Kharkov
Stalingrad
Astrakhan
UKRAINE
Donets R.
Don R.
Dnepropetrovsk
Dnieper R.
Odessa
CRIMEA
RUMANIA
Bucharest
Danube R.
Sofia
BULGARIA
Black Sea
Caspian Sea
TRANSCAUCASIA
Baku
Ankara
TURKEY
IRAN
IRAQ
SYRIA
GREECE
Aegean Sea
R.M.Chapin, Jr.

the way for a conference held during October of the same year in the little Swiss town of Locarno. For the first time since 1919 the distinction between conquered and conqueror seemed forgotten, and the German delegation was cordially received. Referring to previous conferences, a German statesman at Locarno said, "They treated us decently but never permitted us to forget that we were Huns."[7]

After twelve days of negotiation five treaties emerged from the conference, the most important being a treaty of mutual guarantee. Signed by Germany, Great Britain, Belgium, France, and Italy, this agreement guaranteed the existing frontiers along the Rhine (this was a reaffirmation of the provision in the Treaty of Versailles), provided for a demilitarized German zone fifty kilometers east of the Rhine, and pledged France, Germany, and Belgium not to invade or resort to war against each other except under certain specified conditions. In case of the violation of these pledges the nations signing the treaty agreed to assist the injured party. There were also four arbitration treaties and two bilateral treaties of guarantee.

The Locarno agreements heralded a new era in European affairs. Germany accepted an invitation to join the League of Nations, and there were good grounds for believing that the hatreds of the past war were now on the wane. In referring to the Locarno agreements, Briand eloquently declared:

"Peace for Germany and for France: that means that we have done with the long series of terrible and sanguinary conflicts which have stained the pages of history. We have done with black veils of mourning for sufferings that can never be appeased, done with war, done with brutal and sanguinary methods of settling our disputes. True, differences between us still exist, but henceforth it will be for the judge to declare the law. . . . Away with rifles, machine guns, cannon! Clear the way for conciliation, arbitration, peace!"[8]

The Kellogg-Briand Pact. Three years after the meeting at Locarno an event occurred which seemed to register another triumph for peace and international good will. This was the appearance of the Kellogg-Briand Pact, a general plan for the renunciation of war. Getting the nations of the world to agree to outlaw war was first initiated as a practical movement by a Chicago lawyer whose ideas were presented for the first time in the *New Republic* in March 1918 and whose program to outlaw war secured the support of many eminent men in America.

In April 1927 Briand made a speech in Paris proposing that war be renounced or outlawed between France and the United States. Encouraged by several prominent Americans, Briand sent the draft of a treaty incorporating these ideas to Washington. Mr. Kellogg, then secretary of state, persuaded Briand to make the treaty cover all the great powers. After several months of negotiation, the representatives of fifteen states gathered at the Quai d'Orsay (the location of the French foreign office) to sign the pact. In 1932 President Hoover announced that the treaty had been signed by sixty-two nations. While the Kellogg-Briand Pact (August 27, 1928) had its origin in the movement for the outlawry of war, it merely provided for the renunciation of war as an instrument of national policy. Moreover, there were no provisions for enforcing the agreements made in the pact.

Disarmament proposals. Article VIII of the League's Covenant plainly stated that it was the intention of the members to reduce arms to the lowest point consistent with security. It further empowered the Council of the League to formulate plans for disarmament. The Article also condemned the manufacture of munitions by private enterprise and declared that, as a means of avoiding suspicion and fear, the various members of the League should keep each other informed of their armament plans. The question of disarmament was raised in 1922, but any progress in this direction was blocked by the passage of a resolution stating that no disarmament would be possible until the members were guaranteed security and protection from attack. Thereupon the League attempted to provide security for its members, and when this failed, it tried once more to achieve results by a direct method of limitation. The Council, as stipulated in the Covenant, created a permanent advisory commission on armaments whose members were mainly military experts. These specialists floundered in a maze of military technicalities and made little progress.

When the sixth Assembly of the League met in 1925, it was the common feeling at Geneva that something had to be done about disarmament. Germany had been disarmed in

"It is for peace that this hammer works," read the caption on this French cartoon published in postwar times. The Frenchman (probably Briand) smashes his guns while the English (personified by Sir Austen Chamberlain, left) and the Germans (represented by Stresemann) wait their turn.

1919 with the understanding that other nations would follow suit. The Assembly therefore requested the Council to make a preparatory study of the problem to pave the way for an international conference on disarmament. A preparatory commission was consequently set up to meet at Geneva in 1926.

At the end of a year's study, Great Britain and France each presented a draft convention to serve as a basis for further discussion at meetings of the commission. These tentative proposals for disarmament clashed on nearly every vital point. In counting soldiers France objected to the inclusion of trained reserves, while states which depended on volunteer armies maintained that reserves should be counted as part of a nation's military power. After much wrangling over this question of "When is a soldier not a soldier?" the Commission was again divided on problems relating to naval limitation. The United States and Great Britain wanted total-tonnage restriction, plus a definite tonnage limit for each type of ship. This was opposed by France and Italy. Soviet Russia proposed complete disarmament, a position supported by Germany and Turkey. This proposal did not get very far because the English delegates were suspicious of the Russian government's sincerity. Germany, in the meantime, became more and more rebellious. She had already been disarmed, and she demanded to know why her neighbors could not agree to reduce their armaments. Finally, in 1930 a general scheme for an international disarmament conference was adopted, but so many reservations were made that few people hoped for much in the way of accomplishment when the conference convened.

Progress in the direction of naval disarmament was a little more encouraging. At the end of the war a naval race between Great Britain and the United States was in prospect. Up to this time England had followed the policy of maintaining a fleet equal to the combined navies of the next two naval powers. Following the war she accepted naval parity with the United States, whom she regarded as a friendly power. Differences of opinion, however, still persisted. In 1921, the same year that Great Britain dropped her two-power standard, President Harding called a conference at Washington to consider the problem of disarmament and that of the Pacific.

The Washington disarmament conference. The Washington Conference was a dramatic event in international relations. Apparently without any warning, Secretary of State Charles Evans Hughes dramatically proposed that Great Britain, Japan, and the United States should together scrap seventy-nine capital ships. The United States would have made the greatest sacrifice, thirty of these vessels being hers. This proposal was too radical for adoption, but it served as an effective means of getting the discussion started. In all, seven treaties were signed at the conference, two of which concerned naval armaments. The total tonnage of aircraft carriers and capital ships was limited for the United States, Great Britain, Japan, Italy, and France, in such a way as to make the ratio of naval strength in this class of vessel 5:5:3:1.67:1.67. The powers agreed to a ten-year naval holiday in capital ships and agreed further that no battleship was to be built unless it replaced a vessel twenty years old.

Hence the Washington Conference registered a definite advance in naval disarmament. The largest type ships were kept down to a reasonable limit, but much was left undone. France refused to discuss the limitation of submarines, and no limit was placed upon the building of smaller type naval units, such as light cruisers and destroyers.

The Geneva and London conferences. In 1927 President Coolidge called another conference to convene at Geneva. France and Italy refused to take part in the deliberations. At this conference a serious dispute occurred between the United States and Great Britain on the question of cruisers. Having few naval bases, the United States pressed for the limitation of cruisers which in her opinion ought to be of a large type. With bases all over the world, England maintained that she ought to have small cruisers upon which there should be no limitation in number.

In 1930 another naval conference met in London. This meeting was signalized by a bitter dispute between France and Italy, wherein Italy was unsuccessful in securing naval parity with France. The United States, Great Britain, and Japan settled the problem of relative cruiser strength among themselves, and agreements were also made as to tonnage in cruisers and submarines. That the work of the conference did not rest upon too firm a foundation is apparent from the appearance of the famous "escalator clause," in the treaty. This gave any one of the signatories the right to increase its tonnage of any class of ships in the event it believed that its security demanded such action.

Europe's "high period." The years from 1925 to 1929 have been called Europe's diplomatic high period. Germany entered the League, economic prosperity appeared to be returning to Europe, the frontier along the Rhine was settled by the Locarno agreement, and the nations of the world renounced war. These achievements in postwar international affairs were primarily the work of three men: Gustav Stresemann, German foreign minister from 1923 to 1929; Aristide Briand, French foreign minister almost continuously from 1925 to 1930; and Sir Austen Chamberlain, foreign minister of Great Britain from 1924 to 1929. Stresemann echoed the sentiments of all these statesmen when he said, "Each one of us must first be a citizen of his own country —a good Frenchman, a good Englishman, a good German—as a member of his own nation, but each one also is a citizen of Europe, linked together by the great conception of civilization which imbues our continent."

Undercurrents of trouble. The promise of Europe's high period, however, was not fulfilled. There were many straws in the wind in 1930 indicating that progress in the direction of international amity and cooperation was only superficial. Germany loudly and repeatedly protested against the failure of her neighbors to disarm and simultaneously proceeded to rearm secretly. She had also expected that Locarno and her entry into the League would mean changes in the Treaty of Versailles. France, however, thought that German acceptance of Locarno meant that Germany had resigned herself to the terms of Versailles. Nothing could have been further from the truth.

When the Kellogg-Briand Pact was signed, the nations of the world were lauded for their change of heart. A careful examination of the treaty hardly justifies such enthusiasm. The pact was a declaration only. It contained no provisions for its enforcement. So many informal reservations were made by the various nations as to render it meaningless. Wars of self-defense were not renounced or wars in fulfillment of obligations under a military alliance. Further, such states as Great Britain and the United States both retained freedom of action to exercise force in maintaining their vital interests in certain regions of the world. The United States, for example, would not permit the Kellogg-Briand Pact to interfere with the Monroe Doctrine. Hence a nation could interpret almost any war as being either defensive or related to its vital interests.

By 1930 it was apparent that in the field of politics the statesmen of the world had fallen far short of the expectations of the war-weary world of 1919 and that neither security nor disarmament was in sight.

Problems of Reconstruction and Economic Stability

The cost of the war. The most obvious of the economic consequences of the First World War was the tremendous cost. In 1918 the average daily cost was $224,000,000, or about ten million dollars every hour in the day. The total cost was estimated to be $337,000,000,000. The significance of this sum is not so much in the fact that it had been spent but rather that it had been invested in destruction rather than in the creation of equipment capable of producing wealth.

The shift to a peace economy. The armistice found the world's commercial and industrial structure geared to a war basis. There was an urgent need for getting back to a peacetime economy, which meant the production of peacetime goods instead of munitions, the demobilization of millions of soldiers, and their absorption in the business structure.

It was not easy to return to the prosperous and stable world economy that had been operating before 1914. The conflict had brought about many changes in world trade. Europe in particular had suffered a serious decline in its share of the world's commerce because of war blockades, the reduction of purchasing power on the part of consumers, the loss of shipping and other transportation facilities, and the capture of overseas markets during the war by the United States, Latin America, and Japan. This loss was keenly felt by Germany and Great Britain.

The huge increase in the public debt was a further economic consequence of the war. Germany's national debt increased twenty times between 1913 and 1918 and that of France and Great Britain also mounted, although to a lesser extent. These increases were accompanied in many nations by the circulation of large amounts of paper money not backed by adequate reserves. Tension sprang up between economic groups in the various nations. War profiteers were particularly detested by the people, and labor unions that frequently had made important gains in wages during the war were determined not to give up these advantages when it ceased. For a brief period many of these economic problems were obscured by an artificial postwar boom from 1919 to 1920. The peak of prosperity was reached in 1920. It was followed by a diminution of world trade and industrial activity. Strikes, unemployment, and other industrial problems multiplied, and for the next five years the nations, particularly in Europe, tried to extricate themselves from this economic morass.

The statesmen at Paris had paid little heed to matters of economics. The existence of world economic unity and interdependence had been forgotten or disregarded in the preoccupation with political matters. National boundaries were multiplied by the creation of new states and soon became obstacles to the flow of goods. Moreover, impossible economic burdens were placed upon Germany, one of the world's most important industrial nations.

German reparations. The Treaty of Versailles stipulated that Germany was to pay a preliminary sum of about five billion dollars. In the meantime, the reparations commission was to determine what the total reparations payments should be. By 1921 Germany claimed she had paid, in money and goods, the equivalent of the preliminary sum demanded in the treaty. The Allied powers answered that less than half of the necessary payment had been made. As a means of bringing pressure upon Germany, three of her cities were added to the area of Allied occupation, and a customs wall was erected around the Rhineland in order to obtain additional payments from Germany. The reparations commission (in 1921) fixed the total German reparations as $32,000,000,000. The reparations payments were apportioned among the various Allied nations, France being given 52 per cent and the British Empire 22 per cent.

In August 1921, Germany made a payment of $250,000,000. This reacted disastrously upon her currency system. It was commonly believed that the reparations were impossibly high and that higher tariffs the world over were keeping out German goods. Furthermore Germany had already lost many of her most important economic resources. In 1922 some relief was granted her by the Allies, and she then asked them to extend this relief until the end of 1924. The alarming economic conditions prevailing in central Europe, and Germany in particular, caused Lloyd George to support this idea. Great Britain believed that her own economic difficulties could not be removed until prosperity was reëstablished in Germany.

The French, however, were outraged at Germany's request. They estimated that France had been spending $5700 a minute to restore her devastated regions and pay war pensions while Germany had been paying reparations at the rate of only $381 a minute. The French believed that Germany was able to pay and was deliberately seeking to escape her obligations. Raymond Poincaré, the French prime minister, thought that although France had won the war there was a danger she might lose the peace.

France invades the Ruhr. Searching for a justification to employ force in compelling Germany to make the full reparations payments, Poincaré discovered that the Germans had not delivered to France the stipulated number of telegraph poles as laid down in the Versailles Treaty. Germany was likewise in arrears in the matter of coal and cattle deliveries. This default was termed microscopic by the British, who impolitely referred to Poincaré as "Monsieur Shylock." Undeterred by this British opposition, French, Belgian, and Italian troops marched into the Ruhr district of Germany in January 1923. A sorry state of affairs then ensued. The Germans were scandalized by having French black colonial troops quartered in their towns. The French were determined that the inhabitants should work the industries and mines of the Ruhr for the benefit of France. Defying the French army of occupation, the Germans went on a general strike. All economic life stopped, and many German officials were thrown into prison by the French authorities. Nothing hardened the resolve of Germans to revise the Treaty of Versailles more than this invasion of the Ruhr.

During the winter of 1923-1924 France endeavored to establish a separatist state in the Rhineland which the Germans called a "revolver republic." Subsidized by the French, political agitators were shipped into the Ruhr from all parts of Germany and encouraged to carry on a separatist movement which, if successful, would create a buffer state between Germany and France.

The chaotic conditions in the Ruhr gave the *coup de grace* to the German economic system. The currency completely collapsed. Inflation skyrocketed the marks into the stratosphere. In January 1923, one American dollar was worth 8695 marks; in November of the same year it took 6,666,666,666,667 marks to equal one dollar! Public opinion all over the world was shocked at Poincaré's strong-armed tactics in the Ruhr, and Great Britain was particularly critical. The French, meanwhile, were learning that they "could not dig German coal with French bayonets." Following the fall from power of Poincaré in 1924, the French government signified its desire to settle its difficulties with Germany, whose leaders were equally anxious to negotiate.

The Dawes Plan for reparations. An international committee of economic experts was accordingly set up under the chairmanship of the American banker Charles Dawes to examine the whole reparations problem. In the fall of 1924 the Dawes Plan came into operation. No figure was set for the total reparations bill, but the individual payments were decreased and extended over a longer period. A large loan was also floated to aid Germany's economic recovery. On her part Germany ended her currency inflation, and the French reciprocated by evacuating the Ruhr.

The war debt problem. The adoption of the Dawes Plan and the evacuation of the Ruhr eased the tension in Europe. Germany recommenced her reparations payments, made possible only by huge loans from abroad, chiefly America. Referring to the Dawes Plan, James Ramsay MacDonald optimistically declared, "Now we are agreed. Satan only can divide us."

This soon proved to be a vain hope. The reparations burden continued to be denounced by Germans as excessive, and there were many in Europe who shared this view. But the Allied powers would not reduce German payments unless the United States reduced their obligations to her, known as the war debts. During and after the war more than ten billion dollars had been loaned by the government of the United States to the Allies for the prosecution of the war and for purposes of reconstruction. Great Britain, who owed the United States over four billion dollars, had also extended credit to her European allies amounting to more than ten billion dollars. She therefore proposed in 1922 that there should be a general cancellation of all war debts. To this proposal the United States would not agree, but between 1923 and 1925 a series of debt settlements, involving in certain instances generous reductions of interest but not of principal, was made with the debtor European nations. The total amount to be paid to the United States by her debtors amounted to $22,188,000,000.

The question of the war debts proved to be one of the most serious problems in postwar international relations. The Allied powers contended that reparations and war debts were inseparably connected.

They felt that, if Germany's reparations payments were reduced, a similar reduction should be made in the debts owed to the United States. Our stand on the debt question, whether wise or not, undoubtedly made France determined to exact the full reparations bill from Germany. Most Americans were apparently not interested in this phase of the question and accepted Coolidge's comment, "They hired the money, didn't they?"

Tariff Barriers and the War Debts

The disappearance of free trade. During the nineteenth century in spite of the growth of tariffs one could still speak of a world economy in which free trade existed throughout much of the British empire and in which people, goods, and capital moved in comparative freedom over national frontiers in other parts of the world.

Immediately after the war, barriers, mainly in the form of tariffs, began to appear as obstacles to international trade. Instead of buying manufactured goods or commodities where they could be produced most cheaply, nations tried to manufacture or grow them at home even though the cost was greater. They strove for self-sufficiency, or what the economists call autarchy. Those who had suffered from an inability to secure vital foodstuffs and other materials from old sources of supply now determined not to find themselves in the same predicament again. The search for national political security in postwar Europe was accompanied by an attempt to found economic nationalism as well.

The old freedom of international trade was also hampered by the gradual weakening of the international gold standard. During the war many nations had been forced to go off the gold standard. Paper currencies of doubtful value were created, and stability was never completely regained for any great period.

The effect of rising tariffs and other barriers on world trade was particularly strong in the general interplay of international finance and more especially in the problem of reparations and war debts. This happened largely because of the revolution in the relative position of the great powers as debtors or creditors in the field of international finance. Before 1914 France, England, and Germany were all creditor nations with billions of dollars invested over the world, but the United States was a debtor nation to the extent of five billion dollars. After the war the United States became a creditor nation. Germany also changed her position, in this case from creditor to debtor, when the reparations payments were imposed upon her. For the former allies of the United States, outside perhaps of Great Britain, to pay their war debts from accumulated capital (that is, investments made abroad, or gold and silver) was not possible. The only other course available was to sell goods. The United States, however, did not want foreign goods to compete with those produced in her own factories.

United States tariffs. The revolution in the world creditor-debtor situation demanded a shift in trade relationships in order that the debtors could obtain funds to meet their heavy obligations. Unfortunately this shift was not made. Tariffs were raised, and the United States—the greatest creditor nation—led the movement. In 1922 our moderate Underwood Tariff Act was superseded by the Fordney-McCumber Tariff Act, which levied the highest tariff rates in our history. This act had three results, according to most economists: it fostered monopolies at home, it made it difficult for our former allies to pay their war debts, and it brought on tariff reprisals from other countries. Between 1926 and 1930 fifty-seven important tariff revisions were made by the nations of the world, and in most instances the rates were raised. The climax came in 1930 when, contrary to the advice of President Hoover, objections from the American Bankers Association, and a vigorous protest from 1028 American economists, Congress enacted the Smoot-Hawley Tariff Act, which was described by a League of Nations committee as the highest in the world with the single exception of Spain. Within two years twenty-five nations retaliated with discriminatory tariffs against us and against each other, and world trade steadily decreased in volume. In particular, American foreign trade seriously declined.

It should be noted that economists and other groups which opposed the Smoot-Hawley Tariff Act were not attacking the principle of protection in the United States. Although in theory free trade might be a desirable goal for the nations of the world to try ultimately to achieve, under existing circumstances some protection was considered essential. What was criticized was the mounting rate of the tariff in the United States, a great creditor nation.

During the 1920's our former allies paid their war debt installments to us, the funds for this purpose being obtained mainly from German reparations payments. Germany, in turn, was able to meet her reparations payments only because millions of dollars from the United States and Great Britain had been made available in private loans. In view of our high tariff, it was only this economic ring-around-the-rosy that kept reparations and war-debt payments going.

In 1929 Germany's creditors set up the Young Plan to supersede the Dawes Plan. The new plan, which was to run until 1988, provided that Germany should pay a principal sum of $8,800,000,000. The experts who drew up the new schedule of payments believed that Germany would have no difficulty in meeting her obligations thereafter. But within two years the whole world was reeling from the impact of the worst depression of all time, in which the entire structure of reparations and war debts collapsed. Nevertheless, one significant organization developed out of the Young Plan—The Bank for International Settlements. It acted as a channel for the payment of reparations and distribution to the various governments, and although this function ceased when the payments ceased, it continued to serve as a means whereby central banks in various countries could cooperate.

Depression and Economic Nationalism

The collapse of world economy. By 1926 there were signs of a forthcoming collapse of the world economy. Following the economic depression of 1920-1921 in Europe there had been some improvement, but by 1926 unemployment began to be widespread in many European countries. Throughout the world production was in excess of demand, and an alarming glut developed in the wheat, rubber, tin, and copper markets. The condition of the United States was an outstanding exception to the general trend. Prices increased, consumer demand kept pace with supply, and business confidence was unbounded. A wave of optimistic speculation occurred on the stock market. From February 1928 to September 1929 the value of stocks on the New York Stock Exchange increased fifty-one billion dollars.

As long as prosperity existed in the United States, the forces of economic disaster in the rest of the world, especially in Europe, were arrested. American capital in large amounts was readily obtainable by foreign businessmen. These loans, as already noted, were the foundation of the whole system of reparations and war debts, and they also enabled Germany to expand and modernize her industrial production facilities.

The prosperity of the United States, however, was more apparent than real. A large volume of unemployment persisted throughout the 1920's, and an acute condition in agriculture made it increasingly difficult for many farmers to remain on the land when their commodities brought lower and lower prices. The buying power of consumers had been kept up in part by installment buying, much of the wealth was unevenly distributed, foreign trade was decreasing, and stock speculation had become a mania. The crash came in

October 1929, and in a few weeks stocks declined 40 per cent in value, fortunes were wiped out, business confidence was blasted, and the demand for goods was seriously curtailed.

The stock crash had repercussions in Europe. Many short-term American loans in Austria were called in, and this demand threatened the famous Austrian Credit Anstalt Bank with failure. In June 1931 this was averted only by grant of a large credit by the Bank of England. Meanwhile Germany was confronted with a serious economic crisis as foreign investors, disturbed at the trend of events, began to call in their loans. Between July 1930 and July 1931 the German government was forced to issue dozens of emergency decrees, but the economic situation became more and more desperate. By June 1931, the Reichsbank had lost 40 per cent of its gold reserve. In the face of impending disaster President Hoover in June 1931, succeeded in obtaining a moratorium of one year on all intergovernmental debts. In July 1932, at the Lausanne Conference, German reparations payments were practically canceled, the creditors agreeing that future reparations should be reduced to $714,000,000. This drastic step was taken with the hope that the American government would also make a substantial concession in reducing war debts. But our government refused to concede that there was any logical connection between reparations and war debts. And as the depression deepened, our debtors refused to continue their war debt installments. France and other debtors refused outright in 1932, Great Britain and four other nations made "token payments" for a time, then stopped entirely in 1934, and only Finland continued to meet her schedule of payments. Meanwhile Germany had stopped her payment of reparations.

Budget deficits, unemployment, bank failures, decline in industrial production, collapse in commodity prices, and stagnation in trade characterized the world economic picture from 1930 to 1933. The people of many countries suffered from a lowered standard of living and frequently from dire want. This economic collapse was largely the result of conditions created by the First World War—more specifically, to the disturbing effects of the reparations and war debts muddle and the growth of economic nationalism.

Experiments in international finance. During the height of the depression, from 1930 to 1933, each nation tried earnestly to reduce its imports and increase its exports in order to improve its economic position. Competitive devaluation of currency played an important role in this international economic warfare. Japan in particular felt impelled to increase her exports, and to assist in gaining this objective, she depreciated the yen. This move meant that other currencies now had relatively more gold back of them. Being more valuable than the yen, the dollar and the British pound now could command or buy more Japanese goods; or, in other words, the price of Japanese exports was lowered.

Devaluation brought only temporary advantage in most instances. Other countries could play the same game, and so most countries devaluated their currency. In 1934 the United States reduced the gold content of the dollar by about forty per cent. All nations tried to increase exports and at the same time reduce imports. Quota systems were put into operation to control the influx of goods from abroad, and tariffs were boosted to even higher levels. In 1932 Great Britain, after almost a century of free trade, enacted a high tariff. In the summer of 1933, at the World Economic Conference in London, Great Britain, the various dominions, and the colonies agreed to continue the principle of imperial preference initiated at the Ottawa Imperial Economic Conference of the previous year. Imperial preference provided for lower tariffs within the empire than were given to outside nations. The net effect was to encourage trade already in existence between members of the empire but to make it more difficult for non-imperial trade to hurdle the tariff barriers now set up around the British Empire.

The abandonment of gold. Before the First World War, the flow of goods from one country to another had meant that in the last analysis each country imported about the same value of goods and services as it exported. When this balance of international payments was disturbed, a nation would export gold to her creditors to make up the difference. The loss of gold was not serious, however, as creditor nations were eager to lend capital. If a country had an unfavorable trade balance in one area of the world it was quite likely to be more than made up in another.

The depression, by preventing the natural flow of world trade, caused nations to husband their gold reserves. This trend was also strengthened by the fact that the world's gold supply was most unequally divided: the United States had more than half, and another quarter of the gold was held by Great Britain and France. By going off gold, nations could devalue their currencies, thus encouraging foreign buying and stimulating exports. These conditions led to the abandonment of the gold standard by many nations, including Great Britain in 1931 and the United States in 1933. Without gold as the controlling medium of exchange in world trade the practice of barter became more and more prevalent in international trade. This technique was especially utilized by Germany.

Attempts at recovery. The disastrous consequences of world depression led to the calling of the International Economic Conference in London in 1932. Here a report was presented showing that thirty million persons were then unemployed in the world, that the price of raw materials had depreciated more than fifty per cent, and that wheat in particular had dropped to the lowest price in the last four centuries. Little was accomplished, however, by the delegates in London. Currencies were not stabilized, the reparations and war-debt problem was not ironed out, and nothing was done to encourage the return of economic good will among the nations.

During the next six years, 1933 to 1939, recovery was sought not through cooperation but rather by attempts on the part of each nation to fend for itself. Most of them refused to buy except what was absolutely essential, yet all of them tried to achieve the maximum of exports. Seeking economic recovery, particular nations experimented with various national programs—the British with tariffs and subsidized agriculture and the United States with the New Deal. In other countries more drastic politico-economic programs were launched. Most important, the dire economic emergency was seized upon as a justification, and perhaps an excuse, for programs of military aggression.

Capitalism on Trial

Capitalist economy questioned. The depression had serious effects not only upon the international economic structure but upon the domestic economies of the various nations as well. Confusion reigned in economic relations between countries, and within the boundaries of nations people became dismayed and embittered by their misfortunes. In particular, there was growing criticism of capitalism. In the fifty years before 1914 capitalism had been subjected to a certain amount of regulation to adjust gross inequalities of wealth, assure some measure of economic security to the workers, and protect the general public from fraud. These reforms were useful to a certain degree, but they were largely nullified by the disturbing consequences of the First World War—by unemployment, poverty, and business depression. Many critics of capitalism in the postwar period decided that tinkering with the old system would not do and that capitalism must be superseded by an entirely new system.

World depression produced radical criticism and also led many with moderate views to admit that serious weaknesses existed in capitalism. Five weaknesses were singled out.

The business cycle. The first criticism aimed at capitalism was the persistence of the business cycle. Under the capitalist system, economic activity has followed a definite rhythmic pattern in which periods of economic prosperity and collapse alternate. In America, for example, there have been fourteen important business cycles since 1875, and each follows the same course of events: (1) prosperity, (2) the crisis, (3) depression, (4) recovery, and a return to prosperity which forms the first phase of another cycle. Without warning to most people the "crash" comes with suddenness and intensity, bringing unemployment, sweeping away savings, and even reducing millions to the point of starvation. Then out of depression springs recovery, and another business cycle is born. Much study has been given to this cyclical aspect of business, and many theories have been advanced in explanation. Some economists find the cause in fluctuations of the climate; others emphasize the rather intangible psychological factor of periodic waves of business optimism and pessimism. Perhaps the most important school, however, sees the business cycle with all its attendant evils as a natural outcome of the capitalistic system. The workers produce more goods than can be consumed with their inadequate wages. Surplus stocks of goods pile up, and a depression results. This last school sees a more or less planned economy as the only means of checking the ups and downs of business.

Unemployment. Unemployment was the second serious evil in the existing economic system. In 1929 it was estimated that in the past ten years there had been an average of 2,300,000 persons unemployed in the United States. Numerous factors explain this serious condition: (1) cyclical unemployment because of periodic depressions, (2) "stop-watch unemployment" caused by the introduction of efficiency-expert controls into industry, (3) amalgamation unemployment brought about by the fusion of small business units into one great merger, and (4) above all, technological unemployment through the displacement of man-power by new machines. A United States Senate committee of investigation, in referring to technological unemployment, declared that "seven men now do the work which formerly required 60 to perform in casting pig iron; 2 men now do the work which formerly required 128 to perform in loading pig iron; 1 man replaces 42 in operating open-hearth furnaces. A brickmaking machine in Chicago makes 40,000 bricks per hour. It formerly took one man eight hours to make 4501." This explains why, in spite of the fact that American industry increased its productivity at least fifty per cent between 1919 and 1929, there was a definite decline in the number of workers employed. During the period of apparent prosperity in the United States from 1923 to 1928 there was a drop of twelve per cent in employment in the manufacturing industries.

Control by a few. A third serious evil in the economic structure was the increasing tendency for business under finance capitalism to be controlled by a few great corporations which in turn were dominated by a relatively few stockholders. It has been shown that out of 200 of the largest corporations in the United States only 0.7 per cent control half of the corporation assets, one third of the business wealth, and about one fifth of the national wealth. Further, within these great corporations power is often wielded by a small inner group. Frequently the possession of as little as five per cent of a corporation's total stock permits the holders to dictate policy and also wax fat on the profits.

The maldistribution of wealth. Closely connected with this evil was the fourth problem, the unequal distribution of the wealth. It is generally agreed that the standard of living of the people of America is higher than that in any other part of the world. Yet in 1918 the following figures show a surprising maldistribution of the national income. In this year 152 persons received a million dollars or more in income, and 5442 received incomes of one hundred thousand dollars or more. Less than 900,000 got more than five thousand dollars, and only five and one-quarter million persons obtained more than two thousand dollars. Thirty-two and one-quarter million citizens received incomes of less than two thousand dollars. Recent studies show little improvement. In 1928 more than sixty per cent of American families received less than two thousand dollars a year in income, yet the United States government has estimated that no family of five can maintain itself reasonably well on an income of less than two thousand dollars. The critics of the capitalist system especially emphasize the twin evils of unemployment and inequality of wealth and point out how illogical poverty and want are in countries such as America, where foodstuffs are abundant and where the factories could produce an output of goods sufficient for all.

Industrial warfare. The fifth great weakness of the capitalist system was adjudged to be industrial warfare. In most of the industrialized countries of the world a continuous struggle has been going on between the workers and the owners of business. To obtain wage increases the workers have organized unions. This collective action has been met by management through the formation of trade and manufacturing associations in order to present a united front. Strikes by the workers have been answered by lockouts by the employers, and the use of strikebreakers by management has led to picketing by the strikers. Often bloodshed resulted. There has been no neutral body armed with sufficient authority to say what a fair return to management and labor should be in most of the industrialized countries of the world. The only alternative was industrial warfare, which utilized the same weapons of violence and might as were employed in the international sphere in disputes between sovereign states. It is true that certain countries, especially Australia and

New Zealand, were experimenting with compulsory arbitration in labor disputes, but the progress was slow.

By the end of the first decade after the war, neither nations nor men had found lasting economic security or prosperity. The nations of the world were growing further and further apart economically after a half century of growing economic interdependence, and people everywhere began to question capitalism.

Summary

The most interesting as well as most promising development in the decade following the First World War was the establishment of the League of Nations. During the decade from 1920 to 1930 the League acted successfully on several occasions to remove threats to peace. When a crisis arose involving a great power, however, as in the Corfu affair with Italy, the League was less successful. On the whole the record of the League in trying to establish and maintain world peace was not spectacular, but there were sufficient achievements to justify some optimism for its ultimate success. If the political activities of the League were not all they might have been, in the realm of nonpolitical affairs a much more convincing record appeared. Work in the field of public health, the efforts of the International Labor Conference to improve the conditions of labor the world over, control of the drug traffic, and many other solid achievements all testified to the League's contributions in eliminating evils which had been obstructing man's social welfare.

Encouraging as some of the League's activities were, this new body did not bring about the elimination of power politics. France, in particular, confronted by a restless and potentially powerful Germany, put her trust in her army and in a great system of alliances. Great Britain put her main reliance in her fleet. As the first postwar decade ended, it was obvious that international good will and the prospects for a lasting peace were both on the wane. Several disarmament conferences failed, and Germany resented the refusal of the great powers to rectify some of the injustices of Versailles. Then, too, she wanted to regain her former position of prestige and power and strove by every means possible to gain that end.

In the sphere of international economics, recovery in the postwar period was considerably hindered by the problem of reparations and war debts. The strain placed upon international finance by this debt tangle had much to do with the intensification of economic nationalism and the rise of tariff walls. This in turn helped bring on the world economic depression which further increased economic rivalry between nations. International trade decreased, quotas and tariffs were used to restrict imports, and devaluation was resorted to in order to increase exports. The depression also had serious repercussions in the sphere of domestic economy. As unemployment increased and actual poverty and want became widespread, an increasing chorus of criticism was raised against the capitalist system.

If international cooperation had failed to secure a signal success in the political realm, the same failure in the early 1930's was even more evident in the collapse of international trade. The statesmen of the world had failed both to remove the factors that had brought on the First World War in 1914 and, equally disturbing, they had not succeeded in re-creating the relatively free world economy that had characterized business before 1914. This twin failure, in politics and economics, had much to do with the rise of such new national political systems as Russian Communism, Italian Fascism, and German Nazism.

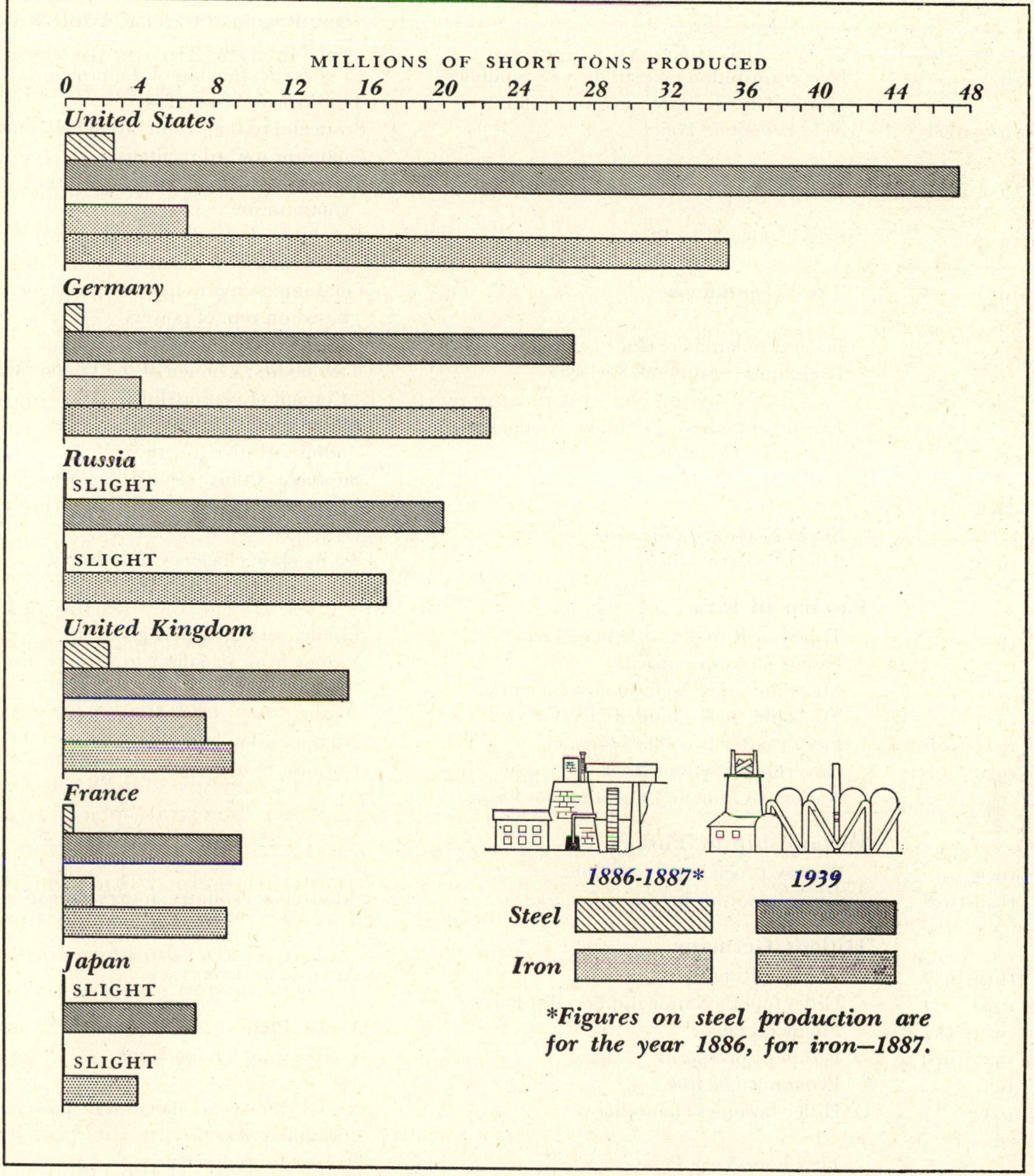

	Communism in Russia	
1917	Revolution	Provisional government under Kerenski
	Lenin's coup d'état	Bloodshed, massacre of czar and family
1918-1920	War Communism period	Allies cooperate with whites, Trotsky organizes Communistic forces
1922	Union of Soviet Socialist Republics created	Four republics: Russian Soc. Federated Sov. Republic, Ukraine, White Russia, Transcaucasia
1924	New constitution takes in the new republics	Creates dictatorship of the proletariat
	Death of Lenin, succeeded by Stalin	Trotsky's ambitions fail
1927-1928	New Economic Policy	Strategic retreat from absolute communism toward capitalism
1928-1933	First Five-Year Plan	Plan for industrialization and return to communism
1933	Second Five-Year Plan	Emphasized production of consumer goods and electrification
1936	Third Constitution	Guarantees more liberal government based on rep. of powers
	Federal union increased to eleven republics	R.S.F.S.R. has dominant position
	Legislature—Supreme Soviet	Two bodies: Council of the Union and Council of Nationalities
	Executive bodies—Presidium, Council of People's Commissars	Latter has highest executive and administrative functions
	Judiciary	Supreme Court elected by Supreme Soviet
	Stalin's "purge" of leaders	
1938	Third Five-Year Plan	To increase efficiency of industry
	Fascism in Italy	
1920	Treaty of Rapallo with Yugoslavia	Fiume, seized earlier, given up
1921	Fascist party organized	Swings from socialism to conservatism
1922	Mussolini asked to form government	
1924	Mussolini makes himself dictator	
1925-1926	Fascist party becomes supreme	No opposition allowed
1926	Government syndicalized	Corporate state established
1930-1931	National Council of Corporations formed	
	Dictatorship in Turkey	
1923	Turkey proclaimed a republic	
1923-1928	Kemal Ataturk becomes dictator	Modernizes country, fosters education
	Hitler's Germany	
1918-1932	Weimar Republic	Attempt at democracy
1920	Hitler founds Nationalist Socialist Party	
1923-1924	Financial chaos	Dawes Plan
1925-1929	Period of prosperity	Founded on foreign loans
1931	Economic collapse	
1933	Hitler becomes chancellor	Voted four-year dictatorial power—Enabling Act
	First Four-Year Plan	To restore prosperity
1934	Blood purge	Hitler becomes president
	Persecution of Jews and religion	Control of education
1936	Second Four-Year Plan	To set up autarchic state

CHAPTER 11

New Patterns in Statecraft

ONE of the immediate results of the First World War was the apparent triumph of democracy. In 1918 there was a firm belief that the extension of this form of government would bring peace and prosperity to the world. Hence out of the ruins of war in Europe there emerged a dozen or more new democratic states, including Germany, all with parliaments and other adjuncts of democracy.

The world as remade by the statesmen of 1919, however, soon proved to be unsatisfactory for the struggling new governments. The preceding chapter showed that developments from 1920 to 1930 largely added up to two failures: first, failure to reduce national rivalries and to substitute an effective system of collective security in the hands of the League of Nations; second, failure to remove barriers to world trade and international cooperation in the sphere of world economics.

It was partly out of this unhappy situation and partly out of the First World War itself that new patterns of government emerged. Confronted by unemployment and starvation and often by the ineffectiveness of their elected leaders, the people of some countries turned to totalitarian régimes. These countries had certain basic similarities. They were similar in that they created strong, authoritarian leaders, men who were able to secure a following by their persuasive oratory, by their ability to organize a new party, or by the formation of attractive programs of reform. Another common feature was the submergence of the individual into the mass and the glorification of the state over everything else. Political liberty was reduced, and obedience to the leader and to the party became the first charge of every citizen. The exaltation of nationalism, as we shall see in a later chapter, led in some cases to aggression and conquest.

This chapter deals mainly with the development of the three most important authoritarian states in Europe, but it will also discuss briefly the achievements of dictatorship in Turkey. The advance of dictatorship in Japan will be considered in Chapter 13. We shall see how the collapse of the czar's government in 1917 paved the way for Russian Communism, how the difficulties of postwar adjustment in Italy led to Fascism, and how the German republic, after a struggle to establish itself, collapsed in 1933 during the world depression and was superseded by National Socialism.

Communism in Russia

The régime of Nicholas II. As the First World War drew to a close the triumph of democracy seemed assured. Soon after fighting ceased, however, a reaction against democratic institutions arose in Europe and elsewhere. In the Balkans, Russia, Poland, Turkey, Italy, Iran, and finally Germany, some form of strong centralized government prevailed sooner or later. The earliest and one of the most significant of these was the government of Russia, a gigantic socio-economic experiment. About one hundred seventy million people are embraced by this new state, in an area more than twice the size of the United States and having natural resources greater than all the rest of Europe (see map, page 409).

In 1914 the Russian government was still in the hands of an irresponsible clique of nobles. The czar, supposedly all-powerful, was in reality often controlled by a small circle in the imperial court. Most notorious of his advisers was Rasputin, who exercised a malignant influence over the royal family. This evil person, reputed to be a monk, was able at times to control government policy through his influence over the czarina. When an army general complained of Rasputin's influence, the czar is reported to have said that he would rather have "five Rasputins to one hysterical woman."

In any event, Nicholas II showed little capacity for guiding his country. Instead of soliciting the support of the Russian legislature, the *Duma,* he ignored and weakened it. Growing Russian industries had created a working class restless and rebellious because of low wages and intolerable working conditions. Strikes took place more and more frequently, and in July 1914 serious labor troubles broke out. The peasants were also dissatisfied. Land reform, in their opinion, was necessary to break up large estates and to distribute agricultural returns more equitably. Several political parties had developed in opposition to the existing régime. Most important of these was the Social Democratic party organized about 1890 by George Plekhanov.

Mensheviks and Bolsheviks. The Social Democratic party espoused Marxian Socialism and worked not only for the overthrow of the czar's government but also for the destruction of capitalist society in Russia. The party carried effective propaganda to the workers and organized meetings in other countries where the delegates would be safe from the Russian secret police. In 1903 an important conference was held in London. Here the organization split into two factions over the methods required to attain the Socialist state. The Mensheviks, led by Plekhanov, believed Socialism should grow gradually and peacefully, that it should "sprout under the shell of capitalism," using constitutional means. The Bolsheviks, led by Nikolay Lenin, advocated forcible methods because they believed the Socialist state could never be achieved through seeking parliamentary majorities. Lenin thought that the capitalist system, including parliamentary government as it then existed, must be overthrown by revolution. To gain this end, the Bolsheviks must bore from within, filling the workers with discontent against their employers, the bourgeoisie. Lenin's goal was rule by the working class, or, in a phrase borrowed from Karl Marx, "the dictatorship of the proletariat." When this was achieved, the capitalist class would be eliminated and all industry would be taken over by the workers' government. It was believed that the best time to accomplish a workers' revolution was during a national crisis, especially during wartime.

Although the Bolsheviks, or Communists as they were called after 1918, repudiated the democratic state and planned to establish a dictatorship, they differed fundamentally from the Fascists in Italy and the Nazis in Germany. Italy and Germany, as we shall see, would maintain a permanent dictatorship of the state and severely restrict the exercise and scope of individual freedom. The Russians, however, held that the dictatorship of the proletariat was only a temporary condition and that the final goal was a society in which the state would practically disappear. Lenin, following the ideas of Karl Marx, published his famous work, *The State and the Revolution*, in 1917. Here he made it clear that the dictatorship of the proletariat was only a transitional stage between capitalism and pure communism. Lenin asserted that "the toilers need a state merely for the suppression of the resistance of the exploiters."[1] Gradually the state would "wither away," dictatorship would disappear, and an absolutely classless society, with practically no machinery of government, would emerge. "In a classless society . . . the state, that instrument of coercion, will be both unnecessary and impossible."[2] When this stage is reached, according to Lenin, it will be possible "for society to inscribe on its banners: 'from each according to his ability: to each according to his needs.' "[3] In other words, the Fascists and Nazis looked upon dictatorship as an end in itself, while the Bolsheviks considered it as a means to an end.

The Russian revolution. The First World War pitilessly exposed the inefficiency of the czarist government. The battle of Tannenberg, in 1914, was only the first of a series of defeats for the Russian armies. Medical supplies were inadequate, and the plight of the wounded was horrible. An adequate supply of munitions was not always available. The railroads were disorganized, and the transport system was unable to carry the burdens imposed upon it by the war. As early as 1915 it became apparent that the czar's régime was nearing disaster, but a request from the *Duma* for more power in order to improve conditions in the field and at home met with a brusque refusal from the czar.

On March 3, 1917, a strike occurred in a factory in Petrograd. Within a week nearly all the workers in the city were idle, and fighting broke out in the streets. On March 11 the czar ordered the members of the *Duma* to go home and the strikers to go back to work. These orders precipitated the revolution. The *Duma* refused to disband, the strikers held great mass meetings in defiance of the government, and the army openly sided with the workers. Encouraged by the army's support, the *Duma* selected a committee to head the revolution. At the same time the radical Socialists in Petrograd formed a Soviet (Council) of workers and soldiers' deputies to oppose the czar. On March 14 a provisional government headed by the moderate liberal, Prince Lvov, was named by the *Duma*, and the following day the czar abdicated in favor of his brother, Grand Duke Nicholas, who refused to accept the throne.

Thus far the revolution had been, on the whole, peaceful. Dominated by liberal middle-class representatives, the *Duma* hoped to achieve a political but not an economic revolution. On the other hand the Bolsheviks in the Petrograd Soviet were determined that there should be a thoroughgoing change in keeping with the teachings of Marx. Nevertheless, for a few months the radical Soviet cooperated with the provisional government. In July Lvov was succeeded by A. F. Kerenski, who was more progressive than his predecessor but not radical enough for the Bolsheviks. While the government of Kerenski marked time, the Soviet in Petrograd extended its organization. All over the country local Soviets were set up. Assisted in part by funds from Germany, the Bolsheviks created effective propaganda under the slogan of: "Peace, Land, and Bread."

Lenin's coup d'état. It was fortunate for the Bolsheviks that at this time they had two great leaders. Nikolay Lenin was spirited out of Switzerland by the German government and taken in a sealed railroad car across the Russian border. Leon Trotsky, another refugee, managed to make his way to Petrograd from the United States, where he was living when the 1917 revolution occurred. In addition to these two capable leaders, the Bolshevik cause was materially strengthened by the presence of such men as Stalin, Bukharin, Kamenev, Kalinin, and Rykov.

In April 1917, Lenin declared in the Russian press that the war was an imperialist conflict between bourgeois interests, that the provisional government must go, and that its place must be taken by a republic of Soviet workers. After much maneuvering behind the scenes and several false starts, the Soviets carried out a *coup d'état* on November 6 and 7. The provisional government was overthrown, Kerenski was driven from power, and a central executive committee of the Soviets assumed control. Lenin had accomplished an amazing feat. With a party estimated to have had only thirty thousand members, he had gained control of a country of more than one hundred fifty million people, using audacity, splendid organization, and astute propaganda.

During the course of the second revolution in Petrograd, disorder and massacre were prevalent throughout Russia. Soldiers shot their officers, members of the nobility were liquidated, and peasants massacred their landlords. The royal family had been arrested in March 1917 and later sent to Siberia. In the summer of 1918 the approach of a pro-czar White army sealed the fate of the royal prisoners. On July 18, the royal family were herded into a cellar, so the story goes, and shot.

War Communism. The history of Russian Communism can be divided into four periods. The introductory period, lasting from October 1917 to the middle of 1918, saw the Bolshevik Revolution and Lenin's rise to power. The second period, extending from July 1918 to 1921, is known as the epoch of War Communism. In July 1918, the Communists established a constitution based on the following principles: (1) the dictatorship of the proletariat, (2) the nationalization of the land, (3) the nationalization of the banks, (4) compulsory labor, (5) free education for all, and (6) the establishment of absolute Communism.

Having set up the new structure of government, the Communists made peace with Germany in the treaty of Brest Litovsk in 1918 and turned to domestic problems. Industry was chaotic, many people were starving, and hostile armies, the so-called White forces, were being formed to overthrow the Communist régime. The Allies blockaded Russia and landed troops to cooperate with the White Russians. At the height of the crisis Lenin appointed Trotsky to organize and direct the Communist forces. Allied intervention caused the patriotic Russians to forget their differences, while skillful propaganda spurred the morale of the people to great heights. By 1920 the White armies had been scattered or destroyed. Much of this success is attributed to Trotsky who, like Carnot of the French Revolution, was the "organizer of victory."

The period from 1918 to 1921 was thus one of suffering and travail for all classes of Russian people. The nobility lost its estates, businessmen were deprived of their positions, private property was abolished, and refugees were scattered over the face of the earth. The peasant and the worker faced starvation and disease. That the Russian people as a whole were able to overcome what seemed to be insurmountable obstacles is a tribute to the leadership of Lenin and Trotsky.

Lenin's leadership. Lenin was born in 1870 in the southeastern part of Russia. His parents were fairly well-to-do. In 1887 his elder brother, whom he greatly admired, was hanged for plotting to assassinate the czar, and this tragedy undoubtedly stimulated young Lenin's antipathy against the government. After being expelled from a Russian university for radical views, he went to St. Petersburg, where he passed the state bar examinations.

The profession of law had no real attraction for Lenin, who soon became engaged in political activities. After a period of banishment to Siberia from 1897 to 1900, he wandered as an exile all over Europe, plotting against the czar's government. In 1917 the German government, hoping to weaken Russian resistance by encouraging civil war, assisted Lenin's return to Russia so that he would be able personally to direct the course of revolution.

When the time came, Lenin successfully undertook the immense task of governing Russia, almost without previous experience in statecraft. But for more than forty years he had been preparing for this opportunity. His success was due in part to his unswerving determination, his firm methods, his absolute integrity, and his devotion to the Communist cause and to the principles of Karl Marx. When he died the Soviet Congress declared: "His vision was colossal, his intelligence in organizing the masses was beyond belief. He was the greatest leader of all countries, of all times, of all peoples."

Trotsky's background. Leon Trotsky was born in Russia in 1879, the son of prosperous Jewish peasants. He ran afoul of the czar's government after his graduation from high school, when he was arrested for organizing a workers' union. Attendance at a university only whetted his impulse toward Socialist agitation, and between 1898 and 1917 he spent four years in prison, was twice sent to Siberia, and for twelve years roamed as an exile. Trotsky was an excellent orator, but he was exceedingly vain and erratic. It is said that Lenin appreciated his gifts but never quite trusted him.

The New Economic Policy. From 1918 to 1921 the Communists attempted to apply undiluted Communist principles to the Russian economy. Banks, railroads, and shipping were nationalized, money economy was restricted, and all private property was abolished. Strong opposition to this program soon developed. The peasants wanted cash and resented having to surrender their surplus grain to the government. Many laborers grumbled at being conscripted to work in the factories, and former business managers showed little enthusiasm for administering enterprises for the benefit of the state. In the face of such opposition the Russian economic system was threatened with collapse. Mutinies became more frequent, and cries of "Down with the Soviet Government" were heard. Despite strenuous opposition from his colleagues, Lenin decided to make a strategic retreat. He felt that the Communists had been too eager to change everything at once, and he therefore inaugurated the New Economic Policy (NEP), which permitted a return to certain practices of the capitalist system.

This retreat from War Communism is the third phase in Russian Communism. The NEP was in operation from 1921 to 1928. The peasants, after paying a tax, were permitted to sell their surplus produce. Retail trading was also permitted. Small factories were returned to the management of private individuals, and a graduated wage scale was granted to the workers. This compromise proved highly beneficial. Industry revived, but there was criticism from the simon-pure Communists against the wealthy peasants, the *kulaks,* who benefited from the new order of things, and against the private businessmen, who were dubbed Nepmen.

The introduction of the New Economic Policy was Lenin's last work. For three years he worked unceasingly. In May 1922, a stroke stopped him, but he rallied and managed to carry on. In March 1923, a second stroke shattered his health, and he died in January 1924. The tomb where his body was placed became the Mecca for thousands of devout followers who came each year to pay their homage at the leader's bier

The rivals: Trotsky and Stalin. The death of Lenin brought with it the great question of his successor. Trotsky was the best known Communist after Lenin and naturally expected to step into his shoes. But Joseph Stalin had his own views on this subject. Born in the Caucasus in 1879, the son of a lowly shoemaker, Stalin was sent as a youth to a seminary to be educated for the priesthood. Socialist propensities resulted in his expulsion. Young Stalin thereupon became a member of the Social Democratic party and between 1902 and 1913 was arrested and imprisoned at least six times. When Lenin died, disagreement over matters of policy broke out between Stalin and Trotsky. Stalin quietly placed his supporters in key posts of the government and assumed the powerful chairmanship (formerly held by Lenin) of the *Politburo,* an executive body of ten members of the Communist party.

On the surface Trotsky seemed more intelligent and brilliant than Stalin, but the stolidness of Stalin concealed great strength of will. Stalin had little trouble in removing his rival. At first he placed him and his followers in minor posts. Then they were sent to remote parts of Russia and finally in 1929 were deported to Turkey. For a time Trotsky lived in Constantinople. Then he moved to France and finally to Mexico City, where he set up a barrage of censure against Stalin and all his works. In August 1940, Trotsky was murdered in his guarded villa by a political enemy.

Russian governmental structure. During the third phase of the evolution of Soviet Russia, that of the New Economic Policy, the system of government assumed certain distinctive characteristics. The Communists started out in 1918 with a constitution establishing a state known as the Russian Socialist Federated Soviet Republic (R.S.F.S.R.). As the power of this government grew and the anti-Bolshevik forces were destroyed, the jurisdiction of the R.S.F.S.R. expanded. In 1922 the Union of Soviet Socialist Republics (U.S.S.R.) was created consisting of four constituent republics: the original R.S.F.S.R., the Ukraine, White Russia, and Transcaucasia. A new constitution was adopted in 1924.

The Soviets. The new constitution established a federal system of government, based on a succession of Soviets, that is, councils of

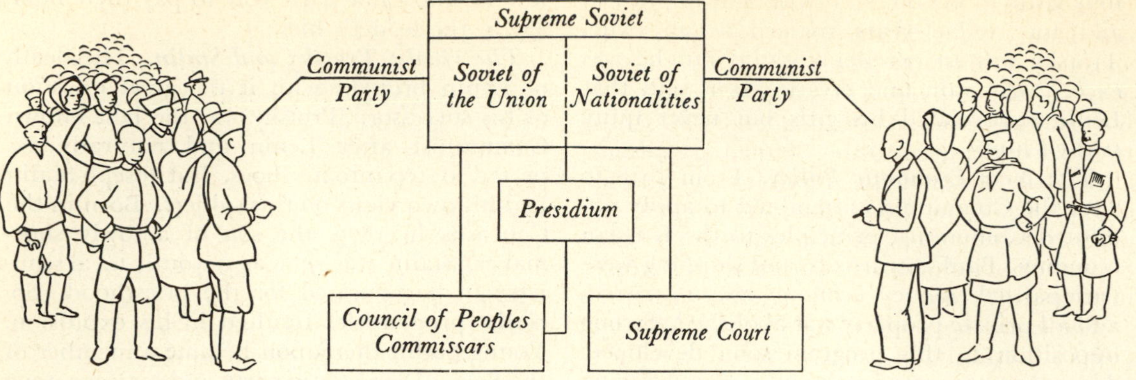

deputies, which were set up in the villages, the factories, cities, and in larger regions. This pyramid of Soviets, found in each constituent republic, was duplicated in the federal government of the Soviet Union. At the apex of the entire governmental structure was the Union Congress of Soviets. The constitution of 1924 brought about the dictatorship of the proletariat. Many persons, such as ministers, monks, members of the former royal family, and private traders, were not permitted to vote. The power of the various Soviets was negligible. They met infrequently and had little to do. There was no separation of powers among the executive, judicial, and legislative branches as exists in the United States. All these functions were exercised by the Union Congress of Soviets and the various bodies it appointed.

While the Union Congress apparently exercised sovereign political power, this body was in reality controlled by the Communist party. The *Politburo* laid down all matters of policy and was the most powerful body in the U.S.S.R. Joseph Stalin held no governmental post; it was his leadership of the party which made him virtual dictator of Russia. Practically all government posts were filled by graduates of the Communist Youth Organization: the Octobrists, the Pioneers, and the Komsomol, which enlist the youth of Russia from the age of eight to twenty-four.

The third constitution. In 1936 Soviet Russia adopted a third constitution, which brought about some notable changes in the machinery of government. This constitution defines the U.S.S.R. as "a Socialist State of Workers and Peasants" (Chapter I, Article 1). Further it declares that "All power in the U.S.S.R. belongs to the toilers of town and country as represented by the Soviets of Toilers' Deputies" (Chapter I, Article 3).

The constitution of 1936 contained provisions guaranteeing a more liberal form of government than had hitherto existed. Articles 118 and 133 constituted a kind of Bill of Rights in which the people were granted and guaranteed such political rights as freedom of speech, of the press, and of assembly. The provisions regulating elections provide for "universal, equal, and direct suffrage by secret ballot," and that all citizens, men and women, who have reached the age of eighteen "irrespective of race or nationality, religion, standard of education, domicile, social origin, property status or past activities, have the right to vote in the election of deputies and to be elected." Many people hailed these guarantees as proof that Soviet Russia was introducing the principles of democratic government as understood in the United States.

The role of the R.S.F.S.R. In structure Soviet Russia is a federal system. By 1936 the original four constituent republics had grown to eleven. (In 1940 the sixteenth was admitted.) Each of these is self-governing in regard to matters of local interest, and each contains smaller administrative areas such as autonomous republics, autonomous regions, territories, provinces, counties, and so on. The government of these local areas is carried on by a hierarchy of Soviets. Because of its much greater size and because it is the center of the most important cities, in practice the R.S.F.S.R. plays a dominant role in the federal union.

How legislation is accomplished. Legislative power in the federal government is exercised by the Supreme Soviet of the U.S.S.R., consisting of a Union Council and a Council of Nationalities. The Union Council is elected by territorial districts throughout the union, one deputy being returned for every area with 300,000 population. The Council of Nationalities is made up of various political divisions. For example, each constituent republic sends twenty-five deputies to the Council of Nationalities, the autonomous republics each send eleven, five come from each autonomous region, and so on. The total membership of the Supreme Soviet with its two houses is slightly in excess of 1100.

The executive bodies. The Supreme Soviet elects a Presidium of thirty-six members which is a kind of executive committee of the larger body. The Presidium carries on the functions of the Supreme Soviet when it is not in session. In case of a deadlock in the Supreme Soviet the Presidium arranges new elections. It convenes this legislature twice a year and ratifies important treaties. The president of the Presidium is the titular head of the Soviet Union and performs some of the ceremonial functions exercised by presidents in western democracies, such as receiving ambassadors.

Similar to the British cabinet is the Council of People's Commissars, which possesses the highest executive and administrative functions. This body is responsible to the Supreme Soviet or to the Presidium when the former is not in session. The members of the Council of People's Commissars act as the heads of the various federal departments, such as defense, foreign affairs, foreign trade, railways, and so on.

The judiciary. The highest judicial tribunal is the Supreme Court of the U.S.S.R., whose members are elected by the Supreme Soviet for a term of four years. The constitution of 1936, unlike its predecessors, is based on the principles of the separation of powers. The Supreme Soviet is responsible for legislation, the Council of People's Commissars is the executive body of the federal government, and the judicial functions are in the hands of the Supreme Court.

The Communist party in Russia. Joseph Stalin has declared that "no one dares to question that our constitution is the most democratic in the world." It is still true, however, that Soviet Russia is a one-party state, with the Communist party effectively dictating the policy of government. This fact is accepted by Stalin in his statement to the Congress of Soviets in November 1936:

"I must admit that the draft of the new Constitution actually leaves in force the régime of the dictatorship of the working class as well as it preserves unchanged the present leading position of the Communist Party."[4]

Article 126 of the constitution gives citizens the right to political expression. The Communist party, however, is the only agency listed through which this expression can be made. At the present time there are about 2,500,000 members in the Communist party, only about 1.5 per cent of the total population. In practice a candidate for a government office is rarely elected unless he is approved by the Communist party. Because Soviet Russia is in essence a one-party state numerous critics maintain there is not much democracy as we know it in Russia. To judge the situation fairly, however, the following facts should be kept in mind.

The Russian ideal. In the United States and Great Britain, as well as in other western democracies, the practice has been to focus guarantees on political bills of rights. In the Soviet Union the main emphasis at present is upon what we may think of as an economic and social bill of rights. Citizens are guaranteed the "right to work." The right to rest and leisure is ensured by a seven-hour working day, annual vacations with pay, and rest homes and clubs for workers. Russians are guaranteed the right to "maintenance in old age and also in the case of sickness or loss of capacity to work." They are granted the right to education, a right ensured "by universal, compulsory elementary education; by the fact that education, including higher education, is free of charge; by the system of state scholarships for the overwhelming majority." Many people recognize that in the western democracies political rights have often been guaranteed in advance of social and economic rights. In Soviet Russia it may perhaps be said that the process is being reversed, that economic rights are taking precedence over political rights. Of course this view assumes that the Soviet state will gradually be democratized politically.

In defending the preëminence of the Communist party, Soviet officials maintain that it would have been impossible to introduce a mature democratic system in the Russia of 1917. Illiterate and confused, the peasants had to be given a program calculated to improve

Students in the Cherepovetz Technical College of Industrial Agriculture (Russia) spend their summers on the state farms, acting as instructors in the use of farm machinery. Here they assemble a tractor.

their status. This program the leaders provided. They were quite sure their program was what Russia needed and, therefore, that its fundamental objectives and procedures could not be questioned. "Thus all discussion and debate must keep within the bounds of the program of the Revolution. There can no longer be any debate as to the possibility of building Socialism, or as to whether what is being built is Socialism. Similarly, the collectivization of agriculture must be accepted as an established policy."[5] Within the framework, however, of the Russian Soviet plan much opportunity is given for criticism and suggestion. Administration of factories can be criticized by the workers, suggestions for improving manufacturing techniques are welcomed, and inadequacies of any industry may be aired. Thus "the mechanical working of the new institutions can be criticized constructively and this discussion is in fact constantly going on. Criticism . . . is developing organically within each group, and throughout these groups on a broader scale. It leads to changes of methods of internal organization, to new emphasis, always however within the established framework. It may in this gradual way bring considerable alterations in the structure and functioning of the various institutions and organizations."[6]

The trials of 1936. Many observers were of the opinion that the constitution of 1936 marked the beginning of a mellowing process in Russia. This belief was somewhat shaken when an epidemic of treason trials began in Russia that year. Violence had never been completely absent in the internal politics of Russia, but in 1936 it suddenly became intensified. Some of the most famous Communist leaders, including several generals, were sent to prison and executed. Stalin has been charged with weeding out these men simply because they differed with him in policy. He is said to have refused them the privilege of just trials. On the other hand, it has been suggested that Stalin found definite evidence that these men were fifth-columnists working with Hitler for the overthrow of the Socialist experiment. Those who explain the purges in this manner point out that when Hitler invaded Russia in the summer of 1941 there were no "Quislings" in the Soviet ranks. Perhaps there is some truth in the French statesman's remark: "In Russia they shot their fifth columnists. In France we put them in the Cabinet."[7] At any rate, the real reason for the executions is not yet a matter of certain knowledge.

Stalin's first Five-Year Plan (1928-1933). Lenin had been forced to give up the experiment in pure socialism and to introduce the NEP, but Stalin was determined that this compromise with capitalism should be swept away as soon as possible. In 1928 he was ready to introduce a program of economic reform which would not only destroy the last vestiges of capitalism in Russia but would industrialize the country almost overnight. His Five-Year Plan envisaged the following: (1) the collectivization of 55,000,000 acres of land into huge government farms, (2) the removal of illiteracy, and (3) the increase of industrial products by 136 per cent, of agricultural output by 55 per cent, of oil and coal by 100 per cent, and of power by 300 per cent. This vast economic program was devised by a State Planning Commission, the Gosplan. Each factory and each farm was given the opportunity to criticize its share in the plan, either to increase or decrease it. For the first time in modern history an economic blueprint controlling the entire business life of a nation had been set in motion. With the initiation of the first Five-Year Plan began a new period, the fourth in Soviet history, called the period of Socialist reconstruction. It was characterized by the advent of economic planning, the collectivization of farming, and the adoption of the new constitution in 1936.[8]

Such a program was bound to impose severe hardships on the people, for they were being asked to concentrate upon industrial equipment and drastically curtail the production of consumer goods. But the leaders succeeded in arousing a militant enthusiasm that gave the Five-Year Plan the appearance of a crusade. Remarkable results were attained. The number of industrial workers doubled, and the total industrial output in 1932 was 334 per cent above that in 1914. The largest tractor factory in the world was erected at Chelyabinsk, the greatest electric power station was constructed at Dnepropetrovsk, and the largest automobile plant was set up at Gorki. All the industries of the country were organized into great government trusts, and the process of collectivizing was pushed in agriculture.

The collective farm, or *kolkhoz*, was created by doing away with the units of land owned by the *kulaks*, established peasants. In the new type of farm thus created, the members work their land as one great unit under the direction of a board of directors. Each family retains its house, its personal effects, and a small garden. Each *kolkhoz* is allowed to work out its own system of payments to members based on what is known as the "labor day unit." At the end of the year the collective farm computes its net earnings in cash and in kind and makes payments to the members on the basis of the number of labor days with which each has been credited.

The *sovkhoz* is the state farm. Unlike the *kolkhoz*, it does not represent the collective effort of a number of peasant farmers but is an outright state farm run by paid laborers. At the present time these state and collective farms comprise nearly ninety per cent of the land under cultivation in Russia.

While the first Five-Year Plan made notable gains, it also produced a number of disturbing results. The quality of industrial products deteriorated, and in 1932 there was a serious shortage of farm products. Erecting new factories was not so difficult, but it was almost impossible to train overnight the technicians necessary to run the new machines. The process of collectivization on the farms caused disorder and opposition among the peasants. During the hectic days of the first Five-Year Plan, huge amounts of Russian grain and raw materials were dumped on foreign markets in order to secure the necessary funds to pay for the importation of industrial equipment.

Cotton farmers belonging to an agricultural union in Turkestan, Asiatic Russia, examine their supply of seed. Part of Turkestan belongs to China, part to Afghanistan, this part (in Usbekistan) to Russia.

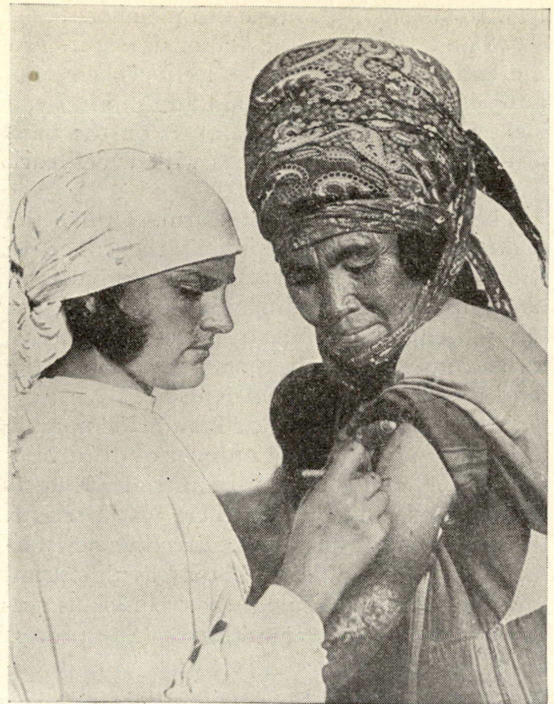

In 1932 Russian doctors vaccinated peasants like this woman from a collective farm in Asiatic Russia as part of the Soviet program for education in modern health methods.

Much of the grain and other products could have been used at home, but the people were convinced that sacrifices had to be made in order to make Russia more wealthy and powerful in the future. In the later stages of the first Five-Year Plan measures were introduced to cope with some of its obvious weaknesses. Differential wage scales were offered the workmen to encourage individual initiative, the unwieldy state farms were reduced in number and the collective farms were increased, and in industry the principle of piecework as a basis for pay was also extended.

The second and third Five-Year Plans. In 1933 a second Five-Year Plan was introduced which had as its goal greater concentration on the production of goods that the people could use and less concentration on making industrial equipment. Special emphasis was laid upon the electrification of the country. Factories were to be expanded for the manufacture of shoes, textiles, canned goods, and candies. A third Five-Year Plan was initiated in 1938, concerned mainly with increasing the efficiency of the industrial equipment setup under the first and second Five-Year Plans.

Many books have been written in denunciation or defense of Soviet national economic planning as exemplified in the three Five-Year Plans. Despite certain failures and weaknesses, it can be said that economic productivity in Russia during the past decade and a half has increased at an amazing pace. Joseph E. Davies, United States ambassador to Russia (1936-1938), writes: "They have painted on a ten-league canvas with a brush of comet's hair."[9]

Russian accomplishments. According to Soviet figures the three Five-Year Plans have resulted in the following accomplishments:

"The share of the U.S.S.R. in total world production amounted in 1926 to 4.7 per cent. In 1936 the level of the world industrial production remained at the 1923 level. But the level of production in the U.S.S.R. increased by 4.6 times, and the share of the U.S.S.R. in world total production now amounts to about 20 per cent. The U.S.S.R. has surpassed Germany in production and now occupies the second place in the world. It is interesting to note the growth in individual branches of industry: in the production of electric power, the U.S.S.R. rose from fifteenth place in the world in 1913, to third place in 1937; in machine building, the U.S.S.R. rose from fourth to second place, having surpassed England and Germany; in tractors the U.S.S.R. occupies second place; and in the production of locomotives, cars and combines, first place in the world."[10]

One of the most important aspects of Soviet Russian policy and one on which it will perhaps ultimately be judged is its national economic planning. The following evaluation of the Russian economic experiment would seem to be an unprejudiced and fair analysis:

"The details of the economic organization which the Communists are evolving—the consolidation of industry into self-governing trusts and syndicates, the cooperative stores and factories, the nationalization of railways, banks, and agriculture—these deserve to be studied and watched without bias and with the closest attention. Above all, the attempt to coordinate the entire industry of a nation as vast as Russia into a unified system, under the agency of the Gosplan (the national economic planning agency), is a daring and gigantic experiment which may prove of great value to the world; for there can be very little doubt that in every nation there is going on an evolution toward greater unification of industry, whether along socialistic or capitalistic lines, and the experience of Russia in attempting to handle so tremendous an organization is sure to reveal much by which others can profit."[11]

The new social life in Russia. Communism has not only revolutionized the economic life of 170,000,000 people through breathtaking industrialization and collectivization; it has, at the same time, brought about equally drastic changes in the environment of men, women, and children, and in their attitudes toward life.

In czarist Russia women in general did not enjoy equality with men. Their education was neglected and their tasks were almost exclusively homemaking and childbearing. The Soviet government encourages girls to secure an education and to go to higher institutions of learning if they wish and if they are qualified. Homemaking is now frequently subordinated to a woman's independent career in the factory or office. As part of the emancipation of women, the government at one time endeavored to diminish the importance of the family as an institution. Efforts were made to shift the center of the people's social life from the home to the Soviet club, an important educational and recreational institution. This policy has been modified in recent years.

To make women more independent of home and family many interesting methods of caring for small children have been introduced. Those with working mothers have been placed in nurseries where they are given scientific supervision, including balanced diets and medical inspection, and are taught to play in groups. Getting a divorce used to be easy in the Soviet Union. In recent years, however, Soviet leaders have felt that this course was sociologically undesirable. Hence divorces are more difficult to obtain today.

Religion in Russia. The Soviet Union has been sharply criticized in the western world for its attitude toward religion. Lenin maintained that religion is "the opiate of the people." Russian churches were stripped of political and educational privileges and deprived of state support. Many critics of Communism called it godless, an attitude which should be qualified. There is little doubt that the Soviet leaders discouraged participation in organized religion, but the churches were not closed. At the outbreak of the Russo-German war in 1941, the patriarch of Moscow prayed for victory for the Russian cause, asking that his followers support Stalin.

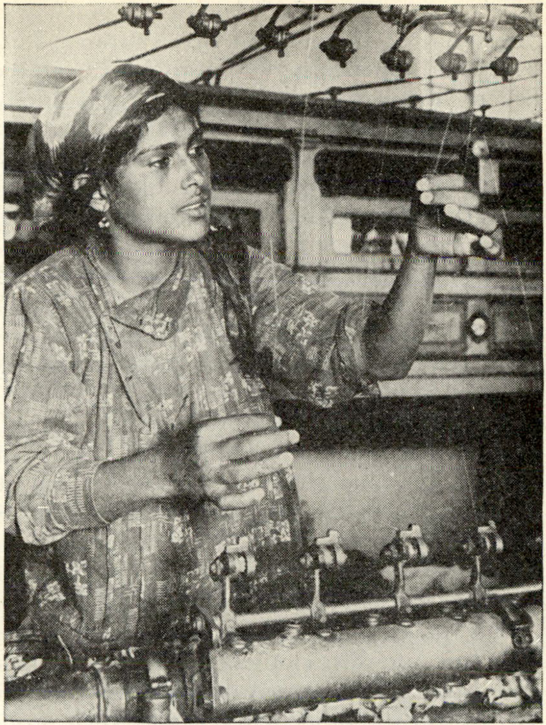

This Turkestan girl has discarded her veil to work in a factory at Samarkand. Here she spins the fine strands from the cocoon into silk thread.

The Orthodox Church of pre-revolution days, thanks to Peter the Great and his successors, was subordinated to the czarist régime and had become its complete tool. In the eyes of the intellectuals the Church stood for the perpetuation of everything reactionary—including resistance to mass education and the condonement of gross superstition, especially among the peasants. Reformers therefore believed that a new social order could be successfully introduced only if all vestiges of the old system were swept away. Today, the Church has no educational or political power, and the leaders of the U.S.S.R. are apparently more tolerant of its religious teachings. The constitution of 1936 declares that "freedom of religious worship and freedom of antireligious propaganda is recognized for all citizens" (Article 124).

The importance of education. Lenin once said, "Give me four years to teach the children, and the seed I shall have sown will never be uprooted." The abolition of illiteracy was made one of the goals in 1927. By 1933 illiteracy had practically disappeared in a country where illiteracy had always been appallingly high. In 1918 8,000,000 children were in school. In 1938 the attendance was estimated to be 38,000,000. Where possible the educational authorities have tried to introduce the latest educational techniques of other countries. The primary purpose of the educational system, it should be kept in mind, is to inculcate Communist ideals. "The educational system frankly rests upon class purposes and is conducted along class lines."[12]

Ownership in Russia. Although capitalism, that is, the private ownership of the means of production, has been abolished in Soviet Russia, citizens can still own certain forms of private property. "The Soviet leaders draw a sharp distinction between ownership of capital for private gain, and ownership of various forms of personal property—houses, books, domestic utensils, clothes, furniture, automobiles, and so on—for private use."[13] A Russian citizen, on the other hand, cannot own property which is utilized to make profits by the hiring of people. The only employer is the state. Real estate for personal use, automobiles, and even government bonds are classed as personal property and may be willed to the owner's children. Outside the cities the average peasant is a member of a collective farm, but he too may own his own home and even have his own garden and a few animals. Eggs, vegetables, and meat produced by the peasant on his own garden plot may be sold and the revenue reserved for his use.

Other reforms. The life of the Russian people has been affected in numerous other ways. The old policy of persecuting national minorities has given way to one of tolerance for the more than two hundred different minority groups, such as Armenians, Jews, Uzbeks, Turks, and Georgians. "Complete cultural autonomy is granted each group; teaching in the schools is in the language of the particular group; newspapers are printed in the various languages; and, for those primitive tribes who had no written language, one has been worked out."[14] Other commendable features of the Soviet system have been the extension of public health programs, the development of large housing projects, and the patronage of science, music, and drama. The number of doctors has increased from about 26,000 before the First World War to over 100,000, and the death rate has decreased from 27 per thousand to 18, with child mortality reduced from 360 to 130.[15]

Mussolini and Italian Fascism

Nineteenth-century Italy. At the end of the nineteenth century Italy faced the future with some fear and disquiet. Political unification had been achieved, and all Italians now lived under the House of Savoy; but unification had not solved the country's most pressing difficulties. Parliamentary government was often ineffectual and sometimes corrupt. The population increased rapidly, and the task of feeding the people was a considerable problem in itself. Moreover, Italy lacked the coal, oil, and iron to make her a strong industrialized nation, although industry had advanced to some extent. Italy, famous for its beautiful ruins, matchless scenery, and brilliant singers, was also the country of the Neapolitan slums—as bad as those anywhere in Europe—of mass illiteracy and grinding poverty.

Italy entered the First World War on the side of the Allies hoping that participation would improve her lot. During the conflict Italy lost 650,000 men. The wounded numbered nearly a million. War expenditures amounted to fifteen billion dollars. But the termination of the war did not bring a solution for Italian problems. On the contrary, it only aggravated them. At the peace conference Italian claims to territory along the eastern Adriatic and in the Near East and Africa were not fully realized. Italian diplomats wasted their efforts on the Adriatic question to the neglect of more important subjects. They insisted that the valuable port of Fiume on the Adriatic Sea should be Italian. While the dispute raged between the Italians on the one hand and the British, French, and Americans on the other, the famous Italian poet and nationalist, D'Annunzio, seized Fiume. In 1920, when a compromise was reached by the Treaty of Rapallo with Yugoslavia, and the Italian government ejected D'Annunzio's forces from the disputed city, ardent nationalists in Italy were infuriated at what they considered an abject surrender of their government to Great Britain and the United States. Many others felt in 1919 that the Allies had been niggardly in the distribution of the spoils. Italian gains in Africa were almost negligible, although the nation acquired nearly 9000 square miles in Europe and more than a million and a half additional subjects.

Incompetent government. Following the armistice in 1918, Italy had five prime ministers in a period of four years. Not one of these leaders demonstrated a capacity for real statesmanship. For example, A. J. Zurcher says of one of them: "Under Facta the Italian cabinet simply abdicated. It had no policy, foreign or domestic; it had not even the firmness necessary to enforce elementary respect for law."[16] In this year a swing toward radical socialism was apparent in the country. The Socialists gained 156 seats in the parliament. Communist propaganda made its appearance in Italy, and "Long live Lenin" was heard frequently in the streets. People refused to pay their rent, workers seized factories, and numerous strikes, accompanied in many cases by bloodshed, occurred.

Conditions went from bad to worse. It was difficult to find employment for the demobilized soldiers, foreign trade was at a low ebb, war profiteers called *pescicani* (sharks) had grown rich at the expense of the masses, the trade unions controlled the railways, and the internal debt advanced six hundred per cent. A desire for strong government grew steadily. The propertied classes wanted protection against radicalism, and the jobless wanted jobs.

Mussolini's background. Italy was soon to have a strong leader, Benito Mussolini. Mussolini was born on July 29, 1883. By hard work and sacrifice he managed to secure an education and finally entered a normal school. He started his career by teaching school at a salary of $10.25 a month.

Mussolini was too tempestuous and ambitious to be cooped up in a country schoolhouse, however. At nineteen he went to Switzerland, partly to see more of the world and partly to escape compulsory military training, for Mussolini was an antimilitarist critic of nationalism and the self-styled friend of the proletariat. In Switzerland he attended several universities and engaged in Socialist activities. After getting into trouble with the Swiss authorities, in 1904, the young agitator returned to his native country. During the next ten years, before the outbreak of the First World War, he made his living from teaching and journalistic activities. He ran afoul of the law in the Tyrol and was ejected from this region by the Austrian authorities. He was imprisoned by the Italian police in 1908 and again in 1911, in the latter case because of his opposition to the war against Turkey in Tripoli, which he criticized as a purely imperialist venture.

By this time Mussolini had attracted considerable attention. Radicals all over the world were following his career with considerable interest. In 1912, in recognition of his accomplishments, he was made editor of the most influential Socialist newspaper in Italy, *Avanti.* When war broke out in 1914, the young editor advocated a policy of strict neutrality. But in a few months he had forgotten about international socialism and become an ardent Italian nationalist. He now demanded that Italy join the war on the side of the Allies. Angered by this about-face, the Socialists ejected Mussolini from the party and from the editorship of *Avanti.* Undaunted, Mussolini proceeded to found another paper, *Il Popolo d'Italia,* and began again to urge Italian entrance into the war. When this event took place, he joined the army, saw active service, and was wounded by the explosion of a trench mortar. After several months in the hospital Mussolini returned to civilian life. Life in the trenches had left its mark on the former idealist and radical, for now Mussolini came back more than ever the nationalist, apparently believing fiercely in his country's destiny.

Mussolini's gifts of oratory, his swagger and bombast, and his physical magnetism were of decided value in his dealings with the Italian people. He revealed himself as much more than a mere demagogue. For a decade and more he proved to be a shrewd diplomat and a capable administrator, although his lust for power and his adulation of war eventually brought misery to the Italian people and contempt for himself from much of the rest of the world.

The birth of Italian Fascism. Fascism in Italy began with organized bands of young interventionists, which appeared late in 1914. These groups were called *fasci,* a name derived from the Latin *fasces,* a bundle of rods bound about an ax, symbolizing the authority of the *lictor* in the days of ancient Rome. In March 1919 Mussolini organized the *fascio* of Milan into a group called the *fasci di combattimento* (the fighting group). A revolutionary program formulated by Mussolini stressed universal suffrage, a heavy inheritance tax, a minimum wage law, a national assembly to work out a new constitution, control of certain industries by the workers, and the annexation of Fiume and Dalmatia. It is interesting that at the outset of Mussolini's career as a Fascist he leaned in the direction of the proletariat rather than toward the bourgeoisie. In November 1921, in a national congress held at Rome, a national Fascist party was established. By this time the Fascists had borrowed from the followers of the poet D'Annunzio the distinctive uniform of the black shirt.

Communists, whose number had continued to increase, now brawled with Fascists, in the autumn of 1920 and throughout 1921. In one city on a single day, twenty-one Communists were killed by the Black Shirts. Fascist squadrons roamed all over the country. Sometimes they acted as genuine preservers of law and order, but just as often they pounced on innocent citizens, insulted them, and even rounded up the police and put them in their own jails. Although Mussolini's original program contained some elements of Socialism, the Fascists soon were posing as the instruments of law and order and the implacable foes of radicalism. According to Mussolini the Socialists had gone too far. Now "it was his *fasci* who became the sword and buckler of the middle class and capitalist counter-offensive against Socialism."[17]

Mussolini comes to power. Amid the fights between Black Shirts and Socialists the established government remained impotent. Mussolini called it "a worn-out democracy." In October 1922 he declared at Naples: "Either the government will be given to us or we shall seize it by marching on Rome."[18] Facta, the prime minister, resigned, and the king telephoned Mussolini in Milan, requesting him to form a government. On October 30 Mussolini entered Rome, where his Fascist militia already were in control, and assumed the head of the ministry.

Although the Fascists are fond of claiming that they saved the country from Communism, authorities are able to show now that there was no real likelihood of Italy's becoming Communist. By 1922 radicalism was declining, and economic conditions actually were on the upgrade. To point out these facts, however, is not to ignore the fact that the Italian people were restlessly seeking some new government. The crosscurrents of public opinion in Italy following the war have been described thus: "The landlords and property holders were much affected by the incidents of the brief reign of radicalism. They were determined that Italy should have a government strong enough to protect private property. The university people, the professionals, and many of the young men were disgusted with the whole trend of events since 1914. They wanted to see a general governmental housecleaning and the emergence of a strong and patriotic administration. The nationalists and ex-soldiers were angered by the thought that the net result of their participation in the war might be an anarchic Italy. They too wanted to see new men at the governmental helm."[19]

Mussolini actually had only six per cent of the seats in parliament to support his policies. His opponents hoped that he would soon make some blunder which would discredit the whole Black Shirt movement. But Mussolini, who had been waiting a long time for this opportunity, played his cards shrewdly and carefully. In 1923 he succeeded in getting a law passed whereby the party with the largest number of votes in a national election was entitled to two thirds of the seats in the Chamber of Deputies. Largely as a result of this law, the Fascists obtained a sizable majority in 1924. It was a year of crisis for Mussolini. The chief opponents of Fascism in parliament were the Socialists. Their leader, Matteotti, constantly denounced the dubious methods of the Fascists. In June 1924, Matteotti was murdered, presumably by Mussolini's clique. A wave of digust swept the country. Nearly all the non-Fascists left the legislature (the so-called Aventine Secession), declaring they would not return until it was purged of Fascist members. Mussolini, however, cleverly wriggled out of the mess and proceeded to make himself a full-fledged dictator.

Mussolini organizes Fascist government. During 1925 and 1926 the cities were deprived of their right of local self-government. Parliament was stripped of its power to initiate laws. Mussolini—now premier—obtained the right to issue decrees having the force of law. He became head of all the Italian armed forces. As the power of the parliamentary system declined, that of the Fascist organization increased. At the top of the new system the Fascist Grand Council became the principal source of authority. The leading member of this body, Mussolini, now assumed the title of *Il Duce*, the leader. Members of the Council occupied the government's ministerial posts, and at one time Mussolini himself had eight cabinet posts. The Fascist party began to run the nation. Membership in the party was open only to those who had come up from, and hence were trained in, the various Fascist organizations; political offices were open only to party members in good standing. Ten thousand local *fasci* had appeared throughout the country, each with a secretary to keep in touch with the central organization.

The Senate and Chamber of Deputies became relatively unimportant, being under the thumb of the Grand Council. The Senate, while completely dominated by the Fascist régime, was permitted to retain its original form. In 1938, however, the national lower house—the Chamber of Deputies—was abolished and the Chamber of Fasces and Corporations established in its place. After this body's 800 members had been selected by the Fascist Grand Council and the Corporations, the Italian voters were given the opportunity of registering their "popular approval in a plebiscite."

Italian Fascism defined. In brief, Fascism today is (1) antidemocratic, (2) an example of what we call the corporate state, (3) ultranationalist, and (4) pledged to imperialism. Fascism has been defined as "the cult of state worship." In the Italian totalitarian state the individual has no existence, no significance, and no rights, except as a member of the state. Blind devotion and unquestioning obedience are exacted from all. In the words of Mussolini, "All in the state, nothing without the state, nothing against the state."

Fascist political theory holds that mere members must not be allowed to rule the state, as in a democracy, but must instead be guided by capable rulers. This élite group of rulers is furnished by the Fascist party. It follows, also, that Fascists cannot tolerate any opposition to their policies. All parties not Fascist have been ruthlessly suppressed, and critics of

At Camp Dux, Rome, Il Duce's monumental bust stands many times the height of a man. The obelisk-like structure is reminiscent of the massive portrait sculpture of the Egyptians.

the new régime have been banished to penal settlements on islands off the southern Italian coast. Censorship of the press has of course been established, and a tribunal for defense of the state set up to punish any individuals not conforming with Fascist practices.

In the Fascist state all the units of local and provincial government are welded into a unified structure dominated from Rome. Fascism, therefore, means the ultra-centralization of government. A new Fascist penal code has been drawn up to insure the security of the Fascist system.

The corporate state. In economic matters Fascism has borrowed from Syndicalism. The Syndicalists, whose main authority was Sorel in France, advocated an economic basis for a nation's political structure. Industrial unions were to be the "cells" of society, and a confederation of these unions, or syndicates, would become the governing body of the state. In such a confederation there was to be no

In pre-World War II days Mussolini's government did all possible to increase the birth rate in Italy, offering bonuses to newly married couples and establishing gifts of money for babies. Interestingly enough, this is a German cartoon.

place for the capitalist because the workers would run the government. In 1926 the Fascists passed a law in which Syndicalism was adapted to their own needs. The economic structure of the country was divided into thirteen syndicates, each representing a major economic activity. Six of these syndicates were formed from the ranks of labor, and an equal number represented capital or management. A thirteenth syndicate was set up for professional men. All syndicates, whether they represented capital or labor, came under the control of the government. Strikes and lockouts became illegal. In the event of an industrial dispute the matter was to be taken to a Labor Court, whose decision was binding.

In 1930 and 1931 a National Council of Corporations was set up, consisting of seven corporations, or divisions, whose members were obtained from the thirteen syndicates mentioned above. In 1934 the nation was reorganized into twenty-two corporations, each of which consisted of syndicates of workers and employers. Every corporation was controlled by the government. Its activities were subject to the approval of the Fascist Grand Council of which Mussolini was the chief official. In addition to the twenty-two corporations there was also created a Central Corporative Committee to harmonize the activities of all corporations. At the head of this economic pyramid sat the Minister of Corporations, a position also controlled by Mussolini.

There is a marked difference in economic theory between the Communist and Fascist states. The Communist state is determined to destroy private capital and liquidate the capitalist-managerial class. The Fascist state, sometimes defined as state capitalism, aims to abolish the class war through cooperation between capital and labor, by the compulsion of the state if need be. In Communist theory labor is the state itself; in Fascism labor and capital are both instruments of the state.

Some of the main economic objectives of Fascism have been to make Italy more self-sufficient, especially in the matter of food; to increase the power resources of the nation; and to expand Italy's foreign trade. A campaign called the "battle of the wheat" increased the home yield of this cereal seventy per cent. Extensive marsh land has been reclaimed and hydro-electric power resources have been increased. To some extent the intention to increase Italy's natural resources was commendable, but the drive was carried on to an extreme and uneconomic degree. Mussolini's desire to attain national self-sufficiency, a policy known in international economics as autarchy, was primarily motivated not by the exigencies of economics but rather by those of war. Many projects were launched to provide for a home supply of materials which could be obtained much more cheaply abroad. But as Mussolini saw the situation:

"Political independence—that is, the possibility of pursuing an independent foreign policy—cannot be conceived without a corresponding capacity for economic self-sufficiency. . . . We must secure in the shortest possible time the maximum degree of economic independence for the nation. . . . This plan is dominated by one premise—the inevitability of war. When? How? No one can say, but the wheel of destiny turns quickly."[20]

Fascism's extreme nationalism. The Fascist state is not only antidemocratic in politics and corporative in economics but ultra-nationalist as well. Passionate faith in and blind devotion to the great destiny of Italy are expected of the Fascist citizen. These requirements are best illustrated by the educational system, which is a medium of national propaganda. The first sentence read by the little children in school is, "Let us salute the flag in the Roman fashion; hail to Italy; hail to Mussolini." All the Italian textbooks have been rewritten to conform with Fascist ideology. These texts teach the greatness of Italy, the nobility of the vocation of a soldier, the virtue of having many children, the necessity of obedience to the state, and the idea that Il Duce is always right.

Italian imperialism. Another important aspect of Italian Fascism is the stress on imperial destiny. Italy must expand or explode, as Mussolini once tersely expressed it. A high birth rate, together with a rather limited territory and meager natural resources, does give a logical cast to Italian imperialism. But it is not so much economic necessity that drives the Fascist state to expand as the belief that such expansion is a manifestation of Italy's vitality and a glorification of Italian nationalism. In the words of Il Duce: "If Italy wants to count for something, she must appear on the threshold of the second half of the century with a population of not less than 60,000,000 inhabitants. If we fall off, gentlemen, we cannot make an empire, we shall become a colony."[21]

Fascism necessitates militarism. The exaggerated nationalism of modern Italy and the determination of its leaders to expand necessitated a strong army and navy, by which Fascism hoped to attain its objectives. War was glorified. Peace became the manifestation of national decadence. In Mussolini's own words: "Only war carries human energies to the highest level and puts the seal of nobility upon people who have the courage to undertake it."[22] The cult of militarism demanded that the youth of the nation be trained and disciplined. Three organizations accordingly were established for this purpose. The *Wolf Balilla* enrolled boys from the age of six to eight, the *Balilla* enrolled those between eight and fourteen, and the Advance Guard included youths between the ages of fourteen and eighteen. What effect the militaristic-imperialistic policy had on modern Italian history will be told as part of a larger story in a later chapter.

The reclamation of the Pontine marshes, malaria-infested since Roman times, is on the credit side of Fascist Italy. Farm crops, vegetables, poultry, and livestock are now raised in this region, within easy reach of Rome. This is a drainage canal.

Fascism has been described thus:

"Signor Mussolini's . . . dictatorship, like others in history has destroyed respect for political morality and constitutional restraint. It has been responsible for the corrosion of civic initiative and the decay of all forms of local self-government. . . . To the dictatorship, too, must be charged the moral or physical exile of Italy's leading intellectuals and the reduction of the people as a whole to a condition of political tutelage which is more characteristic of a medieval despotism than of a twentieth-century commonwealth."[23]

Efficient Turkish Dictatorship

Mustafa Kemal. Simultaneous with Italian Fascism, another authoritarian system developed in a Mediterranean land. This was the dictatorship in Turkey established by Mustafa Kemal, one of the most remarkable persons of twentieth-century Europe. Born in

Sacred to the memory of Kemal Ataturk is this small square with its statue of the great man of Turkey. It stands in the center of a boulevard in Ankara, the modern capital his efforts produced.

1880, Kemal was educated in a military academy and in the staff college in Constantinople. As a young army officer he participated in the revolution of 1908 and distinguished himself as a military expert of the first rank in the war against Italy in 1911 and in the Balkan wars of 1912-1913. In the Gallipoli campaign his leadership had much to do with the successful defense of the Straits against British troops. After the defeat of Turkey the Allies forced the Treaty of Sèvres on the sultan, who sent Mustafa Kemal to demobilize the Turkish troops in Asia Minor. Disregarding his instructions, Kemal reorganized the troops and prepared to defy the Allies. A new government was set up at Ankara. Kemal was selected as president and commander-in-chief. In 1922 a Greek army, invited by the Allies to take over a part of Asia Minor, was forced to withdraw. In the same year the sultan was deposed, and in 1923 Turkey was proclaimed a republic.

Kemal's reforms. The new constitution was democratic in form, but in reality Mustafa Kemal was a dictator who brooked no interference with his plans. His main objective was to modernize Turkey, and under his rule the old institutions and customs of a backward oriental state were transformed or replaced within a few short years. The caliphate, the sultan's spiritual leadership of the Mohammedan world, was abolished. Education was taken out of the hands of the Church and the courts of the Church were discontinued. New law codes were promulgated. Use of the fez and of the veil for women was forbidden. Polygamy was prohibited. In addition the western Gregorian calendar, European numerals, and Latin script were introduced.

A frontal attack was made on illiteracy. Attendance at school was made compulsory until the student had reached the age of sixteen. No field of activity was overlooked by the indefatigable leader, who erected a new capital at Ankara. Turkey was rejuvenated and made more progress in the two decades after the close of the First World War than she had done during the entire nineteenth century. Because of his achievements Mustafa Kemal was called Ataturk, meaning the Father of the Turks.

In modern times such a wholesale adoption of new culture traits is nowhere duplicated except perhaps in Japan. The dictatorship Ataturk established was more palatable than most to those who believe in democratic government, because there is much to show that Ataturk did not think of his dictatorship as an end in itself but as a necessary means to raise his people to that level of education and social well-being which democratic government required. The beloved maker of modern Turkey died in 1938, admired all over the world for his constructive statesmanship.

The Rise of Hitler's Third Reich

The republic of Germany. On November 9, 1918, when the German kaiser abdicated and fled to neutral Holland, the British and French people received the news with deep satisfaction. It was their belief that, if a liberal democratic government could be substituted in Germany for the old imperial autocratic régime, the cause of peace and international good will in Europe would be greatly strengthened. The revolution that caused the kaiser to pack his bags began in the fleet on November 4. The news spread like lightning throughout Germany, and everywhere the authority of the old government crumpled. Five days after the revolt Prince Max, the chancellor, turned his authority over to Friedrich Ebert, the leader of the majority Socialists and a self-taught man of the people. The same day the republic was officially proclaimed.

Germany at this time was in a state of bewilderment. The collapse of the old imperial government, symbolized in the abdication of the kaiser, provoked much disagreement as to what should be substituted in its place. The Communists wanted a complete social as well as a political revolution. The followers of Ebert favored the path of moderation in order to establish a democratic system in which the rights of private property and individual economic initiative would be safeguarded. In December clashes occurred between the Communists, known as the Spartacists, and the followers of Ebert. Early in January desperate fighting took place in Berlin, ending in the annihilation of the Spartacists and the death of their two leaders, Karl Liebknecht and Rosa Luxemburg.

The following week, in a national election to select the members of a constitutional convention, the moderate Liberals, the Catholic Center Party, and the Socialists gained the most votes. The representatives selected by the people then convened to draw up the so-called Weimar constitution. By midsummer of 1919 their work was complete. The new constitution was a remarkable document, the work of men who believed in social and political democracy. It provided for a president, a chancellor who was responsible to the Reichstag, and national referendums. The rights of labor were guaranteed, personal liberties safeguarded, and compulsory education planned for everyone up to the age of eighteen.

Troubles of the new republic. It soon became apparent that it was easier to write a constitution than to make it work. Even while the document was being drafted, in the spring of 1919, counter-revolutions broke out in many parts of the country. These uprisings, mostly the work of Communists, were put down, but not before ten thousand persons had lost their lives. In March 1920 a reactionary leader named Wolfgang Kapp seized Berlin. This revolt, or *Putsch* as it is called in Germany, was a failure. In 1923 Munich became the scene for what appeared to be a comic-opera revolt engineered by a comparatively unknown Austrian named Adolf Hitler. The revolt was promptly subdued and its instigator sent to prison.

No sooner had internal political stability been secured than the new republic found itself confronted with financial problems. In accordance with the Treaty of Versailles, Germany had already made considerable reparation payments to the Allied governments, but these payments were stopped in 1922. During the dreadful days of 1923 when French and Belgian troops occupied the Ruhr, much that was wholesome and substantial in German society was wiped out. Middle-class savings declined because of the inflation of the mark, the moderates in political circles lost their influence to ultra-nationalists and reactionaries, and the republic began to falter. But

Not so long ago Berlin open-air cafes held gaiety and unconcern. Table overflowed table, and greetings were called across the flagstone courtyards. The Kroll Garden was not unlike the restaurant in the plaza at Rockefeller Center, New York City.

the republic was saved and Germany rescued from economic disruption when the French evacuated the Ruhr in 1924, and by the Dawes Plan, which made it easier for Germany to meet her schedule of payments and enabled her to obtain large loans from abroad.

Foreign affairs. There were, too, certain encouraging developments in the field of foreign affairs. From 1923 to 1929 the German foreign minister, Gustav Stresemann, earnestly sought a reconciliation with Germany's former enemies. We have already noted how this statesman cooperated with Briand and Sir Austen Chamberlain in bringing about the Locarno agreements in 1925. In 1926 Germany entered the League of Nations, peace in Europe seemed assured, and the happy prospect was emphasized by the grant of the Nobel peace prize to Briand, Sir Austen Chamberlain, and Stresemann.

The fading of German liberalism. The stability of the new German republic was more apparent than real. Almost from the beginning of the republic the Socialist parties began to lose ground, while the conservatives advanced slowly but steadily. In 1925 the loyal President Ebert died. Into his place stepped no republican. The election of 1925 resulted in the selection of Paul von Hindenburg, a war hero, as Ebert's successor. Many people believed that the new president, a member of the proud Prussian aristocracy, would undermine the republic. But to the surprise of the whole world Hindenburg supported the constitution. The fact remained, however, that the conservative element in Germany had been able to place one of its representatives in the presidential chair.

German democratic inexperience. One of the most important reasons for the failure of the German republic was lack of experience in handling democratic institutions. The principle of proportional representation was carried so far that innumerable separate parties were formed. Only by coalition could government majorities be formed. The liberal elements in Germany were too diverse to remain united and to follow a consistent policy. Moreover, the republic dealt too gently with its enemies, who utilized democratic privileges to get into power and, once in, destroyed the institutions that had allowed them to grow.

Prosperity and depression. During the years from 1925 to 1929, in spite of the political fumbling of the republic, Germany was nevertheless quite prosperous. Tremendous sums borrowed mainly from the United States exceeded the amounts paid by Germany in reparations and enabled the country to go on a spending spree. Extensive housing activity took place, public works projects including city halls, post offices, stadiums, and roads were undertaken, and industry was expanded and modernized. Germany, next to the United States, became the second most powerful industrial nation in the world.

But the collapse of world economy in 1931 brought on an acute financial crisis in Germany as many investors tried to liquidate their German holdings. In July 1931 all the banks were forced to close and disorders took place in many cities. Unemployment rapidly increased until it reached almost 6,000,000 working families. In order to balance the national budget, emergency decrees slashed unemployment benefits and cut wages in some trades as much as 40 per cent. Desperate, jobless workers roamed the streets shouting, "Give us bread." Night after night in Berlin and Munich shootings and fighting took place on the streets as the police and military forces battled hungry mobs.

Ingredients of dictatorship in Germany. It has been customary to ascribe the triumph of Hitler to the economic misery which accompanied the depression. But other nations had depressions as bad as Germany's and did not invariably turn to dictatorship as the way out. The truth is that Nazi Germany is a compound of numerous ingredients, many of which have been in existence in Germany for centuries. Such men as Hegel the philosopher and Treitschke the historian had exalted the state at the expense of the individual. The weakness of the tradition of political liberalism in German history made the success of the Weimar republic doubtful from the outset.

Furthermore, of decisive importance in discrediting the German republic was the legend fostered by the Prussian military clique to the effect that the German army had not really been defeated on the field of battle in 1918. It had, so went the view, been stabbed in the back by pacifist liberals and decadent democrats on the home front. According to one student of German post-war affairs:

"In spite of the elaborate precautions of the constitution to forestall resurrection of a super-government of the army, the militaristic machine remained in fact unaffected by political change. Nothing could please the army leaders more than the 'stabbing-in-the-back' legend invented by nationalistic propaganda, making the Socialists and pacifists alike a convenient scapegoat for the failures of the General Staff. The German people were incapable of accepting defeat and making the best of it. Had Marshal Foch dictated the peace in Berlin, thus driving home the collapse of the army to the masses, perhaps the Germans would have learned their lesson for once."[24] For centuries the German people have been conditioned to accept and even enjoy regimentation. In many Germans, also, there has been evident a strong current of morbidity and mysticism, which was fertile soil for Nazi philosophy with its cult of the Leader, its racial dogmas, and its emphasis upon the injustices of Versailles.

Versailles in particular produced a persecution complex in the minds of many embittered Germans. The mistaken policy of France, as illustrated by Poincaré's invasion of the Ruhr, sowed seeds of hate. The reparations and the war guilt clause in the peace treaty caused further resentment. Some of the vexations and unjust features of Versailles had of course been eliminated by the time Hitler came to power—such problems as reparations, Germany's exclusion from the League of Nations, and the Allied occupation of the Rhineland. But the war guilt clause, Germany's enforced disarmament, the lost colonies, and other grievances still remained. Behind scenes worked the German industrialists, convinced that the republic was not competent to discourage, and if need be stifle, the strong trend toward Communism in certain quarters of the country.

Adolf Hitler's rise to prominence. The historian must take cognizance of all these factors as he mulls over the rise of National Socialism. Perhaps, however, the factor that explains its rise more than any other is Adolf Hitler, its creator and high priest. While it is perhaps magnifying the importance of Hitler, some authorities go so far as to assert that "The National Socialist party and the Third Reich would never have arisen without Hitler."[25]

The future creator of Nazism was born in Austria in 1889. His father was a minor customs official. An orphan at seventeen, Adolf Hitler went to Vienna with ambitions of becoming an architect or artist. Rejected as a pupil by the Academy of Art, he was forced to make his living by painting postcards and doing odd jobs. In 1911 he went to Munich where he earned a scanty living by selling small paintings. When war broke out he joined a German regiment and was sent to France where he served during the entire period of hostilities.

The armistice of 1918 found him in a hospital. When the news of Germany's defeat came he says that he turned his face to the wall and wept bitterly. The authorities in Munich were worried about Communist and other radical plots and hired Hitler after his release from the army as a special investigating agent. In the line of duty he was asked to check on a small organization called the German Workers' party.

After attending several of its meetings, Hitler joined this group. It was not long before he became the leader. In speaking before their meetings, held in various beer halls, he discovered that he possessed remarkable oratorical powers. Hitler's speeches were always compounded of the same elements: hatred of the Jews and Communists, the injustice of Versailles, and the contention that the German army had not been defeated in 1918 but had been betrayed by pacifists and Jews behind the lines.

Birth of the National Socialist party. At a mass meeting in a large Munich beer house, in 1920, Hitler announced to 2000 followers the 25-point program of the National Socialist party, the successor to the small and ineffectual German Workers' party. Among other things the program promised land reform, the nationalization of trusts, and the abolition of all income that was not actually earned. The economic proposals were clothed in generalities, but the demands for a greater Germany which should include all the German-speaking peoples of Europe, the abrogation of Versailles, and the acquisition of land and colonies for the needs of the German people were clearly stated. Thus by the end of 1922 Hitler had become a fairly important political figure. Sometimes he would hire a dozen beer halls and dash from one to the other in an automobile, delivering fiery and eloquent harangues before the various audiences. The swastika, an ancient symbol used by many primitive people throughout the world, was adopted as the emblem of the National Socialist party, now known as the Nazi party. (Nazi is a contraction of *National-sozialistische Partei,* meaning National Socialist party.)

Hitler's Mein Kampf. Meanwhile the Nazi organization grew, and a newspaper, the *Volkische Beobachter* (Racial Observer), was obtained as a party mouthpiece. The brown-shirted Storm Troops were recruited. In November 1923, after the failure of Hitler's Munich *Putsch,* he was sentenced to prison for a term of five years. His quarters were quite pleasant, and, assisted by some of his followers, among them his close friend and confidant, Rudolf Hess, he began to write *Mein Kampf* (My Battle). Before his work was finished his sentence was cut short, and he became a free man in December 1924.

Mein Kampf is an autobiography, a long and involved treatment of the principles and philosophy of Nazism, a statement of the objectives of Hitler's party, and a discussion of the techniques which must be utilized to achieve the desired ends. The book contains a number of observations of interest to us here. (1) History is made by great races. The greatest of these is the Aryan and its most perfect and noble exemplification is the German people whose destiny it is to be the world's foremost people. (2) Mixed nations always deteriorate and come into existence through contact with inferior peoples such as the Poles, Slavs, and, above all, the Jews. In the mind of Hitler the Jew is the arch-criminal of all time. (3) *Mein Kampf* breathes contempt for what it calls decadent democracy and challenges the menace of Communism. The first is the agency of fools, the second the weapon of nefarious criminals. (4) Hitler has little faith in the common people. Only through a great leader can they realize whatever destiny may be theirs. Writes Hitler: "The German has not the faintest idea of how a nation must be swindled if one wants to have masses of supporters." (5) In the realm of foreign policy, expansion is upheld as the rightful outlet of German energy until Greater Germany becomes a state of 250 million souls. (6) Before this aim is attained France, the arch-enemy of Germany, must be destroyed. (7) The main area of German expansion must be to the east, in the Russian Ukraine, and the two main allies utilized by Germany should be Great Britain and Italy. (8) Again and again, *Mein Kampf* heaps scorn on pacifism. War and force are held up as the only method to be used by the

In March 1936 Hitler ordered German troops, here passing in review, to march into the demilitarized Rhineland. The Fuehrer's move disregarded the last repressive clauses of the Versailles Treaty and the Locarno Pact.

strong. (9) Recourse to war had not been proved a mistaken policy by the defeat suffered in 1918, for it was not the collapse of the kaiser's armed forces that led to German defeat but the cowardice and treachery of weak souls within Germany itself.

Nazism grows in power. After his release from prison, Hitler and a devoted group of followers began the huge task of converting Germany to Nazism. His success at first was negligible. In 1925 the Nazi party had no more than 27,000 followers. In the national election of 1928 Hitler won only twelve seats in the Reichstag. So trivial did the Nazi movement seem at the time that when Lord D'Abernon, former British ambassador to Berlin, published his important memoirs entitled *An Ambassador of Peace* he made the following reference to Hitler in a footnote: "He was finally released after six months and bound over for the rest of his sentence, thereafter fading into oblivion."[26] In 1929 a distinguished German scholar, Arnold Wolfers, delivered an address in London on "Germany and Europe" without mentioning Nazism. There was hardly any need to, since Hitler's deputies in the Reichstag at this time numbered twelve. Yet in September of 1930 this number rose to 107!

Once the Nazi movement began to take hold, Hitler and his master propagandist, Joseph Goebbels, utilized every art of persuasion to convert the mass of the people to Nazism. Seldom, if ever, has there been such a propaganda campaign. All over Germany huge meetings were organized. Over each stadium a Nazi aviator thrilled the crowd with his aerobatics. Then thousands of Storm Troops marched in to form a great swastika. Martial music, the roll of drums, the trumpeting of bugles—all these sounds impregnated the air with a stirring martial appeal. No speaker was at first seen on the platform. Suspense grew as a huge spotlight was turned upon the rostrum. Into this beam of light stepped the slight Goebbels. For two hours he poured forth a torrent of eloquence: "Germany is in ruins"—"This is the result of reparations"—"The Jews are behind all our woes"—"It is only the Nazi party that can make Germany strong and prosperous, that will repudiate the reparations, obtain lost colonies, and make Germany's army and navy the fear of all Europe."

Hitler created chancellor. In 1932 when the Austrian-born Hitler became a German citizen, he ran against von Hindenburg for the

Chancellor Hitler greets the aged President von Hindenburg as Germany honors her war dead on National Heroes' Memorial Day, 1934. That is Goering at the left; Admiral Raeder is standing behind Hitler.

presidency of the German republic. Hitler was defeated, but the Nazi party continued to grow. The other political parties refused to join ranks, and it became increasingly difficult for the German ministries based on weak coalition to carry on the government. On two occasions von Hindenburg asked Hitler to join a coalition, but Hitler refused, demanding instead what was equivalent to dictatorial power. At this point a clique of aristocratic nationalists and powerful industrialists of the Ruhr conspired to place Hitler in power as the chancellor. This act they prevailed upon the aged Hindenburg to carry out, and a mixed cabinet of nationalists was created in January 1933 with Hitler at the head. The industrialists and nationalists mistakenly hoped by this maneuver to use Hitler as a means of blocking the growth of radicalism.

Dictator Hitler. Hitler, because he could not control the Reichstag, called a general election for March 5, 1933. During the campaign broadcasting stations were monopolized by Nazi propaganda. Storm Troops bullied and coerced the voters. Just before the election was held, fire gutted the Reichstag building. The mysterious conflagration was blamed upon the Communists, although it was almost certainly caused by the Nazis themselves. After the votes were counted, Hitler controlled 44 per cent of the deputies. To this large bloc was added the support of the Nationalists, another 8 per cent, giving the Nazis a bare majority.

Quickly the Nazi majority passed a law giving Hitler dictatorial power for the next four years. During the debate one of the opponents to the bill cried: "Take our liberty, take our lives, but leave us our honor. If you Nazis really want social reconstruction you would need no law such as this." The world at large, shocked at the creation of the Nazi dictatorship, was nevertheless happy to note that Adolf Hitler in addressing the Reichstag had said: "In the field of foreign relations we desire to live at peace with all nations, but only on a basis of equality. Our hand is stretched out to every people willing to forget the sad past."

Nazi terrorism. Assisted by such lieutenants as Goering, Goebbels, Himmler (head of the dread Gestapo, or secret police), Hess, and Von Ribbentrop, Hitler now ruthlessly smashed and uprooted the democratic institutions by which he was brought to power. All rival po-

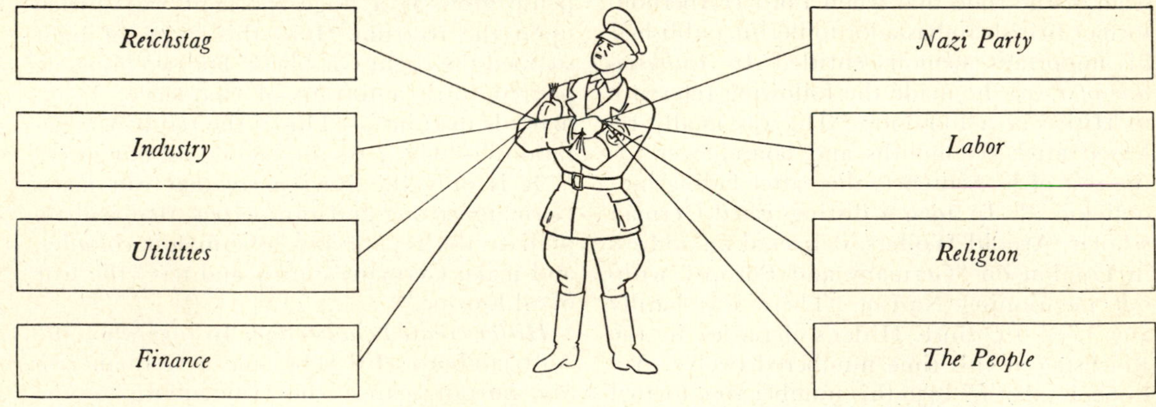

litical parties were disbanded by force, and individuals who had spoken out against Nazism mysteriously disappeared. It has been estimated that 19,000 persons committed suicide in 1933 and that 16,000 died from unexplained causes. Concentration camps were built to house thousands of prisoners, and tales of horrible persecution leaked out of Germany.

In June 1934 the world was horrified at the news of a terrible blood purge in Germany. Disagreement had apparently broken out between Hitler and his old friend and supporter, Captain Ernst Roehm, Chief of the Storm Troops. Without warning Hitler and Goering struck. Roehm, Gregor Strasser, General von Schleicher and his wife, and other leaders were wiped out without trial or ceremony. In the same year President von Hindenburg died, and Hitler became both chancellor and president. It now became common to use the title Führer (leader) in referring to Hitler, and the new régime was described as the Third Reich. Its two predecessors were the ones created by Otto the Great in 962 and by Bismarck in 1871.

It is interesting to note that the old Weimar constitution of the republic has never been formally abolished. The basic constitutional document of the Nazi régime is the so-called Enabling Act, passed by the Reichstag in March 1933. This act gave the executive branch of government the right to legislate by decree. Such decrees could deviate from the Weimar constitution. The Reichstag continued as a phantom legislature, called on rare occasions to pass on acts or policies already in existence. As in Fascist Italy, practically all political power in practice was lodged in and exercised by one political organization, the National Socialist party. "The actual power of the party lies in the fact that it controls the state, while it is itself immune from supervision or interference by the state."[27]

Nazi persecution. In domestic affairs Hitler ruthlessly put into practice his ideas of racial superiority. A national boycott against the Jews was proclaimed in April 1933, and they were barred from public service. Discrimination of all sorts followed. Many noted scholars either were sent to concentration camps or fled the country. Among those fortunate enough to escape were such Nobel prize winners as Albert Einstein and James Franck, physicists, and Fritz Haber, the chemist.

In 1933 fire burst out in twenty different places in the Reichstag, German parliament house, inscribed "The German People." The Nazis are generally credited with starting the fire, although police blamed Communists. Communist or not, a hundred members of the Reichstag were arrested.

Hitler was not contented with racial discrimination alone. All labor unions were disbanded. A new organization, the Labor Front, was set up under Robert Ley, to enroll both workers and employers. The right to strike or to call a lockout was made illegal. Both capital and labor were now subordinated to the state.

Since Nazi doctrine elevated the state above all else, a movement was instigated to subordinate religion to the Hitler régime. Revolting against such pressure, German Protestants, led by the Reverend Martin Niemoeller, naval officer in the First World War, repudiated the attempts of Hitler to interfere with religious freedom. The movement was crushed, and Niemoeller was placed in a concentration camp in the spring of 1938. Perhaps most disturbing to German Christians was the intention of some Nazi extremists to paganize the church. Speaking in 1938 Karl Barth, the noted Swiss theologian, declared: "It is impossible to understand National Socialism, unless we see it in fact as a new Islam, its myth as a new Allah, and Hitler as this new Allah's prophet."

Nazi youth organizations did not train their members in hurling the discus or throwing javelins, but specialized in hand-grenade throwing. It was peacetime, so shovels took the place of guns.

German propaganda and education. Education and public opinion were coordinated for Nazi needs. A Reich culture cabinet was set up to control literature, the press, broadcasting, drama, music, art, and the cinema. All of these agencies were to reflect only one attitude, one pattern of thought, and one stream of esthetic appreciation. Goebbels was given the task of controlling the minds and hearts of the German people with his department of propaganda. From this department, broadcasting stations sent programs abroad, jamming the air lanes to disrupt the broadcasts of other nations. Goebbels also provided radio fare for the German listener and spied on the people to see whether they listened to forbidden foreign broadcasts.

Education especially felt the heavy hand of the Nazis. The German universities, once famous throughout the world for their academic freedom and objectivity of thought, became agencies for propagating such ideas as the racial myths of Nazism. Enrollment in the universities was limited to good Nazi material, and professors were dismissed from their chairs by the score. The school system was integrated with the German Youth Movement, which drilled and regimented boys and girls between the ages of ten and fourteen. The boys were taught above all else to be ready to fight and die for their Führer, the girls, that it was their place to mother the many babies needed by the Third Reich. Care was taken to foster the cult of athleticism. Everywhere physical culture was stressed, many of those physically unfit were sterilized so they could not reproduce their kind, and a race of super-Aryans was supposed to be in the process of creation.

The economy of Nazism. In theory and in outward form Nazism has retained capitalism and perpetuated the institution of private property. Businessmen may still take risks and be rewarded by profits, but both business and labor are rigidly controlled by and subordinated to the state. In the beginning the Nazi program was strongly socialist in tone, but the 25-point program of 1920 was so ambiguous that it enticed the support of the big industrialists, the small businessmen, and a large number of workers. It soon became evident, however, that Hitler had no intention of carrying out all the points of his program. Somewhat as Mussolini had done, he placed the state above both the laborer and the capitalist.

Between 1933 and 1939 unemployment was reduced, but the means to this end are questionable. The middle class was bowed down under a huge tax load, and the national debt was increased one third in order to give employment to the masses, who were put to work in armament factories or drafted for the army. This was, naturally, only a temporary solution of the economic problem. It led logically to the utilization of these vast armaments in aggression against other states, in order to solve other economic difficulties which have continued to grow under the Third Reich.

Nazi Germany, in the field of economics, introduced a program in 1933 whose purpose was to try to restore prosperity to the nation. In 1936 the famous Four-Year plan, overlapping the first program, was initiated. The objective of this last plan was more sinister. Briefly, it was to set up an autarchic state in which Germany would be practically self-sufficient. In 1936 Hitler stated: "Within four years Germany must be independent of foreign countries with regard to all those materials that can be produced in any way by

Giant swastikas bordered the closely-packed May Day (1937) crowd as Hitler told 50,000 chosen Nazi party members that he would not tolerate church interference in German politics. He is speaking in front of the Kaiser Wilhelm Art Gallery in Berlin.

German ability, by our chemistry and our machines and mining industries themselves."[28] In many cases the chemically-created commodities cost much more and were inferior in quality to those purchasable on the world market. "The Nazi leaders, however, insisted that economic independence and military preparedness more than outweighed the resulting lower standard of living."[29]

Summary

In reviewing the rise of Communism in Russia it is important to remember that the ideology of Communism is derived from the teachings of Karl Marx and has been subsequently modified by other leaders and writers. The Russian system is based on governmental control and ownership of all economic enterprise and the utilization of national economic planning. Although it advocates the dictatorship of the proletariat as a preliminary phase, Communist theory does not exalt the state as against the individual but looks to the time when the absolutism of the state and the restraints of government can be removed. The Communists, unlike Hitler's Nazis, have not resorted to a racial philosophy which seeks to exalt Russian Slavs as a super-race. The Communist state visualizes all its citizens as belonging to one class, that of the workers.

In industrialization, education, and social welfare tremendous innovations have been brought about. The schools have been expanded to a remarkable degree. Divorces, at one time easy to obtain, are being made more difficult. Home and family life are being strengthened rather than deprecated. The new constitution of 1936 registers in theory at least many gains in political freedom. Russia still remains a one-party state, where the trend so far has been to emphasize a social and economic, rather than a political, Bill of Rights. The most important aspect of Communism and the one on which it probably will ultimately be judged is its system of national economic planning.

Italian Fascism is less complex in theory and practice than Communism and is therefore somewhat easier to describe. Some of its most significant features are: (1) its ultranationalist character, (2) its emphasis on imperialist expansion, (3) the military nature of Mussolini's new state, (4) the national regimentation of economic life by and for the state, and (5) its antidemocratic character, which teaches that the individual has no rights except as a cog in the Fascist machine.

The followers of Mussolini were wont to maintain in the early 1930's that his régime had restored order to a distraught country, that governmental administration had been improved, educational facilities expanded, and the country made more self-sufficient. They maintained, in a word, that Fascism has restored national self-respect. Many Italians, it has been said, supported Fascism because it was apparently "a means of recovering their sense of human importance." There was some truth in these assertions, but the changes brought about by Mussolini were achieved only at the cost of considerable sacrifice from the people. The price of Fascism has been too high for the advantages it supposedly bought. Education is the mere tool of Fascist propaganda. A more malignant result has been the glorification of war. This, as we shall see in a later chapter, involved Italy in a conflict which not only loaded grievous losses upon the people but completely shattered whatever constructive achievement the Fascist régime could claim for Italy.

Superficially, German Nazism seems the result of world depression, of Versailles, of an outraged nationalism, and of a lack of confidence in the weak Weimar Republic. These causes supplied the opportunity and the justification for Nazism, but did not necessarily create Nazism itself. One must look farther back in history than the First World War. Rulers like Frederick the Great had made the ideal of benevolent despotism acceptable to those who lived under it. Men like Hegel and Treitschke exalted the position of the state at the expense of the individual. Beginning in Brandenburg and Prussia, pride in a military tradition and the accomplishment of arms eventually fixed itself in the German mind. None of these sentiments were necessarily peculiar to Germany, but in other countries they were eventually discarded or became relatively unimportant.

Nazism is built on a fanatical racial ideology. It places the German people on the pedestal of a super-race. Like Fascism it glorifies war and welcomes the opportunity to expand its power by the force of arms. A later chapter will describe the part played by the Nazis in plunging the world into a Second World War. While Communism sees the dictatorship of the proletariat as a temporary measure preparing the way to ultimate democracy and freedom for the individual, both Nazism and Fascism repudiate completely and finally all democratic practices.

In its early phases Nazism succeeded in removing some of the features of Versailles regarded by many Germans as humiliating and unfair. Some of the strong measures taken by Hitler to meet the depression in Germany might have been justified. But what started out allegedly as a means to an end, as an instrument to serve the needs of the

German people, soon became an end in itself, and one may reasonably question whether this was not the original intention. What began as a means to correct the few remaining inequalities of Versailles quickly changed to an attempt to impose on others inequalities that made those of the 1918 peace conference pale into insignificance.

	France	
1919-1924	National Bloc government	Reconstruction of country
1924-1926	Left Cartel government	Dangerous monetary policy
1926-1932	National Union under Poincaré	Strengthened finances
1932-1936	Constant shift of French ministries	Paris riots, Stavisky scandal
1936-1937	Popular Front under Léon Blum	Leftist government
1937-1939	Conservative government	Growing cleavage between classes
	The Succession States	
1919-1939	Czechoslovakian republic prospers	Political liberalism under Masaryk
1926-1935	Poland, a dictatorship under Pilsudski	Problem of minorities
1918-1921	Republic in Hungary	Communist régime of Bela Kun
1921-1931	Regent Horthy dictator in Hungary	Monarchy without a monarch
1919-1939	Yugoslavia wrestles with Serb-Croat rivalry	King assassinated by Croat
	Elsewhere in Europe	
1919-1934	Socialist government in Austria	Civil war and defeat of Socialists
1934	Dollfuss becomes dictator	
1919-1938	Rumania struggles with minorities	
1938	King Carol becomes dictator	Growth of pro-Fascist Iron Guard
1919-1923	Radical peasant party forms Bulgarian dictatorship	
1934	Dictatorship under King Boris	Moderate régime swept away
1932	Salazar becomes Portuguese dictator	
1936	Metaxas dictatorship in Greece	
1919	Finland a republic	
	Socialized democracy in Scandinavia	
	Democracy holds its own in Switzerland, Belgium, Holland	
1923-1930	Spanish dictator Rivera bolsters corrupt system	Alfonso abdicates
1930-1936	Republic in Spain	Overthrown by Fascist revolt
	Great Britain	
1921-1924	Postwar economic depression	
1924-1929	Conservative government under Baldwin	Economic crisis
1929-1931	Labor government under MacDonald	
1931	Statute of Westminster establishes British Commonwealth of Nations	Gives dominions autonomy
1931-1935	MacDonald heads coalition	Accused of treason to Labor party
1935	Conservative government under Baldwin	An "old-man" government
	United States	
1919	Withdrawal from world affairs	Refusal to join League
1920-1923	Return to normalcy under Harding	High tariff, graft
1923-1928	Coolidge and the era of big business	Immigration restrictions
1928-1933	Hoover and the great depression	High tariff, isolationism
1933-1935	Roosevelt and the New Deal	Relief, recovery, reform
	Latin America	
1919-1939	Postwar period; industrialization	Rise of middle class, especially in Mexico
1919-1929	Attempt at diversification instead of specialization in economics	
	Trade rivalry: German tactics	
	Race fusion and distinctive culture	Art—Orozco, Rivera; Music—Chavez
	Pan-Americanism: Good Neighbor Policy	Hull's influence, reciprocity treaties

CHAPTER 12

Democracy on Trial

THE states surveyed in the previous chapter—Russia, Italy, Germany—were sure of themselves, assertive, and dynamic. They were the countries of a new order as contrasted with those which one may regard as belonging to an established order, an order pledging allegiance to certain traditions and concepts in the process of development since the Renaissance and Religious Revolt. The countries of the established order placed their faith in democracy and capitalism, which in turn rested upon the principles of individual liberty, representative government, religious freedom, and *laissez-faire* economics. These countries were in a majority in continental western Europe, in the British Commonwealth of Nations, and in the Western Hemisphere. Certain nations, such as the United States, Great Britain, the British Dominions, the Scandinavian countries, and Czechoslovakia, were clearly democracies. Several other states, including certain Latin-American republics, only imperfectly realized the democracy guaranteed in their constitutions. On the fringe of the established order were such countries as Poland, Yugoslavia, and Bulgaria, where dictatorships loomed.

The record of the nations of the established order makes melancholy reading in the decade and a half following the peace conference. In this chapter we shall see how nearly all the new states created in 1919 scrapped their liberal constitutions in favor of some form of dictatorship. We shall observe how, even in Great Britain and France, traditional champions of democracy, there was a growing lack of confidence in representative government. Here and there European democracy seemed to flourish, as in the Scandinavian countries and Switzerland. The overthrow of the Spanish monarchy, too, was for a time a hopeful sign that the liberal political tradition was not dying in Europe.

The United States in 1919 seemed in a logical position to assume leadership among the nations of the established order. She was now the most powerful and wealthy of them all. But after participating in the defeat of Germany and her allies and after her leader had proposed a League of Nations to enforce peace, the United States chose to withdraw from international affairs. During the next two decades America went through an era of industrial boom and stock speculation, a depression, and a period of partial recovery and reform.

South of the Rio Grande were the Latin-American republics. After the First World War their ample natural resources became more and more important to the rest of the world. The history of Latin America from 1919 to 1939 reflects some social and economic reform, some advance of trade and industry. The republics drew a little closer to the United States, whom they had formerly feared, when their northern neighbor chose to exchange the policy of Dollar Diplomacy for that of the Good Neighbor. Presidents Hoover and Roosevelt made a determined effort to woo the esteem and friendship of Latin America and succeeded to an encouraging degree.

The Period of French Reconstruction

The National Bloc. As November 1918 brought victory to France and her allies, the republic set about binding up its wounds and repairing the ravages of war. More than one million Frenchmen had been killed; 13,000 square miles of French land had been devastated. During the war with Germany, France had been governed by a coalition known as the Sacred Union. After the elections of 1919 the country was ruled by the National Bloc, a political group made up of conservatives, in which money interests were strongly represented. The most important leaders of the National Bloc were Clemenceau, Poincaré, and Millerand. These men, ultranationalists, believed in the rigid enforcement of the provisions of the Versailles Treaty. They hated Germany and feared Russia. The main task of the National Bloc, the restoration of the devastated regions of France, was accomplished in record time. It had been expected by the French government that the huge costs of rebuilding the destroyed towns in the north of France would be covered by the reparation payments from Germany. But these payments ceased in 1923, and accordingly French troops marched into the Ruhr. From January 1922 to May 1924 Raymond Poincaré was premier of France and leader of the National Bloc. More than any other man he symbolized the policy of making Germany pay for the war and keeping her disarmed.

Leadership of the Left Cartel. Poincaré's policy did not gain the approval of the British, who favored a more moderate and conciliatory attitude toward Germany. Many Frenchmen also began to see that as long as Germany was held down and her economic life throttled it would be impossible for her to pay reparations. The National Bloc therefore fell from power in 1924 and was succeeded by the Left Cartel. This coalition under the leadership of Edouard Herriot advocated the extension of government control of industry, an increase in income taxes, and a liberal foreign policy. The Left Cartel guided the destinies of France until 1926. Herriot had an enviable record in foreign affairs, for the Dawes Plan had now apparently solved the reparations tangle, French troops had evacuated the Ruhr, and Germany had signed the Locarno agreements. In the field of domestic affairs the Left Cartel was not so successful. This was especially true in the case of public finance. Although France had practically no unemployment after the war and her foreign trade by 1922 surpassed that before 1913, her monetary policy threatened to plunge the franc into the same abyss that engulfed the German mark in 1923.

To meet this emergency Poincaré was called back to power to head a National Union government and save the franc. Drastic measures were taken by the new government. Taxes were increased and expenditures curtailed.

In 1936 various groups in France succeeded in organizing the first Popular Front ministry, headed by Léon Blum (center, seated). The Popular Front championed a forty-hour week, collective bargaining, pay raises, and paid vacations for French workers. But the ministry was not strong enough to survive the attack of vested interests, and the reforms were not achieved.

Poincaré's policies gave French finances a new lease on life, and progress in other fields brought the enactment of workmen's insurance and the completion of the task of rebuilding the devastated areas. In 1929 Poincaré retired from public life. His passing from the political scene coincided with the appearance of a world depression and a period of storm and stress that menaced the republic.

French parliamentary government. Unlike the British system of parliamentary government, which usually operates through two major political parties, the French system has worked with a dozen or more political parties. When a premier desired to form a new government he could not depend upon the support of one dominant and cohesive party as in England but must build a cabinet of several diverse political elements. Such a bloc, as it is called, may possess unanimity of policy when it is formed. But on the slightest provocation disagreement may develop, the unity of the bloc disappears, and the premier is usually forced to resign. French cabinets were thus highly unstable political compounds. From 1917 to 1937 thirty-four separate governments held office in France.

Constant shift of French ministries. The Coalition government was faced with serious problems shortly after the retirement of Poincaré. For three years it tried to cope with rising unemployment, budget deficits, and heavy military expenditures. In 1932 France repudiated the conservative Coalition and placed a more liberal group in power. The Left Cartel, again under Herriot, now sought to solve its country's ills. But the question of paying the war debt to the United States brought about the collapse of the Herriot ministry. In the following thirteen months (December 1932 to January 1934) a period of parliamentary demoralization ensued in which five governments were placed in office. Public impatience with politicians was heightened by a railroad disaster in December 1933, when two hundred were killed. There was evidence of negligence on the railroad's part, but the government's investigation was half-hearted.

Disgust with the government was increased even more by the affair of Stavisky, who cheated French investors out of some 600,000,000 francs. Many politicians were involved in the scandal, but the ministry in power refused to authorize an investigation. The wrath of the people smoldered, then flared forth in Paris on the evening of February 6, 1933. Thousands of angry citizens thronged the streets and tried to storm the Chamber of Deputies. In the fighting the police killed a score of rioters and injured a hundred others. The riot was quelled, and a National Union was formed under Gaston Doumergue. He demanded that the position of the prime minister be strengthened and that other constitutional changes be made so that the constant coming and going of ministries be ended. But Doumergue's suggestions were not heeded, and he resigned in November 1934.

Sentiment against the government. Pierre Laval and Pierre Etienne Flandin tried to carry on the National Union, which by now had become ultra-conservative and the agent of the wealthy and privileged classes, but the deterioration of parliamentary institutions continued. By this time the mass of French people believed their politicians to be thoroughly corrupt. The Third French Republic was assailed by enemies from all sides. The Fascist organization, the Croix de Feu, demanded: "Take France away from the politicians and give it back to the French people." Communists worked for a revolution to sweep away the bourgeoisie. Monarchists agitated for the restoration of a king. In the winter of 1934-1935, the *Petit Journal* of Paris conducted a contest to increase circulation. The paper asked its readers to answer the question "If France were to have a dictator, whom would you choose?" There was no dearth of choices—forty persons were named.

From June 1935 to January 1936 Pierre Laval was premier of France. The fall of this wily politician came when the French people repudiated the Hoare-Laval agreement in which France and Great Britain agreed to partition Abyssinia to suit Mussolini. A stop-gap ministry followed Laval but it too was forced out of office in May 1936.

The Popular Front. At this point emerged the Popular Front, a coalition composed of parties of the Left—Radical Socialists, Socialists, and Communists—united to oppose the conservative elements in the government. In June the Popular Front won a national election securing 381 of the 615 seats in the Chamber of Deputies. Léon Blum, a noted lawyer and writer, became premier. For the first time the Socialist party became the largest single party in France.

Under Blum the Popular Front endeavored to stem the influence of Fascism, to improve the country's finances, to better the condition of the workers, and to bring about certain fundamental economic reforms. In particular, Léon Blum promised to "break the power of the two hundred families who control the economic life of the nation."[1] In foreign policy the Popular Front was friendly to Great Britain and supported the League of Nations.

An epidemic of sit-down strikes at first embarrassed the new government, but gradually labor was conciliated by the passage of laws introducing a forty-hour week, higher wages, collective bargaining, and vacations with pay. Furthermore, the government extended its control over the Bank of France and initiated a public-works program. "The Blum government, in short, was for the laborer and against monopoly and Big Business. But it was equally against collectivism."[2]

Growing rift between classes. Socialists and Communists had not got along too well in the coalition, and in June 1937 Blum was forced to resign. Unfavorable trade balances, an enormous public debt, and an unbalanced budget proved too much for the Popular Front government. France swung in the direction of conservatism. The forty-hour week was ended, and strikes were energetically suppressed. A deplorable feature of French society in the late 1930's was the growing chasm between the upper and lower classes. Businessmen and financiers were horrified at the prospects of Communism and were inclined to flirt with Fascism. The working classes believed that the reforms of the Popular Front had been sabotaged and that a France dominated by a wealthy clique was hardly worth fighting for. This cleavage between classes was secretly encouraged by subtle propaganda from the totalitarian countries. And while Frenchmen quarreled, while France's economic strength and productivity were being sapped, Hitler's Germany, regimented and feverishly productive, was rapidly outstripping France in the production of armaments. The tragic ingredients explaining the fall of France in the spring of 1940 had now been supplied.

Czechoslovakia, Poland, Hungary, and Yugoslavia

The new Czech republic. The nations which arose in 1919 out of the débris of the once great Austro-Hungarian empire were called the Succession States (see map, page 317). The most important of these new countries was Czechoslovakia. Four hundred years of Austrian rule had not diminished the patriotic zeal of the Czechs, who during the First

World War were planning the emergence of a new Czech state should Austria-Hungary be defeated. The most important of these Czech patriots was Thomas G. Masaryk, who was instrumental in the creation of the new Czech and Slovak state. With the approval and support of President Wilson he published the Czechoslovakian declaration of independence in Washington. In November 1918, after the collapse of Austria, the Slovaks and Czechs joined in establishing a republic; by 1920 a constitution was adopted. Masaryk became president and Dr. Eduard Benes foreign minister of the new state.

Within an area of about 50,000 square miles Czechoslovakia had a population of fifteen million. These people were of many different racial stocks and nationalities. In addition to Czechs and Slovaks, there were such minority groups as Germans in the Sudeten area, Russians (Ruthenians), and Hungarians (see map, page 321). Altogether these minorities constituted one third of the total population. Despite the problem of the minorities Czechoslovakia prospered. She inherited most of the industries of the old Austrian empire, her soil was rich, her timber resources ample, and her minerals valuable. From the Czechoslovakian factories poured a stream of goods: glass, armaments, shoes, toys, and textiles. A large foreign trade was built up, and the government assisted small farmers by breaking up large estates. The people of the new state demonstrated that they were industrious, conscientious citizens and sincere lovers of political liberalism. Now free, the Czechs and Slovaks eagerly turned to enrich their own culture.

Difficulties of Polish independence. To the north of Czechoslovakia lay Poland. With Germany on the west and Russia on the east, Poland extended from Rumania to the Baltic Sea. She had, in the eighteenth century, been partitioned three times; in 1795 she disappeared as a national political entity. But Polish nationalism persisted despite the alien rule of the Germans, Austrians, and Russians. During the First World War there was much confusion among the Poles. Some wished to fight for Russia, others for Austria. Some saw no reason for fighting on either side. But all were agreed on the necessity for obtaining independence. With the collapse of Russia, Austria-Hungary, and Germany it became possible in 1918 to declare a Polish republic. The

Ignace Jan Paderewski, Polish pianist-patriot, was one of the organizers of the Polish republic (1918-1919). When he died in 1941, the United States placed his body with those of her war heroes in Arlington Cemetery.

two men most instrumental in its creation were Ignace Paderewski, the famous pianist, and Marshal Jozef Pilsudski, a strong-willed and capable army officer. A democratic government was set up in 1921, but it soon became evident that the Poles were not too successfully running their democracy. Corruption, deadlock, and economic instability characterized the early twenties. In 1926 Pilsudski came out of retirement to engineer a *coup d'état.* The government was overthrown, and the old warrior became dictator and remained so until his death in 1935. A new constitution was adopted in 1935 which legalized a form of dictatorial government.

Poland also had large minorities (German, Lithuanian, and Ruthenian Russian—see map, page 321). She was primarily an agricultural nation, in which the wealth was controlled by a small landed and capitalist minority. The poverty of Poland was accentuated by the high birth rate. In 1919 the population was estimated to be 20 million; in 1939 it was 34 million.

Dictatorship in Hungary. The creation of new states after the First World War resulted in grievous losses to Hungary, whose territory was reduced seventy-five per cent. More than half her population was given to her neighbors. Immediately after the armistice in 1918 a short-lived republic was set up. The peace terms imposed by the Allies and subsequent unfavorable economic conditions discredited the new government, which was followed by a Soviet republic established by the Communist Bela Kun. After only a few months this régime was overthrown by a Rumanian army, which helped itself to any plunder that could be carried away by train or truck. After the Rumanians left the country, Admiral Horthy, head of a Hungarian army, established law and order. During 1921 several unsuccessful attempts were made by Charles, the former emperor of Austria-Hungary, to regain the throne. Constitutionally, however, Hungary remained a monarchy although the throne was vacated. Admiral Horthy ruled merely as the regent of the kingdom. To all intents a dictator, the regent relied from 1921 to 1931 upon a shrewd statesman, Count Stephen Bethlen, to run the government in the capacity of premier.

Dominating all thought in Hungary was the question of revision of the Treaty of Trianon. Everywhere maps of old Hungary surrounded by a crown of thorns were displayed showing the areas lost to other countries. Like Poland, Hungary was essentially a land of peasants, but the poverty and debasement of the peasantry was even worse than that in Poland. A feudal aristocracy owned most of the land on which tenants eked out a miserable existence.

Racial rivalries in Yugoslavia. Along the eastern shores of the Adriatic Sea emerged a new state called the Kingdom of Yugoslavia, a nation slightly less than 100,000 square miles in area, with a population of thirteen million. The Croats and Slovenes of the former Hapsburg empire joined with their brother Slavs in Serbia and Montenegro, mainly Serbs, to form the state of Yugoslavia. From the outset King Alexander had difficulty in reconciling the rivalries between Serbs, Croats, and Slovenes. Political differences reached a climax in 1928 when a riot broke out in the parliament in which Radich, the Croatian leader, was mortally wounded. In 1929 the king was forced to establish a dictatorship. Five years later he was assassinated in France by one of a group of Croatian terrorists. Prince Paul, a cousin of the murdered king, now became regent until young Peter, Alexander's son, should become old enough to take over the affairs of state. In addition to the rivalry between Croat and Serb there was an acute agrarian problem in Yugoslavia, because the country had too many large estates.

Austria, Rumania, Bulgaria, and Spain

Austria tries Socialism. The Treaty of St. Germain reduced Austria's population and territory three fourths, leaving a feeble little nation about the size of Maine, with less than seven million inhabitants (see map, page 317). Vienna, once the prosperous capital of a large empire, was now a great city without an adequate hinterland to nourish it. The area of the new Austria was but 32,000 square miles, and more than one quarter of the country's population lived in Vienna. In place of the old Hapsburg monarchy a republic was established somewhat after the federal system of Switzerland. For ten years afterward Austria was faced with the specter of financial bankruptcy and widespread unemployment. There was some talk of an economic union (*Anschluss*) with Germany as a way out of these difficulties, but this was forbidden by the Allies. In 1919 nearly fifty thousand children were sent from Austria to other countries to be saved from starvation, and in 1920 many additional thousands were also sent abroad. Through the efforts of the League of Nations in 1922 extensive loans were secured for Austria which did much to ease her economic distress.

During the days of unemployment and starvation the people of Vienna turned to Socialist leadership as a way out. The Socialist administration in Vienna introduced many remarkable reforms. Slums were torn down, and nearly 100,000 dwellings were built for the working class. Clinics and kindergartens were established. It was said that the city government now watched over the interests of a citizen from his birth in a municipal hospital to his death and subsequent burial by a municipal funeral. But the Socialist experiment in Vienna aroused the fears of the conservative elements in Austria, and in 1934 class antagonism flared into civil war. The Socialists were

Karl Marx Hof in Vienna cost $4,000,000. The apartment building housed 2000 Socialist families before revolt swept Austria in February 1934. While Socialists fought back with machine guns, government artillery killed hundreds and pounded down the middle arch of the building.

defeated in savage fighting, mainly in Vienna. Austria was further rent by the rapid development of a Nazi movement, which looked toward union with Germany. Another group, called the *Heimwehr,* inclined to be pro-Fascist, looked to Italy for support and worked for the restoration of the Hapsburg monarchy. With resentment in the hearts of the cowed proletariat, with a program of union with Germany held out by the rising Nazi party, and with the Heimwehr demanding a monarchy, Austria was threatened with dissolution. To stave off civil war and because he was thought sympathetic to Fascist ideas, Engelbert Dollfuss, the chancellor, became dictator in April 1934. Parliament was forced out of existence.

Rumania takes a dictator. Rumania, between Russia on the north and Yugoslavia and Bulgaria on the south, was a kingdom of a little more than 100,000 square miles, with a population of nearly twenty million. This country profited nearly as much by the war as Hungary had lost, for her population and area were doubled (see page 317). But only seventy per cent of the people in the enlarged state were Rumanian (see map, page 321). Like most of the Succession States, Rumania enjoyed little tranquillity after 1919. Despite a liberal constitution granted in 1923, her peasants were restless, and large minority groups, especially the Hungarians, were a troublesome element. The domestic difficulties of Rumania were complicated by Crown Prince Carol, who had married Princess Helen of Greece. Carol fell under the influence of the now notorious Magda Lupescu. Public disapproval of this affair caused Carol to give up his rights to the throne and go, with Lupescu of course, to Paris as an exile. In 1927 Carol's father, King Ferdinand, died, and the crown went to Prince Michael. In 1930 young Michael stepped aside when his father returned to Rumania to assume the kingship.

In the next few years internal harmony was threatened by the growth of anti-Semitism and the rise of the Iron Guard, a Fascist organization. In 1938 King Carol himself became dictator of Rumania, and a new constitution was drawn up giving him the sole power to introduce legislation into parliament and the power to veto any of the parliament's actions.

Boris of Bulgaria becomes dictator. Bulgaria lost relatively little land or population as a result of the peace treaty of 1919. But the cumulative effect of being on the losing side in the second Balkan War (1913) and the First World War had whittled Bulgaria down to only forty thousand square miles, with a population of less than six million people. King Ferdinand was forced by Alexander Stambuliski to abdicate in favor of his son Boris shortly after the conclusion of peace in 1919. Stambuliski, the leader of a radical peasant party, was the head of a dictatorial government from 1919 to 1923. Important land reforms were carried out which antagonized the upper classes, who succeeded in overturning the Stambuliski government in 1923. Repression of the peasants and lower classes followed. Stambuliski was subsequently shot, and an era of disorder ensued. This period culminated in a bomb outrage in the cathedral in Sofia in 1925, in which 150 persons were killed and more than 300 wounded.

For a brief period, from 1926 to 1931, a moderate government sought to restore civil liberties, to free political prisoners, and to balance the budget. Whatever chances of success this régime might have had were swept away by the shock of the world depression. Conservative elements, fearful of the spread of Communism, forced King Boris to head a dictatorship in 1934.

Dictators in other countries. In other small European states, the story was much the same—the waning of democracy and the rise of dictatorship. Greece ended the war as a monarchy, changed to a republic in 1924, had a king once more in 1935, and the following year got a dictator in the person of General John Metaxas. The three Baltic republics of Latvia, Lithuania, and Estonia underwent similar changes. Each of these states, formerly part of the old Russian empire, had established a republican form of government after achieving independence. But the existence of universal suffrage and one-house legislatures in each of these Baltic republics did not prevent the growth of dictatorship. Portugal was still another failure. In 1910 Portugal became a republic. Since that time she has had twenty-four revolutions. In 1932 Dr. Antonio de Oliveira Salazar became dictator, a new constitution was introduced, and the republic was superseded by a government suggestive of Italian Fascism.

Finland and the Scandinavian countries. The record of political instability and the rise of dictatorship in much of central and southern Europe disappointed the hopes of many who had fought from 1914 to 1918 for a better world. But the picture was not entirely black. In some sections of Europe representative government and political liberalism were enjoying a prosperous existence. In Finland a republic had been declared when independence was secured from Russia in 1919. The government immediately set about passing laws which provided for the compulsory purchase of large estates to be divided into small acreages for little farmers. Child labor was banned, the eight-hour day legalized, and education, from the elementary school through the university, was made free. The ideal of the Finnish leaders seemed to be to create a sturdy race of small independent farmers constituting an educated citizenry.

The Scandinavian countries enjoyed a particularly happy existence. In Denmark and Sweden the standard of living was said to be the highest in the world. In these countries as well as in Norway important social and economic reforms strengthened and vitalized the democratic way of life. Much was done for the small farmer, cooperative movements were encouraged for the benefit of both producer and consumer, and legislation was enacted to provide social insurance for the people. In Scandinavia democratic government exhibited a lustiness and an efficiency which stood out in sharp contrast to the muddle in many of the countries of central Europe. In Sweden an interesting experiment of controlled capitalism under democracy was being carried out. This experiment, called the "Middle Way," meant government control of many forms of economic activity and government operation of

Stockholm is probably the only city in the world which has wholeheartedly accepted modern architecture for her municipal buildings. These apartment houses are located on one of the numerous waterways. There are no slums in Stockholm.

mines, electric power plants, communications, and many other activities. "Disparity between rich and poor was reduced to a minimum and Sweden seemingly became a kind of Middle-class paradise."[3]

Other democratic successes. Democracy also held its own in Switzerland, Holland, and Belgium. In Switzerland some four million people living in an area about the size of the state of Maryland enjoyed reasonable prosperity and stable government following the First World War. While the parliamentary régimes in many states in Europe toppled or were discredited, government by the people prospered; so much so that it could be well said in the 1930's "the probability is that Switzerland will remain a promontory of democracy and free government projecting into a portion of Europe which seems to have forgotten all about such institutions, and that she will continue to afford a practical example of the way in which man may redeem himself from the curse of war, social strife, and racial bigotry."[4]

Holland and Belgium, while not so democratic as the Scandinavian countries or Switzerland, nevertheless possessed stable parliamentary institutions. In Belgium a disturbing factor was the growth of a form of Fascism known as the Rexist movement. Here the language question was also a complicating feature. Some two million Belgians speak only French, about the same number speak only Flemish, and nearly one million are bilingual. Both linguistic groups were determined to perpetuate their "national culture," a fact which endangered the unity of the country.

Monarchy and dictatorship in Spain. Perhaps the most encouraging incident in post-war Europe was the elimination of the backward and corrupt Spanish government that had exploited an impoverished Spain. Throughout Spanish history there had been three privileged classes—the landowners, the clerics, and the army officers. These classes represented the bulk of the wealth and political power. The landless workers and the small farmers were left to fend for themselves. The illiteracy rate was at least forty-five per cent. One per cent of the population possessed more than half of the land. And this land supported 21,000 officers, one for every six ordinary soldiers, more than the entire German army had in 1914.

From 1914 to 1918 Spain enjoyed a temporary prosperity by supplying food and other materials to the warring nations. After the war, industry and trade lagged; industrial unrest and political instability ensued. To make matters worse, severe fighting broke out in Spanish Morocco, where the Spaniards endeavored to suppress a revolt led by a capable Berber chief named Abd-el-Krim. Graft and inefficiency characterized the conduct of the campaign. In 1921 the Spanish people were

The popular front in Spain exhibited such posters as these in the troubled days of November 1933. The city is Barcelona; the language is Catalan.

horrified to learn that an entire army of 10,000 men had been wiped out by the Moors. An investigation of this military disaster threatened to expose many in high positions in the government, and it was rumored that even the deposition of the king would be demanded. To ward off this exposé and to save the position of the privileged classes and the monarchy, Primo de Rivera set up a dictatorship in 1923 which operated until 1930. For seven years he tried to bolster up the old system by removing its most flagrant abuses and making a few concessions to the people. After the dictator's downfall, King Alfonso tried to continue the traditional arbitrary rule, but popular opposition proved too much for him. Municipal elections held in April 1931 resulted in a clearcut victory for the Republicans. Alfonso, realizing that the time had come to step down, fled the country and made his way to Paris.

The republic of Spain. The leader of the Republicans, Alcalá Zamora, became the head of a provisional government and called an election for the selection of representatives to attend a constituent assembly. Again the Liberals won a sweeping victory. The Monarchists and Conservatives held only a few scattered regions. The constituent assembly then drafted a new constitution which provided for a one-house *Cortes* elected for four years by universal suffrage. The chief executive was to be a president elected for a term of six years. The prime minister was to be responsible to the legislature.

Armed with the new constitution the Spanish Liberals turned to the task of reorganization. The Jesuit order was dissolved, and its property, worth thirty million dollars, was taken over by the state. The Church was prohibited from engaging in education, and all its schools were closed. The Republican *Cortes* next authorized the construction of nearly 10,000 school buildings, then turned to the land problem. It passed a bill giving the government authority to take 52,000,000 acres from the large landowners in order to redistribute it in small parcels. The next major effort of the new government was the reform of the army. Officers were asked to take an oath of allegiance to the republic, their number was drastically reduced, and the size of the army itself was decreased one third. The driving force behind the new republic was President Zamora and the prime minister, Manuel Azaña, a noted writer.

To many liberals in Europe the Spanish revolt was an encouraging sign that perhaps the democratic tradition would win out after all and that dictatorship, now rampant in central Europe, was only a temporary condition. That they were mistaken was demonstrated between 1930 and 1940, when the republics in Spain and Germany were overthrown and two dictatorial régimes, Fascist Italy and Nazi Germany, began a campaign of conquest to undermine democracy in Europe and elsewhere.

Great Britain and the British Empire

Great Britain after the war. After the First World War the English parliamentary system appeared listless, even worn out. It lacked dynamic leadership. A Liberal ministry had been at the helm since 1905, but in 1915 the critical state of the war brought about a coalition composed of representatives of Labor, Liberals, and Conservatives. Asquith, who had taken the country into the war, was superseded in 1916 by Lloyd George. The new prime minister, heading a coalition government, promised his people that after the war "England would be made a land fit for heroes" fresh from the trenches in France. A brief period of prosperity followed the armistice. Then England's foreign trade collapsed; unemployment reached huge proportions. In July 1921 there were two million persons unemployed, and Great Britain faced an uncertain future. Sixty per cent of her food had to be imported, and its cost could be met only by the sale of manufactured articles abroad. The war debt was forty billion dollars. Seven hundred thousand young men had not returned from the battlefield.

In spite of many serious problems Great Britain's parliamentary system somehow muddled along. Following the decision of the Conservative party to withdraw, in 1922, Lloyd George lost his majority in the Commons. He was succeeded by Andrew Bonar Law, the leader of the Conservatives, who presently retired because of ill health. Bonar Law was in turn followed by another Conservative, Stanley Baldwin, who remained in office as prime minister until the end of 1923. In the general election of this year the Conservatives gained the largest number of representatives in the House of Commons. By swinging their support to the Labor party, however, the Liberals gave James Ramsay MacDonald a majority and in January 1924 made him Great Britain's first Laborite prime minister.

MacDonald's Labor government. The British Labor party espoused the policy of gradualism; that is, it wished to see Socialism introduced slowly. Declared MacDonald: "Our labor movement has never had the least intention to try short cuts to the millennium."[5] Dependent upon the support of the Liberal party, the Labor government had to move cautiously. Hence its record in domestic affairs was not outstanding. In foreign affairs its accomplishments were more substantial. MacDonald believed in helping Germany get back on her feet. Accordingly he favored the Dawes Plan, urged the entry of Germany into the League of Nations, and supported disarmament. By working with Herriot he managed to improve relations with France. But failure to cure the country's economic ills, together with the accusation that the Labor government was pro-Communist, brought about the fall of MacDonald's ministry in October 1924.

Prime Minister Ramsay MacDonald bids farewell to Aristide Briand, French foreign minister, as the seven-power German debt holiday plan is completed in London (July 1931).

The Conservative Baldwin government. From 1924 to 1929 a Conservative government led again by Stanley Baldwin was in power. During this period the economic crisis continued unabated; in 1926 a general strike threatened to disrupt the economy of the nation.

Although the Baldwin government extended the system of social insurance and enfranchised all women between twenty-one and thirty who had not received the right to vote by the electoral act of 1918, its general tone was conservative and at times even reactionary. In 1927 the Baldwin government passed the Trade Disputes Act, making it difficult for unions to obtain funds from their members for political campaigns. Meanwhile economic difficulties continued. In the summer of 1928, twenty-nine per cent of the mine workers in Great Britain, twenty-eight per cent of the ship workers, twenty-one per cent of the men in steel industries, and fifteen per cent of those in textile industries were unemployed.

The second Labor ministry. This failure to solve unemployment brought MacDonald back to Number 10 Downing Street in May 1929. Again the Labor party had little to show for its two years in power (1929-1931) as far as internal problems were concerned, although in foreign affairs its record was again praise-

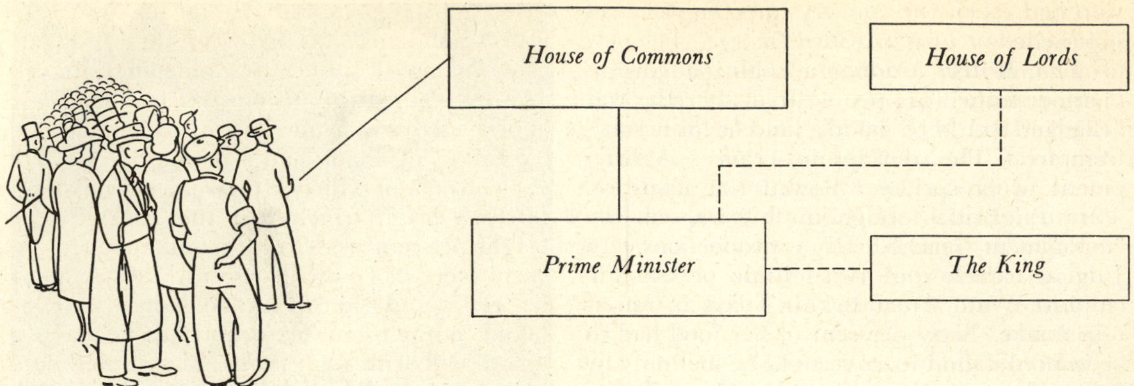

worthy. MacDonald journeyed to the United States to talk with President Hoover about peace and disarmament. The Labor government also signed the "optional clause" (Article 36 of the Statute of the World Court), which bound Great Britain to place before the Court any dispute which involved the interpretation of a treaty or international law.

The National government. The world economic crisis, forcing Great Britain off the gold standard and further increasing her unemployment, brought the second Labor ministry to an end in 1931. But instead of giving up the prime ministership, MacDonald became the leader of a National Coalition government composed of practically all the Conservatives, a goodly number of the Liberals, and a few Laborites. The rank and file of the Labor party accused MacDonald of being a traitor and renegade. The formation of the National government under MacDonald's leadership complicated party divisions, for there were now National Laborites, National Liberals, and National Conservatives (all in the Coalition) opposed by a small number of Laborites and Liberals. During the next four years the National government became in reality more and more the agent of the Conservative party, and in 1935 MacDonald resigned. His place as prime minister was taken by Baldwin. The fiction of the National government was, however, continued. By 1935 the enactment of tariff legislation, the encouragement of home agriculture, and a policy of economic cooperation with the self-governing elements in the British Empire improved England's economic condition.

Great Britain's "old-man" government. Considering the multiplicity of Great Britain's problems and the adverse conditions which confronted her statesmen in the disillusioning post-war years, perhaps her government did as well as could be expected. But in examining the two decades which ended one war and brought in another (1919-1939) it is evident that democratic government in Great Britain lacked vitality. The leadership was, in the main, uninspiring and mediocre. Stanley Baldwin is a perfect symbol of British leadership after the war. He entered Parliament in 1908 at the age of forty-one and in almost ten years in the House of Commons made only five speeches. In 1921 he became a member of the cabinet and was made chancellor of the exchequer in 1923. When he was made prime minister later in the same year, Baldwin was fifty-nine. In 1928 the average age of Baldwin's cabinet members was sixty years; that of MacDonald's colleagues in 1931 was sixty-three and one half. No wonder that many Englishmen complained about the "tired-old-man" atmosphere in the British government. In the fateful years from 1935 to 1939, when Great Britain was suffering defeat after defeat in the arena of international affairs at the hands of the totalitarian states, the men leading the government were old and lethargic, seemingly unaware of the changing world around them.

A more serious menace to British democracy than the well-intentioned ineptness of its leaders was the alarming fact that an influential group of citizens had apparently lost their faith in the efficacy of democratic government to solve British problems. Faced with the possible breakdown of the capitalist system, fearful of Russian Communism, and disgusted with conditions in France, they began during the middle 1930's to admire more and more the strength, resoluteness, and superficial efficiency of the new régime in Germany.

The British Commonwealth. During the period from 1914 to 1939 many important changes had been taking place in the British Empire. The development of self-government, which had been a feature of nineteenth-century British imperial history, in such colonies as Canada and Australia reached its logical conclusion as a result of the First World War. During this conflict Canada, Australia, New Zealand, and South Africa rendered valuable service to the mother country. The war effort not only obligated Great Britain to reward these people but also stimulated nationalism in these areas, by this time known as dominions.

In 1926 a British Imperial Conference declared that the mother country and the dominions were "autonomous Communities within the British Empire, equal in status, in no way subordinate one to another. . . ."[6] In 1931 the Statute of Westminster was passed by the British Parliament which, in effect, was a constitution for the British Commonwealth of Nations. From now on the dominions and Great Britain were held together by economic interests, by loyalty to the crown, and by similar ideals of language, law, and tradition.

The Dominion of Canada. The oldest and most important dominion was Canada. After 1918 this country experienced an uneasy and difficult period of national reconstruction. But by 1927 prosperity had again returned to the Canadians. In that year they celebrated the Diamond Jubilee of Confederation. The future seemed promising. Stocks boomed, exports increased, and the railroads profited.

In 1939 Canada had a population of about 11,000,000, of which fifty-two per cent were of British origin (including the Irish), twenty-eight per cent were French, and about five per cent were of German descent. Less than half of the population of Canada considered England as their mother country. Canada is almost embarrassingly large, larger than continental United States. W. L. Mackenzie King, Canadian prime minister, once said: "If some countries have too much history, we have too much geography." Overshadowed by the immensity of the country, the small Canadian population mainly stretches in a narrow band less than three hundred miles wide along the border of the United States from the Atlantic to the Pacific. This narrow band consists of four main economic regions: the Maritime Provinces (Nova Scotia, New Brunswick, and Prince Edward Island), Quebec, Ontario, the Prairie Provinces (Alberta, Saskatchewan, and Manitoba), and British Columbia on the western side of the Rocky Mountains (see maps, page 236). Each of these regions has its peculiar economic characteristics, often conflicting with those of the others.

Canada is one of the richest countries in the world in natural resources. Although she

In Quebec harbor on the St. Lawrence stands this immense grain elevator. With its loading galleries at either end, it is nearly a half mile long. Here Canada's magnificent wheat crops are stored prior to exporting.

lacks much oil, and her coal deposits are situated at the extreme ends of the country, she produces tremendous quantities of wheat, is the third nation in the production of gold, and has almost a world monopoly on asbestos. Pulpwood, silver, and nickel are also important Canadian products. Just before the depression of 1929 Canada ranked fifth among the nations of the world in value of exports. Canadian per capita exports were about three and a half times as large as those of the United States.

In 1929 the depression struck Canada with a paralyzing shock, and the government tried with little success to cope with rising unemployment, the plight of the farmers, and an alarming number of business failures. In 1934 it is estimated that 1,200,000 Canadians were either on relief or in labor camps. In this emergency the prime minister, Richard B. Bennett, advocated a far-reaching program of reform. Bennett declared, "If we cannot abolish the dole, we should abolish the system." "This is the end of an economic era. Capitalism will never work again."[7]

In 1935 Bennett secured the passage of eight acts in the Canadian Parliament. Their purpose was to secure a more equitable division of the nation's income and provide a greater share of social justice for the average Canadian. In 1937, after being taken to the court of the Privy Council in London, the majority of these acts were declared unconstitutional. Meanwhile depression and drought were attacking the Canadian western provinces, labor unrest troubled the east, and there was much criticism directed against the Canadian constitution, described by some as suitable only "for the horse and buggy period." After 1937 the weight of depression in Canada was somewhat lifted, but it was commonly agreed that fundamental problems relating to economic justice, the plight of the western farmers, and the improvement of the federal system of government still remained to be solved. The easy optimism of the late 1920's had now been superseded by a spirit of national stocktaking.

British South Africa. The Union of South Africa, a settlement of Dutch and British people, proved loyal to Great Britain during the First World War. However, after the conflict friction occurred on several occasions between the British and Dutch communities. The latter pressed for complete recognition of South Africa's independent status, while the former was determined that the Union, while independent, must remain a member of the British Commonwealth.

Basic to South African economy are the great gold and diamond mines which furnish a large share of the government's revenues. Without this mineral wealth the country would be helpless. The arid soil and the distance from the world's markets complicate South Africa's economic development, but perhaps the fundamental problem of the country is that of its native policy.

There are more than six and a half million natives in the Union and barely two million whites. The native question is really a series of questions: What educational facilities should be offered? What political opportunities should be given? Should the native be kept on his tribal lands, or should contact between European and black be encouraged? But underlying all these is the element of fear. The Europeans wonder whether political and economic dominance will one day pass from the white minority to the black majority. No one can prophesy what will be the outcome. Much has been done in South Africa to study the native question scientifically; and recent legislation, while not removing by any means certain disabilities suffered by the natives, has undoubtedly improved their lot, especially in the direction of providing them with land.

Australia and New Zealand. Following the war Australia and New Zealand went through the usual throes of postwar adjustment, but from 1923 to 1929 both countries were prosperous. The effects of the ensuing depression were especially severe in these dominions, for both were agricultural countries with large debts held by outside investors. Only by stringent measures did the two governments avoid default on their obligations.

In the early thirties Australia and New Zealand became more and more concerned with foreign affairs. The next chapter will discuss these at greater length. Here it is sufficient to note that both countries were apprehensive of Japanese expansion. The Australians in particular had adopted a "White Australia" policy by which they were resolved to keep their population exclusively European, preferably British. The great fear of the Australians came from a realization that they might be hard put to maintain the

"White Australia" policy in a continent so underpopulated as their own, in the face of an overpopulated Japan. This circumstance explains why Australia and New Zealand, unlike South Africa, worried very little about their exact constitutional status. Dependence upon the British fleet and the fortress of Singapore bound these South Pacific dominions closely to their mother country.

Elsewhere in the Empire. In the post-war years the tropical dependencies of the British Empire also posed many problems. India demanded self-government, as did Ceylon and Burma. The Egyptians were irked by British control of the Suez Canal, and in other African colonies the British government found difficulty in reconciling the conflicting interests of European settlers and natives.

The end of the First World War brought no peace to Palestine, which had been turned over to Great Britain as a mandate in 1920. The Arab inhabitants were resolved that the Jewish immigrants should not obtain control, while the latter were equally determined that what had once been their ancient kingdom should become a modern homeland for Jewry.

Like France, Czechoslovakia, Austria, and other European states, Great Britain and the dominions enjoyed little tranquillity after 1919. Great Britain's problems, however, were more numerous and complex, scattered as they were in many lands populated by diverse peoples.

The United States

America after the war. The First World War left its mark on the Western Hemisphere as well as on the European countries and the British Empire. Although the Latin-American republics, for example, experienced important economic developments, it was the United States whose position was most radically altered by the conflict.

While the European nations were destroying and depleting the sources of their wealth from 1914 to 1917, the United States was expanding its factories and pouring goods into Europe and South America. By 1919 it had attained first place in industrial equipment, wealth, and prestige, and it had also become the world's greatest creditor nation. The United States, so suddenly grown great and rich, had been the most conspicuous defender of democratic ideals. The country was therefore looked upon by many as the leader, both at home and abroad.

There was much to be done. The new League needed American support, and the tangle of war debts, reparations, and trade disruption demanded sympathetic attention. But the expected leadership was not forthcoming. Almost overnight the American people seemed to have forgotten the Wilsonian ideal. They quite definitely turned away from the international scene to concentrate upon domestic affairs. An industrial boom completely absorbed the nation. While many parts of the world were struggling with serious economic problems, the United States enjoyed almost unbelievable prosperity. The League of Nations was a vague memory, nationalism triumphed over internationalism, conservatism over liberalism.

The period of readjustment. While the basic result of the war upon the United States had been to increase the nation's wealth enormously, Americans nevertheless experienced several years of confused economic and social readjustment. Industrial warfare between capital and labor characterized the years 1919-1922. The managers of industry endeavored to recover some of the ground lost to labor during the war through collective bargaining and better wages; the ranks of labor were equally determined to hold these gains. In 1919, 3000 strikes involved four million workers.

Industrial strife was further stimulated by the business depression of 1920 and 1921. The prosperous war years had been made possible largely by huge exports to Europe. By 1919 the warring nations had used up their funds and credit. In consequence American foreign trade declined. At home, too, there was a revolt of the consumer against "the high cost of living." A buyers' strike curtailed American production. The result was a depression in 1920 and 1921 in which manufacturers tried to cut down costs, especially by lowering wages. The repercussion was the strike of 600,000 coal miners and 300,000 railway shopmen in 1922. But now the post-war boom had commenced, at first slowly, then with breathtaking momentum.

In addition to economic troubles in the im-

In 1922 the eighteenth "prohibition" amendment had become law and New York drys dumped 50,000 barrels of whiskey into the street.

mediate post-war years, there was an unfortunate upsurge of exaggerated nationalism, manifesting itself in a hunt against persons or groups accused of radicalism. In particular the attorney-general made numerous arrests and carried out deportations of anyone suspected of "red" sympathies. Five members were expelled from the New York legislature because they were Socialists, an action vigorously denounced by Charles E. Hughes, one of the country's most eminent statesmen. The most exaggerated form of intolerance was the activity of a new Ku Klux Klan which singled out for its attention immigrants, Catholics, Jews, the League of Nations, and pacifism. Its membership in 1924 was over four million, but it declined after this date.

In politics the two most important events were the ratification of the eighteenth amendment in January 1919 and the passing of the nineteenth amendment in the summer of 1920. The eighteenth amendment prohibited the sale of intoxicating liquor; the nineteenth gave women the right to vote. Both of these measures had been brought about largely by the war. In order to conserve grain during the war, the production of beer and other alcoholic beverages had been restricted or entirely forbidden. The nineteenth amendment came into being because women in America had played an important part in the war effort. They made increasing demands for the right to vote. Woman's suffrage was the nation's answer.

The "return to normalcy." In 1920 Warren G. Harding, the Republican candidate, was elected to the presidency on the platform of a "return to normalcy." The inauguration of Harding as president in 1921 ushered in twelve years of Republican dominance in American politics. It soon became apparent that by "normalcy" President Harding meant conservatism in domestic affairs and resistance to the liberal progressivism embodied before the war in such measures as the Clayton Anti-Trust Act and the Underwood Tariff Act. In foreign affairs the new president was bent on isolation and repudiation of the League of Nations. Speaking confidently of America's ability to take care of itself, Harding declared in his inaugural address, "We seek no part in directing the destinies of the world." Other Republican leaders announced that the League issue was "as dead as slavery." In accordance with this policy the American ambassador in London was "instructed to inform the League's authorities that as the United States had not joined the League she was not in a position to answer letters from it."[8]

In 1922 Congress enacted the Fordney-McCumber Tariff Act, establishing the highest rates in American history. A similar high tariff had been passed in 1921 by Congress but vetoed by President Wilson, who maintained, "If there ever was a time when America had anything to fear from foreign competition that time has passed. If we wish Europe to settle her debts, governmental or commercial, we must be prepared to buy from her."[9] In 1922 a bill calling for payment of a bonus to soldiers of the First World War (fifty dollars for each month in service), was passed by Congress. Vetoed by Harding, the bonus issue appeared again before Congress and became a political football.

Less than a year after its inauguration, Harding's administration became the storm center of an exposé of graft and corruption. While the ugly truth was being uncovered, the president, in ill health, had taken a trip to Alaska. On his return his condition became grave, and he died in San Francisco. The knowledge that those whom he had placed in high office had betrayed his confidence probably aggravated his illness. Congressional investigating committees at length

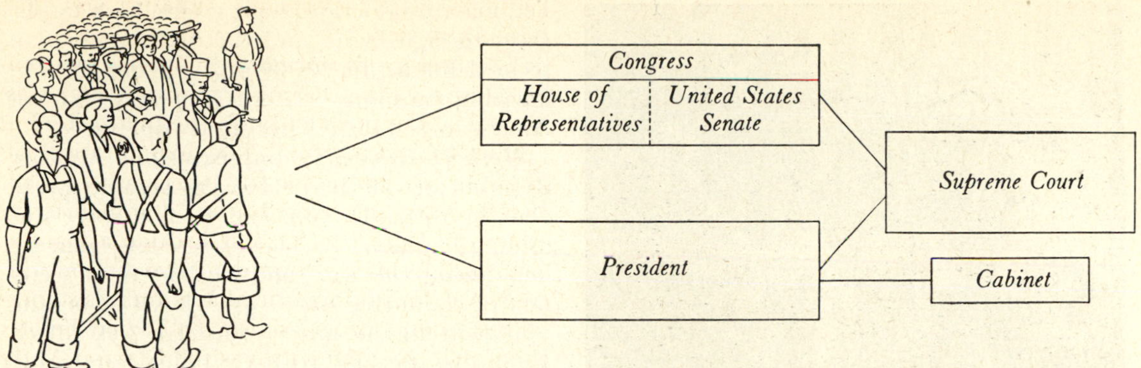

uncovered the whole sordid affair. The most infamous scandal had to do with government oil reserves at Teapot Dome. The Secretary of the Interior obtained at least $400,000 for himself from the oil companies in this shady deal.

It hardly seems likely that Harding had any direct hand in the scandals. The truth apparently is that his friends and political cronies used him as an innocent dupe. Harding was beyond his depth in the White House.

The era of Big Business. In 1923, after the death of Harding, the then Vice-President Calvin Coolidge became the chief executive. As governor of Massachusetts he had gained the reputation of being both safe and sound. He assured the people that the scandals were now over.

Even more than Harding, Coolidge stood for a return to conservatism. The progressive movement of the first decade of the twentieth century had little appeal for him. He favored high tariffs, the reduction of taxes, and governmental assistance to industry. The philosophy of President Coolidge was best summed up in his own dictum: "The business of the United States is business!"

In 1924 a Soldiers' Bonus Bill, providing insurance to war veterans, was introduced into Congress and passed over Coolidge's veto. The Johnson Immigration Act became law in 1924. Immigration had been restricted in 1921 by a law which introduced the so-called quota system. The number of aliens admitted from any country was to equal three per cent of the total number of persons of that nationality living in the United States in 1910. About 350,000 immigrants could thus come into the country each year by the terms of the act. The law of 1924 reduced the quota to two per cent and in addition provided that as soon as possible the so-called national-origins principle should control future immigration. By this scheme, finally adopted in 1929, immigration was limited to 150,000 each year; and the number of emigrants from each nation was to be so fixed that the national origin of the American people in 1920 would not be changed. One vexing feature of the Johnson Act was the express exclusion of the Japanese. This end had been practically secured by the Gentlemen's Agreement of 1907, and the new arrangement was keenly resented by Japan. It did much to poison Japanese-American amity.

The American people were satisfied with Coolidge's record as the presidential election neared in 1924. The Democrats tried vainly to raise the issue of corruption so rampant during Harding's régime. But under the warm glow of rising prosperity all was forgiven, and with such slogans as "Keep cool with Cal" and "Coolidge or Chaos," the Republicans won easily, gaining 54 per cent more votes than the combined votes of Robert LaFollette, the leader of a Progressive party, and John W. Davis, the Democratic aspirant.

During the second Coolidge administration there were few outstanding pieces of legislation. The national debt was lowered, and efforts were made at farm relief. Like the bonus, the problem of what to do for the farmer confronted Congress throughout the postwar decade. Agriculture failed to revive after the depression of 1920-1921. During the war, motivated by high prices for agricultural products, American farmers had bought thousands of tractors and land at boom prices. In

New Yorkers put out flags, cheered, waved, and threw tons of paper and ticker tape into the jammed streets when Admiral Richard Byrd returned from his flight over the South Pole in November 1929.

1919 the total farm debt was four billion dollars. With the depression, prices tumbled; wheat that brought $2.14 a bushel in 1919 was down to $.93 in 1923. Farm income declined from fifteen and one half to five and one half billion dollars. Yet fixed payments on debts had to be continued. After several unsuccessful attempts to aid the farmer, Congress finally passed the McNary-Haugen Bill in 1927 and again in 1928. Each time it was vetoed by President Coolidge.

Notwithstanding the depression in agriculture, the United States continued to enjoy what seemed to be dazzling prosperity in 1927 and 1928. Trade with the outside world kept factories at the peak of production. Radios, automobiles, rayon, cloth, moving pictures, and electric refrigerators were produced in great quantities, and the people had plenty of money to spend for them. Business optimism was reflected in an era of stock speculation that became a virtual mania. The stock market, mass production, high wages, high tariffs, great foreign loans, and the installment plan seemed for a time to be working together in amazing harmony. It was the high tide of American self-satisfaction and content.

Herbert Hoover's administration. Another Republican, Herbert Hoover, became president in 1929. Hoover had been a successful mining engineer, he had directed Belgian relief during the war, and he had been secretary of commerce since 1921. His Democratic opponent in the bitter campaign was Alfred E. Smith, the first Irish Catholic ever to obtain the presidential nomination. A liberal in politics, Smith was a product of the "sidewalks of New York." While governor of New York state he had made a name for himself as a progressive sponsor of social legislation. He came out boldly for repeal of prohibition. However laudable the aims of prohibition, it was true that the amendment had given rise to a new set of problems which seemed to many people more dangerous to the public than the evil which prohibition aimed at abolishing. Police forces were corrupted, and otherwise respectable citizens became lawbreakers. The taint of the "pay off" was found among government officials, while the bootlegger grew rich in defiance of law and order.

Hoover won the day on what one historian termed "Prosperity, prohibition, and prejudice." When the new president assumed office in 1929, he had behind him a Republican Congress and a country enjoying unbounded prosperity. The president indicated to Congress the necessity of action in three fields: tariff revision, farm relief, and law enforcement.

Hoover desired downward revision of the tariff, but after what one newspaper termed "the unrestrained play of selfishness and of petty politics," the Smoot-Hawley Tariff Act was passed in 1930. Tariff rates were raised on an average of 20 per cent over those already created by the act of 1922. More than one thousand economists from nearly two hundred colleges and universities joined in sending a protest to Hoover urging him to veto the bill. The bill was not vetoed.

In June 1929, an agricultural-marketing act was passed to bring relief to the farmer. This established a Federal Farm Loan Board controlling a fund of half a billion dollars to stabilize prices. The hoped-for results did not follow, and farm prices continued their downward trend. A special commission was created to study the problem of prohibition enforcement. But the commission's answer, couched in the Wickersham Report (1931) was disappointingly vague and divided, implying merely that some change in the machinery of prohibition was essential.

Foreign policy. From the beginning of Coolidge's term in 1923 to the end of the Hoover administration in 1933, the general trend of American foreign policy was isolationist. But some broadening of American interest and activity in international affairs took place. The United States, which had originally ignored messages from the League, began early in the 1920's to send unofficial observers to League meetings. In 1923 and again in 1927 American financial experts had taken a leading part in arranging for reparation payments. As early as 1921 Harding had called an international conference at Washington to study the problems of the Pacific. The famous Nine-Power Treaty grew out of this conference.

Presidents Harding, Coolidge, and Hoover all tried to get the United States to join the World Court, but none was successful. Other instances of American activity in the international scene were attendance at the Disarmament Conference at Geneva in 1927, the signing of the Kellogg-Briand Pact in 1928, and representation at the London Naval Conference in 1930. In 1932 an American representative sat on the Lytton Commission of the League of Nations which denounced Japanese aggression in Manchuria.

The great depression. In shocking contrast to the golden days of prosperity was the heavy fog of depression which settled on the United States in October 1929, when a catastrophic stock-market crash paralyzed American business. Farm foreclosures came by the thousands. By 1932 business failures numbered at least 30,000; the number of unemployed was somewhere between 12 and 15 million; foreign trade had fallen from 9 to 3 billion dollars. Five thousand banks closed their doors in the years 1929-1932.

The depression was a plain warning that the easy-going ways of a young and carefree nation were outdated. It was realized now that natural resources had to be safeguarded, that the banking system and security exchanges should

This is one of the twelve large dams built by the Tennessee Valley Authority for the development of electrical power in the Tennessee River basin.

be controlled in the public interest, and that purchasing power had to be given to all the people to keep industry moving. It was apparent also that citizens in a democracy had to pay at least as much attention to their duties in a democratic state as they had been paying to their rights and privileges.

The New Deal. In the midst of this stocktaking Franklin D. Roosevelt, the Democratic standardbearer, became President of the United States. Under his leadership a program to cope with the national emergency was put forth in 1933. Called the New Deal, it had three objectives: relief, recovery, and reform. Many millions of dollars were appropriated for the relief of the unemployed, and vast sums were expended for the construction of public works in the hope that such activity would stimulate economic recovery. The Civilian Conservation Corps offered employment and educational opportunities to thousands of young men. Federal Housing Administration encouraged building activity and gave, especially to lower-income groups, an opportunity to finance home building under liberal terms. Some plainly significant, as well as controversial, measures were taken to reform the economic structure. Measures were instituted to guarantee the bank deposits of small investors. The sale of stocks and bonds was regulated by a Securities Exchange Commission. The Tennessee Valley Authority was created by the government to produce power at reasonable rates that would constitute a "yardstick" for public utilities. The National Labor Relations Board was designed to protect labor and give it the right to collective bargaining. Most important of all was the Social Security Act, passed in 1935. For the first time in the history of the United States a comprehensive scheme for unemployment insurance and a plan for old-age retirement were introduced.

The full significance of the New Deal cannot be estimated at this early date. Its opponents contend that it has given too much power to the labor unions, that it has created a vast and irresponsible bureaucracy at Washington, that it has spent public funds in a profligate fashion, and that it seeks to destroy the capitalist system. Its supporters, on the other hand, maintain that the New Deal represents a reasonable compromise between the old and discredited system of *laissez faire* with its unbridled opportunities for exploitation and, at the other extreme, the tyranny of an all-powerful state under a totalitarian régime. They say that its aim is not to destroy capitalism but rather to preserve it by adapting it to new circumstances.

Latin America (1919-1939)

Latin America and the war. Latin America itself did not figure very prominently in the First World War, but the epochal struggle nevertheless quietly inaugurated a new era of trade in the Western Hemisphere. The fighting nations had made huge demands for Latin-American products, such as her cereals, meats, wool, hides, nitrates, copper, manganese, and oil. But export restrictions, high prices, and lack of ships made it difficult to get goods into Latin America from abroad. This unequal situation tended to encourage home-made products. The consequent development of industry and the increased buying power of Latin America resulted in a considerable increase in her foreign trade, which grew from less than three to more than five billion dollars. The mileage of railways was doubled, new highways were constructed, and public utilities were installed.

Fundamentally, however, Latin-American economy was not firmly established. There still remained several inescapable weaknesses. One was the lack of resources for an industrial economy, mainly iron and coal. A second was the predominantly agricultural basis of economic life. A third was the dangerous specialization of Latin-American economy.

Economic specialization. Although a vast storehouse of natural riches, Latin America compromised her economic future by drawing political boundaries which forced many of her countries to depend for their sustenance upon one product alone. Hence no distribution of economic risk has been possible. The welfare of most of the Latin-American countries has been so bound up with the export of particular agricultural or mineral resources that these countries have become enslaved by world market prices. Brazil is dependent upon a world market for its coffee, which accounts for one half of Brazil's annual exports. To check production and keep up the price of coffee, Brazil has been forced to burn nearly a sixth of the coffee crop each year. Costa Rica also is mainly a coffee-exporting country. The other Central American states are so bound up with the world's demand for one particular commodity that they have been popularly dubbed "the banana republics." In Chile the national economy has been dependent upon the export of nitrates and copper. In Argentina and Uruguay it has been meat and wheat. Cuban prosperity has been dependent upon sugar exports, and Mexico relies upon foreign sales of oil and silver. Economically far off balance, Latin America has been less equipped against loss of foreign markets through wars or depressions than almost any other region in the world.

Prosperity and depression. During the decade 1919 to 1929 Latin America carried forward economic diversification and industrialization. Local industries grew, and comparative prosperity prevailed. Seven nations adopted new constitutions of a liberal nature, and political stability seemed to be more prevalent, for six out of the twenty-one republics were tranquil from 1913 to 1929. The Indian was given greater attention, laws were passed for his protection, and land was made available for his use. This hopeful period of progress, however, was abruptly ended by the onset of the depression in 1929. Depending upon the export of one or more raw materials, such as oil or copper, for their prosperity, the Latin-American countries suffered critical economic conditions when world prices collapsed. These difficulties in turn increased political instability.

The depression took its usual fatal course in most of the states, leading to bankruptcies, unemployment, business stagnation, decline in public revenues, excessive governmental borrowing, government debt defaults, and even political revolutions. Within a year after February 1930, seven of the twenty Latin-American republics had revolutions. Recuperation was slow and painful, but the economic disasters had at least served to accelerate the vast socio-economic revolution which had been stirring since the First World War.

The economic outlook. Recent observers look to the growing industries of Latin America for a more promising future. In Argentina, the leading manufacturing nation in Latin America, industry had so progressed by 1939 that factory products almost equaled in value the agricultural products that had hitherto founded Argentine economy. Cities like Buenos Aires in Argentina, São Paulo and Rio de Janeiro in Brazil, Santiago in Chile, Mexico City, and Havana are rapidly developing into important manufacturing centers in Latin America's drive toward industrialization. Yet the relative scarcity of iron and coal, as well as a notable lack of local available capital, does not encourage the development of extensive manufacturing. The greatest progress has been made in the manufacture of consumer goods, and while all of the leading Latin-American states visualize the development of heavy industry, only Chile and Mexico seem sufficiently endowed with the necessary natural resources. Over $10,000,000,000 of foreign capital have been invested already in Latin America, but it appears unlikely that our southern neighbors will be able to realize their plans for industrialization without obtaining even more foreign capital and encouraging the further backing of enterprise by European and United States investors.

When former President Calles returned to Mexico in 1935, some voters, loyal to a subsequent administration, pinned a caricature of Calles on a mule's face and paraded through the streets of Mexico City. "This mule is for sale," the rider announced.

The fact has not been substantially altered, despite recent industrialization, that the prosperity of Latin America depends largely upon its ability to sell agricultural and mineral products abroad, mainly to Europe and the United States. The desire of the Latin Americans to trade abroad has always been met by an equivalent eagerness on the part of Europe and the United States to exchange manufactured goods for Latin-American raw materials. Trade rivalry among the great powers in Latin America has been, consequently, intense.

Although for thirty years the United States has been the largest single trader with Latin America, in normal times Europe as a whole represents Latin America's most important market. Of the total Latin-American trade in 1938, Europe took approximately fifty-four per cent of the exports and supplied forty-four per cent of the imports. The United States took thirty-one per cent of Latin America's exports and provided thirty-four per cent of its imports in the same year. The importance of a European market for Latin America has been even greater than the figures show, for the United States has done most of its Latin-American trading with the Caribbean states, leaving the great states of South America proper far more dependent upon Europe than

By 1936 Brazil had begun to modernize her methods of coffee production. Here a youth spreads coffee berries to commence drying on prepared soil. When they are half dried, they will be removed to ventilators for completion of the process.

the over-all view would indicate. Unfortunately, the dangers, both to the United States and to South America, which are inherent in the reliance of South America upon European trade cannot be solved by any great diversion of South American trade to the United States, for with the exception of such items as Brazilian coffee, Bolivian tin, and some few others, the United States also produces most of the materials prominent in South America's export trade.

Trade rivalry. The United States has always been greatly concerned over the political ramifications of Latin America's economic reliance upon Europe. Until recently, keen trade and investment competition between the United States and Great Britain has dominated the Latin-American economic scene. At the turn of the century, Germany began to loom in importance as a trade rival, and after a temporary eclipse because of the First World War and postwar economic debility, Germany again surged forward, dangerously challenging the Anglo-American trade ascendency in Latin America. Most of Germany's trade gains were made at the expense of the British; since 1910, in fact, only the United States and Germany have made any substantial gains in the Latin-American market. While on the eve of the Second World War the United States still had a greater annual market in Latin America than both Germany and England combined, it was highly significant that by then Germany had dethroned England as the nearest competitor of the United States.

Concern over the ascending prominence of German trade was necessarily intensified by the realization that Nazi-German rivalry was neither friendly, honorable, nor purely economic. Thanks to governmental sponsorship, Germany long before the Nazi régime was able to grant longer terms and better and easier conditions in its business transactions with Latin America. The Nazi system was even more effective. By resorting to barter, Nazi Germany had competitors at her mercy. Barter deals based upon the notorious *Aski* mark proved the most formidable weapon. Germany would offer to take great quantities of the staple export of some short-sighted Latin-American state and then pay for it with *Aski* marks, good only to buy German exports. The system at first appeared highly attractive to Latin America, but in the long run its advantages were typically one way. Prevented by the *Aski* mark from gaining foreign exchange, committed to buy German goods and only those goods—at artificial prices chosen by the Nazis—the disillusioned Latin Americans were being undersold with their own goods in the world market. Moreover, the Nazi methods became exceedingly dangerous when the Germans began capitalizing upon their ability to draw Latin America into a foreign-trade slavery. The threat of being able to create an accompanying political subservience became so great that by 1936 the Americas had already begun to unite in an effort to counteract it.

Social reform. There is a close correlation between the economic revolution which began at the close of the First World War and an accompanying social revolution. It had been hoped that the increase of factories, with their higher wages, would eventually raise social as well as economic standards and create a middle class that would act as a stabilizer for Latin-American governments. That hope is at present being realized in the more advanced republics. Modern Mexico has perhaps outstripped all the others in the process of social change. While certain other Latin-American states have gone further in some aspects, Mexico may justly claim to have epitomized the social revolution which has affected all of

Latin America in one way or another. As one authority has pointed out:

"In Mexico may be observed in process the rise of the *mestizo* and middle class into control of the state and toward ampler economic boundaries; the rise of the Indian, the revalidation of his culture and his participation in political life; the development of a conscious proletarian movement; the defeat of its landholding class and the partial solution of the agrarian problem; the growing freedom of women; the smashing of the political and economic power of the Church; the increasing strength of organized civilian life against militarism, still very dominant; the winning of unabridged national sovereignty and increasing economic independence from foreign imperialism; the rapid expansion of popular education; the painful advance toward greater political stability."[10]

Social reform in all of Latin America has grown out of socio-economic problems which have existed for centuries. Most prominent among these problems have been those of the land, illiteracy, sanitation, and clerical influence. The land problem has been especially acute. Vast feudal estates have re-created a medieval serfdom in most of Latin America. Statistics show that Brazil has 45,000,000 people and fewer than 800,000 landowners; four fifths of the arable land is owned by 3000 people. In Argentina, nearly thirty per cent of the total area under cultivation is in estates of 25,000 acres or over. The arable soil of Chile is owned by seven per cent of the population. In 1934 thousands of Colombian peasants, driven to desperation under the age-old system of absentee landlordism, rose up to demand titles to the holdings on which they and their forefathers had toiled under virtual feudal bondage. Only in Mexico, where before the First World War it took an entire day on a railroad train to cross some farms, has there been any extensive land reform.

Some of the oldest and finest universities in the world are located in Latin America. Generally, however, educational opportunities have been lacking for the poor. Illiteracy is prevalent throughout Latin America, varying from twenty-five per cent in countries like Argentina or Costa Rica, to seventy-five per cent in Brazil, and to even a higher proportion in some of the countries of the Caribbean area. With the recent democratic movements, however, more attention has been given to education, especially in Argentina, Chile, Uruguay, Paraguay, Mexico, Cuba, and Costa Rica. Latin America is beginning to believe that its promises for the future must be won largely in the schools.

Health and sanitation problems have been particularly challenging to Latin America, where ignorance, poverty, and often debilitating climate have combined to create deplorable conditions. It has been said that as many as two thirds of the people of Spanish America suffer from one or another of the many tropical scourges of the hemisphere. The mass of the people know little about sanitation and personal hygiene, and the death rate, especially among children, is extremely high. In the past ten years, however, the Latin-American countries, particularly Bolivia, Chile, Mexico, and Venezuela, have spent increasing sums for public health.

The problem of the Church has been politico-economic. In Latin America certain officials of the Church have combined with the landed interests to oppose the liberals. The clerical-liberal struggle became a government-clerical struggle wherever the liberals won power, for the liberal government officials found they could make few moves without encroaching upon some prerogative claimed by the Church as its special field. In the majority of the countries, Church and state have now been separated, but the problem is yet far from solved.

Social trends summarized. In summary, the socio-economic revolution has opened new horizons to Latin America. The gradual development of a middle class, where before there had been only a few extremely rich and the extremely poor, is the accompaniment of industrialization and land reform. The realization of practical democracy and stable government is the accompaniment of the more equal distribution of wealth. Rising political, economic, and social standards will bring greater health and sanitation. Latin America is perhaps just now passing over the threshold to the realization of its greater potentialities. Before this is accomplished, however, Latin America will have many problems to deal with, and their solution will in no small measure depend upon the moral and even material support of the United States.

Netherlands investors built up great oil refineries like this one at Curacao in the Dutch West Indies, guarded in the Second World War against sabotage by Allied troops.

Race fusion and distinctive culture. If Latin America's economic and political problems are solved there is every reason to believe that a rich and distinctive culture will be created, able to play an even more notable role in world civilization. Important racial factors are now working in this direction. Latin America is the outstanding example of the fusion of European stock with non-Europeans.

Latin-American culture has always been much more European in nature than that of the United States because the whites, looking toward Latin Europe for cultural inspiration, were the dominant group. During the past three hundred years, the European culture transplanted to Latin America has made important contributions in literature and thought. The most promising aspect of Latin-American culture, however, is not that modeled in the past, very largely upon European forms, but a distinctively new culture which utilizes native patterns, especially in art and music. Unlike the situation in the United States, where the North American Indian contributed little toward the new national culture, in Latin America after a long period of European domination the great mass of pure Indian and half-breed blood is beginning to assert itself. Thus after many generations of neglect the Indian's folk music, dances, art, and handicrafts are coming into prominence.

Latin America is now creating a new musical idiom, independent of European tradition. The themes and rhythmic patterns of aboriginal music joined often to Negro forms are giving rise to much musical creativeness. Latin America has two world-famous musicians who are active in its musical Renaissance. Carlos Chavez has done much research in native music and has been in charge of the Mexican National Conservatory of Music. Heitor Villa-Lobos is a prolific composer, a native of Brazil, whose main aim has been to make his countrymen a nation of music lovers. One of the ways by which he hopes to achieve this is the arrangement of masterpieces for choral singing.

The modern art of Latin America is especially noteworthy, showing many signs of multiple race-culture contributions from such sources as the Negro, the Spanish, and above all the Indian. Many Latin-American painters are finding inspiration in native types and scenery. Portinari is one well-known Brazilian artist who paints the life around him instead of copying European models (see page 497). Cesáreo Bernaldo de Quirós, long a painter in Europe, returned to Argentina to paint a series of canvases depicting the life of the *gaucho* and country scenes. José Clemente Orozco became known for his interpretation of political struggles in Mexico. Diego Rivera, another famous Latin-American painter, has used the Indian as a symbol of his country's culture (see page 496).

Literature is also finding it need not go abroad for its models. Of late, Latin-American writing has become more realistic and more rooted in the life of the country. Since 1920 prose writing has shown much interest in the exploitation of the Indian, has utilized native folklore, and has evidenced much concern for the oppressed.

Pan American policies. The profound revolution in Latin-American political, economic, and social life has fortunately been paralleled by an equally profound revolution in the relations of the United States to Latin America. The First World War and the subsequent era of prosperity, however, did not bring any modification of the policies of Dollar Diplomacy and Theodore Roosevelt's Big Stick. Actually, the postwar Washington administration avidly capitalized upon investment opportunities in Latin America to strengthen the political and economic hegemony of the United States. At an inter-American conference held in Havana in 1928, the Latin-American delegates took the opportunity to display their resentment of what appeared to be the increasing "interventionism" of the United States. Certainly, the era of good will and inter-American solidarity seemed as far from realization at Havana as it ever had been.

A change began to take place in the Latin-American policy of the United States under Secretary of State Stimson in the Hoover administration. The formerly vigorous protection of the lives, property, and investments of United States citizens was appreciably modified; the Marines were withdrawn from Nicaragua, and preparations were made for their withdrawal from Haiti; the depression revolutions of Latin America were given a free hand, thus marking the general repudiation of the Wilson policy of supporting only constitutionally established régimes in Latin America. As one authority has stated, however:

> "Such modifications in our Latin-American policy were in many ways a forecast of the good-neighbor policy later proclaimed by Franklin D. Roosevelt. But they were piecemeal and almost surreptitious. They seemed to be made unenthusiastically and reluctantly under the pressure of strong opposition to former aggressiveness."[11]

The Good Neighbor policy. Despite praiseworthy beginnings under President Hoover, it was the Roosevelt-Hull administration that secured the program known as the Good Neighbor policy. In his 1933 inaugural speech President Roosevelt committed the United States to "the policy of the good neighbor—the neighbor who resolutely respects himself, and because he does so, respects the rights of others—the neighbor who respects his obligations and respects the sanctity of his agreements in and with a world of neighbors."

Avenue 18th of July is "Main Street" in Montevideo, Uruguay. Contrast the nineteenth-century "eclectic," domed skyscraper in the rear with the modern office building in the foreground.

The new policy was given further definition by Sumner Welles of the state department when he said later:

"Our new policy of the Good Neighbor has been predicated upon the belief of this government that there should exist an inter-American political relationship based on a recognition of actual and not theoretical equality between the American republics; on a complete forbearance from interference by any one republic in the domestic concerns of any other; on economic cooperation; and finally on the common realization that, in the world at large, all of the American republics confront the same international problems, and that, in their relations with non-American powers, the welfare and security of any one of them cannot be a matter of indifference to the others."[12]

Adding significantly that acts and not words were required, Welles was soon able to prove the good intentions of the Roosevelt administration. Late in 1933 Secretary of State Hull signed at Montevideo an agreement by which he committed the United States to uphold the principle that "no state has the right to intervene in the internal or external affairs of another." In February 1934 an Export-Import Bank was established in Washington to help finance and facilitate foreign trade, especially with Latin America. In May 1934 a treaty was signed with Cuba expressly abrogating the Platt Amendment and the right of the United States thereunder to intervene in that country. In August 1934 the Marines were withdrawn from Haiti. In September 1934 the United States signed with Cuba its first reciprocal trade agreement; six more were signed in the next two years with Latin-American countries. Only little over a year had passed since Franklin D. Roosevelt first proclaimed the Good Neighbor policy, but by the end of 1934 his sincerity had been amply proved by deeds.

Consistency has been the keynote of the Roosevelt Good Neighbor policy ever since its inception. The changes in the policy of the United States were welcomed by the Latin Americans, who soon began to view the United States with an unprecedented confidence and esteem. In the words of one authority: "The stern policeman and the imperialistic colossus had become the Good Neighbor. At the end of 1938 the economic position of the United States in Latin America was stronger than ever and it possessed the friendship of most of its neighbors."[13]

Summary

Confidence in democratic institutions seemed unbounded at the conclusion of the First World War. Nearly all the states emerging from the débris of the vanquished German and Austrian empires started their national existence with liberal constitutions. In practically all of them—Rumania, Poland, Austria, and others—self-governing institutions soon gave way to dictatorial régimes.

In 1919 France apparently had everything a nation could desire. The old enemy across the Rhine had been crushed, and Alsace-Lorraine had been returned to the fold. France was certainly the undisputed master of Europe and after the war enjoyed a measure of economic prosperity. But the heavy burden of rebuilding her devastated war regions, the cessation of German reparations payments, and the onerous financial burden of subsidizing many allies in eastern and central Europe gradually undermined economic stability. National budgets were not balanced; chronic political instability and corruption among politicians gradually weakened the French position as the leader of Europe.

Great Britain soon began to realize that her victory in 1918 was largely illusory. Successive prime ministers tried in vain to solve the ensuing problems. In 1924 the people turned from the Conservative party under Baldwin and placed MacDonald in power. This leader of the British Labor party shared with his rival, Baldwin, the political spotlight in England's troubled decade after the war. Neither of them made much headway in overcoming England's difficulties. The depression in 1931 gave Great Britain a National government, which did manage to make some progress in economic recovery. While it would be incorrect to assert that democratic institutions were waning in Great Britain, there were numerous disturbing indications that British leadership was not sufficiently dynamic to adapt itself to the conditions of a new age.

In the Western Hemisphere the Latin-American republics had democratic institutions which were often a façade for dictatorial régimes. In these states much remained also to be done—to divide the land more equally, to offer more adequate educational opportunities, and to raise the standard of living of the people. Progress was made in this direction in several of the republics, but here too the onslaught of the depression in 1930 retarded and even undid some of the achievements.

The United States in 1919 had two more years of leadership by Woodrow Wilson. No constructive governmental measures were enacted during this period, for the Congress and the American people were merely marking time until they could have a chief executive who would lead the way back to "normalcy." Such a man was Warren G. Harding, whose short term, however, was blighted by corruption among his highest officials. His successors at the White House, Calvin Coolidge and Herbert Hoover, were better qualified to give the nation what it wanted: prosperity, isolation, and national confidence. For six years, from 1923 to 1929, the American scene was tranquil. The country seemed to be securing what it wanted without recourse to the wishes or needs of the rest of the world. In 1929 depression came to shatter the illusion of glittering prosperity and to reënforce the fact that in the long run the world is economically interdependent. Twelve years of Republican dominance closed in 1933 when Franklin D. Roosevelt, a Democrat, became President of the United States. With decision and speed the new President inaugurated a scheme of relief, reform, and recovery—the New Deal—which took the United States far from the conservative policies of the early twenties.

India

1919	New constitution	Did not satisfy nationalists
	Rowlatt Acts give police power	
1920	Gandhi's civil disobedience campaign	Bloodshed and noncooperation
1930-1932	Round Table Conferences accomplish little	Non-participation of Congress
1935	Government of India Act	Federal government with many restrictions
1941	National Congress demands independence	Leadership of Nehru
1942	Failure of Cripps Mission	

Eastern Asia and Western Powers

	Great Britain: Hong Kong, Singapore	Largest Chinese investor
	France: Indo-China, Kwangchow	Small investment
	Holland: Netherlands East Indies	Economic exploitation
	United States: Philippines	Not heavy investments in China, Japan
	Russia: geographical consideration	Political, not economic stake
	Oceania: strategic value	Wake, Guam, Fiji, mandates

China

1898-1918	Reactionary government of Tzu Hsi	Last of Manchu rulers
1900	Boxer rebellion against foreigners	Harsh treaty imposed by west
1912-1915	Sun Yat-sen forms Chinese republic	Yuan Shih-Kai and reaction
1916-1926	Disorder and disunity	Rival governments
1926-1930	Chiang Kai-Shek unites country	Economic and educational advance

Japan

1894-1895	Victory in war with China	Treaty of Shimonoseki
1902	Alliance with Great Britain	
1904-1905	War with Russia nets gains in Korea, Manchuria	Treaty of Portsmouth
1910	Annexation of Korea, or Chosen	
1915	Twenty-one Demands on China	To reduce China to protectorate
1922	Nine Power Treaty to protect China	
1922-1931	Economic and Industrial advance	
1931	Attack on Chinese	Nonintervention by powers
1932	Puppet régime set up in Manchuria	Called Manchukuo
1936	Japan joins Axis	
1937	Invasion of China	
1938	"New Order" proclaimed	Economic self-sufficiency

The Line-Up

1939	Allies: Australia, New Zealand, India, Burma, Malaya, Indo-China, Chinese concessions, Oceania	India protests inclusion in war without independence
	Axis: Japan, Thailand	
	Neutral: Russia, Netherlands East Indies	

CHAPTER 13

The Orient Astir

On Sunday morning, December 7, 1941, Japanese airplanes suddenly appeared over the American naval base at Pearl Harbor in Hawaii. This action was a tragic surprise to the naval and military forces of the United States and to the American people as well. For many months they had been looking apprehensively at Europe, the main theater of the Second World War. In that direction, as always in the past, seemed to lie the chief threat to American security and peace. The great problems which precipitated the war had their center in Europe, and the Atlantic had become increasingly smaller with the development of air power. Yet it was from Japan, with whom America had never fought a battle, and in the vast expanse of the Pacific, that war came once more to a shocked American people.

Wars are seldom the result of sudden whims on the part of nations, and when the Japanese government decided to strike at Pearl Harbor, it had reasons it deemed important. This chapter shows in part what these reasons were and traces the sequence of events in the Pacific area during the twentieth century up to 1939. The tragedy which occurred at Pearl Harbor was the outcome of historical forces which for the past fifty years had been revolutionizing the entire structure of oriental civilization.

The pages to follow have significance in another way. From early times the orient and occident, despite numerous contacts, tended to evolve along paths of mutual exclusiveness. Then, in the eighteenth and nineteenth centuries especially, the barrier of isolation was broken down under the impact of western culture upon such countries as India, China, and Japan. The eventual triumph of westernization set in motion new historical forces which today are creating sweeping changes in the world pattern.

But we should bear in mind that the westernizing process did not affect all Asiatic countries equally. Whereas western machines and education only partially modified life in China and India, they brought about a vast economic and social revolution in Japan. Therefore, while India and China did not learn the means of attaining power to command international respect, Japan made herself powerful enough to embark upon a program of imperialistic aggression, the full effects of which were felt only in the Second World War.

India Seeks to Rule Herself

The Morley-Minto reforms. In 1857, as earlier described, the British government had to cope with a rebellion in India known as the Sepoy mutiny. While the British put down this threat to their dominance and introduced numerous reforms to improve the political situation, Indian nationalism did not wither. On the contrary, by 1880 it was apparent that nationalism was growing rapidly. During the next quarter of a century it grew even more self-assertive. Confronted by the spread of violence, the British government between the years 1907 and 1909 carried out the Morley-Minto reforms. Up to this time the government had been almost completely bureaucratic. Now the various provincial legislatures in India were given elected Indian majorities, and an Indian was permitted to sit in the executive council of the governor-general. The legislature of the central government remained under British control. Moderate nationalists were satisfied for the time being, but they were presently repudiated by many more aggressive nationalists who regarded the others as old-fashioned and who were determined to obtain complete independence for India. Violence continued until 1914, the year of the outbreak of the First World War.

Indian loyalty to Great Britain. Many observers had predicted that when such a conflict came Great Britain would find India a serious liability. But when hostilities commenced in the summer of 1914, nearly all unfriendly acts against Great Britain ceased. The native princes sent large sums of money to London for the purchase of war equipment, and at the moment when the German army was threatening to break through to British lines in Belgium, an Indian expeditionary force of some fifty thousand men arrived in France and was hurried to the battlefield, where it soon proved its worth. As the war continued, Indian regiments were sent to east Africa, and other contingents participated in the campaigns fought in the Near East.

Moves for self-government. For the first three years of the war there was little unrest in India, but by the spring of 1917 it was obvious that the Indian people expected compensation from Great Britain in the way of more self-government. In the summer of 1917 it was announced in the British Parliament that the goal to be attained in India was the gradual development of self-government as part of the British Empire. India expected that as soon as the war ended steps would be taken to put this policy into effect. When victory came in 1918 to Great Britain and her allies, India eagerly awaited the reforms which had been promised. A commission had already been sent to India to frame a new constitution, and its proposals were made public in 1919. These did not provide for full self-government, as Indian nationalists had hoped, but represented only a step in that direction.

No one can say whether the proposed governmental reforms might have proved satisfactory in a tranquil atmosphere, but any chance of their acceptance in India was swept away by the outbreak of a struggle between the British and the Indian nationalists. Unrest developed, and in an ill-advised moment the British decided to pass the Rowlatt Acts, giving the police and other officials extraordinary powers to ferret out subversive activity. Disappointment with the political situation, epidemics, the high cost of living, and the Rowlatt Acts made many nationalists demand sweeping changes.

Gandhi. The chief nationalist was Mohandas K. Gandhi. Born in 1869 of middle-class parents, Gandhi had been sent to London to study law. Upon his return home he found the practice of law disappointing, and thereupon went to South Africa, where he built up a lucrative practice. So far he had been a normal businessman, but suddenly his outlook on life and his standard of values were completely revolutionized. The new Gandhi repudiated wealth, condemned violence, practiced ascetic self-denial, and above all believed that true happiness can be achieved only by service.

Gandhi began his career as reformer and champion of his people in South Africa. The Indians in this British dominion were victimized by numerous laws which restricted their freedom of movement, prevented them from buying property, and imposed special taxation. Gandhi forced the government to remove some of these restrictions. His method was not force but rather passive resistance or noncooperation. With Gandhi as their leader the Indians in South Africa carried on various strikes—including hunger strikes; they refused work, held mass demonstrations, and marched into areas where their presence was forbidden by law. Some of his followers were beaten, and many were thrown into prison, but Gandhi persisted in noncooperation and continued to secure concessions for his countrymen.

When he returned to his native land shortly after the First World War broke out in 1914, Gandhi was welcomed as a hero. Something in his character appealed strongly to the Indian people, who for centuries past had revered the mystic and the ascetic. During the war Gandhi cooperated with the British government, but the Rowlatt Acts and the disappointing concessions of the new constitution led him to announce his determination to force the British to give India self-rule.

The civil-disobedience campaign. In the spring of 1919 Gandhi actively introduced his campaign. A mass *hartal,* or strike, was announced in which all work was to cease and the population was to pray and fast. Contrary to Gandhi's plan, riots took place, Europeans were killed, and a body of soldiers was sent to try to restore order. By command of General Dyer a large body of unarmed Indians assembled contrary to the general's orders was dispersed by gunfire, several hundred being killed. All hope of cooperation between Indian and Briton was temporarily at an end. During these tragic days the new governmental system was set up, but members of the powerful National Congress who were behind Gandhi refused to take office under the new constitution. Gandhi, although at the peak of his popularity in 1921, suffered a temporary

A crowd of admirers surrounded Mohandas Gandhi as he arrived by ricksha at the viceroy's palace in September 1940. His visit followed the British offer to give India dominion status if she would aid the British war effort.

eclipse when his program failed to obtain *Swaraj* (independence) from the British. For his civil-disobedience campaign Gandhi was sentenced in 1922 to six years' imprisonment. However, he was released in 1924 when Ramsay MacDonald became prime minister.

Round Table Conferences. There was little peace in India in the 1920's, and during 1928 and 1929 a group of experts from Great Britain, the Simon Commission, toured the country preparatory to making recommendations for changes in the structure of government. In June 1930 the Simon Commission issued a survey of the Indian situation which suggested only a cautious advance in the direction of self-government. Meanwhile Gandhi had initiated another campaign demanding self-government. A new and promising road opened in 1930 when a series of Round Table Conferences was arranged in London. At the first of these conferences the world was electrified by the news that the Indian princes had agreed in principle to the idea of creating a great federal union in India. Up to this time India had consisted of two great political divisions: British India, ruled directly by the British, and the native India of the princes, composed of a number of distinct political units each ruled by a rajah or other Indian ruler under the final protection and authority of the British government. Unfortunately, the safeguards needed to protect the Mohammedan minority under the new government were not settled to the satisfaction of either Hindus or Moslems, and in the second conference (1931) the native princes and the delegates from British India could not agree as to the best type of federation. Vigorous anti-British demonstrations broke out in India, becoming very serious in 1932. Neither the second conference nor a third one (in November 1932) achieved tangible results.

The Government of India Act. In March 1933 a proposed constitution was made public. For two years this was heatedly discussed by members of the British Parliament and by Indian leaders. After prolonged debate the Government of India Act became a law in August 1935. Although the new constitution provided for a substantial degree of self-government, it did not give India complete independence but created a federal government consisting of the viceroy and a legislature composed of a council of state and a legislative assembly. To these houses both the Indian princes and the eleven provinces of British India were to send representatives. In the provinces the government was under the control of the Indian lawmakers, subject to certain safeguards in the hands of a British governor. In the central government all the departments of government were transferred to the Indian legislators except those of defense, religious affairs, and foreign relations. These remained in British hands. In addition a supreme court was established. The Government of India Act expanded the franchise, thereby giving the vote to about thirty-five million persons in provincial elections. By 1941 that part of the act dealing with the provinces of British India was in force, but the federal system had not been launched, owing to the hesitancy of many of the native states to come under the central government.

Nationalist policies and the war. That a vast number of Indians were dissatisfied with existing political conditions was indicated by the insistent demands of the Indian National Congress during 1941 for Indian self-rule. These nationalists, led by the dynamic Pandit Jawaharlal Nehru, were convinced that Great Britain's record in the past did not justify Indian participation in the Second World War, that the paramount issue for India was freedom.

The success of Japan in the South Pacific in the opening months of 1942 demonstrated that not only British interests in Asia but the political future of India itself were menaced.

The sacred cattle of India leisurely roam the principal bazaar street in Delhi. It is a poor country, and the animals are underfed. They are literally not worth their salt, but Hindu law forbids the natives to kill them.

On March 23, 1942, Sir Stafford Cripps arrived in India. For many years a champion of Indian home rule, Cripps brought with him a proposal from the British cabinet for full dominion status for India after the war. Cripps held numerous conferences with Hindu and Moslem leaders, but unfortunately no agreement was reached among the interested parties. The British government maintained that it must have the final decision regarding the defense of India at such a critical time; the nationalist leaders wanted more active Indian participation. The Moslems demanded assurances that under the proposed scheme they as a minority would be protected, while the Hindu leaders would not accede to a plan calling for virtual Moslem autonomy.

When Cripps finally departed for London, his mission had achieved no immediate success. A short time later, as the Japanese armies overran Burma and struck dangerously toward India proper, Gandhi announced that the Indian people should meet the invaders with a policy of noncooperation. He also demanded that the British grant India freedom at once.

The social aspect of India. India, it must be remembered, is not a country in the ordinarily accepted sense of that term, nor is it a nation. Rather, it is a vast subcontinent, as large as all of Europe excluding Russia, and a congeries of nations. Mere size is not necessarily a bar to progress, but India has a complexity of religions and a social stratification not found elsewhere in the world. In 1500 the population was estimated at 100 million; today it is over 400 million, and in 1950 it may exceed 450 million. As most of the people are engaged in tilling the soil, the tremendous increase in population has caused the farms to be fragmented into uneconomical holdings. A high birth rate is accompanied by a high death rate. In New Zealand the expectation of life is 62 years; in India it is 28.

India's millions do not form one homogeneous unit. It is estimated that there are at least 225 different languages in use, to say nothing of minor dialects. Arbitrary divisions in Indian social and economic life exist because of the deep-seated antagonism between the Hindu community (about 280 million) and the Moslems (some 90 million). Within Hinduism itself there are about 2000 castes and sub-castes. Politically there exist the dualism of the provinces of British India (the territory of which was annexed to the Crown) and the 600 native states in the India of the rajahs. Some of these states are as large as the entire British Isles and have a population of several million. Each of these states, small or large, follows its own customs and form of government. It was the aim of the Government of India Act of 1935 to merge these states with the provinces in a national political structure, but, as has been stated, the rajahs have not yet come under the proposed federal government.

Although India is predominantly agricultural, she has turned over most of her factories to war production and is making nearly all her own war materials. These workmen are shaping a piece of white-hot metal.

Economic life in India. Ninety per cent of India's population lives a rural life in the 700,000 villages which dot the countryside. For thousands of years rulers and régimes have come and gone in India, but the peasant, the *ryot*, has paid little attention to politics. His mind is concerned with the state of his crops, a current religious ceremony, or payments to the moneylender. The Indian peasant typically celebrates certain important occasions, such as the marriage of a son, with lavishness which he can ill afford. This custom plays into the hands of unscrupulous moneylenders who charge as high as thirty-seven per cent interest for their loans.

Hundreds of thousands of peasant families barely manage to survive on their diminutive farms. An average peasant's budget shows an annual income of about one hundred dollars. Farm produce valued at sixty-one dollars provides the food budget of the peasant and his family. The left-over crops (when sold) bring in about thirty-nine dollars in actual cash. Out of this sum six dollars is paid out for land tax, leaving thirty-three dollars to be spent on education, clothing, medicine, and the like. But interest often amounting to as much as twenty dollars is due yearly to the moneylender. It is evident that such a budget does not provide a decent standard of living.

A basic feature of Hindu religion—in contrast to some other religions in India—is its belief in the sacredness and unity of all animal life and its refusal to kill animals or eat meat. This aspect of Hinduism has important economic consequences. The refusal to take any form of animal life results in the accumulation of immense numbers of unproductive cattle. India maintains 215 million out of the total 690 million cattle in the entire world. The barren, maimed, and aged cattle are kept, and they eat much of the all-too-scarce fodder which might be used to feed better stock. Although there are about sixty cattle for every one hundred persons in India, the milk consumption per person is very low.

The conflict of forces in India. The Indian problem is one of the most important and complex in the world. Indian leaders see in parliamentary self-government the answer to India's problems. Gandhi has succeeded in arousing his countrymen from their lethargy and in kindling for the first time in the long history of India a dynamic feeling of national unity in a large part of the population. India must sooner or later be its own master. But when? What kind of social, political, and economic structure should be created? Gandhi would apparently return India to the handicraft days of the family spinning wheel and shun the factories that are becoming more and more common in the larger Indian cities.

But economists believe that industrialization is necessary for India in order to raise the standard of living of its teeming masses. Pandit Jawaharlal Nehru, realizing that much of Indian poverty springs from evils in the native social and economic structure, is attacking not only British rule but also the exploitation of the peasant by the moneylender and landowner. Nehru advocates the doctrine of socialism. If India's poverty is to be ameliorated, there must be an improvement of village life. Already the government has worked out certain regulations and plans: (1) each village must have a school, (2) villagers are discouraged from spending large sums on marriage ceremonies, (3) vaccination is required, (4) small model houses are being built and village drains and supplies improved, and (5) the milk and egg supplies have been increased.

India is on the march. It is probable that sweeping changes, peaceful and violent, will occur. No one can predict their form or content. India today is a disturbing complex of forces ancient and modern, religious and secular, capitalistic and socialistic, eastern and western. But since even more complex problems have been solved throughout history, it is reasonable to hope that India will be able to work out her own unique pattern of life.

The Great Powers in Eastern Asia

W***estern interests in eastern Asia.*** No Asiatic country has been left unaffected by the impact of western, that is European and American, interests. In India, Burma, the Netherlands East Indies, the Philippines, and Indo-China the control has been more or less direct. In China, Persia (Iran), and Siam (Thailand), the control has been less obvious, perhaps because the economic domination has not been accompanied by out-and-out direct rule or political suzerainty. Japan is unique in that it adopted the techniques of the west without accepting domination. In fact, Japan is now attempting to oust western power from eastern Asia and convert the area to her "New Order." It is therefore necessary to review the political and economic interests of the major powers in this part of the world.

Great Britain's stake in the Far East. Exclusive of its control of India, Great Britain was still probably the greatest investor in Asia during the period at hand and therefore had

ASIA
GREENLAND
ALASKA
-94° F.
Cold pole of the world
EUROPE
U. S. S. R.
Sakhalin
MANCHUKUO
JAPAN
textiles
coal and iron
MONGOLIA
TURKEY
SYRIA
IRAQ
TURKESTAN
textiles
CHINA
PERSIA
rugs
AFGHANISTAN
TIBET
silk, rice, and tea
AFRICA
ARABIA
NEPAL
textiles
INDIA
PHILIPPINES
BURMA
FR. INDOCHINA
SIAM
rubber
tin
EAST INDIES
NETHERLANDS
Indian Ocean
Equator (marked at 500 mi. intervals)
R.M. Chapin, Jr.

the most at stake. That helps explain why the British taxpayer was called on to construct huge naval strongholds at Hong Kong and Singapore at a cost of hundreds of millions of dollars. The British flag waved over Burma, the Malay Peninsula, British North Borneo, British New Guinea, and numerous smaller sites of strategic importance, such as various islands in the Pacific. Nine million Britishers had established permanent homes in Australia and New Zealand. Hundreds of millions of English pounds were invested in tea and rubber plantations, gold and tin mines, oil wells, rice fields, and spices. It is estimated that the British had invested half a billion dollars in southeastern Asia (including $150,000,000 in the Netherlands East Indies). From British Malaya came forty per cent of the world's rubber and tin, eleven per cent of its copra, and nine per cent of its tungsten. And southeastern Asia paid British and other western shareholders large dividends.

Great Britain and China. British economic interests were even more strongly involved in China. It is estimated that in 1900 the total British investments in China amounted to about $260,300,000. In 1914 this figure had jumped to $607,500,000, while in 1930 British investments stood at $1,189,200,000.[1] Twenty-five per cent of this amount was involved in import, export, and general trade, 21 per cent in real estate, 18 per cent in manufacturing, 14 per cent in transportation, 12 per cent in banking and finance, and the rest in public utilities, mining, and miscellaneous items. In 1902, British money represented 33 per cent of the total foreign investment in China; in 1930 it stood at 36.7 per cent.[2] British investments centered principally in the prosperous Shanghai area and the Yangtze valley.

Great Britain has been interested in protecting these investments as much as possible and has favored on the whole comparatively little change in the status quo. During the thirties the British government was conciliatory to the point of appeasement. It made no effort to slow down Japanese expansion so long as these were confined to Manchuria and northern China. The defensive attitude of the British in eastern Asia prior to 1939, and to some extent later, was due to their fear that they were not strong enough in the Far East to cope with a Japan which could threaten British interests in China and British Malaya and perhaps even in Australia and New Zealand.

French activity. France has not played so dramatic a role in eastern Asia as other occidental powers. Its possessions centered about French Indo-China, an area which contained about twenty-one million people in 1931. Indo-China is immensely rich in mineral and agricultural resources. France also used Indo-China as a springboard to advance its interests in southern China, such as building a railroad into that area. The French secured a leasehold at Kwangchow and concessions at certain treaty ports. To protect their investments in eastern Asia as well as possessions in the Pacific, the French established a naval base on the east coast. French investments in China in 1902 were worth $91,000,000; in 1914, $171,400,000; and in 1930, $192,400,000. Compared with some other countries, French investments were small, representing but 5.9 per cent of the total foreign investment.[3]

With Great Britain, France played an important part in the internal affairs of Siam (Thailand), lying between French Indo-China and Burma (see map, page 409). France and Great Britain attempted to prevent the domination of Thai affairs by the Japanese, a domination which would critically affect French and British interests in the adjoining territories.

The Netherlands East Indies. In 1941 the Netherlands East Indies had an estimated population of 70,000,000 distributed over some 3000 islands possessing an area of 735,267 square miles. The Netherlands East Indies extend east and west for a distance longer than continental United States and are sixty times the size of Holland itself. Java is the most densely populated area in the world. In 1941 it was estimated that Europeans numbered only 250,000 out of this huge population. The Chinese numbered well over 1,200,000, and other foreign Asiatics, more than 110,000. The rest were natives, of the ethnological group known as Indonesians, a highly industrious people of the Mohammedan faith. The spread of education has fostered in these natives an increasing desire for self-government. And Dutch administrators have had to face the problem of a growing trade unionism.

The Netherlands East Indies play a strategic role in the world economy, whether in times of peace or war. Besides producing great quantities of copper, manganese, petroleum, and phosphates, the islands supply 90 per cent of the world's quinine requirements, 85 per cent of its pepper, 33 per cent of its rubber, 18 per cent of its tin, 17 per cent of its tea, and 12 per cent of its sugar.[4] The Indies have been a lucrative field for many foreign investors, although the Dutch have had by far the greatest stake in these islands.

"Western capital is invested in banking, shipping, mining, and agriculture, with agriculture taking the lion's share. The amount of outside capital invested in the East Indies is estimated at from four to six billion florins. Three fourths of this capital is estimated as Dutch. The Dutch East Indies Government bonds, now aggregating about a billion and a half florins, are held abroad, practically all by the Dutch. Before 1930 the profits on these investments ran as high as 400,000,000 florins yearly. During the worst of the depression years these profits practically disappeared and today are only a fraction of what they were in 1930."[5]

Dutch policy in the Indies. The possession of the Indies has had a striking effect upon Holland and her economy. Millions in profits have gone to the governing country. As a result, the Dutch have ruled the Indies from an economic rather than from a political or social standpoint. This does not mean that they have not been concerned with such colonial problems as hygiene, education, and the general well-being of the natives. But their principal aim has been to govern the islands so as to exploit their economic resources as efficiently as possible.

Holland maintained a small but efficient navy and army in the Netherlands East Indies, although the Dutch realized always that their strength would avail them nothing against such powerful neighbors as the British or the Japanese. Great Britain has had rich adjoining territory in the Malay Peninsula and Burma and so could supply herself with the vital products of southeastern Asia. From the British, the Dutch have had little or nothing to fear. But with the Japanese, the situation has been different. Modern and semi-industrialized Japan is lacking in those mineral and agricultural resources which bring so much wealth to the investors in the Netherlands East Indies. Furthermore, Japan showed herself during the thirties as more than willing to use her powerful navy and army to obtain hegemony over an area extending from Manchuria to Java. The Dutch were powerless to resist conquest alone and depended on the British as allies in such an emergency. As the Second World War drew near, an apprehensive Dutch gaze was constantly turned toward the northern horizon, where war clouds were gathering.

In Tarakan, Borneo, Dutch oil wells were built native style, with thatched roofs. These fields fell to Japan in 1942.

United States interests. The United States, too, has had an important role in eastern Asia during the present century. An American, John Hay, was intimately associated with the famous Open Door policy at the turn of the century to insure China's territorial integrity and make possible equal privileges for all nations trading with the Chinese. President Theodore Roosevelt aided in the negotiating of the Treaty of Portsmouth, which concluded the Russo-Japanese War. American business interests created a link across the Pacific which could be broken only at a painful price. Furthermore, as a result of the Spanish-American War, the United States found herself in pos-

A native worker taps a rubber tree on a Sumatra plantation in the Netherlands East Indies. Rubber sap flows at the rate of two drops a second.

session of the rich and coveted Philippines.

The United States, however, has never been so heavy an investor in the orient as Great Britain. In 1931 American investments in China amounted to only $196,800,000, or 6.1 per cent of the total foreign investment, as compared with Japan's 35.1 per cent and Great Britain's 36.7 per cent.[6] "Consequently, if it is investment interest that determines the strength or weakness, from the power standpoint, of national policy, it is clear that there had been relatively little incentive to the United States to utilize effectively its power to establish its China policies."[7] On the other hand, American investments were greater in Japan than in China.

The question of Philippine independence. The Tydings-McDuffie Act of March 24, 1934, provided that the islands were to get their complete independence on July 4, 1946. This act, while striving to please the Nationalists, stipulated that the United States was to retain power over such matters as foreign relations and military affairs until 1946 arrived and was therefore committed to maintaining order in the Philippines up to that time. Economic ties were as strong as political ties. Whereas in 1899 American goods being shipped to the islands were valued at only $1,150,000, in 1929 these products were worth $92,592,959. By 1934, eighty-four per cent of Philippine exports was going to the United States.

Other factors entered into the question of what to do with the islands. Certain American economic interests in competition with Philippine interests favored the severing of political ties. American naval and military strategists argued the value of the Philippines as a protection of those trade routes whereby America got its much-needed supplies of rubber, tin, and other products. Still another question was the threat of the Japanese, who coveted the islands for their resources and as an outlet for surplus population at home.

U. S. policy in the orient. When the entire far-eastern picture is taken into account, a truer view of the position of the United States during the period up to 1939 results. The United States asked no territorial acquisitions and did not seek war. It did not have enough economic stake in China to feel that there was vital need to take drastic action against Japanese aggression. Nevertheless the United States was committed to oppose any power which threatened to dominate by force all of Asia and the western Pacific. An embargo against Japan might provoke war and would certainly result in a loss of profitable commerce. It is true that the United States government refused to recognize Japan's puppet state of Manchukuo in 1932, which had been created at the expense of China, but it did not prevent American materials of war from being sold to Japan. It thus helped Japan to humiliate China, kill innumerable Chinese, injure Americans and American properties—and blast Pearl Harbor.

Other European powers. Other occidental powers have long been involved in eastern Asia, but their influence has not been so great as those already mentioned. Prior to the First World War Germany won important concessions in the Shantung peninsula and elsewhere in China, besides gaining control of the Caroline and Marshall Islands in the South Seas. Germany's defeat destroyed its imperialist position in eastern Asia, but the post-

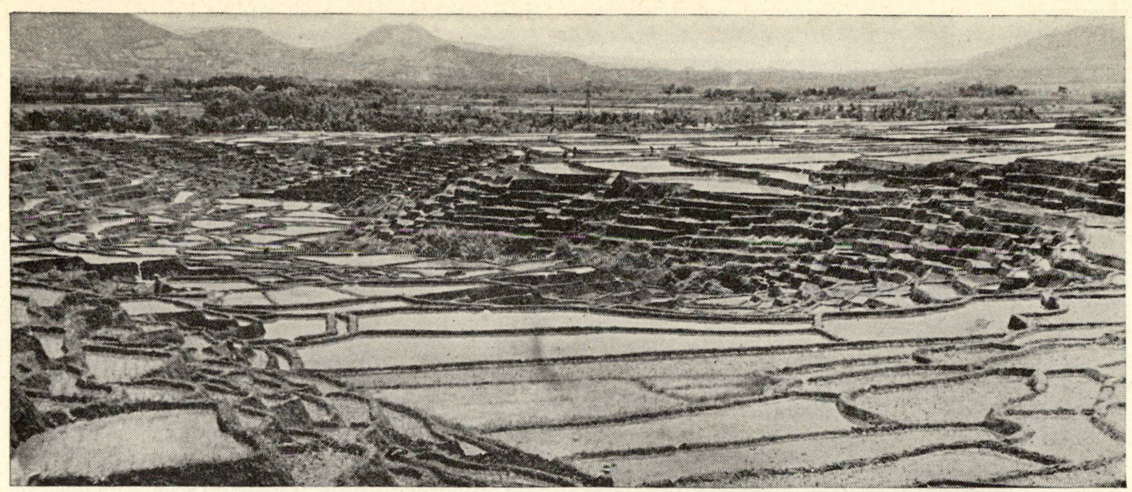

Terraced rice paddies covered with water lace the countryside in Java, part of the rich Netherlands East Indies. Thrifty natives also raise fish in the shallow ponds between their fields.

war years saw German-Chinese relations become friendly. German officers were sent to train China's national army. This political friendship was reflected in the growth of German trade in China. In return for tungsten, antimony, cotton, wool, hog casings, and so on, Germany exported to China dyes, munitions, iron manufactures, and machinery. Before the reopening of the Sino-Japanese struggle on July 7, 1937, Germany had taken the place of Great Britain as the third most important nation in China's trade.

Italy has never had territorial acquisitions in the Far East. Most Italians living in China have done missionary work, and Italian investments there have been insignificant. During the late thirties Italy's attitude toward eastern Asia was conditioned by its growing ideological solidarity with Japan. Belgium became a larger investor in China, especially in railways. Portugal kept as a colony only the small port of Macao on the south China coast.

Russia. The Soviet Union has occupied a unique position in eastern Asia because its territory stretches continuously from the Baltic Sea in Europe to the Pacific Ocean (see map, page 409). Russia adjoins China and Japan's puppet state of Manchukuo. Because of its economic system, the Soviet Union stresses self-sufficiency. Foreign investments are condemned as capitalistic and imperialistic. Therefore the stake of the Soviet Union in eastern Asia has primarily depended upon its geographical position and is political rather than economic. Russians have bought and sold on a basis of mutual advantage with all the countries of eastern Asia. On the political front, however, the Soviet Union witnessed periods of crisis during the years leading up to 1939. Early in the twenties China and Russia entered into favorable relations, and Russian advisers came to China. After 1927, however, Chiang Kai-shek became increasingly anti-Communist. In the decade that followed, his armies tried to destroy Chinese forces designated as Communist which opposed him. Thereafter, the Soviet Union took a less friendly attitude toward the Chinese, although it allowed war materials to proceed to China in her fight against Japan.

With Japan the Soviet Union has had many altercations. Russia looks on the island kingdom as a great potential enemy in the east, and during the thirties the two nations attempted to jockey into favorable positions. The Soviet Union viewed the establishment of Manchukuo with apprehension, fearing that it might become a springboard for activities in eastern Siberia. There have been numerous clashes along the border, owing in part to lack of definite boundary lines. Problems relating to fishing rights have also been a sore spot between the two powers for a long time.

The Pacific islands. Spread throughout the vast expanse of the Pacific (see map, page 272) is Oceania—innumerable small or large island possessions of the great powers. These outposts are important principally for strategic reasons:

On Luzon island in the Philippines a native farmer plows his small muddy plot with a water buffalo. This plantation has belonged to one family for several generations.

they can be used as naval and air bases. New Caledonia, one of France's most prized oceanic possessions, is an area of considerble economic importance because of its rich nickel deposits. The German-owned Caroline and Marshall islands were turned over to Japan at the end of the First World War as mandates. Other islands in the Pacific have also been fortified by the Japanese. The British controlled such centers as Fiji, and the Australians controlled groups of small islands south of the equator which used to belong to Germany but were later given as mandates to Australia. The United States has made use of her oceanic possessions for purposes of strategy and commercial air travel. The Hawaiian Islands were fortified to serve as an outlying defense for continental America, although this group of islands is also economically desirable for its sugar and pineapple production. Wake Island and Guam lie advantageously on the route to Manila and for this reason were used as key centers in the air service which was inaugurated between the Philippines and the United States.

Western contributions in the orient. To this point the treatment of the role of the great powers in eastern Asia has stressed the importance of their financial stakes in that area and has shown how these investments have helped shape national policies. That the actions of Europe and America in China and neighboring lands have been motivated by economic interests of sometimes the most selfish and ruthless nature cannot be gainsaid. But the picture would be incomplete without a mention of other aspects of occidental activity in eastern Asia. Many colleges and schools have been established by various western organizations for the increase of education among the peoples of eastern Asia. This work has been done largely by missionaries, many of whom have given unceasingly of their energy for the betterment of the people of Asia. Western powers have also cooperated in sending to the Far East engineering experts to construct needed public works. Doctors have proved invaluable in establishing hospitals and clinics, in helping to check epidemics, and in educating the populace to the necessity of public health measures. And, as we shall see later, the western powers pledged themselves in the 1920's to respect the territorial integrity of China. Many occidental leaders tried to strengthen the political status of India by encouraging home rule.

China Tries to Change

Chinese losses to Japan. From the period of the first Anglo-Chinese War (1839-1842) to the end of the nineteenth century, China was forced to kowtow to the demands of foreign powers. European nations exploited her mercilessly, stripping her of strategic ports, wresting important economic concessions, and imposing upon her such humiliations as extraterritoriality, customs regulations, and the stationing of foreign warships in Chinese waters. A weak central government and lack of national unity made it impossible for China to resist these encroachments upon her rights.

But the real blow came not from occidental nations but from that small land which China had always regarded with amused contempt. What China had to learn was that a nation as small as Japan could defeat her easily because, in an industrial and military sense, her aggressive neighbor was thoroughly westernized. Trouble brewed for some time between the two nations, especially over the control of Formosa and Korea. Finally a dispute arose over China's claim to suzerainty in Korea, war broke out in 1894, and the brief Sino-Japanese struggle resulted in a humiliating defeat for China. By the Treaty of Shimonoseki in 1895, China was forced to relinquish claim to Korea (which Japan later annexed in 1910), hand over the rich Liaotung peninsula and Formosa, pay an indemnity of $150,000,000 to Nippon for a war which the latter had brought on, and grant the Japanese further commercial and extraterritorial privileges.

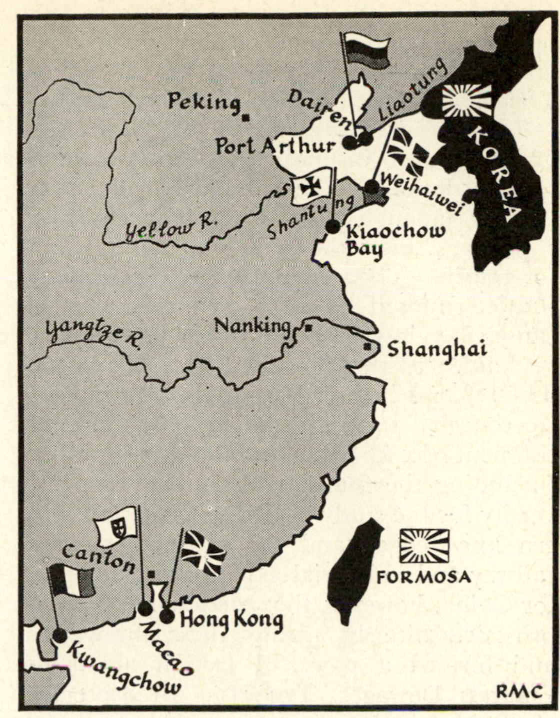

Europe exploits China. China's defeat was the signal for the renewal of aggressive actions by western powers, which robbed Japan of the advantages of her recent victory by forcing her to give back the Liaotung peninsula in return for an extra indemnity from China. These nations were afraid to let Japan take the strategic peninsula, and Russia in particular was at that time trying to obtain control of all Manchuria for herself. That their motive was utterly selfish is proved by their subsequent actions. In 1895 France confirmed her mining and railroad concessions in Indo-China, and Great Britain obtained an extension of the boundaries of Burma and additional trading privileges. Germany in the meanwhile had been trying to get the fine harbor of Kiaochow and mining rights in Shantung peninsula. The murder by brigands of two Roman Catholic missionaries of German nationality in 1897 gave the kaiser's government an excuse to seize territory, including a ninety-nine year lease to Kiaochow Bay plus some two hundred square miles of adjacent territory. Germany was also given exclusive mining and railroad rights throughout all of Shantung province.

Russia, Great Britain, and France now made their demands. Russia obtained a twenty-five-year lease to Dairen and Port Arthur on the tip of the Liaotung peninsula with the right to build a railroad across Manchuria, known as the Chinese Eastern Railway, allowing Russia to dominate Manchuria completely. In 1898 Great Britain obtained the lease of Weihaiwei, a naval base, to protect her interests in northern China against growing Russian control. In the same year France leased Kwangchow in southern China for ninety-nine years.

The Open Door policy. China was now in imminent danger of disintegrating completely. Manchuria and Mongolia were under Russian domination; the Shantung peninsula was virtually a possession of Germany; much of southern China was controlled by France. Hong Kong, Weihaiwei, and the rich Yangtze valley, created as a special "sphere of influence" to be exploited economically, belonged to Great Britain. A halt, or at least a hesitation in the disintegrating process, was provided by the United States, not solely because of high-minded desires but largely out of the aim of Washington to safeguard its own interests in the orient. It is probably true that American imperialism had been less obnoxious in China than that of any of the large European powers, but the United States had taken little or no action in China at this time, in part because its energies had been devoted to acquiring the Philippine Islands. However, in 1899 Secretary of State John Hay asked the major powers to agree (1) not to interfere with any "sphere of interest" or any leased territory, (2) to have the Chinese tariff apply to all merchandise in such regions and to allow the Chinese government to collect this tariff, and

(3) to permit all nations to enjoy the same harbor dues and railroad charges. In 1900 several powers had agreed to Hay's request. The famous Open Door policy was born.

The "hundred days of reform." At this time China was rousing herself to cope with these foreign dangers. The humiliation of her defeat by Japan had particularly incensed the younger Chinese thinkers, who now agitated for reform. The young Kuang Hsu emperor showed himself to be sympathetic to their cause when in 1898 he instituted what came to be known as the "hundred days of reform." The reforms included an attempt to modernize the civil service examinations, the establishment of a school system along western lines (including the founding of an imperial university for the study of both ancient and modern knowledge), and the encouragement of railway and industrial expansion. Unhappily for China, however, the reactionaries at court protested bitterly against these innovations and formed a powerful faction about the Empress Dowager, Tzu Hsi. In September 1898, she seized and imprisoned the emperor, executed some of the leading reformers, and took over the government. With Tzu Hsi in control, an attempt was soon made to lead China to salvation by reaction.

The Boxer Rebellion. China has for centuries had many secret societies of a religious or political purpose. After the suppression of the reform movement a group of secret societies united in an organization known as the "Righteous Harmony Fists"—called by westerners "Boxers." At first the Boxers were strongly anti-Manchu because of the reactionary measures of "Old Buddha" (Tzu Hsi), but by 1899 their chief object of hatred had become the foreign nations who were stripping China of her possessions and power. With the addition of rowdy elements to their ranks, the Boxers started a campaign to rid China of all Christians and "foreign devils." Many Europeans were killed, including the German minister, and the legations at Peking were besieged. For months foreign residents there and elsewhere were in constant peril, and not until August 1900 did an international army force its way to Peking and effect the release of the foreigners besieged there. After Peking was captured, many Europeans, Japanese, and Americans who composed the force committed grievous acts of vandalism, plundering the palaces of their priceless art objects, burning private dwelling places, and putting numerous Chinese to death. In the protocol of 1901, which concluded the Boxer Rebellion, China had to agree to apologize for the murder of the German minister and other foreign officials, allow the outside nations to police a larger area around Peking, fulfill many other irritating obligations, and pay to the foreign powers an indemnity of about $333,000,000. The United States returned most of the indemnity which China owed her, and the Chinese government set this sum aside for sending students to American universities.

Cultural revolution in China. China had failed to save herself by conservatism. Now a growing number of Chinese thinkers were becoming convinced that China's only salvation lay in adopting some of those western techniques by which smaller enemies had been able to humiliate her. The old cultural structure underwent profound changes. This period of transition is by no means over; in fact, the mammoth cultural revolution in which the most dynamic elements of the occident are being integrated with the permanent values of the orient is perhaps only now getting into full swing. At any rate, the young Chinese intellectuals at the beginning of the century saw the necessity for radical change. Moreover they believed that so long as the reactionary officials, Chinese and Manchu, of the Manchu dynasty headed the government, China could never hope for real progress. Not only were the military and civil leaders incompetent and inefficient in the main, but they and their subordinates were corrupt.

Hostility concentrated upon the Manchus persisted despite their attempts to institute various reform measures. In 1905 the Manchus discontinued the old civil-service examinations and introduced tests designed to include economics and political science as well as the traditional questions. The army was partially reorganized, and a constitution was promised to the people. Provincial assemblies were convoked in 1909 and a national assembly in 1910. Unfortunately for the Manchus, their last relatively able but unenlightened leader passed away in November 1908. With the death of Tzu Hsi, the dynasty soon crumbled. The heir apparent was but a child.

In the meantime the young rebellious elements had much to complain about. In 1904

Morrison Street in the Tatar city section of Peiping, China, is one of its most modern thoroughfares. The wide sidewalks bordered with Chinese signs and the spacious boulevards with their cyclists are a far cry from the dark and twisted streets of older China.

the government of British India was threatening China's shadowy suzerainty over Tibet. At this time also China was unable to prevent the Russians and Japanese from making use of her territory as a private battlefield. The ranks of the reformers increased, and the revolutionary fervor of the Young China party was heightened by youthful intellectuals who had studied western subjects in China and abroad.

Reformer Sun Yat-sen. Ultimately the most important leader of the movement was Sun Yat-sen (1867-1925). This outstanding revolutionist was born in a village about forty miles from Canton, the son of a tenant farmer. When about thirteen he went to Hawaii, where an older brother lived. There Sun Yat-sen received a western education. In 1879 he was put in an Anglican school, where he became a Christian convert. His shocked brother had him recalled to China, but the youthful Sun began to disfigure and destroy the images in the village temple. As a result of these sacrilegious acts, Sun had to flee to Canton, where an American Protestant missionary doctor helped him. Once more he resumed his studies with Protestant missionaries in Hong Kong.

In 1892, Sun Yat-sen received a diploma in medicine. Taking up practice in Macao, he set about organizing a reform society. The Portuguese government ordered him to leave, not because of his political actions, it is said, but because he was competing with Portuguese physicians. Going to Canton, Sun sent a petition to Peking asking that agricultural schools be founded. When this request was refused, he helped organize a revolt against the Manchus. The discovery of the plot forced him to flee in 1895 to Hong Kong and then to Japan, the United States, and Great Britain. Wherever he went, he sought aid in his now almost fanatical desire to create a new China. He came near being executed in 1896 when the Chinese legation captured him in London. But the British government ordered his release, and Sun Yat-sen was free to continue agitating against his Manchu enemies.

The Republic of China is born. Sun's great opportunity arrived in 1912 when the 268-year-old Manchu dynasty abdicated, and China for the first time in its long history became, in name, a republic. The revolution which brought about this dramatic turn of events was won with relatively little bloodshed. A revolt had broken out in September 1911, over a foreign loan to finance certain railways. The outbreak spread unexpectedly when some imperial troops mutinied in the Yangtze valley and joined the new movement. Soon a republic was declared in the region, and several cities fell to these forces. General Yuan Shih-kai, whom the Manchus summoned to quell the revolt, was dissatisfied with the government, and he procrastinated sufficiently long to allow the revolution to spread like wildfire through the provinces. The revolutionists assembled at Nanking where, on December 28, 1911, they elected Sun Yat-sen president of the republic. He had been out of the country when the revolt began but had now returned triumphantly to China.

Before Sun Yat-sen arrived home, however, the revolutionists had been negotiating with Yuan Shih-kai, the most powerful military figure in the country. He soon persuaded the imperial clan and others surrounding the young emperor that the Manchu dynasty was doomed. On February 12, 1912, edicts were promulgated by which the emperor abdicated, and Yuan Shih-kai was asked to form a republic. It was agreed on both sides that the emperor was to live at peace in his palace in the northern part of the Forbidden City of Peking in possession of his title and a large annuity. To prevent internal dissension, Sun Yat-sen declined the presidency, and the republican group at Nanking elected Yuan Shih-kai. China now faced the future as a republic.

Dissension in the government. Yuan possessed the largest army and the blessing of foreign powers and republicans alike, but he had not the idealism of Sun Yat-sen and shortly began scheming to restore the monarchy with himself as emperor. The provisional constitution adopted in March 1912 had put the office of president under the jurisdiction of parliament. The first parliament was controlled by the radicals who had engineered the revolution and organized themselves into the Kuomintang (Nationalist party). In 1913 trouble broke out when Yuan concluded a large loan with banking groups of Great Britain, France, Germany, and Russia, thus placing the government under their influence. Furthermore, he replaced certain military commanders in the south with his own henchmen. The outcome was a new rebellion, endorsed by Sun Yat-sen. With the suppression of the revolt by Yuan, Sun had to flee to Japan. Yuan, now firmly entrenching himself as president, dismissed the Kuomintang members from parliament in November 1913, dismissed parliament itself in January 1914, and in 1915 announced the imminent restoration of the monarchy with himself as emperor. Rebellion spread in the last month of 1915, Yuan's prestige evaporated, and in June 1916, the discredited dictator died.

A decade of disorder. Dissension in the government continued for the next decade (1916-1926). Squabbles at home and incidents abroad brought added misery to the struggling republic. It is impossible here to trace the confusion that existed in Chinese political circles during these years. In 1917 one military chieftain actually declared to a surprised world that the Manchu dynasty had been restored, but the "restoration" did not last. For a time the country was divided between two would-be governments, one at Peking, the other at Canton. The one in the south was composed largely of the radicals who had engineered the Revolution of 1911-1912 and who had adhered to the constitution of 1912. The Canton government, not nearly so powerful as the conservative Peking administration, elected Sun Yat-sen as president in 1921. Meanwhile the Peking government was enfeebled as rivalries developed between cliques and warlords fought for control.

Sun Yat-sen's philosophy. A social philosopher who was abler as a propagandist and revolutionist than as a political administrator, Sun Yat-sen and his Kuomintang government did little to reunite the country. However, the social ideology which he formulated during this period had important results for the future. In 1923, unable to obtain aid from the foreign powers in his attempt to overcome the Peking government, he called in certain Soviet advisers. The chief of these Russian helpers was the influential and brilliant thinker, Michael Borodin. Owing to the confidence placed in Borodin and his associates, the Kuomintang soon adopted many of the planks of the program subscribed to by the Communist party in the Soviet Union.

After his death on March 12, 1925, Sun Yat-sen became a national hero. Weekly memorial services were held before his picture. To the present day Sun Yat-sen maintains his exalted position in the minds of many Chinese republicans of various shades of thought. Sun left a will and certain books which were adopted as infallible guides for the country. One of these volumes, *San Min Chu I*, or the *Three People's Principles*, became the manual of the Kuomintang. The three Principles are (1) nationalism—the liberation of China from foreign domination; (2) democracy—"government by the people and for the people"; and (3) livelihood—economic security for all the people.

China united under Chiang Kai-shek. In 1926 the armies of the Kuomintang began to drive northward. Their chief Chinese leader, a young man of military ability, was Chiang Kai-shek. The armies encountered little real opposition, and by early spring, 1927, the Yangtze valley was reached, and important cities such as Shanghai were occupied. But dissension broke out in the Kuomintang itself between radical and conservative elements. Because the Communists frankly opposed organized religion and Confucian morality to the shocked antagonism of much of the nation and because of Chiang Kai-shek's own leanings toward conservatism, a split became inevitable. The murder of several foreigners at Nanking and attacks upon others by certain radicals in March 1927 brought about the cleavage. The moderates under Chiang created a government at Nanking, and before the end of 1927 public opinion had crystallized behind this régime. Back to the Soviet Union went the Communist advisers; many radicals were driven into exile (including the widow of Sun Yat-sen), and the Nanking government came to depend for financial support upon the foreign bankers at Shanghai. Meanwhile, in 1927, Chiang Kai-shek married Mei-ling Soong, a sister of Madame Sun Yat-sen, and so further cemented his position among his countrymen. The next summer, the Nationalist armies moved northward again and by June had entered Peking. With peace between the northern war leaders and the Kuomintang, China appeared once more to be united.

The world at large now looked forward to a time of internal harmony and growing stabilization in China. There was little doubt that China's chances for success were the brightest since the Revolution of 1911-1912. The country was being administered by men trained in, or influenced by, the west. The Nationalist government was enacting measures designed to unite all China and integrate the techniques of the occident with the ideals of the orient. The new capital, Nanking, was alive with bustle and plans for the future, and

The historic meeting of Jawaharlal Nehru, Madame Chiang Kai-shek, and General Chiang Kai-shek took place in India in February 1942. Here leaders of the two greatest Asiatic countries met to discuss problems of Indian independence.

the foreign situation had improved. China was protected by the Nine-Power Treaty of 1922; she was a member of the League of Nations; many of those in America and Europe who wished China well advocated the abolition of extraterritoriality and other concessions against which the Chinese were protesting effectively by employing an ancient weapon, the boycott; and Japan appeared, on occasion, relatively conciliatory in her attitude to China.

Anti-Nanking groups. But the sympathizers of the young republic were overlooking several aspects of national life which caused endless friction. In many places the people were being tyrannized by bandits, especially where the strength of the Nanking government was least effective. Famine in the northwest cost the lives of millions. In 1929 certain military leaders who were dissatisfied with the policies of the Kuomintang broke away. By the following year, however, they had been defeated, and the government of Chiang Kai-shek was secure from attack from this source.

But trouble was arising now between the Nanking régime and the Chinese so-called Communists. During 1930-1933 extensive areas were in the hands of these anti-Nanking

In February 1936 the stand of a wealthy (by Chinese standards) tea vendor in Canton looked like this. The best of its kind in the city, the stand was patronized by well-to-do merchants.

groups. While many of the Chinese Communists were active believers in the principles of Marx and had attended a university at Moscow which the Soviet Union had started in 1925 for Chinese students, other groups involved in the revolt were in reality local military forces or even bandits. The Communist banner attracted many landless peasants who did not understand the dialectics of Marx but who had suffered greatly from personal privation and who now understandably wanted to wrest land from the rich proprietors. Chiang Kai-shek turned with great severity upon these elements, and untold numbers of so-called Communists were put to death. In fact the criticism has been levied against Chiang that he was more interested in 1931 in fighting his countrymen than in warring against the aggressors from Japan. However serious this internal trouble might have become for the Nanking government, it was overshadowed by developments in Manchuria in 1931 which will be discussed later in this chapter.

The economic evolution of China. In the early twentieth century commerce increased rapidly, for the Chinese represented the largest potential market in the world, and the foreign powers were interested in taking whatever advantage they could of this fact. China's total foreign trade was seven times as great in 1929 as it had been in 1894. Nevertheless, China still is almost entirely self-contained, and her civil warfare, currency insecurity, inefficient transportation system, and national poverty have all combined to keep her virtually undeveloped in the economic world. Some progress has been made with the building of factories and the adoption of western machinery. The manufacturing of cotton goods, for example, has reached impressive proportions. Unfortunately, however, these cotton mills and other factories are largely owned or controlled by foreign entrepreneurs to whom go the sizable profits. Exports which have also added to China's growing economic life include silk, tea, vegetable oils, and products from the mines. China has colossal economic potentialities, but until they are exploited for the advantage of the Chinese people, the inhabitants of the republic will continue to suffer.

The progress of Chinese education. The intellectual changes that have taken place in modern China are phenomenal. In the words of Kenneth S. Latourette, "In some respects, between 1895 and 1933 the mental life of China moved farther from its old moorings than that of the west had done between the thirteenth and the twentieth centuries. It was in greater turmoil than at any time since the Chou."[8] Whereas at the beginning of the century the educated class was extremely small and concerned almost exclusively with classical subject matter, by 1931 China had 34 universities and colleges with 17,285 students, some 1300 secondary schools with 234,811 pupils, and innumerable primary schools affording the basic elements of education to about 9,000,000 persons. When the total population of China is considered, this figure may not appear impressive until one remembers the remarkable advances made in only a very few years. The Chinese people venerate learning. Even during the present conflict, in which whole university centers have been destroyed, their students have trekked sometimes hundreds of miles inland to reorganize their college life. New institutions, in fact, have been created during the past few years.

Other cultural changes. The intellectual pattern of the land has been modified in other ways. The printing of books has increased manyfold, and hundreds of important western treatises have been translated and disseminated. Scholarly journals have made their appearance, contributed to by some of China's most energetic minds. One of her outstanding scholars is the brilliant and far-seeing intellectual, Dr. Hu Shih. Hu Shih is American-educated and when in China lectures and writes continually. He is associated with the renaissance of modern Chinese thought, emphasizing the value of the physical and social sciences rather than the precepts of Confucius, and championing the use of a new and simplified written language, *pai hua*, or "plain speech." Scholars such as Hu Shih have also labored for the adoption of Mandarin as a national speech so that scholars and laymen from all parts of China can converse intelligently.

Modern China's social changes. The social life, morals, and customs of modern China have been considerably altered. The movies have both helped and hindered the Chinese to visualize western life. The larger cities have installed telephones, electric lights, and modern water systems. Newspapers, factories, railways, movie houses, and neon signs are also to be seen. Occidental dress has made its way among the people. Chinese fashions such as long fingernails (to indicate that the aristocratic bearer did not soil his hands with work), the queue which the Manchus made the Chinese wear as a mark of national inferiority, and the bound feet of women, a cruel self-imposed fashion which was supposed to add to the appeal of the ladies by making them that much more helpless, are now disappearing. Folk ways are changing at the same time, as are ancient family traditions, the deference (and even submission) of youth to age, the acceptance of concubinage, and the former social stratification. China is in the process of a significant social revolution. However, it will take many decades to create the new China with its blending of the orient and occident, for in the rural districts especially the people are slow to change ancient customs.

Japan Expands

Japan's imperialism. The island kingdom of Nippon made phenomenal advances in the decades following the visit of Commodore Perry in 1853. There was a complete reorganization in the government, army, and navy which created a westernized nation.

The next big event in the nation's history took place in 1894 with the outbreak of hostilities against China. The issue concerned Korea, and although the outside world looked for a Chinese victory because of overwhelmingly superior numbers, the well-trained Japanese army and navy inflicted upon the forces of China a swift and utter defeat. By the terms of the Treaty of Shimonoseki, signed on April 14, 1895, China had to recognize the independence of Korea, cede the Liaotung peninsula to Japan (which, as we saw previously, three of the great powers made her return), cede also the island of Formosa, open various cities in China to Japanese trade, and pay a huge war indemnity. That victory marked the beginning in modern times of Japanese imperialist expansion on the Asiatic continent and the rise of the military clique in Japan.

Japan was by now on the way to recognition as a first-class power, a reputation accentuated in 1900 during the Boxer Rebellion, when Japanese soldiers, in conjunction with western military forces, performed heroic feats at the relief of the Peking legations. In January 1902, Japan scored a diplomatic triumph by an alliance with Great Britain. Both parties looked upon such an alliance as a threat to Russian expansion, while the prestige it gave the Japanese in European eyes was considerable. If either party became involved in a war, the other would use its influence to prevent other nations from attacking its ally. If a third power entered the fray, Japan or Great Britain, as the case might be, would come to the assistance of its ally.

The Russo-Japanese war. With the diplomatic horizon cleared and the army and navy growing in size and efficiency, Nippon entered into its next conflict with quiet confidence. This time the war was directed against Russia. Soon after Russia, Germany, and France had forced Japan to hand back the Liaotung peninsula to China, the Russians had negotiated with the imperial government of China for the lease of Dairen and Port Arthur on the tip of the peninsula, as well as the right to build a railroad across Manchuria to connect with the Trans-Siberian line. Japan had not let this incident go unnoticed and was only biding her time to challenge the strength of czarist Russia. This rivalry of imperialistic ambitions brought on a war early in 1904. Japan was conceded only the slimmest chance to de-

Women were fighting to obtain civic rights in the Japan of February 1931. Here a Buddhist woman's organization is engaged in lettering signs to be used in the campaign.

feat a nation which appeared to be almost impregnable. But to the world's surprise, Russia proved herself almost unbelievably corrupt and incompetent at this time. Russia's poor showing was in part the result of the universal unpopularity of the struggle among the Russian people, who staged an unsuccessful rebellion at home shortly afterward. A disastrous naval defeat sealed Russia's hopes. When President Theodore Roosevelt at the request of Tokyo offered to negotiate peace terms on June 9, 1905, both combatants agreed.

By the Treaty of Portsmouth, signed September 5, 1905, Japan acquired the southern half of the island of Sakhalin (instead of an indemnity of $580,000,000 as had been demanded), the leaseholds to the Liaotung peninsula and Port Arthur, and various Russian railway and mining rights in southern Manchuria. Japan's paramount position in Korea was also conceded, paving the way to annexation of that peninsula in 1910. Nippon was fully accepted as a first-class power, a position attested by the renewal of the Anglo-Japanese alliance on August 12, 1905.

Further acquisitions on the mainland. Holding an important position in far-eastern affairs, Japan merely had to bide her time once more before embarking upon further imperialism. Korea was next in line with Japanese aims and, as earlier stated, was annexed to the empire on August 29, 1910. Korea's old name of Chosen, "Land of the Morning Freshness," was officially adopted. When the First World War broke out in 1914, Japan told Germany on August 15 to take all warships out of the Far East and to turn over the Kiaochow territory to Japan "with a view to the eventual restoration of the same to China." When Germany did not reply to this request, the Japanese government declared war on August 23 and seized the territory.

The Twenty-One Demands. Then, on January 18, 1915, the president of China was presented with terms which startled the world by disclosing the aim of Japanese imperialists on the Asiatic continent. These were the notorious Twenty-One Demands, which would have made of China little more than a Japanese protectorate. The other powers did little to hinder the success of Japanese ambitions, preoccupied as they were with the gigantic struggle in Europe. China was swept with indignation but had not the physical means to protest effectively. On May 25, 1915, the Chinese government under threats of coercion had to accede to the first sixteen demands, while the rest were reserved for later consideration. "Among other things these treaties confirmed Japan's newly won position in Shantung province and extended her railway and territorial rights in south Manchuria to the end of the century. American protests helped block the most sweeping of the demands, which would have made China a Japanese protectorate."[9]

The European powers secretly agreed in 1917 to support Japanese claims in the peace conference that would follow the First World War. The United States, while not agreeing to support these claims, admitted, by the Lansing-Ishii agreement of November 2, 1917, that Japan deserved "special interests in China" owing to her "territorial propinquity." The Allies had evidently chosen to forget that China had also entered the war on their side and was entitled to respect and consideration.

Postwar Japan. Japan's role in the Far East was secure after the war; she controlled in one way or another Shantung, Manchuria, southern Mongolia, and the German islands north of the equator, besides those territories and concessions she had wrested from China and Russia prior to the war. By this time the power of Japan had increased to such proportions that the United States and the British Dominions in the Pacific area were frankly alarmed. Various acts were passed discriminating against Japanese ownership of land in several of the American states. In 1921 Great Britain allowed her treaty with Japan to terminate without renewal.

The table[10] at the bottom of this page shows the phenomenal increase of Japan's economic power invested in China since 1902 and why the other powers were alarmed at this development.

The Washington Conference. Great Britain and the United States drew together to restrain Japan's expansionist program, especially in naval matters, and the United States called the Washington Conference in 1921. The conference was attended by delegates from Great Britain, France, Italy, Holland, Portugal, China, Belgium, Japan, and the United States. The purpose of the conference was to decide not only upon naval matters but also upon problems affecting the entire Pacific area. The three leading naval powers, Great Britain, the United States, and Japan, consented to reduce the tonnage of their capital ships so as to achieve a respective ratio of 5-5-3. While this agreement made official the inferiority of the Japanese fleet to those of the other two powers, it recognized the position of the Japanese navy as the third most powerful in the world. By the Four-Power Treaty the United States, Great Britain, Japan, and France agreed "to respect their rights in relation to their insular possessions and insular dominions in the region of the Pacific Ocean."

In 1922 the well-known Nine-Power Treaty was signed at Washington. All the signatories agreed to respect the independence, sovereignty, territoriality, and administrative integrity of China. Furthermore, they were to use their influence to preserve the Open Door Policy and "to refrain from taking advantage of conditions in China in order to seek special rights or privileges which would abridge the rights of subjects or citizens of friendly states, and from countenancing action inimical to the security of such states." It is impossible to square Japan's acts in China today with the pact which she signed in 1922, just as it is difficult for the other signatories to excuse their apathy toward China until they were themselves drawn into war against Japan in December 1941.

Earthquakes and politics. From 1922 to 1931 the spotlight switched largely from foreign to domestic issues. In September 1923, Japan was devastated by a terrible earthquake which destroyed large areas of Tokyo, Yokohama, and other densely populated centers. Hundreds of thousands were killed or injured, while billions of dollars of property damage

	1902		1914		1931	
	Millions of dollars	Per cent of total	Millions of dollars	Per cent of total	Millions of dollars	Per cent of total
Great Britain	260.3	33.0	607.5	37.7	1,189.2	36.7
Russia	246.5	31.3	269.3	16.7	273.2	8.4
Germany	164.3	20.9	263.6	16.4	87.0	2.7
France	91.9	11.6	171.4	10.7	192.4	5.9
United States	19.7	2.5	49.3	3.1	196.8	6.1
Japan	1.0	0.1	219.6	13.6	1,136.9	35.1

resulted from the national catastrophe. Universal sympathy was aroused, and millions of dollars were subscribed by Americans and others to relieve the distressed areas. The ingenuity and courage of the Japanese people came to the fore at once, and reconstruction of Tokyo and other cities along the most modern lines was soon set in operation.

In March 1925 the Manhood Suffrage Bill was passed, granting the franchise with few exceptions to every male above twenty-five. By this bill the number enfranchised jumped from 3,000,000 to 12,000,000. "This change forced Diet members to spend large sums in electioneering, and made them more dependent on capitalist support. Consequently, it strengthened the capitalists' control over the Minseito and the Seiyukai (political parties). At the same time it made possible the rise of labor and left-wing parties, which began to win Diet seats."[11]

The increase in suffrage did relatively little to democratize the nation. The cabinets in power were not subject to the same control by the lower house as they were, say, in British parliamentary procedure. In Japan the cabinets continued to be made and broken largely by the House of Peers, or the Privy Council, or the military clique. We must not forget that the army and navy authorities were virtually independent of civil control, and they could—and frequently did—force the country to do their bidding.

Economic progress in Japan. In the economic sphere, Japan forged ahead rapidly. Thousands of factories were built, and the manufacturers of the country undersold foreign competitors in the world market, owing in part to the low standard of wages prevailing in Japan and to the modern machine techniques which the Japanese industrialists were swift to adopt. In the field of textiles especially, Japan captured one market after another. Commerce and industry were controlled by a few great concerns in whose hands the greater part of the country's wealth was concentrated. The two greatest financial powers were the houses of Mitsui and Mitsubishi. The Mitsui interests, for example, controlled banks, trust companies, industrial plants, department stores, shipping lines, mines, power companies, paper plants, and so on.

Japanese economic prosperity, however, was more apparent than real. It depended upon the maintenance of a large volume of exports, the sale of which gave funds to buy raw materials and foodstuffs abroad. For Japan now had a population of 65 million living on an area smaller than the state of California, of which only one fifth could be cultivated.

Japan Prepares for a "New Order"

Japanese designs on China. The problems which Japan faced in 1931 could not easily be solved. The population was growing rapidly, and it would take increased industrialization at home and increased commerce abroad to take care of unemployment. But Japan was lacking in resources, and her home market was limited. The solution appeared to rest with China, rich in resources and possessing an unlimited market. Perhaps both nations might have profited mutually through cooperation, whereby China would have been encouraged to sell raw products to Japan, getting manufactured goods in return. But the situation in both countries seemed to make cooperation impossible. China had not forgotten the Sino-Japanese war of 1894, the annexation of Korea, or the Twenty-One Demands. Meanwhile Japanese leaders were alarmed at the progress China was making toward unification, modernization, and utilization of economic resources.

By 1930, because of social and economic conditions, the Japanese army had gained control of governmental leadership. Japan was in the throes of a critical depression. Whereas in 1929 her export and import trade had been worth 4,365,000,000 yen, in 1931 it had fallen almost by half to 2,383,000,000. Unemployment, wage-cuts, strikes, rural misery, and a growing acceptance of Marxist beliefs characterized the crisis. The militarists chose a policy not of internal reform and reconstruction but of foreign conquest. By this means they hoped to allay unrest at home, unite the country, and somehow rectify Japan's economic problems through the forcible acquisition of new territory and markets. Furthermore, a successful military campaign would enhance the prestige of the army. The venture stood a better chance of succeeding if it occurred before China had become unified.

The Manchurian campaign. Without warn-

This is the Japanese colony of Bokuryo in Manchukuo, looking not unlike Alaskan towns on our own continent. Manchukuo was a "wild west" to the Japanese, and they planned to devote twenty years to its development.

ing, in September 1931, the Japanese army attacked Chinese forces in Manchuria. It is possible that this action was taken by army leaders without the authorization of the Tokyo government. Unable to cope with the invader, the Chinese government appealed to the League of Nations. This body appointed a committee of inquiry, known as the Lytton Commission, which later made a report condemning aggression in Manchuria while trying not to affront Japan. Beyond expressing regret at the invasion of Manchuria, no action was taken by the League. The government of the United States declared in the so-called Stimson Doctrine that it would not recognize conquests made in violation of existing treaties. But this action failed to elicit positive response from other great powers, which were in the throes of the world-wide economic depression.

Without allies and apparently with only fair-weather friends the Chinese resorted to a nation-wide boycott of Japanese goods. This led to armed reprisal by Japan. An expedition was sent to Shanghai, in January 1932, to teach the Chinese a lesson. Much to the surprise of the Japanese militarists it took more than a month to capture the great city. On February 18, 1932, Manchuria was renamed Manchukuo and recognized in September 1932 by Japan. The abdicated Manchu emperor of China became its first ruler.

As 1933 opened, the Japanese began to push farther to the south into Chinese territory. A portion of north China was occupied, and armies were sent into districts south of the Great Wall. Helpless in the face of this aggression, the Chinese leaders decided to make a temporary truce with Japan to slow down the invasion and give China a chance to prepare for the critical struggle for national existence which was bound to come. In May 1933, therefore, the T'ang-ku Truce was signed, whereby the Nanking government reluctantly recognized Japanese conquests in Manchuria and north China.

Meanwhile, Japan found its position in the League of Nations untenable in the face of the Lytton Report. On February 17, 1933, Japan gave formal notice of its intention to withdraw. How fateful the Manchurian campaign was can now be recognized. It showed that a great power could embark with impunity upon a course of aggression; it marked the beginning of the collapse of the League of Nations' prestige. From then on, it seemed, the world was to be governed by considerations of national interests and power politics exclusively.

Problems in Manchukuo. The Japanese hoped that the new puppet state of Manchukuo would prove economically profitable, and they poured vast sums of money into their new investment. The results were disappointing. The hoped-for immigration by Japanese settlers did not come up to expectations. New industries in Manchukuo competed with industries in Japan. The problem of maintaining law and order remained acute; so-called "bandits" (often Chinese patriots) made life so miserable for the authorities that the Japanese army had to create "protected villages"—villages surrounded by high walls into which the population of the countryside was herded. Less than half as much money was expended on education as the Chinese had spent, and the Chinese colleges were disbanded. Furthermore, the new educational philosophy placed emphasis on Confucian doctrines of right conduct and submission to one's superior.

But an even graver charge has been leveled at the Japanese attempts to break the spirit of their Chinese subjects in Manchuria. In Manchukuo and north China in 1933 an opium monopoly was established, and the use of narcotics was actually encouraged in those areas where the Japanese army had control. In the words of an American representative to the League's Opium Advisory Committee: "[Manchukuo and north China] constitute the one region in the world where the governing authority not only makes no effort to prevent the use of narcotic drugs but actually profits by the rapid increase of narcotic addiction."[12] Meanwhile the Japanese peasant at home had to work longer to help pay for the economic fiasco in Manchukuo.

A united front in China. Between 1933 and 1936 there was comparative peace between Japan and China. The Japanese were trying to consolidate their position in the north, while the Chinese national government under the leadership of Generalissimo Chiang Kai-shek was attempting to cope with internal problems. Unhappily for China, virtual civil war raged between Chiang Kai-shek's forces and those of the Chinese Communists. Chiang tried to subjugate the Red armies but only succeeded in driving them away from the Nanking area to the northwest, where they were now in closer contact with the Soviet Union. Chiang opposed the Chinese Communists' economic doctrines, while they in turn charged that Chiang was more willing to fight his own countrymen than he was to fight the Japanese invaders. This last view was in some measure held by regional leaders in Canton also. In 1935 the heads of the Chinese Communists demanded a united front against the Japanese, stating that the first objective of all China should be wholehearted resistance against foreign imperialism and aggression. On December 12, 1936, Chiang was actually kidnapped by rebels for two weeks. Instead of killing him as they might easily have done, they asked him to lead a united China against the common

Terrified Chinese flee the invading Japanese on the outskirts of Peiping, China, in June 1933, just before the signing of the Sino-Japanese truce. Hundreds of Japanese troops reënforced the Peiping Japanese legation guard.

enemy. The rebels were also influenced by the obvious national feeling of solidarity behind Chiang that showed itself during his period of abduction. The result was that Chiang returned safely to Nanking, and the basis was laid for a common working agreement between the national government and the Communists. China was unified in time to meet the next Japanese thrust.

Background of the "incident." The next Sino-Japanese military "incident," as the Japanese have preferred to term an affair which has caused millions of casualties and lasted for several years, broke out on July 7, 1937. Mr. Y. Suma of the Japanese Foreign Office described the renewal of hostilities in this manner: "You see there is China, a very beautiful girl. And here is Japan, a very strong young man. . . . And the young man is determined to marry that girl. You understand . . . determined . . . to . . . marry her."[13]

Back of that plot lay many factors. Japan's costly venture in 1931 had not paid the expected dividends. Militarists and industrialists in Japan hoped that the control of China's richer areas in the south would bring the prosperity they had expected from Manchukuo. The situation at home was unhealthy. Agricultural rents were rising while living costs among the industrial workers were also mounting. The workers were agitating against their landlords and employers, but the patriotic, patient Japanese mind is such that it would not protest against a national war sanctioned by the emperor. Japanese capitalists were alarmed by the foreign trade situation. In 1937 Japan faced the prospect of having to export gold to pay for a billion yen adverse balance, brought about by the heavy increase in imports from abroad and a loss of exports resulting from mounting costs of production and an increasing world hostility toward Japanese policies. All these elements, and the desire of Japanese military and naval leaders to increase their power, underlay the "incident" of July 7, 1937.

The outbreak of hostilities. Fighting broke out in the north. Meanwhile in August, 1937, the Japanese attacked Shanghai by land, sea, and air. Despite a heroic resistance for which the Japanese had not bargained, the Chinese finally lost the city and had to begin retreating inland. The Japanese advance up the Yangtze valley went rapidly, and Nanking, the capital, was captured December 15, 1937. The horror of the story of Nanking's destruction, looting, and raping by Japanese soldiers shocked the world and served to steel Chinese resistance. In the north the Chinese armies were also forced to retreat, and the Japanese set up a provisional government at Peiping (formerly Peking). The Chinese, instead of capitulating after the fall of Nanking, established a new capital farther up the Yangtze. In October 1938, this city in turn fell to Japanese forces. In the same month the Nipponese captured Canton, whence military supplies had been shipped to the Chinese armies. Canton fell easily because the Chinese thought that the enemy would not attack so close to Hong Kong. However, British prestige had hit a new low a month before with the Munich appeasement settlement, and so the Japanese boldly set foot in Canton. The Chinese, despite their forced withdrawal from the coast, moved their capital still further inland to Chungking on the upper Yangtze and continued the war against the extended Japanese lines.

The incident became a war, and the weeks which were expected to end it have lengthened into years. It is estimated that the war in China has cost Japan at least $5,000,000 a day besides hundreds of thousands, if not millions, of casualties. As a result of the crisis, the military forces in Japan have become virtual masters of the country's political and economic structure. But it would be folly to expect the Japanese people to rebel soon under such war conditions. Their whole history and conditioning have bred in them a reverence for authority and an almost unbelievable indifference to hardship and even death in any cause designed to enhance the glory of the Sun Goddess' empire.

The "New Order" proclaimed. On November 3, 1938, the "New Order in eastern Asia" was proclaimed. Its objectives were stated to be the destruction of the Chiang Kai-shek régime in China, the expulsion of western interests in eastern Asia, and the establishment of "a self-sufficient economy through the formation of a close Japan-Manchukuo-China closed-door bloc."[14] When the democracies found themselves embroiled in a second great international war in September 1939, Japan still had as its principal objective the creation of its cherished "New Order in eastern Asia."

The Pacific Situation: 1939

Alignment of the Pacific powers. When Europe plunged into war in September 1939, the effect upon the Pacific area was to differentiate more clearly the alignments which had been developing there during the preceding years. The presence of war in Europe made its spread to eastern Asia highly probable, if not almost certain, because of the strong economic and colonial ties between the European powers and the Asiatic countries.

In terms of alignment there were the following categories: on the Allied side were the possessions and interests of the British Empire and France, including Australia, New Zealand, India, Burma, British Malaya, Indo-China, numerous concessions in China, and British and French Oceania. These areas were actively at war with Germany and Italy. The situation in India was obscured by growing demands on the part of the Indian Nationalists for independence. In a second category were the economic interests of Germany and Italy in the Far East, which were relatively unimportant. In the third category were numerous neutral nations, divided on ideological grounds at least. Japan was bound by common interests to the Axis alignment in Europe and was engaged actively in an expansionist program against China. Thus Japan would favor German and Italian interests in eastern Asia and work against the Allies and their sympathizers. Thailand was likewise pro-Japanese and anti-Ally in sympathy. Sympathetic to Great Britain and France in their war (and possible future allies) were the Netherlands East Indies, China, and the United States. Holland was trying desperately to remain neutral as war broke out in Europe in 1939, but in eastern Asia the Dutch knew that only by collaboration with the British could they withstand Japanese aggression against the Netherlands East Indies. The United States was openly sympathetic to the Allies and China, and anti-Axis and anti-Japanese feeling mounted steadily.

The situation of the Soviet Union was by no means so clear-cut. Russia and Japan had for generations regarded each other as dangerous enemies, and the Soviet Union had sent war supplies to China to aid her against the Japanese. But the signing of a non-aggression pact with Germany prior to the outbreak of war in 1939 altered matters considerably. Japan was linked by an anti-Communist pact with Germany and Italy, and now that Hitler and Stalin apparently had settled their differences, the Japanese were forced to retreat in bewilderment from their former strong anti-Russian attitude. It looked in 1939, however, as though the Soviet Union would adopt a policy of wait-and-see in eastern Asia.

In view of the history of the various powers in far-eastern affairs it was only logical to suppose that the large powers in the Pacific would adopt the course of action they did. Obviously, the course of events in the Pacific area rested primarily with Japan, for since 1931 (in fact since the Sino-Japanese war of 1894) Japan had been the prime disturber of the status quo.

Similarities in Nazi and Japanese policy. The Japanese and Nazi militarists have much in common. Economically they look upon themselves as "have-not" nations which can gain resources only at the expense of such "have" powers as Great Britain, France, and the United States. Both have strong views of racial superiority; Hitler rhapsodizes about the Aryan type, while the Japanese maintain that they are the descendants of the Sun Goddess and have a divine mission to perform in bringing their superior culture to the rest of Asia—in fact to the entire world, according to certain chauvinists. After Japan had successfully defied the League of Nations in its Manchurian conquest and had served as an example to Hitler, the two nations spent the next decade in cajoling and threatening smaller nations with remarkable success. German and Japanese techniques have often been similar. A typical approach is the establishment of puppet régimes, with the army as the real master. Both nations have taken advantage of the apathy of the larger powers or have appealed to them on the grounds that they were fighting Communism and were the enemies of the Soviet Union.

Axis "squeeze play." The Germans, Japanese, and to a lesser degree the Italians were executing a gigantic "squeeze play." Unqualified revisionists and expansionists, they were, on the surface at least, ideologically in strong agreement. The weakness of the League in connection with the Manchuria affair showed Hitler that he could ignore the Treaty of Ver-

Occasion for this "huddle in Berlin" was Adolf Hitler's reception of the Japanese ambassador, Saburo Kurusu, on the occasion of the 2600th anniversary of the founding of the Japanese empire. Foreign Minister von Ribbentrop is at the ambassador's right, and Hitler is flanked by his interpreter, a man named Schmidt. It happened in December 1940.

sailles with impunity. Like Japan, Germany left the League of Nations in 1933. As will be seen in the next chapter, the Abyssinian conquest of 1935-1936, the reoccupation of the Rhineland by Germany in 1936, and the Spanish Civil War all dragged the system of collective security into the dust in Europe.

In 1936 the Rome-Berlin Axis was formed, as was the Japanese-German Anti-Comintern Pact. This latter agreement was directed against Communism and served to link the co-signers closer together. The "incident" of 1937, which began in July, was followed in November by Italy's adherence to the Anti-Comintern Pact and Mussolini's notice of withdrawal from the League of Nations, given in December 1937. In 1938 the annexation of Austria by Hitler took place, and in September came the Munich appeasement, by which the prestige of the democracies fell to hitherto unplumbed depths. One month later the Japanese ignored the danger of a possible clash with the British at Hong Kong and captured nearby Canton. Hitler and Mussolini had the democracies "on the run" in the west; the Japanese press was now insisting that Asia should be for the Asiatics and that it was high time that the western powers cleared out of China.

In March 1939, Hitler took over Czechoslovakia, and within a few months the Japanese had blockaded British and French concessions at Tientsin and were subjecting British subjects to gross insults. The "squeeze play" resulted ultimately in war in Europe in 1939. What would happen in eastern Asia?

Reactions of the democracies. Certainly the democracies were not completely blind to the dangerous position of their interests in the Far East. The British people seethed with rage at the humiliation to which they were subjected by the Japanese, and more and more Americans began to protest the selling of high-octane gasoline and war materials to Japan. The Netherlands East Indies, Australia, New Zealand, Indo-China, and the Philippines studied each new aggressive act with apprehension. The British government spent millions of pounds on the naval base at Singapore so as to create in southeastern Asia a key defense center for its rich possessions. The Dutch augmented their naval forces and reduced the length of army service in order to build up reserves of manpower having military training. The Soviet Union was realistic enough to station a large well-trained army in Siberia as well as great numbers of airplanes and submarines at Vladivostok.

The reaction of the United States to the Pacific situation was especially based on its complex relations with Japan. The American people had long been sympathetic toward the Chinese. As a whole they resented the Twenty-One Demands which the Japanese foisted upon a hapless China in 1915. The growth of Nippon's power as a result of the war was disturbing to the United States, and in the Washington Conference (1921-1922) the United States and Great Britain fixed the naval ratio of the three naval powers at 5-5-3, with Japan on the short end. The Nine-Power Treaty guaranteeing China's territorial integrity was more acceptable to America than to Japan.

Relations between the two countries were considerably improved by the generous help given by Americans after the disastrous earthquake of 1923. But this was offset by the passage in 1924 of an act which excluded Japanese immigrants from the United States. The Chinese had been excluded since 1882 except under certain conditions. The Japanese people took the exclusion act as a deep affront. In 1931 Secretary Stimson led the way in proposing nonrecognition of Japan's conquest of Manchuria. Relations deteriorated even further during the thirties because of increased hostility of Americans toward Japan's expansion and the open friendship and aid given by our government to China.

On the economic front, also, relations were strained. Japan's lower standard of living enabled it to produce and sell many goods more cheaply than the United States, with the result that Japanese businessmen captured more than one market that used to bring profits to American manufacturers. And the danger which Japan's expansion in southeastern Asia might prove to their supply of rubber, tin, and tea stimulated many interests in America to devise strong strategic policies and plans of action.

Summary

This chapter has briefly traced the development of the major areas of eastern Asia during this century up to the year 1939. We have seen how India attempted to gain self-government but had not succeeded in solving its religious, social, or economic problems at home, or in persuading Great Britain to go far toward granting it home rule. Likewise we have seen how China tried to extricate herself from exploitation by creating a republican form of government, unifying her various social and political groups, and resisting Japanese aggression. The evolution of Japan into one of the foremost world powers, culminating in a dynamic expansionist program during the years 1931-1939, has also been traced. Attention has also been given to the numerous colonial possessions and interests held in eastern Asia by the major western powers and how they have been affected by events in the orient.

The most eventful decade in the recent history of eastern Asia was that from September 18, 1931, to December 7, 1941, and the motivating power was Japan. The events which transpired in that part of the world prove beyond any doubt that an inseparable tie-up now exists—and will continue to exist—between east and west. During the period we have studied, Japan allied herself with the Axis powers in a campaign which had a sweeping revisionist and expansionist program for its purpose. Concomitantly in Europe and Asia they were trying to forge "New Orders." On the other hand, China found herself linked to the cause of the western democracies, and everywhere it was the same struggle to resist aggression and ruin.

This chapter is extremely significant in our survey of world history. The civilizations that sprang up along the Indus and Ganges, the Wei and Hwang Ho, and in the archipelago off eastern Asia seemed for centuries so remote from those of Egypt, Greece, Rome, and Europe that the world appeared to be split for all time into "East" and "West." But while these two great cultural segments evolved largely in mutual exclusiveness (though not nearly so exclusively as has been believed in the past), it was inevitable that men would in some age smash the cultural barriers. Improved transportation gradually drew the areas together, and the Industrial Revolution enormously hastened the process. Now we know there is no going back to the isolation of the past.

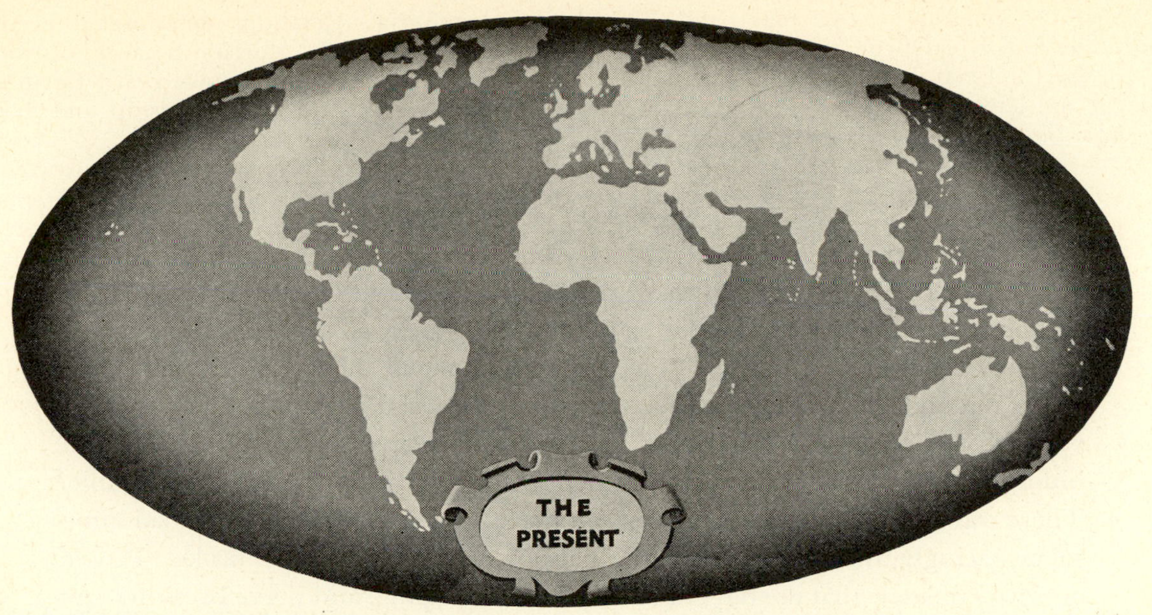

PART FIVE

Ordeal of Our Time

CHAPTER 14

A World Divided

CHAPTER 15

Forging a New World

On September 1, 1939, Hitler's legions marched into Poland, and the Second World War began. On that fateful day an era in world history closed. It had been an era which tried to find a solution for war by creating an ill-supported League of Nations—and failed. The era had witnessed the rise of dynamic new ideologies and the apathy of the static nations toward what was to menace their very existence. It had watched a resurgent, aggressive nationalism bluff and bludgeon an appeasing democratic system into a position no longer tolerable. There was a feeling almost of relief when the clouds of total war, which had hung so menacingly and so long over the nations of Europe, finally broke. People everywhere knew that the old era of blundering, groping, and nerve-breaking tension was at last over. For good or for ill, it was to be replaced by something new.

What that "something" will be cannot yet be known. It may be, as George Bernard Shaw pointed out, that the really important things which will develop out of the war will be those which we could never have foreseen. Certainly history has taught us to expect the unexpected.

But in the course of the war, certain developments were taking place which deserved notice. One was its global nature, far more apparent than was true of the First World War. Battlefronts existed in the Soviet Union, in western Europe, in China, Africa, the Aleutians, and the South Sea Islands. Journalists wrote about the Battle of the Atlantic, of the Pacific, of the Caribbean, of the Mediterranean. Virtually no segment of the earth's surface escaped the holocaust which started in the Polish Corridor.

Another development to be considered was the totality of the Second World War. Civilians had to face air bombardments and starvation blockades as though they, too, were soldiers. Women participated on a scale hitherto unknown. Belligerents converted their industrial systems into "all-out" war machines. The dangers which entire populations had to face in common started to bring about undreamed-of social change. Duties which rich and poor performed alike—air-raid work, fire fighting, and airplane spotting—brought about a new sense of common purpose and solidarity.

A third important development was the ideological nature of the Second World War. People everywhere felt that this was not just a war of rival imperialisms. They saw the rise of a foe who based his actions upon a carefully thought-out political and social philosophy. It was a war between the "Four Freedoms" of democracy and the New Order of Germany, Italy, and Japan. Fascism openly avowed that war is beneficial, that nationalism and not internationalism is desirable, and that democracy is inherently decadent. In this war also was highlighted the struggle between the opposing viewpoints of equality of races and a superior or ruling race—a *Herrenvolk.* A dynamic reaffirmation of their belief in democracy began to find voice in the peoples of the United States and the British Commonwealth of Nations. This new-found enthusiasm for an old and cherished ideal expressed itself in many groping plans for the creation of a truly democratic world in the postwar era.

THE SECOND WORLD WAR, with its gigantic processes of change, would undoubtedly usher in a new era—whatever that new era might be. But even in the midst of war the people were not unaware of changes that had been brought about by peaceful means in their century. Certain discoveries had revolutionized scientific and philosophical thought. Nineteenth-century physicists had thought that the atom was indivisible and was composed of "solid matter." But their successors learned more about its composition, began to understand something of its energy contents, and in smashing the atom began to open up a new material world. The universe as explained by the laws of Newton was radically modified by the relativity theory of Einstein. Radio-active substances and cosmic rays were discoveries of significant import. Sweeping public-health measures, endocrinology, and the conquering of some of the most destructive diseases added many years to the human life span and pointed the way to an era of better health for all.

Literature, music, and art reflected very clearly the tendencies of this age. The disillusionment following the First World War was mirrored in the works of British and American writers. The depression years brought into focus maladjustments of the social environment, and authors and dramatists inveighed against prevailing injustice. Twentieth-century music broke quite sharply with the past. Composers invented new tone patterns and attempted to catch the spirit of the contemporary scene. In architecture the emphasis on functionalism was a healthy sign. Experimentation in painting produced cubism and surrealism.

Where this prolific experimentation in sciences and the arts might lead was as unpredictable as the full results of the Second World War. But it was symptomatic of great changes to come in the world culture pattern. There was no going back. The twentieth century was forging a new world.

	Abyssinia and Spain	
1935-1936	Italy invades, conquers Abyssinia	Failure of League sanctions
1936	Hitler remilitarizes Rhineland	Violation of Versailles Treaty
1936-1939	Civil war in Spain. Fascist victory with Axis aid	Nonintervention of Great Britain, France
	Road to Munich	
1936	Mussolini announces Rome-Berlin Axis	
1936-1937	Anti-Comintern Pact against Russia	Germany, Italy, Japan
1938	Nazi purge	Removes restraining influences
	Hitler takes over Austria, demands Sudetenland	Chamberlain's appeasement efforts
1939	Munich conference	
	Complete capitulation of Czechoslovakia	
	Second World War	
March 1939	Hitler demands Danzig and part of Corridor	
August	Russo-German Pact	Complete reversal of alignment
September	Poland invaded, conquered	Germany and Russia divide country
	England, France declare war	
1939-1940	Standstill in the west	Maginot vs. Siegfried Line
	Russo-Finnish war	
1940	Fall of the western nations: Norway, Low Countries, France	Dunkirk, occupied and unoccupied France
1940-1941	The battle of Britain	All-out bombing fails of purpose
	Italian invasion of Africa, Greece stopped	British raid on Italian navy
	German drive to the Near East	
	Dismemberment of Rumania	
	Annihilation of Yugoslavia	Greece overwhelmed
	Invasion of Crete	British retreat
	Blitzkrieg against Russia slowed	
1942	War in the Pacific	Fall of Hong Kong, Singapore, Java, Burma, Australia threatened
	All-out Axis drive	Battle for Russia
	United States and the War	
1939	New neutrality legislation revised	
1940	The draft: Selective Service Act	First peacetime conscription
Jan. 1941	Lend-Lease Bill	Cash and carry favored Allies
March	Occupation of Iceland	
November	Repeal of neutrality law	
December	Japs attack Pearl Harbor	
Jan. 1942	Pan American Conference at Rio	
Jan.-May	Fall of Philippines	Heroic battle of Bataan
May-June	Battles of Coral Sea, Midway	
July	Increasing American participation	

CHAPTER 14

A World Divided

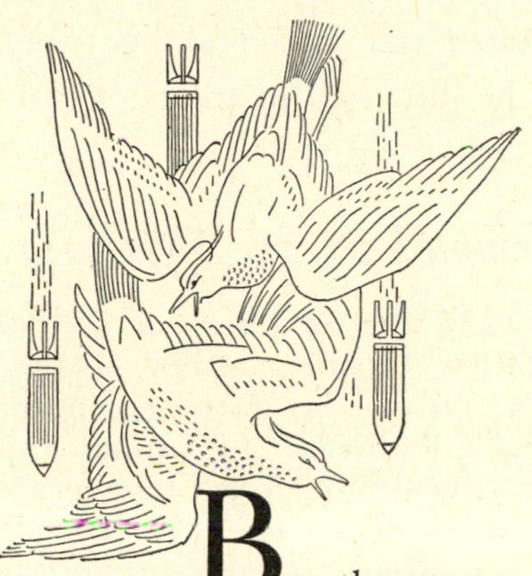

By the postwar settlement of 1919, in the activities of the League of Nations, and in the Locarno agreements of 1925, Germany, Great Britain, and France appeared to have settled their differences. The League seemed to be achieving encouraging if not brilliant success in promoting international harmony, and the signature of the Kellogg-Briand Pact renouncing war as an instrument of national policy in 1928 seemed to promise a new era of peaceful cooperation among nations.

Never have hopes been more thoroughly dashed than in the decade from 1930 to 1940. The restraints and guarantees embodied in collective security, the Nine-Power Treaty, the Locarno agreements, and the Kellogg-Briand Pact all disappeared before the onslaught of undeclared wars, unprovoked aggression, and irresistible blitzkriegs. The period of international disorder was inaugurated by Japanese aggression in Manchuria in 1931, when the League of Nations received its first serious setback. War between China and Japan raged intermittently throughout the next decade. While China was fighting for her national existence, western Europe experienced the Italian conquest of Abyssinia, the Fascist revolt in Spain, and a succession of diplomatic crises. All this foreshadowed the Second World War that came in September 1939.

In 1934, "the year of blood," the world was given a preview of the shape of things to come. In February the Stavisky scandal caused rioting in Paris, and in the same month the Socialist experiment in Vienna was brought to a bloody conclusion when Chancellor Dollfuss turned the Austrian army on the workers. In June Hitler carried out his blood purge, murdering Ernst Roehm and other prominent Nazi leaders.

In July the world was given another example of frightfulness when, in an attempted plot to seize Austria, the Nazis killed Dollfuss. The trail of blood next led to the streets of Marseilles, in France, where King Alexander of Yugoslavia was murdered by a Croatian terrorist from the king's own country. As the year 1934 drew to a close, a news dispatch disclosed that Abyssinian and Italian troops had fought a battle on the Abyssinian border. Europe, and indeed the world, was to have little tranquillity from then on.

In tracing the background for the war which came in September 1939, particular emphasis will be placed upon the following: (1) the Italian conquest of Abyssinia (known also as Ethiopia), (2) the Spanish Civil War, (3) the annexation of Austria, (4) the Munich Agreement, and (5) the dismemberment of Czechoslovakia. These events led to the Polish crisis that precipitated war in September 1939. What may be termed the Second World War will then be discussed in terms of eight fundamental phases, to the summer of 1942.

Fascism Triumphant in Abyssinia and Spain

The conquest of Abyssinia. Italy was the first European nation to follow Japan's lead in aggression. As Mussolini became increasingly convinced of the imperial destiny of his régime, his speeches grew more and more bellicose, bristling with such statements as: "War is to man what maternity is to woman." "Perpetual peace negates the fundamental virtues of mankind, which are revealed only on the bloodstained battlefield in the full light of the sun." The logical spot for Mussolini to strike was Abyssinia, the only important independent native state left in Africa. Furthermore, the Italians had suffered a humiliating defeat at the hands of Abyssinia in 1896.

On December 5, 1934, fighting broke out between Abyssinians and Italians over a section of land on the frontier. On the fourteenth of the same month Emperor Haile Selassie sent an urgent message to the League of Nations, expressing his fears. In May 1935 the League gave the affair serious consideration and tried to arrange for arbitration of the dispute. In the meantime large forces of Italian troops were passing through the Suez Canal on their way to eastern Africa.

In July 1936, before going into exile, Haile Selassie arrived at Geneva to plead before the League of Nations the hopeless cause of his conquered country.

In July 1935 Abyssinia appealed vainly for support from the United States. Outside the framework of the League, France and Great Britain were trying desperately to dissuade Italy from carrying out her plans. Fear of Germany made France want to keep Italy as a friend, and if France had to honor her League pledges against aggression, the invasion of Abyssinia would undoubtedly terminate Italian friendship. Great Britain also was anxious to settle the dispute without invoking pressure by the League in order to present a unified front against Germany. But in Great Britain the Conservative government was faced with the fact that in a recent poll several million votes had been cast in favor of supporting the League at all cost, even war, in order to maintain international law and order. The government of Great Britain was thus forced to agree to certain measures against Italy instituted by the action of the League. France tried to retain the friendship of Great Britain by supporting the League but attempted also to make this support as ineffectual as possible so that Italy would not be offended. Under such circumstances the League action was doomed to failure.

On October 2, 1935, Italian troops invaded Abyssinia. Despite the audacious argument of the Italian delegates to the League that Abyssinia, not Italy, was the aggressor, the League voted to impose sanctions against Italy. This action meant prohibiting shipment of certain goods to Italy and denying her credits. Sanctions were put in force on November 18, but oil, the all-important commodity without which no modern army and navy can fight, was not included in the list of prohibited articles.

While the League was endeavoring to apply pressure against Italy, Italian troops were advancing with little difficulty into Abyssinia. Their progress was facilitated by the use of bombing planes, mustard gas, and tanks. Fighting valiantly, Haile Selassie's warriors were driven back, crushed, and scattered. In May 1936 the Italians entered Addis Ababa, the Abyssinian capital, and the conquest was practically completed. The whole sorry story ended in July 1936, when sanctions were removed, and the League of Nations admitted another catastrophic setback. Collective security had failed against Japan and now had fared no better with Italy. Haile Selassie, an emperor without a country, became an exile in England, the first of several royal exiles.

Military occupation of the Rhineland. The Treaty of Versailles provided that the German Rhineland should be permanently unfortified, and in the Locarno agreements of 1925 Germany pledged herself to abide by this arrangement. When Hitler came to power in 1933, an ambitious disarmament conference was in session at Geneva. Little progress was made, however, and in October 1933 Germany not only withdrew from this conference with the plain intention of rearming herself but withdrew from the League as well. In March 1935, in defiance of the Treaty of Versailles, Hitler introduced conscription. But the conflict over Abyssinia gave him his first big opportunity. His opponents were divided. While the sanction wrangle was in progress, German troops marched into the Rhineland on March 7, 1936.

France mobilized 150,000 troops and considered using force to compel the German troops to evacuate the Rhineland, but Great Britain refused to support such a measure. Many Englishmen thought it hardly worth while to risk war over the demand of a country to fortify its own territory. There were others, however, who recognized the danger in allowing Hitler to break an agreement with little or no protest. As one speaker put it, "What we all wanted to know was 'What is Germany's limit?' You might take the view that Hitler's system required him to have about two stunts a year, and if he were to govern Germany for another twenty-five years, this would mean about fifty more stunts. But if you took the other view—that Germany might stabilize and settle down—then there might come a point . . . when she might say that she had now got restitution and would therefore now stop."

Spanish unrest and revolution. Germany's repudiation of Locarno was followed shortly by the Civil War in Spain, which not only shattered that country but threatened to involve all of Europe. The Spanish constitution of 1931, established after the downfall of the monarchy, had not brought prosperity and stability to Spain. On the contrary it caused serious clashes between the forces of the right and the left. During 1934 and 1935 there was danger that reactionary groups would gain control of the government and nullify most of the progressive legislation enacted in the early days of the republic. In 1936 a coalition of liberal and leftist elements obtained control of the government. Fascist sympathizers were imprisoned, and many military officers who had been engaging in political activities were pensioned. The government tried to steer a middle course, but it satisfied neither the leftists, who were anxious to have revolutionary social changes immediately, nor the ultraconservatives, who were against all reforms. The government was powerless to maintain order. Conservatives and radicals fought and murdered each other early in July, and on July 17 regiments in Spanish Morocco revolted against the government.

Dress rehearsal in Spain. From the outset it was apparent that the totalitarian powers, Italy and Germany, were behind the uprising. Large numbers of Italian planes were made available at once to the Fascist insurgents, whose leader was General Francisco Franco. The Franco Rebels planned a quick campaign. Most of the regular troops were faithful to Franco, and little trouble was anticipated. But the Spanish people in many sections rose *en*

Soldiers of the Spanish Loyalist Army relax during a lull in the fighting before Madrid. Though ill-equipped, they were tough and resourceful fighters.

masse. The Loyalists, representing the people, quickly formed a militia, and volunteers from Austria, Poland, Germany, the United States, and Great Britain flocked to Spain to fight against Fascism. The Rebels got to the outskirts of Madrid, but there they were held. During 1937 the Rebels captured several important strongholds, but the Loyalists dealt a serious blow to a large Italian contingent at Guadalajara.

More and more the struggle in Spain became a proving ground for the coming clash between the totalitarian and democratic powers. Franco claimed he was fighting for Christian civilization against Bolshevism. Both Germany and Italy sent thousands of troops and tons of war equipment to the Rebels. Russia sent large amounts of material and some personnel to the Loyalist government at Madrid. On the Spanish battlefields Germany, Italy, and Russia tried out their new cannon and combat planes. It was a dress rehearsal for the real drama of war even then in the making.

Instead of permitting arms to be sent to the recognized Loyalist government which had the right to purchase them in self-defense under international law, Great Britain and France tried to avoid unpleasantness with the dictators by creating a nonintervention system for Spain. The nations of Europe agreed not to send weapons to either side. But while France and Great Britain held scrupulously to this bargain, Italy and Germany flagrantly sent assistance to Franco. Russia also sent assistance to the Loyalists at Madrid but not on a scale to offset German and Italian aid. All through 1938 the struggle raged, and in December Franco's army of 300,000 men struck at the Loyalist stronghold of Barcelona. The city was captured, and thousands of refugees escaped to France, where those who were not turned back were interned. In March 1939 Madrid fell, and the Spanish republic was no more.

The outcome. Peace brought only famine to distracted Spain. Cities were wrecked, the countryside pillaged, and the farms neglected. Some 500,000 political prisoners were placed in custody, and many were subsequently executed. Most of the reforms instituted by the republic under the constitution of 1931 were repealed, labor unions were abolished, and a Fascist system similar to that in Italy was estab-

Even women rallied as full warriors to the Spanish Loyalist cause. Ernest Hemingway has immortalized fighters like these in "For Whom the Bell Tolls."

lished. The head of the state was Francisco Franco, the *caudillo* (leader), endowed with absolute power.

The affair in Abyssinia represented a setback for Great Britain and France, but the triumph of Franco was even more damaging to their prestige and security. Athwart the frontiers of France and at one end of Great Britain's Mediterranean lifeline the totalitarian powers had established their own creature who might, if need be, arise to do their bidding.

Milestones to Munich

The Rome-Berlin Axis proclaimed. In announcing the military reoccupation of the Rhineland in the spring of 1936, Hitler had stated, "We have no territorial demands to make in Europe." But the course of events during the next two years in Europe increased Hitler's strength enormously. The period of revisionism against the Treaty of Versailles gave way to Nazi determination to undermine and destroy all opposition in Europe.

Italy was a decisive factor in the new course of events. Up to the end of 1934 Mussolini had posed as the guardian of Austrian independence, and in January 1935 a French-Italian colonial agreement had been signed although it was never ratified. France gave Italy certain areas in Africa, and both nations pledged support to each other in European affairs. In July 1935 General Gamelin of the French army went to Rome to map a common plan of action in the event of war with Germany.

Up to this point Germany was diplomatically isolated in Europe, an avowed enemy of Russia and confronted by Great Britain, Italy, and France. But the Abyssinian incident and the imposition of sanctions changed all this, and Italy became the friend of Germany. In November 1936 a Rome-Berlin Axis was announced by Mussolini, and both Axis countries, as we have seen, pursued a common policy in supporting Franco in Spain. Axis solidarity steadily grew throughout the next year, 1937, and in September Mussolini made a visit to Berlin.

British appeasement and Axis strength. By 1937 it was evident that Europe was entering a new and very dangerous phase in international relations. The united front against Germany had been broken. Great Britain, which had allowed its armaments to drop, was alarmed by this development and announced in February 1937 an arms program which would require the expenditure of seven and a half billion dollars in the next five years.

In May 1937 Stanley Baldwin gave up his post as British prime minister and was succeeded by Neville Chamberlain. Great Britain's new leader had a horror of war and was determined to explore every possibility for reaching some equitable understanding with the dictators. Despite criticism at home and snubs from those he wished to placate, Chamberlain persisted throughout 1937 in trying to ease international tension.

Late in 1936 Germany had made an Anti-Comintern Pact with Japan against Russia, and in 1937 Italy subscribed to this pact. Chamberlain was confronted with a Rome-Berlin-Tokyo Axis, the three members of which were increasingly strenuous in their demands for more living space for their people. Germany began to insist upon her right to colonies and *Lebensraum* (living space) in Europe, Italy declared that the Mediterranean should be under Italian control, and Japan began to talk about a New Order which would allow her to dominate China and southern Asia. The words of Mussolini boded no good for Chamberlain's appeasement policy: "The struggle between two worlds can permit no compromise. Either we or they."

The year 1938 marked the termination of the first phase in Hitler's foreign policy and inauguration of a new and much more daring program. By this time the German army had amazing strength. In the air the *Luftwaffe* far exceeded the air fleets of Great Britain and France.

Hitler's Austrian coup. One of the cardinal principles in Hitler's *Mein Kampf* was the union within the Reich of all German-speaking peoples in Europe. In 1934 Hitler attempted to annex Austria, which had more than six million German-speaking people. An uprising was organized for July 25. Nazi agents took over the Vienna broadcasting station, and another group occupied the governmental offices, where they murdered the Austrian chancellor, Engelbert Dollfuss. Mussolini be-

Signs of the times. Not long after the Austrian Anschluss, a photographer found this workman changing the name of the former City Hall Square in Vienna.

gan to mobilize troops at the Austrian frontier, however, and resistance within Austria against the Nazi *Putsch* strengthened. The conspiracy collapsed, and in 1936 Hitler signed a pact with Austria recognizing "the full sovereignty of the Austrian Federal State."

On February 4, 1938, a Nazi purge took place. The minister of war and several other high officers were removed because they refused to countenance some of Hitler's proposed actions. The restraining influence of these officers was superseded by the leadership of Joachim von Ribbentrop, who became one of Hitler's right-hand men. Early in February the Austrian chancellor, Kurt Schuschnigg, received an invitation, or a command, from Berlin to visit Hitler in his mountain retreat. The stories about this interview seem to agree that Hitler suddenly broke into a rage, accusing the chancellor of mistreating Nazis in Austria.

Hitler demanded the inclusion of several prominent Nazi sympathizers in the Austrian cabinet and the release of Austrian Nazis who had been imprisoned, especially Dr. Seyss-Inquart. Schuschnigg steadfastly refused to adhere to this view. On his return to Vienna, the chancellor made Seyss-Inquart minister of the interior but declined to go any further. By the end of February the world became aware that a crisis was brewing in Austria.

The blow fell on Friday, March 11. American radio listeners were told at 2:15 p.m. that Schuschnigg had resigned, at 2:45 that German troops were crossing the frontier, and at 3:43 that the swastika had been hoisted over the Austrian chancellery. Meanwhile Nazi agents in Austria took over the government, and on Saturday, March 12, German troops occupied most of the country.

Germany aspires to the Sudetenland. Austria disappeared from the international pond with scarcely a ripple. Maxim Litvinov, the Russian foreign minister, suggested a conference among the United States, Great Britain, France, and Russia to discuss preventing further aggression, but nothing came of it.

After the Austrian coup, Hitler moved on to his next objective, the annexation of the Sudetenland. (This was the name given to the area around the edges of Czechoslovakia peopled mainly by Germans; see map, page 321.) In 1919 the Sudeten area had been turned over to the new republic of Czechoslovakia for three reasons: (1) although German-speaking, Germans in the Sudeten area had never been part of Germany but part of the Austro-Hungarian empire; (2) the area formed a strategic eastern frontier for Czechoslovakia; (3) it was economically integrated with the rest of Czechoslovakia. Suspecting the Nazis' next move, France promised protection to the Czechs, and Great Britain said that war in this area could not be localized.

In a speech before the Nuremberg Congress on September 12, 1938, Hitler attacked President Benes of Czechoslovakia as a liar and labeled his government criminal. The Sudetens, he declared, "are being oppressed in an inhuman and intolerable manner." Continuing, Hitler screamed into the microphone, "And I say that if these tortured creatures cannot obtain rights and assistance by themselves, they can obtain both from us." Immediately after this speech Chamberlain arranged for a conference with the Führer, and on September 15 sped from England in an airplane to

On his arrival at the Munich airport on September 29, 1938, Prime Minister Chamberlain (center) was invited to review a picked group of Hitler's Storm Troops. He is flanked by Foreign Minister von Ribbentrop and Sir Nevile Henderson and accompanied by Nazi army bigwigs.

Germany. Hitler bluntly informed him that he was determined to secure self-determination for the Sudeten Germans. This was not an easy task, for not less than 400,000 Czechs lived in the districts which were mainly German and not less than 750,000 Germans in the predominantly Czech areas. Returning to London, Chamberlain met with Daladier, the French premier, and both agreed to accept Hitler's demand. A note was sent to the Czech government by France and Great Britain. The plan agreed upon required Czechoslovakia to cede all areas in which the Germans numbered more than fifty per cent. Plebiscites were to be held in other areas where Germans lived, Czechoslovakia was to become a neutral country, and France and Great Britain were to guarantee its new borders. After heated discussion the Czech cabinet acquiesced.

On September 22 Chamberlain again met Hitler in Germany. To Chamberlain's surprise and consternation Hitler presented new demands that the Czechs evacuate within one week all areas marked on a prepared map and that all military material, goods, and livestock in these areas be turned over to the Germans immediately. Chamberlain returned to London without obtaining a settlement. The Czechs were advised that Great Britain and France would help them if they resisted Hitler's newest demands. Tuesday evening, September 27, Chamberlain gave a radio message to the world in which he expressed his desire for peace but warned that Great Britain would fight if "any nation had made up its mind to dominate the world by fear of its force."

The Munich Conference. On Wednesday, September 28, the British House of Commons assembled to hear a report by the prime minister. As he neared the end of his address, a messenger delivered a note from Hitler inviting him to attend a conference at Munich. The following day four men met at the Nazi headquarters in Munich, and for thirteen hours these men—Hitler, Mussolini, Daladier, and Chamberlain—worked out the details of the surrender of the Sudetenland. No Czech representative was present. The terms of the Munich Agreement provided that the Czechs were to withdraw from the disputed area in four stages between October 1 and October 8 and that in the remaining areas where large German groups lived an international commission should conduct a plebiscite. The four powers agreed to guarantee the new frontier.

An interval of uneasiness. The Munich Agreement brought relief to millions of Europeans half-crazed with fear of war, but it

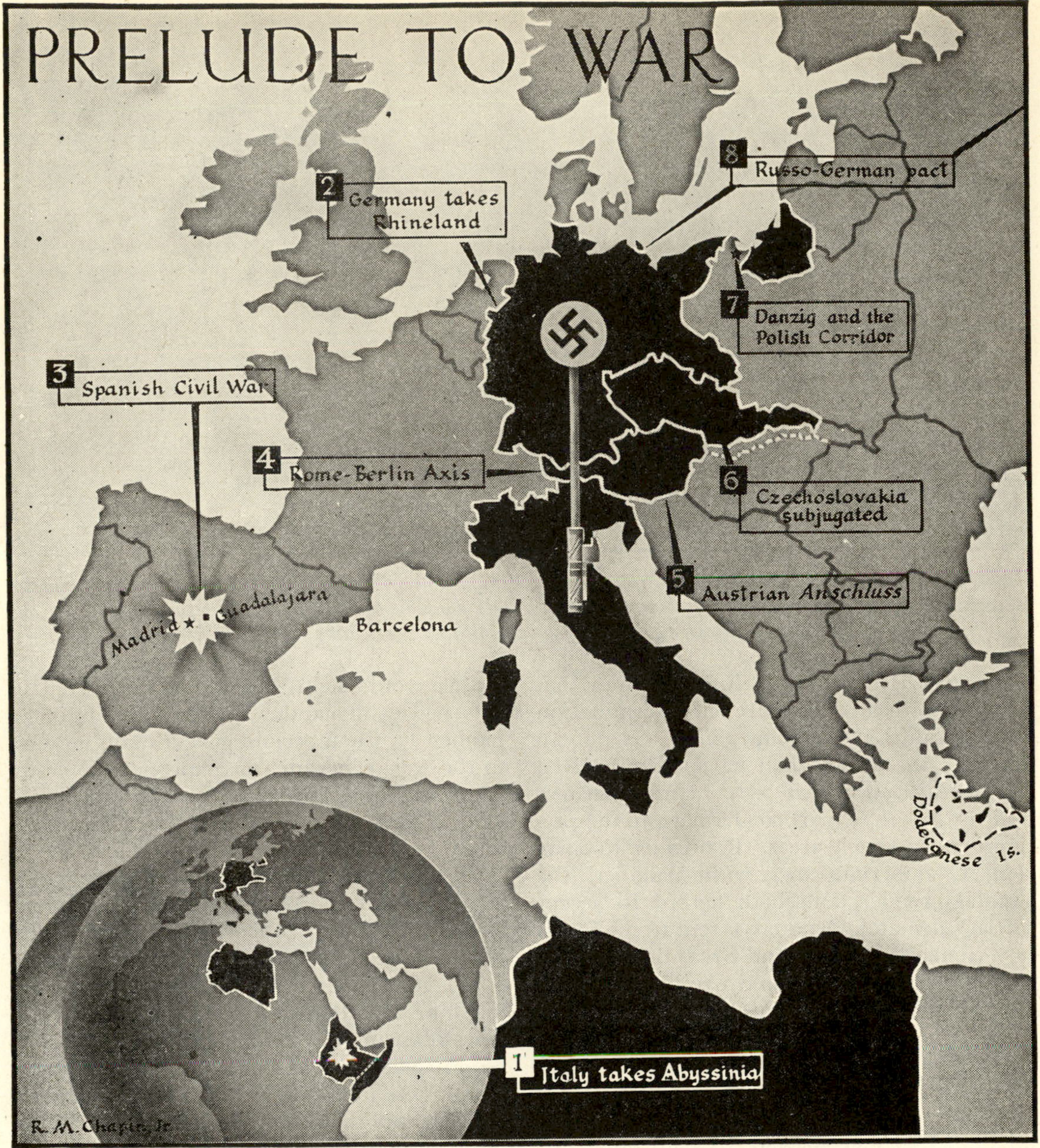

was still a question whether this settlement was to be followed by another crisis. Many hoped for the best but feared the worst. Anthony Eden declared, "Foreign affairs cannot indefinitely be continued on the basis of stand and deliver. Successive surrenders only bring successive humiliations." Alfred Duff Cooper, the first lord of the admiralty, resigned his post and declared, "The premier believes he can come to a reasonable settlement with Herr Hitler on all outstanding questions. He may be right. I hope he is. But I cannot believe it." Winston Churchill in a denunciation of the Munich Agreement said, "The utmost the prime minister was able to gain for Czechoslovakia has been that the German dictator, instead of snatching his victuals from the table, has been content to have them served to him course by course."

Not long afterward it became manifest that

the surrender at Munich by Great Britain and France had purchased only a brief respite from additional Nazi demands. With callous disregard for the rights of the Czechs, the German government took over the Sudetenland and the border areas. Only ten days after the Munich conference, Hitler gave a speech which showed little trace of conciliation. He boasted of the military power of Germany, told France and Great Britain not to meddle with Germany's affairs, and warned the British in particular that trouble would follow if a "war-monger" like Churchill was given a post in the British cabinet.

In November a terrible wave of Jewish persecution swept over Germany. For a whole day Storm Troops and ruffians burned and looted Jewish shops and synagogues. Thousands were sent to concentration camps.

Expansionism announced. Meanwhile the success of Franco in Spain had made Mussolini and Hitler more contemptuous than ever of France and Great Britain. Mussolini openly demanded the cession of French territory in Africa and the Mediterranean. On November 30, 1938, there were shouts in the Italian Chamber of Deputies for Tunisia, Corsica, Savoy, and Nice. In January 1939, in a speech before the Reichstag, Hitler warned the world that Germany would not be content to remain deprived of some of the great land areas controlled by nations such as Great Britain and France. The plain truth, he said, was that Germany was overpopulated and must have room to expand.

Czechoslovakia's total capitulation. The mounting fears of French and British statesmen were confirmed in March 1939. After the Munich Agreement, President Benes had resigned in order that his anti-Nazi views would not embarrass the Czech government. In November the Czech government had given a large measure of self-government to the Slovaks and Ruthenians. The country was then really a loose federation of three peoples. But the new arrangement was not allowed to work. Disorder and treachery among the Slovaks and Ruthenians were fostered by Nazi agents. The Czech president, Emil Hacha, took energetic measures to maintain order and dismissed the Slovakian premier, who went at once to Berlin.

Early in March a bitter attack against the Czech government was inaugurated by the German press. Another coup was in the making. On March 14 Hitler summoned President Hacha and his foreign minister to Berlin. Arriving late in the evening, Hacha and his aid were taken to the German chancellery to be interviewed by Hitler. The conference lasted until 4:15 a.m. For several hours the Czech officials were subjected to all kinds of threats in order to make them sign a document placing their country under the so-called protection of Germany. Finally Hacha capitulated. His signature was a mere formality, however, for German troops were already crossing the Czech frontier. The Nazis entered Prague, capital of Czechoslovakia, on the evening of March 15.

Emergency measures in England and France. The shock of the final conquest of Czechoslovakia and Hitler's callous violation of pledges made at Munich ended the appeasement policy of France and Great Britain. Chamberlain, the chief advocate of appeasement, was embittered by Hitler's latest action. In April, for the first time in Great Britain's long history, the government authorized the conscription of young men for military training in time of peace.

Meanwhile a tremendous arms program was launched for which Great Britain began to spend five million dollars a day. Plans were made to expand the fleet, air-raid shelters were built, a barrage balloon system for the chief cities was introduced, and the Royal Air Force was increased. In Paris Daladier obtained special emergency powers to push forward national defense.

Hitler Looks toward Poland

The Polish Corridor. Nazi Germany under the leadership of Hitler had thus far enjoyed amazing success. In the last coup of March 1939, the Nazis without firing a shot had obtained three hundred million dollars in gold and in foreign credits from the Czechs, the Skoda munitions works, valuable timber resources, and large stocks of arms. Apparently certain of his ability to annex territory and conquer nations without resorting to actual fighting, Hitler turned to the next item on his list: the Polish Corridor. It will be recalled

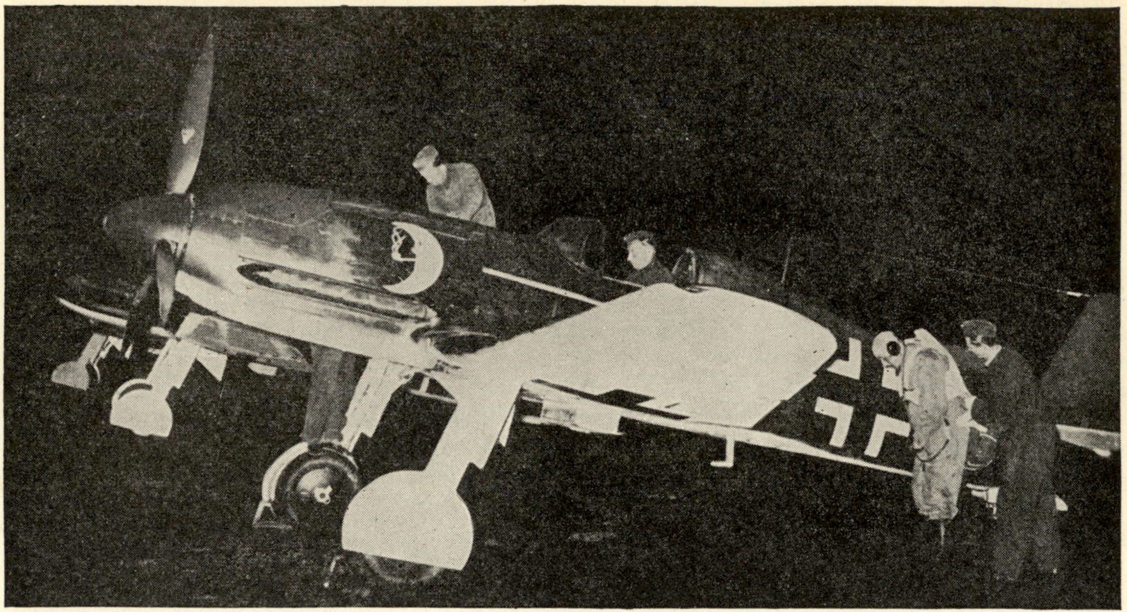

During the battle for Britain the Germans were obliged to keep constant patrol against retaliating British bombers. Here a night fighter's crew readies his plane for a sortie. Notice the night fighter's emblem on the motor.

that in the eighteenth century Poland had been partitioned among three states: Prussia, Russia, and Austria. In 1919 the Treaty of Versailles had turned over West Prussia to Poland in order to give the new Polish state an outlet to the sea (see map, page 317). This Polish Corridor was ninety per cent Polish, but Danzig, at the mouth of the Vistula and the Corridor's chief seaport, had a population of 400,000, nearly all German. In spite of Germany's dislike of the corridor between Germany proper and East Prussia, Hitler had made a ten-year nonaggression pact with Poland in 1934.

Hitler demands and the "Stop Hitler Front." Late in March 1939 it became known that Hitler had proposed to Poland that she cede Danzig to Germany and that permission be given the Nazi government to occupy a narrow strip of land connecting Germany with East Prussia—a corridor across the corridor. On March 31, Chamberlain warned the Nazi government in a speech to the House of Commons that "in the event of any action which clearly threatened Polish independence" and in case the Poles resisted, the British would "at once lend the Polish government all support in their power." France concurred in this declaration.

The Polish question which precipitated the Second World War went through three separate stages. From March through April, Hitler made known his demands, and there was much diplomatic maneuvering as Great Britain and France attempted to organize a "Stop Hitler Front." In April French and British guarantees against aggression were given to Rumania and Greece, and in May the British succeeded in winning Turkey as a quasi-ally. In this same month Hitler abrogated his nonaggression pact with Poland.

The courtship of Russia. The second phase in the Polish question was an interim period from May to August in which the main activity was a duel between Germany on the one hand and Great Britain and France on the other for a Russian alliance. When Great Britain made her guarantee to Poland, it was thought in London that this would be sufficient to restrain Hitler, but as the summer of 1939 wore on, it became evident that war was likely. In such an event it was imperative that Great Britain secure a strong ally in eastern Europe to join her in aiding Poland. In April negotiations with Russia were started by France and Great Britain, and in July a Franco-British military mission was sent to consult with the Russian staff. Since 1934, when she joined the League of Nations, Russia had condemned German aggression and supported the League principle of collective security. But Great Britain in particular up to this time had not been anxious to cooperate closely with Russia because British leaders were suspicious of Russian policy, had a dread of Communism, and were not greatly impressed with the Russian army.

At Munich Russia was completely disregarded in the partition of Czechoslovakia. As the power of Hitler grew and that of France and Great Britain waned, Stalin, the Russian leader, evidently decided to change his policy. The first indication of this decision was the replacement of Foreign Minister Litvinov in May. In August the world was amazed, and Great Britain and France in particular were stunned, at the news that Russia and Germany had signed a nonaggression pact on August 24. With the pact in his pocket Hitler believed that Great Britain and France would not dare to oppose his Polish ambitions. For their part France and Great Britain realized that if they wished to stop Germany from dominating all of Europe they must fight.

Last-minute peace moves. A third stage in the Polish dispute began. Prime Minister Chamberlain wrote a personal letter to Hitler, saying that Great Britain would not countenance the solution of the Danzig question by the use of force. From several quarters appeals were made for peace—from the Pope, the king of Belgium, and President Roosevelt. During the last two weeks of August the British government also made strenuous efforts to bring about a peaceful solution of the Polish question.

The German ultimatum. On August 29 the German government demanded that the Poles send an emissary with full power to make an agreement with Hitler. The Polish government hesitated in complying, for it knew all too well the treatment meted out to Schuschnigg and Hacha. Near midnight of August 30, the British ambassador, Sir Nevile Henderson, saw Von Ribbentrop, the German foreign minister, who rapidly read aloud a list of sixteen terms which were to have been presented to Poland. But since no emissary had arrived, "it was now too late," in Von Ribbentrop's own words. Poland meanwhile was ready to undertake negotiations but not to accept demands at a moment's notice, and her ambassador went to see Von Ribbentrop the night of August 31. The Polish ambassador was thereupon given the demands, which he tried to communicate to Warsaw, only to find that the wires had been cut and the war had already begun. The German government then read its terms over the radio and declared that they had been rejected.

The invasion of Poland. Before either the British or the Polish governments had had a chance to examine the German demands, Nazi troops had crossed the Polish frontier early in the morning of September 1. Fighting began without a declaration of war, and the German air force began its blast of Polish cities. In the afternoon Nevile Henderson notified the Nazi government that unless fighting ceased Great Britain would fulfill her treaty obligations to Poland.

On the morning of September 3 Chamberlain with the full consent of his cabinet sent an ultimatum to Germany, demanding that the invasion of Poland be halted. The time limit was given as 11 a.m. of the same day. At 11:15 the British prime minister broadcast a message to his people stating that the country was at war. France took similar action.

After an interval of only twenty-five years since the First World War Europe was again at war. In 1914 there was enthusiasm on both sides when the conflict commenced, and few sacrifices or concessions had been made by the various countries in order to arrest war. On the other hand, 1939 saw the vast majority of people in Europe, and indeed the world, dreading war and seeking to preserve peace. Many efforts had been made to satisfy what Nazi Germany called her "legitimate aspirations."

Concessions gained at Munich had been ruthlessly exploited to dismember Czechoslovakia. Despite the warnings of British and French statesmen and the anxiety of people all over the world the Nazi régime next applied its coercive techniques against Poland. The causes of war are usually complex and the conflict of 1939 is no exception. But there can be little doubt that the immediate and most important cause was the Nazi government's determination to get what it wanted regardless of consequences. Brusquely sweeping aside all suggestions of conciliation and arbitration, Hitler attacked Poland. This country naturally fought back to maintain its existence; Great Britain and France took up arms because the very existence of a free Europe was at stake.

The Second World War

Stages of the war. The conflict that followed can truly be thought of as the Second World War, so widespread was its action. It may be helpful to think of the first three years of the war (September 1939 to July 1942) as involving eight phases of development:

(1) Blitzkrieg in Poland: September 1939.
(2) Standstill in the west: October 1939 to April 1940.
(3) The battle for Europe and the fall of the western nations: April to June 1940.
(4) Great Britain under fire: July 1940 to May 1941.
(5) The Italian campaigns: October 1940 to April 1941.
(6) The German drive to the Near East: beginning in April 1941.
(7) Blitzkrieg versus Russia: beginning June 1941.
(8) The war enters the Pacific: December 7, 1941.

Blitzkrieg in Poland. About five a.m., September 1, 1939, without any declaration of war, German columns crossed the Polish frontier from four angles, while squadrons of bombing planes dropped their deadly missiles upon hangars and landing fields. The Poles fought with great courage, but from the outset they were overwhelmed. The Polish army numbered over a million men, but it was built upon nineteenth-century conceptions of warfare. It had the best cavalry regiments in Europe but little mechanized or motorized equipment and an inadequate air force. In a few days the world witnessed the drama of a new military technique in operation. This was the blitzkrieg, or lightning war, which unleashed tanks, motorized artillery, parachutists on Polish soil, and blackened Polish skies with bomber squadrons. In a few days the Polish air force was destroyed, communications were disrupted, and the Polish army was demoralized.

In view of later developments when Nazi Germany attacked the Soviet Union, it is probable that Russian leaders suspected Hitler's aggressive designs early in 1939. Russian troops, therefore, were sent into eastern Poland to secure a protective strip of territory between German-conquered Poland and the Soviet Union.

For several weeks Warsaw held out even though its inhabitants were subjected to an almost constant bombardment from German artillery and German planes. But resistance was hopeless, and the city capitulated on September 27, signalizing the end of all fighting in the country except by a few patriotic "bitter-enders" here and there. At the end of hostilities a Russo-German treaty partitioned Poland for the fourth time, giving each nation approximately half the country.

Standstill in the west. An unreal and perplexing period of inaction now began along the Franco-German frontier, where two gigantic fortress systems faced each other—the Maginot and Siegfried lines. The Poles had expected assistance from their allies, but France and Great Britain could do nothing. Planes might have been sent, but the destruction of Polish airdromes and landing fields by the Nazi *Luftwaffe* rendered this impossible. General Gamelin tried an offensive feint here and there against the Siegfried Line and in a fortnight captured about 100 square miles of German territory, which was lost as soon as Nazi reinforcements arrived from their triumphs in Poland. Until the spring of the next year, 1940, action along the western front was practically limited to night patrols in the no-man's-land between the two lines.

Great Britain and France had nestled their armies snugly behind the Maginot Line. There was to be no repetition of the slaughter of the First World War. British and French generals believed that it would be suicidal for any army to try to storm either the Maginot or the Siegfried Line. According to many experts modern warfare was to be one of position, not of movement, in which the nations with the greatest economic resources would eventually emerge triumphant. British and French leaders expected to blockade Germany with the superior Allied navy and gradually starve her out. For more than six months the war followed this pattern, and many people both in Europe and America were suspicious of the genuineness of the struggle.

The Russo-Finnish war. In this phase of the war the only real fighting, ironically enough, was not between the major contestants but between Finland and Russia. Late in September 1939 Russia demanded and obtained mutual assistance pacts with the three Baltic republics of Latvia, Lithuania, and Estonia. Soviet troops were given the right to occupy certain strategic areas in the three countries. The three republics were joined to the Soviet Union (in August 1940). Russia then made similar demands of Finland, but the Finns refused to turn over the required territory. Soviet troops thereupon crossed the Finnish frontier.

Much to the astonishment of the world the Finns put up stiff resistance. A strongly fortified system called the Mannerheim Line barred the path of the Russians across the Karelian isthmus. In the open country of northeastern Finland, bands of Finnish ski troops harassed and broke up numerically superior enemy forces. But no nation of four million could be expected to hold out against a foe the size of Russia, and in January 1940 sheer weight of numbers began to tell. The League denounced Russian aggression, many volunteers from the non-totalitarian countries flocked into Finland, and there was talk of an Anglo-French expeditionary force. Norway and Sweden, however, refused to grant transit rights to any such force.

On March 12, 1940, Russian terms of peace were accepted. Finland promised to make no alliance contrary to Russian interests, guaranteed Russia the use of the railroad across Finland to Norway and Sweden, leased important naval sites to Russia, and ceded a large area of her territory.

At the time of Russia's invasion of Finland condemnation of this action was widespread in many countries, especially in Great Britain, France, and the United States. As in the case of eastern Poland, however, the trend of opinion in many quarters following Hitler's later attack on the Soviet Union was to regard Russian policy toward Finland as having been a drastic but understandable measure taken to create a zone of defense against probable Nazi aggression.

The battle for Europe. Great Britain and France might have planned to carry on a long war of attrition against Germany, but the Nazi leaders had a different plan, daring, ruthless, and drawn up with consummate skill. The tremendous power of the greatest military machine in history again struck like lightning. Early on the morning of April 9, German troops occupied Denmark. At the same time small Norwegian defense units were overwhelmed by swarms of Nazi troops who came ashore from innocent-looking merchant vessels or who had been on Norwegian soil for some time in the guise of tourists.

The Germans were assisted by a Norwegian Nazi sympathizer, Vidkun Quisling, who had been Norwegian minister of defense. With clocklike precision the German invasion of Norway was carried out as the Nazi forces took over the main strategic points: Narvik, Bergen, and Oslo. Units of the British fleet attempted to intercept German transports carrying troops, and some of these vessels and their escorting warships were sunk. But this effort failed, and in three weeks some eighty thousand German troops had been landed by plane or naval transport.

On April 15 a British force arrived at the Norwegian port of Narvik, and in the next few days other Allied troops were disembarked at other harbors. The expeditionary force lacked equipment, especially anti-aircraft guns, and after two weeks was forced to evacuate under heavy bombardment from Nazi aircraft. The justification for German invasion of Norway and Denmark was, according to the Reich government, the fact that both these countries were in imminent danger of attack by Great Britain and France and hence needed German "protection." Hitler's move had given him a valuable larder of food, timber resources, easy access to the valuable iron mines of northern Sweden, and important air bases from which to menace the British Isles. The Nazi success also demonstrated to certain neutral European powers the alleged invincibility of German arms.

Invasion of the Low Countries. On the evening of May 9, 1940, Hitler and his leading Nazi aids attended various musicals and movies in Berlin. There was nothing to indicate that one of the greatest battles in world history was to commence at dawn the next morning. As 4 a.m. approached, German armies received orders to attack Belgium, Luxemburg, and Holland. As the troops moved forward, swarms of Nazi bombers attacked forts, railroad junctions, airfields, and cities in these three countries and in northern France as well.

Holland was the scene of the heaviest fighting, and her great cities were pounded by German bombing planes. Two hours after the invasion had begun, the German minister to the Dutch government presented an ulti-

Overlooking nothing, the Nazi blitzkrieg army uses a convenient canal barge as a pontoon bridge to invade Holland. Bicycle and motorcycle troops are crossing by it, prepared to infiltrate the Low Countries.

matum demanding the surrender of the country. As in the case of Norway and Denmark, the Reich claimed to possess "irrefutable evidence of an immediately threatening invasion by British and French forces . . . prepared a long time beforehand with the knowledge of the Netherlands and Belgian Governments." The demand to surrender was summarily rejected, and the Dutch armed forces braced themselves for the struggle against the invader. Again, resistance was hopeless. On May 13 the Dutch royal family headed by Queen Wilhelmina fled to England. On May 14 the Dutch military authorities surrendered to the Germans.

On the same day that had brought war to Holland, the conflict burst upon Belgium. Again the attack came without warning. On the morning of May 10 British and French were already on their way to support the Belgian defense line. The following day, however, the Germans captured a supposedly impregnable fortress, the pivot in Belgian defense. A week after the fighting began, German forces captured Brussels.

Invasion of France: Dunkirk. After French forces had been hurried north to assist the hard-pressed Belgians, the German high command struck at a weak spot in the French line, and by May 19 a gap of sixty miles had been made in the northern part of the Maginot Line. Large numbers of heavy tanks supported by dive bombers rapidly cut a swath to the west. German panzer divisions next reached a point on the English Channel, and the Allied troops in Belgium were cut off from the main French army.

In this hour of national peril the French premier, Paul Reynaud, replaced General Gamelin with General Weygand. The new supreme commander tried to rally his troops with the message, "The future of France depends upon your tenacity. Hold tight the soil of France. . . . Look only forward." But bad news came from Belgium on May 28 when King Leopold announced the surrender of his army. In danger of encirclement, the Allied forces in Belgium retreated to Dunkirk on the seacoast. While picked suicide squads slowed up the German advance, thousands of Allied troops waded into the surf and were picked up by boats of every description. Out of an original force of 400,000, 335,000 men were successfully evacuated.

The fall of France. With the conquest of Luxemburg, Holland, and Belgium completed, the German forces directed a final blow at France. The assault commenced June 5. In five days the invader was within thirty-five miles of Paris, and the French government fled. Anxious to get in at the kill and satisfied that both Great Britain and France would be out of the war in a few weeks, Mussolini declared war against France on June 10. In explaining this action, Il Duce declared:

"This gigantic conflict is only a phase of the logical development of our revolution. It is the conflict of poor, numerous peoples who labor against starvers who ferociously cling to a monopoly of all riches and all gold on earth.

"It is a conflict of fruitful, useful peoples against peoples who are in a decline. It is a conflict between two ages, two ideas."

In vain did General Weygand improvise new tactics to stop the German forces. The French were outnumbered in men, in motorized equipment, and above all, in airplanes. On June 14 Paris fell, and Weygand informed the French government at Bordeaux that the situation was hopeless. Premier Reynaud wished to continue the struggle, but the majority of his cabinet believed further resistance was impossible. Reynaud thereupon resigned, and Marshal Pétain, 84-year-old hero of Verdun in the First World War, became premier.

While the French leaders initiated negotiations with the Germans, the Maginot Line was captured, and southern France was threatened. Actual negotiations began on June 21. In the same old dining car in which Marshal Foch had imposed armistice terms on the Germans in 1918, the French representatives received the Nazi terms. On June 22 the French delegation signed the armistice agreement. Nearby stood a granite block on which now ironically was inscribed:

"Here on the Eleventh of November, Succumbed the Criminal Pride of the German Empire, Vanquished by the Free Peoples Which It Tried to Enslave."

France was split into two zones, occupied and unoccupied. All the French coast was controlled by Germany. The cost of occupation was to be paid by France. All French forces were to be demilitarized, and the French fleet was to be turned over to the Axis powers with the understanding that the surrendered naval units would not be employed against Great Britain. More than two million French prisoners were to be held until the end of the war. An armistice agreement was also made with Italy, and a small strip of France on the Italian border was occupied by the forces of Il Duce. In unoccupied France the French government was to manage its own affairs, supposedly free from any interference. In reality France became the puppet of the Nazi government.

The Vichy government. The Third French Republic, born in 1871 as the result of a defeat suffered in the Franco-Prussian War, now perished in another defeat administered by the same enemy. Meeting in the city of Vichy on July 9 the French parliament signed the death warrant of the republic. It was a stormy and tragic meeting. As the names of some of the French leaders who had only recently guided the destinies of France were read during the roll call, jeers and hisses filled the room. The parliament voted to give power to Marshal Pétain to draw up a new constitution. On July 11 the Marshal was made chief of the French state with dictatorial powers. The new government soon showed that it had buried the old democratic principles of Liberty, Equality, and Fraternity. In their place the people were to be guided by Labor, Family, Fatherland. Outright Fascism had come to France.

Symbol of German military exactness, the seated soldier seems to be, as for all practical purposes he is, part of the gun on which he rides.

The naval battle of Oran. The impact of the German blitzkrieg left France demoralized, impotent, her republican institutions discredited, but across the Channel the British people seemed suddenly to discover a new reservoir of power and confidence. The genesis of this new spirit came with the resignation of Neville Chamberlain as prime minister and the appearance of Winston Churchill in his stead. Chamberlain resigned his office just as

Under bombing with such results as are shown here, the people of London never relaxed in their dogged insistence that Germany be defeated. This view was taken from the top of St. Paul's Cathedral.

Nazi troops poured into the Low Countries.

The major part of the French fleet, cooped up in the harbor of Oran in Morocco, was sought out early in July by a British squadron from Gibraltar. Fearing that the Nazi government might obtain the French vessels and use them in the fight against Great Britain, British naval chiefs demanded that the French fleet either continue the struggle against Germany or agree to demobilization. Upon the refusal of this ultimatum, the British squadron opened fire and destroyed four French battleships and several destroyers.

Great Britain under fire. From July to October the war entered its fourth phase. Great Britain was at bay, faced by invasion. With most of the tanks and guns of the British army lost at Dunkirk, only the British navy and a numerically weak air force barred the way across the narrow English Channel. In June heavy daily air raids were commenced by the Germans. Increasing in intensity, the raids assumed vast proportions early in August. Waves of German planes crossing the Channel from convenient bases in France tried to blast British airdromes and disrupt communications. Apparently failing in this purpose the German *Luftwaffe* then concentrated upon the bombing of London. During the first two weeks of September thousands of bombs were dropped on the city. Hundreds of buildings were destroyed, with a heavy loss of life.

The main objective of Nazi tactics was to secure air superiority over Great Britain, to drive the Royal Air Force from the sky as a prelude to German invasion. But the R.A.F. showed unexpected strength. On August 15 alone, 180 German airplanes were shot down by British fighter planes, and between September 6 and October 5 Germany lost almost 900 planes. Meanwhile heavy bombers from Great Britain ranged over Germany and particularly over French channel ports where barge concentrations, assembled for invasion, were destroyed. By the end of October it became evident that German hopes for an early invasion of Great Britain had been frustrated. Nevertheless the bombings continued, as we shall see.

The Italian campaigns. The failure of the summer bombings of England was followed by the fifth phase of the war, the Italian period. By autumn of 1940 it was apparent that Mussolini was determined to secure a few victories of his own. They would not only add to the glory and prestige of Fascism but would also provide more bargaining power when the final peace terms were imposed on Great Britain and France.

The grand plan of Fascist strategy was to inclose the British possessions, the Sudan, and British Somaliland, as well as Egypt, in a vast encircling movement. Italian troops under Marshal Graziani were to proceed east from Libya, cross the Egyptian border, and then capture Cairo and the Suez Canal. Once the canal was captured, the British lifeline via the Mediterranean to India and the Far East would be cut. From Italian east Africa other Italian armies were to strike in the north and west making their way to southern Egypt and the British Sudan. If this plan succeeded, Mussolini would gain a great African empire.

Italian troops assisted by native soldiers seized British Somaliland during August. This placed Italy in a position to threaten the entrance to the Red Sea. Early in September

Marshal Graziani headed an army of 300,000 men against Egypt and captured a point a few miles within Egyptian territory. But here the invading army stalled. In the meantime Mussolini made plans to obtain a virtual protectorate over Greece. This would have given the Italian fleet valuable bases, such as Crete and Corfu, enabling them to challenge the British naval squadron in the eastern Mediterranean. But on October 28 the Greek government refused to accede to a three-hour ultimatum from Italy. Much to the amazement of the world, Greece stopped the invading Italians and pushed them back into Albania. Harried by British aircraft, the Italians were forced to retreat across Albania, and by November more than 1000 square miles of Albanian soil had been conquered by the Greek army.

The British retake Africa. The next setback Italy received was the raid on the naval base at Taranto by British torpedo-carrying planes. When the smoke cleared, half of the battleships in the Italian navy had been put out of action. Meanwhile the British army of the Nile, under General Archibald Wavell, had been quietly preparing a counterstroke against Graziani in Egypt. On December 9 a large number of British tank units attacked, and in a few days the Italians had been forced back into Libya. Thousands of prisoners were taken as Wavell's men pushed deeper into Libya. At the same time fresh imperial troops from India and the Union of South Africa attacked Italian forces in eastern Africa. Italian Somaliland was overrun, British Somaliland was recaptured, Eritrea was conquered in April, and the British entered Addis Ababa, the capital of Abyssinia. As a crowning discomfiture to the Italian command, the British fleet managed to entice the Italians into the Aegean Sea in April. Here the Italian fleet suffered serious losses—at least three heavy cruisers and several destroyers.

Germany meanwhile. The fifth phase of the war saw little major activity on the part of Germany. It was Italy's affair, although Hitler's partner had nothing to show but defeats and setbacks. But Hitler was far from unoccupied. The submarine war was carried on against British shipping, especially in the North Atlantic. The British were at a disadvantage because the Irish Free State refused to allow the British fleet to use its ports. The convoy system did much to reduce the submarine hazard, but in the spring of 1941 it was plain that the Battle of the North Atlantic was now the most serious threat to Great Britain.

The failure of German mass raids in the summer of 1940 and the surprising strength of the British air force caused Air Marshal Goering to alter his tactics. Daylight raids had been too costly. In the autumn months of 1940, therefore, increasing use was made of indiscriminate night bombing. Neither Germany nor Great Britain was able to counter this attack effectively. On the night of November 15, the English city of Coventry was almost completely gutted by high explosive and incendiary bombs. The important ports of Bristol, Plymouth, and Southampton were bombed again and again, and on the night of December 29, the German air force tried to destroy London by fire. Some 10,000 two-pound incendiary bombs were dropped. The damage was severe. The old Guildhall, a dozen famous historic churches, many large office buildings, and most of Bookseller's Row containing 6,000,000 books were destroyed. Throughout the spring of 1941 night bombing on Great Britain continued. In May it was announced that since the start of the raids 35,000 civilians had been killed and many more severely wounded. Throughout the ordeal the British people, inspired in part by the dogged leadership of Winston Churchill, remained steadfast in their determination to oppose Hitlerian Germany.

The German drive to the Near East. The first three rounds of the war went to the Germans and the fourth and fifth to the British, who held off the *Luftwaffe* and with the aid of Greece inflicted numerous defeats upon Italy. In April 1941 Hitler initiated another great offensive, the sixth phase of the war. This was designed to succor his hard-pressed Italian ally in Albania, to get control of the Balkans, and to use the Balkan peninsula as a stepping stone to mastery of the Near East with its Suez Canal and the rich oil fields of northern Iraq.

Rumania dismembered. While Italy was trying to invade Greece, the Nazi high command was laying the groundwork for its projected drive toward the Near East. As long as France remained strong, Rumania tried to evade any commitments until it became more

As Britain began to challenge with good results the vaunted invincibility of the German Luftwaffe, such planes as these were put into the skies. In the foreground is a Wellington bomber, in the background a Spitfire fighter.

evident which side would win in Europe. When France collapsed, Rumania decided that she must cooperate with the Nazi régime. King Carol II of Rumania, in June 1940, made his country a totalitarian state by decree, and British oil properties were seized. While Germany was preoccupied in the west, Russia demanded, on June 26, that Rumania cede to her a large slice of territory, most of which had been taken from Russia in 1918. King Carol appealed to Germany and Italy for assistance, but these powers, anxious to prevent a major war in the Balkans at this time, advised capitulation.

After the cession of the territory, two other neighbors of Rumania decided to present their claims. Bulgaria demanded territory which she had lost to Rumania in 1913, and Hungary asked for the area taken from her in 1920. Again a Balkan war appeared imminent, and during the summer months of 1940 Berlin and Rome, acting as arbiters, forced Rumania to cede most of the disputed territory. One of the results of the dismemberment of Rumania was the abdication of King Carol II, who fled the country. Another, and much more important, consequence was that Rumania became a puppet state of Germany. Between November 20 and 24 both Hungary and Rumania came into the Axis camp by accepting the terms of the alliance signed by Germany, Italy, and Japan in September 1940. In March 1941 the Nazi diplomats also brought Bulgaria into the Axis.

The invasion of Yugoslavia. Two Balkan nations still remained to be taken care of, Greece and Yugoslavia. Although Greece was inflicting heavy losses on Italian forces in Albania, it was desirable to secure control over Yugoslavia before sending aid to the hard-pressed Italians. In preparation for the advance into Greece large quantities of material and thousands of men were sent into Bulgaria and massed on the Greek frontier. When Berlin presented its demands to Yugoslavia late in March 1941, Prince Paul and his two co-regents decided there was no recourse but acceptance. On March 25 Yugoslavian delegates at Vienna agreed to permit the passage of German supplies through the country and to undertake certain measures of economic cooperation. Two days after the pact was signed, the government of Prince Paul was overthrown, and King Peter, just seventeen, was placed on the throne by an anti-Axis government. This startling development was welcomed in Greece, and Great Britain pledged her aid in the event of German aggression.

On April 6 German armies attacked Greece and Yugoslavia simultaneously. The motorized equipment, Stuka bombers, and fighter planes of the blitzkrieg were again in action. The Yugoslavs had waited too long before deciding to defy Hitler. Their army was not fully mobilized, and staff talks for cooperation had not been carried on with the Greek command.

In what was evidently meant as an object lesson to the people of Europe who might have ideas of defying German policies, the *Luftwaffe* carried out a terrible bombing attack against the open and unfortified capital of Yugoslavia, Belgrade. At the same time German tank divisions, moving with unexpected rapidity over mountain passes, destroyed the Yugoslavian forces. It had been thought that the rugged terrain might slow down German operations, but the panzer divisions seemed as much at home on the mountainous mule tracks of Yugoslavia as on the plains of France.

Greece overwhelmed. The collapse of the Yugoslavian armies allowed a strong German force to push in the direction of the great Greek port of Salonika. Another Nazi army punched its way across Thrace and reached the Aegean Sea, thus trapping a Greek army at the Turkish border. Assisted by British troops the Greeks put up a magnificent fight. But the Allied troops were hopelessly outnumbered in tanks, in planes, and in men. During the last week in April the position of the Greeks and British became desperate. On April 23, the Greek army that had kept the Italians on the run in Albania but was now caught between both the Italian army and a German force was compelled to surrender. The British managed "another Dunkirk." The navy evacuated some 48,000 British soldiers to Crete and Alexandria.

By May 1, after a campaign of just three weeks, Hitler had conquered two more countries, and King George of Greece had set up his government on the island of Crete. Great Britain had been forced to weaken the army of the Nile in order to send troops and equipment to Greece. This weakness became apparent during April when German and Italian forces in Libya suddenly assumed the offensive while the battle for Greece was going on. In the space of a few days Libyan posts were recaptured, and the enemy had again reached the Egyptian frontier.

Revolt engineered in Iraq. With perfect timing the Nazi high command also presented Great Britain with another military problem. On April 4 the pro-British government in Iraq was overthrown by an Arab leader with pro-Axis leanings. From Iraq's rich oil fields a pipe line more than one thousand miles long carried this essential fuel to Palestine, where it was available for the British fleet operating in the Mediterranean and for the British army of the Nile. Shortly after the new leader came to power, a British contingent was landed at Basra to protect the oil fields in accordance with treaty arrangements between Iraq and Great Britain, arrangements which gave the latter the right to maintain troops and air fields in Iraq.

On May 2, the day after the termination of the Greek campaign, severe fighting broke out in Iraq between British and Iraqi forces. The pattern of Nazi strategy was evident. German troops would arrive by air from Greek airdromes. But before this could be carried out with good chance of success, the island of Crete had to come into German hands, and arrangements had to be made with the French government to permit German transport planes en route to Iraq to use facilities in French Syria.

The invasion of Crete. On May 19 thousands of German parachutists dropped from transport planes on Crete. Desperate fighting took place as British troops tried to prevent the few air fields on the island from falling into the hands of the aerial invaders. At the same time units of the British fleet sought to prevent the ferrying of troops from Greece. After two weeks of fighting, superior power in the air crushed British resistance, and during the first weeks of June the small British force had to be evacuated by a British fleet under constant attack from German dive bombers.

By June 1941 it appeared that Hitler had won the battle for the Mediterranean and that his armies were in a position to launch an offensive against the Near East and the Suez Canal. Axis troops were menacing the eastern frontier of Egypt. With Crete in German hands an all-out attack appeared logical against both Turkey and French Syria, if they resisted the powerful Nazi war machine. In this way Palestine and Egypt could be attacked from the north by way of Greece and Crete and from the west by way of Libya.

The United States and the War

American isolation. Before discussing the seventh phase of the war, it is necessary to consider the effect of the conflict upon the United States. As the battle for the Near East and the Mediterranean reached a climax and Japan, as will be shown later in this chapter, attempted to establish her New Order in Asia, the eyes of all the remaining neutrals—especially those in the New World—anxiously followed the tide of conflict. This was especially true in the United States. After the First World War the United States had lapsed into her traditional isolation, critical of the Treaty of Versailles, which she refused to sign, and indifferent to the League of Nations, which she refused to join.

Between 1920 and 1930 the desire of the American people to avoid international complications grew rather than diminished. The repudiation of the war debts by her former allies strengthened the belief that participation in the war in 1917 and 1918 had been a mistake. From 1934 to 1936 a Senate investigating committee under Senator Nye studied the role played by armament makers in the First World War and exposed huge profits. This in itself fell far short of explaining the United States' entrance into the conflict in 1917, but many Americans believed, more than ever, that the nation had been stimulated by the desire for profits on the part of a few financiers. In April 1937 the American Institute of Public Opinion revealed in one of its polls that seventy per cent of people canvassed believed that it had been a mistake for the United States to go to war in 1917. In 1934 Congress passed the Johnson Act prohibiting debt-defaulting governments from marketing their securities in the United States, and in January 1935 the Senate refused to sanction American entry into the World Court.

Neutrality legislation. As war clouds appeared on the horizon in 1935 in the shape of the Italo-Abyssinian dispute, Congress enacted neutrality legislation designed to keep the country out of war. Various amendments were made in 1935, 1936, and 1937, and in them isolationist sentiment reached an all-time high. The traditional policy of freedom of the seas, of the right of a neutral to carry on legitimate trade with belligerents, was scrapped. It became unlawful for any nation at war to obtain munitions from the United States, American citizens could not travel on the ships of belligerents, and the "cash and carry" provision permitted any nation to purchase certain raw materials and goods, provided that nation took them away in its own ships. Congress hoped the legislation would keep war at a distance. The State Department, however, pointed out that this legislation did not make any discrimination between aggressor and nonaggressor nations. In the event of war no nation could buy arms in this country.

As the menace of the totalitarian nations became greater in both Europe and the Far East after 1935, there was a strong minority group in the United States that believed the neutrality legislation was a mistake, that it encouraged aggression in other parts of the world, and that such aggression in the long run would become so serious as to demand American participation for purposes of national security. With the hope of arousing the American people to the dangers in the world situation, President Roosevelt in October 1937 gave his famous "quarantine speech" in Chicago. In it he declared:

"The peace, the freedom, and the security of 90 per cent of the population of the world is being jeopardized by the remaining 10 per cent, who are threatening a break-down of all international order and law. Surely the ninety per cent who want to live in peace under law and in accordance with moral standards . . . can and must find some way to make their will prevail. . . . There must be positive endeavors to preserve peace."

After this speech was delivered, however, it was obvious that American public opinion would not countenance any action involving the United States in the "quarrels of other nations."

United States attempts at arbitration. The Sudeten crisis in September 1938 confronted the American government with the alarming prospect of a war which might spread to the Far East, in view of the fact that Japan had been an ally of Germany since 1936. On September 26 President Roosevelt sent a cable to Hitler, urging that he utilize peaceful negotiation, rather than war, in the Sudeten crisis. The following day another appeal was cabled to both Hitler and Mussolini by President Roosevelt.

After the Munich Agreement American public opinion was profoundly shocked by the anti-Jewish riots which broke out in November 1938. In an unusually blunt statement the American Chief Executive declared, "I myself could scarcely believe that such things could occur in a twentieth-century civilization." Then came the final partition of Czechoslovakia in March 1939. With the approval of the President, Sumner Welles, Undersecretary of State, issued an official statement declaring that "acts of wanton lawlessness and of arbitrary force are threatening world peace and the very structure of modern civilization." Again President Roosevelt sent messages to the leading nations of the world asking if they would give a pledge not to attack any one of thirty specified states for a period of ten years. Other nations eagerly gave this pledge, but none was forthcoming from Germany or Italy.

The neutrality policy questioned. In the spring of 1939 revision of the neutrality legislation became an important issue in Congress. Secretary of State Cordell Hull wanted the law amended to permit this country to sell munitions to any belligerent that could pay cash and carry them on its own ships. The shipping of the United States would still be denied access to war zones. Since Great Britain and France controlled the seas with their superior navies, in practice this would mean that Germany and Italy would be denied the purchase of American munitions. Amendment of the neutrality law along these lines, according to Mr. Hull, would serve as a warning to Germany and Italy that in the event of war American arms would be made available to Great Britain and France. Amendment of our neutrality legislation, however, was blocked by the isolationist faction in the Senate, which threatened to hold up action by resorting to a filibuster. In the opinion of many members of Congress there was no prospect of war in Europe, and hence no need to change the American neutrality policy.

United States reaction to the war. The Polish crisis of August 1939 saw President Roosevelt again trying to serve the interests of peace. Appeals were sent to Hitler, to the king of Italy, and to the president of Poland. As we have already seen, these efforts availed nothing, and war came on September 1. Unlike the situation in the war that came in 1914, the

As war clouds gathered on the American horizon, this earnest audience sought a formula to keep the United States at peace. Within three or four months the Japanese would bomb Pearl Harbor, ending such efforts.

American people—that is, the great majority—took sides from the very day that war broke out. It was the general opinion that war had been brought about by Germany and Italy, and sympathy lay with Great Britain and France. The American people detested Nazi ideology and methods and hoped for an Allied victory. But the overwhelming opinion was that America should not interfere in the struggle. This attitude was taken with few qualms, as most Americans believed that Great Britain and France alone would defeat Germany.

It was acknowledged, however, that certain changes should be made in existing neutrality legislation. In November 1939, therefore, a new act was passed providing for the exclusion of American citizens, planes, and vessels from combat zones and for the sale of munitions to any belligerent able to carry such goods away and pay cash. Having made this concession to the Allied cause, America waited for the expected defeat of the Nazi régime.

But defeat was not forthcoming, and in April 1940, there came instead the conquest of Norway and Denmark and then in May the blitzkrieg in the Low Countries and France. The Nazi victories made a profound impression on America. For the first time the full implications of a totalitarian victory began to be seen by American public opinion. With a hostile Japan in the Pacific and the French fleet conceivably in the hands of Germany, the whole strategic outlook for America had been revolutionized. Isolation was coming with a vengeance, but it was the kind of isolation which meant being alone in a troubled world, devoid of allies and surrounded by warlike and expansionist powers.

Rearmament and aid to Great Britain. While Great Britain battled for existence as the *Luftwaffe* tried to take command of the English sky, steps were taken by the United States in answer to what had become in reality a national crisis. Arms were sent immediately to Great Britain to take the place of those lost at Dunkirk. A rearmament program was introduced contemplating the expenditure of more than seventeen billion dollars. In particular a gigantic naval building program was initiated, providing for the construction of two navies—one for the Pacific, the other for the Atlantic. In May 1940 a National Defense Advisory Board was entrusted with the organization of the rearmament effort. Later in the year a special office for production management for defense was set up. In June President Roosevelt moved to broaden the base of his cabinet by adding two outstanding Republicans: Colonel Frank Knox, a newspaper publisher, who accepted the post of Secretary of the Navy, and Henry L. Stimson, a former Secretary of State, who assumed the post of Secretary of War.

On August 18, 1940, it was announced that the President and Premier Mackenzie King had agreed to establish a permanent joint board on defense to coordinate the defense measures of Canada and the United States. In September much discussion was aroused by President Roosevelt's revelation that he had authorized the exchange of 50 over-age destroyers to Great Britain for the right to construct naval bases in Newfoundland, the British West Indies, and British Guiana. In the event of the defeat of Great Britain these bases would constitute an invaluable protective screen, especially in the Caribbean area, where the protection of the Panama Canal was of crucial concern to American strategy.

During the summer of 1940 the main issue was that of conscription during peace time. Although it was foreign to historical tradition, the gravity of the international situation convinced most of the people that compulsory military training was vital in developing a trained army. On September 16 the Selective Service Act became law, and the following month more than 16,000,000 men between the ages of twenty-one and thirty-six registered for the draft.

As the autumn months of 1940 unfolded, there was much discussion and controversy on the problem of how far to go in assisting Great Britain. The presidential campaign of November made little political capital of this issue. Both President Roosevelt and the Republican aspirant for the presidency, Wendell L. Willkie, were in favor of all aid "short of war." Both before and after the election, however, radios and countless auditoriums throughout the land echoed the arguments of the America First Committee, which branded aid to Great Britain as the open door to war, and the Committee to Defend America by Aiding the Allies, which urged all possible support of Great Britain. On December 29, 1940, the United States took

THE ATLANTIC CHARTER

THE PRESIDENT of the United States of America and the Prime Minister, Mr. Churchill, representing His Majesty's Government in the United Kingdom, being met together, deem it right to make known certain common principles in the national policies of their respective countries on which they base their hopes for a better future for the world.

First, Their countries seek no aggrandizement, territorial or other;

Second, They desire to see no territorial changes that do not accord with the freely expressed wishes of the peoples concerned;

Third, They respect the right of all peoples to choose the form of government under which they will live; and they wish to see sovereign rights and self-government restored to those who have been forcibly deprived of them;

Fourth, They will endeavor, with due respect for their existing obligations, to further the enjoyment by all States, great or small, victor or vanquished, of access, on equal terms, to the trade and to the raw materials of the world which are needed for their economic prosperity;

Fifth, They desire to bring about the fullest collaboration between all nations in the economic field with the object of securing, for all, improved labor standards, economic adjustment and social security;

Sixth, After the final destruction of the Nazi tyranny, they hope to see established a peace which will afford to all nations the means of dwelling in safety within their own boundaries, and which will afford assurance that all the men in all the lands may live out their lives in freedom from fear and want;

Seventh, Such a peace should enable all men to traverse the high seas and oceans without hindrance;

Eighth, They believe that all of the nations of the world, for realistic as well as spiritual reasons, must come to the abandonment of the use of force. Since no future peace can be maintained if land, sea or air armaments continue to be employed by nations which threaten, or may threaten, aggression outside of their frontiers, they believe, pending the establishment of a wider and permanent system of general security, that the disarmament of such nations is essential. They will likewise aid and encourage all other practicable measures which will lighten for peace-loving peoples the crushing burden of armaments.

another step in the direction of aiding Great Britain. In a fireside chat to the nation President Roosevelt declared:

"We must be the great arsenal of democracy. For us this is an emergency as serious as war itself. We must apply ourselves to our task with the same resolution, the same sense of urgency, the same spirit of patriotism and sacrifice as we would show were we at war."

Two weeks later the Lend-Lease Bill was introduced into Congress, giving the President power to manufacture, sell, lease, lend, or exchange any arms to any country "whose defense the President deems vital to the defense of the United States." The bill became law on March 11, 1941, after much debate in and out of the halls of Congress, and the country now prepared to make available to Great Britain and others billions of dollars of war material. In April the United States assumed the defense of the Danish possession of Greenland.

Pan-American cooperation. The United States was now pursuing three definite policies: rearmament at home on a truly colossal scale, all-out aid to Great Britain, and cooperation with the Latin-American republics. In conferences called for the purpose of mapping common action, the twenty-one American republics set up a neutral zone extending 300 to 1000 miles from the shores of the Western Hemisphere into the North and South Atlantic. They warned belligerent warships not to come into this neutral zone. Further, an agreement was drawn up for the provisional administration of European colonies in the Western Hemisphere, in the event that such a step became necessary, to prevent Germany from securing French and Dutch colonies in the Caribbean area. After 1940 the realization of the common danger faced by all the peoples of the Western Hemisphere tended to draw the twenty-one republics closer and closer together.

Sharpening of U. S. policy. Early in the spring of 1941, alarming British shipping losses presented the administration at Washington with the prospect that supplies made available to the British under the terms of the Lend-Lease Bill might find their way to the bottom of the sea rather than to England. This emergency precipitated the convoy issue. Wendell L. Willkie and members of the President's cabinet gave strong support to the idea of convoying merchant vessels to Great Britain with American warships.

While the majority of citizens did not support the isolationist point of view, there was much confusion of thought, and the time had come for a clear and unequivocal statement of the government's policy. There could be little doubt where the American government stood and what it proposed to do when the President's fireside chat of May 28 ended. President Roosevelt accused the totalitarian states of aiming at world domination. He stressed the suicidal folly of waiting idly until the totalitarian attack actually began to rain bombs on American cities. The President said: "When your enemy comes at you in a tank or a bombing plane, if you hold your fire until you see the whites of his eyes, you will never know what hit you. Our Bunker Hill of tomorrow may be several thousand miles from Boston." Coming to the convoy issue, President Roosevelt stated: "Our patrols are helping now to insure delivery of the needed supplies to Britain. All additional measures necessary to deliver the goods will be taken."

As a means of speeding up production and uniting public opinion behind the great task of making America an arsenal of democracy the President announced the existence of an unlimited national emergency. No one could deny that America had now made her choice. The United States had committed herself and dedicated vast resources to the task of defeating Hitler and his totalitarian allies.

During the summer and fall of 1941 the United States accelerated and expanded her support to all nations fighting aggression. A military mission was sent to China to facilitate more aid to that country, and American military observers also assisted the British in the Near East. During July troops occupied Iceland, where the United States established a military base. In August President Roosevelt and Prime Minister Churchill, with their chief advisers, met secretly "somewhere in the Atlantic" and drafted the Atlantic Charter (see page 457).

The war draws closer. While the intensification of American aid to Great Britain and China was taking place, several American ships had been sunk by Nazi submarines. In May 1941, the *Robin Moor* was sunk in the South Atlantic, outside of any war zone.

Other merchantmen were sunk during August and September. On September 11 the President announced a policy of "shooting at sight" any Axis vessels found in the Atlantic defense zones. After an attack on an American destroyer early in October which, however, made port safely in Iceland, another destroyer, the *Reuben James,* was sunk by a submarine in the North Atlantic, with heavy loss of life. This event led Congress, upon the recommendation of President Roosevelt, to repeal the major provisions of the neutrality law prohibiting American ships from entering belligerent waters and from being armed. The American public did not realize how close the war had come to them. But by November 1941, if the country was not yet a belligerent, it certainly was not a neutral.

The War Encircles the Globe

Blitzkrieg versus Russia. Following the successful invasion of Crete in May 1941, a widespread German offensive against Palestine and Egypt appeared logical. Instead, on June 22, a gigantic panzer attack was launched by Hitler's armies against Russia, despite the nonaggression pact signed between the German Reich and Russia in August 1939. Thus began the seventh major phase of the war. In a proclamation to the German people, Hitler charged that the Russians were plotting to conquer Europe. He said that one hundred sixty Russian army divisions had been stationed along the German frontier, menacing the security of the Reich. In Hitler's words, "to safeguard Europe from the Jewish rulers of the Bolshevik center in Moscow" Germany was forced to attack Russia.

Hitler's decision was probably influenced by several factors. To carry on a long war, Germany had to secure new stocks of raw materials. All of Hitler's needs could be served by two areas in Russia. The Ukraine, a district somewhat larger than California, called the Soviet breadbasket, produced tremendous crops of wheat, corn, and rye. In the eastern Ukraine the industrialized Donets Basin produced more than seventy per cent of Russian coal and large amounts of iron. The Donets Basin was also important for its automobile factories, chemical plants, and steel mills.

The second Russian area of value to Hitler was the Caucasus, a wide neck of land between the Black and Caspian seas, one of the world's richest oil regions. The oil wells of the Caucasus produced 90 per cent of Russia's oil. With stocks of oil being rapidly depleted, a new source of this vital fuel could be had here for the Nazi army.

In addition to the need for raw materials, Hitler probably feared Russia. She was getting too strong for his comfort. Before United States' aid in war supplies to Great Britain challenged the resources of the Reich, all possibility of Russian "danger" had to be removed. The Nazi leaders also hoped to sell their attack on Russia as a crusade against Communism. Since many people in the subjugated European countries feared and disliked Communism, it was thought that the attack might rally these groups behind Hitler.

The Germans accordingly launched a major offensive against Russia from the Baltic to the Black seas. Assisted by Rumanian and Finnish forces, the panzer divisions had little difficulty in pushing Soviet forces out of the

These German prisoners, taken when the Russians struck back on the Kalinin front, do not appear to like the Russian cold. Unprepared, Hitler appealed to the German people for clothes for the troops.

THE WORLD

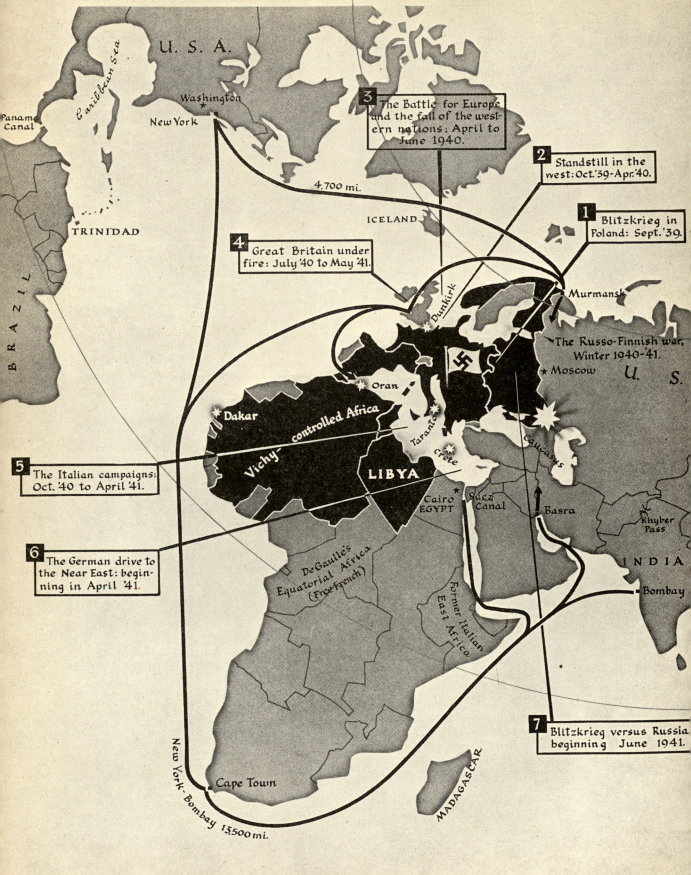

U. S. A.
Caribbean Sea
Washington
New York
Panama Canal
TRINIDAD
BRAZIL
ICELAND
4,700 mi.

1 Blitzkrieg in Poland: Sept. '39.

2 Standstill in the west: Oct. '39-Apr. '40.

3 The Battle for Europe and the fall of the western nations: April to June 1940.

4 Great Britain under fire: July '40 to May '41.

5 The Italian campaigns: Oct. '40 to April '41.

6 The German drive to the Near East: beginning in April '41.

7 Blitzkrieg versus Russia beginning June 1941.

Murmansk
Dunkirk
The Russo-Finnish war, Winter 1940-41.
Moscow
U. S.
Oran
Dakar
Vichy-controlled Africa
Taranto
Crete
LIBYA
Caucasus
Cairo EGYPT
Suez Canal
Basra
Khyber Pass
INDIA
Bombay
DeGaulle's Equatorial Africa (Free French)
Former Italian East Africa
MADAGASCAR
Cape Town
New York-Bombay 13,500 mi.

R. M. Chapin, Jr.
September 1942

AT WAR

U. S. A.
Seattle
San Francisco
ALASKA
6,500 mi. by air
Dutch Harbor
Kiska
Pearl Harbor
Arctic Circle
Kamchatka
Midway
S. R.
SIBERIA
Sakhalin
8 The war enters the Pacific: Dec. 7, '41.
MANCHUKUO
Vladivostok
MONGOLIA
Tokyo
Wake
China "incident" beginning 1937
Marianas Is.
Marshall Is.
CHINA
Gilbert Is.
Guam
Caroline Is.
Chungking
Hong Kong
BURMA
Bataan
Calcutta
Equator
Solomon Is.
Coral Sea
NEW GUINEA
New Caledonia
Port Moresby
Wellington
Singapore
Macassar Strait
NEW ZEALAND
JAVA
AUSTRALIA
Sydney
Calcutta-San Francisco 15,000 mi.

border area acquired by Russia from 1939 to 1941. Estonia, Lithuania, Latvia, and other regions were conquered by the German forces.

On the borders of Russia proper, a second German offensive struck in the direction of Leningrad in the north, Moscow at the center, and Kiev to the south. The summer saw a titanic battle in progress, both sides claiming to have inflicted hundreds of thousands of casualties on their foes. The Russians had to give ground. Yet to the astonishment of the world, the blitzkrieg at times seemed to falter and prove ineffective. Russian morale was high, and a scorched-earth policy destroyed everything of value left behind by the Russian army. Hitler had a difficult problem in maintaining his long lines of communication.

New allegiances. Since 1939 British statesmen, and indeed the world in general, had regarded Russia as virtually the ally of Nazi Germany. Following the German attack, however, Churchill declared that any nation fighting against Hitler was the ally of Great Britain. In July 1941 a mutual assistance pact was signed in Moscow between Russia and Great Britain. At the same time the government of the United States declared that Lend-Lease material would be provided to Russia. Late in September an Anglo-American war mission arrived in Moscow to work out a program of war aid for the Soviet Union.

Continued Nazi advance. During the summer, Soviet forces had been compelled to surrender the key city of Smolensk guarding the approaches to Moscow, and Leningrad was almost encircled. Kiev, in the south, the gateway to the Ukraine, had fallen. German pressure continued during September, and early in October a smashing attack designed to knock out and destroy Russian resistance was begun. In his proclamation to the German armies, Hitler claimed that already 2,400,000 Russians had been captured and that victory was at hand.

Mud as well as snow slowed up the Nazi blitzkrieg in Russia. This German soldier, wearing a camouflaged raincoat, plans to tow one tank with another.

In October and November victory for the Nazi armies appeared imminent. Leningrad was surrounded, and fighting was carried on in the suburbs. The Nazi forces penetrated to within forty miles of Moscow, and the Russian government was moved to the temporary capital of Kuibyshev, far to the east. In the south the Ukraine had been overrun, the Dnieper River crossed, and Kharkov captured. The strategic Crimean peninsula had also fallen with the exception of the naval base at Sevastopol. Late in November the gateway to the Caucasus and its oil fields, Rostov on the Don River, was captured. Stalin appealed to Great Britain to ease German pressure by opening a new front in western Europe, but the only aid forthcoming from Great Britain was an energetic air offensive against the Channel ports and western Germany, which perhaps diverted some Nazi air squadrons from the Russian front. The British, however, did dispatch tanks and other supplies to Russia.

The turn of the tide. The Russian situation improved suddenly late in November 1941, when the Russian winter with its blinding snowstorms and subzero temperatures began to derange Nazi communications and slow down the drive. During the first week of December the Russian armies counterattacked along the entire 1500-mile front. Rostov was recaptured, and the Russians advanced into the Ukraine. Before Moscow the Germans were forced to give ground, and the pressure on Leningrad was relieved. On December 21 Hitler removed his supreme commander and himself assumed command. The Nazi chief announced that the Russian war had "exceeded all past notions" and that his soldiers must hold on till spring. The "ever victorious" German army appeared to be on the defensive.

By mid-January 1942, the Russians had recaptured more than 100,000 square miles and were less than 100 miles from the Latvian frontier between Leningrad and Moscow. This brilliant counterstroke of the Soviet armies raised hopes in all countries fighting Nazi Germany that perhaps the debacle of Napoleon's invasion of Russia in 1812 was to be repeated.

Great Britain in the Near East. The Russian campaign had meanwhile given Great Britain an opportunity to strengthen her defenses in the Mediterranean and the Near East. Following the conquest of Crete by Nazi parachutists at the end of May, no new German advance was made. This gave British troops the chance to gain full control of Iraq. Just before the Russo-German war broke out, the British turned their attention to French Syria. The situation in this country can be understood only by reference to the position of France.

Unoccupied France. Following the armistice with Germany in June 1940, the status of France was little short of pitiable. Marshal Pétain was willing to cooperate to a limited extent with the German victor as long as this did not necessitate taking up arms actively against his former ally, Great Britain. But there were many French leaders in high places who apparently were quite willing to do anything Germany proposed. The situation was further complicated by the Free French movement under General Charles de Gaulle. Following the collapse of France, General de Gaulle established a Free French government in London to carry on the war by the side of Great Britain. About one quarter of the French empire sided with De Gaulle and repudiated the Vichy government of Pétain. Support for De Gaulle came from Frenchmen all over the world who deplored the renunciation of democracy at Vichy and believed that from such colonies as Morocco, and with the aid of the French fleet, Pétain should have continued the struggle against Germany.

Until April 1941 Pétain had been able to hold in check those in the Vichy government who were in favor of full collaboration with Nazi Germany. The collapse of Yugoslavia and Greece, the British reverses in north Africa, and the lack of national unity in the United States on the question of "all-out aid to Great Britain" persuaded Pétain that France now had no choice other than to do Germany's bidding. By the middle of May Vichy announced full cooperation with the Nazi régime, and German planes en route to Iraq began to use air bases in French Syria. In retaliation these fields were bombed by British air squadrons, and open conflict seemed imminent between France and Great Britain.

British successes in Syria, Iran, Egypt. The prospect of full French collaboration with Germany in turning over strategic bases in Syria caused the British government to act decisively. On June 8 British troops supported by a Free French contingent entered Syria. Only "a token resistance" was anticipated, but the Syrian forces, on orders from Vichy, resisted savagely. Only after two weeks of fighting did Syria fall to the Allied forces.

There was yet another area of great strategic value in the Near East, especially after Russia became an ally of Great Britain. This was Iran, formerly known as Persia, which constituted a vital corridor through which supplies could be sent to Russia via the Persian Gulf and then north through Iran to the Russian Caucasus. Both Great Britain and Russia became alarmed, however, at the pro-Axis sentiments of Iran's ruler and the fact that the country was filling up with German technicians. On August 25, 1941, following the refusal of authorities in Iran to expel the German agents, British and Russian forces invaded the country. Four days later all resistance ceased. The decision of the Nazi government to attack Russia had enabled Great Britain to gain control of a great block of territory stretching from the Mediterranean to the Persian Gulf and thence to India.

During September and October when Germany was fully occupied with her great offensive in Russia, the British forces in Egypt were receiving large consignments of American Lend-Lease material. By the middle of November the British commander in the Near East, General Auchinleck, was in a position to plan an offensive against the Nazi forces under General Rommel that had been menacing the Egyptian border since April. On November 21 the British, using in large measure American tanks and American pursuit planes, struck at Rommel's forces. By the end of December the British army had pushed the German army with its Italian allies more than eight hundred miles to the west, had captured the important base of Bengasi, and had taken more than 36,000 prisoners. The Near East and now Egypt had been rendered secure, for the time being, from Nazi pressure.

Japan in the Pacific. During the years of the Abyssinian and Spanish wars, Munich, the Polish crisis, and finally war in western Europe, the Far East (as we have noted in a previous chapter) followed a similar pattern of lawlessness. Japan, successful in the conquest of Manchuria, determined to press forward to additional victories while the great powers in Europe were quarreling among themselves and the United States was attempting to isolate itself.

In 1938 Japan informed the United States that she was determined to establish a régime in Asia in accordance with her own interests, implying that all the former treaties safeguarding American commercial rights were henceforth inoperative. Answering this declaration, the American government bluntly informed Japan that it refused to recognize the New Order in Asia and that it would not relinquish any of its rights.

The outbreak of war in Europe in 1939 gave Japan a golden opportunity to press her drive against China to a successful conclusion and, with this done, even perhaps to capture the colonies in the Far East controlled by the western powers. Late in 1939 several strong offensives against the Chinese forces holding the hinterland were carried out, but the lines held. Unable to smash Chinese resistance, Japan now turned to other promising fields of endeavor. In the spring of 1939 she commenced a squeeze play in the orient by seizing the Chinese island of Hainan. This island dominated French Indo-China and gave Japan valuable bases in the event of attack against British Malaya or the Dutch East Indies. It was this action that caused the United States government to move its fleet to Pacific bases in April 1939.

Japanese pressure on European powers. After the collapse of France in the spring of 1940, a Japanese diplomat candidly declared: "We should not miss the present opportunity or we shall be blamed by posterity." Raw materials such as oil and iron were becoming difficult to procure as a result of the European war, and the rise of anti-Japanese sentiment in America also made this country an uncertain source for raw materials. By controlling Indo-China, the Netherlands East Indies, and perhaps British Malaya, Japan's fears on this score would be largely removed, and enriched by her booty she could deal with the obstinate Chinese at her leisure.

Throughout 1939 Japan made open threats against Great Britain in the Far East and even blockaded British and French business districts in Chinese cities. In June 1940 Japanese troops concentrated near Hong Kong, the British colony on the Chinese coast, and in July the British decided to close the Burma Road—the vital artery of supply for the Chinese armies. In the summer of 1940 pressure was also extended to the Netherlands East Indies. No action was forthcoming, however, perhaps because Secretary of State Hull warned that the United States would not tolerate any change in their status.

Defeated France also felt Japanese pressure. Pétain consented in June 1940 to permit Japanese observers to watch traffic in Indo-China. The object of this demand, of course, was to prevent supplies from reaching the Chinese forces via French territory. In the fall of 1940 France had to allow Japan to set up air bases in Indo-China and land a limited number of soldiers. In the meantime an amateur in aggression was encouraged by Japan to distract France still further. This was Thailand, formerly Siam, which demanded the return of territory originally taken from her by France and added to the colony of Indo-China. After several months of wrangling, Japan stepped in as mediator in March 1941 and brought both Thailand and Indo-China under her control.

Growing concern of occidental powers. Contrary to Japanese expectations, Great Britain had not been conquered in the summer of 1940. The United States clearly manifested a determination to keep both China and Great Britain in the field. Thus Great Britain was able to reopen the Burma Road in the fall of 1940, and the United States made large loans to China. The totalitarian states were now plainly worried. Japan feared the intervention of the United States in the Pacific, and Germany was not at all sure that the United States would keep out of the European struggle. In September 1940 Germany, Italy, and Japan had signed a military alliance "to assist one another with all political, economic, and military means when one of the three is attacked by a power at present not involved in

As the truth of America's greatest naval defeat began to come home to the people, the Navy released this tragic picture showing the U. S. S. Arizona down and aflame after the Japanese attack on Pearl Harbor.

the European war or in the Chinese-Japanese conflict." This pact, directed at the United States, was ample evidence that the European war was becoming a world conflict.

The A.B.C.D. powers. Confronted with Japan's ambitious Asiatic intentions, America, Great Britain, China, and the Netherlands East Indies in the spring of 1941 began to consult with each other on common measures to be taken to check further Japanese agression. These conferences created what was known as the "A.B.C.D." front against Japan. Backed by friends, the Dutch felt able to reject Japanese pressure for oil and more liberal trade concessions in June 1941. In July Japanese strategy became apparent when under a new pact with the Vichy government for "common defense" additional Japanese troops were sent into Indo-China. Domination of this French colony placed Japanese forces in a position (1) to strike at Burma through Thailand and cut off the one remaining route of supplies to China and (2) to march through Thailand south into the Malay Peninsula and launch an attack against the English naval base of Singapore.

In retaliation for Japan's action in Indo-China, America, Great Britain, and the Dutch froze all Japanese funds late in July, making it impossible for that country to obtain additional vital materials from members of the A.B.C.D. front. The freezing order was followed by parallel warnings by Great Britain and the United States against Japanese designs on Thailand.

Japan was faced with the alternative of backing down or casting the die, whatever the stakes, in favor of a great empire in southeast Asia. She made the latter choice. In October her premier was replaced by General Tojo. An avowed militarist now headed the cabinet of Japan. While additional troops were being sent to Singapore by Great Britain, and arrangements were being made to recall all American marines in China, and while the pro-Axis Tojo cabinet became more and more truculent, a special envoy was dispatched in November from Tokyo to Washington. The envoy was Saburo Kurusu, a veteran diplomat, whose task it was to convince the American State Department that Japanese policy in the Pacific was in no way prejudicial to the interests of the United States.

The attack on Pearl Harbor. On November 26 the United States, acting for the A.B.C.D. powers, presented proposals to Kurusu for a peaceful agreement in the Pacific, requiring Japanese withdrawal from China and the termination of Tokyo's collaboration with the Axis. News of Japanese

Bombers like these were assigned the task of protecting America's coastline against marauding Axis submarines, a contest that developed into major proportions. Such planes were also used to give Tokyo its first bombing.

troop movements toward Thailand (Siam) early in December caused President Roosevelt to send an urgent appeal to the Japanese emperor on December 6. The following day, Sunday, while Kurusu and the Japanese Ambassador Nomura were delivering a note to the American Secretary of State, announcing Japan's refusal to continue negotiations, word was received from the Hawaiian Islands that Japanese planes based on aircraft carriers had carried out a destructive bombardment of the naval base at Pearl Harbor. It was shortly admitted that this attack had brought about the loss of two battleships, several smaller craft, and many planes.

The issue joined. On December 8, following the President's recommendation, Congress declared war on Japan. Germany and Italy followed the Japanese attack by declaring war on the United States on December 12, and the following day Congress declared war on these two powers. Great Britain, her Dominions, the conquered and refugee governments of Europe, and the Caribbean and Central American republics also declared war on Japan. In all twenty-six nations now stood arrayed against Germany, Japan, Italy, and their satellites. The greatest global struggle in all history was now under way.

Initial Japanese successes. Any complacency that existed in America was considerably reduced after Pearl Harbor by Japan's initial successes in the Pacific. On December 8 and 9 Japanese attacks were made against the Malay Peninsula, the Philippines, Hong Kong, and the three American naval bases of Guam, Wake, and Midway. The defense of Singapore was made much more difficult by the loss of two British battleships, destroyed by Japanese bombing planes. Almost at will, without fear of naval attack, Japanese troops could now be landed from transports along the Malayan coast.

Heavy fighting followed the landing of Japanese forces in the Philippines on December 9. For three weeks the American army of General MacArthur was able to hold the enemy before Manila. On January 2 this city fell, and further American resistance was confined to a small area in the Bataan peninsula and on the heavily fortified island of Corregidor. Throughout January the world watched with admiration the outnumbered forces under MacArthur hold their lines against heavy attack. After heroic resistance a small detachment of marines was overwhelmed on Wake Island, Guam also was lost, and on December 26 the British crown colony of Hong Kong had surrendered.

During January the Japanese arc of operations expanded, for the real prize was the Malay Peninsula and the Netherlands East Indies. Landings were made in British North Borneo. Other points of attack in the Netherlands East Indies were harbors along the eastern coast of Borneo and points on the island of Celebes. Japanese contingents landed on New Guinea and other nearby islands. From these islands the Japanese could now make plans to attack Australia. Meanwhile British imperial forces were being forced back in Malaya. Mid-January saw the Japanese less than 100 miles from Singapore. At the same time a Japanese army driving west from Thailand was menacing the vital Burma Road. To offset these numerous Japanese successes the A.B.C.D. powers had, after almost two months of war, gained only one outstanding success. This was the sinking of numerous vessels of a Japanese convoy in the Macassar Strait presumably taking troops to invade Java.

The United Nations. The initial success of Japanese arms was due largely to her surprise attack and to her state of full military preparedness. The one great power capable of defeating Japan was the United States. Both Great Britain and Russia were occupied in Europe with Germany and Italy. The power of the United States, however, was largely inert and could not be immediately exerted against Japan. It was also apparent that the best way for the United States, Great Britain, China, and their associated allies to achieve victory was to work out a scheme of grand strategy in which every nation would be alloted the task best suited to its resources and capacity. Such a plan was undertaken hardly more than a fortnight after the Pacific phase of the Second World War began.

On December 22 Prime Minister Churchill arrived in Washington, accompanied by high-ranking officials, to discuss the conduct of the war with President Roosevelt and his aids. At the same time Anthony Eden was closeted with Joseph Stalin in Moscow on a similar errand. A few days after the British and American statesmen had begun their discussions, it was announced that twenty-six nations had signed an agreement which pledged each signatory to use all of its resources to defeat the Axis powers, not to sign a separate peace, and, finally, to accept the provisions of the Atlantic Charter (page 457) agreed to by Roosevelt and Churchill during the preceding summer. On January 2, 1942, a unified command in the southwestern Pacific theater of war was announced.

On January 6 President Roosevelt, in his annual message to Congress, laid down the gigantic war program considered essential for Allied victory. During 1942 the government asked for the production of 60,000 planes, 45,000 tanks, and 8,000,000 tons of merchant shipping. In 1943 production was to be even greater. The armament program called for an expenditure of fifty-six billion dollars in 1942, more than half the national income of the United States. To insure the utilization of material and munitions where they would do the most good against the enemy, Great Britain and the United States agreed to pool all their resources. A series of boards was set up in January 1942 to decide upon the allocation and priority of supplies.

The conference at Rio. Shortly after going to war with Japan the United States tested the fruits of the Good Neighbor policy inaugurated with Latin America about 1930. In January 1942 a Pan-American Conference of the twenty-one American republics met at Rio de Janeiro to discuss their attitude following an unprovoked attack upon one of their number —the United States. There had been a time, only a decade or so ago, when not one Latin-American republic would have raised a finger to assist the United States. But during the past ten years the United States had spared no effort in earning the good will of her southern neighbors. The conference at Rio de Janeiro was the first real test of the new policy.

The United States wanted a unanimous rupture of diplomatic relations with the Axis powers. This objective was supported by several other nations, especially Mexico. Unanimous action was not obtained at the conference because of the opposition of Chile and Argentina. The final declaration recommended severance of relations with Japan, Germany, and Italy. By the end of January nineteen Latin-American republics had either broken off relations or were at war with the enemies of the United States. Only Chile and Argentina held aloof.

While not complete, a victory for the Good Neighbor policy had been won at Rio de Janeiro. The United States made arrangements to send Lend-Lease aid to her Latin-American friends, to assure them of needed industrial supplies, and to work out unified plans for combating Axis espionage in the Western Hemisphere.

The Japanese plunge ahead. The initial efforts of the United Nations to mobilize their fighting strength and attain unity of purpose

The crew of a Curtiss Commando, giant troopship, welcomes a U. S. army scout car, the familiar "jeep." The ship is designed to transport field artillery, aircraft engines, tractors, and fully equipped troops.

did little to halt the expansion of Japanese forces in the Pacific theater of war. On February 15, after a furious battle in which British troops had been unable to halt the Japanese, the Singapore fortress fell. Thousands of British troops were taken as prisoners.

The latter part of February saw the Japanese closing in on Java, the most valuable island in the Netherlands East Indies. A small naval flotilla comprised of Dutch, American, and British units tried to destroy Japanese naval concentrations, but Allied force was insufficient, and in a great battle the Japanese wiped out practically all opposition. Without fear of naval interference, the Japanese now landed large bodies of men on the beaches of Java and pressed into the interior. The Dutch, assisted by a few contingents of Australian and American soldiers, fought valiantly. But outnumbered and without adequate air power, the resistance quickly crumpled.

While the Japanese were carrying out their conquest of Java, they had also initiated a drive against the British colony of Burma, terminus of the Burma Road. A successful campaign would close this vital artery to China and interfere with supplies being sent by Great Britain and the United States to the forces of Generalissimo Chiang Kai-shek. Japanese forces converged on Burma in mid-January from Thailand and the Malay Peninsula. Rangoon, the capital, was captured early in March. The Japanese then launched an offensive toward the north in order to secure Lashio, the southern end of the Burma Road. Chinese troops under the command of an American officer, General Joseph W. Stilwell, reinforced the British army, but the Japanese could not be halted. Lashio fell on April 30, and in the first part of May the Chinese forces were pushed out of Burma. The Japanese also gained some territory in China along the Burma Road. A few thousand British troops managed to escape into India. Burma joined the long list of Japanese conquests.

In the Philippines General Douglas MacArthur had carried out brilliant defensive tactics against Japanese forces much superior to his own. Despite gallant resistance American opposition gradually was worn down.

Food and medicinal supplies were depleted. On April 9 the remnants of the army on Bataan surrendered, and some 40,000 American and Philippine troops were captured. Corregidor fortress still held out with its satellite island forts in Manila Bay, but it too was stormed, and the garrisons were forced to capitulate on May 7.

Threats to India and Australia. The fall of Singapore, the conquest of the Netherlands East Indies, and the end of American resistance in the Philippines placed India and Australia in jeopardy. By April Japan was threatening to control the Bay of Bengal. The Andaman Islands were captured, thus giving Japan air bases near enough to bomb the important Indian city of Calcutta and the strategic British island of Ceylon. At this juncture the British government sent to India a special emissary, Sir Stafford Cripps, to try to obtain full support of the Indian people in the war effort. After several weeks of negotiation Sir Stafford failed to secure agreement with Indian leaders over the vexed problem of self-government. While active support of the all-important Indian National Congress in prosecuting the war was not obtained, the Indian leaders did not at this time seriously hinder Great Britain's efforts to defend India.

Battles of the Coral Sea and Midway. During the battle of Bataan the American government transferred General MacArthur to Australia to assume full command in this area. Large numbers of American troops and quantities of equipment were convoyed across the Pacific to bolster Australian defenses. The position in the Bay of Bengal and the Indian Ocean, as well as the defenses of Australia, was materially improved by two important naval victories of American naval task forces. Early in May a savage encounter between Japanese and American fleets and aircraft took place in the Coral Sea. This engagement destroyed fifteen of the enemy's ships and damaged twenty more. The United States lost the aircraft carrier *Lexington,* a destroyer, and a tanker.

The second important naval encounter occurred in early June when United States forces, mainly aircraft, intercepted large Japanese fleet concentrations apparently sent to capture the strategic base of the Midway Islands. A severe defeat was suffered by the enemy. Four aircraft carriers were sunk, two large cruisers were disposed of, and several battleships were severely damaged. American losses were negligible.

Other encouraging developments were the British capture of the important Vichy island of Madagascar, a potential naval base for the Japanese in the Indian Ocean; the bombing of Tokyo and other Japanese cities by American flyers led by Brigadier General James Doolittle; and heavy air attacks from Allied bases in Australia against Japanese bases in the Dutch East Indies, especially Timor, and on the island of New Guinea.

The Japanese attack on Midway was part of a larger engagement aimed at attaining still greater strength in the Pacific. It had been preceded by the bombing of Dutch Harbor in Alaska. Then, toward the end of June, the Japanese succeeded in occupying two small islands at the end of the Aleutian chain, off Alaska.

Summer 1942. In the summer of 1942 the war was being fought in all parts of the globe. In the Japanese-dominated Pacific General Douglas MacArthur's forces in Australia were harrying Jap bases. In Russia the Nazis were again on the offensive. The war in Africa, opened by the Italians in the fall of 1940 and taken over by the Germans in 1941, again became active as General Erwin Rommel's forces drove the British back in Egypt. Japanese planes bombed Dutch Harbor in the Aleutians, and Japanese troops secured a foothold on the island of Kiska, threatening Alaskan shores. The supply lines of the Allies stretched long and far over the globe (see map, pages 460-461). In contrast, Axis holdings, compact and often contiguous, made enemy problems of communication and supply relatively easy. Late spring and midsummer of 1942 saw inaugurated a mighty Axis drive for victory.

The battle for Russia. During the winter months the Nazi armies had been forced to assume defensive tactics in Russia. Intense cold and constant harrying by the Russians caused much loss in men and material. With the coming of spring and better weather Nazi armies inaugurated the long-awaited drive for victory against Russia. The initial effort was made in the Crimean peninsula, the eastern part of which fell to the Germans on May 23. To divert German strength Marshal Timoshenko had opened an offensive against the

As the United States went into production as the arsenal for democracy, this picture was taken in the Boeing Aircraft plant at Seattle. It shows the final assembly of the nose and center fuselage sections of the famous Flying Fortresses.

enemy in the vicinity of Kharkov, but the German drive in the Ukraine continued. The mighty fortress of Sevastopol, the last remaining Russian foothold in the Crimean peninsula, was attacked constantly by German forces during June and fell to the Nazis on July 1. German pressure then switched north, to the neighborhood of Kursk, where one of the heaviest attacks of the entire war was hurled against Russian positions. The objective was to reach the Don River and cut the vital railroad line connecting Moscow with south Russia. After bitter fighting the Germans crossed the Don and pushed east from their original positions and south toward the oil fields of the Caucasus.

If a major defeat were suffered by Russia, this would prolong the war and menace both the United States and Great Britain. This fact was fully realized in both Washington and London. In the spring and early summer there had been much talk of a second front in Europe to aid Russia. American troops in considerable force reached prepared billets in Northern Ireland, and high-ranking American officers went to London to discuss the strategy of the war. A form of second front was introduced when industrial centers in Germany were raided by British air forces consisting at times of more than a thousand planes. The crucial importance of Russia also brought the Soviet Foreign Commissar V. Molotov to both London and Washington. An important treaty was negotiated with Great Britain, and the United States and Russia signed a mutual aid agreement.

The Axis drive on Egypt. As part of the Axis victory campaign for 1942, the German Africa Corps under General Erwin Rommel launched an offensive against the British Eighth Army in Libya in May. For nearly three years the contending armies had seesawed back and forth over the desert. Rommel's latest push was the sixth campaign fought in Libya between the British on the one hand and the Germans and Italians on the other. Early in June the British army seemed to be holding its own. But after a defeat on June 18, the battered British forces began a rapid retreat. A garrison left to hold Tobruk was captured by Rommel with some twenty-five thousand British troops, according to Berlin claims, on June 21. The successful German army crossed the Egyptian border and by July 1 was only seventy miles from Alexandria. In the first week of July the British commander, General Auchinleck, reorganized his troops and commenced a heavy air offensive against Rommel's long lines of communication. The immediate threat to Alexandria, base of the British Mediterranean fleet, had been halted.

The Japanese persist in China. Checked in the mid-Pacific at Midway and unable to advance any closer to Australia, Japanese forces turned their attention to their first intended victim—China. In May Japanese troops opened an offensive in south China designed primarily to secure possession of the main railroad lines. Possession and control of these lines would give Japan an all-land network of communications extending from north China to Singapore. Troops and supplies could be moved along this route without fear of attack from American warships. By June the Japanese had captured the disputed railroad line and were pushing west into the heart of China. Denied the use of the Burma Road, the Allied nations found it increasingly difficult to send supplies to China.

The outlook for the United Nations. In July 1942 the Second World War was approaching the end of its third year. Involving at least eight distinct phases, the conflict had begun primarily as a war between Germany on the one hand and Great Britain and France on the other. By the end of the third year the war had become a global conflict involving the three Axis powers with their satellite allies and twenty-nine United Nations.

While crucial battles were being fought in Egypt and Russia, a less dramatic but equally heroic struggle was taking place in Europe. In the face of all forms of intimidation—forced labor, mass execution of hostages, extermination of villages—the conquered peoples of Europe refused to cooperate in Hitler's New Order. Sabotage, espionage, and assassinations showed that the Dutch, Norwegians, Poles, Serbs, French, and others were only waiting the day when they could rise and assist the armies of the United Nations to overthrow Nazi tyranny.

Great Britain had limited manpower but extensive productive capacity in the war; Russia had much greater manpower but inadequate industrial equipment for her vast armies; and China had virtually nothing except manpower. The United States was the heart of the opposition to the Axis, for she had manpower and immense productivity. But she was, in a sense, on the fringe of the battle areas, and so in a more limited way was Great Britain. The task of the British and even more of Americans was to transport men and supplies from the fringe to the center of the struggle (see map, pages 460-461). This war, therefore, was called "the perimeter war," in which Allied lines of communication were three to fifteen times longer than those of the Axis. In addition to the terrific assault against Egypt and Russia, the Germans also carried on a less spectacular offensive against the United States, a submarine campaign which accounted for more than 400 Allied vessels by the summer of 1942.

While the situation from the standpoint of the United Nations in the summer of 1942 appeared critical, if Russia could beat down the German onslaught without losing too much to Hitler; if the Near East and Egypt could be held, thus insuring a route of supply via the Persian Gulf and Iran to Russia and preventing Germany from reaching India and joining hands with Japan; and if Chinese resistance could hold out against increasing Japanese pressure, it was thought that the tremendous industrial potential of the United States might be able to operate toward the end of 1942 in favor of the United Nations.

United States war effort. Granted the continuation of the heroism of Russian, Chinese, and British soldiers, plus the Free French and guerilla bands of patriots in conquered Yugoslavia, the United States would be given a few more vital months to put her fighting forces into action fully equipped. America at war in the midsummer of 1942 gave every indication of a nation stripped for action. There were many evidences that the full power of the United States would soon be thrown into battle areas throughout the world. Naval units were in the Mediterranean; flying corps were being built up in Egypt, India, Australia, England, and China. Technicians were working in supply depots and transportation services in Iran, Egypt, and the Red Sea area. Large contingents were manning bases along the supply routes to Australia and in the Atlantic from Iceland to the Caribbean.

Defense factories, army cantonments, shipyards busy on merchant marine or warship construction rapidly increased their facilities. By the end of June President Roosevelt revealed that in the previous month 4000 planes, 2000 pieces of artillery, and more than 100,000 machine guns had been produced. This prodigious war effort was of necessity influencing the life of the people in every direction. The manufacture of private automobiles had ended, dim-outs were in operation along the Pacific and Atlantic coasts, gasoline rationing and rigid rationing of tire sales restricted the use of automobiles. Mounting taxes, shortages in many commodities heretofore abundantly available, and the requirements of civilian defense became the lot of Americans within a few months after Pearl Harbor.

Basic issues of the war. The sacrifices and derangement of normal living routines were willingly accepted by a vast majority of American people. The reason was to be found in the basic meaning of the Second World War. What were the issues? What were the United States and her allies fighting for and fighting against? The most obvious issue was self-preservation. The United Nations were fighting to prevent three powers—Germany, Japan, and Italy—from securing world domination and with it the control of the trade and raw materials of the world, for their own use. But apart from self-preservation, the United Nations were also fighting against countries which championed a philosophy repugnant to their way of life. The United States, the British Commonwealth of Nations, and other states believed in the dignity and worth of the individual. In the Axis nations the state alone was important. Such a philosophy denied to the individual religious freedom, voluntary participation in government, and freedom in thought and speech.

That the Axis powers, particularly Nazi Germany, gave allegiance to views that struck at the very heart of the humanistic tradition of western civilization was a fundamental fact. The Axis glorified war, ridiculed pacifism, and exalted martial Spartanism. Its militarism was conveniently tied to a super-race idea which rationalized the use of force, for force was considered the instrument that elevates nature's elect to the pedestal of world mastery.

Many people in the twenty-nine nations pledged to oppose the Axis realized there was much in the world before 1939 that had been illogical and unfair. They realized that the United Nations were not fighting to maintain and perpetuate a perfect world. But these men saw in an Axis triumph only an intensification of such old evils as militarism, excessive nationalism, and intolerance. Only by the defeat of Germany, Italy, and Japan could certain human values, already in existence, be preserved, strengthened, and made the basis for a better civilization after peace had been secured.

Summary

This chapter has shown how, in the early 1930's, efforts toward collective security were halted by a series of defeats. In the face of the rapidly growing military power of Germany and Italy, Great Britain and France seemed impotent, incapable of action. After Hitler's accession to power in 1933 a span of five years followed in which Germany succeeded in scrapping most of the remaining provisions of the Treaty of Versailles. This period of Revisionism, from 1933 to 1938, was followed by German attempts to achieve continental domination in Europe. During the period of Revisionism four factors largely explain Hitler's success. First, Great Britain and France were unable to see eye to eye. British statesmen were inclined to believe that France was endeavoring to dominate Europe and that, in the long run, her policy of keeping Germany down could not be successful. Second, pacifist sentiments were very pronounced in both France and Great Britain. The average citizen in these countries was resolved that war should be avoided at all costs. This resolution enabled Hitler to succeed, because he realized that, although the democracies might threaten to use force, in the last analysis they could be made to back down. Third, Italy threw her strength on the side of the Third Reich. This move made it increasingly difficult for the democracies to oppose Hitler. Finally, influential elements in Great Britain were inclined to regard Germany as a buffer against Russia. Both German Nazism and Russian Communism were regarded with suspicion by British statesmen, but it was preferable—so they thought—to placate Germany so that she would destroy Russia. Out of these elements the policy of "Appeasement" was born, a policy which existed with full vigor from 1933 until Munich in 1938. Appeasement was scrapped early in 1939, when both Great Britain and France realized that the true intentions of the Hitler régime were not merely to rectify the injustices of Versailles but to dominate Europe and the world as well.

During the decade from 1930 to 1940 Europe was once more the scene of two great antagonistic camps—Great Britain and France on the one side and Germany and Italy on the other. This rivalry became a world-wide conflict when Japan became a member of the Axis. Gradually the world became divided into two hostile groups: the democratic powers and the totalitarian states.

War broke out in Europe in 1939. Beginning with the conquest of Poland, the war spread throughout Europe, into Africa, Asia, and the Far East. By the spring of 1941 the swastika flew over Norway, Denmark, Holland, Belgium, and France. Great Britain had survived an all-out bombing. Italy controlled Albania. Rumania and Bulgaria were German puppets. Greece and Yugoslavia had been crushed. In north Africa the Axis and British forces seesawed in the desert for control of Egypt and Suez. In the summer of 1941 the Nazi blitzkrieg descended on Russia but was soon slowed. The global nature of the war was indeed becoming more pronounced. For the first year of the war the United States tried to maintain a policy of neutrality; during the second year she tried to remain a nonbelligerent while sending all possible aid to Great Britain. By the summer of 1941 collaboration had reached the point of a Churchill-Roosevelt meeting resulting in the Atlantic Charter, which, though couched in general terms, contained the long-awaited statement of war aims. Conflicting interests with Japan in the Pacific area would probably have drawn the United States into the war sooner or later. But the unprovoked Japanese attack on Pearl Harbor catapulted the United States into full belligerency in December 1941.

The year 1942 brought the Japanese conquest of the Philippines, Java, and Burma with the consequent threat to Australia and India. The necessity of a global strategy was recognized by the establishment of a United Nations command in the Pacific and the creation of various joint boards for shipping and supply. While Japan was sweeping through the Far East, Germany launched two all-out attacks, one on Russia to gain the coveted Caucasus oil fields, the other in Libya to secure the British fleet base at Alexandria. As for the United States, by July 1 her participation was being increasingly felt on the far-flung battlelines of the Second World War.

Science

Astrophysics and electromagnetics
Quantum theory: Max Planck
Einstein's theory of relativity
New atomic theory: Rutherford
Cosmic ray research: Millikan, Anderson
Principle of uncertainty or indeterminacy: Heisenberg
Chemical synthesis: Von Bayer, Haber, Carver
Biochemistry—vitamins, endocrinology: Hopkins, Banting
Biology—discovery of chromosomes by Morgan
Psychology—conditioned reflexes: Pavlov; behaviorism: Watson; *Gestalt* psychology: Wertheimer, Köhler, Koffka; psychology of unconscious: Freud, Jung, Adler
Medicine—serology, disease control: Ross, Reed

Philosophy

American pragmatism—James, Dewey
Bergson's philosophy of change
Croce's philosophy of history
Other thinkers—Santayana, Russell

Education

Increase in compulsory, free schooling
Philosophy—Montessori, Dewey

Religion

Totalitarian opposition to religion
Separation of Church and state
Increasing social emphasis

Literature

Romantics: Yeats, Masefield, Noyes
Realistic romantics: Galsworthy, Bennett, Conrad
Individualist: G. B. Shaw
Dramatists—Pinero, Barrie, Dunsany
American poets—Robinson, Frost, Lowell
American prose: William James, Santayana, Henry Adams, O. Henry
American novelists: Garland, Norris, London, Sinclair
War poets: Brooke, Owen, Sassoon
Postwar "Waste Land": Eliot, Jeffers
Disillusion: Hemingway, Huxley
Influence of James Joyce, O'Neill and abnormal psychology
American satire—Sinclair Lewis
Affirmation of democracy—Sandburg
Social consciousness in the thirties—Steinbeck, Odets
French literature—Romain, Rolland, Proust, Gide
German writers: Feuchtwanger, Wassermann, Remarque, Mann
Other nations—Undset, Gorki, Tagore

Art

Matisse the pioneer
Influence of Picasso on cubism
Surrealism deifies subsconscious—Dali
American realism—Grant Wood
Mural renaissance—Rivera, Orozco, Poor
Sculpture—Milles, Epstein, Maillol
Functionalism in architecture—skyscrapers, Wright, city planning, industrial arts

Music

Experiments in tonality—Debussy
Ballet music—Ravel, Stravinsky
Radicals—Schönberg, Hindemith, Shostakovich
Traditionalists—Sibelius, Strauss
Development of jazz—Gershwin

CHAPTER 15

Forging a New World

As the twentieth century approaches its half-way point, we are obliged to contemplate the record of two great wars, resulting chiefly from imperialistic ambitions and economic rivalries. Millions have lost their lives, billions of dollars' worth of property have been destroyed, and artistic and historic riches of the past have in countless instances been lost for all time. There are those who see in this record a decline of the civilization so slowly and laboriously built up from the past.

While the twentieth century has certainly presented mankind with some of its most perplexing problems—especially in economics, government, and social relations—the outlook is not wholly discouraging. Their solution remains uncertain, of course, but many men see in them a challenge which holds out immense rewards in human betterment. To consider these problems in their largest and longest perspective is one of the functions of the study of history; not to provide answers—that is scarcely possible—but to see what light can be thrown on them out of the infinitely detailed record of man's past. The foregoing chapters have highlighted some of the problems and furnished some background for thinking them through.

While twentieth-century developments in politics, economics, and society have been world-shaking, and final statements cannot be made about them, we are able to see in the intellectual and artistic aspects of his culture that mankind has made in our century some of its most significant contributions. Although science has often been prostituted to purposes of violent destruction, it has also worked out the quantum and relativity theories, revolutionary notions about the structure of the atom, and a host of other discoveries that indicate a new and promising material environment, waiting only for man to improve his institutions so as to take advantage of them. Medical science has added appreciably to the years of man by bringing under control many scourges that baffled earlier days. Finally, no less than the past, our age has produced philosophers, poets, essayists, dramatists, novelists, artists, and composers. All these, too, will help to shape the world to come.

Science

Twentieth-century scientific contributions. Whereas the eighteenth century saw the special advance of mathematics and chemistry, and the nineteenth witnessed the predominance of discoveries in biology and physics, it appears so far that the twentieth century has made its most notable scientific contributions in astrophysics and electromechanics. The study of astrophysics, a combination of mathematics, astronomy, and physics, has yielded some truly phenomenal results. Electromechanics is the study of the structure and activity of the atom; discoveries in this field rival in importance those of astrophysics. Thus one line of investigation takes the universe with its myriad galaxies and nebulae as its special sphere, while the other contents itself with examining a structure which no man has even seen but which may hold the ultimate secret of the universe. Astrophysics and electromechanics may appear to be worlds apart; in reality, they bear a close affinity, for the atom in many respects is a solar system in miniature.

Scientists at the end of the nineteenth century were smug. The laws of Newton had been thoroughly correlated by experiment, and the laws of thermodynamics had been evolved. Maxwell had developed an electromagnetic theory of wave propagation which linked up light and electricity and showed the way to the discovery of X-rays, the ultra-violet rays, visible, infra-red, and radio waves. In the year 1900 several outstanding physicists were of the opinion that science in the future must content itself with adding only a decimal place or two to existing equations. The basic discoveries, they thought, had already been made.

The quantum theory. Scientific thought was jolted out of its complacency when three bombshells were hurled at classical physics: the quantum theory, the relativity theory, and the new concept of the structure of the atom. The quantum theory, the work of a German, Max Planck, was put forward in 1901 to account for a discrepancy that had occurred in regard to so-called black-body radiation. A black body is one which absorbs all the radiant energy it receives. Planck explained the distribution of black-body radiation in the spectrum and was awarded the Nobel prize in 1918. But science can be hidebound, as Planck found out in presenting his new hypothesis. When the first public statement of it was made at a meeting of the Prussian Academy of Sciences, one irate professor left the room after declaring, "Gentlemen, this is *not* physics." But it was physics of the highest caliber and was soon corroborated by other scientists.

One of these scientists was Einstein, who used the quantum theory to make clear the energy relation within the atom and to explain a point on which experiment and classical theory did not agree, that is, the question of specific heats of bodies at low temperatures. The quantum theory has received further corroboration in other fields.

Albert Einstein. At the beginning of the century an even greater bombshell was ready to explode, one whose philosophical reverberations have never ceased. It was the all-important theory of relativity, which deals particularly with problems of velocity, time, and space. The theory of relativity has the most profound implications in mathematics, astronomy, and physics. The man to whom the world is primarily indebted for its new concepts of space and time is at present living in the United States as a result of racial and political persecution in his native land. He is Albert Einstein, who deserves to be known to us as a person. Einstein is that scientific explorer who, in the words of George Bernard Shaw, "discovered a new universe."

Einstein was born in 1879, the son of a Jewish merchant in Germany. Financial difficulties and anti-Semitic discrimination early jeopardized young Einstein's career. Finding his teachers in Munich to be "like non-commissioned officers," Einstein at sixteen traveled to Switzerland, where he obtained his doctorate. At twenty-three he became a technical expert in the Swiss Patent Office. In time he was made a member of the faculty at the University of Bern, and while he was professor of theoretical physics there in 1905, he presented his famous paper asking for a new approach to the concepts of time and space. Later Einstein became director of the physics institute at Berlin, where he remained until 1931. In the meantime he had been awarded the Nobel prize for physics in 1921 in recognition of his momentous contributions to that science.

The anti-Semitic campaign of the Nazis, during which Einstein's house was searched for weapons because of his allegedly dangerous radicalism, convinced the physicist that Germany was no longer a place suitable for him as an individual or scientist. So he accepted a position temporarily at Oxford, then came to the United States in 1933. Here he has been associated with Princeton University. Modest regarding his great accomplishments, shunning publicity, never capitalizing on his fame, and forever seeking to verify and perfect his theories, Einstein is a living symbol of the true scientist who has dedicated his life to the furtherance of knowledge. In the midst of race persecution, nationalistic greed, and social and economic unrest, there are living today worthy successors to Aristotle, Archimedes, Copernicus, and Newton. Einstein is one of them.

Einstein's theory of relativity. The story is current that few people in the world fully comprehend Einstein's theories. However, Newton had indicated that space, time, and motion are all absolute and that intervals of time are identical in all situations. Einstein disagrees, maintaining that absolute motion through space cannot be detected or measured. However, the speed of light appears to be constant, that is, irrespective of where an observer may be or how he may be moving, light seems to be traveling at the rate of 186,000 miles per second. Mass varies with velocity—rigid bodies contract in the direction in which they are moving—and a gravitational field alters the nature of space so as to cause light rays to bend. Not only mass but time varies with velocity.

The universe of Einstein is not Newton's three-dimensional figure of length, breadth, and thickness but a "four-dimensional space-time continuum." Thus, to the ordinary three dimensions Einstein adds the fourth dimension of time, fusing them all into "space-time." Such a concept shows the relative interrelationship of space, motion, and time and, since it cannot be explained by the old Euclidean geometry, necessitates a new, or non-Euclidean, system. While Newton's mechanics still continue to be of satisfactory use in everyday science and engineering, the new concepts of Einstein have completely reoriented our attitude toward the structure and mechanics of the cosmos.

Atomic structure and activity. A third great revolution in twentieth-century science must be added to those created by the quantum and relativity theories. This revolution came about from new views on the structure and activity of the atom. The nineteenth century looked upon the atom as indivisible and "solid." However, near the close of the century new concepts of a radical nature were being developed. Hendrik Lorentz and Joseph Thomson came to the conclusion that the atoms contain smaller units called electrons. X-rays were discovered in 1895 by Wilhelm Roentgen, and radioactivity was observed in regard to uranium by Becquerel in 1896. Soon afterward Pierre and Marie Curie extracted radium from pitchblende, and the world took cognizance of this strange new science of radioactivity. Then in 1911 a New Zealander, Sir Ernest Rutherford, correlated this radioactive phenomenon with the electron theory and conceived of a fuller explanation. His new atomic theory proposed that each atom has a nucleus (proton) charged with positive electricity around which revolve negatively charged particles called electrons. The result was to postulate for the atom a structure analogous to that of the solar system.

The cosmic ray and atom smashing. Another important development has been the study of a new type of wave which had been observed to bombard the earth even at night and which therefore could not emanate from the sun. Because it seemed to come from "out beyond" and not the sun, the name cosmic ray was given it. The cosmic ray possesses an exceedingly short wave-length and can penetrate lead to a distance of many yards, whereas X-rays can force their way to a depth of only a quarter of an inch. Particular work has

The pear-shaped tank of this atom smasher is erected over a two-story building at the East Pittsburgh research laboratories of Westinghouse Electric. The structure houses an electrostatic direct-current generator and a forty-foot vacuum tube through which particles are shot in the bombardment of various types of matter.

been done on cosmic rays by two American physicists, Robert Millikan and Carl Anderson, whose efforts in unraveling at least a portion of their mystery have earned both men the Nobel prize.

Still more knowledge is being gained by the process of atom smashing. Huge machines, called cyclotrons, bombard atoms with electrons, creating new combinations of atoms which would not otherwise result. The possibilities in this new field of research are so enormous that no one can make predictions as to what new marvels will be uncovered in the future.

In keeping with Einstein's relativity theory, which throws out the old concept of absolutes, is a new principle put forward in 1927 by a German physicist, Werner Heisenberg, the principle of uncertainty or indeterminacy. Heisenberg points out that, just as the electrons in the atom follow no set rule but are unpredictable, so throughout the whole realm of physics we have to work as much with unknowable as knowable quantities. Thus our future cannot be predetermined but only estimated according to probability and is subject to change without notice.

The progress of chemical synthesis. The twentieth century has also witnessed much progress in chemical synthesis. The chemist has been able to create literally thousands of synthetic substances. The economic importance of such discoveries is enormous. Let us take as an example the history of synthetic indigo. In 1880 some 1,400,000 acres of land were being cultivated in India for the purpose of growing natural indigo. But in that same year Von Bayer synthesized this dye. The result was that by 1912 only 214,000 acres in India were being cultivated, while in Germany, on the other hand, the synthetic production of indigo rose from 2500 tons in 1900 to about 39,000 tons in 1914.

Germany managed to sustain her munitions program throughout the First World War despite an Allied blockade that prevented her obtaining Chilean nitrates, because Fritz Haber found out how to make practical use of the inert nitrogen in the atmosphere.

Until recently cottonseed was discarded as useless. Now scores of products are obtained from this once despised source, including smokeless powder, photographic films, felt, soap, salad oil, and washing-powder. The outstanding Negro scientist, Dr. George W. Carver, has found dozens of uses for the peanut, while the soybean runs the gamut of synthetic products from food to steering wheels.

The new biochemistry. The twentieth century has also seen the development of a new science called biochemistry, dealing with the "study of the life processes which take place in plants or animals" and concerned, for example, with the investigation of living tissue. As a result of their study of problems of nutrition, biochemists have established rates regarding the energy or caloric value of fats, proteins, carbohydrates, and minerals. It was known that the absence of certain elements in the human diet would cause such deficiency diseases as scurvy and beri-beri. The British navy had long been aware that a salt-meat and hard-tack diet over a protracted period of time caused scurvy to break out among its sailors and early in the nineteenth century insisted that every ship leaving port must bear its proper amount of fresh limes—thus giving the name "limeys" to the British tars. But not until just prior to the First World War did a British biochemist, Sir Frederick Hopkins, show conclusively that health can be maintained only if the daily diet contains accessory factors—vitamins, as they were later called. Today some six vitamins have been isolated and studied with great promise for the future health of mankind.

Biochemistry has also performed valuable research in discovering the presence and purpose of the mysterious ductless glands, which have much to do with controlling our bodies. This study of glands, known as endocrinology, has thrown light on how internal secretion controls metabolism, the growth of the body, sex characteristics, and the emotions. In 1901 a Japanese biologist, Takamine, isolated adrenalin in the suprarenal glands and discovered that it was of value in regulating the action of the heart. The pituitary gland was found to condition physical growth. When overactive, the secretion of the gland produced giants, when underactive, dwarfs. The thyroid gland was found to affect metabolism, and in 1919 an American biochemist, Edward C. Kendall, crystallized its active principle and named it thyroxin. A Canadian scientist, Frederick Banting, was the chief discoverer of the use of insulin, an extract taken from the pancreas of sheep, prescribed for diabetes.

Biology. In the twentieth century there has been further confirmation of the great evolutionary hypothesis, although certain aspects of Darwin's theory have had to be modified. Similarly, Mendel's laws of heredity have been finally confirmed and amplified by modern biologists, while Thomas H. Morgan has studied with great exactness the mechanism of heredity. Through his careful research into the cell structure of the fruit fly, Morgan discovered within each cell nucleus certain thread-like bodies known as chromosomes, which transmit hereditary characteristics. The various combinations of these chromosomes make possible literally millions of different kinds of cells—hence the infinite variety of forms throughout nature.

Psychology. Still another science which has attracted widespread attention in our century is psychology, the study of human thought, behavior, and emotions. Perhaps the youngest of the major sciences, psychology is being placed upon as exact a basis as possible, for it is realized how inseparably linked are our thinking and emotions with our physical bodies. The study of psychology in terms of physiological factors was given impetus by a Russian scientist, Ivan Pavlov. Pavlov was concerned with demonstrating the importance to behavior of physical stimuli and reactions, and this psychology of "conditioned reflexes" with its denial of the validity of so-called subjective factors in human conduct was furthered by an American psychologist, John B. Watson. Watson's psychology is known as behaviorism and considers man more or less as a machine who responds mechanically to physical stimuli. Behaviorism stressed experimentation and observational techniques with the result that it did much to create relatively valid intelligence and aptitude tests.

In Germany the *Gestalt* or "form" psychology, like behaviorism in America, rose consciously as a protest against the "older psychology." Max Wertheimer is generally regarded as its founder, though Wolfgang Köhler and Kurt Koffka have been no less active in working out the concepts of the *Gestalt* school, which believes that the perception of an object has a character of totality, a *Gestalt* or form, and is not merely the sum of all the parts of the object.

Even more radical in the development of psychology have been the contributions of the Austrian Sigmund Freud, his pupil Carl Jung, and the Viennese Alfred Adler. Freud, father of the psychoanalyst school, was the first to bring into consideration the psychology of the "unconscious." He was, however, mainly concerned with the mechanics of man's "libido." Jung broke definitely with Freud, explaining man's libido as "life energy" rather than sexual urge. An important contribution of Jung is his typology of man, from which originated the popular expressions "introvert" and "extrovert." Adler, conceiving of the individual as an indivisible unity whose behavior can be understood only in his relation to society, brought out the purposiveness of all human behavior. To him life was a definite striving for a "goal" which is each individual's own idea of security and is a compensation for his "inferiority feelings."

Advance in medical science. The field of serology (serums) in medicine has received considerable attention. For example, the Schick test and the administration of toxin-antitoxin to those found susceptible to diphtheria has reduced the mortality from this disease by almost seventy-five per cent. Serums against scarlet fever, whooping cough, colds, and other maladies are now available, although they are still not one hundred per cent effective. The alleviation of distress resulting from diabetes by the use of Banting's insulin has already been mentioned.

Many other scourges of mankind have been checked by modern medical science. In 1898 Sir Ronald Ross, who had carried on investigations in India, announced that he had discovered the sequence of stages in the transmission of bird malaria by the mosquito. Italian investigators used this knowledge to solve the problem of human malaria, and one of the worst tropical diseases had at last been understood. In 1900 an American commission in Cuba under the direction of Walter Reed made the discovery that a certain common mosquito can transmit the unknown virus of yellow fever.

Today, after such maladies as small-pox, diabetes, diphtheria, tuberculosis, malaria, and yellow fever are being brought under control, we have yet to conquer the most dreaded disease confronted by mankind—cancer. While doctors do not know very much about the cause or nature of this scourge, certain curative effects have been attained. They involve the use of radium and other radioactive substances, for it has been shown that radium can destroy the cancerous cells. Medical science throughout the world is bending every effort to the eradication of cancer, and it is possible that human society will surmount this obstacle in the not too distant future.

Philosophy

Philosophy from early times. The original meaning of the word philosopher is "a lover (or seeker) of wisdom." But whereas the scientist has confined his efforts particularly to the realm of observation and analysis, the philosopher has entered the realm of speculation and synthesis. The desire to speculate about the nature of reality was found in early India, where the Indo-Aryans worked out an elaborate cosmological system. Some of their basic philosophical concepts included the unity of all life, the transitory nature of the physical world, the reabsorption of the individual soul into the universal soul, the spiritual evolution of humanity through the process of reincarnation, and the governing of all actions by a universal moral law called *karma*. This philosophy, found in the *Upanishads*, has become the heritage of the modern Indians.

Meanwhile the early Chinese had evolved philosophies in keeping with their racial and environmental history. Whereas the Indians were concerned with mysticism and metaphysics, the practical Chinese concentrated on humanism and nonmetaphysical philosophy. It is true that Lao-tse emphasized the intuitional rather than the intellectual approach to reality, but the most popular philosopher has been Confucius, advocate of the virtuous, obedient, sympathetic life. He and his followers, placing emphasis upon tradition and duty, have retained a strong influence upon all later generations and have taught the Chinese to live rational, ethical lives here on earth. In one way or another these two great philosophical attitudes, the mystical in India and the humanist in China, have also vied for favor in western thought.

The first people in the west to speculate about the nature of the universe were the Greeks. Out of a maze of conflicting concepts came some important contributions. Pythagoras showed the importance of mathematics in approaching the study of philosophy. Heraclitus maintained that everything in life is in constant flux, and Democritus put forth an "atomic" theory to explain the structure of the universe. As time went on, certain Greeks studied man and his purpose in living. The Sophists proclaimed that "man is the measure of all things" and that there were no universal standards—everything was relative. Socrates disagreed, stating that such standards do exist, and he and his disciple, Plato, set forth a theory of Ideas, such as perfect Beauty, Truth, and Goodness. But Plato's great pupil, Aristotle, disagreed with his master as to the nature of these Ideas. Plato had stated that Real Being was to be found in universal ideas, but Aristotle said it was to be found in the particular, the individual, and the concrete. Plato's views concerning an ideal state of society are recorded in his *Republic.* Aristotle gave the world the concept of the "golden mean" in his ethics and the syllogism in his deductive logic.

The Romans did little original philosophical thinking, preferring to take over the systems of the Greeks. During the Middle Ages philosophy was much concerned with theology. Medieval thinkers, known as Scholastics, split into two schools of thought called Nominalism and Realism. The Scholastics tried unsuccessfully to reconcile permanently the new discoveries in science and scholarship with church dogmas. Scholasticism was doomed to failure in such an age as the Renaissance, which emphasized the new values of present-worldliness and experimental science. And so we find Francis Bacon criticising the philosophy of the Scholastics and stressing an inductive approach.

Philosophy aligned with science. Philosophy now departed from the orbit of theology and came under the influence of science, a situation which still exists. Descartes with his acceptance of the scientific attitude gave modern philosophy its initial impetus. Some of his successors, Spinoza and Leibnitz included, were strongly influenced by mathematics and built up systems of rationalism. Meanwhile English philosophers were taking Bacon's inductive method to heart and were formulating systems of empiricism. Among the most outstanding of these empiricists were Locke, Hobbes, and Hume.

A new departure came with Kant. He agreed that sensations are at the basis of human knowledge, but he maintained that science itself can investigate only the realm of physical nature. This system of thought, in which the object of perception is held to consist of ideas of either the perceiving mind or a universal mind, found later followers in Germany: Fichte, Schelling, and Hegel. Hegel glorified the state as the ultimate social reality, a phase of philosophical idealism of the greatest consequence to Karl Marx and to Fascist ideologists.

While German philosophy was engaged in dealing with transcendentalism and absolutes, the practical British were continuing to create empirical systems of thought. The industrialism that has permeated the country since the invention of the steam engine profoundly strengthened this trend. Jeremy Bentham and James and John Stuart Mill worked out Utilitarianism, the theory of the greatest good for the greatest number of people.

Twentieth-century pragmatism. Our age has not produced so many philosophers as the eighteenth and nineteenth centuries, but certain thinkers deserve notice. John Dewey, educational authority and champion of science, has furthered pragmatism, an American philosophy stimulated by William James which considers the validity of an idea according to its ability to "work" in human experience. He has consistently sought to establish the scientific method in philosophy. He is not concerned with deductions about absolutes, nor does he attempt to prognosticate. Dewey asks only that the method of experimental science be used so that intelligence and experience together can solve our individual and social problems.

Bergson and Croce. One of the most significant philosophers of the century was Henri Bergson. A French Jew, professor of philosophy and writer of some of the most stimulating books in the history of philosophy, Bergson created a tremendous stir in the early years of the century by his revolutionary views. Protesting against the mechanistic concepts of the day, Bergson based his views largely on a biological concept of life in which mutation and the unpredictable were prominent. To Bergson nature is always creating afresh, and change is at the bottom of everything. In this respect the French philosopher goes back to the Greek Heraclitus. Bergson called this fundamental creative impulse the *élan vital* and with it built up a dynamic philosophy of change which to him is reality itself. Because his views on change are correlated with time (which he considers indivisible), Bergson's philosophy has points of contact with Einstein's relativity theory.

Benedetto Croce is an Italian philosopher who has evolved a famous philosophy of history. He does not look upon past events as dead but considers them to have been brought into the present age as experience. We are inseparably bound up with our past, and every new change today must affect our interpretation of yesterday. Thus history must be constantly revaluated, and every new interpretation of it should add fresh significance both to our history and to our present philosophy.

Santayana and Russell. The Spanish-born George Santayana has emphasized esthetics. Santayana writes a somber philosophy which embodies the atomic theory of Democritus and the golden-mean ethics of Aristotle. The greatest work of Santayana is his five-volume *The Life of Reason,* although his first philosophical essay—*The Sense of Beauty*—brought him initial fame.

Probably the best-known English philosopher of recent times is Bertrand Russell. Coming from one of England's most aristocratic and famous families, Russell has distinguished himself by combining a practical interest in science and social criticism with a mathematician's love of eternal logical forms.

The relation of science and philosophy. Modern philosophers show heavy indebtedness to science, as is indicated by the titles of their books. J. B. S. Haldane of England published in 1933 an outstanding work called *Science and Human Life,* while a distinguished Harvard thinker, Alfred North Whitehead, published in 1926 *Science and the Modern World,* in which science and philosophy were correlated not in terms of mechanism and matter but more in keeping with the latest developments in the physiological sciences and the field of electromagnetics. During this century science has tended to become more philosophical and philosophy more scientific. Some of our greatest mathematicians and physicists have written treatises on the implications of their discoveries, so that what began as statements of fact have developed into metaphysical speculations.

Since the later nineteenth century an attempt has been made by followers of St. Thomas Aquinas to renew the philosophy of the schools by using it to illuminate and solve modern problems and to give them entity. Foremost today among these revitalizers of the Aristotelian-Thomist tradition are Catholic philosophers everywhere, especially Jacques Maritain and Etienne Gilson.

Education

Modern increase in education. During our century education has made its most rapid progress. All major countries have enacted laws making schooling compulsory for both sexes for a prescribed period of time. Millions of people, both children and adults, are being given the opportunity for the first time to enjoy educational advantages in such countries as the Soviet Union, Turkey, China, Iraq, and the African colonial possessions. Added to the increase in elementary schooling are the scores of institutions of higher learning which have been established all over the world. In the United States can be found indication of the phenomenal growth of universities. In 1900 scarcely one American institution had over a thousand students. Today the twenty-five largest universities each have an enrollment of over 5000 full-time students. In many places junior colleges have been established to give higher education to thousands who cannot afford university tuition or who want a two-year college course.

New thought in education. Many new concepts have arisen in the field of educational philosophy, especially in the United States. The "spare the rod and spoil the child" theory has been proved disastrous as well as inefficient. Maria Montessori, the eminent Italian educator, showed that a repressive system of education inhibited the child and that more satisfactory results could be obtained by allowing him to develop naturally and spontaneously. Each child, she maintained, should be treated as an individual with distinctive potentialities and interests. According to her theory, punishment should not be meted out, for the failure of the child to accomplish an assignment indicated his mental inability or unpreparedness to grasp the subject at that time.

American educators have advanced along this line of thought. Most prominent among the American educational philosophers has been John Dewey, the pragmatist thinker. To Dewey education is not even a preparation for life but life itself. He shows that its purpose is to reconstruct experience into purposeful values. Education is a process of continuous growth and has a precise social function: to adjust the individual to his environment and, at the same time, to create a more purposeful environment for the individual. The dovetailing of the individual and the group into a harmonious pattern means for Dewey a functional, dynamic educational system. He sees education as the bulwark of true democracy, where not only equal political rights but also equal social and economic rights are assured to everyone.

The potentialities of the child have been determined by the use of intelligence tests, while vocational tests are administered to help him make a rational decision as to the kind of employment best suited to his abilities and temperament. Another important step has been taken in educational philosophy with the introduction of such new programs as "integration" and "fusion." Among other features is the emphasis placed upon integrating such subjects as history, civics, economics, and literature into a basic social-studies course, rather than treating them as unrelated and separate.

Religion

Early religions. Religion has always been a basic human concern throughout history. Primitive man was naturally concerned with how and why he came to be alive and with his relationship to the world about him. He had no understanding of thunder, lightning, earthquakes, volcanoes, and tidal waves, and at first he had little control over disease and famine. Much (if not all) of his religious emotion was permeated with fear. The forces with which he could not cope and the sense of danger lurking in the mysterious and unknown created within our primitive ancestors many superstitions, along with the desire to supplicate those unseen forces which controlled earthly destiny. They established various rituals and forms of worship, giving reverence to animals or stones or other manifestations of nature. Man now believed that the world was controlled by spirits, and it was natural for him to ascribe to good spirits all the beneficial things that happened to him and to evil spirits all the unfortunate affairs. Primitive society sought the favor of the good spirits and attempted to nullify the efforts of the bad ones by sacrifice, taboos, and fetishism.

Concept of one god develops. As civilization advanced, man began to ascribe, for example, not a separate spirit for every sea but a single spirit, or god, for all the seas. He came to think that individual gods controlled his emotional and mental state. The Greeks, for instance, paid their respect to Minerva, the goddess of wisdom, and Venus, the goddess of love. All the ancient civilizations had gods in one form or another, whether we examine Egypt, China, India, Mesopotamia, Greece, or Rome. In some of the cultures, however, there gradually developed the concept of one god who was greater than all the rest or even one from whom all others were derived. The religious history of the Indo-Aryans shows this evolution quite clearly. The Indo-Aryans came into India with such gods as Surya (the sun), Agni (the fire-god), and Indra (the god of war). To these gods the Indo-Aryans paid sacrificial rites including the drinking of *soma* juice and the pouring of liquid butter into the sacred fire. But slowly there evolved the belief in a Something greater even than these gods. Eventually Indian philosophers spoke of Brahma, that unborn, impersonal, all-pervading force which not only created the universe but was the universe.

Other peoples came to have a belief in a universal power. The Zoroastrians divided that power between two warring cosmic powers, Mazda, who symbolized righteousness, and Ahriman, the summation of everything evil. The poems of the Mayas obliquely ascribe the supreme power to an abstract force which they term the "cause of all." But in the west the first definite attribution of power to a single universal source came from the Jews. The Old Testament repeats over and over again that there is only one God, Jehovah. The two other large religions of the west, Christianity and Mohammedanism, also fervently affirmed their faith in monotheism. Meanwhile Buddhism cast aside the polytheism of Hinduism and adhered to a principle of cosmic law.

Pattern of main religions. The vitality of the most important religions has been amazing. Hinduism, Buddhism, Judaism, Zoroastrianism (almost extinct now except for the Parsee sect in India), and Confucianism are all at least two thousand years old. Christianity is almost two thousand years old, while Mohammedanism has a history stretching over thirteen hundred years. Literally thousands of millions have lived and died in these faiths, accepting their teachings as a suitable explanation of the mystery of life.

Each of the great world religions has experienced much the same sort of evolution. First came the founder, who taught his followers the truth as he saw it. After a period in which his teachings were transmitted orally, they were written down in permanent form, acquiring a holy reputation. Then as disputes arose over the interpretation of various of his teachings, religious or political leaders would decide on doctrinal differences. Thus a definite theology developed which the orthodox members of the faith accepted. The members who dissented would either be forced to conform or, if the opportunity came, might break away and form new sects.

Place of religion in our century. It is difficult to assess the exact status of religion in the twentieth century. In the western world, while the great majority still adhere to the teachings of Christianity, it is none the less true that the traditional faith of our forefathers—like their economic and political beliefs—is undergoing a serious period of stress and uncertainty. There are many today whose faith in organized religion has been weakened by the spectacle of western civilization rent by war, by so-called Christians locked in a death struggle on the battlefield. On the other hand there are many who are inclined to turn once more to the supernatural for solace. Then, too, within the past twenty-five years it has often been difficult to reconcile new trends of science with prevailing beliefs of Christianity.

Furthermore, various national states have attacked organized Christianity. Lenin maintained (as had Marx before him) that "religion is the opiate of the people," and the Soviet government ended the function of the Greek Orthodox Church as an official Russian institution. Not only have the Soviet leaders refused to countenance the old status of the Church, which they maintained had been a tool of czarism since the days of Peter the Great, but they have allowed anti-religious propaganda to be disseminated. However, church services are not officially banned in the Soviet Union, and there seems even to be a revival of religion among the people.

Nazi Germany has clashed with the Roman Catholic Church, owing principally to the totalitarian concept that allegiance should be undivided and that the German people ought to obey their national government rather than any international body. The Nazis have also interfered with Protestant groups whenever they felt these sects were teaching doctrines inimical to the political ideology. One section of the Nazi party has tried to revive the pagan worship of old Germanic gods. The Jewish people of Germany have suffered under Nazi attacks. The savage persecution of Jews has aroused world-wide sympathy for their cause and animosity for Hitler's new so-called Aryan régime.

The Catholic Church in Italy concluded the Lateran Treaty in 1929 which reëstablished an independent temporal sovereignty for the papacy at Vatican City. However, totalitarianism under Mussolini has again tried to capture first place in the hearts of the Catholic population. The civil war in Spain between the Loyalists and the forces of General Franco had religious implications. The Loyalists believed in a popular-front form of government in which the Catholic Church would be divorced from power in the political, economic, and educational fields. The victory of Franco was also a victory for the Church in Spain. Mexico under President Cárdenas embarked upon a policy whereby the state would control the educational facilities of the country and curb the power of the landowners, high church officials, and foreign economic groups. In Protestant countries during the century there has been a strengthening of the belief that the state and Church should be kept separate.

There has been a tendency among the important religions of the world to get rid of certain older theological attitudes. Such notions as that of God as a wrathful deity or a universe full of demons, hells, and cruel torments have not withstood the scrutiny of science and education. A growing number of adherents of the major faiths—Christian, Jewish, Buddhist, Mohammedan, Hindu—have come to believe that the value of religions is to focus more attention upon their inspiring doctrines.

An interesting trend in current religious thought is the rising concern about social problems. In 1941 the Church of England held a convocation known as the Malvern Conference. At this meeting the Archbishop of York, Dr. William Temple (later Archbishop of Canterbury), expressed his belief that the Church should endeavor to work wholeheartedly for the social and economic betterment of all of England's working people.

The Methodist Church in the United States has formulated a program for postwar reconstruction, and leaders of other denominations in America are also considering the responsibility of church leadership in social reconstruction. Many of these churchmen envisage the church as a community center where religious, psychological, social, economic, and educational matters will be synthesized into a pattern for more dynamic living. By this means they say that the Church could perform invaluable service in molding character and adjusting personality.

Literature

Literature in the nineteenth century. Nineteenth-century literature mirrored faithfully the main intellectual and social currents of the period. In an age of rapid industrial growth, scientific achievement, and colonial and imperial expansion, our Victorian forebears were wont to take an optimistic and even smug attitude toward the world in which they lived. There were indeed problems, such as the rise of hideous factory towns and the growing misery of the laboring classes, which some of the more outspoken writers dared to consider. But by and large the average middle-class Englishman or American of the nineteenth century was quite satisfied with his age and as a result demanded literature which should be amusing, pleasant, moral, and "edifying."

As the century drew to a close, however, men of letters could not ignore the many social problems needing to be solved. Some English writers began to express dissatisfaction with their age, but others continued to follow a romantic vein. In the nineties, however, it had become fashionable to decry the conventionality and smugness of the older Victorian school. Leaders of this trend, like Oscar Wilde and his friends, rebelled against the stultification of their age but went off into flights of esthetic murmurings and excesses.

No spectacular literary changes appeared with the birth of the present century. Change was in the air, but it was yet in a nebulous shape. As the century opened, Kipling was still singing the glories of an imperialistic expansion which was largely over so far as such countries as Great Britain, the United States, and France were concerned. Other writers sighed nostalgically for the good old days, the days of Victorian stability when the words "goodness" and "nobility" were highly fashionable, when man's motives were not interpreted simply in terms of Watson or Freud.

Early twentieth-century literature. In the early years of the twentieth century there were some writers in the United States and England who frankly accepted the dicta of science and rebelled at the maladjustments of a social and economic system that was showing signs of internal pressure. But the realism so prevalent in recent literature was long condemned as being vulgar, inartistic, and perverted. Its struggle for acceptance as a valid channel of literary expression was owing largely to the inability of a majority of writers to wake up to the realities of the age. The First World War provided the necessary jolt.

Prewar British poets. A poet who lived at this time and whose interests centered not in immediate problems or literary trends but in a quest after unalloyed beauty and the world of the imagination was William Butler Yeats. Until his death a few years ago, Yeats was perhaps the most significant Irish poet. He also gained fame for his playwriting and his efforts on behalf of the Irish Literary Theater, which he helped found. These contributions and his rich lyrical gifts won him the Nobel prize for literature in 1923. Yeats's writings are characterized by a deep mysticism, a rich imagination, and an extraordinary sensitiveness to beauty which marks the best of Celtic poets.

Among other British poets who made their chief contribution prior to the First World War was John Masefield, who became poet laureate in 1930. Masefield is a mixture of the realist and mystic, due perhaps to his varied career. When fourteen he ran off to sea and became a common sailor; later he was a dish-washer in O'Connor's saloon in New York City. Like Yeats, Masefield has searched endlessly after beauty, finding it in seascapes and slums alike. He was greatly influenced by Chaucer and no doubt captured from him his fondness for the narrative poem. Such narrative poems as *The Widow in the Bye Street* and *The Everlasting Mercy* brought Masefield renown prior to the First World War. Yet, despite realistic settings and phraseology, Masefield has remained primarily a romantic poet.

Alfred Noyes and A. E. Housman also became famous prior to World War I. Noyes places reliance upon musical cadences and romantic themes, while his philosophy of poetry is frankly conservative. Housman was more austere in his poetry and possessed a melancholy personal philosophy. His fame grew after the publication of *A Shropshire Lad* (1896). All of his work is marked by classical simplicity, economy of words, and persistent pessimism. Noyes and Housman, despite their wide personal differences, are alike in that their poetry has little, if anything, that pertains exclusively to the spirit and concepts of the twentieth century.

Prewar English novelists. The early years of the present century saw in England the flourishing of numerous novelists. John Galsworthy wrote novels of social importance, specializing in an analysis of upper middle-class life. In 1906 he began a long series of such studies in the *Forsyte Saga* (1906-1922). Its main theme is the acquisitive instinct as personified by Soames Forsyte, a man with a compulsion to own all desirable objects.

Arnold Bennett is noted not so much for his analysis of society as for his keen descriptions of it. Much of his work is placed in the "Five Towns," the pottery center of England, whose features are woven skillfully into the stories which Bennett created. His fame rests chiefly on *The Old Wives' Tale*.

Joseph Conrad, the novelist, was a Pole by birth and a sailor during his younger years. He excelled in his sea yarns and descriptions. Something like Masefield in his love of the sea and his mixture of realism and romanticism, Conrad won fame for such novels as *Lord Jim*, *Victory*, and *The Nigger of the Narcissus*.

British dramatists. Probably the most colorful figure of twentieth-century English drama has been George Bernard Shaw. Famous as "a conscientious objector to practically everything," as a Fabian Socialist, a vegetarian, and an Irish playwright who would not live anywhere but in London, Shaw has written a score of successful plays. But Shaw's most influential period may well have been prior to the First World War, for during the nineties and the following decade he lambasted bourgeois society for its prudishness, shortsightedness, and inability to cope effectively with economic and social problems. And he is still doing it. Among his most outstanding plays are *Androcles and the Lion*, which satirizes organized Christianity, *Man and Superman*, attacking the contemporary economic structure, *Back to Methuselah*, which ridicules traditionalism and the British Empire, *Arms and the Man*, which satirizes war, and *Saint Joan*, a sympathetic portrayal of the heroine Joan of Arc. Shaw has also written a long treatise embodying his socialistic doctrines, *The Intelligent Woman's Guide to Socialism and Capitalism*. Recently Shaw began to adapt some of his stage successes to the movie screen. His first two adaptations were *Pygmalion* and *Major Barbara*.

Lesser British dramatists of the period were neither as trenchant as Shaw in their attacks upon society nor as influential. Sir Arthur Wing Pinero wrote numerous plays which enjoyed popularity during the early years of the century. The finest of Pinero's dramas is *The Second Mrs. Tanqueray* (1893), a play dealing with the question of whether a woman "with a past" can be accepted by polite society. Sir James Matthew Barrie became noted as an exponent of whimsy and the fantastic in drama. The world knows Barrie best for his creation of Peter Pan, "who never grew up." Sentiment pervades *Quality Street*, mild satire *What Every Woman Knows*, while some critics judge *The Admirable Crichton* to be Barrie's best play.

In Ireland prior to the war there evolved a strong interest in a national theater. Yeats, as noted earlier, was one of the leading figures in the fostering of this movement, and he even contributed some romantic plays to it. Lord Dunsany, like so many of his countrymen, displayed a splendid Celtic wit coupled with strong imaginative powers. *The Glittering Gate*, produced first at the famous Abbey Theater in Dublin in 1909, heralded a prolific output by Dunsany. Irish drama assumed its most realistic and trenchant forms following the First World War and remains to this day a brilliant, original contribution to the twentieth-century theater.

Prewar American literature. American literature went along much the same path as that of England during the first decade of the present century. The old standards of virtue and progress had been severely shaken in the face of upheavals in the scientific and industrial world. However, economic conditions in the United States were more favorable than in the British Isles, the American people were believing more and more that their culture was equal to that of Europe, and an air of easy optimism permeated the country. With the exception of Walt Whitman and some outstanding nineteenth-century humorists, the writers of this country had followed patterns imported from England. But in the twentieth century American poets, playwrights, and novelists were to achieve a vigorous independence. This maturity and originality of thought were to appear because of the impact of World War I.

American poets. One of the more conservative poets of the prewar era was Edwin Arlington Robinson. This Maine poet and many times Pulitzer prize winner achieved recognition for his ability to incorporate spoken language into his rhymes and for his interest in philosophical problems. Another important New England poet who gained fame before 1915 was Robert Frost. True to his background, Frost has interpreted the spirit of staunch Puritan self-reliance and individualism. In his studies of the New England scene he perceives the dignity of the farmer in his constant struggle against the forces of nature. He is suspicious and fearful of the changes brought about by industrialism in his New England, and he apparently does not look upon the future with much confidence.

Amy Lowell came from a distinguished New England family. It was her custom to introduce herself as "Amy Lowell of Brookline, Massachusetts." She traveled much and developed varied tastes for European and oriental art. As a leader in the imagist school of poetry she cultivated unorthodox patterns in subject matter and style. But she did little if anything new in breaking away from traditional literary themes. In addition to many volumes of poetry she published a definitive life of John Keats and an analysis of his poetry.

Prose writing in prewar America. American prose was prolific from 1890 to 1910. William James was not only an outstanding philosopher but also a gifted essayist with a warm and pungent style whose thoughts were concerned with American democracy "that worked." George Santayana may not appear prewar because of the phenomenal success of his autobiographical novel, *The Last Puritan* (1936), but his writings began in the nineties. Santayana is a materialist and skeptic who at the same time clings tenaciously to an affection for classical beauty. Henry Adams was one of the most far-seeing intellectual figures in New England. He is justly famous for his *Mont-Saint-Michel and Chartres,* a keen analysis of the spirit which motivated medieval art and society, and his *Education of Henry Adams,* a criticism of contemporary American life. Henry Adams saw clearly the crass materialism in which American society was then wallowing, and he prophesied that "a new social mind" would be required to restore sanity to our thought and coherence to our actions.

The novelists prior to the First World War were varied in their approach to writing. Hamlin Garland, representative of the regional type of novelist, portrayed faithfully and simply scenes of the middle west far from fashionable New England and New York. Quite a few novelists arose to call attention to maladjustments in society, and their influence was not inconsiderable. Frank Norris had a short life, but he embodied in his work the naturalism of Zola and wrote with powerful intensity. Such works as *The Octopus* and *The Pit* expressed the need for social justice in the American scene.

Jack London wrote exciting yarns and used the theme of survival-of-the-fittest to good advantage. *The Sea Wolf* is still widely read. Jack London is also remembered for such novels as *The Iron Heel,* portraying in all its most terrible forms a Fascist type of society—long before Fascism itself appeared on the political horizon. Another American novelist with a distinct flair for "social significance" is Upton Sinclair. His most influential book was *The Jungle.* This vivid account of the sordid state of affairs existing at that time in the stockyards of Chicago had much to do with the passage of more stringent regulations for the safeguarding of public health.

Prior to the First World War American literature produced its most facile, if not most brilliant, exponent of the short story, William Sydney Porter, known as O. Henry. His humor and the ability to conclude his tales with a sudden and quite unexpected turn of situation achieved national popularity for his stories. O. Henry analyzed concretely and sometimes with startling clearness the sort of existence which the average American led, and he has given us much of the spirit of the New York of about 1907 in his famous collection of short stories, *The Four Million.*

Effects of the war. The First World War could not fail to bring radical changes in the literary world. If these changes were not immediately observable, it was because the writers who were to be primarily conditioned by the conflict were in the trenches. The older writers continued to write largely in terms of a nostalgic longing for the now fleeting values of Victorian stability. The younger writers came out of the holocaust embittered, disillusioned, and eager to condemn the traditional standards of society. The youths who had been promised that the war was to save the world for democracy and to create a world fit for heroes to live in emerged from the trenches to find their illusions shattered.

Poetry during the war. Little worth-while poetry was written during the years 1914-1918 by either English or Americans. Rupert Brooke, a Cambridge graduate who loved life with the exuberance of youth, was able to compose some noteworthy war sonnets before succumbing to fever in the Mediterranean. Wilfred Owen, another victim of the war, was one of the most gifted of all the war poets. Despite the fact that he won the Military Cross for conspicuous bravery, Owen hated war intensely. Still another English war poet who came to hate the futility that the First World War appeared to represent was Siegfried Sassoon, a holder of the Distinguished Service and Military crosses. Sassoon has also written poetry and prose on other subjects, but his most brilliant and biting work resulted from the fact that the last great struggle failed to create a better world or to act as the war to end all wars.

New trends and techniques. With the war over, those writers who were left returned to experiment with new literary theories and techniques. Imagist poetry, an attempt by means of word pictures to objectify personal moods, and free verse, an abandonment of the techniques of versification, came into prominence. At the same time writers openly abandoned the manners and moral standards prevailing prior to the war. Theodore Dreiser analyzed man in terms of body chemistry and animal instincts and wants. The postwar world had come into a new phase—the age of jazz and of bathtub gin.

Poetry of disillusionment. From the literary standpoint, the twenties in America have been called the "Waste Land age." The name is derived from T. S. Eliot's poem *The Waste Land,* which was published in 1923. This work epitomized the atmosphere of skepticism and negation which pervaded the intellectual world both in England and the United States. Eliot, a Harvard-educated American, was the standard-bearer of the new movement.

"He, better than anyone else, summed up in his poetry the pessimism current in the literature of both countries. First of all he set out to negate all that the romantic poets had insisted upon as truth about life. In his early poems he attacked religion and love. Religion was the opium of the people, and love was a pathological sickness. As for tragedy, there was none save the tragedy of being born. Once you were born, life was a living death to be gone through in utter boredom. Men had lost their passion. If Eliot wrote a spring song, it was to state that spring no longer awakened man to delight. If he wrote a love song, it had to do with a bored young man in spats who could not make up his mind to declare himself."[1]

Other poets acclaimed Eliot's tone of disillusionment and followed suit. E. E. Cummings took pleasure in satirizing established institutions. Cummings has been called "the playboy of the Waste Land." Another poet who sought escape from his social environment and who had little faith in his fellow man was Robinson Jeffers. Jeffers has written his poetry in a stone tower which he built for himself on the Pacific coast. Writing dramatic poetry in which violence and unusual human emotions predominate, Jeffers finds comfort in associating himself with the elements in all their tempestuous strength. Like other Waste Landers, Jeffers decries the commercialism of modern society, nor does he accept the political philosophy that men are created equal and deserve equal rights. There is a defeatist attitude among the poets of this school which mirrors the disillusionment of postwar years, a bankruptcy of constructive ideas. It has been suggested, however, that this period of negation was a necessary prelude to attitudes of constructive thinking.

Novels of the Waste Land era. The novelists who rose to prominence after the war in America and the British Isles were as disillusioned and skeptical as the poets. Freud's psychology heightened interest in the complexes affecting human personality, and novelists hastened to dissect the psychological patterns of the characters which they created. As a result these writers often delved into the abnormal and neurotic, and a spirit of moral disintegration frequently characterized their studies of character and society alike.

Ernest Hemingway rocketed to fame after the war with vivid and dynamic novels peopled with a strange assortment of derelict characters. The disillusionment which is apparent in Hemingway's early stories was doubtless acquired in large part during the last war when as an ambulance worker on the Italian front he was indelibly affected by the carnage about him. Two of his novels deal with the effects of the First World War, *The Sun Also Rises* (1926) and *A Farewell to Arms* (1929). A revolutionary at heart, Hemingway recently wrote a best-seller about the Spanish Civil War entitled *For Whom the Bell Tolls* (1940). In so far as he interests himself in attacking social injustice and hopes for a better world for man to live in, Hemingway has separated himself from the sterile Waste Land school.

An English novelist who emphasizes the spirit of disillusionment and frustration is Aldous Huxley, the grandson of the famous Darwin champion, Thomas Huxley. Aldous Huxley has written verse, essays, and novels. In all media he has displayed facile wit, clever satire and cynicism, and a deep-seated feeling of skepticism regarding society's ability to act intelligently. Among his most widely read novels are *Crome Yellow* (1921), *Point Counter Point* (1928), and *A Brave New World* (1932).

James Joyce, one of the most influential novelists of the century, was a native of Dublin, which is the setting of his most famous story, *Ulysses*, as well as of the carefully woven short stories, *The Dubliners*, and of the spiritual autobiography, *Portrait of the Artist As a Young Man*. Joyce was unusually gifted in his ability to set down the flow of images surging through the subconscious mind, and he added to his "stream-of-consciousness" technique a universality of learning and a frank and even startling realism that displayed itself in earthiness of vocabulary. *Ulysses* is a vivid analysis of the experiences in the lives of a mixed group of characters during a single day in Dublin. Through this cross-section of humanity Joyce points out the disorder and complexity of modern civilization. The work is permeated with an atmosphere of frustration and even decadence.

O'Neill's dramas of pessimism. A dramatist who during the twenties also spoke pessimistically of the age and who probed mercilessly into the psychological abnormalities of human nature was Eugene O'Neill. This American playwright has shattered academic concepts regarding play structure. Some of O'Neill's plays, like *Mourning Becomes Electra* (1931), take many hours to present. In *Mourning Becomes Electra*, O'Neill reintroduced the Elizabethan device of the aside, whereby his characters speak twice, once to give the conventional remark, once to convey to the audience the real thoughts in the character's mind. O'Neill has been concerned with many topics: *The Long Voyage Home* portrays the life of the common sailor in a freighter's forecastle, *Anna Christie* is a story of human regeneration, and *Emperor Jones* is a study of primitive mentality. In 1936 O'Neill received the Nobel prize for literature.

Lewis' satirical novels. Sinclair Lewis was the first American author to be awarded the Nobel prize for literature (1930). He earned this distinction because of the group of brilliant novels satirizing American life. In *Main Street* (1920) Lewis showed that, contrary to the accepted view that the big city was a den of iniquity while the small town was the harbor of virtue and high thinking, the latter was sometimes the repository of petty and even vicious social attitudes. In *Babbitt* (1922) Lewis laid bare the superficiality of an average successful businessman with his false values and poverty of ideas. So incisive was Lewis' satire that the terms "Main Street" and

"Babbitt" have passed into our everyday vocabulary. Sinclair Lewis emphasized the shallowness, artificiality, materialism, and hypocrisy which existed in so much of American life during the twenties and did much to deflate the egotism of the era.

Literature in the thirties. The great period of stock-taking and the evolution of writers from a state of social negation to a sense of social responsibility did not take place until after the crash of 1929 and the ensuing depression. During the years of unemployment, bank failures, hunger marches, and the rise of dangerous totalitarian movements in Europe, authors began to see that there was more to write about than the boredom of the Four Hundred or the psychological maladjustments of abnormal characters.

The thirties produced a large number of books imbued with "social significance." But long before this trend set in, there had been writers in America who perceived the need of social adjustment and who, because of their faith in the intelligence of the average people, believed that democracy could work.

Carl Sandburg. One of these was the colorful poet, Carl Sandburg, champion of the industrial era in America and its potentialities for the common people. Sandburg called one of his books *The People, Yes* (1937), and that phrase embodied much of his philosophy. To him, the people are the most vital of all subject matter and most worthy of consideration, and their existence—despite its mixture of idealism, beauty, and ugliness—is worth recording. Sandburg has no use for sham or for those institutions which in any way exploit the people. Besides writing virile poetry about the American scene, Sandburg has made two further contributions of note: in *The American Songbag* (1927) he compiled a rich collection of American folk ballads. He has also found time to write the several-volumed, important biography of Lincoln—*The Prairie Years* and *The War Years.*

Literature with a purpose. The thirties produced many writers who dealt with the romance of groups and masses rather than of persons and who stressed collectivism instead of individualism. To improve the lot of the "one-third ill-housed, ill-clothed, and ill-nourished" had become their goal. Much of their work was propaganda of the most obvious sort, but it had a vitality and purpose lacking in the Waste Landers of the twenties. The novels of John Steinbeck and the plays of Clifford Odets, two examples chosen at random, are compositions of outstanding power and appeal.

It is not possible to forecast what literary trends may develop in the present decade. As the whole world became embroiled in the Second World War, however, it seemed that most writers were determined to grapple with its more profound implications and perhaps to avoid the sometimes shallow cynicism of the twenties.

French writers. The First World War exacted a heavy toll among France's men of letters, but men still carried on the French literary traditions. The novelists stand out, especially such men as Jules Romains, Romain Rolland, Marcel Proust, and André Gide. Romains has been interested in showing how men totally unknown to each other are bound together by secret and powerful ties. In *Mort de Quelqu'un* he indicates how the death of an ignorant tenant in a large Paris apartment house affects all the other lodgers.

Romain Rolland has been a staunch internationalist and during the First World War severely criticised France as well as the other combatants for engaging in it. Rolland's finest effort is *Jean Christophe* (1907-1912) which, while depicting the biography of a musical genius, at the same time throws strong light on contemporary social and intellectual patterns. Rolland is an idealist much influenced by the Russian Tolstoy and by the music of Germany's Wagner and Richard Strauss—all of which help to account for his internationalism.

Marcel Proust has been attacked by some critics for making his novels look like "the contents of a chiffonier scattered helterskelter on the floor." Despite such criticism, Proust excelled as a psychological novelist. He delighted in vivisecting men's motives, especially in *Remembrance of Things Past* (1913-1927). André Gide is still another master of the psychological novel and brings to it a genius at observation. So concerned is he with intimate problems of conduct that he has been termed "a moral immoralist."

French drama has seen two important figures in this century: Eugène Brieux and Edmond Rostand. Brieux's plays are penetrating social analyses. Some are concerned with problems of marriage, while *The Red Robe* (1900) exposes the machinations of those members of the legal profession who place success above the innocence of their victims. Rostand was both a poet and a playwright. The world today knows him best for his *Cyrano de Bergerac.* This masterpiece of humor and pathos, in which the long-nosed hero, a mixture of swashbuckler and poet, attempts with great gallantry to attain the unattainable, has a quality about it which never fails to excite sympathy on the part of the audience.

German men of letters. Among the most outstanding German novelists of the twentieth century are Lion Feuchtwanger, Jakob Wassermann, Erich Maria Remarque, and Thomas Mann. Nearly all competent German writers have fled from their homeland to escape the chauvinistic and bigoted cultural concepts of the Third Reich. Feuchtwanger has written some novels whose setting lies in the Middle Ages but which reflect rather the disillusionment of postwar Germany. Wassermann's most famous work is *The World's Illusion,* revealing a penetrating psychological power reminiscent of Dostoevski, by whom he was much influenced. Remarque's *All Quiet on the Western Front* (1929) swept through the western world and told it the unvarnished facts about the brutality and bestiality of modern warfare.

Thomas Mann is the greatest living German writer. His fame was established in 1903 with the publication of *Buddenbrooks: Ruin of a Family,* a masterly analysis of character extending over a period of generations. Perhaps Mann's masterpiece, however, is *The Magic Mountain* (1924), a beautifully written, moving novel about life in a tuberculosis sanitarium in the Alps. In such an environment Mann shows how completely relative both time and human values become, and he conveys deftly the strange atmosphere pervading such a place. In recent years Mann has written a trilogy centering around the Old Testament figure Joseph, and he expands the simple story of Joseph and his brothers into a fascinating psychological study. In 1929 Mann was honored with the Nobel prize for literature.

Writers of other nations. Mention can be made here of only a few of the outstanding literary figures in other countries. Norway produced Sigrid Undset, who won the Nobel prize in 1928 for her famous series of novels about fourteenth-century Norway. The finest prose writer in recent Russia has been Maxim Gorki, a staunch supporter of the new régime and much honored by it for his literary efforts. Gorki, a realist, wrote numerous stories showing the tragically primitive conditions under which the peasants lived during the czarist days. Out of regard for the novelist, his birthplace Nizhni Novgorod (famous since medieval times as a great fair site) was renamed Gorki.

Two Italian literary figures are Gabriele d'Annunzio and Giovanni Papini. D'Annunzio was an egotist who was pictured as a romantic character; after the Peace Conference in 1919 had denied Fiume to Italy, he occupied it himself in protest. A man of many love affairs, a poet of beauty and sensuality, d'Annunzio proclaimed himself an ardent patriot who championed the Fascist cause and as an old man offered his services in a military capacity to Il Duce. Papini has written some lovely prose, notably a devotional *Life of Christ,* in which he shows his inherent mysticism and emotionalism.

A great Spanish prose writer was Vicente Blasco Ibáñez, who concerned himself with economic and social problems of his native land and who achieved world renown in 1916 for his great war novel, *The Four Horsemen of the Apocalypse.* A non-European poet who won worldwide distinction for the beauty and thought of his verse was Sir Rabindranath Tagore, the Bengali poet who received the Nobel prize in 1913.

Art and Music

New directions in art. Discontent with old types of artistic expression appeared, as we have seen, in the nineteenth century, particularly in France. Impressionists, breaking away from the academic, evolved a new color formula and a less realistic approach. Cézanne, Gauguin, and Van Gogh, keeping the unacademic approach and the color of the Impressionists, emphasized structure and composition in their pictures.

The search for new types of expression has continued among contemporary artists. Henri

Matisse exemplifies the leadership of France in the early twentieth century. Matisse simplifies forms and expresses them with an almost oriental line, using flat, brilliant colors. His painting has none of the didactic about it. Compare his work with that of a social commentator like Orozco (page 497) and notice the difference in approach.

Matisse is more interested in beauties of line, pattern, and color than in teaching a lesson or stating an opinion. He has been influenced by the art of eastern and primitive peoples and has incorporated their brilliant color and design in his technique. His all-over patterns, his denial of western perspective, and his use of line show the eastern influence.

The series of photographs of a Matisse painting, "Blue Dress" (pages 492-493), shows the development of the painting from a sketch to a carefully composed design of flat colors with lines scratched into the paint. The illustration at the right, page 493, is the finished painting. One can see the way the artist has seized upon certain features and emphasized them to carry out his design. Note the way in which the settee, the ruffles on the front of the dress, and the flowers behind the model's head have all been composed to emphasize the design.

For those who consider the flat pattern and strong stylization of Matisse's work extremely modern, it is interesting to turn back to Egyptian and Cretan murals (Volume One, pages 47 and 111) and notice their distorted and decorative figures. Renaissance painters with their interest in the scientific and realistic representation of objects (see Da Vinci, Volume One, page 449, and Van Eyck, Volume One, page 459) left in Europe a conception of painting which lasted until the late nineteenth century. Many modern painters feel that this type of expression is not representative of twentieth-century life. They feel that the photograph takes the place of the painting as an exact record of people, events, and customs and that the painter's task lies elsewhere.

Many influences from all parts of the world and all periods are to be seen in modern art. The contemporary artist, through better communication and better reproduction of works of art, is surrounded by influences of all kinds. The multiplicity of influences in part accounts for the many types of modern painting. The primitive influence has been strong. Men like

MATISSE: SKETCH AND FURTHER DEVELOPMENT FOR "BLUE DRESS"

Picasso and Matisse were interested in primitive African art, and distortions such as those seen on African masks (page 258) appear in many modern paintings.

Cubist experimentation. After the First World War the reaction against academic painting continued. A certain group of artists followed Cézanne in the portrayal of an object by planes and gradually simplified the object into a series of geometric planes. Pablo Picasso, a Spaniard who settled in Paris, was the most famous exponent of the new "cubism." An object was no longer of interest for its own sake; rather the artist was concerned with the problem of representing the planes of an object in space on a two-dimensional surface.

This problem of course exists whether the object is simplified into geometric planes or whether it is dealt with in a more realistic manner. The cubists chose to experiment with the more simplified planes. Compare Picasso's "Woman with Mandolin" (page 494) with Cézanne's "The Portrait of a Peasant" (page 210) to see this development. After Picasso had tired of this approach, other cubist painters in Paris continued to experiment and modify along this line.

Abstract painting. The cubist experiments with abstract relationships started many different types of "abstract painting." Of these Fernand Leger, in murals and smaller paintings, represents the more mechanical type. In his expertly designed canvases the influence on art of modern technological developments is apparent. Leger has clearly been influenced by the machine. His "Accordion" (page 494) shows this influence in the machine-like forms represented. Some abstract painters, such as the Russian Wassily Kandinsky, have found a freer, more lyric expression, while in others, like Georges Braque, the object is still recognizable. Although this preoccupation with artistic problems with little interest in subject matter has perhaps not been understood by the public and has led to a certain alienation of the artist from the public, the experiments have produced much excellent painting and have been of great value to other artists.

Picasso's influence. Picasso abandoned the cubist approach later and passed through many phases. He has been the greatest artistic experimenter of an age full of experiments and has had an important influence on other artists. An excellent draftsman, Picasso has abandoned realism for abstractionism, dis-

MATISSE: SUCCESSIVE SKETCH AND FINISHED PAINTING, "BLUE DRESS"

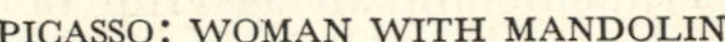

PICASSO: WOMAN WITH MANDOLIN

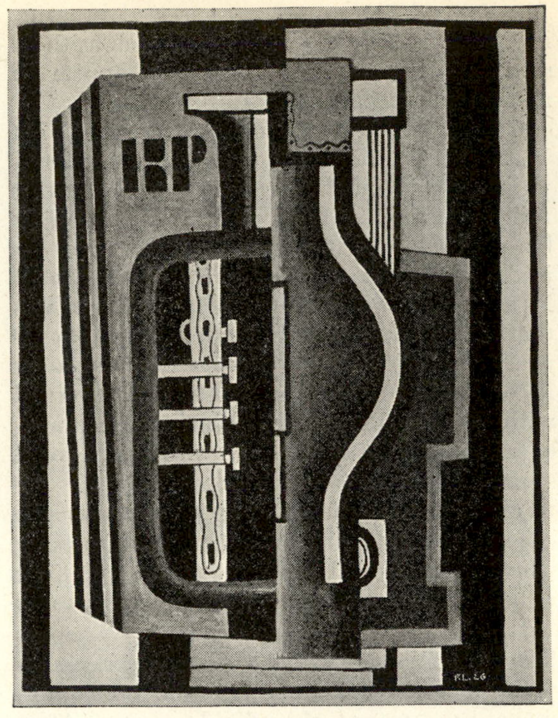

LEGER: ACCORDION

tortion, surrealism, and numerous other devices. Some younger painters without Picasso's artistic knowledge have copied his techniques without any understanding of his purpose, but for others this prolific painter has opened many new channels for study. In the process he has himself produced works of great artistic value. The Guernica mural was painted to express Picasso's horror at the Fascist air raids on a small defenseless Spanish town. Painted only in black, grey, and white, it is a mass of distortion, conveying vividly the horror of the scene. Compare it with the painting "Massacre of Scio" by Delacroix (page 208), a romantic's interpretation of an equally horrible event, the massacre of Christians by the Turks during the Greek wars of independence.

Surrealism. Another modern development is surrealism, with its acceptance of the validity of the subconscious and dream world. The surrealist, in contrast to the abstractionist, chooses a more realistic technique to express fanciful scenes. Surrealist pictures depend for their effect on unexpected combinations of objects. Very carefully planned and thoughtfully painted, they are extremely subjective expressions of one man's dream world, and for this reason they may lack a necessary universal appeal. One well-known surrealist artist is Salvador Dali, a Spaniard, whose canvases filled with weird combinations of objects are strong in mood and craft even if sometimes hard to decipher in symbolism. "The Persistence of Memory" shows this meticulous craft, with the tiny flies and ants on the watches painted in every detail. These objects, combined with the vast expanses of empty space, give the painting a mood of strangeness.

American painting. In America, the twentieth century has brought a new interest in the arts, and painting has made great advances. We have seen that painting in this country to the end of the nineteenth century was greatly influenced by European models. Since 1900, however, the American artist has grasped his medium with increasing sureness and originality. Many painters reacted against what they considered the too refined, too abstract approach of the French school. They turned to their own country and its people for subject matter and depicted its everyday life. This reaction against the more abstract approach of the French school may have led

PICASSO: GUERNICA MURAL

some artists too far toward making the story-telling element over-important, but it was a necessary reaction which has freed us from a copying of European art. It is natural that American art should show the influence of Europe, partly because of the many nations and races represented in our population, but these influences are being blended, not copied.

An example of the American artist's interest in his own country is Grant Wood,

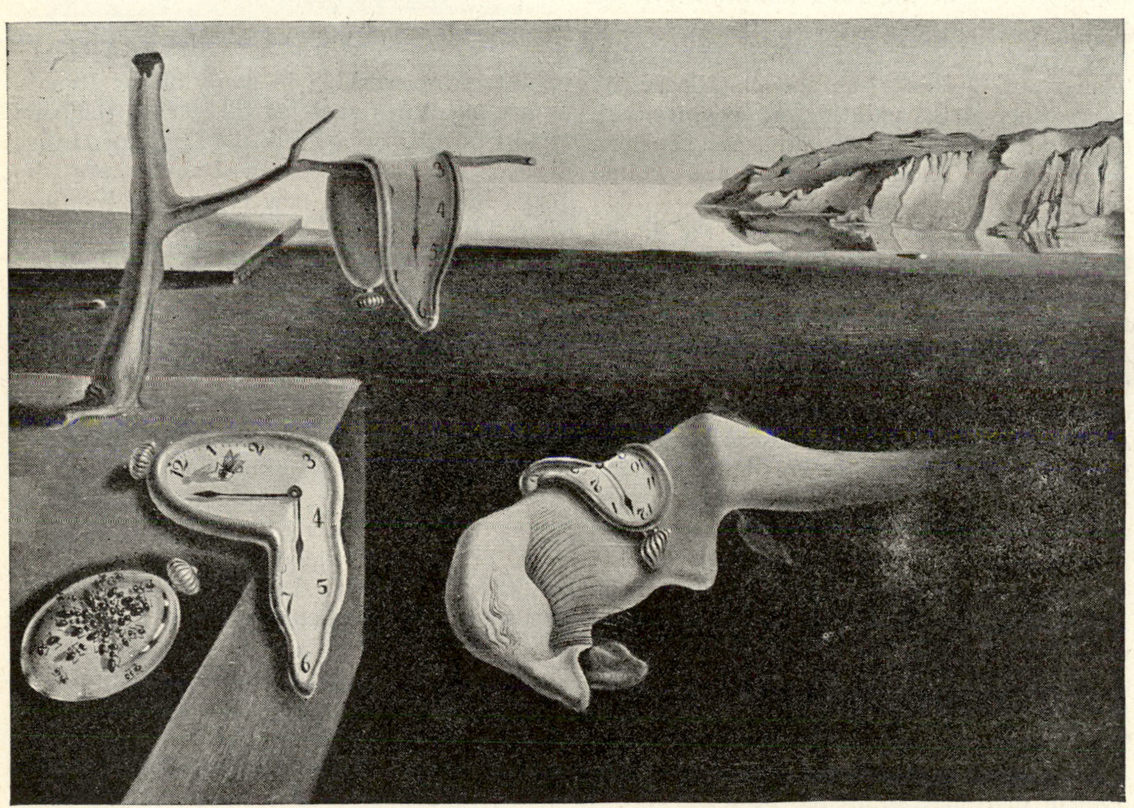

DALI: THE PERSISTENCE OF MEMORY

WOOD: AMERICAN GOTHIC

RIVERA: THE MARKET

the portrayer of the Iowa landscape. Wood was also an excellent satirist and won recognition (and hostility) for such canvases as "American Gothic" (see above). There are many other artists painting our country with great skill and understanding, among them John Sloan, Thomas Benton, and Zoltan Sepeshy.

South American painting. In the Latin-American countries the influence of Europe remained strong until very recently. The colonial period, like its counterpart in North America, produced a few "primitive" local painters, but it was not until the twentieth century that the South American countries became fully aware of their national identity. Painters such as Cândido Portinari in Brazil broke away from the Spanish-Renaissance type of painting and experimented with techniques better suited to express the more vigorous life of the New World (see "Morro," page 497). Portinari's use of dark earth-colors contrasted with vivid reds and yellows and his rebellion against the polished European technique combine to make him a vigorous exponent of South American life.

Interest in the artist's craft. Another development in American art has been the revival of interest in the artist's craft. Contemporary painters are working in many of the Renaissance mediums such as oil glazes, tempera, and fresco, as opposed to the almost exclusive use of impasto oil paint. Painters are also experimenting with new types of paints produced by modern chemists. Graphic arts (lithography, wood cutting, etching, and so on) are becoming popular as a means of reaching more people. A method of making color prints used formerly in commercial work (silk screen) is being tried as an artistic medium. Thus the artist is seeking to reach a larger public, and many scientific discoveries of the last two centuries are helping him.

Mural painting. An important feature of modern art is the renaissance in mural painting. This development has been made significant in the United States by the numerous artists employed by the federal government to decorate schools, libraries, post offices, and other public buildings. Much inspiration for mural work has come from Mexico, where this type of decoration has made great forward strides led by such men as Diego Rivera and José Clemente Orozco. Rivera is notable for his successful revival of the fresco tech-

OROZCO: THE FIRST BATTLE OF THE REVOLUTION

nique in mural painting. Not only is he a competent designer and a forceful storyteller, but he has skillfully blended the folk art of Mexico with concepts of the present-day industrial age.

Orozco designs his social documents freely. Compare his "First Battle of the Revolution" with Rivera's "The Market" to see the differences of technique and composition. The work of Rivera is stylized and carefully patterned. Notice the patterning of the hats and balloons in the market scene (page 496). The paint is applied carefully and in large areas. Contrast this with the more emotional work of Orozco, who applies paint in a free manner, with emphasis on the brush strokes.

It is also interesting to compare these two Mexican muralists with such Renaissance mural painters as Giotto and Raphael (Volume One, pages 440 and 450) and with Roman, Cretan, Egyptian, and Indian mural designers (Volume One, pages 173, 111, 47 and 48, and 265) to see different ways of handling mural decoration. It is important to remember that, although the social background of the period changes, the problems confronting a painter in the actual handling of the wall space—such as composition, appropriate color, and observance of architectural requirements—are the same in any age. Compare the way in which different cultures have solved, or tried to solve, these problems.

PORTINARI: MORRO

POOR: DEPARTMENT OF JUSTICE MURAL

MILLES: THE ORPHEUS FOUNTAIN

Fresco is a medium which has been neglected since the Renaissance. Many of the murals sponsored by the federal government are done in fresco and in tempera. Henry Varnum Poor's murals in the Department of Justice building in Washington illustrate the use of the arts in interpreting such American concepts as justice, freedom, and equality. The three panels around the door show the operation of justice after a man is sentenced to prison. In the top panel (above) he is taught skills to help him find work upon his release. In the right-hand panel he rejoins his wife.

Recognition of the artist as a member of the community with a definite contribution to offer is an important step toward ending the period of "splendid isolation" of the artist, an attitude which developed during the nineteenth century. We are moving again toward the Renaissance conception of the artist as a recognized part of society.

Modern sculpture. Sculpture is once again becoming one of the major arts, as it was in Egypt, Greece, and the Italian Renaissance. Whereas it remained relatively static throughout the nineteenth century except for the efforts of Rodin, sculpture has again entered upon a dynamic phase. Artists are using an increasing number of mediums, including plastics, with interesting and novel results. Sculpture is being used more and more in connection with architecture, and the two arts are being blended sympathetically. It is no longer bound by the academic tradition of a mere realistic depiction of the model.

The result is a new sculpture, much more abstract, geometrical, and symbolic than heretofore.

Some of the European countries have produced excellent sculptors, such as Sweden's Carl Milles (now working in the United States), who is renowned for his many fountains of bronze in Sweden and America. Milles combines a fine sense of the architectural setting of his sculpture and a respect for his material with a very lyrical approach. The Orpheus Fountain (opposite) in the marketplace in Stockholm shows his lyricism and architectural sense.

A much-discussed figure in modern sculpture is Jacob Epstein, an American living in London. He has executed many bronze portraits which have created controversy because of their abstract quality and distortion. His sculpture on the British Medical Building shows one attempt to make sculpture a decorative part of architecture.

Aristide Maillol is a French sculptor in whom the true classic tradition is strong. With no attempt to imitate classic motifs, his monumental simplicity and restraint produce in this French sculptor an expression akin to the Mediterranean Greeks. The war memorial at Banyuls is an example of the way in which Maillol respects the material he works in. The simple, strong treatment of the stone is most impressive and adds greatly to the emotional quality of the monument.

EPSTEIN: BRITISH MEDICAL BUILDING SCULPTURE

Constantin Brancusi is a Rumanian who worked in Paris. He is searching for new ways to express ideas which have appealed to the sculptor for centuries. This discontent with realism appears throughout contemporary art. "Bird in Space" (page 500) is the work of a man who, upon completing careful traditional studies, felt he must go further in his searching.

As in painting, there is a multiplicity of influences in sculpture, and there is also interest in the forms of primitive sculpture such as that of the Negroes, South Sea Island-

MAILLOL: WAR MEMORIAL AT BANYULS

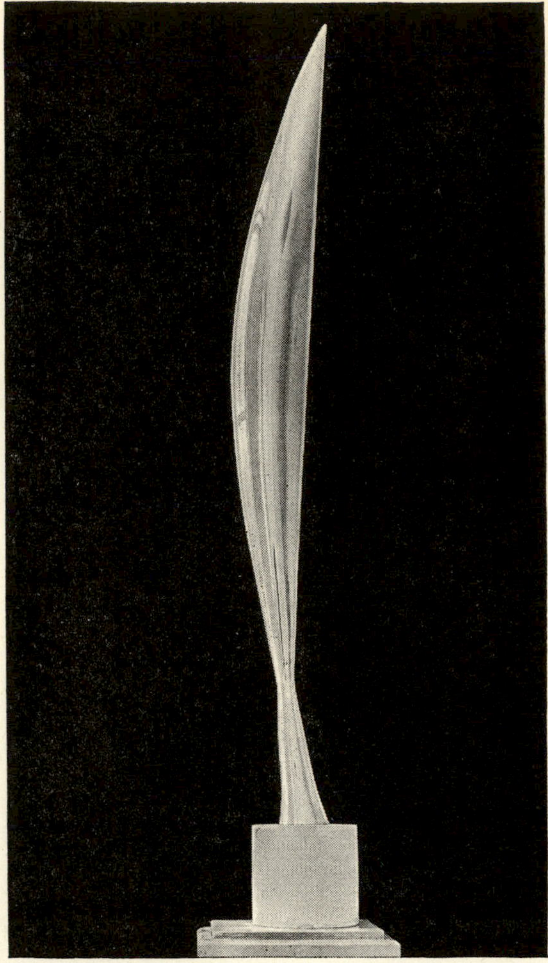

BRANCUSI: BIRD IN SPACE

ers, and other primitive peoples. America is quickly realizing the importance of sculpture as architectural decoration and is making strides in this field. Again, government competitions for public building have provided opportunity and encouragement. The New York World's Fair and similar exhibits called for sculptural decoration, giving impetus to the development of the art.

New trends in architecture. Architecture has also made spectacular advances in the twentieth century. New materials, such as steel, reënforced concrete, and glass, have made new types of construction possible. New uses for buildings such as factories, new community needs, new commercial needs, and new types of transportation have presented hitherto unknown problems to the architect. Many still fail to face the new problems

THE SUPREME COURT BUILDING

frankly and continue to escape by grafting old styles onto twentieth century buildings. This use of old styles has been very popular and has been called "eclecticism." It is far from dead yet, and many of our public buildings are still built in styles which have little to do with our civilization. An example of these is the Supreme Court Building in Washington, the façade of which is styled after a Greek temple with Roman columns (above). The general proportions of the building are well handled, but it is a question whether this borrowing of old styles is expressive of our national life.

We have heard much of the word "functionalism." It is not a new idea. The Gothic cathedral was functional in its plan and in its expression of use. A modern functional building also expresses its plan, its use, and the methods of construction used.

In the early twentieth century the functional architect felt that a building should be simplified and stripped of all decoration. This resulted in the so-called "international style," examples of which are the group of workers' houses by J. J. Oud at Hook of Holland (page 501), the Karl Marx Hof in Vienna (page 381), and the modern apartment building in Montevideo illustrated on page 399. Such men as Le Corbusier in France and Walter Gropius in Germany (now in America) were greatly influenced by the mechanical developments of the time. The Scandinavians developed from their tradition of craftsmanship a functional architecture with decorative detail. Contrast the Karl Marx Hof (page 381) with the Stockholm apartment buildings (page 383) and notice the greater use of contrasting planes and levels in the Swedish buildings to give variety and interest.

The United States has also witnessed many departures from traditional architecture. The most spectacular development in American architecture has been the skyscraper. Louis Sullivan was one of the earliest exponents of functionalism, and his early skyscrapers were the first to treat the new construction in a frank manner. Built primarily in large cities where real estate space is at a premium and dependent upon such modern innovations as structural steel and elevators, the skyscraper has evolved into a unique edifice in which efficient height, strength, and simplicity of line have been successfully harmonized. The skyscraper is an example of the steel structure which is now the framework for all large modern buildings. Such buildings as the RCA Building in Rockefeller Center (at right) express this structure frankly, using stone and cement merely as insulation and protection against the weather (see diagram, page 503). In the illustration of the RCA Building the clean vertical lines, emphasizing the structure rather than masking it, contrast vividly with

THE RCA BUILDING

OUD: WORKERS' HOUSES AT HOOK OF HOLLAND

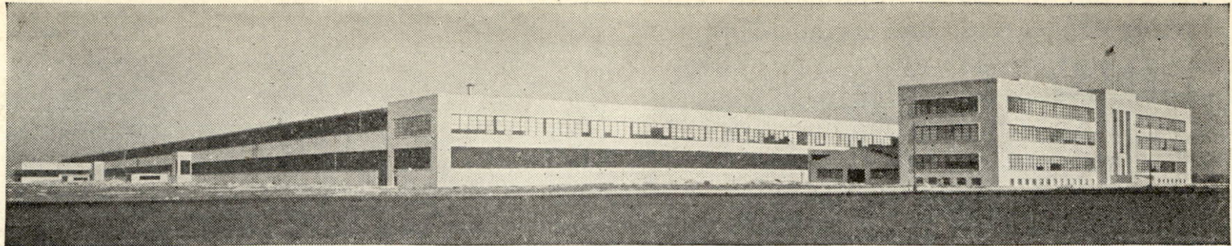

KAHN: MODERN INDUSTRIAL PLANT

the profile of the pseudo-Gothic church in the foreground. Many skyscrapers have been built with modern methods of construction covered with Gothic, Byzantine, classic, or other such decorations. Modern architects are questioning the use of this type of decoration on structures built for twentieth-century uses. New types of construction, such as reënforced concrete and the development of the cantilever, used crudely in Mycenae (Lion Gate, Volume One, page 112), have encouraged new architectural forms. "Falling Water" (page 503) is an example of the contemporary use of the cantilever principle.

America has also developed new architectural forms from her industries. The ugly industrial buildings of the nineteenth century have now become well designed and efficient.

TVA GENERATORS

The new industrial building makes no attempt to hide its function by pretending to be something else, but it uses the new structures needed in industry to create interesting design. This can be seen in the grain elevator shown on page 387. New demands have necessitated the construction of huge factories which are being designed in a dramatic manner making frank use of the structures developed for new industrial methods. Albert Kahn is an outstanding architect of industrial plants. (See the plant pictured above.) Other feats of American engineering, which in their frank design may well be classed as architecture, are such great dams as those of the TVA (see illustration, page 393). The great generators in these dams (below) are excellent examples of the exciting design which can be produced with modern engineering equipment.

The domestic architect of private houses has also developed a new approach and new forms. Men like Frank Lloyd Wright have demonstrated the value of applying functional principles to the building of dwellings and of harmonizing the home with its environment. A house such as "Falling Water" (opposite) is built to harmonize with its surroundings and to make use of the features of its site to dramatize the house. In the use of new materials, and local materials where that is possible, in the scientific planning for living, and in the sound design of all elements of the composition, modern domestic architects are challenging the appropriateness of Old English, Hispano-Mooresque, and such importations for the houses of the twentieth century.

City planning. An important development in contemporary architecture has been the interest in logical city planning and in the planning of residential districts. Nineteenth-century cities grew up with no rhyme or

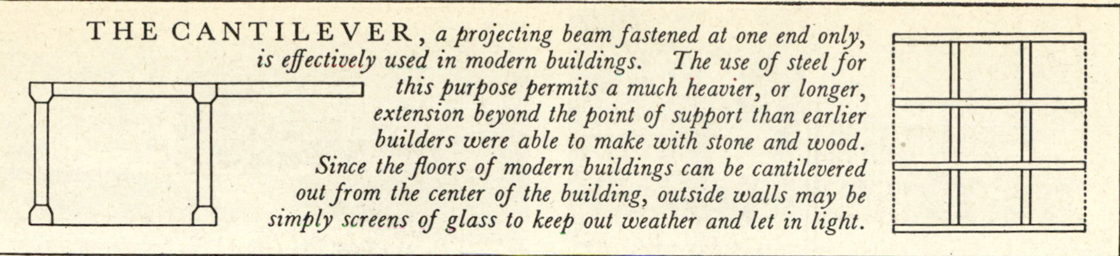

THE CANTILEVER, *a projecting beam fastened at one end only, is effectively used in modern buildings. The use of steel for this purpose permits a much heavier, or longer, extension beyond the point of support than earlier builders were able to make with stone and wood. Since the floors of modern buildings can be cantilevered out from the center of the building, outside walls may be simply screens of glass to keep out weather and let in light.*

reason and now present problems of transportation and housing. On page 504 is a section of the congested area in New York. Although Manhattan is probably one of the most extreme cases of overcrowding, the problem exists in urban areas throughout the country.

The tendency of modern city planning is toward decentralization and development of small self-sufficient residential communities, with large arteries routed around them (see Greenbelt, page 504). An attempt is being made to place these communities so that they will be conveniently near industry without being surrounded by the grime and unpleasantness of industrial sections. In the communities themselves attempts are made to place houses in green settings and not in rows on streets. Problems such as pedestrian traffic are specially provided for, and some communities are planned so that a pedestrian can reach any section without crossing a street.

New defense housing needs are also providing opportunities for architects to meet the housing needs of our working people. Well-known architects such as Walter Gropius and Eliel Saarinen are being called on for such projects. It may be that in spite of the destructive implications of defense industries we may realize good from their demands in efficient planning of communities. Architects

WRIGHT: FALLING WATER

CONGESTED AREA IN NEW YORK

HOUSING IN GREENBELT, MARYLAND

will have a great program of reconstruction to face after the war, and it is to be hoped that they can bring to it a full realization of the necessity for the esthetic as well as the scientific in a community.

Household arts. The minor arts in the twentieth century have been greatly changed by the industrialization of our civilization. What was once done by hand is now turned out by mass production. In the last few years good design based on functionalism has been applied to our industrial arts. Our everyday

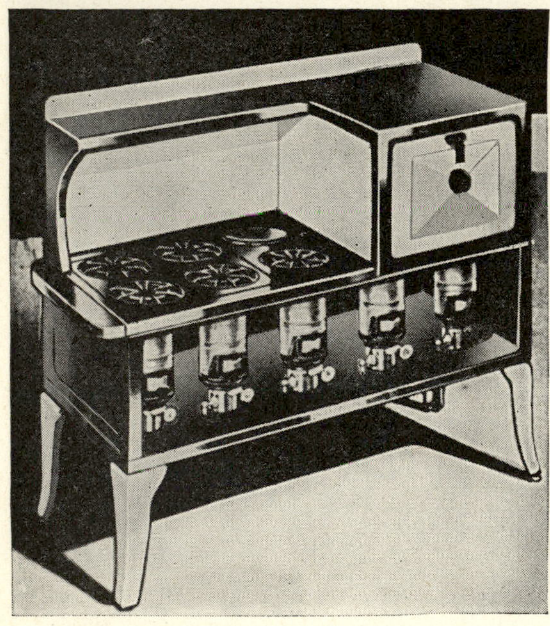

OLD-TYPE KEROSENE STOVE

MODERN KEROSENE STOVE

MODERN TEXTILES MADE AT CRANBROOK ACADEMY

household appliances show this change; we are beginning to realize that there is no reason why an object of practical use should be ugly or covered with decoration which is better suited to a baroque picture frame. Industrial designers are not only producing more efficient appliances but are making use of good proportions and simple surfaces to make them more attractive. A comparison of two stoves illustrated opposite shows the manner in which industry has recently begun to combine functionalism with good proportions to produce household appliances which are both better looking and more useful. (Notice the greater storage and work space, for example.) The glassware illustrated is another example of functionalism applied to household objects. Industry is also becoming aware of color and is using it to enhance simple objects.

Although mass production takes the place of a great many handicrafts, people still enjoy the beauties of handmade objects. Crafts of various regions in America, such as the Kentucky mountains, are being encouraged, and refugees from Europe are bringing with them high standards of artistry. But perhaps the most typical expression of our civilization at present is the object produced by the machine, and it is encouraging to note the new appreciation of good design in industry. Contemporary pottery craftsmen, metal-workers, and weavers are making experiments with new techniques and are designing in new ways suggested by these techniques. Experimentation with texture is shown in the picture of weaving samples above. Articles of everyday use—irons, cars, books, dishes, and thousands of others—are all more interesting when frankly and appropriately designed.

Music. While poets, architects, painters, and sculptors have been groping for new patterns to express the spirit of the twentieth century, the same searching process has characterized modern music, which has rebelled against the conventional forms and attitudes of the past. The results have been significant. Music has broken with the nineteenth-century ideal of a fixed tonality and instead is experimenting now with the absence of any fixed tonic key, called atonality, or the superimposing of one key upon another, called polytonality. Music has thereby achieved a fresh freedom and vitality, abetted by experiment in new rhythmic patterns.

KITCHEN GLASSWARE

The chaos of our present social and economic world is often reflected in the use of harsh dissonances by many composers, but it is significant to note that what is condemned as radical by one generation may be often accepted without question by its successor. Much modern music strikes some of us as ugly because we do not understand the purpose of its composer, but he may well be vindicated by a later age which he foreshadows in his work, just as Beethoven and Wagner had to wait for music lovers of future decades to appreciate them fully. As Paul Bekker, the music critic, points out concerning modern trends: "We forget that Bach, Haydn, Mozart, and Beethoven were just as modern in their times as our young composers are today. We forget that these young composers write music that is different not because they want to but because they *must*. And they must, because different perceptive powers live and thrive within them, and because in this very state of being different the creative energy of life finds its expression."[2]

Claude Debussy. One of the most significant and popular of modern composers has been Claude Debussy, the French impressionist. A master of orchestration and tone color, Debussy maintained that the music of his day had become too conventionalized and was no longer expressing the spirit of the age. He made such radical innovations in modern music as using at times oriental scales, a whole-tone scale, and varieties of harmony such as some of the medievalists knew. He does not subordinate chords and themes, and his harmonies are brought into the piece complete in themselves. Once heard, his music is immediately recognizable. Debussy is famed for his nocturnes, which include *Clouds* and *Festivals,* his symphonic poem *La Mer* (*The Sea*), such preludes as *The Engulfed Cathedral* and *Afternoon of a Faun,* numerous piano works which include *Clair de Lune,* and an opera *Pélléas et Mélisande.*

Maurice Ravel. A French composer whom Debussy affected strongly was Maurice Ravel. Born in the Pyrenees not far from Spain, Ravel was attracted to Basque rhythms and harmonies, which he incorporated with great success into his compositions. The world knows him best for a typically Spanish piece, *Bolero,* a sensuous, rhythmic, hypnotic masterpiece of orchestration. However, Ravel has composed better works, including numbers for the piano, much chamber music, the popular *Mother Goose Suite,* and sensuous music for the ballet *Daphnis et Chloë.*

Russian composers. Another modern composer noted for ballet music is Igor Stravinsky, a Russian who has lived much of his life in Paris. Stravinsky is known the world over for the clashing dissonances and shifting rhythms with which his colorful music abounds. He is a great exponent of polytonality. Most famous among his ballet suites are *The Firebird, Petrushka,* and the bacchanalian *Rite of Spring.* He has written other compositions as well, including piano and violin concertos, and in recent years has become engrossed in composing music of a much more classical form than those pieces which brought him fame.

Three other Russian composers should be mentioned also. Alexander Scriabin was a musical mystic who evolved a "Mystic Chord," a new system of harmony. Among his best-known numbers are *Ecstasy* and *Poem of Fire.* Serge Prokofieff, versatile as a composer, pianist, and conductor, has composed a *Classical Symphony,* as well as piano music and an opera called *The Love of Three Oranges.* A young Soviet composer who has attracted wide fame for his unusual talent is Dmitri Shostakovich, whose first and fifth symphonies especially are standard numbers in the repertoire of all first-class orchestras. Shostakovich shows brilliant mastery of orchestration as well as rich imaginative gifts. Imbued with Socialist ideology, Shostakovich maintains there is no such thing as "art for art's sake" but that the composer is bound to interpret his milieu and social philosophy. While the Nazis were bombing Leningrad, he completed his *Seventh Symphony* in the midst of his wartime duties.

Modern German composers. Two Germanic composers have added lustre to the great musical tradition behind them. Richard Strauss is in some respects a disciple of Wagner and has composed several excellent operas, notably *Der Rosenkavalier* (1911). Strauss has a brilliant ability to create rich melodies and orchestrate them in a sumptuous fashion. Among his most popular tone poems for orchestra are *Death and Transfiguration, Till Eulenspiegel's Merry Pranks,* and *A Hero's Life.*

Arnold Schönberg, a Viennese composer, is perhaps the most radically minded musician of importance living today. He is a master theorist in the field of harmony and is famous for having devised a twelve-note system of tones unrelated to any key center. Such a system is argued to be simply a mathematical progression of existing musical theory, but its effects upon contemporary audiences are notable. Perhaps Schönberg is right and will be vindicated by future decades, but at present his attack upon classical concepts of tonality has won him more enemies than admirers. Paul Hindemith is another German modernist who, like Schönberg, has experimented widely in problems of tonality.

Finland's Sibelius. A man considered by some critics to be the twentieth century's most outstanding composer is Jean Sibelius, of Finland. He has attracted attention not for tonal idiosyncrasies but for his rich, sincere compositions. To use his own figure of speech, the Finnish composer is not interested in giving the public sparkling champagne but cold, clear water. Yet this cold, clear water constitutes some of the most satisfying music to have come out of our age. Besides writing numerous songs, Sibelius has composed such tone poems as *The Swan of Tuonela, En Saga,* and *Pohjola's Daughter.* But perhaps his finest work has been in the field of symphonic composition. Sibelius has written seven symphonies, of which the most widely known are the First, Second, Fifth, and Seventh. The Seventh is written in one continuous movement and shows Sibelius' interest in following an important trend in modern music: brevity.

Other noted modern composers. Ottorino Respighi, an Italian composer, has won distinction for such symphonic poems as the *Fountains of Rome* (1916) and the *Pines of Rome* (1924). A gifted Spanish musician is Manuel de Falla, who has written in his native style such compositions as *Night in the Gardens of Spain* and *Three Cornered Hat.* England, never prominent for its composers, has contributed two gifted musicians: Frederick Delius, a blind composer who wrote such pieces as *On Hearing the First Cuckoo in Spring,* and Cyril Scott, an English disciple of Debussy, who is noted for many piano pieces and songs. Two of the most gifted living American composers are Roy Harris, a composer of symphonies, and John Alden Carpenter, the author of *Adventures in a Perambulator* (1915).

Jazz. A vigorous development in modern American music is jazz. This type of music derives largely from Negro rhythms. With this form of dance music has evolved another characteristically American institution, the popular dance band, with emphasis upon clarinets, saxophones, traps, and trumpets. Jazz has been elevated at times to a dignified level by certain American composers, notably George Gershwin, who became famous in New York with his musical comedies. Gershwin first attempted to create jazz in a serious vein with the writing of *Rhapsody in Blue* in 1923. Later Gershwin composed his *Piano Concerto in F* (1925) and *An American in Paris* (1928). No one can foretell the ultimate role of jazz in serious music—whether or not it represents the folk song of our age—but no one can ignore its importance in modern culture.

Summary

Some physicists about 1900 were rash enough to state that the basic discoveries in their field had already been made and future generations could hope to add only a decimal place or two to existing equations. But this complacent attitude was annihilated early in the twentieth century by the quantum theory of Max Planck, the relativity theory of Albert Einstein, and Sir Ernest Rutherford's new atomic theory in which protons and electrons were found to make up the "indivisible" and "solid" atom. The results of these discoveries are so far-reaching that we do not yet know their ultimate consequences, but already the world has seen giant strides made in astrophysics, cosmic rays, and "atom smashing" by which it may be possible to create a whole world of new marvels by disturbing and rearranging the structures of atoms.

Biochemistry developed during the century, and the British biochemist, Sir Frederick Hopkins, did valuable research in the study of vitamins. Knowledge was also gained as to the function of the little-known ductless glands, while Sir Frederick Banting was foremost in using an extract made from sheep's pancreas, insulin, to prolong the lives of sufferers from diabetes. Sir Ronald Ross discovered the role of the mosquito in transmitting malaria, American doctors conquered yellow fever, and other scientists developed serums against many other diseases. Preventive medicine has become increasingly important in the twentieth century, and public health measures have helped stamp out the recurrence of many of the scourges which periodically used to decimate vast portions of the population.

Artists, tired of old forms, are seeking ways to express contemporary life. Matisse and other Frenchmen sought new techniques of expression early in the century, while Picasso began to construct patterns along geometric lines, the movement becoming known as cubism. Interest in mural painting has revived, and artists are experimenting in new mediums. There is an added interest in the arts, and the artist is beginning to be recognized again as an important member of society. In architecture the keynote is functionalism. Houses, offices, and factories are frankly designed according to use. The architect has become more aware of the social implications of his work and has made progress in the planning of whole communities and of building for community life, to suit the needs of residents. In all the arts artists are attempting to find types of expression suited to our civilization, instead of being content with old styles disguising the real spirit of our times.

Modern science has influenced contemporary philosophical views. William James and other American thinkers applied the experimental method of science to philosophy to get a body of ideas that "work" in everyday living. Henri Bergson, the French philosopher, created a school of thought based largely on biological discoveries and showing points of contact with the relativity theory. Bertrand Russell and Alfred North Whitehead are two other philosophers who have sought to correlate philosophical views with present-day scientific discoveries. Jacques Maritain is the leader of the Thomists, Catholic philosophers who stress the unifying value of their views.

Contemporary educational standards have increased enormously, with great new areas of the world receiving mass instruction in reading and writing for the first time. New philosophies of education have made their appearance in our times, notably in the United States. Educators make attempts to use scientifically devised tests to ascertain the intelligence and aptitude quotients of students and by new techniques to stimulate the child's potentialities.

Religious organizations have also shown a tendency to stress social values. In many cases the older aspects of theology have been discarded, and religious bodies tend to concentrate more on those ethical concepts in which the teachings of the great religious teachers so richly abound.

Twentieth-century literature has struck out along new paths, leaving behind many of the standards and patterns which the Victorian age thought indispensable. Poets and novelists have mirrored in their works the changing social environment, and the periods of skepticism, disillusionment, and cynicism brought about by the upheavals in the political and economic spheres have been reflected in contemporary literature. During the postwar years many American and British writers moved in a wasteland of despair and negation, but the economic crisis of the thirties galvanized writers into action against social injustice.

Still another science that has made great progress is psychology. Probably the youngest of the major sciences, psychology is being placed on as exact a basis as possible. The pioneer research of the Russian Pavlov, led to Watson's psychology of behaviorism which stresses man's mechanical reaction to stimuli. A different emphasis is that of the *Gestalt* psychology worked out by the Germans Wertheimer, Köhler, and Koffka. Probably the most radical development, however, has been that of Freud, the founder of psychoanalysis, Jung, and Adler who base man's actions on the operation of the unconscious.

Music has not escaped the changes in standards which occurred in science, literature, and art. There early arose a strong reaction against the romanticism of the previous century, and composers experimented with new concepts in tonality. Claude Debussy was a dominant figure in modern music, for he was a guiding spirit of the new school of musical impressionism. Debussy made use of chords which united far-removed intervals, such as chords of the eleventh and thirteenth intervals. The result was brilliant tone color which has become an important element in twentieth-century music. Our age has produced many other gifted composers, including Jean Sibelius, Richard Strauss, Igor Stravinsky, and Dmitri Shostakovich.

Aids to Further Study

Chart of Contemporary Events

Occasional reference to this chart from the chronological tables at the head of each chapter will indicate the parallelism of events throughout the world.

Date	England and The British Empire	France	Germany	Italy	Smaller European Countries	Russia	North and South America	India, China, Japan, Oceania
1500			Hanseatic League in decline	Decline of Venice	Portuguese commerce supreme			
	←MARTIN LUTHER AND THE RELIGIOUS REVOLT→						Spanish exploration Conquest of Mexico and Peru	
	Henry VIII establishes Church of England		Fuggers, bankers					
	←THE COUNTER REFORMATION→						French exploration of Canada	
1550	←NATIONAL STATE SYSTEM CRYSTALLIZED→						Brazil colonized by Portugal	
	Elizabethan Age in literature Defeat of Spanish Armada	Henry IV	Peace of Augsburg		Spanish empire and commerce supreme			
	←RISE OF DIPLOMATIC PRACTICE→							
1600	East India Company				Dutch East India Co.	Beginning of Romanov dynasty	Colonization of Atlantic coast	Netherlands East Indies exploited
	←BEGINNING OF THIRTY YEARS' WAR→							
	Beginning of scientific method Age of mercantilism Puritan Revolt Commonwealth Period				Dutch trade supreme		Great migration to New England	British open trading post at Madras
1650	←PEACE OF WESTPHALIA→							
	Restoration Great fire in London First insurance company Hudson's Bay Company	Louis XIV and Absolutism East, West India Companies	←DISUNIFICATION→		Commercial wars—Holland vs. England Period of Spanish decline			
1675	Habeas Corpus Act Glorious Revolution Bill of Rights William and Mary Bank of England	Revocation of Edict of Nantes			Great age in Spanish painting			
1700	Union of Scotland and England *Asiento* gained from Spain Hanoverian rulers Walpole Prime Minister	Treaty of Utrecht ends wars of Louis XIV				Peter the Great westernizes Russia	13 American Colonies established	English East India Co. founds trading post in India Decline of Mogul Empire in India
1725		Age of Voltaire, Rousseau, and Montesquieu	Frederick William I					
	←AGE OF REASON→							
1750	Commercial supremacy							

	England and The British Empire	France	Germany	Italy	Smaller European Countries	Russia	North and South America	India, China, Japan, Oceania
1750	← BEGINNING OF INDUSTRIAL REVOLUTION →							
1750–1775	Seven Years' War with France New inventions in textiles Watt's steam engine	Loses Canada, India to British			Poland partitioned by great powers	Catherine the Great gains Black Sea port	Canada gained by British from French	India gained by British
1775–1800	First settlement in Australia	Turgot's attempt to break up guilds French Revolution Reign of Terror Directorate Napoleon rules			Third partition of Poland		Quebec Act in Canada American Revolution Articles of Confederation Constitution	Dutch control Netherlands East Indies Manchu decline in China
1800	Ceylon acquired	Sale of Louisiana to U. S. Defeat of Waterloo				Napoleonic invasion fails	War, U. S. vs. England	
	← CONGRESS OF VIENNA →							
1825	Singapore secured Burma annexed	Bourbon restoration	Germanic Confederation		Norway given to Sweden	Alexander forms Holy Alliance	Mexican independence Brazilian independence Monroe Doctrine Jacksonian democracy in U. S.	British East India Company supreme in India
1825–1850	First railroad Faraday's dynamo First Reform Bill New Zealand settled	Louis Philippe, King Revolution of 1848 Second Republic	Zollverein formed Abortive revolt	Young Italy formed by Mazzini Constitution granted	Greek independence Belgium gains constitution			Chinese rivers, ports opened
1850	← AGE OF INTELLECTUAL OPTIMISM →							
1850–1875	Bessemer process in steel Second Reform Bill Gladstone, Disraeli, prime ministers	Louis Napoleon and Second Empire Indo-China acquired Acquisition of Algeria Franco-Prussian War Third Republic	Bismarck's work Unification complete Three Emperors' League	Cavour annexes Lombardy, Sicilies, Venetia Unification complete	Alexander II crushes Polish revolt Austria defeated by Bismarck	Crimean War Alexander tries liberalism Liberation of serfs	Age of dictators in Latin America Civil War in U. S. Maximilian abdicates in Mexico Federal union, Canada	Perry opens up Japan Sepoy Mutiny in India End of East India Co. rule in India *Shogunate* overthrown in Japan Japan westernized
1875–1900	Suez Canal acquired Intervention in Egypt Third Reform Bill Labor Party formed Boer War	Protectorate over Tunisia Dreyfus case Control over Indo-China	Congress of Berlin Large areas claimed in Africa	Joins Triple Alliance Defeat in Abyssinia	Leopold of Belgium claims Congo	War with Turkey over Balkans Foreign investments Alliance with France Social Democratic Party organized	First Pan-American conference U. S. annexes Hawaii Spanish-American War	Indian National Congress formed Sino-Japanese War Treaty of Shimonoseki Foreign concessions in China
1900	Australian Commonwealth Japanese Alliance Triple Entente Union of South Africa Parliament Act	Separation of Church and State Algeciras Conference Moroccan protectorate		War with Turkey Tripoli acquired	Austria annexes Bosnia-Herzegovina Portuguese republic Balkan wars	War with Japan Peasant revolt Trans-Siberian railway	Venezuela dispute Gentleman's Agreement, U. S. and Japan Panama Canal opened	Open Door Policy Boxer Rebellion Morley-Minto reforms End of Manchu rule in China Japan annexes Korea
	← FIRST WORLD WAR →							
1918			Republic established	Italy joins Allies		Communist Revolution Czar murdered	U. S. enters war Wilson's Fourteen Points	Japan's Twenty-One Demands on China

Year	England and The British Empire	France	Germany	Italy	Smaller European Countries	Russia	North and South America	India, China, Japan, Oceania	Year
1919	LEAGUE OF NATIONS								1919
		National Bloc government	Treaty of Versailles Reparations imposed Weimar Constitution	Fiume seized by D'Annunzio	Poland recreated Czechoslovakia and Yugoslavia formed Finland independent	Civil war between Reds and Whites	Eighteenth amendment in U. S. Social reform in Mexico	Treaty of Sèvres with Turkey Rowlatt Acts in India	
1920	Brief economic boom		Hitler organizes National Socialist Party	Treaty of Rapallo with Yugoslavia	Aland dispute settled by League Masaryk president of Czechoslovakia	War Communism period	U. S. refuses to join League or World Court Nineteenth amendment in U. S.	Gandhi's civil disobedience campaign	1920
1921	Postwar depression			Fascist party formed	Horthy dictator in Hungary Irish Free State	New Economic Policy	Rise of middle class in Mexico	Sun Yat-sen president in China	1921
	NINE POWER TREATY								
1922	Bonar Law, premier	Little Entente Alliance with Poland	Reparations payments stopped	Mussolini assumes government	Austria receives financial aid from U. S.	U. S. S. R. created	Fordney-McCumber Tariff Act in U. S.	Greco-Turkish war	1922
1923	Leadership of Baldwin	Occupation of Ruhr	Inflation, financial collapse Hitler's Munich *Putsch*	Corfu dispute with Greece	Rivera, Spanish dictator		Teapot Dome oil scandal in U. S.	Earthquake in Japan Treaty of Lausanne revises Sèvres Ataturk, dictator	1923
1924	MacDonald, first Labor prime minister Conservative government takes over	Alliance with Czechoslovakia Evacuation of Ruhr Left Cartel ministry	Dawes Plan Hitler begins *Mein Kampf*	Murder of Matteoti		New constitution Death of Lenin Stalin wins over Trotsky as leader	Johnson Immigration Act in U. S.		1924
1925	LOCARNO TREATIES								1925
		Dangerous monetary policy		Fascist Party supreme			Coolidge, U. S. president	Death of Sun Yat-sen Manhood Suffrage Bill in Japan	
1926	General strike Imperial Conference	Pact with Rumania National Union government		Syndicalism established in economic structure	Pilsudski dictator in Poland			Chiang Kai-shek dictator in China	1926
1927	Trade Disputes Act								1927
1928	KELLOGG-BRIAND PACT								1928
		Treaty with Yugoslavia				First Five-Year Plan	McNary-Haugen bill in U. S. Hoover, president Pan-American Conference	Simon Commission tours India	
1929	MacDonald heads Labor government	Poincaré's retirement	Young Plan				Stock market crash in U. S. Strict immigration act in U. S.		1929
1930	WORLD ECONOMIC DEPRESSION								1930
	London Naval Conference				Carol reascends Rumanian throne		Smoot-Hawley Tariff Act in U. S.		
1931	Off gold standard National Coalition under MacDonald Statute of Westminster		Hoover Moratorium	National Council of Corporations set up	Abdication of Alfonso		Wickersham Report in U. S.	Round Table conferences in London Manchuria invaded by Japan	1931
1932	Free trade abolished Ottawa Imperial Economic Conference International Economic Conference				Salazar dictator in Portugal			Japan puts puppet ruler in Manchukuo	1932

	England and The British Empire	France	Germany	Italy	Smaller European Countries	Russia	North and South America	India, China, Japan, Oceania	
1933		Stavisky scandal Paris riots National Union government	Withdrawal from League Reichstag fire Enabling Act makes Hitler dictator Anti-Jew boycott			Second Five-Year Plan Decreased illiteracy	Pan-American Conference U. S. abandons gold standard Good Neighbor policy	T'ang-ku Truce Japan leaves League	*1933*
1934			Blood purge of Nazi leaders Non-aggression pact with Poland	Reorganization of Corporate state	Assassination of Alexander of Yugoslavia Civil war in Austria Boris' dictatorship	Joins League	Export-Import Bank established Platt Amendment abrogated by U. S.	Tydings-McDuffie Act for Philippines	*1934*
1935	Baldwin, prime minister	Laval, premier Hoare-Laval agreement over Abyssinia		Conquest of Abyssinia	New Polish constitution legalizes dictatorship		Social Security Act in U. S. Neutrality law in U. S.	Government of India Act	*1935*
1936		Popular Front under Blum Socialist legislation	Four-Year Plan Rome-Berlin Axis Anti-Comintern Pact Rhineland remilitarized		Metaxas dictator in Greece Fascist revolt in Spain	New democratic constitution Treason trials	Pan-American Conference, Buenos Aires	Kidnaping of Chiang Kai-shek	*1936*
1937	Chamberlain, prime minister	New conservative government	Demand for *Lebensraum* Niemoeller in concentration camp	Withdrawal from League Mussolini visits Hitler Adheres to Anti-Comintern Pact				Reopening of Sino-Japanese war Fall of Nanking	*1937*
1938			Nazi purge Invasion of Austria	Chamber of Fasces and Corporations formed	Carol dictator in Rumania	Third Five-Year Plan	Pan-American Conference at Lima	Fall of Canton Japan declares "New Order in Asia"	*1938*
	←MUNICH AGREEMENT→				Sudetenland occupied				
1939			Jewish persecution Non-aggression pact with Russia Invasion of Poland		Final victory of Franco Czechoslovakia capitulates	Pact with Germany	Revision of U. S. neutrality law U. S. fleet to Pacific	Japan dominates Indo-China	*1939*
	←SECOND WORLD WAR→								
1940	Retreat from Dunkirk Churchill, premier Battle of Britain	Nazi invasion and conquest Vichy government	Occupation of Denmark and Norway Low Countries invaded Military alliance with Japan, Italy	War declared against France Invasion of Greece Defeat in Africa	Rumania dismembered		Selective Service Act in U. S. Third term for Roosevelt	Burma Road closed, reopened	*1940*
1941	Atlantic Charter Pact with Russia Occupation of Syria Nazis routed in Africa Fall of Hong Kong	Cooperation with Nazis	Submarine warfare Revolt engineered in Iraq Invasion of Crete		Bulgaria joins Axis Yugoslavia attacked Greece overwhelmed	Nazi blitzkrieg Invasion of Iran	Lend-Lease Bill Atlantic Charter Repeal of neutrality	Thailand under Japanese control	*1941*
							←PEARL HARBOR→		
1942	Air raids on Germany		Drive in Egypt			Nazi advance to Caucasus oil	Fall of Philippines, Wake, Guam Rio Conference Coral Sea, Midway Battles All-out production	Cripps Mission to India Java, Burma fall Aleutian moves	*1942*
1943									*1943*

Tables of Cultural History

A survey of the history of man—his governmental, economic, social, religious, intellectual, and esthetic activities—from the earliest times to the present, in Europe, in Asia, in Africa, and in the Americas.

Religion

Intellectual Activities

Science

Education

Philosophy

Government and Politics

Economics

Social Life and Customs

Esthetic Activities

Architecture

Sculpture

Painting

Music

Literature

The Reading of History

The right book. "If I could only lay my hands on just the right book" is a plaintive statement heard in many libraries. But the right book is often elusive and hard to find. Information regarding every aspect of human activity—politics, business, religion, art, literature, etc.—has been accumulating for several thousand years. The bulk of this lore now resides in books of which there exist hundreds of thousands in each of the major divisions of man's pattern of culture. The field we have been dealing with in this volume —a kind of panorama or bird's-eye view of the whole business of human living throughout the ages—is of course very wide and the literature available for its study, enormous. It is the purpose of this section to aid the reader in obtaining that "right book," and more particularly to introduce him to various short cuts to desired information, to acquaint him with a few standard books in each of the major fields of the history of civilization.

Where to look. The first step in acquiring an understanding of some particular topic is usually to consult a reliable bibliography. These are legion; in fact one can consult bibliographies of bibliographies. Perhaps the most valuable general list of books dealing with world history is the *Guide to Historical Literature,* edited by G. M. Dutcher and others (1931). In the main it deals with political history supplemented by some references to social and economic aspects of world history. This reference book is divided into sections such as General History, Africa, United States, France, etc. Each section contains a comprehensive list of books. These are briefly described and evaluated and in addition attention is called to the original reviews which came out when the books appeared.

L. J. Paetow's *Guide to the Study of Medieval History,* revised edition (1931), will smooth the path of anyone seeking information in the study of medieval civilization. This famous bibliography is not exclusively political but contains lists of the most valuable sources in the science, religion, art, and social life of the middle ages. Skimming through its pages one notes such sections—each with a descriptive outline and a bibliography—as the Crusades, the City of Paris, Medieval Art, and the Life of the Nobles.

A well-chosen selection of books on European developments from 1500 down to the present can be found in Ferdinand Schevill's *History of Europe,* revised edition (1940), pp. 781-789. This list is particularly well suited to the general reader, not the specialist, for in Schevill's own words he has listed only "spark-plug books, that is, volumes which, having literary as well as historical merit, make easy and pleasurable reading." This bibliography contains references to science, literature, art, and economics in addition to the usual political topics. In American history useful bibliographies can be found in most of the standard one- or two-volume surveys on this subject. A case in point is S. E. Morison and H. S. Commager, *The Growth of the American Republic* (1930). This two-volume work contains two bibliographies amounting in all to eighty pages. Many of the books listed are briefly described and evaluated.

Political history and international relations during the past quarter of a century are two of the most important and challenging fields in world history, constituting the immediate background for the gigantic movements that have changed the political map of the world in the past few years. One of the most helpful guides to reading in these subjects is W. C. Langsam's bibliography in *The World Since 1914,* 4th edition (1940).

Useful aids. The need often arises for one to check the sequence of events in some particular period of world history. Several excellent books are at hand to fill such a need. *A Dictionary of Dates,* edited by Ernest Rhys (1940), G. P. Putnam's *Handbook of Universal History* (1936), and *Ploetz's Dictionary of Dates* (1935) are the best known. The last named was first issued in 1880 in Germany. The work of a sound historian, it soon became famous and was translated into English. It is now out of print, but this old standard reference book has been modernized under the direction of W. L. Langer under the title of *An Encyclopedia of World History* (1940).

Good sources for maps are all too scarce. Perhaps the most useful volume in this connection is W. R. Shepherd, *Historical Atlas,* 7th edition (1929). Putnam's *Historical Atlas* (1927) will be found helpful as will also the volume exclusively devoted to maps in the *Cambridge Modern History* series, Volume XIV (1912).

There seems to be rather general agreement that the *Encyclopaedia Britannica* is the best encyclopedia for all purposes. The fourteenth edition (1929) contains the latest information available in this source, but the eleventh edition (1911) is more detailed and hence more valuable for the general reader except for those new trends and topics which have emerged during the past twenty-five years. The *Americana* (1941) encyclopedia is another outstanding reference especially good for its articles on science. One of the most significant events in recent American scholarship was the completion, during the years 1929-1935, of the *Encyclopaedia of the Social Sciences* in fifteen volumes. Eminent scholars from all over the world contributed in this undertaking. Although many articles are technical, written for specialists, the beginner and general reader should always consult this source.

In the field of biography two works of high merit and great usefulness should be noted. The first is *The Dictionary of National Biography,* 25 volumes, edited by Davis and Weaver (last edition 1939), in which can be found scholarly biographies of deceased British men of note. The second is *The Dictionary of American Biography,* 20 volumes, edited by Allen Johnson and Dumas Malone (1928-1936), which presents adequate surveys of our American worthies. The last two volumes to be listed as useful aids can solve many problems. I. G. Mudge, *Guide to Reference Books,* 6th edition (1939), has been a standard work for over a decade. Louis Shores, *Basic Reference Books* (1939), issued under the auspices of the American Library Association, is more recent and more readable.

Important cooperative works. The neophyte in world history should become familiar as soon as possible with several great cooperative works in this field. Among the most important in the field of European political history are the three monumental English series: *The Cambridge Ancient History,* 9 volumes (1923-1939), *The Cambridge Medieval History,* 7 volumes (1911-1936), and *The Cambridge Modern History,* 14 volumes (1903-1928). Another important English cooperative undertaking is the "Legacy" series. So far the following titles have appeared: *The Legacy of Islam,* edited by Sir Thomas Arnold and A. Guillaume (1931), *The Legacy of Greece,* edited by R. W. Livingstone (1921), *The Legacy of India,* edited by G. T. Garratt (1937), *The Legacy of Rome,* edited by C. Bailey (1923), *The Legacy of the Middle Ages,* edited by Crump and Jacob (1926), and *The Legacy of Egypt,* edited by S. R. K. Glanville (1941). These volumes are rich in all manifestations of civilization. America has also found time to produce noteworthy cooperative histories. One such set is *The American Nation: A History* (largely political), edited by A. B. Hart, 28 volumes (1906-1918). More recent and much more concerned with social, economic and intellectual aspects is the twelve-volume set, *The History of American Life,* edited by A. M. Schlesinger and D. R. Fox.

The raw stuff of history. History as read by the layman is usually in the convenient form of an account prepared by the professional historian in which events, causes, results, and interpretations are blended into a complete whole. Sometimes, however, it is essential and worth while to go back of the secondary account to what we know as primary sources. These consist of government documents, memoirs, letters, tattered newspapers, diaries, etc., the raw material from which the historian reconstructs the past. Benjamin Franklin's *Autobiography,* for example, throws much light on conditions in colonial America, as does Francis Bailey, *Journal of a Tour in Unsettled Parts of North America in 1796 and 1797.* The *Chronicles* of Sir John Froissart is an invaluable source for the period when knighthood was in flower in France and England. Chauncey Canfield's *Diary of a Forty-Niner* (1920) gives a vivid account of the gold rush in California. The student may obtain a fascinating glimpse into medieval university life from C. H. Haskins' study of the life of medieval students as seen in their letters in his *Studies in Medieval Culture* (1929).

Numerous collections of source material

have been prepared by scholars. *Historical Selections* by Hutton Webster (1929) gives representative documentary material covering the entire span of world history. The general field of European history is covered by J. H. Robinson and C. A. Beard, *Readings in Modern European History,* 2 volumes (1908-1909), and J. H. Robinson, *Readings in European History,* 2 volumes (1904; 1906). The volume by J. F. Scott and A. Baltzly, *Readings in European History Since 1814* (1930) will prove of value. Two source collections may also be noted in the American history field: H. S. Commager, *Documents of American History,* 2 volumes (1935), and William Macdonald, *Documentary Source Book of American History, 1606-1926,* 3rd edition (1926). In medieval history J. F. Scott, A. Hyma, and A. H. Noyes have made available their *Readings in Medieval History* (1923). W. C. Langsam, *Documents and Readings in the History of Europe Since 1918* (1939) is valuable for the study of contemporary developments. As a background for studying the first and second world wars W. H. Cooke and E. P. Stickney, *Readings in European International Relations Since 1879* (1931) will be found most useful. Future primary materials that will occupy the study of future generations of scholars and general readers are in process of creation even now: *Mein Kampf* (1939 edition) by one Adolf Hitler, the speeches of Winston Churchill, letters smuggled out of occupied France, perhaps William Shirer's *Berlin Diary* (1941), and Clarence Streit's *Union Now with Britain* (1941).

Surveys of world history. H. G. Wells, the famous English sociologist and novelist, made history in 1920 when his *Outline of History: A Plain History of Life and Mankind* was published. This work was immediately popular and had a tremendous sale. It was a pioneer attempt to break away from the previous preoccupation of most historians with political developments, and to make history include all the aspects of human activity. Although Wells' *Outline* is inadequate for many topics and periods of world history and although some of his interpretations are not sound, it still remains one of the most satisfactory and brilliant syntheses of world history. One-volume editions are now available. In 1926 *A Short History of Civilization* by Lynn Thorndike, an American scholar, appeared. This remained one of the basic texts in this subject for a decade. More recently the excellent survey of Harry E. Barnes titled *The History of Western Civilization,* two volumes (1935), was a significant contribution to the literature produced in America on the history of civilization. The most valuable cooperative survey of world history and one that concerns itself with the development of civilization in the broadest sense is *The Universal World History,* 10 volumes, edited by Sir J. A. Hammerton (1937). This set, profusely illustrated, simply written, is the work of eminent authorities.

Geographical areas.

A. WESTERN EUROPE. For ancient history one of the most valuable general surveys is A. A. Trever, *History of Ancient Civilization,* 2 volumes (1936). J. W. Thompson and E. N. Johnson, *An Introduction to Medieval Europe* (1937) is a standard treatment. Robert Ergang, *Europe from the Renaissance to Waterloo* (1939) adequately covers early modern times. The nineteenth century is treated in the well-known volume *Modern and Contemporary European History* by J. S. Schapiro (1931). Two recent excellent surveys of the nineteenth and twentieth centuries are W. P. Hall and W. S. Davis, *The Course of Europe Since Waterloo* (1941) and J. E. Gillespie, *Europe in Perspective* (1942). The latest phase of European history is surveyed in J. S. Swain, *Beginning the Twentieth Century* (1933) and W. C. Langsam, *The World Since 1914* (1937). Reference should also be made to H. A. L. Fisher, *A History of Europe* (1936). Written by an eminent English scholar this work is regarded as one of the most brilliant single surveys of European development.

B. GREAT BRITAIN. For a survey of British history in a single volume G. M. Trevelyan, *A History of England* (1928) has few rivals. W. E. Lunt, *History of England* (1928) is particularly good for its emphasis upon constitutional development and social and economic history. *The History of British Civilization* (1928) by Esmé Wingfield-Stratford is an outstanding interpretive survey in which politics, economics, and thought are dovetailed into an absorbing narrative.

C. THE BRITISH EMPIRE. The most comprehensive account in one volume of the development of the British Empire is James A. Williamson, *Short History of British Expan-*

sion (1930). For references on the British self-governing Dominions the following sources are recommended: *A History of Canada* (1941) by Carl Wittke, an American scholar, is perhaps the best one-volume survey yet written. *The Canadians* (1938) by George Mackinnon Wrong is a readable survey written by one of Canada's most famous historians. The most complete history of South Africa in a single volume is Eric A. Walker, *History of South Africa* (1941). J. H. Hofmeyr, *South Africa* (1931) is particularly good for its lucid and interesting description of this country's social, political, and economic problems. W. K. Hancock, *Australia* (1931) is a splendid description of the growth and present characteristics of Australian culture. A good brief account is Ernest Scott, *A Short History of Australia* (1927). W. P. Reeves, *The Long White Cloud* (1924) is valuable for New Zealand. On Indian history H. G. Rawlinson, *India: A Short Cultural History* (1938) is excellent for its treatment of political and other aspects of India's culture. Of value also is the excellent condensation of the monumental *Cambridge History of India*, 6 volumes (1922-1937), the *Cambridge Shorter History of India*, edited by H. H. Dodwell (1934).

D. LATIN AMERICA. A reliable and standard treatment containing a comprehensive political treatment together with valuable chapters on art, literature, and thought, is Mary W. Williams, *The People and Politics of South America* (1938). Another excellent survey is Charles E. Chapman, *The Development of Hispanic America* (1938). An interesting discussion of the economic, social, artistic, and intellectual trends in Latin America will be found in a series of papers contained in *Concerning Latin American Culture*, edited by C. C. Griffin (1940).

E. THE UNITED STATES. For general purposes the history of Morison and Commager, already referred to in connection with the bibliographies, is an adequate survey. This work is not exclusively political and its style is much more readable than the average history text. Another good standard survey is H. C. Hockett and A. M. Schlesinger *The Political and Social Growth of the American People*, 2 volumes (1941). For a fascinating study of American history in which political, social, and economic trends are woven into an absorbing narrative, Charles and Mary Beard, *The Rise of American Civilization*, 2 volumes (1927), is in a class by itself. *America in Midpassage* (1939) by the same authors, brings the narrative up to 1939.

F. CHINA AND JAPAN. Two reliable surveys are E. T. Williams, *Short History of China* (1928) and H. H. Gowan, *Outline History of Japan* (1927). A work whose merit is universally recognized is the two-volume survey *The Chinese, Their History and Culture* (1934) by K. S. Latourette. *History of the Far East* (1936) by G. Nye Steiger is the best single-volume political survey. The development of culture in China and Japan from earliest times is capably examined in C. P. Fitzgerald, *China, A Short Cultural History* (1938) and G. C. Sansom, *Japan, A Short Cultural History* (1938). A good treatment of the Far East with special reference to international relations is H. M. Vinacke, *A History of the Far East in Modern Times* (1941).

Special topical readings. Thus far we have listed books in relation to specific geographical areas. In this section references will be listed for each of the six basic divisions of the culture pattern.

A. ART AND MUSIC. Taking the esthetic first, the following are excellent one-volume surveys of world art: Helen Gardner, *Art Through the Ages* (1926) and R. S. Stites, *The Arts and Man* (1940). In architecture, Sir Banister Fletcher, *History of Architecture*, 10th edition (1938), is the standard work. Talbot Hamlin, *Architecture Through the Ages* (1940) is also a noteworthy study. In music the general reader will find Karl Nef, *An Outline of the History of Music* (1935), brief, readable, and scholarly. Comprehensive also is W. S. Pratt, *History of Music* (1935). Paul Bekker, *The Story of Music* (1927) is also useful. It is generally agreed that the finest historical treatment of music is Paul Henry Láng, *Music in Western Civilization* (1941).

B. LITERATURE. In the field of literature reference should be made to John Drinkwater, *Outline of World Literature*, 3 volumes (1923-1924). It is inclusive and readable. A splendid help is Mark Van Doren, *An Anthology of World Poetry* (1939). Botta, *Handbook of Universal Literature* (1923) is a good concise summary. Two anthologies may be mentioned which contain types of world literature together with descriptive material: P. M. Buck, *An Anthology of World Literature* (1940) and

T. P. Cross and C. T. Goode, *Heath Readings in the Literature of Europe* (1927). In the former, for example, are readings in Homer, Greek tragedy, Greek lyric poetry, and ancient philosophy. Examples of Indian, Arabic, Jewish, and Persian literature are also given. Specimens of early European vernacular literature are given, followed by examples of eighteenth- and nineteenth-century writing. Each main section of the anthology has a brief descriptive essay explaining the historical development of the material. In the field of the drama, Sheldon Cheney, *The Theatre: Three Thousand Years of Drama, Acting, and Stage Craft* (1930) is an excellent, well-written survey.

For American literature the layman will find V. L. Parrington, *Main Currents in American Thought*, 2 volumes (1927-1930), worth while, as well as P. H. Boynton, *Literature and American Life* (1936). Osgood, *Voice of England* (1935) is an excellent introduction to the history of English literature. An encyclopedic survey is the one-volume *Concise Cambridge History of English Literature* (1941) by George Sampson.

C. RELIGION. Several excellent treatments of the history and teachings of the world's great religions are available. One such is Robert Hume, *World's Living Religions* (1930). E. W. Hopkins, *The History of Religions* (1918) is rather old but is readable and comprehensive. More recent, brief, and not technical is C. S. Braden, *The World's Religions* (1939). A well-known popular but accurate survey is Lewis Browne, *This Believing World* (1926).

D. SCIENCE, PHILOSOPHY, AND EDUCATION. Science, philosophy, and education constitute the intellectual division of the culture pattern. In science we have a comprehensive and readable one-volume history by W. T. Sedgwick and H. W. Tyler, *A Short History of Science* (1939). It contains a very useful bibliography. Students will also find helpful R. J. Harvey-Gibson, *Two Thousand Years of Science* (1929) and Sir William Dampier, *A History of Science* (1929). In philosophy the following surveys are standard and not too difficult: A. K. Rogers, *A Student's History of Philosophy* (1935) and H. E. Cushman, *A Beginner's History of Philosophy* (1910-1911). An outstanding survey of the intellectual history of western Europe with special attention to the development of ideas is J. H. Randall, *The Making of the Modern Mind* (1940). The development of schools is a topic of major importance in intellectual history. In this regard E. P. Cubberley, *History of Education* (1920) is the best single source. Reference can be made also to E. C. Moore, *The Story of Instruction* (1936).

E. POLITICAL ORGANIZATION. The development of political organization is a topic usually taken care of in most standard histories, hence the references above to general United States, English, European, etc., history take care of this aspect. A few additional references may be cited, however: C. W. C. Oman, *A History of the Art of War* (1905) and R. G. Albion, *Introduction to Military History* (1929) are two valuable treatments. To bring this regrettable aspect of man's culture up to date mention should also be made of Hermann Foertsch, *The Art of Modern Warfare* (1940). Written by a colonel in Hitler's army, it is one of the best accounts of blitzkrieg tactics. On the history of political theory are W. A. Dunning, *A History of Political Theories*, 3 volumes (1924) and T. I. Cook, *History of Political Philosophy* (1936).

F. ECONOMIC HISTORY. A sound and yet nontechnical treatment of economic history is Herbert Heaton, *Economic History of Europe* (1936). Another parallel study is S. B. Clough and C. W. Cole, *The Economic History of Europe* (1941). Clive Day, *History of Commerce* (1907) and E. Osgood, *History of Industry* (1921) are indispensable. H. U. Faulkner, *American Economic History* (1935) is a standard one-volume study. Few have attempted to cover world history as an economic unit, but a promising start in this direction is H. E. Barnes, *Economic History of the Western World* (1937).

G. SOCIAL HISTORY. In the field of social history, comprising marriage, family, clothing, health, etc., the following references may be cited: W. Goodsell, *A History of Marriage and the Family* (1934) is the best brief treatment of this subject. See also Meyrick Booth, *Woman and Society* (1920). E. R. Mowrer, *The Family* (1932) discusses the problems of the modern family. Robert Graves and Alan Hodge, *The Long Week End: A British Social History, 1918-1939* (1941) is a graphic picture of fashions, novels, inventions, etc., in Great Britain between two wars. The best general introduction to contemporary American social life is Robert and Helen Lynd,

Middletown (1929) and *Middletown in Transition* (1937). In the field of health and medicine the following sources are helpful: H. W. Haggard, *Devils, Drugs, and Doctors* (1929). The macabre pictures in this volume intrigue most readers. R. H. Major, *Disease and Destiny* (1936), discusses the major plagues in world history and their effects. The standard one-volume history of medicine for some time has been F. H. Garrison, *Introduction to the History of Medicine* (1913). Arturo Castiglioni's *History of Medicine* (1927), written in Italian, has been translated into English (1941) by E. B. Krumbahr, a well-known American pathologist and medical historian. Profusely illustrated, it is a splendid introduction to medical history for the layman.

H. HISTORICAL NOVELS. No discussion of books relating to the history of civilization would be complete without reference to historical novels. As Thomas Carlyle once wrote, "Historical novels have taught all men this truth: . . . that the bygone ages of the world were actually filled by living men, not by protocols, state papers, controversies, and abstractions of man." Such historical novels have done much in the past to create interest in history and often have presented an accurate re-creation of some period of history. In this connection one recalls Tolstoy's *War and Peace,* Wallace's *Ben Hur,* Reade's *Cloister and the Hearth,* and Victor Hugo's *Les Misérables.* In recent years historical novels have become more popular and more significant. We cite a few examples of more recent outstanding historical fiction: Robert Graves, *I. Claudius* (1937), C. S. Forester, *Captain Horatio Hornblower* (1939), Margaret Mitchell, *Gone with the Wind* (1936), and Kenneth Roberts, *Oliver Wiswell* (1940). The student of history cannot afford to ignore the drama. Noel Coward, *Cavalcade* (1932), Maxwell Anderson, *Elizabeth, the Queen* (1936), Robert Sherwood, *There Shall Be No Night* (1940), and F. H. Brennan, *The Wookey* (1941), a story of London during the bombing blitz, are all plays which deal with some aspect of the human drama we call history. There are two valuable guides to historical fiction: E. A. Baker, *A Guide to Historical Fiction* has been the standard reference since 1914. This may be supplemented by the excellent *Guide to the Best Historical Novels and Tales* (1929) by Jonathan Nield.

I. BIOGRAPHY. The biographical approach to history is popular, and rightly, with many readers and especially those who believe that it is human personality which determines in large part the course of historical events. Such studies as Emil Ludwig's *Bismarck* (1927), Harvey Cushing's *Sir William Osler* (1940), L. Strachey's *Queen Victoria* (1921), Carl Sandburg's *Lincoln* (1926-1939), and Carl Van Doren's *Benjamin Franklin* (1938) are outstanding examples of how the relationship between men and historical events can be worked out. Any good bibliographical list will indicate the best biographical studies for a particular period.

Keeping abreast of the times. New books, plays, and even movies are constantly seeing the light of day, many of which are valuable case studies to those interested in understanding as much as possible about our modern civilization. This volume and its predecessor, which have traced the major events, achievements, and failures of mankind from the earliest times to the Second World War, form but an essential background for future reading. During the next few decades it is likely that major political changes will be brought about, new inventions will radically change the mode of living, and new personalities will appear as champions of some suggested change or plan of action. Reading is one of the principal instruments by which an individual is enabled to keep posted. It is, therefore, the essential agent for intelligent adaptation to a rapidly changing world. Reading is a lifelong process, and the *New York Times Book Review* (in the Sunday edition), the *Saturday Review of Literature,* the *Book Review Digest,* and the excellent reviews in such magazines as the *Yale Review, Harpers,* and *Atlantic Monthly* are usually available to help you find "just the right book."

For Further Reading

A list of books, classified and annotated, for further information or leisure reading.

1: New Ways of Life

1. The Growth of Commerce: A good brief account of this subject is found in L. B. Packard, *The Commercial Revolution, 1400-1776* (1927), Chapter 1. A detailed analysis of the effects of colonial life upon English economy and society is ably put forward in J. E. Gillespie, *The Influence of Overseas Expansion on England to 1700* (1920), Chapters 4-6. French commercial and industrial developments have been studied carefully by the French scholar, Henri Sée, in *Economic and Social Conditions in France During the Eighteenth Century* (1927), Chapters 7 and 8. The effects of precious metals upon Europe's commercial economy have been best studied in E. J. Hamilton, *American Treasure and the Price Revolution in Spain, 1501-1650* (1934). Preserved Smith, *The Age of the Reformation* (1920), Chapter 11, has a good account of early capitalistic policies. J. K. Wright analyzes the shift of Europe's economy from a thalassic to an oceanic setup in *The Geographical Basis of European History* (1928).

2. Banking and Commercial Practices: The student is encouraged to look into N. S. B. Gras, *Business and Capitalism* (1939). See especially Chapters 3 and 4, "Mercantile Capitalism." A brief account of English commercial practices during the period from 1500 to 1700 is found in Clive Day, *Economic Development in Europe* (1942), Chapter 6. Source materials regarding joint-stock company formations as well as monopolies have been set forth in A. E. Bland, P. A. Brown, R. H. Tawney, *English Economic History, Select Documents,* 3rd impression (1919), Part II, Section V, "The Encouragement of Industry and Commerce." A. P. Usher has written "The Origins of Banking: The Primitive Bank of Deposit" for *Economic History Review,* April, 1934, while an excellent account of the growth of insurance practices is found in C. E. Fayle, *A History of Lloyd's* (1928), a study of a fascinating institution.

3. Industry and Agriculture: Important in this field is J. L. and Barbara Hammond, *The Rise of Modern Industry* (1926). For the enclosure movement, see N. S. B. Gras, *A History of Agriculture* (1925), Chapter 7, while Chapter 9 of this work deals with "The Agricultural Revolution, chiefly in England." A worth-while résumé of the rise of the putting-out industry and changes in agriculture will be found in Harry E. Barnes, *The History of Western Civilization* (1935), Volume II, Chapter 2.

4. Social Life and Customs: See Laurence B. Packard, *The Age of Louis* XIV (1929), Chapter 3, a short account of the artistic and intellectual achievements of the age of the Sun King. A delightful insight into eighteenth-century London life as revealed by the literature of the age can be gleaned from William H. Irving, *John Gay's London* (1928). Another important source is Sir Walter Besant, *London in the Time of the Stuarts* (1903). The section on "Manners and Customs" throws much light on food, dress, theaters, amusements, sports, crimes, etc., pp. 287-362. Besant, *London in the Eighteenth Century* (1925), pp. 229-610, continues his study of social conditions for a later period.

2: Science, Reason, and Enlightenment

1. Science and Medicine: Excellent treatments of the rise of science in early modern times are given in Sir William Dampier, *History of Science* (1929), and W. T. Sedgwick and H. W. Tyler, *A Short History of Science* (1939). Other volumes of special interest are: J. M. Stillman, *The Story of Early Chemistry* (1924); D. E. Smith, *History of Mathematics* (1925); and B. Jaffe, *Crucibles, the Lives and Achievements of the Great Chemists* (1930).

F. H. Garrison, *An Introduction to the History of Medicine* (1929) is a standard work.

*2. **Religion, Thought, Education:*** For education see Preserved Smith, *A History of Modern Culture* (1934), Volume I, Chapter 11, and Volume II, Chapter 12. A good discussion of educational theory and method will be found in E. P. Cubberley, *The History of Education* (1920). "The Religion of Reason" and "The Morality of Reasonableness" are two excellent chapters in J. H. Randall, *The Making of the Modern Mind* (1929). A popular account of the work of Bacon, Spinoza, and Voltaire is given by Will Durant, *The Story of Philosophy* (1926). Preserved Smith, cited above, has a simple but adequate discussion of philosophy, Volume I, Chapter 7 and Volume II, Chapter 5. Brief interpretations will be found in Henry Thomas and Dana Lee Thomas, *Living Biographies of Famous Philosophers* (1940). See also E. S. Haldane, *Descartes, his life and times* (1905).

*3. **Literature:*** J. Macy, *The Story of the World's Literature* (1925), contains a condensed and popular survey of the literature of seventeenth- and eighteenth-century Europe. George Sampson, *The Concise Cambridge History of English Literature* (1941) is an excellent terse survey. See Chapter 9, "From Steele and Addison to Pope and Swift." Further material may be perused in Preserved Smith, cited above, Volume I, Chapter 18 and Volume II, Chapters 9 and 10. A delightful work is L. Stephen, *English Literature and Society in the Eighteenth Century* (1904). See also Kuno Francke, *History of German Literature*, 4th edition (1901), and Arthur Tilley, *From Montaigne to Molière* (1923).

*4. **Esthetic Activities:*** Superb reproductions of the most important paintings are given in Thomas Craven, *A Treasury of Art Masterpieces* (1939). See also this author's work: *Men of Art* (1931). Dependable surveys of art in the eighteenth century are contained in such works as: E. Faure, *History of Art* (1924), Volume IV; H. W. Van Loon, *The Arts* (1937), Chapters 24-27; and R. S. Stites, *The Arts and Man* (1940). Other works recommended are: M. S. Briggs, *The Architect in History* (1927); S. F. Kimball and G. H. Edgell, *A History of Architecture* (1918); and C. Whitaker-Wilson, *Sir Christopher Wren* (1932). For music the following are useful: Cecil Gray, *History of Music* (1928), Chapters 8 and 9; Paul Bekker, *The Story of Music* (1927), Chapters 8-11; W. S. Pratt, *The History of Music* (1922), Parts III-VI; and Henry and Dana Lee Thomas, *Living Biographies of Great Composers* (1940).

*5. **General Surveys:*** A brief but good account will be found in F. Schevill, *A History of Europe* (1938), Chapter 19. Another excellent introduction to the subject is given in Chapters 3 and 11 in C. J. H. Hayes, *A Political and Cultural History of Modern Europe* (1932), Volume I. Two volumes on the eighteenth century will be found stimulating and enjoyable: R. B. Mowat, *The Age of Reason* (1934), and P. Russell, *The Glittering Century* (1936). Very worth while also is the discussion by Preserved Smith, cited above, Volume II, Chapter 1.

*6. **Other References:*** The history of science may be interestingly followed in the pages of numerous biographies. A few such works can be mentioned: J. J. Fahie, *Galileo, his Life and Work* (1903); Zsolt Harsányi, *The Star Gazer,* Galileo in the form of a biographical novel (1939); J. L. E. Dreeyer, *Tycho Brahe* (1890); A. Holt, *Life of Joseph Priestley* (1931); G. S. Brett, *Sir Isaac Newton* (1929); B. Fay, *Benjamin Franklin* (1929); Paul de Kruif, *The Microbe Hunters* (1926); and F. Masson, *Robert Boyle* (1914). For the part played by disease in history see Ralph H. Major, *Disease and Destiny* (1936). Logan Clendening, *Behind the Doctor* (1933) has interesting sections on William Harvey, pp. 69-91; Vesalius, pp. 55-68; Paré, pp. 113-122; and the use of the microscope, pp. 92-112. Chapter 10 in Walter Libby, *The History of Medicine* (1922) contains discussions of Auenbrugger and Laënnec.

3: When in the Course of Human Events

*1. **The Ascendancy of France:*** A brief, excellent account is Laurence B. Packard, *The Age of Louis* XIV (1929). A good survey of the reign of Louis XIV is David Ogg, *Europe in the Seventeenth Century* (1925), pp. 281-364. The foundation of French absolutism with emphasis on the work of Richelieu and Mazarin is given in the *Cambridge Modern History* (1907), Volume IV, pp. 118-157 and 592-622. H. O. Wakeman, *The Ascendancy* *of France, 1598-1715* (1894), is a good account of politics, wars, and diplomacy.

2. ***Diplomacy and Politics:*** G. Brunn, *The Enlightened Despots* (1929) is an excellent brief résumé. A. H. Johnson, *The Age of the Enlightened Despot, 1660-1789,* revised edition (1933), is a brief and clear outline of politics. A. H. Buffington, *The Second Hundred Years' War* (1929) is a condensed account of Anglo-French rivalry. A. Hassal, *The Balance of Power, 1715-1789* (1896) is a standard short study of European power politics.

3. ***Rise of Prussia and Russia:*** F. Nowak, *Medieval Slavdom and the Rise of Russia* (1930) is a good introduction. An excellent study of Russian beginnings and the reigns of Peter the Great and Catherine the Great is given by Bernard Pares, *A History of Russia* (1926), Chapters 11-15. A short classic treatment of the rise of Prussia is S. B. Fay, *The Rise of Brandenburg-Prussia to 1786* (1937). The best one-volume treatment of Prussia is J. A. R. Marriott and C. G. Robertson, *The Evolution of Prussia* (1915).

4. ***English Politics:*** G. B. Adams, *Constitutional History of England* (1934), Chapters 11-16, presents a clear account of the Puritan Revolution, the Glorious Revolution, the growth and perfection of the cabinet. The general course of English history from the Restoration to 1815 is dealt with in a vigorous and vivid fashion by W. P. Hall and R. G. Albion, *A History of England and the British Empire* (1937), Chapters 14-19. Another good account is A. L. Cross, *A Shorter History of England and Greater Britain* (1939), Chapters 32-47. Arthur Bryant, *The Postman's Horn* (1936) is an anthology of letters illustrating various phases of life in Restoration England.

5. ***The American Revolution:*** Carl Becker, *The Declaration of Independence* (1922), is a stimulating discussion of origins, drafting, and philosophy. R. W. Pettengill, *Letters From America: 1776-1779* (1924) contains letters written by German soldiers, mainly Hessians, which throw interesting light upon the course of the Revolution. S. E. Morison and H. S. Commager, *The Growth of the American Republic* (1937), Volume I, has an excellent summary of the Revolution, Chapters 4 and 5. A spirited interpretation of the American Revolution will be found in Charles and Mary Beard, *The Rise of American Civilization* (1927), Volume I. An eminent authority discusses various aspects of this topic in *England and America: Rivals in the American Revolution* (1927). E. Channing, *History of the United States* (1912), Volume III, is a scholarly one-volume treatment of the Revolution.

6. ***The French Revolution:*** A brief, useful study is Leo Gershoy, *The French Revolution, 1789-1799* (1935); and a longer study by the same author is *The French Revolution and Napoleon* (1933). A somewhat popular and interpretive approach is Pierre Gaxotte, *The French Revolution* (1932). The Revolution through the eyes of men who were there is E. L. Higgins, *The French Revolution as Told by Contemporaries* (1938). Impressions of an American diplomat in Paris are given in Gouverneur Morris, *A Diary of the French Revolution,* edited by B. C. Davenport (1939). A French historian discusses outstanding personalities in Louis Madelin, *The Revolutionaries* (1930). Napoleon's escape from Elba and Waterloo are described in Philip Guedalla, *The Hundred Days* (1934). The first complete account of Napoleon's Russian campaign is given in Eugene Tarlé, *Napoleon's Invasion of Russia—1812* (1941).

7. ***General Surveys:*** Useful accounts of the course of politics in the seventeenth- and eighteenth-centuries will be found in J. E. Gillespie, *A History of Europe* (1928), Chapters 17, 18, 19, 24-26; Albert Hyma, *Europe From the Renaissance to 1815* (1931), Chapters 9-18; and Robert Ergang, *Europe From the Renaissance to Waterloo* (1939), Chapters 12-26.

8. ***Other References:*** Good biographies are: Pierre Gaxotte, *Frederick the Great* (1942); Gina Kaus, *Catherine, the portrait of an empress* (1935), stresses the ruler's loves and lovers; Arthur Bryant, *King Charles* II (1936), a well-written account of the "merry monarch"; A. G. Macdonell, *Napoleon and His Marshals* (1934), an interesting description of the military exploits and final defeat of Napoleon; J. M. Whitham, *A Biographical History of the French Revolution* (1931), terse biographical sketches; Karl Bartz, *Louis* XIV (1937); S. Zweig, *Marie Antoinette* (1933); W. F. Reddaway, *Frederick the Great* (1919); Margaret Goldsmith, *Maria Theresa of Austria* (1937); H. A. L. Fisher, *Napoleon* (1924); P. Guedalla, *Wellington* (1932); P. F. Willert, *Henry of Navarre* (1902); J. Buchan, *Life of Oliver Cromwell* (1934); C. H. Firth, *Oliver Cromwell* (1935); E. Schuyler, *Peter the Great,*

2 volumes (1884); J. H. Rose, *The Life of Napoleon* I (1913); R. M. Johnston, *Napoleon; a Short Biography* (1910).

9. Historical Novels: Gertrude Atherton, *The Conqueror,* career of Alexander Hamilton; Winston Churchill, *Richard Carvell,* events leading to the American Revolution; Lion Feuchtwanger, *Power,* an outstanding novel of a German state from 1730 to 1740; Phyllis Bentley, *The Power and the Glory,* English Civil War; Henry Sienkiewicz, *With Fire and Sword, The Deluge,* and *Pan Michael,* a trilogy dealing with seventeenth-century Poland, Russia, and Sweden; W. M. Thackeray, *Henry Esmond,* a vivid picture of the life and times of Queen Anne; Hervey Allen, *Anthony Adverse,* in part deals with the Napoleonic period; V. Sheean, *San Felice,* the revolution in Naples; Alessandro Manzoni, *The Betrothed,* a classic novel on seventeenth-century Italy; Alexandre Dumas, *The Three Musketeers,* France in 1626-1628; Sir Walter Scott, *The Fortunes of Nigel,* London in the early seventeenth century; Anatole France, *The Gods Are Athirst,* the revolution in France, 1793-1794; Jane Porter, *Thaddeus of Warsaw,* Poland's struggle for independence; and R. D. Blackmore, *Lorna Doone,* the west of England, 1673-1688; Leo Tolstoy, *War and Peace,* Russia in the Napoleonic wars; and Charles Dickens, *A Tale of Two Cities,* a famous story of the French Revolution.

4: Factories, Owners, and Workers

1. Technological Changes: A worth-while account can be found in Abbott P. Usher, *A History of Mechanical Inventions* (1929). See especially Chapter 9, textile machines, Chapter 10, steam and pumping engines, and Chapter 13, the production of power since 1832. In J. L. and Barbara Hammond, *The Rise of Modern Industry* (1926), Chapters 7, 9, and 11, is more material on changes in steam, iron, and textiles. A brief résumé of canal- and railroad-building is set forth in F. C. Dietz, *The Industrial Revolution* (1927), Chapter 2; Clive Day, *Economic Development in Europe* (1942), Chapter 8; H. E. Barnes, *The History of Western Civilization* (1935), Volume II, Chapter 8. The history of transportation is dealt with in A. W. Kirkaldy and A. D. Evans, *History and Economics of Transport* (1915). For an excellent bibliography consult Eileen Power, *The Industrial Revolution, 1757-1850* (1927).

2. Industrialism: The spread of industrialism is admirably presented in E. W. Zimmermann, *World Resources and Industries* (1933). Clive Day, cited above, has separate chapters for developments in various countries: France, Chapters 14-16; Germany, 17-19; Russia, 22-27; Italy, 29; Spain, 30 and 31. Along this line such works as F. A. Ogg and W. R. Sharp, *Economic Development of Modern Europe* (1926) and Herbert Heaton, *Economic History of Europe* (1936) should also be consulted. For industrial conditions in the United States, see E. L. Bogart, *Economic History of the American People* (1930), and for a reliable treatment of industrialism in the Orient, see H. M. Vinacke, *A History of the Far East in Modern Times,* 4th edition (1941).

3. Consequences of Industrialism: For source materials regarding the condition of industrial workers see J. F. Scott and A. Baltzly, *Readings in European History Since 1814* (1934), Chapter 3; Friedrich Engels, *The Condition of the Working-Class in England in 1844* (1926); and, especially for the employment of children in factories and mines, A. E. Bland, P. A. Brown, R. H. Tawney, *English Economic History, Select Documents* (1919), pp. 502-519. Child labor in mills, mines, and chimneys is also graphically discussed in J. L. and Barbara Hammond, *The Town Labourer, 1760-1832* (1917), Chapters 8 and 9. Chapter 11 shows the acceptance of the principles of Adam Smith and Ricardo, and Chapter 14 discusses the growing antipathy of the poor toward their employers. The student should look into Adam Smith's classic, *Wealth of Nations* and Malthus' *Essay on Population.*

4. The Challenge of the Workers: A study of Christian socialism is furnished by Hugh Martin, Editor, *Christian Reformers of the Nineteenth Century* (1927). The student should contrast the work of Adam Smith with that of Karl Marx by reading some of the latter's *Capital.* For selections from the works of Louis Blanc, Marx and Engels, and Kropotkin, see J. F. Scott and A. Baltzly, cited above, Chapter 11. Chapter 6 has materials on the recognition of social problems and the progress of trade unionism in Great Britain.

5: Nationalism and Democracy Advance

1. Congress of Vienna: Arthur May, *The Age of Metternich, 1814-1848* (1933) is an admirable brief study. See F. B. Artz, *Reaction and Revolution, 1814-1832* (1934), Chapters 1 and 2, for social conditions after 1815. The Congress is treated fully in C. K. Webster, *The Congress of Vienna* (1919). Other accounts are in C. P. Higby, *History of Modern Europe* (1932), Chapter 2; C. D. Hazen, *Europe Since 1815* (1910), Chapter 1; and the *Cambridge Modern History* (1902-1912), Volume IX, Chapters 19 and 21.

2. Continental Europe, 1815-1870: The collapse of the Metternich system is described by Artz, cited above, Chapters 7-9. The revolutions of 1848 are treated in the following: G. M. Priest, *Germany since 1740* (1915), Chapters 8 and 9; E. Feuter, *World History, 1815-1920* (1924), Chapters 21 and 23; and A. C. Flick, *Modern World History Since 1775* (1935), Chapter 11. The unification of Italy is covered in the *Cambridge Modern History,* Volume XI, Chapters 4, 14, 19, and 25. See also T. W. Riker, *A Short History of Modern Europe* (1935), Chapter 13; and Bolton King, *A History of Italian Unity* (1912). The work of Garibaldi is described in Chapters 31 and 32 and the war of 1859 in Chapter 27. The unification of Germany is succinctly treated in E. Achorn, *European Civilization and Politics* (1934), Chapter 5. Political developments are fully treated in R. C. Binkley, *Realism and Nationalism, 1852-1871* (1935). A very readable account of the unification of Germany is W. P. Hall and W. S. Davis, *The Course of Europe Since Waterloo* (1941), Chapters 12 and 13.

3. Great Britain and France: A splendid survey of nineteenth-century French history is J. S. Schapiro, *Modern and Contemporary European History* (1934), Chapters 5, 12, 13, and 18. The *Cambridge Modern History* has a very good chapter on the Third French Republic, Volume XII, Chapter 5. One of the best studies of modern France is D. W. Brogan, *France Under the Republic: The Development of Modern France, 1870-1939* (1940). See Book I, "The Birth of the Republic," and Book VII, "The Dreyfus Case." Sidney Huddleston, *France* (1927) has interesting sections on "What France Is," and "Between Two Wars" (1871-1914). The history of Great Britain is treated clearly in L. M. Larson, *A History of England and the British Commonwealth* (1932), Chapters 22-25. British history from 1850 to 1914 is admirably surveyed by J. Gillespie, *Europe in Perspective* (1942), Chapter 11. An important topic is discussed in M. Hovell, *The Chartist Movement* (1918). The constitution and political history of France before 1914 are ably treated by R. K. Gooch in *Governments of Continental Europe,* edited by J. T. Shotwell (1940), pp. 59-67 and 232-259.

4. Russia, Austria-Hungary, Germany, 1870-1914: For Russia see the *Cambridge Modern History,* Volume XII, Chapters 12 and 13. M. M. Karpovich, *Imperial Russia* (1932) is a convenient summary. B. Pares, *History of Russia* (1926) presents an adequate narrative, pp. 391-448. Russia at the end of the nineteenth century is admirably interpreted in J. W. Swain, *Beginning the Twentieth Century* (1933), Chapter 6. The *Cambridge Modern History,* Volume XII, has a brief account of Austria-Hungary, Chapter 7, as has Swain, cited above, Chapter 7. For Germany consult the following: G. P. Gooch, *Germany* (1927), Chapters 2, 3, and 5; Ferdinand Schevill, *The Making of Modern Germany* (1916), Chapters 4, 5, and 6; the *Cambridge Modern History,* Volume XII, Chapter 6; and Hall and Davis, cited above, Chapter 18.

5. Nationalist Sore Spots, 1870-1914: Submerged nationalities and their aspirations are dealt with in: R. W. Seton-Watson, *The Rise of Nationality in the Balkans* (1917); *Cambridge Modern History,* Volume XII, Chapter 4, "Ireland and the Home Rule Movement"; and for the same topic see V. L. and M. H. Albjerg, *From Sedan to Stresa* (1937), Chapter 6; J. W. Wuorinen, *Nationalism in Modern Finland* (1931); W. M. Gewehr, *Nationalism in the Balkans, 1800-1930* (1933); and N. Hill, *Poland and the Polish Question* (1915).

6. Italy, Spain, and Portugal: This Latin trio is well treated in Albjerg and Albjerg, cited above, Chapter 4. See also *Cambridge Modern History,* Volume XII, Chapters 8 and 10. Swain, cited above, has a good chapter on "Italy and the Lesser Powers."

7. The Small States: Holland, Scandinavia, Switzerland, and Belgium are briefly and interestingly discussed in Schapiro, cited above,

Chapter 22; Gillespie, cited above, Chapter 14; Albjerg and Albjerg, Chapter 7.

*8. **General Surveys:*** For the nineteenth century, readable summaries are: H. A. L. Fisher, *A History of Europe* (1936), Chapters 9-28; F. Schevill, *A History of Europe* (1938), Sections IV and V. Also see F. C. Palm and F. E. Graham, *Europe Since Napoleon* (1934), Chapters 1-21. The two basic movements discussed in this chapter, nationalism and democracy, are discussed in: E. B. Krehbiel, *Nationalism, War, and Society* (1916); J. Holland Rose, *Nationality in Modern History* (1916); C. J. H. Hayes, *Essays on Nationalism* (1926) and *The Historical Evolution of Modern Nationalism* (1931); H. E. Barnes, *The History of Western Civilization* (1935), Volume II, Chapter 14; and A. F. Hattersley, *Short History of Democracy* (1930).

*9. **Other References:*** Entertaining and instructive biographies are: O. Burdett, *W. E. Gladstone* (1928); Sir E. Clarke, *Benjamin Disraeli: the Romance of a Great Career* (1926); A. Maurois, *Disraeli* (1927); L. Strachey, *Queen Victoria* (1921); A. Herman, *Metternich* (1932); A. Hassall, *Viscount Castlereagh* (1908); P. Guedalla, *Wellington* (1932) and *Palmerston* (1926); A. D. White, *Seven Great Statesmen* (1927), good account of Bismarck and Cavour; E. Pears, *Life of Abdul Hamid* II (1917); C. G. Robertson, *Bismarck* (1919); P. E. L. Deschanel, *Gambetta* (1920); and G. M. Trevelyan, *Garibaldi and the Making of Italy* (1928).

*10. **Historical Novels:*** Valuable for reconstructing the spirit and conditions of the nineteenth century are: W. M. Thackeray, *Vanity Fair;* Emile Zola, *The Downfall,* Franco-Prussian War; Maxim Gorki, *The Specter;* Victor Hugo, *Les Misérables,* one of the greatest historical novels; G. Meredith, *Vittoria,* Italy in 1848; T. Mann, *Buddenbrooks,* a famous study of a German trading family; B. Disraeli, *Coningsby,* English politics in the 1830's; P. Bentley, *Inheritance;* G. Eliot, *Felix Holt, the Radical,* English social conditions about 1830; F. M. Crawford, *Don Orsino,* nineteenth-century Italy; J. Galsworthy, *Forsyte Saga,* notable novel of the English middle class; I. Turgenev, *Fathers and Sons,* the impact of new ideas in Russia; A. Daudet, *Monday Tales,* the Franco-Prussian War; and M. B. Whitney, *The Torchbearers,* Italian politics at the end of the nineteenth century.

6: All's Right with the World

*1. **Science:*** The history of science in the nineteenth century is dealt with admirably in the *Cambridge Modern History,* Volume XII, Chapter 4, and in J. E. Hammerton, Editor, *Universal History of the World,* Chapter 170. W. T. Sedgwick and H. W. Tyler, *A Short History of Science* (1939), Chapter 15, sets forth some of the principal achievements in mathematics, and Roberto Bonola discusses a new and most important phase in *Non-Euclidian Geometry* (1912). Sedgwick and Tyler, cited above, Chapter 16, discusses the evolution of contemporary physics, and Chapter 17, biological developments. For the history of psychology see Gardner Murphy, *Historical Introduction to Modern Psychology* (1929).

*2. **Philosophy:*** The writings of some of the century's philosophers, such as Nietzsche, Schopenhauer, and Carlyle, should be read. A brief treatment of contemporary trends will be found in A. K. Rogers, *Student's History of Philosophy* (1932), p. 425 and following The intellectual aspects of the world-shaking theory of evolution are discussed in John Langdon-Davies, *Man and His Universe* (1930), Chapter 7.

*3. **Literature:*** Again a study should be made primarily of the actual writings of the century. Among the English poems one should read Tennyson's "In Memoriam," Browning's novel in poetic form, "The Ring and the Book," and Matthew Arnold's elegies. Walt Whitman is perhaps the most significant American poet of the day and his "Leaves of Grass" should not be neglected. Fairly good translations of the poetry of Alfred de Musset, Victor Hugo, and Heinrich Heine can be found in most libraries. The nineteenth century produced many excellent novelists. William M. Thackeray, *Vanity Fair,* Charles Dickens, *Pickwick Papers,* Charles Reade, *The Cloister and the Hearth* are but examples of the type of English novel which should not be overlooked. Translations are obtainable: Victor Hugo, *Les Misérables,* Gustave Flaubert, *Madame Bovary,* Anatole France, *Penguin Island,* Feodor Dostoevski, *The Brothers Karamozov,* and Leo Tolstoy, *War and Peace.*

*4. **Esthetic Activities:*** A. ART. For good treatments of the most outstanding figures in nineteenth-century art see Sheldon Cheney, *The Story of Modern Art* (1941). See his accounts of Turner, pp. 57-66, Corot, 77-87, Courbet, 126-132, Manet, 132-143, Impressionists and Renoir, 175-204, and Van Gogh, 269-298. For an amusing insight into the famous "feud" waged between James McNeill Whistler and his critics read Whistler, *The Gentle Art of Making Enemies* (1925).

B. MUSIC. Perhaps the finest of all studies of the historical development of music is Paul Henry Láng, *Music in Western Civilization* (1941). For a discussion of classicism versus romanticism in music see pp. 734-740; for Beethoven, see pp. 750-776; for Wagner, pp. 873-894; for Brahms, pp. 895-904; and for Verdi, pp. 909-915. An excellent and vivid account of the personality and genius of Wagner is furnished in Deems Taylor, *Of Men and Music* (1937).

7: New Europes Overseas

*1. **The United States:*** The student will enjoy the brilliant survey of Charles and Mary Beard, *The Rise of American Civilization* (1930). Max Farrand, *The Development of the United States* (1918), is an excellent terse synthesis of American history. A good reliable history in two volumes is *Political and Social Growth of the American People;* Volume I, 1492-1865, by H. C. Hockett and Volume II, 1865-1940, by A. M. Schlesinger, 3rd edition (1940). Foreign relations are discussed in a vivid fashion in T. A. Bailey, *A Diplomatic History of the American People* (1940). The colonial period may be perused in the simply and charmingly told narrative by Frank J. Klingberg, *The Morning of America* (1941). See Chapter 11, "The Significance of the American Revolution," Chapter 12, "The Social Results of the Revolution," and Chapter 14, "Travel, Marketing and Living Conditions." Of interest also are Chapters 17 and 18, "Colonial Society and Culture and Religion" in Curtis P. Nettels, *The Roots of American Civilization* (1939). The social and economic aspects are presented graphically in *A History of American Life,* edited by A. M. Schlesinger and D. R. Fox (1927-1934). See for example in Volume I (Thomas J. Wertenbaker, *The First Americans*), Chapter 2, "The New England Town and Its People," Chapter 7, "The Practice of Physic," and Chapter 10, "The Beginnings of an Intellectual Life." Other readings on a variety of topics are: Carl Wittke, *We Who Built America, The Saga of the Immigrant* (1939); Arthur K. Train, *The Story of Everyday Things* (1941); F. R. Dulles, *America Learns to Play, A History of Popular Recreation* (1940). For the progressive movement see H. U. Faulkner, *The Quest for Social Justice, 1898-1914* (1931); and an interesting approach in D. F. Cohen, *Good Old Days, A History of American Morals and Manners as seen through the Sears, Roebuck Catalogues, 1905 to the Present* (1940).

*2. **Canada:*** A delightful nontechnical account of Canadian development is given in George M. Wrong, *The Canadians, the Story of a People* (1938). The best one-volume history is Carl Wittke, *A History of Canada* (1941). A shorter account is Paul Knaplund, *The British Empire, 1815-1939* (1941). See Chapters 12, 20, and 29. An admirable survey profusely illustrated is *A Short History of Canada for Americans* (1942). A study of Canadian literature is presented in Lionel Stevenson, *Appraisals of Canadian Literature* (1926).

*3. **South Africa:*** A convenient, brief summary is given in Knaplund, cited above, Chapters 6, 14, 22, and 31. A very readable account of South African history and problems is J. H. Hofmeyr, *South Africa* (1931). The standard one-volume history is E. A. Walker, *A History of South Africa* (1935).

*4. **Australia and New Zealand:*** The best summary of Australian history is E. Scott, *Short History of Australia,* 5th edition (1927). For New Zealand, W. P. Morrell, *New Zealand* (1935), is a good succinct treatment. Another good account is W. P. Reeves, *The Long White Cloud,* 3rd edition (1924). Other valuable references are: E. O. G. Shann, *An Economic History of Australia* (1930); E. Jenks, *A History of the Australasian Colonies* (1912); and *The Maori People Today,* edited by I. L. G. Sutherland (1941).

*5. **Latin America:*** An excellent introduction to the subject is Delia Goetz and Varian Fry, *The Good Neighbors, The Story of the Two Americas* (1939). For foreign relations see G. H. Stuart, *Latin America and the United States* (1922). See Chapters 10-12 for American imperialism in the Caribbean. A reliable survey is A. Curtis Wilgus, *The Development of Hispanic America* (1941); the culture of the colonial period is discussed in Chapters 9-15. Another standard work is C. E. Chapman, *Hispanic America; Colonial and Republican,* 2 volumes (1938). A convenient summary of Latin-American literature and art is in M. W. Williams, *The People and Politics of Latin America* (1930).

6. ***Other References:*** For the United States there is a vast biographical literature. From it a few suggestive titles are given: Allan Nevins, *Grover Cleveland* (1932); H. F. Pringle, *Theodore Roosevelt* (1931); Carl Van Doren, *Benjamin Franklin* (1939); Gamaliel Bradford, *Lee the American* (1927); N. W. Stephenson, *Lincoln* (1924), the best one-volume study. All students will enjoy a few chapters from one of the volumes in Carl Sandburg, *Abraham Lincoln,* a monumental study of the great emancipator. For Canada the following studies of the Dominion's two outstanding statesmen in the nineteenth century are recommended: J. W. Dafoe, *Laurier, A Study in Canadian Politics* (1922) and G. R. Parkin, *Sir John Macdonald* (1908). This will prove worth while for South Africa: Basil Williams, *Cecil Rhodes* (1931). For Australia, the life of the famous explorer is described in J. H. Carruthers, *Captain James Cook* (1930). For Latin America these biographies may be cited: Emil Ludwig, *Bolivar* (1942); Carleton Beals, *Porfirio Diaz* (1932); U. R. Burke, *A Life of Benito Juarez* (1894); Salvador de Madariaga, *Hernán Cortés; Conqueror of Mexico* (1941); H. Angell, *Simon Bolivar* (1930); J. J. Mehegan, *O'Higgins of Chile* (1913); and Anna Schoellkopf, *Don José de San Martín* (1924).

7. ***Historical Novels:*** Among historical novels dealing with the American scene the following may be mentioned: Kenneth Roberts, *Oliver Wiswell;* Upton Sinclair, *The Jungle,* an example of muckraking literature; Theodore Dreiser, *The Financier* and *The Titan,* novels dealing with frenzied finance; a series of notable historical novels written by the American author, Winston Churchill: *Richard Carvel, The Crossing,* and *The Crisis.* W. D. Howells, *The Rise of Silas Lapham* is one of the first realistic studies of the American middle class; Hamlin Garland, *A Son of the Middle Border,* a saga of the western pioneer. Stephen Vincent Benét, *John Brown's Body,* is an impressive and moving epic poem. An epic of French Canada is the novel *Maria Chapdelaine* by Louis Hémon. Evelyn Eaton, *Quietly My Captain Waits* is a rather melodramatic story of seventeenth-century Canada. Two well-known novels dealing with life in the province of Ontario are: Ralph Connor, *The Man from Glengarry* and *Glengarry School Days.* For Africa, there are Stuart Cloete, *Turning Wheels,* a novel of Boer life; Olive Schreiner, *The Story of an African Farm;* and Deneys Reitz, *Commando,* a stirring tale of the Anglo-Boer war. For Australia, two good novels are: Nordhoff and Hall, *Botany Bay,* a fast-moving novel about the first settlement in Australia, and Henry Kingsley, *Geoffrey Hamlyn.* Latin American novels in English translation will be found in the bibliography for Chapter 12.

8: Dominion over Palm and Pine

1. ***The Rise of Modern Imperialism:*** A valuable explanation of the causes and background of imperialism is found in R. L. Buell, *International Relations* (1925), Chapter 13. An excellent summing up of the pros and cons of imperialism is presented in P. T. Moon, *Imperialism and World Politics* (1926), Chapter 19. Helpful also is the essay on imperialism in G. A. Hedger, Editor, *An Introduction to Western Civilization* (1932), Chapter 23. Another useful account is "The Background of Modern Imperialism," in James Gillespie, *Europe in Perspective* (1942).

2. ***Imperialism in Africa:*** H. L. Hoskins, *European Imperialism in Africa* (1930), a terse summary; Sir Charles Lucas, *The Partition of Africa* (1922), the best one-volume survey; Sir Harry Johnston, *History of the Colonization of Africa by Alien Races* (1913), a standard work by an authority. The following are also helpful: Ifor L. Evans, *The British in Tropical Africa* (1929); R. L. Buell, *The Native Problem in Africa,* 2 volumes (1928), a standard work, fine surveys for all African countries; *Cambridge Modern History,* Volume XII, Chapters 15-20, 22, 25.

*3. **The British in India:*** A survey of nineteenth-century Indian history will be found in J. Allan, T. W. Haig, and H. H. Dodwell, *The Cambridge Shorter History of India* (1934), Chapters 10-18. A less advanced treatment is found in Howard Robinson, *The Development of the British Empire* (1926), Chapters 12 and 13. The following chapters are worth noting in Edward Thompson and G. T. Garratt, *Rise and Fulfilment of British Rule in India* (1934), Book V, Chapter 6, "The Mutiny," Book VI, Chapter 1, "The Effect of the Mutiny," and Book VII, Chapter 2, "The Growth of Nationalism." C. M. P. Cross, *Development of Self-Government in India, 1858-1914* (1922) traces the rise of political nationalism. One of the best introductions to Indian life and customs is the official British document: *Report of the Indian Statutory Commission* (Cmd. 3568, 1930), Volume 1.

*4. **Imperialism and America:*** A good brief treatment is D. S. Muzzey, *The United States of America* (1924), Volume II, Chapter 5. P. T. Moon, cited above, has helpful discussions of United States expansion, as does Charles and Mary Beard, *The Rise of American Civilization* (1927), Volume II, Chapter 26. Other references: D. P. Barrows, *History of the Philippines* (1924); D. R. Williams, *The United States and the Philippines* (1924); W. S. Robertson, *Hispanic-American Relations with the United States* (1923); M. W. Williams, *The People and Politics of Latin America* (1930); Tancredo Pinochet, *The Gulf of Misunderstanding; or North and South America as seen by each other* (1920).

*5. **Southeastern Asia:*** For a general account of British colonies in this region consult Howard Robinson, cited above, Chapter 19, and J. A. Williamson, *A Short History of British Expansion* (1931), pp. 143-151 and 193-195. Also recommended are: H. W. Codrington, *A Short History of Ceylon* (1926); Rupert Emerson, *Malaysia* (1937); Amry Vandenbosch, *The Dutch East Indies* (1933); J. S. Furnivall, *Netherlands Indies* (1933); and H. A. van Coenen Torchiana, *Tropical Holland, Java and Other Islands* (1923). A vivid description of the people of the Dutch East Indies is in E. R. Embree and others, *Island India Goes to School* (1934).

*6. **China and the Great Powers:*** A good readable political account is G. Nye Steiger, *A History of the Far East* (1936), Chapter 23, "China's First Half-Century under the Treaties, 1844-1894."

*7. **Japan and the West:*** A scholarly work is E. Herbert Norman, *Japan's Emergence as a Modern State* (Institute of Pacific Relations, 1940), Chapter 2, "Background of the Meiji Restoration," and Chapter 3, "The Restoration." A good political account also is Steiger, cited above, Chapter 25, "The Development of Modern Japan."

*8. **Other References:*** T. W. Holderness, *Peoples and Problems of India* (1912), one of the best introductory treatments. R. Grant Brown, *Burma as I Saw It, 1889-1917* (1926). Basil Williams, *Cecil Rhodes* (1921), an interesting life of the "Empire Builder"; and Lord Roberts, *Forty-One Years in India* (1898). For Singapore see R. Coupland, *Raffles, 1781-1826* (1926), and H. E. Egerton, *Life of Sir Stamford Raffles* (1900). Interesting works all dealing with some aspect of European expansion are: A. B. Gould and C. A. Bampfylde, *A History of Sarawak under Its Two White Rajahs* (1909); Lord Ronaldshay, *The Life of Lord Curzon*, 3 volumes (1927-1928); Sir Harry H. Johnston, *The Story of my Life* (1923); D. Livingstone, *Missionary Travels in Africa* (n.d.); H. Schnee, *German Colonization, Past and Future* (1926); H. M. Stanley, *In Darkest Africa* (1897); and S. N. Banerjea, *A Nation in the Making; Reminiscences of Fifty Years of Public Life in Bengal* (1926).

9: Explosion in Europe

*1. **The Diplomatic Background:*** Short and interesting accounts are given in C. J. H. Hayes, *A Generation of Materialism* (1941), Chapters 1 and 8; J. S. Schapiro, *Modern and Contemporary European History* (1934), Chapter 33; W. P. Hall and W. S. Davis, *The Course of Europe Since Waterloo* (1941), Chapter 27; V. L. and M. H. Albjerg, *From Sedan to Stresa* (1937), Chapter 19; and G. P. Gooch, *History of Modern Europe* (1923), Chapter 13, "Anglo-German Rivalry," and Chapter 16, "The Breaking of the Storm."

*2. **The Peace Movement:*** See I. S. Bloch, *The Future of War* (1902); A. J. Grant and Harold Temperley, *Europe in the Nineteenth and Twentieth Centuries* (1932), Chapter 35;

and especially the famous work, Norman Angell, *The Great Illusion* (1910). A brief account of the peace movement is given by C. J. H. Hayes, *A Political and Cultural History of Modern Europe* (1937), Volume II, pp. 742-749.

3. Causes of the War: For the standard and definite account see S. B. Fay, *The Origins of the World War,* 2 volumes in 1 (1930). A graphic and objective account will be found in J. W. Swain, *Beginning the Twentieth Century* (1933). Illustrative of the school inclined to place the war guilt on Russia and France is H. E. Barnes, "The World War of 1914-1918," in *War in the Twentieth Century,* edited by Willard Waller (1940). Another good account, more objective and restrained is W. C. Langsam, *The World Since 1914* (1937), Chapter 1, "Into the Valley of Death."

4. The First World War: The best one-volume account is C. R. M. F. Crutwell, *History of the Great War* (1936). Two others recommended are: C. J. H. Hayes, *A Brief Outline of the Great War* (1920), and L. Hart, *The War in Outline* (1936). Langsam, cited above, has a fine summary, Chapters 2 and 3.

5. The United States: See T. A. Bailey, *A Diplomatic History of the American People* (1940), Chapters 37 and 38. A good account will be found in A. M. Schlesinger, *Political and Social Growth of the American People, 1865-1940* (1941), Chapters 15 and 16. More in detail is C. Seymour, *American Diplomacy During the World War* (1934), and J. B. McMaster, *The United States in the World War,* 2 volumes (1927). Provocative is Walter Millis, *The Road to War* (1935).

6. Other References: There has been no better account of the British army in France than this first-hand description by a famous journalist: Sir Philip Gibbs, *Now It Can Be Told* (1920). A pictorial introduction to war is afforded by L. Stallings, Editor, *The First World War, A Photographic Study* (1933). The grim details of life in the French trenches are outlined in Henri Barbusse, *Under Fire* (1917). Potential arm-chair strategists will be interested in W. S. Woods, *Colossal Blunders of the War* (1931). The rôle of the civilian and the condition of the home fronts are well described in F. P. Chambers, *The War Behind the War* (1939). The war in the Near East is described in two classical accounts by an enigmatic genius: T. E. Lawrence, *Revolt in the Desert* (1927) and *Seven Pillars of Wisdom* (1935). The following memoirs will be found of value: Prince Lichnowsky, *My Mission to London* (1918); Viscount E. Grey, *Twenty-Five Years,* 2 volumes (1925); P. von Hindenburg, *Out of My Life* (1920). L. Renn, *War* (1929), the frank record of experiences in the German army. Siegfried Sassoon, *The Memoirs of George Sherston* (1937), stresses the horrors of war. G. P. Gooch in *Before the War: Studies in Diplomacy,* 2 volumes (1936 and 1938), discusses the diplomacy of ten leading statesmen, such as Lansdowne, Delcassé, Iswolsky, etc.

7. Novels: E. M. Remarque, *All Quiet on the Western Front,* a grippling novel dealing with the common German soldier. A famous novel of the Argentine and wartime France is Blasco Ibáñez, *The Four Horsemen of the Apocalypse.* Humphrey Cobb, *Paths to Glory,* is a realistic war story. The Russian front is portrayed in Sir Hugh Walpole, *The Dark Forest,* and in Richard Boleslavski, *The Way of the Lancer.* The effect of the war upon England is brilliantly portrayed by H. G. Wells in *Mr. Britling Sees It Through.* Two well-known dramas of the war are: R. C. Sheriff, *Journey's End* and L. Stallings and M. Anderson, *What Price Glory?* The Italian front is portrayed in Ernest Hemingway, *A Farewell to Arms.* Arnold Zweig's novels are classic studies of the First War: *Young Woman of 1914, The Case of Sergeant Grischa,* and *Education Before Verdun.*

10: A Quest for World Order

1. The Peace Treaties: W. C. Langsam, *The World Since 1914* (1937) is especially fine for the making of the peace. See Chapters 4 and 5. A good account is also given by W. P. Hall and W. S. Davis, *The Course of Europe Since Waterloo* (1941), Chapter 30. Erik Achorn, *European Civilization and Politics Since 1815* (1934) severely castigates the Treaty of Versailles. See Chapter 16, "Carthago Delenda Est." Another critical evaluation of the Treaty is found in H. E. Barnes, *The History of Western Civilization* (1935), Volume II, Chapter 18. A well-balanced appraisal of the Treaty of Versailles is given in Paul Birdsall,

Versailles Twenty Years After 1914 (1941). The German technique of making peace may be studied in J. W. Wheeler-Bennett, *Brest-Litovsk, The Forgotten Peace* (1939).

2. The League of Nations: Brief excellent treatments of the League, its genesis, organization, and function are in Langsam, cited above, Chapter 6; Achorn, cited above, Chapter 21; and F. L. Benns, *Europe Since 1914* (1930), Chapter 9. Adequate summaries of American foreign policy and the attitude toward the League immediately after the Versailles Conference are in S. E. Morison and H. S. Commager, *The Growth of the American Republic* (1937), Volume II, Chapter 21; and A. M. Schlesinger, *Political and Social Growth of the American People* (1941), Volume II, Chapter 17. The rôle played by the United States in the affairs of the League of Nations is treated in D. F. Fleming, *United States and the League of Nations* (1932), good for the conflict over joining the League; see also Fleming's *United States and World Organization, 1920-1933* (1938). Activities of the League are covered in J. S. Bassett, *The League of Nations* (1928); P. J. N. Baker, *The League of Nations at Work* (1926), a popular account. F. L. Schuman, *International Politics* (1937) has a good discussion of the League; and C. Howard-Ellis, *The Origin, Structure, and Working of the League of Nations* (1928) covers the whole subject in a capable manner.

3. World Problems: For an elementary yet splendid summary treatment see Thomas Brockway, *Battles Without Bullets, the Story of Economic Warfare* (1939). A standard treatment of the war debt question is found in H. G. Moulton and Leo Pasvolsky, *World War Debt Settlements* (1926). See also by the same authors: *War Debts and World Prosperity* (1932). Sumner H. Schlichter, *Modern Economic Society* (1928), Chapter 30, "International Economic Policies." Other important sources on the economic results of the war and the peace are: J. M. Keynes, *The Economic Consequences of the Peace* (1920); H. Schacht, *The End of Reparations* (1931); and G. P. Auld, *The Dawes Plan and the New Economics* (1927). The advent of the great depression is treated in the following: P. Einzig, *The World Economic Crisis, 1929-1932* (1932), a nontechnical account; E. M. Patterson, *The World's Economic Dilemma* (1930); S. B. Clough and C. W. Cole, *Economic History of Europe* (1941), Chapter 24, "In Our Time."

4. Diplomacy, Pacts, Disarmaments: R. L. Buell, *The Washington Conference* (1922), a standard work; J. T. Shotwell, *War as an Instrument of National Policy and its Renunciation in the Pact of Paris* (1929), a very comprehensive treatment; J. W. Wheeler-Bennett, *Disarmament and Security Since Locarno* (1932), a valuable work by a prolific writer on peace and disarmament. A valuable brief discussion of postwar diplomacy is given in Langsam, cited above, Chapter 8; and in Gillespie, cited above, Chapter 28. The best single volume on international relations is G. M. Gathorne-Hardy, *Short History of International Affairs* (1938). William Orton, *Twenty Years' Armistice* (1938) is "a rapid view of the period as a whole."

5. Other References: Helpful memoirs and biographies are: G. A. Riddell, *Lord Riddell's Intimate Diary of the Peace Conference and After, 1918-1923* (1934); Allan Nevins, *Henry White: Thirty Years of American Diplomacy* (1930); R. Lansing, *The Big Four and Others at the Peace Conference* (1921); J. H. Edwards, *David Lloyd George* (1929); H. H. Tiltman, *J. Ramsay MacDonald: Labor's Man of Destiny* (1929); Sisley Huddleston, *Poincaré* (1924); Valentine Thomson, *Briand, Man of Peace* (1930); A. Vallentin, *Stresemann* (1931); H. C. Englebrecht and F. C. Hanighen, *Merchants of Death* (1934), a study of the armament industry. An intimate and vivid account of men and events at the Paris Peace Conference is given in J. T. Shotwell, *At the Peace Conference* (1937). A rather depressing brief account of the complexities and squabbles of the Conference is presented by Herbert Hoover, *America's First Crusade* (1942).

6. Novels: Upton Sinclair, *World Without End*, deals with postwar international relations; Sir Philip Gibbs, *Blood Relations*, a moving story woven around the marriage of an English girl to an idealistic German; E. M. Remarque, *The Road Back*, a vivid and depressing picture of what happened to many German demobilized soldiers in 1919; Sylvia Thompson, *Hounds of Spring;* Sholom Asch, *The War Goes On*, the effects of inflation in Germany; Sir Philip Gibbs, *The Cross of Peace*, a splendid picture of postwar years in France, Germany, England.

11: New Patterns in Statecraft

*1. **Soviet Russia:*** A good summary of events since 1917 is given in George Vernadsky, *A History of Russia* (1929), the last eight chapters. Nontechnical and not too detailed accounts of the rise of Communism, its political and economic structure, its accomplishments and failures, may be found in Earl R. Sikes, *Contemporary Economic Systems* (1940), Part III; and W. N. Loucks and J. W. Hoot, *Comparative Economic Systems* (1938), Part V. The draft of the Soviet constitution is given in Sikes, pp. 648-669; and in Loucks and Hoot, pp. 766-787. Two important anti-Soviet studies are W. H. Chamberlain, *Russia's Iron Age* (1936), and Eugene Lyons, *Assignment in Utopia* (1937). In contrast two works of a highly favorable nature may be cited: Sidney and Beatrice Webb, *Soviet Communism: A New Civilization* (1936); A. R. Williams, *The Soviets* (1937). An interesting and valuable work, by a former American ambassador to Russia, is Joseph E. Davies, *Mission to Moscow* (1941). See especially "Brief on the Facts," pp. 375-426, a confidential report sent to the Secretary of State in 1938. A sympathetic account of Russian justice is Mary S. Calcott, *Russian Justice* (1935). An important discussion of Soviet aims and ideology is A. I. Stetsky, "The Liquidation of Classes in the USSR," *Source Book of European Governments,* edited by W. E. Rappard *et al* (1939), pp. 130-165.

*2. **The Third German Reich:*** For the Weimar Republic see H. Quigley and R. T. Clark, *Republican Germany* (1928). Karl Lowenstein in *Governments of Continental Europe,* edited by J. T. Shotwell (1940), has a comprehensive treatment of the Republic, pp. 339-404. See especially "The Balance Sheet of the Weimar Republic," pp. 400-404. A standard work on National Socialism is K. Heiden, *A History of National Socialism* (1931). E. A. Mowrer, *Germany Puts the Clock Back,* new edition (1939), is a classic treatment of the rise to power of Nazism. Other valuable works dealing with the passing of the republic are: C. B. Hoover, *Germany Enters the Third Reich* (1933), R. T. Clark, *The Fall of the German Republic* (1935), and Douglas Reed, *The Burning of the Reichstag* (1934). Three outstanding and very readable studies of Hitler's régime are Stephen H. Roberts, *The House That Hitler Built* (1937), F. L. Schuman, *The Nazi Dictatorship,* 2nd edition (1936), and H. Lichtenberger, *The Third Reich* (1937). A. S. Duncan-Jones, *The Struggle for Religious Freedom in Germany* (1938) and E. Y. Hartshorne, *The German Universities Under National Socialism* (1937), discuss Nazi repression in the fields of religion and education. The concentration camp is covered in G. Seger, *A Nation Terrorized* (1935), and K. Billinger, *Fatherland* (1935).

*3. **Fascist Italy:*** An excellent brief account is C. T. Schmidt, *The Corporate State in Action* (1939). An outstanding discussion of Fascist politics is Herman Finer, *Mussolini's Italy* (1935). H. W. Schneider, *Making the Fascist State* (1928), and A. Rossi, *The Rise of Italian Fascism* (1938), are thorough studies of the rise of dictatorship in Italy. The Fascist political structure is treated, not too extensively, in R. L. Buell, *New Governments in Europe* (1934), and F. A. Ogg, *European Governments and Politics,* 2nd edition (1939). The repressive features of Fascism are presented in P. Nenni, *Ten Years of Tyranny in Italy* (1932), and F. F. Nitti, *Escape* (1930). C. M. Creswell, *The Keystone of Fascism: A Study of the Ascendancy of Discipline* (1929), is an enthusiastic evaluation. Gaetano Salvemini, *The Fascist Dictatorship in Italy* (1927), is one of the best accounts hostile to Mussolini.

*4. **Modern Turkey:*** The regeneration and transformation of Turkey is ably and interestingly treated in the following: A. J. Toynbee and K. P. Kirkwood, *Turkey* (1927); H. F. Armstrong, *Turkey and Syria Reborn* (1930); H. E. Allen, *The Turkish Transformation* (1935); and D. E. Webster, *The Turkey of Ataturk* (1939).

*5. **General Surveys:*** Concise, introductory treatments of postwar Russia, Germany, and Italy are: George Vernadsky, *The Russian Revolution, 1917-1931* (1932); T. W. Riker, *A Short History of Modern Europe* (1935); Frederick L. Schuman, *Germany Since 1918* (1937); F. L. Benns, *Europe Since 1914* (1931); W. C. Langsam, *The World Since 1914* (1934); J. E. Gillespie, *Europe in Perspective* (1942).

*6. **Other References:*** D. von Mikusch, *Mustapha Kemal: Between Europe and Asia* (1931), an invaluable study; H. E. Wortham, *Mustapha Kemal of Turkey* (1931), an interesting sketch. For Italy the following may be recommended: B. Mussolini, *My Autobiography* (1928); Gaudens Megaro, *Mussolini in the Making* (1938); M. Sarfatti, *The Life of Benito Mussolini* (1925), a eulogy which may be corrected by referring to George Seldes, *Sawdust Caesar* (1935). The following will be found interesting: Louis Fischer, *Soviet Journey* (1935), very sympathetic; André Gide, *Return from the U.S.S.R.* (1937), a French novelist finds Russia somewhat disappointing; Sir Walter Citrine, *I Search for Truth in Russia* (1936), the personal account of a British labor union leader; and J. D. and Bess Littlepage, *In Search of Soviet Gold* (1937), the reaction of American engineers to Soviet industrial methods. For Lenin, Trotsky, and Stalin see: D. S. Mirsky, *Lenin* (1931); G. Vernadsky, *Lenin, Red Dictator* (1931); Leon Trotsky, *My Life: An Attempt at an Autobiography* (1930); S. Graham, *Stalin* (1931); and I. D. Levine, *Stalin* (1931). J. H. Wheeler-Bennett, *Hindenburg, the Wooden Titan* (1936) is an excellent study of the famous German idol. Two important Nazis tell their part in creating the New Order, in Joseph Göbbels, *My Part in Germany's Fight* (1935) and Hermann Göring, *Germany Reborn* (1934). For Hitler see S. Wallach, *Hitler* (1933); John Gunther, *Inside Europe* (1938); Adolf Hitler, *My Battle* (*Mein Kampf*), several editions, an invaluable insight into Hitler's personality and policies; and K. Heiden, *Hitler: A Biography* (1936). The following are intensely interesting: Margaret Kent, *I Married a German* (1938); G. E. R. Gedye, *Betrayal in Central Europe* (1939); C. W. Domville-Fife, *This Is Germany* (1939); Martha Dodd, *Through Embassy Eyes* (1939).

*7. **Novels:*** Two novels of modern Italy are Ignazio Silone, *Fontamara*, and *Bread and Wine*. Maurice Hindus, *Moscow Skies*, a novel of Soviet life at the beginning of the Five-Year Plan; Mikhail Sholokhov, *The Silent Don* (combining in one volume *And Quiet Flows the Don* and *The Don Flows to the Sea*), deals with the First World War and the Russian Revolution. Valuable fictionalized accounts are: L. Feuchtwanger, *The Oppermanns*, the Jews under Hitler; Ethel Vance, *Escape;* Nora Waln, *Reaching for the Stars;* Ernst Glaeser, *The Last Civilian;* André Malraux, *Days of Wrath*, a story of Nazi persecution of German Communists; Ida A. Wylie, *To the Vanquished*, revolt of a group of Nazi youths.

12: Democracy on Trial

*1. **Continental Europe:*** Readable scholarly surveys of the various European countries after 1919 are in J. E. Gillespie, *Europe in Perspective* (1942), and W. P. Hall and W. S. Davis, *The Course of Europe Since Waterloo* (1941). More comprehensive but suitable for the general reader are W. C. Langsam, *The World Since 1914* (1937), and F. L. Benns, *Europe Since 1914* (1934). The background of the Spanish Civil War is given in E. A. Peers, *The Spanish Tragedy* (1936). For other countries see: M. W. Childs, *Sweden, the Middle Way* (1936); A. J. Barnouw, *The Dutch: A Portrait Study of the People of Holland* (1940); M. W. Fodor, *Plot and Counterplot in Central Europe* (1937); R. L. Buell, *Poland: Key to Europe* (1939); M. Derrick, *The Portugal of Salazar* (1939); P. Vaucher, *Post-War France* (1934); D. W. Brogan, *France Under the Republic* (1940); André Simone, *J'Accuse* (1941), an exposé of French politicians; A. J. Toynbee and K. P. Kirkwood, *Turkey* (1927); J. S. Roucek, *Contemporary Rumania and Her Problems* (1932); *The Cambridge History of Poland*, edited by W. F. Reddaway, J. H. Penson, O. Halecki, R. Dyboski (1941); G. M. Gathorne-Hardy, *Norway* (1925); J. R. Harris, *Progressive Norway* (1939); P. Manniche, *Denmark, A Social Laboratory* (1939); and J. H. Jackson, *Finland* (1938). A valuable reference book giving much information on postwar Europe is René Albrecht-Carrié and others, *Contemporary Europe, A Study of National, International, Economic, and Cultural Trends* (1941).

*2. **Great Britain:*** A good survey of Great Britain following the Treaty of Versailles will be found in J. A. Spender, *Great Britain, Empire and Commonwealth* (n. d.), Chapters 51-59 and 65-67. The social history of Great Britain is interestingly presented in Robert Graves and Alan Hodge, *The Long Week End* (1941). An account of efforts in England to counter economic depression is given in H. Heaton, *The British Way to Recovery* (1934). Postwar trends are described in D. C. Somervell, *The Reign of George* v (1935). A concise account of England after 1919 is Sir John

Marriott, *Modern England* (1934), Chapters 25-29. An interpretation of British life and institutions by a German scholar is W. Dibelius, *England* (1930). An interesting account of British colonial problems in Africa is J. Huxley, *Africa View* (1936). British imperial problems are in R. Coupland, *The Empire in These Days* (1935). Recent developments in the British Dominions are in Howard Robinson, *The Development of the British Empire* (1936). American students will find Alfred L. Burt, *A Short History of Canada for Americans* (1942) very worth while. One of the best brief surveys of the British Empire is R. G. Trotter, *The British Empire-Commonwealth* (1933).

3. The United States: James Truslow Adams, *The March of Democracy* (1933), Volume II. The last two chapters give an interesting interpretation of recent American history. The same period is covered in Charles and Mary Beard, *The Rise of American Civilization* (1927), Volume II, the last 2 chapters; Charles and Mary Beard, *America in Midpassage* (1939); L. M. Hacker, *American Problems of Today* (1938); R. L. Dumond, *Roosevelt to Roosevelt* (1937); and A. M. Schlesinger, *Political and Social Growth of the American People* (1941). John D. Hicks, *The American Nation* (1941), Chapters 23-30, is a vivid well-written story of the twenties and thirties. F. L. Allen, *Only Yesterday* (1931), is an interesting picture of America in the 1920's. See also F. L. Allen, *Since Yesterday* (1940).

4. Latin America: A journalistic account with shrewd interpretations and a mass of digestible information is John Gunther, *Inside Latin America* (1941). Reliable accounts of Latin America between two wars are: F. A. Kirkpatrick, *Latin America* (1939); Charles E. Chapman, *Republican Hispanic America* (1938); J. F. Rippy, *Historical Evolution of Hispanic America* (1940); A. C. Wilgus, *The Development of Hispanic America* (1941); W. L. Schurz, *Latin America* (1941). See Part V, "The Economy" and Part VII, "The Way of Life." A valuable interpretation of Latin-American trends and culture is given by S. G. Inman, *Latin America, Its Place In World Life* (1937). The bibliographies are especially good in this work. A handy panoramic view of Latin-American culture and development is given in J. B. Trend, *South America: With Mexico and Central America* (1941). Contemporary conditions in Latin America are discussed by experts in *Modern Hispanic America*, edited by A. C. Wilgus (1933). See Chapter 5 on political life, 6 on economics, 12 on education, and 21 on Inter-American relations. Additional sources for current problems are Carleton Beals, *The Coming Struggle for Latin America* (1939) and Frank Tannerbaum, *Whither Latin America* (1934). For specific areas: Luis Goldames, *A History of Chile* (1941); Ernest Gruening, *Mexico and Its Heritage* (1940); and F. A. Kirkpatrick, *A History of the Argentine Republic* (1931).

5. Other References: Stuart Chase, *A Study of the Two Americas* (1931), Indian and Anglo-Saxon American culture contrasted. G. L. Sanchez, *Mexico, A Revolution by Education* (1936). A good anthology of poetry is Alice S. Blackwell, *Some Spanish American Poets* (1929). Harold Nicolson, *Life of Dwight Morrow* (1935), one of our most important ambassadors to Mexico. M. V. Hughes, *A London Family Between Two Wars* (1940) is a valuable sociological document. R. H. Lockhart, *Retreat from Glory* (1934) is a readable biography covering the period 1918 to 1934. An Englishman sizes up the "States" in D. W. Brogan, *U.S.A.* (1941). S. H. Adams, *Revelry* (1926), the Harding scandal. Marie, Queen of Rumania, *The Story of My Life* (1934). H. A. Gibbons, *Venizelos* (1923).

6. Novels: Upton Sinclair, *Between Two Worlds*, a novel dealing with the international scene, mainly Europe, in the 1920's. Liam O'Flaherty, *The Informer* deals with civil war in Ireland. For the American scene in the 1920's see Sinclair Lewis, *Main Street* and *Babbitt;* also Theodore Dreiser, *An American Tragedy*. For the life of soldiers during the Mexican revolutions see Mariano Azuela, *Underdogs*, and M. L. Guzman, *The Eagle and the Serpent*.

13: The Orient Astir

1. India: The problems of the Nationalist movement have been set forth in A. Besant, *India: A Nation*, 4th edition (1930), and, more recently, in J. Nehru, *An Autobiography* (1936). The writings of M. K. Gandhi should be consulted for his philosophical views concerning noncooperation and nonviolence. See especially *Young India, 1924-1926* (1927). A sympathetic interpretation of Gandhi himself is furnished by C. F. Andrews, *Mahatma Gandhi's Ideas, Including Selections from His Writings* (1930). A work that stirred up much controversy in its analysis of Indian social life was K. Mayo, *Mother India* (1927). In connection with this work the student is counseled to consult authors holding contrary viewpoints, such as D. G. Mukerji, *A Son of Mother India Answers* (1928). One of the most interesting accounts of Indian developments following 1918 is found in W. P. Hall, *From Empire to Commonwealth* (1928), Chapter 11. A useful series of short essays on political conditions and problems will be found in *Political India,* edited by Sir John Cumming (1932). Social and economic conditions are treated in *Modern India,* edited by Sir John Cumming (1931). Works written by Indian nationalists critical of British rule are: Lajpat Rai, *Young India* (1916), and by the same author *England's Debt to India* (1918); *Mahatma Gandhi, His Own Story,* edited by C. F. Andrews (1930); and Annie Besant, *India, Bond or Free* (1926). In W. Durant, *The Case for India* (1933), an American author presents the Indian case. C. H. Van Tyne, *India in Ferment* (1923) is a first-hand objective account by an American historian. The concluding chapters of E. Thompson and E. T. Garratt, *The Rise and Fulfilment of British Rule in India* (1934) represent an unbiased summary of recent events. W. E. Duffett, A. R. Hicks, G. R. Parkin, *India Today* (1942) is an excellent brief account of Indian problems and politics. Another valuable analysis of contemporary India is Sir George Schuster and Guy Wint, *India and Democracy* (1941).

2. China: The student should read for himself source materials relating to modern Chinese history: Harley F. MacNair, *Modern Chinese History, Selected Readings* (1923). See especially Chapters 15, 16, and 17. Sun Yat-sen's ideas are set forth in *San Min Chu I; The Three Principles of the People* (1927), while an excellent account of Sun Yat-sen's work itself is given in L. Sharman, *Sun Yat-Sen; His Life and Its Meaning* (1934). C. F. Remer has written the most definitive study of the subject in *Foreign Investments in China* (1933). For a general picture of conditions, see pp. 58-80; regarding American, British, and Japanese investments, see Part II, Chapters 15, 16, 17 respectively. A work containing documents is W. W. Willoughby, *The Sino-Japanese Controversy and the League of Nations* (1935). On the subject of the work of the Chinese Communists and their military successes, see V. A. Yakhontoff, *The Chinese Soviets* (1934) and Edgar Snow, *Red Star Over China* (1938).

3. Japan: An admirable and readable brief account of the rise of Japanese power is given in T. A. Bisson, *Shadow over Asia* (1941). A work of social and economic importance is G. C. Allen, *Modern Japan and Its Problems* (1928), while an up-to-date account of the political and social evolution of the country is found in Hugh Borton, *Japan Since 1931* (1940). Japan's most powerful financial house is described in Oland D. Russel, *The House of Mitsui* (1939). How the army has strengthened its position in the political framework of Japan is told in Kenneth W. Colegrove, *Militarism in Japan* (1936).

4. Other References: A delightful study of the temperament of the Chinese people has been written by Lin Yutang in *My Country and My People* (1935). For keeping informed about the Far East, the student should consult the following journals: *Far Eastern Survey, Pacific Affairs,* and *Asia.*

5. Novels: Pearl Buck has written some magnificent novels about modern China: *The Good Earth, Sons, A House Divided,* and *The Patriot.* Another very worth-while novel is the recent book by Lin Yutang, *A Moment in Peking.*

14: A World Divided

1. Immediate Background: The most complete discussion of the background of World War II will be found in F. L. Schuman, *Night Over Europe, The Diplomacy of Nemesis, 1939-1940* (1941). The German explanation is given by Alfred von Wegerer, *The Origins of World War II* (1941). A prophetic picture of what Nazi policy aimed to achieve is found in *Ambassador Dodd's Diary,* edited by W. E. and Martha Dodd (1941). G. G. Armstrong, *Why Another World War* (1941) points out the tragic lost opportunities of collective security. Otto D. Tolischus, *They Wanted War* (1940) is an indictment of the militaristic ambitions of Nazi Germany. F. J. C. Hearnshaw, *Germany the Aggressor* (1940) endeavors to show that conquest is a deep-seated German tradition. J. F. Kennedy, *Why England Slept* (1940) attempts to show how muddle and appeasement in Great Britain played their rôle in bringing on World War II. The works of Winston Churchill are valuable for an understanding of British policy. See *Step by Step, 1936-1939* (1939) and *While England Slept* (1938). A graphic description of British diplomacy in Germany is contained in Sir Nevile Henderson, *Failure of a Mission* (1940).

2. ***Issues of the War:*** Norman Angell, *For What Do We Fight?* (1939); Harold Nicholson, *Why Britain Is at War* (1939); H. A. L. Fisher and others, *The Background and Issues of the War* (1940), lectures delivered at the University of Oxford; Arthur Greenwood, *Why We Fight: Labour's Case* (1939).

3. ***World War II:*** Much useful information is presented in John De Wilde, D. H. Popper, and Eunice Clark, *Handbook of the War* (1940). The first two years of war are clearly covered in Edgar McInnis, *The War: First Year* (1940) and *The War: Second Year* (1941). The collapse of France is graphically narrated in Gordon Waterfield, *What Happened to France* (1940); C. D. Freeman and D. Cooper, *The Road to Bordeaux* (1941); and André Maurois, *Tragedy in France* (1940). Other works that may be consulted are: E. N. Van Kleffens, *Juggernaut Over Holland* (1941); Alan Moorehead, *Mediterranean Front* (1942); David Garnett, *War in the Air: September 1939-May 1941* (1941); Maurice Hindus, *Hitler Cannot Conquer Russia* (1942); M. Dobb, *Soviet Economy and the War* (1941); and Lucien Zacharoff, Editor, *The Voice of Fighting Russia* (1942), vivid pictures of the conflict in Russia.

4. ***Military Tactics:*** See Hermann Foertsch, *The Art of Modern Warfare* (1940), by a German colonel; Donald Portway, *Military Science Today* (1941), a popular account; and two widely discussed books: Lieutenant Colonel W. F. Kernan, *Defense Will Not Win the War* (1942), and Major Alexander P. de Seversky, *Victory Through Air Power* (1942).

5. ***Europe in Wartime:*** Halvdan Koht, *Norway: Neutral and Invaded* (1941); Lars Moën, *Under the Iron Heel* (1941), Belgium under the Nazis; Quentin Reynolds, *The Wounded Don't Cry* (1941), France and mainly Great Britain in war time; Paul Einzig, *Europe in Chains* (1941). German techniques in gaining control of France's economic resources are in Thomas Kernan, *France on Berlin Time* (1941). Wallace R. Deuel, *People Under Hitler* (1942); Allan Nevins, *This Is England Today* (1941). The systematic spoilation of conquered areas is described in Thomas Reveille, *The Spoil of Europe* (1941).

6. ***The United States:*** J. H. Latané and D. W. Wainhouse, *A History of American Foreign Policy* (1941); William C. Bullitt, *Report to the American People* (1940), the danger of Nazi conquest. General Hugh S. Johnson, *Hell-Bent for War* (1941), against American involvement; Ralph Ingersoll, *America Is Worth Fighting For* (1941); H. R. Luce, *The American Century* (1941).

7. ***War in the Pacific:*** W. C. Johnstone, *Why Japan Chose War* (1942); H. C. Bywater, *The Great Pacific War*, first written in 1925, prophesied the United States-Japanese imbroglio; F. R. Dulles, *America in the Pacific* (1938); J. L. Christian, *Modern Burma* (1942). See Chapters 12-14 on the Burma Road, foreign relations, and the rise of Nationalism. Edgar Snow, *The Battle for Asia* (1940); Wilfrid Fleisher, *Our Enemy Japan* (1942). The strategic pattern of the Pacific is described in W. D. Puleston, *The Armed Forces of the Pacific* (1941); F. M. Keesing, *The South Seas in the Modern World* (1941), economic, social, political conditions in South Pacific islands.

8. ***General Surveys:*** Brief surveys may be found in the following: W. P. Hall and W. S. Davis, *The Course of Europe Since Waterloo* (1941), Chapter 37; J. E. Gillespie, *Europe in Perspective* (1942), Chapter 36; W. C. Langsam, *Since 1939, A Narrative of War* (1941); F. Lee Benns, *Europe's Return to War* (1940); and *War in the Twentieth Century*, edited by Willard Waller (1940), Chapters 2, 3, 8, and 9. Longer accounts are in: Walter Millis, *Why Europe Fights* (1940), a popularly written but helpful summary; Editors of *Fortune*, *Background of War* (1937); William Orton, *Twenty Years' Armistice* (1938); and V. M. Dean, *Europe in Retreat* (1939). Two excellent treatments of the diplomatic history preceding the outbreak of war are G. M. Gathorne-Hardy, *A Short History of International Affairs* (1938) and D. E. Lee, *Ten Years* (1942).

9. Other References: Oswald Garrison Villard, *Within Germany* (1940); Leland Stowe, *No Other Road to Freedom* (1941); Hans Habe, *A Thousand Shall Fall* (1941); Thomas B. Morgan, *Spurs On the Boot* (1941), first-hand account of Fascist Italy; Winston Churchill, *Blood, Sweat, and Tears* (1941), speeches of the British prime minister; H. R. Wilson, *Diplomat Between Wars* (1941); John Cudahy, *The Armies March* (1941); P. Barrès, *Charles De Gaulle* (1941); Eric Estorick, *Stafford Cripps: Prophetic Rebel* (1941); Philip Guedalla, *Mr. Churchill* (1942); Louis Fischer, *Men and Politics* (1941); Vincent Sheean, *Not Peace but a Sword* (1939); Vera Brittain, *England's Hour* (1941); E. B. Hitchcock, *"I Built A Temple For Peace," The Life of Eduard Benes* (1940); W. L. Shirer, *Berlin Diary* (1941); E. R. Murrow, *This Is London* (1941); Sir Walter Citrine, *My American Diary* (1941); Virginia Cowles, *Looking For Trouble* (1941), exciting memoirs of a correspondent; Henry Torrès, *Pierre Laval* (1941); Patricia Strauss, *Bevin and Company* (1941); Fritz Thyssen, *I Paid Hitler* (1941); and René Kraus, *The Men Around Churchill* (1941).

10. Novels: Eric Knight, *This Above All,* a widely discussed novel of England in war time. Helen MacInnes, *Assignment in Brittany,* an excellent spy story; John Steinbeck, *The Moon Is Down,* a gripping story of life in a conquered country.

15: Forging a New World

1. Science: A provocative work which concerns itself with the philosophical implications of modern science is Alfred North Whitehead, *Science and the Modern World* (1926). A good brief account of the theory of relativity is Bertrand Russell, *The A.B.C. of Relativity* (1925). The student interested in the latest trends in science should consult a journal such as *Nature.*

2. Religion and Philosophy: A good study of comparative religion is William E. Hocking, *Living Religions and a World Faith* (1940). One of the finest novels of modern American literature, and an autobiographical account of one of America's foremost philosophers, is George Santayana, *The Last Puritan* (1935). Recommended are: the pungent essays of the famous American pragmatist, William James; Henri Bergson, *Creative Evolution* (1911), for excellent literary style and provocative reading matter; the works of Benedetto Croce.

3. Literature: The student is advised to learn about twentieth-century literature by reading its "classics." Thomas Mann has written a masterpiece in *Magic Mountain* (1939), and his trilogy on Joseph is a fascinating elaboration of the Old Testament story. *Ulysses* (1940) by James Joyce will repay the diligent reader, and good translations of the novels of Proust can be obtained. Sinclair Lewis' works such as *Babbitt* (1932), *Arrowsmith* (1935), and *Main Street* (1939), deserve to be read also. The poetical philosophy of T. S. Eliot can be found in *The Use of Poetry and the Use of Criticism* (1933), and one should not neglect his *Poems* (1909-1925). Many good anthologies of modern British and American verse can be procured without trouble, and an excellent selection of poetry translated from the world's major literatures is Mark Van Doren, *An Anthology of World Poetry* (1928). For brilliant literary essays consult those of Aldous Huxley, while for clever essays in the humorous vein read the works of such men as Stephen Leacock and James Thurber. Modern dramatists who should be read are George Bernard Shaw, a witty satirist of society, and Eugene O'Neill, the brilliant innovator and psychological dramatist.

4. Esthetic Activities: The philosophy of art and its modern ramifications is discussed interestingly by D. T. Rice, *The Background of Art* (1939). Modern trends in painting are discussed in Sheldon Cheney, *The Story of Modern Art* (1941). However, nothing can take the place of actual visits to art galleries and museums. Fine centers in the United States are the Metropolitan Museum and the Frick Collection in New York, the National Gallery in Washington, D. C., the Art Institute in Chicago (one of whose chief treasures is its collection of ancient Chinese bronzes), and the Henry E. Huntington Library in San Marino, California (the home of many famous English paintings). Toronto, Ontario is a rich Canadian art center and possesses one of the world's finest collections of Chinese ceramics. In the field of music the student will find profitable Deems Taylor, *Of Men* *and Music* (1937), while Oscar Levant, *A Smattering of Ignorance* (1940) is amusing. Again, the student will learn more about musical masterpieces and contemporary trends by listening to music. Cities such as New York, Boston, Philadelphia, Chicago, Cincinnati, Cleveland, St. Louis, San Francisco, and Los Angeles are noted for their fine symphony orchestras.

5. General Surveys: The twentieth century has been richly productive not only in thought and art but in self-examination. Magazines like *Harper's* and the *Atlantic Monthly* should be dipped into periodically for an appraisal of current intellectual trends. Works of real interest which evaluate the sociological trends of modern America include R. S. and H. Lynd, *Middletown* (1937) and *Middletown in Transition* (1937). The ramifications of our modern urban culture are focused in Lewis Mumford, *Technics of Civilization* (1934), and *Culture of Cities* (1940). A delightful humanistic study of modern life from the Chinese point of view, for example, is Lin Yutang, *The Importance of Living* (1941), while a more serious evaluation of contemporary intellectual patterns is found in John H. Randall, *Our Changing Civilization* (1929).

6. Tomorrow's Problems: As a basis for understanding problems that will face the peacemakers after World War II, students will find much of interest in Paul Birdsall, *Versailles Twenty Years After* (1941). Two brief but significant studies on the future of democracy are: Carl Becker, *Modern Democracy* (1941) and C. E. Merriam, *On the Agenda of Democracy* (1941). The pertinent racial, geographical, and economic facts of modern Europe are graphically presented in J. H. Jackson and Kerry Lee, *Problems of Modern Europe* (1941). Probable economic and social trends resulting from the war are touched upon in: Harold J. Laski, *Where Do We Go From Here* (1940); Vera M. Dean, *Toward a New World Order* (Foreign Policy Reports, May 15, 1941); and, with respect to Great Britain, Allan Nevins, *This Is England Today* (1941), and J. B. Priestley, *Out of the People* (1941). A readable and dependable survey of social and economic trends in contemporary United States will be found in C. H. Pegg and others, *American Society and the Changing World* (1942). One of the best single-volume treatments of social trends is H. E. Barnes, *Society in Transition* (1939). Sir George Schuster and G. Vint, *India and Democracy* (1941) analyzes India's political and social aspects today. The most helpful introduction to the colonial problem is W. C. Langsam, *In Quest of Empire, The Problem of Colonies* (1939). Also of value are G. Clark, *A Place in the Sun* (1936); and Royal Institute of International Affairs, *Raw Materials and Colonies* (1936).

7. New Proposals: The most convenient introduction to the complex problem of proposed new world organization is Vera M. Dean, *The Struggle For World Order* (1941). Other works dealing with various phases of this subject are: *Winning both the War and the Peace* (The Annals of the American Academy of Political and Social Science, 1942); Payson S. Wild, Jr., *Machinery of Collaboration Between the United Nations* (Foreign Policy Reports, July 1, 1942); Liston Pope, *Religious Proposals for World Order* (The Church Peace Union and World Alliance, 1941); J. E. Mead, *The Economic Basis of a Durable Peace* (1940); John MacCormac, *America and World Mastery* (1942). P. E. Corbett, *Post-War Worlds* (1942) discusses the various plans that have been formulated; and Nicholas Doman, *The Coming Age of World Control* (1942) proposes a world system of democratic control.

8. Other References: Additional readings of value are: N. Peffer, *Prerequisites to Peace in the Far East* (1940); N. J. Speakman, *America's Strategy in World Affairs* (1942); H. G. Wells, *The New World Order* (1940); Lionel Gelber, *Peace by Power* (1942); Carl Wittke and others, *Democracy Is Different* (1941).

Bibliography and Acknowledgments

1: New Ways of Life

Specific References

1. Herbert Heaton, *Economic History of Europe,* 1936, p. 238. Reprinted by permission of Harper & Brothers.
2. *Ibid.,* p. 239. Reprinted by permission of Harper & Brothers.
3. Laurence B. Packard, *The Commercial Revolution, 1400-1776,* Henry Holt and Company, 1927, p. 23.
4. Heaton, p. 255.
5. G. F. Renard and G. Weulersse, *Life and Work in Modern Europe,* Alfred A. Knopf, 1926, p. 38, and London, Kegan Paul, Trench, Trubner & Co.
6. *Ibid.,* p. 43.
7. Quoted by Renard and Weulersse, p. 49.
8. Quoted by Packard, p. 46.
9. See F. A. Ogg and W. R. Sharp, *Economic Development of Modern Europe,* The Macmillan Company, 1926, p. 77.
10. See Heaton for a discussion of French economic drawbacks, pp. 298-300.
11. See Ogg and Sharp, pp. 75-76.
12. From "A True Report of the late Discoveries and Possessions Taken in the Sight of the Crown of England of the Newfound Lands by . . . Sir Humphrey Gilbert; Hakluyt's Principal Voyages of the English Nation," reprinted in *English Economic History, Select Documents,* compiled by A. E. Bland, P. A. Brown, R. H. Tawney, 3rd impression, London, George Bell & Sons, 1919, p. 435.
13. Edward P. Cheney, *The Dawn of a New Era, 1250-1453,* 1936, pp. 59-61. Reprinted by permission of Harper & Brothers.
14. Clive Day, *A History of Commerce,* 4th ed., Longmans, Green & Co., 1938, p. 152.
15. See Heaton, pp. 366-381.
16. N. S. B. Gras, *Business and Capitalism,* F. S. Crofts & Co., 1939, p. 119.
17. *Merchant of Venice,* Act I, Scene 3.
18. See H. E. Barnes, *The History of Western Civilization,* Harcourt, Brace and Company, 1935, II, pp. 70-72.
19. Heaton, p. 363. Reprinted by permission of Harper & Brothers.
20. *Ibid.,* p. 309.
21. Gras, *A History of Agriculture in Europe and America,* F. S. Crofts & Co., 1925, p. 212.
22. *Ibid.,* p. 213.
23. Heaton, p. 430. Reprinted by permission of Harper & Brothers.
24. Gras, p. 162.
25. From Sir Walter Besant, *London in the Time of the Stuarts,* 1903, p. 303. By permission of The Macmillan Company and London, A. & C. Black, publishers.

General References

Indebtedness for this chapter is owed especially to Herbert Heaton, *Economic History of Europe,* Harper & Brothers, 1936; G. F. Renard and G. Weulersse, *Life and Work in Modern Europe,* Alfred A. Knopf, 1926, and London, Kegan Paul, Trench, Trubner & Co.; F. A. Ogg and W. R. Sharp, *Economic Development of Modern Europe,* The Macmillan Company, 1926; Clive Day, *A History of Commerce,* 4th ed., Longmans, Green & Co., 1938; and H. E. Barnes, *The History of Western Civilization,* II, chaps. 1-3, Harcourt, Brace and Company, 1935. A work of brief compass helpful for general background was Laurence B. Packard, *The Commercial Revolution, 1400-1776,* Henry Holt and Company, 1927. The authors found information on France's commercial and industrial development in Henri Sée, *Economic and Social Conditions in France During the Eighteenth Century,* Alfred A. Knopf, 1927. The effect of the import of bullion in Europe, and Spain's economic decline are covered in E. J. Hamilton, *American Treasure and the Price Revolution in Spain, 1501-1650,* Harvard University Press, 1934. For the background of the rise of capitalism the authors were helped by M. M. Knight, H. E. Barnes, and Felix Flügel, *Economic History of Europe,* Houghton Mifflin Company, 1928, and Preserved Smith, *The Age of the Reformation,* Henry Holt and Company, 1920. For many of the ideas expressed in regard to the agricultural revolution the authors want to thank N. S. B. Gras, whose *History of Agriculture in Europe and America,* F. S. Crofts & Co., 1925, they found most helpful, while the same author's *Business and Capitalism,* F. S. Crofts & Co., 1939, proved excellent in its treatment of mercantile capitalism. Consulted for contemporary source material was A. E. Bland, P. A. Brown, R. H. Tawney, *English Economic History, Select Documents,* 3rd impression, The Macmillan Company, 1919. The social history of London was based principally on William H. Irving, *John Gay's London,* Harvard University Press, 1928; and Sir Walter Besant, *London in the Time of the Stuarts,* The Macmillan Company, 1903, and his *London in the Eighteenth Century,* London, A. & C. Black, 1925.

2: Science, Reason, and Enlightenment

Specific References

1. Quoted by John E. Bentley, *Outline of Philosophy,* Longmans Green & Co., 1939, p. 53.
2. C. H. LaWall, *Four Thousand Years of Pharmacy,* J. B. Lippincott Company, 1927, p. 204.
3. Quoted by H. E. Sigerist, *The Great Doctors,* W. W. Norton & Company, 1933, p. 112.
4. Logan Clendening, *Behind the Doctor,* Alfred A. Knopf, 1933, p. 270.
5. Preserved Smith, *A History of Modern Culture,* Henry Holt and Company, 1930, II, p. 574.

General References

For European science and thought in the 17th and 18th centuries, the authors are indebted to Preserved Smith, *A History of Modern Culture,* 2 vols., Henry Holt and Company, 1930. Valuable suggestions regarding intellectual trends were also drawn from J. H. Randall, *The Making of the Modern Mind,* Houghton Mifflin Company, 1926. The following general works, containing useful and succinct treatments of the Age of Reason, were frequently consulted in planning the general structure of this chapter: Ferdinand Schevill, *A History of Europe,* Harcourt, Brace and Company, 1938; Carlton J. H. Hayes, *A Political and Cultural History of Modern Europe,* The Macmillan Company, 1932; Albert Hyma, *Europe from the Renaissance to 1815,* F. S. Crofts & Co., 1931; and James E. Gillespie, *A History of Europe, 1500-1815,* Alfred A. Knopf, 1928. In the field of science, W. T. Sedgwick and H. W. Tyler, *A Short History of Science,* rev. ed., The Macmillan Company, 1939, was a trustworthy guide. Sir William Dampier, *A History of Science and its relations with philosophy and religion,* Cambridge University Press, 1929, was also of much assistance. The discussion of the rise of scientific societies was based on Martha Ornstein, *The Role of Scientific Societies in the Sevententh Century,* University of Chicago Press, 1928. Two works supplied useful biographical items in the field of science: Phillipp E. Lenard, *Great Men of Science,* The Macmillan Company, 1933; and E. R. Trattner, *Architects of Ideas,* Carrick & Evans, 1938. There are numerous scholarly yet easily understood works on the developments in medical science. In this category is preeminently F. H. Garrison, *An Introduction to the History of Medicine,* W. B. Saunders Company, 1929. Mention should also be made of Arturo Castiglioni, *History of Medicine,* trans. by E. B. Krumbahr, Alfred A. Knopf, 1941. The dramatic and often horrific aspects of medical history are well portrayed in Logan Clendening, *Behind the Doctor,* Alfred A. Knopf, 1933; and Howard W. Haggard, *Devils, Drugs, and Doctors,* Harper & Brothers, 1929. The discussion on early drugs and nostrums was found mainly in Charles H. LaWall, *Four Thousand Years of Pharmacy,* J. B. Lippincott Company, 1927. The discussion of art owes much to three excellent treatments: Thomas Craven, *Men of Art,* Simon and Schuster, 1936; Sheldon Cheney, *A World History of Art,* The Viking Press, 1937; and R. S. Stites, *The Arts and Man,* McGraw-Hill Book Company, 1940. The treatment of architecture was checked against the authoritative work by Sir Banister Fletcher, *A History of Architecture,* 9th ed., Charles Scribner's Sons, 1931. Reference was also made to Fiske Kimball and G. H. Edgell, *A History of Architecture,* Harper & Brothers, 1918. Valuable guides in preparing the material on music were Waldo S. Pratt, *The History of Music,* G. Schirmer, 1935, and Karl Nef, *An Outline of the History of Music,* Columbia University Press, 1935. Useful for an interpretive viewpoint was Hugo Leichtentritt, *Music, History, and Ideas,* Harvard University Press, 1938. In literature the most convenient summary was John Drinkwater, *The Outline of Literature,* 3 vols., G. P. Putnam's Sons, 1923-1924. In English literature the authors are indebted to L. F. Cazamian and Emile H. Legouis, *A History of English Literature,* rev. ed., The Macmillan Company, 1929. Pedagogical trends were treated in E. P. Cubberley, *History of Education,* Houghton Mifflin Company, 1920, an authoritative and interesting account. A charming interpretation of European manners and taste in the eighteenth century was found in R. B. Mowat, *The Age of Reason,* Houghton Mifflin Company, 1934.

3: When in the Course of Human Events

Specific References

1. Quoted by Frederick L. Schuman, *International Politics: The Western State System in Transition,* 3rd ed., McGraw-Hill Book Company, 1941, p. 33.
2. Quoted by Schuman, p. 49.
3. W. P. Hall and R. G. Albion, *A History of England and the British Empire,* Ginn and Company, 1937, p. 394.
4. John C. Hamilton, Ed., *The Works of Alexander Hamilton,* 7 vols., Houghton, Osgood and Co., 1851, II, p. 80.
5. H. A. L. Fisher, *A History of Europe,* Houghton Mifflin Company, 1936, p. 769.
6. L. M. Larson, *A History of England and the British Commonwealth,* rev. ed., Henry Holt and Company, 1932, p. 529.
7. Quoted by Robert Ergang, *Europe from the Renaissance to Waterloo,* D. C. Heath and Company, 1939, p. 621.
8. E. J. Lowell, *The Eve of the French Revolution,* Houghton Mifflin Company, 1892, p. 24.
9. Ergang, p. 329.
10. From Carlton J. H. Hayes, *History of Modern Europe,* 1932, I, p. 614. By permission of The Macmillan Company, publishers.
11. James E. Gillespie, *A History of Europe, 1500-1815,* W. W. Norton & Company, 1928, p. 537.
12. Albert Hyma, *Europe from the Renaissance to 1815,* F. S. Crofts & Co., 1931, p. 513.
13. Gillespie, p. 544.
14. Ergang, p. 717.
15. *Ibid.,* p. 752.

General References

For political developments from 1650 to 1815, this chapter is indebted to Robert Ergang, *Europe from the Renaissance to Waterloo,* D. C. Heath and Company, 1939. Other works spanning this period were utilized: H. A. L. Fisher, *A History of Europe,* London, Edward Arnold and Company, 1937; Albert Hyma, *Europe from the Renaissance to 1815,* F. S. Crofts & Co., 1931; and James E. Gillespie, *A History of Europe, 1500-1815,* Alfred A. Knopf, 1929. Helpful ideas on the rise of the national state system and the advent of modern diplomatic techniques were found in Frederick L. Schuman, *International Politics,* McGraw-Hill Book Company, 1933. The making of French absolutism is clearly discussed in J. B. Perkins, *Richelieu and the Growth of French Power,* G. P. Putnam's Sons, 1900. One of the best accounts of Louis XIV was Arthur Hassal, *Louis* XIV *and the Zenith of the French Monarchy,* G. P. Putnam's Sons, 1895. The narrative for seventeenth-century England is indebted to G. M. Trevelyan, *England Under the Stuarts,* London, Methuen and Company, 1919; and G. N. Clark, *The Later Stuarts,* Oxford University Press, 1934. Numerous phases of the 17th century were admirably treated in David Ogg, *Europe in the Seventeenth Century,* London, A. & C. Black, 1925. The following works were relied upon in the treatment of Great Britain and the American colonies in the 18th century: L. M. Larson, *History of England and the British Commonwealth,* rev. ed., Henry Holt and Company, 1932; T. P. Taswell-Langmead, *English Constitutional History,* 9th ed., Houghton Mifflin Company, 1929; James A. Williamson, *A Short History of British Expansion,* 2nd ed., The Macmillan Company, 1931. For the American Revolution the bulk of facts were drawn from Edward Channing, *A History of the United States,* I-III, The Macmillan Company, 1905, 1912. In interpreting the American Revolution valuable suggestions were drawn from C. H. Van Tyne, *Causes of the War of Independence,* Houghton Mifflin Company, 1922; and Charles and Mary Beard, *The Rise of American Civilization,* 2 vols., The Macmillan Company, 1927. Ernest F. Henderson, *A Short History of Germany,* The Macmillan Company, 1919, was helpful in treating the rise of Prussia. C. R. Beazley, N. Forbes, and G. A. Birkett, *Russia from the Varangians to the Bolsheviks,* Oxford University Press, 1918, was referred to for the rise of the house of the Romanovs. The following works were referred to for material on the French Revolution and Napoleon: Charles D. Hazen, *The French Revolution,* 2 vols., Henry Holt and Company, 1932, clear and well-balanced; Louis R. Gottschalk, *The Era of the French Revolution,* Houghton Mifflin Company, 1929, especially good for the background of the revolution; Shailer Mathews, *The French Revolution,* Longmans, Green & Co., 1930, excellent, concise narrative; and the *Cambridge Modern History,* ed. by Sir A. W. Ward, Sir G. W. Prothero, and Sir Stanley Leathes, VIII and IX, Cambridge University Press, 1902-1912.

4: Factories, Owners, and Workers

Specific References

1. Quoted by H. E. Barnes, *The History of Western Civilization,* Harcourt, Brace and Company, 1935, II, p. 272. Cf. F. A. Ogg and W. R. Sharp, *Economic Development of Europe,* The Macmillan Company, 1926, pp. 128-130.
2. From Clive Day, *Economic Development in Europe,* 1942, p. 134. By permission of The Macmillan Company, publishers.
3. *Ibid.,* p. 138. By permission of The Macmillan Company, publishers.
4. J. L. and Barbara Hammond, *The Rise of Modern Industry,* 1926, p. 184. By permission of J. L. and B. Hammond; London, Methuen & Co.; Harcourt, Brace and Company.
5. From Day, p. 141. By permission of The Macmillan Company, publishers.
6. *Ibid.,* p. 142. By permission of The Macmillan Company, publishers.
7. Abbott P. Usher, *A History of Mechanical Inventions,* McGraw-Hill Book Company, 1929, pp. 311-312.
8. Quoted by Andrew Carnegie, *Life of James Watt,* Doubleday Doran and Company, 1933, p. 53. By permission of Mrs. Andrew Carnegie.
9. Usher, p. 363.
10. *Ibid.,* p. 365.
11. Friedrich C. Dietz, *The Industrial Revolution,* Henry Holt and Company, 1927, pp. 86-87.
12. From Day, p. 146. By permission of The Macmillan Company, publishers.
13. See Herbert Heaton, *Economic History of Europe,* Harper & Brothers, 1936, p. 520.
14. See Heaton, pp. 524-530.
15. See Ogg and Sharp, pp. 227 and following.
16. Hammond, p. 70.
17. Heaton, p. 540. Reprinted by permission of Harper & Brothers.
18. Samuel Smiles, *The Story of the Life of George Stephenson,* London, John Murray, 1859, quoted by J. H. Robinson and C. A. Beard, *Readings in Modern European History,* Ginn and Company, 1909, II, p. 410.
19. Heaton, p. 563. Reprinted by permission of Harper & Brothers.
20. J. F. Reigart, *The Life of Robert Fulton,* C. G. Henderson, 1856, quoted by Robinson and Beard, p. 407.
21. From Day, p. 273. By permission of The Macmillan Company, publishers.
22. *Ibid.,* p. 390. By permission of The Macmillan Company, publishers.
23. See Barnes, II, pp. 337-341; Ogg and Sharp, pp. 315-324.
24. Quoted by Barnes, II, p. 368.
25. J. L. and Barbara Hammond, *The Town Labourer, 1760-1832,* Longmans, Green & Co., 1917, p. 160.
26. Quoted by Friedrich Engels, *The Condition of the Working-Class in England in 1844,* London, George Allen and Unwin, 1926, p. 63.
27. *Ibid.,* p. 68.
28. From Charles and Mary Beard, *The Rise of American Civilization,* 1927, II, pp. 386-387. By permission of The Macmillan Company, publishers.
29. Heaton, p. 403. Reprinted by permission of Harper & Brothers.
30. W. P. Hall and W. S. Davis, *The Course of Europe Since Waterloo,* D. Appleton-Century Company, 1941, pp. 262-263.
31. Cf. J. S. Schapiro, *Modern and Contemporary European History, 1815-1934,* Houghton Mifflin Company, 1934, pp. 569-573.
32. Quoted by Schapiro, p. 581.
33. Quoted by Schapiro, p. 576.
34. From Ogg and Sharp, p. 551. By permission of The Macmillan Company, publishers.
35. Ferdinand Schevill, *History of Europe,* Harcourt, Brace and Company, 1938, p. 481.

General References

In preparing this chapter, use was made of the following: F. A. Ogg and W. R. Sharp, *Economic Development of Modern Europe,* The Macmillan Company, 1926; Herbert Heaton, *Economic History of Europe,* Harper & Brothers, 1936; Clive Day, *Economic Development in Europe,* The Macmillan Company, 1942; and H. E. Barnes, *The History of Western Civilization,* II, chaps. 7-12, Harcourt, Brace and Company, 1935. For a general view of the Industrial Era, F. C. Dietz, *The Industrial Revolution,* Henry Holt and Company, 1927, was consulted. The technological developments of the age were set forth clearly in A. P. Usher, *A History of Mechanical Inventions,* chaps. 9, 11-13, McGraw-

Hill Book Company, 1929. Valuable accounts of the rise of the factory system and the social consequences of the Industrial Revolution were two works by J. L. and Barbara Hammond, *The Town Labourer, 1760-1832,* Longmans, Green & Co., 1917, and *The Rise of Modern Industry,* Harcourt, Brace and Company, 1926; and a vivid account of social life in English towns during the 1840's was found in Friedrich Engels, *The Condition of the Working-Class in England in 1844,* London, George Allen & Unwin, 1926. Among the primary source collections consulted were: A. E. Bland, P. A. Brown, and R. H. Tawney, *English Economic History, Select Documents,* The Macmillan Company, 1919; J. H. Robinson and C. A. Beard, *Readings in Modern European History,* II, Ginn and Company, 1909; L. C. Marshall, *Readings in Industrial Society,* University of Chicago Press, 1929; and J. F. Scott and A. Baltzly, *Readings in European History Since 1814,* F. S. Crofts & Co., 1934.

5: Nationalism and Democracy Advance

Specific References

1. F. C. Palm and F. E. Graham, *Europe Since Napoleon,* Ginn and Company, 1934, p. 38.
2. Charles Downer Hazen, *Europe Since 1815,* Henry Holt and Company, 1923, p. 17.
3. Alexander C. Flick, *Modern World History Since 1775,* rev. by Witt Bowden, F. S. Crofts & Co., 1935, p. 176.
4. J. Salwyn Schapiro, *Modern and Contemporary European History, 1815-1934,* rev. ed., Houghton Mifflin Company, 1934, p. 77.
5. From Carlton J. H. Hayes, *A Political and Cultural History of Modern Europe,* 1937, II, pp. 109-110. By permission of The Macmillan Company, publishers.
6. Victor L. and M. H. Albjerg, *From Sedan to Stresa, Europe Since 1870,* D. Van Nostrand Company, 1937, p. 93.
7. Schapiro, p. 344.
8. Hazen, p. 330.
9. Schapiro, p. 181.
10. From William B. Munro, *The Governments of Europe,* 1931, p. 728. By permission of The Macmillan Company, publishers.
11. James E. Gillespie, *Europe in Perspective,* Harcourt, Brace and Company, 1942, p. 324.
12. G. M. Paléologue, *Cavour,* trans. by I. F. D. and M. M. Morrow, 1927, p. 276. Reprinted by permission of Harper & Brothers.
13. Schapiro, p. 222.
14. H. A. L. Fisher, *A History of Europe,* Houghton Mifflin Company, 1936, p. 924.
15. Schapiro, p. 237.
16. *Ibid.,* p. 412.

General References

The political history of nineteenth-century Europe is so complex that this treatment had to be based mainly upon standard secondary surveys. A good source, exclusively political, was Charles Downer Hazen, *Europe Since 1815,* rev. ed., Henry Holt and Company, 1923. The influence of the middle class was emphasized in F. C. Palm and F. E. Graham, *Europe Since Napoleon,* Ginn and Company, 1934. An outstanding work of historical objectivity was Eduard Fueter, *World History,* trans. by S. B. Fay, Harcourt, Brace and Company, 1922. A good survey meshing political and social developments was J. S. Schapiro, *Modern and Contemporary European History,* rev. ed., Houghton Mifflin Company, 1934. The period from 1870 was treated admirably in V. L. and M. H. Albjerg, *From Sedan to Stresa,* D. Van Nostrand Company, 1937, especially good for the inclusion of literary, scientific, and intellectual data. Many helpful ideas were found in the fascinating treatment in W. P. Hall and W. S. Davis, *The Course of Europe Since Waterloo,* D. Appleton-Century Company, 1941. The discussion of the advance of nationalism is indebted to the following: Carlton J. H. Hayes, *Essays on Nationalism,* The Macmillan Company, 1926; J. Holland Rose, *Nationality in Modern History,* The Macmillan Company 1916; and Harry E. Barnes, *The History of Western Civilization,* II, especially chap. 13, Harcourt, Brace and Company, 1935. In the field of political science, particularly the subject of democracy, the following works were consulted: James Bryce, *Modern Democracies,* The Macmillan Company, 1921; Barnes, cited above, chap. 14; William B. Munro, *The Governments of Europe,* The Macmillan Company, 1931; and James T. Shotwell, Ed., *Governments of Continental Europe,* The Macmillan Company, 1940. Profitable were Frederick B. Artz, *Reaction and Revolution, 1814-1832,* Harper & Brothers, 1934; and R. C. Binkley, *Realism and Nationalism, 1852-1871,* Harper & Brothers, 1935. An outstanding interpretation of the English Victorian period was Esmé Wingfield-Stratford, *The History of British Civilization,* Harcourt, Brace and Company, 1928. The most complete single volume on the reign of Victoria and the first decade of the 20th century was found to be R. C. K. Ensor, *England, 1870-1914*, Oxford University Press, 1936. Other works which are recommended from which ideas and suggestions were drawn were: F. Schevill, *The History of the Balkan Peninsula*, Harcourt, Brace and Company, 1922; S. R. Tompkins, *Russia Through the Ages*, Prentice-Hall, 1940; W. C. Atkinson, *Spain: a Brief History*, London, Methuen and Company, 1934; L. Salvatorelli, *A Concise History of Italy*, London, George Allen & Unwin, 1940; G. P. Gooch, *Germany*, Charles Scribner's Sons, 1927; and D. W. Brogan, *France Under the Republic: The Development of Modern France, 1870-1939*, Harper & Brothers, 1940.

6: All's Right with the World

Specific References

1. Cf. J. Salwyn Schapiro, *Modern and Contemporary European History, 1815-1930*, Houghton Mifflin Company, 1934, chap. 26, pp. 512-513.
2. Cf. Carlton J. H. Hayes, *A Political and Cultural History of Modern Europe*, The Macmillan Company, 1933, II, pp. 333-334.
3. Quoted by Hayes, II, p. 335. By permission of The Macmillan Company, publishers.
4. This study of the antecedents of Darwin's views is principally taken from H. E. Barnes, *The History of Western Civilization*, Harcourt, Brace and Company, 1935, II, pp. 655-657.
5. Quoted by Hayes, II, p. 345. By permission of The Macmillan Company, publishers.
6. From A. K. Rogers, *A Student's History of Philosophy*, 1932, p. 455. By permission of The Macmillan Company, publishers.
7. Paul H. Láng, *Music in Western Civilization*, W. W. Norton & Company, 1941, p. 776.
8. David Ewen, Ed., *From Bach to Stravinsky*, W. W. Norton & Company, 1933, p. 230.
9. Láng, p. 815.
10. From *The Story of Modern Art*, pp. 131-132. Copyright 1941 by Sheldon Cheney. By permission of The Viking Press, Inc., New York.

General References

Among the books found especially helpful for the general background of this chapter were: Carlton J. H. Hayes, *A Political and Cultural History of Modern Europe*, The Macmillan Company, 1933; J. Salwyn Schapiro, *Modern and Contemporary European History, 1815-1934*, rev. ed., Houghton Mifflin Company, 1934; Alexander C. Flick, *Modern World History Since 1775*, rev. by Witt Bowden, F. S. Crofts & Co., 1935; and appropriate chapters in J. A. Hammerton, Ed., *Universal World History*, Wm. H. Wise & Co., 1937. The scientific advancements of the age were dealt with succinctly in W. T. Sedgwick and H. W. Tyler, *A Short History of Science*, The Macmillan Company, 1939. Two books were valuable in regard to nineteenth-century developments in music: David Ewen, Ed., *From Bach to Stravinsky*, W. W. Norton & Company, 1933; and Paul H. Láng, *Music in Western Civilization*, W. W. Norton & Company, 1941. Deems Taylor, *Of Men and Music*, Simon and Schuster, 1937, was also consulted. For a study of the period's art, the authors made extensive use of Sheldon Cheney, *The Story of Modern Art*, The Viking Press, 1941; Helen Gardner, *Art Through the Ages*, Harcourt, Brace and Company, 1936; Thomas Craven, *Men of Art*, Simon and Schuster, 1936; and R. S. Stites, *The Arts and Man*, McGraw-Hill Book Company, 1940. Among the works consulted in literature were G. B. Woods, H. A. Watt, G. K. Anderson, *The Literature of England*, II, Scott, Foresman and Company, 1941; M. E. Speare, *The Political Novel*, Oxford University Press, 1924; and C. H. C. Wright, *History of French Literature*, Oxford University Press, 1925. Invaluable for source material were such works as J. F. Scott and Alexander Baltzly, *Readings in European History Since 1814*, F. S. Crofts & Co., 1930; J. H. Robinson and C. A. Beard, *Readings in Modern European History*, II, Ginn and Company, 1909. For the social milieu of the period, the authors went to Sir Walter Besant, *London in the Nineteenth Century*, The Macmillan Company, 1909.

7: New Europes Overseas

Specific References

1. Quoted by Howard Robinson, *The Development of the British Empire*, Houghton Mifflin Company, 1922, p. 38.
2. Quoted by S. E. Morison and H. S. Commager, *The Growth of the American Republic*, 2 vols., Oxford University Press, 1937, I, p. 205.
3. Quoted by Max Farrand, *The Development of the United States*, Houghton Mifflin Company, 1918, p. 164.
4. Morison and Commager, II, p. 240.

5. *Ibid.*, II, p. 3.
6. Carl Wittke, *A History of Canada,* 3rd ed., F. S. Crofts & Co., 1941, p. 115.
7. Quoted by *The Cambridge History of the British Empire,* 1933, VII, Part II, *New Zealand,* p. 242. By permission of The Macmillan Company and London, Cambridge University Press, publishers.
8. Manuel Ugarte, *The Destiny of a Continent,* Alfred A. Knopf, 1925, p. 288.
9. J. Lloyd Mecham, "Conflicting Ideals of Pan-Americanism," *Current History,* The New York Times (former owners) and Events Publishing Co., December, 1930, p. 402.

General References

The discussion of the growth of the United States owes much to such interpretive surveys as James Truslow Adams, *The Epic of America,* Little, Brown and Co., 1932; Max Farrand, *The Development of the United States,* Houghton Mifflin Company, 1918; and Charles and Mary Beard, *The Rise of American Civilization,* 2 vols., The Macmillan Company, 1927. For the verification of historical facts the two following standard treatments were relied upon: Edward Channing, *A History of the United States,* 6 vols., The Macmillan Company, 1905-1925; and James Fordes Rhodes, *A History of the United States from the Compromise of 1850 to the End of the Roosevelt Administration,* 9 vols., The Macmillan Company, 1892-1922. Helpful in the treatment of early colonial society was Curtis P. Nettels, *The Roots of American Civilization,* F. S. Crofts & Co., 1939. Many valuable suggestions were obtained from the scholarly and readable two-volume work: S. E. Morison and H. S. Commager, *The Growth of the American Republic,* Oxford University Press, 1937. The section on Latin America was based on the following standard treatments: M. W. Williams, *The People and Politics of Latin America,* Ginn and Company, 1930; E. G. Inman, *Latin America, Its Place in World Life, Willert Clark,* 1937; F. A. Kirkpatrick, *Latin America,* The Macmillan Company, 1939; and J. E. Rippy, *Historical Evolution of Hispanic America,* F. S. Crofts & Co., 1932. An excellent survey was found in Delia Goetz and Varian Fry, *The Good Neighbors, The Story of the Two Americas,* Foreign Policy Association, 1941. The standard work used for the British Dominions was the *Cambridge History of the British Empire,* ed. by J. H. Rose, A. P. Newton, and E. A. Benians, Cambridge University Press. The following volumes were used: VI, *Canada and Newfoundland,* 1930; VII, Part I, *Australia,* 1933; VII, Part II, *New Zealand,* 1933; and VIII, *South Africa, Rhodesia, and the Protectorates,* 1936. Other accounts, more general in scope, to which acknowledgment is given are: Howard Robinson, *The Development of the British Empire,* rev. ed., Houghton Mifflin Company, 1936; C. F. Mullett, *The British Empire,* Henry Holt and Company, 1938; and Paul Knaplund, *The British Empire, 1815-1939,* Harper & Brothers, 1941. The section on Canada is especially obligated to Carl Wittke, *A History of Canada,* 3rd ed., F. S. Crofts & Co., 1941.

8: Dominion over Palm and Pine

Specific References

1. F. C. Palm and F. E. Graham, *Europe Since Napoleon,* Ginn and Company, 1934, p. 391.
2. Quoted by S. E. Morison and H. S. Commager, *The Growth of the American Republic,* Oxford University Press, 1937, II, p. 324.
3. Quoted by P. T. Moon, *Imperialism and World Politics,* 1928, p. 317. By permission of The Macmillan Company, publishers.
4. Cf. Thomas A. Bailey, *A Diplomatic History of the American People,* F. S. Crofts & Co., 1940, p. 467.
5. Cf. Moon, p. 401.
6. G. Nye Steiger, *A History of the Far East,* Ginn and Company, 1936, p. 562.
7. Quoted by Steiger, p. 596.
8. *Ibid.*, pp. 612-613.

General References

The two most valuable sources covering the general topic of imperialism were: P. T. Moon, *Imperialism and World Politics,* The Macmillan Company, 1926; and Mary E. Townsend (with the collaboration of C. H. Peake), *European Colonial Expansion Since 1871,* J. B. Lippincott Company, 1941. Other useful treatments utilized were: R. L. Buell, *International Relations,* Henry Holt and Company, 1925; Frederick Schuman, *International Politics,* McGraw-Hill Book Company, 1933; Leonard Woolf, *Economic Imperialism,* Harcourt, Brace and Company, 1920; and J. A. Hobson, *Imperialism, A Study,* London, George Allen and Unwin, 1939. A brief but helpful résumé was found in G. A. Hedger, Ed., *An Introduction to Western Civilization,* Doubleday, Doran and Company, 1931. Another excellent summary is given in H. E. Barnes, *The History of Western Civilization*, II, Harcourt, Brace and Company, 1935. For imperialism in Africa the authors are indebted to Reginald Coupland, *The Exploitation of East Africa, 1856-1890*, London, Faber & Faber, 1939; and to N. D. Harris, *Europe and Africa*, Houghton Mifflin Company, 1927. The best condensation of British African colonization was found to be Ifor L. Evans, *The British in Tropical Africa*, Cambridge University Press, 1929. Two works somewhat old but still valuable were consulted: J. S. Keltie, *The Partition of Africa*, London, E. Stanford, 1895; and Sir Harry H. Johnston, *History of the Colonization of Africa by Alien Races*, Cambridge University Press, 1905. A good introduction to the operation of imperialism was found in D. R. Bhandarkar, Ed., *India*, Part II of the *Annals of the American Academy of Political and Social Science*, CXLV, 1929. The following works were referred to for the eighteenth century: Sir Richard Burn, Ed., *The Cambridge History of India*, IV, Cambridge University Press, 1937. E. T. Thompson and G. T. Garratt, *Rise and Fulfilment of British Rule in India*, London, The Macmillan Company, 1934; and Sir Alfred Lyall, *Rise of the British Dominion in India*, London, John Murray, 1914. Good surveys of nineteenth-century development were obtained in H. Dodwell, *A Sketch of the History of India from 1858-1918*, Longmans, Green & Co., 1925; *The Cambrige History of the British Empire*, V, The Macmillan Company, 1929-1933; and Sir Verney Lovett, *History of the Indian Nationalist Movement*, London, John Murray, 1920. Material relating to French, German, and Dutch colonial empires was obtained from the following: Alleyne Ireland, *The Far Eastern Tropics*, Houghton Mifflin Company, 1905; Amry Vandenbosch, *The Dutch East Indies: Its Government, Problems and Politics*, University of California Press, 1942; S. H. Roberts, *History of French Colonial Policy* (1870-1925), P. S. King & Son, 1929; M. E. Townsend, *The Rise and Fall of Germany's Colonial Empire, 1884-1918*, The Macmillan Company, 1930. The details concerning American imperialism were based on the following books: P. T. Moon, cited above; Thomas A. Bailey, *A Diplomatic History of the American People*, F. S. Crofts & Co., 1940; S. F. Bemis, *Diplomatic History of the United States*, Henry Holt and Company, 1936; and the provocative study by Albert K. Weinberg, *Manifest Destiny*, Johns Hopkins Press, 1935.

9: *Explosion in Europe*

Specific References

1. H. A. L. Fisher, *A History of Europe*, Houghton Mifflin Company, 1936, p. 1114.
2. Quoted by R. J. Sontag, *European Diplomatic History, 1871-1932*, D. Appleton-Century Company, 1933, p. 213.
3. Quoted by Hermann Foertsch, *The Art of Modern Warfare*, Oskar Piest, 1940, p. 3.
4. J. Salwyn Schapiro, *Modern and Contemporary European History*, rev. ed., Houghton Mifflin Company, 1934, p. 687.
5. From C. J. H. Hayes, *A Political and Cultural History of Modern Europe*, 1937, II, p. 774. By permission of The Macmillan Company, publishers.
6. *Ibid.*, p. 776. By permission of The Macmillan Company, publishers.
7. *Ibid.*, p. 778. By permission of The Macmillan Company, publishers.
8. Royal Institute of International Affairs, *Political and Strategic Interests of the United Kingdom*, London, Oxford University Press, 1939, p. 14.
9. J. W. Swain, *Beginning of the Twentieth Century*, W. W. Norton & Company, 1933, p. 377.
10. From W. C. Langsam, *The World Since 1914*, 3rd ed., 1937, p. 38. By permission of The Macmillan Company, publishers.
11. S. E. Morison and H. S. Commager, *The Growth of the American Republic*, Oxford University Press, 1937, II, pp. 453-454.
12. Quoted by L. M. Hacker and B. B. Kendrick, *The United States Since 1865*, 3rd ed., F. S. Crofts & Co., 1940, p. 520.

General References

The treatment of this complex and controversial subject had to be general without benefit of the mass of material found in many historical monographs. The authors found the following surveys terse and accurate: J. E. Gillespie, *Europe in Perspective*, Harcourt, Brace and Company, 1942; B. E. Schmitt, *Triple Alliance and Triple Entente*, Henry Holt and Company, 1934; G. P. Gooch, *History of Modern Europe, 1878-1919*, Longmans, Green & Co., 1923; Erik Achorn, *European Civilization and Politics Since 1815*, Harcourt, Brace and Company, 1933; J. W. Swain,

Beginning the Twentieth Century, W. W. Norton & Company, 1933; and R. J. Sontag, *European Diplomatic History, 1871-1932,* D. Appleton-Century Company, 1933. More specialized works consulted on specific problems were: S. B. Fay, *The Origins of the World War,* 2 vols. in 1, rev. ed., The Macmillan Company, 1930; H. E. Barnes, *The Genesis of the World War,* Alfred A. Knopf, 1929; B. E. Schmitt, *The Coming of the War,* 2 vols., Charles Scribner's Sons, 1930; and G. Lowes Dickinson, *The International Anarchy,* D. Appleton-Century Company, 1926. A penetrating interpretation of the period from 1870 to 1914 was obtained in Benedetto Croce, *History of Europe in the Nineteenth Century,* especially chap. 10, "International Politics, Activism, and the World War," Harcourt, Brace and Company, 1933. A moderate, scholarly account of the German side was found in Erich Brandenburg, *From Bismarck to the World War,* Oxford University Press, 1927. A brief excellent account of Balkan nationalism was W. M. Gewehr, *Nationalism in the Balkans, 1800-1930,* Henry Holt and Company, 1931. The costs of the war were fully treated in E. L. Bogart, *Direct and Indirect Costs of the War,* Oxford University Press, 1920. A dramatic, well-written account of Great Britain at war was furnished by Winston Churchill, *The World Crisis,* Charles Scribner's Sons, II, 1923, and III, two parts, 1927. For the United States the following were consulted: T. A. Bailey, *A Diplomatic History of the American People,* F. S. Crofts & Co., 1940; Walter Millis, *The Road to War,* Houghton Mifflin Company, 1935; and C. H. Grattan, *Why We Fought,* Vanguard Press, 1929. For a general study of military affairs C. R. M. F. Crutwell, *History of the Great War,* Oxford University Press, 1936; and C. J. H. Hayes, *A Brief History of the Great War,* The Macmillan Company, 1920, were indispensable guides. For a discussion of action at sea H. J. Newbolt, *A Naval History of the War,* Hodder & Stoughton, 1920, was consulted.

10: A Quest for World Order

Specific References

1. From W. C. Langsam, *The World Since 1914,* 3rd ed., 1937, p. 111. By permission of The Macmillan Company, publishers.
2. Quoted by Erik Achorn, *European Civilization and Politics Since 1815,* Harcourt, Brace and Company, 1934, p. 470.
3. From Karl Lowenstein in *Governments of Continental Europe,* ed. by J. T. Shotwell, 1940, p. 400. By permission of The Macmillan Company, publishers.
4. Quoted by Achorn, p. 473.
5. S. E. Morison and H. S. Commager, *The Growth of the American Republic,* Oxford University Press, 1937, II, p. 497.
6. League of Nations Document C. 77. M. 37. 1939. VII., quoted in "The United States and World Organization During 1938," *International Conciliation,* Carnegie Endowment for International Peace, September, 1939, No. 352, pp. 390-391.
7. F. Lee Benns, *Europe Since 1914,* rev. ed., F. S. Crofts & Co., 1934, p. 312.
8. *Ibid.,* p. 314.

General References

The most useful treatment of postwar diplomacy was G. M. Gathorne-Hardy, *Short History of International Affairs,* Oxford University Press, 1938. For Great Britain and France much reliance was placed upon Arnold Wolfers, *Britain and France Between Two Wars,* Harcourt, Brace and Company, 1940. A brief and lively discussion of international affairs was given in William A. Orton, *Twenty Years' Armistice,* Farrar & Rinehart, 1938. Of special value in linking diplomacy with economic factors was F. H. Symonds and Brooks Emeny, *The Great Powers in World Politics,* American Book Company, 1937. R. Palme Dutt, *World Politics, 1918-1936,* Victor Gollancz, 1936, was characteristic of the school which blames world strife mainly upon capitalism. The following were also consulted: W. C. Langsam, *The World Since 1914,* The Macmillan Company, 1937; J. E. Gillespie, *Europe in Perspective,* Harcourt, Brace and Company, 1942; and F. Lee Benns, *Europe Since 1914,* rev. ed., F. S. Crofts & Co., 1934. Simplified accounts whose summary of international economic and political trends was most helpful were: Varian Fry, *The Peace That Failed,* 1939; Varian Fry, *Bricks Without Mortar, the Story of International Cooperation,* 1939; and Thomas Brockway, *Battles Without Bullets, the Story of Economic Warfare,* 1939—all three published by The Foreign Policy Association. For the conference of Paris and the Peace Treaties the following works were consulted: René Albrecht-Carrié, *Italy at the Peace Conference,* Columbia University Press, 1938; R. S. Baker, *Woodrow Wilson and World Settlement,* 3 vols., Doubleday, Page & Company, 1922. One of the most penetrating studies of the Paris Peace Conference was found in Harold Nicolson, *Peacemaking,* Houghton Mifflin Company, 1933. E. M. House and C. Seymour, Eds., *What Really Happened At Paris,* Charles Scribner's Sons, 1921, was also consulted. A valuable recent study of the Treaty of Versailles was Paul Birdsall, *Versailles Twenty Years After,* Reynal & Hitchcock, 1941. Valuable also were: S. P. H. Duggan, Ed., *The League of Nations: the Principle and the Practice,* Little, Brown & Company, 1919; J. S. Bassett, *The League of Nations,* Longmans, Green & Co., 1928; G. N. Barnes, *History of the International Labor Office,* Williams and Norgate, 1926. A good account of the peace settlement and the fight for the League in the United States was given in Thomas A. Bailey, *A Diplomatic History of the American People,* F. S. Crofts & Co., 1940, chaps. 39 and 40. Used in preparing the economic sections of this chapter were: H. G. Moulton and Leo Pasvolsky, *World War Debt Settlements,* Brookings Institution, 1926; J. M. Keynes, *The Economic Consequences of the Peace,* Harcourt, Brace and Company, 1920; and S. B. Clough and C. W. Cole, *Economic History of Europe,* D. C. Heath and Company, 1941. Consulted for the problem of disarmament were: J. W. Wheeler-Bennett, *Disarmament and Security Since Locarno,* The Macmillan Company, 1932, and Salvador de Madariaga, *Disarmament,* Coward-McCann, 1929.

11: New Patterns in Statecraft

Specific References

1. From Michael T. Florinsky, in *Governments of Continental Europe,* ed. by James T. Shotwell, 1940, p. 816. By permission of The Macmillan Company, publishers.
2. *Ibid.,* p. 817. By permission of The Macmillan Company, publishers.
3. Quoted by W. N. Loucks and J. W. Hoot, *Comparative Economic Systems,* 1938, p. 240. Reprinted by permission of Harper & Brothers.
4. From Florinsky, p. 855. By permission of The Macmillan Company, publishers.
5. Samuel N. Harper, *The Government of the Soviet Union,* D. Van Nostrand Company, 1938, pp. 169-170.
6. *Ibid.,* p. 170.
7. Quoted by Vera M. Dean, *Russia At War,* The Foreign Policy Association, 1942, p. 71.
8. Based on Florinsky, p. 838.
9. Joseph E. Davies, *Mission to Moscow,* Simon and Schuster, 1941, p. 94.
10. From *Soviet Russia Today,* November, 1937, quoted in Loucks and Hoot, p. 485. Reprinted by permission of Harper & Brothers.
11. R. T. Bye and W. W. Hewett, *Applied Economics,* F. S. Crofts & Co., 1934, p. 642.
12. H. E. Barnes, *The History of Western Civilization,* Harcourt, Brace and Company, 1935, II, p. 1019.
13. Dean, p. 56.
14. Earl R. Sikes, *Contemporary Economic Systems,* Henry Holt and Company, 1940, p. 370.
15. Cf. A. R. Williams, *The Soviets,* Harcourt, Brace and Company, 1937, p. 309.
16. From Arnold J. Zurcher, in *Governments of Continental Europe,* p. 613. By permission of The Macmillan Company, publishers.
17. *Ibid.,* p. 610. By permission of The Macmillan Company, publishers.
18. F. Lee Benns, *Europe Since 1914,* rev. ed., F. S. Crofts & Co., 1934, p. 356.
19. From Walter C. Langsam, *The World Since 1914,* 1937, p. 379. By permission of The Macmillan Company, publishers.
20. Sikes, p. 430.
21. From Langsam, p. 401. By permission of The Macmillan Company, publishers.
22. *Ibid.,* p. 401. By permission of The Macmillan Company, publishers.
23. From Zurcher, p. 748. By permission of the Macmillan Company, publishers.
24. From Karl Lowenstein, in *Governments of Continental Europe,* p. 403. By permission of The Macmillan Company, publishers.
25. *Ibid.,* p. 406. By permission of The Macmillan Company, publishers.
26. Quoted by G. M. Gathorne-Hardy, *A Short History of International Affairs, 1920 to 1934,* London, Oxford University Press, 1934, p. 252.
27. From Lowenstein, p. 473. By permission of The Macmillan Company, publishers.
28. Max Ascoli and Arthur Feiler, *Fascism For Whom?,* W. W. Norton & Company, 1938, p. 207.
29. Sikes, p. 509.

General References

The general framework of this chapter is based on F. Lee Benns, *Europe Since 1914,* F. S. Crofts & Co., 1930, and W. C. Langsam, *The World Since 1914.* The Macmillan Company, 1937. In addition "New Dictatorships and Old Democracies" in H. A. L. Fisher, *A History of Europe*, London, Edward Arnold and Company, 1936, was most helpful. Also good in providing interesting items were: *Ambassador Dodd's Diary*, W. E. and Martha Dodd, Eds., Harcourt, Brace and Company, 1941; W. L. Shirer, *Berlin Diary*, Alfred A. Knopf, 1941; and John Gunther, *Inside Europe*, Harper & Brothers, 1938. The discussion of Nazi Germany was written only after a careful study of Hitler's *Mein Kampf*, unabridged ed., Reynal & Hitchcock, 1939. One of the best summaries of postwar Germany is given in F. L. Schuman, *Germany Since 1918*, Henry Holt and Company, 1937; and in V. L. and M. H. Albjerg, *From Sedan to Stresa*, chap. 27, D. Van Nostrand Company, 1937. Henri Lechtenberger, *The Third Reich*, Greystone Press, 1937, an objective study by a French scholar and noted student of German life and culture, was especially helpful. Other works consulted were: K. Heiden, *A History of National Socialism*, Methuen and Company, 1934; and by this same authority on Nazism, *Hitler*, Alfred A. Knopf, 1934; Stephen A. Roberts, *The House That Hitler Built*, Harper & Brothers, 1938, especially good for the characterization of Hitler and his lieutenants; E. A. Mowrer, *Germany Puts the Clock Back*, rev. ed., William Morrow & Co., 1939; F. L. Schuman, *The Nazi Dictatorship*, Alfred A. Knopf, 1939; and Calvin B. Hoover, *Germany Enters the Third Reich*, The Macmillan Company, 1933, particularly good on the early phases of National Socialism. H. Powys Greenwood, *The German Revolution*, George Routledge & Sons, 1934, represented a certain section of English society that admired Nazism in its early phases. Special obligation is expressed to Karl Lowenstein for his informative section on Germany in *Governments of Continental Europe*, ed. by J. T. Shotwell, The Macmillan Company, 1940. For the general trend of developments in Italy the authors express their indebtedness to Benns, Langsam, and Albjerg, all cited above. Benito Mussolini, *My Autobiography*, London, Hutchinson & Co., 1939, was an interesting approach to a complex personality. Much reliance was placed upon Arnold J. Zurcher's section on Italy in *Governments of Continental Europe*, cited above. H. A. Steiner, *Government in Fascist Italy*, McGraw-Hill Book Company, 1938, gave many details on the emergence of Fascism. Useful in the appraisal of the Fascist movement was Hugh Quigley, "Fascism Fails in Italy," *Current History*, Events Publishing Co., June, 1934. The economic structure of Italian Fascism was ably presented by Earl Sikes, *Contemporary Economic Systems*, Henry Holt and Company, 1940. M. T. Florinsky's study of Soviet Russia in *Governments of Continental Europe*, cited above, was helpful for all phases. Joseph E. Davies, *Mission to Moscow*, Simon and Schuster, 1941, containing reports to the United States Department of State, presented useful material. An excellent condensation of Soviet Russia was Vera M. Dean, *Russia at War*, The Foreign Policy Association, 1942. The best succinct treatment of the economics of Communism was in W. N. Loucks and J. W. Hoot, *Comparative Economic Systems*, Harper & Brothers, 1938. Other sources were: H. E. Barnes, *The History of Western Civilization*, II, chap. 25, Harcourt, Brace and Company, 1935; A. R. Williams, *The Soviets*, Harcourt, Brace and Company, 1937; W. H. Chamberlain, *Collectivism: A False Utopia*, The Macmillan Company, 1937; R. T. Bye and W. W. Hewett, *Applied Economics*, chap. 29, F. S. Crofts & Co., 1934.

12: *Democracy on Trial*

Specific References

1. Quoted by W. C. Langsam, *Major European and Asiatic Developments Since 1935*, 1938, p. 15. By permission of The Macmillan Company, publishers.
2. *Ibid.*, p. 17. By permission of The Macmillan Company, publishers.
3. W. P. Hall and W. S. Davis, *The Course of Europe Since Waterloo*, D. Appleton-Century Company, 1941, p. 745.
4. From J. T. Shotwell, Ed., *Governments of Continental Europe*, 1940, p. 1036. By permission of The Macmillan Company, publishers.
5. F. Lee Benns, *Europe Since 1914*, rev. ed., F. S. Crofts & Co., 1934, p. 481.
6. *Cmd. 2768* (of 1926), London, p. 14. Quoted by Sir J. A. R. Marriott, *Modern England, 1885-1932*, London, Methuen and Company, 1934, p. 466.
7. Carl Wittke, *A History of Canada*, F. S. Crofts & Co., 1941, p. 400.
8. Quoted by W. C. Langsam, *The World Since 1914*, 1937, p. 752. By permission of The Macmillan Company, publishers.
9. S. F. Morison and H. S. Commager, *The Growth of the American Republic*, Oxford

University Press, 1937, II, p. 531.
10. Carleton Beals, *America South,* J. B. Lippincott Company, 1937, p. 359.
11. J. F. Rippy, *Historical Evolution of Hispanic America,* F. S. Crofts & Co., 1940, pp. 539-540.
12. From *A New Doctrine for the Americas,* pp. 93-94. Copyright 1941 by Charles Wertenbaker. By permission of The Viking Press, Inc., New York.
13. Rippy, p. 541.

General References

The framework of the discussion of postwar United States was based upon the following standard historical surveys: John D. Hicks, *The American Nation: A History of the United States from 1865 to the Present,* Houghton Mifflin Company, 1941; F. L. Paxson, *Recent History of the United States: 1865 to the Present,* Houghton Mifflin Company, 1926; A. M. Schlesinger, *Political and Social Growth of the American People,* The Macmillan Company, 1941; and S. E. Morison and H. S. Commager, *The Growth of the American Republic,* II, Oxford University Press, 1937. Also helpful were: D. L. Dumond, *Roosevelt to Roosevelt: The United States in the Twentieth Century,* Henry Holt and Company, 1937; Charles and Mary Beard, *America in Midpassage,* The Macmillan Company, 1939; D. W. Brogan, *U. S. A.: An Outline of the Country, Its People and Institutions,* Oxford University Press, 1941; and Sir Walter Citrine, *My American Diary,* George Routledge & Sons, 1941. The study of Great Britain after World War I owes much to the excellent survey in Sir John Marriott, *Modern England, 1885-1932,* London, Methuen and Company, 1934; to the comprehensive discussion in J. A. Spender, *Great Britain, Empire and Commonwealth, 1886-1935,* Cassell & Co., n. d.; and to the concluding chapter in W. P. Hall and R. G. Albion, *A History of England and the British Empire,* Ginn and Company, 1937. For developments in the British Empire the following sources were consulted: Sir Arthur Willert, B. K. Long, and H. V. Hodson, *The Empire in the World,* Oxford University Press, 1937; A. E. Zimmern, *The Third British Empire,* 3rd ed., Oxford University Press, 1934; and R. Coupland, *The Empire in These Days,* The Macmillan Company, 1935. For the British Dominions the concluding chapters of Carl Wittke, *A History of Canada,* F. S. Crofts & Co., 1941, were particularly helpful. A brief but penetrating interpretation of modern Canada was found in B. K. Sandwell, *The Canadian Peoples,* Oxford University Press, 1941. Readable and scholarly was A. L. Burt, *A Short History of Canada for Americans,* The University of Minnesota Press, 1942. The following works were frequently consulted for Australasia: E. Scott, *Short History of Australia,* Oxford University Press, 1927; W. P. Morrell, *New Zealand,* London, Ernest Benn, 1935; and *The Cambridge History of the British Empire,* VII, two parts, *Australia* and *New Zealand,* Cambridge University Press, 1933. The discussion of South Africa owes much to the standard history by E. Walker, *History of South Africa,* Longmans, Green & Co., 1939, and to the popularly written but reliable survey by J. H. Hofmeyr, *South Africa,* London, Ernest Benn, 1931. The discussion of Latin America was based upon the following authorities: A. C. Wilgus, *The Development of Hispanic America,* Farrar & Rinehart, 1941; S. G. Inman, *Latin America, Its Place in World Life,* Willett, Clark & Company, 1937; J. Fred Rippy, *Historical Evolution of Hispanic America,* F. S. Crofts & Co., 1940; C. E. Chapman, *Republican Hispanic America: A History,* The Macmillan Company, 1937. For social and economic trends the following work was especially provocative: Carleton Beals, *America South,* J. B. Lippincott Company, 1937. Many facets of Latin American culture were explored by various authorities in the admirable *Modern Hispanic America,* ed. by A. Curtis Wilgus, The George Washington University Press, 1933. Inter-American relations were discussed with penetration by Charles Wertenbaker, *A New Doctrine for the Americas,* The Viking Press, 1941. In tracing European developments after 1919 the following works were consulted: A. J. Zurcher, *The Experiment With Democracy in Central Europe,* Oxford University Press, 1933; R. L. Buell, *Poland: Key to Europe,* Alfred A. Knopf, 1939, the best short survey in English; W. J. Rose, *Poland,* Middlesex, Penguin Books, 1939; J. H. Jackson, *Finland,* London, George Allen & Unwin, 1938, the standard work in English; M. W. Childs, *Sweden, The Middle Way,* Yale University Press, 1936, an excellent discussion of Swedish cooperatives; E. C. Bellquist, *Some Aspects of the Recent Foreign Policy of Sweden,* University of California Press, 1939; R. J. Kerner, Ed., *Czechoslovakia, A Record of Two Decades,* University of California Press, 1940; Salvador de Madariaga, *Spain,* Charles Scribner's Sons, 1930; Louis Pierard, *Belgian Problems Since the War,* Yale University Press, 1929; A. J. Barnouw, *The Dutch: A Portrait Study of the People of Holland,* Columbia University Press, 1940.

13: *The Orient Astir*

Specific References

1. See C. F. Remer, *Foreign Investments in China,* The Macmillan Company, 1933, p. 406.
2. *Ibid.,* p. 397.
3. *Ibid.,* p. 636.
4. As of 1942, according to J. Anton de Haas, *Our Allies! The Netherlands East Indies,* London, Oxford University Press, 1942, p. 6. But for 1940 figures, consult Amry Vandenbosch, *The Dutch East Indies,* 2nd ed., University of California Press, 1941, p. 5.
5. Vandenbosch, p. 28.
6. Cf. Remer, pp. 338, 407, 553.
7. Harold M. Vinacke, *A History of the Far East in Modern Times,* 4th ed., F. S. Crofts & Co., 1941, p. 478.
8. From Kenneth S. Latourette, *The Chinese, Their History and Culture,* 2nd rev. ed., 1934, I, p. 487. By permission of The Macmillan Company, publishers.
9. T. A. Bisson, *Shadow Over Asia,* The Foreign Policy Association, 1941, p. 60.
10. From Remer, p. 76. By permission of The Macmillan Company, publishers.
11. Bisson, p. 69.
12. Quoted by Claude A. Buss, *War and Diplomacy in Eastern Asia,* 1941, p. 54. By permission of The Macmillan Company, publishers.
13. Quoted by Buss, p. 118. By permission of The Macmillan Company, publishers.
14. Vinacke, p. 585.

General References

The authors are indebted to Harold M. Vinacke for his excellent survey *A History of the Far East in Modern Times,* 4th ed., F. S. Crofts & Co., 1941. Also consulted for its survey value was G. Nye Steiger, *A History of the Far East,* Ginn and Company, 1936; while appropriate chapters in K. S. Latourette, *The Chinese, their History and Culture,* 2 vols. in 1, 2nd ed. rev., The Macmillan Company, 1934; and Walter C. Langsam, *The World Since 1914,* 4th ed., The Macmillan Company, 1940, were found valuable. Of particular value in connection with the Netherlands Indies was Amry Vandenbosch, *The Dutch East Indies,* 2nd ed., University of California Press, 1941. T. A. Bisson, *American Policy in the Far East, 1931-1940;* Irving S. Friedman, *British Relations with China, 1931-1940;* and Hugh Borton, *Japan since 1931,* all three published by the Institute of Pacific Relations, 1940, proved valuable in their fields. An excellent and authoritative study of the strength of European, American, and Japanese economic interests in China was C. F. Remer, *Foreign Investments in China,* The Macmillan Company, 1933. A short but reliable account of the rise of militant Japan was found in T. A. Bisson, *Shadow Over Asia,* The Foreign Policy Association, 1941. The authors made use of Claude A. Buss, *War and Diplomacy in Eastern Asia,* The Macmillan Company, 1941, for an over-all picture of the relative positions and strength of the major powers in the Pacific area, and also examined W. D. Pulestan, *The Armed Forces of the Pacific,* Yale University Press, 1941. They consulted for treaty stipulations, Harley F. MacNair, *Modern Chinese History, Selected Readings,* Shanghai, Commercial Press, 1923. Numerous articles in such journals as *Far Eastern Survey, Pacific Affairs, Amerasia,* and *Asia* were helpful. For political conditions and developments in India from 1914 to 1939, A. B. Keith, *Constitutional History of India, 1600-1935,* London, Methuen and Company, 1936, was valuable. E. Thompson and G. T. Garratt, *The Rise and Fulfilment of British Rule in India,* The Macmillan Company, 1934, was also consulted. In economics the following were especially helpful: V. Anstey, *Economic Development of India,* Longmans, Green & Co., 1937, and D. M. Bucchanan, *The Development of Capitalist Enterprise in India,* The Macmillan Company, 1935. One of the best surveys of politics, economics, and social life was found in the *Indian Statutory (Simon) Commission Report,* I, London, 1930. The constitutional reforms of 1919 were discussed at length in E. A. Horne, *The Political System of British India,* Oxford University Press, 1922. For the nationalist movement the following were especially useful: C. H. Van Tyne, *India in Ferment,* D. Appleton-Century Company, 1923; Sir V. Lovett, *History of the Indian Nationalist Movement,* London, John Murray, 1921; E. J. Thompson, *Reconstructing India,* Dial Press, 1930.

14: *A World Divided*

General References

The authors placed main reliance upon the following works: F. L. Schuman, *Europe On the Eve: the Crisis of Diplomacy, 1933-1939,* Alfred A. Knopf, 1939; E. H. Carr, *The Twenty Years' Crisis, 1919-1939,* The Macmillan Company, 1939; D. E.

Lee, *Ten Years*, Houghton Mifflin Company, 1942, a clear and objective synthesis of diplomacy from 1930 to 1942; Sir John Marriott, *The Tragedy of Europe*, Glasgow, Blackie & Son, 1941, a suggestive interpretation of prewar trends in Europe; William Orton, *Twenty Years' Armistice: 1918-1938*, Farrar & Rinehart, 1938, a popular account but helpful in giving "a rapid view of the period as a whole." R. P. Dutt, *World Politics, 1918-1936*, Victor Gollancz, 1936, highly critical of the foreign policy of British conservatives. One of the best surveys of international affairs is the standard work by G. M. Gathorne-Hardy, *A Short History of International Affairs, 1920-1938*, Oxford University Press, 1938. A penetrating examination of foreign policy was Arnold Wolfers, *Britain and France between Two Wars*, Harcourt, Brace and Company, 1940. W. C. Langsam, *The World Since 1914*, The Macmillan Company, 1937, with a supplement *Since 1939: A Narrative of War*, The Macmillan Company, 1941; and F. Lee Benns, *Europe Since 1914*, F. S. Crofts & Co., 1934, with supplement *Europe's Return to War*, F. S. Crofts & Co., 1941, constitute a reliable survey of international developments. The most comprehensive study dealing with the immediate background and causes of the war was F. L. Schuman, *Night Over Europe: The Diplomacy of Nemesis, 1939-1940*, Alfred A. Knopf, 1941, a brilliant treatment. A good example of the German viewpoint was found in Alfred von Wegerer, *The Origins of World War II*, Richard R. Smith, 1941. Among the many personal accounts dealing with the coming of the conflict, Sir Nevile Henderson, *Failure of a Mission, Berlin 1937-1939*, G. P. Putnam's Sons, 1940, was found to be one of the most significant. The official British explanation of the outbreak of war is contained in *Documents Concerning German-Polish Relations and the Outbreak of Hostilities between Great Britain and Germany on September 3, 1939*, London, H. M. Stationery Office, 1939. The course of the war was clearly outlined in Edgar McInnis, *The War: First Year*, Oxford University Press, 1940, and *The War: Second Year*, Oxford University Press, 1941. Of much assistance also were the various bulletins of the governments of the United Nations. The *Yale Review*, Yale University Press and *Foreign Affairs*, Council of Foreign Affairs, contained articles by eminent scholars and publicists on various aspects of the Second World War. One of the most useful expositions of the strategic situation in the Pacific was Captain W. D. Puleston, *The Armed Forces of the Pacific*, Yale University Press, 1941. The historical background to the Pacific conflict was presented effectively in F. R. Dulles, *America in the Pacific*, Houghton Mifflin Company, 1942. The various factors behind the attack on Pearl Harbor are explained in W. C. Johnstone, *Why Japan Chose War*, Oxford University Press, 1942. The treatment of the foreign policy of the United States and the reaction of public opinion to the blitzkrieg in Europe was based on a study of current American periodicals and press notices, as well as books. The isolationist view was capably presented in General Hugh S. Johnson, *Hell-Bent for War*, Bobbs-Merrill Company, 1941. The much discussed book of Anne M. Lindbergh, *The Wave of the Future*, Harper & Brothers, 1940, also belongs in the isolationist category. R. H. Markham, *The Wave of the Past*, University of North Carolina Press, 1941, is an answer to the latter work. A good consensus of the interventionist viewpoint was found in William A. White, Ed., *Defense For America*, The Macmillan Company, 1940. The effect of Hitler's victories on American opinion is well treated in W. H. Shepardson and W. O. Scroggs, *The United States In World Affairs, 1940*, Harper & Brothers, 1941. H. R. Luce, *The American Century*, Farrar & Rinehart, 1941, is a stirring appeal for intervention.

15: Forging a New World

Specific References

1. George K. Anderson and Eda Lou Walton, Editors, *This Generation*, Scott, Foresman and Company, 1939, pp. 288-289. Reprinted by permission of Eda Lou Walton.
2. Paul Bekker, "Late Romanticism and Modern Trends," *From Bach to Stravinsky*, W. W. Norton & Company, 1933, p. 314.

General References

Ideas about the cultural activities of this century have been gathered from innumerable books, journals, magazine articles, and newspaper accounts. Some of the works to which the authors feel especially indebted are enumerated. A splendid short account of the major scientific discoveries and trends was found in V. L. and M. H. Albjerg, *From Sedan to Stresa*, D. Van Nostrand Company, 1937. Other books consulted in this regard were Carlton J. H. Hayes, *A Political and Cultural History of Modern Europe*, II, The Macmillan Company, 1937; H. E. Barnes, *The History of Western Civilization*, II, chap. 26, Harcourt, Brace and

Company, 1935. Religious problems and trends are discussed in William Ernest Hocking, *Living Religions and a World Faith,* The Macmillan Company, 1940. Of much assistance in the development of modern British and American literature was George K. Anderson and Eda Lou Walton, *This Generation,* Scott, Foresman and Company, 1939. Still another work helpful in this matter was Ludwig Lewisohn, *The Story of American Literature,* Modern Library, Random House, 1939. Paul Láng, *Music in Western Civilization,* W. W. Norton & Company, 1941, was consulted for the evolution of music to the present century, while several essays in David Ewen, Ed., *From Bach to Stravinsky,* W. W. Norton & Company, 1933, threw light on modern trends. The authors are indebted to the authority of Sheldon Cheney as demonstrated in *The Story of Modern Art,* The Viking Press, 1941, and also to R. S. Stites, *The Arts and Man,* McGraw-Hill Book Company, 1940; and Helen Gardner, *Art Through the Ages,* Harcourt, Brace and Company, 1926. Monographs and studies on Picasso, the Cubists, and Surrealism were helpful. Twentieth-century architecture was discussed in Talbot Hamlin, *Architecture Through the Ages,* G. P. Putnam's Sons, 1940, and in articles by Frank Lloyd Wright which appeared in various journals.

For material on postwar planning and reconstruction the following works are recommended: Clarence Streit, *Union Now,* Harper & Brothers, 1939, and *Union Now With Britain,* Harper & Brothers, 1941; Vera M. Dean, *Toward a New World Order,* in the *Foreign Policy Reports,* May 15, 1941, and *The Struggle For World Order,* Foreign Policy Association, 1941; P. E. Corbett, *Post-War Worlds,* Farrar & Rinehart, 1942; W. B. Curry, *The Case for Federal Union,* Middlesex, Penguin Books, 1939; H. G. Wells, *The New World Order,* Alfred A. Knopf, 1940; *The United States in a New World,* No. I., *Relations With Britain* from *Fortune,* May, 1942, Time Inc.; W. P. Maddox, *European Plans for World Order,* American Academy of Political and Social Science, 1940; W. Ivor Jennings, *A Federation for Western Europe,* The Macmillan Company, 1940; Herbert Hoover and Hugh Gibson, *The Problems of Lasting Peace,* Doubleday, Doran and Company, 1942; and *The World's Destiny and the United States,* World Citizens Association, 1941. A brief but splendid exposition of a program for dynamic democracy is outlined in Charles E. Merriam, *On the Agenda of Democracy,* Harvard University Press, 1941. Postwar democracy is discussed in the address of Vice-President Henry A. Wallace, "The Price of Free World Victory," published by L. B. Fisher, 1942. Another helpful discussion is to be found in Carl Becker, *Modern Democracy,* Yale University Press, 1941. The publications of the Commission To Study the Organization of Peace are helpful in suggesting specific postwar problems. The periodical *New Europe and World Reconstruction,* largely the channel for the expression of views of émigré European scholars, presents much valuable material as do publications of the United Nations governments, such as the *Inter-Allied Review* and *Bulletins from Britain.* The colonial problem is well treated in W. C. Langsam, *In Quest of Empire, The Problem of Colonies,* Foreign Policy Association, 1939, and more extensively in Royal Institute of International Affairs, *The Colonial Problem,* Oxford University Press, 1937. The rôle of the United States in the postwar world is provocatively treated by Nicholas John Spykman, *America's Strategy in World Politics,* Harcourt, Brace and Company, 1942. Economic trends in America are covered in the popular but suggestive brief volume: Stuart Chase, *The Road We Are Travelling, 1914-1942,* Twentieth Century Fund, 1942.

General Index

For the convenience of the reader the outstanding references have been put in boldface type whenever it was possible and practical to do so.

Suggested pronunciations for difficult or unusual words are respelled according to the table below, which is repeated in simplified form at the bottom of each right hand page of the *Index*. The mark ′ is placed after a syllable with primary or strong accent; the mark ′ shows a secondary or light accent, as in **civilization** (siv′i li za′tion).

The local pronunciations of many foreign words are too unusual for persons untrained in linguistics, and the aim has therefore been to provide pronunciations commonly acceptable in unaffected, educated American speech.

a	hat, cap	j	jam, enjoy	u	cup, butter
ā	age, face	k	kind, seek	u̇	full, put
ã	care, air	l	land, coal	ü	rule, move
ä	father, far	m	me, am	ū	use, music
		n	no, in		
b	bad, rob	ng	long, bring		
ch	child, much	o	hot, rock	v	very, save
d	did, red	ō	open, go	w	will, woman
		ô	order, all	y	you, yet
e	let, best	oi	oil, voice	z	zero, breeze
ē	equal, see	ou	house, out	zh	measure, seizure
ėr	term, learn				
		p	paper, cup		
f	fat, if	r	run, try	ə	represents:
g	go, bag	s	say, yes	a	in about
h	he, how	sh	she, rush	e	in taken
		t	tell, it	i	in pencil
i	it, pin	th	thin, both	o	in lemon
ī	ice, five	ᴛʜ	then, smooth	u	in circus

FOREIGN SOUNDS

Y as in French du. Pronounce ē with the lips rounded as for English ü in **rule**.

œ as in French peu. Pronounce ā with the lips rounded as for ō.

N as in French bon. The N is not pronounced, but shows that the vowel before it is nasal.

H as in German ach. Pronounce k without closing the breath passage.

A

hat, āge, cãre, fär; let, ēqual, tėrm; it, īce; hot, ōpen, ôrder; oil, out; cup, pu̇t, rüle, ūse, ch, child; ng, long; th, thin; ᴛʜ, then; zh, measure; ə represents *a* in about, *e* in taken, *i* in pencil, *o* in lemon, *u* in circus.

B

C

hat, āge, cãre, fär; let, ēqual, tėrm; it, īce; hot, ōpen, ôrder; oil, out; cup, půt, rüle, ūse; ch, child; ng, long; th, thin; ᴛʜ, then; zh, measure; ə represents *a* in about, *e* in taken, *i* in pencil, *o* in lemon, *u* in circus.

D

hat, āge, cãre, fär; let, ēqual, tėrm; it, īce; hot, ōpen, ôrder; oil, out; cup, pu̇t, rüle, ūse; ch, child; ng, long; th, thin; ᴛʜ, then; zh, measure; ə represents *a* in about, *e* in taken, *i* in pencil, *o* in lemon, *u* in circus.

E

H

I

hat, āge, cãre, fär; let, ēqual, tėrm; it, īce; hot, ōpen, ôrder; oil, out; cup, pu̇t, rüle, ūse; ch, child; ng, long; th, thin; ᴛʜ, then; zh, measure; ə represents *a* in about, *e* in taken, *i* in pencil, *o* in lemon, *u* in circus.

J

K

L

M

N

O

P

S

hat, āge, cãre, fär; let, ēqual, tėrm; it, īce; hot, ōpen, ôrder; oil, out; cup, pu̇t, rüle, ūse; ch, child; ng, long; th, thin; TH, then; zh, measure; ə represents *a* in about, *e* in taken, *i* in pencil, *o* in lemon, *u* in circus.

T

U

V

W

X

Y

Z

SUPPLEMENT *to Civilization—Past and Present, Volume Two*
by T. Walter Wallbank and Alastair M. Taylor

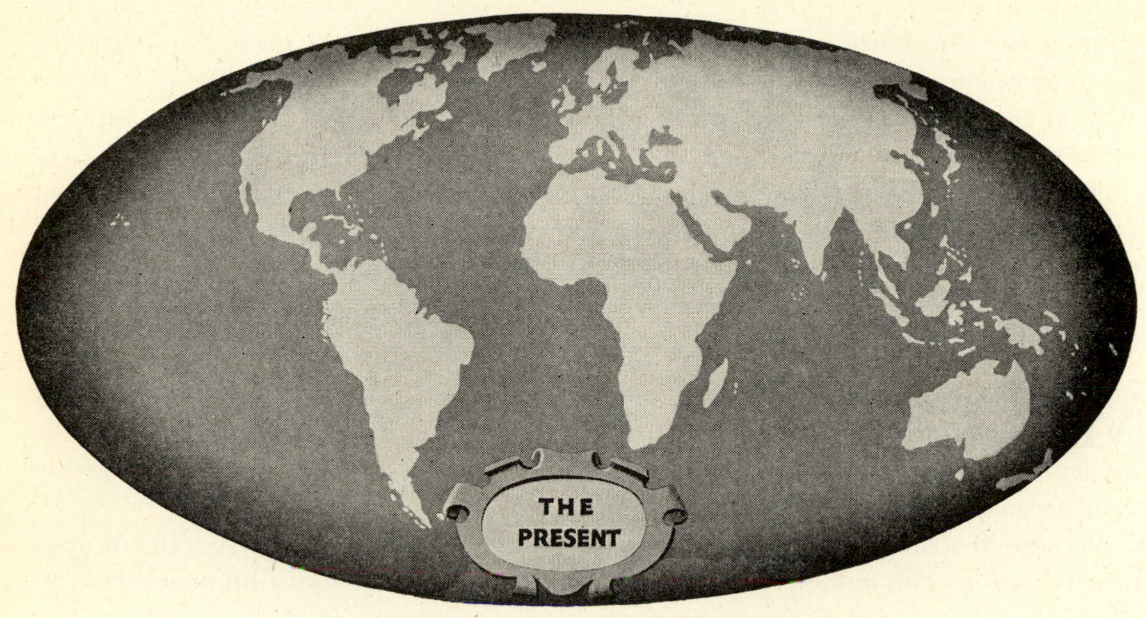

Days of Decision

Scott, Foresman and Company CHICAGO ATLANTA DALLAS NEW YORK

Preface

TO SUPPLEMENT

FROM THE POINT where Volume Two of *Civilization—Past and Present* stopped—the summer of 1942—this supplement carries forward the story of the Second World War. It covers the tremendous world-wide actions of 1942-1943 (through the Moscow Conference), developments on the home fronts, and postwar planning.

The reader is asked to bear in mind that some of the issues discussed here are most complex, that the full facts about a recent event are not always available, that historical judgment in some cases may be years in crystallizing. But some understanding of the general pattern we are helping to shape is demanded. *Days of Decision* attempts to show this pattern as objectively, as accurately as possible.

MR. CARROLL BINDER, Foreign Editor of *The Chicago Daily News,* and Professor S. William Halperin of the University of Chicago have read and criticized the supplement. Although we assume full responsibility for the material, we are indebted to them for many helpful suggestions.

Because Mr. R. M. Chapin, Jr., map-maker for *Time,* did the extensive series of maps for *Civilization—Past and Present,* Time, Inc. made possible a similar illumination of this supplement by agreeing to our using maps that have appeared in their columns during the past year. We are grateful to both Mr. Chapin and the publishers of *Time.*

We express our thanks also to Miss Winifred Pawliger for the initial drawings.

The following publishers have generously allowed the use of quotations from their materials. Such quotations are indicated in detail in the Bibliography beginning on page 69: The Christian Science Publishing Society, Boston; Doubleday, Doran and Company, New York; Editorial Publications, Inc., New York; L. B. Fischer, New York; Foreign Affairs, New York; Foreign Policy Association, New York; Harcourt, Brace and Company, New York; Harvard University Press, Cambridge; International Labor Review, Montreal; International Publishers, New York; Alfred A. Knopf, New York; Newsweek, New York; New Zealand Legation, Washington, D. C.; Press Association, Inc., New York; Soviet Russia Today, New York; The Curtis Publishing Company, Philadelphia; The Macmillan Company, New York; The University of Chicago Press, Chicago; Time, Inc., New York.

Finally, acknowledgment for permission to reprint the illustrations is made to Acme Newspictures, Inc.: 11, 16, 20, 22, 25, 38, 39, 46, 58; British Combine: 12, 33; Graphic Associates for Public Affairs Committee: 28; National Film Board of Canada: 23, 36 (2); Pictograph Corporation for Public Affairs Committee: 56; Pix: 41; Sovfoto: 5, 43; St. Louis Star-Times: 54.

T. W. W.
A. M. T.

Los Angeles, California
November 15, 1943

Copyright, 1943, by Scott, Foresman and Company

SECTION 1

Since Stalingrad

By the summer of 1942 the Second World War had been raging for three years. The actions were more widespread than ever, the fighting more intense, and the issues for which men died more fateful and clearcut. In July 1942 the armies of the United Nations everywhere were on the defensive, but a truly amazing transformation in the military fortunes of the war took place during the subsequent months. Events carried the United States and her allies from defense to offense, from imminent defeat to the growing prospect of victory.

The War in Retrospect, 1939-1942

Basic features of the war. In this study of the phases of the war since Stalingrad, it will be helpful to review the outstanding features of the global conflict thus far: (1) the surprising military strength of Russia; (2) the complete military and political collapse of France, and DeGaulle's efforts to rebuild it in exile; (3) the failure of Italian Fascism; (4) the astonishing striking power of Japan; (5) the pertinacity and fighting spirit of the British; (6) the inability of the Nazis to secure the co-operation of subjugated Europeans; (7) the rapidity of total war mobilization in the United States; (8) the unity existing between Latin and North America; (9) the growing importance of air power; and (10) the tremendous distances involved in transportation and supply for the Allies (see the maps, pp. 2 and 3).

The military score. In summer, 1942, the score stood heavily against the Allies: (1) The Nazis in Russia had completed their conquest of the Crimea. (2) Hitler's Africa Corps stood poised in North Africa to deliver final blows and take Alexandria. (3) The Japanese were consolidating their positions in the Solomons and New Guinea. (4) They had taken possession of several Aleutian Islands, particularly Attu and Kiska. (5) Burma was in the hands of the Japanese. The danger of Japanese invasion of India was rendered more acute by the internal crisis in India. (6) China was again feeling the brunt of Japanese attack. Supplies from abroad could only trickle in.

Crest of Axis Power

R*ussia: Hitler's objective.* In 1942 there was still time for Hitler to strive for the prize which he had sought unsuccessfully in the summer of 1941—the defeat of Russia, which would leave him free to turn against Great Britain and the United States.

It seems apparent that the German objective was not to destroy the Russian armies. This had proved impossible in 1941. But the Nazi High Command did expect to cripple the Russians and, more important, cut off their vital war supplies. By striking in the south and securing the control of the Ukraine region and the Caucasus, the Germans would deprive the Russians of oil, iron, manganese, and great food-producing areas. Such a military success would also cut the Russian forces in two. At the same time such conquests, it was hoped, would rectify the acute Nazi shortage in raw materials, especially oil.

The Germans possessed almost overwhelming strength. The *Luftwaffe* was supreme in the air; the Nazi generals had at their disposal more than a million superbly equipped and

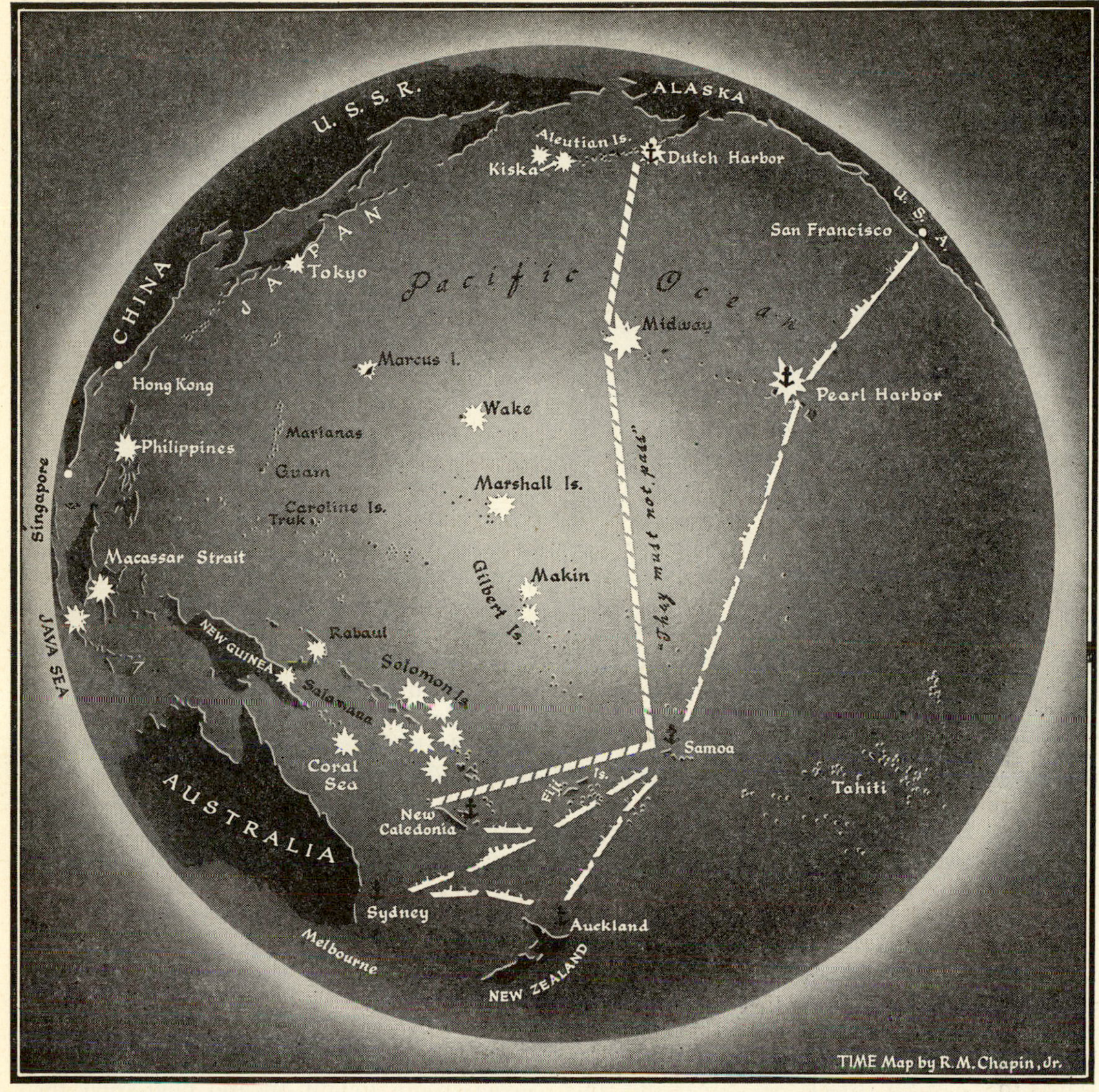

trained troops. Russia, on the other hand, began the 1942 campaign weakened by the loss of many important industrial regions and by the subjugation of one third of her population.

Drive on Voronezh. On June 28, 1942 the Germans began a heavy attack from Kursk. The main objective of Field Marshal Fedor Von Bock was the city of Voronezh on the Don River, the wheat center of the Don region and a railway center for Russian defense. The new offensive was based on what the Germans chose to call *Motpulk,* mechanized mass movement. The Nazi forces used heavier tanks, better mobile guns, and more dive bombers than they had in previous operations of their dreaded *Blitzkrieg.*

After two weeks of fighting, German forces reached the vicinity of Voronezh and managed to cross the Don River at several points. The Russian defenders of the city, under the direction of Marshal Timoshenko, kept the German pontoon bridges and rubber boats under heavy fire, and squadrons of Soviet *Stormovik* planes strafed the attacking troops. Although Von Bock's forces succeeded in breaking into the city on several occasions, their hold was precarious, and by July 16 Russian counterattacks began to push these

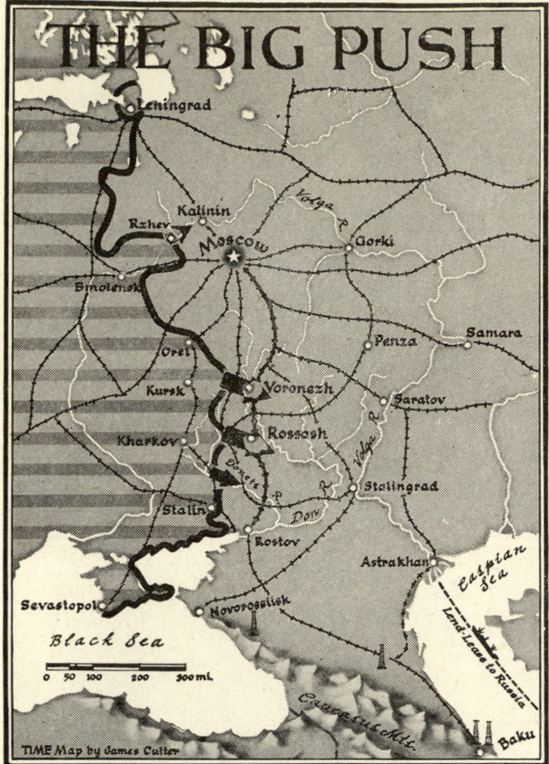

spearheads out of Voronezh, then a mass of ruins. To the south other German units had pushed eastward, reaching the Don about halfway between Voronezh and Stalingrad. It was this penetration into Russian territory enclosed within the great bend of the Don that menaced both the important city of Rostov and the entire Caucasus region to the south. (See the map above.)

Nazi push in Caucasus. Halted at Voronezh, Von Bock's soldiers opened a strong drive toward the eastern Black Sea area and the Caucasus. The rich iron and coal region of the Donets Basin was overrun first, and on July 23 the Nazi forces reached the outskirts of Rostov. Five days later the city fell to Von Bock. Pressing forward, the Nazis entered the northern Caucasus region. Baku, producing 70 per cent of all Russia's oil, was only 700 miles away. The Grozny and Maikop oil fields, contributing 18 per cent, were much nearer.

Advancing as much as eighteen miles a day the German armies captured Maikop on August 9. Most of its wells had already been destroyed by the Russian defenders. On September 6 the Nazis, edging down the east coast of the Black Sea, captured Novorossiisk. This was Russia's last good naval base on the Black Sea. Pushing eastward along the fringes of the Caucasus Mountains, the victorious Germans drove the desperate Russian forces back toward the Caspian Sea and Baku. The latter part of September, however, witnessed a change in the fortunes of war. German tanks could not be used effectively in the rough terrain. October saw Von Bock's troops held just fifty miles from Grozny, and the rich prize of Baku had not been secured.

The epic of Stalingrad. While the Germans were carrying on their Caucasus campaign, which had been halted just short of its goal, other Nazi armies were striving to crush all Russian resistance in the Don River bend, to capture the important industrial city of Stalingrad, and to push east to Astrakhan on the Caspian. Stalingrad was a symbol of the first Five-Year Plan. From a mere country town it had grown into a great industrial city of 500,000. Stretching twenty miles along the Volga were its numerous factories, one of which produced more than 50,000 tractors a year. On August 22 a Nazi spearhead was established across the Don, and a week later an all-out assault was hurled against the Stalingrad defenses.

This battle was the fiercest of the war to date; more than one million men were locked in a gigantic struggle. On September 12, the Germans battered their way into the city, but the defense was carried on from street to street by both Soviet soldiers and civilians whose motto was "Ni shaya nazad" (Not one step back). Nazi *stukas* might pulverize buildings, but from cellars and crannies in the ruins Soviet troops fought on and held their own. Losses were estimated to run as high as 6000 for the Russians and 2000 for the Germans daily. On September 22 a grand assault paced by 200 tanks reached the center of the city but was finally forced to withdraw. By October, although the Germans still retained their possession of parts of the city, it was obvious that they did not have sufficient strength to effect its complete capture.

Stalingrad had become in World War II what Verdun was to the Allied cause in World War I: a symbol of indomitable courage.

The battle for Egypt. When the Nazi High Command launched its summer campaign against the Russian positions before Voronezh,

A Red Army soldier takes his stand behind a chest of drawers during fierce street fighting in Stalingrad. The soldiers are firing tommy guns to dislodge Germans from houses in the background.

an equally important German drive was in progress on the borders of Egypt. Early in June the British had lost a crucial tank battle against Rommel's Africa Corps, and on June 21, 25,000 British troops were forced to surrender at Tobruk. Rommel raced ahead into Egypt, taking Matruh, while the retreating British forces under General Auchinleck prepared to make a stand at el Alamein. On this 35-mile front, with the Mediterranean guarding one flank and a marshy depression the other, Auchinleck's men halted Rommel's advance toward Alexandria, only 70 miles away.

Throughout July sporadic fighting was carried on in the desert. Neither side was strong enough to break through, and the whole outcome depended on the flow of supplies and reinforcements. The United States supplied ships to help send 50,000 British troops to Egypt, and hundreds of Sherman tanks from American armament plants were rushed around the southern tip of Africa to Egypt. Rommel contrived to get large forces from southern Italy, and Axis shipping landed much equipment in Africa.

In this battle of supply the small British island outpost of Malta was important as it menaced the Axis supply route. The Germans and Italians made every effort to destroy Malta; by the fall of 1942 it had suffered 2537 raids.

By the end of August, Rommel felt strong enough to stab again at the British troops. The British Eighth Army, meanwhile, had been strongly reinforced and placed under the direct command of Lieutenant General Bernard Montgomery. Auchinleck had been succeeded by General Harold Alexander, who assumed direction of all British forces in the Near East. On August 31 the Germans, assisted by Italian divisions, attacked the southern flank of Montgomery's men entrenched behind minefields, desert "boxes," and wire barricades. The attack penetrated twenty-five miles but was later forced back to its initial starting point. It was in this battle, at el Alamein, that United States tank crews had their first experience in desert fighting.

It is important to keep in mind that Rommel made his attack at the same moment when Von Bock was thrusting against Stalingrad. The two movements were in reality parts of gigantic pincers which, if successful, would advance toward each other from the north and south and squeeze out all United Nations resistance in the Caucasus and in the Middle East. The next Axis move could then be an advance toward India from the west, with the Japanese in a position to attack that country from conquered Burma.

Russian resistance at Voronezh and Stalingrad and the halt of Rommel at el Alamein ended for the time being the great summer drive of the Axis powers in the western theaters of war. But in this global struggle, thousands of miles away from the Nile or the Don other fighting of a decisive nature was taking place in the Pacific.

Japan halted in China. In China, Japanese armies in the late spring of 1942 attacked strongly in the southeast provinces. The aim was to secure control of important railways and to obtain the major air bases from which, otherwise, Japan might be bombed when adequate bomber forces arrived from the United States. Fear of such an attack had been active in Japanese quarters since the famous Doolittle raid on Tokyo and other cities on April 18, 1942. In June and July, the Japanese carried forward their advance. Capture of the important strip of railway between Hangchow and Nanchang brought closer the Japanese plan of establishing an all-rail communication route from Shanghai to Singapore. At the same time the Japanese secured a few important air bases.

The loss of the Burma route had practically closed China to the outside world. The most pressing need of the Chinese was for heavy artillery and airplanes, without which defeat in the long run seemed inevitable. A small American air force, the A.V.G's, or Flying Tigers, had rendered great assistance to China and Burma. In June 1942 it was announced that a new United States Army Air Force was to be established in China under the command of Brigadier General Claire L. Chennault. On July 6 a communiqué described the first operations of America's new air squadrons in China. Chennault's pilots frustrated a heavy bombing raid on the Chinese capital, Chungking, on July 27, and his bombers made heavy raids on the Japanese bases at Hong Kong, Hankow, Canton, and Foochow. The Japanese made determined efforts to destroy American air bases but were not successful and lost numerous planes. Encouraged by the advent of this new air power, the Chinese struck back and checked the Japanese drives. The Japanese were driven from the vital Hangchow-Nanchang railway and from some of their recently won air bases.

The collapse of the Japanese offensive was puzzling to many military observers, as China's air power was weak and her armies lacked equipment. Some believed Japan failed because of a growing need for supplies and manpower in other war theaters, especially the South Pacific. The important thing, however, was that China after five years of war had been able to hold and then hurl back a determined Japanese offensive; and there was now prospect of more and more assistance from her allies, as the huge armament program of the United States got into high gear.

Crisis in India. Aid to China could hardly reach her unless India were held as a great base for military operations of the United Nations. From India, when Allied strength became sufficient, the reconquest of Burma could be undertaken and the lifeline to China reopened. And perhaps from India sufficient armies might be mustered not only to recapture Burma but to drive the Japanese out of Malaya and southeast Asia. In the spring of 1942, however, the Chinese cause was seriously menaced by the danger of internal collapse in India. Mohandas Gandhi pressed his demand for Indian independence from Great Britain with more vigor. Impressed by the successes of the Japanese in the Pacific, in Malaya, and in Burma, Gandhi apparently believed that before the Japanese were actually in a position to invade India from Burma the British troops and government officials should leave the country. The connection between India and Great Britain should be immediately severed. He argued, "The presence of the British in India is an invitation to Japan to invade India. Their withdrawal would remove the bait. Assume, however, that it does not, free India would be better able to cope with invasion. Unadulterated non-cooperation would then have full sway."[1] On April 27, 1942, Gandhi urged the Congress Party to adopt a resolution which demanded the evacuation of all foreign soldiers from Indian soil. India then would follow the policy of pacifism and attempt to negotiate with Japan. Gandhi argued in his resolution that "Britain is incapable of defending India. Japan's quarrel is not with India; she is warring against the British Empire." There were numerous Indians, however, who doubted whether moral force and passive resistance would have much influence upon the Japanese once they were inside India.

Gandhi's resolution of outright pacifism was rejected by the Congress, but its leaders decided to adopt his proposal for a program of civil disobedience if Britain would not withdraw immediately from the country. Further, Gandhi's ideas of negotiating with Japan were scrapped for a policy of a free India, once British control had been removed, "throwing all her great resources into the struggle against aggression of Nazism, Fascism, and Imperialism."[2] On August 8 the Congress Party endorsed a resolution demanding Britain's withdrawal from India, calling on all Indians to engage in a mass struggle on non-violent lines. The following day Gandhi, Nehru, and about 200 other leading Indian nationalists were taken into custody by the British government. Rioting, sabotage, and strikes then followed in many parts of the country. Railway stations and lines in particular were destroyed. In general, however, the mass of people failed to respond to the call for mass civil disobedience. Several weeks elapsed before order was restored in the main centers of revolt.

The failure of Gandhi's mass movement was due in part to the belief in many circles of Indian public opinion that such a program with the Japanese ready to batter at the gates of India was suicidal. In particular Mohammed Jinnah, leader of the Indian Mohammedans, called Gandhi's demand fantastic and warned that he would cease to cooperate with the government if it gave in to the Congress. While Gandhi's Congress Party declined in influence the Moslem League, led by Jinnah, advanced. Known as Pakistan, Jinnah's plan called for the creation of a Moslem state separate from Hindu India.

Although some semblance of order had been restored, the situation remained quite unsatisfactory, and certainly pleasing to Japan. If all parties concerned—British, Hindus, and Mohammedans—had exhibited more moderation and the spirit of compromise, some solution might have been found. Even in certain British quarters there was a demand that America and China "should help to compose a quarrel which injures every one (of the United Nations)." The crisis in India posed an almost insuperable problem: how to satisfy Great Britain's determination to be responsible for defending India from Japanese invasion; how to meet the demand of the Congress Party for immediate independence; and how to reconcile the various opposing factions in India.

Japan's New Guinea campaign. Following the Japanese conquest of Burma, Malaya, and Bataan in the Philippines, and the Dutch East Indies, the number one question in the Southwest Pacific was: will Japan attack Australia? She seemed in a good position to embark on such an undertaking from bases at Rabaul in New Britain and Lae and Salamaua in New Guinea. The danger would be immediate if Japanese units succeeded in capturing Port Moresby, capital of Australian Papua in southwestern New Guinea. The Japanese were also strengthening their position in the Solomon Islands, notably on Guadalcanal, which pointed menacingly toward the United Nations' bases on New Hebrides and New Caledonia. The defense of these bases was essential to maintain the supply route from the United States to Australia.

With Port Moresby as their objective, Japanese landing parties were put ashore in July 1942 at Buna and Gona on the western side of the long tip of southern New Guinea. Their goal was only 120 miles away, but they would have to cross the mountains, follow a rough trail over a 7000-foot pass, before they reached it. Nevertheless the Japanese troops made good progress. Adept in jungle fighting and painted green for camouflage, the invaders advanced across the mountains and reached Kokoda by the first week of August. In the next month the Japanese had penetrated to within 34 miles of Port Moresby. Less success was achieved when they landed at a bay below Gona and Buna with the plan of streaking across southern New Guinea at its narrowest point. They were met by Australian troops; these would have annihilated them entirely if naval craft had not managed to evacuate a small remnant.

In view of the imminent menace to Port Moresby and later to Australia itself, General MacArthur concentrated all his available air power to disrupt the Japanese attack. Heavy bombing raids were made against Buna, Lae, and Salamaua. The lines of supply of the advancing Japanese column were heavily damaged. Without adequate supplies and reinforcements the Japanese strength diminished, and counterattacks forced a Japanese retreat as September ended. A threat to western Australia via southern New Guinea was ended.

Struggle for Guadalcanal. The first offensive of the United Nations in the Pacific was undertaken in the southern Solomons. On the night of August 7 a combined force of United States naval units and transports moved against the islands of Guadalcanal, Tulagi, and Gavutu. Japanese positions were first bombarded by the warships and bombed from the air. Then marines in steel-walled barges were landed on the beach. Tanks, tractors, light cannon, and machine guns were quickly set on shore. In Tulagi and Gavutu the fighting was fierce but brief. Small Japanese detachments fought to the last man. On the island of Guadalcanal the Japanese were more numerous. With great difficulty the marines succeeded in obtaining control of a small area seven miles wide along the beach, which included a vital air field.

During the months of August, September, and October fighting on the land, on the sea, and in the air continued with unparalleled ferocity at Guadalcanal. On the night of August 9 a Japanese naval squadron surprised an Allied force and sank four cruisers guarding the troops and supply ships unloading in the harbor. In the days that followed, Japanese planes bombed the marines' beachhead continuously, and light naval forces bombarded their positions from the sea. A fortnight later a Japanese task force was driven off by American air power with the loss to the Japanese of a small carrier and damage to other vessels. In mid-September the Japanese again made a determined attack with warships, supported by a simultaneous offensive by the Japanese troops on Guadalcanal. Marine positions were penetrated, but the attack was finally repulsed. During this action the United States lost the modern aircraft carrier *Wasp*, by submarine attack.

October saw no diminution in the struggle. The Japanese succeeded in landing reinforcements, and naval action off Guadalcanal was continuous. In one battle—the battle of Cape Esperance—a United States task force with the loss of one destroyer disposed of two heavy

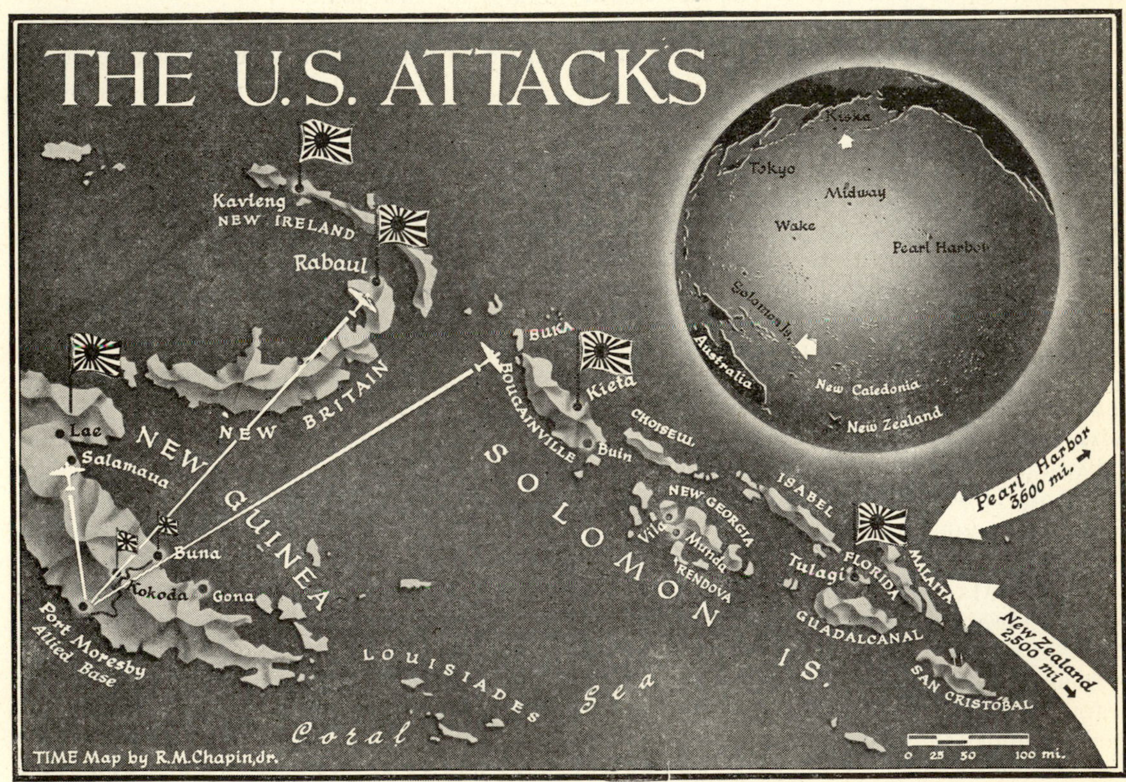

cruisers, one light cruiser, and three destroyers. In another—the battle of Santa Cruz Islands—United States forces sank two destroyers and inflicted damage on two battleships, two carriers, and four cruisers. The United States' loss, however, was heavy: a destroyer and the carrier *Hornet*.

The marines on land were proving more than a match for the Japanese, although the manner of fighting was new to them; it was a return to the fighting by stealth which characterized the French and Indian War of the eighteenth century. The battle was waged in dense jungle country. Here the Japanese waited in dense grass or strapped high as snipers in coconut palms. No American soldier in previous wars had ever met such an opponent. It was kill or be killed. But the fate of Guadalcanal hinged not so much on land action as on events that might take place on the sea. The naval losses sustained by the United States, especially in aircraft carriers, had been serious, and if command of the sea was obtained by Japan, defeat on Guadalcanal was a foregone conclusion.

Crusade for a second front. During the fateful summer of 1942 the people of the United Nations staggered but somehow maintained their fortitude and belief in final victory. This period of crisis was characterized by an insistent demand in many quarters for more energetic measures against Nazi Germany. This became a veritable crusade for the Russian concept of a second front, an invasion against Nazi Europe to relieve the desperate plight of the Russians.

The only offensive, and that of a limited character, had been the spectacular British Commando raid on the French coast, at Dieppe. Resistance was unexpectedly strong, and the Commandos, mostly Canadians, withdrew after suffering heavy casualties. This was a foretaste of what hazards the invasion of Nazi Europe involved.

Controversy over a second front, however, largely subsided for a while (see p. 28) with a new turn of events late in October. In Russia, North Africa, the South Pacific, and the Aleutian Islands, the tide of victory changed rapidly in favor of the United Nations.

Emergence of Allied Strength

British offensive in North Africa. On October 23 the British Eighth Army assumed the offensive. Its commander, General Montgomery, announced: "For three years we have been trying to plug holes all over the world. Now, thank God, that period is over." On a forty-mile front at el Alamein an artillery barrage was opened up that rocked buildings in Alexandria, seventy miles away. Sappers advancing through the German mine fields cleared a corridor for the infantry, who were then followed by the tanks. By November 6 the German forces with their Italian allies were in full retreat westward across the Egyptian border.

As the defeated forces fled, they were harried from the air by continuous bombardment. Supply trucks, tanks, and columns of troops were blasted by waves of British and American bombers. Many German troops of the Africa Corps were captured, and six divisions of Italians were abandoned by Rommel. Advancing into Libya, the British Eighth Army captured Tobruk, the best port between Alexandria and Tunis. As November ended, the British had occupied and passed beyond Bengasi and were half way to their final objective of Tripoli. Fortified by American planes, Canadian trucks, and immense supplies from Great Britain, the army of Montgomery pursued the scattered remnants of the Africa Corps. The Eighth Army showed great power, organization, and mobility.

During the first half of December there was a lull in the fighting as the British army advanced on el Aghéila, a natural defense position protected by wide salt-flats. Here Rommel was expected to make a stand after retreating 700 miles from el Alamein. This strong position, however, was evacuated by the German forces, and by December 21 Rommel's decimated battalions were again in full retreat. On January 23 the Eighth Army entered Tripoli, thus capturing the last remnant of the Italian empire; Rommel's army crossed into French Tunisia and barricaded itself in the Mareth Line, a defensive position originally built by the French on the Tunisian border. Other German forces were already in Tunisia. How they came to be there will constitute part of the story of the next phase of the North African front.

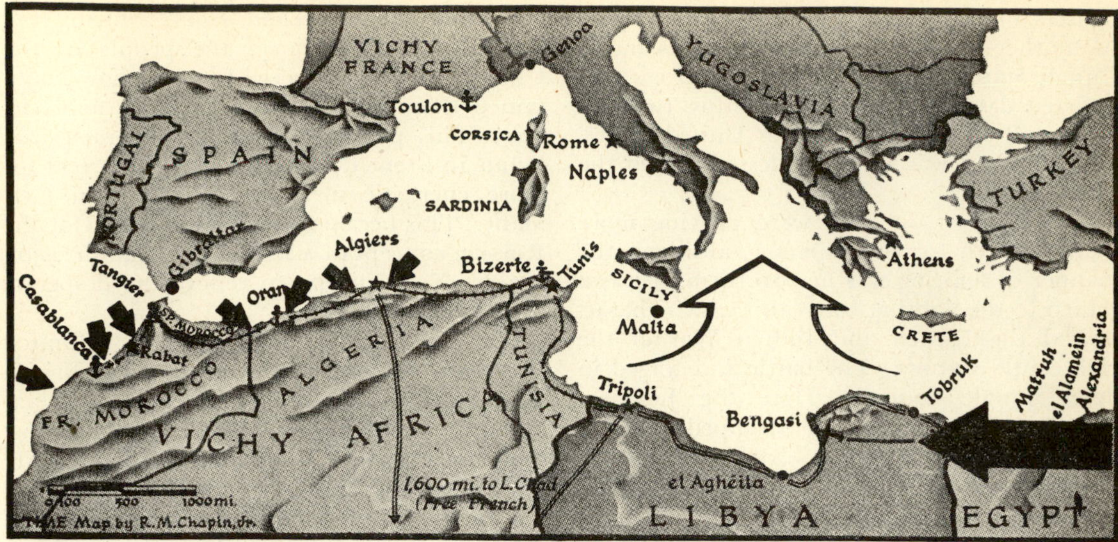

Allied invasion of French North Africa. Early in November, American troops from a huge convoy of 850 ships were landed at various points along the French North African coast. (Study the map above.) The troops were under the unified command of Lieutenant General Dwight D. Eisenhower. Their immediate objectives were Algiers, Oran, and Casablanca. The operation was brilliantly carried out in coordination with the British Eighth Army's offensive against Rommel in Egypt. Morocco and Algeria were invaded. Tunisia, it was expected, could be quickly overrun following the occupation of these territories. French North Africa, administered by Vichy officials, was groaning under the heavy demands made upon it for raw materials and food stuffs by the Nazis. Everything, therefore, was done to assure the French people that the forces of the United Nations came not as conquerors but as deliverers.

On the whole, resistance was half-hearted and the casualties of the American expedition were light. Algiers fell in one day, and Admiral Darlan, a high Vichy official, was captured. At Oran the fighting was more bitter, but hostilities ceased on November 10. Casablanca also saw fierce fighting and a French fleet put out of action. On November 11 Admiral Darlan ordered all commanders in French North Africa to cease hostilities. He then assumed the civil administration of the territory in the name of Marshal Pétain, head of the French state. The new régime was accepted by the American military authorities, since Darlan for his part was now ready to cooperate with the United Nations. There were many people in Great Britain and the United Nations who resented this "deal" with a Vichy official who had been notoriously anti-British and in favor of collaboration with Germany, but authorities insisted it was necessary on the grounds of expediency. Explaining his action, Admiral Darlan stated that in 1940 he believed an Axis victory was possible; in 1941 he believed no victory could be achieved by either side; but at the end of 1942 he was convinced that Germany would lose.[3] To facilitate military cooperation with General Eisenhower, Darlan appointed General Henri Giraud as commander of the French North African forces.

Repercussions of the invasion of Africa. The response of Hitler to the occupation of French North Africa was swift. On November 11 German troops took over what had been known as Unoccupied France, and the fiction of the Vichy government as an independent administration was, at long last, practically ended. At the same time Italian forces took over the French island of Corsica.

There was still another repercussion of the North African invasion. Contrary to the Armistice of 1940, Hitler decided to reach for the French fleet, lying in the harbor of Toulon. Just before daybreak, November 27, Nazi armored units overpowered the French guards and raced to the docks. From the flagship of Vice Admiral Jean de Laborde was flashed the command: "Carry out Order B." Immediately

This picture, smuggled out of France, shows part of the French fleet sinking to the bottom of Toulon Harbor. The scuttling of the French fleet was one of the most dramatic incidents of the war.

ship after ship exploded and settled to the bottom. Over sixty warships were destroyed, including the famous *Dunkerque, Strasbourg,* and *Algerie.* Only four submarines succeeded in escaping from Toulon. General de Gaulle, referring to the heroism of the French crews, among which loss of life was heavy, stated that in their supreme test the sailors had followed the course of true patriotism, that "in one brief moment they saw through the odious veil of lies which since June 1940 hung before their eyes."

Climax in Africa: Tunisia. Two days following the first American landings, the British First Army under Lieutenant General Kenneth A. Anderson disembarked at Algiers and started a rapid advance into Tunisia. It was expected that the Tunisian campaign would be an all-British affair. Anderson's First Army would sweep to Bizerte and Tunis from the west while Montgomery's Eighth was advancing from the east in the direction of the Tunisian border. If Anderson had been successful, the Tunisian campaign would have been over in a few weeks. As it was it took six months of savage fighting. Immediately following the American occupation of North Africa, the German High Command commandeered every type of air transport available in southern Europe and flew thousands of soldiers to Tunisia, where the French could offer little resistance. Lines of communication from Bizerte to Sicily were only 200 miles, and over this short stretch of water tanks, artillery, and troops were ferried.

The First Army entered Tunisia on November 17 and two days later contact was made with the Germans. The British were hindered by lack of airfields and the unusually heavy rains, the heaviest in several years. By December, Anderson's troops had reached a point about a dozen miles from Tunis; but the Germans, who by this time outnumbered the British in men and had the advantage of operating from all-weather airfields and shorter supply lines, counterattacked and drove them back. For the next few months the line of battle in northern Tunisia remained fixed, with intermittent sparring for important positions in the hilly country.

Until the Eighth Army of Montgomery could break through the Mareth Line, the combined forces of von Arnim in northern Tunisia and Rommel could concentrate superior strength on the Allied armies, even though the latter had been reinforced by French and American contingents. The Germans struck first at the French and inflicted heavy losses. Early in February Rommel attacked American positions and drove through

Faid Pass. His next objective was Kasserine Pass, and he gained this. In the engagement the American forces lost 100 tanks and four times the casualties suffered by the Germans. Rommel was then in a position to outflank the First Army in the north. Instead, because all available reinforcements were sent to aid the Allies, Rommel was checked and then forced to retreat from the Kasserine Pass.

The construction of new air bases, improvement of lines of communication, a change of generals, and arrival of vast quantities of artillery and tanks began to turn the tide in March. United States forces regained most of the ground lost in February, and the British drove through the Mareth Line. Command of the air passed to the armies of General Eisenhower. While von Arnim's and Rommel's fighter planes were knocked out of the sky over Tunisia, Allied bombers destroyed Axis shipping that was bringing supplies from Sicily. Sweeps were also made over targets in Sicily and southern Italy, and harbor installations and air fields were destroyed.

The climax to the Tunisian campaign came in April. During this final phase, American, British, and French troops attacking from the east, west, and south relentlessly forced the Axis divisions back to the sea. American soldiers performed magnificently in capturing vital points in victories that helped soften the sting of their defeat at Kasserine. Unchallenged in the air, Allied fighters and bombers broke up and shattered Axis resistance. In one day Allied planes sank twenty-five Axis ships, unloaded 1,250,000 pounds of bombs, and made 2500 sorties. Bizerte and Tunis were captured simultaneously on May 8. A remnant of the Axis armies hoped to make a stand on the peninsula east of Tunis, but Allied troops broke into the promontory before lines of defense could be set up. There was no prospect of a German imitation of the British at Dunkirk. Allied naval craft patrolled the coastline of Tunis and sank or captured any boats that attempted to evacuate troops. On May 12 Allied headquarters announced the end of all organized Axis resistance.

One of the most astonishing features of the final round in the Battle of Tunisia was the sudden capitulation of the Axis forces. They surrendered by the thousands, not emulating their brethren at Stalingrad, who just four months before had fought to the end when

Everyone seems to be having a good time as these members of the R.A.F., somewhere in North Africa, relax during time off from strenuous duties. Note the bullet holes in the box on the far right.

surrounded by Russian armies. To some observers this meant the Nazi soldier was losing his early blind faith in ultimate victory; he no longer believed in useless sacrifice. But Germans in Africa had fought fiercely until it became apparent that U. S. preponderance in planes and tanks was overwhelming. The military box score in Tunis was 266,000 Axis prisoners, with casualties estimated at some 323,000. To these figures must be added the prisoners taken in the Eighth Army's victory over Rommel in Egypt. As for the Allies, their casualties were less than 70,000.

Summing up the Tunisian campaign, and the other African campaigns which preceded it, Winston Churchill, speaking before Congress on May 19, declared:

"All the vast territories from Madagascar to Morocco, from Cairo to Casablanca, from Aden to Dakar, are under British, American, or French control. One continent at least has been cleansed and purged forever from Fascist or Nazi tyranny. The African excursions of the two dictators have cost their countries in killed and captured 950,000 soldiers."

Defense to offense in Russia. While Nazi and Fascist divisions were being defeated and captured by the thousands in North Africa, momentous events were taking place along the 1500-mile Russian front. It will be recalled that in October 1942 the *Wehrmacht* of Hitler was prevented only by the slightest margin from capturing the key city of Stalingrad and from obtaining the precious oil of the Caucasus. During their great summer drive the Nazis had lost many men and used up vast quantities of equipment. Hitler's determination not to withdraw from Stalingrad, despite the warnings of his generals, placed his armies in an extended bulge which was vulnerable to Soviet flank attack. Furthermore, any successful Russian attack from Stalingrad southwestward to Rostov would menace the German forces in the Caucasus with encirclement. In the event of large-scale fighting, the Nazi High Command would find it difficult to rush in reinforcements—especially aircraft—because of the gravity of the situation in Egypt, where Rommel was retreating.

Such were the circumstances when the Russians began a savage offensive on November 19. Soviet divisions pressed forward northwest and southwest of Stalingrad. New reserves had come up quietly to the front and crossed the Volga at night. The prime objective of the offensive was to surround and destroy 300,000 Germans around Stalingrad. In three days the Russian troops drove fifty miles to the Don and sped westward another ninety miles. In little more than a week 66,000 prisoners were taken, together with much booty, such as heavy guns and tanks.

Another Russian attack was opened west of Moscow. At this point the Nazis held a menacing salient only 130 miles from the Russian capital. The two key fortified German points in this area were Rzhev and Vyazma. The second offensive, therefore, was directed against Rzhev. This powerful Nazi position, or hedgehog as it was termed, was by-passed, surrounded, and its 75,000 defenders threatened with extinction.

In mid-December a third Russian offensive broke on the Voronezh front. Spearheads pushed southwestward and surrounded a strong German position. The strategy of this drive was to make a junction with other Soviet divisions pushing southwest of Stalingrad. A closing of the pincers would trap large numbers of the enemy in the bend of the River Don, would doom the Nazi army before Stalingrad, and at the same time menace Rostov. While Nazi troops attempted to hold their own around Stalingrad, at Rzhev, and southwest of Voronezh, two additional offensives were initiated at the extreme ends of the eastern front. In the far north a determined effort was made to break the German ring around Leningrad. This was accomplished in January when a narrow corridor was punched through to the long-beleaguered city. At the same time Russian armies northwest of Rzhev exerted pressure in the direction of the old Latvian border. At the other end of the battle line, far to the south, a Russian offensive drove against the Nazi positions in the Caucasus. Early in January considerable progress was being made northeast of the important Grozny oil area. Russian forces also edged their way north along the Black Sea in the direction of the Sea of Azov.

January 1943 was the most disastrous month so far in the war for the Nazis. All along the eastern front the dearly won German gains of the last summer were being nullified. In the desperate engagements the Rus-

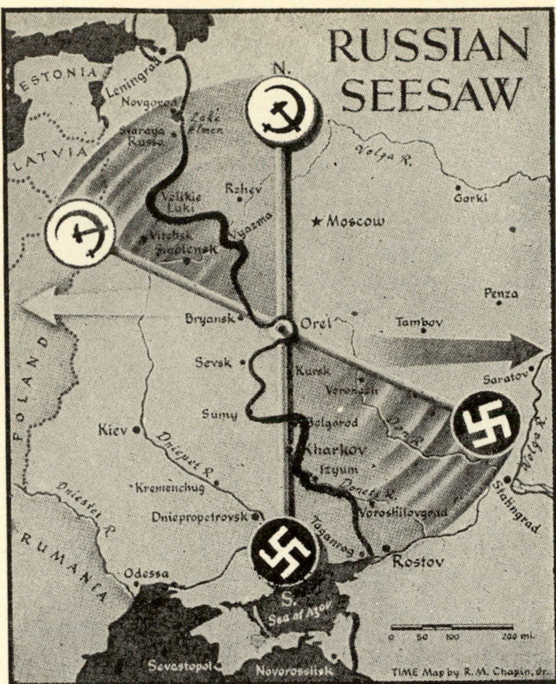

sians were aided by their "General Winter." Skis were placed on much equipment, the troops wore long white robes and capes, and above all, the men were warmly clad. On the other hand the severe winter disrupted Nazi communications and found German troops insufficiently clad in spite of the fact that furs and blankets had been confiscated for the Russian front from conquered territories.

It was in January that the Nazi forces before Stalingrad, hemmed in between the Don and Volga rivers, were trapped. On the eighth of this month the Soviets demanded that the encircled troops surrender. They refused. Two days later the final drive began which was to hack the Nazi divisions to shreds. By the end of the month only a few isolated pockets of Nazi resistance remained in Stalingrad. On the last day of January the Nazi commander, General von Paulus, surrendered with a pitiful remnant of his men. Since November 19, when the Stalingrad battle had begun, 300,000 Nazis had been killed or captured. Stalingrad in October 1942 had become the symbol for unexcelled fortitude and heroism for the United Nations; by the following January it had also become the grave for an immense Axis army and the first real catastrophe suffered by the Nazis.

The various offensives undertaken by the Russian High Command in addition to the mopping-up activities at Stalingrad were pushed vigorously throughout January. The Caucasus was being rid of Nazi armies, the bend of the Don where there had been such savage fighting in the summer of 1942 was completely cleared of them, and a new offensive was launched directly east of Voronezh toward Kursk and Kharkov. During February several strategic Nazi positions were taken, including Kursk, an important city midway between Voronezh and Kiev; Rostov, the city which was the only land corridor through which Nazi forces in the north Caucasus could escape; and Kharkov, the third largest city in the Soviet Union and key to the whole rich industrial Donets Basin.

These conquests proved to be the high point of the Russian winter campaign. Other gains were made. The danger to Moscow was eased by the capture of Rzhev and Vyazma, and penetrations were made south of Leningrad. The last crucial battle of the winter took place west of Kharkov. Here Russian divisions pushed toward the Dnieper River in a drive that threatened to entrap German forces strung along the Sea of Azov. Success in this region of the southern Ukraine would also deprive the Third Reich of any opportunity of utilizing its rich resources: water power of the Dnieper, the vast grainfields, and the coal of the Donets Basin. The Nazi High Command determined, therefore, to throw back this Russian offensive at any cost. About 325,000 reserve troops, presumably assembled originally for a new Nazi offensive, were now thrown into the battle by the Germans, together with a tank force estimated to be 1000 strong. An unusually early spring thaw hindered the Russians, whose lines of communications were extended in comparison with their enemy's. The result for the Russians was a serious setback; outnumbered, they fell back. Kharkov fell again to the Germans on March 16. With difficulty Russian troops were finally able to hold the German offensive along the Donets River.

If the high hopes of forcing the German armies out of the southern Ukraine were dashed by this counterstroke, it yet remains true that the Russian winter campaign of 1942-1943 was a brilliant achievement and one which cost the Axis dearly in men and materiel. There has always been much controversy concerning statistics of losses and gains on the Russian front. Even if the following Russian figures, given at the end of March, be substantially discounted, the score remains very impressive: 850,000 men killed, 343,000 captured, 183,000 square miles of land liberated, 5000 planes destroyed, 9000 tanks put out of action or captured, and 20,000 guns seized or destroyed. The Russian offensive may be credited with the following major achievements: (1) destruction of a complete Axis army at Stalingrad, (2) capture of Rzhev and Vyazma, potential bases for a German offensive against Moscow, (3) breaking of the Nazi cordon around Leningrad, and (4) removal of the serious menace to the Caucasus oil fields.

May brought little change in the positions along the Russian front from Leningrad to Rostov. While the spring thaws were taking place, both sides waited for the ground to harden and mustered their reserves. Most observers in the United Nations were of the belief that Hitler would make another supreme bid for victory in Russia in the early summer of 1943.

Japan turned back in the Solomons. In the Solomons, as we have seen, desperate fighting both on land and sea in October left the issue still largely in doubt. Another crisis came in mid-November with the most determined Japanese effort up to then to conquer the American beachhead on Guadalcanal. A large Japanese fleet of transports was assembled at the bases of Rabaul and Buin. Another fleet of fighting craft, which included 2 battleships, 4 cruisers, and 10 destroyers, sailed from the base of Truk and made for Guadalcanal. The Japanese strategy was to destroy the U. S. fleet and thus enable the transports to land their troops unopposed from the sea. The battle was joined just after midnight, November 13. The American fleet commanded by Rear Admiral Daniel Callaghan audaciously rushed between two Japanese ship columns. In this melee the U. S. cruisers and destroyers engaged Japanese battleships at close range. One battleship was so badly damaged that it sank by morning. The *U. S. S. San Francisco,* flagship and spearhead of the attack, was severely damaged, and Rear Admiral Callaghan and the captain were killed on her bridge.

The fighting continued until the morning of November 15. For the first time American battleships tried their striking power against Japanese sea power. One of America's new battleships, the *South Dakota,* proved her worth by sinking three Japanese cruisers at long range. Despite the absence of carriers, which left them with no protection from attacks by United States land-based planes, the Japanese persisted in trying to land men from their transports. The result was a field day for the American air forces and the almost complete annihilation of the Japanese convoy. In this decisive battle the Japanese losses were: 2 battleships, 8 cruisers, 6 destroyers, 8 transports, and 4 cargo ships. American losses were 2 light cruisers and 7 destroyers. This victory was an outstanding achievement not only for the American officers and men who so well turned back the Japanese threat but also for Admiral William F. Halsey, commander of the U. S. naval forces in the South Pacific. Guadalcanal was now "saved." The balance of naval power had been tipped to the American side.

Failing by frontal attack to regain Guadalcanal, the Japanese for the time being resorted to swift night convoys which landed small bodies of troops on the beaches of the island. On the last day of November the night convoy was intercepted. One United States cruiser was sunk; the Japanese loss was heavy—2 cruisers, 4 destroyers, and 2 transports. In all, 12,000 Japanese troops were killed. During the first week of February the Japanese, realizing that the game was up on Guadalcanal, switched from trying to infiltrate reinforcements to the island to evacuating some of its personnel. For a week at least a dozen air battles and motor torpedo-boat engagements took place in which an American cruiser was sunk and several Japanese destroyers were lost. The objective of evacuating the Guadalcanal force only partially succeeded. By February 10 all organized resistance on the island had ceased.

On this small patch of land, only 100 miles long, bitter fighting had raged for six months. The Japanese had fought to "save their face" and also to prevent the United States from securing what would probably become a strategic springboard for a great offensive against Japanese strongholds in the South Pacific. The losses sustained by American forces, especially the navy, were heavy, but the Japanese had suffered much more. Their losses in the entire campaign were estimated to be: 166

Battle-weary U. S. Marines plod their way through the fire-blacked remains of a captured village on Guadalcanal. Some of the bloodiest fighting of the war took place on this island.

warships and transports, 800 planes, and at least 60,000 men.

Japan checked in New Guinea. In the narrow peninsula in southwestern New Guinea the Japanese were retreating over the mountains as fast as they had advanced in their original drive on Port Moresby. A widespread air offensive under the command of Lieutenant General George C. Kenney was undertaken by the Allies. Heavy bombing attacks were carried out against such important Japanese bases as Rabaul, Lae, Salamaua. These prevented further Japanese reinforcements from reaching the New Guinea coast in the vicinity of Buna. A gigantic job of air transportation was carried out under Lieutenant General Kenney's direction. American troops from their bases in Australia were flown 600 miles to New Guinea. Eighteen thousand were then ferried by air over the mountains. As the Japanese were pressed down from the crest of the mountains, they fought stubbornly to keep from being pushed into the sea between their two strong points of Buna and Gona. Australian and American airmen brought in artillery, jeeps, and even a field hospital accommodating 250 beds. An average of a thousand tons of supplies was carried to the jungle battlefield by air each week.

General MacArthur arrived in New Guinea in November to direct personally the operations, which were now reaching the crucial stage. In the first part of December both Buna and Gona were captured. Early the next month all Japanese resistance in southwestern New Guinea had been rooted out. The fighting there surpassed in savagery even that on Guadalcanal. Around Buna and Gona in the thick jungle the Japanese had a web of trenches and machine-gun nests which had to be taken one by one. One correspondent observed that nowhere in the world at that time were American soldiers engaged in such desperate, merciless, bitter, bloody fighting.

The naval victory in November, the mopping up of the last remnants of Japanese resistance on Guadalcanal in February, and the ousting of the Japanese from southwestern

New Guinea ended a phase of the war in the South Pacific in which the United Nations had, on the whole, the better of the fighting. But no decisive victory had been won which guaranteed the supremacy of the United Nations in the South Pacific. The Japanese might again try to recover Guadalcanal, might set in motion an offensive against southwestern New Guinea. Even if this were not done, if the offensive rested with the forces of General MacArthur, there would likely be desperate fighting as the fleets and armies of the United Nations pushed northward against Lae, Rabaul, Truk, and other Japanese strongholds.

Reversal of roles in the Aleutians. From October 1942 to May 1943 important action was taking place in the North Pacific, fully six thousand miles from the Solomon Islands. In June 1942, when Japanese aggression in the Pacific was at high crest, the American people were disturbed to learn that Japanese forces had been landed on Attu and Kiska, islands in the Aleutian group. Wake Island and the Philippines were remote, far removed from America proper, but the occupation of Kiska and Attu was a different matter. The Japanese were coming dangerously close to the North American mainland.

Meanwhile careful and secret preparations were being made by the United States High Command to stage an offensive in the Aleutians. Large quantities of equipment were sent north to Alaskan bases. To keep the general public at home and also, of course, the Japanese from knowing what was coming, this project of Alaskan supply was dubbed the "Blair Packing Company." In August American troops began round one in the Aleutian battle by landing on Adak Island some 200 miles from Kiska. A fighter base was immediately set up at Adak. Round two followed, in which American planes kept up a constant bombing of Kiska throughout the fall months. In January another round was completed when United States troops occupied Amchitka, an island in the Rat group of the Aleutians. This gave a base only sixty miles from Kiska.

The fourth round in the Aleutian campaign was started on May 11 and lasted for three weeks. During this period the island of Attu was captured and practically its entire Japanese garrison was annihilated. The Attu victory made almost inevitable the fall of

Kiska, the last Japanese base in the long island chain. This island was now outflanked; Attu is 172 miles west, and Amchitka, 63 miles east. Another significant result of the reconquest of Attu was that the role of menacing invader in the Aleutians had been reversed. Instead of the Japanese looking toward the Alaskan mainland, the Americans now looked toward Paramoshiri, the nearest Japanese naval base.

The burden on China. From the fall of 1942 to the spring of 1943 the general trend of the war in Russia, in the South and North Pacific, and in the Mediterranean was favorable to the United Nations. In two main areas of the global struggle, however, no clear-cut victories had been registered by the United Nations, and the Japanese still enjoyed an unchallenged strategic initiative. These areas were China and the India-Burma theater.

In the world conflict the United Nations between October 1942 and April 1943 had concentrated mainly upon the Axis powers in the west. Some serious setbacks had been inflicted upon Japan, but these operations had been designed only to keep open the supply lines of the United Nations and to forestall any growing menace to the safety of Australia. While such strategy brought success in general, it placed a heavy burden upon war-weary China.

China continually felt the offensive power of the Japanese invaders as they stabbed here and there trying to uncover a weak link in the

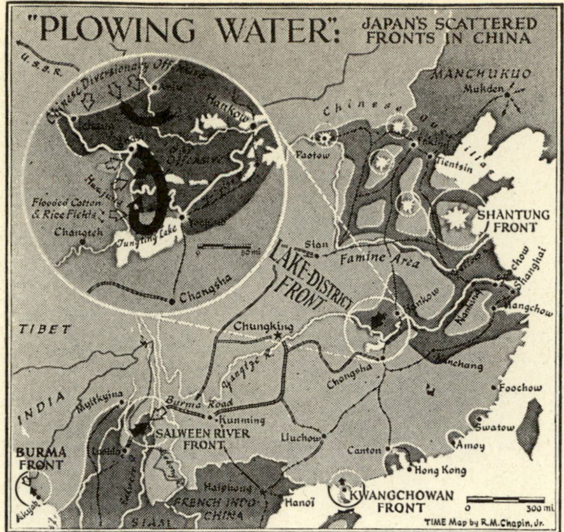

Chinese chain of resistance. The scattered Japanese drives lacked force, however, and made only limited gains. Valuable assistance to the armies of Chiang Kai-shek was given by the American air force under Chennault.

While China heroically maintained an effective resistance on the battlefield, disquieting developments in the spring of 1943 were apparent. There was natural impatience over the failure of Great Britain and the United States to send large-scale aid to the Chinese theater, and criticism of the United Nations' strategy of defeating Germany first. On the Chinese domestic front the Japanese blockade had resulted in a serious scarcity of all goods. Said Mrs. Wellington Koo, wife of the Ambassador to Britain, "China is nearer collapse on the economic front than at any other time during the course of the war." Notwithstanding her serious internal problems China continued to resist; during her long struggle with Japan, resistance to what appeared hopeless odds had become almost a national instinct. As Madame Chiang Kai-shek put it: "From five and a half years of experience we are convinced it is the better part of wisdom not to accept failure ignominiously, but to risk it gloriously."

The fate of China was largely bound up with events in the India-Burma area. The Burma Road, artery of Chinese supplies, had not been reopened after the Japanese overran it in the spring of 1942. A Japanese invasion of India in the fall of 1942 seemed likely. But losses in the South Pacific halted such an offensive and, further, under the direction of Sir Archibald Wavell a large army had been assembled on the Burma-India border. This force was largely Indian, reinforced by British troops and American air units.

During the winter of 1942-1943 heavy and constant air raids were carried out from India on Japanese installations in Burma. In retaliation the Japanese raided the great Indian city of Calcutta and other points, but in general, air superiority was maintained by the Allies. So improved were the defenses of India by December 1942 that Wavell essayed a limited offensive against the Japanese. The objective was the important port of Akyab on the Gulf of Bengal. After a promising start this offensive bogged down and initial gains were lost to the Japanese at heavy cost to the British. As in China, the striking power of the United Nations was not sufficiently strong to challenge the Japanese.

Pattern for Victory

Conferences and action. In the latter part of May 1943 the war leaders of Britain and the United States met in Washington to survey a brightening panorama. This was the fifth meeting of President Roosevelt and Prime Minister Churchill. Four months earlier the two chief executives had met at Casablanca in North Africa for a conference which resulted in the famous "unconditional surrender" formula for the Axis nations.

Following the conference unusual Allied activity was reported in the Mediterranean area. On May 30, 300 United States planes bombed Naples and objectives at the tip of the Italian peninsula. Early in June, air attacks and naval bombardment by units of the British fleet commenced against Pantelleria, a small fortified Italian island between Tunisia and Sicily. In all, 3500 tons of bombs were dropped on the naval base. On the eighteenth day of the siege, following three Allied ultimatums, the white flag was hoisted and the Italian commander signaled, "Beg surrender through lack of water." This was the first time in history that a major fortress had been crushed completely by the sole use of air power. In a few days three Italian islands near Pantelleria surrendered.

Suspense in Europe. Throughout June 1943 the entire world of the United Nations was in suspense, while the Axis countries were on edge from "invasion jitters."

In the face of an Allied invasion that might come from England the Nazis hesitated to commit too many troops in a Russian offensive. However, the growing might of the

Reich's other foes demanded that Russia be crushed while there was yet time. The German High Command was forced, therefore, to launch a summer offensive against Russia on the fifth of July. Four days later the Allies began to invade—not Germany's Atlantic bastion, but the Italian island of Sicily.

Invasion of Sicily. The first Allied soldiers to reach Sicily were American paratroopers, whose assignment was to knock out pillboxes, seize airfields, and spread confusion back of the Axis lines. While the paratroopers were carrying out their tasks, a huge armada of 3266 ships left the coast of North Africa and began to disembark troops about 3 a.m., the morning of July 10. Battleships, cruisers, destroyers, transports, and special landing boats were used in the greatest amphibious invasion in all history. Within 48 hours, 80,000 men had landed on Sicilian beaches, together with 7000 vehicles, 300 tanks, and 700 guns.

The invasion was directed at the southern shore of Sicily, with the American Seventh Army forming the left wing, Canadians in the center, and the British Eighth Army on the right flank. The initial landings were accomplished with little loss and beachheads were quickly consolidated. Patton's men were met by a fierce tank assault which almost succeeded in driving them into the sea. Desperate resistance and the arrival of heavy guns saved the day. Another large factor was the gunfire from Allied warships that went near shore to blast German tanks. Following this success Patton's men began to knife inland, fighting their way to the northern shore. To the east the British and Canadian forces pushed forward along the east coast but met a stone wall, for the moment, at Catania. Here the Axis defense line was supported by towering Mt. Etna, from which guns could command the Catanian plain below. After eight days of fighting, more than 3000 square miles had been conquered, 200 miles of coast cleared, and 30,000 prisoners taken. In a brilliant maneuver General Patton's army cut Sicily in two and captured Palermo, the island's capital, on the northern coast. All Axis troops to the west were now cooped in a small area. Leaving adequate forces to mop up these nests of resistance, the American army then drove east along the north coast, with Messina as the objective. Resistance of the Italians and Germans was confined to the northeastern tip of Sicily, with Italy only two miles behind them across a narrow strait.

On the lookout for enemy snipers, an American reconnaissance unit marches through smoke from burning buildings in captured Messina.

The Sicilian catastrophe had a chilling effect on Italian morale. It grew worse after a mass raid on Rome's transportation system was carried out on July 19 by 500 U. S. planes.

Fall of Mussolini. In desperation Mussolini and Hitler conferred about Italy's plight. Taking advantage of Italian discouragement and war weariness, President Roosevelt and Prime Minister Churchill offered peace, declaring: "The time has come for you to decide whether Italians shall die for Mussolini and Hitler—or live for Italy, and for civilization." On July 25 a startled world heard the news that Mussolini had been removed from office by the king and that Marshal Pietro Badoglio had been appointed premier. A long string of defeats—in Greece, Abyssinia, Libya, and Sicily—had finally toppled the "Sawdust Caesar" who had prated so long about the nobility of war. The fall of Mussolini and the disbanding of the Fascist Party set off peace demonstrations all over Italy, but Badoglio declared that Italy would continue to resist alongside Germany.

Meanwhile the Sicilian campaign drew to a close. The British Eighth Army captured Catania and edged around the slopes of Mt. Etna. Finally on August 17 Messina was captured by American troops, joined shortly by their British comrades.

The Sicilian balance sheet showed a victory over 300,000 Axis troops and the conquest of 10,000 square miles of territory. Of these troops an Italian army of 225,000 had been captured or destroyed; of the 75,000 crack German soldiers some 40,000 had managed to escape to Italy. A huge amount of booty had been captured; a superb fighting machine of some 300,000 Americans, British, and Canadians had gained a fighting efficiency unsurpassed in this war. Furthermore the Mediterranean was now virtually an Allied lake. Transports and supplies en route to the Near and Far East could now ply its waters, which also could be used for amphibious operations against the Fortress of Europe.

Tables turned in Russia. Meanwhile on the Russian front decisive action was coming. In previous summer drives the Germans had just fallen short of victory. In the summer of 1941 Moscow had almost fallen; in the summer of 1942 Stalingrad and the Caucasus had nearly been overwhelmed. The summer of 1943 was likely the last opportunity for a victory drive against Russia. In June the Soviet army was told by its leaders, "The hour of decisive events is approaching"; but they were not discouraged. They were encouraged, in fact, for their air squadrons had begun to achieve supremacy during the savage air fighting in May and early June. Offensive action was undertaken by the Nazis in several areas during June, but as we have seen, it was not until July 5 that their real summer drive was opened on a 165-mile front between Orel and Belgorod.

This battle has been referred to as the greatest tank battle in history. The German forces made a few gains, but after ten days they were halted; the Russians assumed the offensive. The great Nazi defense bastion of Orel was captured on August 5, and on the same day Belgorod was entered. It was then evident that a great Soviet offensive was in progress on a 450-mile front. The next objective was Kharkov, and this likewise was captured, two weeks later. The sledge-hammer blows had so far been aimed at the middle and southern sections of the long battle line. A third attack was directed against Smolensk, in the north; but to attain this objective the Russians had first to storm the vital center of Bryansk. By August 17, Soviet forces were only 15 miles from this stronghold. They had shown that the *Wehrmacht* was no longer the strongest single force in Europe.

The German drive had been halted and forced into reverse gear. The Russians' month-old offensive had resulted in the recapture of 5000 square miles of territory, control over the vital Moscow-Kharkov railroad, and a possibility of encircling German troops along the Sea of Azov. These facts, together with the results of the Sicilian campaign, meant that the offensive in Europe had definitely passed to the United Nations.

Allied air offensive. In the Churchill-Roosevelt conference of May 1943, it was decided that Allied air power was great enough to permit an all-out air blitz. The first crippling blow in the air attack against the Axis came that same month when a specially trained group of British Lancaster bombers made a night attack on three key dams in the German Ruhr district. The results were disastrous. Towns were inundated, power stations flooded, and industry halted. During June the tempo of air attack was stepped up, with the British attacking at night and American squadrons during the day. The growing power of the United Nations in the air was also shown in June by bombing raids over Axis targets in Greece.

What was referred to as "the third front against the Axis," that is, the air offensive, was carried on during the first half of July and reached a new intensity in the final days of that month. Hamburg, the Reich's second city and most important port, attacked night and day, was hit with 10,000 tons of bombs. This was more than had been dropped on London in an entire month by the *Luftwaffe* during the Nazi blitz of 1940. Hamburg was practically destroyed and thousands of its people buried under a mass of rubble. Berlin was next to feel the shock of Allied bombs. In several consecutive night raids thousands of tons of bombs were dropped on the Reich capital. The final city to be pulverized as August ended was Nurenberg, the site of important industry and a key railroad center for communication with Italy. Far to the east in the Balkans a serious air blow was delivered against the center of Rumania's oil industry.

The Allied third front required the services of British and American personnel on a huge scale. The bombing of Hamburg, for example, was equivalent to fighting a full-scale land battle in Germany. For one raid on this target over 5000 men to man the planes, 100,000 ground technicians, and some fifty air fields were necessary. It was estimated that one such air attack inflicted damage equal to the work of 77,000 Germans for one month.

Showdown in the Solomons. Early in the spring of 1943, when the Tunisian campaign was monopolizing attention, there were signs of another showdown in the South Pacific. Following their failure to hold Guadalcanal, the Japanese tried to build up air strength in New Guinea and in the central Solomons.

To smash Japanese strength in the Solomons and at the same time to seize air fields as future springboards against Japanese bases north of the Solomons, United States forces carried out the biggest offensive to date in the South Pacific. The attack began on the night of June 29. One force landed in Japanese-held territory not far from Salamaua. Another convoy landed unopposed on two groups of islands lying between Guadalcanal and southern New Guinea. To the northeast another force captured the island of Rendova after brief but sharp fighting, and troops landed under heavy fire on the southern tip of New Georgia Island.

The objective of the Solomons push was the capture of an important Japanese air base, Munda, 200 miles northwest of Guadalcanal. The fighting on New Georgia was as fierce as the battle for Guadalcanal, but now Allied troops were experienced jungle fighters clad in splotched green-yellow coveralls for protection against Japanese snipers. The fighting continued for two months until, late in August, the remnants of the Japanese garrison fled to a nearby island still in their hands. At the same time savage fighting was taking place as Allied troops advanced toward Salamaua.

As important as the land fighting in the central Solomons were the American victories on the sea and in the air. The most serious Japanese loss was in ships.

Occupation of Kiska gets under way, with each member of the landing party doing a specific job. To help landers avoid sharp underwater rocks, the earthen ramp was extended from the rock-covered beach into the water.

Securing the Aleutians. In the North Pacific Kiska was bombed and shelled continuously during the summer. On August 15 American forces landed unopposed on the island to discover the flight of several thousand Japanese troops under cover of darkness and heavy fog. From the Aleutians American air power began to reach out in the direction of Japan proper.

The Quebec Conference. In August 1943 Churchill and Roosevelt had their sixth meeting, in historic Quebec. Here the two leaders of the English-speaking world with their Chiefs of Staff took stock of the global war and made plans for the fifth year.

Despite China's success in halting recent Japanese drives it was apparent in the summer of 1943 that the naval blockade and the cutting of the Burma Road were beginning to have deadly effect on Chinese resistance. The leaders at Quebec, fully aware of the gravity of the situation, created a new military southeast Asia command based in India and Ceylon. Direction of this new post was given to Lord Louis Mountbatten, a naval officer who had won distinction as leader of the British Commandos. It was generally believed that Mountbatten's objective would be to drive the Japanese out of Burma in order to reopen the Burma Road.

As a result of the Conference the French Committee of National Liberation was recognized, partially by the United States and Britain, fully by Russia. Following the conquest of North Africa acrimonious disputes had taken place between General de Gaulle's Free French organization in London and General Henri Giraud, the head of French administration in North Africa. Differences had finally been reduced and the two factions had merged. After much regrettable controversy, the united participation of Frenchmen in the cause of the United Nations seemed assured.

During the summer of 1943 there were numerous rumors of misunderstandings and rivalries between Russia and her two great allies. These tales seemed to be confirmed when Stalin did not attend the Quebec Conference.

Russia, longing for relief from her great struggle and looking for unquestionable expression of good faith from her capitalistic allies, continued to urge Britain and America to open a second front in western Europe. In answer to criticism, the United States and Britain could point out that while Russia had a single foe to contend with, they had not only Germany but Japan. This required diversion of men and supplies to the Pacific area which might otherwise have been sent to the European theater. Even so, great quantities of food and military supplies had been sent to Russia, appreciatively acknowledged in a message from Stalin: "Our friends who are participating in the manufacture of the ammunition and supplies of provisions are rendering great support in the fight against our common enemy." If Britain and the United States for their part were reluctant to open a premature second front across the English Channel, Russia herself was equally reluctant to open another front by providing air bases for American bombers to use in the war against Japan. Also, while Russia found her enemy on her own soil, the United States in particular was forced to transport men and materiel thousands of miles to the war areas. The truth seemed to be that Russia on one hand, and Britain and the United States on the other, each had certain distinctive problems which dictated their military strategy. The contribution of the British and American strategy became more evident in the fall of 1943 when the first major phase was successfully concluded (see page 24).

The leaders of the Quebec Conference in a jovial mood. That is the Earl of Athlone, Governor General of Canada, on President Roosevelt's left. Mackenzie King, Canada's Prime Minister, is standing to the right of Winston Churchill with the omnipresent hat and cigar.

Meeting in Moscow. In September the world began to hear more and more about a forthcoming meeting of British, American, and Russian representatives. Late in October Secretary Hull and Foreign Minister Eden flew to Moscow for sessions with Foreign Minister Molotov. The conference, with the Chinese ambassador to Russia participating—and large staffs of diplomatic and military experts—surprised the world with results that apparently settled such questions as the second front, the conduct of the war, and the nature of the peace. (See page 30.)

The submarine war. In the "silent war" against the Nazi submarines, gratifying results had been achieved by September 1943. From January to October 1942 the undersea craft had been so dangerously successful that energetic measures were introduced against them in the fall of 1942. Convoy methods were improved, more ships were built, and vessels were better armed. In particular, the use of air power checkmated the undersea menace. Long-range reconnaissance planes from shore bases scoured the sea lanes and small "flat tops"—carriers—were used to afford convoys air protection even when in mid-Atlantic. As a result of these measures it was announced in September that no ship had been sunk by submarine in the North Atlantic during the past four months.

The air offensive. Air power was not only instrumental in solving the submarine menace; it was also increasingly utilized as a major destructive weapon against the German Fortress of Europe. During the fall of 1943 strategic centers and industrial establishments were bombed night and day by the R.A.F. and the U.S. Eighth Air Force. On October 10 they penetrated the continent as far as East Prussia and Poland; five days later another force flew deep into Germany to bomb an important ball-bearing industry. In this last raid 60 bombers were lost with their crews, estimated at 593 men dead or captured. This was a high price to pay, but evidence was accumulating that the steady air war against the Third Reich was undermining German morale and seriously curtailing production. These raids were also forcing the Nazis to withdraw air power from the fighting fronts. The air offensive was therefore of tremendous assistance to the Russian offensive, ensuring Russian supremacy in the air on the eastern front.

Russian gains. Most spectacular of the military operations was the progress of the Russian summer offensive. Hurled as a counterattack against a faltering Nazi offensive begun in July, the Soviet drive gained momentum late in August and in September.

In the south, along a fringe of the northeastern coast of the Black Sea, German troops fought desperately to maintain their bridgehead in the Caucasus, but were finally driven out in October. Farther north the Russian forces had retrieved the rich industrial Donets Basin and had taken the city of Dniepropetrovsk, site of Russia's greatest dam, which in 1941 had fallen a victim of the scorched-earth policy. These advances meant that the entire Ukraine was rapidly being recaptured. Early in October Soviet armies surrounded the historic Ukrainian capital of Kiev. By November they had captured it.

Some 700 miles north of the Black Sea the "Gateway to Moscow" had been taken from the Germans in the recapture of Smolensk. This advance brought Russian armies close to the old Latvian border and threatened to cut off Nazi forces in a pocket around Leningrad. The Nazi High Command hoped to be able to make a stand at the Dnieper. Since July 12, 1943, Soviet armies had reconquered 195,000 square miles.

The surrender of Italy. Meanwhile Italy was going through a tragic ordeal of retribution for its unprovoked attack upon France and Great Britain in the spring of 1940. Two weeks after the conquest of Sicily, Montgomery and his Eighth Army, protected by air power, landed in southern Italy opposite Messina. One of the most dramatic events of the war came the evening of September 8 when General Eisenhower announced over the Algiers radio that Italy had been granted a military armistice, effective immediately. An hour later Premier Marshal Pietro Badoglio announced over the Rome radio, "Italian forces will cease all acts of hostility against the Anglo-United States forces. . . . They will, however, oppose attack from any other quarter."

The desperate position of Italy was frankly admitted in a message sent by Badoglio to his former Axis allies, which ended: "In order to avoid complete ruin, Italy is therefore obliged to ask her enemies for an armistice."

The armistice carried thirteen provisions, the most important of which were: the end of all Italian resistance, the surrender of United Nations prisoners held in Italy, transfer of the Italian fleet, use of the Italian mer-

Like that of Sicily, the invasion of the Italian mainland was largely an amphibious one. Eager Yanks, pouring from landing craft at Salerno, are met by enemy fire. Note the machine guns trained skyward, and the MP ducking instinctively in the foreground.

chant marine if necessary, and free use of ports and air bases in the fight against Germany.

The Nazis quickly proceeded to make Italy a vassal state. German troops occupied the main cities, especially Genoa, Rome, Milan, and Naples, and sporadic fighting ensued between Nazi forces and Italian soldiers. To prevent the Germans from consolidating their hold over central Italy, a second amphibious attack was directed by General Mark Clark's Fifth Army just south of the great port of Naples. Landing on the beaches took place on the morning of September 9. In the meantime the British Eighth Army was punching its way north from the toe and heel of Italy.

The fight for Naples was one of the fiercest yet experienced by American troops. For two days they and the British Allies enlarged their bridgehead. But counterattacks followed. Nazi tank units drove the Allied forces back, in some instances almost to the sea. After six days of savage fighting, the Fifth Army held and was soon joined by the British Eighth coming up from the south. In the next two weeks the combined armies forced their way through the German lines, and on October 1, the once beautiful, now war-torn port city was entered.

In accordance with the armistice terms, units of the Italian navy left port and made their way to Malta and other Allied ports. While en route the great Italian battleship *Roma* was sunk by German bombs.

The sinking of the *Roma* and the determination of the Germans to make Italy their battlefield brought a dramatic transformation in Italo-German relations, and on September 20 Badoglio announced to the Italians: "We are cooperating side by side with the Anglo-Americans, who are now accepting our assistance in the task of driving the Germans from the country." The situation was further complicated by the "rescue" of Mussolini by Nazi troops. Il Duce was thereupon made the head of an Italian puppet régime by his Nazi masters. While the status of Italy, which had signed an unconditional surrender, remained for a time obscure, it was quite apparent that at least she was more than a mere conquered ex-foe. Since Italy had turned against the Germans there were references to her as a "co-belligerent," and on October 13 Badoglio formally stated Italy was at war with Germany.

Elsewhere in the Mediterranean Hitler's outposts of the *Festung Europa* fell: Sardinia, Corsica, and several eastern Mediterranean islands.

The surrender of Italy had repercussions favorable to the United Nations everywhere in the global struggle: (1) Conquest of the Mediterranean shortened lines of communication to the Near and Far East. This meant more tools of war to Russia, to North Africa, and to India. (2) With the surrender of the Italian fleet, considerable British and American naval forces were freed for action in the Bay of Bengal and the Pacific. (3) Possession of important air bases in Italy brought eastern Germany and Austria within more effective bombing range. (4) The invasion of Italy opened up the way for Allied fleets in the Adriatic. These could bring badly needed supplies for the heroic Yugoslav guerrillas or perhaps even convoy an Allied invasion force to open up a Balkan front. (5) The collapse of Italy naturally was a great psychological help to the Allied cause throughout the world.

Pacific operations. While the world's attention was centered on the dramatic events in Italy and Russia, there were marked advances in the Pacific battle. In September the United States Navy defied the Japanese high seas fleet by raiding the Japanese island base of Marcus, only four hours from Tokyo by air. There was a fourth air attack against Paramoshiri, nearest Japanese base to the Aleutians. The most important operation in the South Pacific early in the fall of 1943 was the offensive against Japanese bases in central New Guinea and further advances in the Solomons. By the use of paratroopers and amphibious landing operations, Salamaua and Lae were cut off, partially destroyed, and eventually captured. The important position held by the Japanese at Finschhafen in New Guinea was also surrounded, and in October it was taken. Later air and sea attacks in the direction of Rabaul and Truk gave promise of new advances.

Position of neutrals. The cumulative effect of Axis reverses was plainly marked in the behavior of the European neutrals who previously, willingly or not, had danced to whatever tune Hitler played. In 1943 neutral countries basically sympathetic to the Allied cause adopted a more independent attitude. Sweden, for example, forbade the transit of German troops across its territory to Norway, and Portugal turned over valuable naval and air bases in the Azores to Britain. While there was little for Switzerland to do except hope for a German defeat, there were increasing signs that Turkey was more committed to the Allied cause. As for Fascist Spain, its dictator, Franco, viewed the prospect of Nazi defeat with unmitigated dismay. During the high tide of German victory, Franco had cooperated to the full with the Nazis. Spain was a hotbed of Nazi espionage; and during the Tunisian campaign the Spanish government maintained menacing concentrations of troops in Spanish Morocco. Allied successes at least made Fascist Spain more discreet and less able, if stili willing, to do Hitler's bidding.

Summary

In September 1943 the Second World War entered its fifth year. For the first three years the Axis powers had enjoyed the military initiative and in June 1942 had begun a world-wide offensive which was to fall just short of success. This was the high mark of totalitarian strength. With the turning point of Stalingrad the United Nations emerged in growing military might and started on a series of outstanding victories.

Allied forces cleared the Aleutians of the Japanese. In the South Pacific they eliminated the Nipponese from central New Guinea and all of the Solomons. In North Africa and the Mediterranean region striking successes were achieved. Sicily was conquered; Mussolini was overthrown and Fascism discredited. Italy turned against Germany. The long-heralded German offensive had backfired, and the Russians were making substantial gains all along the eastern front. While the Allies pointed toward Europe proper in the west, Germans at home were for the first time experiencing the horrors of war; the savage air blitz of the British Isles carried out in the fall and winter of 1940-1941 was being turned back on Germany with ample interest. On every front there were signs of Axis weakness and imminent further offensives by the United Nations.

SECTION 2

On the Home Fronts

As no other war in history, the Second World War has broken down the old lines of demarcation between the firing and home fronts. For this is total war—war involving total populations. Not only is it total war because of the new dangers which civilian populations have faced, but because the very nature of modern warfare demands the closest integration of domestic and military interests. Every country, Allied or Axis, has been concerned about the proper allocation of manpower: to the farm, the factory, and the firing front. This section, therefore, although it emphasizes the impact of the war upon the civilian populations, desires to set up no false boundary between soldier and civilian. They are in it together. And together after the war they will face the problem of constructing a durable peace.

The United States

T***he arsenal of democracy.*** The United States has built up in the Second World War a production machine whose size surpasses anything in the world's history. The output of American mines, blast furnaces, shipyards, mills, and plants has been in figures which are almost beyond comprehension. For example, steel production in 1943 is estimated at more than 90,000,000 tons, almost twice as much as the best year in the First World War, and more than that of all the rest of the world put together. Five ocean-going ships were sliding down the ways every twenty-four hours in 1943. Whereas in the First World War the United States turned out 80 tanks, by the end of the first year alone of the Second World War the nation had produced 20,000. In 1943 the goal of 10,000 war planes a month—scoffed at by the Axis—was sighted. Every month in 1943 the munitions plants were making almost 2,000,000,000 small-arms cartridges, 18,000,000 artillery shells, 66,000 machine guns, and 2500 75-mm. field guns.

In June 1943 Donald Nelson could report

to the President: "The record certainly makes it clear that the American industrial system can be justifiably proud of an astonishing display of economic muscle. In the main, the productive achievement of the American war economy in 1942 met the requirements of our war strategy; and the prospects for 1943 are for a quantity and quality of production that will realize to the full the tremendous potential of American industry."[1] Mr. Nelson's confident views were fortified by convincing statistics. Whereas the overall military program in 1942 amounted to $59,000,000,000, the program for 1943 was set at $106,000,000,000—an increase of 80 per cent.

But these results did not come overnight, nor were they unaccompanied by serious problems and domestic dissension. Like her English-speaking allies, the United States did not comprehend the full gravity of the war for the first six months or more. A series of stinging defeats in the Pacific was needed to awaken the man in the street to the perilous military situation. Then, despite the complacency of the average citizen and the confusion of overcrowded Washington, the country in 1942 converted its industries in a huge all-out effort. While the armed forces expanded from two million men to seven million, industrial centers began to change. Millions of war workers poured into cities to find ready jobs and ready money—but not ready houses in which to live. New factories rose on the outskirts of towns and operated on a twenty-four hour schedule, so that "swing shift" and "graveyard shift" became nationally understood terms.

Danger of inflation. Serious shortages soon developed in materials and manpower. Manufacturers frantically sought the highest priorities at Washington, and industry and agriculture argued with the army and navy about the indispensability of workers. Civilians found that the war was something more than repeating "Remember Pearl Harbor."

OUR CHIEF PRESSURE GROUPS

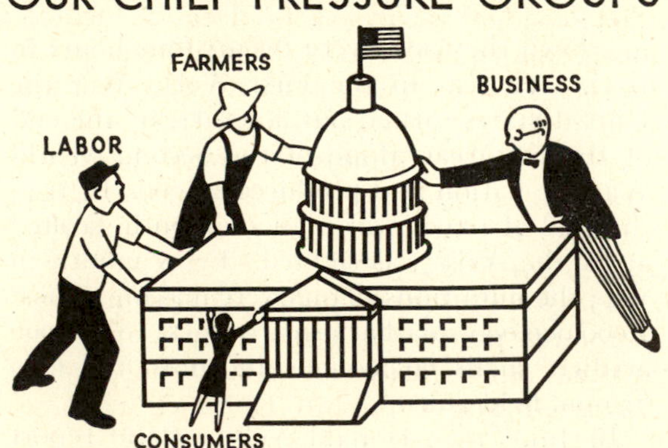

As shortages in civilian goods became more acute the nation's purchasing power increased. Incomes for 1944 were expected to be over twice the figures for 1940. With unprecedented amounts of money in circulation and less civilian goods available, the cost of living rose to a point roughly estimated as 25 per cent above that of 1939. Strict governmental controls in the forms of higher taxes, more stringent rationing, and effective price and wage ceilings became necessary measures in the battle against inflation.

President Roosevelt had called on Congress to assist the Office of Price Administration by limiting wages, farm prices, and profits and by passing a fiscal program to drain off surplus purchasing funds. By the end of 1942, stabilization measures had saved the government and the American consumer many billions of dollars. Price control measures, though, however beneficial to the nation as a whole, often proved irksome to the public and unprofitable to some pressure groups. The result was that the OPA lost favor in Congressional circles, and price controls sagged in effectiveness. As the country embarked on its 1943 course, the danger of inflation mounted.

There was an insistent voice in the cost-of-living struggle, a voice which could not be ignored. It belonged to organized labor, which in 1943 complained unceasingly that the Administration was in effect "freezing" wages, yet allowing the cost of living to mount alarmingly. Labor had held pretty well to its no-strike pledge (99.95 per cent compliance according to one source[2]), but its dissatisfaction with wage ceilings, corporation profits, executive salaries, and constantly rising prices resulted in more than one dramatic outburst. The most spectacular strikes in 1943 centered about John L. Lewis' demands for portal-to-portal payments for his coal miners, wage increases which he maintained were necessary if the miners were to cope with the rise in living costs.

The War Food Administration and the Office of Price Administration were directed in September 1943 to proceed with the payment of roll-back subsidies on important food commodities. This program, estimated to cost $1,000,000,000 yearly, was depended upon to lower living costs between 4 and 5 per cent. It was a step in the Administration's commitment to reduce living costs to the level of September 15, 1942. However, the program to hold down the cost of living by the payment of subsidies, successful in Britain and Canada, faced strong Congressional opposition, with the farm bloc especially emphatic in its disapproval of ceilings on foodstuffs.

In 1943, then, perhaps the most serious domestic economic problem was that of inflation, involving as it did the increase in national income, the decrease in consumer goods (with the natural result of greater willingness to pay more for a commodity), the freezing of wages in certain quarters, and a cost of living which had risen in the United States far more than in Britain or Canada. However, toward the end of the year, Price Administrator Prentiss Brown (prior to resigning) voiced his belief that the danger of inflation had been halted.

The public debt. Meanwhile the war was costing the United States the greatest amounts in the world's history. In the fiscal year 1942, expenditures for war activities amounted to 26 billion dollars. In 1943, the figure jumped to 75 billion. According to the President's statement in July 1943, on the summation of the 1944 Federal budget, total war expenditures for the fiscal year just starting would come to approximately 100 billion.[3] By June 1943, monthly war expenditures had risen to 7.7 billion.

Concomitant with the increase in war expenditures was the rise of the public debt. According to the President's figures, at the beginning of the 1942 fiscal year, the public debt stood at 48 billion. In 1943 it had risen to 72 billion. At the beginning of the 1944 fiscal year (June 30, 1943) the direct public debt (excluding obligations of government corporations) amounted to 137 billion dollars, and Roosevelt warned that unless additional tax legislation was enacted, the debt would increase to 206 billion dollars by June 30, 1944.[3]

The President and many Congressional leaders anxiously urged the immediate adoption of "a truly stiff program of additional taxes, savings, or both." It was maintained that individual tax rates in 1943, much lower than in Britain and Canada, had not advanced with the increase in incomes, and also that many American corporations were still making huge profits, compared with British and Canadian companies, subject to a 100 per cent tax on excess profits. To end war profiteering, Congress passed the Contract Renegotiation Act in April 1942, giving power to four executive agencies to renegotiate contracts and subcontracts whenever excessive profits would otherwise result. This Act was not ineffective. In 1943, however, pressure was being exerted in some Congressional quarters for repeal, or at least strong modification, of the Renegotiation Act, on the grounds that postwar reconversion necessitated the setting aside of large reserves which should be included as costs. Advocates of the Act replied that war industries were already guaranteed against postwar losses and, furthermore, that corporations had set aside by the end of 1943 war years' reserves which amounted to almost four times the total accumulated reserve for the 1936-1939 period. A special 1943 study of 29 large corporations showed that 23 of them had at least doubled their normal peacetime profits in 1942—after taxes were paid.[4]

Politics within. On the domestic political front, both major parties were jockeying into position for the 1944 presidential election. The more conservative Congress elected in 1942 was much less sympathetic toward the New Deal and much more independent of the President. During 1943 Congress showed not too gentle concern for Mr. Roosevelt's program for controlling the cost of living, and overrode his veto of the Smith-Connally Anti-Strike Bill. Congress also lifted the $25,000 salary ceiling which the President favored; abolished such agencies as the NYA (June), WPA (June), CCC (April), and the National Resources Planning Board (August); and appropriated for the Farm Security Administration funds which the President's supporters deemed "ridiculously inadequate." Lack of concerted action by the executive and legislative branches was heightened by cleavages within the ranks of the President's own party—cleavages that made clear-cut legislation difficult, and at times drove the country's allies to worry over the apparent lack of political policy.

Search for a foreign policy. On the question of foreign policy, the issues in 1943 appeared at times dangerously confused. True enough, Roosevelt and Churchill had met again at Quebec in August, and reported that all was going well with the war. But there was growing criticism in many circles that these conferences were not satisfactory: (1) because China and the Soviet Union were not coparticipants; (2) because they featured an Anglo-American pattern for the postwar era; and (3) because they seemed—at least to some critics—to show an inadequate understanding of the sociological and ideological problems of the peoples of Europe.

The defeat of Italy in 1943 brought the problem into prominence. Critics contended that while all through the Mussolini régime there had existed a strong democratic underground opposed to Fascism, the American government appeared less interested in supporting this people's movement than in "playing ball" with the House of Savoy and Marshal Badoglio, who, despite his coolness toward Il Duce in former days, had nevertheless led the Fascist forces into Ethiopia. American liberals were worried. They had been disturbed earlier by the sometimes cordial relations with Franco's Spain and Pétain's Vichy France, and by the apparently unsatisfactory relations with the Soviet Union. The State Department was emphatic in maintaining that American-Russian relations were excellent, but in the summer of 1943 its critics remained unconvinced.

To add further to the political confusion in the autumn of 1943, as we have seen, was the still burning question of a second front. (See p. 23.) In October, however, new hopes for a solution of this and related problems were born. Accompanied by diplomatic and military experts, the foreign ministers of the United States, Britain, and Russia met in Moscow and after twelve days of conferences came forth with what promised to be historic new patterns of collaboration. Among the Moscow decisions, in which China was represented too, were the agreements to act together in the war; not to conclude a separate peace; and to establish as soon as possible an international organization of all peace-loving nations. The three countries, in addition, set up a European council and a Mediterranean council (in which France was to have a place) to make studies and recommendations on future political questions; called for the establishment of democratic government and principles in Italy; laid down a pattern for the salvation of Austria and, presumably, other countries; warned Axis leaders and followers that those guilty of atrocities would eventually be punished as war criminals.

The year 1943 had been marked by divergent views as to the postwar role America should play. "Neo-isolationist" groups in the Midwest and certain newspaper chains had strongly opposed "foreign entanglements." More than one important voice was heard suggesting what some said would be American imperialism, involving a favored position in Latin America, a five-ocean navy, and ownership of air bases from Asia to Greenland and Dakar. Leaders like Willkie and Wallace outspokenly advocated complete international participation. The Congress went on record as favoring participation.

The Moscow declarations, however, were bold, clarifying strokes. If they could be followed by a meeting of Stalin, Churchill, and Roosevelt—late in November such a meeting seemed assured, possibly with Chiang Kai-shek also present—the United Nations, indeed the world, might be embarked on a new era of cooperation looking toward an early end of the war, a solidly established peace.

Race problems at home. While discussion of the United States foreign policy continued, a grave social problem flared to ugly dimensions within the country itself in 1943. This was the race problem, conspicuous for a time in Los Angeles and Detroit especially. As a result of expanded war production with its accompanying high wages, many classes of Americans found themselves with more money than they had ever possessed before. With the improved financial status came a conscious or unconscious demand for greater social recognition than they had hitherto received.

In Los Angeles the race problem involved a portion of the Mexican population, known (because of the exaggerated garb they wore) as "zoot-suiters." Mexican youths became embroiled in street brawls with members of the armed services. Probably blame must be apportioned to both sides. That the officials involved acted with legal impartiality was debated throughout the country, however. Significantly enough, some psychologists made the analysis that the "zoot-suiters" by their costume and acts were expressing an inner drive to break free of the inferiority complex caused by an unhealthy social and material environment; the war and its new social pattern afforded them that chance.

Much more serious was the bitter race riot

in Detroit. That city had become dangerously overcrowded and ill-housed, and long hours at production lathes did little to improve the people's tempers. Furthermore, the offer of lucrative jobs attracted thousands of workers from the South—both Negroes who had earned little, if any, hard cash before, and "poor whites," almost as poverty-stricken, many of whom were imbued with a deep Negro animosity. Both classes found themselves thrown into the same depressed neighborhoods, with more money than they needed. Out of the complex of old hatreds, new money, bad living conditions, and sultry summer days and nights suddenly flared the worst race riots in modern American history. The entire nation was shamed. The full causes of the riot were the subject of much debate, but one thing appeared tragically certain in 1943: little had been done apparently to cure the evil, and there seemed nothing to indicate that it would not break out again.

Looking over America in 1943, one could see disturbing indications that many people were not yet taking a sufficiently profound and sober view of the war and its larger meanings. How the country would handle the great social and political problems still before it, remained to be seen. But of this there could be no doubt—the natural resources, the skilled labor, the inventive genius, the will to win the war were all present, indeed were all in action.

Great Britain

Social revolution. It is commonplace to describe the significance of the Second World War with the words "vast social revolution." Whatever may be the case for other countries, that term applies clearly for Great Britain. The British people have been in the struggle since September 3, 1939, and deep in it. One home in every five has been damaged or destroyed; whole areas have been obliterated.

Class stratification has been fundamentally shaken by the war. There is agitation from many quarters for a new education "deal"—one which will do away with the evils of social discrimination inherent in two distinct school systems, the public school and the private school. In the past the majority of top-ranking positions in British society were held by the "old school tie"—those fortunate persons to whom the accident of birth had bequeathed title or wealth. All Parliamentary parties are now agreed that British education must be broadened to give every group a longer and more adequate schooling, and that educational opportunity must be based on ability rather than social status. Another significant educational development has been the strong emphasis placed upon adult education in the armed forces. American observers in Britain have remarked that, although the American doughboys stationed there are better clothed, better fed, and better entertained than the British Tommies, they lack the latter's political and ideological training. In other words, the British soldier has a good idea of what he's fighting against and what he's fighting *for*—and it is this factor which may help revolutionize postwar Britain.

The blitz bombings and the stringent food rationing have proved blessings in some ways. Many of the slums of London, Glasgow, and the Lancashire cities—slums which nineteenth-century industrialism begot—were blown or burned up when the Nazis tried to smash the industries which the slums encircled. England has been planning a housing system even vaster than the prewar building program, which saw 60,000 slum dwellings demolished every year. Decentralization of industry and the creation of model "garden cities" in the countryside have already been started. The British people in 1942 were healthier than before the outbreak of war; the birth rate was up and the death rate down. And this encouraging condition prevailed despite the strict rationing of foodstuffs. For Britons in 1942 were enjoying more balanced diets with more dairy products and vegetables. However, in 1943 experts saw the cropping up of dietary deficiencies and a certain lowering of health levels.

The cultural life of the British people was at a new high in 1943, if adult education classes, discussion groups, and interest in literature and the arts were at all indicative. The CEMA—Council for the Encouragement of Music and the Arts—brought concerts, plays, and art exhibitions to villages and war factories, and the finest stage talent was enlisted. Civilians and soldiers have also turned out by the scores of thousands for the traveling shows in which Ministry of Information films provide entertainment of an educational nature.

Every available economic and human resource has been mobilized. Characteristics of prewar business—the leisurely pace, the long weekend, the complacent attitude, the sharp social stratification, the "old school tie" leadership—have largely had to go. To get the maximum results, the National Service Act has absolute control over manpower. Consequently, at least two out of every three persons between the ages of 14 and 65 are working full time in the armed forces, industry, or civil defense. The age limit in the armed forces had been raised to 51 by 1943. An important aspect of present-day British life has been the mobilization of women in industry; by May 1943, over 7,000,000 women were engaged steadily in the war program, while millions more (such as housewives) were working part time. Also, seven out of every ten girls and boys between 14 and 17 were doing war work.

The British people know that there is no going back to the England of prewar days. This fact was emphasized by the American historian Commager upon his return from an extended visit in 1942. The British also realize that their postwar plans are contingent upon the victory aims of the United States.

Production increases. The intensive mobilization of manpower in Great Britain has enabled the country to challenge the industrial might of Germany. Aircraft production, three times as great in 1942 as in 1939, has shattered all previous records. Shipping has always been Britain's lifeline, and never have the people relaxed in constructing both naval and merchant craft. Up to March 1943, they had completed and added to the Royal Navy over 900 ships, thus making the fleet stronger, despite its heavy losses, than at the outbreak of war. Merchant tonnage was already twice as great by 1941 as in 1939. The British people did not intend to starve because of shipping losses in this war as they came so perilously close to doing in the last conflict. Britain has been a huge tank arsenal for the Allies, turning out by the middle of 1942 some 257,000 tanks and mechanical vehicles a year—or more than five times the number produced during the dark days of Dunkirk. Army supplies and stores kept pace with this swift armament expansion, so that toward the end of 1943, artillery and ammunition were being turned out in twice the quantities of the preceding year.

Important progress has also been made on the agricultural front. Prior to the war, British farming was in a bad way, with decaying farmhouses and neglected fields. Britain's agriculture was able to support only a third of her population. But the war brought radical changes, for the shipping strain had to be reduced by all possible means. As the Minister of Agriculture put it in 1942, the plan was to convert the island "from a mainly grazing to a mainly arable country, to save a round voyage for a ship with every 10,000 tons of food we could grow."[5] The government paid substantial subsidies for the plowing up of untouched grasslands, for draining and ditching, and for the making of tools. Markets were assured by the Ministry of Food, and national minimum wages for farm workers were laid down. By the end of 1942 some 6,000,000 more acres were under cultivation than in 1939, and a record harvest resulted. Britain was now not one-third but two-thirds self-sufficient.

Two factors had much to do with the record production. One was the tremendous increase in the use of tractors, so that in 1943 British agriculture had become the most highly mechanized in the world. The second factor was the creation of a large farm labor front including notably the Women's Land Army and the use of the armed forces to help with the harvesting. Italian prisoners of war were also employed in draining and reclamation projects, while hundreds of thousands of city dwellers had their own gardens or went out to the countryside to work at harvest time. British agriculture is today in a healthier condition than it has been for decades.

The economic transformation. The war has proved a heavy financial obligation to the British people. In 1940 the cost of running the war was £5,000,000 a day; in 1943 it had risen to £15,000,000. The national debt has reached astronomical proportions. Because the government has been a strong advocate of pay-as-you-go, the British taxpayer has had to carry a load unsurpassed by any of his allies. For example, the income tax is fixed on the standard rate of 10 shillings on the pound (20 shillings), while the maximum rate of tax runs as high as 19 shillings, sixpence. Excess profits are taxed 100 per cent, while the Purchase Tax—a sales tax on consumers' goods—ranges from 12 to 50 per cent on retail prices.

But personal savings have increased during the war because of the rationing of goods, the high peak of employment, and the cutting down of pleasure spending. The country in 1943 had over 300,000 Savings Groups compared with 45,000 in 1939. An important result will be apparent in the postwar era when, to quote Prime Minister Churchill, "there will be seven or eight million people in the country with two or three hundred pounds apiece."

That postwar Britain is in for striking economic changes can be deduced from existing conditions. Naturally such problems as reconversion of expanded industry to peacetime production, absorption of fighting personnel into agriculture and industry, women workers, and a huge national debt must affect Britain and her allies alike. But there are problems of a particularly national significance. One is the matter of foreign investments. Prior to the war British investors owned valuable assets in every nook and cranny of the world—rubber plantations in Malaya, oil fields in Rumania, and railroads in South America. Axis occupation destroyed British investments in many lands, at least temporarily, and it is problematical whether the *status quo ante bellum* will be restored. But even British investments in Allied nations have altered drastically. To pay for vast military supplies from the United States and Canada, for example, Britain sold hundreds of millions of dollars' worth of securities pertaining to those countries. In the postwar era Britain will not have this investment income once so important in her economy.

Britain's lucrative carrying trade has changed considerably also. At one time British ships carried most of the world's commerce; after the war they will have to compete with huge merchant fleets of the United States, Canada, and the Soviet Union. Nor will British shipyards be able to maintain their former virtual monopoly.

Foreign markets are yet another vital problem. The United Kingdom lived by its sale of manufactured goods to Canada, Australia, South America, China, and other countries. After the war, Canada and Australia will be much more industrially self-sufficient, and already Britain's position in the markets of South America, in comparison with that of the United States, has suffered considerably. In fact, some economists feel that Britain's greatest postwar economic problem is that of exports; she must export manufactured products if she is to exist. This may help explain why the country as a whole was apparently quite willing in 1943 to embark upon new economic developments, involving international cooperation.

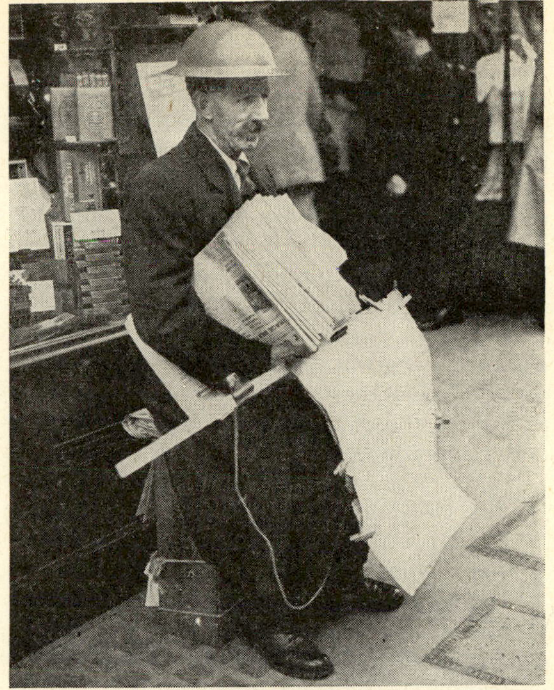

Air raid warnings did not keep this newsman from supplying the people with news. With a tin hat for security, he sticks to his post. Determination to "get on with it" has been a marked characteristic of the English during four years of war.

Too alarming a picture of Britain's future economic life should not be painted; the country has access to vast resources, and its industry will make adjustments needed to cope with world conditions. British economists are well aware of the sweeping economic changes in store. Furthermore, the British people anticipate these changes and are already prepared to go a long way. The direction they favor is to the left (though not along Marxist lines), toward a cooperative international order, and toward a progressively cooperative economy.

However, despite an unmistakable approval of the postwar objective of social reconstruction, there was no certainty in 1943 how the basic pattern would look. Great numbers of landowners and industrialists favored social concessions sufficient to weather the postwar storms but not radical enough to alter Britain's basic capitalistic and nationalistic institutions. Articulate elements of labor, especially the trade union groups, were warning of the dangers of what they called a "Tory victory." They pointed out, for example, that although every party in the House of Commons had paid lip service to the principles of the Beveridge Report, the Conservative-dominated government had flatly refused to put any of those principles into law during the war.

And labor groups, while endorsing the uncompromising war program of Churchill, have reported that they will want a dissolution of the present agreement between Conservatives and Labor once the war has been won. For they continue to believe that Churchill is the man to win the war—but apparently fear that he may not be socially constructive enough to win the peace.

British morale in 1943 was stronger than at any time since the outbreak of war. Gone were the foreboding days of Dunkirk and the heavy air raids; victory appeared inevitable. But the home front, in the conflict since the first day, refused to be unrealistic about the length of the war. The British worker and farmer preferred to say, "Let's get on with it," meanwhile paying the greatest attention to postwar planning. In 1943 Britons believed—as perhaps no other people except the Russians—that they were fighting a "people's war."

Canada

From complacency to action. Madame Chiang Kai-shek, speaking before the House of Commons in Ottawa in June 1943, stated that Canada's war effort was the greatest per capita among the United Nations.

Canada entered the war in September 1939, but its industrial mobilization did not become immediately effective. Following the typical history of the democracies, the country basked in the complacency of the "sitzkrieg," satisfied with sending Great Britain and her allies increased supplies of raw materials and agricultural products. But with the fall of France in June 1940, Canada went to work in earnest.

Canada's Industrial Revolution. Prime Minister Mackenzie King has pointed out that during the first three years of the Second World War the Dominion underwent an Industrial Revolution. Instead of concentrating upon the export of wheat, nonferrous metals, wood products, and fish, as in the past, Canada embarked upon one of the most ambitious industrial programs in modern history.

First there had to be rapid expansion of capital equipment. At the same time the government had to check all inflationary tendencies caused by this expansion and restrict specific commodities in domestic consumption. By March 1941, however, the newly constructed factories were beginning to turn out their war products in sizable quantities, and in the war years which followed, Canadian production, employment, and wages mounted to unprecedented heights. The Second World War has brought swift maturity to the country.

Canada in 1943 was the fourth largest producer of war supplies among the United Nations. More than 50 per cent of the mechanized transport used by the British army in North Africa was manufactured in Canada.

The shipbuilding industry shows expansion as great as that of the automotive industry. At the outbreak of war Canada was constructing virtually no ships at all. As of June 1943, there were in various stages of production 167 cargo ships of the 10,000-ton category, and 15 ships of the 4700-ton class. In addition, Canadian shipyards are turning out corvettes and frigates in a steady stream for the all-important convoy duty of the R.C.N. Before the war, Canada's aircraft industry employed only 1000 people, who turned out 40 planes a year. In July of 1943 almost 100,000 workers had built about 10,000 planes since the outbreak of war.

Food exports. In the last war Canada's great contribution to her allies was in agriculture, especially the export of wheat. In this war there is more emphasis upon the shipment of cheese, eggs, bacon, and pork. In addition the entire 1942 catch of salmon and herring went to the United Kingdom. Food objectives for 1943 call for a 22 per cent increase in hog production and a 29 per cent increase in eggs, and an 18 per cent decrease in wheat acreage because of a wheat surplus of almost 800,000,000 bushels beyond domestic needs—a surplus which will nevertheless be valuable to Europe in the postwar reconstruction years. Canadian delegates took an active part at the United Nations Food Conference held at Hot Springs,

Virginia, from May 18 to June 3, 1943. The importance of Canada in the international food situation was given full recognition.

Financing the war. How is the Second World War affecting the Canadians from a financial point of view? Some of the features of Canada's financial plans have been closely analyzed by American economists.

Government expenditures for 1943-1944 are estimated at approximately eleven times as much as the average of the years just before the war. Naturally, such heavy expenditures mean heavy obligations for the taxpayer. Both direct and indirect taxes have been increased steadily since the outbreak of the war. When rates of taxes paid by the average man in the United States, Britain, and Canada are compared, it will be seen that the Canadian consistently paid in 1943 half as much again as the American, and about as much as the Englishman.[6] Income taxes, on a pay-as-you-owe basis, are deducted from pay envelopes or collected in quarterly installments. Part of the sum is a compulsory saving to be refunded after the war, with 2 per cent interest. Exponents of the plan maintain that this arrangement not only reduces civilian purchasing power and combats inflation but also sets aside for the taxpayer funds which will be welcomed during the trying postwar period. Corporation and luxury taxes were also at a record high in 1943.

In spite of the heavy taxation, the national debt rose from $3,152,000,000 in 1939 to $4,045,000,000 in 1942, and economists estimate that it will jump to $9,215,000,000 in 1944. To meet this condition, the government has relied primarily on borrowing through Victory Loans.

Control of inflation. To prevent inflation, the Wartime Prices and Trade Board introduced price ceilings on November 30, 1941. The ceiling decided upon was the level of retail prices between September 15 and October 11, 1941. To keep prices from rising despite increased consumer purchasing power and mounting production costs, the Canadian government has consistently paid subsidies.

Price control and rationing have worked well. During the first war, when prices were unchecked, they rose 57.6 per cent above the prewar level. In World War II the cost-of-living index by December 1941 had risen but 14.7 per cent—and since the enforcement of price ceilings it has mounted only another 1.5 per cent. Canadian economists look with apprehension at American difficulties with price controls. For, if inflation should have its way in the United States, it must inevitably cross the boundary, so closely interdependent have the economies of the two countries become.

Other wartime controls include the National War Labor Board, which both regulates wages and administers cost-of-living bonuses so that wages will not lag behind wartime price levels.

The Air Training Plan. In some ways Canada's most spectacular military contribution—and certainly one out of all proportion to its population—has been its air force and air training plan. The British Commonwealth Air Training Plan is jointly the project of Canada, Great Britain, Australia, and New Zealand, but is administered by the R.C.A.F. This training scheme, which on May 1, 1943 involved 150,000, grew up soon after the outbreak of the war in 1939. Huge airfields and training schools mushroomed across the entire length of Canada, and young recruits from all over the Empire reported for duty. Each month has seen an increase in the number of air crew personnel graduated and sent overseas. Sixty per cent of the Plan's graduates are Canadians, and the Dominion has paid about the same proportion of its cost and upkeep.

This aerial revolution in Canada portends a strategic postwar role in aviation. Thousands of skilled fliers and technicians, superb new facilities and aircraft manufacturing plants, huge military bases on both coasts, and especially the new airfields in the Northwest promise an important future in commercial air travel along the great northern route to Europe and Asia. Well aware of postwar possibilities, the government has officially stated that the development of Canadian aviation will not be left to chance or the plans of rival commercial companies, but will be fostered and supervised mainly by the government.

Canada comes of age. The growing stature of Canada as a nation is reflected in its relations with other members of the United Nations. The country is no longer an acquiescing, timid stepchild of Great Britain. To Ottawa go the diplomatic and economic representatives of a score of countries to deal with the government on a new plane of parity. To Quebec went Roosevelt and Churchill in August 1943. In both war and postwar plans Canadians show frankness and independence.

Demonstrating United States-Canadian cooperation and solidarity, Canadian builders hand over this sleek corvette, adorned with the American flag and goodwill messages, to the United States Navy.

Canadian-American relations have always been a model of international amity and cooperation. The war has, if anything, strengthened them; the two nations have pooled their resources and planning initiative, especially in the Permanent Joint Board on Defense.

Canada's economic relations with Great Britain have assumed an unprecedented importance. The mother country has had to make heavy purchases in the Dominion, and the Canadian government entered into various arrangements to facilitate payment by Britain. Then in 1942 the Dominion made an outright gift of $1,000,000,000 in materials, munitions, and foodstuffs to the United Kingdom. This gift was followed by the passage on May 20, 1943, of the United Nations Mutual Aid Bill, providing for the distribution to Canada's allies of material, foodstuffs, and equipment worth $1,000,000,000. These supplies are not being sold but contributed, for Canadians agree that postwar debts among nations will only lead to grave international friction.

Debit and credit. But the national picture is not without its discordant elements. Canadians did the usual grumbling about rationing, the various black markets, the coal shortage—especially as much-needed shipments of hard coal from the United States were threatened by the coal situation there—and manpower difficulties. There was strong criticism in various quarters that too much manpower has been allowed to continue in the less essential industries, while many indispensable industries suffered from a dearth of labor.[7]

Labor's reaction to the manpower problem in 1943 was emphatic. Canadian labor had a record of few strikes, but it maintained that this existed in spite of inadequate representa-

In November 1943 the first United States-Alaska land route formally opened. Faster and less vulnerable than the old water route, the 1500-mile Alaska Highway has strategic importance now and postwar industrial value for the Western Hemisphere.

tion in Ottawa's wartime administration. Some labor groups were convinced that Selective Service had been a means of "freezing" workers at their posts and depriving them of better wages. By and large, Ottawa's handling of the manpower situation could bear favorable comparison with conditions in Great Britain and the United States; but there was enough dissatisfaction among the working groups to explain the results of the August 4, 1943 provincial election in Ontario. The new labor party, the C.C.F. (Cooperative Commonwealth Federation), jumped from a no-seat group to almost a majority group in the legislature. This election had peculiarly national implications because Premier King had personally endorsed the incumbent Ontario government—which was almost obliterated at the polls. The political temper throughout Canada in 1943 was an unmistakable swing to the left, with the C.C.F. and its policy of national planning and public ownership forging ahead in nearly every province. In fact, a Gallup poll taken in the fall of 1943 indicated that the C.C.F. then slightly led the Liberals and Progressive-Conservatives in popular favor. C.C.F. critics of the government charged that the government's production policy was all to the advantage of large financial and industrial groups. They warned that unless steps were taken, Canada after the war would be the victim of big business monopolies.

One problem, which troubled Canada in the last war also, has been English-French relations. The problem is highly complex, because the tensions which have developed over decades are at once social, political, economic, and religious. The French-Canadians are exceedingly loyal in their love of Canada, but their conditioning has tended to make and keep them strongly isolationist. The result is that a foreign war has little appeal for Quebec, even though the rest of the Dominion maintains that the security of Canada—and therefore of Quebec itself—depends upon an Allied victory overseas. The government, wishing at all costs to avoid the unfortunate misunderstanding in French-English relations during World War I, has compromised on certain basic issues. One of these is conscription. Conscription of all eligible males for military service was in force in 1943, but only those soldiers who volunteered for general service needed to serve overseas. This system satisfied the Quebec element, but appeared to be highly distasteful to the rest of the Dominion, who insisted volubly that conscription must be both universal and complete. Actually, the vast majority of Canadian soldiers have volunteered for general service, but the presence of many French-Canadians among the trainees called up only for home defense has created a delicate situation.

There were still other issues which gave rise to anxiety among various groups, but, when a national balance is struck, Canada's domestic condition appeared very sound. The Canadian people had no Utopian ideas about the reconstruction years; but already they were trying to plan a postwar social and economic order of plenty—for their country had come of age.

Australia, New Zealand, South Africa

Australia. Unlike the First World War, during which the enemy was 10,000 miles away, the Second World War has brought the fearful possibility of invasion and national annihilation to Australia's very doorstep. It has been the most critical period of the nation's history. Statistics show that every other man between the ages of 18 and 45 is in the fighting services. Altogether 800,000 men have been inducted—the equivalent of more than 15,000,000 Americans in uniform. Australian feats in the Second World War live up to the proud record of 1914-1918, "Cobbers" having distinguished themselves in Libya, Egypt, Syria, Greece, Crete, Malaya, the Netherlands East Indies, and New Guinea.

The home front had to overcome grave handicaps to meet the threat from abroad. Since Australia has a population of only 6½ million, the foremost handicap was manpower. To create a proper balance between the fighting and production fronts, the government established a Manpower Directorate.

Another handicap was that prior to this war Australia was primarily an agricultural country, relying heavily upon manufactured imports. After 1939 the country had to set its energies to turning out the tools and munitions of war.

Australia saw the danger of concentrating her industries in two or three large cities on the east coast as the threat of Japanese bomb-

Even the very young are doing their part for the home front. These small members of an Australian "Cub Pack" are obviously pleased with their collection of scrap metal to be turned into arms for the Allies.

ing grew greater. Much of industry was therefore decentralized and spread out into the interior; at the same time use of more local labor and resources became possible. The conversion of the country's industry from a peacetime to a wartime economy has been the special job of the Department of War Organization of Industry.

As in other Allied countries, the surplus purchasing power created by consumer restrictions was taken up by a heavy increase in taxation and by government loan programs. In spite of action taken early in the war, living costs in Australia have risen sharply, but it was felt in 1943 that the adoption of the Canadian principle of paying subsidies to producers of war essentials to maintain price ceilings would do much to check inflation.

Australian workers are enthusiastic trade unionists and as such enjoy a strong economic and political bargaining power. The trade unionists were largely instrumental in electing a Labor Government under Premier John Curtin in 1941, and they have accepted the drastic government action to step up the total war effort. The special regulations passed in February 1942 were designed to peg wage rates in all industries, freeze all workers in their jobs, suspend all holidays, and impose penalties on absenteeism. In the general election held August 21, 1942, Curtin's government won a smashing victory, capturing about two thirds of the 75 seats in the House of Representatives, and all 19 Senate seats, for which voting took place.

In 1943 American soldiers filled the streets of Sydney; American planes filled the skies of "Down Under." Doughboys were marrying Australian girls in surprising numbers, and Yankees and "Cobbers" vied with each other in outlandish slang, beer drinking, and a mania for betting on anything and everything. The fighting qualities of each nation were fully approved by the other, and the Aussies were cooperating splendidly with General MacArthur. American men and materials had been transported many thousands of miles to the Australian war theater, and the Commonwealth was deeply appreciative of America's Lend-Lease aid.

What we may not realize is that Australia was repaying this aid with a reciprocal aid program of her own. At the end of 1942, American forces had received 30 million pounds of meat and 50 million pounds of vegetables and fruits from the Australian government, which provides rations for every American soldier stationed on its soil. Likewise the government provided camp accommodations, services, hospitals, and large quantities of army and civilian stores. It is said that on a population basis, Australian aid was approximately seven times as great as United States aid to Australia.[8] Australia promises to come out of the war stronger and more united, more industrialized, and more aware than ever of her responsibilities in the family of nations. The cooperation demonstrated by Australia and the United States was a portent of the kind of world that democratic action could create.

New Zealand. Within a matter of minutes after Britain's declaration of war on September 3, 1939, New Zealand's cabinet unanimously followed suit. Since that day, this country of but 1,640,000 inhabitants has made a military contribution on an all-out scale, and her men have distinguished themselves on battlefronts the world over. A New Zealander was the first Allied war ace, and the New

Zealand cruiser *Achilles* helped to destroy the *Graf Spee* in the battle of the River Plate.

In normal times New Zealand's prosperity is largely based on the export of great quantities of butter, cheese, meat, and wool, its best customer being the United Kingdom. Faced with the possibility of invasion and the cutting of her supply lines, New Zealand simply had to embark upon a rapid industrial program, even though she must import all her steel. What plant facilities there were had to be converted, and workers trained to do precision work unknown in the Dominion before. By 1943 an industrial transformation had resulted, and armored vehicles, Bren gun carriers, mortars, and ammunition were swelling the supplies of the United Nations. In the words of one New Zealander, addressing American readers: "It isn't much to set beside your giant factories. But remember we start from scratch—and the more we can produce here the less is the strain on your shipping."[9]

New Zealanders and Americans stationed in the Dominion in 1943 were establishing a basis for greater cooperation in the postwar era. It was not impossible that returning doughboys would help spread news of the progressive quality of the social security program of New Zealand—"the test tube of the democracies."

South Africa. In September 1939, one outstanding leader of South Africa, General Hertzog, held that since the Dominion was a sovereign independent state not bound to participate in a war simply because Britain was involved, it should adhere to a policy of benevolent neutrality. But General Smuts, who maintained that in this crisis the destinies of all democracies were inseparably linked, carried the day and formed a new pro-war government. Pro-war leaders had 84 seats in the House of Assembly against the 66 seats mustered by the anti-war forces. The difference constituted a fairly comfortable working majority, and with it General Smuts began a vigorous policy of war participation.

Nevertheless, the opposition continued to give voice to its strong disapproval of South Africa's foreign policy. And so, on July 7, 1943, a general election was held, with the war as the principal issue. Interest ran high throughout the Union, and about 75 per cent of the eligible population voted. Ballots were sent to the soldiers scattered in North Africa, Britain, India, and elsewhere, and then flown back for tabulation. The results were an overwhelming victory for the pro-war parties; so that they then held 107 seats in the House of Assembly to the anti-war groups' 43.

New Zealand soldiers fought—and fought well—alongside their allies in the North African campaign. Here New Zealanders man slit trenches in the Battle of Egypt.

South Africa's war effort has been valiant. The Union has a white population of only 2,230,000, yet has more than 200,000 well-equipped "Springboks" under arms. The industrial front has made rapid strides. At the outbreak of the war, South Africa had but three factories capable of producing military materials; after two years, she could boast of more than six hundred.

The Dominion's conversion program was the result of efficient governmental planning, largely directed by a special civilian agency known as the War Supplies Board. The production of steel was rapidly stepped up, as was the mining of coal. It became possible to manufacture indispensable military tools. An entirely new and important machine tool industry has been created. The workshops of the state-controlled South African Railways and Harbors, the largest organization in the Dominion, are turning out armored cars, troop-carrier bodies, airplane hangars, electric generators, gun sights, and precision instruments. The country's shoe and textile industries now not only fulfill all their own army's needs but make large deliveries of boots and blankets to Britain and other Allies.

On June 13, 1942 was held the inaugural meeting of the Social and Economic Planning Council, created to handle postwar reconstruction plans. A fundamental postwar problem is that of the status of the colored population. The British and Boers are far outnumbered by the Negroes and the latter have virtually no say in the government. Articulate Negro elements have been increasingly persistent in demanding for their people greater educational facilities, a higher economic status, and more political representation. The democratic ideals to which the war aims of the Union are pledged demand, observers point out, an eventual settlement of this complicated question.

In 1943, then, the political horizon was not without clouds, but, as in its sister Dominions, Canada and Australia, the Union's swiftly growing industrialization had brought a new maturity and promise.

Latin America

Good Neighbor cooperation. The twenty-one sovereign republics of the Western Hemisphere have a total population of some 270,000,000. The problems which they share in common—hemispheric defense, health and education, standards of living, trade, and mutual understanding—necessitated the creation of special machinery. Thus, since 1923, inter-American conferences have been held every five years, and three special meetings have been called since 1939—at Panama in 1939, Havana in 1940, and Rio de Janeiro in 1942.

The last conference recommended that the American nations sever relations with the Axis powers (which all Latin American republics with the exception of Argentina have now done), and it set up an Inter-American Defense Board as well as an Emergency Advisory Committee for Political Defense to stamp out fifth-column activities. United States Lend-Lease has assisted many republics in buying army and navy equipment; and the State Department has enforced the regulations of the Proclaimed List of Blocked Nationals—a blacklist of 3000 Axis firms, and firms operating with the Axis, in Latin America.

Economic importance. Since the loss of southeastern Asia to Japan, the United Nations have had to rely almost entirely on South American sources for shipments of natural rubber, tin, quinine, antimony, and other needed war materials. Besides these products, they depend on Latin America for a diversity of goods, ranging from sugar to iron. To coordinate the production and distribution of these vital war materials swiftly and effectively has been a large job. After the conference at Rio de Janeiro, the United States concluded agreements with various South American countries to furnish them with machinery and financial and technical assistance in return for their products. Necessary loans are made through the Export-Import Bank and the Reconstruction Finance Corporation. Transportation of the products to the United States is under the cooperative direction of various Washington agencies, such as the State Department, the War Production Board, and the War Shipping Administration.

Thus, even though from a military point of view the Latin American countries have played to date a purely defensive role, patrolling their shores, events in the Pacific war theater and the technological demands of modern combat have combined to make the South American economy especially important and strategic. The Axis powers realized the economic significance of Latin America long ago. For years prior to 1939 all three nations—Germany, Italy, and Japan—were busily engaged in pouring money and nationals into the southern continent in an effort to gain a stranglehold over its economic and political life. Today their economic power is virtually annihilated, and Axis political influence is being combatted. Meanwhile, the Allies have become increasingly aware of the role Latin America can play now and in the postwar era.

Latin American difficulties. The present economic condition of the republics to the south is not a simple one of progress and prosperity. Distressing problems confront the Good Neighbors, and a solution to some of them must be discovered soon.

The cost of living in almost all the Latin American countries has been mounting steadily, and from 1941 has risen alarmingly. For example, taking the cost of living index in

Good Neighbor policy in action at the conference table in Rio de Janeiro. The United States representative, Sumner Welles, former Undersecretary of State, is seated at the far right.

Brazil as 100 for 1929, in 1938 it was 125, and by March 1943 had soared to 163 in Rio de Janeiro. Wages have not kept pace with the inflation of prices; so a progressively reduced standard of living has resulted. The story is similar for most of the other republics, and in Bolivia the situation has already become highly critical. There the cost-of-living index for the capital city, La Paz, jumped from 100 in 1931 to 1497 in December 1942. Many of the countries have created special price controls to aid in stabilization, but apparently these measures have not been successful.

The shipping shortage has been acute and has brought in its wake pressing economic problems. Brazil has accelerated its industrial development in steel, aluminum, rayon, and chemical products, but this entire development depends upon shipments of petroleum and coal from the United States. Limited shipping space meant a limitation in imports and a serious threat to Brazil's war effort.

The shipping problem affects almost all the other republics as well. Chile has had a shortage of needed petroleum, while in 1942 Colombia could not fill its coffee quota as established in the Inter-American Coffee Agreement, even though production was sufficient. Uruguay's construction industry, employing a large proportion of the industrial population, has been held back because it has not been possible to import sufficient iron and steel. Venezuela's oil production has been curtailed drastically because of a shortage in tankers; unemployment in this important industry has increased markedly. Cuba could not export all its 1942 sugar crop. The "banana republics," unable to ship their chief product abroad, have suffered sharp economic reverses.

The war has cut off important European and, to a lesser degree, Asiatic markets; some countries have been hit hard. In 1942 Argentina's imports were by volume less than half those of 1938, while its exports were also less, although slightly greater in actual value. Since cereals can no longer be exported as formerly, the government has had to pay continued subsidies to their growers.

A significant feature of South American trade at present is the growing importance of the United States' position. Naturally, the war has decimated the lucrative commerce enjoyed by Germany and Italy, and the United States has been by all odds the chief gainer, even in comparison with Britain. With probably no exception, every Latin American republic has shown the ascendancy of the United States in its trade. It will be interesting to see whether the United States continues to enjoy this favorable economic position.

Despite the many difficulties, the Second World War is helping to industrialize Latin America; this development in turn holds forth the promise of a higher standard of living. Much remains to be done, however, before the vast majority of the people south of the Rio Grande enjoy anything like a proper economic existence. Dietary deficiencies, nutritional diseases, lack of sanitation, illiteracy, and abject poverty have to be combated vigorously. In this vast socio-economic struggle, the United States is contributing its exports and resources. In Peru, for example, the American government has authorized an Export-Import Bank loan of 25 million dollars, and is rendering financial and technical assistance for a cooperative sanitation and health program. An American mission is planning a cooperative food production program for the country. In Costa Rica, American money and technical aid are helping to complete the Pioneer Road, which will link finished sections of the Pan-American Highway. A health program has been inaugurated to accompany the road building. These Good Neighbor contributions bode well for the future of the Western Hemisphere.

Political Latin America. By and large, the political front in Latin America has shown both stability and solidarity. Perhaps the most prominent political upheaval in 1943 was the Argentine revolt of June 4 against the government of President Ramon S. Castillo, who had pursued an appeasing policy of "prudent neutrality." It was hoped that the revolt would result in the formation of a more pro-Allied government, but the first cabinet appointed by Ramirez appeared to be strongly nationalist and included leaders with pro-Axis leanings. The present political struggle is being closely followed by the United States and the Argentine's neighbors.

The balance sheet shows that Latin America as a whole is linked to the United Nations and their cause. Eleven republics have declared war on the Axis powers, seven have severed relations with them, and two have assumed a nonbelligerent position, allowing the Allies—but not the Axis—to use their ports. Pan-American relations have been further cemented in 1943 by the special trips of Latin American Presidents for conferences and negotiations in Washington and by Vice-President Wallace's extensive tour of every South American republic. Wherever he went, Mr. Wallace received heartfelt ovations, evidence of the growing approval of American foreign policy.

Russia

M*eeting the crisis.* The position of Russia in 1943 amazed the world. That the country did not capitulate from economic necessity and psychological despair after the Nazi invasions will go down in history as a tribute to the tenacity of the Russian populace. That the Russians were able to drive the Germans back beyond the Dnieper by fall seemed almost miraculous. Certainly part of the success was due to the Soviet leaders' foresight and planning.

On July 3, 1941, eleven days after the Nazis poured across the borders, Stalin declared: "To the enemy must not be left a single engine, a single railway car, not a single pound of grain or a gallon of fuel."[10] The world expected that this now-famous "scorched-earth" policy would result in the systematic destruction of all factories and installations. What the world did not expect was the wholesale removal of entire plants. For example, the Russians removed to new foundations a thousand miles eastward in the Urals the tractor works of Kharkov, the farm implement factory of Rostov, the aircraft plants of Taganrog, and huge armament works. The great industrial trek to the East, involving hundreds of large and small plants, was accompanied by the transfer of an estimated million workers with their families. Prewar planning by Stalin and his engineers made the trek possible; because of it the USSR was able to catch its second wind. The transfer of industry held important postwar implications as well. The Urals and western Siberia are fabulously rich in mineral resources, the twin-peaked Magnet Mountain, for example, being an almost solid mass of magnetite, 60 per cent pure iron. Lenin long foretold the industrial potentialities of this vast hinterland. The words of ex-ambassador Joseph E. Davies are significant:

" . . . I saw great cities—boom cities, laid out in squares like our prairie towns, dotted with factories, huge plants and chimneys, all over the place—one small Pittsburgh after another. . . .

The impression of power, innate strength, vigor, and pioneer energy, which one gets from this great section, is extraordinary."[11]

The efforts of the industrial workers, whose output has increased daily, have been matched by the farmers, despite loss for a time of all the Ukraine and the fertile Don region. Some 5,000,000 acres of uncultivated land have been made productive to compensate for the millions of acres lost to the Nazis. Soviet agriculture has faced dangerous shortages in manpower, machines, and animals as well. The sowing and harvesting have been taken over principally by women, men too old for military service, and hundreds of thousands of school children and students. The country has suffered but has averted the starvation which Hitler must undoubtedly have relied upon.

A marked characteristic of the Russian home front in 1943 was the growing proportion of women in industry. Even before the war the world saw pictures of Soviet women driving locomotive engines, tractors, and subway trains, performing operations, welding, bricklaying, or unloading ships. The socialist philosophy stresses complete equality of the sexes. By 1943 there were 15,000,000 women in industry, and of course women were playing an unprecedented role of importance in Soviet agriculture. In addition a half million women were serving in the Red Cross and Red Crescent Societies at the front. Nor have Americans forgotten meeting in 1942 the mild-mannered young lady who, as one of many women snipers, had accounted for 309 Nazis.

Putting finishing touches on ammunition for the Red Army, these Soviet women typify the unprecedented role of women in industry on all home fronts.

The war brought serious social problems to the country. Untold numbers of civilians in overrun territory had been slain or left to starve. As the Red armies drove victoriously westward in 1943, the government had to grapple with the tremendous job of reconstructing areas of desolation. For example, the city of Kharkov was left burning by the retreating Germans, the streets blocked by piles of broken glass, bricks, and twisted iron. The Ukrainian Academy of Sciences had developed plans—while the city was still occupied by the Nazis—for the reconstruction of Kharkov, utilizing the best available materials, making provision for subways and a new drainage system. In 1943 these plans had already begun to take form.[12]

Also in 1943, as the southern regions of the Soviet Union were liberated, the collective farmers began to repair the destruction wrought by German occupation. Since almost all farm machinery and buildings had been demolished, the government at once sent in about 11,000 specialists and hundreds of tractors and other machines. Agricultural research is being resumed.[13]

These liberated areas have required not only the services of engineers but those of doctors, educators, and social workers. The invasion necessitated the stepping up of hospital facilities and medical personnel. Although there were 160,000 doctors in 1940 (as contrasted with 20,000 at the time of the Revolution), the needs of the war forced the medical schools to speed their graduation rate from 12,000 yearly to an estimated 42,000 for the first sixteen months of the war. With the liberation of Russian territory came Russian doctors and nurses to aid the sick.

One poignant aspect has been the problem of war orphans. Whenever land has been reconquered, the government has immediately set aside special stores of foods, medicines, and school supplies, and has established special homes and nurseries for orphaned children. A popular movement has been the adoption of orphans by citizens living all over the Soviet Union. But, like Britain, Russia faces a large problem in readjusting psychologically thousands of these young minds, scarred by the terrors of modern warfare.

The national budget. In a socialistic state the annual budget naturally must be reckoned in tremendous figures. The Soviet budget in 1941, for example, reached 216 billion rubles. The 1931 budget was 19 billion rubles. That the war has been a heavy burden on the Russian people is shown by the fact that in 1931 less than one billion rubles were appropriated for the army, whereas in 1941 the appropriation came to 70 billion, or about one third of the annual budget. No doubt the critical years, 1942 and 1943, have witnessed a still greater percentage set aside for military operations. A breakdown of the 1941 budget affords other interesting insights into the country's economic condition. Of the 216 billion total, 33 per cent was appropriated for capital construction in industry, agriculture, and transportation. Government operations, police and court administration, social security reserves, and emergency funds required about 12 per cent. However, despite the critical foreign situation with its heavy demands on defense preparations, the 1941 budget called for appropriations amounting to 22 per cent to be spent on the nation's educational system, health program, and scientific research.[14] Budget statistics like these help explain what the Russian people were fighting for as they met Hitler's challenge.

In 1943 the government allotted over 67,000,000 rubles to the People's Commissariat of Education to restore and reëquip schools in liberated regions. It was pointed out in an article in *Izvestia* that of 18,000 schools in twelve liberated areas, 10,500 had already been restored.[15] However, it will be a long time before the losses suffered by schools and libraries are fully replaced.

Political differences. As has been indicated, the world in 1943 was unstinting in its praise of Russia's military accomplishments and resiliency of its economic and social institutions. But Russia's allies were more hesitant when it came to evaluating the Soviet's foreign policy and political frame of mind. What was Russia's real postwar objective? What was Russia's true evaluation of her allies?

Because until November there was no closely knit program of political activity among the four principal United Nations, there seemed little possibility in 1943 of getting definitive answers to these questions. But it is important to bear in mind that in 1943 the Russian people were also troubled by the same questions: what were the true postwar objectives of Britain and the United States?

The principal source of trouble in 1943 was the second front which the Russians were asking the Allies to establish. (See pages 23 and 30.) Similarly, in the fall of 1943 many Americans were asking aloud what Russia was going to do about Japan. They felt that she could at least provide bases in Siberia for her Allies. Roosevelt was of the opinion, however, that Soviet policy regarding Japan was dictated by purely practical reasons; in 1943 her hands were tied in the west.

In other matters also, on the political and diplomatic fronts, Soviet leaders in 1943 were not seeing eye to eye with the British and Americans. Washington and London gave partial recognition to the French Committee of National Liberation; Moscow recognized it fully. London and Washington seemed interested in plans suggested by Polish leaders for a postwar East European Federation (to be made up of Poland, Czechoslovakia, Hungary, Rumania); Moscow came out flatly against this. *War and the Working Class*, a new semiofficial Moscow periodical, perceived in the whole idea an unfriendly move by Polish reactionaries and warned about trying to establish another "cordon sanitaire" against Russia.

At the same time government-approved groups in Moscow were supporting a Free Germany Committee. Some observers abroad saw in this new movement a Soviet desire either to bring about a negotiated peace with Germany or to pave the way for the eventual establishment of bolshevism in German territory. Defenders of the movement replied that it was designed to encourage and aid the strong anti-Hitler underground forces in Germany to throw off the Nazi leadership; that its objectives were similar to those of the French Committee of National Liberation and of Roosevelt and Churchill regarding Italy, i.e., encouragement of anti-Fascist governments which would bring about the regeneration of the countries.

Promising signs. The Moscow Conference, as we have seen (p. 30), promised much for more complete understanding and cooperative action among the Allies. Another step toward creating a friendlier international atmosphere was the abolition of the Comintern by Stalin. With the historic termination of this world-wide organization for the propagation of communism, Russia's allies had further evidence that she was not trying to sabotage their capitalistic institutions.

Meanwhile, the smashing victories on the front were celebrated with cannon salutes in Moscow and fireworks. Victory seemed at last in sight. The people at home had no abundance of food, but there was no famine—and no inflationary increase in the cost of living, and no war profiteering. The theaters were more widely patronized than ever, although many of Russia's finest theater and ballet companies were spending most of their time entertaining the soldiers at the front. Sports contests were widely held and well attended. The Archbishop of York, visiting Moscow in September, reported publicly that he found complete freedom of religion there, that antireligious propaganda had ceased, that fifty to sixty churches were open in the Moscow area alone.

Russian people presumably had their differences of opinion, their domestic conflicts, their great problem of providing a high degree of individual liberty within a way of life regulated by the state. But however serious these difficulties might or might not be, the Russians stood before the world as a unified people throwing back an aggressor.

China

After twelve years. On September 19, 1931, Japanese troops marched into Manchuria and set in motion a train of events culminating in the Second World War. On September 19, 1943, the Chinese people looked back over twelve heart-breaking years of fighting Japanese aggression. On them had fallen a tremendously heavy yoke. In those twelve years the richest regions of the land—the teeming seaports and industrial cities, the fertile river valleys—had been occupied by the Japanese, millions of Chinese soldiers and civilians had perished, and the supplies promised by China's allies, on which the nation's fate depended, were in the fall of 1943 still only trickling in between the Japanese-held areas. The gravity of China's position had not gone unnoticed abroad; the Quebec Conference drafted plans for an ambitious campaign in southeastern Asia. But the situation was ominous—and the Chinese were weary.

Three-point program. Yet in one of China's darkest hours, Madame Sun Yat-sen, the widow of the nation's great modern reformer, set forth a three-point program for the future: (1) China must attain political, economic, and cultural equality with other nations; (2) the Japanese must be forced out of Chinese territory; and (3) China must become a true democracy by the national election of a People's Congress to replace the one-party government of the Kuomintang.[16]

Toward Madame Sun Yat-sen's first goal, historic action was taken simultaneously in Washington and Chungking on January 11, 1943. In the former capital, the United States and China signed a treaty ending the special rights enjoyed by the United States in certain Chinese cities, including special courts at Shanghai for the trial of Americans.[17] At Chungking British and Chinese officials signed a similar treaty abrogating the extraterritorial rights and privileges of the British Empire. Thus ended a century of political humiliation for China. In addition the Chinese government in February 1943 unilaterally abrogated the treaty of 1899, by which France had leased Kwangchowwan on China's southern coast. The Vichy government was powerless to take counter measures.

The second goal, as expressed by Madame Sun Yat-sen, was perhaps brought a little closer in 1943 as the Chinese won minor battles against the Japanese. Dr. T. V. Soong, China's Foreign Minister, was explicit regarding his country's attitude toward the regaining of lost

Camouflaged Chinese troops ford a river near the front, as the Japanese are held at China's "back door."

areas, stating that China had no territorial ambitions and claimed no special privileges. He expected Manchuria and Formosa to be returned to China, but thought Korea ought to be independent.[18]

China's struggle toward democracy—the third goal—was marked during 1943 by both disturbing and promising developments. Another dangerous rift appeared between the Central Government and the Chinese Communists. The Central Government strongly opposed the Communists' possession of an autonomous government, army, currency, and taxation system in the border provinces. The Communists, on the other hand, have for years criticized what they deem the inefficiency and half-heartedness of the Central Government's war against the Japanese. Furthermore, the Communists wanted full recognition as a political party, but were afraid to give up their military organization until their political aims were granted. Actual clashes broke out in the summer of 1943, the official Central News revealed.

But this serious internal crisis seemed likely to be satisfactorily settled by the Kuomintang and Generalissimo Chiang Kai-shek. On August 1, 1943, the venerable and respected President of China, Lin Sen, died. In September, the Central Executive Committee of the Kuomintang selected Chiang Kai-shek as Lin Sen's successor, thus legalizing Chiang Kai-shek's position as the military and political leader of China. Chiang told the Central Executive Committee to maintain a "policy of leniency and forbearance" toward the Communists, and stated that the problem "should be solved by political means."[19]

The new President went farther, encouraging the Central Executive Committee to pass a resolution stating that a People's Congress to adopt a constitution must be held within a year after the war. The Kuomintang was responding to the note struck in Chiang's new book, *China's Destiny*. Though in the past China's fate depended on foreign policy, now "it depends on our ability to secure inner political unification and concentration of national power. China stands at the watershed of her fate."[20]

Economic and political developments. The Kuomintang's Central Executive Committee also passed a 16-point resolution blueprinting China's postwar economic aims. The resolution allowed for both private and public enterprise. Those industries which are inherently monopolistic and public utilities are to be owned by the state. On the other hand, "industry which may be entrusted to individuals or which will be less suitable for the state to operate shall be privately operated."[21]

In addition to the democratic economic planning, a new system of self-government, known as the *hsien* system, has developed widely in Free China during the war. "These *hsien* governments are very close to the people, . . . and are giving the farmers an increasing share in the running of local affairs."[22]

The ability of the Chinese to keep fighting the aggressor has been due largely to the removal of strategic industries into the still-free regions, as in Russia. With government help, 450 private factories with their personnel have been moved despite the appalling transport difficulties. Hundreds of thousands of farmers and their equipment and most of China's student body have moved inland, also.

The government has played an important role in establishing and subsidizing new industrial enterprises and regulating prices, wages, credit, and foreign trade. Light industry—for instance, textiles and medical supplies—with emphasis upon decentralization and high mobility, has been fostered by the Chinese Industrial Cooperatives. Only a few years old, these cooperatives numbered 1700 in 1941, and they promised to play an increasingly important role in postwar China.

Critical domestic condition. Nevertheless, China's domestic condition was extremely critical in 1943. The Japanese blockade was proving all too effective; shortages of food and necessary medical and military supplies in Free China were becoming alarming. Transportation facilities in Free China were so bad that it required superhuman efforts to ship food from one region to another. China's coastal and river shipping dropped from 1,500,000 or 2,000,000 tons, before the war, to 110,000 tons.[23] In order to keep the troops fed at all adequately, many of China's armies were forced to grow their own rice, wheat, and vegetables. Milk and medicine were even scarcer, and the people as a whole were suffering from serious undernourishment. The acute shortage in Free China of everything from munitions to milk resulted in the skyrocketing of prices, adding to the woes of the people.

Yet in 1943 the Chinese spirit still seemed indomitable. The universities which they had transported hundreds of miles upstream into Free China still carried on. A further indication of China's age-old veneration for learning was the announcement in March 1943 that the *Encyclopaedia Britannica* was about to be translated *in toto* into Chinese.

Italy

Grievances of the people. From 1922 to July 25, 1943, Mussolini had been the absolute head of the Italian people substituting for the democratic tradition a Machiavellian philosophy based on aggression, state absolutism, and the subordination of individual rights. By 1943, however, his attempt to construct a new Roman Empire had brought Italy to the point of national exhaustion, war weariness, and bankruptcy. World-shaking changes were inevitable—and Il Duce went out, and Badoglio came in.

Italy's natural resources are relatively poor, and the country is not equipped to be a first-rate military power, though superficially it might appear to be. Yet for years Mussolini had been forcing his people in an unnatural attempt to dominate the Mediterranean. The Italian people were given only the most glowing accounts of victories. Finally, as Italy's military prestige sank lower and lower, the impotent rage of the masses against the leader who had so tragically misled them reached new peaks of intensity.

The Italian people nursed other grievances at home as well. Mussolini had linked his fate irrevocably with Hitler's, resulting in what from the historical point of view must be considered an unnatural alliance. However, it was not an alliance of equals, but of master and servant.

Hundreds of thousands of Italian workers, as well as shipments of agricultural products needed by the underfed populace in Italy, were sent to Germany. In April 1943 reports from Switzerland, Russia, and Britain indicated that the Italian diet was poor compared with that of the Germans. For example, the normal bread ration in Italy was 37 ounces per week as contrasted with 80 ounces in Germany; the normal adult meat ration was 5-7 ounces weekly as against the Nazis' 12½ ounces.[24] The Italians knew that they were vastly worse fed than their "blood brothers" and they bitterly resented further exporting of foods. Meanwhile, much-needed imports from Germany fell far below expectations in 1943, the Nazis, for example, admitting their inability to supply Italy's war industries with the 1,000,000 tons of coal per month that agreements called for. Thus in 1943 the raw materials and food situation grew desperate. Added to this was an inflationary rise in prices and a widespread black market which harmed the poorer classes especially. Long before the summer of 1943 the Italians had come to the realistic conclusion that whether the Allies or Germany won, they had lost.

The political struggle. Therefore, when military desperation forced the resignation of Mussolini (and his subsequent flight to Germany), the Italian masses gave vent to their feelings by spontaneous demonstrations of enthusiasm in the large cities. This spirit had already been manifested when the Allies conquered Sicily and the boot of the peninsula. All Fascist insignias disappeared; workers in the northern cities went on strike in the war factories; demands arose for the rededication of Italy to democratic principles of government.

From Germany the fallen Duce proclaimed the formation of a new Fascist Republican State. In a radio speech he exhorted "loyal" Italians to take up arms again on the side of Germany and Italy, to reorganize the armed forces and militia, to eliminate the "traitors" collaborating with the Allies, and to reëstablish Fascist order.

The Italian people had no desire to heed Mussolini's exhortations. They had a new government, led by Badoglio, who clamped down strict censorship on the press and put the railway, postal, radio, and telegraph operators under military control. They had to worry about the problems attending "unconditional surrender" and the terms of the armistice. They were now battling their former Axis partners in the streets of Naples and Rome, and soon the southern half of the peninsula was aflame. The Italians were caught between two fires.

They were caught between other fires as well, republican and monarchial, revolutionary and reactionary. Throughout the Fascist régime a strong underground had persisted in the northern industrial centers. Composed of workers who had seen Fascism destroy ruthlessly the rights of labor and murder its leaders, this underground came to the surface immediately upon Mussolini's fall. The movement favored a clean break not only with Germany and all vestiges of the old Fascist order, but also with the House of Savoy and the group around Badoglio. It called for a popular front, democratic elections, and favored collaboration with the United Nations.

The American and British governments, however, announced (in the words of Churchill), "We certainly do not seek to reduce Italian life to a condition of chaos and anarchy, and find ourselves without any authority with whom to deal." There were many in high governmental circles in Washington and London who saw in the popular movement the danger of a communist revolution. The House of Savoy was commended (by General Eisenhower) for getting rid of Mussolini, and active support was given Badoglio in establishing government and order. The Marshal favored a government recognizing all shades of political thought, and intimated that his own views were those of a moderate. In October 1943 Italy joined the Allies as a cobelligerent, declaring war on its former ally.

However, Italian progressives in exile like Count Sforza and Professor Salvemini decried the maintenance of so many of the old Fascist régime, including petty party bureaucrats; they doubted whether the regeneration of the country could come at the price of so much compromise. For it was well known that Badoglio's own record was in almost direct contrast to the avowed purposes of the democracies; "Since 1936 he had been a member of the Fascist Party. He had acted as the unofficial leader of its right wing. He had paid public tribute to the Duce, master-minded the Fascist victory in Spain, defeated the Ethiopians and accepted from the grateful Mussolini the title of Viceroy and Duke of Addis Ababa."[25] Many Laborites in the British House of Commons deplored what appeared to them a "deal" made with Italian Quislings, and American liberal journals declared that Anglo-American policies were thwarting the democratic ambitions of the Italians.

However, the upholders of the official Allied attitude toward the House of Savoy and Marshal Badoglio were quick to point out that much British and American blood had been saved. Italian soldiers and workers, they said, would relieve Allied troops for combat by unloading ships, guarding railways, building roads. The Italian fleet had come over almost intact to the side of the Allies, without firing a shot. The State Department and Foreign Office appeared reasonably satisfied that the promise of Badoglio to work out a democratically constructed government seemed hopeful —and certainly worth a trial.

Germany

Propaganda and facts. Reports leaking out of the Reich in July 1943 gave credence to the joke current there: "We'd better enjoy the war while we can. The peace is going to be terrible."[26] Whether apocryphal or not, the story was apt in that it pointed up the people's realization that for them the war had shifted from a victorious offensive to a bitter defensive. The German population had come to think of the Russian campaign as a living nightmare. To steel home-front resistance, the propaganda agencies drummed into the minds of the people the alleged barbarities of Communist life and the merciless fate awaiting a defeated Germany at the hands of Stalin. In a somber speech in May 1943 the Fuehrer neither minced words nor predicted victory; to lull the German populace by soft words at that stage might prove fatal. Emphasis was placed upon a new propaganda word: *Notgemeinschaft,* unity because of necessity.

The havoc wreaked by the *Luftwaffe* on European cities and historic shrines had been returned ten-fold by 1943—to virtually obliterate Hamburg and many great industrial Ruhr towns, and even begin the destruction of Berlin itself. Hitler in the prewar years continually glorified war; but the temper of the German home front was expressed by one Cologne newspaper after that city had been bombed over a hundred times: "Anyone who lives in a district threatened by air raids experiences a feeling of physical disgust when he meets a comrade who today still glorifies war."[27] Eyewitness accounts relayed from Stockholm and Berne agreed that the destruction wrought in the large industrial areas was well-nigh unbelievable; that families by the thousands were destitute, homeless, and without food; that the transportation and production systems of the Reich were critically shaken.

In addition to the effects of the boomeranging Russian campaign and the Allied aerial offensive, the German people in 1943 were hard hit by the defection of Italy. For months Hitler had maintained a strict silence, but the psychological effects of the collapse of Italy necessitated his reporting to the home front. He attempted to minimize from a military standpoint the withdrawal of Italy from the Axis. He also tried to minimize the fact that the German people were nearly alone in their struggle by maintaining that they could now proceed "free of all burdensome encumbrances."[28] It is interesting to recall his remarks to the Reichstag in 1940: "We could not allow Italy to be defeated. We know that if Fascist Italy were to go down it would be the end of Nazi Germany." To keep the home front in order, Hitler in August 1943 formally appointed Heinrich Himmler (Chief of the Gestapo) both Minister of the Interior and Chief of the Reich Administration. As head of the powerful black-uniformed SS (Schutz-Staffel) troops since 1929, the new home-front "czar" was expected to be able to take care of any possible trouble in his usual efficient, ruthless fashion.

Working conditions inside Germany. The German people were spending long hours in factories during 1943, turning out vital supplies amid the crash of block-busters. They were faced by a serious manpower shortage; the heavy losses on the eastern front necessitated scouring the bottom of the manpower barrel for all possible recruits. By inducements and force the Nazis have recruited workers from occupied countries. According to one report, in September 1943, some 30 per cent of all labor forces in Germany were composed of foreigners.[29] Without a doubt this vast labor army freed able-bodied Germans to fight in the armed services. However, forced labor could scarcely be expected to work enthusiastically, and the setbacks of the "master race" in Russia and Italy undoubtedly contributed to a further decline in this foreign labor's will to work. Certain classes of the recruited workers were being treated decently, but other classes were not so fortunate. For example, the *International Labor Review* reported the Nazis have systematically maintained their "discriminatory racial policy against the millions of Soviet workers placed in German industry and agriculture," that the Soviet workers were housed in special barracks, given only limited medical care, were isolated from other groups, and grossly underpaid and overworked.[30] Much of Germany's forced labor was existing in a state of near-slavery.

The German home front did not suffer from an acute food shortage in 1943, although certain commodities (soap, for example) were very scarce. The Nazis had commandeered food supplies from occupied countries to make sure that the needs of the German population were met first. Germany's farm crop prospects in 1943 appeared normal. The first priority on food was held by the armed forces, followed by the hospitals, the people in bombed areas, children, and expectant mothers.

Outlook for the Germans. Allied capitals in the fall of 1943 were rife with rumors that Germany might be closer to capitulation than military experts would admit. In November Berlin was subjected to bombings of the intensity which had practically destroyed Hamburg, and the indicated meeting of Stalin, Churchill, Roosevelt might result in further impairment of German morale. But experts had to assume that the German armies would fight bitterly to build and maintain a wall of steel around their fatherland. German home production was still at an exceptionally high peak, and the output was good both in quantity and quality. The German worker and farmer were at once hard-working and patient, and their tenacity was further strengthened by their deep dread of a victorious Russia—and by the specter of a flaming revolt of the peoples in Europe. Furthermore, during most of 1943 the German home front hoped that dissension and cross-purposes among its major enemies would yet allow the Reich to win. The Moscow Conference did much to challenge that hope.

Japan

Military and economic consolidation. For the Japanese the question in 1943 was whether they could retain their recently occupied territories long enough to consolidate their military position, at the same time exploiting the resources of the new lands to a degree sufficient to make the war economy at home virtually impregnable. In large measure it was a race against time, because the naval and military offensive had passed to the United Nations.

On the home front the chief objective was to step up war production to the maximum level before the vast arsenal of the United States hit its full stride. In the spring of 1943 the Japanese Diet passed bills centralizing unprecedented power in Tojo. He was given authority to take over any Cabinet Minister's duties pertaining to "labor, materials, motive power and capital,"[31] to centralize those Japanese economic resources not already absorbed by the military socialism long developing in Japan. In October 1943 the industrial subsidiaries owned by the House of Mitsubishi were ordered to double their capital and sell half their stock to the government.[32] Observers in Washington assumed that this step paved the way for government control of the other large Japanese financial and industrial houses also. The Mitsubishi interests include shipbuilding, aircraft production, and steel—and these are three "Achilles heels" to Japan. Without adequate ships, aircraft, and steel she is bound to lose the war—and in all three she had serious shortages in 1943.

Production difficulties. The very existence of the Japanese Empire is contingent upon ships—ships to carry the raw materials of Malaya, the Philippines, the Dutch East Indies to the mother country, and to take back the finished products of Tokyo and Osaka, and ships to transport and provision the Emperor's armies. At the outbreak of war, Japan was estimated to have 6,300,000 tons of cargo shipping. With further construction and the seizure of vessels, the Japanese brought their shipping total to about 7,500,000 tons. However, on September 3, 1943, Secretary of the Navy Knox announced that of this 7,500,000 total, some 2,500,000 had been sent to the bottom.[33] The Japanese have done everything to overcome this heavy damage, including the construction of wooden ships, but the shipping shortage in 1943 seemed a problem which neither the naval nor the industrial chiefs were able to eliminate.

One of the reasons for the shipping shortage lay in the lack of adequate supplies of iron and steel. Whereas the United States in 1943 was producing around 95,000,000 tons of steel, Japan could only turn out some 8,000,000 tons. In a desperate effort to step up production, Tojo's economic planners have attempted the expansion of production facilities in Manchuria, Korea, China, and Japan proper, but it is reported that difficulties have been encountered in building blast furnaces. Prior to the outbreak of hostilities Japan fed her war machine to an important extent on the scrap iron purchased from the United States, and the countries which she has overrun have been systematically stripped. One of these sources of supply is now entirely cut off, while another possesses only limited iron and steel.

Before Pearl Harbor the world underrated the power and effectiveness of Japan's air force. The Zero fighter plane and its skilled pilot necessitated a change of attitude. Nevertheless American airplanes proved to be better armed and better protected, and Japanese planes were shot down in 1942 and 1943 in great numbers. The country's air force declined seriously, and it was evident in the fall of 1943 that the aircraft factories of Nagoya and Kobe could not begin to match the output of their enemies. The United States alone produces many times the maximum Japanese output. Allied experts who have studied Japan's industrial potential agree that a drastic shortage of machine tools will hinder any important increase in Japan's productive capacity in 1944.[34]

The home front had more to worry about than just the construction of airplanes. The country's heavy industry has been highly concentrated along a narrow southern coastal belt extending south some 600 miles from Tokyo to Nagasaki. The ability of the island empire to wage war depends upon the continuous-producing capacity of these industrial centers. The cities are largely of the "tinderbox" construction, and hence very inflammable. The Japanese have long realized their vulnerability. Accounts seeping through censorship indicated in 1943 that the Japanese population greatly feared repetition of the bombing raid carried out by Doolittle's men. Knowing the potency of the psychological as well as the military factor involved, many persons in the United States pressed for more and heavier bombings of Japan's principal cities. The Japanese realize that they will presently be subject to attack from bases in China, and the Philippines, and from aircraft carriers, whatever the stand of Russia on the use of her far-eastern bases. As a result, Tojo's planners have been engaged in working out a decentralization program for industry, and some of Japan's vital factories have been moved to Manchuria and China.

The Japanese were working much longer hours, and their living costs had at least doubled. All classes and ages were being drafted either for military purposes or essential war work. Students formerly exempted from the draft had their deferments canceled, and reports maintained that even Koreans and Formosans, hitherto regarded as untrustworthy, were to be conscripted. Many occupations were open to women only. Yet, despite the growing severity of wartime restrictions and sacrifices, and the admissions by high-ranking politicians and militarists that the war had entered a critical stage, the Japanese people apparently showed little or no signs of cracking.

Preparing for a long war. The enemies of Japan were forced to realize in 1943 that with her gains Japan was no longer a "have-not" nation. True, the Japanese war machine was handicapped by shortages in copper and nickel. But now the resources of Japan had been powerfully augmented by the rice of Indo-China and Thailand, sugar and chrome from the Philippines, lead and zinc from Burma, oil from the Dutch East Indies, antimony from China, and the prospect of nickel from the Celebes. Furthermore, Japan had at her command a potential slave labor force of a billion people, whom she was exploiting ruthlessly, but not without disguise. Every day the peoples of East Asia were bombarded by the constant refrain of "Asia for the Asiatics," by reference to Occidental imperialism before the war, by the promise (however hypocritical) of "co-prosperity" and "co-administrative" rule, and by the establishment in occupied lands of native puppet governments.

In November 1943 the "Co-Prosperity Sphere of Greater Asia" had scarcely been attained—but neither was Japan yet defeated. The Allies' attempts to wrest back their lost possessions island by island were about to be replaced by larger naval air operations against Japan proper and land operations via Burma, China, etc. The Japanese guessed this and were preparing for a long war. And in this struggle they were fanatical in the divine mission of their cause. Their whole conditioning and environment had made them unswerving, loyal subjects of the Emperor—and therefore of the military caste and industrial hierarchy which directed the policies of the Emperor. In the opinion of Ambassador Grew and others familiar with Japan, the Japanese would not crack until the bitter end. And it would be well to remember that they were always buoyed up by the proudest of national traditions: Japan had never lost a war. However, she had never fought a first-class foe—certainly never a coalition of first-class foes.

Summary

In reviewing events on the home fronts during 1942 and 1943, the fact that this has been a total war stands out in bold relief. True, the visitation of death and destruction has fallen upon particular peoples. But—and this is important in the broad historical perspective—all the peoples of the world have been subjected to the crucible of war.

Certain socio-economic trends can be discerned in all countries. One is the vast expansion and stepping-up of industrial processes. To thoughtful students everywhere this worldwide industrialization poses serious questions. If the prewar world suffered from technological unemployment, what is to happen in the postwar world where industrial facilities have been almost doubled? At the same time, no one doubts that, if properly handled, this unprecedented expansion makes possible a postwar standard of living capable of giving every man, woman, and child throughout the world a decent way of life.

Another unavoidable trend has been the growing importance of government controls and enterprise. In Allied and Axis lands alike, the state has been forced either to regulate basic industries and utilities, or to take them over outright. Many far-reaching decisions confront the people after the war as to their permanent disposition. For example, American taxpayers have paid out billions of dollars for plant expansion. Will those government-built facilities be maintained by the people, will they be turned over to private enterprise, or will there be some sort of joint management? This is symptomatic of a fundamental issue confronting every country after the war—the relative merits of economic individualism and collectivism.

A further interesting change in the industrial field has been that of decentralization. The whole trend has been toward spreading factories—and cities too—throughout the countryside; modern industrial life has demonstrated surprising mobility. One beneficial social result will probably be the continued growth of suburban and "garden" towns, and a more healthful environment for factory workers.

The exigencies of modern warfare have made for an intensification of the goal of national self-sufficiency. But this situation guarantees some serious postwar problems. More than one student is wondering whether the trend toward self-sufficiency does not carry with it the seeds of unbridled nationalism as well.

The problems which civilian populations have faced are to an unusual degree universal. Perhaps this is all to the good; for one day the war will be over, and all the peoples of the earth will have to learn to cooperate in building a new world society. The sacrifices which they have shared in common will motivate them toward a new understanding—without which even the most striking military victory must result only in social defeat.

SECTION 3

Preparing for Tomorrow

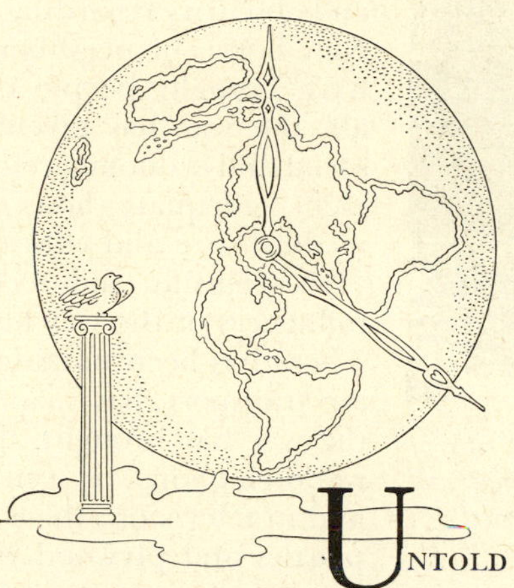

UNTOLD numbers of men and women in the United Nations ponder why two horrible world wars have occurred in less than thirty years. They are considering what may be done to lessen the danger of such periodic catastrophes and what can be accomplished toward general economic and social reform. Beyond victory they seek a way of life worth all the blood, sweat, and tears of the agonizing war years.

The First Steps

Peace agencies. Numerous agencies have been set up to study postwar problems, even among the handicapped refugee governments in London. In the United States at least 150 groups have been active, such as the Commission to Study the Organization of Peace, the Harvard-Radcliffe Bureau of International Research, the Institute of Pacific Relations, the Universities Committee on Postwar International Problems, and the Foreign Policy Association. In American business circles the Committee on Economic Development was set up in 1942 to study the gigantic problem of switching America's war industries to a peacetime economy. In the Federal Government the National Resources Planning Board, the Federal Reserve Board, the Treasury, and the State Department also carried on studies relating to the establishment of a lasting peace.

Outstanding in importance has been the work of the Church—Protestant, Catholic, and Jewish—in studying postwar problems. For example, the Protestant Federal Council of Churches of Christ has met twice and, with fourteen nations represented, produced the "Six Pillars of Peace," a specific program of collaboration for the postwar period.

New forces after the war. Wars are not detached military episodes significant only on the battlefield and unimportant as instruments of change in human affairs. They release new forces, accelerate the development of emerging ideas and institutions.

"Wars . . . sweep away the half-rotted structure of an old social and political order, and lay the foundations of a new. New trends germinating unseen beneath the surface are brought to a sudden maturity in the forcing-house of war. War begets new needs and new

"A platform is no good without steps" is the title of this cartoon by Bishop. Each must be strong, and there must be enough of them, to insure peace.

loyalties which help to determine social and political forms for the coming century."[1]

These words of the English historian E. H. Carr do not mean that war necessarily brings only desirable results, or that of itself it solves existing problems. The "new loyalties" and the "new trends" may contain serious negative qualities. The truth is that great conflicts leave behind them a complex pattern of results both good and bad, permanent and ephemeral. The important thing to keep in mind is that whether good or bad the consequences of war mean considerable modification of the traditional forms of society. As the British economist R. H. Tawney wrote: "The crisis confronting the world is not a mere interlude from which it can turn, when the last bomb has been dropped, to re-knit, with a sigh of relief, the broken threads of its existence."[2]

On the debit side of war there is the staggering expenditure of money for purely destructive purposes. The human cost in misery, lives lost, bodies maimed, and homes uprooted cannot be estimated. And with peace will come additional problems: the demobilization of soldiers, the scrapping or conversion of the huge war industrial installations, the resumption of world trade, the emergence of subjugated peoples' long-smoldering hatreds against their totalitarian oppressors—these and other problems.

But war has its credit side too. The horrors of total war have brought about in the minds of many men and women a new appreciation of the importance of international law and some cooperative way of enforcing it. Also in many lands the totalitarian menace to democracy has removed some of the complacency and obscurity regarding the aims of democracy. New bonds of neighborliness and mutual aid have brought people closer together. Above all, the war has given impetus to plans for social and economic reform: stabilized employment, adequate housing, and provision for medical care and educational services.

In scientific and technological realms, the influences of the war have been revolutionary. There has been notable progress in medicine; air transport has made unbelievable strides; the war has brought about rapid progress in radiotelephony, as seen in the "walkie-talkie," and in television; the war boom in transparent plastics and plywood will lead to many startling applications in furniture, automobile body design, and home building; the need of housing for war workers has accelerated experimentation in prefabrication; radar, the detector so vital in wartime, will in peacetime keep airplanes from flying blindly into mountains and keep ships from colliding; and finally processes of food concentration have been advanced.

The war, then, is both the means of self-protection and the opportunity for self-improvement. What can be gained from it depends upon the vision and purpose of the victors. More specifically, it depends upon their having a conscious desire to be prepared for the task of reconstruction. Mental unpreparedness for war almost fatally handicapped the Allies when Axis aggression came; unpreparedness for peace could prove even more disastrous, paving the way for future conflicts. On this point President Roosevelt has declared:

"In the process of our working and fighting for victory, we must never permit ourselves to forget the goal which is beyond victory. The defeat of Hitlerism is necessary so that there may be freedom; but this war, like the last war, will produce nothing but destruction unless we prepare for the future now."

The Period of Transition

Immediate and long-range aims. Most students of postwar conditions visualize a settling-down process after the war in two distinct stages. The first, a relatively brief period of from three to ten years, will be concerned largely with the problems of disarming the Axis powers, evacuating them from conquered countries, policing their territory, punishing war criminals, returning refugee governments and prisoners to their countries, and bringing relief to millions of needy people all over the world. The second, growing out of the first period, will be concerned with setting up healthy trade relations throughout the world, rehabilitating industry and agriculture in war-devastated areas, cooperating with liberal and peace-desiring elements in the vanquished countries in order to establish stable governments, and, above all, building up the international machinery to reduce the factors which have led to war in the past and, if necessary, to coerce nations which break the peace and embark on aggression.

Kinds of treaties. Some authorities believe two types of treaties should be arranged.[3] The first would be a Preliminary Treaty imposed on the Axis countries, and would take care of insistent conditions: disarmament, demobilization, relief, and provisional boundaries. The Final Treaty, drawn up at an International Congress, would be not imposed but negotiated with the defeated powers. Boundaries would be definitely fixed; specific conditions laid down for the return of defeated powers to full nationhood; long-range plans made for international cooperation in trade, emigration of peoples, and access to raw materials. At this congress steps would also be taken to set up some form of league, federation, or alliance to enforce the Final Treaty. This two-stage treaty process would have a distinct advantage over the procedure in 1919, when all problems regardless of their short- or long-time character were settled in one conference.

Problems of the Transition. Whatever treaty plan is followed, the Transitional Period will be concerned with the following major problems: (1) relief in war devastated areas; (2) restoration of legal governments in Axis conquered lands; (3) occupation and policing of Axis territory; and (4) transition from a war to a peace economy in all nations.

Relief and rehabilitation. The problem of relief and rehabilitation following the war will be the most acute in the history of the world. During the first two years of war the Axis powers overran thirty-five countries with a population of more than half a billion people. The Chinese have suffered worse than the people of the South Pacific battle areas, who may rely on jungle products and who do not need warm clothing; but the Europeans have suffered worst of all.

In Europe needed raw materials can no longer be imported, and what is available in Europe is taken by the Nazis. Factories have been dismantled by the Germans for scrap and machinery to be used in making armaments. Whole districts, once good farmland, are no longer cultivated, for the farm workers have been sent as forced labor to Germany. Agricultural machinery has rusted or been taken to Germany. Livestock has been slaughtered to provide meat for the Nazi army. In July 1943 Herbert Lehman wrote, "Never before has the world witnessed so ruthless a despoliation of so many in so short a time."[4] Malnutrition in Europe is universal. Thousands have already died of disease and lingering starvation. Unless provision is made for the immediate distribution of food, clothing, and medical supplies, a horrible period of famine and plague seems likely.

It will be recalled that in 1941 representatives of eleven Allied countries approved the Atlantic Charter, agreeing "That it is their common aim to secure that supplies of food, raw materials, and articles of prime necessity should be made available for the postwar needs of the countries liberated from Nazi oppression."[5] The conference created an Inter-Allied Relief Committee. The entry of the United States into the war, and behind it the resources of the entire Western Hemisphere, accelerated the relief movement inaugurated in London. During the summer of 1942, members of the Committee conferred with American officials in Washington. The next step was the creation of a Joint Wheat Council, consisting of representatives of the great wheat countries—the United States, Canada, Australia, and Argentina. It has been given charge of a relief pool of one hundred million bushels of wheat.

SOME JOBS FOR THE UNITED NATIONS RELIEF ORGANIZATION

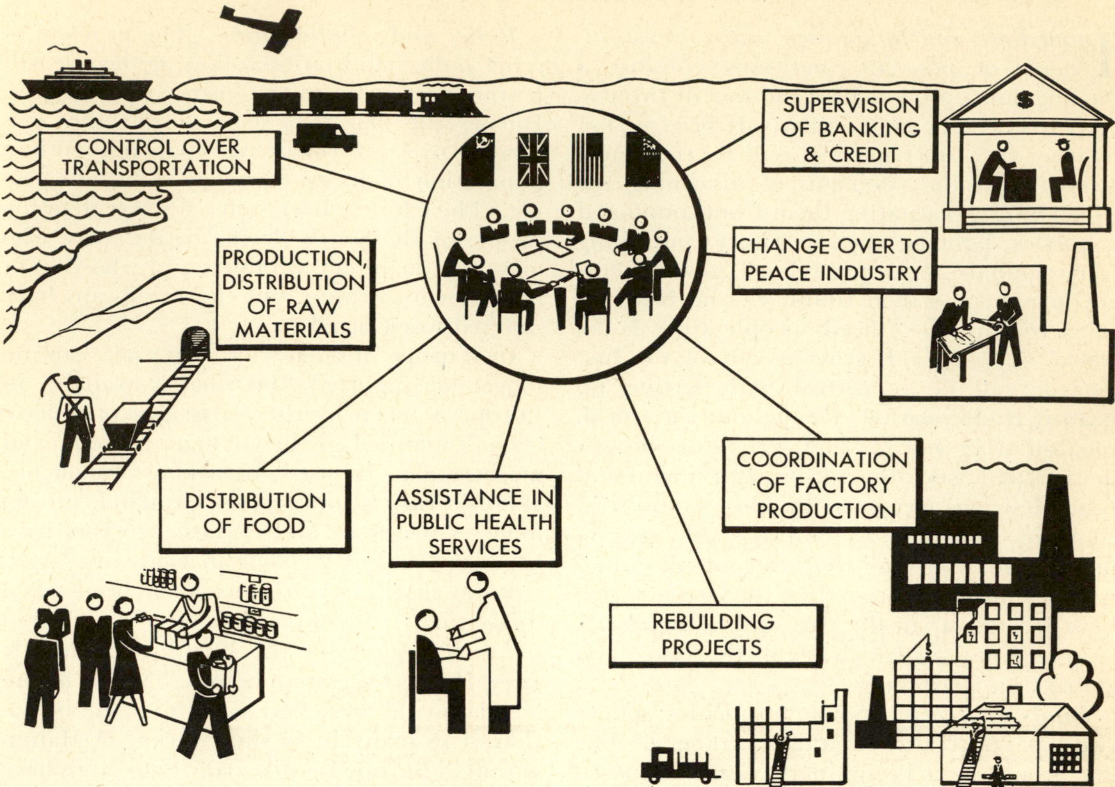

Late in 1942, President Roosevelt created a special agency to take over plans for relief, the Office of Foreign Relief and Rehabilitation (abolished in September 1943, its functions being shifted to a newly-created Foreign Economic Administration). In May 1943 he further advanced postwar relief plans by convening a United Nations Conference on Food and Agriculture. This Conference, held at Hot Springs, Virginia, was attended by over 500 delegates representing 45 nations. While immediate postwar needs were considered, the Food Conference dealt with more fundamental and long-range problems concerning freedom from want. It was emphasized that many peoples of the world do not have sufficient food even in peace time, that a world agricultural policy is essential.

The planning for a United Nations Relief and Rehabilitation Administration was heartening. The agency was to provide "food, fuel, clothing and other basic necessities, housing facilities, medical and other essential services" for victims of war in any area under United Nations control.

The UNRRA, as the agency is called, would consist of a Director General, a Council, and a Central Committee. Representatives of all interested nations would make up the Council, dealing largely with matters of policy. The Central Committee, consisting of representatives of the United States, Great Britain, China, and Russia, would represent the Council when that body was not in session.

The agency was definitely formed when representatives of 44 nations signed an agreement in Washington and on November 12 convened at Atlantic City.

There are some people who criticize proposals to feed the hungry abroad on the basis that "charity begins at home" and that the United States should hardly be expected "to give away" her own food and clothing. Others agree with Herbert Lehman:

"If we have learned anything from the decades just behind us it is this: that we cannot, even if we would, make ourselves secure in a world in which millions of men, women, and children are dying of want or epidemic.

. . . If the United States is to have any hope of lasting peace and a stable world economy, it must help see to it that the liberated peoples of the world are restored as rapidly as possible to a self-sustaining basis."[6]

Restoration of governments. The second major problem of the Transitional Period is the restoration of government in lands freed from Axis rule. The majority of these countries already have exile governments which have adhered to the principles of the Atlantic Charter, kept in constant touch with underground movements in their occupied lands, and contributed substantial amounts of money and men in the common cause. The exile governments of Poland, Czechoslovakia, Yugoslavia, Belgium, the Netherlands, Luxemburg, Greece, Norway, and France have been recognized by the Big Four (the United States, Britain, Russia, and China). Will such governments be acceptable to the people, who perhaps have developed new leaders and new ideas about government during the period of Axis domination? Such exile governments as have been recognized by the Big Four may be restored with their aid until the wishes of the people have been determined. In the interim it is likely that some form of United Nations occupation will be sought to maintain order, administer relief, and supervise the creation of a legitimate government acceptable to the majority of people. Where the political desires of a people are complicated and rent with factionalism, this work will be difficult.

Following World War I, there was a tendency of the newly-formed central European states to defy or ignore recommendations made in the general peace. Minor wars ensued and territorial arrangements were set aside. It has been suggested that the exile governments be restored "only in accordance with (1) their acceptance throughout the period of transition of the supreme authority of the United Nations; (2) their willingness to get along with their neighbors; (3) their acceptability to their people and their chances of keeping order."[7]

Administering Axis territory. The occupation and administration of Axis territory will be a third major task during the Transition. Disarmament of the Axis powers as described in the Atlantic Charter would be impossible without successful policing of this territory. Following World War I, Allied troops of occupation were stationed in the German Rhineland district until 1930, and certain Allied commissions operated in Germany until 1927. It is likely that occupation forces will cover a much wider area in Germany after this war. In addition there will be Japan, if not Italy, to consider. The U. S. Army School of Military Government at Charlottesville, Virginia, has trained a large number of officers for this work. The British Army has a Civil Affairs Service whose personnel also is prepared to take over this job of administration.

A preview of AMG (Allied Military Government) was given in Sicily. Within a week of the British-American amphibious invasion of Sicily, the system was established on this island. It was a combined American and British régime, secretly planned long before the invasion took place. The proclamation setting up the new administration assured Sicilians that rule was to be benevolent, that when possible, administration would be through the peoples' own officials, although all Fascist officials would be removed from office. It also promised the people food, rationed by AMG. It is worth while noting additional provisions:

"Freedom of religious worship will be upheld and the position of the Catholic Church and all religious institutions will be respected.

All laws which discriminate on the basis of race, creed, or color will be annulled.

Physical symbols of the culture of true Italy, buildings, libraries, monuments, archives, and works of art will be protected from damage.

Within military necessity free press and free speech will be promulgated.

Those accused of crimes against the Allies will be tried by Allied military courts under AMG."

Mediterranean operations have been an all British, Canadian, and American performance and AMG reflects this fact. In the administration of Germany, however, conditions will be different. In 1943 it appeared certain that Soviet forces would conquer and occupy larger areas of at least eastern and central Europe than would American and British forces. This raises the question of whether the system of military occupation will vary from area to area depending on what United Nations force is in occupation, or whether agreement among all the United Nations will

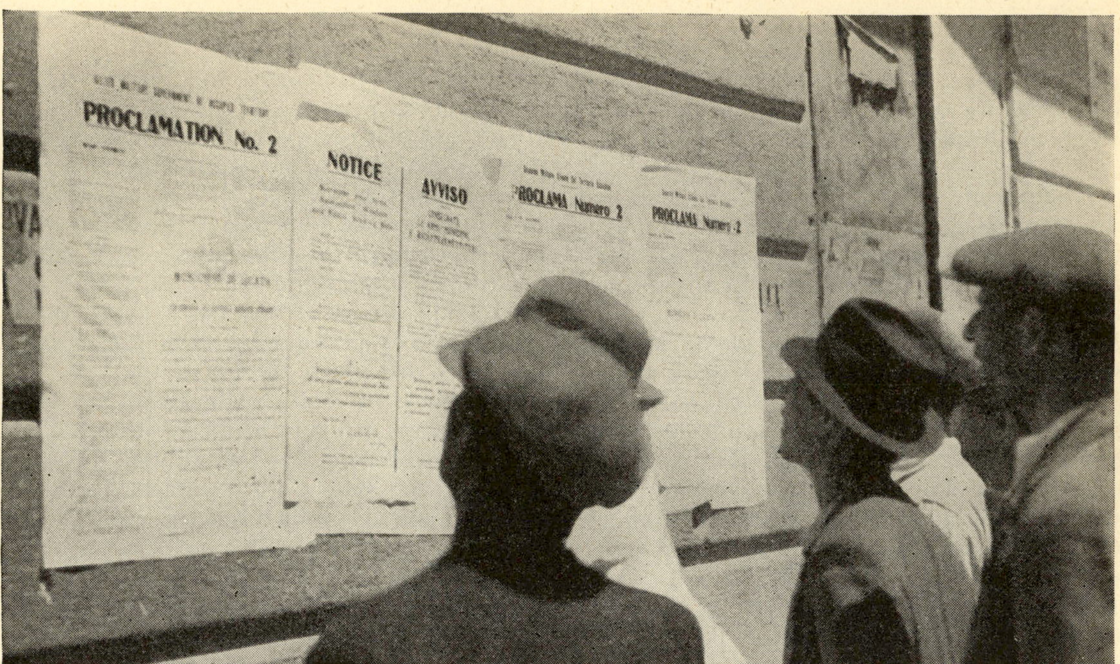

Italian citizens of Sicily are interested in the proclamation put up by the AMG. The Italians are being assured of good treatment if Allied orders are obeyed.

result in a common system. No word on this important point had been given to the public in the fall of 1943.

Transition to a peace economy. Success in the Transitional Period will depend largely upon how soon and how smoothly the economy of the world is shifted from production for war to production for peace. There can be little assistance to the rest of the world if the United Nations, especially the United States, have millions of demobilized soldiers and former war workers unemployed in their own countries.

Broadcasting to the British Empire and the United States in the spring of 1943, Churchill proposed a Four-Year Economic Plan for the period of transition and reconstruction. Numerous organizations in Britain, such as the Association of British Chambers of Commerce, the Federation of British Industries, and the National Institute of Economic and Social Research, have also made specific recommendations to ensure speedy return to a healthy economic condition after the war.

The problem of economic transition will be most difficult in the United States, however, where the largest industrial resources in the world were geared and expanded. In midsummer 1943, it was estimated that 60 per cent of the United States industrial capacity was devoted to war needs, and that despite the millions of men in the armed services, employment figures for men and women reached 52 million.

The United States, like Britain, has been looking ahead to these problems. There are, for example, the peace agencies already mentioned (p. 53). There are also many far-seeing business executives who are laying plans for the changeover from weapons to refrigerators, automobiles, radios, helicopters, and other consumer goods of peace.

Perhaps the most comprehensive study of postwar economic problems in the United States was that made by the National Resources Planning Board. In the spring of 1943 the findings of the N.R.P.B. were sent to Congress in two reports. These dealt with the general topic of social security and the role government should take in the postwar economic situation. The most controversial aspect of the Board's recommendations was that the federal government should consider various types of partnership in such war-expanded industries as aluminum, shipbuilding, aircraft, and magnesium. In the fall of 1943 it was not clear how Congress would finally act on the

Board's proposals, but the Congress of 1943 had voted against a continuation of the Board.

Considerable attention was also given to President Roosevelt's recommendations for the demobilization of the U.S. armed forces, made in a nation-wide broadcast on July 28, 1943:

1. Mustering-out pay to every member of the armed forces and merchant marine when he or she is honorably discharged, large enough to cover a reasonable period of time between his discharge and the finding of a new job.

2. In case no job is found after diligent search, then unemployment insurance if the individual registers with the United States Employment Service.

3. An opportunity for members of the armed services to get further education or trade training at the cost of their government.

4. Allowance of credit to all members of the armed forces, under unemployment compensation and Federal old-age and survivors' insurance, for their period of service. They should be treated as if they had continued their employment in private industry.

5. Improved provisions for the hospitalization of the armed forces and merchant marine.

6. Sufficient pensions for disabled members of the armed forces.

Many students of economics urge that some of the war agencies and wartime controls should not be disbanded immediately following peace. To do so would invite the sudden dislocation of a complex system of production and distribution. It is likely, therefore, that the United Nations will continue cooperatively to control shipping, foreign exchange, and the allocation of certain raw materials. Within each of the victorious nations it is possible that rationing and price ceilings will be kept for a limited period.

Relief in the war areas, restoration of governments, occupation and policing of Axis territory, shift from a war to a peace economy—these are the immediate problems of the Transitional Period. Beyond these, observers say, lie at least five long-term aims: (1) reduction of the hazard of war, (2) perfection and encouragement of democracy, (3) advancement of colonial peoples, (4) achievement of freedom from want, (5) economic cooperation.

Reduction of the Hazard of War

First aim of the United Nations. The question of boundaries and political self-determination, the treatment of Axis states, and the establishment of some form of international cooperation to preserve peace constitute the crux of the first postwar aim of the United Nations—reduction of the hazard of war.

Boundary questions. The map of the world will show many changes involving more than a mere return to the *status quo* before 1939. In certain cases there will be little difficulty for the boundary fixers. For example, the historic outlines of Norway, Denmark, Holland, Greece, Belgium, and France will probably be re-created. But there are many areas where clear-cut decisions will be difficult to make. Undoubtedly an independent Czechoslovakia will emerge after the war; but will the German-speaking Sudeten region be joined to the Czech state as it was in 1919? In Poland it seems likely that Russia may claim the eastern portions taken in the summer of 1939 when the Nazis overran the country from the west. This claim would be based on certain historic and racial factors. Again—will Austria remain with Germany or will it prefer to be set up anew as an independent state? Here perhaps a plebiscite might be resorted to in settling the problem. The status of the Lilliputian Baltic states—Lithuania, Latvia, and Estonia—is at present confused. The Soviet Union after ejecting the German armies may well wish to absorb these states into the Union rather than see them return to their precarious independence of 1919-1940. The ghost of the Polish Corridor will also rise at the Peace Conference. Poles have historic arguments for such a corridor as well as the logic of immediate economic needs; on the other hand a corridor between eastern and western Prussia would be objectionable to the Germans.

The problems involved in determining the dimension and the status of nations are most complex in Europe, but a global war raises similar problems all over the world. Manchuria will in all likelihood be given back to China after the dozen or so years of Japanese rule. But how about Hong Kong? The Chinese government may not urge its immediate cession to China by Great Britain following the ejection of the Japanese, but the gradual liquidation of British control over this Chinese island seems inevitable. After over a quarter century of Japanese rule, the Koreans are more than ever resolved to be free and masters of their own destiny. An independent Korean state, therefore, may join the family of nations as a result of the Allied victory.

Political determination. Changes in political status will occur in what may be termed the Colonial World. The United States has pledged itself to underwrite a free Philippine Commonwealth; Britain has promised to give India independence after the war; and Ethiopia will continue to be free of Italian Fascist rule. Certain strategic islands in the Pacific mandated to Japan in 1919 after the First World War may well be taken from her to be administered by members of the United Nations. The future of Italy's African colonies, Tripoli, Libya, Somaliland, Eritrea, remains uncertain; their disposal may be left primarily to Great Britain and the United States, the powers most responsible for ridding Africa of Axis rule. As for such Axis-conquered colonies as Burma, British Malaya, the Dutch East Indies, and Dutch-Australian New Guinea, it appears to be taken for granted by the former imperial powers that victory will see their colonial rule reëstablished. The question of colonies is further examined on page 64.

Treatment of the Axis countries. While there is wide acceptance of unconditional surrender, disarmament, and punishment of war criminals as factors in the treatment of defeated nations, there is much disagreement over many other issues. Germany usually has been singled out as the most serious problem. Even before the events of September 1943, Italy was not generally regarded as a menace. Comparatively little has been said about what should be done to Japan, though she is considered the most fanatical. Perhaps this is because the great powers of the West naturally regard as most dangerous the aggressive tendencies of a state among their own number. Probably they feel, also, that a victorious Russia and a constantly more progressive China can easily keep Japan in check. Furthermore, they know that in industrial potential, Japan—unless she is permitted to utilize the great resources of her new colonial empire—is far behind Germany, Russia, Britain, and the United States.

On the treatment of Germany, opinion is divided. There are two main schools. The first believes that the Germans' astounding rise to political and economic power from 1870-1914 made them a "bumptious, conceited, aggressive people"; and that long before the Nazis came along a philosophy had taken root, compounded of the master-race idea, the decadence of democracy, the nobility of war, and the rightness of ruthlessness for a chosen people to achieve its "destiny." This school believes further that: (1) the Germans should be defeated on their own soil; (2) disarmament must be complete; (3) a system of policing must prevent rearmament; (4) all property stolen or destroyed by the Germans must be restored; (5) liberated peoples should be fed first, before Germany; (6) Germans accused of crimes must be tried and punished if found guilty.[8] (A blacklist of 4000 Nazi criminals has been prepared; it is based on evidence obtained by the Polish underground and smuggled into London.) In effect, in the words of Bernadotte Schmitt, "The only sensible course is to give the Germans a strong dose of their own medicine. . . . We cannot bribe the Germans to behave. They must learn, from hard and bitter experience, that their political philosophy leads them only to misery and disaster."[9]

The second school, while not eliminating retribution and punishment where merited, supports a moderate treatment. It believes that Germany was led to war by a relatively small clique that bullied and hypnotized the masses. The German nation, it is argued, should not be partitioned; pernicious elements within it must be destroyed, but for the bulk of the people there should be the opportunity to participate with other great nations in the common tasks of civilization.

Supporting this moderate approach to the German problem, the English historian E. H. Carr has written: "The modern world is not so richly endowed with ability and resourcefulness that it can light-heartedly cast out from its midst as irredeemably bad, a nation possessing, in combination with many grave defects, so many valuable attributes."[10] Even Joseph Stalin has declared that the aim of Russia is the destruction of the Hitlerite state and its leaders only, and he adds, "It is impossible to destroy Germany, just as it is impossible to destroy Russia."

The second school believes that the principle of monetary payments, which after World War I placed a tremendous burden on Germany, should be abandoned for one utilizing German labor and technical facilities in rebuilding the war-torn areas of Europe. Above all, the United Nations should carry on "the most stupendous experiment for reëducation the world has ever witnessed."[11] The task would be "to encourage the work of groups and individuals in Germany who share the ideas of the United Nations and can advance them in terms understandable to the German people."[12] It should be explained to the Germans that as soon as they proved they no longer followed the Nazi ideology, ample opportunity would be offered to join the United Nations on a basis of equality. This view seems to be held by the majority of Englishmen.

Some observers advocate the fragmentation of Germany. Other students point out that the splitting up of Germany would seriously disrupt the economic unity of Central Europe.

The problem seems well-nigh insoluble. European peace apparently demands a weak, divided Germany, but the reconstruction and future prosperity of the continent is dependent in large measure upon the industry of a strong, united Germany. The solution may well be the strengthening of liberal elements, as mentioned above. Perhaps the best approach does not involve so much emphasis upon Germany's territorial extent but upon Allied supervision of Germany's industrial potential. German business could be prevented from serving war and could be directed to constructive purposes for the greater benefit of the German people.

The demarcation of boundaries and the solution of German and Japanese problems have direct bearing on the prospects of peace. The most challenging question, however, is what political arrangements for national security and world peace should be made.

The Hemispherists' plan. The Hemispherists repudiate any allegiance to a re-created League of Nations. They believe that security for the United States will be achieved best by a policy of hemisphere solidarity, of building up and maintaining the armed forces of the United States and securing common defense arrangements with the Latin American republics as well as Canada. At the same time the peace of the world would be served by the Americas' non-interference in the great regional political systems set up elsewhere for the same purposes.

The Geopoliticians' plan. Opposed to the Hemispherists' plan, the Geopoliticians believe that American foreign policy must be predicated on a broader geographical basis than the Western Hemisphere. In a world compressed by modern invention, the United States must seek its friends and thwart its enemies all over the globe. The primary purpose would be the maintenance of a balance of power throughout the world favorable to the United States. Alliances would be made with any nation whose interests paralleled our own, and following the war care would be taken not to make China or Russia too strong. Thus N. J. Spykman observes: "The danger of another Japanese conquest of Asia must be removed, but this does not inevitably mean the complete elimination of Japan and the surrender of the Western Pacific to China or Russia."[13]

The Geopoliticians side with the Hemispherists, however, in repudiating membership in any world organization. "If the foreign policy of a state is to be practical," asserts Spykman, "it should be designed not in terms of some dream world but in terms of the realities of international relations, in terms of power politics. The international community is without government, without a central authority to preserve law and order, and it does not guarantee the member states either their territorial integrity, their political independence, or their rights under international law."[14]

Plans for international organization. In contrast with the ideas of the Hemispherists and Geopoliticians there are the plans which insist upon the creation of some form of international organization with cooperative machinery to maintain world peace. Interest in such a program has been widespread. The Atlantic Charter pledged the United States and Great Britain to work for "the establishment of a wider and permanent system of general security." In the Moscow Conference of October 1943, representatives of Russia, China, England, and the United States expressed their approval of a world organization. On October 6, leaders of the Protestant, Catholic, and Jewish faiths in the United States united in a statement of seven main principles, advocating international collaboration.

The adherents of international organization for peace condemn Nazi Germany for plunging the world into war in 1939. But they place the blame, more fundamentally, on the perpetuation of the national state system, in which the states do not have to answer for their acts to a higher body representing the collective interests of mankind. It is argued that the real responsibility for the Second World War is shared by men and women in all lands, who failed to create an effective system of collective security after the first war, allowing the Axis powers to terrorize the world. The lawbreaker bears the most obvious responsibility, but behind it is the absence of cooperative effort to limit lawlessness.

Plan to revive the League. Among the various plans for the establishment of some form of world organization, one proposal calls for the resuscitation and strengthening of the old League of Nations. In spite of handicaps imposed by the war this organization still continues its valuable work on a diminished scale. A skeleton staff of about eighty remains at Geneva to keep up the records. One department has been removed to Princeton and another to Montreal, where they are working on postwar economic problems. The League of Nations is, then, very much alive; forty-five members still pay their annual dues. In the 1942 *Report* of the Acting Secretary-General of the League, it was stated that the various agencies of this body are "ready at the appropriate moment to take their respective parts in the reconstruction of the world or to serve as the foundations on which the new order can be built."[15]

Although there are strong supporters for a revived League, majority opinion among those advocating international organization seems to be opposed to it. In place of its loose system of sovereign states which failed to achieve united action in the face of emergency, a more binding system is desired. This calls either for world federation outright or at least for regional federation with the machinery of each geographical unit loosely tied to some international body.

Plans for world federation. One of the outstanding publicists of federation has been Clarence Streit. In *Union Now*, published in 1939, he advocated the federation of fifteen democracies—the democracies of Europe, the members of the British Commonwealth, and the United States. After Nazi Germany's conquests in Europe in 1940-1941, Mr. Streit in *Union Now With Britain* urged the immediate union of the United States with the British Commonwealth as a nucleus for a wider union after the war. In these federal plans the member states definitely cede powers relating to citizenship, defense, trade, currency, and some powers of taxation to the federal government consisting of a two-house legislature, a five-man executive board, and a high court.

More ambitious is the plan of Ely Culbertson, which would set up a super-federal government for the entire world. In it eleven regional federations, such as American, British, Latin-European, North European, Middle Eastern, are suggested. These would then be a part of a World Federation made up of a Legislature, a World Supreme Court, a World Court of Equity, and a World Police Force.

Another scheme for federalism on a global scale was advanced by Harold E. Stassen while Governor of Minnesota. This calls for the continuance of the present alliance of the United Nations and its expansion into a United Nations of the World. In his words:

"Through a gradual development over a period of years, we should reach a point eventually where a United Nations government of limited powers would function in seven major fields: (1) temporary administration of Axis, backward, or disputed territories; (2) maintenance of a police force; (3) regulation of international airways; (4) supervision of sea gateways; (5) stimulation of trade; (6) promotion of health and literacy; and (7) enforcement through a court of a basic code of justice."[16]

Plans for interlocking regional federations. Less ambitious than outright world federation are the plans for regional federation which envisage groups of states in an interlocking association in preference to a single league or union. One such proposal, called the World Commonwealth plan,[17] would set up (1) an Inter-American System; (2) the Soviet Union; (3) Europe; (4) a Far Eastern Association consisting of China, Japan, India, and an Indonesian Union (the Philippines, Burma, Dutch East Indies, British Malaya, Thailand, and Indo-China); (5) perhaps a Mohammedan League in the Near East; and (6) a possible British Commonwealth System in which Great

Britain would to some extent withdraw from the European System. Such groupings would be represented in an international organization. This would consist of an Assembly and World Court, together with various other bodies dealing with international economics, human welfare, colonies, and scientific and cultural cooperation. The regionalists depend upon each regional federation to maintain peace within its own political orbit. Each federation, therefore, would have a central governmental body empowered to enforce its will in stipulated matters over its member states. No provision is made for an international police force with authority over the member federations. The hope would be that consultations and negotiations between the various federations in the international Assembly would discourage war between regional groupings.

Plans have been advanced especially for the federation of Europe. Some of these proposals call for the complete federation of the entire continent. While these are only paper schemes as yet, already definite steps have been made by some European states in the direction of limited European regional federation. In 1942 the Polish and Czechoslovakian governments in exile drew up a plan for confederation in Central Europe; and in the Greek-Yugoslav agreement made in the same year, plans were also drawn for a Balkan Union.

Dominance of the Big Four. In the planning for postwar political organization there is general agreement on one point. Postwar international politics will begin with the dominance of the leading powers of the United Nations: the United States, Russia, China, and Britain. After disarmament and occupation of Axis countries, power in the world will be in their hands. Some observers, then, believe future world organization should grow out of the hegemony of the United Nations. In *U. S. Foreign Policy: Shield of the Republic,* Walter Lippmann asserts the interests of the United States and the peace of the world can best be served by the formation of a "nuclear alliance" between Britain, China, Russia, and the United States.

Anthony Eden and other British statesmen have pointedly stressed that the Big Four mean to hold the peace after victory. At the same time it is agreed that as soon as possible other states must be allowed to play their part, the dominance of the Big Four thus giving way to an expanded international system.

Some contend that it may be wiser, though not so spectacular, to follow this policy of gradualism. Payson S. Wild expresses it thus:

"Out of the links now connecting the United Nations may be forged firm bonds for permanent collaboration. International government created in this unspectacular fashion may lack the glamour that might be associated with a great charter or a solemn covenant, but it should be remembered that international arrangements developing in an *ad hoc* manner may prove stronger and have a far sounder basis for the future than a special new edifice created at one stroke of the pen."[18]

Already the United Nations have established an amazing structure of international collaboration in shipping, military strategy, standardization of military equipment, and monetary policy. Plans for postwar economic collaboration have also been laid down in the various Lend-Lease agreements made by the Allies.

It is argued on the other hand that the situation of the world today may be parallel to the situation of America in 1787, when the loosely joined states—finally realizing their great need for a strong union—assembled in convention, argued out their differences (including questions of "sovereignty"), and within a relatively brief period created the system of federal government embodied in the American Constitution.

In conclusion, the trend of public opinion in both the British Commonwealth of Nations and the United States appears to be in favor of association with some international organization rather than a return to isolationism or the operation of power politics. Isolationism, so long entrenched in United States philosophy, has not of course been one hundred per cent superseded. But Gallup Polls; the polls of *Fortune* and the National Opinion Research Center of the University of Denver; the developments in the Republican Party (which in 1919 opposed United States entry in the League); and Congressional action, in particular the adoption by overwhelming majorities of the strengthened Connally resolution in the Senate and the Fulbright resolution in the House—all indicate support of United States adherence to a world system of collective security.

Perfection and Encouragement of Democracy

Second aim of the United Nations. The United Nations' second aim, to perfect and encourage democracy, is closely related to the first—the prevention of war. Only when we have ultimately a universal democracy protecting all individuals and groups will we have an enduring world state and lasting peace.

Democracy, like everything else in life, can suffer from complacency. In the 1920's and early 1930's the democracies of the world were severely criticized for their lack of leadership, for the apathy of the electorate, for putting politics above patriotism, for giving democracy a too narrow definition, or for their lack of dynamic political faith. Such accusations were true in greater or less degree in many of the countries possessing representative institutions.

The future of democracy at home and abroad depends upon the answers given to the following questions: (1) What can be done to strengthen and perfect democracy at home? In particular what can be done to extend economic democracy along with political democracy? (2) What can be done to encourage the growth of democratic institutions in the Axis countries? (3) What can be done to foster self-government among the so-called backward and colonial peoples of the world? The latter question will be taken up in the general discussion of the advancement of colonial peoples.

Democracy in the democracies. The Second World War has done much to quicken a new respect for democratic government among those people who have been fortunate enough to retain their representative institutions and among those conquered people who look to the day when such governments can be restored. Democracy has therefore to a large extent been revitalized and has met the challenge laid down by one of its champions, the eminent German novelist, Thomas Mann, who declared: "It should put aside the habit of taking itself for granted, of self-forgetfulness. It should . . . renew and rejuvenate itself by again becoming aware of itself."[19]

Renewal of faith is fundamental, but important too is a determination to broaden the definition and improve the techniques of democracy. The democratic way of life cannot be static but must be prepared to adapt itself to the demands of a rapidly changing world. In one country this may mean working for a better civil service, in another higher pay for legislators, in another greater protection of minority groups, in another new techniques to interest the electorate in governmental issues. As Charles E. Merriam expressed it, "Democracy is not merely something to be defended and preserved . . . but an ideal to be developed and enriched, a constant approximation to higher standards of living and higher levels of the good life."[20]

Democracy for other countries. Should the United States, following victory, attempt to universalize democratic government? It is argued that the world is too small for totalitarianism and democracy to exist side by side, and that one or the other will have to go. However, it is admitted that every people should have the right to choose its own form of government and that no democratic country should force its own way of life upon unwilling peoples, that the object of universalizing democracy does not necessarily involve coercion. Much can be done by assisting liberal elements everywhere and by showing that the democratic system is the way of the richer and more abundant life.

Advancement of Colonial Peoples

Third aim of the United Nations. The third basic aim toward which the United Nations are working is the protection and advancement of the world's colonial peoples. The question of self-government for these peoples has been raised in the discussion of democracy. While the Allies fight to free subjugated peoples from Axis imperialism, it is natural that a great deal of criticism should be leveled against any form of empire in which colonial subjects are denied the right of self-government. From many quarters there has come the demand that imperialism of any sort must go.

As has been said, India and the Philippines have been promised self-government. There are other colonial areas where self-government may soon be possible, as in Ceylon and Burma.

In British Malaya, however, 37 per cent of the population are Malays, 42 per cent are Chinese, and 13 per cent are Indians. In this area the question would be: self-government for whom and according to which set of ideas? A similar mixed racial situation exists in other colonial areas. In Fiji the native people are outnumbered by the Chinese and Indians. In Africa, the native populations of the tropical colonies are split into dozens of tribes with no tradition of cooperation to hold them together. Would self-government mean independence for each of these many tribes? Furthermore, such tribes are only just emerging from a primitive culture and are utterly unable to cope with the complexities of the modern world now.

Except in the more advanced areas, then, supervision and protection of colonial areas must be continued in some form. Such colonies could be pooled and placed under the control of some supervisory body connected with a world organization. Or the colonial powers could continue the administration of their colonies but in cooperation with some international agency.

Colonial Charter. An influential body of opinion in Britain has advocated the creation of a Colonial Charter to be formulated and agreed to by all members of the United Nations. The Charter would stipulate that (1) colonies should be administered on the basis of benevolent guardianship; (2) the people should be trained for eventual self-government where possible; (3) the colonies should be developed economically both for the interests of the native people and for the world in general; and (4) the principle of the Open Door should permit economic equality for all nations in such colonial areas. The important consideration is to ensure that control and administration are free from exploitation.

The principles of the Colonial Charter are not entirely new. They were contained in the machinery of colonial mandates set up by the League of Nations in 1919. However, the League did not possess sufficient supervisory power over such mandates, though it provided that "There should be an annual examination of the mandatory by the Mandates Commission."

Colonial trusteeship has been developed independently, too, especially by Britain. In 1923, for example, Britain refused to grant local self-government to the British settlers in the African colony of Kenya because the members of the British government "regard themselves as exercising a trust on behalf of the African population, and they are unable to delegate or to share this trust, the object of which may be defined as the protection and advancement of the Native races."[21] British colonies are no longer regarded as "possessions." Increased attention has been given to native education, agriculture, and medical needs for which the Colonial Development Fund provides. The system of Indirect Rule has been successful in providing natives with increased responsibilities in self-government.

The future of colonies constitutes one of the great basic contemporary problems. If an effective and truly international league with a colonial pool fails to eventuate with the peace—the ideal solution for colonies not yet prepared for the responsibility of self-government—the alternative is the perpetuation of colonial systems administered by nation states. If such powers progressively expand the principle of colonial trusteeship or the technique of a Colonial Charter underwritten by all members of the United Nations, the tutelage of colonial peoples will be benevolent and their prospects for ultimate equality in the family of nations certain.

Freedom from Want

Fourth aim of the United Nations. Postwar political relationships both within and between nations have been considered so far. Of comparable importance is the improvement of the economic structure, within countries and between countries. Thus the fourth and fifth basic objectives of the United Nations are freedom from want and improvement of international economic cooperation.

The Second World War has accelerated the process of inquiry and reform in economic systems. From every side have come appeals to eliminate or reduce economic evils. Pope Pius XII, speaking to the world on Christmas Day, 1940, urged that every state be given "the medium necessary for insuring the proper standard of living for its own citizens of every rank."[22] Mr. Eden, the British statesman, has said, "Never again must we tolerate chronic unemployment, extremes of wealth and poverty, slums, and the lack of opportunity for so many which disfigured our national life in the past."[23] Vice-President Henry A. Wallace has declared, "The peace must mean a better standard of living for the common man";[24] and President Roosevelt's Four Freedoms include "freedom from want" for his own and as far as possible for all peoples.

The laissez-faire approach. There are three main types of plans to eliminate poverty and unemployment. The first would leave the capitalist system more or less as it is at present, and perhaps even eliminate recent innovations interfering with the laissez-faire principle, which calls for the very minimum of governmental control. It is asserted that governmental supervision and regulation of business results in capricious and uninformed bureaucracy; that the taxation of the ambitious and successful elements in society for the provision of economic security has a dangerous tendency to subsidize the shiftless and penalize the efficient and productive; that anything beyond certain minimum governmental controls slows down initiative and results in bureaucratic centralization menacing individual freedom. The kernel of argument is the so-called Fifth Freedom—"To be free, men must choose their callings, bargain for their own services, save and provide for their families and old age. And they must be free to engage in enterprise just so long as each does not injure his fellow man."[25]

The collectivists' approach. At the other extreme is the collectivist plan, which would substitute for individual capitalistic enterprises a state-owned, state-planned, state-directed system of production and distribution. It is argued that the people would have the final control through democratic elections; that ultimately the individual would have more real expression and liberty than he can have under a set-up which permits uncontrolled concentrations of power; that only by all-out planning and elimination of wasteful competition can a nation achieve a full standard of living. The collectivists have little faith in international organization as a means of discouraging war as long as capitalism is allowed to operate. For "capitalism is itself the general underlying cause of war."[26] In the words of one of its advocates, collectivism "is the only alternative to capitalism. It is the transfer of the national economy to the ownership and control of the entire people, incorporated into the working class."[27]

The "middle road." There is another road leading to economic improvement. Those who advocate following it emphatically deny that collectivism is the only alternative to capitalism. This may be thought of as a middle road economy between pure laissez-faire doctrine and collectivism. Walter Lippmann has called it a "compensated economy," and it is referred to by the editors of *Fortune* as a new "democratic capitalism—a synthesis of the conflicting elements in our recent past."[28] It seeks to perpetuate the profit motive and individual enterprise within a fabric of governmental control and support. The chief objects are (1) the restriction of activities by business elements, whether employers or employees, deemed injurious to the public good; (2) the support by governmental action of the economic structure when necessary in order to maintain full and continuous employment for all; and (3) the guarantee to all of basic economic and social essentials, such as medical care, education, housing, accident compensation, unemployment insurance, and old-age pensions.

Social security. Although the principle of social security usually plays an important part in the middle road solution, it is by no means the exclusive possession of this school of economic thought. In Britain it is supported by Churchill and by the traditionally conservative newspaper, the *Times*. And in the United States, support is found in labor circles, among important employer groups, and in the press from union weeklies to *Fortune*. This is not to say that a majority of people in the United States have come to believe in a comprehensive system of social security. The issue is still hotly debated. But the principle has already been accepted widely enough to make it one of the major possibilities in postwar society.

The Beveridge plan. In Great Britain a Committee on Social Reconstruction headed by Sir William Beveridge presented a noteworthy report to Parliament in December 1942. A plan was submitted guaranteeing the British people a national minimum of subsistence "from the cradle to the grave." The program was a considerable expansion of already existing social services and caught the imagination of the people. The Beveridge report overnight became a "best seller."

Some of the specific recommendations were: (1) $11.20 a week unemployment insurance for an indefinite period; (2) $11.20 a week for nonindustrial disability; (3) $8 a week for old age pensions; and (4) a comprehensive medical service for all citizens.[29] Support for the Beveridge report came from all sections. The *Times,* for example, declared it was "A momentous document which should and must exercise a profound and immediate influence on the direction of social change in Britain."

Canada also was tendered a kind of Beveridge plan—the Marsh plan—in the spring of 1943 when a committee appointed by the Canadian Prime Minister, W. L. Mackenzie King, submitted two reports on a national social insurance plan.

The N.R.P.B. report on security. In the United States, interest in social security was accelerated by the report of the National Resources Planning Board presented to Congress in March 1943. The Board, while covering economic questions (see page 58), examined the limited social security measures which have existed in the country during the past ten years and made recommendations for their expansion. These were based on the socio-economic philosophy that it should be the policy of the national government:

"To underwrite full employment for the employables:

To guarantee a job for every man released from the armed forces and the war industries at the close of the war, with fair pay and working conditions;

To guarantee and, when necessary, underwrite:

Equal access to security.

Equal access to education for all.

Equal access to health and nutrition for all.

Wholesome housing conditions for all."[29]

The Wagner plan. In June 1943 the so-called Wagner plan was introduced into both Houses of Congress. This plan went much farther than the report of the N.R.P.B., extending social security to 15 million persons now excluded from such benefits in the United States. Like the Beveridge plan the Wagner program calls for payments both from the employer and the employee to help finance the system. The proposed plan, in the words of its creator, "covers broadly the major economic hazards of average people throughout their lifetime—loss of income in unemployment, sickness, temporary and permanent disability, and old age."[30]

Improvement of International Economic Cooperation

Fifth aim of the United Nations. The problem of raising standards of living and guaranteeing economic security for the average man cannot be managed entirely within domestic fields. Equally important are matters relating to trade and monetary relations between nations. All proposals for postwar organization, therefore, emphasize a fifth objective—the improvement of international economic cooperation. Wendell Willkie has pointedly declared: "Political internationalism without economic internationalism is a house built upon sand. For no nation can reach its fullest development alone."[31] Technological progress has made the nations so interdependent that no nation can cavalierly adopt economic policies without reference to the effect upon its neighbors.

War debts. It is now believed by many economists that following the First World War, healthy world trade and harmonious economic relations between nations were obstructed by the legacy of war debts. These deranged and confused the monetary and trade structure of the world.

Under Lend-Lease agreements the United States has sent to its allies, principally the British Empire and Russia, billions of dollars of war supplies and food. Lend-Lease is not a one-way affair; the Allies have contributed large quantities of material to the United States armies. In the final analysis, however, the major measurable contribution in the Lend-Lease system will be made by this government. Even so, "there must be an all-round cancellation of obligations in respect to Lend-Lease goods actually consumed in war effort, on the theory that each of the United Nations will have contributed, to the best of its ability, to the common effort and, having given of its best, will owe nothing to the others."[32]

Trade and currency. To facilitate economic cooperation between nations, the majority of political plans for international organization provide for agencies which would remove obstacles to the free movement of world trade, such as unreasonably high tariffs, quotas, ruthless competition for markets, and the manipulation of currencies. Advocated also are Migration and Settlement Commissions to ease the strain of overpopulation in certain areas and Development Commissions to administer international funds for public works.

In March 1943 appeared two important plans designed to secure stable exchange rates in the world's monetary system, to help free world trade, and to encourage fiscal cooperation. The White plan was the work of an official of the United States Treasury, and the Keynes scheme was devised by Lord Keynes, adviser to the British Treasury. Both would set up an international treasury to control the fluctuation of currencies in the world and establish a new international monetary unit.

The whole subject of international trade and currency becomes highly technical; the important thing to understand is that there is growing agreement among the world's best economic thinkers that no machinery devised for political cooperation can succeed unless at the same time it provides for comparable economic cooperation. Economic nationalism has been a prolific cause of international disputes and war in the past. Yet the world's business is not something to be fought over by various national units but a common task and opportunity leading toward benefits for all.

Summary

The most perplexing and difficult postwar problems have to do with long-range attempts to ensure the kind of world the people of the United Nations are fighting for. Such a world has been described in general terms in the Atlantic Charter and in the speeches of statesmen of the United Nations. The United Nations seek five ideals for the postwar world, three of them political and two economic: (1) reduction of the hazard of war—freedom from aggression means freedom from fear; (2) perfection of democracy in every way possible at home; encouragement and expansion of democracy abroad; (3) protection and advancement of the so-called backward or colonial people; (4) achievement of the highest possible level of individual economic prosperity and security in all countries; (5) realization of a high degree of economic cooperation between nations.

The United Nations may not succeed in bringing about a painless and an entirely smooth transition from war to peace. But apparently the basic needs and problems have been recognized and plans to meet them have been set in motion. Whether in the end these will amount to a people's peace depends, in the final analysis, on the people.

Bibl[illegible]ography and Acknowledgments

1: Since Stalingrad

1. S[illegible]tatement published by the Government on the Congress Party's responsibility for the Disturbances in India, 1942-1943*, London, 1943, p. 5.
2. *Ibid.*, p. 4.
3. See *Time*, Dec. 28, 1942, p. 21.

2: On the Home Fronts

1. Office of War Information Release, No. 2022, p. 1.
2. See Julius Hochman, "Let's Look at Labor," VII, "The Opportunity for Leadership," *Nation*, Sept. 11, 1943.
3. See *New York Times*, Aug. 1, 1943.
4. See Helen Fuller, "The Rich Get Richer," *The New Republic*, Sept. 20, 1943. See also *Survey of Current Business*, U.S. Department of Commerce, Sept. 1943, pp. 57.
5. *Home Front Handbook*, Q2227, British Ministry of Information, April 1943, p. 4.
6. See *Canada at War*, Ottawa, Wartime Information Board, June 1943, p. 54.
7. See Editorial, *Toronto Globe and Mail*, June 28, 1943.
8. See *The Job Australia Is Doing*, Australia News and Information Bureau, 1943, p. 13.
9. *Meet New Zealand*, distributed by New Zealand Legation, 1943, p. 24.
10. Quoted by Albert Rhys Williams, *The Russians*, Harcourt, Brace and Company, 1943, p. 128.
11. Joseph E. Davies, in *Soviet Russia Today*, Aug. 1943, p. 9.
12. See *Information Bulletin*, Embassy of the USSR, Sept. 14, 1943, p. 7; and *Information Bulletin*, Sept. 18, 1943, p. 8.
13. See *Information Bulletin*, Sept. 14, 1943, p. 8.
14. See Williams, pp. 162 and following.
15. See *Information Bulletin*, Aug. 24, 1943, p. 7.
16. See *Time*, Feb. 15, 1943, p. 34.
17. See *New York Times*, Jan. 12, 1943.
18. See *Ibid.*, Aug. 5, 1943.
19. See *Ibid.*, Sept. 13, 1943.
20. See *Time*, Sept. 20, 1943, p. 27.
21. *Ibid.*, p. 27.
22. Editorial, "Democracy in China," *The New Republic*, Sept. 27, 1943, p. 412.
23. See Brooks Atkinson, to *New York Times*, from Chungking, July 8, 1943.
24. See *New York Times*, April 23, 1943.
25. *Time*, Aug. 2, 1943, p. 25.
26. "Nazi Desperation Reflected by Switch of Propaganda Line," *Newsweek*, July 12, 1943, p. 46.
27. William L. Shirer, in *Montreal Standard*, from London, July 3, 1943.
28. See *New York Times*, Sept. 11, 1943.
29. See *Ibid.*, Sept. 26, 1943.
30. *International Labor Review*, Montreal, Canadian Press, May 2, 1943.
31. See *Time*, April 5, 1943.
32. German Transocean Agency broadcast, reported in *Chicago Tribune*, Oct. 17, 1943.
33. See *New York Times*, Sept. 4, 1943.
34. See A. T. Steele, to *The Chicago Daily News*, from New Delhi, Oct. 29, 1943.

3: Preparing for Tomorrow

1. E. H. Carr, *Conditions of Peace*, 1942, p. 3. By permission of The Macmillan Company, publishers.
2. R. H. Tawney, *Why Britain Fights*, London, 1941, p. 45. By permission of The Macmillan Company, publishers.
3. See for example Herbert Hoover and Hugh Gibson, *The Problems of Lasting Peace*, Dou-

bleday, Doran and Company, 1942, chap. 14; and Harold Nicolson, *Why Britain Is at War,* Penguin Books, Ltd., 1939, pp. 148-149.

4. Herbert H. Lehman, *Relief and Rehabilitation,* Foreign Policy Reports, July 15, 1943, p. 102.
5. See "Allies Chart Post War Plans," *Inter-Allied Review,* Oct. 15, 1941, p. 1.
6. Lehman, p. 105.
7. "The United States in a New World," IV, "Relations With Europe," *Fortune,* May 1942, p. 10.
8. See Bernadotte E. Schmitt, *What Shall We Do With Germany?* Public Policy Pamphlets, No. 38, The University of Chicago Press, 1943, pp. 16-20.
9. *Ibid.*, p. 21.
10. Carr, p. 221.
11. See Robert Ergang, "Subjugate or Conciliate Germany," *Current History,* Events Publishing Company, Feb. 1943, p. 473.
12. V. M. Dean, *What Future For Germany,* Foreign Policy Reports, Feb. 1, 1943, p. 295.
13. N. J. Spykman, *America's Strategy in World Politics,* Harcourt, Brace and Company, 1942, p. 460.
14. *Ibid.*, p. 447.
15. Quoted by R. L. Buell, "Draftsmen of the New World," *Fortune,* Feb. 1943, p. 152.
16. Harold E. Stassen, "We Need a World Government," *The Saturday Evening Post,* May 22, 1943, p. 41.
17. See P. E. Corbett, *Post-War Worlds,* Farrar and Rinehart, 1942, pp. 189-190.
18. [illegible] Payson S. Wild, *Machinery of Collaboration Between the United Nations,* Foreign Policy Reports, July 1, 1942, p. 106.
19. Thomas Mann, *The Coming Victory of Democracy,* Alfred A. Knopf, 1938, p. 14.
20. Charles E. Merriam, *On The Agenda of Democracy,* 1941, p. 14. Reprinted by permission of the President and Fellows of Harvard College.
21. CMD, 1922, *Indians in Kenya,* London, 1923.
22. See *Toward a New World Order,* Foreign Policy Reports, May 15, 1941, p. 54.
23. Quoted from *As Britain Sees the Post-War World,* Foreign Policy Reports, Oct. 15, 1942, p. 192.
24. Henry A. Wallace, *Free World Victory,* L. B. Fischer, 1942, p. 19.
25. Hoover and Gibson, p. 209.
26. Earl Browder, *The Way Out,* International Publishers, 1941, p. 15.
27. *Ibid.*, p. 106.
28. See "The United States in a New World," III, "The Domestic Economy," supplement to *Fortune,* Dec. 1942, p. 17.
29. Details of the Beveridge and the N.R.P.B. plans were taken from a convenient summary in *Bulletin of the Commission to Study the Organization of Peace,* May-June, 1943.
30. Quoted from *Christian Science Monitor,* June 4, 1943, p. 1.
31. Speech before *New York Herald-Tribune* Forum, Nov. 17, 1942.
32. J. B. Condliffe, *Implications of Lend-Lease,* Foreign Affairs, April 1943, p. 501.

6 7 8 9 10 11 12 13 14 15 16 17 18 19 20 21 22 23 24 25 55 54 53 52 51 50 49 48 47 46

ASIA

PACIFIC OCEAN

EUROPE

ARCTIC OCEAN

NORTH AMERICA

ATLANTIC OCEAN

NORTHERN HEMISPHERE